OXFORD WORLD'S CLASSICS

JOHN MILTON

JOHN MILTON was born on 9 December 1608 in Cheapside, London. He published little until the appearance of *Poems of Mr. John Milton, both English and Latin* in 1646, when he was thirty-seven. By this time he was deeply committed to a political vocation, and became an articulate and increasingly indispensable spokesman for the Independent cause. He wrote the crucial justifications for the trial and execution of Charles I, and, as Secretary for Foreign Tongues to the Council of State, was the voice of the English revolution to the world at large. After the failure of the Commonwealth he was briefly imprisoned; blind and in straitened circumstances he returned to poetry, and in 1667 published a ten-book version of *Paradise Lost*, his biblical epic written, as he put it, after 'long choosing, and beginning late'. In 1671, *Paradise Regained* and *Samson Agonistes* appeared, followed two years later by an expanded edition of his shorter poems. The canon was completed in 1674, the year of his death, with the appearance of the twelve-book *Paradise Lost*, which became a classic almost immediately. His influence on English poetry and criticism has been incalculable.

STEPHEN ORGEL is the Jackson Eli Reynolds Professor in Humanities at Stanford University. His most recent books are *The Authentic Shakespeare* (2002) and *Impersonations: The Performance of Gender in Shakespeare's England* (1996). He is the author of *The Illusion of Power* (1975), *Inigo Jones* (1973, with Sir Roy Strong), and *The Jonsonian Masque* (1965). His editions include Marlowe's poems and translations, Ben Jonson's masques, *The Tempest*, and *The Winter's Tale* in the Oxford Shakespeare, and *Macbeth*, *King Lear*, *Pericles*, *The Taming of the Shrew*, and *The Sonnets* in the New Pelican Shakespeare, of which he is general editor.

JONATHAN GOLDBERG is Arts and Sciences Distinguished Professor of English at Emory University. Among his many books on early modern literature and culture are: *James I and the Politics of Literature* (1983), *Writing Matter: From the Hands of the English Renaissance* (1990), *Sodometries: Renaissance Texts, Modern Sexualities* (1992), *Desiring Women Writing: English Renaissance Examples* (1997), and *Shakespeare's Hand* (2002). He is editor of *Queering the Renaissance* (1994) and *Reclaiming Sodom* (1994). He is also the author of *Willa Cather and Others* (2001).

Melpo'mene   Erato.

Pri· ΙΟΑΝΝΙS ΜΙLΤΟΝΙ ΑΝGLI ΕFFIGIES

ÆTATIS niGelt.

ANNA

Urania.

Ἀμαθεῖ γεγράφθαι χειρὶ τήνδε μὲν εἰκόνα
Φαίης τάχ' ἄν, πρὸς εἶδος αὐτοφυὲς βλέπων·
Τὸν δ' ἐκτυπωτὸν ὀκ ἐπιγνόντες φίλοι
Γελᾶτε φαύλȣ δυσμίμημα ζωγράφȣ.

W·M· ſculp :

Poems 1645, frontispiece. Engraving by William Marshall. For the Greek
epigram, see p. 162.

OXFORD WORLD'S CLASSICS

====

John Milton
The Major Works

====

Edited with an Introduction and Notes by
STEPHEN ORGEL *and* JONATHAN GOLDBERG

OXFORD
UNIVERSITY PRESS

OXFORD

UNIVERSITY PRESS

Great Clarendon Street, Oxford OX2 6DP

Oxford University Press is a department of the University of Oxford.
It furthers the University's objective of excellence in research, scholarship,
and education by publishing worldwide in

Oxford New York

Auckland Bangkok Buenos Aires Cape Town Chennai
Dar es Salaam Delhi Hong Kong Istanbul Karachi Kolkata
Kuala Lumpur Madrid Melbourne Mexico City Mumbai Nairobi
São Paulo Shanghai Singapore Taipei Tokyo Toronto

Oxford is a registered trade mark of Oxford University Press
in the UK and in certain other countries

Published in the United States
by Oxford University Press Inc., New York

Introduction and editorial material © Stephen Orgel and Jonathan Goldberg 1991
Exracts from *Second Defence of the English People* and
Christian Doctrine from *The Complete Prose Works of John Milton*
(Vol. 7, ed. M. Kelly. Latin trans. J. Carey, and Vol. 4, ed. D. M. Wolfe)
© Yale University Press

The moral rights of the author have been asserted

Database right Oxford University Press (maker)

First published 1991 in hardback and simultaneously in paperback edition
First published, with revisions, as an Oxford World's Classics paperback 2003
Reissued 2008

All rights reserved. No part of this publication may be reproduced,
stored in a retrieval system, or transmitted, in any form or by any means,
without the prior permission in writing of Oxford University Press,
or as expressly permitted by law, or under terms agreed with the appropriate
reprographics rights organization. Enquiries concerning reproduction
outside the scope of the above should be sent to the Rights Department,
Oxford University Press, at the address above

You must not circulate this book in any other binding or cover
and you must impose this same condition on any acquirer

British Library Cataloguing in Publication Data

Data available

Library of Congress Cataloging in Publication Data

Milton, John, 1608–1674.
[Selections. 1990]
John Milton/edited by Stephen Orgel and Jonathan Goldberg.
p. cm.—(Oxford world's classics)
Includes bibliographical references.
I. Orgel, Stephen. II. Goldberg, Jonathan. III. Title. IV. Series.
PR3552.074 1990 821'.4—dc20 90–34107

ISBN 978–0–19–953918–5

1

Printed in Great Britain by
Clays Ltd, St Ives plc

On the Fifth of November   124
To my Father   134
To Salzilli   140
Manso   142
Damon's Epitaph   148

GREEK POEM ADDED IN 1673

On the Engraver of his Portrait   162

UNCOLLECTED LATIN POEM

Elegaic Verses   163

PROSE WORKS

From *The Reason of Church Government*   165
From *An Apology for Smectymnuus*   173
The Doctrine and Discipline of Divorce   182
Of Education   226
Areopagitica   236
The Tenure of Kings and Magistrates   273
From *Second Defence of the English People*   308
The Ready and Easy Way to Establish a Free Commonwealth   330

MAJOR POEMS

Paradise Lost   355
Paradise Regained   619
Samson Agonistes   671

FAMILIAR LETTERS 1674

To Charles Diodati, 1637   717
To Benedetto Buonmattei, 1638   719
To Leonard Philaris, 1654   721

From *Christian Doctrine*   723

CONTENTS

Notes   735
Further Reading   960
Index of Titles and First Lines   963

INTRODUCTION

IN THE spring of 1674, some six months before Milton died, and only a few months before the second edition of *Paradise Lost* appeared, John Dryden completed an opera, *The State of Innocence*; the Poet Laureate had chosen Milton's epic as the basis for his extravaganza. Operas were a distinctively modern genre in late seventeenth-century England, and their librettos were often derived from classic texts, including works that were coming to be claimed as English classics. Shakespeare's *The Tempest*, which had been rewritten by Davenant and Dryden in 1667, was playing in a rival operatic revision early in 1674, and Dryden had undertaken his opera in response to the success of that production. In choosing to base *The State of Innocence* on *Paradise Lost*, Dryden was declaring that Milton's poem had the status of a classic. The claim was an extraordinary one, for Milton was still living. If his epic seemed to come from an earlier age (in subsequent criticism and verse, Dryden would couple it with Homer and Virgil), Milton's name could not be dissociated from a recent and, from Dryden's perspective, threatening past—the years of the English Revolution that had seen Charles I deposed and executed in 1649 and the ascendancy of Oliver Cromwell. Thanks to his defence of regicide in *The Tenure of Kings and Magistrates*, Milton had been appointed Cromwell's Latin Secretary. His position involved the handling of diplomatic correspondence, but he would have been best known for such tracts as *Eikonoklastes* (1649), with its point-for-point demolition of the royal image, and for the series of defences he had written in the 1650s in which he had made himself the spokes-man for the revolution. Consequently, with the restoration of Charles II in 1660 Milton's life had been in danger.

Dryden's choice of *Paradise Lost* for his operatic libretto therefore was not an uncomplicated act of poetic homage: Charles II's Poet Laureate sought to recast Milton's poem to serve new poetic, and polit-ical, designs. Milton's only recorded response to Dryden's operatic plan was a comment on what might seem merely a question of poetic technique: Dryden's decision to recast Milton's blank verse as rhymed couplets. Milton is reported to have said, 'Well, Mr Dryden, it seems you have a mind to tag my points, and you have my leave to tag them.'[1]

[1] William Riley Parker, *Milton: A Biography*, 2 vols. (Oxford: Clarendon Press, 1968), i. 635.

The old poet referred sardonically to Dryden's rhymes as the equivalent of fashionable metal stays, and went on to remark that some of his lines were 'so awkward and old-fashioned' that they could not be updated and might as well be left as Dryden found them.

Milton's response was not simply a recognition of changing poetic fashions. For the 1669 printing of the first edition of *Paradise Lost* (1667) he had provided an introductory note about his versification, describing his choice of blank verse as a political decision: it was to serve as an exemplary instance of 'ancient liberty recovered to Heroic Poem from the troublesome and modern bondage of Rhyming'. Milton's note, indeed, may well have been a reply to Dryden, who, in the dedication to his play, *The Rival Ladies* (1664), had insisted that the 'wild and lawless' imagination of a poet required the 'clogs' of rhyme to restrain and circumscribe it. The debate, which engaged a number of other authors, was continued, too, in the prefatory poem that Andrew Marvell provided for the 1674 edition of *Paradise Lost*. Alluding to the Poet Laureate and his fashionable 'tags', Marvell commended Milton for writing in blank verse. Dryden and Marvell were political opponents, taking sides that within a few years would be called Tory and Whig.

To begin with this episode is to be reminded of a number of things: that literary history is something constructed; that the question of classic and canonical status for a text is often a matter of contestation; that literary history cannot be separated either from history in the broader sense, or even from the more narrow sphere of party politics. If Dryden's choice of *Paradise Lost* as the basis for his operatic libretto functioned as an act of poetic recognition, it was also intended to serve as an attempt at poetic and political appropriation. It can stand as an initial instance in the afterlife of Milton's epic—the first of those rewritings through which literary history is constructed. But it does so in relation to other literary histories, among them the one glanced at in Milton's own allusion to the 'ancient liberty' with which he affiliated his poem. Milton's implied sense of his epic is not necessarily or obviously more correct than Dryden's; after all, coming in 1669, it may be a response to Dryden. And its appearance in a note solicited by the publisher of *Paradise Lost* is no guarantee that the choice of blank verse had been politically charged in the same way when Milton began to write the poem a quarter of a century earlier. As much as Dryden's rewriting of the epic, which occurred before the poem had even reached its definitive twelve-book form, Milton's note suggests the poet's revisionary relationship to his own text and career.

The Poet of the 1640s

Such relationships can be seen throughout Milton's life, and most explicitly when Milton's subject is his own career, as it is a number of times in his verse and prose. The prose passages in particular have often shaped later accounts of Milton's life and works; read critically, they allow one to examine the revisionary processes at work in Milton's writings. When, for example, Milton presents himself in his first signed publication, *The Reason of Church Government* (1642), it is as a poet who uses only his 'left hand' in writing prose. In the account he gives, his entire life appears to have been spent in training as a poet; the prose he writes in response to the present religious and political turmoil is represented as an interruption of a career that he intends to resume, even promising his reader 'a work not to be raised from the heat of youth'. These pages read resoundingly now, and the hope to write something 'to aftertimes, as they should not willingly let it die' sounds like a forecast of *Paradise Lost*; but in 1642, the name 'John Milton' had never appeared on any published poem. The fact is obscured, if not deliberately suppressed, in this prose declaration of an already existing corpus of works of his right hand soon to be crowned with immortal fame. If any of what was to become *Paradise Lost* had been written by 1642, it was as some lines of a drama entitled 'Adam Unparadised' that Milton showed to his nephews, John and Edward Phillips, at around this time—lines that, twenty-five years later, would form part of Satan's soliloquy at the beginning of book 4.

On 2 January 1646 a volume of *Poems of Mr John Milton, Both English and Latin*, dated 1645, appeared. If it was meant to fulfil the promise made in 1642, it notably failed to do so. A citation from Virgil's seventh eclogue on the title-page said as much: 'Baccare frontem/Cingite, ne vati noceat mala lingua futuro' ('Wreathe my brow with valerian, lest an evil tongue harm the poet yet to be'), imploring the safety of the poet who is still to come—'vati . . . futuro'. The fulfilment of the 1642 promise was thereby deferred. The 1645 volume included no epic or drama 'doctrinal and exemplary to a nation' such as Milton had envisioned in *The Reason of Church Government*; it was, in many respects, a perfectly familiar compilation of lyrics of the sort that had been published throughout the century. It exhibited skill in a number of the prevailing forms and modes: pastoral invitation in 'L'Allegro' and 'Il Penseroso', elegies in English and Latin, metrical psalms, epigrams, sonnets. And if, in *Lycidas*, Milton drew on the traditional capacity of pastoral to comment on ecclesiastical corruption (something that can be seen in numerous

Renaissance precursors, among them Spenser's *Shepheardes Calender*),
the poem in 1645 no doubt also spoke powerfully to the present situation, the ousting of the bishops and the substitution of a Presbyterian Church government. None the less, the longest poem in the 1645
Poems was written in the most royalist of forms, the masque, and the
title-page to the volume announced that it contained songs set by
Henry Lawes, 'Gentleman of the King's Chapel, and one of his Majesty's Private Music'. Testimonials that preceded the section of Latin
poems came from the hands of the Italian—and Catholic—literati
who had acknowledged Milton's talent during his trip to Italy in
1638–9.

Milton's self-presentation in the prose of 1642 scarcely suggests the
heterogeneity that can be seen in the 1645 collection of his poetry; the
disparity between them makes clear that the career Milton was pursuing cannot entirely be understood through his own later designs. The
volume in which Milton emerged as a self-acknowledged poet not only
deferred the major work forecast in 1642. It also, inevitably, invoked
another self: by 1645, Milton was well known, not as a poet but as the
author of pamphlets on divorce. These were regarded as scandalous
even by Milton's fellow Presbyterians—the publisher of *Poems of Mr
John Milton* may, indeed, have been hoping to cash in precisely on the
notoriety of Milton's name. As a collection of verse, the 1645 volume
points backwards to the many directions Milton's career might have
taken; it displays Milton trying on the mantle of many predecessors,
and never in uncomplicated ways. But it also suggests that there is
more to his biography than Milton allowed in *The Reason of Church
Government.*

This is the case even at a personal level. To the 'ceaseless diligence
and care' of his father, acknowledged there, might be juxtaposed the
tense eloquence of the poem *Ad Patrem*, which suggests that the poetic
career Milton chose in the mid-1630s was not his father's choice; the
smooth progression toward the profession of poetry described in *The
Reason of Church Government* ignores the conflicts that were occasioned
by Milton's decision. This is by no means to suggest that the elder Milton was a philistine. He was an accomplished musician and composer,
and (on the evidence of *Ad Patrem*) fostered his son's interests, even
when they seemed opposed to his own. He was above all socially
ambitious for all his children, and generous to them: he had settled a
considerable dowry on his daughter Anne when she married Edward
Phillips in 1623; Milton's younger brother Christopher was being
trained as a lawyer; Milton himself, the elder son, had been from child-

hood 'destined', as he puts it in *The Reason of Church Government*, to a Church career. The ecclesiastical destiny also reflects what little we know about his mother, Sara, whose piety Milton praises elsewhere. The education that John Milton accorded his namesake bespeaks those plans: private tutoring; grammar school education at the prestigious St Paul's School; university education at Cambridge, culminating with an MA in 1632. His studies subsequently extended beyond the university, and were pursued at his father's expense.

The elder John Milton was a professional scrivener, lucrative work in the seventeenth century. Scriveners were employed to draw up legal documents, and were thereby made privy to financial transactions. Milton's father, in fact, made his money by lending money. He amassed enough not only to provide his son with the education of a gentleman and scholar, but to permit him the leisure of several years of independent study, first at the family estate at Hammersmith, to which the elder Milton had retired in 1632, and then at Horton, in Buckinghamshire, where he took up residence in 1635. In 1638–9 Milton capped his education with a trip to the continent, although the motives behind this Grand Tour were clearly complicated, both by his decision not to fulfil his parents' plans for him to enter the Church and by the death of his mother in April 1637. *Lycidas*, an elegy for a drowned Cambridge contemporary who had entered the priesthood, was completed by November 1637. In its situation, and from its initial declaration of poetic unripeness to its final lines heading towards 'pastures new', it echoes against the cross purposes of Milton's life in the 1630s.

There is no reason to doubt that Milton's decision not to enter the Church was made on the basis of religious principles; but one must also recognize that he was able to arrive at it because he was under no pressure to earn a living throughout this period. Nevertheless, when he came back from the continent he did not return to his father's estate but set up on his own in London; and in his first move towards independence he took on pupils, among them his sister's children, John and Edward Phillips. His financial circumstances remained relatively comfortable, though it would not be until almost a decade later, in 1649, when he became Cromwell's Latin Secretary, that the 40-year-old Milton would receive a regular salary.

The letter to a friend written about the same time as *Ad Patrem* expresses Milton's doubts about his vocation, and we can see from the 1645 *Poems* that in the 1630s Milton had pursued the kind of employment that a young man of means and leisure who wished to be a poet might have sought. He found a patron in the Dowager Countess of

Derby, for whom he composed the courtly entertainment *Arcades*; Henry Lawes, the king's musician and an acquaintance of Milton's father, had very likely provided the music on that occasion, and it was probably at his suggestion that the Countess's son-in-law, the Earl of Bridgewater, commissioned a masque from Milton to commemorate his installation as Lord Lieutenant of Wales. Between these two events, Milton's first published poem, 'On Shakespeare', had appeared, anonymously, in the second Shakespeare Folio (1632). There is no evidence of how the 24-year-old Milton found his way into that volume, but the fact suggests that he had ambitions quite separate from those for a career as a Churchman—or as a courtly poet. For this sort of professional aspiration, Ben Jonson offered almost the only living example, though by this time he was reduced to poverty and was sadly neglected. His example, nevertheless, was a powerful one: it would have demonstrated first of all the need for aristocratic or courtly patronage. But more important, through the publication of his *Workes* in folio in 1616, Jonson had presented himself as an English classic, and thereby had laid the ground both for the literary claims of Shakespeare's plays as they too appeared in authoritative folio editions, and for those of all future English writers who, like Milton, sought for their work the status of classics.

In the sixth of his Latin elegies, addressed to Charles Diodati, the close friend he made at Cambridge, Milton had described *On the Morning of Christ's Nativity* as his own poetic coming of age; the poem stands first in the 1645 volume, followed by psalm translations and poems on Christian themes. These are, however, precisely the sorts of poems a future Churchman might have written and may be compared to the religious verse of Donne or Herbert. They are not the poems of a would-be laureate. In the letter written to an unknown friend some years later than the elegy to Diodati, Milton included a copy of his seventh sonnet, a declaration of poetic immaturity, but also, in that context, a defence of his belatedness. The contradiction between the announced arrival in the poem to Diodati and the subsequent deferral in the letter to the friend registers a critical change of direction, as Milton abandoned the Church career for which he had been trained and moved towards a poetic career whose terms and possibilities were necessarily transformed by the events of the 1640s.

Thus, while the 1645 *Poems* may look like the kind of collection produced by any number of poets in the 1630s, in that revolutionary time there could no longer be the hope that any of the sorts of poetic careers promised in that volume might be realized. The urgent work, Milton came quickly to recognize, was the work of his left hand: the defence of embattled friends, the call for the reformation that seemed within reach. The declaration of immaturity and the anxieties expressed in the 1630s, in the letter to the friend, or in 'How soon hath time', or in *Lycidas*, none the less recur throughout the 1640s, and later, continually recontextualized by events Milton could not have anticipated. The poetic career, as Milton writes it, is always being postponed, is always in preparation. In 'How soon hath time', to enhance that claim, and to take charge of circumstances that were not always in his control, Milton described himself as both feeling and appearing younger than he really was; there, as in *The Reason of Church Government*, recalling the biblical parable that haunted the imagination of the scrivener's son, he presents himself as not yet ready to deliver on the talent with which he had been invested.

The Prose Career

Such strategies can still be seen as late as the *Second Defence* (1654). Although totally blind, his eyes, he insists, appear 'as clear and bright, without a cloud, as the eyes of men who see most keenly'; and although he is well on towards middle age, 'past forty', 'there is', he continues, 'scarcely anyone to whom I do not seem younger by about ten years'. It would be mistaken to read these remarks merely as signs of vanity; Milton's defensive self-construction occurs here, after all, more than a dozen years after he had promised his readers the poem 'doctrinal and exemplary to a nation'. These self-protective gestures are means to ensure the possibility that the promise might yet be kept. But they are also in the service of the self forged during his years as Latin Secretary, as his earlier notions of immediate revolutionary reform were challenged, and his blindness could be taken as a reason for, and a sign of abandonment. In the *Second Defence*, what had become a long digression from the poetic career is reread and reinterpreted.

This can be clearly seen in the tract when Milton reviews his career as a prose writer. No allowance is made for historical contingency or multiplicity; history, rather, is treated as a kind of logical problem and his prose takes place within what is represented as an entirely straightforward and rationalized exploration of various kinds of liberty:

Since, then, I observed that there were, in all, three varieties of liberty without which civilized life is scarcely possible, namely ecclesiastical liberty, domestic or personal liberty, and civil liberty, and since I had already written about the first, while I saw that the magistrates were vigorously attending to the third, I took as my province the remaining one, the second or domestic kind. This too seemed to be concerned with three problems: the nature of marriage, the education of the children, and finally the existence of freedom to express oneself.

Milton had written his first prose tract, *Of Reformation*, in response to religious issues; yet there is an insistent politicization as one proceeds from *Of Reformation* to the *Apology* and *The Reason of Church Government* that is virtually effaced in his later account. His defences in the 1640s of Presbyterianism as the only true form of Protestantism entangled him in political debate and strife, moving him ever further from hopes of reform within the Church and with the support of the king. The 'reason' of Church government, like the logic of liberty in the *Second Defence*, is not so self-contained as Milton would have it. There is none the less the most intimate relationship between Milton's self-presentation and the kinds of claims he makes for such intrinsic logics. Similarly, the decision to treat domestic liberty, with its focus on the issue of divorce, can hardly have been the entirely rational choice that Milton represents; indeed, it is difficult to imagine that the moment of thought represented in the *Second Defence* ever took place except in that retrospective recounting. The point here is not to impugn Milton's veracity, but to see throughout his career, and as perhaps the single constant in it, Milton's overwhelming attempt to give a coherent shape to his life. The terms change, and different constraints are denied for the sake of the controlling design. If we pause over the acts of suppression involved in these acts of forecasting and retrospective recasting, it is only because such attention makes Milton's career and the texts he wrote legible beyond those Miltonic designs.

The tracts Milton wrote on domestic liberty from 1642 to 1645 are far more complex than the single progression through a tripartite structure that he describes. They represent particular responses to a range of situations, both political and personal. Behind the divorce tracts lies not only the anomaly that England was the sole Protestant nation that forbade divorce; there also lies the fact that Milton was separated from his wife throughout those years. He had married Mary Powell suddenly, or so the story goes: 'home he returns a married man, that went out a bachelor' is the memorable sentence in the first biography of Milton, written by his nephew Edward Phillips,[2] a description almost as startling as Milton's own endorsement of marriage in the *Apology*, after

[2] Merritt Y. Hughes (ed.), *John Milton: Complete Poems and Major Prose* (New York: Odyssey Press, 1957), 1031. Phillips's biography was almost certainly written at Milton's dictation; it shows signs, too, of having been influenced by Milton's accounts in his prose.

paragraphs lauding chastity. What is not mentioned in Phillip's *Life* is the fact that the elder Milton had loaned money to the Powells; Milton's trip to the country, when he met Mary Powell, was undertaken to collect interest on the loan. Shortly after their marriage, Mary Powell Milton returned to her parents, supposedly for a visit; she was absent for the next three years. But what separated the Miltons was not merely personal: Powell was a royalist. In the four divorce pamphlets Milton wrote in these years, incompatibility is repeatedly presented as grounds for divorce. Milton argues as if he were articulating a universal, time-transcending principle of freedom, yet we cannot ignore personal and political dimensions to his motives. We must also come to terms with the fact that the right of divorce insisted upon is solely a male prerogative: no provision is imagined for women with marital grievances. Finally, while Milton associates this liberty with the principle of Christian liberty proclaimed by St Paul, it is hard won against the biblical texts upon which Milton attempted to rest his case.

So too with *Areopagitica*, written to defend the liberty of the press against the 1643 licensing order that asserted the government's right of pre-censorship. Milton's liberty, however, is explicitly only for Protestants and not for Catholics; and although he attacks pre-censorship, he does not question post-publication censorship. Moreover, rather than representing a seamless development from the pamphlets on religious freedom, *Areopagitica* registers Milton's move away from the Presbyterians who had assumed power; it is their policies that he calls into question. Glossed over, then, by Milton's category of domestic liberty are the personal and political motives in his writing—and those categories are not easily separated. Similarly, the tract *On Education* arises from experiences Milton chose not to acknowledge there nor to recount in the *Second Defence*: that he first earned a living in the 1640s by taking on pupils. Although Dr Johnson is hardly the most sympathetic biographer of Milton, he is perhaps worth listening to here: 'Let not our veneration for Milton forbid us to look with some degree of merriment on great promises and small performance, on the man who hastens home, because his countrymen are contending for their liberty, and, when he reaches the scene of action, vapours away his patriotism in a private boarding-school.'[3] Johnson had no sympathy with Milton's politics; he none the less points accurately to the several years between Milton's return from the continent and his first prose writings, years

[3] *The Lives of the Poets* in *The Works of Samuel Johnson*, 9 vols. (Oxford: Talboys and Wheeler, 1825), vii. 75.

suppressed in Milton's account. One could be more sympathetic to Milton at this point in his life; he was establishing a home of his own; dealing with the death of his best friend, Diodati, memorialized in the *Epitaphium Damonis*; casting about for a large poetic subject (as that poem indicates); facing, even at a personal level, the national schism—his brother Christopher chose to side with the king. None the less, the point holds: the *Second Defence* presents a far more single-minded Milton, and years disappear in it.

Of Education is a complex document, testifying to Milton's interest in educational reforms, but also marking his adherence to the humanist education he had received at St Paul's, and which he attempted to pass on to his nephews. When, in 1673, Milton republished the 1645 poems with some further additions of poems both early and late (another attempt to organize his poetic career), he included *Of Education* in the volume, treating it thereby as a kind of poetics. The tract can be seen in that way; but it also imagines education not merely as an intellectual pursuit but as a kind of military training. It points, as does *Areopagitica*, towards Milton's break with the Presbyterians and his alliance with the Independents who assumed power after the trial and execution of Charles I in January 1649. They were enabled to do so only because Colonel Pride with an armed troop had entered Parliament the month before and forcibly ejected the Presbyterians. When, a month later, Milton defended the inevitability of the removal of the unjust king in *The Tenure of Kings and Magistrates*, he did not address the question of the illegality of Pride's Purge: the king would not have been executed had the Presbyterians been allowed to vote.

The 'ancient liberty' with which Milton associated his versification in *Paradise Lost* has its connections with the principle of liberty announced in the *Second Defence*, and practised in Milton's strenuous engagements with the Bible in the divorce tracts (the principle behind such interpretive strategies is laid out in a chapter on the scriptures in *Christian Doctrine*). It allies the poem with the highly politicized version of individual male prerogative forged in Milton's prose, and perhaps most resolutely stated in the most desperate of situations: in *The Ready and Easy Way*, for example, written shortly before the Restoration, Milton virtually dictates solutions to the nation; the principle of liberty leads him to propose ignoring the will of the people. It is not difficult to find in the heroic self-portrait of the blind bard and prophet offered in the *Second Defence* the creation of the voice of the poet of *Paradise Lost*. The extraordinary strength of the self-presentation in the prose of the 1650s is part of the most literal act of revision, as the claims for sight and foresight are made in the face of personal ruin or of impending political collapse. And it is worth noting, too, that in these tracts, Milton had stopped promising the poem 'doctrinal and exemplary to a nation'; the prose has come to stand in that place, explicitly so at the end of the *Second Defence*. Taking control of the career had come to be an abandonment of that career as it had been laid out in the early 1640s; what remained was to 'stand and wait'.

The Last Revision: the 1660s

In 1660, with his life in danger, Milton went into hiding, only to emerge after the Act of Oblivion, which pardoned those who had served under Cromwell. He was made to pay an exorbitant fee for the costs of his imprisonment; his works were burned, and he lived a far more straitened life than he had ever known. Instead of the steady supply of amanuenses to take down his words, or to read to him, he now had only his three daughters, whom he required, notoriously, to read texts to him in languages they could not understand. These were the surviving children of his marriage to Mary Powell, who had died in 1652 (there were no surviving children from his brief second marriage to Katherine Woodstock, and none from his third marriage to Elizabeth Minshull, whom he married in 1663). In the changed circumstances of the 1660s, *Paradise Lost* reached its final form, appearing first as a ten-book epic in 1667. The poem is striated by its years of composition. Doubtless it is not only Satan's soliloquy at the beginning of book 4 that dates from the 'Adam Unparadised' of the 1640s, or from other early drafts of epics and tragedies. Some passages seem to draw upon political experiences from the 1640s and 1650s—the war councils and battles, for all their Homeric and Virgilian overtones, must also have had their counterparts in the years of revolution. But the 'evil days' of the opening of book 7 seem to allude to the collapse of the Revolution and the restoration of the Stuarts; and, more intimately, references to Milton's blindness must postdate the 1640s, and are likely to be later than 1652, when he lost his sight completely.

If *Paradise Lost* at last fulfils the promise to write a poem 'doctrinal and exemplary', it does so in ways that could not have been anticipated in the early 1640s, when the poem, imagined as a national epic, would have served as an arm of the state and its religion. That the poem is heavily censored even in its theology can be seen by comparing it with the *Christian Doctrine*, a work that occupied Milton for the last twenty years of his life, and in which his religious beliefs are detailed. These include heresies, among them the rejection of the Trinity and a conviction that the soul dies with the body—Milton's religion was hardly one that any Christian nation would have embraced as doctrinal. *Paradise Lost* barely allows its heretical views to be seen; it similarly suppresses its politics. If the poem managed to have an immediate afterlife it was as much due to what was being denied as to its recasting of the founding myth of Christian culture.

In his final years, Milton also completed *Samson Agonistes*, a poem whose roots lie in the 1640s and 1650s, and *Paradise Regained*, explicitly written as a sequel to the earlier epic. These are poems whose strengths, too, lie in powerful denials; the negativity of the Jesus of *Paradise Regained* baffles Satan almost as much as it has puzzled modern readers.[4] Milton published these two poems together in 1671, followed them with a reissue of his shorter poems, with additions, in 1673, and with the revised twelve-book version of *Paradise Lost* in 1674, shortly before his death; he attempted thereby to give a final and definitive shape to his career. After years in which postponement had been the key to poetic production, and in which contingencies—whether political or personal—were constantly being made to serve as parts of a willed design, the poet finally delivered himself, complete. The opening lines of *Paradise Regained*, in a gesture reminiscent of the Virgil citation on the title-page of the 1645 *Poems*, refer back to *Paradise Lost* as if the earlier epic had been the pastoral prelude and this the epic fulfilment. Yet even *Paradise Regained* returns its hero home to await a deferred, if inevitable, destiny. Jesus and Samson are palpably versions of Milton, and it is through the latter that the poet at last delivered himself and his talent over to posterity, and to death—and to those subsequent revisions, of which Dryden's *State of Innocence* has served as a first example.

Early Critical Views: The Sublimity of Paradise Lost

Dryden's opera was never staged, however, and its appearance in print in 1677 seems to have made little impact. Unlike Restoration versions of Shakespeare plays, which claimed the stage for over a century, Dryden's operatic recasting of *Paradise Lost* did not replace the poem. But Dryden's engagement with Milton did have other consequences, most immediately for Dryden's style and his own epic ambitions, but perhaps more importantly for a long history of critical pronouncements, beginning with the preface to the *State of Innocence*, which praised Milton's epic as 'one of the greatest, most noble, and most sublime poems which

---

[4] For a noteworthy exception, see Stanley Fish's 'Things and Actions Indifferent: the Temptation to Plot in *Paradise Regained*', *Milton Studies*, 17 (1983).

either this age or nation has produced'.[5] Dryden laid down terms for discussing Milton that were rarely to be absent from criticism for at least a century afterwards.

Dryden's terms cannot be treated in isolation, and they are not simply stylistic comments. Consider, for example, his epigram on Milton that appeared beneath his portrait in the 1688 edition of *Paradise Lost*:

> Three poets, in three distant ages born,
> Greece, Italy, and England did adorn.
> The first in loftiness of thought surpassed,
> The next in majesty, in both the last:
> The force of Nature could no further go;
> To make a third, she joined the former two.

There are hesitations in this celebration of Milton's genius: to confirm his classic status, Dryden locates Milton in a past that seems as 'distant' as that of Homer and Virgil. This serves Dryden's conservative bias,-as does his inability to find new terms for Milton's epic; 'art' is never invoked, and 'Nature' takes its place. The reasons for this are not far to seek, and not merely as a response to the threat that Milton might have represented to Dryden's own art and aspirations. The new edition of *Paradise Lost* was appearing, after all, in the same year that the Stuarts once again had been removed from the throne; the Glorious Revolution reaffirmed Protestant England, and Milton's epic read differently in that context. (Indeed, Milton's final prose work, *Of True Religion* [1673], had attempted to capitalize on the emergent political situation.) Dryden's epigram, like *The State of Innocence*, attempts to assimilate the poem to his politics; its terms of a timeless 'loftiness' and 'majesty' were more fitting to the claims of James II and his Catholic Poet Laureate than to the reign of Parliament's choice, the Protestant William III— who would shortly replace Dryden as Poet Laureate with Thomas Shadwell, the rival excoriated in *MacFlecknoe*.

Dryden's critical estimation of *Paradise Lost* underwent revision even when subsequent critics seemed simply to repeat his terms. Dryden's claim of the poem's 'sublimity' offers a good example, for the shifting meanings of the term resituate the value of *Paradise Lost* in changing historical and social circumstances. The word is used by Addison in 1712 in a series of important essays in *The Spectator*. 'Milton's chief talent, and, indeed, his distinguishing excellence, lies in the sublimity

---

[5] W. P. Ker (ed.), *Essays of John Dryden*, 2 vols. (Oxford: Clarendon Press, 1900), i. 179.

of his thoughts', Addison writes.[6] Although Addison is as insistent as Dryden was in praising Milton's classicism, for him the poem is sublime and exceeds its 'pagan' models because there is nothing more elevating than its Christian subject. Whereas Dryden had associated sublimity with a classicism that safely distanced Milton's religious beliefs, for Addison it is Milton's 'thoughts' that are sublime. Dryden, on the other hand, had claimed that Milton's epic ran into 'a flat of thought' precisely when it got too close to scripture.[7] Addison reads in Milton a reflection of his own culture's normative Protestantism, and the classicism he finds in Milton is similarly regularized.

Johnson, in his account of Milton (in *Lives of the Poets*), appears to echo Addison: 'the characteristic quality of his poem is sublimity', he writes. It is not what is normative in the poem that engages Johnson, however, and the term sublimity is now attached to the imaginative power that grasped 'a subject on which too much could not be said'. Johnson stresses the ways in which Milton invents beyond the scope of his biblical and classical models; but he also notes the strain that the epic imposes upon the reader: '*Paradise Lost* is one of the books which the reader admires and lays down, and forgets to take up again. None ever wished it longer than it is.' Developing an observation of Addison's about Milton's style, 'our language sunk under him' (*Spectator* No. 297), Johnson declares that 'criticism sinks in admiration'. Milton oppresses with the weight of his capacious imagination: 'he crowds the imagination'.

Milton is valuable, and troubling, to Johnson, precisely for his individual imaginative powers. No longer safely assimilated to the socialized norms of classicism or Christianity, Milton is cast in a new model, one that might be characterized as proto-Romantic. Sublimity is still the word for this quite altered characterization. Johnson brilliantly describes the poem's violations of normative categories, its intermingling of the material and the spiritual, the figurative and the literal. But he also resists Milton, denigrating his politics and, in so far as he can, his poems (many of the early poems are treated dismissively). However, by the time that Coleridge wrote that 'sublimity is the pre-eminent characteristic of the *Paradise Lost*', that sentence, which sounds so like Dryden or the eighteenth-century critics, represents an almost entirely opposite judgement. Coleridge's sentence appears shortly after his characteriza-

---

[6] No. 279, 19 January 1712.
[7] See 'A Discourse concerning the Original and Progress of Satire', *Essays of John Dryden*, ii. 29.

tion of Satan as the image of 'a grandeur of sufferance, and a ruined splendour, which constitute the very height of poetic sublimity'.[8] With Coleridge one is close to Blake's famous estimation in *The Marriage of Heaven and Hell* that Milton 'was of the Devil's party without knowing it', or Shelley's remark in the *Defence of Poetry* that 'Milton's devil as a moral being is . . . far superior to his God'. Dryden, admittedly, had thought Satan the hero of *Paradise Lost*; but for him, that was one of the faults of the poem.[9]

Paradise Lost *in Our Times*

Commentary on *Paradise Lost* has often been directed at its style; but, as this brief survey of the changing implications of sublimity—or, indeed, as Dryden's desire to turn blank verse into rhyme might suggest—a great deal more is involved. Perhaps at no time has this been clearer than in the twentieth century, when the movement that came to be called modernism marked its modernity by the repudiation of Milton. 'Milton's dislodgment, in the past decade, after his two centuries of predominance, was effected with remarkably little fuss', F. R. Leavis in 1936 coolly opened a chapter on 'Milton's Verse' in *Revaluation*, a book that sought to redefine the canon of English literature. Leavis followed the lead provided by T. S. Eliot's 1921 essay, 'The Metaphysical Poets', in which Milton was made responsible for what Eliot termed the 'dissociation of sensibility'. Eliot argued that poets before Milton had unproblematically united thought and feeling, and that Milton had divided them, and in a style whose remoteness from living speech also implied a remoteness from felt experience. 'We dislike his verse', Leavis announced magisterially. Yet more than versification was involved, and from a number of perspectives. Leavis wrote in the early years of the institutionalization of English studies; his remarks were embroiled in academic politics; they were written in support of a canon revision that would have made Eliot the logical heir of the English tradition. But beyond that, the name 'Milton' summed up not merely all of English literature, but values which, in the hands of Tennyson or Matthew Arnold, had come to be associated with Victorian respectability. 'Milton is English', Arnold had intoned,[10] 'English' meaning both the

---

[8] James Thorpe (ed.), *Milton Criticism: Selections from Four Centuries* (New York: Octagon Books, 1966), 95.

[9] See 'Dedication of the Aeneis', *Essays*, ii. 165. Characteristically, as part of his normalization of Dryden's remarks, Addison had insisted that Jesus was the hero of the poem.

[10] *Essays in Criticism, Second Series* (London: Macmillan, 1898), 66.

language and the nation. For Leavis and Eliot, another sense of England was involved, one that harkened back to the Elizabethans and a supposedly more 'organic', pre-'dissociated' civilization. For all of Leavis's complaints about the ritualistic monotony and Latinate style of *Paradise Lost* as opposed to the 'sensuousness' of Shakespeare or Donne, or Eliot's insistence in his 1936 essay, 'Milton', that Milton had always been blind, the real complaint was that Milton had shattered a world that modernism sought to reassemble.

The most telling sign of this occurs in a footnote to 'In Defence of Milton', Leavis's response to those, like Sir Herbert Grierson or E. M. W. Tillyard, who had resisted the 'dislodgment' of Milton, and had implied that Leavis, not being a 'professional' Miltonist, was insufficiently versed in Milton's work: 'Perhaps I had better put it on record', Leavis wrote, 'that the pocket Milton I have referred to writing this essay is falling to pieces from use, and that it is the only book I carried steadily in my pocket between 1915 and 1919.'[11] Leavis's Milton had been carried as if a talisman for all the values brought to the Great War and shattered there. Leavis, however, was almost alone in his final anti-Miltonic essays; by then Eliot had followed his 1936 piece on Milton with a second one (in 1947) that partially recanted the first. If his initial revulsion from Milton had been motivated by his politics and religion, when Eliot came to embrace the established Church, he grudgingly found room for a fellow believer, even if Milton had been a radical Puritan.

Eliot's move was symptomatic of Milton criticism in the period after the Second World War. The defenders of Milton saw in him not only the humanism Leavis found in Shakespeare, but also those specifically Christian virtues that Eliot came to endorse. Thus Douglas Bush, an avowedly Christian humanist critic, argued, in a book significantly titled *Paradise Lost in Our Time* (1945), that Milton was the repository of timeless values necessary in the face of a collapsing world. Such critics were, surprisingly, joined in the celebration of Milton by their apparent opposites, the New Critics, who championed the close reading of poems. Although they were seemingly concerned only with poetic technique and linguistic analysis, their formalism raised works of art to the status of eternal artefacts, as the title of Cleanth Brooks's *The Well-Wrought Urn* (1947) suggests, and they assumed in Milton, without ever arguing it, a comfortable, if energetic Christianity. Brooks's volume includes an essay on 'The Light Symbolism in "L'Allegro" and "Il Penseroso"'; the companion poems are seen to balance and commingle light and dark in a

---

[11] *The Common Pursuit* (London: Chatto & Windus, 1952), 43, n. 1.

union of opposites which, it is claimed, exists on a symbolic level that foreshadows 'the celestial light' of *Paradise Lost*.[12] In 1952, Brooks and John Edward Hardy collaborated on a detailed study of Milton's 1645 *Poems* that included Brooks's earlier essay and extended its mode of analysis to the volume as a whole. The authors begin by dismissing Bush on Milton as 'an apologist for Christianity, for the humanist tradition, and sometimes merely for the genteel tradition'; similarly, C. S. Lewis's *Preface to Paradise Lost* is declared 'pure Anglo-Catholic apologetics'.[13] But to the discerning eye of William Empson, the most brilliant reader of Milton in the twentieth century, it was not difficult to recognize that post-war Milton criticism, whether nominally Christian-humanist or New Critical, represented a united front, which he called 'neo-Christianity'. It remains the prevailing mode of interpretation.

Empson had first written about Milton in *Some Versions of Pastoral* (1935), in an essay that took off from the annotations to *Paradise Lost* by its eighteenth-century editor, Richard Bentley. Bentley had balked at moments when the poem violated his sense of the discreteness of moral categories, differences between matter and spirit, the literal and the figurative. Empson, rather like Johnson, took these confusions seriously; they allowed him to recognize complexities in Milton that more monolithic readings of his sublimity had failed to notice. (Empson's insights were subsequently methodized in Christopher Ricks's *Milton's Grand Style* [1963], which provided a taxonomy of the varieties of Miltonic figuration.) In 1961, Empson published *Milton's God*, an assault on the ferocity of Christianity, and the consequent 'moral confusions' of *Paradise Lost* and their effects on poetic representation. For Empson, these signalled Milton's conflicted relationship to received belief. 'God is on trial', Empson wrote, quoting a sentence from one of Milton's Christian critics, but turning his argument on its head. 'You may still say, even after accepting this argument, that Milton does not make God come out of the trial as well as he should; and the poet could answer that it was not his immediate business to invent a new theology.'[14] Rather, in Empson's account, God was guilty of Satan's fall, and Eve, too, had been set up.

Empson's work still rankles those Miltonists bent on representing

---

[12] *The Well-Wrought Urn* (New York, 1947), 65.
[13] *Poems of Mr John Milton: The 1645 Edition with Essays in Analysis* (New York, 1952), iii.
[14] *Milton's God* (London: Chatto & Windus, 1961), 94. There are some powerful additions to Empson's book in its final 1981 edition, published by Cambridge University Press.

the poet as the repository of universal and benign Christian humanist values. But such views have been challenged. Stanley Fish's *Surprised by Sin* (1967), for example, explored the dilemmas imposed upon the reader of Milton's poem, insisting on the difficulties that must be faced to arrive at God's point of view. For Fish, as for Johnson, the reader is harassed by the poem. Johnson even more explicitly stands behind Harold Bloom's description of Milton in *A Map of Misreading* (1975), as a poet who so encompasses earlier literature as almost to forestall any imitators. Like Empson, Bloom (from *The Anxiety of Influence* on) has embraced Satan's strong misreading of the divine plan; Bloom, however, finds in it an epitome of the situation of the post-Miltonic poet. In his reversal of Eliot's and Leavis's history of English literature, Bloom has reaffirmed the canonical centrality of Milton, and made it inescapable. The influence of Milton, which Johnson had registered as a heavy weight, and which Leavis had thought pernicious, becomes, for Bloom, the site of an oedipal struggle among male poets that has defined English literary history.[15]

Such arguments forcefully recast the terrain of Milton criticism, redefining the poet and his epic, and its place in literary history. They make necessary the rethinking of many basic questions, about the nature of poetry, for example, or poetic influence, or about relationships between ideas and psychology, whether of the poet or his readers. These questions are congruent with those asked by critics writing in a more political vein to interrogate Milton's relationship to the foundations of modernity. In such criticism, Milton is seen less as the man who single-handedly changed literary history and more as someone fully embedded in larger upheavals that affected not only Milton's sense of himself, his politics, and his poems, but that also recast relationships between society and the individual. Many of these critics have been inspired by the work of Christopher Hill, who has aligned Milton's thought with that of some of the most radical Puritans of the period, and in *Milton and the English Revolution* (1977) read *Paradise Lost* as a virtual allegory of Milton's relationship to the Revolution. For such readers, the seventeenth-century 'dissociation of sensibility' must be re-understood. In literary terms, as in John Guillory's *Poetic Authority* (1983), it is seen as a conflicted moment in the secularization of the poetic imagination. For Francis Barker, in *The Tremulous Private*

---

[15] In a psychoanalytic reading inspired in part by Bloom, *The Sacred Complex* (1983), William Kerrigan returns such an oedipal reading to Milton's relationship to God.

Body (1984), Miltonic self-representation in *Areopagitica* is situated at the centre of a broad social and psychic transformation, and cannot be understood outside of the larger history, both of the times and of an emerging modern subjectivity.[16] Catherine Belsey, arguing that Milton's texts 'record and participate in the historical turning-point which marks the installation of the modern epoch', provides an excellent introduction to the issues implied in her title, *John Milton: Language, Gender, Power*.[17]

Under scrutiny in Belsey's account is the emergence of a peculiarly modern notion of the human, and her argument leads to the conclusion that Milton can no longer be taken uncritically as the poet of enduring values, for these are historically determined expressions of individual, male, middle-class prerogatives. Recent essays by such critics as Guillory and Mary Nyquist pursue the point, examining Milton's place within the history of the construction of gender and gender relations.[18] But because historical determinism does not 'end' the story, only situating Milton within histories that continue to communicate with contemporary understandings, whether of the issues Milton's texts engage, or of the place of literature in the apparatuses of culture, the question no longer is whether Milton belongs as a central figure in the English literary canon, but what the history of canon formation means, in what interests it has been formed and reformed. These questions start with a recognition that Milton's relationship to his writing is only the initial instance in a history of rewritings. What follows, as Nyquist and Margaret W. Ferguson conclude in their 'Preface' to *Re-membering Milton*, an anthology of recent criticism, should be 'a more engaged, as well as more theoretically and historically informed, critical literature on Milton'.[19]

[16] Similarly, in *Milton: A Study in Ideology and Form* (1986), Christopher Kendrick considers Milton's theology and formal choices in a materialist and psychoanalytic framework.

[17] Oxford, 1988, p. 8; the volume is in Terry Eagleton's *Rereading Literature* series.

[18] See John Guillory, 'Dalila's House: *Samson Agonistes* and the Sexual Division of Labor', in *Rewriting the Renaissance*, ed. Margaret W. Ferguson, Maureen Quilligan, and Nancy J. Vickers (Chicago: University of Chicago Press, 1986); 'The Father's House: *Samson Agonistes* in its Historical Moment', in *Re-membering Milton*, ed. Mary Nyquist and Margaret W. Ferguson (New York and London: Methuen, 1987); Mary Nyquist, 'Textual Overlapping and Dalilah's Harlot-lap', in *Literary Theory/Renaissance Texts*, ed. Patricia Parker and David Quint (Baltimore: Johns Hopkins University Press, 1986); 'Gynesis, Genesis, Exegesis, and the Formation of Milton's Eve', in *Cannibals, Witches, and Divorce: Estranging the Renaissance*, ed. Marjorie Garber (Baltimore: Johns Hopkins University Press, 1987); 'The Genesis of Gendered Subjectivity in the Divorce Tracts and in *Paradise Lost*', in *Re-membering Milton*.

[19] London: Methuen, 1987, p. xvi.

ACKNOWLEDGEMENTS

Like every editor of Milton, our greatest debt is to previous editors. In particular, the *Variorum Milton*, the editions of Merritt Y. Hughes, John Carey, and Alastair Fowler, and the relevant volumes of the great Yale Milton *Prose* have been our constant companions. Our work has been greatly assisted by Fellowships at the Humanities Research Centre of the Australian National University in Canberra, and at the J. Paul Getty Center in Santa Monica; we gratefully acknowledge the superlative working conditions, the hospitality of our hosts, and the opportunity to discuss Milton over an extended period with two distinguished groups of Fellows. For enlightenment on particular points we are indebted to Philip Brett, Ian Donaldson, J. Martin Evans, Marcie Frank, Stanley Fish, Christopher Highley, Robert Mandelbaum, Bradley Rubidge, and Gary Spear. John Shawcross deserves a sentence to himself for his invaluable assistance on bibliographical matters. The general editor has been an unfailingly helpful guide, and many of his suggestions have been silently incorporated. Finally, the care, goodwill, and especially the patience of Judith Luna at the Oxford University Press seem to us beyond praise.

CHRONOLOGY

1608   9 December: John Milton born in Cheapside, London, first son of John Milton, scrivener and musician, and his wife Sara.

c.1615/17–24   Attends St Paul's School, London.

1625   Enters Christ's College, Cambridge.

1626   Probably rusticated (suspended) from Cambridge for part of Lent term.

1629   BA.

1632   MA; Milton's first published poem, 'On Shakespeare', appears in the dedicatory verses to the second Shakespeare folio.

1632–4   Lives at the family home in Hammersmith.

1634   *A Masque Presented at Ludlow Castle* ('*Comus*') performed.

1635–8   Lives at the family's country house at Horton, Bucks.

1637   Death of Sara Milton. Milton's Cambridge contemporary Edward King drowned.

1638–9   Travels in Italy.

1638   Publication of *Lycidas* in a volume of elegies for Edward King. Milton's closest friend, Charles Diodati, dies in August and is memorialized in *Epitaphium Damonis*.

1639   Milton returns to England and lives and teaches in London.

1640   Long Parliament convened 3 November.

1641   Publication of Milton's first political tracts: *Of Reformation*, *Of Prelatical Episcopacy*, *Animadversions upon the Remonstrant's Defence against Smectymnuus*.

1642   Civil War begins 22 August. Publication of *The Reason of Church Government*, *Apology for Smectymnuus*. Milton marries Mary Powell, who soon after returns to her family.

1643   Publication of *The Doctrine and Discipline of Divorce*.

1644   *Of Education*, *The Judgement of Martin Bucer Concerning Divorce*, *Areopagitica*, and a revised and enlarged edition of *Doctrine and Discipline* published.

1645   Publication of *Tetrachordon* and *Colasterion*. Mary Powell Milton returns to live with Milton.

1646   *Poems of Mr John Milton* (dated 1645) published. Milton's daughter Anne born.

1647   Death of John Milton, Sen.

1648   Milton's daughter Mary born.

1649   King Charles executed. Publication of *The Tenure of Kings and Magistrates* and *Eikonoklastes*. Milton appointed Secretary for Foreign Tongues to the Council of State.

1651   Publication of *Defensio pro Populo Anglicano*. Milton's son John born.

1652   Milton becomes totally blind. His wife Mary dies after giving birth to their daughter Deborah. His son John dies.

1654   *Defensio Secunda* published. Cromwell becomes Protector.

1655   *Pro Se Defensio* published.

1656   Marries Katherine Woodcock.

1657   Birth of a daughter, who dies six months later.

1658   Death of Katherine Woodcock Milton. Death of Cromwell.

1659   Publication of *A Treatise of Civil Power* and *Considerations touching the Likeliest Means to Remove Hirelings out of the Church*.

1660   Publication of *The Ready and Easy Way to Establish a Free Commonwealth*. Charles II enters London. Milton arrested and imprisoned; released some months later.

1663   Marries Elizabeth Minshull.

1667   *Paradise Lost* published in a ten-book version.

1670   *The History of Britain* published.

1671   *Paradise Regained* and *Samson Agonistes* published.

1673   Revised and enlarged edition of *Poems* (1645) published. *Of True Religion* published.

1674   *Paradise Lost* published in a twelve-book version. Milton dies 8 November.

NOTE ON THE TEXT

MODERNIZATION of Milton's spelling has been carried out according to the principles established by Stanley Wells in *Modernizing Shakespeare's Spelling* (Oxford, 1979). This has meant a loss of quaintness—e.g., sovran, quire, and faery have become sovereign, choir, and fairy—but it is hoped that most readers will agree with us that Milton in his own time was not quaint. In the spelling of proper names, an uneasy compromise has been attempted. Where the modern spelling leaves pronunciation and rhythm unaffected, we have modernized; but Milton's biblical names are those of the Latin Bible, not the Authorized Version, and his geography cannot be brought up to date. Hence we retain Dalila, Fesole, Rhene, Danaw, but we use Moloch (not Moloc), Moscow (not Mosco), Astrakhan (not Astracan). In general, the sound of English has changed so much since Milton's time that it has seemed pointless, if not positively misleading, to retain old spellings merely because they seem to preserve a particular Miltonic pronunciation. Punctuation is a more complex matter, and one to which Milton paid careful attention. His practice is not entirely consistent, but to modernize it is to lose not only a good deal of rhetorical force, but often his most individual syntax. Here again, the language has changed, and grammatical structures that were possible, and even commonplace, in the seventeenth century are now solecisms. For example, a question mark does not invariably indicate the end of a sentence for Milton; to capitalize the lower-case word following the question mark, as most modern editors routinely do, constitutes a grammatical change. In general, we have undertaken to alter the original punctuation only when it seemed patently incorrect or when not to modernize it would be confusing or misleading. We have not attempted to produce a Milton in modern syntax.

In our arrangement of the poems, we have undertaken to follow the order established by Milton himself, in so far as it was feasible to do so, rather than the arrangement according to dates of composition, often putative, usual in modern editions. We have undertaken, that is, to present Milton as he presented himself, feeling that this is an essential element in understanding his career. We have, therefore, kept the 1645 *Poems* together as a unit, and have in most instances preferred its readings to those of the 1673 text, which editorial opinion has generally considered less authoritative. In the case of the *Ode on the Morning of*

Christ's Nativity, however, the 1673 text includes revisions that are clearly authorial, and therefore that is the text we have followed (the variants are given in the notes). For the text of *A Masque* (*Comus*), we have been persuaded by the editorial argument most forcefully maintained by John Shawcross that the 1673 revision of lines 166–9 is unlikely to be Milton's, and we have therefore retained the 1645 reading. Poems added in the 1673 edition, and the few uncollected poems, have been placed after the 1645 poems, though it has seemed sensible to keep the English and Latin poems separate so that the 1673 English poems here follow the 1645 English poems rather than the Latin poems, which conclude the 1645 volume. We have not included Milton's occasional translations from the classics found in the prose works.

The degree sign (°) indicates a note at the end of the book. More general headnotes are not cued.

Letter to a Friend (?1633)

Sir,

Besides that in sundry other respects I must acknowledge me to profit by you whenever we meet, you are often to me, and were yesterday especially, as a good watchman° to admonish that the hours of the night pass on (for so I call my life, as yet obscure and unserviceable to mankind), and that the day with me is at hand wherein Christ commands all to labour while there is light. Which because I am persuaded you do to no other purpose than out of a true desire that God should be honoured in everyone, I therefore think myself bound, though unasked, to give you account, as oft as occasion is, of this my tardy moving, according to the precept of my conscience, which I firmly trust is not without God. Yet now I will not strain for any set apology,° but only refer myself to what my mind shall have at any time to declare herself at her best ease.

But if you think, as you said, that too much love of learning is in fault, and that I have given up myself to dream away my years in the arms of studious retirement like Endymion° with the moon, as the tale of Latmos goes, yet consider that if it were no more but the mere love of learning, whether it proceed from a principle bad, good, or natural, it could not have held out thus long against so strong opposition on the other side of every kind; for if it be bad, why should not all the fond° hopes that forward youth and vanity are fledge° with, together with gain, pride and ambition, call me forward more powerfully than a poor, regardless° and unprofitable sin of curiosity° should be able to withold me, whereby a man cuts himself off from all action, and becomes the most helpless, pusillanimous and unweaponed creature in the world, the most unfit and unable to do that which all mortals most aspire to, either to defend and be useful to his friends, or to offend his enemies? Or if it be to be thought a natural proneness, there is against it a much more potent inclination inbred which about this time of a man's life solicits most, the desire of house and family of his own, to which nothing is esteemed more helpful than the early entering into credible employment, and nothing more hindering than this affected solitariness; and though this were enough, yet there is to this another act if not of pure, yet of refined nature, no less available to dissuade prolonged obscurity: a desire of honour and repute and immortal fame seated in the breast of every true scholar, which all make haste to by the readiest ways of publishing and divulging conceived merits, as well those°

that shall as those that never shall obtain it—nature therefore would presently° work the more prevalent way if there were nothing but the inferior bent° of herself to restrain her.

Lastly, this love of learning, as it is the pursuit of something good, it would sooner follow the more excellent and supreme good known and presented, and so be quickly diverted from the empty and fantastic chase of shadows and notions to the solid good flowing from due and timely obedience to that command in the gospel set out by the terrible seizing of him that hid the talent.° It is more probable, therefore, that not the endless delight of speculation but this very consideration of that great commandment does not press forward as soon as may be to undergo, but keeps off with a sacred reverence and religious advisement how best to undergo, not taking thought of being late so it give advantage to be more fit; for those that were latest lost nothing when the master of the vineyard° came to give each one his hire. And here I am come to a stream-head copious° enough to disburden itself like Nilus° at seven mouths into an ocean; but then I should also run into a reciprocal contradiction of ebbing and flowing at once, and do that which I excuse myself for not doing, preach and not preach. Yet that you may see that I am something suspicious of myself, and do take notice of a certain belatedness in me, I am the bolder to send you some of my nightward thoughts some while since (because they come in not altogether unfitly) made up in a Petrarchan stanza, which I told you of.

[Sonnet 7 was included here.]

By this I believe you may well repent of having made mention at all of this matter; for if I have not all this while won you to this, I have certainly wearied you to it. This therefore alone may be a sufficient reason for me to keep me as I am, lest having thus tired you singly, I should deal worse with a whole congregation, and spoil all the patience of a parish; for I myself do not only see my own tediousness, but now grow offended with it that has hindered me thus long from coming to the last and best period° of my letter, and that which must now chiefly work my pardon, that I am

Your true and unfeigned friend.

POEMS 1645

On the Morning of Christ's Nativity

I

This is the month, and this the happy morn
Wherein the son of heaven's eternal king,
Of wedded maid, and virgin mother born,
Our great redemption from above did bring;
For so the holy sages once did sing,°
   That he our deadly forfeit should release,°
And with his father work us a perpetual peace.

II

That glorious form, that light unsufferable,°
And that far-beaming blaze of majesty,
Wherewith he wont at heaven's high council-table,°   10
To sit the midst of trinal unity,°
He laid aside; and here with us to be,
   Forsook the courts of everlasting day,
And chose with us a darksome house of mortal clay.°

III

Say heavenly muse, shall not thy sacred vein°
Afford a present to the infant God?°
Hast thou no verse, no hymn, or solemn strain,
To welcome him to this his new abode,
Now while the heaven by the sun's team untrod,°
   Hath took no print of the approaching light,   20
And all the spangled host keep watch in squadrons bright?°

IV

See how from far upon the eastern road
The star-led wizards haste with odours sweet,°
O run, prevent them with thy humble ode,°

And lay it lowly at his blessèd feet;
Have thou the honour first thy Lord to greet,
    And join thy voice unto the angel choir,
From out his secret altar touched with hallowed fire.°

The Hymn

I

It was the winter wild,
While the heaven-born-child   30
    All meanly wrapped in the rude manger lies;
Nature in awe to him
Had doffed her gaudy trim,
    With her great master so to sympathize:
It was no season then for her
To wanton with the sun her lusty paramour.°

II

Only with speeches fair
She woos the gentle air
    To hide her guilty front with innocent snow,°
And on her naked shame,   40
Pollute with sinful blame,°
    The saintly veil of maiden white to throw,°
Confounded, that her maker's eyes
Should look so near upon her foul deformities.

III

But he her fears to cease,°
Sent down the meek-eyed Peace,
    She crowned with olive green, came softly sliding°
Down through the turning sphere°
His ready harbinger,
    With turtle wing the amorous clouds dividing,°   50
And waving wide her myrtle wand,°
She strikes a universal peace through sea and land.

IV

No war, or battle's sound
Was heard the world around
    The idle spear and shield were high up hung,

The hookèd chariot stood°
Unstained with hostile blood,
  The trumpet spake not to the armèd throng,
And kings sat still with awful eye,°
As if they surely knew their sovereign Lord was by.   60

V

But peaceful was the night
Wherein the prince of light
  His reign of peace upon the earth began:
The winds with wonder whist,°
Smoothly the waters kissed,
  Whispering new joys to the mild ocean,
Who now hath quite forgot to rave,
While birds of calm sit brooding on the charmèd wave.°

VI

The stars with deep amaze
Stand fixed in steadfast gaze,   70
  Bending one way their precious influence,°
And will not take their flight,
For all the morning light,°
  Or Lucifer that often warned them thence;°
But in their glimmering orbs did glow,
Until their Lord himself bespake, and bid them go.

VII

And though the shady gloom
Had given day her room,°
  The sun himself withheld his wonted speed,
And hid his head for shame,   80
As his inferior flame,°
  The new enlightened world no more should need;
He saw a greater sun appear
Than his bright throne, or burning axle-tree could bear.°

VIII

The shepherds on the lawn,
Or ere the point of dawn,°
  Sat simply chatting in a rustic row;

Full little thought they then,
That the mighty Pan°
   Was kindly come to live with them below;°   90
Perhaps their loves, or else their sheep,
Was all that did their silly thoughts so busy keep.°

IX

When such music sweet
Their hearts and ears did greet,
   As never was by mortal finger strook,°
Divinely-warbled voice
Answering the stringèd noise,
   As all their souls in blissful rapture took:
The air such pleasure loth to lose,
With thousand echoes still prolongs each heavenly close.°   100

X

Nature that heard such sound
Beneath the hollow round
   Of Cynthia's seat, the airy region thrilling,°
Now was almost won°
To think her part was done,
   And that her reign had here its last fulfilling;
She knew such harmony alone
Could hold all heaven and earth in happier union.

XI

At last surrounds their sight
A globe of circular light,   110
   That with long beams the shamefaced night arrayed,
The helmèd cherubim
And sworded seraphim,°
   Are seen in glittering ranks with wings displayed,
Harping in loud and solemn choir,
With unexpressive notes to heaven's newborn heir.°

XII

Such music (as 'tis said)
Before was never made,
   But when of old the sons of morning sung,

While the creator great   120
His constellations set,°
And the well-balanced world on hinges hung,°
And cast the dark foundations deep,
And bid the welt'ring waves their oozy channel keep.°

XIII

Ring out, ye crystal spheres,
Once bless our human ears
  (If ye have power to touch our senses so),°
And let your silver chime
Move in melodious time;
  And let the base of heaven's deep organ blow,°   130
And with your ninefold harmony°
Make up full consort to the angelic symphony.°

XIV

For if such holy song
Enwrap our fancy long,
  Time will run back, and fetch the age of gold,°
And speckled vanity°
Will sicken soon and die,
  And lep'rous sin will melt from earthly mould,
And hell itself will pass away,
And leave her dolorous mansions to the peering day.°   140

XV

Yea Truth, and Justice then°
Will down return to men,
  Orbed in a rainbow; and like glories wearing
Mercy will sit between,°
Throned in celestial sheen,
  With radiant feet the tissued clouds down steering,°
And heaven as at some festival,°
Will open wide the gates of her high palace hall.

XVI

But wisest fate says no,
This must not yet be so,   150
  The babe lies yet in smiling infancy,

That on the bitter cross
Must redeem our loss;
   So both himself and us to glorify:
Yet first to those ychained in sleep,°
The wakeful trump of doom must thunder through the deep.

XVII

With such a horrid clang
As on Mount Sinai rang
   While the red fire, and smould'ring clouds out brake:
The agèd earth aghast   160
With terror of that blast,
   Shall from the surface to the centre shake;
When at the world's last session,°
The dreadful judge in middle air shall spread his throne.°

XVIII

And then at last our bliss
Full and perfect is,
   But now begins; for from this happy day
The old dragon underground°
In straiter limits bound,
   Not half so far casts his usurpèd sway,   170
And wroth to see his kingdom fail,
Swinges the scaly horror of his folded tail.°

XIX

The oracles are dumb,°
No voice or hideous hum
   Runs through the archèd roof in words deceiving.
Apollo from his shrine
Can no more divine,
   With hollow shriek the steep of Delphos leaving.°
No nightly trance, or breathèd spell,
Inspires the pale-eyed priest from the prophetic cell.   180

XX

The lonely mountains o'er,
And the resounding shore,
   A voice of weeping heard, and loud lament;

From haunted spring, and dale
Edged with poplar pale,
  The parting genius is with sighing sent,°
With flower-inwoven tresses torn
The nymphs in twilight shade of tangled thickets mourn.

XXI

In consecrated earth,
And on the holy hearth,   190
  The lars, and lemures moan with midnight plaint,°
In urns, and altars round,
A drear and dying sound
  Affrights the flamens at their service quaint;°
And the chill marble seems to sweat,
While each peculiar power forgoes his wonted seat.°

XXII

Peor, and Baalim,°
Forsake their temples dim,
  With that twice battered god of Palestine,°
And moonèd Ashtaroth,°   200
Heaven's queen and mother both,
  Now sits not girt with tapers' holy shine,
The Libyc Hammon shrinks his horn,°
In vain the Tyrian maids their wounded Thammuz mourn.°

XXIII

And sullen Moloch fled,°
Hath left in shadows dread,
  His burning idol all of blackest hue;
In vain with cymbals' ring,
They call the grisly king,
  In dismal dance about the furnace blue;   210
The brutish gods of Nile as fast,°
Isis and Orus, and the dog Anubis haste.°

XXIV

Nor is Osiris seen
In Memphian grove, or green,
  Trampling the unshowered grass with lowings loud:

Nor can he be at rest
Within his sacred chest,
   Nought but profoundest hell can be his shroud,°
In vain with timbrelled anthems dark
The sable-stolèd sorcerers bear his worshipped ark.°   220

XXV

He feels from Judah's land
The dreaded infant's hand,
   The rays of Bethlehem blind his dusky eyn;°
Nor all the gods beside,
Longer dare abide,
   Not Typhon huge ending in snaky twine:°
Our babe to show his Godhead true,
Can in his swaddling bands control the damnèd crew.

XXVI

So when the sun in bed,
Curtained with cloudy red,   230
   Pillows his chin upon an orient wave,°
The flocking shadows pale,
Troop to the infernal jail,
   Each fettered ghost slips to his several grave,
And the yellow-skirted fays,
Fly after the night-steeds, leaving their moon-loved maze.°

XXVII

But see the virgin blest,
Hath laid her babe to rest.
   Time is our tedious song should here have ending:°
Heaven's youngest teemèd star,°   240
Hath fixed her polished car,
   Her sleeping Lord with handmaid lamp attending:
And all about the courtly stable,
Bright-harnessed angels sit in order serviceable.°

A Paraphrase on Psalm 114

When the blest seed of Terah's faithful son,°
After long toil their liberty had won,

And passed from Pharian fields to Canaan land,°
Led by the strength of the Almighty's hand,
Jehovah's wonders were in Israel shown,
His praise and glory was in Israel known.
That saw the troubled sea, and shivering fled,
And sought to hide his froth-becurlèd head
Low in the earth, Jordan's clear streams recoil,
As a faint host that hath received the foil.°   10
The high, huge-bellied mountains skip like rams
Amongst their ewes, the little hills like lambs.
Why fled the ocean? And why skipped the mountains?
Why turnèd Jordan toward his crystal fountains?
Shake earth, and at the presence be aghast
Of him that ever was, and ay shall last,
That glassy floods from rugged rocks can crush,
And make soft rills from fiery flint-stones gush.

Psalm 136

Let us with a gladsome mind
Praise the Lord, for he is kind,
    For his mercies ay endure,°
    Ever faithful, ever sure.

Let us blaze his name abroad,
For of gods he is the God;
    For, &c.

O let us his praises tell,
Who doth the wrathful tyrants quell.   10
    For, &c.

That with his miracles doth make
Amazèd heaven and earth to shake.
    For, &c.

That by his wisdom did create
The painted heavens so full of state.°
    For, &c.   20

That did the solid earth ordain
To rise above the watery plain.
    For, &c.

That by his all-commanding might,
Did fill the new-made world with light.
   For, &c.

And caused the golden-tressèd sun,
All the day long his course to run.   30
   For, &c.

The hornèd moon to shine by night,
Amongst her spangled sisters bright.
   For, &c.

He with his thunder-clasping hand,
Smote the first-born of Egypt land.
   For, &c.   40

And in despite of Pharaoh fell,°
He brought from thence his Israel.
   For, &c.

The ruddy waves he cleft in twain,
Of the Erythraean main.°
   For, &c.

The floods stood still like walls of glass,
While the Hebrew bands did pass.   50
   For, &c.

But full soon they did devour
The tawny king with all his power.
   For, &c.

His chosen people he did bless
In the wasteful wilderness.
   For, &c.   60

In bloody battle he brought down
Kings of prowess and renown.
   For, &c.

He foiled bold Seon and his host,°
That ruled the Amorean coast.
   For, &c.

And large-limbed Og he did subdue,°
With all his over-hardy crew.   70
   For, &c.

And to his servant Israel,°
He gave their land therein to dwell.
   For, &c.

He hath with a piteous eye
Beheld us in our misery.
   For, &c.   80

And freed us from the slavery
Of the invading enemy.
   For, &c.

All living creatures he doth feed,
And with full hand supplies their need.
   For, &c.

Let us therefore warble forth
His mighty majesty and worth.
   For, &c.   90

That his mansion hath on high
Above the reach of mortal eye.
   For his mercies ay endure,
   Ever faithful, ever sure.

The Passion

I

Erewhile of music, and ethereal mirth,°
Wherewith the stage of air and earth did ring,
And joyous news of heavenly infant's birth,
My muse with angels did divide to sing;°
But headlong joy is ever on the wing,
   In wintry solstice like the shortened light
Soon swallowed up in dark and long out-living night.

II

For now to sorrow must I tune my song,
And set my harp to notes of saddest woe,

Which on our dearest Lord did seize ere long,   10
Dangers, and snares, and wrongs, and worse than so,
Which he for us did freely undergo.
    Most perfect hero, tried in heaviest plight
Of labours huge and hard, too hard for human wight.°

III

He sovereign priest stooping his regal head°
That dropped with odorous oil down his fair eyes,
Poor fleshly tabernacle enterèd,°
His starry front low-roofed beneath the skies;°
O what a mask was there, what a disguise!
    Yet more; the stroke of death he must abide,   20
Then lies him meekly down fast by his brethren's side.

IV

These later scenes confine my roving verse,°
To this horizon is my Phoebus bound,°
His godlike acts, and his temptations fierce,
And former sufferings otherwhere are found;
Loud o'er the rest Cremona's trump doth sound;°
    Me softer airs befit, and softer strings
Of lute, or viol still, more apt for mournful things.°

V

Befriend me night best patroness of grief,
Over the pole thy thickest mantle throw,°   30
And work my flattered fancy to belief,
That heaven and earth are coloured with my woe;
My sorrows are too dark for day to know:
    The leaves should all be black whereon I write,
And letters where my tears have washed a wannish white.°

VI

See see the chariot, and those rushing wheels,
That whirled the prophet up at Chebar flood,
My spirit some transporting cherub feels,
To bear me where the towers of Salem stood,°
Once glorious towers, now sunk in guiltless blood;   40
    There doth my soul in holy vision sit
In pensive trance, and anguish, and ecstatic fit.

VII

Mine eye hath found that sad sepulchral rock°
That was the casket of heaven's richest store,
And here though grief my feeble hands up lock,
Yet on the softened quarry would I score°
My plaining verse as lively as before;°
   For sure so well instructed are my tears,
That they would fitly fall in ordered characters.°

VIII

Or should I thence hurried on viewless wing,°   50
Take up a weeping on the mountains wild,
The gentle neighbourhood of grove and spring
Would soon unbosom all their echoes mild,
And I (for grief is easily beguiled)
   Might think the infection of my sorrows loud,
Had got a race of mourners on some pregnant cloud.°

This subject the author finding to be above the years he had when he wrote it, and nothing satisfied with what was begun, left it unfinished.

On Time

Fly envious Time, till thou run out thy race,
Call on the lazy leaden-stepping hours,
Whose speed is but the heavy plummet's pace;°
And glut thyself with what thy womb devours,°
Which is no more than what is false and vain,
And merely mortal dross;
So little is our loss,
So little is thy gain.
For whenas each thing bad thou hast entombed,°
And last of all, thy greedy self consumed,   10
Then long eternity shall greet our bliss
With an individual kiss;°
And joy shall overtake us as a flood,
When everything that is sincerely good
And perfectly divine,
With truth, and peace, and love shall ever shine
About the supreme throne
Of him, t' whose happy-making sight alone,°

When once our heavenly-guided soul shall climb,
Then all this earthy grossness quit,°   20
Attired with stars, we shall for ever sit,
   Triumphing over Death, and Chance, and thee O Time.

Upon the Circumcision

Ye flaming powers, and wingèd warriors bright,°
That erst with music, and triumphant song°
First heard by happy watchful shepherds' ear,
So sweetly sung your joy the clouds along
Through the soft-silence of the listening night;
Now mourn, and if sad share with us to bear
Your fiery essence can distil no tear,
Burn in your sighs, and borrow
Seas wept from our deep sorrow,
He who with all heaven's heraldry whilere°   10
Entered the world, now bleeds to give us ease;
Alas, how soon our sin
   Sore doth begin
     His infancy to seize!
O more exceeding love or law more just?
Just law indeed, but more exceeding love!
For we by rightful doom remediless°
Were lost in death, till he that dwelt above
High-throned in secret bliss, for us frail dust°
Emptied his glory, even to nakedness;   20
And that great cov'nant which we still transgress°
Entirely satisfied,
And the full wrath beside
Of vengeful justice bore for our excess,
And seals obedience first with wounding smart
This day, but O ere long
Huge pangs and strong
     Will pierce more near his heart.°

At a Solemn Music

Blest pair of sirens, pledges of heaven's joy,°
Sphere-born harmonious sisters, Voice, and Verse,°
Wed your divine sounds, and mixed power employ
Dead things with inbreathed sense able to pierce,
And to our high-raised fantasy present,°
That undisturbèd song of pure concent,°
Ay sung before the sapphire-coloured throne°
To him that sits thereon
With saintly shout, and solemn jubilee,
Where the bright seraphim in burning row   10
Their loud uplifted angel trumpets blow,
And the cherubic host in thousand choirs
Touch their immortal harps of golden wires,
With those just spirits that wear victorious palms,°
Hymns devout and holy psalms
Singing everlastingly;
That we on earth with undiscording voice°
May rightly answer that melodious noise;
As once we did, till disproportioned sin
Jarred against nature's chime, and with harsh din   20
Broke the fair music that all creatures made
To their great Lord, whose love their motion swayed
In perfect diapason, whilst they stood°
In first obedience, and their state of good.
Oh may we soon again renew that song,
And keep in tune with heaven, till God ere long
To his celestial consort us unite,°
To live with him, and sing in endless morn of light.

An Epitaph on the Marchioness of Winchester

This rich marble doth inter°
The honoured wife of Winchester,
A viscount's daughter, an earl's heir,°
Besides what her virtues fair
Added to her noble birth,
More than she could own from earth.

Summers three times eight save one
She had told, alas too soon,°
After so short time of breath,
To house with darkness, and with death.   10
Yet had the number of her days
Been as complete as was her praise,
Nature and fate had had no strife
In giving limit to her life.
Her high birth, and her graces sweet,
Quickly found a lover meet;°
The virgin choir for her request°
The god that sits at marriage-feast;°
He at their invoking came
But with a scarce-well-lighted flame;   20
And in his garland as he stood,
Ye might discern a cypress bud.
Once had the early matrons run°
To greet her of a lovely son,°
And now with second hope she goes,
And calls Lucina to her throes;°
But whether by mischance or blame°
Atropos for Lucina came;°
And with remorseless cruelty,
Spoiled at once both fruit and tree: 30
The hapless babe before his birth
Had burial, yet not laid in earth,
And the languished mother's womb
Was not long a living tomb.
So have I seen some tender slip°
Saved with care from winter's nip,
The pride of her carnation train,°
Plucked up by some unheedy swain,
Who only thought to crop the flower
New shot up from vernal shower;   40
But the fair blossom hangs the head
Sideways as on a dying bed,
And those pearls of dew she wears,
Prove to be presaging tears
Which the sad morn had let fall
On her hastening funeral.
Gentle lady may thy grave

Peace and quiet ever have;
After this thy travail sore°
Sweet rest seize thee evermore,°   50
That to give the world increase,
Shortened hast thy own life's lease;
Here, besides the sorrowing
That thy noble house doth bring,
Here be tears of perfect moan
Wept for thee in Helicon,°
And some flowers, and some bays,°
For thy hearse to strew the ways,
Sent thee from the banks of Came,°
Devoted to thy virtuous name;   60
Whilst thou bright saint high sit'st in glory,
Next her much like to thee in story,
That fair Syrian shepherdess,°
Who after years of barrenness,
The highly favoured Joseph bore
To him that served for her before,°
And at her next birth much like thee,
Through pangs fled to felicity,
Far within the bosom bright
Of blazing majesty and light,   70
There with thee, new welcome saint,
Like fortunes may her soul acquaint,
With thee there clad in radiant sheen,
No marchioness, but now a queen.

Song. On May Morning

Now the bright morning star, day's harbinger,°
Comes dancing from the east, and leads with her
The flowery May, who from her green lap throws
The yellow cowslip, and the pale primrose.
  Hail bounteous May that dost inspire
  Mirth and youth and warm desire,
  Woods and groves are of thy dressing,
  Hill and dale doth boast thy blessing.
Thus we salute thee with our early song,
And welcome thee, and wish thee long.   10

On Shakespeare. 1630

What needs my Shakespeare for his honoured bones,
The labour of an age in pilèd stones,
Or that his hallowed relics should be hid
Under a star-ypointing pyramid?°
Dear son of memory, great heir of fame,
What need'st thou such weak witness of thy name?
Thou in our wonder and astonishment
Hast built thyself a live-long monument.
For whilst to th' shame of slow-endeavouring art,
Thy easy numbers flow, and that each heart°   10
Hath from the leaves of thy unvalued book,°
Those Delphic lines with deep impression took,°
Then thou our fancy of itself bereaving,
Dost make us marble with too much conceiving;°
And so sepulchred in such pomp dost lie,
That kings for such a tomb would wish to die.

On the University Carrier

WHO SICKENED IN THE TIME OF HIS VACANCY, BEING FORBID TO GO TO LONDON, BY REASON OF THE PLAGUE

Here lies old Hobson, Death hath broke his girt,°
And here alas, hath laid him in the dirt,
Or else the ways being foul, twenty to one,
He's here stuck in a slough, and overthrown.
'Twas such a shifter, that if truth were known,°
Death was half glad when he had got him down;
For he had any time this ten years full,
Dodged with him, betwixt Cambridge and the Bull.°
And surely, Death could never have prevailed,
Had not his weekly course of carriage failed;   10
But lately finding him so long at home,°
And thinking now his journey's end was come,
And that he had ta'en up his latest inn,°
In the kind office of a chamberlain°
Showed him his room where he must lodge that night,
Pulled off his boots, and took away the light:

If any ask for him, it shall be said,
Hobson has supped, and 's newly gone to bed.

Another on the Same

Here lieth one who did most truly prove,
That he could never die while he could move,
So hung his destiny never to rot
While he might still jog on and keep his trot,°
Made of sphere-metal, never to decay°
Until his revolution was at stay.°
Time numbers motion, yet (without a crime°
'Gainst old truth) motion numbered out his time:
And like an engine moved with wheel and weight,°
His principles being ceased, he ended straight,°   10
Rest that gives all men life, gave him his death,
And too much breathing put him out of breath,°
Nor were it contradiction to affirm
Too long vacation hastened on his term.°
Merely to drive the time away he sickened,
Fainted, and died, nor would with ale be quickened;°
Nay, quoth he, on his swooning bed outstretched,
If I may not carry, sure I'll ne'er be fetched,°
But vow though the cross doctors all stood hearers,°
For one carrier put down to make six bearers.°   20
Ease was his chief disease, and to judge right,
He died for heaviness that his cart went light,°
His leisure told him that his time was come,
And lack of load made his life burdensome,
That even to his last breath (there be that say't)
As he were pressed to death, he cried more weight;°
But had his doings lasted as they were,
He had been an immortal carrier.
Obedient to the moon he spent his date
In course reciprocal, and had his fate°   30
Linked to the mutual flowing of the seas,
Yet (strange to think) his wain was his increase:°
His letters are delivered all and gone,
Only remains this superscription.°

L'Allegro

Hence loathèd Melancholy°
  Of Cerberus, and blackest Midnight born,
In Stygian cave forlorn°
  'Mongst horrid shapes, and shrieks, and sights unholy,
Find out some uncouth cell,°
  Where brooding Darkness spreads his jealous wings,
And the night-raven sings;
  There under ebon shades, and low-browed rocks,
As ragged as thy locks,
  In dark Cimmerian desert ever dwell.°   10
But come thou goddess fair and free,
In heaven yclept Euphrosyne,°
And by men, heart-easing Mirth,
Whom lovely Venus at a birth
With two sister Graces more
To ivy-crownèd Bacchus bore;
Or whether (as some sager sing)°
The frolic wind that breathes the spring,
Zephyr with Aurora playing,°
As he met her once a-Maying,   20
There on beds of violets blue,
And fresh-blown roses washed in dew,
Filled her with thee a daughter fair,
So buxom, blithe, and debonair.°
Haste thee nymph, and bring with thee
Jest and youthful jollity,
Quips and cranks, and wanton wiles,°
Nods, and becks, and wreathèd smiles,°
Such as hang on Hebe's cheek,°
And love to live in dimple sleek;   30
Sport that wrinkled Care derides,
And Laughter holding both his sides.
Come, and trip it as ye go
On the light fantastic toe,°
And in thy right hand lead with thee,
The mountain nymph, sweet Liberty;
And if I give thee honour due,
Mirth, admit me of thy crew

To live with her, and live with thee,°
In unreprovèd pleasures free;° 40
To hear the lark begin his flight,°
And singing startle the dull night,
From his watch-tower in the skies,
Till the dappled dawn doth rise;
Then to come in spite of sorrow,
And at my window bid good morrow,°
Through the sweet-briar, or the vine,
Or the twisted eglantine.
While the cock with lively din,°
Scatters the rear of darkness thin,° 50
And to the stack, or the barn door,°
Stoutly struts his dames before,
Oft list'ning how the hounds and horn
Cheerly rouse the slumb'ring morn,
From the side of some hoar hill,°
Through the high wood echoing shrill.
Sometime walking not unseen
By hedgerow elms, on hillocks green,
Right against the eastern gate,
Where the great sun begins his state,° 60
Robed in flames, and amber light,
The clouds in thousand liveries dight,°
While the ploughman near at hand,
Whistles o'er the furrowed land,
And the milkmaid singeth blithe,
And the mower whets his scythe,
And every shepherd tells his tale°
Under the hawthorn in the dale.
Straight mine eye hath caught new pleasures
Whilst the landscape round it measures, 70
Russet lawns, and fallows grey,°
Where the nibbling flocks do stray,
Mountains on whose barren breast
The labouring clouds do often rest:
Meadows trim with daisies pied,°
Shallow brooks, and rivers wide,
Towers, and battlements it sees
Bosomed high in tufted trees,
Where perhaps some beauty lies,

The cynosure of neighbouring eyes.°   80
Hard by, a cottage chimney smokes,
From betwixt two agèd oaks,
Where Corydon and Thyrsis met,
Are at their savoury dinner set
Of herbs, and other country messes,°
Which the neat-handed Phyllis dresses;
And then in haste her bower she leaves,
With Thestylis to bind the sheaves;°
Or if the earlier season lead
To the tanned haycock in the mead,   90
Sometimes with secure delight°
The upland hamlets will invite,°
When the merry bells ring round,
And the jocund rebecks sound°
To many a youth, and many a maid,
Dancing in the chequered shade;
And young and old come forth to play
On a sunshine holiday,°
Till the livelong daylight fail,
Then to the spicy nut-brown ale,   100
With stories told of many a feat,
How fairy Mab the junkets eat,°
She was pinched, and pulled she said,
And he by friar's lantern led°
Tells how the drudging goblin sweat,°
To earn his cream-bowl duly set,
When in one night, ere glimpse of morn,
His shadowy flail hath threshed the corn,
That ten day-labourers could not end;
Then lies him down the lubber fiend.°   110
And stretched out all the chimney's length,°
Basks at the fire his hairy strength;
And crop-full out of doors he flings,°
Ere the first cock his matin rings.
Thus done the tales, to bed they creep,
By whispering winds soon lulled asleep.
Towered cities please us then,
And the busy hum of men,
Where throngs of knights and barons bold,
In weeds of peace high triumphs hold,°   120

With store of ladies, whose bright eyes°
Rain influence, and judge the prize°
Of wit, or arms, while both contend
To win her grace, whom all commend.
There let Hymen oft appear°
In saffron robe, with taper clear,°
And pomp, and feast, and revelry,
With masque, and antique pageantry,
Such sights as youthful poets dream
On summer eves by haunted stream.   130
Then to the well-trod stage anon,
If Jonson's learnèd sock be on,°
Or sweetest Shakespeare fancy's child,°
Warble his native wood-notes wild,
And ever against eating cares,
Lap me in soft Lydian airs,°
Married to immortal verse°
Such as the meeting soul may pierce°
In notes, with many a winding bout°
Of linkèd sweetness long drawn out,   140
With wanton heed, and giddy cunning,
The melting voice through mazes running;
Untwisting all the chains that tie
The hidden soul of harmony.
That Orpheus self may heave his head°
From golden slumber on a bed
Of heaped Elysian flowers, and hear
Such strains as would have won the ear
Of Pluto, to have quite set free°
His half-regained Eurydice.°   150
These delights, if thou canst give,
Mirth with thee, I mean to live.

Il Penseroso

Hence vain deluding joys,
    The brood of folly without father bred,
How little you bestead,°
    Or fill the fixèd mind with all your toys;°

Dwell in some idle brain,
   And fancies fond with gaudy shapes possess,°
As thick and numberless
   As the gay motes that people the sunbeams,
Or likest hovering dreams
   The fickle pensioners of Morpheus' train.°   10
But hail thou goddess, sage and holy,
Hail divinest Melancholy,
Whose saintly visage is too bright
To hit the sense of human sight;°
And therefore to our weaker view,
O'erlaid with black staid wisdom's hue.°
Black, but such as in esteem,
Prince Memnon's sister might beseem,°
Or that starred Ethiop queen that strove°
To set her beauty's praise above   20
The sea-nymphs, and their powers offended.
Yet thou art higher far descended,
Thee bright-haired Vesta long of yore,°
To solitary Saturn bore;°
His daughter she (in Saturn's reign,
Such mixture was not held a stain)
Oft in glimmering bowers, and glades
He met her, and in secret shades
Of woody Ida's inmost grove,
While yet there was no fear of Jove.°   30
Come pensive nun, devout and pure,°
Sober, steadfast, and demure,
All in a robe of darkest grain,°
Flowing with majestic train,
And sable stole of cypress lawn,°
Over thy decent shoulders drawn.
Come, but keep thy wonted state,
With even step, and musing gait,
And looks commercing with the skies,°
Thy rapt soul sitting in thine eyes: 40
There held in holy passion still,
Forget thyself to marble, till°
With a sad leaden downward cast,°
Thou fix them on the earth as fast.°
And join with thee calm Peace, and Quiet,

Spare Fast, that oft with gods doth diet,
And hears the muses in a ring,
Ay round about Jove's altar sing.°
And add to these retired Leisure,
That in trim gardens takes his pleasure;   50
But first, and chiefest, with thee bring,
Him that yon soars on golden wing,
Guiding the fiery-wheelèd throne,°
The cherub Contemplation,
And the mute Silence hist along,°
'Less Philomel will deign a song,°
In her sweetest, saddest plight,
Smoothing the rugged brow of night,
While Cynthia checks her dragon yoke,°
Gently o'er th' accustomed oak;   60
Sweet bird that shunn'st the noise of folly,
Most musical, most melancholy!
Thee chauntress oft the woods among,
I woo to hear thy even-song;
And missing thee, I walk unseen
On the dry smooth-shaven green,
To behold the wandering moon,
Riding near her highest noon,°
Like one that had been led astray
Through the heaven's wide pathless way;   70
And oft, as if her head she bowed,
Stooping through a fleecy cloud.
Oft on a plat of rising ground,°
I hear the far-off curfew sound,
Over some wide-watered shore,
Swinging slow with sullen roar;°
Or if the air will not permit,°
Some still removèd place will fit,°
Where glowing embers through the room
Teach light to counterfeit a gloom,   80
Far from all resort of mirth,
Save the cricket on the hearth,
Or the bellman's drowsy charm,°
To bless the doors from nightly harm:
Or let my lamp at midnight hour,
Be seen in some high lonely tower,

Where I may oft outwatch the Bear,°
With thrice great Hermes, or unsphere°
The spirit of Plato to unfold°
What worlds, or what vast regions hold   90
The immortal mind that hath forsook
Her mansion in this fleshly nook:°
And of those daemons that are found°
In fire, air, flood, or underground,
Whose power hath a true consent
With planet, or with element.°
Sometime let gorgeous Tragedy
In sceptred pall come sweeping by,°
Presenting Thebes, or Pelops' line,°
Or the tale of Troy divine.   100
Or what (though rare) of later age,
Ennobled hath the buskined stage.°
But, O sad virgin, that thy power
Might raise Musaeus from his bower,°
Or bid the soul of Orpheus sing
Such notes as warbled to the string,
Drew iron tears down Pluto's cheek,
And made hell grant what love did seek.°
Or call up him that left half-told°
The story of Cambuscan bold,   110
Of Camball, and of Algarsife,
And who had Canace to wife,
That owned the virtuous ring and glass,°
And of the wondrous horse of brass,
On which the Tartar king did ride;
And if aught else, great bards beside,
In sage and solemn tunes have sung,
Of tourneys and of trophies hung;
Of forests, and enchantments drear,
Where more is meant than meets the ear.   120
Thus Night oft see me in thy pale career,°
Till civil-suited Morn appear,°
Not tricked and frounced as she was wont,°
With the Attic boy to hunt,
But kerchiefed in a comely cloud,°
While rocking winds are piping loud,
Or ushered with a shower still,°

When the gust hath blown his fill,
Ending on the rustling leaves,
With minute drops from off the eaves.   130
And when the sun begins to fling
His flaring beams, me goddess bring
To archèd walks of twilight groves,
And shadows brown that Sylvan loves°
Of pine, or monumental oak,
Where the rude axe with heavèd stroke,
Was never heard the nymphs to daunt,
Or fright them from their hallowed haunt.
There in close covert by some brook,
Where no profaner eye may look,   140
Hide me from day's garish eye,
While the bee with honied thigh,
That at her flowery work doth sing,
And the waters murmuring
With such consort as they keep,°
Entice the dewy-feathered Sleep;
And let some strange mysterious dream,
Wave at his wings in airy stream,
Of lively portraiture displayed,
Softly on my eyelids laid.   150
And as I wake, sweet music breathe
Above, about, or underneath,
Sent by some spirit to mortals good,
Or th' unseen genius of the wood.°
But let my due feet never fail,°
To walk the studious cloister's pale,°
And love the high embowèd roof,°
With antic pillars' massy proof,°
And storied windows richly dight,°
Casting a dim religious light.   160
There let the pealing organ blow,
To the full-voiced choir below,
In service high, and anthems clear,
As may with sweetness, through mine ear,
Dissolve me into ecstasies,
And bring all heaven before mine eyes.
And may at last my weary age
Find out the peaceful hermitage,

The hairy gown and mossy cell,
Where I may sit and rightly spell,°　　　　　　170
Of every star that heaven doth shew,
And every herb that sips the dew;
Till old experience do attain
To something like prophetic strain.
These pleasures Melancholy give,
And I with thee will choose to live.°

Sonnet 1

O nightingale, that on yon bloomy spray
　　Warblest at eve, when all the woods are still,
　　Thou with fresh hope the lover's heart dost fill,
While the jolly hours lead on propitious May,°
Thy liquid notes that close the eye of day,
　　First heard before the shallow cuckoo's bill°
　　Portend success in love; O if Jove's will°
Have linked that amorous power to thy soft lay,
Now timely sing, ere the rude bird of hate°
　　Foretell my hopeless doom in some grove nigh:　　　　10
　　As thou from year to year hast sung too late
For my relief; yet hadst no reason why,
　　Whether the muse, or Love call thee his mate,
　　Both them I serve, and of their train am I.

Sonnet 2

Donna leggiadra il cui bel nome onora
　　L'erbosa val di Reno, e il nobil varco,
　　Ben è colui d'ogni valore scarco
Qual tuo spirto gentil non innamora,
Che dolcemente mostrasi di fuora
　　De'suoi atti soavi giammai parco,
　　E i don', che son d'amor saette ed arco,
Là onde l'alta tua virtù s'infiora.
Quando tu vaga parli, o lieta canti
　　Che mover possa duro alpestre legno,　　　　10
　　Guardi ciascun agli occhi, ed agli orecchi

SONNET 3

L'entrata, chi di te si trova indegno;
Grazia sola di sù gli vaglia, innanti
Che'l disio amoroso al cuor s'invecchi.

Charming lady, whose beautiful name honours the grassy Reno valley°
and its famous ford [2],° surely that man has no merit at all who is not in
love with your noble spirit, which is sweetly revealed in her gracious,
generous ways, and her gifts, which are the arrows and bow of love,
there, where your great power flourishes. When in your beauty you
speak or joyously sing, so that even the tough mountain trees might
respond, then let whoever feels unworthy of you guard the gates of his
eyes and ears. May heaven's grace alone help him, lest a lover's desire
grow fixed in his heart.

Sonnet 3

Qual in colle aspro, al'imbrunir di sera,
   L'avezza giovinetta pastorella
   Va bagnando l'erbetta strana e bella,
   Che mal si spande a disusata spera,
Fuor di sua natia alma primavera,
   Così Amor meco insù la lingua snella
   Desta il fior nuovo di strania favella,
   Mentre io di te, vezzosamente altera,
Canto, dal mio buon popol non inteso,
   E'l bel Tamigi cangio col bel Arno.   10
Amor lo volse, ed io a l'altrui peso
Seppi ch'Amor cosa mai volse indarno.
Deh! foss'il mio cuor lento e'l duro seno
A chi pianta dal ciel sì buon terreno.

As on a rugged mountain at dusk a young shepherdess skilfully waters a
lovely foreign plant, which scarely spreads its leaves in the alien
environment, far from its own nurturing springtime; so in me love
wakens upon my quick tongue the strange flower of a foreign language
as I sing of you, graciously proud, and, not understood by my own good
people, exchange the fair Thames for the fair Arno [10].° Love willed
it, and I knew from the distress of others that Love never willed anything in vain. Ah, that my dull heart and hard breast were as good a soil
for heaven's gardener!

Canzone

Ridonsi donne e giovani amorosi,
M'accostandosi attorno, e perchè scrivi,
Perchè tu scrivi in lingua ignota e strana
Verseggiando d'amor, e come t'osi?
Dinne, se la tua speme sia mai vana,
E de' pensieri lo miglior t'arrivi,
Così mi van burlando, altri rivi,
Altri lidi t'aspettan, ed altre onde
Nelle cui verdi sponde
Spuntati ad or, ad or a la tua chioma   10
L'immortal guiderdon d'eterne frondi:
Perchè alle spalle tue soverchia soma?
  Canzon, dirotti, e tu per me rispondi:
Dice mia donna, e'l suo dir è il mio cuore,
Questa è lingua di cui si vanta Amore.

Amorous young men and ladies gathering about me laugh and ask, 'Why, why do you write your love poems in an unknown foreign language; how do you dare to do it? Tell us, so that your hopes may not be in vain, and your best wishes come true.' Thus they tease me: 'Other rivers, other shores await you, on whose green banks already grows the immortal reward of everlasting leaves to crown your head—why do you take this heavy burden on your shoulders?'

Song, I will tell you, and you may answer for me: my lady says, and her words are my heart, 'This is the language of which Love is proud.'

Sonnet 4

Diodati, e te'l dirò con maraviglia,
  Quel ritroso io ch'amor spreggiar soléa
  E de' suoi lacci spesso mi ridéa
  Già caddi, ov' uom dabben talor s'impiglia.
Nè treccie d'oro, nè guancia vermiglia
  M'abbaglian sì, ma sotto nuova idea
  Pellegrina bellezza che'l cuor bea,
  Portamenti alti onesti, e nelle ciglia

Quel sereno fulgor d'amabil nero,
Parole adorne di lingua più d'una,   10
E'l cantar che di mezzo l'emisfero
Traviar ben può la faticosa luna,
E degli occhi suoi avventa si gran fuoco
Che l'incerar gli orecchi mi fia poco.

Diodati—and I say it to you with amazement—I, the obstinate one who
used to despise Love and often laughed at his snares, have now fallen
where good men are sometimes caught. Neither golden hair nor rosy
cheeks dazzle me so, but a foreign beauty modelled on a rare pattern
[6],° which thrills my heart; fine manners, modest, and that calm
radiance of lovely blackness in her eyes, speech graced by more than
one language, and singing that might well draw the labouring moon out
of her path in mid-sky; and from her eyes darts such fierce fire that
sealing my ears with wax [14]° would be of little use.

Sonnet 5

Per certo i bei vostr'occhi, donna mia,
Esser non può che non sian lo mio sole,
Si mi percuoton forte, come ei suole
Per l'arene di Libia chi s'invia,
Mentre un caldo vapor (nè senti' pria)
Da quel lato si spinge ove mi duole,
Che forse amanti nelle lor parole
Chiaman sospir; io non so che si sia:
Parte rinchiusa, e turbida si cela
Scossomi il petto, e poi n'uscendo poco,   10
Quivi d'attorno o s'agghiaccia, o s'ingiela;
Ma quanto a gli occhi giunge a trovar loco
Tutte le notti a me suol far piovose
Finchè mia Alba rivien colma di rose.

Surely, lady, your lovely eyes can only be my sun; they beat upon me as
powerfully as the sun upon a traveller in the Libyan desert, while a hot
vapour (I have never felt it before) bursts from that side [6]° where my
pain is: I know not what it is—perhaps what lovers in their language call
a sigh. Part of it, compressed within me, hides shivering, shaking my

breast; then a little escaping, it is either chilled or turns to ice. But the part that finds its place in my eyes makes all my nights rainy, until my dawn returns crowned with roses.

Sonnet 6

Giovane piano, e semplicetto amante
   Poichè fuggir me stesso in dubbio sono,
   Madonna a voi del mio cuor l'umil dono
Farò divoto; io certo a prove tante
L'ebbi fedele, intrepido, costante,
   Di pensieri leggiadro, accorto, e buono.
   Quando rugge il gran mondo, e scocca il tuono,
S'arma di se, e d'intero diamante,
Tanto del forse, e d'invidia sicuro,
   Di timori, e speranze al popol use   10
   Quanto d'ingegno, e d'alto valor vago,
E di cetra sonora, e delle muse:
   Sol troverete in tal parte men duro
   Ove amor mise l'insanabil ago.

Since I am a young, simple and candid lover, in doubt how to escape from myself, lady, I will devoutly give you the humble gift of my heart; in so many trials I have proved it faithful, fearless, constant, in its thoughts gracious, prudent and good. When the whole world roars and thunders, it arms itself within, and with total adamant [8],° as safe from chance and envy and ordinary fears and hopes as it is eager for genius and high courage, and the sounding lyre and the muses. You will find the armour less hard only where love's incurable dart has pierced.

Sonnet 7

How soon hath time the subtle thief of youth,
   Stol'n on his wing my three and twentieth year!
   My hasting days fly on with full career,°
   But my late spring no bud or blossom shew'th.
Perhaps my semblance might deceive the truth,°
   That I to manhood am arrived so near,
   And inward ripeness doth much less appear,
   That some more timely-happy spirits endueth.°

Yet be it less or more, or soon or slow,°
  It shall be still in strictest measure even,°   10
  To that same lot, however mean or high,
Toward which time leads me, and the will of heaven;
  All is, if I have grace to use it so,
  As ever in my great task-master's eye.

Sonnet 8

Captain or colonel, or knight in arms,°
  Whose chance on these defenceless doors may seize,
  If ever deed of honour did thee please,°
Guard them, and him within protect from harms,
He can requite thee, for he knows the charms°
  That call fame on such gentle acts as these,
  And he can spread thy name o'er lands and seas,
Whatever clime the sun's bright circle warms.
Lift not thy spear against the muses' bower,
  The great Emathian conqueror bid spare°   10
  The house of Pindarus, when temple and tower
Went to the ground: and the repeated air
  Of sad Electra's poet had the power°
  To save the Athenian walls from ruin bare.

Sonnet 9

Lady, that in the prime of earliest youth,°
  Wisely hast shunned the broad way and the green,°
  And with those few are eminently seen,
  That labour up the hill of heavenly truth,
The better part with Mary and with Ruth,°
  Chosen thou hast, and they that overween,°
  And at thy growing virtues fret their spleen,°
  No anger find in thee, but pity and ruth.
Thy care is fixed, and zealously attends
  To fill thy odorous lamp with deeds of light,   10
  And hope that reaps not shame. Therefore be sure
Thou, when the bridegroom with his feastful friends
  Passes to bliss at the mid-hour of night,
  Hast gained thy entrance, virgin wise and pure.°

Sonnet 10

Daughter to that good earl, once president
 Of England's council, and her treasury,
 Who lived in both, unstained with gold or fee,
 And left them both, more in himself content,
Till the sad breaking of that parliament°
 Broke him, as that dishonest victory°
 At Chaeronea, fatal to liberty°
 Killed with report that old man eloquent,°
Though later born, than to have known the days°
 Wherein your father flourished, yet by you,   10
 Madam, methinks I see him living yet;
So well your words his noble virtues praise,
 That all both judge you to relate them true,
 And to possess them, honoured Margaret.

Arcades

*Part of an entertainment presented to the Countess Dowager of Derby at Harefield, by
some noble persons of her family, who appear on the scene in pastoral habit, moving
toward the seat of state,° with this song.*

I. SONG

Look nymphs, and shepherds look,
What sudden blaze of majesty
Is that which we from hence descry
Too divine to be mistook:
    This this is she
To whom our vows and wishes bend,
Here our solemn search hath end.

Fame that her high worth to raise,
Seemed erst so lavish and profuse,°
We may justly now accuse   10
Of detraction from her praise,
    Less than half we find expressed,
    Envy bid conceal the rest.

Mark what radiant state she spreads,
In circle round her shining throne,
Shooting her beams like silver threads,
This this is she alone,
    Sitting like a goddess bright,
    In the centre of her light.

Might she the wise Latona be,°   20
Or the towered Cybele,°
Mother of a hundred gods;
Juno dares not give her odds;°
    Who had thought this clime had held
    A deity so unparalleled?

As they come forward, the Genius° of the Wood appears, and turning toward them, speaks.

    Gen. Stay gentle swains, for though in this disguise,°
I see bright honour sparkle through your eyes,
Of famous Arcady ye are, and sprung
Of that renownèd flood, so often sung,
Divine Alpheus, who by secret sluice,°   30
Stole under seas to meet his Arethuse;
And ye the breathing roses of the wood,°
Fair silver-buskined nymphs as great and good,°
I know this quest of yours, and free intent
Was all in honour and devotion meant
To the great mistress of yon princely shrine,
Whom with low reverence I adore as mine,
And with all helpful service will comply
To further this night's glad solemnity;
And lead ye where ye may more near behold   40
What shallow-searching Fame hath left untold;
Which I full oft amidst these shades alone
Have sat to wonder at, and gaze upon:
For know by lot from Jove I am the power°
Of this fair wood, and live in oaken bower,
To nurse the saplings tall, and curl the grove
With ringlets quaint, and wanton windings wove.°
And all my plants I save from nightly ill,
Of noisome winds, and blasting vapours chill.°
And from the boughs brush off the evil dew,   50
And heal the harms of thwarting thunder blue,°

Or what the cross dire-looking planet smites,°
Or hurtful worm with cankered venom bites.°
When evening grey doth rise, I fetch my round°
Over the mount, and all this hallowed ground,
And early ere the odorous breath of morn
Awakes the slumb'ring leaves, or tasselled horn
Shakes the high thicket, haste I all about,
Number my ranks, and visit every sprout°
With puissant words, and murmurs made to bless,°   60
But else in deep of night when drowsiness
Hath locked up mortal sense, then listen I
To the celestial sirens' harmony,°
That sit upon the nine enfolded spheres,°
And sing to those that hold the vital shears,°
And turn the adamantine spindle round,°
On which the fate of gods and men is wound.
Such sweet compulsion doth in music lie,
To lull the daughters of Necessity,
And keep unsteady Nature to her law,   70
And the low world in measured motion draw
After the heavenly tune, which none can hear
Of human mould with gross unpurgèd ear;°
And yet such music worthiest were to blaze°
The peerless height of her immortal praise,
Whose lustre leads us, and for her most fit,
If my inferior hand or voice could hit
Inimitable sounds, yet as we go,
Whate'er the skill of lesser gods can show,
I will assay, her worth to celebrate,   80
And so attend ye toward her glittering state;°
Where ye may all that are of noble stem°
Approach, and kiss her sacred vesture's hem.

II. SONG

O'er the smooth enamelled green
Where no print of step hath been,
    Follow me as I sing,
    And touch the warbled string.°
Under the shady roof
Of branching elm star-proof,
    Follow me,   90

I will bring you where she sits,
Clad in splendour as befits
    Her deity.
Such a rural queen
All Arcadia hath not seen.

III. SONG

Nymphs and shepherds dance no more
    By sandy Ladon's lilied banks.°
On old Lycaeus or Cyllene hoar,°
    Trip no more in twilight ranks,
Though Erymanth your loss deplore,   100
    A better soil shall give ye thanks.
From the stony Maenalus,
Bring your flocks, and live with us,
Here ye shall have greater grace,
To serve the lady of this place.
    Though Syrinx your Pan's mistress were,°
    Yet Syrinx well might wait on her.
    Such a rural queen
    All Arcadia hath not seen.

Lycidas

In this monody the author bewails a learned friend, unfortunately drowned in his passage from Chester on the Irish Seas, 1637. And by occasion foretells the ruin of our corrupted clergy then in their height.

Yet once more, O ye laurels, and once more°
Ye myrtles brown, with ivy never sere,°
I come to pluck your berries harsh and crude,°
And with forced fingers rude,°
Shatter your leaves before the mellowing year.°
Bitter constraint, and sad occasion dear,°
Compels me to disturb your season due:
For Lycidas is dead, dead ere his prime,
Young Lycidas, and hath not left his peer:
Who would not sing for Lycidas? he knew°   10
Himself to sing, and build the lofty rhyme.°
He must not float upon his watery bier
Unwept, and welter to the parching wind,°

Without the meed of some melodious tear.°
  Begin then, sisters of the sacred well,
That from beneath the seat of Jove doth spring,
Begin, and somewhat loudly sweep the string.°
Hence with denial vain, and coy excuse,°
So may some gentle muse°
With lucky words favour my destined urn,°   20
And as he passes turn,°
And bid fair peace be to my sable shroud.
For we were nursed upon the self-same hill,
Fed the same flock; by fountain, shade, and rill.
  Together both, ere the high lawns appeared°
Under the opening eyelids of the morn,
We drove afield, and both together heard
What time the grey-fly winds her sultry horn,°
Battening our flocks with the fresh dews of night,°
Oft till the star that rose, at evening, bright°   30
Toward heaven's descent had sloped his westering wheel.°
Meanwhile the rural ditties were not mute,
Tempered to the oaten flute,°
Rough satyrs danced, and fauns with cloven heel,
From the glad sound would not be absent long,
And old Damaetas loved to hear our song.°
  But O the heavy change, now thou art gone,
Now thou art gone, and never must return!
Thee shepherd, thee the woods, and desert caves,
With wild thyme and the gadding vine o'ergrown,°   40
And all their echoes mourn.
The willows, and the hazel copses green,
Shall now no more be seen,
Fanning their joyous leaves to thy soft lays.
As killing as the canker to the rose,
Or taint-worm to the weanling herds that graze,°
Or frost to flowers, that their gay wardrobe wear,
When first the whitethorn blows;°
Such, Lycidas, thy loss to shepherd's ear.
  Where were ye nymphs when the remorseless deep   50
Closed o'er the head of your loved Lycidas?°
For neither were ye playing on the steep,
Where your old bards, the famous Druids lie,
Nor on the shaggy top of Mona high,°

Nor yet where Deva spreads her wizard stream:°
Ay me, I fondly dream!°
Had ye been there . . . for what could that have done?
What could the muse herself that Orpheus bore,°
The muse herself, for her enchanting son
Whom universal nature did lament,   60
When by the rout that made the hideous roar,°
His gory visage down the stream was sent,
Down the swift Hebrus to the Lesbian shore.°
   Alas! What boots it with uncessant care°
To tend the homely slighted shepherd's trade,°
And strictly meditate the thankless muse,
Were it not better done as others use,
To sport with Amaryllis in the shade,°
Or with the tangles of Neaera's hair?°
Fame is the spur that the clear spirit doth raise°   70
(That last infirmity of noble mind)
To scorn delights, and live laborious days;
But the fair guerdon when we hope to find,°
And think to burst out into sudden blaze,
Comes the blind Fury with th' abhorrèd shears,°
And slits the thin-spun life. But not the praise,
Phoebus replied, and touched my trembling ears;°
Fame is no plant that grows on mortal soil,
Nor in the glistering foil°
Set off to the world, nor in broad rumour lies,   80
But lives and spreads aloft by those pure eyes,
And perfect witness of all-judging Jove;
As he pronounces lastly on each deed,
Of so much fame in heaven expect thy meed.
   O fountain Arethuse, and thou honoured flood,°
Smooth-sliding Mincius, crowned with vocal reeds,°
That strain I heard was of a higher mood:°
But now my oat proceeds,°
And listens to the herald of the sea°
That came in Neptune's plea,°   90
He asked the waves, and asked the felon winds,°
What hard mishap hath doomed this gentle swain?
And questioned every gust of rugged wings
That blows from off each beakèd promontory;
They knew not of his story,

And sage Hippotades their answer brings,°
That not a blast was from his dungeon strayed,
The air was calm, and on the level brine,
Sleek Panope with all her sisters played.°
It was that fatal and perfidious bark   100
Built in th' eclipse, and rigged with curses dark,°
That sunk so low that sacred head of thine.
    Next Camus, reverend sire, went footing slow,°
His mantle hairy, and his bonnet sedge,°
Inwrought with figures dim, and on the edge°
Like to that sanguine flower inscribed with woe.°
Ah! who hath reft (quoth he) my dearest pledge?°
Last came, and last did go,
The pilot of the Galilean lake,°
Two massy keys he bore of metals twain   110
(The golden opes, the iron shuts amain),°
He shook his mitred locks, and stern bespake,°
How well could I have spared for thee, young swain,
Enow of such as for their bellies' sake,°
Creep and intrude, and climb into the fold?
Of other care they little reckoning make,
Than how to scramble at the shearers' feast,
And shove away the worthy bidden guest.
Blind mouths! that scarce themselves know how to hold°
A sheep-hook, or have learned aught else the least   120
That to the faithful herdman's art belongs!
What recks it them? What need they? They are sped;°
And when they list, their lean and flashy songs°
Grate on their scrannel pipes of wretched straw,°
The hungry sheep look up, and are not fed,
But swoll'n with wind, and the rank mist they draw,°
Rot inwardly, and foul contagion spread:
Besides what the grim wolf with privy paw°
Daily devours apace, and nothing said,
But that two-handed engine at the door,   130
Stands ready to smite once, and smite no more.°
    Return Alpheus, the dread voice is past,°
That shrunk thy streams; return Sicilian muse,
And call the vales, and bid them hither cast
Their bells, and flowrets of a thousand hues.°
Ye valleys low where the mild whispers use,°

Of shades and wanton winds, and gushing brooks,°
On whose fresh lap the swart star sparely looks,°
Throw hither all your quaint enamelled eyes,
That on the green turf suck the honied showers,   140
And purple all the ground with vernal flowers.
Bring the rathe primrose that forsaken dies,°
The tufted crow-toe, and pale jessamine,°
The white pink, and the pansy freaked with jet,°
The glowing violet,
The musk-rose, and the well-attired woodbine,
With cowslips wan that hang the pensive head,
And every flower that sad embroidery wears:
Bid amaranthus all his beauty shed,
And daffodillies fill their cups with tears,   150
To strew the laureate hearse where Lycid lies.
For so to interpose a little ease,
Let our frail thoughts dally with false surmise.
Ay me! Whilst thee the shores, and sounding seas
Wash far away, where'er thy bones are hurled,
Whether beyond the stormy Hebrides
Where thou perhaps under the whelming tide°
Visit'st the bottom of the monstrous world;
Or whether thou to our moist vows denied,°
Sleep'st by the fable of Bellerus old,°   160
Where the great vision of the guarded mount°
Looks toward Namancos and Bayona's hold;°
Look homeward angel now, and melt with ruth.°
And, O ye dolphins, waft the hapless youth.°
    Weep no more, woeful shepherds weep no more,
For Lycidas your sorrow is not dead,
Sunk though he be beneath the watery floor,
So sinks the day-star in the ocean bed,°
And yet anon repairs his drooping head,
And tricks his beams, and with new spangled ore,°   170
Flames in the forehead of the morning sky:
So Lycidas sunk low, but mounted high,
Through the dear might of him that walked the waves,
Where other groves, and other streams along,
With nectar pure his oozy locks he laves,
And hears the unexpressive nuptial song,°
In the blest kingdoms meek of joy and love.

There entertain him all the saints above,
In solemn troops, and sweet societies
That sing, and singing in their glory move,   180
And wipe the tears for ever from his eyes.
Now Lycidas the shepherds weep no more;
Henceforth thou art the genius of the shore,°
In thy large recompense, and shalt be good°
To all that wander in that perilous flood.

 Thus sang the uncouth swain to th' oaks and rills,°
While the still morn went out with sandals grey,
He touched the tender stops of various quills,°
With eager thought warbling his Doric lay:°
And now the sun had stretched out all the hills,   190
And now was dropped into the western bay;
At last he rose, and twitched his mantle blue:°
Tomorrow to fresh woods, and pastures new.

A Masque of the same Author
Presented at Ludlow Castle, 1634
Before the Earl of Bridgewater
Then President of Wales
['Comus']

THE PERSONS

The Attendant Spirit, afterwards in the habit of Thyrsis.
Comus, with his crew.
The Lady.
First Brother.
Second Brother.
Sabrina the Nymph.

The chief persons which presented, were
The Lord Brackley,
Master Thomas Egerton his brother,
The Lady Alice Egerton.

  The first scene discovers° a wild wood.
   The Attendant Spirit° descends or enters.

Before the starry threshold of Jove's court
My mansion is, where those immortal shapes°
Of bright aerial spirits live ensphered°
In regions mild of calm and serene air,
Above the smoke and stir of this dim spot,
Which men call earth, and, with low-thoughted care
Confined, and pestered in this pinfold here,°
Strive to keep up a frail, and feverish being
Unmindful of the crown that virtue gives
After this mortal change, to her true servants   10
Amongst the enthroned gods on sainted seats.°
Yet some there be that by due steps aspire
To lay their just hands on that golden key
That opes the palace of eternity:
To such my errand is, and but for such,
I would not soil these pure ambrosial weeds,°
With the rank vapours of this sin-worn mould.°
    But to my task. Neptune besides the sway
Of every salt flood, and each ebbing stream,°
Took in by lot 'twixt high and nether Jove,°   20
Imperial rule of all the sea-girt isles
That like to rich and various gems inlay
The unadornèd bosom of the deep,
Which he to grace his tributary gods°
By course commits to several government,°
And gives them leave to wear their sapphire crowns,
And wield their little tridents, but this isle
The greatest, and the best of all the main°
He quarters to his blue-haired deities,°
And all this tract that fronts the falling sun   30
A noble peer of mickle trust, and power°
Has in his charge, with tempered awe to guide°
An old, and haughty nation proud in arms:°
Where his fair offspring nursed in princely lore,
Are coming to attend their father's state,°
And new-entrusted sceptre, but their way
Lies through the perplexed paths of this drear wood,°
The nodding horror of whose shady brows°
Threats the forlorn and wandering passenger.
And here their tender age might suffer peril,   40
But that by quick command from sovereign Jove

I was dispatched for their defence, and guard;
And listen why, for I will tell you now
What never yet was heard in tale or song
From old, or modern bard in hall, or bower.
    Bacchus that first from out the purple grape,°
Crushed the sweet poison of misusèd wine
After the Tuscan mariners transformed°
Coasting the Tyrrhene shore, as the winds listed,°
On Circe's island fell (who knows not Circe°   50
The daughter of the Sun? Whose charmèd cup°
Whoever tasted, lost his upright shape,
And downward fell into a grovelling swine);°
This nymph that gazed upon his clustering locks,
With ivy berries wreathed, and his blithe youth,
Had by him, ere he parted thence, a son
Much like his father, but his mother more,
Whom therefore she brought up and Comus named,°
Who ripe, and frolic of his full-grown age,°
Roving the Celtic, and Iberian fields,°   60
At last betakes him to this ominous wood,
And in thick shelter of black shades embowered,
Excels his mother at her mighty art,
Offering to every weary traveller,
His orient liquor in a crystal glass,°
To quench the drought of Phoebus, which as they taste°
(For most do taste through fond intemperate thirst)°
Soon as the potion works, their human countenance,
The express resemblance of the gods, is changed
Into some brutish form of wolf, or bear,°   70
Or ounce, or tiger, hog, or bearded goat,°
All other parts remaining as they were,
And they, so perfect is their misery,°
Not once perceive their foul disfigurement,
But boast themselves more comely than before
And all their friends, and native home forget
To roll with pleasure in a sensual sty.
Therefore when any favoured of high Jove,
Chances to pass through this advent'rous glade,°
Swift as the sparkle of a glancing star,   80
I shoot from heaven to give him safe convoy,
As now I do: but first I must put off

These my sky-robes spun out of Iris' woof,°
And take the weeds and likeness of a swain,°
That to the service of this house belongs,
Who with his soft pipe, and smooth-dittied song,
Well knows to still the wild winds when they roar,°
And hush the waving woods, nor of less faith,°
And in this office of his mountain watch,
Likeliest, and nearest to the present aid°   90
Of this occasion. But I hear the tread
Of hateful steps, I must be viewless now.°

Comus enters with a charming-rod in one hand, his glass in the other, with
him a rout of monsters, headed like sundry sorts of wild beasts, but otherwise
like men and women, their apparel glistering, they come in making a riotous
and unruly noise, with torches in their hands.

Comus. The star that bids the shepherd fold,°
Now the top of heaven doth hold,
And the gilded car of day,°
His glowing axle doth allay°
In the steep Atlantic stream,°
And the slope sun his upward beam°
Shoots against the dusky pole,°
Pacing toward the other goal   100
Of his chamber in the east.
Meanwhile, welcome joy, and feast,
Midnight shout, and revelry,
Tipsy dance, and jollity.
Braid your locks with rosy twine
Dropping odours, dropping wine.
Rigour now is gone to bed,
And Advice with scrupulous head,
Strick Age, and sour Severity,
With their grave saws in slumber lie.°   110
We that are of purer fire
Imitate the starry choir,°
Who in their nightly watchful spheres,
Lead in swift round the months and years.°
The sounds, and seas with all their finny drove°
Now to the moon in wavering morris move,°
And on the tawny sands and shelves,°
Trip the pert fairies and the dapper elves;

By dimpled brook, and fountain-brim,
The wood-nymphs decked with daisies trim,   120
Their merry wakes and pastimes keep:°
What hath night to do with sleep?
Night hath better sweets to prove,°
Venus now wakes, and wakens Love.
Come let us our rites begin,
'Tis only daylight that makes sin
Which these dun shades will ne'er report.
Hail goddess of nocturnal sport
Dark-veiled Cotytto, to whom the secret flame°
Of midnight torches burns; mysterious dame   130
That ne'er art called, but when the dragon womb°
Of Stygian darkness spits her thickest gloom,°
And makes one blot of all the air,
Stay thy cloudy ebon chair,°
Wherein thou rid'st with Hecat', and befriend
Us thy vowed priests, till utmost end
Of all thy dues be done, and none left out,°
Ere the blabbing eastern scout,
The nice morn on th' Indian steep°
From her cabined loophole peep,°   140
And to the tell-tale sun descry°
Our concealed solemnity.°
Come, knit hands, and beat the ground,
In a light fantastic round.°

The Measure°

Break off, break off, I feel the different pace
Of some chaste footing near about this ground.
Run to your shrouds, within these brakes and trees;°
Our number may affright: some virgin sure
(For so I can distinguish by mine art)
Benighted in these woods. Now to my charms,   150
And to my wily trains; I shall ere long°
Be well stocked with as fair a herd as grazed
About my mother Circe. Thus I hurl
My dazzling spells into the spongy air,°
Of power to cheat the eye with blear illusion,°
And give it false presentments, lest the place°
And my quaint habits breed astonishment,°

And put the damsel to suspicious flight,
Which must not be, for that's against my course;
I under fair pretence of friendly ends,   160
And well-placed words of glozing courtesy°
Baited with reasons not unplausible
Wind me into the easy-hearted man,°
And hug him into snares. When once her eye
Hath met the virtue of this magic dust,°
I shall appear some harmless villager
Whom thrift keeps up about his country gear;
But here she comes, I fairly step aside°
And hearken, if I may, her business here.°

The Lady enters

Lady. This way the noise was, if mine ear be true,   170
My best guide now, methought it was the sound
Of riot, and ill-managed merriment,
Such as the jocund flute, or gamesome pipe
Stirs up among the loose unlettered hinds,°
When for their teeming flocks, and granges full,°
In wanton dance they praise the bounteous Pan,°
And thank the gods amiss. I should be loath
To meet the rudeness, and swilled insolence°
Of such late wassailers; yet O where else°
Shall I inform my unacquainted feet°   180
In the blind mazes of this tangled wood?
My brothers when they saw me wearied out
With this long way, resolving here to lodge
Under the spreading favour of these pines,
Stepped as they said to the next thicket-side
To bring me berries, or such cooling fruit
As the kind hospitable woods provide.
They left me then, when the grey-hooded Even°
Like a sad votarist in palmer's weed°
Rose from the hindmost wheels of Phoebus' wain.°   190
But where they are, and why they came not back,
Is now the labour of my thoughts; 'tis likeliest
They had engaged their wand'ring steps too far,°
And envious darkness, ere they could return,
Had stole them from me, else O thievish Night
Why shouldst thou, but for some felonious end,

In thy dark lantern thus close up the stars,°
That Nature hung in heaven, and filled their lamps
With everlasting oil, to give due light
To the misled and lonely traveller?   200
This is the place, as well as I may guess,
Whence even now the tumult of loud mirth
Was rife, and perfect in my listening ear,°
Yet nought but single darkness do I find.°
What might this be? A thousand fantasies
Begin to throng into my memory
Of calling shapes, and beckoning shadows dire,
And airy tongues, that syllable men's names
On sands, and shores, and desert wildernesses.
These thoughts may startle well, but not astound°   210
The virtuous mind, that ever walks attended
By a strong siding champion Conscience—°
O welcome pure-eyed Faith, white-handed Hope,
Thou hovering angel girt with golden wings,
And thou unblemished form of Chastity,°
I see ye visibly, and now believe
That he, the Supreme Good, t' whom all things ill
Are but as slavish officers of vengence,
Would send a glistering guardian if need were
To keep my life and honour unassailed.   220
Was I deceived, or did a sable cloud
Turn forth her silver lining on the night?
I did not err, there does a sable cloud
Turn forth her silver lining on the night,
And casts a gleam over this tufted grove.
I cannot hallo to my brothers, but
Such noise as I can make to be heard farthest
I'll venture, for my new-enlivened spirits
Prompt me; and they perhaps are not far off.

SONG

Sweet Echo, sweetest nymph that liv'st unseen°   230
   Within thy airy shell°
  By slow Meander's margent green,°
And in the violet-embroidered vale
  Where the love-lorn nightingale°
Nightly to thee her sad song mourneth well,

Canst thou not tell me of a gentle pair
  That likest thy Narcissus are?
    O if thou have
  Hid them in some flowery cave,
    Tell me but where   240
  Sweet queen of parley, daughter of the sphere.°
  So mayst thou be translated to the skies,
And give resounding grace to all heaven's harmonies.

Comus. Can any mortal mixture of earth's mould°
Breathe such divine enchanting ravishment?
Sure something holy lodges in that breast,
And with these raptures moves the vocal air°
To testify his hidden residence;°
How sweetly did they float upon the wings
Of silence, through the empty-vaulted night   250
At every fall smoothing the raven down°
Of darkness till it smiled: I have oft heard
My mother Circe with the Sirens three,°
Amidst the flowery-kirtled Naiades°
Culling their potent herbs, and baleful drugs,
Who as they sung, would take the prisoned soul,
And lap it in Elysium; Scylla wept,°
And chid her barking waves into attention,
And fell Charybdis murmured soft applause:°
Yet they in pleasing slumber lulled the sense,   260
And in sweet madness robbed it of itself,
But such a sacred, and home-felt delight,°
Such sober certainty of waking bliss
I never heard till now. I'll speak to her
And she shall be my queen. Hail foreign wonder°
Whom certain these rough shades did never breed
Unless the goddess that in rural shrine°
Dwell'st here with Pan, or Sylvan, by blest song°
Forbidding every bleak unkindly fog
To touch the prosperous growth of this tall wood.   270
Lady. Nay gentle shepherd ill is lost that praise
That is addressed to unattending ears,
Not any boast of skill, but extreme shift°
How to regain my severed company
Compelled me to awake the courteous Echo

To give me answer from her mossy couch.
Comus. What chance good lady hath bereft you thus?
Lady. Dim darkness, and this leafy labyrinth.
Comus. Could that divide you from near-ushering guides?
Lady. They left me weary on a grassy turf.   280
Comus. By falsehood, or discourtesy, or why?
Lady. To seek i' the valley some cool friendly spring.
Comus. And left your fair side all unguarded lady?
Lady. They were but twain, and purposed quick return.
Comus. Perhaps forestalling night prevented them.
Lady. How easy my misfortune is to hit!°
Comus. Imports their loss, beside the present need?°
Lady. No less than if I should my brothers lose.
Comus. Were they of manly prime, or youthful bloom?
Lady. As smooth as Hebe's their unrazored lips.°   290
Comus. Two such I saw, what time the laboured ox
In his loose traces from the furrow came,°
And the swinked hedger at his supper sat;°
I saw them under a green mantling vine°
That crawls along the side of yon small hill,
Plucking ripe clusters from the tender shoots,
Their port was more than human as they stood;°
I took it for a fairy vision°
Of some gay creatures of the element°
That in the colours of the rainbow live   300
And play i' the plighted clouds. I was awestruck,°
And as I passed, I worshipped; if those you seek
It were a journey like the path to heaven,
To help you find them.
Lady.   Gentle villager
What readiest way would bring me to that place?
Comus. Due west it rises from this shrubby point.
Lady. To find out that, good shepherd, I suppose,
In such a scant allowance of starlight,
Would overtask the best land-pilot's art,
Without the sure guess of well-practised feet.   310
Comus. I know each lane, and every alley green,
Dingle, or bushy dell of this wild wood,°
And every bosky bourn from side to side°
My daily walks and ancient neighbourhood,
And if your stray attendance be yet lodged,°

Or shroud within these limits, I shall know°
Ere morrow wake, or the low-roosted lark
From her thatched pallet rouse; if otherwise,°
I can conduct you lady to a low
But loyal cottage, where you may be safe   320
Till further quest.
Lady.   Shepherd I take thy word,
And trust thy honest-offered courtesy,
Which oft is sooner found in lowly sheds
With smoky rafters, than in tap'stry halls
And courts of princes, where it first was named,°
And yet is most pretended: in a place°
Less warranted than this, or less secure
I cannot be, that I should fear to change it;
Eye me blest Providence, and square my trial°
To my proportioned strength. Shepherd lead on.—   330

The two Brothers

Eld. Bro. Unmuffle ye faint stars, and thou fair moon
That wont'st to love the traveller's benison,°
Stoop thy pale visage through an amber cloud,
And disinherit Chaos, that reigns here°
In double night of darkness, and of shades;°
Or if your influence be quite dammed up
With black usurping mists, some gentle taper
Though a rush-candle from the wicker hole°
Of some clay habitation visit us
With thy long levelled rule of streaming light,°   340
And thou shalt be our star of Arcady,
Or Tyrian Cynosure.°
Sec. Bro.   Or if our eyes
Be barred that happiness, might we but hear
The folded flocks penned in their wattled cotes,°
Or sound of pastoral reed with oaten stops,°
Or whistle from the lodge, or village cock
Count the night-watches to his feathery dames,
'Twould be some solace yet some little cheering
In this close dungeon of innumerous boughs.°
But O that hapless virgin our lost sister   350
Where may she wander now, whither betake her
From the chill dew, amongst rude burrs and thistles?

Perhaps some cold bank is her bolster now
Or 'gainst the rugged bark of some broad elm
Leans her unpillowed head fraught with sad fears;
What if in wild amazement, and affright,
Or while we speak within the direful grasp
Of savage hunger, or of savage heat?
Eld. Bro. Peace brother, be not over-exquisite°
To cast the fashion of uncertain evils;°   360
For grant they be so, while they rest unknown,°
What need a man forestall his date of grief,°
And run to meet what he would most avoid?
Or if they be but false alarms of fear,
How bitter is such self-delusion!
I do not think my sister so to seek,°
Or so unprincipled in virtue's book,°
And the sweet peace that goodness bosoms ever,°
As that the single want of light and noise°
(Not being in danger, as I trust she is not)   370
Could stir the constant mood of her calm thoughts,
And put them into misbecoming plight.°
Virtue could see to do what Virtue would
By her own radiant light, though sun and moon
Were in the flat sea sunk. And Wisdom's self°
Oft seeks to sweet retired solitude,°
Where with her best nurse Contemplation
She plumes her feathers, and lets grow her wings°
That in the various bustle of resort°
Were all to-ruffled, and sometimes impaired.°   380
He that has light within his own clear breast
May sit i' the centre, and enjoy bright day,°
But he that hides a dark soul, and foul thoughts
Benighted walks under the midday sun;
Himself is his own dungeon.
Sec. Bro.   'Tis most true
That musing Meditation most affects°
The pensive secrecy of desert cell,°
Far from the cheerful haunt of men, and herds,°
And sits as safe as in a senate-house,
For who would rob a hermit of his weeds,°   390
His few books, or his beads, or maple dish,°
Or do his grey hairs any violence?

But Beauty like the fair Hesperian tree°
Laden with blooming gold, had need the guard
Of dragon-watch with unenchanted eye,°
To save her blossoms, and defend her fruit
From the rash hand of bold Incontinence.°
You may as well spread out the unsunned heaps°
Of miser's treasure by an outlaw's den,
And tell me it is safe, as bid me hope   400
Danger will wink on opportunity,°
And let a single helpless maiden pass
Uninjured in this wild surrounding waste.
Of night, or loneliness it recks me not,°
I fear the dread events that dog them both,
Lest some ill-greeting touch attempt the person
Of our unowned sister.°
Eld. Bro.   I do not, brother,
Infer, as if I thought my sister's state°
Secure without all doubt, or controversy:
Yet where an equal poise of hope and fear°   410
Does arbitrate the event, my nature is°
That I incline to hope, rather than fear,
And gladly banish squint suspicion.°
My sister is not so defenceless left
As you imagine, she has a hidden strength
Which you remember not.
Sec. Bro.   What hidden strength,
Unless the strength of heaven, if you mean that?
Eld. Bro. I mean that too, but yet a hidden strength
Which if heaven gave it, may be termed her own:
'Tis chastity, my brother, chastity:°   420
She that has that, is clad in complete steel,
And like a quivered nymph with arrows keen°
May trace huge forests, and unharboured heaths,°
Infamous hills, and sandy perilous wilds,
Where through the sacred rays of chastity,
No savage fierce, bandit, or mountaineer°
Will dare to soil her virgin purity,
Yea there, where very desolation dwells°
By grots, and caverns shagged with horrid shades,°
She may pass on with unblenched majesty,°   430
Be it not done in pride, or in presumption.°

Some say no evil thing that walks by night
In fog, or fire, by lake, or moorish fen,°
Blue meagre hag, or stubborn unlaid ghost,°
That breaks his magic chains at curfew time,°
No goblin, or swart fairy of the mine,°
Hath hurtful power o'er true virginity.
Do ye believe me yet, or shall I call
Antiquity from the old schools of Greece°
To testify the arms of chastity?   440
Hence had the huntress Dian her dread bow
Far silver-shafted queen for ever chaste,
Wherewith she tamed the brinded lioness°
And spotted mountain pard, but set at nought°
The frivolous bolt of Cupid; gods and men°
Feared her stern frown, and when was queen o' the woods.
What was that snaky-headed Gorgon shield
That wise Minerva wore, unconquered virgin,°
Wherewith she freezed her foes to congealed stone?
But rigid looks of chaste austerity,   450
And noble grace that dashed brute violence
With sudden adoration, and blank awe.
So dear to heaven is saintly chastity,
That when a soul is found sincerely so,
A thousand liveried angels lackey her,
Driving far off each thing of sin and guilt,
And in clear dream, and solemn vision
Tell her of things that no gross ear can hear,
Till oft converse with heavenly habitants°
Begin to cast a beam on the outward shape,   460
The unpolluted temple of the mind,
And turns it by degrees to the soul's essence,
Till all be made immortal: but when lust°
By unchaste looks, loose gestures, and foul talk,
But most by lewd and lavish act of sin,
Lets in defilement to the inward parts,
The soul grows clotted by contagion,
Embodies, and imbrutes, till she quite lose°
The divine property of her first being.
Such are those thick and gloomy shadows damp   470
Oft seen in charnel-vaults, and sepulchres
Lingering, and sitting by a new-made grave,

As loath to leave the body that it loved,
And linked itself by carnal sensuality
To a degenerate and degraded state,°
Sec. Bro. How charming is divine philosophy!
Not harsh, and crabbèd as dull fools suppose,
But musical as is Apollo's lute,
And a perpetual feast of nectared sweets,°
Where no crude surfeit reigns.° 480
Eld. Bro. List, list, I hear
Some far-off hallo break the silent air.
Sec. Bro. Methought so too; what should it be?
Eld. Bro. For certain
Either some one like us night-foundered here,°
Or else some neighbour woodman, or at worst,
Some roving robber calling to his fellows.
Sec. Bro. Heaven keep my sister, again, again, and near,
Best draw, and stand upon our guard.
Eld. Bro. I'll hallo,
If he be friendly he comes well, if not,
Defence is a good cause, and heaven be for us.

The Attendant Spirit habited like a shepherd.

That hallo I should know, what are you? speak; 490
Come not too near, you fall on iron stakes else.°
Spir. What voice is that, my young lord? speak again.
Sec. Bro. O brother, 'tis my father's shepherd sure.
Eld. Bro. Thyrsis? Whose artful strains have oft delayed°
The huddling brook to hear his madrigal,°
And sweetened every musk-rose of the dale,
How cam'st thou here good swain? hath any ram
Slipped from the fold, or young kid lost his dam,
Or straggling wether the pent flock forsook?
How couldst thou find this dark sequestered nook? 500
Spir. O my loved master's heir, and his next joy,°
I came not here on such a trivial toy°
As a strayed ewe, or to pursue the stealth
Of pilfering wolf; not all the fleecy wealth
That doth enrich these downs is worth a thought
To this my errand, and the care it brought.°
But O my virgin Lady, where is she?
How chance she is not in your company?

Eld. Bro. To tell thee sadly shepherd, without blame,°
Or our neglect, we lost her as we came.   510
Spir. Ay me unhappy then my fears are true.°
Eld. Bro. What fears good Thyrsis? Prithee briefly show.°
Spir. I'll tell ye, 'tis not vain or fabulous°
(Though so esteemed by shallow ignorance),
What the sage poets taught by the heavenly Muse,
Storied of old in high immortal verse
Of dire chimeras and enchanted isles,°
And rifted rocks whose entrance leads to hell,
For such there be, but unbelief is blind.
   Within the navel of this hideous wood,°   520
Immured in cypress shades a sorcerer dwells
Of Bacchus, and of Circe born, great Comus,
Deep skilled in all his mother's witcheries,
And here to every thirsty wanderer,
By sly enticement gives his baneful cup,
With many murmurs mixed, whose pleasing poison
The visage quite transforms of him that drinks,
And the inglorious likeness of a beast
Fixes instead, unmoulding reason's mintage
Charactered in the face; this have I learnt°   530
Tending my flocks hard by i' the hilly crofts,°
That brow this bottom glade, whence night by night°
He and his monstrous rout are heard to howl
Like stabled wolves, or tigers at their prey,°
Doing abhorrèd rites to Hecate°
In their obscurèd haunts of inmost bowers,
Yet have they many baits, and guileful spells
To inveigle and invite the unwary sense
Of them that pass unweeting by the way.°
This evening late by then the chewing flocks   540
Had ta'en their supper on the savoury herb
Of knot-grass dew-besprent, and were in fold,°
I sat me down to watch upon a bank
With ivy canopied, and interwove
With flaunting honeysuckle, and began°
Wrapt in a pleasing fit of melancholy°
To meditate my rural minstrelsy,°
Till fancy had her fill, but ere a close°
The wonted roar was up amidst the woods,

And filled the air with barbarous dissonance 550
At which I ceased, and listened them a while,°
Till an unusual stop of sudden silence
Gave respite to the drowsy frighted steeds°
That draw the litter of close-curtained sleep;
At last a soft and solemn-breathing sound
Rose like a steam of rich distilled perfumes,
And stole upon the air, that even Silence
Was took ere she was ware, and wished she might°
Deny her nature, and be never more
Still to be so displaced. I was all ear,° 560
And took in strains that might create a soul
Under the ribs of death, but O ere long
Too well I did perceive it was the voice
Of my most honoured lady, your dear sister.
Amazed I stood, harrowed with grief and fear,
And O poor hapless nightingale thought I,
How sweet thou sing'st, how near the deadly snare!
Then down the lawns I ran with headlong haste
Through paths, and turnings often trod by day,
Till guided by mine ear I found the place 570
Where that damned wizard hid in sly disguise
(For so by certain signs I knew) had met
Already, ere my best speed could prevent,
The aidless innocent Lady his wished prey,
Who gently asked if he had seen such two,
Supposing him some neighbour villager;
Longer I durst not stay, but soon I guessed
Ye were the two she meant, with that I sprung
Into swift flight, till I had found you here,
But further know I not. 580
Sec. Bro.   O night and shades,
How are ye joined with hell in triple knot
Against the unarmed weakness of one virgin
Alone, and helpless! Is this the confidence
You gave me brother?
Eld. Bro.   Yes, and keep it still,
Lean on it safely, not a period°
Shall be unsaid for me: against the threats
Of malice or of sorcery, or that power
Which erring men call chance, this I hold firm,

Virtue may be assailed, but never hurt,
Surprised by unjust force, but not enthralled,   590
Yea even that which mischief meant most harm
Shall in the happy trial prove most glory.
But evil on itself shall back recoil,
And mix no more with goodness, when at last
Gathered like scum, and settled to itself
It shall be in eternal restless change
Self-fed, and self-consumed; if this fail,
The pillared firmament is rottenness,
And earth's base built on stubble. But come, let's on;°
Against the opposing will and arm of heaven   600
May never this just sword be lifted up,
But for that damned magician, let him be girt
With all the grisly legions that troop
Under the sooty flag of Acheron,°
Harpies and hydras, or all the monstrous forms°
'Twixt Africa and Ind, I'll find him out,°
And force him to restore his purchase back,°
Or drag him by the curls, to a foul death,°
Cursed as his life.
Spir.   Alas good venturous youth,
I love thy courage yet, and bold emprise,°   610
But here thy sword can do thee little stead,°
Far other arms, and other weapons must
Be those that quell the might of hellish charms,
He with his bare wand can unthread thy joints,
And crumble all thy sinews.
Eld. Bro.   Why prithee shepherd
How durst thou then thyself approach so near
As to make this relation?
Spir.   Care and utmost shifts°
How to secure the Lady from surprisal,°
Brought to my mind a certain shepherd lad
Of small regard to see to, yet well skilled°   620
In every virtuous plant and healing herb°
That spreads her verdant leaf to the morning ray,
He loved me well, and oft would beg me sing,
Which when I did, he on the tender grass
Would sit, and hearken even to ecstasy,
And in requital ope his leathern scrip,°

And show me simples of a thousand names°
Telling their strange and vigorous faculties;
Amongst the rest a small unsightly root,
But of divine effect, he culled me out;   630
The leaf was darkish, and had prickles on it,
But in another country, as he said,
Bore a bright golden flower, but not in this soil:
Unknown, and like esteemed, and the dull swain
Treads on it daily with his clouted shoon,°
And yet more med'cinal is it than that moly
That Hermes once to wise Ulysses gave;°
He called it haemony, and gave it me,°
And bade me keep it as of sovereign use
'Gainst all enchantments, mildew blast, or damp   640
Or ghastly Furies' apparition;
I pursed it up, but little reckoning made,
Till now that this extremity compelled,
But now I find it true; for by this means
I knew the foul enchanter though disguised,
Entered the very lime-twigs of his spells,°
And yet came off: if you have this about you°
(As I will give you when we go) you may
Boldly assault the necromancer's hall;
Where if he be, with dauntless hardihood,   650
And brandished blade rush on him, break his glass,°
And shed the luscious liquor on the ground,
But seize his wand, though he and his cursed crew
Fierce sign of battle make, and menace high,
Or like the sons of Vulcan vomit smoke,°
Yet will they soon retire, if he but shrink.
Eld. Bro. Thyrsis lead on apace, I'll follow thee,°
And some good angel bear a shield before us.

*The scene changes to a stately palace, set out with all manner of deliciousness:
soft music, tables spread with all dainties. Comus appears with his rabble, and
the Lady set in an enchanted chair, to whom he offers his glass, which she puts
by, and goes about to rise.°*

Comus. Nay lady sit; if I but wave this wand,
Your nerves are all chained up in alabaster,°   660
And you a statue, or as Daphne was
Root-bound, that fled Apollo.°

Lady.   Fool do not boast,
Thou canst not touch the freedom of my mind
With all thy charms, although this corporal rind°
Thou hast immanacled, while heaven sees good.
Comus. Why are you vexed Lady? why do you frown?
Here dwell no frowns, nor anger, from these gates
Sorrow flies far: see, here be all the pleasures
That fancy can beget on youthful thoughts,°
When the fresh blood grows lively, and returns   670
Brisk as the April buds in primrose season.
And first behold this cordial julep here°
That flames, and dances in his crystal bounds°
With spirits of balm, and fragrant syrups mixed.°
Not that nepenthes which the wife of Thone,
In Egypt gave to Jove-born Helena,°
Is of such power to stir up joy as this,
To life so friendly, or so cool to thirst.
Why should you be so cruel to yourself,
And to those dainty limbs which Nature lent   680
For gentle usage, and soft delicacy?
But you invert the covenants of her trust,
And harshly deal like an ill borrower
With that which you received on other terms,
Scorning the unexempt condition°
By which all mortal frailty must subsist,
Refreshment after toil, ease after pain,
That have been tired all day without repast,°
And timely rest have wanted, but fair virgin
This will restore all soon.
Lady   'Twill not false traitor,   690
'Twill not restore the truth and honesty
That thou hast banished from thy tongue with lies,
Was this the cottage, and the safe abode
Thou told'st me of? What grim aspects are these,°
These ugly-headed monsters? Mercy guard me!
Hence with thy brewed enchantments, foul deceiver,
Hast thou betrayed my credulous innocence
With vizored falsehood, and base forgery,°
And wouldst thou seek again to trap me here
With lickerish baits fit to ensnare a brute?°   700
Were it a draught for Juno when she banquets,

I would not taste thy treasonous offer; none
But such as are good men can give good things,
And that which is not good, is not delicious
To a well-governed and wise appetite.
Comus. O foolishness of men! that lend their ears
To those budge doctors of the Stoic fur,°
And fetch their precepts from the Cynic tub,°
Praising the lean and sallow Abstinence.
Wherefore did Nature pour her bounties forth,   710
With such a full and unwithdrawing hand,
Covering the earth with odours, fruits, and flocks,
Thronging the seas with spawn innumerable,
But all to please, and sate the curious taste?°
And set to work millions of spinning worms,
That in their green shops weave the smooth-haired silk°
To deck her sons, and that no corner might
Be vacant of her plenty, in her own loins
She hutched the all-worshipped ore, and precious gems°
To store her children with; if all the world°   720
Should in a pet of temperance feed on pulse,°
Drink the clear stream, and nothing wear but frieze,°
The all-giver would be unthanked, would be unpraised,
Not half his riches known, and yet despised,
And we should serve him as a grudging master,
As a penurious niggard of his wealth,
And live like Nature's bastards, not her sons,
Who would be quite surcharged with her own weight,
And strangled with her waste fertility;
The earth cumbered, and the winged air darked with plumes,° 730
The herds would over-multitude their lords,
The sea o'erfraught would swell, and the unsought diamonds
Would so emblaze the forehead of the deep,°
And so bestud with stars, that they below
Would grow inured to light, and come at last
To gaze upon the sun with shameless brows.
List Lady be not coy, and be not cozened°
With that same vaunted name virginity,°
Beauty is Nature's coin, must not be hoarded,
But must be current, and the good thereof°   740
Consists in mutual and partaken bliss,
Unsavoury in the enjoyment of itself,

If you let slip time, like a neglected rose
It withers on the stalk with languished head.
Beauty is Nature's brag, and must be shown°
In courts, at feasts, and high solemnities
Where most may wonder at the workmanship;
It is for homely features to keep home,
They had their name thence; coarse complexions
And cheeks of sorry grain will serve to ply°   750
The sampler, and to tease the housewife's wool.°
What need a vermeil-tinctured lip for that,°
Love-darting eyes, or tresses like the morn?
There was another meaning in these gifts,
Think what, and be advised, you are but young yet.
Lady. I had not thought to have unlocked my lips
In this unhallowed air, but that this juggler
Would think to charm my judgement, as mine eyes
Obtruding false rules pranked in reason's garb.°
I hate when vice can bolt her arguments,°   760
And virtue has no tongue to check her pride:
Imposter do not charge most innocent Nature,
As if she would her children should be riotous
With her abundance, she good cateress
Means her provision only to the good
That live according to her sober laws,
And holy dictate of spare temperance:
If every just man that now pines with want
Had but a moderate and beseeming share°
Of that which lewdly-pampered luxury°   770
Now heaps upon some few with vast excess,
Nature's full blessings would be well-dispensed
In unsuperfluous even proportion,
And she no whit encumber with her store,°
And then the giver would be better thanked,°
His praise due paid, for swinish gluttony
Ne'er looks to heaven amidst his gorgeous feast,
But with besotted base ingratitude
Crams, and blasphemes his feeder. Shall I go on?
Or have I said enough? To him that dares   780
Arm his profane tongue with contemptuous words
Against the sun-clad power of chastity;°
Fain would I something say, yet to what end?

Thou hast nor ear, nor soul to apprehend
The sublime notion, and high mystery°
That must be uttered to unfold the sage
And serious doctrine of virginity,
And thou art worthy that thou shouldst not know
More happiness than this thy present lot.
Enjoy your dear wit, and gay rhetoric   790
That hath so well been taught her dazzling fence,°
Thou art not fit to hear thyself convinced;
Yet should I try, the uncontrollèd worth°
Of this pure cause would kindle my rapt spirits°
To such a flame of sacred vehemence,
That dumb things would be moved to sympathize,
And the brute Earth would lend her nerves, and shake,°
Till all thy magic structures reared so high,
Were shattered into heaps o'er thy false head.
Comus. She fables not, I feel that I do fear   800
Her words set off by some superior power;
And though not mortal, yet a cold shuddering dew
Dips me all o'er, as when the wrath of Jove°
Speaks thunder, and the chains of Erebus°
To some of Saturn's crew. I must dissemble,°
And try her yet more strongly. Come, no more,°
This is mere moral babble, and direct
Against the canon laws of our foundation;°
I must not suffer this, yet 'tis but the lees°
And settlings of a melancholy blood;°   810
But this will cure all straight, one sip of this°
Will bathe the drooping spirits in delight
Beyond the bliss of dreams. Be wise, and taste.—

*The Brothers rush in with swords drawn, wrest his glass out of his hand, and
break it against the ground; his rout make sign of resistance but are all driven
in. The Attendant Spirit comes in.*

    Spir. What, have you let the false enchanter scape?
O ye mistook, ye should have snatched his wand
And bound him fast; without his rod reversed,°
And backward mutters of dissevering power,°
We cannot free the Lady that sits here
In stony fetters fixed, and motionless;
Yet stay, be not disturbed, now I bethink me,   820

Some other means I have which may be used,
Which once of Meliboeus old I learnt,°
The soothest shepherd that e'er piped on plains.°
    There is a gentle nymph not far from hence,
That with moist curb sways the smooth Severn stream,°
Sabrina is her name, a virgin pure,
Whilom she was the daughter of Locrine,°
That had the sceptre from his father Brute.°
The guiltless damsel flying the mad pursuit
Of her enragèd stepdame Guendolen,   830
Commended her fair innocence to the flood°
That stayed her flight with his cross-flowing course,°
The water nymphs that in the bottom played,
Held up their pearlèd wrists and took her in,
Bearing her straight to agèd Nereus' hall,°
Who piteous of her woes, reared her lank head,°
And gave her to his daughters to imbathe°
In nectared lavers strewed with asphodel,°
And through the porch and inlet of each sense°
Dropped in ambrosial oils till she revived,°   840
And underwent a quick immortal change°
Made goddess of the river; still she retains
Her maiden gentleness, and oft at eve
Visits the herds along the twilight meadows,
Helping all urchin blasts, and ill-luck signs°
That the shrewd meddling elf delights to make,°
Which she with precious vialed liquors heals.
For which the shepherds at their festivals
Carol her goodness loud in rustic lays,°
And throw sweet garland wreaths into her stream   850
Of pansies, pinks, and gaudy daffodils.
And, as the old swain said, she can unlock°
The clasping charm, and thaw the numbing spell,
If she be right invoked in warbled song,
For maidenhood she loves, and will be swift
To aid a virgin such as was herself
In hard-besetting need, this will I try,
And add the power of some adjuring verse.°

SONG

Sabrina fair
   Listen where thou art sitting   860
Under the glassy, cool, translucent wave,
   In twisted braids of lilies knitting
The loose train of thy amber-dropping hair,°
   Listen for dear honour's sake,°
   Goddess of the silver lake,°
      Listen and save.

Listen and appear to us
In name of great Oceanus,°
By the earth-shaking Neptune's mace,°
And Tethys' grave majestic pace,°   870
By hoary Nereus' wrinkled look,°
And the Carpathian wizard's hook,°
By scaly Triton's winding shell,°
And old soothsaying Glaucus' spell,°
By Leucothea's lovely hands,°
And her son that rules the strands,°
By Thetis' tinsel-slippered feet,°
And the songs of sirens sweet,°
By dead Parthenope's dear tomb,°
And fair Ligea's golden comb,°   880
Wherewith she sits on diamond rocks
Sleeking her soft alluring locks,
By all the nymphs that nightly dance
Upon thy streams with wily glance,°
Rise, rise, and heave thy rosy head
From thy coral-paven bed,
And bridle in thy headlong wave,
Till thou our summons answered have.
          Listen and save.

Sabrina rises, attended by water nymphs, and sings.

By the rushy-fringèd bank,   890
Where grows the willow and the osier dank,
   My sliding chariot stays,°
Thick set with agate, and the azurn sheen°
Of turquoise blue, and emerald green
   That in the channel strays,

Whilst from off the waters fleet°
Thus I set my printless feet
O'er the cowslip's velvet head,
  That bends not as I tread,
Gentle swain at thy request   900
  I am here.
Spir. Goddess dear
We implore thy powerful hand
To undo the charmèd band°
Of true virgin here distressed,
Through the force, and through the wile
Of unblessed enchanter vile.°
Sabr. Shepherd 'tis my office best
To help ensnared chastity;
Brightest Lady look on me,   910
Thus I sprinkle on thy breast
Drops that from my fountain pure
I have kept of precious cure,°
Thrice upon thy finger's tip,
Thrice upon thy rubied lip,
Next this marble venomed seat
Smeared with gums of glutinous heat°
I touch with chaste palms moist and cold,
Now the spell hath lost his hold;
And I must haste ere morning hour   920
To wait in Amphitrite's bower.°

Sabrina descends, and the Lady rises out of her seat.

Spir. Virgin, daughter of Locrine,
Sprung of old Anchises' line,°
May thy brimmèd waves for this°
Their full tribute never miss
From a thousand petty rills,°
That tumble down the snowy hills;
Summer drought, or singèd air°
Never scorch thy tresses fair,
Nor wet October's torrent flood°   930
Thy molten crystal fill with mud,
May thy billows roll ashore
The beryl, and the golden ore,°
May thy lofty head be crowned

With many a tower and terrace round,
And here and there thy banks upon
With groves of myrrh, and cinnamon.
Come Lady while heaven lends us grace,
Let us fly this cursèd place,
Lest the sorcerer us entice   940
With some other new device.°
Not a waste or needless sound°
Till we come to holier ground,
I shall be your faithful guide
Through this gloomy covert wide,
And not many furlongs thence
Is your father's residence,
Where this night are met in state
Many a friend to gratulate°
His wished presence, and beside   950
All the swains that there abide,
With jigs, and rural dance resort,
We shall catch them at their sport,
And our sudden coming there
Will double all their mirth and cheer;
Come let us haste, the stars grow high,
But night sits monarch yet in the mid sky.

*The scene changes, presenting Ludlow town and the President's castle; then
come in country dancers, after them the Attendant Spirit, with the two
Brothers and the Lady.*

SONG

Spir. Back, shepherds, back, enough your play,
Till next sunshine holiday,°
Here be without duck or nod°   960
Other trippings to be trod°
Of lighter toes, and such court guise°
As Mercury did first devise°
With the mincing Dryades°
On the lawns, and on the leas.°

This second song presents them to their father and mother.

Noble lord, and lady bright,
I have brought ye new delight,

Here behold so goodly grown
Three fair branches of your own,
Heaven hath timely tried their youth,° 970
Their faith, their patience, and their truth.°
And sent them here through hard assays°
With a crown of deathless praise,
To triumph in victorious dance
O'er sensual folly, and intemperance.

The dances ended, the Spirit epiloguizes.

Spir. To the ocean now I fly,
And those happy climes that lie
Where day never shuts his eye,
Up in the broad fields of the sky:
There I suck the liquid air° 980
All amidst the gardens fair
Of Hesperus, and his daughters three
That sing about the golden tree:°
Along the crispèd shades and bowers°
Revels the spruce and jocund Spring,°
The Graces, and the rosy-bosomed Hours,°
Thither all their bounties bring,
That there eternal summer dwells,°
And west winds, with musky wing°
About the cedarn alleys fling° 990
Nard, and cassia's balmy smells.°
Iris there with humid bow,°
Waters the odorous banks that blow°
Flowers of more mingled hue
Than her purfled scarf can show,°
And drenches with Elysian dew°
(List mortals if your ears be true)°
Beds of hyacinth, and roses,
Where young Adonis oft reposes,°
Waxing well of his deep wound° 1000
In slumber soft, and on the ground
Sadly sits the Assyrian queen;°
But far above in spangled sheen
Celestial Cupid her famed son advanced,°
Holds his dear Psyche sweet entranced

After her wandering labours long,
Till free consent the gods among
Make her his eternal bride,°
And from her fair unspotted side
Two blissful twins are to be born,   1010
Youth and Joy; so Jove hath sworn.°
   But now my task is smoothly done,
I can fly, or I can run
Quickly to the green earth's end,
Where the bowed welkin slow doth bend,°
And from thence can soar as soon
To the corners of the moon.°
   Mortals that would follow me,
Love Virtue, she alone is free,
She can teach ye how to climb   1020
Higher than the sphery chime;°
Or if Virtue feeble were,
Heaven itself would stoop to her.

ENGLISH POEMS ADDED
IN 1673

On the Death of a Fair Infant Dying of a Cough

I

O fairest flower no sooner blown but blasted,°
Soft silken primrose fading timelessly,°
Summer's chief honour if thou hadst outlasted
Bleak winter's force that made thy blossom dry;
For he being amorous on that lovely dye
    That did thy cheek envermeil, thought to kiss°
But killed alas, and then bewailed his fatal bliss.°

II

For since grim Aquilo his charioteer°
By boisterous rape the Athenian damsel got,°
He thought it touched his deity full near,   10
If likewise he some fair one wedded not,
Thereby to wipe away the infamous blot
    Of long-uncoupled bed, and childless eld,°
Which 'mongst the wanton gods a foul reproach was held.

III

So mounting up in icy-pearlèd car,
Through middle empire of the freezing air°
He wandered long, till thee he spied from far,
There ended was his quest, there ceased his care.°
Down he descended from his snow-soft chair,°
    But all unwares with his cold-kind embrace°   20
Unhoused thy virgin soul from her fair biding place.

IV

Yet art thou not inglorious in thy fate;
For so Apollo, with unweeting hand°
Whilom did slay his dearly lovèd mate

Young Hyacinth born on Eurotas' strand,°
Young Hyacinth the pride of Spartan land;
　　But then transformed him to a purple flower—
Alack that so to change thee winter had no power.

V

Yet can I not persuade me thou art dead
Or that thy corpse corrupts in earth's dark womb,°   30
Or that thy beauties lie in wormy bed,
Hid from the world in a low-delvèd tomb;
Could heaven for pity thee so strictly doom?
　　O no! for something in thy face did shine
Above mortality that showed thou wast divine.

VI

Resolve me then O soul most surely blest
(If so it be that thou these plaints dost hear),
Tell me bright spirit where'er thou hoverest,
Whether above that high first-moving sphere°
Or in the Elysian fields (if such there were),°   40
　　O say me true if thou wert mortal wight°
And why from us so quickly thou didst take thy flight.

VII

Wert thou some star which from the ruined roof
Of shaked Olympus by mischance didst fall;°
Which careful Jove in nature's true behoof°
Took up, and in fit place did reinstall?
Or did of late Earth's sons besiege the wall°
　　Of sheeny heaven, and thou some goddess fled°
Amongst us here below to hide thy nectared head?

VIII

Or wert thou that just maid who once before°   50
Forsook the hated earth, O tell me sooth,
And cam'st again to visit us once more?
Or wert thou that sweet smiling youth?°
Or that crowned matron sage white-robèd Truth?
　　Or any other of that heavenly brood
Let down in cloudy throne to do the world some good?

IX

Or wert thou of the golden-wingèd host,°
Who having clad thyself in human weed,°
To earth from thy prefixèd seat didst post,°
And after short abode fly back with speed,   60
As if to show what creatures heaven doth breed,
   Thereby to set the hearts of men on fire
To scorn the sordid world, and unto heaven aspire?

X

But O why didst thou not stay here below
To bless us with thy heaven-loved innocence,
To slake his wrath whom sin hath made our foe,°
To turn swift-rushing black perdition hence,
Or drive away the slaughtering pestilence,°
   To stand 'twixt us and our deservèd smart?
But thou canst best perform that office where thou art.   70

XI

Then thou the mother of so sweet a child
Her false imagined loss cease to lament,
And wisely learn to curb thy sorrows wild;
Think what a present thou to God hast sent,
And render him with patience what he lent;°
   This if thou do he will an offspring give,°
That till the world's last end shall make thy name to live.

At a Vacation Exercise in the
College, part Latin, part English

The Latin Speeches ended, the English thus began

Hail native language, that by sinews weak
Didst move my first endeavouring tongue to speak,
And mad'st imperfect words with childish trips,
Half unpronounced, slide through my infant lips,
Driving dumb silence from the portal door,
Where he had mutely sat two years before:
Here I salute thee and thy pardon ask,
That now I use thee in my latter task:°

Small loss it is that thence can come unto thee,
I know my tongue but little grace can do thee.   10
Thou need'st not be ambitious to be first,
Believe me I have thither packed the worst:°
And, if it happen as I did forecast,
The daintiest dishes shall be served up last.
I pray thee then deny me not thy aid
For this same small neglect that I have made;
But haste thee straight to do me once a pleasure,
And from thy wardrobe bring thy chiefest treasure;°
Not those new-fangled toys, and trimming slight°
Which takes our late fantastics with delight,   20
But cull those richest robes, and gayest attire°
Which deepest spirits, and choicest wits desire:
I have some naked thoughts that rove about
And loudly knock to have their passage out;
And weary of their place do only stay
Till thou hast decked them in thy best array;
That so they may without suspect or fears°
Fly swiftly to this fair assembly's ears;
Yet I had rather, if I were to choose,
Thy service in some graver subject use,   30
Such as may make thee search thy coffers round,
Before thou clothe my fancy in fit sound:°
Such where the deep transported mind may soar°
Above the wheeling poles, and at heaven's door°
Look in, and see each blissful deity
How he before the thunderous throne doth lie,°
Listening to what unshorn Apollo sings°
To the touch of golden wires, while Hebe brings°
Immortal nectar to her kingly sire:
Then passing through the spheres of watchful fire,°   40
And misty regions of wide air next under,
And hills of snow and lofts of pilèd thunder,°
May tell at length how green-eyed Neptune raves,
In heaven's defiance mustering all his waves;
Then sing of secret things that came to pass
When beldam Nature in her cradle was;
And last of kings and queens and heroes old,
Such as the wise Demodocus once told°
In solemn songs at King Alcinous' feast,

While sad Ulysses' soul and all the rest   50
Are held with his melodious harmony
In willing chains and sweet captivity.°
But fie my wandering muse how thou dost stray!
Expectance calls thee now another way,°
Thou knowest it must be now thy only bent
To keep in compass of thy predicament:°
Then quick about thy purposed business come,
That to the next I may resign my room.°

Then ENS *is represented as father of the Predicaments his ten sons, whereof the
eldest stood for* SUBSTANCE *with his Canons, which* ENS *thus speaking,
explains.*

Good luck befriend thee son; for at thy birth
The fairy ladies danced upon the hearth;   60
Thy drowsy nurse hath sworn she did them spy
Come tripping to the room where thou didst lie;
And sweetly singing round about thy bed
Strew all their blessings on thy sleeping head.
She heard them give thee this, that thou shouldst still°
From eyes of mortals walk invisible,°
Yet there is something that doth force my fear,
For once it was my dismal hap to hear
A sibyl old, bow-bent with crooked age,°
That far events full wisely could presage,   70
And in time's long and dark prospective glass°
Foresaw what future days should bring to pass,
Your son, said she (nor can you it prevent),
Shall subject be to many an accident.°
O'er all his brethren he shall reign as king,
Yet every one shall make him underling,
And those that cannot live from him asunder
Ungratefully shall strive to keep him under,
In worth and excellence he shall outgo them,
Yet being above them, he shall be below them;   80
From others he shall stand in need of nothing,
Yet on his brothers shall depend for clothing.
To find a foe it shall not be his hap,
And peace shall lull him in her flow'ry lap;
Yet shall he live in strife, and at his door
Devouring war shall never cease to roar:

Yea it shall be his natural property
To harbour those that are at enmity.
What power, what force, what mighty spell, if not
Your learnèd hands, can loose this Gordian knot?°   90

The next QUANTITY *and* QUALITY, *spake in prose, then* RELATION *was called by his name.*

Rivers arise; whether thou be the son,°
Of utmost Tweed, or Ouse, or gulfy Dun,°
Or Trent, who like some earth-born giant spreads
His thirty arms along the indented meads,
Or sullen Mole that runneth underneath,°
Or Severn swift, guilty of maiden's death,°
Or rocky Avon, or of sedgy Lea,
Or coaly Tyne, or ancient hallowèd Dee,°
Or Humber loud that keeps the Scythian's name,°
Or Medway smooth, or royal towered Thame.   100

The rest was prose.

Sonnet 11

A book was writ of late called *Tetrachordon*;°
And woven close, both matter, form and style;
The subject new: it walked the town awhile,
Numbering good intellects; now seldom pored on.°
Cries the stall-reader, Bless us! what a word on°
A title-page is this! And some in file
Stand spelling false, while one might walk to Mile-°
End Green. Why is it harder sirs than Gordon,°
Colkitto, or Macdonnel, or Galasp?°
Those rugged names to our like mouths grow sleek°   10
That would have made Quintilian stare and gasp.°
Thy age, like ours, O soul of Sir John Cheke,°
Hated not learning worse than toad or asp;
When thou taught'st Cambridge, and King Edward Greek.

Sonnet 12
On the Same

I did but prompt the age to quit their clogs°
  By the known rules of ancient liberty,°
  When straight a barbarous noise environs me
  Of owls and cuckoos, asses, apes and dogs.°
As when those hinds that were transformed to frogs
  Railed at Latona's twin-born progeny
  Which after held the sun and moon in fee.°
  But this is got by casting pearl to hogs;°
That bawl for freedom in their senseless mood,
  And still revolt when truth would set them free.°   10
  Licence they mean when they cry liberty;
For who loves that, must first be wise and good;
  But from that mark how far they rove we see°
  For all this waste of wealth, and loss of blood.°

Sonnet 13
To Mr H. Lawes, on his Airs

Harry whose tuneful and well-measured song
  First taught our English music how to span
  Words with just note and accent, not to scan°
  With Midas' ears, committing short and long;°
Thy worth and skill exempts thee from the throng,
  With praise enough for envy to look wan;
  To after age thou shalt be writ the man,
  That with smooth air couldst humour best our tongue.°
Thou honour'st verse, and verse must lend her wing
  To honour thee, the priest of Phoebus' choir°   10
  That tun'st their happiest lines in hymn, or story.°
Dante shall give fame leave to set thee higher
  Than his Casella, whom he wooed to sing°
  Met in the milder shades of Purgatory.

Sonnet 14

When faith and love which parted from thee never,
  Had ripened thy just soul to dwell with God,
  Meekly thou didst resign this earthy load
Of death, called life; which us from life doth sever.°
Thy works and alms and all thy good endeavour
  Stayed not behind, nor in the grave were trod;
  But as faith pointed with her golden rod,
Followed thee up to joy and bliss forever.°
Love led them on, and faith who knew them best
  Thy handmaids, clad them o'er with purple beams   10
  And azure wings, that up they flew so dressed,
And speak the truth of thee on glorious themes
  Before the judge, who thenceforth bid thee rest
  And drink thy fill of pure immortal streams.

Sonnet 15
On the Late Massacre in Piedmont

Avenge O Lord thy slaughtered saints, whose bones°
  Lie scattered on the Alpine mountains cold,
  Even them who kept thy truth so pure of old
  When all our fathers worshipped stocks and stones,°
Forget not: in thy book record their groans°
  Who were thy sheep and in their ancient fold
  Slain by the bloody Piedmontese that rolled
  Mother with infant down the rocks. Their moans
The vales redoubled to the hills, and they
  To heaven. Their martyred blood and ashes sow°   10
  O'er all the Italian fields where still doth sway
The triple tyrant: that from these may grow°
  A hundredfold, who having learnt thy way
  Early may fly the Babylonian woe.°

Sonnet 16

When I consider how my light is spent,°
  Ere half my days, in this dark world and wide,°
  And that one talent which is death to hide,
  Lodged with me useless, though my soul more bent
To serve therewith my maker, and present
  My true account, lest he returning chide,°
  Doth God exact day-labour, light denied,°
  I fondly ask; but patience to prevent°
That murmur, soon replies, God doth not need
  Either man's work or his own gifts, who best   10
  Bear his mild yoke, they serve him best, his state°
Is kingly. Thousands at his bidding speed°
  And post o'er land and ocean without rest:
  They also serve who only stand and wait.

Sonnet 17

Lawrence of virtuous father virtuous son,
  Now that the fields are dank, and ways are mire,
  Where shall we sometimes meet, and by the fire
  Help waste a sullen day; what may be won°
From the hard season gaining: time will run
  On smoother, till Favonius reinspire°
  The frozen earth; and clothe in fresh attire
  The lily and rose, that neither sowed nor spun.°
What neat repast shall feast us, light and choice,°
  Of Attic taste, with wine, whence we may rise°   10
  To hear the lute well touched, or artful voice
Warble immortal notes and Tuscan air?°
  He who of those delights can judge, and spare
  To interpose them oft, is not unwise.°

Sonnet 18

Cyriack, whose grandsire on the royal bench
  Of British Themis, with no mean applause°
  Pronounced and in his volumes taught our laws,°
  Which others at their bar so often wrench;°
Today deep thoughts resolve with me to drench°
  In mirth, that after no repenting draws;
  Let Euclid rest and Archimedes pause,
  And what the Swede intend, and what the French.°
To measure life, learn thou betimes, and know°
  Toward solid good what leads the nearest way;   10
  For other things mild heaven a time ordains,°
And disapproves that care, though wise in show,
  That with superfluous burden loads the day,
  And when God sends a cheerful hour, refrains.

Sonnet 19

Methought I saw my late espousèd saint°
  Brought to me like Alcestis from the grave,°
  Whom Jove's great son to her glad husband gave,
  Rescued from death by force though pale and faint.
Mine as whom washed from spot of childbed taint,°
  Purification in the old law did save,°
  And such, as yet once more I trust to have
  Full sight of her in heaven without restraint,
Came vested all in white, pure as her mind:°
  Her face was veiled, yet to my fancied sight,°   10
  Love, sweetness, goodness in her person shined
So clear, as in no face with more delight.
  But O as to embrace me she inclined°
  I waked, she fled, and day brought back my night.

The Fifth Ode of Horace, Lib. I

Quis multa gracilis te puer in rosa

Rendered almost word for word without rhyme according to the Latin measure, as near as the language will permit.

What slender youth bedewed with liquid odours°
Courts thee on roses in some pleasant cave,
 Pyrrha for whom bind'st thou
 In wreaths thy golden hair,
Plain in thy neatness; O how oft shall he
On faith and changèd gods complain: and seas
 Rough with black winds and storms
 Unwonted shall admire:°
Who now enjoys thee credulous, all gold,°
Who always vacant always amiable   10
 Hopes thee; of flattering gales°
 Unmindful? Hapless they
To whom thou untried seem'st fair. Me in my vowed
Picture the sacred wall declares t' have hung°
 My dank and dropping weeds
 To the stern god of sea.

On the New Forcers of Conscience
under the Long Parliament

Because you have thrown off your prelate lord,°
 And with stiff vows renounced his liturgy
 To seize the widowed whore plurality°
From them whose sin ye envied, not abhorred,
Dare ye for this adjure the civil sword°
 To force our consciences that Christ set free,
 And ride us with a classic hierarchy°
 Taught ye by mere A. S. and Rutherford?°
Men whose life, learning, faith and pure intent
 Would have been held in high esteem with Paul° 10
 Must now be named and printed heretics

By shallow Edwards and Scotch What-d'ye-call:°
    But we do hope to find out all your tricks,
    Your plots and packing worse than those of Trent,°
        That so the Parliament
May with their wholesome and preventive shears
Clip your phylacteries, though balk your ears,°
        And succour our just fears
When they shall read this clearly in your charge,°
New *Presbyter* is but old *Priest* writ large.°   20

UNCOLLECTED ENGLISH POEMS

On the Lord General Fairfax at the Siege of Colchester

Fairfax, whose name in arms through Europe rings°
  Filling each mouth with envy, or with praise,
  And all her jealous monarchs with amaze,
  And rumours loud, that daunt remotest kings,
Thy firm unshaken virtue ever brings°
  Victory home, though new rebellions raise°
  Their hydra heads, and the false north displays°
  Her broken league, to imp their serpent wings,°
O yet a nobler task awaits thy hand;°
  For what can war, but endless war still breed,   10
  Till truth, and right from violence be freed,
And public faith cleared from the shameful brand
  Of public fraud. In vain doth valour bleed
  While avarice, and rapine share the land.

To the Lord General Cromwell

Cromwell, our chief of men, who through a cloud°
  Not of war only, but detractions rude,
  Guided by faith and matchless fortitude
  To peace and truth thy glorious way hast ploughed,°
And on the neck of crownèd fortune proud
  Hast reared God's trophies and his work pursued,°
  While Darwen stream with blood of Scots imbrued,°
  And Dunbar field resounds thy praises loud,°
And Worcester's laureate wreath; yet much remains°
  To conquer still; peace hath her victories°   10
  No less renowned than war, new foes arise
Threatening to bind our souls with secular chains:°
  Help us to save free conscience from the paw
  Of hireling wolves whose gospel is their maw.°

To Sir Henry Vane the Younger

Vane, young in years, but in sage counsel old,°
  Than whom a better senator ne'er held
  The helm of Rome, when gowns not arms repelled°
  The fierce Epirot and the African bold:°
Whether to settle peace or to unfold
  The drift of hollow states, hard to be spelled,°
  Then to advise how war may best, upheld,
  Move by her two main nerves, iron and gold°
In all her equipage: besides to know°
  Both spiritual power and civil, what each means,   10
  What severs each, thou hast learned, which few have done.
The bounds of either sword to thee we owe;°
  Therefore on thy firm hand Religion leans
  In peace, and reckons thee her eldest son.

To Mr Cyriack Skinner Upon
his Blindness

Cyriack, this three years' day these eyes, though clear°
  To outward view, of blemish or of spot,
  Bereft of light their seeing have forgot,°
  Nor to their idle orbs doth sight appear
Of sun or moon or star throughout the year,
  Or man or woman. Yet I argue not°
  Against heaven's hand or will, nor bate a jot
  Of heart or hope; but still bear up and steer°
Right onward. What supports me dost thou ask?
  The conscience, friend, to have lost them overplied°   10
  In liberty's defence, my noble task,
Of which all Europe talks from side to side.
  This thought might lead me through the world's vain mask°
  Content though blind, had I no better guide.

LATIN POEMS

ELEGIARUM LIBER

Elegia Prima

AD CAROLUM DIODATUM

Tandem, care, tuae mihi pervenere tabellae,
    Pertulit et voces nuntia charta tuas;
Pertulit occidua Devae Cestrensis ab ora
    Vergivium prono qua petit amne salum.
Multum, crede, iuvat terras aluisse remotas
    Pectus amans nostri, tamque fidele caput,
Quodque mihi lepidum tellus longinqua sodalem
    Debet, at unde brevi reddere iussa velit.
Me tenet urbs reflua quam Thamesis alluit unda,
    Meque nec invitum patria dulcis habet.   10
Iam nec arundiferum mihi cura revisere Camum,
    Nec dudum vetiti me laris angit amor.
Nuda nec arva placent, umbrasque negantia molles.
    Quam male Phoebicolis convenit ille locus!
Nec duri libet usque minas perferre magistri,
    Caeteraque ingenio non subeunda meo.
Si sit hoc exilium, patrios adiise penates,
    Et vacuum curis otia grata sequi,
Non ego vel profugi nomen sortemve recuso,
    Laetus et exilii conditione fruor.   20
O utinam vates nunquam graviora tulisset
    Ille Tomitano flebilis exul agro!
Non tunc Ionio quicquam cessisset Homero,
    Neve foret victo laus tibi prima, Maro.
Tempora nam licet hic placidis dare libera Musis,
    Et totum rapiunt me, mea vita, libri.
Excipit hinc fessum sinuosi pompa theatri,
    Et vocat ad plausus garrula scena suos.
Seu catus auditur senior, seu prodigus haeres,
    Seu procus, aut posita casside miles adest,   30
Sive decennali foecundus lite patronus
    Detonat inculto barbara verba foro;
Saepe vafer gnato succurrit servus amanti,
    Et nasum rigidi fallit ubique patris;
Saepe novos illic virgo mirata calores

A BOOK OF ELEGIES

Elegy 1

TO CHARLES DIODATI

At last, dear friend, your letter has reached me, and the messenger tablet has borne me your words from the western shore of Chester's Dee, where with swift falling stream it seeks the Vergivian sea.° Great joy it is, believe me, that distant lands have fostered a heart that loves me and a head so true, and that the remote region which withholds my charming companion will soon at my behest return him to me.

I am now in the city that is washed by the ebbing and flowing Thames, tarrying, not unwilling, under my father's kindly roof. Meanwhile I care not to revisit reedy Cam; I suffer from no longing for my forbidden hearth; I find no pleasure in bare fields that afford no gentle shade. How ill that place befits the cult of Phoebus!° Nor does it suit me always to endure the threats of a harsh master, and other wrongs to which my nature will not submit. If this be exile, to have retired to my father's house, and there carefree to live in pleasant leisure, then I refuse neither the name nor the lot of an exile, and gladly enjoy such banishment. Would that no heavier blow had fallen on the lamentable bard who was exiled to the land of Tomis.° In naught would he then have yielded to Ionian Homer, nor would the first praise be yours, O vanquished Maro.

Here I may freely give my time to the tranquil muses; and here my books, which are my life, absorb me wholly. When I am weary with these, the splendours of the changing theatre° call me forth, and the babbling stage summons me to its applause. Sometimes it is the grasping old man or spendthrift heir who speaks, the lover or the soldier with helmet doffed who is here; again it is an attorney grown rich on a ten year's suit who thunders forth his barbarous jargon to the untutored court. Often the sly servant aids the enamoured son, and on every side cheats the stern father under his very nose; there often the maiden, marvelling at the unwonted glow of passion, knows not what love is—

Quid sit amor nescit, dum quoque nescit amat.
   Sive cruentatum furiosa Tragoedia sceptrum
   Quassat, et effusis crinibus ora rotat.
Et dolet, et specto, iuvat et spectasse dolendo.
   Interdum et lacrymis dulcis amaror inest: 40
Seu puer infelix indelibata reliquit
   Gaudia, et abrupto flendus amore cadit;
Seu ferus e tenebris iterat Styga criminis ultor,
   Conscia funereo pectora torre movens;
Seu maeret Pelopeia domus, seu nobilis Ili,
   Aut luit incestos aula Creontis avos.
Sed neque sub tecto semper nec in urbe latemus,
   Irrita nec nobis tempora veris eunt.
Nos quoque lucus habet vicina consitus ulmo,
   Atque suburbani nobilis umbra loci.   50
Saepius hic, blandas spirantia sidera flammas,
   Virgineos videas praeteriisse choros.
Ah quoties dignae stupui miracula formae
   Quae possit senium vel reparare Iovis!
Ah quoties vidi superantia lumina gemmas,
   Atque faces quotquot volvit uterque polus;
Collaque bis vivi Pelopis quae brachia vincant,
   Quaeque fluit puro nectare tincta via,
Et decus eximium frontis, tremulosque capillos,
   Aurea quae fallax retia tendit Amor;   60
Pellacesque genas, ad quas hyacinthina sordet
   Purpura, et ipse tui floris, Adoni, rubor!
Cedite laudatae toties Heröides olim,
   Et quaecunque vagum cepit amica Iovem;
Cedite Achaemeniae turrita fronte puellae,
   Et quot Susa colunt, Memnoniamque Ninon;
Vos etiam Danaae fasces submittite Nymphae,
   Et vos Iliacae, Romuleaeque nurus;
Nec Pompeianas Tarpeia Musa columnas
   Iactet, et Ausoniis plena theatra stolis.   70
Gloria virginibus debetur prima Britannis;
   Extera, sat tibi sit, foemina, posse sequi.
Tuque urbs Dardaniis, Londinum, structa colonis,
   Turrigerum late conspicienda caput,
Tu nimium felix intra tua moenia claudis
   Quicquid formosi pendulus orbis habet.

yet, not knowing, loves. Then raging Tragedy° brandishes her gory
sceptre, and rolls her eyes beneath dishevelled locks. As I look upon
her, the sight pains me, yet in the pain there is pleasure. Sometimes in
tears the sweet and the bitter are mingled: as when perchance an
unhappy boy leaves his joy untasted, and torn from his love, perishes
lamented; or when the cruel avenger again has crossed the Styx from
the abode of the shades, stirring with baleful torch the hearts that are
conscious of sin; or when the house of Pelops,° or of noble Ilus,°
mourns, or Creon's° house suffers for its incestuous sires.

   But I do not always live secluded within doors, nor even within the
city; neither do I let the spring pass by in vain. I visit, too, the neighbouring grove thick-set with elms, and near the city a place celebrated
for its shade. There one may often see the bands of maidens pass, stars
that breathe seductive flames. Ah, how often have I stood amazed at the
marvellous beauty of a form which might rejuvenate even the old age of
Jove; ah, how often have I seen eyes brighter than jewels, brighter than
all the stars that turn about either pole; necks which surpass the arms of
twice-living Pelops,° and the galaxy that flows with pure nectar; how
often seen the surpassing beauty of brow and light-blown hair, golden
snares set by deceiving Love; and how often seen alluring cheeks, to
which hyacinthine purple, and even the blush of your flower, O
Adonis,° are pale. Give place, O heroines, once so often lauded,° and
whatever mistress captivated wandering Jove. Give place, O Achaemen-
ian° maidens with foreheads high-turreted, and all you who dwell in
Susa and Memnonian Nineveh;° and even you, O Grecian nymphs,
and you Trojan and Roman women, acknowledge yourselves inferior.
Let not the Tarpeian muse° boast of Pompey's porch,° and of the
theatre thronged with Ausonian° stoles. To the virgins of Britain first
glory is due; and as for you, O foreign women, let it be enough that you
may follow after. And you, London, a city built by Dardanian colonists,°
with tower-crowned head conspicuous far and wide, happy are you
beyond measure in holding within your walls whatever beauty this

Non tibi tot caelo scintillant astra sereno,
    Endymioneae turba ministra deae,
Quot tibi conspicuae formaque auroque puellae
    Per medias radiant turba videnda vias.   80
Creditur huc geminis venisse invecta columbis
    Alma pharetrigero milite cincta Venus,
Huic Cnidon, et riguas Simoentis flumine valles,
    Huic Paphon, et roseam posthabitura Cypron.
Ast ego, dum pueri sinit indulgentia caeci,
    Moenia quam subito linquere fausta paro;
Et vitare procul malefidae infamia Circes
    Atria, divini Molyos usus ope.
Stat quoque iuncosas Cami remeare paludes,
    Atque iterum raucae murmur adire Scholae.   90
Interea fidi parvum cape munus amici,
    Paucaque in alternos verba coacta modos.

Elegia Secunda

Anno Aetatis 17

IN OBITUM PRAECONIS ACADEMICI CANTABRIGIENSIS

Te, qui conspicuus baculo fulgente solebas
    Palladium toties ore ciere gregem,
Ultima praeconum praeconem te quoque saeva
    Mors rapit, officio nec favet ipsa suo.
Candidiora licet fuerint tibi tempora plumis
    Sub quibus accipimus delituisse Iovem,
O dignus tamen Haemonio iuvenescere succo,
    Dignus in Aesonios vivere posse dies,
Dignus quem Stygiis medica revocaret ab undis
    Arte Coronides, saepe rogante dea.   10
Tu si iussus eras acies accire togatas,
    Et celer a Phoebo nuntius ire tuo,
Talis in Iliaca stabat Cyllenius aula
    Alipes, aetherea missus ab arce Patris;
Talis et Eurybates ante ora furentis Achillei
    Rettulit Atridae iussa severa ducis.
Magna sepulchrorum regina, satelles Averni,
    Saeva nimis Musis, Palladi saeva nimis,

pendulous orb contains. Not so many stars, ministrant troops of Endymion's goddess,° shine upon you from heaven serene, not so many as the maidens bright with gold and beauty who are seen shining through your streets. Hither, it is believed, came kindly Venus, borne by her twin doves, and attended by her quiver-bearing soldiery, preferring this to Cnidus and the valleys watered by Simöis, to Paphos and to rosy Cyprus.°

But as for me, while yet the indulgence of the blind boy° permits, I am preparing with what haste I can to leave these happy walls, and with the aid of divine moly° to guide my steps far from the infamous halls of faithless Circe. It is also fixed that I return to the sedgy marshes of Cam, and once more enter the hoarse murmur of the schools. Meanwhile accept the small tribute of a faithful friend, even these few words coaxed into alternate measures.°

Elegy 2

At the Age of Seventeen

ON THE DEATH OF THE CAMBRIDGE UNIVERSITY BEADLE

Conspicuous with your shining staff,° you were wont so often to summon the Palladian band;° but, beadle as you were, fell Death, the last of all beadles, has seized you, and shows no favour even to his own office. Although your temples were whiter than the plumes under which we have heard that Jove° disguised himself, O yet were you worthy to renew your youth with a Haemonian potion,° worthy like Aeson to relive your early days, worthy that Coronides, at the frequent prayer of a goddess, should with his healing art recall you from the waves of Styx.° If you were ordered by your Apollo to go as a swift messenger to summon the gowned ranks, you stood like wing-footed Cyllenius in the Trojan halls,° sent from the ethereal citadel of his father; stood like Eurybates,° when before the face of angry Achilles he announced the stern commands of his lord, the son of Atreus. O great queen° of sepulchres, attendant of Avernus,° too cruel to the muses, too cruel to

Quin illos rapias qui pondus inutile terrae?
   Turba quidem est telis ista petenda tuis.   20
Vestibus hunc igitur pullis, Academia, luge,
   Et madeant lacrimis nigra feretra tuis.
Fundat et ipsa modos querebunda Elegeia tristes,
   Personet et totis naenia moesta scholis.

Elegia Tertia

Anno Aetatis 17

IN OBITUM PRAESULIS WINTONIENSIS

Moestus eram, et tacitus, nullo comitante, sedebam.
   Haerebantque animo tristia plura meo,
Protinus en subiit funestae cladis imago
   Fecit in Angliaco quam Libitina solo;
Dum procerum ingressa est splendentes marmore turres
   Dira sepulchrali Mors metuenda face,
Pulsavitque auro gravidos et iaspide muros,
   Nec metuit satrapum sternere falce greges.
Tunc memini clarique ducis, fratrisque verendi,
   Intempestivis ossa cremata rogis;   10
Et memini Heroum quos vidit ad aethera raptos,
   Flevit et amissos Belgia tota duces.
At te praecipue luxi, dignissime praesul,
   Wintoniaeque olim gloria magna tuae;
Delicui fletu, et tristi sic ore querebar:
   'Mors fera, Tartareo diva secunda Iovi,
Nonne satis quod silva tuas persentiat iras,
   Et quod in herbosos ius tibi detur agros,
Quodque afflata tuo marcescant lilia tabo,
   Et crocus, et pulchrae Cypridi sacra rosa?   20
Nec sinis ut semper fluvio contermina quercus
   Miretur lapsus praetereuntis aquae?
Et tibi succumbit liquido quae plurima caelo
   Evehitur pennis, quamlibet augur, avis,
Et quae mille nigris errant animalia silvis,
   Et quod alunt mutum Proteos antra pecus.
Invida, tanta tibi cum sit concessa potestas,

Pallas! Why not seize those who are useless burdens to the earth? At that crowd should you aim your arrows. Therefore, Cambridge, mourn in sable robes for this man, and let his dark bier be wet with your tears. Let complaining Elegy pour forth her sad measures, and let a melancholy dirge sound through all the schools.

Elegy 3

At the Age of Seventeen

ON THE DEATH OF THE BISHOP OF WINCHESTER

Silent and alone I sat in sorrowful mood, and many griefs laid hold upon my soul, when, lo! suddenly arose the phantom of the deadly plague which Libitina° sent upon England, when bitter Death, fearful with her sepulchral torch, entered the gleaming marble palaces of the great, smote the walls heavy with jasper and gold, and feared not with her scythe to mow down troops of nobles. Then I remembered that famous duke and his revered brother,° whose bones were consumed on untimely pyres; I remembered the heroes that all Belgia° saw caught up to heaven, the lost leaders whom she wept.

But I chiefly lamented for you, most noble Bishop, once the crowning glory of Winchester. I melted in tears, and thus sadly complained:

'O cruel Death, goddess next in power to Tartarean Jove,° is it not enough that the forests suffer under your wrath, that power is given you over the grass of the field, that the lily, the crocus, and the rose sacred to lovely Cypris,° droop at the touch of your withering breath? Nor do you permit the oak that stands by the river to gaze forever at the flow of the passing water. And the birds, as many as are borne on wings through the liquid heaven—although they are diviners of the future; all the thousand wild beasts that wander in the dark forests; the dumb herds that find shelter in the caves of Proteus;° all succumb to you. You

Quid iuvat humana tingere caede manus?
Nobileque in pectus certas acuisse sagittas,
  Semideamque animam sede fugasse sua?'   30
Talia dum lacrymans alto sub pectore volvo,
  Roscidus occiduis Hesperus exit aquis,
Et Tartessiaco submerserat aequore currum
  Phoebus, ab Eöo littore mensus iter.
Nec mora, membra cavo posui refovenda cubili;
  Condiderant oculos noxque soporque meos,
Cum mihi visus eram lato spatiarier agro—
  Heu! nequit ingenium visa referre meum.
Illic punicea radiabant omnia luce,
  Ut matutino cum iuga sole rubent;   40
Ac veluti cum pandit opes Thaumantia proles
  Vestitu nituit multicolore solum;
Non dea tam variis ornavit floribus hortos
  Alcinoi Zephyro Chloris amata levi.
Flumina vernantes lambunt argentea campos,
  Ditior Hesperio flavet arena Tago.
Serpit odoriferas per opes levis aura Favoni,
  Aura sub innumeris humida nata rosis:
Talis in extermis terrae Gangetidis oris
  Luciferi regis fingitur esse domus.   50
Ipse racemiferis dum densas vitibus umbras
  Et pellucentes miror ubique locos,
Ecce mihi subito praesul Wintonius astat!
  Sidereum nitido fulsit in ore iubar;
Vestis ad auratos defluxit candida talos;
  Infula divinum cinxerat alba caput.
Dumque senex tali incedit venerandus amictu.
  Intremuit laeto florea terra sono;
Agmina gemmatis plaudunt caelestia pennis;
  Pura triumphali personat aethra tuba.   60
Quisque novum amplexu comitem cantuque salutat,
  Hosque aliquis placido misit ab ore sonos:
'Nate, veni, et patrii felix cape gaudia regni;
  Semper abhinc duro, nate, labore vaca.'
Dixit, et aligerae tetigerunt nablia turmae;
  At mihi cum tenebris aurea pulsa quies;
Flebam turbatos Cephaleia pellice somnos.
  Talia contingant somnia saepe mihi!

are envious? But, endowed with such power, what joy is it to stain your hands with human blood, to sharpen your unerring bolts to pierce a noble breast, and to drive a soul half divine from its home?'

While thus in tears I pondered such matters deep in my heart, dewy Hesperus° arose from the western wave,° and Phoebus, having finished his course from the shores of dawn, had submerged his chariot in the Iberian ocean. Straightway I laid myself on my yielding bed to find repose, and night and sleep had closed my eyes, when, as it seemed, I was wandering in a wide field—but, alas! I have no gift to tell what I saw. There all things glowed with a purple light, as when the mountain-peaks grow red in the morning sun; and, even as when Iris° has scattered her rich offspring, the earth was luxuriant in many-coloured robes. Chloris,° the goddess beloved of gentle Zephyr, did not adorn the garden of Alcinous° with flowers so varied. Through verdant fields flowed silver streams whose sands shone a richer gold than those of Hesperian Tagus.° Through the fragrant leaves the soft breath of Favonius° trembled, the moist breath born beneath countless roses. Such a place, it is supposed, is the home of royal Lucifer,° in a land on the farthest shores of the Ganges. As I gazed in wonder at these sunlit spaces everywhere, and the deep shadows under the clustering vines, lo! suddenly before me stood the Bishop of Winchester. From his face shone a heavenly light° like the radiance of the stars, his robe of dazzling white swept down to his golden sandals, and a white fillet encircled his divine head. As the venerable man in such raiment advanced, the flowery earth trembled with joyous sound. The heavenly hosts clapped their jewelled wings, and the clear air resounded with the triumphal horn. Each saluted his new companion with embrace and song, and one with placid lips uttered these words:

'Come, my son, partake of the joy and gladness of your Father's kingdom, and from hard labour henceforth and forever be free.'

He spoke, and the winged companies touched their harps. But my golden peace was dispelled with the night, and I wept for my dreams shattered by the mistress of Cephalus.° May such dreams often return.°

Elegia Quarta

Anno aetatis 18

AD THOMAM IUNIUM,
PRAECEPTOREM SUUM, APUD MERCATORES ANGLICOS HAMBURGAE
AGENTES PASTORIS MUNERE FUNGENTEM

Curre per immensum subito, mea littera, pontum;
    I, pete Teutonicos laeve per aequor agros;
Segnes rumpe moras, et nil, precor, obstet eunti,
    Et festinantis nil remoretur iter.
Ipse ego Sicanio fraenantem carcere ventos
    Aeolon, et virides sollicitabo Deos,
Caeruleamque suis comitatam Dorida Nymphis,
    Ut tibi dent placidam per sua regna viam.
At tu, si poteris, celeres tibi sume iugales,
    Vecta quibus Colchis fugit ab ore viri;   10
Aut queis Triptolemus Scythicas devenit in oras,
    Gratus Eleusina missus ab urbe puer.
Atque, ubi Germanas flavere videbis arenas,
    Ditis ad Hamburgae moenia flecte gradum,
Dicitur occiso quae ducere nomen ab Hama,
    Cimbrica quem fertur clava dedisse neci.
Vivit ibi antiquae clarus pietatis honore
    Praesul, Christicolas pascere doctus oves;
Ille quidem est animae plusquam pars altera nostrae;
    Dimidio vitae vivere cogor ego.   20
Hei mihi, quot pelagi, quot montes interiecti,
    Me faciunt alia parte carere mei!
Carior ille mihi quam tu, doctissime Graium,
    Cliniadi, pronepos qui Telamonis erat;
Quamque Stagirites generoso magnus alumno,
    Quem peperit Lybico Chaonis alma Iovi.
Qualis Amyntorides, qualis Philyrëius Heros
    Myrmidonum regi, talis et ille mihi.
Primus ego Aonios illo praeeunte recessus
    Lustrabam, et bifidi sacra vireta iugi,   30
Pieriosque hausi latices, Clioque favente
    Castalio sparsi laeta ter ora mero.
Flammeus at signum ter viderat arietis Aethon

Elegy 4

At the Age of Eighteen

TO HIS TUTOR, THOMAS YOUNG, NOW PERFORMING THE DUTIES OF CHAPLAIN TO THE ENGLISH MERCHANTS AT HAMBURG

Away, my letter, speed through the boundless sea; go, seek the Teut-onic lands over the smooth expanse of the deep; have done with linger-ing delays, and let nothing, I pray, thwart your going, nothing stay the haste of your course. I shall myself implore Aeolus, who restrains the winds in his Sicilian cave, and the green gods, and cerulean Doris° with her company of nymphs, to give you a peaceful journey through their realms. But procure for yourself, if you may, the swift team wherewith Medea° in flight rode from the face of her husband, or that with which young Triptolemus° reached the Scythian shores, a welcome mes-senger from the city of Eleusis. And when you descry the yellow sands of Germany, turn your course to the walls of rich Hamburg, which, as the legend runs, derives its name from Hama,° slain, it is said, with a Cimbrian club. There dwells a pastor, renowned for his simple piety, instructed to feed the flocks of Christ. In truth he is more than half my soul,° and I am forced to live half my life without him. Alas, how many seas, how many mountains, intervene and part me from my other dearer self! Dearer is he to me than were you, Socrates, wisest of the Greeks, to Alcibiades of the stock of Telamon;° dearer even than the great Stagirite to his noble pupil,° whom a Chaonian mother bore to Libyan Jove. What the son of Amyntor and what the half divine son of Philyra° were to the king of the Myrmidons, such is this man to me. He was my guide when I was first threading the Aonian shades,° and the sacred greenswards of the cloven hill; he first led me to drink of the Pierian water,° and favoured by Clio° I thrice wet my lips with Castalian wine.° But thrice° has flaming Aethon passed the sign of the Ram, and

Induxitque auro lanea terga novo,
Bisque novo terram sparsisti, Chlori, senilem
Gramine, bisque tuas abstulit Auster opes;
Necdum eius licuit mihi lumina pascere vultu,
Aut linguae dulces aure bibisse sonos.
Vade igitur, cursuque Eurum praeverte sonorum;
Quam sit opus monitis res docet, ipsa vides.   40
Invenies dulci cum coniuge forte sedentem,
Mulcentem gremio pignora cara suo;
Forsitan aut veterum praelarga volumina Patrum
Versantem, aut veri Biblia sacra Dei,
Caelestive animas saturantem rore tenellas,
Grande salutiferae religionis opus.
Utque solet, multam sit dicere cura salutem,
Dicere quam decuit, si modo adesset, herum.
Haec quoque, paulum oculos in humum defixa modestos,
Verba verecundo sis memor ore loqui.   50
'Haec tibi, si teneris vacat inter praelia Musis,
Mittit ab Angliaco littore fida manus.
Accipe sinceram, quamvis sit sera, salutem;
Fiat et hoc ipso gratior illa tibi.
Sera quidem, sed vera fuit, quam casta recepit
Icaris a lento Penelopeia viro.
Ast ego quid volui manifestum tollere crimen,
Ipse quod ex omni parte levare nequit?
Arguitur tardus merito, noxamque fatetur,
Et pudet officium deseruisse suum.   60
Tu modo da veniam fasso, veniamque roganti;
Crimina diminui quae patuere solent.
Non ferus in pavidos rictus diducit hiantes,
Vulnifico pronos nec rapit ungue leo.
Saepe sarissiferi crudelia pectora Thracis
Supplicis ad moestas deliquere preces;
Extensaeque manus avertunt fulminis ictus,
Placat et iratos hostia parva Deos.
Iamque diu scripsisse tibi fuit impetus illi;
Neve moras ultra ducere passus Amor;   70
Nam vaga Fama refert—heu nuntia vera malorum!
In tibi finitimis bella tumere locis,
Teque tuamque urbem truculento milite cingi,
Et iam Saxonicos arma parasse duces.

newly clothed his fleecy back with gold; and twice, Chloris, you have
bestrewn the old earth with new grass, and twice Auster has swept away
your wealth, since my eyes were permitted to feast on his face, or my
ears to drink in the sweet music of his voice.

Go, then, and in your course outstrip the roaring east wind. Whatever admonition you may need, circumstances will teach, and you yourself will see. You will find him perhaps sitting with his charming wife,
fondling on his knee the pledges of their love; or perchance turning
over some stout volume of the ancient Fathers,° or the holy scriptures
of the one true God; or shedding the heavenly dew upon the souls of
feeble men, which is religion's sublime work of healing. But only let it
be your care to greet him, as the custom is, and to speak as would befit
your master were he present. Fix your shy glances for a brief space on
the ground, then remember with modest lips to speak these words:

'If in the midst of battles° there is leisure for the gentle muses, a
faithful hand sends you these verses from the shores of England.
Though it be late, accept this cordial greeting; and may it be the more
welcome because it is late. Late indeed, but true, was the greeting that
chaste Penelope, daughter of Icarius, received from her tardy husband.° But why should I wish to blot out so manifest a fault, which even
the offender himself could in no way excuse? He is justly charged with
delay; he confesses his fault, and is ashamed to have left a duty unfulfilled. But forgive me, since I thus confess and crave your favour, for
sins confessed are half atoned. The wild beast with gaping jaws does
not rend its trembling prey; the lion with wounding claw will not tear
his cowering victim. Even the cruel hearts of Thracian lancers have
often yielded to the sorrowful appeals of a suppliant. Uplifted hands
will stay the thunderbolt, and a little offering appease the angry gods.

'He has long been moved to write to you, and now love will suffer
him no longer to delay, for uncertain rumour—alas! a truthful messenger of evils—reports the districts round about you rife with war, you
and your city besieged by ravaging armies, and the Saxon leaders
already prepared for conflict. Enyo° is devastating the surrounding

Te circum late campos populatur Enyo,
    Et sata carne virum iam cruor arva rigat.
Germanisque suum concessit Thracia Martem;
    Illuc Odrysios Mars pater egit equos.
Perpetuoque comans iam deflorescit oliva;
    Fugit et aerisonam Diva perosa tubam,   80
Fugit, io! terris, et iam non ultima Virgo
    Creditur ad superas iusta volasse domos.
Te tamen interea belli circumsonat horror,
    Vivis et ignoto solus inopsque solo;
Et, tibi quam patrii non exhibuere penates,
    Sede peregrina quaeris egenus opem.
Patria, dura parens, et saxis saevior albis
    Spumea quae pulsat littoris unda tui,
Siccine te decet innocuos exponere foetus,
    Siccine in externam ferrea cogis humum,   90
Et sinis ut terris quaerant alimenta remotis
    Quos tibi prospiciens miserat ipse Deus,
Et qui laeta ferunt de caelo nuntia, quique
    Quae via post cineres ducat ad astra docent?
Digna quidem Stygiis quae vivas clausa tenebris,
    Aeternaque animae digna perire fame!
Haud aliter vates terrae Thesbitidis olim
    Pressit inassueto devia tesqua pede,
Desertasque Arabum salebras, dum regis Achabi
    Effugit, atque tuas, Sidoni dira, manus.   100
Talis et, horrisono laceratus membra flagello,
    Paulus ab Aemathia pellitur urbe Cilix;
Piscosaeque ipsum Gergessae civis Iesum
    Finibus ingratus iussit abire suis.
At tu sume animos, nec spes cadat anxia curis,
    Nec tua concutiat decolor ossa metus.
Sis etenim quamvis fulgentibus obsitus armis,
    Intententque tibi millia tela necem,
At nullis vel inerme latus violabitur armis,
    Deque tuo cuspis nulla cruore bibet.   110
Namque eris ipse Dei radiante sub aegide tutus;
    Ille tibi custos, et pugil ille tibi;
Ille Sionaeae qui tot sub moenibus arcis
    Assyrios fudit nocte silente viros;
Inque fugam vertit quos in Samaritidas oras

fields far and wide, and blood drenches the earth now sown with the flesh of men. Thrace has yielded Mars to Germany, and thither the father of war now urges his Odrysian° horses. The ever verdant olive now withers, and the goddess of peace° who hates the blare of the brazen trumpet has fled from the earth; and, lo! the just virgin° is believed not to have been the last to flee to a home in the heavens. Yet where you dwell alone and helpless in a foreign land, about you still resounds the horror of war. Poor, you must seek in foreign parts the sustenance that your fatherland denies you. O fatherland, ruthless parent, harsher than the white cliffs where the foaming waves beat on your shores, does it become you thus to cast off your innocent children, thus, O heart of iron, to drive them forth upon a foreign soil? And will you permit those whom God himself in his providence sent to bear you glad tidings from heaven, and to teach you the way that leads through death to heaven— will you permit them to seek their sustenance in lands remote? You are worthy then to live confined in Stygian° darkness, and to perish from the everlasting hunger of the soul! Even so the Tishbite prophet° trod of old with unaccustomed feet the lonely paths of the desert and the rugged wastes of Arabia, when he fled from the hand of King Ahab and from you, O relentless Jezebel. Thus Cilician Paul,° tortured and bleeding from the stripes of the harsh-sounding scourges, was cast out of the Aemathian city. Thus the ungrateful fisher people of Gergessa° bade even Jesus depart out of their coasts.

'But take courage; and, though hope be spent with care, let it not fail; let not wan fear send a shudder through your bones. For though you are beset with gleaming arms, and a thousand darts threaten death, yet no weapon shall wound your defenceless breast, no spear shall drink your blood. You shall dwell in safety under the radiant aegis of God. He will be your protector and your champion—he who in the silence of night overthrew the hosts of Assyria beneath the walls of the citadel of Zion,° and put to flight those whom venerable Damascus from her

Misit ab antiquis prisca Damascus agris;
Terruit et densas pavido cum rege cohortes,
Aere dum vacuo buccina clara sonat,
Cornea pulvereum dum verberat ungula campum,
Currus arenosam dum quatit actus humum, 120
Auditurque hinnitus equorum ad bella ruentum,
Et strepitus ferri, murmuraque alta virum.
'Et tu—quod superest miseri—sperare memento,
Et tua magnanimo pectore vince mala;
Nec dubites quandoque frui melioribus annis,
Atque iterum patrios posse videre lares.'

Elegia Quinta

Anno aetatis 20

IN ADVENTUM VERIS

In se perpetuo Tempus revolubile gyro
Iam revocat Zephyros, vere tepente, novos;
Induiturque brevem Tellus reparata iuventam,
Iamque soluta gelu dulce virescit humus.
Fallor? an et nobis redeunt in carmina vires,
Ingeniumque mihi munere veris adest?
Munere veris adest, iterumque vigescit ab illo—
Quis putet?—atque aliquod iam sibi poscit opus.
Castalis ante oculos, bifidumque cacumen oberrat,
Et mihi Pyrenen somnia nocte ferunt; 10
Concitaque arcano fervent mihi pectora motu,
Et furor, et sonitus me sacer intus agit.
Delius ipse venit—video Peneide lauro
Implicatos crines—Delius ipse venit.
Iam mihi mens liquidi raptatur in ardua caeli,
Perque vagas nubes corpore liber eo;
Perque umbras, perque antra feror, penetralia vatum;
Et mihi fana patent interiora deum;
Intuiturque animus toto quid agatur Olympo,
Nec fugiunt oculos Tartara caeca meos. 20
Quid tam grande sonat distento spiritus ore?
Quid parit haec rabies, quid sacer iste furor?

ancient plains sent forth upon the fields of Samaria. He made their king tremble, and terrified their dense cohorts, when on the empty air the clear-voiced trumpet sounded, when horny hoofs beat the dusty plain, and the routed chariot shook the sandy ground, and there was heard the neighing of horses rushing to battle, the clash of steel, and the deep roar of men's voices.

'But remember still to hope—for hope is left even to the wretched—and with high-souled courage conquer your misfortune. Doubt not that in future you will enjoy happier times, and once more see your native home.'

Elegy 5

At the Age of Twenty

ON THE APPROACH OF SPRING

Time as it moves in its ceaseless round now with the warmth of spring recalls the zephyrs. Earth refreshed assumes her brief youth, and the ground released from the frost turns softly green. Is it only my fancy, or does fresh strength return to my song, and is it the gift of spring to inspire my genius? Yes, from spring comes genius waxing strong; and—who would believe it?—my powers are already demanding for themselves some new task. Before my eyes hover the Castalian spring and the twin peaks of Parnassus, and dreams by night bear to me the fountain of Pirene.° My heart burns, stirred by a secret throb, and a divine rapture and tumult within impel me. Phoebus himself comes; I see his locks encircled with the laurel of Daphne;° Phoebus himself descends. My mind is quickly caught up into the heights of the limpid heavens, and free from the body I pass through the wandering clouds. Amid the shades and through the innermost shrines of the poets I am borne, and the secret fanes of the gods lie open before me. My soul perceives all that is done on Olympus, and the dark secrets of Tartarus escape not my sight. What lofty utterance will my soul pour from parted lips? What will this madness, what this sacred frenzy, bring forth? Spring, that gave

Ver mihi, quod dedit ingenium cantabitur illo;
    Profuerint isto reddita dona modo.
Iam, Philomela, tuos, foliis adoperta novellis,
    Instituis modulos, dum silet omne nemus.
Urbe ego, tu silva, simul incipiamus utrique,
    Et simul adventum veris uterque canat.
Veris, io! rediere vices; celebremus honores
    Veris, et hoc subeat Musa perennis opus.   30
Iam sol, Aethiopas fugiens Tithoniaque arva,
    Flectit ad Arctoas aurea lora plagas.
Est breve noctis iter, brevis est mora noctis opacae,
    Horrida cum tenebris exulat illa suis.
Iamque Lycaonius plaustrum caeleste Boötes
    Non longa sequitur fessus ut ante via;
Nunc etiam solitas circum Iovis atria toto
    Excubias agitant sidera rara polo,
Nam dolus, et caedes, et vis cum nocte recessit,
    Neve Giganteum dii timuere scelus.   40
Forte aliquis scopuli recubans in vertice pastor,
    Roscida cum primo sole rubescit humus.
'Hac,' ait, 'hac certe caruisti nocte puella,
    Phoebe, tua celeres quae retineret equos.'
Laeta suas repetit silvas, pharetramque resumit
    Cynthia, luciferas ut videt alta rotas,
Et tenues ponens radios, gaudere videtur
    Officium fieri tam breve fratris ope.
'Desere,' Phoebus ait, 'thalamos, Aurora, seniles;
    Quid iuvat effoeto procubuisse toro?   50
Te manet Aeolides viridi venator in herba;
    Surge; tuos ignes altus Hymettus habet.'
Flava verecundo dea crimen in ore fatetur,
    Et matutinos ocius urget equos.
Exuit invisam Tellus rediviva senectam,
    Et cupit amplexus, Phoebe, subire tuos.
Et cupit, et digna est; quid enim formosius illa,
    Pandit ut omniferos luxuriosa sinus,
Atque Arabum spirat messes, et ab ore venusto
    Mitia cum Paphiis fundit amoma rosis?   60
Ecce, coronatur sacro frons ardua luco,
    Cingit ut Idaeam pinea turris Opim;
Et vario madidos intexit flore capillos,

me inspiration, will my inspiration celebrate in song. His gifts repaid
shall be his reward.

Now, O Philomela,° hidden by the opening leaves you begin your
song, while as yet all the woods are still. I in the city, you in the forest,
together let us begin our song on the coming of spring. Lo, changing
spring has returned; let us sing praises in his honour; and let the muse
once more assume her perennial task. The sun now fleeing from Ethiopia and the Tithonian° fields turns his golden reins to the regions of
the north. Brief is now the course of night, few the hours of her darkness, when she dwells in exile in her horrid shades. And northern
Boötes now weary pursues through a shorter span the heavenly wain.°
Now even less numerous stars through all the heavens keep watch as
wonted sentinels about the courts of Jove; for fraud, murder, and violence retreat with the night, and the gods fear not the onslaughts of the
giants.° Perhaps some shepherd says as he reclines at the summit of a
crag, while the dewy earth grows red beneath the rising sun:

'This night, surely this night, O Phoebus, you have lacked the fair
one who restrains your swift steeds.'

When from on high Cynthia° sees the bright rays of the sun, she lays
aside her own pale beams, gladly returns to her forests, and resumes
her quiver, seeming to rejoice that by her brother's aid her task is made
so brief.

'Come, O Aurora, leave the chamber of your aged husband,' Phoebus cries; 'what joy is it to lie in that cold bed? The Aeolian hunter°
awaits you on the green. Up! Lofty Hymettus holds your flame.'

With blushing cheek the goddess shyly confesses her fault, and urges
to greater speed the horses of the morning. Earth with new life casts off
her hated age, and is eager, O Phoebus, to receive your loving caresses.
She desires them, and is worthy of them; what indeed is more fair than
she when voluptuously she bares her all-sustaining breast, and breathes
of the harvests of Arabia, and, with the delicate scent of the balsam,
from her lovely lips pours forth the fragrance of Paphian° roses.
Behold, her lofty brow is crowned with a sacred wood, as the tower of
pines encircles Ops° on Ida; she entwines her dewy hair with various

Floribus et visa est posse placere suis.
Floribus effusos ut erat redimita capillos,
    Taenario placuit diva Sicana deo.
Aspice, Phoebe; tibi faciles hortantur amores,
    Mellitasque movent flamina verna preces;
Cinnamea Zephyrus leve plaudit odorifer ala,
    Blanditiasque tibi ferre videntur aves.   70
Nec sine dote tuos temeraria quaerit amores
    Terra, nec optatos poscit egena toros;
Alma salutiferum medicos tibi gramen in usus
    Praebet, et hinc titulos adiuvat ipsa tuos.
Quod si te pretium, si te fulgentia tangunt
    Munera—muneribus saepe coemptus amor—
Illa tibi ostentat quascunque sub aequore vasto,
    Et superiniectis montibus, abdit opes.
Ah, quoties, cum tu clivoso fessus Olympo
    In vespertinas praecipitaris aquas,   80
'Cur te,' inquit, 'cursu languentem Phoebe diurno
    Hesperiis recipit caerula mater aquis?
Quid tibi cum Tethy? quid cum Tartesside lympha?
    Dia quid immundo perluis ora salo?
Frigora, Phoebe, mea melius captabis in umbra.
    Huc ades; ardentes imbue rore comas.
Mollior egelida veniet tibi somnus in herba.
    Huc ades, et gremio lumina pone meo.
Quaque iaces circum mulcebit lene susurrans
    Aura per humentes corpora fusa rosas.   90
Nec me, crede mihi, terrent Semeleia fata,
    Nec Phaetonteo fumidus axis equo.
Cum tu, Phoebe, tuo sapientius uteris igni,
    Huc ades, et gremio lumina pone meo.'
Sic Tellus lasciva suos suspirat amores;
    Matris in exemplum caetera turba ruunt.
Nunc etenim toto currit vagus orbe Cupido,
    Languentesque fovet solis ab igne faces.
Insonuere novis lethalia cornua nervis,
    Triste micant ferro tela corusca novo.   100
Iamque vel invictam tentat superasse Dianam,
    Quaeque sedet sacro Vesta pudica foco.
Ipsa senescentem reparat Venus annua formam,
    Atque iterum tepido creditur orta mari.

flowers, and has seemed to be able to please her lover with her flowers, just as the Sicanian goddess,° when she had wreathed her flowing locks, pleased the god of Taenarus. Look, O Phoebus, a willing love awaits you; the breezes of spring are laden with honey-sweet prayers. Fragrant Zephyr softly claps his cinnamon-scented wings, and the very birds seem to offer you their flattery. Not without a dowry does Earth rashly seek your love, nor in want does she beg the longed-for bridals; she kindly gives you the healing herbs for medicines, sustaining thereby your renown as a healer. If splendid recompense, if illustrious gifts, can move you—for love is often bought with gifts—she lays before you all the wealth hidden beneath the vast deep and under the towering mountains. Ah, how often, when, wearied by the steep ascent of heaven, you have plunged headlong into the western sea, how often does she cry:

'Why, O Phoebus, fainting after your daily course, must the cerulean mother° receive you in the Hesperian waters? What have you to do with Tethys? What are the Tartessian waves° to you? Wherefore do you bathe your hallowed face in the unclean sea? You will court a better coolness in my shades, O Phoebus. Come hither, and cool your glowing locks with dew. A sweeter sleep will fall upon you in the cool grass. Come hither, and lay your splendours on my breast. Where you lie a softly whispering breeze will caress our bodies stretched among dewy roses. Believe me, the fate of Semele,° and the smoking chariot drawn by Phaethon's° steeds do not terrify me. O Phoebus, when you have put your fires to a wiser use, come hither and lay your splendours on my breast.'

Thus wanton Earth breathes her amorous desires, and all her children haste to follow her example. Wandering Cupid now courses over the whole world, and rekindles his flickering torch in the fire of the sun. With new strings his deadly bow resounds, and with new points his trembling arrows cruelly gleam. Now he essays to conquer unconquerable Diana and even pure Vesta who sits by the sacred hearth. Venus herself each year renews her ageing form, and seems once more just risen from the warm sea.° Through the marble halls of cities, youths

Marmoreas iuvenes clamant *Hymenaee* per urbes,
    Litus *io Hymen* et cava saxa sonant.
Cultior ille venit, tunicaque decentior apta;
    Puniceum redolet vestis odora crocum.
Egrediturque frequens ad amoeni gaudia veris
    Virgineos auro cincta puella sinus.   110
Votum est cuique suum; votum est tamen omnibus unum—
    Ut sibi quem cupiat det Cytherea virum.
Nunc quoque septena modulatur arundine pastor,
    Et sua quae iungat carmina Phyllis habet.
Navita nocturno placat sua sidera cantu,
    Delphinasque leves ad vada summa vocat.
Iupiter ipse alto cum coniuge ludit Olympo,
    Convocat et famulos ad sua festa deos.
Nunc etiam Satyri, cum sera crepuscula surgunt,
    Pervolitant celeri florea rura choro,   120
Sylvanusque sua cyparissi fronde revinctus,
    Semicaperque deus, semideusque caper.
Quaeque sub arboribus Dryades latuere vetustis
    Per iuga, per solos expatiantur agros.
Per sata luxuriat fruticetaque Maenalius Pan;
    Vix Cybele mater, vix sibi tuta Ceres;
Atque aliquam cupidus praedatur Oreada Faunus,
    Consulit in trepidos dum sibi nympha pedes,
Iamque latet, latitansque cupit male tecta videri,
    Et fugit, et fugiens pervelit ipsa capi.   130
Dii quoque non dubitant caelo praeponere silvas,
    Et sua quisque sibi numina lucus habet.
Et sua quisque diu sibi numina lucus habeto,
    Nec vos arborea, dii, precor, ite domo.
Te referant, miseris te, Iupiter, aurea terris
    Saecla! quid ad nimbos, aspera tela, redis?
Tu saltem lente rapidos age, Phoebe, iugales
    Qua potes, et sensim tempora veris eant;
Brumaque productas tarde ferat hispida noctes,
    Ingruat et nostro serior umbra polo!   140

shout *Hymenaee*; and shore, and cave, and rock resound with the cry, *Io,
Hymen!*° In gala attire he comes, all fitly clad in a new tunic, his fragrant
robes shedding the perfume of the purple crocus. Maidens in troops,
their virgin breasts cinctured with gold, go forth to the joys of lovely
spring. Each makes her own prayer, but the prayers are all the same—
that Cytherea° grant each the husband she desires. Now, too, the shepherd pipes on his seven reeds, and Phyllis° has a song to suit his strain.
With nightly chant the mariner greets his stars, and calls the swift dol-
phins° to the tops of the waves. Jupiter himself on high Olympus makes
merry with his spouse, assembles even the menial gods to his feast.
Now, when late twilight falls, even the satyrs in nimble bands dance
over the flowery fields, and with them Sylvanus,° cypress-crowned, a
god half goat and goat half god. The dryads that hide under ancient
trees roam over the mountains and the lonely meadows. Maenalian
Pan° riots through the crops and the thickets; there mother Cybele and
Ceres° are hardly safe from him. Wanton Faunus would ravish some
oread,° who with trembling feet seeks safety. Now she hides, but ill-
concealed in her hiding wishes to be seen; she flees, but fleeing longs to
be caught. The gods themselves are not slow to prefer the forests of
earth to heaven, and every grove has its own deity.

Long let each grove have its deity! Leave not, O gods, your homes
amid the trees. O Jupiter, let the age of gold restore you to the unhappy
world! Why do you return to the clouds, your harsh armoury?° At least,
O Phoebus, do you rein in as you can your fleet steeds, and slowly let
the vernal season pass. Let rainy winter be slow to bring us again nights
long drawn out, and let the shadows fall later about our pole.

Elegia Sexta

AD CAROLUM DIODATUM, RURI COMMORANTEM

(Qui cum idibus Decemb. scripsisset, et sua carmina excusari postulasset si solito minus essent bona, quod inter lautitias quibus erat ab amicis exceptus haud satis felicem operam Musis dare se posse affirmabat, hunc habuit responsum.)

Mitto tibi sanam non pleno ventre salutem,
  Qua tu distento forte carere potes.
At tua quid nostram prolectat Musa Camenam,
  Nec sinit optatas posse sequi tenebras?
Carmine scire velis quam te redamemque colamque?
  Crede mihi, vix hoc carmine scire queas,
Nam neque noster amor modulis includitur arctis,
  Nec venit ad claudos integer ipse pedes.
Quam bene solennes epulas, hilaremque Decembrim,
  Festaque caelifugam quae coluere Deum,   10
Deliciasque refers, hiberni gaudia ruris,
  Haustaque per lepidos Gallica musta focos!
Quid quereris refugam vino dapibusque poesin?
  Carmen amat Bacchum, carmina Bacchus amat.
Nec puduit Phoebum virides gestasse corymbos,
  Atque hederam lauro praeposuisse suae.
Saepius Aoniis clamavit collibus *Euoe*
  Mista Thyoneo turba novena choro.
Naso Corallaeis mala carmina misit ab agris;
  Non illic epulae, non sata vitis erat.   20
Quid nisi vina, rosasque, racemiferumque Lyaeum,
  Cantavit brevibus Teia Musa modis?
Pindaricosque inflat numeros Teumesius Euan.
  Et redolet sumptum pagina quaeque merum,
Dum gravis everso currus crepat axe supinus,
  Et volat Eleo pulvere fuscus eques.
Quadrimoque madens lyricen Romanus Iaccho
  Dulce canit Glyceran, flavicomamque Chloen.
Iam quoque lauta tibi generoso mensa paratu
  Mentis alit vires ingeniumque fovet.   30
Massica foecundam despumant pocula venam,
  Fundis et ex ipso condita metra cado.

Elegy 6

TO CHARLES DIODATI, STAYING IN THE COUNTRY

(He had written to the author on the thirteenth of December, and asked him to excuse his verses, if they were not so good as usual, because, amid the festivities with which he had been received by his friends, he was unable favourably to devote himself to the muses; he received the following reply.)

I who am not surfeited with feasting wish you good health, which, perhaps you may need because of an overtaxed stomach. But why should your muse lure mine forth and not permit it to seek the shades it loves? You would hear in song how much I love and cherish you? But believe me, you can hardly learn that from a song, for neither is my love bound in strict measures, nor does it come unimpaired on halting feet.°

How well you describe the banquets, the December merriment, the pleasures and the cheer, that do honour to the god who flees from heaven and seeks the earth! How well you recount the joys of winter in the country, and the French wine quaffed by the comfortable fireside! But why do you complain that poetry shuns wine and feasting? Song loves Bacchus, and Bacchus loves song. Nor was Phoebus ashamed to have worn the green ivy wreath and to have preferred the ivy to his own laurel. Often on the Aonian hills have the nine muses in a crowd shouted *Euoe*,° and mingled with the Bacchic revels. Naso° sent bad verses from the Corallian fields, because there he had no dainties, and there no vine was planted. Of what but wine and roses, and Bacchus crowned with clusters, did the Teian bard° sing in his brief measures? Teumesian Euan° inspires the Pindaric numbers, and every page breathes the fragrance of wine he drank, as with loud crash the heavy chariot lies overturned, and the horseman speeds on swarthy with the Elean° dust. The Roman lyrist° drank deep of the four-year-old wine when he sweetly sang of Glycera and golden-haired Chloe. The rich board with its sumptuous provision now fosters the strength of your mind and your genius. Your Massic° cups foam rich with song, and from the jar itself you pour the treasures of your verse. To these

Addimus his artes, fusumque per intima Phoebum
    Corda; favent uni Bacchus, Apollo, Ceres.
Scilicet haud mirum tam dulcia carmina per te,
    Numine composito, tres peperisse deos.
Nunc quoque Thressa tibi caelato barbitos auro
    Insonat arguta mollitur icta manu;
Auditurque chelys suspensa tapetia circum
    Virgineos tremula quae regat arte pedes.   40
Illa tuas saltem teneat spectacula Musas,
    Et revocent quantum crapula pellit iners.
Crede mihi, dum psallit ebur, comitataque plectrum
    Implet odoratos festa chorea tholos,
Percipies tacitum per pectora serpere Phoebum,
    Quale repentinus permeat ossa calor;
Perque puellares oculos digitumque sonantem
    Irruet in totos lapsa Thalia sinus.
Namque elegia levis multorum cura deorum est,
    Et vocat ad numeros quemlibet illa suos;   50
Liber adest elegis, Eratoque, Ceresque, Venusque,
    Et cum purpurea matre tenellus Amor.
Talibus inde licent convivia larga poetis,
    Saepius et veteri commaduisse mero.
At qui bella refert, et adulto sub Iove caelum,
    Heroasque pios, semideosque duces,
Et nunc sancta canit superum consulta deorum,
    Nunc latrata fero regna profunda cane,
Ille quidem parce, Samii pro more magistri,
    Vivat, et innocuos praebeat herba cibos.   60
Stet prope fagineo pellucida lympha catillo,
    Sobriaque e puro pocula fonte bibat.
Additur huic scelerisque vacans et casta iuventus,
    Et rigidi mores, et sine labe manus;
Qualis veste nitens sacra, et lustralibus undis,
    Surgis ad infensos augur iture deos.
Hoc ritu vixisse ferunt post rapta sagacem
    Lumina Tiresian, Ogygiumque Linon,
Et lare devoto profugum Calchanta, senemque
    Orpheon edomitis sola per antra feris.   70
Sic dapis exiguus, sic rivi potor Homerus
    Dulichium vexit per freta longa virum
Et per monstrificam Perseiae Phoebados aulam,

influences add the arts, and give Phoebus freedom of the inmost heart;
Bacchus, Apollo, and Ceres as one lend their favour. Small wonder
then that your songs are so sweet, brought forth as they were by the
common will of three gods.

For you too now sounds the Thracian° lute, inwrought with gold, and
gently touched by the nimble hand. In tapestried rooms is heard the
lyre that guides in sprightly rhythm the maidens' feet. At least let such
sights as these stay your muse, and let them recall whatever inspiration
idle indulgence in wine has banished. Be assured, when the ivory keys°
resound, and the accompanying festive band fills the perfumed
chambers, you will feel Phoebus silently steal into your breast, like a
sudden glow that penetrates the very bones; and, through the eyes and
hands of the girlish player, swift Thalia° will fill your whole breast.

Truly light elegy is the care of many gods, and summons to its
measures whom it will; to elegy Bacchus comes, and Erato,° Ceres, and
Venus, and tender Love° with his blushing mother, all will come. Such
poets then may have abundant feasting, and full often may mellow
themselves on old wine; but the poet who tells of wars, and of heaven
under Jove to manhood grown, of pious heroes, and of demigods, the
leaders of men—who sings now of the sacred decrees of the gods
above, and now of that deep realm guarded by the barking dog°—he
indeed must live sparely, after the manner of the Samian master,° and
herbs must supply his harmless food. Let only the crystal-clear water in
a beechen bowl stand near him, and let him drink temperate draughts
from the pure spring. More than this, his youth must be chaste and free
from sin, his manners strict, and his hand without stain, even like you,
O priest, when in sacred vestment and gleaming with the cleansing
waters° you rise as augur to face the angry gods. After this manner, they
say, wise Tiresias° lived when the light of his eyes was gone; and
Ogygian Linus,° and Calchas,° a fugitive from the doom of his household,
and aged Orpheus when in their lonely caves he tamed the wild beasts.
Thus sparing of food and drinking but water, Homer bore Odysseus
over the reaches of the sea, through Perseian Circe's° magic hall, past

Et vada foemineis insidiosa sonis,
Perque tuas, rex ime, domos, ubi sanguine nigro
  Dicitur umbrarum detinuisse greges:
Diis etenim sacer est vates, divumque sacerdos.
  Spirat et occultum pectus et ora Iovem.
At tu si quid agam scitabere—si modo saltem
  Esse putas tanti noscere siquid agam—   80
Paciferum canimus caelesti semine regem,
  Faustaque sacratis saecula pacta libris;
Vagitumque Dei, et stabulantem paupere tecto
  Qui suprema suo cum patre regna colit;
Stelliparumque polum, modulantesque aethere turmas,
  Et subito elisos ad sua fana deos.
Dona quidem dedimus Christi natalibus illa;
  Illa sub auroram lux mihi prima tulit.
Te quoque pressa manent patriis meditata cicutis;
  Tu mihi, cui recitem, iudicis instar eris.   90

Elegia Septima

Anno aetatis undevigesimo

Nondum blanda tuas leges, Amathusia, noram,
  Et Paphio vacuum pectus ab igne fuit.
Saepe Cupidineas, puerilia tela, sagittas,
  Atque tuum sprevi maxime numen, Amor.
'Tu puer imbelles,' dixi, 'transfige columbas,
  Conveniunt tenero mollia bella duci;
Aut de passeribus tumidos age, parve, triumphos;
  Haec sunt militiae digna trophaea tuae.
In genus humanum quid inania dirigis arma?
  Non valet in fortes ista pharetra viros.'   10
Non tulit hoc Cyprius—neque enim deus ullus ad iras
  Promptior—et duplici iam ferus igne calet.
Ver erat, et summae radians per culmina villae
  Attulerat primam lux tibi, Maie, diem;
At mihi adhuc refugam quaerebant lumina noctem,
  Nec matutinum sustinuere iubar.
Astat Amor lecto, pictis Amor impiger alis;
  Prodidit astantem mota pharetra deum;

the shoals made treacherous by the siren's song, and through your house, infernal king, where with an offering of dark blood he is said to have held spellbound flocks of shades. Truly the bard is sacred to the gods; he is their priest, and both his heart and lips mysteriously breathe the indwelling Jove.

But if you will know what I am doing—if indeed you think it of consequence to know that I am doing anything—I am singing of the peace-bearing king of heavenly race, and of that happy age promised in the sacred books, of the infant cries of Jesus, and his shelter beneath the humble roof, who with his father now dwells in the realms above. I sing of the star-bearing firmament and melodious hosts in the heavens, of the gods suddenly shattered in their fanes. This is the gift that I have offered to Christ on his birthday, when the first light of dawn brought me my theme. These strains composed on my native pipes await you in close keeping, and when I recite them to you, you will be my judge.

Elegy 7

In His Nineteenth Year

Not yet, O genial Amathusia,° had I learned your laws, and my heart was still void of the Paphian° fire. Often I scorned Cupid's arrows as childish weapons, and most of all made light of your divinity, O Love.

'Go, child,' said I, 'and shoot timid doves, for only easy battles become a tender warrior; or win swelling triumphs, little one, over sparrows; these are martial trophies worthy of your valour. Why direct vain arms against mankind? That quiver of yours has no power against strong men.'

This the Cyprian boy° could not endure—for no god is more prompt to wrath than he—and fiercely burned with double fire.

It was spring, and the light streaming over the topmost roofs of the village had ushered in the first of May; but my eyes still sought the retreating night, nor could they endure the brightness of morning. Suddenly Love stood by my bed, unwearied Love in painted wings. The swinging quiver betrayed the god where he stood; his face, his

Prodidit et facies, et dulce minantis ocelli,
  Et quicquid puero dignum et Amore fuit. 20
Talis in aeterno iuvenis Sigeius Olympo
  Miscet amatori pocula plena Iovi;
Aut, qui formosas pellexit ad oscula nymphas,
  Thiodamantaeus Naiade raptus Hylas.
Addideratque iras, sed et has decuisse putares;
  Addideratque truces, nec sine felle, minas.
Et 'Miser exemplo sapuisses tutius,' inquit;
  'Nunc mea quid possit dextera testis eris.
Inter et expertos vires numerabere nostras,
  Et faciam vero per tua damna fidem. 30
Ipse ego, si nescis, strato Pythone superbum
  Edomui Phoebum, cessit et ille mihi;
Et, quoties meminit Peneidos, ipse fatetur
  Certius et gravius tela nocere mea.
Me nequit adductum curvare peritius arcum,
  Qui post terga solet vincere, Parthus eques.
Cydoniusque mihi cedit venator, et ille
  Inscius uxori qui necis author erat.
Est etiam nobis ingens quoque victus Orion,
  Herculeaeque manus, Herculeusque comes. 40
Iupiter ipse licet sua fulmina torqueat in me,
  Haerebunt lateri spicula nostra Iovis.
Caetera quae dubitas melius mea tela docebunt,
  Et tua non leviter corda petenda mihi.
Nec te, stulte, tuae poterunt defendere Musae;
  Nec tibi Phoebaeus porriget anguis opem.'
Dixit, et, aurato quatiens mucrone sagittam,
  Evolat in tepidos Cypridos ille sinus.
At mihi risuro tonuit ferus ore minaci,
  Et mihi de puero non metus ullus erat. 50
Et modo qua nostri spatiantur in urbe Quirites,
  Et modo villarum proxima rura placent.
Turba frequens, facieque simillima turba dearum,
  Splendida per medias itque reditque vias;
Auctaque luce dies gemino fulgore coruscat.
  Fallor? an et radios hinc quoque Phoebus habet?
Haec ego non fugi spectacula grata severus,
  Impetus et quo me fert iuvenilis agor;
Lumina luminibus male providus obvia misi.

sweetly threatening eyes, and whatever else becomes a boy, and Love betrayed him. Thus the Sigeian youth° appears as on eternal Olympus he mixes brimming cups for amorous Jove; or Hylas,° son of Theodamas, who, snatched away by a naiad, enticed the beautiful nymphs to his kisses. He had assumed a wrathful countenance, but you would have thought that it became him; and he uttered harsh threats full of bitterness.

'Wretch,' said he, 'it had been better for you to learn from the example of others; but now you shall be testimony of what my right hand can do; you shall be numbered among those who have felt my powers, and by your sufferings I shall win the faith of men. I, even I, if you know it not, overcame Phoebus,° haughty after his conquest of the serpent Python; to me even he did yield. As oft as he remembers Peneus' daughter, he confesses that my darts inflict surer and deadlier wounds than his own. The Parthian horseman° who conquers as he flees can draw the bow no more skilfully than I. The Cydonian° hunter yields to me, and he who unwittingly was the author of his own wife's death.° Huge Orion° too I conquered, and the hand of Hercules,° and Hercules' friend.° Jupiter himself may turn his bolts against me, but my arrows will pierce his side. Whatever doubts you still may have, my darts will resolve more surely than my words; and not lightly shall I seek your heart. Neither can your muses defend you, foolish one, nor will the serpent° of Apollo offer you aid.' Thus he spoke, and, shaking his gold-pointed arrow,° flew away to the warm bosom of his Cyprian mother. But I almost laughed at these blustering threats, and had no fear of the boy.

I took my pleasures, now in those parts of the city where our citizens walk, and now in the villages of the surrounding country. A great crowd, most like it seemed to a radiant troop of goddesses, came and went along the walks; the day brightened with a double splendour. Am I deceived, or does Phoebus too find here his rays? I did not turn

Neve oculos potui continuisse meos.   60
Unam forte aliis supereminuisse notabam;
  Principium nostri lux erat illa mali.
Sic Venus optaret mortalibus ipsa videri,
  Sic regina deum conspicienda fuit.
Hanc memor obiecit nobis malus ille Cupido,
  Solus et hos nobis texuit ante dolos.
Nec procul ipse vafer latuit, multaeque sagittae,
  Et facis a tergo grande pependit onus.
Nec mora; nunc ciliis haesit, nunc virginis ori,
  Insilit hinc labiis, insidet inde genis;   70
Et quascunque agilis partes iaculator oberrat,
  Hei mihi! mille locis pectus inerme ferit.
Protinus insoliti subierunt corda furores;
  Uror amans intus, flammaque totus eram.
Interea misero quae iam mihi sola placebat
  Ablata est, oculis non reditura meis.
Ast ego progredior tacite querebundus, et excors,
  Et dubius volui saepe referre pedem.
Findor; et haec remanet, sequitur pars altera votum.
  Raptaque tam subito gaudia flere iuvat.   80
Sic dolet amissum proles Iunonia caelum,
  Inter Lemniacos praecipitata focos;
Talis et abreptum solem respexit ad Orcum
  Vectus ab attonitis Amphiaraus equis.
Quid faciam infelix, et luctu victus? Amores
  Nec licet inceptos ponere, neve sequi.
O utinam spectare semel mihi detur amatos
  Vultus, et coram tristia verba loqui!
Forsitan et duro non est adamante creata,
  Forte nec ad nostras surdeat illa preces!   90
Crede mihi, nullus sic infeliciter arsit;
  Ponar in exemplo primus et unus ego.
Parce, precor, teneri cum sis Deus ales amoris;
  Pugnent officio nec tua facta tuo.
Iam tuus O certe est mihi formidabilis arcus,
  Nate dea, iaculis nec minus igne potens;
Et tua fumabunt nostris altaria donis,
  Solus et in superis tu mihi summus eris.
Deme meos tandem, verum nec deme, furores;
  Nescio cur, miser est suaviter omnis amans.   100

austerely from the pleasing sights, but was borne on where youthful ardour led. Imprudently I let my gaze meet theirs, nor could I then withhold my eyes. One by chance I noticed who surpassed the others, and that glance was the beginning of my ills. Like her even Venus might wish to appear to mortals; fair like her must the queen° of the gods have been. Mischievous Cupid, mindful of his threat, cast her in my path; he alone laid this snare before me. Not far off lurked the crafty god himself with the mighty weight of his torch and his many arrows suspended from his back. Without a moment's loss he clung now to the eyelids, and now to the mouth of the maiden; thence in he darted between her lips, then settled on her cheeks; and wherever the nimble archer flitted, alas! from a thousand points he wounded my defenceless breast. Forthwith strange passions assailed my heart. The fire of love within consumed me; I was all aflame. Meanwhile, she who now was my only pleasure in misery was snatched from my sight to return no more.

Yet, silent and sorrowing, I pursued my way, my understanding dulled, and in doubt I often wished to retrace my steps. I am torn asunder: my body remains here; my soul pursues the object of its desire. It is my solace to weep for the joys so suddenly snatched away. Thus Juno's son,° cast down among the hearths of Lemnos, mourned for the heaven he had lost; thus Amphiaraus,° borne down by his frightened horses to Orcus, looked back on the vanishing sun. What shall I do, wretched and overcome as I am with grief? I cannot put aside the love begun, nor yet may I follow after it. O, would it were given me but once again to see her loved countenance and to speak a few sad words with her face to face. Perhaps she is not wrought in adamant; perhaps she would not be deaf to my prayers. Surely none has ever burned so unhappily. I may stand as the first and only example. Spare me, I pray, since you are the winged god of love, and love is tender. Let not your acts conflict with your office. Now, O son of Venus, with your darts no less potent than fire, now in truth is your bow a terror to me. Henceforth your altars will smoke with my offerings, and you alone will be for me supreme among the gods. Take away my longings then; yet nay, take them not; I know not why, but all love is sweet pain. But if any

Tu modo da facilis, posthaec mea sique futura est,
 Cuspis amaturos figat ut una duos.

———————

Haec ego mente olim laeva, studioque supino,
 Nequitiae posui vana trophaea meae.
Scilicet abreptum sic mea malus impulit error,
 Indocilisque aetas prava magistra fuit;
Donec Socraticos umbrosa Academia rivos
 Praebuit, admissum dedocuitque iugum.
Protinus, extinctis ex illo tempore flammis,
 Cincta rigent multo pectora nostra gelu;
Unde suis frigus metuit puer ipse sagittis,
 Et Diomedeam vim timet ipsa Venus.

maiden hereafter will be mine, in kindness let one arrow pierce us both, and make us lovers.

[*Epilogue to the Elegies*]

These vain trophies of my idleness I once set up in foolish mood and with supine endeavour. Injurious error, truly, led me astray, and untutored youth was a bad teacher; until the shady Academy offered its Socratic streams,° and freed me from the yoke to which I had submitted. At once these flames were extinguished, and thenceforth my breast has been stiff with encircling ice, whence Cupid has feared a frost for his arrows, and Venus fears my Diomedean strength.°

SYLVARUM LIBER

In Quintum Novembris

Anno aetatis 17

Iam pius extrema veniens Iacobus ab arcto
Teucrigenas populos, lateque patentia regna
Albionum tenuit, iamque inviolabile foedus
Sceptra Caledoniis coniunxerat Anglica Scotis:
Pacificusque novo, felix divesque, sedebat
In solio, occultique doli securus et hostis:
Cum ferus ignifluo regnans Acheronte tyrannus,
Eumenidum pater, aethereo vagus exul Olympo,
Forte per immensum terrarum erraverat orbem,
Dinumerans sceleris socios, vernasque fideles,   10
Participes regni post funera moesta futuros.
Hic tempestates medio ciet aere diras;
Illic unanimes odium struit inter amicos.
Armat et invictas in mutua viscera gentes,
Regnaque olivifera vertit florentia pace;
Et quoscunque videt purae virtutis amantes,
Hos cupit adiicere imperio, fraudumque magister
Tentat inaccessum sceleri corrumpere pectus,
Insidiasque locat tacitas, cassesque latentes
Tendit, ut incautos rapiat, ceu Caspia tigris   20
Insequitur trepidam deserta per avia praedam
Nocte sub illuni, et somno nictantibus astris.
Talibus infestat populos Summanus et urbes,
Cinctus caeruleae fumanti turbine flammae.
Iamque fluentisonis albentia rupibus arva
Apparent, et terra Deo dilecta marino,
Cui nomen dederat quondam Neptunia proles,
Amphitryoniaden qui non dubitavit atrocem,
Aequore tranato, furiali poscere bello,
Ante expugnatae crudelia saecula Troiae.   30
  At simul hanc, opibusque et festa pace beatam,
Aspicit, et pingues donis Cerealibus agros,
Quodque magis doluit, venerantem numina veri
Sancta Dei populum, tandem suspiria rupit
Tartareos ignes et luridum olentia sulphur.

Selections from A BOOK OF SYLVAE

On the Fifth of November

At the Age of Seventeen

Scarce had pious James come from the distant north and assumed the rule of the Troy-sprung people° and wide-spreading kingdom of Albion;° scarce had the inviolable treaty joined the Anglican and the Caledonian sceptres, and the pacific king in wealth and happiness was seated on his new throne, secure from foe and secret guile, when the fierce tyrant° who rules by the fiery flood of Acheron,° the father of the furies, a wandering exile from ethereal Olympus, had chanced to be roving through the immense orb of the earth, counting over his companions in evil, and his faithful slaves, who after their unhappy burials shall share his kingdom. Here in mid-air° he rouses terrible tempests; there among friends of one mind he scatters hatred. He arms invincible nations to war against each other's vitals; he throws in tumult kingdoms that flourish with the olive of peace; whomsoever he sees in love with purity and virtue, these he is fain to join to his rule; a master of deception, he strives to corrupt the hearts as yet untouched of evil. He lays secret snares, and stretches hidden nets to catch the unwary, as the Caspian tiger follows its trembling prey through pathless deserts under the moonless night and the drowsily twinkling stars. Even with such destruction does Summanus,° girt with whirlings of smoke and blue flame, overwhelm cities and peoples.

And now appear the white fields compassed by wave-beaten cliffs,° and the land beloved of the sea-god, to which of old the son of Neptune gave his name, he who, having crossed the sea, did not hesitate to demand murderous war of Amphitryon's fierce son° before the cruel days of conquered Troy. Soon as he beheld this land blest with riches and festal peace, and the fields fat with the gifts of Ceres° and—what grieved him more—the people worshipping the sacred majesty of the one true God; then sighs, and Tartarean flames, and brimstone, lurid

Qualia Trinacria trux ab Iove clausus in Aetna
Efflat tabifico monstrosus ab ore Typhoeus.
Ignescunt oculi, stridetque adamantinus ordo
Dentis, ut armorum fragor, ictaque cuspide cuspis;
Atque 'Pererrato solum hoc lacrymabile mundo   40
Inveni,' dixit, 'gens haec mihi sola rebellis,
Contemtrixque iugi, nostraque potentior arte.
Illa tamen, mea si quicquam tentamina possunt,
Non feret hoc impune diu, non ibit inulta.'
Hactenus; et piceis liquido natat aere pennis;
Qua volat, adversi praecursant agmine venti,
Desantur nubes, et crebra tonitrua fulgent.
    Iamque pruinosas velox superaverat Alpes,
Et tenet Ausoniae fines. A parte sinistra
Nimbifer Apenninus erat, priscique Sabini;   50
Dextra veneficiis infamis Etruria, nec non
Te furtiva, Tibris, Thetidi videt oscula dantem;
Hinc Mavortigenae consistit in arce Quirini.
Reddiderant dubiam iam sera crepuscula lucem,
Cum circumgreditur totam Tricoronifer urbem,
Panificosque deos portat, scapulisque virorum
Evehitur; praeeunt submisso poplite reges,
Et mendicantum series longissima fratrum;
Cereaque in manibus gestant funalia caeci,
Cimmeriis nati in tenebris vitamque trahentes.   60
Templa dein multis subeunt lucentia taedis—
Vesper erat sacer iste Petro—fremitusque canentum
Saepe tholos implet vacuos, et inane locorum.
Qualiter exululat Bromius, Bromiique caterva,
Orgia cantantes in Echionio Aracyntho,
Dum tremit attonitus vitreis Asopus in undis,
Et procul ipse cava responsat rupe Cithaeron.
    His igitur tandem solenni more peractis,
Nox senis amplexus Erebi taciturna reliquit,
Praecipitesque impellit equos stimulante flagello,   70
Captum oculis Typhlonta, Melanchaetemque ferocem,
Atque Acherontaeo prognatam parte Siopen
Torpidam, et hirsutis horrentem Phrica capillis.
    Interea regum domitor, Phlegetontius haeres,
Ingreditur thalamos—neque enim secretus adulter
Producit steriles molli sine pellice noctes;

and odorous, burst from him, such as the ghastly monster Typhoeus,°
imprisoned by Jove in Trinacrian Aetna belches from his noisome
mouth. His eyes kindle, and the gnashing of his iron teeth sounds like
the clash of arms, like the shock of lance against lance.

'This,' he said, 'is the only distressful sight I have found in my wanderings over the world. This people alone rebels against me, spurning
my yoke and too powerful for my art. Yet if my efforts can aught avail,
they shall not long do this with impunity, shall not long go without vengeance.'

Thus much he spoke, and on pitch black wings floats on through the
limpid air; wherever he flies contrary winds in gusts precede him,
clouds grow thick, and quick come the flashes of lightning.

Now in swift flight he had passed the snowy Alps, and had reached
the borders of Ausonia.° On the left lay the stormy Apennines and the
ancient land of the Sabines; on the right was Etruria notorious for its
sorcerers. You too, O Tiber, he saw giving furtive kisses to Thetis.°
Flying thence he alighted on the citadel of Quirinus,° son of Mars. The
uncertain light of evening had returned, when he who wears the triple
crown was going about the whole city carried on men's shoulders, and
bearing the gods made of bread.° Before him went kings with humbly-
bending knees, and an endless line of medicant friars bearing in their
hands waxen tapers. Blind fools are they, born and drawing out their
lives in Cimmerian° darkness. Then they entered the temple that was
bright with many torches—it was the eve of St Peter—and frequent
thunders of song filled the hollow domes and empty spaces, like the
howlings of Bacchus and his troop as they sing in their orgies on
Boeotian Aracynthus,° while bewildered Asopus° trembles in his clear-
flowing stream, and from afar Cithaeron° sends an echoing answer
from his hollow cliff.

When at last with the usual solemn pomp these rites were ended,
silent Night left the embrace of aged Erebus,° and with goading whip
urged her steeds headlong across the sky—blind Typhlos, and fierce
Melanchaetes, and torpid Siope born of an infernal sire, and shaggy
Phrix with the long mane.

Meanwhile the subduer of kings,° the heir to the throne of Phlegethon, entered his chamber—nor does the secret adulterer pass his
nights alone without some gentle concubine—but scarce had sleep

At vix compositos somnus claudebat ocellos
Cum niger umbrarum dominus, rectorque silentum
Praedatorque hominum, falsa sub imagine tectus
Astitit. Assumptis micuerunt tempora canis;   80
Barba sinus promissa tegit; cineracea longo
Syrmate verrit humum vestis; pendetque cucullus
Vertice de raso; et, ne quicquam desit ad artes,
Cannabeo lumbos constrinxit fune salaces.
Tarda fenestratis figens vestigia calceis.
Talis, uti fama est, vasta Franciscus eremo
Tetra vagabatur solus per lustra ferarum,
Silvestrique tulit genti pia verba salutis
Impius, atque lupos domuit, Libycosque leones.
    Subdolus at tali Serpens velatus amictu   90
Solvit in has fallax ora execrantia voces:
    'Dormis, nate? Etiamne tuos sopor opprimit artus?
Immemor O fidei, pecorumque oblite tuorum!
Dum cathedram, venerande, tuam diademaque triplex
Ridet Hyperboreo gens barbara nata sub axe,
Dumque pharetrati spernunt tua iura Britanni.
Surge, age! surge piger, Latius quem Caesar adorat,
Cui reserata patet convexi ianua caeli.
Turgentes animos et fastus frange procaces,
Sacrilegique sciant tua quid maledictio possit,   100
Et quid Apostolicae possit custodia clavis;
Et memor Hesperiae disiectam ulciscere classem,
Mersaque Iberorum lato vexilla profundo,
Sanctorumque cruci tot corpora fixa probrosae,
Thermodontea nuper regnante puella.
At tu si tenero mavis torpescere lecto,
Crescentesque negas hosti contundere vires,
Tyrrhenum implebit numeroso milite pontum,
Signaque Aventino ponet fulgentia colle.
Relliquias veterum franget, flammisque cremabit,   110
Sacraque calcabit pedibus tua colla profanis,
Cuius gaudebant soleis dare basia reges.
Nec tamen hunc bellis et aperto Marte lacesses;
Irritus ille labor; tu callidus utere fraude.
Quaelibet haereticis disponere retia fas est.
Iamque ad consilium extremis rex magnus ab oris
Patricios vocat, et procerum de stirpe creatos,

closed his peaceful eyes, when the black lord of shades, the ruler of the dead, the destroyer of men, in a false shape° stood at his bedside. His temples were silvered with false grey hair; a long beard covered his breast; an ashen-grey garment swept the ground with its trailing skirts; a cowl hung from his shaven crown, and, lest he should lack aught in his artifice, he had bound his lustful loins with a hempen cord. Slowly he walked, his feet clad in laced sandals. So, the story runs, Francis wandered alone in the desert among the waste and noisome haunts of wild beasts, and, himself a sinner, bore to the creatures of the forest the pious words of salvation, and subdued the wolves and Libyan lions.

Thus garbed, the crafy serpent, the deceiver, spoke these words from his detestable lips:

'Are you asleep, my son?° And is drowsiness overpowering even *your* limbs? You unmindful of the faith, and forgetful of your flocks! Even now, Holy Father, that barbaric people born beneath the northern sky derides your throne and triple diadem. Even now the quivered Britons scorn your laws. Up, bestir yourself! Arise from your sloth, you whom even the Roman emperor° adores, you to whom the locked gates of vaulted heaven fly open. Break their swelling spirits and their shameless pride; then the sacrilegious wretches may know the power of your malediction and what the keeper of the apostolic keys° can do. Remember to avenge the scattered Hesperian fleet,° and the ensigns of Iberia engulfed in the depths of the sea, and the bodies of so many saints hanged on the ignominious gallows during the recent reign of the Thermodontean virgin.° But if you choose to drowse on your soft bed, and if you refuse to shatter the waxing strength of the enemy, then will that enemy soon fill the Tyrrhenian sea° with his soldiery, and plant his gleaming standards on the Aventine hill.° He will break the relics of your fathers, will burn them with fire. He will tread with unholy feet upon your sacred neck, yours whose shoes kings once rejoiced to kiss. Yet do not attack him with war and open conflict; that would be fruitless labour; rather make skilful use of fraud. Right is it to set any sort of snares to catch heretics. Their great king is now summoning to council the dignitaries from the kingdom's remotest shores, the hereditary

Grandaevosque patres trabea canisque verendos;
Hos tu membratim poteris conspergere in auras,
Atque dare in cineres, nitrati pulveris igne　　　　　120
Aedibus iniecto, qua convenere, sub imis.
Protinus ipse igitur quoscunque habet Anglia fidos
Propositi factique mone, quisquamne tuorum
Audebit summi non iussa facessere Papae?
Perculsosque metu subito, casuque stupentes,
Invadat vel Gallus atrox, vel saevus Iberus.
Saecula sic illic tandem Mariana redibunt,
Tuque in belligeros iterum dominaberis Anglos.
Et, nequid timeas, divos divasque secundas
Accipe, quotque tuis celebrantur numina fastis.'　　130
　　Dixit, et adscitos ponens malefidus amictus
Fugit ad infandam, regnum illaetabile, Lethen.
　　Iam rosea Eoas pandens Tithonia portas
Vestit inauratas redeunti lumine terras;
Maestaque adhuc nigri deplorans funera nati
Irrigat ambrosiis montana cacumina guttis;
Cum somnos pepulit stellatae ianitor aulae
Nocturnos visus et somnia grata revolvens.
　　Est locus aeterna septus caligine noctis,
Vasta ruinosi quondam fundamina tecti,　　　　　140
Nunc torvi spelunca Phoni, Prodotaeque bilinguis,
Effera quos uno peperit Discordia partu.
Hic inter caementa iacent praeruptaque saxa
Ossa inhumata virum, et traiecta cadavera ferro;
Hic Dolus intortis semper sedet ater ocellis,
Iurgiaque, et stimulis armata Calumnia fauces,
Et Furor, atque viae moriendi mille, videntur,
Et Timor, exanguisque locum circumvolat Horror,
Perpetuoque leves per muta silentia Manes
Exululant, tellus et sanguine conscia stagnat.　　150
Ipsi etiam pavidi latitant penetralibus antri
Et Phonos et Prodotes, nulloque sequente per antrum,
Antrum horrens, scopulosum, atrum feralibus umbris,
Diffugiunt sontes, et retro lumina vortunt.
Hos pugiles Romae per saecula longa fideles
Evocat antistes Babylonius, atque ita fatur:
　　'Finibus occiduis circumfusum incolit aequor
Gens exosa mihi, prudens natura negavit

peers,° and the venerable sages with their white hair and robes of state;°
these limb from limb you can blow to the sky, and blast to ashes by
firing nitrous powder under the buildings where they shall convene.
Therefore do you yourself warn whatever faithful souls there are in
England both of the purpose and the deed; and will any of your children dare to disobey the commands of his lord the Pope? Then, when
the nation is seized with panic and stunned by the catastrophe, let
either the ruthless Gaul or the fell Iberian° invade the land. Thus at
length will the spirit of the Marian° age return among them, and you
will rule again over the valiant English. Fear nothing, but accept the
favour of all the gods and goddesses, as many deities as are celebrated
in your festivals.'°

So spoke the fiend, and, laying aside the vesture he had assumed,
fled to the abominable realm of joyless Lethe.

Now when the porter° of the starry hall had driven sleep away and
rolled back the nocturnal shapes and pleasant dreams, rosy Dawn,°
opening the gates of the east, was tinging the earth again with golden
light, and, still mourning for the unhappy death of her swarthy offspring, was bedewing the mountain tops with ambrosial tears.

There is a place° begirt with the darkness of an eternal night, the vast
foundations of a building long in ruins, now the den of cruel Murder
and double-tongued Treachery, whom raging Discord brought forth at
one birth. Here amid chips of stone and broken rocks lie unburied the
bones of men and corpses pierced with steel; here dark Guile ever sits
with distorted eyes; here are seen Strife, and Calumny with fanged
jaws, and Fury, and Death in a thousand forms, and Fear. About the
place flies Horror; and the bodiless shades perpetually cry through the
deep silence. The conscious earth is stagnant with blood. In the innermost recesses of the cave Murder and Treason lie fearfully lurking, and
though none pursues them through the cavern—cavern of horrors and
jagged rocks, dark with funereal shadows—with backward glances the
guilty pair retreats. The high priest of Babylon° summons these Roman
bullies who have been faithful through long years, and thus addresses
them:

'On the western frontiers of the world, surrounded by the ocean,
there lives a people that I hate, and that prudent nature did not consider

Indignam penitus nostro coniungere mundo.
Illuc, sic iubeo, celeri contendite gressu,   160
Tartareoque leves difflentur pulvere in auras
Et rex et pariter satrapae, scelerata propago,
Et quotquot fidei caluere cupidine verae
Consilii socios adhibete, operisque ministros.'
Finierat, rigidi cupide paruere gemelli.

Interea longo flectens curvamine caelos
Despicit aetherea Dominus qui fulgurat arce,
Vanaque perversae ridet conamina turbae,
Atque sui causam populi volet ipse tueri.

Esse ferunt spatium, qua distat ab Aside terra   170
Fertilis Europe, et spectat Mareotidas undas;
Hic turris posita est Titanidos ardua Famae,
Aerea, lata, sonans, rutilis vicinior astris
Quam superimpositum vel Athos vel Pelion Ossae.
Mille fores aditusque patent, totidemque fenestrae,
Amplaque per tenues translucent atria muros.
Excitat hic varios plebs agglomerata susurros;
Qualiter instrepitant circum mulctralia bombis
Agmina muscarum, aut texto per ovilia iunco,
Dum Canis aestivum caeli petit ardua culmen.   180
Ipsa quidem summa sedet ultrix matris in arce,
Auribus innumeris cinctum caput eminet olli,
Queis sonitum exiguum trahit, atque levissima captat
Murmura, ab extremis patuli confinibus orbis.
Nec tot, Aristoride, servator inique iuvencae
Isidos, immite volvebas lumina vultu,
Lumina non unquam tacito nutantia somno,
Lumina subiectas late spectantia terras.
Istis illa solet loca luce carentia saepe
Perlustrare, etiam radianti impervia soli.   190
Millenisque loquax auditaque visaque linguis
Cuilibet effundit temeraria; veraque mendax
Nunc minuit, modo confictis sermonibus auget.

Sed tamen a nostro meruisti carmine laudes,
Fama, bonum quo non aliud veracius ullum,
Nobis digna cani, nec te memorasse pigebit
Carmine tam longo. Servati scilicet Angli
Officiis, vaga diva, tuis tibi reddimus aequa.
Te Deus, aeternos motu qui temperat ignes,

worthy to be conjoined with our world. Thither swiftly bend your course—such is my command; and as many as are inflamed with zeal for the true faith receive as associates in the plot and aids in its execution; then with Tartarean powder let king and nobles alike, and the whole accursed race, be blown into thin air.'

He ended, and the ruthless twins eagerly obeyed him. Meanwhile the Lord who turns the great sphere of the heavens, and sends out lightning from his ethereal citadel, looks down, and smiles° at the vain efforts of the perverse crowd, and will himself defend his people's cause.

There is a place,° men say, that looks toward the waters of Mareotis,° equally distant from Asia and the fertile land of Europe; here stands the lofty tower of Fame, the Titanian goddess, brazen, wide, resounding, nearer to the golden stars than Athos, or Pelion piled upon Ossa.° A thousand doors and a thousand windows stand open, and the spacious courts within shine through the thin walls. Here a swarming crowd raises a confused murmur, like the buzzing of flies about milk pails or wattled sheepfolds, when in the heat of summer the Dog Star seeks the summit of the heavens. Fame herself, who avenges her mother,° sits upon the topmost height, and lifts her head that is girt with numberless ears, with which she gathers the slightest whisper, and catches the airiest murmur from the ends of the widespread earth. Not even you, Argus,° false guard of the heifer Io, rolled so many eyes in your savage face, eyes that never grow drowsy in silent sleep, eyes gazing far and wide over the lands beneath, eyes with which she often searches places devoid of light, places inaccessible even to the rays of the sun. What she has heard and seen, with a thousand babbling tongues she heedlessly pours out to any one; now with lies she lessens the truth, now with invented speeches she augments it.

Nevertheless, O Fame, you deserve the praises of our song for one good deed, than which there was never a better; you are worthy of our song, nor will it repent me to have celebrated you at such length. We English, saved forsooth by your good offices, capricious goddess, render you our just thanks. God, who tempers the motion of the eternal

Fulmine praemisso, alloquitur, terraque tremente: 200
  'Fama, siles? an te latet impia Papistarum
Coniurata cohors in meque meosque Britannos,
Et nova sceptrigero caedes meditata Iacobo?'
  Nec plura, illa statim sensit mandata Tonantis,
Et, satis ante fugax, stridentes induit alas
Induit et variis exilia corpora plumis;
Dextra tubam gestat Temesaeo ex aere sonoram.
Nec mora, iam pennis cedentes remigat auras,
Atque parum est cursu celeres praevertere nubes;
Iam ventos, iam solis equos, post terga reliquit   210
Et primo Angliacas, solito de more, per urbes
Ambiguas voces incertaque murmura spargit,
Mox arguta dolos et detestabile vulgat
Proditionis opus, nec non facta horrida dictu
Authoresque addit sceleris, nec garrula caecis
Insidiis loca structa silet. Stupuere relatis,
Et pariter iuvenes, pariter tremuere puellae,
Effoetique senes pariter, tantaeque ruinae
Sensus ad aetatem subito penetraverat omnem.
Attamen interea populi miserescit ab alto   220
Aethereus Pater, et crudelibus obstitit ausis
Papicolum. Capti poenas raptantur ad acres;
At pia thura Deo et grati solvuntur honores;
Compita laeta focis genialibus omnia fumant;
Turba choros iuvenilis agit: Quintoque Novembris
Nulla dies toto occurrit celebratior anno.

Ad Patrem

Nunc mea Pierios cupiam per pectora fontes
Irriguas torquere vias, totumque per ora
Volvere laxatum gemino de vertice rivum;
Ut, tenues oblita sonos, audacibus alis
Surgat in officium venerandi Musa parentis.
Hoc utcunque tibi gratum, pater optime, carmen
Exiguum meditatur opus, nec novimus ipsi
Aptius a nobis quae possint munera donis
Respondere tuis, quamvis nec maxima possint
Respondere tuis, nedum ut par gratia donis   10

fires, hurled his thunderbolt, and while the earth yet trembled addressed you thus:

'Are you silent, O Fame? And does that evil band of Papists, who have conspired against me and my Britons, lie hidden from you? Have you not heard of the strange murder designed against King James?'

Nor said he more, but she forthwith gave heed to the commands of the Thunderer;° and though she were swift enough before she now put on buzzing wings, and clothed her slender body with varied plumage; in her right hand she carried a resounding trumpet of Temesan° brass. She tarried not, but beat the yielding air with her wings. It was not enough for her to outstrip the swift clouds, for now she left behind her the winds, and now even the horses of the sun. First, as is her wont, she scattered through the cities of England doubtful tales and uncertain whisperings; anon, waxing louder, she published the plot and the whole abominable work of treachery, and not only the deed, horrid to tell, but she even names the authors of the crime, and in her garrulity is not silent about the places prepared for an ambush. Aghast at these rumours young men and maidens and worn old men alike are seized with terror, and the sense of so great a disaster suddenly strikes at the hearts of all. But meanwhile the Heavenly Father from on high was moved to pity for this people, and thwarted the daring cruelty of the Papists. The conspirators were captured and dragged off for severe punishment. Honours and sacred incense are offered in gratitude to God; all the joyous crossways smoke with genial fires; the youths in tumult dance, for no day occurs in all the year more celebrated than the Fifth of November.

To My Father

I would that the Pierian fountains° might now pour their inspiring waters through my breast, and the stream that flows from the twin peaks° roll all its flood upon my lips, so that my muse, unmindful of her trivial strains, might rise on adventurous wing to do honour to my revered father. I know not, dearest father, how this trifling song that I am meditating will please you, yet I know not what offerings from me can better repay your gifts, though not even the greatest can repay them, nor can any gratitude expressed by the vain return of empty

Esse queat vacuis quae redditur arida verbis.
Sed tamen haec nostros ostendit pagina census,
Et quod habemus opum charta numeravimus ista,
Quae mihi sunt nullae, nisi quas dedit aurea Clio
Quas mihi semoto somni peperere sub antro,
Et nemoris laureta sacri, Parnassides umbrae.
   Nec tu vatis opus divinum despice carmen,
Quo nihil aethereos ortus, et semina caeli,
Nil magis humanam commendat origine mentem,
Sancta Prometheae retinens vestigia flammae.   20
Carmen amant Superi, tremebundaque Tartara carmen
Ima ciere valet, divosque ligare profundos,
Et triplici duros Manes adamante coercet.
Carmine sepositi retegunt arcana futuri
Phoebades, et tremulae pallentes ora Sibyllae;
Carmina sacrificus sollennes pangit ad aras,
Aurea seu sternit motantem cornua taurum,
Seu cum fata sagax fumantibus abdita fibris
Consulit, et tepidis Parcam scrutatur in extis.
Nos etiam, patrium tunc cum repetemus Olympum,   30
Aeternaeque morae stabunt immobilis aevi,
Ibimus auratis per caeli templa coronis,
Dulcia suaviloquo sociantes carmina plectro,
Astra quibus geminique poli convexa sonabunt.
Spiritus et rapidos qui circinat igneus orbes
Nunc quoque sidereis intercinit ipse choreis
Immortale melos et inenarrabile carmen;
Torrida dum rutilus compescit sibila serpens,
Demissoque ferox gladio mansuescit Orion,
Stellarum nec sentit onus Maurusius Atlas.   40
   Carmina regales epulas ornare solebant,
Cum nondum luxus, vastaeque immensa vorago
Nota gulae, et modico spumabat coena Lyaeo.
Tum de more sedens festa ad convivia vates,
Aesculea intonsos redimitus ab arbore crines,
Heroumque actus imitandaque gesta canebat,
Et Chaos, et positi late fundamina mundi,
Reptantesque deos, et alentes numina glandes,
Et nondum Aetnaeo quaesitum fulmen ab antro.
Denique quid vocis modulamen inane iuvabit   50
Verborum sensusque vacans, numerique loquacis?

words be equal to the obligation. Nevertheless this page displays my resources, and all my wealth is set forth on this paper; but I have nothing save what golden Clio° has given me, what dreams have brought me in the distant caves of sleep, and what the laurel copses of the sacred wood and the shades of Parnassus bestowed.

Scorn not the poet's song, a work divine, which more than aught else reveals our ethereal origin and heavenly race. Nothing so much as its origin does grace to the human mind, possessing yet some sacred traces of Promethean fire. The gods love song, song that has power to move the trembling depths of Tartarus, to bind the nether gods, and restrain the cruel shades with triple adamant. The priestesses of Apollo and the pale trembling Sibyl disclose in song the secrets of the distant future. The sacrificing priest composes verses before the festal altars, whether he slays the bull that tosses its gilded horns, or sagely consults the destinies hidden in the reeking flesh, and reads fate in the entrails still warm with life. When I too return to my native Olympus, and when the changeless ages of eternity stretch forever before me, I shall go through the temples of heaven crowned with gold,° accompanying my sweet songs with the gentle beat of the plectrum, wherewith the stars and the arch of heaven shall resound. Even now that fiery spirit° who encircles the swift orbs himself sings with the starry choirs in an immortal melody, an ineffable song, while the glittering serpent° checks his angry hissing, and fierce Orion with lowered sword grows gentle, and Maurusian° Atlas no longer feels the burden of the stars.°

Poems were wont° to grace the banquets of kings, when as yet luxury and the vast gulf of gluttony were unknown, when at dinner Bacchus flowed in moderation. Then, according to custom, the bard, seated at the festal board, his unshorn locks wreathed with a garland from the oak, used to sing the feats of heroes and their emulable deeds, sang of chaos and the broadly laid foundations of the world, of the creeping gods° that fed upon acorns,° and of the thunderbolt not yet brought from the cavern of Aetna.° And finally, what will the empty modulation of the voice avail, void of words and sense, and of eloquent numbers?

Silvestres decet iste choros, non Orphea, cantus.
Qui tenuit fluvios, et quercubus addidit aures,
Carmine, non cithara, simulacraque functa canendo
Compulit in lacrymas; habet has a carmine laudes.
  Nec tu perge, precor, sacras contemnere Musas,
Nec vanas inopesque puta, quarum ipse peritus
Munere mille sonos numeros componis ad aptos,
Millibus et vocem modulis variare canoram
Doctus, Arionii merito sis nominis haeres.   60
Nunc tibi quid mirum si me genuisse poetam
Contigerit, caro si tam prope sanguine iuncti
Cognatas artes studiumque affine sequamur?
Ipse volens Phoebus se dispertire duobus,
Altera dona mihi, dedit altera dona parenti,
Dividuumque deum genitorque puerque tenemus.
  Tu tamen ut simules teneras odisse Camenas,
Non odisse reor. Neque enim, pater, ire iubebas
Qua via lata patet, qua pronior area lucri,
Certaque condendi fulget spes aurea nummi;   70
Nec rapis ad leges, male custoditaque gentis
Iura, nec insulsis damnas clamoribus aures.
Sed magis excultam cupiens ditescere mentem,
Me procul urbano strepitu, secessibus altis
Abductum, Aoniae iucunda per otia ripae,
Phoebaeo lateri comitem sinis ire beatum.
  Officium cari taceo commune parentis;
Me poscunt maiora. Tuo, pater optime, sumptu
Cum mihi Romuleae patuit facundia linguae,
Et Latii veneres, et quae Iovis ora decebant   80
Grandia magniloquis elata vocabula Graiis,
Addere suasisti quos iactat Gallia flores,
Et quam degeneri novus Italus ore loquelam
Fundit, barbaricos testatus voce tumultus
Quaeque Palaestinus loquitur mysteria vates.
Denique quicquid habet caelum, subiectaque caelo
Terra parens, terraeque et caelo interfluus aer,
Quicquid et unda tegit, pontique agitabile marmor,
Per te nosse licet, per te, si nosse libebit.
Dimotaque venit spectanda scientia nube,   90
Nudaque conspicuos inclinat ad oscula vultus
Ni fugisse velim, ni sit libasse molestum.

That song will do for the sylvan choirs, but not for Orpheus, who with song and not with lute held back the rivers, and gave ears to the oaks, and moved the shades of the dead to tears; these praises he has from song.

Do not, I pray, persist in contemning the sacred muses; think them not vain and poor, by whose gift you yourself are skilled in setting a thousand sounds to fitting numbers, and are trained to vary the singing voice through a thousand modulations, you who by merit should be heir to the name of Arion.° Now, if it has happened that I have been born a poet, why is it strange to you that we, so closely joined by the loving bond of blood, should pursue related arts and kindred ways of life? Phoebus,° wishing to divide himself in two, gave some gifts to me, others to my father; and we, father and son, possess the divided god.

Although you pretend to hate the gentle muses, I believe you do not hate them, for you did not bid me go, father, where the broad way lies open, where the field of gain is easier, and where the certain hope of laying up money shines golden; neither do you drag me to the bar,° to the laws of the nation so ill observed, nor do you condemn my ears to silly clamourings. But, wishing my already nurtured mind to grow more rich, you permit me in deep retreats, far from the city's uproar, to pass my pleasant leisure by the Aonian stream,° and to go a happy companion by Apollo's side.

I pass in silence over the common kindness of a loving parent—greater matters call me. When at your cost, dear father, I had become fluent in the tongue of Romulus, and had mastered the graces of Latin, and the lofty words of the magniloquent Greeks, which became the lips of Jove himself; you then persuaded me to add to these the flowers that Gallia boasts, and the language which the modern Italian pours from his degenerate mouth—a witness by his speech of the barbarian tumults°—and the mysteries which the prophet of Palestine utters.° Finally, whatever is contained in the heavens, in mother earth beneath, and in the air that flows between earth and heaven, whatever is hidden by the waves and the restless surface of the sea—this through you I may learn, through you, if I care to learn. From the parted cloud appears science,° and naked bends her lovely face to my kisses, unless I wish to flee, and if it be not dangerous to taste.

I nunc, confer opes, quisquis malesanus avitas
Austriaci gazas Perüanaque regna praeoptas.
Quae potuit maiora pater tribuisse, vel ipse
Iupiter, excepto, donasset ut omnia, caelo?
Non potiora dedit, quamvis et tuta fuissent,
Publica qui iuveni commisit lumina nato,
Atque Hyperionios currus, et fraena diei,
Et circum undantem radiata luce tiaram.   100
Ergo ego iam doctae pars quamlibet ima catervae
Victricis hederas inter laurosque sedebo,
Iamque nec obscurus populo miscebor inerti,
Vitabuntque oculos vestigia nostra profanos.
Este procul vigiles Curae, procul este Querelae,
Invidiaeque acies transverso tortilis hirquo,
Saeva nec anguiferos extende, Calumnia, rictus;
In me triste nihil, foedissima turba, potestis,
Nec vestri sum iuris ego; securaque tutus
Pectora vipereo gradiar sublimis ab ictu.   110
At tibi, care pater, postquam non aequa merenti
Posse referre datur, nec dona rependere factis,
Sit memorasse satis, repetitaque munera grato
Percensere animo, fidaeque reponere menti.
Et vos, O nostri, iuvenilia carmina, lusus,
Si modo perpetuos sperare audebitis annos,
Et domini superesse rogo, lucemque tueri,
Nec spisso rapient oblivia nigra sub Orco,
Forsitan has laudes, decantatumque parentis
Nomen, ad exemplum, sero servabitis aevo.   120

Ad Salsillum

POETAM ROMANUM, AEGROTANTEM
SCAZONTES

O Musa gressum quae volens trahis claudum,
Vulcanioque tarda gaudes incessu
Nec sentis illud in loco minus gratum
Quam cum decentes flava Dëiope suras
Alternat aureum ante Iunonis lectum,
Adesdum, et haec s'is verba pauca Salsillo
Refer, Camena nostra cui tantum est cordi,

Go, gather wealth, fool, whoever you are, that prefer the ancient treasures of Austria, and of the Peruvian realms.° But what more than learning could my father have given, or Jove himself had he given all but heaven? He who committed to his young son° the common lights, the chariot of Hyperion, the reins of day, and the tiara radiant with light, gave not more potent gifts, even had they been safe. Therefore, since I am one, though the humblest, of the learned company, I shall sit among the victor's ivy and laurels, and no longer obscurely mingle with the dull rabble; my footsteps will avoid the gaze of profane eyes. Away sleepless cares, away complaints, and the wry glance of envy with side-long goatish leer. Fierce Calumny, open not your serpent's jaws. O most detestable band, you can cause me no unhappiness; I am not under your law. Safe may I walk, my breast secure, high above your viper stroke.

But as for you, dear father, since it is not granted me to make a just return for your deserts, nor to recompense your gifts with my deeds, let it suffice that I remember, and with gratitude count over, your repeated gifts, and treasure them in a faithful mind.

You too, my youthful verses, my pastime, if only you dare hope for endless years—dare think to survive your master's pyre and look upon the light—and if dark oblivion does not drag you down to crowded Orcus,° perchance you will treasure these praises and a father's name rehearsed in song as an example to a distant age.

To Salzilli

THE ROMAN POET, IN HIS ILLNESS
SCAZONS°

O muse, who willingly drag a halting pace,° and rejoice in the limping gait of Vulcan,° and think that not less pleasing in its place than fair Deiopea,° when in the dance her graceful feet move before the golden couch of Juno, come now, I pray, bear these few words to Salzilli, who thinks so well of my poetry that undeservedly he prefers it to that of the

Quamque ille magnis praetulit immerito divis.
Haec ergo alumnus ille Londini Milto
Diebus hisce qui suum linquens nidum 10
Polique tractum, pessimus ubi ventorum,
Insanientis impotensque pulmonis,
Pernix anhela sub Iove exercet flabra,
Venit feraces Itali soli ad glebas,
Visum superba cognitas urbes fama,
Virosque, doctaeque indolem iuventutis,
Tibi optat idem hic fausta multa, Salsille
Habitumque fesso corpori penitus sanum;
Cui nunc profunda bilis infestat renes,
Praecordiisque fixa damnosum spirat. 20
Nec id pepercit impia quod tu Romano
Tam cultus ore Lesbium condis melos.
    O dulce divum munus, O Salus Hebes
Germana! Tuque Phoebe morborum terror
Pythone caeso, sive tu magis Paean
Libenter audis, hic tuus sacerdos est.
Querceta Fauni, vosque rore vinoso
Colles benigni, mitis Evandri sedes,
Siquid salubre vallibus frondet vestris,
Levamen aegro ferte certatim vati. 30
Sic ille caris redditus rursum Musis
Vicina dulci prata mulcebit cantu.
Ipse inter atros emirabitur lucos
Numa, ubi beatum degit otium aeternum,
Suam reclivis semper Aegeriam spectans.
Tumidusque et ipse Tibris, hinc delinitus,
Spei favebit annuae colonorum;
Nec in sepulchris ibit obsessum reges,
Nimium sinistro laxus irruens loro;
Sed fraena melius temperabit undarum, 40
Adusque curvi salsa regna Portumni.

Mansus

(Ioannes Baptista Mansus, Marchio Villensis, vir ingenii laude, tum literarum studio, nec non et bellica virtute apud Italos clarus in primis est. Ad quem Torquati Tassi dialogus extat de Amicitia scriptus; erat

great divines. These things, therefore, Milton, a native of London, wishes you, he who of late left his own nest and that region of the heavens where the worst of the winds,° with raging lungs, swift and unbridled, drives the gusty blasts beneath the sky, he who has come to the fruitful fields of Italy to see its cities, known to proud renown, its men, and the genius of its learned youth; this same Milton wishes you, Salzilli, many favours and complete good health for your ailing body, whose liver is now infested with excessive bile,° which, deep-seated, spreads disease through your vitals. The accursed bile did not spare you for all the Lesbian strain° that you elegantly pour from your Roman lips.

O sweet gift of the gods! Health,° Hebe's° sister! And you Phoebus— or Paean° if that name better suits you—the terror of diseases after the death of Python, this man is your own priest. Oak groves of Faunus, and you hills rich with vinous dew, seats of gentle Evander,° if any healing plant puts forth leaves in your valleys, let each strive to be the first to bring comfort to the sick poet. Thus restored again to his beloved muses, he will delight the neighbouring plains with sweet song. Numa° himself shall wonder, where amid the dark groves he spends his blessed eternity of leisure, as he reclines with gaze forever fixed on his Egeria. Swollen Tiber° himself, charmed by the song, will favour the annual hope of the husbandmen; nor will he rush on unchecked with too loose a rein on the left and overwhelm even the kings in their sepulchres; he will better control the course of his waters as far as the salt realms of curving Portumnus.°

Manso

(Giovanni Battista Manso, Marquis of Villa, is a man in the first rank of renown among the Italians by reason not merely of his genius in literary pursuits, but also of his military valour. There is extant a dialogue on

enim Tassi amicissimus; ab quo etiam inter Campaniae principes cele-
bratur, in illo poemate cui titulus Gerusalemme conquistata, lib. 20:

> Fra cavalier magnanimi e cortesi
> Risplende il Manso.

Is authorem Neapoli commorantem summa benevolentia prosecutus
est, multaque ei detulit humanitatis officia. Ad hunc itaque hospes ille
antequam ab ea urbe discederet, ut ne ingratum se ostenderet, hoc carmen misit.)

Haec quoque, Manse, tuae, meditantur carmina laudi
Pierides; tibi, Manse, choro notissime Phoebi,
Quandoquidem ille alium haud aequo est dignatus honore,
Post Galli cineres, et Maecenatis Etrusci.
Tu quoque, si nostrae tantum valet aura Camenae,
Victrices hederas inter laurosque sedebis.
  Te pridem magno felix concordia Tasso
Iunxit, et aeternis inscripsit nomina chartis.
Mox tibi dulciloquum non inscia Musa Marinum
Tradidit; ille tuum dici se gaudet alumnum,   10
Dum canit Assyrios divum prolixus amores,
Mollis et Ausonias stupefecit carmine nymphas.
Ille itidem moriens tibi soli debita vates
Ossa, tibi soli supremaque vota reliquit.
Nec manes pietas tua cara fefellit amici;
Vidimus arridentem operoso ex aere poetam.
Nec satis hoc visum est in utrumque, et nec pia cessant
Officia in tumulo; cupis integros rapere Orco,
Qua potes, atque avidas Parcarum eludere leges,
Amborum genus, et varia sub sorte peractam   20
Describis vitam, moresque, et dona Minervae;
Aemulus illius Mycalen qui natus ad altam
Rettulit Aeolii vitam facundus Homeri.
Ergo ego te, Clius et magni nomine Phoebi,
Manse pater, iubeo longum salvere per aevum,
Missus Hyperboreo iuvenis peregrinus ab axe.
Nec tu longinquam bonus aspernabere Musam,
Quae nuper, gelida vix enutrita sub Arcto,
Imprudens Italas ausa est volitare per urbes.
Nos etiam in nostro modulantes flumine cygnos   30

friendship addressed to him by Torquato Tasso, whose devoted friend he was, and by whom he is also celebrated among the nobles of Campania in that poem entitled *Gerusalemme Conquistata*, Book 20:

> Fra cavalier magnanimi e cortesi
> Risplende il Manso.

Manso honoured the present author during his stay in Naples with the greatest kindness, and did him many acts of courtesy. Therefore, that he might not seem ungrateful, his guest before he left the city sent him this poem.)

These verses too,° Manso, the Pierides° intend for your praise, for you, Manso, already so well known to Phoebus' choir, seeing that he has deemed scarce another worthy of equal honour since the deaths of Gallus° and Etruscan Maecenas.° If the breath of my muse so much avails, you too shall sit among the victor's ivy and laurels.

Happy friendship once joined you with great Tasso, and inscribed your names on everlasting pages. Afterward the knowing muse delivered to you sweet-tongued Marino,° who rejoiced to be called your foster son, while he sang at great length° the Assyrian loves of the gods, and gently stupefied the Ausonian° nymphs with song. So this poet when dying left to you alone his doomed bones, to you alone his latest wishes. Nor has your loving piety deceived the shade of your friend, for we see the poet smiling from the wrought bronze.° But in the case of neither poet did this seem enough; your pious offices did not cease at the tomb, for, wishing to snatch them unharmed from Orcus,° and, as far as you could, to cheat the greedy laws of the fates, you described the ancestry of both, their lives harassed by varying fortune, their characters, and their gifts from Minerva. You were emulous of him, the eloquent one° born on high Mycale,° who related the life of Aeolian Homer. Therefore, father Manso, in the name of Clio° and of mighty Phoebus, I, a youthful traveller sent from beneath the Hyperborean° heaven, wish you good health through a long life. You are kind and will not spurn a foreign muse, which, sparely nourished under the frozen Bear, of late has indiscreetly ventured to fly through the cities of Italy. Methinks through the dusky shades of night I too have heard the swans

Credimus obscuras noctis sensisse per umbras,
Qua Thamesis late puris argenteus urnis
Oceani glaucos perfundit gurgite crines.
Quin et in has quondam pervenit Tityrus oras.
  Sed neque nos genus incultum, nec inutile Phoebo,
Qua plaga septeno mundi sulcata Trione
Brumalem patitur longa sub nocte Boöten.
Nos etiam colimus Phoebum, nos munera Phoebo,
Flaventes spicas, et lutea mala canistris,
Halantemque crocum, perhibet nisi vana vetustas,   40
Misimus, et lectas Druidum de gente choreas.
Gens Druides antiqua, sacris operata deorum,
Heroum laudes imitandaque gesta canebant.
Hinc quoties festo cingunt altaria cantu
Delo in herboso Graiae de more puellae
Carminibus laetis memorant Corineïda Loxo,
Fatidicamque Upin, cum flavicoma Hecaërge,
Nuda Caledonio variatas pectora fuco.
  Fortunate senex! ergo quacunque per orbem
Torquati decus et nomen celebrabitur ingens,   50
Claraque perpetui succrescet fama Marini,
Tu quoque in ora frequens venies plausumque virorum,
Et parili carpes iter immortale volatu.
Dicetur tum sponte tuos habitasse penates
Cynthius, et famulas venisse ad limina Musas.
At non sponte domum tamen idem, et regis adivit
Rura Pharetiadae caelo fugitivus Apollo;
Ille licet magnum Alciden susceperat hospes;
Tantum, ubi clamosos placuit vitare bubulcos,
Nobile mansueti cessit Chironis in antrum,   60
Irriguos inter saltus frondosaque tecta
Peneium prope rivum. Ibi saepe sub ilice nigra,
Ad citharae strepitum, blanda prece victus amici,
Exilii duros lenibat voce labores.
Tum neque ripa suo, barathro nec fixa sub imo
Saxa stetere loco; nutat Trachinia rupes,
Nec sentit solitas, immania pondera, silvas;
Emotaeque suis properant de collibus orni,
Mulcenturque novo maculosi carmine lynces.
  Diis dilecte senex, te Iupiter aequus oportet   70
Nascentem, et miti lustrarit lumine Phoebus,

singing in our own river, where silvery Thames with clear urns lets her
gleaming locks flow wide in the waters of ocean. Indeed Tityrus° once
came to these shores.

But we, a race that through long nights endures the wintry Boötes in
that region of the world that is furrowed by the sevenfold Triones, we
are not untaught and useless to Phoebus. We even worship Phoebus,
and—unless age renders void the tale—we have sent him gifts, yellow-
ing ears, rosy apples in baskets, crocuses breathing fragrance, and
troops of maidens chosen from the Druid race. The Druids,° an
ancient people skilled in the rites of the gods, used to sing the praises of
heroes and their emulable deeds. Hence as often as they° circle the
altars in festive song, as is their wont, the Greek maidens on grassy
Delos in joyful verses commemorate Corinedian Loxo, prophetic Upis,
with yellow-haired Hecaerge, their bare breasts stained with Caledonian paint.

Therefore, fortunate old man,° wherever Torquato's glory and great
name shall be celebrated throughout the world, wherever the brilliant
fame of enduring Marino increases, your praises too will frequently be
on men's lips, and flying by their side you shall enjoy their immortal
flight. Then will it be said that Cynthius° of his own accord has dwelt in
your house, and the attendant muses come as handmaids to your
threshold; yet it was not of his own free will that the same Apollo came,
a fugitive from heaven, to the farm of King Pheretiades,° even though
that host had received great Alcides.° When he wished as much as
possible to avoid the noisy ploughmen, he retired to the well-known
cave of gentle Chiron° amid well-watered pastures and leafy shelters
beside the river Peneus. There, won by his friend's flattering desire, he
used often under the dark ilex to lighten the hard labours of exile with a
song to the sound of the cithern. Then neither the banks nor the rocks
in the lowest chasm beneath stood fixed in their places; the Trachinian
cliff tottered, nor longer felt the usual weight of its forests; the mountain ash trees, uprooted, hastened from their hills; and the spotted
lynxes were soothed by the new song.

Aged man, beloved of the gods, Jupiter must have been friendly to

Atlantisque nepos; neque enim nisi carus ab ortu
Diis superis poterit magno favisse poetae.
Hinc longaeva tibi lento sub flore senectus
Vernat, et Aesonios lucratur vivida fusos,
Nondum deciduos servans tibi frontis honores,
Ingeniumque vigens, et adultum mentis acumen.
O mihi si mea sors talem concedat amicum
Phoebaeos decorasse vircs qui tam bene norit,
Siquando indigenas revocabo in carmina reges,   80
Arturumque etiam sub terris bella moventem,
Aut dicam invictae sociali foedere mensae
Magnanimos Heroas, et—O modo spiritus adsit—
Frangam Saxonicas Britonum sub Marte phalanges!
Tandem ubi non tacitae permensus tempora vitae,
Annorumque satur, cineri sua iura relinquam,
Ille mihi lecto madidis astaret ocellis,
Astanti sat erit si dicam, 'Sim tibi curae.'
Ille meos artus, liventi morte solutos,
Curaret parva componi molliter urna.   90
Forsitan et nostros ducat de marmore vultus,
Nectens aut Paphia myrti aut Parnasside lauri
Fronde comas, at ego secura pace quiescam.
Tum quoque, si qua fides, si praemia certa bonorum,
Ipse ego, caelicolum semotus in aethera divum,
Quo labor et mens pura vehunt atque ignea virtus,
Secreti haec aliqua mundi de parte videbo,
Quantum fata sinunt, et tota mente serenum
Ridens purpureo suffundar lumine vultus,
Et simul aethereo plaudam mihi laetus Olympo.

Epitaphium Damonis

ARGUMENTUM

(Thyrsis et Damon eiusdem viciniae pastores, eadem studia sequuti a pueritia amici erant, ut qui plurimum. Thyrsis animi causa profectus peregre de obitu Damonis nuntium accepit. Domum postea reversus, et rem ita esse comperto, se, suamque solitudinem hoc carmine deplorat. Damonis autem sub persona hic intelligitur Carolus Diodatus ex

you at birth; Phoebus and the grandson° of Atlas must have shone with kindly light; for no one, unless from his birth he were dear to the gods above, could have befriended a great poet. Hence your old age blooms with lingering flowers, and, still full of life, has the benefit of the Aesonian spindles,° keeping the honours of your brow still unshed,° your genius flourishing, and the keenness of your mind in its prime. If ever I recall in song my native kings, and Arthur setting wars in motion even beneath the earth;° if ever I tell of the high-souled heroes in the social bond of the invincible Round Table; and—let the spirit be present to aid me—if ever I break the Saxon phalanxes with British war;° then may my lot grant me such a friend, one who knows so well how to honour the sons of Phoebus. At last when I had measured the span of a life not mute, and, full of years, should leave to ashes their due, with tear-stained eyes he would stand by my bed; and as he stood there I need only say: 'Let me be under your care.' He would provide that my limbs, relaxed in livid death, were gently gathered in a little urn. Perchance he would also draw my features from marble, binding the locks on my brow with Paphian myrtle or with laurel° of Parnassus, and I should rest in peace secure. Then, if there be any faith, and if there be sure rewards for the righteous, I myself, removed to the ethereal realms of the heaven-dwelling gods, whither labour, a pure mind, and ardent courage convey us, even I shall see these things from some part of that secret world—as the fates permit—and with mind all serene, my smiling face suffused with a rosy light, I shall joyfully clap my hands on ethereal Olympus.

Damon's Epitaph

ARGUMENT

(Thyrsis and Damon, shepherds of the same neighbourhood and following the same pursuits, were most intimate friends from boyhood. Thyrsis, who had gone abroad for the improvement of his mind, received news of Damon's death. Having afterward returned home and discovered that the news was true, he deplores himself and his solitude in this poem. Under the guise of Damon is here understood Charles

urbe Etruriae Luca paterno genere oriundus, caetera Anglus; ingenio, doctrina, clarissimisque caeteris virtutibus, dum viveret, iuvenis egregius.)

Himerides Nymphae—nam vos et Daphnin et Hylan,
Et plorata diu meministis fata Bionis—
Dicite Sicelicum Thamesina per oppida carmen:
Quas miser effudit voces, quae murmura Thyrsis,
Et quibus assiduis exercuit antra querelis,
Fluminaque, fontesque vagos, nemorumque recessus,
Dum sibi praereptum queritur Damona, neque altam
Luctibus exemit noctem, loca sola pererrans.
Et iam bis viridi surgebat culmus arista,
Et totidem flavas numerabant horrea messes,   10
Ex quo summa dies tulerat Damona sub umbras,
Nec dum aderat Thyrsis; pastorem scilicet illum
Dulcis amor Musae Tusca retinebat in urbe.
Ast ubi mens expleta domum pecorisque relicti
Cura vocat, simul assueta seditque sub ulmo
Tum vero amissum, tum denique, sentit amicum,
Coepit et immensum sic exonerare dolorem:
   'Ite domum impasti, domino iam non vacat, agni.
Hei mihi! quae terris, quae dicam numina caelo,
Postquam te immiti rapuerunt funere, Damon;   20
Siccine nos linquis, tua sic sine nomine virtus
Ibit, et obscuris numero sociabitur umbris?
At non ille animas virga qui dividit aurea
Ista velit, dignumque tui te ducat in agmen,
Ignavumque procul pecus arceat omne silentum.
   'Ite domum impasti, domino iam non vacat, agni.
Quicquid erit, certe, nisi me lupus ante videbit,
Indeplorato non comminuere sepulchro,
Constabitque tuus tibi honos, longumque vigebit
Inter pastores. Illi tibi vota secundo   30
Solvere post Daphnin, post Daphnin dicere laudes,
Gaudebunt, dum rura Pales, dum Faunus amabit—
Si quid id est, priscamque fidem coluisse, piumque,
Palladiasque artes, sociumque habuisse canorum.
   'Ite domum impasti, domino iam non vacat, agni.
Haec tibi certa manent, tibi erunt haec praemia, Damon.
At mihi quid tandem fiet modo? quis mihi fidus

Diodati, connected on his father's side with the Tuscan city of Lucca, otherwise an Englishman, a youth distinguished while he lived for genius, learning, and other most notable virtues.)

Nymphs of Himera°—for you remember Daphnis and Hylas° and the long lamented fate of Bion°—repeat this Sicilian song through the cities of Thames; tell what words, what murmurs, unhappy Thyrsis poured forth, and with what ceaseless complaints he disturbed the caves, the rivers, the eddying fountains, and the recesses of the groves, while he mourned to himself for Damon snatched away, nor left deep night free from his lamentations as he wandered in lonely places. Twice° the stalk had risen with green ear, and as often had the garners counted the yellow crops, since his last day had borne Damon down to the shades, and Thyrsis was not there the while; love of the sweet muse forsooth detained that shepherd in a Tuscan city.° But when a full mind, and the care of the flock he had left behind, called him home, and when he sat once more beneath his accustomed elm, then, then at last he felt in truth the loss of his friend, and began thus to vent his measureless sorrow:

'Go home unfed, my lambs,° your troubled master is not free to tend you. Ah me! what deities shall I name in earth or heaven, now that they have torn you away, Damon, by inexorable death? Do you leave me thus, and is your virtue to go without a name and be merged with the obscure shades? But nay, let him who with his golden wand marshals the souls° will it otherwise, and may he lead you into a company that is worthy of you, and keep far off the whole base herd of the silent dead.

'Go home unfed, my lambs, your troubled master is not free to tend you. Be sure whatever comes, unless the wolf shall first see me,° you shall not moulder in the tomb unwept; your honour shall endure and long flourish among shepherds. To you next after Daphnis shall they rejoice to fulfil their vows, and next after Daphnis of you to speak their praises, so long as Pales,° so long as Faunus,° love the fields—if it aught avails to have cherished the ancient faith and piety, and the Palladian arts,° and to have had a musical compeer.

'Go home unfed, my lambs, your troubled master is not free to tend you. These rewards for you remain certain, Damon; they shall be yours. But what will become of me; what faithful friend will stay close

Haerebit lateri comes, ut tu saepe solebas
Frigoribus duris, et per loca foeta pruinis,
Aut rapido sub sole, siti morientibus herbis,   40
Sive opus in magnos fuit eminus ire leones.
Aut avidos terrere lupos praesepibus altis?
Quis fando sopire diem cantuque solebit?
    'Ite domum impasti, domino iam non vacat, agni.
Pectora cui credam? quis me lenire docebit
Mordaces curas, quis longam fallere noctem
Dulcibus alloquiis, grato cum sibilat igni
Molle pirum, et nucibus strepitat focus, at malus Auster
Miscet cuncta foris, et desuper intonat ulmo.
    'Ite domum impasti, domino iam non vacat, agni.   50
Aut aestate, dies medio dum vertitur axe,
Cum Pan aesculea somnum capit abditus umbra,
Et repetunt sub aquis sibi nota sedilia nymphae,
Pastoresque latent, stertit sub saepe colonus,
Quis mihi blanditiasque tuas, quis tum mihi risus,
Cecropiosque sales referet, cultosque lepores?
    'Ite domum impasti, domino iam non vacat, agni.
At iam solus agros, iam pascua solus oberro,
Sicubi ramosae densantur vallibus umbrae,
Hic serum expecto; supra caput imber et Eurus   60
Triste sonant, fractaeque agitata crepuscula silvae.
    'Ite domum impasti, domino iam non vacat, agni.
Heu quam culta mihi prius arva procacibus herbis
Involvuntur, et ipsa situ seges alta fatiscit!
Innuba neglecto marcescit et uva racemo,
Nec myrteta iuvant; ovium quoque taedet, at illae
Morerent, inque suum convertunt ora magistrum.
    'Ite domum impasti, domino iam non vacat, agni.
Tityrus ad corylos vocat, Alphesiboeus ad ornos,
Ad salices Aegon, ad flumina pulcher Amyntas: 70
    '"Hic gelidi fontes, hic illita gramina musco,
Hic Zephyri, hic placidas interstrepit arbutus undas."
    'Ista canunt surdo, frutices ego nactus abibam.
    'Ite domum impasti, domino iam non vacat, agni.
Mopsus ad haec, nam me redeuntem forte notarat,
Et callebat avium linguas et sidera Mopsus:
    '"Thyrsi, quid hoc?" dixit, "quae te coquit improba bilis?
Aut te perdit amor, aut te male fascinat astrum.

by my side as you were wont to do in bitter cold through places rough with frost, or under the fierce sun with the grasses dying from drought, whether the task were to go within spear's throw of great lions or to frighten the ravenous wolves from the high sheepfolds? Who will now lull my day to rest with talk and song?

'Go home unfed, my lambs, your troubled master is not free to tend you. To whom may I entrust my heart? Who will teach me to assuage my gnawing cares and to cheat the long night with pleasant conversation, when the mellow pears hiss before the cheery fire, nuts crackle on the hearth, and outside the stormy south wind is throwing all in confusion and comes roaring through the elms.

'Go home unfed, my lambs, your troubled master is not free to tend you. Or in summer when the day turns on mid-axle, when Pan takes his sleep hidden in the oak shade, and the nymphs return to their wonted seats beneath the waters, when shepherds lie concealed, and the husbandman snores beneath the hedge, who will then bring back to me your blandishments, your laughter, Cecropian wit,° culture, and charm?

'Go home unfed, my lambs, your troubled master is not free to tend you. Now I wander in the fields alone, alone through the pastures; wherever the shady branches grow thick in the valleys, there I await the evening, while overhead rain and the south-east wind sadly moan, and the twilight of the forest is broken with gleams of light.

'Go home unfed, my lambs, your troubled master is not free to tend you. Alas, how my fields once tilled are overgrown with trailing weeds, and even the tall corn droops with blight! The cluster of grapes withers unwedded to the stalk. The myrtle groves please me not. I am weary too of my sheep, but even they are sad and turn their faces to their master.

'Go home unfed, my lambs, your troubled master is not free to tend you. Tityrus° calls to the hazels, Alphesiboeus to the mountain ashes, Aegon to the willows, fair Amyntas to the rivers.

' "Here are cool fountains," they cry, "here are mossy greenswards, here are the zephyrs, here the arbutus whispers amid peaceful streams."

'But, deaf to their songs, I gain the thickets and withdraw.

'Go home unfed, my lambs, your troubled master is not free to tend you. Then Mopsus spoke, for he by chance had noticed me returning—Mopsus who was versed in the stars and in the language of birds:

' "What is this, Thyrsis?" said he; "What black melancholy is tormenting you? Either you are wasting with love, or some star is casting an

Saturni grave saepe fuit pastoribus astrum,
Intimaque obliquo figit praecordia plumbo."   80
 'Ite domum impasti, domino iam non vacat, agni.
Mirantur nymphae, et "Quid te, Thyrsi, futurum est?
Quid tibi vis?" aiunt: "non haec solet esse iuventae
Nubila frons, oculique truces, vultusque severi;
Illa choros, lususque leves, et semper amorem
Iure petit; bis ille miser qui serus amavit."
 'Ite domum impasti, domino iam non vacat, agni.
Venit Hyas, Dryopeque, et filia Baucidis Aegle,
Docta modos, citharaeque sciens, sed perdita fastu;
Venit Idumanii Chloris vicina fluenti.   90
Nil me blanditiae, nil me solantia verba,
Nil me si quid adest movet, aut spes ulla futuri.
 'Ite domum impasti, domino iam non vacat, agni.
Hei mihi! quam similes ludunt per prata iuvenci,
Omnes unanimi secum sibi lege sodales,
Nec magis hunc alio quisquam secernit amicum
De grege; sic densi veniunt ad pabula thoes,
Inque vicem hirsuti paribus iunguntur onagri;
Lex eadem pelagi, deserto in littore Proteus
Agmina phocarum numerat, vilisque volucrum   100
Passer habet semper quicum sit, et omnia circum
Farra libens volitet, sero sua tecta revisens;
Quem si fors letho obiecit, seu milvus adunco
Fata tulit rostro, seu stravit arundine fossor,
Protinus ille alium socio petit inde volatu.
Nos durum genus, et diris exercita fatis
Gens, homines, aliena animis, et pectore discors,
Vix sibi quisque parem de millibus invenit unum,
Aut, si sors dederit tandem non aspera votis,
Illum inopina dies, qua non speraveris hora   110
Surripit, aeternum linquens in saecula damnum.
 'Ite domum impasti, domino iam non vacat, agni.
Heu! quis me ignotas traxit vagus error in oras
Ire per aëreas rupes, Alpemque nivosam?
Ecquid erat tanti Romam vidisse sepultam,
Quamvis illa foret, qualem dum viseret olim,
Tityrus ipse suas et oves et rura reliquit,
Ut te tam dulci possem caruisse sodale,
Possem tot maria alta, tot interponere montes,

evil spell over you. Saturn's star has often been baleful to shepherds, and his slant leaden shaft has pierced your inmost breast."

'Go home unfed, my lambs, your troubled master is not free to tend you. The nymphs are amazed and cry:

' "What will become of you, Thyrsis? What do you wish? The brow of youth is not commonly cloudy, the eyes stern, the mien austere; youth seeks dances and nimble sports, and always love as its right. Twice wretched is he who loves late."

'Go home unfed, my lambs, your troubled master is not free to tend you. Hyas came, and Dryope, and Aegle, the daughter of Baucis— Aegle instructed in numbers and skilled on the lyre, but overly proud; Chloris came, a neighbour of the Idumanian river.° Their blandishments, their comforting words, are nothing to me; nothing in the present moves me, nor have I any hope for the future.

'Go home unfed, my lambs, your troubled master is not free to tend you. Ah me! how like one another are the young cattle that frolic through the fields, all comrades to each other under one harmonious law; none seeks from out the herd a special friend. Even so the jackals come in packs to their food, and the shaggy wild asses by turn are joined in pairs. The law of the sea is the same, where on the desert shore Proteus numbers his troops of sea-calves. Even that paltry bird the sparrow always has a mate with whom it happily flies about to every heap of grain, and returns at evening to its own thatch; yet should chance strike one of them dead—whether the kite with hooked beak has brought this fate, or the clown has pierced it with his arrow—the other seeks a new mate to be henceforth its companion in flight. But we men are a stony race, a tribe vexed by stern fates, alien in our minds one from the other, in our hearts discordant. Hardly from among thousands does one find a single kindred spirit, or if fortune not unfriendly gives one such in answer to our prayers, yet in a day and an hour when we least expect it he is snatched away, leaving an everlasting wound.

'Go home unfed, my lambs, your troubled master is not free to tend you. Ah, what wandering fancy lured me to traverse lofty cliffs and snowy Alps to unknown shores! Was there any such need to see buried Rome—even had it been what it was when Tityrus left his sheep and his pastures to see it°—that I could part with so charming a companion, that I could put between us so many deep seas, so many mountains,

Tot silvas, tot saxa tibi, fluviosque sonantes? 120
Ah! certe extremum licuisset tangere dextram,
Et bene compositos placide morientis ocellos,
Et dixisse, "Vale! nostri memor ibis ad astra."
'Ite domum impasti, domino iam non vacat, agni.

Quamquam etiam vestri nunquam meminisse pigebit,
Pastores Tusci Musis operata iuventus,
Hic Charis, atque Lepos; et Tuscus tu quoque Damon,
Antiqua genus unde petis Lucumonis ab urbe.
O ego quantus eram, gelidi cum stratus ad Arni
Murmura, populeumque nemus, qua mollior herba, 130
Carpere nunc violas, nunc summas carpere myrtos,
Et potui Lycidae certantem audire Menalcam!
Ipse etiam tentare ausus sum, nec puto multum
Displicui, nam sunt et apud me munera vestra,
Fiscellae, calathique, et cerea vincla cicutae.
Quin et nostra suas docuerunt nomina fagos
Et Datis et Francinus, erant et vocibus ambo
Et studiis noti, Lydorum sanguinis ambo.
   'Ite domum impasti, domino iam non vacat, agni.
Haec mihi tum laeto dictabat roscida luna, 140
Dum solus teneros claudebam cratibus haedos.
Ah! quoties dixi, cum te cinis ater habebat,
   '"Nunc canit, aut lepori nunc tendit retia Damon
Vimina nunc texit varios sibi quod sit in usus;"
   'Et quae tum facile sperabam ente futura
Arripui voto levis, et praesentia finxi.
   '"Heus bone! numquid agis? nisi te quid forte retardat,
Imus, et arguta paulum recubamus in umbra,
Aut ad aquas Colni, aut ubi iugera Cassibelauni?
Tu mihi percurres medicos, tua gramina, succos, 150
Helleborumque, humilesque crocos, foliumque hyacinthi,
Quasque habet ista palus herbas, artesque medentum."
   'Ah! pereant herbae, pereant artesque medentum,
Gramina, postquam ipsi nil profecere magistro!
Ipse etiam—nam nescio quid mihi grande sonabat
Fistula—ab undecima iam lux est altera nocte—
Et tum forte novis admoram labra cicutis,
Dissiluere tamen, rupta compage, nec ultra
Ferre graves potuere sonos; dubito quoque ne sim
Turgidulus, tamen et referam; vos cedite, silvae. 160

forests, rocks, and roaring streams? Surely had I stayed I might at the last have touched the hand, and closed the eyes, of him who was peacefully dying, might have said, "Farewell, remember me when you go to the stars."

'Go home unfed, my lambs, your troubled master is not free to tend you. Even though I shall never weary of remembering you, O Tuscan shepherds, youths devoted to the muses, yet here too were grace and charm; and you too, Damon, were a Tuscan tracing your lineage from the ancient city of Lucca.° O how elated I was when, stretched by cool murmuring Arno° and the poplar grove that softens the grass, I lay, now plucking violets, now sprays of myrtle, and listened to Menalcas contending with Lycidas in song! Even I myself dared to enter the contest, nor do I think I greatly displeased you, for I still have with me your gifts,° reed baskets, bowls, and shepherd's pipes with waxen stops. Nay, both Dati and Francini,° renowned for their eloquence and their learning, and both of Lydian blood, have taught my name to their beeches

'Go, home unfed, my lambs, your troubled master is not free to tend you. These things the dewy moon used to tell me, when happy and alone I was shutting my tender kids in their wattled cotes. Ah! how often have I said when already you were but dark ashes:

' "Now Damon is singing, or stretching nets for the hare; now he is plaiting osiers for his various uses."

'What I then with easy mind hoped for the future, with the wish I lightly seized and fancied present.

'Say, good friend, are you free? If nothing prevents us, let us go and lie down a while in the mumuring shade, by the waters of Colne,° or in the fields of Cassivellanus.° You shall tell me of your healing herbs and juices, hellebore, the lowly crocus, and the leaf of the hyacinth, whatever plants the marshes yield, and tell me of the physician's art.

'Ah! perish the herbs and the simples, perish the physician's art, since they have profited their master nothing! And I—for I know not what my pipe was grandly sounding°—it is now eleven nights and a day—and then perhaps I had put my lips to new pipes, but they burst asunder, broken at the fastening, and could no more bear the deep tones—I hesitate too lest I seem conceited, yet I will tell the tale—give place then, O forests.

'Ite domum impasti, domino iam non vacat, agni.
Ipse ego Dardanias Rutupina per aequora puppes
Dicam, et Pandrasidos regnum vetus Inogeniae,
Brennumque Arviragumque duces, priscumque Belinum,
Et tandem Armoricos Britonum sub lege colonos;
Tum gravidam Arturo fatali fraude Iogernen,
Mendaces vultus, assumptaque Gorlois arma,
Merlini dolus. O, mihi tum si vita supersit,
Tu procul annosa pendebis, fistula, pinu
Multum oblita mihi, aut patriis mutata Camenis   170
Brittonicum strides! Quid enim? omnia non licet uni,
Non sperasse uni licet omnia. Mi satis ampla
Merces, et mihi grande decus—sim ignotus in aevum
Tum licet, externo penitusque inglorius orbi—
Si me flava comas legat Usa, et potor Alauni,
Vorticibusque frequens Abra, et nemus omne Treantae,
Et Thamesis meus ante omnes, et fusca metallis
Tamara, et extremis me discant Orcades undis.
    'Ite domum impasti, domino iam non vacat, agni.
Haec tibi servabam lenta sub cortice lauri.   180
Haec, et plura simul; tum quae mihi pocula Mansus,
Mansus, Chalcidicae non ultima gloria ripae,
Bina dedit, mirum artis opus, mirandus et ipse,
Et circum gemino caelaverat argumento.
In medio Rubri Maris unda, et odoriferum ver,
Littora longa Arabum, et sudantes balsama silvae;
Has inter Phoenix, divina avis, unica terris,
Caeruleum fulgens diversicoloribus alis,
Auroram vitreis surgentem respicit undis.
Parte alia polus omnipatens, et magnus Olympus.   190
Quis putet? hic quoque Amor, pictaeque in nube pharetrae,
Arma corusca, faces, et spicula tincta pyropo;
Nec tenues animas, pectusque ignobile vulgi,
Hinc ferit; at, circum flammantia lumina torquens,
Semper in erectum spargit sua tela per orbes
Impiger, et pronos nunquam collimat ad ictus.
Hinc mentes ardere sacrae, formaeque deorum.
    'Tu quoque in his—nec me fallit spes lubrica, Damon—
Tu quoque in his certe es; nam quo tua dulcis abiret
Sanctaque simplicitas, nam quo tua candida virtus?   200
Nec te Lethaeo fas quaesivisse sub Orco,

'Go home unfed, my lambs, your troubled master is not free to tend you. I would tell of Dardanian ships along the Rutupian Sea,° and of the ancient realm of Imogen, Pandrasus' daughter, of the leaders Brennus and Arviragus, and old Belinus, and of colonists in Armorica under British laws; then I would tell of Igraine pregnant with Arthur by a fatal fraud, of the seeming face and counterfeit arms of Gorlöis, Merlin's artifice. Ah! then if life remain, you, my pipe, shall hang on some aged pine far off and forgotten, unless forsaking your native songs you shrilly sound a British theme. Why not a British theme? One man cannot do all things, cannot hope to do all things. Sufficient my reward, my honours ample—even if I am for ever unknown and wholly without fame in foreign parts—if yellow-haired Ouse° reads me, and he who drinks the waters of Alaun, and Abra full of eddies, and all the woods of Trent, and above all my own Thames, and Tamar stained with metals, and if the Orkneys and their remotest waves but learn my songs.

'Go home unfed, my lambs, your troubled master is not free to tend you. These things I was keeping for you under the tough bark of the laurel,° these and more besides. Then I thought to show you the two cups° that Manso, not the least glory of the Chalcidian° shore, gave me; a wonderful work of art they are—but Manso himself is wonderful. Round about they are decorated with a double band of carving. In the middle are the waters of the Red Sea and the odoriferous spring, the far off coasts of Arabia and the trees dropping balsam, amidst these the phoenix,° divine bird, alone of its kind on earth, gleaming blue, with wings of many colours, watches Aurora rise over the glassy waves. In another part are great Olympus and the whole expanse of heaven. Yes, and who would believe it? here too is Love, his quiver, flashing arms, and torch, his darts tipped with fiery bronze, all pictured in a cloud. He does not aim at little souls and the ignoble hearts of the rabble, but, rolling his flaming eyes about, unwearied he ever scatters his missiles on high through the spheres, and never aims his shots downward. Hence minds immortal and forms divine are inflamed with love.

'You too are among these, Damon—nor does elusive hope deceive me—surely you too are among these; for whither should your sweet and holy simplicity retire, whither your spotless virtue? It is wrong to

Nec tibi conveniunt lacrymae, nec flebimus ultra.
Ite procul, lacrymae; purum colit aethera Damon,
Aethera purus habet, pluvium pede reppulit arcum;
Heroumque animas inter, divosque perennes,
Aethereos haurit latices et gaudia potat
Ore sacro. Quin tu, caeli post iura recepta,
Dexter ades, placidusque fave, quicunque vocaris,
Seu tu noster eris Damon, sive aequior audis
Diodatus, quo te divino nomine cuncti   210
Caelicolae norint, silvisque vocabere Damon.
Quod tibi purpureus pudor, et sine labe iuventus
Grata fuit, quod nulla tori libata voluptas,
En! etiam tibi virginei servantur honores!
Ipse, caput nitidum cinctus rutilante corona,
Laetaque frondentis gestans umbracula palmae,
Aeternum perages immortales hymenaeos,
Cantus ubi, choreisque furit lyra mista beatis,
Festa Sionaeo bacchantur et Orgia thyrso.'

seek you in Lethean Orcus. Tears become you not, and I shall weep no
more. Away then tears! Damon dwells in the purity of heaven, for he
himself is pure. He has thrust back the rainbow with his foot, and
among the souls of heroes and the everlasting gods he quaffs the
heavenly waters, and drinks of joys with his sacred lips. But now that
the rights of heaven are yours, stand by my side and gently befriend me,
whatever be now your name,° whether you would still be our Damon,
or whether you prefer to be called Diodati, by which divine name all the
dwellers in heaven will know you, but in the forests you will still be
called Damon. Because a rosy blush, and a youth without stain were
dear to you, because you never tasted the pleasure of marriage, lo! for
you are reserved a virgin's honours.° Your noble head bound with a
glittering wreath, in your hands the glad branches of the leafy palm, you
shall for ever act and act again the immortal nuptials, where song and
the lyre, mingled with the blessed dances, wax rapturous, and the joyous revels rage under the thyrsus° of Zion.'

GREEK POEM ADDED IN
1673

In Effigiei eius Sculptor

'Αμαθεῖ γεγράφθαι χειρὶ τήνδε μὲν εἰκόνα
Φαίῃς τάχ' ἄν, πρὸς εἶδος αὐτοφυὲς βλέπων·
Τὸν δ' ἐκτυπωτὸν οὐκ ἐπιγνόντες φίλοι
Γελᾶτε φαύλου δυσμίμημα ζωγράφου.

On the Engraver of his Portrait

Viewing the original, you might say that this picture was done by an inept hand. Friends, since you cannot recognize the man depicted, laugh at the wretched picture of a wretched artist.°

UNCOLLECTED LATIN POEM

Carmina Elegiaca

Surge, age, surge, leves, iam convenit, excute somnos,
    Lux oritur, tepidi fulcra relinque tori.
Iam canit excubitor gallus, praenuncius ales
    Solis, et invigilans ad sua quemque vocat.
Flammiger Eois Titan caput exerit undis
    Et spargit nitidum laeta per arva iubar.
Daulias argutum modulatur ab ilice carmen
    Edit et excultos mitis alauda modos.
Iam rosa fragrantes spirat silvestris odores,
    Iam redolent violae luxuriatque seges.   10
Ecce novo campos Zephyritis gramine vestit
    Fertilis, et vitreo rore madescit humus.
Segnes invenias molli vix talia lecto
    Cum premat imbellis lumina fessa sopor.
Illic languentes abrumpunt somnia somnos
    Et turbant animum tristia multa tuum;
Illic tabifici generantur semina morbi.
    Qui pote torpentem posse valere virum?
Surge, age, surge, leves, iam convenit, excute somnos,
    Lux oritur, tepidi fulcra relinque tori.   20

Elegiac Verses

Get up, quickly, get up! It's time; shake off soft sleep. It's growing light; leave your warm bed. Now the sentinel cock crows, herald of the sun, and keeping watch, summons everyone to work. Flaming Titan° raises his head above the eastern waves and scatters his bright rays over the joyous fields. The Daulian bird° warbles her clear song from the oak branch, and the gentle lark pours forth her artful melody. Now the wild rose exhales perfumes, the odour of violets fills the air and the grain flourishes. Now the fertile wife° of Zephyr clothes the fields with new grass, and waters the earth with shining dew. Lazy, you will never find such pleasures in your soft bed when shameful slumber closes your weary eyes. There dreams interrupt your sleep, and many cares disturb your mind. There the seeds of wasting illness are bred. What strength can there be in a lazy man? Get up, quickly, get up! It's time; shake off soft sleep. It's growing light; leave your warm bed.

PROSE WORKS

From *The Reason of Church Government*

THE SECOND BOOK

How happy were it for this frail and as it may be truly called mortal life
of man, since all earthly things which have the name of good and convenient in our daily use are withal° so cumbersome and full of trouble,
if knowledge, yet which is the best and lightsomest possession of the
mind, were, as the common saying is, no burden; and that what it
wanted° of being a load to any part of the body, it did not with a heavy
advantage overlay upon the spirit. For not to speak of that knowledge
that rests in the contemplation of natural causes and dimensions, which
must needs be a lower wisdom, as the object is low, certain it is that he
who hath obtained in more than the scantiest measure to know anything
distinctly of God, and of his true worship, and what is infallibly good
and happy in the state of man's life, what in itself evil and miserable,
though vulgarly not so esteemed; he that hath obtained to know this,
the only high valuable wisdom indeed, remembering also that God,
even to a strictness, requires the improvement of these his entrusted
gifts,° cannot but sustain a sorer burden of mind, and more pressing,
than any supportable toil or weight which the body can labour under,
how and in what manner he shall dispose and employ those sums of
knowledge and illumination which God hath sent him into this world to
trade with. And that which aggravates the burden more is that, having
received amongst his allotted parcels certain precious truths of such an
orient° lustre as no diamond can equal, which nevertheless he has in
charge to put off° at any cheap rate, yea, for nothing to them that will,
the great merchants° of this world, fearing that this course would soon
discover and disgrace the false glitter of their deceitful wares wherewith
they abuse the people, like poor Indians with beads and glasses, practise by all means how they may suppress the vending of such rarities
and such a cheapness as would undo them and turn their trash upon
their hands. Therefore by gratifying the corrupt desires of men in
fleshly doctrines, they stir them up to persecute with hatred and
contempt all those that seek to bear themselves uprightly in this their

spiritual factory;° which they foreseeing, though they cannot but testify of truth and the excellence of that heavenly traffic which they bring against what opposition or danger soever, yet needs must it sit heavily upon their spirits that being, in God's prime intention and their own, selected heralds of peace and dispensers of treasure inestimable, without price, to them that have no pence, they find in the discharge of their commission that they are made the greatest variance° and offence, a very sword and fire both in house and city over the whole earth. This is that which the sad prophet Jeremiah° laments: 'Woe is me, my mother, that thou hast borne me, a man of strife and contention!' And although divine inspiration must certainly have been sweet to those ancient prophets, yet the irksomeness of that truth which they brought was so unpleasant to them that everywhere they call it a burden. Yea, that mysterious book of Revelation° which the great evangelist was bid to eat, as it had been some eye-brightening electuary° of knowledge and foresight, though it were sweet in his mouth, and in the learning, it was bitter in his belly, bitter in the denouncing. Nor was this hid from the wise poet Sophocles, who in that place of his tragedy where Tiresias is called to resolve King Oedipus in a matter which he knew would be grievous, brings him in bemoaning his lot, that he knew more than other men.° For surely to every good and peaceable man it must in nature needs be a hateful thing to be the displeaser and molester of thousands; much better would it like him doubtless to be the messenger of gladness and contentment, which is his chief intended business to all mankind, but that they resist and oppose their own true happiness. But when God commands to take the trumpet and blow a dolorous or a jarring blast, it lies not in man's will what he shall say or what he shall conceal. If he shall think to be silent as Jeremiah° did, because of the reproach and derision he met with daily, 'and all his familiar friends watched for his halting' to be revenged on him for speaking the truth, he would be forced to confess as he confessed: 'His word was in my heart as a burning fire shut up in my bones; I was weary with forbearing, and could not stay.' Which might teach these times not suddenly to condemn all things that are sharply spoken or vehemently written as proceeding out of stomach,° virulence and ill-nature, but to consider rather that if the prelates have leave to say the worst that can be said and do the worst that can be done, while they strive to keep to themselves to their great pleasure and commodity those things which they ought to render up, no man can be justly offended with him that shall endeavour to impart and bestow, without any gain to himself, those sharp but saving words which would be a terror and a torment in him to keep back. For me, I have determined to lay up as the best treasure and solace of a good old age, if God vouchsafe it me, the honest liberty of free speech from my youth where I shall think it available in so dear a concernment as the church's good. For if I be, either by disposition or what other cause, too inquisitive or suspicious of myself and mine own doings, who can help it? But this I foresee, that should the church be brought under heavy oppression, and God have given me ability the while to reason against that man that should be the author of so foul a deed; or should she, by blessing from above on the industry and courage of faithful men, change this her distracted estate into better days without the least furtherance or contribution of those few talents° which God at that present had lent me, I foresee what stories I should hear within myself all my life after, of discourage and reproach. Timorous and ungrateful,° the church of God is now again at the foot of her insulting enemies, and thou bewailest. What matters it for thee, or thy bewailing? When time was, thou couldst not find a syllable of all that thou hadst read or studied to utter in her behalf. Yet ease and leisure was given thee for thy retired thoughts, out of the sweat of other men. Thou hadst the diligence, the parts, the language of a man, if a vain subject were to be adorned or beautified; but when the cause of God and his church was to be pleaded, for which purpose that tongue was given thee which thou hast, God listened if he could hear thy voice among his zealous servants, but thou wert dumb as a beast; from henceforward be that which thine own brutish silence hath made thee. Or else I should have heard on the other ear: slothful and ever to be set light by, the church hath now overcome her late distresses after the unwearied labours of many her true servants that stood up in her defence; thou also wouldst take upon thee to share amongst them of their joy—but wherefore thou? Where canst thou show any word or deed of thine which might have hastened her peace? Whatever thou dost now talk, or write, or look, is the alms of other men's active prudence and zeal. Dare not now to say or do anything better than thy former sloth and infancy;° or if thou darest, thou dost impudently to make a thrifty purchase of boldness to thyself out of the painful merits of other men; what before was thy sin is now thy duty, to be abject and worthless. These and suchlike lessons as these I know would have been my matins duly, and my evensong. But now by this little diligence, mark what a privilege I have gained with good men and saints,° to claim my right of lamenting the tribulations of the church, if she should suffer, when others that have ventured nothing for her sake have not the honour to be admitted mourners. But if she lift up her drooping head and prosper, among those that have something more than wished her welfare, I have my charter and freehold° of rejoicing to me and my heirs. Concerning therefore this wayward° subject against prelaty, the touching whereof is so distasteful and disquietous to a number of men, as by what hath been said I may deserve of charitable readers to be credited that neither envy nor gall hath entered me upon this controversy, but the enforcement of conscience only, and a preventive° fear lest the omitting of this duty should be against me when I would store up to myself the good provision of peaceful hours: so, lest it should be still imputed to me, as I have found it hath been, that some self-pleasing humour of vainglory hath incited me to contest with men of high estimation, now while green years are upon my head, from this needless surmisal I shall hope to dissuade the intelligent and equal° auditor, if I can but say successfully that which in this exigent° behooves me; although I would be heard only, if it might be, by the elegant and learned reader, to whom principally for a while I shall beg leave I may address myself. To him it will be no new thing, though I tell him that if I hunted after praise by the ostentation of wit and learning, I should not write thus out of mine own season when I have neither yet completed to my mind the full circle of my private studies, although I complain not of any insufficiency to the matter in hand; or were I ready to my wishes, it were a folly to commit anything elaborately composed to the careless and interrupted listening of these tumultuous times. Next, if I were wise only to mine own ends, I would certainly take such a subject as of itself might catch applause, whereas this hath all the disadvantages on the contrary, and such a subject as the publishing whereof might be delayed at pleasure, and time enough to pencil it over with all the curious° touches of art, even to the perfection of a faultless picture; whenas in this argument the not deferring is of great moment to the good speeding, that if solidity have leisure to do her office, art cannot have much.° Lastly, I should not choose this manner of writing wherein knowing myself inferior to myself, led by the genial° power of nature to another task, I have the use, as I may account it, but of my left hand. And though I shall be foolish in saying more to this purpose, yet, since it will be such a folly as wisest men going about to commit, have only confessed and so committed, I may trust with more reason, because with more folly, to have courteous pardon. For although a poet soaring in the high region of his fancies° with his garland and singing robes about him might without apology speak more of himself than I mean to do, yet for me sitting here below in the cool element of prose, a mortal thing among many readers of no empyreal conceit,° to venture and divulge unusual things of myself, I shall petition to the gentler sort, it may not be envy to me.° I must say, therefore, that after I had for my first years, by the ceaseless diligence and care of my father (whom God recompense) been exercised to the tongues,° and some sciences,° as my age would suffer,° by sundry masters and teachers both at home and at the schools, it was found that whether aught was imposed me by them that had the overlooking, or betaken to of mine own choice in English or other tongue, prosing or versing, but chiefly this latter, the style, by certain vital signs it had, was likely to live. But much latelier° in the private academies of Italy, whither I was favoured to resort, perceiving that some trifles which I had in memory, composed at under twenty or thereabout (for the manner is that every one must give some proof of his wit and reading there), met with acceptance above what was looked for; and other things, which I had shifted in scarcity of books and conveniences to patch up° amongst them, were received with written encomiums,° which the Italian is not forward to bestow on men of this side the Alps; I began thus far to assent both to them and divers of my friends here at home, and not less to an inward prompting which now grew daily upon me, that by labour and intense study (which I take to be my portion in this life), joined with the strong propensity of nature, I might perhaps leave something so written to aftertimes as they should not willingly let it die. These thoughts at once possessed me, and these other: that if I were certain to write as men buy leases,° for three lives and downward, there ought no regard be sooner had than to God's glory, by the honour and instruction of my country. For which cause, and not only for that I knew it would be hard to arrive at the second rank among the Latins,° I applied myself to that resolution which Ariosto followed against the persuasions of Bembo,° to fix all the industry and art I could unite to the adorning of my native tongue; not to make verbal curiosities the end (that were a toilsome vanity), but to be an interpreter and relater of the best and sagest things among mine own citizens throughout this island in the mother dialect. That what the greatest and choicest wits of Athens, Rome or modern Italy, and those Hebrews of old did for their country, I in my proportion, with this over and above, of being a Christian, might do for mine; not caring to be once named abroad, though perhaps I could attain to that, but content with these British islands as my world; whose fortune hath hitherto been that if the Athenians, as some say, made their small deeds great and renowned by their eloquent writers, England hath had her noble achievements made small by the unskilful handling of monks and mechanics.°

Time serves not now,° and perhaps I might seem too profuse to give any certain account of what the mind at home, in the spacious circuits of her musing, hath liberty to propose to herself, though of highest hope and hardest attempting; whether that epic form whereof the two poems of Homer and those other two of Virgil and Tasso° are a diffuse, and the book of Job a brief model; or whether the rules of Aristotle° herein are strictly to be kept, or nature to be followed, which in them that know art and use judgment is no transgression, but an enriching of art; and lastly, what king or knight before the conquest might be chosen in whom to lay the pattern of a Christian hero. And as Tasso gave to a prince° of Italy his choice whether he would command him to write of Godfrey's expedition against the infidels, or Belisarius against the Goths, or Charlemagne against the Lombards; if to the instinct of nature and the emboldening of art aught may be trusted, and that there be nothing adverse in our climate° or the fate of this age, it haply would be no rashness, from an equal diligence and inclination, to present the like offer in our own ancient stories; or whether those dramatic consti-tutions° wherein Sophocles and Euripides reign shall be found more doctrinal and exemplary to a nation. The Scripture also affords us a divine pastoral drama in the Song of Solomon, consisting of two per-sons and a double chorus, as Origen° rightly judges. And the Apoca-lypse of St John is the majestic image of a high and stately tragedy, shutting up and intermingling her solemn scenes and acts with a seven-fold chorus of hallelujahs and harping symphonies: and this my opinion the grave authority of Pareus commenting that book is sufficient to con-firm. Or if occasion shall lead, to imitate those magnific odes and hymns wherein Pindarus and Callimachus are in most things worthy, some others in their frame judicious, in their matter most an end° faulty. But those frequent songs throughout the law and prophets beyond all these, not in their divine argument alone, but in the very critical art of composition, may be easily made appear over all the kinds of lyric poesy to be incomparable. These abilities, wheresoever they be found, are the inspired gift of God, rarely bestowed, but yet to some (though most abuse) in every nation; and are of power, beside the office of a pulpit, to inbreed and cherish in a great people the seeds of virtue and public civility,° to allay the perturbations of the mind and set the affections in right tune; to celebrate in glorious and lofty hymns the throne and equipage of God's almightiness and what he works, and what he suffers to be wrought with high providence in his church; to sing the victorious agonies of martyrs and saints, the deeds and tri-umphs of just and pious nations doing valiantly through faith against the enemies of Christ; to deplore the general relapses of kingdoms and states from justice and God's true worship. Lastly, whatsoever in religion is holy and sublime, in virtue amiable° or grave, whatsoever hath passion or admiration° in all the changes of that which is called fortune from without, or the wily subtleties and refluxes° of man's thoughts from within; all these things with a solid and treatable smoothness° to paint out and describe. Teaching over the whole book of sanctity and virtue through all the instances of example, with such delight to those especially of soft and delicious temper,° who will not so much as look upon truth herself unless they see her elegantly dressed; that whereas the paths of honesty and good life appear now rugged and difficult, though they be indeed easy and pleasant, they would then appear to all men both easy and pleasant, though they were rugged and difficult indeed. And what a benefit this would be to our youth and gentry may be soon guessed by what we know of the corruption and bane which they suck in daily from the writings and interludes of libidinous and ignorant poetasters, who having scarce ever heard of that which is the main consistence of a true poem, the choice of such persons as they ought to introduce, and what is moral and decent to each one, do for the most part lap up vicious principles in sweet pills to be swallowed down, and make the taste of virtuous documents harsh and sour. But because the spirit of man cannot demean itself lively° in this body without some recreating intermission of labour and serious things, it were happy for the commonwealth if our magistrates, as in those famous governments of old, would take into their care not only the deciding of our contentious law-cases and brawls but the managing of our public sports and festival pastimes that they might be, not such as were authorized a while since,° the provocations of drunkenness and lust, but such as may inure and harden our bodies by martial exercises to all warlike skill and performance, and may civilize, adorn and make discreet our minds by the learned and affable meeting of frequent academies, and the procurement of wise and artful recitations sweetened with eloquent and graceful enticements to the love and practice of justice, temperance and fortitude, instructing and bettering the nation at all opportunities, that the call of wisdom and virtue may be heard everywhere, as Solomon° saith: 'She crieth without, she uttereth her voice in the streets, in the top of high places, in the chief concourse, and in the openings of the gates.' Whether this may not be not only in pulpits but after another persuasive method, at set and solemn paneguries,° in theatres, porches,° or what other place or way may win most upon the people to receive at once both recreation and instruction, let them in authority consult. The thing which I had to say and those intentions which have lived within me ever since I could conceive myself anything worth to my country, I return to crave excuse that urgent reason hath plucked from me by an abortive and foredated discovery.° And the accomplishment of them lies not but in a power above man's to promise; but that none hath by more studious ways endeavoured, and with more unwearied spirit that none shall, that I dare almost aver of myself, as far as life and free leisure will extend; and that the land had once enfranchised herself from this impertinent° yoke of prelaty, under whose inquisitorious and tyrannical duncery° no free and splendid wit can flourish. Neither do I think it shame to covenant with any knowing reader that for some few years yet I may go on trust with him toward the payment of what I am now indebted, as being a work not to be raised from the heat of youth or the vapours of wine, like that which flows at waste from the pen of some vulgar amorist, or the trencher fury° of a rhyming parasite, nor to be obtained by the invocation of Dame Memory and her siren daughters, but by devout prayer to that eternal Spirit who can enrich with all utterance and knowledge, and sends out his seraphim with the hallowed fire of his altar° to touch and purify the lips of whom he pleases; to this must be added industrious and select reading, steady observation, insight into all seemly and generous arts and affairs; till which in some measure be compassed, at mine own peril and cost I refuse not to sustain this expectation from as many as are not loath to hazard so much credulity upon the best pledges that I can give them. Although it nothing content me to have disclosed thus much beforehand, but that I trust hereby to make it manifest with what small willingness I endure to interrupt the pursuit of no less hopes· than these, and leave a calm and pleasing solitariness fed with cheerful and confident thoughts, to embark in a troubled sea of noises and hoarse disputes, put from beholding the bright countenance of truth in the quiet and still air of delightful studies to come into the dim reflection of hollow antiquities sold by the seeming bulk, and there be fain to club° quotations with men whose learning and belief lies in marginal stuffings, who, when they have, like good sumpters,° laid ye down their horse-loads of citations and fathers at your door with a rhapsody° of who and who were bishops here or there, ye may take off their pack-saddles, their day's work is done, and episcopacy, as they think, stoutly vindicated. Let any gentle apprehension that can distinguish learned pains from unlearned drudgery imagine what pleasure or profoundness can be in this, or what honour to deal against such adversaries. But were it the meanest under-service, if God by his secretary conscience° enjoin it, it were sad for me if I should draw back; for me especially, now when all men offer their aid to help, ease and lighten the difficult labours of the church, to whose service by the intentions of my parents and friends I was destined of a child, and in mine own resolutions; till coming to some maturity of years, and perceiving what tyranny had invaded the church, that he who would take orders must subscribe slave, and take an oath withal, which, unless he took with a conscience that would retch, he must either straight perjure or split his faith, I thought it better to prefer a blameless sile.1ce before the sacred office of speaking, bought and begun with servitude and forswearing. Howsoever, thus church-outed by the prelates, hence may appear the right I have to meddle in these matters, as before the necessity and constraint appeared.

From *An Apology for Smectymnuus*

If, readers, to that same great difficulty of well doing what we certainly know were not added in most men as great carelessness of knowing what they and others ought to do, we had been long ere this, no doubt but all of us, much farther on our way to some degree of peace and happiness in this kingdom. But since our sinful neglect of practising that which we know to be undoubtedly true and good hath brought forth among us, through God's just anger, so great a difficulty now to know that which otherwise might be soon learnt, and hath divided us by a controversy of great importance indeed, but of no hard solution, which is the more our punishment, I resolved (of what small moment soever I might be thought) to stand on that side where I saw both the plain authority of Scripture leading and the reason of justice and equity persuading; with this opinion, which esteems it more unlike a Christian to be a cold neuter° in the cause of the church than the law of Solon° made it punishable after a sedition in the state.

And because I observe that fear and dull disposition, lukewarmness and sloth, are not seldomer wont to cloak themselves under the affected name of moderation than true and lively zeal is customably disparaged with the term of indiscretion, bitterness and choler, I could not to my thinking honour a good cause more from the heart than by defending it earnestly, as oft as I could judge it to behoove me, notwithstanding any false name that could be invented to wrong or undervalue an honest meaning. Wherein although I have not doubted to single forth more than once such of them as were thought the chief and most nominated opposers on the other side, whom no man else undertook; if I have done well either to be confident of the truth, whose force is best seen against the ablest resistance, or to be jealous and tender of the hurt that might be done among the weaker by the entrapping authority of great names titled to false opinions; or that it be lawful to attribute somewhat to gifts of God's imparting, which I boast not, but thankfully acknowledge, and fear also lest at my certain account they be reckoned to me many rather than few; or if lasly it be but justice not to defraud of due esteem the wearisome labours and studious watchings wherein I have spent and tired out almost a whole youth, I shall not distrust to be acquitted of presumption: knowing that if heretofore all ages have received with favour and good acceptance the earliest industry of him that hath been hopeful, it were but hard measure now if the freedom of any timely spirit should be oppressed merely by the big and blunted fame of his elder adversary; and that his sufficiency must be now sentenced, not by pondering the reason he shows, but by calculating the years he brings.

However, as my purpose is not, nor hath been formerly, to look on my adversary abroad, through the deceiving glass of other men's great opinion of him, but at home, where I may find him in the proper light of his own worth, so now against the rancour of an evil tongue, from which I never thought so absurdly as that I of all men should be exempt, I must be forced to proceed from the unfeigned and diligent inquiry of mine own conscience at home (for better way I know not, readers) to give a more true account of myself abroad than this modest confuter,° as he calls himself, hath given of me. Albeit that in doing this I shall be sensible of two things which to me will be nothing pleasant; the one is that not unlikely I shall be thought too much a party in mine own cause, and therein to see least; the other, that I shall be put unwillingly to molest the public view with the vindication of a private name; as if it were worth the while that the people should care whether such a one were thus, or thus. Yet those I entreat who have found the leisure to read that name, however of small repute, unworthily defamed, would be so good and so patient as to hear the same person not unneedfully defended.

I will not deny but that the best apology against false accusers is silence and sufferance, and honest deeds set against dishonest words. And that I could at this time most easily and securely, with the least loss of reputation, use no other defence, I need not despair to win belief; whether I consider both the foolish contriving and ridiculous aiming of these his slanderous bolts, shot so wide of any suspicion to be fastened on me that I have oft with inward contentment perceived my friends congratulating themselves in my innocence, and my enemies ashamed of their partner's folly; or whether I look at these present times, wherein most men, now scarce permitted the liberty to think over their own concernments, have removed the seat of their thoughts more outward to the expectation of public events; or whether the examples of men, either noble or religious, who have sat down lately with a meek silence and sufferance under many libellous endorsements, may be a rule to others, I might well appease myself to put up any reproaches in such an honourable society of fellow-sufferers, using no other defence.

And were it that slander would be content to make an end where it first fixes, and not seek to cast out the like infamy upon each thing that hath but any relation to the person traduced, I should have pleaded against this confuter by no other advocates than those which I first commended, silence and sufferance, and speaking deeds against faltering words. But when I discerned his intent was not so much to smite at me as through me to render odious the truth which I had written, and to stain with ignominy that evangelic doctrine which opposes the tradition of prelaty, I conceived myself to be now not as mine own person, but as a member incorporate into that truth whereof I was persuaded, and whereof I had declared openly to be a partaker. Whereupon I thought it my duty, if not to myself, yet to the religious cause I had in hand, not to leave on my garment the least spot or blemish in good name, so long as God should give me to say that which might wipe it off; lest those disgraces which I ought to suffer, if it so befall me, for my religion, through my default religion be made liable to suffer for me. And, whether it might not something reflect upon those reverent men° whose friend I may be thought in writing the *Animadversions*, was not my last care to consider: if I should rest under these reproaches, having the same common adversary with them, it might be counted small credit for their cause to have found such an assistant as this babbler hath devised me. What other thing in his book there is of dispute or question, in answering thereto I doubt not to be justified; except there be who will condemn me to have wasted time in throwing down that which could not keep itself up. As for others who notwithstanding what I can allege have yet decreed to misinterpret the intents of my reply, I suppose they would have found as many causes to have misconceived the reasons of my silence . . .

Thus having spent his first onset not in confuting, but in a reasonless defaming of the book, the method of his° malice hurries him to attempt the like against the author;° not by proofs and testimonies, but 'having

no certain notice of me', as he professes, 'further than what he gathers
from the *Animadversions*', blunders at me for the rest, and flings out
stray crimes at a venture, which he could never, though he be a serpent,
suck from anything that I have written, but from his own stuffed maga-
zine° and hoard of slanderous inventions, over and above that which he
converted to venom in the drawing. To me, readers, it happens as a
singular contentment, and let it be to good men no slight satisfaction,
that the slanderer here confesses he has 'no further notice of me than
his own conjecture'. Although it had been honest to have inquired
before he uttered such infamous words, and I am credibly informed he
did inquire; but finding small comfort from the intelligence which he
received whereon to ground the falsities which he had provided,
thought it his likeliest course, under a pretended ignorance, to let drive
at random, lest he should lose his odd ends, which from some penurious book of characters° he had been culling out and would fain apply.
Not caring to burden me with those vices, whereof, among whom my
conversation° hath been, I have been ever least suspected; perhaps not
without some subtlety to cast me into envy° by bringing on me a necessity to enter into mine own praises. In which argument I know every
wise man is more unwillingly drawn to speak than the most repining ear
can be averse to hear.

Nevertheless, since I dare not wish to pass this life unpersecuted of
slanderous tongues, for God hath told us° that to be generally praised is
woeful, I shall rely on his promise° to free the innocent from causeless
aspersions: whereof nothing sooner can assure me than if I shall feel
him now assisting me in the just vindication of myself, which yet I could
defer, it being more meet that to those other matters of public debate-
ment in this book I should give attendance first, but that I fear it would
but harm the truth for me to reason in her behalf, so long as I should
suffer my honest estimation to lie unpurged from these insolent suspi-
cions. And if I shall be large, or unwonted in justifying myself to those
who know me not, for else it would be needless, let them consider that a
short slander will ofttimes reach farther than a long apology, and that
he who will do justly to all men must begin from knowing how, if it so
happen, to be not unjust to himself. I must be thought, if this libeller
(for now he shows himself to be so) can find belief, after an inordinate
and riotous youth spent at the 'university', to have been at length
'vomited out thence'.° For which commodious° lie, that he may be
encouraged in the trade another time, I thank him; for it hath given me
an apt occasion to acknowledge publicly with all grateful mind that
more than ordinary favour and respect which I found above any of my

equals at the hands of those courteous and learned men, the fellows of that college wherein I spent some years; who at my parting, after I had taken two degrees, as the manner is, signified many ways how much better it would content them that I would stay; as by many letters full of kindness and loving respect, both before that time and long after, I was assured of their singular good affection towards me. Which being like-wise propense° to all such as were for their studious and civil life worthy of esteem, I could not wrong their judgments and upright intentions so much as to think I had that regard from them for other cause than that I might be still encouraged to proceed in the honest and laudable courses of which they apprehended I had given good proof. And to those ingenuous and friendly men who were ever the countenancers of virtu-ous and hopeful wits, I wish the best and happiest things that friends in absence wish one to another.

As for the common approbation or dislike of that place, as now it is, that I should esteem or disesteem myself or any other the more for that, too simple and too credulous is the confuter if he think to obtain with me,° or any right discerner. Of small practice were that physician who could not judge by what both she or her sister° hath of long time vomited, that the worser stuff she strongly keeps in her stomach, but the better she is ever kecking° at, and is queasy. She vomits now out of sickness; but ere it be well with her, she must vomit by strong physic. In the meanwhile that suburb sink,° as this rude scavenger calls it, and more than scurrilously taunts it with the plague, having a worse plague in his middle entrail, that suburb wherein I dwell shall be in my account a more honourable place than his university. Which as in the time of her better health, and mine own younger judgment, I never greatly admired, so now much less. But he follows me to the city, still usurping and forging beyond his book notice, which only he affirms to have had; 'and where my morning haunts are, he wisses not.'° 'Tis wonder that, being so rare an alchemist of slander, he could not extract that, as well as the university vomit and the suburb sink which his art could distil so cunningly; but because his limbec° fails him, to give him and envy the more vexation, I'll tell him.

Those morning haunts are where they should be, at home; not sleep-ing, or concocting° the surfeits of an irregular feast, but up and stirring, in winter often ere the sound of any bell awake men to labour or to devotion; in summer as oft with the bird that first rouses, or not much tardier, to read good authors, or cause them to be read, till the attention be weary, or memory have his full fraught; then, with useful and gener-ous labours preserving the body's health and hardiness, to render lightsome, clear and not lumpish obedience to the mind, to the cause of religion and our country's liberty, when it shall require firm hearts in sound bodies to stand and cover their stations, rather than to see the ruin of our protestation° and the inforcement of a slavish life.

These are the morning practices: proceed now to the afternoon; 'in playhouses', he says, 'and the bordelloes'. Your intelligence, unfaithful spy° of Canaan? He gives in his evidence, that 'there he hath traced me'. Take him at his word, readers; but let him bring good sureties, ere ye dismiss him, that while he pretended to dog others, he did not turn in for his own pleasure: for so much in effect he concludes against himself, not contented to be caught in every other gin,° but he must be such a novice as to be still hampered in his own hemp. In the *Animadversions*, saith he, I find the mention of old cloaks, false beards, night-walkers and salt lotion; therefore the animadverter haunts playhouses and bordelloes; for if he did not, how could he speak of such gear? Now that he may know what it is to be a child and yet to meddle with edged tools, I turn his antistrophon° upon his own head; the confuter knows that these things are the furniture of playhouses and bordelloes, therefore, by the same reason, *the confuter himself hath been traced in those places.* Was it such a dissolute speech telling of some politicians who were wont to eavesdrop in disguise to say they were often liable to° a night-walking cudgeller, or the emptying of a urinal? What if I had writ as your friend the author of the aforesaid mime *Mundus Alter et Idem* to have been ravished like some young Cephalus or Hylas° by a troop of camping housewives in Viraginea,° and that he was there forced to swear himself an uxorious varlet; then after a long servitude to have come into Aphrodisia, that pleasant country that gave such a sweet smell to his nostrils among the shameless courtesans of Desvergonia? Surely he would have then concluded me as constant at the bordello as the galley-slave at his oar.

But since there is such necessity to the hearsay of a tire,° a periwig or a vizard, that plays must have been seen, what difficulty was there in that? when in the colleges so many of the young divines, and those in next aptitude to divinity, have been seen so often upon the stage, writhing and unboning their clergy limbs to all the antic and dishonest gestures of Trinculos,° buffoons and bawds, prostituting the shame of that ministry which either they had, or were nigh having, to the eyes of courtiers and court ladies, with their grooms and mademoiselles. There, while they acted and overacted, among other young scholars, I was a spectator; they thought themselves gallant men, and I thought them fools; they made sport, and I laughed; they mispronounced, and I misliked; and, to make up the atticism,° they were out, and I hissed. Judge now whether so many good text men were not sufficient to instruct me of false beards and vizards, without more expositors; and how can this confuter take the face to object to me the seeing of that which his reverend prelates allow, and incite their young disciples to act? For if it be unlawful° to sit and behold a mercenary comedian personating that which is least unseemly for a hireling to do, how much more blameful is it to endure the sight of as vile things acted by persons either entered, or presently to enter into the ministry; and how much more foul and ignominious for them to be the actors!

But because as well by this upbraiding to me the bordelloes, as by other suspicious glancings in his book, he would seem privily to point me out to his readers as one whose custom of life were not honest, but licentious, I shall entreat to be borne with, though I digress; and in a way not often trod, acquaint ye with the sum of my thoughts in this matter through the course of my years and studies—although I am not ignorant how hazardous it will be to do this under the nose of the envious, as it were in skirmish to change the compact order, and instead of outward actions, to bring inmost thoughts into front. And I must tell ye, readers, that by this sort of men I have been already bitten at; yet shall they not for me know how slightly they are esteemed, unless they have so much learning as to read what in Greek ἀπειροκαλία° is, which, together with envy, is the common disease of those who censure books that are not for their reading. With me it fares now as with him whose outward garment hath been injured and ill-bedighted; for having no other shift, what help but to turn the inside outwards, especially if the lining be of the same, or, as it is sometimes, much better? So if my name and outward demeanour be not evident enough to defend me, I must make trial if the discovery of my inmost thoughts can: wherein of two purposes, both honest and both sincere, the one perhaps I shall not miss; although I fail to gain belief with others, of being such as my perpetual thoughts shall here disclose me, I may yet not fail of success in persuading some to be such really themselves as they cannot believe me to be more than what I feign.

I had my time, readers, as others have, who have good learning bestowed upon them, to be sent to those places where, the opinion was, it might be soonest attained; and as the manner is, was not unstudied in those authors which are most commended. Whereof some were grave orators and historians, whose matter methought I loved indeed, but as my age then was, so I understood them; others were the smooth elegiac poets, whereof the schools are not scarce, whom both for the pleasing

sound of their numerous° writing, which in imitation I found most easy,
and most agreeable to nature's part in me, and for their matter, which
what it is, there be few who know not I was so allured to read that no
recreation came to me better welcome. For that it was then those years
with me which are excused, though they be least severe, I may be saved
the labour to remember ye. Whence having observed them to account it
the chief glory of their wit, in that they were ablest to judge, to praise,
and by that could esteem themselves worthiest to love those high perfections which under one or other name they took to celebrate, I
thought with myself by every instinct and presage of nature, which is
not wont to be false, that what emboldened them to this task might with
such diligence as they used embolden me; and that what judgment, wit
or elegance was my share, would herein best appear and best value
itself by how much more wisely and with more love of virtue I should
choose (let rude ears be absent) the object of not unlike praises. For
albeit these thoughts to some will seem virtuous and commendable, to
others only pardonable, to a third sort perhaps idle; yet the mentioning
of them now will end in serious.

Nor blame it, readers, in those years to propose to themselves such a
reward as the noblest dispositions above other things in this life have
sometimes preferred: whereof not to be sensible when good and fair in
one person meet, argues both a gross and shallow judgment, and withal
an ungentle and swainish breast. For by the firm settling of these
persuasions I became, to my best memory, so much a proficient, that if
I found those authors anywhere speaking unworthy things of themselves, or unchaste of those names which before they had extolled, this
effect it wrought with me, from that time forward their art I still
applauded, but the men I deplored; and above them all preferred the
two famous renowners° of Beatrice and Laura, who never write but
honour of them to whom they devote their verse, displaying sublime
and pure thoughts, without transgression. And long it was not after,
when I was confirmed in this opinion, that he who would not be frustrate of his hope to write well hereafter in laudable things, ought himself to be a true poem,° that is, a composition and pattern of the best
and honourablest things, not presuming to sing high praises of heroic
men or famous cities unless he have in himself the experience and the
practice of all that which is praiseworthy. These reasonings, together
with a certain niceness of nature, an honest haughtiness, and self-
esteem either of what I was, or what I might be (which let envy call
pride), and lastly that modesty, whereof, though not in the title-page,
yet here I may be excused to make some beseeming profession; all

these uniting the supply of their natural aid together kept me still above those low descents of mind beneath which he must deject and plunge himself that can agree to saleable and unlawful prostitutions.

Next (for hear me out now, readers) that I may tell ye whither my younger feet wandered; I betook me among those lofty fables and romances which recount in solemn cantos the deeds of knighthood founded by our victorious kings, and from hence had in renown over all Christendom. There I read it in the oath of every knight that he should defend to the expense of his best blood, or of his life, if it so befell him, the honour and chastity of virgin or matron; from whence even then I learnt what a noble virtue chastity sure must be, to the defence of which so many worthies, by such a dear° adventure of themselves, had sworn. And if I found in the story afterward any of them by word or deed breaking that oath, I judged it the same fault of the poet as that which is attributed to Homer,° to have written undecent things of the gods. Only this my mind gave me, that every free and gentle spirit, without that oath, ought to be born a knight, nor needed to expect the gilt spur or the laying of a sword upon his shoulder to stir him up both by his counsel and his arm to secure and protect the weakness of any attempted chastity. So that even these books which to many others have been the fuel of wantonness and loose living, I cannot think how, unless by divine indulgence, proved to me so many incitements, as you have heard, to the love and steadfast observation of that virtue which abhors the society of bordelloes.

Thus, from the laureate fraternity of poets, riper years and the ceaseless round of study and reading led me to the shady spaces of philosophy; but chiefly to the divine volumes of Plato, and his equal Xenophon;° where, if I should tell ye what I learnt of chastity and love, I mean that which is truly so, whose charming cup is only virtue, which she bears in her hand to those who are worthy—the rest are cheated with a thick intoxicating potion, which a certain sorceress,° the abuser of love's name, carries about—and how the first and chiefest office of love begins and ends in the soul, producing those happy twins of her divine generation, knowledge and virtue: with such abstracted sublimities as these, it might be worth your listening, readers, as I may one day hope to have ye in a still time, when there shall be no chiding; not in these noises, the adversary, as ye know, barking at the door, or searching for me at the bordelloes, where it may be he has lost himself, and raps up without pity the sage and rheumatic old prelatess, with all her young Corinthian° laity, to inquire for such a one.

Last of all, not in time, but as perfection is last, that care was ever had of me, with my earliest capacity, not to be negligently trained in the precepts of Christian religion: this that I have hitherto related hath been to show that though Christianity had been but slightly taught me, yet a certain reservedness of natural disposition, and moral discipline learnt out of the noblest philosophy, was enough to keep me in disdain of far less incontinences than this of the bordello. But having had the doctrine of holy Scripture unfolding those chaste and high mysteries with timeliest care infused, that 'the body is for the Lord, and the Lord for the body',° thus also I argued to myself, that if unchastity in a woman, whom St Paul terms the glory of man, be such a scandal and dishonour, then certainly in a man, who is both the image and glory of God, it must, though commonly not so thought, be much more deflowering and dishonourable. In that he sins both against his own body, which is the perfecter sex, and his own glory, which is in the woman; and, that which is worst, against the image and glory of God, which is in himself. Nor did I slumber over that place° expressing such high rewards of ever accompanying the Lamb with those celestial songs to others inapprehensible, but not to those who were not defiled with women, which doubtless means fornication; for marriage must not be called a defilement.°

Thus large I have purposely been, that if I have been justly taxed with this crime, it may come upon me, after all this my confession, with a tenfold shame; but if I have hitherto deserved no such opprobrious word or suspicion, I may hereby engage myself now openly to the faithful observation of what I have professed.

The Doctrine and Discipline of Divorce
Restored to the Good of Both Sexes

Many men, whether it be their fate or fond° opinion, easily persuade themselves, if God would but be pleased a while to withdraw his just punishments from us, and to restrain what power either the devil or any earthly enemy hath to work us woe, that then man's nature would find immediate rest and releasement from all evils. But verily they who think so, if they be such as have a mind large enough to take into their thoughts a general survey of human things, would soon prove themselves in that opinion far deceived. For though it were granted us by divine indulgence to be exempt from all that can be harmful to us from without, yet the perverseness of our folly is so bent that we should never

lin° hammering out of our own hearts, as it were out of a flint, the seeds
and sparkles of new miseries to ourselves, till all were in a blaze again.
And no marvel if out of our own hearts, for they are evil; but even out of
those things which God meant us either for a principal good or a pure
contentment, we are still hatching and contriving upon ourselves matter
of continual sorrow and perplexity. What greater good to man than that
revealed rule whereby God vouchsafes to show us how he would be
worshipped? And yet that not rightly understood became the cause that
once a famous man° in Israel could not but oblige his conscience to be
the sacrificer, or if not, the jailor of his innocent and only daughter; and
was the cause ofttimes that armies of valiant men have given up their
throats to a heathenish enemy on the sabbath day,° fondly thinking their
defensive resistance to be as then a work unlawful. What thing more
instituted to the solace and delight of man than marriage? And yet the
misinterpreting of some scripture directed mainly against the abusers
of the law for divorce given them by Moses° hath changed the blessing
of matrimony not seldom into a familiar and coinhabiting mischief; at
least into a drooping and disconsolate household captivity, without
refuge or redemption. So ungoverned and so wild a race doth superstition run us from one extreme of abused liberty into the other of
unmerciful restraint. For although God in the first ordaining of mar-
riage° taught us to what end he did it, in words expressly implying the
apt and cheerful conversation° of man with woman, to comfort and
refresh him against the evil of solitary life, not mentioning the purpose
of generation till afterwards, as being but a secondary end in dignity,
though not in necessity; yet now, if any two be but once handed° in the
church and have tasted in any sort of the nuptial bed, let them find
themselves never so mistaken in their dispositions through any error,
concealment or misadventure, that through their different tempers,°
thoughts and constitutions they can neither be to one another a remedy
against loneliness nor live in any union or contentment all their days,
yet they shall, so they be but found suitably weaponed to the least possibility of sensual enjoyment, be made, spite of antipathy, to fadge°
together, and combine as they may to their unspeakable wearisomeness
and despair of all sociable delight in the ordinance which God established to that very end. What a calamity is this, and, as the wise man,° if
he were alive, would sigh out in his own phrase, what a 'sore evil is this
under the sun!' All which we can refer justly to no other author than the
canon law° and her adherents, not consulting with charity, the interpreter and guide of our faith, but resting in the mere element° of the
text; doubtless by the policy of the devil to make that gracious ordinance

become unsupportable, that what with men not daring to venture upon wedlock, and what with men wearied out of it, all inordinate licence might abound. It was for many ages that marriage lay in disgrace with most of the ancient doctors, as a work of the flesh, almost a defilement, wholly denied to priests, and the second time dissuaded to all, as he that reads Tertullian° or Jerome° may see at large. Afterwards it was thought so sacramental° that no adultery could dissolve it; yet there remains a burden on it as heavy as the other two were disgraceful or superstitious, and of as much iniquity, crossing a law not only written by Moses,° but charactered in us by nature, of more antiquity and deeper ground than marriage itself; which law is to force nothing against the faultless proprieties of nature, yet that this may be colourably° done, our Saviour's words touching divorce are as it were congealed into a stony rigour inconsistent both with his doctrine and his office, and that which he preached only to the conscience is by canonical tyranny snatched into the compulsive censure of a judicial court, where laws are imposed even against the venerable and secret power of nature's impression, to love, whatever cause be found to loathe: which is a heinous barbarism both against the honour of marriage, the dignity of man and his soul, the goodness of Christianity and all the human respects of civility. Notwithstanding that some the wisest and gravest among the Christian emperors,° who had about them, to consult with, those of the fathers then living, who for their learning and holiness of life are still with us in great renown, have made their statutes and edicts concerning this debate far more easy and relenting in many necessary cases, wherein the canon is inflexible. And Hugo Grotius,° a man of these times, one of the best learned, seems not obscurely to adhere in his persuasion to the equity of those imperial decrees, in his notes upon the Evangelists, much allaying the outward roughness of the text, which hath for the most part been too immoderately expounded; and excites the diligence of others to inquire further into this question, as containing many points which have not yet been explained. By which, and by mine own apprehension of what public duty each man owes, I conceive myself exhorted among the rest to communicate such thoughts as I have, and offer them now in this general labour of reformation to the candid view both of church and magistrate, especially because I see it the hope of good men that those irregular and unspiritual courts have spun their utmost date in this land, and some better course must now be constituted.°

He therefore that by adventuring shall be so happy as with success to ease and set free the minds of ingenuous° and apprehensive° men from this needless thraldom; he that can prove it lawful and just to claim the performance of a fit and matchable conversation, no less essential to the prime scope of marriage than the gift of bodily conjunction, or else to have an equal plea of divorce as well as for that corporal deficiency;° he that can but lend us the clue that winds out° this labyrinth of servitude to such a reasonable and expedient liberty as this, deserves to be reckoned among the public benefactors of civil and humane life above the inventors of wine and oil; for this is a far dearer, far nobler and more desirable cherishing to man's life, unworthily exposed to sadness and mistake, which he shall vindicate. Not that licence and levity and unconsented breach of faith should herein be countenanced, but that some conscionable and tender pity might be had of those who have unwarily, in a thing they never practised before, made themselves the bondmen of a luckless and helpless matrimony.

In which argument he whose courage can serve him to give the first onset must look for two several oppositions, the one from those who, having sworn themselves to long custom and the letter of the text, will not out of the road, the other from those whose gross and vulgar apprehensions conceit° but low of matrimonial purposes, and in the work of male and female think they have all. Nevertheless, it shall be here sought by due ways to be made appear that those words of God in the institution promising a meet help against loneliness, and those words of Christ° 'that his yoke is easy and his burden light', were not spoken in vain; for if the knot of marriage may in no case be dissolved but for adultery, all the burdens and services of the law° are not so intolerable. This only is desired of them who are minded to judge hardly of thus maintaining, that they would be still and hear all out,° nor think it equal° to answer deliberate reason with sudden heat and noise; remembering this, that many truths now of reverend esteem and credit had their birth and beginning once from singular and private thoughts while the most of men were otherwise possessed, and had the fate at first to be generally exploded° and exclaimed on by many violent opposers. Yet I may err perhaps in soothing myself that this present truth revived will deserve to be not ungently received on all hands, in that it undertakes the cure of an inveterate disease crept into the best part of human society; and to do this with no smarting corrosive, but with a smooth and pleasing lesson, which received, hath the virtue to soften and dispel rooted and knotty sorrows; and without enchantment or spell used hath regard at once both to serious pity and upright honesty; that tends to the redeeming and restoring of none but such as are the object of compassion, having in an ill hour hampered themselves to the utter dispatch of all their most beloved comforts and repose for this life's term. But if we shall obstinately dislike this new overture° of unexpected ease and recovery, what remains but to deplore the frowardness of our hopeless condition, which neither can endure the estate we are in, nor admit of remedy either sharp or sweet? Sharp we ourselves distaste, and sweet, under whose hands we are, is scrupled and suspected as too luscious. In such a posture Christ found the Jews, who were neither won with the austerity of John the Baptist, and thought it too much licence to follow freely the charming pipe° of him who sounded and proclaimed liberty and relief to all distresses; yet truth in some age or other will find her witness, and shall be justified at last by her own children.

To remove, therefore, if it be possible, this great and sad oppression which through the strictness of a literal interpreting hath invaded and disturbed the dearest and most peaceable estate of household society to the overburdening, if not the overwhelming, of many Christians better worth than to be so deserted of the church's considerate care, this position shall be laid down, first proving, then answering, what may be objected either from Scripture or light of reason:

That indisposition, unfitness, or contrariety of mind arising from a cause in nature unchangeable, hindering and ever likely to hinder the main benefits of conjugal society, which are solace and peace, is a greater reason of divorce than natural frigidity, especially if there be no children and that there be mutual consent.

For all sense and reason and equity reclaims° that any law or covenant how solemn or strait soever, either between God and man or man and man, though of God's joining, should bind against a prime and principal scope of its own institution, and of both or either party covenanting; neither can it be of force to engage a blameless creature to his own perpetual sorrow, mistaken for his expected solace, without suffering charity to step in and do a confessed good work of parting those whom nothing holds together but this of God's joining, falsely supposed against the express end of his own ordinance. And what his chief end was of creating woman to be joined with man his own instituting words declare, and are infallible to inform us what is marriage and what is no marriage, unless we can think them set there to no purpose: 'It is not good', saith he, 'that man should be alone. I will make him a help meet for him.' From which words, so plain, less cannot be concluded, nor is by any learned interpreter, than that in God's intention a meet and happy conversation is the chiefest and the noblest end of marriage; for we find here no expression so necessarily implying carnal knowledge as this prevention of loneliness to the mind and spirit of man. And indeed it is a greater blessing from God, more worthy so excellent a creature as man is, and a higher end to honour and sanctify the league of marriage whenas the solace and satisfaction of the mind is regarded and provided for before the sensitive pleasing of the body. And with all generous° persons married thus it is that where the mind and person pleases aptly, there some unaccomplishment of the body's delight may be better borne with than when the mind hangs off in an unclosing° disproportion, though the body be as it ought; for there all corporal delight will soon become unsavoury and contemptible. And the solitariness of man, which God had namely and principally ordered to prevent by marriage, hath no remedy, but lies under a worse condition than the loneliest single life; for in single life the absence and remoteness of a helper might inure him to expect his own comforts out of himself, or to seek with hope; but here the continual sight of his deluded thoughts, without cure, must needs be to him, if especially his complexion° incline him to melancholy, a daily trouble and pain of loss, in some degree like that which reprobates° feel. Lest therefore so noble a creature as man should be shut up incurably under a worse evil by an easy mistake in that ordinance which God gave him to remedy a less evil, reaping to himself sorrow while he went to rid away solitariness, it cannot avoid to be concluded that if the woman be naturally so of disposition as will not help to remove, but help to increase that same Godforbidden loneliness which will in time draw on with it a general discomfort and dejection of mind not beseeming either Christian profession or moral conversation, unprofitable and dangerous to the commonwealth, when the household estate, out of which must flourish forth the vigour and spirit of all public enterprises, is so ill-contented and procured at home, and cannot be supported; such a marriage can be no marriage, whereto the most honest end is wanting; and the aggrieved person shall do more manly to be extraordinary and singular in claiming the due right whereof he is frustrated than to piece° up his lost contentment by visiting the stews,° or stepping to his neighbour's bed, which is the common shift in this misfortune; or else by suffering his useful life to waste away and be lost under a secret affliction of an unconscionable size to human strength.

How vain, therefore, is it, and how preposterous° in the canon law, to have made such careful provision against the impediment of carnal performance, and to have had no care about the unconversing inability of mind so defective to the purest and most sacred end of matrimony, and that the vessel of voluptuous enjoyment must be made good to him that has taken it upon trust, without any caution; whenas the mind, from

whence must flow the acts of peace and love, a far more precious mixture than the quintessence of an excrement,° though it be found never
so deficient and unable to perform the best duty of marriage in a cheerful and agreeable conversation, shall be thought good enough, however
flat and melancholious it be, and must serve, though to the eternal disturbance and languishing of him that complains him.° Yet wisdom and
charity, weighing God's own institution, would think that the pining of
a sad spirit wedded to loneliness should deserve to be freed, as well as
the impatience of a sensual desire so providently relieved. 'Tis read to
us in the liturgy° that 'we must not marry to satisfy the fleshly appetite,
like brute beasts that have no understanding', but the canon so runs as
if it dreamt of no other matter than such an appetite to be satisfied; for
if it happen that nature hath stopped or extinguished the veins of sensuality, that marriage is annulled. But though all the faculties of the
understanding and conversing part after trial appear to be so ill and so
aversely met through nature's unalterable working as that neither peace
nor any sociable contentment can follow, 'tis as nothing; the contract
shall stand as firm as ever, betide what will. What is this but secretly to
instruct us that however many grave reasons are pretended to the married life, yet that nothing indeed is thought worth regard therein but the
prescribed satisfaction of an irrational heat? Which cannot be but ignominious to the state of marriage, dishonourable to the undervalued soul
of man, and even to Christian doctrine itself, while it seems more
moved at the disappointing of an impetuous nerve than at the
ingenuous° grievance of a mind unreasonably yoked, and to place more
of marriage in the channel of concupiscence than in the pure influence°
of peace and love, whereof the soul's lawful contentment is the only
fountain.°

But some are ready to object that the disposition ought seriously to
be considered before. But let them know again that for all the wariness
can be used, it may yet befall a discreet man to be mistaken in his
choice: the soberest and best governed men are least practised in these
affairs; and who knows not that the bashful muteness of a virgin may
ofttimes hide all the unliveliness and natural sloth which is really unfit
for conversation? Nor is there that freedom of access granted or presumed as may suffice to a perfect discerning till too late; and where any
indisposition is suspected, what more usual than the persuasion of
friends that acquaintance, as it increases, will amend all? And lastly, it is
not strange though many who have spent their youth chastely are in
some things not so quick-sighted while they haste too eagerly to light
the nuptial torch; nor is it, therefore, that for a modest error a man

should forfeit so great a happiness, and no charitable means to release him, since they who have lived most loosely, by reason of their bold accustoming, prove most successful in their matches, because their wild affections unsettling at will have been as so many divorces to teach them experience. Whenas the sober man honouring the appearance of modesty, and hoping well of every social virtue under that veil, may easily chance to meet, if not with a body impenetrable, yet often with a mind to all other due conversation inaccessible, and to all the more estimable and superior purposes of matrimony useless and almost lifeless; and what a solace, what a fit help such a consort would be through the whole life of a man, is less pain to conjecture than to have experience.

And that we may further see what a violent cruel thing it is to force the continuing of those together whom God and nature in the gentlest end of marriage never joined, divers evils and extremities that follow upon such a compulsion shall here be set in view. Of evils, the first and greatest is that hereby a most absurd and rash imputation is fixed upon God and his holy laws, of conniving and dispensing with open and common adultery among his chosen people, a thing which the rankest politician would think it shame and disworship° that his laws should countenance—how and in what manner this comes to pass I shall reserve till the course of method brings on the unfolding of many scriptures. Next, the law and gospel are hereby made liable to more than one contradiction, which I refer also thither. Lastly, the supreme dictate of charity is hereby many ways neglected and violated; which I shall forthwith address to prove. First, we know St Paul° saith, 'It is better to marry than to burn.' Marriage, therefore, was given as a remedy of that trouble: but what might this burning mean? Certainly not the mere motion of carnal lust, not the mere goad of a sensitive° desire: God does not principally take care for such cattle.° What is it then but that desire which God put into Adam in Paradise before he knew the sin of incontinence; that desire which God saw it was not good that man should be left alone to burn in; the desire and longing to put off an unkindly solitariness by uniting another body, but not without a fit soul to his, in the cheerful society of wedlock? Which if it were so needful before the fall, when man was much more perfect in himself, how much more is it needful now against all the sorrows and casualties of this life to have an intimate and speaking help, a ready and reviving associate in marriage? Whereof who misses by chancing on a mute and spiritless mate remains more alone than before, and in a burning less to be contained than that which is fleshly, and more to be considered, as being more deeply rooted even in the faultless innocence of nature. As for that other burning, which is but as it were the venom of a lusty and over-abounding concoction,° strict life and labour, with the abatement of a full diet, may keep that low and obedient enough; but this pure and more inbred desire of joining to itself in conjugal fellowship a fit conversing soul (which desire is properly called love) 'is stronger than death', as the spouse of Christ thought; 'many waters cannot quench it, neither can the floods drown it.'° This is that rational burning that marriage is to remedy, not to be allayed with fasting, nor with penance to be subdued, which how can he assuage who by mishap hath met the unmeetest and most unsuitable mind? Who hath the power to struggle with an intelligible° flame, not in Paradise to be resisted, become now more ardent by being failed of what in reason it looked for, and even then most unquenched when the importunity of a provender burning° is well enough appeased, and yet the soul hath obtained nothing of what it justly desires? Certainly such a one forbidden to divorce is in effect forbidden to marry, and compelled to greater difficulties than in a single life; for if there be not a more human burning which marriage must satisfy, or else may be dissolved, than that of copulation, marriage cannot be honourable for the mere reducing and terminating of lust between two, seeing many beasts in voluntary and chosen couples live together as unadulterously, and are as truly married in that respect. But all ingenuous men will see that the dignity and blessing of marriage is placed rather in the mutual enjoyment of that which the wanting soul needfully seeks, than of that which the plenteous body would jollily give away. Hence it is that Plato° in his festival discourse brings in Socrates relating what he feigned to have learned from the prophetess Diotima, how Love was the son of Penury, begot of Plenty in the garden of Jupiter. Which divinely sorts° with that which in effect Moses tells us,° that Love was the son of Loneliness, begot in Paradise by that sociable and helpful aptitude which God implanted between man and woman toward each other. The same also is that burning mentioned by St Paul whereof marriage ought to be the remedy—the flesh hath other natural and easy curbs which are in the power of any temperate man. When, therefore, this original and sinless penury, or loneliness of the soul, cannot lay itself down by the side of such a meet and acceptable union as God ordained in marriage, at least in some proportion, it cannot conceive and bring forth love, but remains utterly unmarried under a formal wedlock, and still burns in the proper meaning of St Paul. Then enters Hate; not that hate that sins, but that which only is natural dissatisfaction and the turning aside from a mistaken object: if that mistake have done injury, it fails not to dismiss with recompense; for to retain still and not be able to love is to heap more injury. Thence that wise and pious law of dismission, Deut. 24:1, took beginning (of which anon); he, therefore, who lacking of his due in the most native and human end of marriage thinks it better to part than to live sadly and injuriously to that cheerful covenant (for not to be beloved, and yet retained, is the greatest injury to a gentle spirit)—he, I say, who therefore seeks to part, is one who highly honours the married life and would not stain it, and the reasons which now move him to divorce are equal to the best of those that could first warrant him to marry; for, as was plainly shown, both the hate which now diverts him and the loneliness which leads him still powerfully to seek a fit help hath not the least grain of a sin in it, if he be worthy to understand himself.

Thirdly, yet it is next to be feared, if he must be still bound without reason by a deaf rigour, that when he perceives the just expectance of his mind defeated, he will begin even against law to cast about where he may find his satisfaction more complete, unless he be a thing heroically virtuous; and that are not the common lump of men, for whom chiefly the laws ought to be made; though not to their sins, yet to their un-sinning weaknesses, it being above their strength to endure the lonely estate which while they shunned they are fallen into. And yet there follows upon this a worse temptation; for if he be such as hath spent his youth unblamably, and laid up his chiefest earthly comforts in the enjoyment of a contented marriage, nor did neglect that furtherance which was to be obtained therein by constant prayers, when he shall find himself bound fast to an uncomplying discord of nature, or, as it oft happens, to an image of earth and phlegm,° with whom he looked to be the copartner of a sweet and gladsome society, and sees withal that his bondage is now inevitable, though he be almost the strongest Christian, he will be ready to despair in virtue, and mutin° against divine providence: and this doubtless is the reason of those lapses and that melancholy despair which we see in many wedded persons, though they understand it not, or pretend other causes because they know no remedy; and is of extreme danger: therefore when human frailty surcharged is at such a loss, charity ought to venture much, and use bold physic, lest an overtossed faith endanger to shipwreck.

Fourthly, marriage is a covenant the very being whereof consists not in a forced cohabitation and counterfeit performance of duties, but in unfeigned love and peace. Thence saith Solomon in Ecclesiastes,° 'Live joyfully with the wife whom thou lovest all thy days, for that is thy portion.' How then where we find it impossible to rejoice or to love can we obey this precept? How miserably do we defraud ourselves of that comfortable portion which God gives us by striving vainly to glue an error together which God and nature will not join, adding but more vexation and violence to that blissful society by our importunate superstition, that will not hearken to St Paul, 1 Cor. 7, who speaking of marriage and divorce, determines plain enough in general that God therein 'hath called us to peace', and not to bondage. Yea, God himself commands in his law more than once, and by his prophet Malachi° (as Calvin and the best translations read), that 'he who hates, let him divorce'; that is, he who cannot love or delight.

I cannot therefore be so diffident as not securely to conclude that he who can receive nothing of the most important helps in marriage, being thereby disenabled to return that duty which is his with a clear and hearty countenance, and thus continues to grieve whom he would not, and is no less grieved, that man ought even for love's sake and peace to move divorce upon good and liberal° conditions to the divorced.° And it is a less breach of wedlock to part with wise and quiet consent betimes than still° to soil and profane that mystery of joy and union with a polluting sadness and perpetual distemper; for it is not the outward continuing of marriage that keeps whole that covenant, but whosoever does most according to peace and love, whether in marriage or in divorce, he it is that breaks marriage least, it being so often written° that *love only is the fulfilling of every commandment*.

Fifthly, as those priests of old were not to be long in sorrow,° or if they were, they could not rightly execute their function, so every true Christian in a higher order of priesthood is a person dedicate to joy and peace, offering himself a lively sacrifice° of praise and thanksgiving, and there is no Christian duty that is not to be seasoned and set off with cheerfulness; which in a thousand outward and intermitting crosses° may yet be done well, as in this vale of tears: but in such a bosom affliction as this, which grinds the very foundations of his inmost nature, when he shall be forced to love against a possibility, and to use dissimulation against his soul in the perpetual and ceaseless duties of a husband, doubtless his whole duty of serving God must needs be blurred and tainted with a sad unpreparedness and dejection of spirit, wherein God has no delight. Who sees not therefore how much more Christianly it would be to break by divorce that which is more broken by undue and forcible keeping, rather that 'to cover the altar of the Lord with continual tears, so that he regardeth not the offering any more',° rather than that the whole worship of a Christian man's life should languish and fade away beneath the weight of an immeasureable grief and discouragment? And because some think the children of a second matrimony succeeding a divorce would not be a holy seed, why should we not think them more holy than the offspring of a former ill-twisted wedlock, begotten only out of a bestial necessity, without any true love or contentment or joy to their parents? So that in some sense we may call them the 'children of wrath'° and anguish, which will as little conduce to their sanctifying as if they h?d been bastards; for nothing more than disturbance of mind suspends us from approaching to God—such a disturbance especially as both assaults our faith and trust in God's providence, and ends, if there be not a miracle of virtue on either side, not only in bitterness and wrath, the canker of devotion, but in a desperate and vicious carelessness when he sees himself, without fault of his, trained° by a deceitful bait into a snare of misery, betrayed by an alluring ordinance and then made the thrall of heaviness and discomfort by an undivorcing law of God, as he erroneously thinks, but of man's iniquity, as the truth is; for that God prefers the free and cheerful worship of a Christian before the grievous and exacted observance of an unhappy marriage, besides that the general maxims of religion assure us, will be more manifest by drawing a parallel° argument from the ground of divorcing an idolatress, which was, lest she should alienate his heart from the true worship of God: and, what difference is there whether she pervert him to superstition by enticing sorcery, or disenable him in the whole service of God through the disturbance of her unhelpful and unfit society, and so drive him at last, through murmuring and despair, to thoughts of atheism? Neither doth it lessen the cause of separating, in that the one willingly allures him from the faith, the other perhaps unwillingly drives him; for in the account of God it comes all to one that the wife loses him a servant; and therefore by all the united force of the Decalogue she ought to be disbanded,° unless we must set marriage above God and charity, which is a doctrine of devils no less than forbidding to marry.

And here by the way, to illustrate the whole question of divorce, ere this treatise end, I shall not be loath to spend a few lines in hope to give a full resolve of that which is yet so much controverted: whether an idolatrous heretic ought to be divorced. To the resolving whereof we must first know that the Jews were commanded to divorce an unbelieving Gentile for two causes: first, because all other nations, especially the Canaanites, were to them unclean. Secondly, to avoid seducement. That other nations were to the Jews impure, even to the separating of marriage, will appear out of Exod. 34: 16, Deut. 7: 3, 6, compared with Ezra 9: 2, also chap. 10: 10, 11, Neh. 13: 30. This was the ground of that doubt raised among the Corinthians by some of the circumcision,° whether an unbeliever were not still to be counted an unclean thing, so as that they ought to divorce from such a person. This doubt of theirs St Paul removes by an evangelical reason, having respect to that vision of St Peter,° wherein the distinction of clean and unclean being abolished, all living creatures were sanctified to a pure and Christian use, and mankind especially, now invited by a general call to the covenant of grace. Therefore saith St Paul,° 'the unbelieving wife is sanctified by the husband', that is, made pure and lawful to his use, so that he need not put her away for fear lest her unbelief should defile him; but that if he found her love still towards him, he might rather hope to win her. The second reason of that divorce was to avoid seducement, as is proved by comparing those places of the law to that which Ezra and Nehemiah did by divine warrant in compelling the Jews to forego their wives. And this reason is moral and perpetual in the rule of Christain faith without evasion; therefore, saith the apostle, 2 Cor. 6,° 'Misyoke not together with infidels', which is interpreted of marriage in the first place. And although the former legal pollution be now done off, yet there is a spiritual contagion in idolatry as much to be shunned; and though seducement were not to be feared, yet where there is no hope of converting, there always ought to be a certain religious aversation and abhorring, which can no way sort with marriage. Therefore saith St Paul, 'What fellowship hath righteousness with unrighteousness? What communion hath light with darkness? What concord hath Christ with Belial? What part hath he that believeth with an infidel?' And in the next verse but one he moralizes and makes us liable to that command of Isaiah,° 'Wherefore come out from among them, and be ye separate, saith the Lord; touch not the unclean thing, and I will receive ye.' And this command thus gospelized° to us hath the same force with that whereon Ezra grounded the pious necessity of divorcing.

Upon these principles I answer that a right believer ought to divorce an idolatrous heretic, unless upon better hopes; however, that it is in the believer's choice to divorce or not.

The former part will be manifest thus; first, that an apostate idolater, whether husband or wife seducing, was to die by the decree of God, Deut. 13: 6, 9; that marriage, therefore, God himself disjoins; for others born idolaters, the moral reason of their dangerous keeping and the incommunicable antagony° that is between Christ and Belial will be sufficient to enforce the commandment of those two inspired reformers, Ezra and Nehemiah, to put an idolater away as well under the gospel.

The latter part, that although there be no seducement feared, yet if there be no hope given, the divorce is lawful, will appear by this, that idolatrous marriage is still hateful to God, therefore still it may be divorced by the pattern or that warrant that Ezra had, and by the same everlasting reason: neither can any man give an account wherefore, if those whom God joins no man may separate, it should not follow that whom he joins not, but hates to join, those men ought to separate. But saith the lawyer, 'that which ought not have been done, once done, avails.' I answer, 'this is but a crotchet° of the law, but that brought against it is plain scripture.' As for what Christ spake concerning divorce, 'tis confessed by all knowing men, he meant only between them of the same faith. But what shall we say then to St Paul, who seems to bid us not divorce an infidel willing to stay? We may safely say thus, that wrong collections° have been hitherto made out of those words by modern divines. His drift, as was heard before, is plain: not to command our stay in marriage with an infidel, that had been a flat renouncing of the religious and moral law; but to inform the Corinthians that the body of an unbeliever was not defiling if his desire to live in Christian wedlock showed any likelihood that his heart was opening to the faith; and therefore advises to forbear departure so long till nothing have been neglected to set forward a conversion—this, I say, he advises, and that with certain cautions, not commands, if we can take up so much credit for him as to get him believed upon his own word: for what is this else but his counsel in a thing indifferent, 'To the rest speak I, not the Lord'?° For though it be true that the Lord never spake it, yet from St Paul's mouth we should have took it as a command, had not himself forewarned us, and disclaimed; which notwithstanding if we shall still avouch to be a command, he palpably denying it, this is not to expound St Paul, but to outface° him. Neither doth if follow but that the apostle may interpose his judgment in a case of Christian liberty without the guilt of adding to God's word. How do we know marriage or single life to be of choice, but by such like words as these: 'I speak this by permission, not of commandment; I have no command of the Lord, yet I give my judgment'?° Why shall not the like words have leave to signify a freedom in this our present question, though Beza° deny? Neither is the Scripture hereby less inspired because St Paul confesses to have written therein what he had not of command; for we grant that the Spirit of God led him thus to express himself to Christian prudence in a matter which God thought best to leave uncommanded. Beza, therefore, must be warily read when he taxes St Austin° of blasphemy for holding that St Paul spake here as of a thing indifferent. But if it must be a command, I shall yet the more evince it to be a command that we should herein be left free; and that out of the Greek word used in the 12th verse,° which instructs us plainly there must be a joint assent and good liking on both sides—he that will not deprave the text must thus render it: 'If a brother have an unbelieving wife, and she join in consent to dwell with him' (which cannot utter less to us than a mutual agreement), let him not put her away for the mere surmise of Judaical uncleanness; and the reason follows, for the body of an infidel is not polluted, neither to benevolence, nor to procreation. Moreover, this note of mutual complacency° forbids all offer of seducement, which to a person of zeal cannot be attempted without great offence; if, therefore, seducement be feared, this place° hinders not divorce. Another caution was put in this supposed command, of not bringing the believer into 'bondage' hereby, which doubtless might prove extreme, if Christian liberty and conscience were left to the humour of a pagan staying at pleasure to play with, or to vex and wound with a thousand scandals and burdens, above strength to bear. If, therefore, the conceived hope of gaining a soul come to nothing, then charity commands that the believer be not wearied out with endless waiting under many grievances sore to his spirit, but that respect be had rather to the present suffering of a true Christian than the uncertain winning of an obdured heretic; for this also must appertain to the precept, 'Let every man wherein he is called, therein abide with God', v. 24,° that is, so walking in his inferior calling of marriage, as not by dangerous subjection to that ordinance to hinder and disturb the higher calling of his Christianity. Last, whether this be a command or an advice, we must look that it be so understood as not to contradict the least point of moral religion that God hath formerly commanded; otherwise what do we but set the moral law and the gospel at civil war together, and who then shall be able to serve those two masters?

Now whether idolatry or adultery be the greatest violation of marriage if any demand, let him thus consider that among Christian writers touching matrimony, there be three chief ends thereof agreed on: godly society; next, civil; and thirdly, that of the marriage bed. Of these, the first in name to be the highest and most excellent no baptized man can deny, nor that idolatry smites directly against this prime end; nor that such as the violated end is, such is the violation; but he who affirms adultery to be the highest breach, affirms the bed to be the highest of marriage, which is in truth a gross and boorish opinion, how common soever; as far from the countenance of Scripture as from the light of all clean° philosophy or civil nature. And out of question the cheerful help that may be in marriage toward sanctity of life is the purest, and so the noblest end of that contract: but if the particular of each person be considered, then of those three ends which God appointed, that to him is greatest which is most necessary; and marriage is then most broken to him when he utterly wants the fruition of that which he most sought therein, whether it were religious, civil or corporal society. Of which wants to do him right by divorce only for the last and meanest is a perverse injury, and the pretended reason of it as frigid as frigidity itself, which the code and canon° are only sensible of. Thus much of this controversy. I now return to the former argument. And having shown that disproportion, contrariety or numbness of mind may justly be divorced, by proving already that the prohibition thereof opposes the express end of God's institution, suffers not marriage to satisfy that intellectual and innocent desire which God himself kindled in man to be the bond of wedlock, but only to remedy a sublunary° and bestial burning, which frugal diet, without marriage, would easily chasten. Next, that it drives many to transgress the conjugal bed, while the soul wanders after that satisfaction which it had hope to find at home, but hath missed; or else it sits repining, even to atheism, finding itself hardly dealt with, but misdeeming the cause to be in God's law, which is in man's unrighteous ignorance. I have showed also how it unties the inward knot of marriage, which is peace and love (if that can be untied which was never knit), while it aims to keep fast the outward formality; how it lets perish the Christian man to compel impossibly the married man.

The sixth place declares this prohibition to be as respectless of human nature and therefore is not of God. He teaches that an unlawful marriage may be lawfully divorced, and that those who having thoroughly discerned each other's disposition, which ofttimes cannot be till after matrimony, shall then find a powerful reluctance and recoil of nature on either side, blasting all the content of their mutual society, that such persons are not lawfully married (to use the apostle's words),° 'Say I these things as a man; or saith not the law also the same? For it is written, Deut. 22, "Thou shalt not sow thy vineyard with divers seeds, lest thou defile both. Thou shalt not plow with an ox and an ass together" ', and the like. I follow the pattern of St Paul's reasoning: 'Doth God care for asses and oxen' how ill they yoke together?—'or is it not said altogether for our sakes? For our sakes no doubt this is written.' Yea, the apostle himself, in the forecited 2 Cor. 6: 14, alludes from that place of Deut. to forbid misyoking marriage, as by the Greek word is evident; though he instance but in one example of mismatching with an infidel, yet next to that, what can be a fouler incongruity, a greater violence to the reverend secret of nature, than to force a mixture of minds that cannot unite, and to sow the furrow of man's nativity with seed of two incoherent and uncombining dispositions? Surely if any noisomeness° of body soon destroys the sympathy of mind to that work, much more will the antipathy of mind infuse itself into all the faculties and acts of the body to render them invalid, unkindly° and even unholy against the fundamental law book of nature, which Moses never thwarts, but reverences. Therefore he commands us to force nothing against sympathy or natural order, no, not upon the most abject creatures, to show that such an indignity cannot be offered to man without an impious crime. And when he forbids all unmatchable and unmingling natures to consort, doubtless by all due consequence, if they chance through misadventure to be miscoupled, he bids them part asunder, as persons whom God never joined.

Seventhly, the canon law and divines consent that if either party be found contriving against the other's life, they may be severed by divorce, for a sin against the life of marriage is greater than a sin against the bed: the one destroys, the other but defiles. The same may be said touching those persons who, being of a pensive nature and course of life, have summed up all their solace in that free and lightsome conversation which God and man intends in marriage; whereof when they see themselves deprived by meeting an unsociable consort, they ofttimes resent one another's mistake so deeply that long it is not ere grief end one of them. When therefore this danger is foreseen, that the life is in peril by living together, what matter is it whether helpless grief or wilful practice be the cause? This is certain, that the preservation of life is more worth than the compulsory keeping of marriage; and it is no less than cruelty to force a man to remain in that state as the solace of his life which he and his friends know will be either the undoing or the disheartening of his life. And what is life without the vigour and spiritful exercise of life? How can it be useful either to private or public employment? Shall it be therefore quite dejected, though never so valuable, and left to molder away in heaviness for the superstitious and impossible performance of an ill-driven bargain? Nothing more inviolable than vows made to God; yet we read in Numbers° that if a wife had made such a vow, the mere will and authority of her husband might break it: how much more may he break the error of his own bonds with an unfit and mistaken wife, to the saving of his welfare, his life, yea, his faith and virtue, from the hazard of overstrong temptations! For if man be lord of the sabbath° to the curing of a fever, can he be less than lord of marriage in such important causes as these?

Eighthly, it is most sure that some even of those who are not plainly defective in body, yet are destitute of all other marriageable gifts, and consequently have not the calling to marry unless nothing be requisite thereto but a mere instrumental body; which to affirm is to that unanimous covenant a reproach: yet it is as sure that many such, not of their own desire, but by persuasion of friends, or not knowing themselves, do often enter into wedlock; where finding the difference at length between the duties of a married life and the gifts of a single life, what unfitness of mind, what wearisomeness, what scruples and doubts to an incredible offence and displeasure are like to follow between may be soon imagined; whom thus to shut up and immure together, the one with a mischosen mate, the other in a mistaken calling, is not a course that Christian wisdom and tenderness ought to use. As for the custom that some parents and guardians have of forcing marriages, it will be better to say nothing of such a savage inhumanity, but only this: that the law which gives not all freedom of divorce to any creature endued with reason so assassinated,° is next in cruelty.

Ninthly, I suppose it will be allowed us that marriage is a human society, and that all human society must proceed from the mind rather than the body, else it would be but a kind of animal or beastish meeting; if the mind therefore cannot have that due company by marriage that it may reasonably and humanly desire, that marriage can be no human society, but a certain formality, or gilding over of little better than a brutish congress, and so in very wisdom and pureness to be dissolved.

But marriage is more than human, 'the covenant of God', Prov. 2: 17; therefore man cannot dissolve it. I answer, if it be more than human, so much the more it argues the chief society thereof to be in the soul rather than in the body, and the greatest breach thereof to be unfitness of mind rather than defect of body; for the body can have least affinity in a covenant more than human, so that the reason of dissolving holds good the rather. Again, I answer that the sabbath is a higher institution, a command of the first table,° for the breach whereof God hath far more and oftener testified his anger than for divorces, which from Moses till after the captivity° he never took displeasure at, nor then neither if we mark the text;° and yet as oft as the good of man is concerned, he not only permits, but commands to break the sabbath. What covenant more contracted with God and less in man's power than the vow which hath once passed his lips? yet if it be found rash, if offensive, if unfruitful either to God's glory or the good of man, our doctrine forces not error and unwillingness irksomely to keep it, but counsels wisdom and better thoughts boldly to break it; therefore to enjoin the indissoluble keeping of a marriage found unfit against the good of man both soul and body, as hath been evidenced, is to make an idol of marriage, to advance it above the worship of God and the good of man, to make it a transcendent command, above both the second and first table; which is a most prodigious doctrine.

Next, whereas they cite out of the Proverbs that it is the covenant of God, and therefore more than human, that consequence is manifestly false; for so the covenant which Zedekiah made with the infidel king of Babel is called the covenant of God, Ezk. 17: 19, which would be strange to hear counted more than a human covenant. So every covenant between man and man bound by oath may be called the covenant of God, because God therein is attested.° So of marriage he is the author and the witness; yet hence will not follow any divine astriction° more than what is subordinate to the glory of God and the main good of either party; for as the glory of God and their esteemed fitness one for the other was the motive which led them both at first to think without other revelation that God had joined them together, so when it shall be found by their apparent unfitness that their continuing to be man and wife is against the glory of God and their mutual happiness, it may assure them that God never joined them, who hath revealed his gracious will not to set the ordinance above the man for whom it was ordained, not to canonize marriage either as a tyranness or a goddess over the enfranchised life and soul of man; for wherein can God delight, wherein be worshipped, wherein be glorified by the forcible continuing of an improper and ill-yoking couple? He that loved not to see the disparity of several cattle at the plough cannot be pleased with any vast unmeetness in marriage. Where can be the peace and love which must invite God to such a house? May it not be feared that the not divorcing of such a helpless disagreement will be the divorcing of God finally from such a place? But it is a trial of our patience, they say: I grant it; but which of Job's afflictions were sent him with that law that he might not use means to remove any of them if he could? And what if it subvert our patience and our faith too? Who shall answer for the perishing of all those souls perishing by stubborn expositions of particular and inferior precepts against the general and supreme rule of charity? They dare not affirm that marriage is either a sacrament or a mystery, though all those sacred things give place to man; and yet they invest it with such an awful sanctity, and give it such adamantine chains to bind with, as if it were to be worshipped like some Indian deity, when it can confer no blessing upon us, but works more and more to our misery. To such teachers the saying of St Peter° at the council of Jerusalem will do well to be applied: 'Why tempt ye God to put a yoke upon the necks of' Christian men, which neither the Jews, God's ancient people, 'nor we are able to bear', and nothing but unwary expounding hath brought upon us?

To these considerations this also may be added as no improbable conjecture, seeing that sort of men who follow Anabaptism, Familism, Antinomianism,° and other fanatic dreams be such most commonly as are by nature addicted to a zeal of religion, of life also not debauched, and that their opinions having full swing do end in satisfaction of the flesh; it may come with reason into the thoughts of a wise man whether all this proceed not partly, if not chiefly, from the restraint of some lawful liberty which ought to be given men and is denied them. As by physic° we learn in menstruous bodies, where nature's current hath been stopped, that the suffocation and upward forcing of some lower part affects the head and inward sense with dotage and idle fancies. And on the other hand, whether the rest of vulgar men not so religiously professing do not give themselves much the more to whoredom and adulteries, loving the corrupt and venial discipline of clergy-courts, but hating to hear of perfect reformation; whenas they foresee that then fornication shall be austerely censured, adultery punished, and marriage, the appointed refuge of nature, though it hap to be never so incongruous and displeasing, must yet of force be worn out when it can be to no other purpose but of strife and hatred, a thing odious to God. This may be worth the study of skilful men in theology and the reason of things. And lastly, to examine whether some undue and ill-grounded strictness upon the blameless nature of man be not the cause in those places where already reformation is, that the discipline of the church so often, and so unavoidably broken, is brought into contempt and derision. And if it be thus, let those who are still bent to hold this obstinate literality so prepare themselves as to share in the account for all these transgressions when it shall be demanded at the last day by one who will scan and sift things with more than a literal wisdom of enquiry; for if these reasons be duly pondered, and that the gospel is more jealous of laying on excessive burdens than ever the law was, lest the soul of a Christian, which is inestimable, should be overtempted and cast away; considering also that many properties of nature, which the power of regeneration itself never alters, may cause dislike of conversing even between the most sanctified; which continually grating in harsh tune together, may breed some jar and discord, and that end in rancour and strife, a thing so opposite both to marriage and to Christianity, it would perhaps be less scandal to divorce a natural disparity than to link violently together an unchristian dissension, committing two ensnared souls inevitably to kindle one another, not with the fire of love, but with a hatred inconcileable;° who, were they dissevered, would be straight friends in any other relation. But if an alphabetical° servility must be still urged, it may so fall out that the true church may unwittingly use as much cruelty in forbidding to divorce as the church of Antichrist doth wilfully in forbidding to marry.

But what are all these reasonings worth, will some reply, whenas the words of Christ° are plainly against all divorce, 'except in case of fornication'? Let such remember, as a thing not to be denied, that all places of Scripture wherein just reason of doubt arises from the letter are to be expounded by considering upon what occasion everything is set down, and by comparing other texts. The occasion which induced our Saviour to speak of divorce was either to convince° the extravagance of the Pharisees in that point, or to give a sharp and vehement answer to a tempting question. And in such cases, that we are not to repose all upon the literal terms of so many words, many instances will teach us, wherein we may plainly discover how Christ meant not to be taken word for word, but, like a wise physician, administering one excess against another to reduce us to a perfect mean. Where the Pharisees were strict, there Christ seems remiss; where they were too remiss, he saw it needful to seem most severe—in one place° he censures an unchaste look to be adultery already committed, another time° he passes over actual adultery with less reproof than for an unchaste look, not so heavily condemning secret weakness as open malice. So here he may be justly thought to have given this rigid sentence against divorce not to cut off all remedy from a good man who finds himself consuming away in a disconsolate and unenjoyed matrimony, but to lay a bridle upon the bold abuses of those overweening rabbis, which he could not more effectually do than by a countersway of restraint curbing their wild exorbitance almost into the other extreme—as when we bow things the contrary way to make them come to their natural straightness.° And that this was the only intention of Christ is most evident, if we attend but to his own words and protestation made in the same sermon, not many verses before he treats of divorcing, that he came not to abrogate from the law 'one jot or tittle',° and denounces against them that shall so teach.

So that the question of divorce following upon this his open profession must needs confirm us that whatever else in the political law of more special relation to the Jews might cease to us, yet that of those precepts concerning divorce, not one of them was repealed by the doctrine of Christ; for if these our Saviour's words inveigh against all divorce, and condemn it as adultery, except it be for adultery, and be not rather understood against the abuse of those divorces permitted in the law, then is that law of Moses, Deut. 24: 1, not only repealed and wholly annulled against the promise of Christ and his known profession not to meddle in matters judicial, but that which is more strange, the very substance and purpose of that law is contradicted and convinced° both of injustice and impurity, as having authorized and maintained legal adultery by statute. Moses also cannot scape to be guilty of unequal° and unwise decrees,° punishing one act of secret adultery by death and permitting a whole life of open adultery by law. And albeit lawyers write that some political edicts, though not approved, are yet allowed to the scum of the people and the necessity of the times, these excuses have but a weak pulse; for first we read, not that the scoundrel people, but the choicest, the wisest, the holiest of that nation have frequently used these laws, or such as these. Secondly, be it yielded that in matters not very bad or impure a human lawgiver may slacken something of that which is exactly good to the disposition of the people and the times; but if the perfect, the pure, the righteous law of God (for so are all his statutes and his judgments) be found to have allowed smoothly, without any certain reprehension, that which Christ afterward declares to be adultery, how can we free this law from the horrible indictment of being both impure, unjust and fallacious?

Neither will it serve to say this was permitted for the hardness of their hearts, in that sense as it is usually explained; for the law were then but a corrupt and erroneous schoolmaster, teaching us to dash against a vital maxim of religion by doing foul evil in the hope of some uncertain good.

This only° text not to be matched again throughout the whole Scripture, whereby God in his perfect law should seem to have granted to the hard hearts of his holy people under his own hand a civil immunity and free charter to live and die in a long successive adultery, under a covenant of works, till the Messiah, and then that indulgent permission to be strictly denied by a covenant of grace, besides the incoherence of such a doctrine, cannot, must not be thus interpreted to the raising of a paradox never known till then, only hanging by the twined thread of one doubtful scripture, against so many other rules and leading principles of religion, of justice and purity of life. For what could be granted more either to the fear or to the lust of any tyrant or politician than this authority of Moses thus expounded, which opens him a way at will to dam up justice, and not only to admit of any Romish or Austrian° dispenses, but to enact a statute of that which he dares not seem to approve, even to legitimate vice, to make sin itself a free citizen of the commonwealth, pretending only these or these plausible reasons? And well he might, all the while that Moses shall be alleged to have done as much without showing any reason at all. Yet this could not enter into the heart of David, Psalm 94: 20,° how any such authority as endeavours to 'fashion wickedness by law' should derive itself from God. And Isaiah lays 'woe upon them that decree unrighteous decrees', chapter 10: 1. Now which of these two is the better lawgiver, and which deserves most a woe, he that gives out an edict singly unjust, or he that confirms to generations a fixed and unmolested impunity of that which is not only held to be unjust, but also unclean, and both in a high degree—not only, as they themselves affirm, an injurious expulsion of one wife, but also an unclean freedom by more than a patent to wed another adulterously? How can we therefore with safety thus dangerously confine the free simplicity of our Saviour's meaning to that which merely amounts from so many letters, whenas it can consist neither with his former and cautionary words, nor with other more pure and holy principles, nor finally with the scope of charity, commanding by his express commission in a higher strain? But all rather of necessity must be understood as only against the abuse of that wise and ingenuous liberty which Moses gave, and to terrify a roving conscience from sinning under that pretext.

Others think to evade the matter by not granting any law of divorce, but only a dispensation; which is contrary to the words of Christ, who himself calls it a law, Mark 10: 5.° But I answer, admitting it to be a dispensation, yet this is a certain rule, that so long as the cause remains, the dispensation ought—let it be shown, therefore, either in the nature of the gospel or of man why this dispensation should be made void. The gospel indeed exhorts to highest perfection, but bears with weakest infirmity more than the law. The nature of man is as weak, and yet as hard; and that weakness and hardness as unfit and as unteachable to be hardly dealt with as ever. Ay but, say they, there is a greater portion of spirit poured upon the gospel which requires perfecter obedience. But that consequence is deceivable, for it is the law that is the exacter of our obedience even under the gospel; how can it then exact concerning divorce that which it never exacted before? The gospel is a covenant revealing grace, not commanding a new morality, but assuring justification by faith only, contented if we endeavour to square our moral duty by those wise and equal° Mosaic rules which were as perfect, as strict and as unpardonable to the Jews as to us; otherwise the law were unjust, giving grace of pardon without the gospel—or if it give allowance without pardon, it would be dissolute and deceitful, saying in general, 'do this and live',° and yet deceiving and damning with obscure and hollow permissions. We find also by experience that the spirit of God in the gospel hath been always more effectual in the illumination of our minds to the gift of faith than in the moving of our wills to any excellence of virtue, either above the Jews or the heathen. Hence these indulgences in the gospel: 'All cannot receive this saying',° 'Every man hath his proper gift',° with strict charges not to lay on yokes which our fathers could not bear.°

But this that Moses suffered for the hardness of their hearts he suffered not by that enacted dispensation (far be it), but by a mere accidental sufferance of undiscovered hypocrites who made ill use of that law; for that God should enact a dispensation for hard hearts to do that whereby they must live in privileged adultery, however it go for the received opinion, I shall ever dissuade myself from so much hardihood as to believe. Certainly this is not the manner of God, whose pure eyes cannot behold, much less his perfect laws dispense with such impurity; and if we consider well, we shall find that all dispensations are either to avoid worse inconveniences, or to support infirm consciences for a time. But that a dispensation should be as long-lived as a law to tolerate adultery for hardness of heart, both sins of like degree (and yet this obdurate disease cannot be conceived how it is the more amended by this unclean remedy), is a notion of that extravagance° from the sage principles of piety that who considers thoroughly cannot but admire° how this hath been digested all this while. What may we do then to salve this seeming inconsistence? I must not dissemble that I am confident it can be done no other way than this:

Moses, Deut. 24: 1, established a grave and prudent law full of moral equity, full of due consideration towards nature, that cannot be resisted, a law consenting with the laws of wisest men and civilest nations: that when a man hath married a wife, if it come to pass that he cannot love her by reason of some displeasing natural quality or unfitness in her, let him write her a bill of divorce. The intent of which law undoubtedly was this, that if any good and peaceable man should discover some helpless° disagreement or dislike either of mind or body whereby he could not cheerfully perform the duty of a husband without perpetual dissembling of offence and disturbance to his spirit, rather than to live uncomfortably and unhappily both to himself and to his wife, rather than to continue undertaking a duty which he could not possibly discharge, he might dismiss her whom he could not tolerably, and so not conscionably, retain. And this law the spirit of God by the mouth of Solomon, Prov. 30: 21, 23, testifies to be a good and a necessary law, by granting it that to 'dwell with a hated woman' (for *hated* the Hebrew word signifies) 'is a thing that nature cannot endure'. What follows then, but that law must remedy what nature cannot undergo?

Now that many licentious and hardhearted men took hold of this law to cloak their bad purposes is nothing strange to believe. And these were they, not for whom Moses made the law (God forbid!), but whose hardness of heart taking ill advantage by this law he held it better to suffer as by accident, where it could not be detected, rather than good men should lose their just and lawful privilege of remedy. Christ therefore having to answer these tempting Pharisees, according as his custom was, not meaning to inform their proud ignorance what Moses did in the true intent of the law, which they had ill cited, suppressing the true cause for which Moses gave it, and extending it to every slight matter, tells them their own, what Moses was forced to suffer by their abuse of his law. Which is yet more plain if we mark that our Saviour, in Matt. 5,° cites not the law of Moses, but the pharisaical tradition falsely grounded upon that law. And in those other places, chapter 19 and Mark 10,° the Pharisees cite the law, but conceal the wise and humane reason there expressed; which our Saviour corrects not in them, whose pride deserved not his instruction, only returns them what is proper to them: 'Moses for the hardness of your heart suffered you' (that is, such as you) 'to put away your wives; and to you he wrote this precept for that cause', which ('to you') must be read with an impression,° and understood limitedly of such as covered ill purposes under that law; for it was seasonable that they should hear their own unbounded licence rebuked, but not seasonable for them to hear a good man's requisite liberty explained.

And to amaze them the more, because the Pharisees thought it no hard matter to fulfil the law, he draws them up to that unseparable institution which God ordained in the beginning before the fall, when man and woman were both perfect and could have no cause to separate; just as in the same chapter° he stands not to contend with the arrogant young man who boasted his observance of the whole law, whether he had indeed kept it or not, but screws him up° higher to a task of that perfection which no man is bound to imitate. And in like manner, that pattern of the first institution he set before the opinionative° Pharisees to dazzle them, and not to bind us. For this is a solid rule, that every command given with a reason binds our obedience no otherwise than that reason holds. Of this sort was that command in Eden,° 'therefore shall a man cleave to his wife, and they shall be one flesh'; which we see is no absolute command, but with an inference 'therefore': the reason then must be first considered, that our obedience be not misobedience. The first is (for it is not single) because the wife is to the husband 'flesh of his flesh', as in the verse going before. But this reason cannot be sufficient of itself; for why then should he for his wife leave his father and mother, with whom he is far more 'flesh of flesh and bone of bone', as being made of their substance? And besides, it can be but a sorry and ignoble society of life whose unseparable injunction depends merely upon flesh and bones. Therefore we must look higher, since Christ himself recalls us to the beginning, and we shall find that the primitive reason of never divorcing was that sacred and not vain promise of God to remedy man's loneliness by 'making him a help meet for him',° though not now in perfection, as at first, yet still in proportion as things now are. And this is repeated, verse 20, when all other creatures were fitly associated and brought to Adam, as if the divine power had been in some care and deep thought, because 'there was not yet found a help meet for man'. And can we so slightly depress° the all-wise purpose of a deliberating God, as if his consultation had produced no other good for man but to join him with an accidental companion of propagation, which his sudden° word had already made for every beast? Nay, a far less good to man it will be found if she must at all adventures° be fastened upon him individually.° And therefore even plain sense and equity, and, which is above them both, the all-interpreting voice of charity herself cries loud that this primitive reason, this consulted promise of God 'to make a meet help' is the only cause that gives authority to this command of not divorcing to be a command. And it might be further added that if the true definition of a wife were asked in good earnest, this clause of being 'a meet help' would show itself so necessary and so essential in that demonstrative argument that it might be logically concluded, therefore she who naturally and perpetually is no meet help can be no wife; which clearly takes away the difficulty of dismissing such a one.

Hence is manifest that so much of the first institution as our Saviour mentions (for he mentions not all) was but to quell and put to nonplus the tempting Pharisees, and to lay open their ignorance and shallow understanding of the Scriptures. For, saith he, 'have ye not read that he which made them at the beginning, made them male and female, and said, for this cause shall a man cleave to his wife?',° which these blind usurpers of Moses's chair could not gainsay—as if this single respect of male and female were sufficient, against a thousand inconveniences and mischiefs, to clog° a rational creature to his endless sorrow unrelinquishably. What if they had thus answered: 'Master, if thou intend to make wedlock as inseparable as it was from the beginning, let it be made also a fit society, as God intended it, which we shall soon understand it ought to be, if thou recite the whole reason of the law'? Doubtless our Saviour had applauded their just answer. For then they had expounded this command of Paradise even as Moses himself expounds it by his laws of divorce —that is, with due and wise regard had to the premises and reasons of the first command, according to which, without unclean and temporizing permissions, he instructs us in this imperfect state what we may lawfully do about divorce.

But if it be thought that the disciples, offended at the rigour of Christ's answer, could yet obtain no mitigation of the former sentence pronounced to the Pharisees, it may be fully answered that our Saviour continues the same reply to his disciples, as men leavened with the same customary licence which the Pharisees maintained, and displeased at the removing of a traditional abuse whereto they had so long not unwillingly been used—it was no time then to contend with their slow and prejudicial belief, in a thing wherein an ordinary measure of light in Scripture, with some attention, might afterwards inform them well enough. After these considerations, to take a law out of Paradise given in time of original perfection, and to take it barely without those just and equal inferences and reasons which mainly establish it, nor so much as admitting those needful and safe allowances wherewith Moses himself interprets it to the fallen condition of man, argues nothing in us but rashness and contempt of those means that God left us in his pure and chaste law, without which it will not be possible for us to perform the strict imposition of this command; or if we strive beyond our strength, we shall strive to obey it otherwise than God commands it. And lamented experience daily teaches the bitter and vain fruits of this our presumption, forcing men in a thing wherein we are not able to judge either of their strength or their sufferance. Whom neither one vice nor other by natural addiction, but only marriage ruins, which doubtless is not the fault of that ordinance, for God gave it as a blessing, nor always of man's mischoosing, it being an error above wisdom to prevent, as examples of wisest men so mistaken manifest: it is the fault therefore of a perverse opinion that will have it continued in despite of nature and reason, when indeed it was never truly joined. All those expositors upon the fifth of Matthew confess the law of Moses to be the law of the Lord, wherein no addition or diminution hath place; yet coming to the point of divorce, as if they feared not to be called least° in the kingdom of heaven, any slight evasion will content them to reconcile those contradictions which they make between Christ and Moses, between Christ and Christ.

Some will have it no law, but the granted premises of another law° following, contrary to the words of Christ, Mark 10: 5, and all other translations of gravest authority, who render it in form of a law, agreeable to Mal. 2: 16,° as it is most anciently and modernly expounded. Besides, the bill of divorce declares it to be orderly and legal. And what avails this to make the matter more righteous, if such an adulterous condition shall be mentioned to build a law upon without either punishment or so much as forbidding? They pretend it is implicitly reproved in these words, Deut. 24: 4, 'after she is defiled'; but who sees not that this defilement is only in respect of returning to her former husband after an intermixed° marriage? else why was not the defiling condition first forbidden, which would have saved the labour of this after-law? Nor is it seemly or piously attributed to the justice of God and his known hatred of sin that such a heinous fault as this through all the law should be only wiped° with an implicit and oblique touch (which yet is falsely supposed), and that his peculiar° people should be let wallow in adulterous marriages almost two thousand years, for want of a direct law to prohibit them; 'tis rather to be confidently assumed that this° was granted to apparent necessities, as being of unquestionable right and reason in the law of nature, in that it still passes without inhibition, even when greatest cause is given us to expect it should be directly forbidden.

But it was not approved. So much the worse that it was allowed;° as if sin had over-mastered the law of God, to conform her steady and straight rule to sin's crookedness, which is impossible. Besides, what needed a positive grant of that which was not approved? It restrained no liberty to him that could but use a little fraud; it had been better silenced, unless it were approved in some case or other.

Can we conceive without vile thoughts that the majesty and holiness of God could endure so many ages to gratify a stubborn people in the practice of a foul polluting sin, and could he expect they should abstain, he not signifying his mind in a plain command, at such time especially when he was framing their laws and them to all possible perfection? But they were to look back to the first institution; nay, rather why was not that individual° institution brought out of Paradise, as was that of the sabbath, and repeated in the body of the law, that men might have understood it to be a command? For that any sentence that bears the resemblance of a precept, set there so out of place in another world, at such a distance from the whole law, and not once mentioned there,

should be an obliging command to us, is very disputable; and perhaps it
might be denied to be a command without further dispute: however, it
commands not absolutely, as hath been cleared,° but only with reference to that precedent promise of God, which is the very ground of his
institution; if that appear not in some tolerable sort, how can we affirm
such a matrimony to be the same which God instituted? In such an acci-
dent° it will best behoove our soberness to follow rather what moral
Sinai prescribes equal to our strength, than fondly° to think within our
strength all that lost Paradise relates.

Another while it shall suffice them° that it was not a moral but a
judicial law, and so was abrogated: nay, rather was not abrogated
because judicial; which law the ministry of Christ came not to deal
with. And who put it in man's power to exempt, where Christ speaks in
general of not abrogating 'the least jot or tittle', and in special not that
of divorce, because it follows among those laws which he promised
expressly not to abrogate, but to vindicate from abusive traditions? And
if we mark the 31st verse of Matt. 5,° he there cites not the law of
Moses, but the licentious gloss which traduced the law; that therefore
which he cited, that he abrogated, and not only abrogated, but disallowed and flatly condemned; which could not be the law of Moses,
for that had been foully to the rebuke of his great servant. To abrogate
a law made with God's allowance had been to tell us only that such a law
was now to cease; but to refute it with an ignominious note of civilizing°
adultery casts the reproof, which was meant only to the Pharisees, even
upon him who made the law. But yet if that be judicial which belongs to
a civil court, this law is less judicial than nine of the ten commandments; for antiquaries affirm that divorces proceeded among the Jews
without knowledge of the magistrate, only with hands and seals° under
the testimony of some rabbis to be then present. And it was indeed a
pure moral economical° law, too hastily imputed of tolerating sin; being
rather so clear in nature and reason that it was left to a man's own arbitrement to be determined between God and his own conscience. And
that power which Christ never took from the master of family, but recti-
fied only to a right and wary use at home; that power the undiscerning
canonist hath improperly usurped into his court-leet,° and bescribbled
with a thousand trifling impertinences, which yet have filled the life of
man with serious trouble and calamity. Yet grant it were of old a judicial
law, it need not be the less moral for that, being conversant as it is about
virtue or vice. And our Saviour disputes not here the judicature, for
that was not his office, but the morality of divorce, whether it be adultery or no; if therefore he touch the law of Moses at all, he touches the

moral part thereof, which is absurd to imagine, that the covenant of grace should reform the exact and perfect law of works, eternal and immutable; or if he touch not the law at all, then is not the allowance thereof disallowed to us.

Others are so ridiculous as to allege that this licence of divorcing was given them because they were so accustomed in Egypt. As if an ill custom were to be kept to all posterity; for the dispensation is both universal and of time unlimited, and so indeed no dispensation at all; for the overdated° dispensation of a thing unlawful serves for nothing but to increase hardness of heart, and makes men but wax more incorrigible; which were a great reproach to be said of any law or allowance that God should give us. In these opinions it would be more religion to advise° well lest we make ourselves juster than God by censuring rashly that for sin which his unspotted law without rebuke allows, and his people without being conscious of displeasing him have used; and if we can think so of Moses as that the Jewish obstinacy could compel him to write such impure permissions against the rule of God and his own judgment; doubtless it was his part to have protested publicly what straits he was driven to, and to have declared his conscience when he gave any law against his mind; for the law is the touchstone of sin and of conscience, must not be intermixed with corrupt indulgences; for then it loses the greatest praise it has of being certain and infallible, not leading into error as all the Jews were led by this connivance of Moses, if it were a connivance. But still they fly back to the primitive institution, and would have us re-enter Paradise against the sword that guards it. Whom I again thus reply to, that the place in Genesis contains the description of a fit and perfect marriage, with an interdict of ever divorcing such a union; but where nature is discovered to have never joined indeed, but vehemently seeks to part, it cannot be there conceived that God forbids it; nay, he commands it both in the law and in the prophet Malachi, which is to be our rule. And Perkins upon this chapter° of Matthew deals plainly, that our Saviour here confutes not Moses's law, but the false glosses that depraved the law; which being true, Perkins must needs grant that something then is left to that law which Christ found no fault with; and what can that be but the conscionable use of such liberty as the plain words import? So that by his own inference, Christ did not absolutely intend to restrain all divorces to the only cause of adultery. This therefore is the true scope of our Saviour's will, that he who looks upon the law concerning divorce should look also back upon the first institution, that he may endeavour what is perfectest; and he that looks upon the institution should not refuse as sinful and unlawful those allowances which God affords him in his following law, lest he make himself purer than his maker, and presuming above strength, slip into temptations irrecoverably. For this is wonderful, that in all those decrees concerning marriage, God should never once mention the prime institution to dissuade them from divorcing, and that he should forbid smaller sins as opposite to the hardness of their hearts, and let this adulterous matter of divorce pass ever unreproved.

This is also to be marvelled at, that seeing Christ did not condemn whatever it was that Moses suffered,° and that thereupon the Christian magistrate permits usury and open stews,° and here with us adultery to be so slightly punished, which was punished by death to these hard-hearted Jews, why we should strain thus at the matter of divorce, which may stand so much with charity to permit, and make no scruple to allow usury, esteemed to be so much against charity. But this it is to embroil ourselves against the righteous and all-wise judgments and statutes of God; which are not variable and contrarious, as we would make them, one while permitting and another while forbidding, but are most constant and most harmonious each to other. For how can the uncorrupt and majestic law of God, bearing in her hand the wages of life and death, harbour such a repugnance within herself as to require an un-exempted and impartial obedience to all her decrees, either from us or from our mediator, and yet debase herself to falter° so many ages with circumcised° adulteries by unclean and slubbering° permissions?

Yet Beza's° opinion is that a politic law (but what politic law I know not, unless one of Machiavel's) may regulate sin; may bear indeed, I grant, with imperfection for a time, as those canons of the apostles did in ceremonial things; but as for sin, the essence of it cannot consist with rule; and if the law fall to regulate sin, and not to take it utterly away, it necessarily confirms and establishes sin. To make a regularity of sin by law, either the law must straighten sin into no sin, or sin must crook the law into no law. The judicial law can serve to no other end than to be the protector and champion of religion and honest civility, as is set down plainly, Rom. 13,° and is but the arm of moral law, which can no more be separate from justice than justice from virtue. Their office also, in a different manner, steers the same course; the one teaches what is good by precept, the other unteaches what is bad by punishment. But if we give way to politic dispensations of lewd uncleanness, the first good consequence of such a relax will be the justifying of papal stews,° joined with a toleration of epidemic whoredom. Justice must revolt from the end of her authority, and become the patron of that whereof she was created the punisher. The example of usury, which is commonly alleged, makes° against the allegation which it brings, as I touched before. Besides that usury, so much as is permitted by the magistrate and demanded with common equity, is neither against the word of God nor the rule of charity, as hath been often discussed by men of eminent learning and judgment. There must be therefore some other example found out to show us wherein civil policy may with warrant from God settle wickedness by law, and make that lawful which is lawless. Although I doubt not but, upon deeper consideration, that which is true in physic will be found as true in polity, that as of bad pulses those that beat most in order are much worse than those that keep the most inordinate circuit, so of popular vices, those that may be committed legally will be more pernicious than those that are left to their own course at peril, not under a stinted privilege to sin orderly and regularly, which is an implicit contradiction, but under due and fearless execution of punishment.

The political law, since it cannot regulate vice, is to restrain it by using all means to root it out. But if it suffer the weed to grow up to any pleasurable or contented height upon what pretext soever, it fastens the root, it prunes and dresses vice, as if it were a good plant.

Lastly, if divorce were granted, as he° says, not for men, but to release afflicted wives, certainly it is not only a dispensation, but a most merciful law; and why it should not yet be in force, being wholly as needful, I know not what can be in cause but senseless cruelty. Esteeming therefore to have asserted° thus an injured law of Moses from the unwarranted and guilty name of a dispensation to be again a most equal and requisite law, we have the word of Christ himself that he came not to alter the least tittle of it, and signifies no small displeasure against him that shall teach to do so. On which relying, I shall not much waver to affirm that those words which are made to intimate as if they forbade all divorce but for adultery (though Moses have constituted otherwise), those words taken circumscriptly, without regard to any precedent law of Moses, or attestation of Christ himself, or without care to preserve those his fundamental and superior laws of nature and charity, to which all other ordinances give up their seals, are as much against plain equity and the mercy of religion as those words of 'take, eat; this is my body',° elementally° understood, are against nature and sense.

And surely the restoring of this degraded law hath well recompensed the diligence was used by enlightening us further to find out wherefore Christ took off the Pharisees from alleging the law, and referred them to the first institution; not condemning, altering or abolishing this precept of divorce, which is plainly moral, for that were against his truth, his promise and his prophetic office; but knowing how fallaciously they had cited and concealed the particular and natural reason of the law, that they might justify any froward reason of their own, he lets go that sophistry unconvinced;° for that had been to teach them else, which his purpose was not. And since they had taken a liberty which the law gave not, he amuses° and repels their tempting pride with a perfection of Paradise, which the law required not; not thereby to oblige our performance to that whereto the law never enjoined the fallen estate of man; for if the first institution must make wedlock, whatever happen, inseparable to us, it must make it also as perfect, as meetly helpful and as comfortable as God promised it should be, at least in some degree; otherwise it is not equal or proportionable to the strength of man that he should be reduced into such indissoluble bonds to his assured misery, if all the other conditions of that covenant be manifestly altered.

Next he saith, 'they must be one flesh',° which when all conjecturing is done will be found to import no more but only to make legitimate and good the carnal act, which else might seem to have something of pollution in it; and infers thus much over,° that the fit union of their souls be such as may even incorporate them to love and amity; but that can never be where no correspondence is of the mind; nay, instead of being one flesh, they will be rather two carcasses chained unnaturally together, or, as it may happen, a living soul bound to a dead corpse, a punishment too like that inflicted by the tyrant Mezentius,° so little worthy to be received as that remedy of loneliness which God meant us. Since we know it is not the joining of another body will remove loneliness, but the uniting of another compliable mind; and that it is no blessing but a torment, nay, a base and brutish condition to be one flesh, unless where nature can in some measure fix a unity of disposition.

Lastly, Christ himself° tells us who should not be put asunder, namely, those whom God hath joined. A plain solution of this great controversy, if men would but use their eyes: for when is it that God may be said to join? when the parties and their friends consent? No, surely; for that may concur to lewdest ends. Or is it when church rites are finished? Neither; for the efficacy of those depends upon the presupposed fitness of either party. Perhaps after carnal knowledge? Least of all; for that may join persons whom neither law nor nature dares join. 'Tis left that only then when the minds are fitly disposed and enabled to maintain a cheerful conversation, to the solace and love of each other, according as God intended and promised in the very first foundation of matrimony, 'I will make him a help-meet for him'; for surely what God intended and promised, that only can be thought to be of his joining, and not the contrary. So likewise the apostle witnesseth, 1 Cor. 7: 15, that in marriage 'God hath called us to peace.' And doubtless in what respect he hath called us to marriage, in that also he hath joined us. The rest, whom either disproportion, or deadness of spirit, or something distasteful and averse in the immutable bent of nature renders unconjugal, error may have joined, but God never joined against the meaning of his own ordinance. And if he joined them not, then is there no power above their own consent to hinder them from unjoining when they cannot reap the soberest ends of being together in any tolerable sort. Neither can it be said properly that such twain were ever divorced, but only parted from each other, as two persons unconjunctive and unmarriable together. But if whom God hath made a fit help, frowardness or private injuries hath made unfit, that being the secret of marriage, God can better judge than man; neither is man indeed fit or able to decide this matter; however it be, undoubtedly a peaceful divorce is a less evil, and less in scandal than a hateful, hardhearted and destructive continuance of marriage in the judgment of Moses and of Christ, that justifies him in choosing the less evil; which if it were an honest and civil prudence in the law, what is there in the gospel forbidding such a kind of legal wisdom, though we should admit the common expositors?°

Having thus unfolded those ambiguous reasons wherewith Christ (as his wont was) gave to the Pharisees that came to sound him such an answer as they deserved, it will not be uneasy° to explain the sentence itself that now follows:° 'Whosoever shall put away his wife, except it be for fornication, and shall marry another, committeth adultery.' First therefore I will set down what is observed by Grotius upon this point, a man of general learning. Next, I produce what mine own thoughts gave me before I had seen his annotations. Origen, saith he, notes that Christ named adultery rather as one example of other like cases, than as one only exception; and that it is frequent not only in human but in divine laws to express one kind of fact whereby other causes of like nature may have the like plea, as Exod. 21: 18, 19, 20, 26; Deut. 19: 5. And from the maxims of civil law he shows that even in sharpest penal laws the same reason hath the same right; and in gentler laws, that from like causes to like the law interprets rightly. But it may be objected, saith he, that nothing destroys the end of wedlock so much as adultery. To which he answers that marriage was not ordained only for copulation, but for mutual help and comfort of life; and if we mark diligently the nature of our Saviour's commands, we shall find that both their beginning and their end consists in charity, whose will is that we should so be good to others, as that we be not cruel to ourselves: and hence it appears why Mark, and Luke, and St Paul to the Corinthians, mentioning this precept of Christ, add no exception, because exceptions that arise from natural equity are included silently under general terms: it would be considered, therefore, whether the same equity may not have place in other cases less frequent. Thus far he. From hence is what I add: first, that this saying of Christ, as it is usually expounded, can be no law at all, that man for no cause should separate but for adultery, except it be a supernatural law, not binding us as we now are. Had it been the law of nature, either the Jews or some other wise and civil nation would have pressed it; or let it be so, yet that law, Deut. 24: 1, whereby a man hath leave to part, whenas for just and natural cause discovered he cannot love, is a law ancienter and deeper engraven in blameless nature than the other: therefore the inspired lawgiver Moses took care that this should be specified and allowed; the other° he let vanish in silence, not once repeated in the volume of his law, even as the reason of it vanished with Paradise. Secondly, this can be no new command, for the gospel enjoins no new morality, save only the infinite enlargement of charity, which in this respect is called the new commandment by St John,° as being the accomplishment of every command. Thirdly, it is no command of perfection further than it partakes of charity, which is 'the bond of perfection'.° Those commands, therefore, which compel us to self-cruelty above our strength, so hardly will help forward to perfection that they hinder and set backward in all the common rudiments of Christianity, as was proved. It being thus clear that the words of Christ can be no kind of command as they are vulgarly taken, we shall now see in what sense they may be a command, and that an excellent one, the same with that of Moses, and no other. Moses had granted that only for a natural annoyance, defect or dislike, whether in body or mind (for so the Hebrew words plainly note), which a man could not force himself to live with, he might give a bill of divorce, thereby forbidding any other cause wherein amendment or reconciliation might have place. This law the Pharisees depraving extended to any slight contentious cause whatsoever. Christ therefore seeing where they halted,° urges the negative part of that law, which is necessarily understood (for the determinate permission of Moses binds them from further licence), and checking their supercilious drift, declares that no accidental, temporary or reconcilable offence except fornication can justify a divorce. He touches not here those natural and perpetual hindrances of society which are not to be removed; for such as they are aptest to cause an unchangeable offence, so are they not capable of reconcilement, because not of amendment. Thus is Moses's law here solidly confirmed, and those causes which he permitted not a jot gainsaid. And that this is the true meaning of this place, I prove also by no less an author than St Paul himself, 1 Cor. 7: 10, 11;° upon which text interpreters agree that the apostle only repeats the precept of Christ: where while he speaks of the 'wife's reconcilement to her husband', he puts it out of controversy that our Saviour meant matters of strife and reconcilement; of which sort he would not that any difference should be the occasion of divorce, except fornication.

But because we know that Christ never gave a judicial law, and that the word fornication is variously significant in Scripture, it will be much right done to our Saviour's words to consider diligently whether it be meant here that nothing but actual fornication, proved by witness, can warrant a divorce; for so our canon law judges. Nevertheless, as I find that Grotius° on this place hath observed, the Christian emperors Theodosius the Second and Justinian, men of high wisdom and reputed piety, decreed it to be a divorcive fornication if the wife attempted either against the knowledge or obstinately against the will of her husband such things as gave open suspicion of adulterizing, as the wilful haunting of feasts, and invitations with men not of her near kindred, the lying forth of° her house without probable cause, the frequenting of theatres against her husband's mind, her endeavour to prevent or destroy conception. Hence that of Jerome, 'where fornication is suspected, the wife may lawfully be divorced'—not that every motion of a jealous mind should be regarded, but that it should not be exacted to prove all things by the visibility of law-witnessing, or else to hoodwink the mind; for the law is not able to judge of these things but by the rule of equity, and by permitting a wise man to walk the middle way of a prudent circumspection, neither wretchedly jealous, nor stupidly and tamely patient. To this purpose hath Grotius° in his notes. He shows also that fornication is taken in Scripture for such a continual headstrong behaviour as tends to plain contempt of the husband, and proves it out of Judges 19: 2, where the Levite's wife is said to have played the whore against him; which Josephus° and the Septuagint,° with the Chaldean,° interpret only of stubbornness and rebellion against her husband; and to this I add that Kimchi and the two other rabbis° who gloss the text are in the same opinion. Ben Gerson reasons that had it been whoredom, a Jew and a Levite would have disdained to fetch her again.° And this I shall contribute, that had it been whoredom, she would have chosen any other place to run to than to her father's house, it being so infamous for a Hebrew woman to play the harlot, and so opprobrious to the parents. Fornication then in this place of the Judges is understood for stubborn disobedience against the husband, and not for adultery. A sin of that sudden° activity as to be already committed when no more is done but only looked unchastely, which yet I should be loath to judge worthy a divorce, though in our Saviour's language° it be called adultery. Nevertheless when palpable and frequent signs are given, the law of God, Numb. 5,° so far gave way to the jealousy of a man as that the woman, set before the sanctuary with her head un-covered, was adjured by the priest to swear whether she were false or no, and constrained to drink that 'bitter water' with an undoubted 'curse of rottenness and tympany'° to follow, unless she were innocent. And the jealous man had not been guiltless before God, as seems by the last verse,° if having such a suspicion in his head, he should neglect this trial; which if to this day it be not to be used, or be thought as uncertain of effect as our antiquated law of Ordalium,° yet all equity will judge that many adulterous demeanours which are of lewd suspi-cion and example may be held sufficient to incur a divorce, though the act itself hath not been proved. And seeing the generosity of our nation is so as to account no reproach more abominable than to be nicknamed the husband of an adulteress, that our law should not be as ample as the law of God to vindicate a man from that ignoble sufferance is our bar-barous unskilfulness, not considering that the law should be exasper-ated° according to our estimation of the injury. And if it must be suffered till the act be visibly proved, Solomon himself, whose judg-ment will be granted to surpass the acuteness of any canonist, con-fesses, Prov. 30: 19, 20, that for the act of adultery it is as difficult to be found as the 'track of an eagle in the air, or the way of a ship in the sea'; so that a man may be put to unmanly indignities ere it be found out. This therefore may be enough to inform us that divorcive adultery is not limited by our Saviour to the utmost act, and that to be attested always by eye-witness, but may be extended also to divers obvious actions which either plainly lead to adultery, or give such presumption whereby sensible men may suspect the deed to be already done. And this the rather may be thought, in that our Saviour chose to use the word fornication, which word is found to signify other matrimonial transgressions of main breach to that covenant besides actual adultery.

Thus at length we see, both by this and by other places, that there is scarce any one saying in the gospel but must be read with limitations and distinctions to be rightly understood; for Christ gives no full com-ments or continued discourses, but scatters the heavenly grain of his doctrine like pearl here and there, which requires a skilful and laborious gatherer, who must compare the words he finds with other precepts, with the end of every ordinance, and with the general analogy of evangelic doctrine; otherwise many particular sayings would be but strange repugnant riddles, and the church would offend in granting divorce for frigidity, which is not here excepted with adultery, but by them added. And this was it undoubtedly which gave reason to St Paul° of his own authority, as he professes, and without command from the Lord, to enlarge the seeming construction of those places in the gospel by adding a case wherein a person deserted (which is something less than divorced) may lawfully marry again. And having declared his opinion in one case, he leaves a further liberty for Christian prudence to determine in cases of like importance, using words so plain as not to be shifted off, 'that a brother or a sister is not under bondage in such cases', adding also that 'God hath called us to peace' in marriage.

Now if it be plain that a Christian may be brought into unworthy bondage, and his religious peace not only interrupted now and then, but perpetually and finally hindered in wedlock by misyoking with a diversity of nature as well as of religion, the reasons of St Paul cannot be made special to that one case of infidelity, but are of equal moment to a divorce wherever Christian liberty and peace are without fault equally obstructed—that the ordinance which God gave to our comfort may not be pinned upon us to our undeserved thraldom, to be cooped up, as it were, in mockery of wedlock, to a perpetual betrothed loneliness and discontent, if nothing worse ensue. There being nought else of marriage left between such but a displeasing and forced remedy against the sting of a brute desire; which fleshly accustoming° without the soul's union and commixture of intellectual delight, as it is rather a soiling than a fulfilling of marriage rites, so is it enough to imbase the mettle of a generous spirit, and sinks him to a low and vulgar pitch of endeavour in all his actions; or, which is worse, leaves him in a despairing plight of abject and hardened thoughts: which condition rather than a good man should fall into, a man useful in the service of God and mankind, Christ himself° hath taught us to dispense with the most sacred ordinances of his worship, even for a bodily healing to dispense with that holy and speculative rest° of sabbath, much more than with the erroneous observance of an ill-knotted marriage for the sustaining of an overcharged° faith and perseverance.

And though bad causes would take licence by this pretext, if that cannot be remedied, upon their conscience be it who shall so do. This was that hardness of heart and abuse of a good law which Moses was content to suffer, rather than good men should not have it at all to use needfully. And he who,° to run after one lost sheep, left ninety-nine of his own flock at random in the wilderness, would little perplex his thought for the obduring° of nine hundred and ninety such as will daily take worse liberties, whether they have permission or not. To conclude, as without charity God hath given no commandment to men, so without it neither can men rightly believe any commandment given. For every act of true faith, as well that whereby we believe the law as that whereby we endeavour° the law, is wrought in us by charity, according to that in the divine hymn of St Paul, 1 Cor. 13, 'Charity believeth all things'; not as if she were so credulous, which is the exposition hitherto current, for that were a trivial praise, but to teach us that charity is the high govern-ess of our belief, and that we cannot safely assent to any precept written in the Bible, but as charity commends it to us. Which agrees with that of the same apostle to the Eph. 4: 14, 15;° where he tells us that the way to get a sure undoubted knowledge of things is to hold that for truth which accords most with charity. Whose unerring guidance and con-duct having followed as a loadstar° with all diligence and fidelity in this question, I trust, through the help of that illuminating Spirit which hath favoured me, to have done no everyday's work in asserting, after many ages, the words of Christ, with other scriptures of great concernment, from burdensome and remorseless obscurity, tangled with manifold repugnances, to their native lustre and consent between each other; hereby also dissolving tedious and Gordian° difficulties; which have hitherto molested the church of God, and are now decided not with the sword of Alexander, but with the immaculate hands of charity, to the unspeakable good of Christendom. And let the extreme literalist sit down now, and revolve° whether this in all necessity be not the due result of our Saviour's words; or if he persist to be otherwise opinioned, let him well advise, lest thinking to grip fast the gospel, he be found instead with the canon law in his fist; whose boisterous° edicts tyranniz-ing the blessed ordinance of marriage into the quality of a most un-natural and unchristianly yoke, hath given the flesh this advantage to hate it, and turn aside, ofttimes unwillingly, to all dissolute unclean-ness, even till punishment itself is weary and overcome by the incred-ible frequency of trading lust and uncontrolled adulteries. Yet men whose creed is custom I doubt not will be still endeavouring to hide the sloth of their own timorous capacities with this pretext, that for all this 'tis better to endure with patience and silence this affliction which God hath sent. And I agree 'tis true, if this be exhorted and not enjoined; but withal it will be wisely done to be as sure as may be that what man's iniquity hath laid on be not imputed to God's sending, lest under the colour ° of an affected patience we detain ourselves at the gulf's mouth of many hideous temptations, not to be withstood without proper gifts, which, as Perkins well notes,° God gives not ordinarily, no, not to most earnest prayers. Therefore we pray, 'lead us not into temptation';° a vain prayer, if, having led ourselves thither, we love to stay in that perilous condition. God sends remedies as well as evils, under which he who lies and groans that may lawfully acquit himself is accessory to his own ruin; nor will it excuse him though he suffer through a sluggish fearfulness to search thoroughly what is lawful, for fear of disquieting the secure falsity of an old opinion. Who doubts not but that it may be piously said to him who would dismiss frigidity, 'bear your trial; take it as if God would have you live this life of continence'? If he exhort this, I hear him as an angel, though he speak without warrant; but if he would compel me, I know him for Satan. To him who divorces an adulteress, piety might say, 'pardon her; you may show much mercy, you may win a soul': yet the law both of God and man leaves it freely to him; for God loves not to plough out the heart of our endeavours with overhard and sad tasks. God delights not to make a drudge of virtue, whose actions must be all elective and unconstrained. Forced virtue is as a bolt overshot:° it goes neither forward nor backward, and does no good as it stands. Seeing, therefore, that neither Scripture nor reason hath laid this unjust austerity upon divorce, we may resolve that nothing else hath wrought it but that letter-bound servility of the canon doctors, supposing marriage to be a sacrament, and out of the art they have to lay unnecessary burdens upon all men, to make a fair show in the fleshly observance of matrimony, though peace and love, with all other conjugal respects, fare never so ill. And, indeed, the Papists, who are the strictest forbidders of divorce, are the easiest libertines to admit of grossest uncleanness; as if they had a design by making wedlock a supportless° yoke, to violate it most, under colour of preserving it most inviolable; and withal delighting (as their mystery° is) to make men the day labourers of their own affliction, as if there were such a scarcity of miseries from abroad that we should be made to melt our choicest home blessings and coin them into crosses,° for want whereby to hold commerce with patience. If any, therefore, who shall hap to read this discourse hath been through misadventure ill engaged in this contracted evil here complained of, and finds the fits and workings of a high impatience frequently upon him, of all those wild words which men in misery think to ease themselves by uttering, let him not open his lips against the providence of heaven, or tax the ways of God and his divine truth; for they are equal,° easy and not burdensome; nor do they ever cross the just and reasonable desires of men, nor involve this our portion of mortal life into a necessity of sadness and malcontent by laws commanding over the unreducible antipathies of nature, sooner or later found, but allow us to remedy and shake off those evils into which human error hath led us through the midst of our best intentions, and to support our incident extremities° by that authentic precept of sovereign charity, whose grand commission is to do and to dispose over all the ordinances of God to man, that love and truth may advance each other to everlasting. While we, literally superstitious, through customary faintness of heart not venturing to pierce with our free thoughts into the full latitude of nature and religion, abandon ourselves to serve under the tyranny of usurped opinions; suffering those ordinances which were allotted to our solace and reviving to trample over us and hale us into a multitude of sorrows which God never meant us. And where he set us in a fair allowance of way, with honest liberty and prudence to our guard, we never leave subtilizing and casuisting till we have straightened and pared that liberal path into a razor's edge to walk on; between a precipice of unnecessary mischief on either side, and starting at every false alarm, we do not know which way to set a foot forward with manly confidence and Christian resolution through the confused ringing in our ears of panic° scruples and amazements.

Another act of papal encroachment it was to pluck the power and arbitrement of divorce from the master of family, into whose hands God and the law of all nations had put it, and Christ so left it, preaching only to the conscience, and not authorizing a judicial court to toss about and divulge the unaccountable and secret reasons of disaffection between man and wife, as a thing most improperly answerable to any such kind of trial. But the popes of Rome, perceiving the great revenue and high authority it would give them even over princes to have the judging and deciding of such a main consequence in the life of man as was divorce, wrought so upon the superstition of those ages as to divest them of that right, which God from the beginning had entrusted to the husband; by which means they subjected that ancient and natural domestic prerogative to an external and unbefitting judicature. For although differences in divorce about dowries, jointures, and the like, besides the punishing of adultery, ought not to pass without referring, if need be, to the magistrate; yet for him to interpose his jurisdictive power upon the inward and irremediable disposition of man, to command love and sympathy, to forbid dislike against the guiltless instinct of nature, is not within the province of any law to reach; and were indeed an uncommodious rudeness, not a just power. For if nature's resistless° sway in love or hate be once compelled, it grows careless of itself, vicious, useless to friend, unserviceable and spiritless to the commonwealth. Which Moses rightly foresaw, and all wise lawgivers that ever knew man what kind of creature he was. The parliament also and clergy of England were not ignorant of this, when they consented that Harry VIII° might put away his queen Anne of Cleve, whom he could not like, after he had been wedded half a year; unless it were that, contrary to the proverb, they made a necessity of that which might have been a virtue in them to do; for even the freedom and eminence of man's creation gives him to be a law in this matter to himself, being the head° of the other sex which was made for him; whom therefore though he ought not to injure, yet neither should he be forced to retain in society to his own overthrow, nor to hear any judge therein above himself; it being also an unseemly affront to the sequestered and veiled modesty of that sex to have her unpleasingness and other concealments bandied up and down, and aggravated in open court by those hired masters of tongue fence.° Such uncomely exigencies it befel no less a majesty than Henry VIII to be reduced to, who, finding just reason in his conscience to forego his brother's wife,° after many indignities of being deluded and made a boy of by those his two cardinal judges, was constrained at last, for want of other proof that she had been carnally known by prince Arthur, even to uncover the nakedness of that virtuous lady, and to recite openly the obscene evidence of his brother's chamberlain. Yet it pleased God to make him see all the tyranny of Rome by discovering this which they exercised over divorce, and to make him the beginner of a reformation to this whole kingdom by first asserting into his familiary° power the right of just divorce. 'Tis true an adulteress cannot be shamed enough by any public proceeding; but that woman whose honour is not appeached° is less injured by a silent dismission, being otherwise not illiberally dealt with, than to endure a clamouring debate of utterless° things in a business of that civil secrecy and difficult discerning as not to be overmuch questioned by nearest friends. Which drew that answer from the greatest and worthiest Roman of his time, Paulus Emilius,° being demanded why he would put away his wife for no visible reason, 'This shoe', said he, and held it out on his foot, 'is a neat shoe, a new shoe, and yet none of ye know where it wrings me.' Much less by the unfamiliar cognizance of a fee'd gamester° can such a private difference be examined; neither ought it.

Lastly, all law is for some good that may be frequently attained without the admixture of a worse inconvenience; but the law forbidding divorce never attains to any good end of such prohibition, but rather multiplies evil. If it aim at the establishment of matrimony, we know that cannot thrive under a loathed and forced yoke, but is daily violated; if it seek to prevent the sin of divorcing, that lies not in the law to prevent; for he that would divorce and marry again but for the law, hath in the sight of God done it already. Civil or political sin it never was, neither to Jew nor Gentile, nor by any judicial intendment of Christ, only culpable as it transgresses the allowance of Moses in the inward man, which not any law but conscience only can evince. The law can only look whether it be an injury to the divorced, which in truth it can be none as a mere separation; for if she consent, wherein has the law to right her? or consent not, then is it either just and so deserved, or if unjust, such in all likelihood was the divorcer, and to part from an unjust man is happiness, and no injury to be lamented. But suppose it be an injury, the law is not able to amend it unless she think it other than a miserable redress to return back from whence she was expelled, or but entreated to be gone, or else to live apart still married without marriage, a married widow. Last, if it be to chasten the divorcer, what law punishes a deed which is not moral but natural, a deed which cannot certainly be found to be an injury, or how can it be punished by prohibiting the divorce, but that the innocent must equally partake? So that we see the law can to no rational purpose forbid divorce; it can only take care that the conditions of divorce be not injurious.

But what, shall then the disposal of that power return again to the master of family? Wherefore not, since God there put it, and the presumptuous canon thence bereft it? This only must be provided, that the ancient manner be observed in the presence of the minister and other grave selected elders, who after they shall have admonished and pressed upon him the words of our Saviour, and he shall have protested in the faith of the eternal gospel and the hope he has of happy resurrection that otherwise than thus he cannot do, and thinks himself and this his case not contained in that prohibition of divorce which Christ pronounced, the matter not being of malice, but of nature, and so not capable of reconciling; to constrain him further were to unchristian him, to unman him, to throw the mountain of Sinai upon him, with the weight of the whole law to boot, flat against the liberty and essence of the gospel; and yet nothing available° either to the sanctity of marriage, the good of husband, wife or children, nothing profitable either to church or commonwealth. But this would bring in confusion: be of good cheer, it would not: it wrought so little disorder among the Jews that from Moses till after the captivity not one of the prophets thought it worth rebuking; for that of Malachi° well looked into will appear to be not against divorcing, but rather against keeping strange concubines, to the vexation of their Hebrew wives. If, therefore, we Christians may be thought as good and tractable as the Jews were (and certainly the prohibitors of divorce presume us to be better), then less confusion is to be feared for this among us than was among them. If we be worse, or but as bad, which lamentable examples confirm we are, then have we more, or at least as much, need of this permitted law as they to whom God expressly gave it under a harsher covenant. Let not, therefore, the frailty of man go on thus inventing needless troubles to itself, to groan under the false imagination of a strictness never imposed from above, enjoining that for duty which is an impossible and vain supererogating. 'Be not righteous overmuch' is the counsel of Ecclesiastes;° 'why shouldest thou destroy thyself?' Let us not be thus overcurious to strain at atoms,° and yet to stop every vent and cranny of permissive liberty, lest nature, wanting those needful pores and breathing-places which God hath not debarred our weakness, either suddenly break out into some wide rupture of open vice and frantic heresy, or else inwardly fester with repining and blasphemous thoughts under an unreasonable and fruitless rigour of unwarranted law. Against which evils nothing can more beseem the religion of the church or the wisdom of the state than to consider timely and provide. And in so doing let them not doubt but they shall vindicate the misreputed honour of God and his great lawgiver by suffering him to give his own laws according to the condition of man's nature best known to him, without the unsufferable imputation of dispensing legally with many ages of ratified adultery. They shall recover the misattended words of Christ to the sincerity of their true sense from manifold contradictions, and shall open them with the key of charity. Many helpless Christians they shall raise from the depth of sadness and distress, utterly unfitted as they are to serve God or man; many they shall reclaim from obscure and giddy sects, many regain from dissolute and brutish licence, many from desperate hardness, if ever that were justly pleaded. They shall set free many daughters of Israel not wanting much of her sad plight whom 'Satan had bound eighteen years'.° Man they shall restore to his just dignity and prerogative in nature, preferring the soul's free peace before the promiscuous draining of a carnal rage. Marriage, from a perilous hazard and snare, they shall reduce° to be a more certain haven and retirement of happy society, when they shall judge according to God and Moses (and how not then according to Christ?), when they shall judge it more wisdom and goodness to break that covenant seemingly, and keep it really, than by compulsion of law to keep it seemingly, and by compulsion of blameless nature to break it really, at least if it were ever truly joined. The vigour of discipline they may then turn with better success upon the prostitute looseness of the times, when men, finding in themselves the infirmities of former ages, shall not be constrained above the gift of God in them to unprofitable and impossible observances never required from the civilest, the wisest, the holiest nations, whose other excellencies in moral virtue they never yet could equal. Last of all, to those whose mind still is to maintain textual restrictions whereof the bare sound cannot consist sometimes with humanity, much less with charity, I would ever answer by putting them in remembrance of a command above all commands which they seem to have forgot, and who spake it; in comparison whereof, this which they so exalt is but a petty and subordinate precept. 'Let them go', therefore, with whom I am loath to couple them, yet they will needs run into the same blindness with the Pharisees; 'let them go therefore', and consider well what this lesson means, 'I will have mercy and not sacrifice',° for on that 'saying all the law and prophets depend';° much more the gospel, whose end and excellence is mercy and peace. Or if they cannot learn that, how will they hear this? which yet I shall not doubt to leave with them as a conclusion, that God the Son hath put all other things under his own feet,° but his commandments he hath left all under the feet of charity.

Of Education

TO MASTER SAMUEL HARTLIB

MASTER HARTLIB

I am long since persuaded that to say or do aught worth memory and imitation, no purpose or respect should sooner move us than simply the love of God and of mankind. Nevertheless, to write now the reforming of education, though it be one of the greatest and noblest designs that can be thought on, and for the want whereof this nation perishes, I had not yet at this time been induced but by your earnest entreaties and serious conjurements; as having my mind for the present half diverted in the pursuance of some other assertions, the knowledge and the use of which cannot but be a great furtherance both to the enlargement of truth and honest living, with much more peace. Nor should the laws of any private friendship have prevailed with me to divide thus, or transpose my former thoughts, but that I see those aims, those actions, which have won you with me the esteem of° a person sent hither by some good providence from a far country° to be the occasion and the incitement of great good to this island.

And, as I hear, you have obtained the same repute with men of most approved wisdom, and some of highest authority among us; not to mention the learned correspondence which you hold in foreign parts, and the extraordinary pains and diligence which you have used in this matter, both here and beyond the seas; either by the definite will of God so ruling, or the peculiar sway of nature, which also is God's working. Neither can I think that so reputed and so valued as you are, you would, to the forfeit of your own discerning ability, impose upon me an unfit and overponderous argument; but that the satisfaction which you profess to have received from those incidental discourses which we have wandered into hath pressed and almost constrained you into a persuasion that what you require from me in this point I neither ought nor can in conscience defer beyond this time both of so much need at once, and so much opportunity to try what God hath determined.

I will not resist, therefore, whatever it is either of divine or human obligement that you lay upon me; but will forthwith set down in writing, as you request me, that voluntary idea° which hath long in silence presented itself to me of a better education, in extent and comprehension far more large, and yet of time far shorter, and of attainment far more certain, than hath been yet in practice. Brief I shall endeavour to be; for that which I have to say assuredly this nation hath extreme need should be done sooner than spoken. To tell you, therefore, what I have benefited herein among old renowned authors, I shall spare; and to search what many modern *Januas* and *Didactics*,° more than ever I shall read, have projected, my inclination leads me not. But if you can accept of these few observations which have flowered off,° and are as it were the burnishing of many studious and contemplative years altogether spent in the search of religious and civil knowledge, and such as pleased you so well in the relating, I here give you them to dispose of.

The end then of learning is to repair the ruins° of our first parents by regaining to know God aright, and out of that knowledge to love him, to imitate him, to be like him, as we may the nearest by possessing our souls of true virtue, which being united to the heavenly grace of faith makes up the highest perfection. But because our understanding cannot in this body found itself but on sensible things, nor arrive so clearly to the knowledge of God and things invisible as by orderly conning over° the visible and inferior creature,° the same method is necessarily to be followed in all discreet teaching. And seeing every nation affords not experience and tradition enough for all kind of learning, therefore we are chiefly taught the languages of those people who have at any time been most industrious after wisdom; so that language is but the instrument conveying to us things useful to be known. And though a linguist should pride himself to have all the tongues that Babel cleft the world into, yet if he have not studied the solid things in them, as well as the words and lexicons, he were nothing so much to be esteemed a learned man as any yeoman or tradesman competently wise in his mother dialect only.

Hence appear the many mistakes which have made learning generally so unpleasing and so unsuccessful; first, we do amiss to spend seven or eight years merely in scraping together so much miserable Latin and Greek as might be learned otherwise easily and delightfully in one year. And that which casts our proficiency therein so much behind is our time lost partly in too oft idle vacancies° given both to schools and universities, partly in a preposterous° exaction, forcing the empty wits of children to compose themes, verses and orations, which are the acts of ripest judgment, and the final work of a head filled by long reading and observing with elegant maxims and copious invention.° These are not matters to be wrung from poor striplings, like blood out of the nose, or the plucking of untimely fruit. Besides the ill habit which they get of wretched barbarizing against the Latin and Greek idiom, with their untutored Anglicisms, odious to be read, yet not to be avoided without a well-continued and judicious conversing° among pure authors digested, which they scarce taste; whereas if after some preparatory grounds of speech by their certain forms got into memory, they were led to the praxis° thereof in some chosen short book lessoned° thoroughly to them, they might then forthwith proceed to learn the substance of good things and arts° in due order, which would bring the whole language quickly into their power. This I take to be the most rational and most profitable way of learning languages, and whereby we may best hope to give account to God of our youth spent herein.

And for the usual method of teaching arts, I deem it to be an old error of universities not yet well recovered from the scholastic grossness of barbarous ages, that instead of beginning with arts most easy, and those be such as are most obvious to the sense, they present their young unmatriculated° novices, at first coming, with the most intellective abstractions of logic and metaphysics; so that they having but newly left those grammatic flats and shallows where they stuck unreasonably to learn a few words with lamentable construction, and now on the sudden transported under another climate, to be tossed and turmoiled with their unballasted wits in fathomless and unquiet deeps of controversy,° do for the most part grow into hatred and contempt of learning, mocked and deluded all this while with ragged notions and babblements, while they expected worthy and delightful knowledge; till poverty or youthful years call them importunately their several ways, and hasten them, with the sway of friends, either to an ambitious and mercenary, or ignorantly zealous divinity; some allured to the trade of law, grounding their purposes not on the prudent and heavenly contemplation of justice and equity, which was never taught them, but on the promising and pleasing thoughts of litigious terms,° fat contentions and flowing fees; others betake them to state affairs, with souls so unprincipled in virtue and true generous breeding that flattery and court-shifts° and tyrannous aphorisms appear to them the highest points of wisdom, instilling their barren hearts with a conscientious slavery, if, as I rather think, it be not feigned. Others, lastly, of a more delicious° and airy° spirit, retire themselves (knowing no better) to the enjoyments of ease and luxury, living out their days in feast and jollity; which indeed is the wisest and the safest course of all these, unless they were with more integrity undertaken. And these are the errors, and these are the fruits of misspending our prime youth at the schools and universities as we do, either in learning mere words, or such things chiefly as were better unlearned.

I shall detain you now no longer in the demonstration of what we should not do, but straight conduct you to a hillside where I will point ye out the right path of a virtuous and noble education; laborious indeed at the first ascent, but else so smooth, so green, so full of goodly prospect and melodious sounds on every side that the harp of Orpheus° was not more charming. I doubt not but ye shall have more ado to drive our dullest and laziest youth, our stocks and stubs,° from the infinite desire of such a happy nurture, than we have now to hale and drag our choicest and hopefullest wits to that asinine feast of sowthistles and brambles which is commonly set before them as all the food and entertainment of their tenderest and most docible° age. I call therefore a complete and generous education that which fits a man to perform justly, skilfully and magnanimously all the offices, both private and public, of peace and war. And how all this may be done between twelve and one and twenty, less time than is now bestowed in pure trifling at grammar and sophistry, is to be thus ordered.

First, to find out a spacious house and ground about it fit for an academy, and big enough to lodge a hundred and fifty persons, whereof

twenty or thereabout may be attendants, all under the government of
one who shall be thought of desert sufficient, and ability either to do all,
or wisely to direct and oversee it done. This place should be at once
both school and university, not needing a remove to any other house of
scholarship, except it be some peculiar° college of law or physic,° where
they mean to be practitioners; but as for those general studies which
take up all our time from Lily° to the commencing, as they term it,
Master of Art, it should be absolute.° After this pattern, as many edi-
fices may be converted to this use as shall be needful in every city
throughout this land, which would tend much to the increase of learning and civility° everywhere. This number, less or more thus collected,
to the convenience of° a foot company, or interchangeably two troops
of cavalry, should divide their day's work into three parts as it lies
orderly: their studies, their exercise and their diet.

For their studies: first, they should begin with the chief and necessary rules of some good grammar, either that now used, or any better;
and while this is doing, their speech is to be fashioned to a distinct and
clear pronunciation, as near as may be to the Italian, especially in the
vowels. For we Englishmen, being far northerly, do not open our
mouths in the cold air wide enough to grace a southern tongue; but are
observed by all other nations to speak exceeding close and inward, so
that to smatter° Latin with an English mouth is as ill a hearing as law
French.° Next, to make them expert in the usefullest points of grammar, and withal to season them and win them early to the love of virtue
and true labour ere any flattering seducement or vain principle seize
them wandering, some easy and delightful book of education would be
read to them, whereof the Greeks have store, as Cebes,° Plutarch,° and
other Socratic discourses.° But in Latin we have none of classic
authority extant, except the two or three first books of Quintilian,° and
some select pieces elsewhere.

But here the main skill and groundwork will be to temper° them such
lectures and explanations upon every opportunity as may lead and draw
them in willing obedience, inflamed with the study° of learning and the
admiration of virtue, stirred up with high hopes of living to be brave
men and worthy patriots, dear to God and famous to all ages. That they
may despise and scorn all their childish and ill-taught qualities, to
delight in manly and liberal° exercises, which he who hath the art and
proper eloquence to catch them with, what with mild and effectual persuasions, and what with the intimation of some fear, if need be, but
chiefly by his own example, might in a short space gain them to an
incredible diligence and courage, infusing into their young breasts such

an ingenuous and noble ardour as would not fail to make many of them renowned and matchless men. At the same time, some other hour of the day, might be taught them the rules of arithmetic, and soon after the elements of geometry, even playing, as the old manner was.° After evening repast, till bedtime, their thoughts will be best taken up in the easy grounds of religion, and the story of Scripture.

The next step would be to the authors of agriculture, Cato, Varro and Columella,° for the matter is most easy; and if the language be difficult, so much the better, it is not a difficulty above their years. And here will be an occasion of inciting and enabling them hereafter to improve the tillage of their country, to recover the bad soil, and to remedy the waste that is made of good; for this was one of Hercules'° praises. Ere half these authors be read, which will soon be with plying hard and daily, they cannot choose but be masters of any ordinary prose. So that it will be then seasonable for them to learn in any modern author the use of the globes and all the maps, first with the old names and then with the new;° or they might be then capable to read any compendious method of natural philosophy.

And at the same time might be entering into the Greek tongue, after the same manner as was before prescribed in the Latin, whereby the difficulties of grammar being soon overcome, all the historical physiology of Aristotle° and Theophrastus° are open before them, and, as I may say, under contribution.° The like access will be to Vitruvius,° to Seneca's *Natural Questions*,° to Mela, Celsus, Pliny or Solinus.° And having thus passed the principles of arithmetic, geometry, astronomy and geography, with a general compact° of physics, they may descend° in mathematics to the instrumental science of trigonometry, and from thence to fortification, architecture, enginery° or navigation. And in natural philosophy they may proceed leisurely from the history of meteors, minerals, plants and living creatures, as far as anatomy.

Then also in course might be read to them, out of some not tedious writer, the institution of physic,° that they may know the tempers, the humours, the seasons,° and how to manage a crudity;° which he who can wisely and timely do is not only a great physician to himself and to his friends, but also may, at some time or other, save an army by this frugal and expenseless means only, and not let the healthy and stout bodies of young men rot away under him for want of this discipline, which is a great pity, and no less a shame to the commander. To set forward all these proceedings in nature and mathematics, what hinders but that they may procure, as oft as shall be needful, the helpful experiences of hunters, fowlers, fishermen, shepherds, gardeners, apothecaries; and in the other sciences, architects, engineers, mariners, anatomists; who doubtless would be ready, some for reward, and some to favour such a hopeful seminary. And this will give them such a real tincture of natural knowledge as they shall never forget, but daily augment with delight. Then also those poets which are now counted most hard will be both facile and pleasant, Orpheus, Hesiod, Theocritus, Aratus, Nicander, Oppian, Dionysius; and in Latin, Lucretius, Manilius, and the rural part of Virgil.°

By this time years and good general precepts will have furnished them more distinctly with that act of reason which in ethics is called Proairesis,° that they may with some judgment contemplate upon moral good and evil. Then will be required a special reinforcement of constant and sound indoctrinating, to set them right and firm, instructing them more amply in the knowledge of virtue and the hatred of vice, while their young and pliant affections are led through all the moral works of Plato, Xenophon, Cicero, Plutarch, Laertius,° and those Locrian remnants;° but still to be reduced° in their nightward studies, wherewith they close the day's work under the determinate sentence° of David or Solomon, or the evangelists and apostolic scriptures. Being perfect in the knowledge of personal duty, they may then begin the study of economics.° And either now or before this, they may have easily learnt, at any odd hour, the Italian tongue. And soon after, but with wariness and good antidote,° it would be wholesome enough to let them taste some choice comedies, Greek, Latin or Italian; those tragedies also that treat of household matters, as *Trachiniæ*, *Alcestis*,° and the like.

The next remove must be to the study of politics, to know the beginning, end, and reasons of political societies, that they may not, in a dangerous fit of the commonwealth, be such poor, shaken, uncertain reeds, of such a tottering conscience as many of our great councillors have lately shown themselves, but steadfast pillars of the state. After this, they are to dive into the grounds of law and legal justice, delivered first and with best warrant by Moses, and as far as human prudence can be trusted, in those extolled remains of Grecian lawgivers, Lycurgus, Solon, Zaleucus, Charondas,° and thence to all the Roman edicts and tables° with their Justinian,° and so down to the Saxon and common laws of England, and the statutes.

Sundays also and every evening may be now understandingly spent in the highest matters of theology and church history, ancient and modern; and ere this time the Hebrew tongue at a set hour might have been gained, that the Scriptures may be now read in their own original, whereto it would be no impossibility to add the Chaldee° and the Syrian° dialect. When all these employments are well conquered, then will the choice histories, heroic poems, and Attic tragedies of stateliest and most regal argument, with all the famous political orations, offer themselves; which if they were not only read, but some of them got by memory, and solemnly pronounced with right accent and grace, as might be taught, would endue them even with the spirit and vigour of Demosthenes or Cicero, Euripides or Sophocles.

And now, lastly, will be the time to read with them those organic arts° which enable men to discourse and write perspicuously, elegantly, and according to the fitted° style of lofty, mean or lowly. Logic, therefore, so much as is useful, is to be referred to this due place with all her well-couched heads and topics,° until it be time to open her contracted palm° into a graceful and ornate rhetoric, taught out of the rule of Plato, Aristotle, Phalereus, Cicero, Hermogenes, Longinus.° To which poetry would be made subsequent, or indeed rather precedent,° as being less subtle° and fine, but more simple, sensuous, and passionate.° I mean not here the prosody of a verse, which they could not but have hit on before among the rudiments of grammar, but that sublime art which in Aristotle's *Poetics*, in Horace,° and the Italian commentaries of Castelvetro,° Tasso,° Mazzoni° and others, teaches what the laws are of a true epic poem, what of a dramatic, what of a lyric, what decorum is, which is the grand masterpiece to observe. This would make them soon perceive what despicable creatures our common rhymers and playwrights be and show them what religious, what glorious and magnificent use might be made of poetry, both in divine and human things.

From hence, and not till now, will be the right season of forming them to be able writers and composers in every excellent matter, when they shall be thus fraught° with an universal insight into things. Or whether they be to speak in parliament or council, honour and attention would be waiting on their lips. There would then also appear in pulpits other visages, other gestures, and stuff otherwise wrought than what we now sit under, ofttimes to as great a trial of our patience as any other that they preach to us. These are the studies wherein our noble and our gentle youth ought to bestow their time in a disciplinary way from twelve to one and twenty, unless they rely more upon their ancestors dead than upon themselves living. In which methodical course it is so supposed they must proceed by the steady pace of learning onward, as at convenient times, for memory's sake, to retire back into the middleward,° and sometimes into the rear of what they have been taught, until they have confirmed and solidly united the whole body of their perfected knowledge, like the last embattling° of a Roman legion. Now will be worth the seeing what exercises and recreations may best agree and become these studies.

Their Exercise

The course of study hitherto briefly described is, what I can guess by reading, likest to those ancient and famous schools of Pythagoras, Plato, Isocrates, Aristotle, and such others, out of which were bred up such a number of renowned philosophers, orators, historians, poets and princes all over Greece, Italy and Asia, besides the flourishing studies of Cyrene and Alexandria.° But herein it shall exceed them, and supply a defect as great as that which Plato° noted in the commonwealth of Sparta; whereas that city trained up their youth most for war, and these° in their academies and Lycæum all for the gown,° this institution of breeding which I here delineate shall be equally good both for peace and war. Therefore about an hour and a half ere they eat at noon should be allowed them for exercise and due rest afterwards; but the time for this may be enlarged at pleasure, according as their rising in the morning shall be early.

The exercise which I commend first is the exact use of their weapon,° to guard, and to strike safely with edge or point; this will keep them healthy, nimble, strong, and well in breath; is also the likeliest means to make them grow large and tall, and to inspire them with a gallant and fearless courage, which being tempered with seasonable lectures and precepts to them of true fortitude and patience, will turn into a native and heroic valour, and make them hate the cowardice of doing wrong. They must be also practised in all the locks and grips of wrestling, wherein Englishmen were wont to excel, as need may often be in fight to tug, to grapple, and to close. And this perhaps will be enough wherein to prove and heat° their single° strength.

The interim of unsweating themselves regularly, and convenient rest before meat, may both with profit and delight be taken up in recreating and composing their travailed spirits with the solemn and divine harmonies of music, heard or learned; either while the skilful organist plies his grave and fancied descant° in lofty fugues, or the whole symphony° with artful and unimaginable touches adorn and grace the well-studied chords of some choice composer; sometimes the lute or soft organ-stop waiting on elegant voices, either to religious, martial, or civil ditties; which, if wise men and prophets be not extremely out,° have a great power over dispositions and manners to smooth and make them gentle from rustic harshness and distempered passions. The like also would not be unexpedient after meat to assist and cherish° nature in her first concoction,° and send their minds back to study in good tune and satisfaction. Where having followed it close under vigilant eyes till about two hours before supper, they are by a sudden alarum or watchword to be called out to their military motions, under sky or covert° according to the season, as was the Roman wont; first on foot, then, as their age permits, on horseback, to all the art of cavalry; that having in sport, but with much exactness and daily muster, served out the rudiments of their soldiership in all the skill of embattling, marching, encamping, fortifying, besieging and battering, with all the helps of ancient and modern stratagems, tactics and warlike maxims, they may as it were out of a long war come forth renowned and perfect commanders in the service of their country. They would not then, if they were trusted with fair and hopeful armies, suffer them, for want of just and wise discipline, to shed away° from about them like sick feathers, though they be never so oft supplied; they would not suffer their empty and unrecruitable° colonels of twenty men in a company to quaff out or convey into secret hoards the wages of a delusive list° and a miserable remnant; yet in the meanwhile to be overmastered with a score or two of drunkards, the only soldiery left about them, or else to comply with all rapines and violences. No, certainly, if they knew aught of that knowledge that belongs to good men or good governors, they would not suffer these things.

But to return to our own institute: besides these constant exercises at home, there is another opportunity of gaining experience to be won from pleasure itself abroad; in those vernal seasons of the year when the air is calm and pleasant, it were an injury and sullenness against nature not to go out and see her riches, and partake in her rejoicing with heaven and earth. I should not therefore be a persuader to them of studying much then, after two or three year that they have well laid their grounds, but to ride out in companies, with prudent and staid guides, to all the quarters of the land, learning and observing all places of strength, all commodities° of building and of soil, for towns and tillage, harbours and ports for trade. Sometimes taking sea as far as to our navy, to learn there also what they can in the practical knowledge of sailing and of sea-fight.

These ways would try° all their peculiar gifts of nature, and if there were any secret excellence among them would fetch it out and give it fair opportunities to advance itself by, which could not but mightily redound to the good of this nation, and bring into fashion again those old admired virtues and excellencies, with far more advantage now in this purity of Christian knowledge. Nor shall we then need the monsieurs of Paris to take our hopeful youth into their slight and prodigal custodies, and send them over back again transformed into mimics, apes and kickshaws.° But if they desire to see other countries at three or four and twenty years of age, not to learn principles, but to enlarge experience and make wise observation, they will by that time be such as shall deserve the regard and honour of all men where they pass, and the society and friendship of those in all places who are best and most eminent. And perhaps then other nations will be glad to visit us for their breeding, or else to imitate us in their own country.

Now lastly for their diet there cannot be much to say, save only that it would be best in the same house; for much time else would be lost abroad, and many ill habits got; and that it should be plain, healthful and moderate I suppose is out of controversy. Thus, Master Hartlib, you have a general view in writing, as your desire was, of that which at several times I had discoursed with you concerning the best and noblest way of education; not beginning, as some have done, from the cradle, which yet might be worth many considerations, if brevity had not been my scope; many other circumstances also I could have mentioned, but this, to such as have the worth in them to make trial, for light and direction may be enough. Only I believe that this is not a bow for every man to shoot in° that counts himself a teacher, but will require sinews almost equal to those which Homer gave Ulysses;° yet I am withal persuaded that it may prove much more easy in the assay° than it now seems at distance, and much more illustrious; howbeit, not more difficult than I imagine, and that imagination presents me with nothing but very happy and very possible according to best wishes, if God have so decreed, and this age have spirit and capacity enough to apprehend.

Areopagitica

A SPEECH FOR

THE LIBERTY OF UNLICENSED PRINTING

TO THE PARLIAMENT OF ENGLAND

———

Τοὐλεύθερον δ᾽ ἐκεῖνο. Τίς θέλει πόλει
χρηστόν τι βούλευμ᾽ ἐς μέσον φέρειν ἔχων;
καὶ ταῦθ᾽ ὁ χρῄζων λαμπρός ἐσθ᾽, ὁ μὴ θέλων
σιγᾷ τί τούτων ἔστ᾽ ἰσαίτερον πόλει;
                              —Euripid. Hicetid.

'This is true liberty, when free-born men,
Having to advise the public, may speak free,
Which he who can, and will, deserves high praise;
Who neither can, nor will, may hold his peace:
What can be juster in a state than this?'
            —*Euripid. Hicetid.*

They who to states° and governors of the commonwealth direct their speech, high court of parliament, or wanting° such access in a private condition, write that which they foresee may advance the public good, I suppose them, as at the beginning of no mean° endeavour, not a little altered and moved inwardly in their minds; some with doubt of what will be the success,° others with fear of what will be the censure;° some with hope, others with confidence of what they have to speak. And me perhaps each of these dispositions, as the subject was whereon I entered, may have at other times variously affected; and likely might in these foremost° expressions now also disclose which of them swayed most, but that the very attempt of this address thus made, and the thought of whom it hath recourse to, hath got the power within me to a passion, far more welcome than incidental° to a preface.

Which though I stay not to confess ere any ask, I shall be blameless if it be no other than the joy and gratulation which it brings to all who wish and promote their country's liberty; whereof this whole discourse proposed will be a certain testimony, if not a trophy.° For this is not the liberty which we can hope, that no grievance ever should arise in the commonwealth: that let no man in this world expect; but when complaints are freely heard, deeply considered and speedily reformed, then is the utmost bound of civil liberty attained that wise men look for. To which if I now manifest, by the very sound of this which I shall utter, that we are already in good part arrived, and yet from such a steep disadvantage of tyranny and superstition grounded into our principles as was beyond the manhood of a Roman recovery,° it will be attributed first, as is most due, to the strong assistance of God, our deliverer; next, to your faithful guidance and undaunted wisdom, lords and commons of England. Neither is it in God's esteem the diminution of his glory when honourable things are spoken of good men and worthy magistrates; which if I now first should begin to do, after so fair a progress of your laudable deeds, and such a long obligement upon the whole realm to your indefatigable virtues, I might be justly reckoned among the tardiest and the unwillingest of them that praise ye.

Nevertheless, there being three principal things without which all praising is but courtship and flattery: first, when that only is praised which is solidly worth praise; next, when greatest likelihoods are brought that such things are truly and really in those persons to whom they are ascribed; the other, when he who praises, by showing that such his actual persuasion is of whom he writes, can demonstrate that he flatters not; the former two of these I have heretofore endeavoured, rescuing the employment from him° who went about to impair your merits with a trivial and malignant encomium; the latter as belonging chiefly to mine own acquittal, that whom I so extolled I did not flatter, hath been reserved opportunely to this occasion. For he who freely magnifies what hath been nobly done, and fears not to declare as freely what might be done better, gives ye the best covenant of his fidelity; and that his loyalest affection and his hope waits on your proceedings. His highest praising is not flattery, and his plainest advice is a kind of prais-ing; for though I should affirm and hold by argument that it would fare better with truth, with learning and the commonwealth, if one of your published orders, which I should name, were called in; yet at the same time it could not but much redound to the lustre of your mild and equal government, whenas private persons are hereby animated to think ye better pleased with public advice than other statists° have been delighted heretofore with public flattery. And men will then see what difference there is between the magnanimity of a triennial° parliament and that jealous haughtiness of prelates and cabin counsellors° that usurped of late, whenas they shall observe ye in the midst of your vic-tories and successes more gently brooking written exceptions against a voted order than other courts, which had produced nothing worth memory but the weak ostentation of wealth, would have endured the least signified dislike at any sudden proclamation.

If I should thus far presume upon the meek demeanour of your civil and gentle greatness, lords and commons, as what your published order hath directly said that to gainsay,° I might defend myself with ease, if any should accuse me of being new or insolent, did they but know how much better I find ye esteem it to imitate the old and elegant humanity of Greece than the barbaric pride of a Hunnish and Norwegian stateli-ness. And out of those ages to whose polite wisdom and letters we owe that we are not yet Goths and Jutlanders, I could name him° who from his private house wrote that discourse to the parliament of Athens that persuades them to change the form of democracy which was then established. Such honour was done in those days to men who professed the study of wisdom and eloquence, not only in their own country, but in other lands, that cities and signiories heard them gladly and with great respect, if they had aught in public to admonish the state. Thus did Dion Prusaeus,° a stranger and a private orator, counsel the Rhodians against a former edict; and I abound with other like examples, which to set here would be superfluous. But if from the industry of a life wholly dedicated to studious labours, and those natural endowments haply not the worst for two and fifty degrees of northern latitude,° so much must be derogated° as to count me not equal to any of those who had this privilege, I would obtain to be thought not so inferior as yourselves are superior to the most of them who received their counsel; and how far you excel them, be assured, lords and commons, there can no greater testimony appear than when your prudent spirit acknowledges and obeys the voice of reason, from what quarter soever it be heard speaking; and renders ye as willing to repeal any act of your own setting forth as any set forth by your predecessors.

If ye be thus resolved, as it were injury to think ye were not, I know not what should withhold me from presenting ye with a fit instance wherein to show both that love of truth which ye eminently profess, and that uprightness of your judgment, which is not wont to be partial to yourselves, by judging over again that order which ye have ordained 'to regulate printing: that no book, pamphlet or paper shall be henceforth printed unless the same be first approved and licensed by such, or at least one of such, as shall be thereto appointed.' For that part° which preserves justly every man's copy to himself, or provides for the poor, I touch not; only wish they be not made pretences to abuse and persecute honest and painful° men, who offend not in either of these particulars. But that other cause of licensing books, which we thought had died with his brother quadragesimal° and matrimonial° when the prelates expired,° I shall now attend with such a homily as shall lay before ye, first, the inventors of it to be those whom ye will be loath to own; next, what is to be thought in general of reading, whatever sort the books be; and that this order avails nothing to the suppressing of scandalous, seditious, and libellous books, which were mainly intended to be suppressed. Last, that it will be primely to the discouragement of all learning, and the stop of truth, not only by disexercising and blunting our abilities in what we know already, but by hindering and cropping the discovery that might be yet further made both in religious and civil wisdom.

I deny not but that it is of greatest concernment in the church and commonwealth to have a vigilant eye how books demean themselves, as well as men; and thereafter to confine, imprison and do sharpest justice on them as malefactors; for books are not absolutely dead things, but do contain a potency of life in them to be as active as that soul was whose progeny they are; nay, they do preserve as in a vial the purest efficacy and extraction of that living intellect that bred them. I know they are as lively and as vigorously productive as those fabulous dragon's teeth;° and being sown up and down, may chance to spring up armed men. And yet, on the other hand, unless wariness be used, as good almost kill a man as kill a good book: who kills a man kills a reasonable creature, God's image; but he who destroys a good book kills reason itself, kills the image of God, as it were, in the eye. Many a man lives a burden to the earth; but a good book is the precious life blood of a master-spirit, embalmed and treasured up on purpose to a life beyond life. 'Tis true, no age can restore a life, whereof perhaps there is no great loss; and revolutions of ages do not oft recover the loss of a rejected truth, for the want of which whole nations fare the worse. We should be wary, therefore, what persecution we raise against the living labours of public men, how we spill° that seasoned life of man preserved and stored up in books; since we see a kind of homicide may be thus committed, sometimes a martyrdom; and if it extend to the whole impression,° a kind of massacre, whereof the execution ends not in the slaying of an elemental life, but strikes at that ethereal and fifth essence,° the breath of reason itself; slays an immortality rather than a life. But lest I should be condemned of introducing licence while I oppose licensing, I refuse not the pains to be so much historical as will serve to show what hath been done by ancient and famous commonwealths against this disorder, till the very time that this project of licensing crept out of the inquisition,° was catched up by our prelates, and hath caught some of our presbyters.

In Athens, where books and wits were ever busier than in any other part of Greece, I find but only two sorts of writings which the magistrate cared to take notice of; those either blasphemous and atheistical, or libellous. Thus the books of Protagoras° were by the judges of Areopagus commanded to be burnt, and himself banished the territory for a discourse begun with his confessing not to know 'whether there were gods, or whether not.' And against defaming, it was decreed that none should be traduced by name, as was the manner of *vetus comoedia*,° whereby we may guess how they censured libelling; and this course was quick° enough, as Cicero° writes, to quell both the desperate wits of other atheists and the open way of defaming, as the event° showed. Of other sects and opinions, though tending to voluptuousness and the denying of divine providence, they took no heed. Therefore we do not read that either Epicurus,° or that libertine school of Cyrene,° or what the Cynic impudence° uttered, was ever questioned by the laws.

Neither is it recorded that the writings of those old comedians were suppressed, though the acting of them were forbid; and that Plato commended the reading of Aristophanes, the loosest of them all, to his royal scholar, Dionysius, is commonly known, and may be excused, if holy Chrysostom,° as is reported, nightly studied so much the same author, and had the art to cleanse a scurrilous vehemence into the style of a rousing sermon.

That other leading city of Greece, Lacedaemon,° considering that Lycurgus° their lawgiver was so addicted to elegant learning as to have been the first that brought out of Ionia the scattered works of Homer, and sent the poet Thales from Crete to prepare and mollify the Spartan surliness with his smooth songs and odes, the better to plant among them law and civility; it is to be wondered how museless and unbookish they were, minding nought but the feats of war. There needed no licensing of books among them, for they disliked all but their own laconic apothegms, and took a slight occasion to chase Archilochus° out of their city, perhaps for composing in a higher strain than their own soldiery ballads and roundels could reach to; or if it were for his broad° verses, they were not therein so cautious, but they were as dissolute in their promiscuous conversing;° whence Euripides affirms, in *Andromache*,° that their women were all unchaste.

Thus much may give us light after what sort of books were prohibited among the Greeks. The Romans also for many ages trained up only to a military roughness, resembling most the Lacedaemonian guise, knew of learning little but what their twelve tables° and the Pontific College° with their augurs° and flamens° taught them in religion and law; so unacquainted with other learning that when Carneades and Critolaus with the Stoic Diogenes coming ambassadors to Rome took thereby occasion to give the city a taste of their philosophy, they were suspected for seducers by no less a man than Cato the Censor, who moved it in the senate to dismiss them speedily, and to banish all such Attic babblers out of Italy.° But Scipio° and others of the noblest senators withstood him and his old Sabine austerity,° honoured and admired the men; and the Censor himself at last, in his old age, fell to the study of that whereof before he was so scrupulous.° And yet at the same time Naevius and Plautus, the first Latin comedians, had filled the city with all the borrowed scenes of Menander and Philemon.° Then began to be considered there also what was to be done to libellous books and authors; for Naevius was quickly cast into prison for his unbridled pen, and released by the tribunes upon his recantation; we read also that libels were burnt and the makers punished by Augustus.

The like severity, no doubt, was used if aught were impiously written against their esteemed gods. Except in these two points, how the world went in books the magistrate kept no reckoning. And therefore Lucretius, without impeachment, versifies his Epicurism to Memmius, and had the honour to be set forth the second time by Cicero,° so great a father of the commonwealth, although himself disputes against that opinion in his own writings. Nor was the satirical sharpness or naked plainness of Lucilius, or Catullus, or Flaccus by any order prohibited. And for matters of state, the story of Titus Livius,° though it extolled that part which Pompey held, was not therefore suppressed by Octavius Cæsar, of the other faction. But that Naso° was by him banished in his old age for the wanton poems of his youth was but a mere covert° of state over some secret cause; and besides, the books were neither banished nor called in. From hence we shall meet with little else but tyranny in the Roman empire, that we may not marvel if not so often bad as good books were silenced. I shall therefore deem to have been large enough in producing what among the ancients was punishable to write, save only which, all other arguments were free to treat on.

By this time the emperors were become Christians,° whose discipline in this point I do not find to have been more severe than what was formerly in practice. The books of those whom they took to be grand heretics were examined, refuted and condemned in the general councils, and not till then were prohibited or burnt by authority of the emperor. As for the writings of heathen authors, unless they were plain invectives against Christianity, as those of Porphyrius° and Proclus,° they met with no interdict that can be cited, till about the year 400, in a Carthaginian council, wherein bishops themselves were forbid to read the books of gentiles, but heresies they might read; while others long before them, on the contrary, scrupled more° the books of heretics than of gentiles.° And that the primitive councils and bishops were wont only to declare what books were not commendable, passing no further, but leaving it to each one's conscience to read or to lay by, till after the year 800, is observed already by Padre Paolo,° the great unmasker of the Trentine council. After which time the popes of Rome, engrossing what they pleased of political rule into their own hands, extended their dominion over men's eyes, as they had before over their judgments, burning and prohibiting to be read what they fancied not; yet sparing in their censures, and the books not many which they so dealt with; till Martin the Fifth, by his bull,° not only prohibited, but was the first that excommunicated the reading of heretical books; for about that time

Wyclif and Huss,° growing terrible, were they who first drove the papal court to a stricter policy of prohibiting. Which course Leo X° and his successors followed, until the Council of Trent° and the Spanish inquisition, engendering together, brought forth or perfected those catalogues and expurging indexes that rake through the entrails of many an old good author with a violation worse than any could be offered to his tomb.

Nor did they stay in° matters heretical, but any subject that was not to their palate they either condemned in a prohibition, or had it straight into the new purgatory of an index. To fill up the measure of encroachment, their last invention was to ordain that no book, pamphlet or paper should be printed (as if St Peter had bequeathed them the keys° of the press also out of Paradise) unless it were approved and licensed under the hands of two or three glutton friars. For example:

> Let the chancellor Cini be pleased to see if in this present work be contained aught that may withstand the printing.
> > Vincent Rabbata, Vicar of Florence.

> I have seen this present work, and find nothing athwart the Catholic faith and good manners: in witness whereof I have given, &c.
> > Nicolo Cini, Chancellor of Florence.

> Attending the precedent relation, it is allowed that this present work of Davanzati may be printed.   Vincent Rabbata, &c.

> It may be printed, July 15.
> Friar Simon Mompei d'Amelia, Chancellor of the Holy Office in Florence.

Sure they have a conceit,° if he of the bottomless pit had not long since broke prison, that this quadruple exorcism would bar him down. I fear their next design will be to get into their custody the licensing of that which they say Claudius° intended, but went not through with. Vouchsafe to see another of their forms, the Roman stamp:

> Imprimatur,° if it seems good to the reverend master of the Holy Palace,
> > Belcastro, Vicegerent.

> Imprimatur,
> > Friar Nicolo Rodolphi, Master of the Holy Palace.

Sometimes five imprimaturs are seen together, dialogue-wise, in the piazza of one title page, complimenting and ducking each to other with their shaven° reverences, whether the author, who stands by in perplexity at the foot of his epistle, shall to the press or to the sponge.° These are the pretty responsories, these are the dear antiphonies° that so bewitched of late our prelates and their chaplains with the goodly echo they made, and besotted us to the gay imitation of a lordly imprimatur, one from Lambeth House,° another from the west end of Paul's°, so apishly romanizing that the word of command still was set down in Latin, as if the learned grammatical pen that wrote it would cast no ink without Latin; or perhaps, as they thought, because no vulgar tongue was worthy to express the pure conceit of an imprimatur; but rather, as I hope, for that our English, the language of men ever famous and foremost in the achievements of liberty, will not easily find servile letters enough to spell such a dictatory presumption English.

And thus ye have the inventors and the original of book licensing ripped up and drawn as lineally as any pedigree. We have it not, that can be heard of, from any ancient state, or polity, or church, nor by any statute left us by our ancestors elder or later, nor from the modern custom of any reformed city or church abroad; but from the most anti-Christian council and the most tyrannous inquisition that ever inquired. Till then books were ever as freely admitted into the world as any other birth; the issue of the brain was no more stifled than the issue of the womb: no envious Juno° sat cross-legged over the nativity of any man's intellectual offspring; but if it proved a monster, who denies but that it was justly burnt, or sunk into the sea? But that a book, in worse condition than a peccant soul, should be to stand before a jury ere it be born to the world, and undergo yet in darkness the judgment of Radamanth° and his colleagues ere it can pass the ferry backward into light,° was never heard before, till that mysterious iniquity° provoked and troubled at the first entrance of reformation sought out new limbos and new hells wherein they might include our books also within the number of their damned. And this was the rare morsel so officiously snatched up, and so illfavouredly imitated by our inquisiturient bishops and the attendant minorites,° their chaplains. That ye like not now these most certain authors of this licensing order, and that all sinister intention was far distant from your thoughts when ye were importuned the passing it, all men who knew the integrity of your actions and how ye honour truth will clear ye readily.

But some will say, what though the inventors were bad, the thing for all that may be good. It may so; yet if that thing be no such deep invention, but obvious and easy for any man to light on, and yet best and wisest commonwealths through all ages and occasions have forborne to use it, and falsest seducers and oppressors of men were the first who took it up, and to no other purpose but to obstruct and hinder the first approach of reformation, I am of those who believe it will be a harder alchemy than Lullius° ever knew to sublimate° any good use out of such an invention. Yet this only is what I request to gain from this reason, that it may be held a dangerous and suspicious fruit, as certainly it deserves, for the tree that bore it, until I can dissect one by one the properties it has. But I have first to finish, as was propounded, what is to be thought in general of reading books, whatever sort they be, and whether be more the benefit or the harm that thence proceeds.

Not to insist upon the examples of Moses, Daniel and Paul,° who were skilful in all the learning of the Egyptians, Chaldeans and Greeks, which could not probably be without reading their books of all sorts, in Paul especially, who thought it no defilement to insert into holy Scripture the sentences of three Greek poets, and one of them a tragedian; the question was notwithstanding sometimes controverted among the primitive doctors, but with great odds on that side which affirmed it both lawful and profitable, as was then evidently perceived when Julian the Apostate,° and subtlest enemy to our faith, made a decree forbidding Christians the study of heathen learning; for, said he, they wound us with our own weapons, and with our own arts and sciences they overcome us. And indeed the Christians were put so to their shifts° by this crafty means, and so much in danger to decline into all ignorance, that the two Apollinarii° were fain, as a man may say, to coin all the seven liberal sciences out of the Bible, reducing it into divers forms of orations, poems, dialogues, even to the calculating of a new Christian grammar.

But, saith the historian Socrates,° the providence of God provided better than the industry of Apollinarius and his son by taking away that illiterate law with the life of him who devised it. So great an injury they then held it to be deprived of Hellenic learning, and thought it a persecution more undermining and secretly decaying the church than the open cruelty of Decius or Diocletian.° And perhaps it was the same politic drift that the devil whipped St Jerome° in a lenten dream for reading Cicero; or else it was a phantasm bred by the fever which had then seized him. For had an angel been his discipliner, unless it were for dwelling too much upon Ciceronianisms, and had chastised the reading, not the vanity, it had been plainly partial, first, to correct him for grave Cicero, and not for scurrile Plautus, whom he confesses to have been reading not long before; next to correct him only, and let so many more ancient fathers wax old in those pleasant and florid studies without the lash of such a tutoring apparition; insomuch that Basil teaches how some good use may be made of *Margites*,° a sportful poem, not now extant, writ by Homer; and why not then of *Morgante*,° an Italian romance much to the same purpose?

But if it be agreed we shall be tried by visions, there is a vision recorded by Eusebius,° far ancienter than this tale of Jerome, to the nun Eustochium, and besides, has nothing of a fever in it. Dionysius Alexandrinus was, about the year 240, a person of great name in the church for piety and learning, who had wont to avail himself much against heretics by being conversant in their books, until a certain presbyter laid it scrupulously to his conscience how he durst venture himself among those defiling volumes. The worthy man, loath to give offence, fell into a new debate with himself what was to be thought; when suddenly a vision sent from God (it is his own epistle that so avers it) confirmed him in these words: 'Read any books whatever come to thy hands, for thou art sufficient both to judge aright and to examine each matter.' To this revelation he assented the sooner, as he confesses, because it was answerable to° that of the apostle to the Thessalonians:° 'Prove all things, hold fast that which is good.'

And he might have added another remarkable saying of the same author:° 'To the pure all things are pure'; not only meats and drinks, but all kind of knowledge, whether of good or evil: the knowledge cannot defile, nor consequently the books, if the will and conscience be not defiled. For books are as meats and viands are, some of good, some of evil substance; and yet God in that unapocryphal vision° said without exception, 'Rise, Peter, kill and eat', leaving the choice to each man's discretion. Wholesome meats to a vitiated stomach differ little or nothing from unwholesome; and best books to a naughty mind are not unapplicable to occasions of evil. Bad meats will scarce breed good nourishment in the healthiest concoction;° but herein the difference is of bad books, that they to a discreet and judicious reader serve in many respects to discover, to confute, to forewarn and to illustrate. Whereof what better witness can ye expect I should produce than one of your own now sitting in parliament, the chief of learned men reputed in this land, Mr Selden,° whose volume of natural and national laws proves, not only by great authorities brought together, but by exquisite° reasons and theorems almost mathematically demonstrative, that all opinions, yea, errors, known, read and collated are of main service and assistance toward the speedy attainment of what is truest.

I conceive, therefore, that when God did enlarge the universal diet of man's body (saving ever the rules of temperance), he then also, as before, left arbitrary the dieting and repasting of our minds, as wherein every mature man might have to exercise his own leading capacity. How great a virtue is temperance, how much of moment through the whole life of man! Yet God commits the managing so great a trust, without particular law or prescription, wholly to the demeanour of every grown man. And therefore when he himself tabled° the Jews from heaven, that omer, which was every man's daily portion of manna, is computed to have been more than might have well sufficed the heartiest feeder thrice as many meals. For those actions which enter into a man, rather than issue out° of him, and therefore defile not, God uses not to captivate under a perpetual childhood of prescription, but trusts him with the gift of reason to be his own chooser; there were but little work left for preaching if law and compulsion should grow so fast upon those things which heretofore were governed only by exhortation. Solomon° informs us that much reading is a weariness to the flesh; but neither he nor other inspired author tells us that such or such reading is unlawful; yet certainly had God thought good to limit us herein, it had been much more expedient to have told us what was unlawful, than what was wearisome.

As for the burning of those Ephesian books by St Paul's converts, 'tis replied the books were magic, the Syriac° so renders them. It was a private act, a voluntary act, and leaves us to a voluntary imitation: the men in remorse burnt those books which were their own; the magistrate by this example is not appointed; these men practised the books,° another might perhaps have read them in some sort usefully. Good and evil we know in the field of this world grow up together almost inseparably; and the knowledge of good is so involved and interwoven with the knowledge of evil, and in so many cunning resemblances hardly to be discerned, that those confused seeds which were imposed upon Psyche° as an incessant labour to cull out and sort asunder were not more intermixed. It was from out the rind of one apple tasted that the knowledge of good and evil, as two twins cleaving together, leaped forth into the world. And perhaps this is that doom which Adam fell into of knowing good and evil; that is to say, of knowing good by evil.

As therefore the state of man now is, what wisdom can there be to choose, what continence to forbear, without the knowledge of evil? He that can apprehend and consider vice with all her baits and seeming pleasures, and yet abstain, and yet distinguish, and yet prefer that which is truly better, he is the true warfaring° Christian. I cannot praise a fugitive and cloistered virtue unexercised and unbreathed,° that never sallies out and sees her adversary, but slinks out of the race where that immortal garland° is to be run for, not without dust and heat. Assuredly we bring not innocence into the world, we bring impurity much rather; that which purifies us is trial, and trial is by what is contrary. That virtue therefore which is but a youngling in the contemplation of evil, and knows not the utmost that vice promises to her followers, and rejects it, is but a blank virtue, not a pure; her whiteness is but an excremental° whiteness; which was the reason why our sage and serious poet Spenser (whom I dare be known to think a better teacher than Scotus or Aquinas),° describing true temperance under the person of Guyon,° brings him in with his palmer through the cave of Mammon and the bower of earthly bliss, that he might see and know, and yet abstain.

Since therefore the knowledge and survey of vice is in this world so necessary to the constituting of human virtue, and the scanning of error to the confirmation of truth, how can we more safely, and with less danger, scout into the regions of sin and falsity, than by reading all manner of tractates, and hearing all manner of reason? And this is the benefit which may be had of books promiscuously° read. But of the harm that may result hence, three kinds are usually reckoned. First is feared the infection that may spread; but then, all human learning and controversy in religious points must remove out of the world, yea, the Bible itself; for that ofttimes relates blasphemy not nicely,° it describes the carnal sense of wicked men not unelegantly, it brings in holiest men passionately murmuring against Providence through all the arguments of Epicurus; in other great disputes it answers dubiously and darkly to the common reader; and ask a Talmudist what ails the modesty of his marginal *keri*, that Moses and all the prophets cannot persuade him to pronounce the textual *chetiv*.° For these causes we all know the Bible itself put by the Papist into the first rank of prohibited books. The ancientest fathers must be next removed, as Clement of Alexandria,° and that Eusebian book of evangelic preparation° transmitting our ears through a hoard of heathenish obscenities to receive the gospel. Who finds not that Irenaeus, Epiphanius,° Jerome, and others discover more heresies than they well confute, and that oft for heresy which is the truer opinion?

Nor boots it to say for these, and all the heathen writers of greatest infection, if it must be thought so, with whom is bound up the life of human learning, that they writ in an unknown tongue, so long as we are sure those languages are known as well to the worst of men, who are both most able and most diligent to instil the poison they suck, first into the courts of princes, acquainting them with the choicest delights and criticisms° of sin. As perhaps did that Petronius,° whom Nero called his Arbiter,° the master of his revels; and that notorious ribald of Arezzo,° dreaded and yet dear to the Italian courtiers. I name not him, for posterity's sake, whom Harry VIII named in merriment his vicar of hell.° By which compendious way all the contagion that foreign books can infuse will find a passage to the people far easier and shorter than an Indian voyage, though it could be sailed either by the north of Cataio° eastward, or of Canada westward, while our Spanish licensing gags the English press never so severely.

But, on the other side, that infection which is from books of controversy in religion is more doubtful and dangerous to the learned than to the ignorant; and yet those books must be permitted untouched by the licenser. It will be hard to instance where any ignorant man hath been ever seduced by Papistical book in English, unless it were commended and expounded to him by some of that clergy; and indeed all such tractates, whether false or true, are as the prophecy of Isaiah° was to the eunuch, not to be 'understood without a guide'. But of our priests and doctors how many have been corrupted by studying the comments of Jesuits and Sorbonists,° and how fast they could transfuse that corruption into the people, our experience is both late and sad. It is not forgot, since the acute and distinct° Arminius° was perverted merely by the perusing of a nameless discourse written at Delft, which at first he took in hand to confute.

Seeing therefore that those books, and those in great abundance, which are likeliest to taint both life and doctrine cannot be suppressed without the fall of learning and of all ability in disputation, and that these books of either sort are most and soonest catching to the learned (from whom to the common people whatever is heretical or dissolute may quickly be conveyed), and that evil manners are as perfectly learnt without books a thousand other ways which cannot be stopped, and evil doctrine not with books can propagate, except a teacher guide, which he might also do without writing, and so beyond prohibiting; I am not able to unfold how this cautelous° enterprise of licensing can be exempted from the number of vain and impossible attempts. And he who were pleasantly disposed could not well avoid to liken it to the exploit of that gallant man who thought to pound up° the crows by shutting his park gate.

Besides another inconvenience, if learned men be the first receivers out of books, and dispreaders both of vice and error, how shall the licensers themselves be confided in, unless we can confer upon them, or they assume to themselves above all others in the land the grace of infallibility, and uncorruptedness? And again, if it be true that a wise man, like a good refiner, can gather gold out of the drossiest volume, and that a fool will be a fool with the best book, yea, or without book, there is no reason that we should deprive a wise man of any advantage to his wisdom, while we seek to restrain from a fool that which being restrained will be no hindrance to his folly. For if there should be so much exactness always used to keep that from him which is unfit for his reading, we should in the judgment of Aristotle° not only, but of Solomon,° and of our Saviour,° not vouchsafe him good precepts, and by consequence not willingly admit him to good books, as being certain that a wise man will make better use of an idle pamphlet than a fool will do of sacred Scripture.

'Tis next alleged we must not expose ourselves to temptations without necessity, and next to that, not employ our time in vain things. To both these objections one answer will serve out of the grounds already laid, that to all men such books are not temptations nor vanities, but useful drugs and materials wherewith to temper and compose effective and strong medicines which man's life cannot want.° The rest, as children and childish men, who have not the art to qualify° and prepare these working minerals, well may be exhorted to forbear; but hindered forcibly they cannot be by all the licensing that sainted inquisition could ever yet contrive; which is what I promised to deliver next: that this order of licensing conduces nothing to the end for which it was framed; and hath almost prevented° me by being clear already while thus much hath been explaining. See the ingenuity of Truth, who, when she gets a free and willing hand, opens herself faster than the pace of method and discourse can overtake her. It was the task which I began with to show that no nation or well instituted state, if they valued books at all, did ever use this way of licensing; and it might be answered that this is a piece of prudence lately discovered.

To which I return that as it was a thing slight and obvious to think on, so if it had been difficult to find out, there wanted not among them long since who suggested such a course; which they not following, leave us a pattern of their judgment that it was not the not knowing, but the not approving, which was the cause of their not using it. Plato, a man of high authority indeed, but least of all for his Commonwealth, in the book of his Laws,° which no city every yet received, fed his fancy with making many edicts to his airy burgomasters,° which they who otherwise admire him wish had been rather buried and excused in the genial cups of an academic night-sitting.° By which laws he seems to tolerate no kind of learning but by unalterable decree, consisting most of practical traditions, to the attainment whereof a library of smaller bulk than his own dialogues would be abundant. And there also enacts that no poet should so much as read to any private man what he had written until the judges and law keepers had seen it and allowed it; but that Plato meant this law peculiarly to that commonwealth which he had imagined, and to no other, is evident. Why was he not else a lawgiver to himself, but a transgressor, and to be expelled by his own magistrates both for the wanton epigrams and dialogues which he made, and his perpetual reading of Sophron Mimus° and Aristophanes, books of grossest infamy; and also for commending the latter of them, though he were the malicious libeller of his chief friends, to be read by the tyrant Dionysius, who had little need of such trash to spend his time on? But that he knew this licensing of poems had reference and dependence to many other provisos there set down in his fancied republic, which in this world could have no place; and so neither he himself, nor any magistrate or city, ever imitated that course, which, taken apart from those other collateral injunctions, must needs be vain and fruitless.

For if they fell upon one kind of strictness, unless their care were equal to regulate all other things of like aptness to corrupt the mind, that single endeavour they knew would be but a fond° labour—to shut and fortify one gate against corruption, and be necessitated to leave others round about wide open. If we think to regulate printing, thereby to rectify manners, we must regulate all recreations and pastimes, all that is delightful to man. No music must be heard, no song be set or sung, but what is grave and Doric.° There must be licensing dancers, that no gesture, motion or deportment be taught our youth but what by their allowance shall be thought honest; for such Plato was provided of. It will ask more than the work of twenty licensers to examine all the lutes, the violins and the guitars in every house; they must not be suffered to prattle as they do, but must be licensed what they may say. And who shall silence all the airs and madrigals that whisper softness in chambers? The windows also and the balconies must be thought on; there are shrewd° books with dangerous frontispieces set to sale: who shall prohibit them, shall twenty licensers? The villages also must have their visitors° to inquire what lectures the bagpipe and the rebec° reads, even to the balladry and the gamut° of every municipal fiddler; for these are the countryman's *Arcadias*,° and his Montemayors.°

Next, what more national corruption for which England hears ill° abroad than household gluttony? Who shall be the rectors of our daily rioting?° And what shall be done to inhibit the multitudes that frequent those houses where drunkenness is sold and harboured? Our garments also should be referred to the licensing of some more sober work-masters, to see them cut into a less wanton garb. Who shall regulate all the mixed conversation° of our youth, male and female together, as is the fashion of this country? Who shall still appoint what shall be discoursed, what presumed, and no further? Lastly, who shall forbid and separate all idle resort, all evil company? These things will be, and must be; but how they shall be least hurtful, how least enticing, herein consists the grave and governing wisdom of a state.

To sequester out of the world into Atlantic° and Utopian polities which never can be drawn into use will not mend our condition, but to ordain wisely as in this world of evil, in the midst whereof God hath placed us unavoidably. Nor is it Plato's licensing of books will do this, which necessarily pulls along with it so many other kinds of licensing as will make us all both ridiculous and weary, and yet frustrate; but those unwritten, or at least unconstraining laws of virtuous education, religious and civil nurture, which Plato there° mentions, as the bonds and ligaments of the commonwealth, the pillars and the sustainers of every written statute; these they be which will bear chief sway in such matters as these, when all licensing will be easily eluded. Impunity and remissness for certain are the bane of a commonwealth; but here the great art lies to discern in what the law is to bid restraint and punishment, and in what things persuasion only is to work. If every action which is good or evil in man at ripe years were to be under pittance,° and prescription, and compulsion, what were virtue but a name, what praise could be then due to well-doing, what gramercy° to be sober, just or continent?

Many there be that complain of divine Providence for suffering Adam to transgress. Foolish tongues! when God gave him reason, he gave him freedom to choose, for reason is but choosing; he had been else a mere artificial Adam, such an Adam as he is in the motions.° We ourselves esteem not of that obedience, or love, or gift, which is of force; God therefore left him free, set before him a provoking object ever almost in his eyes; herein consisted his merit, herein the right of his reward, the praise of his abstinence. Wherefore did he create passions within us, pleasures round about us, but that these rightly tempered are the very ingredients of virtue? They are not skilful considerers of human things who imagine to remove sin by removing the matter of sin; for, besides that it is a huge heap increasing under the very act of diminishing, though some part of it may for a time be withdrawn from some persons, it cannot from all, in such a universal thing as books are; and when this is done, yet the sin remains entire. Though ye take from a covetous man all his treasures, he has yet one jewel left, ye cannot bereave him of his covetousness. Banish all objects of lust, shut up all youth into the severest discipline that can be exercised in any hermitage, ye cannot make them chaste that came not thither so: such great care and wisdom is required to the right managing of this point.

Suppose we could expel sin by this means; look how much we thus expel of sin, so much we expel of virtue: for the matter of them both is the same; remove that, and ye remove them both alike. This justifies the high Providence of God, who, though he command us temperance, justice, continence, yet pours out before us even to a profuseness all desirable things, and gives us minds that can wander beyond all limit and satiety. Why should we then affect a rigour contrary to the manner of God and of nature by abridging or scanting those means which books freely permitted are, both to the trial of virtue and the exercise of truth?

It would be better done to learn that the law must needs be frivolous which goes to restrain things uncertainly and yet equally working to good and to evil. And were I the chooser, a dram of well-doing should be preferred before many times as much the forcible hindrance of evil-doing. For God sure esteems the growth and completing of one virtuous person more than the restraint of ten vicious. And albeit whatever thing we hear or see, sitting, walking, travelling or conversing, may be fitly called our book, and is of the same effect that writings are, yet grant the thing to be prohibited were only books, it appears that this order hitherto is far insufficient to the end which it intends. Do we not see, not once or oftener, but weekly, that continued court-libel° against the parliament and city, printed, as the wet° sheets can witness, and dispersed among us for all that licensing can do? Yet this is the prime service a man would think wherein this order should give proof of itself. If it were executed, you'll say. But certain, if execution be remiss or blindfold now, and in this particular, what will it be hereafter, and in other books?

If then the order shall not be vain and frustrate, behold a new labour, lords and commons, ye must repeal and proscribe all scandalous and unlicensed books already printed and divulged,° after ye have drawn them up into a list, that all may know which are condemned and which not; and ordain that no foreign books be delivered out of custody till they have been read over. This office will require the whole time of not a few overseers, and those no vulgar men. There be also books which are partly useful and excellent, partly culpable and pernicious; this work will ask as many more officials° to make expurgations and expunctions, that the commonwealth of learning be not damnified.° In fine, when the multitude of books increase upon their hands, ye must be fain to catalogue all those printers who are found frequently offending, and forbid the importation of their whole suspected typography. In a word, that this your order may be exact and not deficient, ye must reform it perfectly,° according to the model of Trent and Seville,° which I know ye abhor to do.

Yet though ye should condescend to this, which God forbid, the order still would be but fruitless and defective to that end whereto ye meant it. If to prevent sects and schisms, who is so unread or uncatechized in story° that hath not heard of many sects refusing books as a hindrance, and preserving their doctrine unmixed for many ages only by unwritten traditions? The Christian faith (for that was once a schism) is not unknown to have spread all over Asia ere any gospel or epistle was seen in writing. If the amendment of manners be aimed at, look into Italy and Spain, whether those places be one scruple the better, the honester, the wiser, the chaster, since all the inquisitional rigour that hath been executed upon books.

Another reason whereby to make it plain that this order will miss the end it seeks, consider by the quality which ought to be in every licenser. It cannot be denied but that he who is made judge to sit upon the birth or death of books whether they may be wafted° into this world or not had need to be a man above the common measure, both studious, learned and judicious—there may be else no mean° mistakes in the censure of what is passable or not, which is also no mean injury. If he be of such worth as behooves him, there cannot be a more tedious and unpleasing journeywork,° a greater loss of time levied upon his head, than to be made the perpetual reader of unchosen books and pamphlets, ofttimes huge volumes. There is no book that is acceptable, unless at certain seasons; but to be enjoined the reading of that at all times, and in a hand scarce legible, whereof three pages would not down° at any time in the fairest print, is an imposition which I cannot believe how he that values time and his own studies, or is but of a sensible° nostril, should be able to endure. In this one thing I crave leave of the present licensers to be pardoned for so thinking, who doubtless took this office up looking on it through their obedience to the parliament, whose command perhaps made all things seem easy and unlaborious to them; but that this short trial hath wearied them out already, their own expressions and excuses to them who make so many journeys to solicit their license are testimony enough. Seeing therefore those who now possess the employment by all evident signs wish themselves well rid of it, and that no man of worth, none that is not a plain unthrift of his own hours, is ever likely to succeed them, except he mean to put himself to the salary of a press corrector, we may easily foresee what kind of licensers we are to expect hereafter, either ignorant, imperious and remiss, or basely pecuniary. This is what I had to show, wherein this order cannot conduce to that end whereof it bears the intention.

I lastly proceed from the no good it can do, to the manifest hurt it causes, in being first the greatest discouragement and affront that can be offered to learning and to learned men. It was the complaint and lamentation of prelates, upon every least breath of a motion to remove pluralities° and distribute more equally church revenues, that then all learning would be for ever dashed and discouraged. But as for that opinion, I never found cause to think that the tenth part of learning stood or fell with the clergy, nor could I ever but hold it for a sordid and unworthy speech of any churchman who had a competency° left him. If therefore ye be loath to dishearten utterly and discontent, not the mercenary crew of false pretenders to learning, but the free and ingenuous sort of such as evidently were born to study and love learning for itself, not for lucre, or any other end but the service of God and of truth, and perhaps that lasting fame and perpetuity of praise which God and good men have consented shall be the reward of those whose published labours advance the good of mankind; then know that so far to distrust the judgment and the honesty of one who hath but a common repute in learning, and never yet offended, as not to count him fit to print his mind without a tutor and examiner lest he should drop a schism, or something of corruption, is the greatest displeasure and indignity to a free and knowing spirit that can be put upon him.

What advantage is it to be a man over it is to be a boy at school, if we have only escaped the ferula° to come under the fescue° of an imprimatur? if serious and elaborate° writings, as if they were no more than the theme of a grammar-lad under his pedagogue, must not be uttered° without the cursory eyes of a temporizing and extemporizing licenser? He who is not trusted with his own actions, his drift not being known to be evil, and standing to the hazard of law and penalty, has no great argument to think himself reputed in the commonwealth wherein he was born for other than a fool or a foreigner. When a man writes to the world, he summons up all his reason and deliberation to assist him; he searches, meditates, is industrious, and likely consults and confers with his judicious friends; after all which done, he takes himself to be informed in what he writes, as well as any that writ before him; if in this, the most consummate act of his fidelity and ripeness, no years, no industry, no former proof of his abilities, can bring him to that state of maturity as not to be still mistrusted and suspected, unless he carry all his considerate diligence, all his midnight watchings and expense of Palladian oil° to the hasty view of an unleisured licenser, perhaps much his younger, perhaps far his inferior in judgment, perhaps one who never knew the labour of bookwriting; and if he be not repulsed or slighted, must appear in print like a puny° with his guardian, and his censor's hand on the back of his title to be his bail and surety that he is no idiot or seducer; it cannot be but a dishonour and derogation to the author, to the book, to the privilege and dignity of learning.

And what if the author shall be one so copious of fancy as to have many things well worth the adding come into his mind after licensing, while the book is yet under the press, which not seldom happens to the best and diligentest writers, and that perhaps a dozen times in one book. The printer dares not go beyond his licensed copy; so often then must the author trudge to his leave-giver, that those his new insertions may be viewed, and many a jaunt will be made ere that licenser, for it must be the same man, can either be found, or found at leisure; meanwhile either the press must stand still, which is no small damage, or the author lose his accuratest thoughts, and send the book forth worse than he had made it, which to a diligent writer is the greatest melancholy and vexation that can befall.

And how can a man teach with authority, which is the life of teaching; how can he be a doctor in his book, as he ought to be, or else had better be silent, whenas all he teaches, all he delivers, is but under the tuition, under the correction of his patriarchal° licenser, to blot or alter what precisely accords not with the hide-bound humour which he calls his judgment? When every acute reader, upon the first sight of a pedantic license, will be ready with these like words to ding° the book a quoit's distance° from him: 'I hate a pupil teacher; I endure not an instructor that comes to me under the wardship of an overseeing fist. I know nothing of the licenser, but that I have his own hand here for his arrogance; who shall warrant me his judgment?' 'The state, sir,' replies the stationer—but has a quick return: 'The state shall be my governors, but not my critics; they may be mistaken in the choice of a licenser, as easily as this licenser may be mistaken in an author. This is some common stuff'; and he might add from Sir Francis Bacon° that 'such authorized books are but the language of the times'. For though a licenser should happen to be judicious more than ordinary, which will be a great jeopardy° of the next succession, yet his very office and his commission enjoins him to let pass nothing but what is vulgarly received already.

Nay, which is more lamentable, if the work of any deceased author, though never so famous in his lifetime, and even to this day, come to their hands for license to be printed or reprinted, if there be found in his book one sentence of a venturous edge, uttered in the height of zeal (and who knows whether it might not be the dictate of a divine spirit?) yet not suiting with every low decrepit humour of their own, though it were Knox° himself, the reformer of a kingdom, that spake it, they will not pardon him their dash;° the sense of that great man shall to all posterity be lost, for the fearfulness or the presumptuous rashness of a perfunctory licenser. And to what an author this violence hath been lately done, and in what book of greatest consequence to be faithfully published, I could now instance, but shall forbear till a more convenient season. Yet if these things be not resented seriously and timely by them who have the remedy in their power, but that such ironmoulds° as these shall have authority to gnaw out the choicest periods of exquisitest books, and to commit such a treacherous fraud against the orphan remainders of worthiest men after death, the more sorrow will belong to that hapless race of men whose misfortune it is to have understanding. Henceforth let no man care to learn, or care to be more than worldly wise; for certainly in higher matters to be ignorant and slothful, to be a common steadfast dunce, will be the only pleasant life, and only in request.

And as it is a particular disesteem of every knowing person alive, and most injurious to the written labours and monuments of the dead, so to me it seems an undervaluing and vilifying of the whole nation. I cannot set so light by all the invention, the art, the wit, the grave and solid judgment which is in England, as that it can be comprehended in any twenty° capacities, how good soever; much less that it should not pass except their superintendence be over it, except it be sifted and strained with their strainers, that it should be uncurrent without their manual stamp. Truth and understanding are not such wares as to be monopolized and traded in by tickets, and statutes, and standards.° We must not think to make a staple commodity° of all the knowledge in the land, to mark and license it like our broadcloth and our woolpacks. What is it but a servitude like that imposed by the Philistines,° not to be allowed the sharpening of our own axes and coulters,° but we must repair from all quarters to twenty licensing forges?

Had anyone written and divulged erroneous things and scandalous to honest life, misusing and forfeiting the esteem had of his reason among men, if after conviction this only censure were adjudged him, that he should never henceforth write but what were first examined by an appointed officer whose hand should be annexed to pass his credit for him, that now he might be safely read, it could not be apprehended less than a disgraceful punishment. Whence to include the whole nation, and those that never yet thus offended, under such a diffident° and suspectful prohibition, may plainly be understood what a disparagement it is. So much the more whenas debtors and delinquents may walk abroad without a keeper, but unoffensive books must not stir forth without a visible jailor in their title. Nor is it to the common people less than a reproach; for if we be so jealous over them as that we dare not trust them with an English pamphlet, what do we but censure them for a giddy, vicious and ungrounded people, in such a sick and weak estate of faith and discretion as to be able to take nothing down but through the pipe of a licenser? That this is care or love of them we cannot pretend, whenas in those Popish places where the laity are most hated and despised, the same strictness is used over them. Wisdom we cannot call it, because it stops but one breach of licence, nor that neither, whenas those corruptions which it seeks to prevent break in faster at other doors which cannot be shut.

And in conclusion it reflects to the disrepute of our ministers also, of whose labours we should hope better, and of the proficiency which their flock reaps by them, than that after all this light of the gospel which is, and is to be, and all this continual preaching, they should be still frequented° with such an unprincipled, unedified and laic° rabble, as that° the whiff of every new pamphlet should stagger them out of their catechism and Christian walking. This may have much reason to discourage the ministers, when such a low conceit° is had of all their exhortations, and the benefiting of their hearers, as that they are not thought fit to be turned loose to three sheets of paper without a licenser; that all the sermons, all the lectures preached, printed, vended in such numbers, and such volumes as have now well-nigh made all other books unsaleable should not be armour enough against one single enchiridion° without the castle of St Angelo° of an imprimatur.

And lest some should persuade ye, lords and commons, that these arguments of learned men's discouragement at this your order are mere flourishes, and not real, I could recount what I have seen and heard in other countries, where this kind of inquisition tyrannizes; when I have sat among their learned men (for that honour I had) and been counted happy to be born in such a place of philosophic freedom as they supposed England was, while themselves did nothing but bemoan the servile condition into which learning amongst them was brought; that this was it which had damped the glory of Italian wits; that nothing had been there written now these many years but flattery and fustian. There it was that I found and visited the famous Galileo°, grown old, a prisoner to the inquisition for thinking in astronomy otherwise than the Franciscan and Dominican licensers thought. And though I knew that England then was groaning loudest under the prelatical yoke, nevertheless I took it as a pledge of future happiness that other nations were so persuaded of her liberty.

Yet was it beyond my hope that those worthies were then breathing in her air who should be her leaders to such a deliverance as shall never be forgotten by any revolution of time that this world hath to finish. When that was once begun, it was as little in my fear that what words of complaint I heard among learned men of other parts uttered against the inquisition, the same I should hear by as learned men at home uttered in time of parliament against an order of licensing, and that so generally that when I had disclosed myself a companion of their discontent, I might say, if without envy,° that he° whom an honest quaestorship had endeared to the Sicilians was not more by them importuned against Verres than the favourable opinion which I had among many who honour ye, and are known and respected by ye, loaded me with entreaties and persuasions that I would not despair to lay together that which just reason should bring into my mind toward the removal of an undeserved thraldom upon learning.

That this is not therefore the disburdening of a particular fancy, but the common grievance of all those who had prepared their minds and studies above the vulgar pitch to advance truth in others, and from others to entertain it, thus much may satisfy. And in their name I shall for neither friend nor foe conceal what the general murmur is: that if it come to inquisitioning again, and licensing, and that we are so timorous of ourselves and so suspicious of all men as to fear each book, and the shaking of every leaf, before we know what the contents are; if some who but of late were little better than silenced from preaching shall come now to silence us from reading, except what they please, it cannot be guessed what is intended by some but a second tyranny over learning; and will soon put it out of controversy that bishops and presbyters are the same to us, both name and thing.

That those evils of prelaty which before from five or six and twenty sees were distributively charged upon the whole people will now light wholly upon learning, is not obscure to us: whenas now the pastor of a small unlearned parish on the sudden shall be exalted archbishop over a large diocese of books, and yet not remove, but keep his other cure° too, a mystical pluralist. He who but of late cried down the sole ordination of every novice bachelor of art,° and denied sole jurisdiction over the simplest parishioner, shall now at home in his private chair assume both these over worthiest and excellentest books and ablest authors that write them. This is not the covenants and protestations° that we have made! This is not to put down prelaty; this is but to chop an episcopacy;° this is but to translate the palace metropolitan° from one kind of dominion into another; this is but an old canonical sleight of commuting our penance.° To startle thus betimes° at a mere unlicensed pamphlet will after a while be afraid of every conventicle,° and a while after will make a conventicle of every Christian meeting.

But I am certain that a state governed by the rules of justice and fortitude, or a church built and founded upon the rock of faith and true knowledge, cannot be so pusillanimous. While things are yet not constituted in religion, that freedom of writing should be restrained by a discipline imitated from the prelates, and learned by them from the inquisition to shut us up all again into the breast of a licenser, must needs give cause of doubt and discouragement to all learned and religious men, who cannot but discern the fineness of this politic drift, and who are the contrivers; that while bishops were to be baited down, then all presses might be open; it was the people's birthright and privilege in time of parliament, it was the breaking forth of light.

But now the bishops abrogated and voided out of the church, as if our reformation sought no more but to make room for others into their seats under another name, the episcopal arts begin to bud again; the cruse of truth must run no more oil;° liberty of printing must be enthralled again under a prelatical commission of twenty, the privilege of the people nullified; and, which is worse, the freedom of learning must groan again, and to her old fetters: all this the parliament yet sitting. Although their own late arguments and defences against the prelates might remember° them that this obstructing violence meets for the most part with an event utterly opposite to the end which it drives at: instead of suppressing sects and schisms, it raises them and invests them with a reputation: 'The punishing of wits enhances their authority,' saith the Viscount St Albans;° 'and a forbidden writing is thought to be a certain spark of truth, that flies up in the faces of them who seek to tread it out.' This order, therefore, may prove a nursing mother to sects, but I shall easily show how it will be a stepdame to truth: and first, by disenabling us to the maintenance of what is known already.

Well knows he who uses to consider that our faith and knowledge thrives by exercise, as well as our limbs and complexion. Truth is compared in Scripture° to a streaming fountain; if her waters flow not in a

perpetual progression, they sicken into a muddy pool of conformity and
tradition. A man may be a heretic in the truth; and if he believe things
only because his pastor says so, or the assembly° so determines, without
knowing other reason, though his belief be true, yet the very truth he
holds becomes his heresy. There is not any burden that some would
gladlier post off to another than the charge and care of their religion.
There be, who knows not that there be? of Protestants and professors°
who live and die in as errant and implicit faith° as any lay Papist of
Loreto.°

A wealthy man addicted to his pleasure and to his profits finds religion to be a traffic so entangled, and of so many piddling accounts, that
of all mysteries° he cannot skill to keep a stock going upon that trade.
What should he do? Fain he would have the name to be religious, fain
he would bear up with his neighbours in that. What does he therefore,
but resolves to give over toiling, and to find himself out some factor° to
whose care and credit he may commit the whole managing of his
religious affairs; some divine of note and estimation that must be. To
him he adheres, resigns the whole warehouse of his religion, with all
the locks and keys, into his custody; and indeed makes the very person
of that man his religion; esteems his associating with him a sufficient
evidence and commendatory° of his own piety. So that a man may say
his religion is now no more within himself, but is become a dividual°
moveable, and goes and comes near him according as that good man
frequents the house. He entertains him, gives him gifts, feasts him,
lodges him; his religion comes home at night, prays, is liberally supped
and sumptuously laid to sleep; rises, is saluted, and after the malmsey,
or some well-spiced brewage, and better breakfasted than he° whose
morning appetite would have gladly fed on green figs between Bethany
and Jerusalem, his religion walks abroad at eight, and leaves his kind
entertainer in the shop trading all day without his religion.

Another sort there be who when they hear that all things shall be
ordered, all things regulated and settled, nothing written but what
passes through the custom-house of certain publicans° that have the
tunaging and poundaging° of all free-spoken truth, will straight give
themselves up into your hands, make 'em and cut 'em out what religion
ye please: there be delights, there be recreations and jolly pastimes, that
will fetch the day about from sun to sun, and rock the tedious year as in
a delightful dream. What need they torture their heads with that which
others have taken so strictly and so unalterably into their own purvey-
ing? These are the fruits which a dull ease and cessation of our knowledge will bring forth among the people. How goodly, and how to be

wished were such an obedient unanimity as this! What a fine conformity would it starch us all into! Doubtless a staunch and solid piece of framework as any January could freeze together.

Nor much better will be the consequence even among the clergy themselves: it is no new thing never heard of before for a parochial° minister who has his reward and is at his Hercules' pillars° in a warm benefice to be easily inclinable, if he have nothing else that may rouse up his studies, to finish his circuit in an English concordance and a topic folio,° the gatherings and savings of a sober graduateship, a harmony and a catena,° treading the constant round of certain common doctrinal heads, attended with their uses, motives, marks and means; out of which, as out of an alphabet or sol-fa,° by forming and transforming, joining and disjoining variously, a little bookcraft and two hours' meditation might furnish him unspeakably° to the performance of more than a weekly charge of sermoning; not to reckon up the infinite helps of interlinearies, breviaries, synopses and other loitering gear.° But as for the multitude of sermons ready printed and piled up, on every text that is not difficult, our London trading St Thomas° in his vestry, and add to boot St Martin and St Hugh, have not within their hallowed limits more vendible ware of all sorts ready made: so that penury he never need fear of pulpit provision, having where so plenteously to refresh his magazine.° But if his rear and flanks be not impaled,° if his back door be not secured by the rigid licenser but that a bold book may now and then issue forth and give the assault to some of his old collections in their trenches, it will concern him then to keep waking, to stand in watch, to set good guards and sentinels about his received opinions, to walk the round and counter-round with his fellow-inspectors, fearing lest any of his flock be seduced who also then would be better instructed, better exercised and disciplined. And God send that the fear of this diligence which must then be used do not make us affect° the laziness of a licensing church.

For if we be sure we are in the right, and do not hold the truth guiltily, which becomes not, if we ourselves condemn not our own weak and frivolous teaching, and the people for an untaught and irreligious gadding rout, what can be more fair than when a man judicious, learned, and of a conscience, for aught we know as good as theirs that taught us what we know, shall not privily from house to house, which is more dangerous, but openly by writing, publish to the world what his opinion is, what his reasons, and wherefore that which is now thought cannot be sound? Christ° urged it as wherewith to justify himself that he preached in public; yet writing is more public than preaching, and more easy

to refutation if need be, there being so many whose business and profession merely it is to be the champions of truth; which if they neglect,
what can be imputed but their sloth or inability?

Thus much we are hindered and disinured by this course of
licensing towards the true knowledge of what we seem to know. For
how much it hurts and hinders the licensers themselves in the calling of their ministry, more than any secular employment, if they will
discharge that office as they ought, so that of necessity they must
neglect either the one duty or the other, I insist not, because it is a
particular, but leave it to their own conscience how they will decide
it there.

There is yet behind of what I purposed to lay open, the incredible
loss and detriment that this plot of licensing puts us to, more than if
some enemy at sea should stop up all our havens, and ports, and creeks;
it hinders and retards the importation of our richest merchandise,
truth: nay, it was first established and put in practice by anti-Christian
malice and mystery, on set purpose to extinguish, if it were possible, the
light of reformation, and to settle falsehood; little differing from that
policy wherewith the Turk upholds his *Alcoran*° by the prohibition of
printing. 'Tis not denied, but gladly confessed, we are to send our
thanks and vows to heaven, louder than most of nations, for that great
measure of truth which we enjoy, especially in those main points
between us and the Pope, with his appurtenances the prelates: but he
who thinks we are to pitch our tent here, and have attained the utmost
prospect of reformation that the mortal glass° wherein we contemplate
can show us till we come to beatific vision, that man by this very opinion
declares that he is yet far short of truth.

Truth indeed came once into the world with her divine master, and
was a perfect shape most glorious to look on; but when he ascended,
and his apostles after him were laid asleep, then straight arose a wicked
race of deceivers, who, as that story° goes of the Egyptian Typhon with
his conspirators, how they dealt with the good Osiris, took the virgin
Truth, hewed her lovely form into a thousand pieces and scattered
them to the four winds. From that time ever since, the sad friends of
Truth, such as durst appear, imitating the careful search that Isis made
for the mangled body of Osiris, went up and down gathering up limb by
limb still as they could find them. We have not yet found them all, lords
and commons, nor ever shall do, till her master's second coming; he
shall bring together every joint and member, and shall mould them into
an immortal feature° of loveliness and perfection. Suffer not these
licensing prohibitions to stand at every place of opportunity forbidding

and disturbing them that continue seeking, that continue to do our obsequies° to the torn body of our martyred saint.

We boast our light; but if we look not wisely on the sun itself, it smites us into darkness. Who can discern those planets that are oft combust,° and those stars of brightest magnitude that rise and set with the sun, until the opposite motion of their orbs bring them to such a place in the firmament where they may be seen evening or morning? The light which we have gained was given us, not to be ever staring on, but by it to discover onward things more remote from our knowledge. It is not the unfrocking of a priest, the unmitring of a bishop and the removing him from off the presbyterian shoulders, that will make us a happy nation; no; if other things as great in the church, and in the rule of life both economical° and political, be not looked into and reformed, we have looked so long upon the blaze that Zuinglius° and Calvin have beaconed up to us, that we are stark blind.

There be who perpetually complain of schisms and sects, and make it such a calamity that any man dissents from their maxims. 'Tis their own pride and ignorance which causes the disturbing, who neither will hear with meekness, nor can convince, yet all must be suppressed which is not found in their syntagma.° They are the troublers, they are the dividers of unity, who neglect and permit not others to unite those dissevered pieces which are yet wanting to the body of Truth. To be still searching what we know not by what we know, still closing up truth to truth as we find it (for all her body is homogeneal, and proportional), this is the golden rule° in theology as well as in arithmetic, and makes up the best harmony in a church; not the forced and outward union of cold, and neutral, and inwardly divided minds.

Lords and commons of England, consider what nation it is whereof ye are, and whereof ye are the governors: a nation not slow and dull, but of a quick, ingenious and piercing spirit; acute to invent, subtle and sinewy to discourse,° not beneath the reach of any point the highest that human capacity can soar to. Therefore the studies of learning in her deepest sciences have been so ancient, and so eminent among us, that writers of good antiquity and ablest judgment have been persuaded that even the school of Pythagoras, and the Persian wisdom, took beginning from the old philosophy of this island.° And that wise and civil Roman, Julius Agricola,° who governed once here for Caesar, preferred the natural wits of Britain before the laboured studies of the French.

Nor is it for nothing that the grave and frugal Transylvanian sends out yearly from as far as the mountainous boarders of Russia, and beyond the Hyrcanian wilderness,° not their youth, but their staid men, to learn our language and our theologic arts. Yet that which is above all this, the favour and the love of heaven, we have great argument to think in a peculiar manner propitious and propending° towards us. Why else was this nation chosen before any other, that out of her, as out of Sion, should be proclaimed and sounded forth the first tidings and trumpet of reformation to all Europe? And had it not been the obstinate perverseness of our prelates against the divine and admirable spirt of Wyclif to suppress him as a schismatic and innovator, perhaps neither the Bohemian Huss and Jerome,° no, nor the name of Luther or of Calvin, had been ever known: the glory of reforming all our neighbours had been completely ours. But now, as our obdurate clergy have with violence demeaned° the matter, we are become hitherto the latest and the backwardest scholars, of whom God offered to have made us the teachers.

Now once again by all concurrence of signs, and by the general instinct of holy and devout men as they daily and solemnly express their thoughts, God is decreeing to begin some new and great period in his church, even to the reforming of reformation itself; what does he then but reveal himself to his servants, and as his manner is, first to his Englishmen? I say, as his manner is, first to us, though we mark not the method of his counsels, and are unworthy. Behold now this vast city, a city of refuge, the mansion-house° of liberty, encompassed and surrounded with his protection; the shop of war hath not there more anvils and hammers waking to fashion out the plates° and instruments of armed justice in defence of beleaguered truth, than there be pens and heads there, sitting by their studious lamps, musing, searching, revolving new notions and ideas wherewith to present, as with their homage and their fealty, the approaching reformation: others as fast° reading, trying all things, assenting to the force of reason and convincement.

What could a man require more from a nation so pliant and so prone to seek after knowledge? What wants there to such a towardly and pregnant soil but wise and faithful labourers to make a knowing people, a nation of prophets, of sages and of worthies? We reckon more than five months yet to harvest; there need not be five weeks, had we but eyes to lift up, the fields are white already.° Where there is much desire to learn, there of necessity will be much arguing, much writing, many opinions; for opinion in good men is but knowledge in the making. Under these fantastic terrors of sect and schism, we wrong the earnest and zealous thirst after knowledge and understanding which God hath stirred up in this city. What some lament of, we rather should rejoice at, should rather praise this pious forwardness among men to reassume the ill-deputed care of their religion into their own hands again. A little generous prudence, a little forbearance of one another, and some grain of charity might win all these diligencies to join and unite into one general and brotherly search after truth, could we but forego this prelatical tradition of crowding free consciences and Christian liberties into canons and precepts of men. I doubt not, if some great and worthy stranger should come among us, wise to discern the mould and temper of a people, and how to govern it, observing the high hopes and aims, the diligent alacrity of our extended thoughts and reasonings in the pursuance of truth and freedom, but that he would cry out as Pyrrhus° did, admiring the Roman docility and courage, 'If such were my Epirots, I would not despair the greatest design that could be attempted to make a church or kingdom happy.'

Yet these are the men cried out against for schismatics and sectaries, as if, while the temple of the Lord was building, some cutting, some squaring the marble, others hewing the cedars, there should be a sort of irrational men who could not consider there must be many schisms and many dissections made in the quarry and in the timber ere the house of God can be built. And when every stone is laid artfully together, it cannot be united into a continuity, it can but be contiguous in this world; neither can every piece of the building be of one form; nay, rather the perfection consists in this, that out of many moderate varieties and brotherly dissimilitudes that are not vastly disproportional arises the goodly and the graceful symmetry that commends the whole pile and structure.

Let us therefore be more considerate builders, more wise in spiritual architecture, when great reformation is expected. For now the time seems come wherein Moses, the great prophet, may sit in heaven rejoicing to see that memorable and glorious wish° of his fulfilled, when not only our seventy elders, but all the Lord's people, are become prophets. No marvel then though some men, and some good men too perhaps, but young in goodness, as Joshua then was, envy them. They fret, and out of their own weakness are in agony lest these divisions and subdivisions will undo us. The adversary again applauds, and waits the hour: when they have branched themselves out, saith he, small enough into parties and partitions, then will be our time. Fool! he sees not the firm root out of which we all grow, though into branches; nor will beware, until he see our small divided maniples° cutting through at every angle of his ill-united and unwieldy brigade. And that we are to hope better of all these supposed sects and schisms, and that we shall not need that solicitude, honest perhaps, though overtimorous, of them that vex in this behalf, but shall laugh in the end at those malicious applauders of our differences, I have these reasons to persuade me.

First, when a city shall be as it were besieged and blocked about, her navigable river infested, inroads and incursions round, defiance and battle oft rumoured to be marching up, even to her walls and suburb trenches, that then the people, or the greater part, more than at other times, wholly taken up with the study of highest and most important matters to be reformed, should be disputing, reasoning, reading, inventing, discoursing, even to a rarity and admiration,° things not before discoursed or written of, argues first a singular good will, contentedness, and confidence in your prudent foresight and safe government, lords and commons; and from thence derives° itself to a gallant bravery and well-grounded contempt of their enemies, as if there were no small number of as great spirits among us as his° was who, when Rome was nigh besieged by Hannibal, being in the city, bought that piece of ground at no cheap rate whereon Hannibal himself encamped his own regiment.

Next, it is a lively and cheerful presage of our happy success and victory. For as in a body when the blood is fresh, the spirits pure and vigorous, not only to vital, but to rational faculties, and those in the acutest and the pertest operations of wit and subtlety, it argues in what good plight and constitution the body is; so when the cheerfulness of the people is so sprightly up as that it has not only wherewith to guard well its own freedom and safety, but to spare, and to bestow upon the solidest and sublimest points of controversy and new invention, it betokens us not degenerated, nor drooping to a fatal decay, but casting off the old and wrinkled skin of corruption to outlive these pangs, and wax young again, entering the glorious ways of truth and prosperous virtue, destined to become great and honourable in these latter ages. Methinks I see in my mind a noble and puissant nation rousing herself like a strong man after sleep, and shaking her invincible locks;° methinks I see her as an eagle mewing° her mighty youth, and kindling her undazzled eyes at the full midday beam, purging and unscaling her long-abused sight at the fountain itself of heavenly radiance, while the whole noise of timorous and flocking birds, with those also that love the twilight, flutter about, amazed at what she means, and in their envious gabble° would prognosticate a year of sects and schisms.

What should ye do then, should ye suppress all this flowery crop of knowledge and new light sprung up and yet springing daily in this city, should ye set an oligarchy of twenty engrossers° over it, to bring a famine upon our minds again when we shall know nothing but what is measured to us by their bushel? Believe it, lords and commons, they who counsel ye to such a suppressing do as good as bid ye suppress yourselves; and I will soon show how. If it be desired to know the immediate cause of all this free writing and free speaking, there cannot be assigned a truer than your own mild, and free, and humane government; it is the liberty, lords and commons, which your own valorous and happy counsels have purchased us; liberty which is the nurse of all great wits: this is that which hath rarefied and enlightened our spirits like the influence of heaven; this is that which hath enfranchised, enlarged and lifted up our apprehensions degrees above themselves. Ye cannot make us now less capable, less knowing, less eagerly pursuing of the truth, unless ye first make yourselves, that made us so, less the lovers, less the founders of our true liberty. We can grow ignorant again, brutish, formal° and slavish, as ye found us; but you then must first become that which ye cannot be, oppressive, arbitrary and tyrannous, as they were from whom ye have freed us. That our hearts are now more capacious, our thoughts more erected to the search and expectation of greatest and exactest things, is the issue of your own virtue propagated in us; ye cannot suppress that unless ye reinforce an abrogated and merciless law,° that fathers may dispatch at will their own children. And who shall then stick closest to ye and excite others? Not he who takes up arms for coat and conduct,° and his four nobles° of Danegelt.° Although I dispraise not the defence of just immunities,° yet love my peace better, if that were all. Give me the liberty to know, to utter, and to argue freely according to conscience, above all liberties.

What would be best advised then, if it be found so hurtful and so unequal° to suppress opinions for the newness or the unsuitableness to a customary acceptance, will not be my task to say; I only shall repeat what I have learnt from one° of your own honourable number, a right noble and pious lord, who had he not sacrificed his life and fortunes to the church and commonwealth, we had not now missed and bewailed a worthy and undoubted patron of this argument. Ye know him, I am sure; yet I for honour's sake, and may it be eternal to him, shall name him, the Lord Brooke. He writing of episcopacy, and by the way treating of sects and schisms, left ye his vote, or rather now the last words of his dying charge, which I know will ever be of dear and honoured regard with ye, so full of meekness and breathing charity, that next to his° last testament who bequeathed love and peace to his disciples, I cannot call to mind where I have read or heard words more mild and peaceful. He there exhorts us to hear with patience and humility those, however they be miscalled, that desire to live purely, in such a use of

God's ordinances as the best guidance of their conscience gives them, and to tolerate them, though in some disconformity to ourselves. The book itself will tell us more at large, being published to the world, and dedicated to the parliament by him who both for his life and for his death deserves that what advice he left be not laid by without perusal.

And now the time in special is,° by privilege to write and speak what may help to the further discussing of matters in agitation. The temple of Janus,° with his two controversal faces, might now not unsignificantly be set open. And though all the winds of doctrine° were let loose to play upon the earth, so truth be in the field, we do injuriously by licensing and prohibiting to misdoubt her strength. Let her and falsehood grapple; who ever knew truth put to the worse in a free and open encounter? Her confuting is the best and surest suppressing. He who hears what praying there is for light and clearer knowledge to be sent down among us would think of other matters to be constituted beyond the discipline of Geneva,° framed and fabricked already to our hands.

Yet when the new light which we beg for shines in upon us, there be who envy and oppose, if it come not first in at their casements. What a collusion is this, whenas we are exhorted by the wise man to use diligence, 'to seek for wisdom as for hidden treasures',° early and late, that another order shall enjoin us to know nothing but by statute? When a man hath been labouring the hardest labour in the deep mines of knowledge, hath furnished out his findings in all their equipage, drawn forth his reasons as it were a battle° ranged, scattered and defeated all objections in his way, calls out his adversary into the plain, offers him the advantage of wind and sun if he please, only that he may try the matter by dint of argument; for his opponents then to skulk, to lay ambushments, to keep a narrow bridge of licensing where the challenger should pass, though it be valour enough in soldiership, is but weakness and cowardice in the wars of truth. For who knows not that truth is strong, next to the Almighty; she needs no policies, nor stratagems, nor licensings to make her victorious; those are the shifts and the defences that error uses against her power: give her but room, and do not bind her when she sleeps, for then she speaks not true, as the old Proteus° did, who spake oracles only when he was caught and bound, but then rather she turns herself into all shapes except her own, and perhaps tunes her voice according to the time, as Micaiah° did before Ahab, until she be adjured into her own likeness.

Yet is it not impossible that she may have more shapes than one? What else is all that rank of things indifferent, wherein truth may be on this side, or on the other, without being unlike herself? What but a vain shadow else is the abolition of 'those ordinances, that handwriting nailed to the cross'?° What great purchase is this Christian liberty° which Paul so often boasts of? His doctrine is that he who eats or eats not, regards a day or regards it not, may do either to the Lord.° How many other things might be tolerated in peace and left to conscience had we but charity, and were it not the chief stronghold of our hypocrisy to be ever judging one another? I fear yet this iron yoke of outward conformity hath left a slavish print upon our necks; the ghost of a linen decency° yet haunts us. We stumble, and are impatient at the least dividing of one visible congregation from another, though it be not in fundamentals; and through our forwardness to suppress, and our backwardness to recover, any enthralled piece of truth out of the grip of custom, we care not to keep truth separated from truth, which is the fiercest rent and disunion of all. We do not see that while we still affect by all means a rigid external formality, we may as soon fall again into a gross conforming stupidity, a stark and dead congealment of 'wood and hay and stubble'° forced and frozen together, which is more to the sudden degenerating of a church than many subdichotomies of petty schisms.

Not that I can think well of every light separation; or that all in a church is to be expected 'gold and silver, and precious stones': it is not possible for man to sever the wheat from the tares,° the good fish from the other fry; that must be the angels' ministry at the end of mortal things. Yet if all cannot be of one mind—as who looks they should be?—this doubtless is more wholesome, more prudent and more Christian, that many be tolerated rather than all compelled. I mean not tolerated Popery, and open superstition, which as it extirpates all religions and civil supremacies, so itself should be extirpate, provided first that all charitable and compassionate means be used to win and regain the weak and the misled: that also which is impious or evil absolutely either against faith or manners, no law can possibly permit that intends not to unlaw itself; but those neighbouring differences, or rather indifferences, are what I speak of, whether in some point of doctrine or of discipline, which though they may be many, yet need not interrupt 'the unity of spirit', if we could but find among us 'the bond of peace'.°

In the meanwhile, if any one would write, and bring his helpful hand to the slow-moving reformation which we labour under, if truth have spoken to him before others, or but seemed at least to speak, who hath so bejesuited us that we should trouble that man with asking licence to do so worthy a deed, and not consider this, that if it come to prohibiting, there is not aught more likely to be prohibited than truth itself:

whose first appearance to our eyes, bleared and dimmed with prejudice and custom, is more unsightly and unplausible than many errors; even as the person is of many a great man slight and contemptible to see to. And what do they tell us vainly of new opinions, when this very opinion of theirs, that none must be heard but whom they like, is the worst and newest opinion of all others, and is the chief cause why sects and schisms do so much abound, and true knowledge is kept at distance from us; besides yet a greater danger which is in it. For when God shakes° a kingdom with strong and healthful commotions to a general reforming, 'tis not untrue that many sectaries and false teachers are then busiest in seducing.

But yet more true it is that God then raises to his own work men of rare abilities and more than common industry, not only to look back and revise what hath been taught heretofore, but to gain further, and go on some new enlightened steps in the discovery of truth. For such is the order of God's enlightening his church, to dispense and deal out by degrees his beam, so as our earthly eyes may best sustain it. Neither is God appointed and confined where and out of what place these his chosen shall be first heard to speak; for he sees not as man sees, chooses not as man chooses, lest we should devote ourselves again to set places and assemblies and outward callings of men, planting our faith one while in the old Convocation House,° and another while in the chapel at Westminster, when all the faith and religion that shall be there canonized is not sufficient without plain convincement and the charity of patient instruction to supple the least bruise of conscience, to edify the meanest Christian who desires to walk in the spirit, and not in the letter of human trust, for all the number of voices that can be there made; no, though Harry the Seventh himself there, with all his liege tombs about him, should lend them voices from the dead to swell their number.

And if the men be erroneous who appear to be the leading schismatics, what withholds us but our sloth, our self-will, and distrust in the right cause, that we do not give them gentle meetings and gentle dismissions, that we debate not and examine the matter thoroughly with liberal and frequent audience; if not for their sakes yet for our own? Seeing no man who hath tasted learning but will confess the many ways of profiting by those who, not contented with stale receipts, are able to manage and set forth new positions to the world. And were they but as the dust and cinders of our feet, so long as in that notion they may yet serve to polish and brighten the armoury of truth, even for that respect they were not utterly to be cast away. But if they be of those whom God hath fitted for the special use of these times with eminent and ample gifts, and those perhaps neither among the priests nor among the Pharisees, and we, in the haste of a precipitant zeal, shall make no distinction, but resolve to stop their mouths because we fear they come with new and dangerous opinions, as we commonly forejudge them ere we understand them, no less than woe to us while, thinking thus to defend the gospel, we are found the persecutors!

There have been not a few since the beginning of this parliament, both of the presbytery and others, who by their unlicensed books to the contempt of an imprimatur first broke that triple ice clung about our hearts, and taught the people to see day; I hope that none of those were the persuaders to renew upon us this bondage, which they themselves have wrought so much good by contemning. But if neither the check that Moses° gave to young Joshua, nor the countermand which our Saviour° gave to young John, who was so ready to prohibit those whom he thought unlicensed, be not enough to admonish our elders how unacceptable to God their testy mood of prohibiting is; if neither their own remembrance what evil hath abounded in the church by this let° of licensing, and what good they themselves have begun by transgressing it, be not enough, but that they will persuade and execute the most Dominican part° of the inquisition over us, and are already with one foot in the stirrup so active at suppressing, it would be no unequal distribution in the first place to suppress the suppressors themselves, whom the change of their condition hath puffed up, more than their late experience of harder times hath made wise.

And as for regulating the press, let no man think to have the honour of advising ye better than yourselves have done in that order° published next before this, 'That no book be printed, unless the printer's and the author's name, or at least the printer's be registered'. Those which otherwise come forth, if they be found mischievous and libellous, the fire and the executioner° will be the timeliest and the most effectual remedy that man's prevention can use. For this authentic Spanish policy of licensing books, if I have said aught, will prove the most unlicensed book itself within a short while; and was the immediate image of a Star Chamber decree° to that purpose made in those very times when that court did the rest of those her pious works, for which she is now fallen from the stars with Lucifer.° Whereby ye may guess what kind of state prudence, what love of the people, what care of religion or good manners there was at the contriving, although with singular hypocrisy it pretended to bind books to their good behaviour. And how it got the upper hand of your precedent order so well constituted before, if we may believe those men whose profession gives them cause to inquire most, it may be doubted° there was in it the fraud of some old patentees and monopolizers in the trade of bookselling; who, under pretence of the poor in their company not to be defrauded, and the just retaining of each man his several copy° (which God forbid should be gainsaid), brought divers glosing colours° to the house, which were indeed but colours,° and serving to no end except it be to exercise a superiority over their neighbours; men who do not therefore labour in an honest profession to which learning is indebted, that they should be made other men's vassals. Another end is thought was aimed at by some of them in procuring by petition this order, that having power in their hands, malignant books might the easier escape abroad, as the event° shows. But of these sophisms and elenches° of merchandise I skill not: this I know, that errors in a good government and in a bad are equally almost incident;° for what magistrate may not be misinformed, and much the sooner, if liberty of printing be reduced into the power of a few? But to redress willingly and speedily what hath been erred, and in highest authority to esteem a plain advertisement° more than others have done a sumptuous bribe, is a virtue (honoured lords and commons) answerable to your highest actions, and whereof none can participate but greatest and wisest men.

The Tenure of Kings and Magistrates

PROVING THAT IT IS LAWFUL, AND HATH BEEN HELD SO THROUGH ALL AGES, FOR ANY WHO HAVE THE POWER TO CALL TO ACCOUNT A TYRANT, OR WICKED KING, AND AFTER DUE CONVICTION TO DEPOSE AND PUT HIM TO DEATH, IF THE ORDINARY MAGISTRATE HAVE NEGLECTED OR DENIED TO DO IT. AND THAT THEY WHO OF LATE SO MUCH BLAME DEPOSING, ARE THE MEN THAT DID IT THEMSELVES.

If men within themselves would be governed by reason, and not generally give up their understanding to a double tyranny of custom from without and blind affections within, they would discern better what it is to favour and uphold the tyrant of a nation. But being slaves within doors, no wonder that they strive so much to have the public state conformably governed to the inward vicious rule by which they govern themselves. For indeed, none can love freedom heartily but good men; the rest love not freedom but licence, which never hath more scope or more indulgence than under tyrants. Hence is it that tyrants are not oft offended,° nor stand much in doubt of bad men, as being all naturally servile; but in whom° virtue and true worth most is eminent, them they fear in earnest, as by right their masters; against them lies all their hatred and suspicion. Consequently, neither do bad men hate tyrants, but have been always readiest with the falsified names of loyalty and obedience to colour over their base compliances.

And although sometimes for shame, and when it comes to their own grievances, of purse especially, they would seem good patriots and side with the better cause, yet when others for the deliverance of their country, endued° with fortitude and heroic virtue to fear nothing but the curse written° against those 'that do the work of the Lord negligently', would go on to remove not only the calamities and thraldoms of a people, but the roots and causes whence they spring; straight these men,° and sure helpers at need, as if they hated only the miseries, but not the mischiefs, after they have juggled and paltered° with the world, bandied° and borne arms against their king, divested him, disanointed him, nay, cursed him all over in their pulpits and their pamphlets, to the engaging of sincere and real men beyond what is possible or honest to retreat from, not only turn revolters from those principles which only could at first move them, but lay the stain of disloyalty, and worse, on those proceedings which are the necessary consequences of their own former actions; nor disliked by themselves, were they managed to the entire advantages of their own faction;° not considering the while that he toward whom they boasted their new fidelity counted them accessory; and by those statutes and laws which they so impotently brandish against others, would have doomed them to a traitor's death for what they have done already.

'Tis true that most men are apt enough to civil wars and commotions as a novelty, and for a flash hot and active; but through sloth or inconstancy and weakness of spirit either fainting ere their own pretences, though never so just, be half attained, or through an inbred falsehood and wickedness betray, ofttimes to destruction with themselves, men of noblest temper joined with them for causes whereof they in their rash undertakings were not capable.

If God and a good cause give them victory, the prosecution whereof for the most part inevitably draws after it the alteration of laws, change of government, downfall of princes with their families, then comes the task to those worthies which are the soul of that enterprise to be sweat and laboured out amidst the throng and noises of vulgar and irrational men. Some contesting for privileges, customs, forms, and that old entanglement of iniquity, their gibberish laws, though the badge of their ancient slavery. Others who have been fiercest against their prince, under the notion of a tyrant, and no mean incendiaries of the war against him, when God, out of his providence and high disposal, hath delivered him into the hand of their brethren, on a sudden and in a new garb of allegiance, which their doings have long since cancelled, they plead for him, pity him, extol him, protest against those that talk of bringing him to the trial of justice, which is the sword of God, superior to all mortal things, in whose hand soever by apparent signs his testified will is to put it.

But certainly if we consider who and what they are, on a sudden grown so pitiful, we may conclude their pity can be no true and Christian commiseration, but either levity and shallowness of mind or else a carnal admiring of that worldly pomp and greatness from whence they see him fallen; or rather, lastly, a dissembled and seditious pity, feigned of industry° to beget new discord. As for mercy, if it be to a tyrant, under which name they themselves have cited him so oft in the hearing of God, of angels and the holy church assembled, and there charged him with the spilling of more innocent blood by far than ever Nero did, undoubtedly the mercy which they pretend is the mercy of wicked men; and 'their mercies', we read,° 'are cruelties'; hazarding the welfare of a whole nation to have saved one whom so oft they have termed Agag,° and vilifying the blood of many Jonathans° that have saved Israel; insisting with much niceness° on the unnecessariest clause° of their covenant wrested,° wherein the fear of change and the absurd contradiction of a flattering hostility had hampered them, but not scrupling to give away for compliments,° to an implacable revenge, the heads of many thousand Christians more.

Another sort there is who, coming in the course of these affairs to have their share in great actions above the form of law or custom, at least to give their voice° and approbation, begin to swerve and almost shiver at the majesty and grandeur of some noble deed, as if they were newly entered into a great sin, disputing precedents, forms and circumstances, when the commonwealth nigh perishes for want of deeds in substance done with just and faithful expedition. To these I wish better instruction and virtue equal to their calling; the former of which, that is to say instruction, I shall endeavour, as my duty is, to bestow on them; and exhort them not to startle° from the just and pious resolution of adhering with all their strength and assistance to the present parliament and army in the glorious way wherein justice and victory hath set them—the only warrants through all ages, next under immediate revelation, to exercise supreme power—in those proceedings, which hitherto appear equal to what hath been done in any age or nation heretofore justly or magnanimously.

Nor let them be discouraged or deterred by any new apostate scarecrows who, under show of giving counsel, send out their barking monitories and mementoes,° empty of aught else but the spleen of a frustrated faction. For how can that pretended counsel be either sound or faithful when they that give it see not, for madness and vexation of their ends lost, that those statutes and scriptures which both falsely and scandalously they wrest against their friends and associates would, by sentence of the common adversary, fall first and heaviest upon their own heads? Neither let mild and tender dispositions be foolishly softened from their duty and perseverance with the unmasculine rhetoric of any puling priest or chaplain sent as a friendly letter of advice, for fashion sake in private, and forthwith published by the sender himself, that we may know how much of friend there was in it, to cast an odious envy° upon them to whom it was pretended to be sent in charity. Nor let any man be deluded by either the ignorance or the notorious hypocrisy and self-repugnance of our dancing divines, who have the conscience and the boldness to come with Scripture in their mouths glossed and fitted for their turns with a double contradictory sense, transforming the sacred verity of God to an idol with two faces looking at once two several ways, and with the same quotations to charge others, which in the same case they made serve to justify themselves. For while the hope to be made classic and provincial° lords led them on, while pluralities° greased them thick and deep, to the shame and scandal of religion, more than all the sects and heresies they exclaim against; then to fight against the king's person and no less a party of his Lords and Commons, or to put force upon both the houses, was good, was lawful, was no resisting of superior powers; they only were powers not to be resisted who countenanced the good and punished the evil.

But now that their censorious domineering is not suffered to be universal, truth and conscience to be freed, tithes and pluralities to be no more, though competent allowance provided, and the warm experience of large gifts, and they so good at taking them; yet now to exclude and seize upon impeached members,° to bring delinquents without exemption to a fair tribunal by the common national law against murder, is now to be no less than Korah, Dathan, and Abiram.° He who but erewhile in the pulpits was a cursed tyrant, an enemy to God and saints, laden with all the innocent blood spilt in three kingdoms, and so to be fought against, is now, though nothing penitent or altered from his first principles, a lawful magistrate, a sovereign lord, the Lord's anointed, not to be touched, though by themselves imprisoned. As if this only were obedience, to preserve the mere useless bulk of his person, and that only in prison, not in the field, and to disobey his commands, deny him his dignity and office, everywhere to resist his power but where they think it only surviving in their own faction.

But who in particular is a tyrant cannot be determined in a general discourse otherwise than by supposition; his particular charge, and the sufficient proof of it, must determine that: which I leave to magistrates, at least to the uprighter sort of them, and of the people, though in number less by many, in whom faction least hath prevailed above the law of nature and right reason, to judge as they find cause. But this I dare own as part of my faith, that if such a one° there be by whose commission whole massacres have been committed on his faithful subjects, his provinces offered to pawn or alienation as the hire of those whom he had solicited to come in and destroy whole cities and countries, be he king, or tyrant, or emperor, the sword of justice is above him, in whose hand soever is found sufficient power to avenge the effusion and so great a deluge of innocent blood. For if all human power to execute, not accidentally but intendedly, the wrath of God upon evildoers without exception, be of God, then that power, whether ordinary, or if that fail, extraordinary, so executing that intent of God is lawful and not to be resisted.° But to unfold more at large this whole question, though with all expedient brevity, I shall here set down, from first beginning, the original of kings, how and wherefore exalted to that dignity above their brethren; and from thence shall prove that turning to tyranny they may be as lawfully deposed and punished as they were at first elected: this I shall do by authorities and reasons not learnt in corners among schisms and heresies, as our doubling° divines are ready to calumniate, but fetched out of the midst of choicest and most authentic learning, and no prohibited authors nor many heathen, but Mosaical, Christian, orthodoxal and, which must needs be more convincing to our adversaries, presbyterial.

No man who knows aught can be so stupid to deny that all men naturally were born free, being the image and resemblance of God himself, and were, by privilege above all the creatures, born to command° and not to obey, and that they lived so—till from the root of Adam's transgression falling among themselves to do wrong and violence, and foreseeing that such courses must needs tend to the destruction of them all, they agreed by common league to bind each other from mutual injury and jointly to defend themselves against any that gave disturbance or opposition to such agreement. Hence came cities, towns and commonwealths. And because no faith in all was found sufficiently binding, they saw it needful to ordain some authority that might restrain by force and punishment what was violated against peace and common right.

This authority and power of self-defence and preservation being originally and naturally in every one of them, and unitedly in them all, for ease, for order, and lest each man should be his own partial° judge, they communicated and derived either to one whom for the eminence of his wisdom and integrity they chose above the rest, or to more than one, whom they thought of equal deserving: the first was called a king; the other, magistrates: not to be their lords and masters (though afterward those names in some places were given voluntarily to such as have been authors of inestimable good to the people) but to be their deputies and commissioners, to execute, by virtue of their entrusted power, that justice which else every man by the bond of nature and of covenant must have executed for himself and for one another. And to him that shall consider well why among free persons one man by civil right should bear authority and jurisdiction over another, no other end or reason can be imaginable.

These for awhile governed well, and with much equity decided all things at their own arbitrement, till the temptation of such a power left absolute in their hands perverted them at length to injustice and partiality. Then did they who now by trial had found the danger and inconveniences of committing arbitrary power to any invent laws, either framed or consented to by all, that should confine and limit the authority of whom they chose to govern them: that so man, of whose failing they had proof, might no more rule over them, but law and reason, abstracted as much as might be from personal errors and frailties. While as the magistrate was set above the people, so the law was set above the magistrate. When this would not serve, but that the law was either not executed, or misapplied, they were constrained from that time, the only remedy left them, to put conditions and take oaths from all kings and magistrates at their first instalment to do impartial justice by law: who, upon those terms and no other, received allegiance from the people, that is to say, bond or covenant to obey them in execution of those laws which they, the people, had themselves made or assented to. And this ofttimes with express warning, that if the king or magistrate proved unfaithful to his trust, the people would be disengaged. They added also councillors and parliaments, nor to be only at his beck, but, with him or without him, at set times, or at all times when any danger threatened, to have care of the public safety. Therefore saith Claudius Sesell,° a French statesman, 'the parliament was set as a bridle to the king'; which I instance rather, not because our English lawyers have not said the same long before, but because that French monarchy is granted by all to be a far more absolute than ours. That this and the rest of what hath hitherto been spoken is most true might be copiously made appear throughout all stories,° heathen and Christian, even of those nations where kings and emperors have sought means to abolish all ancient memory of the people's right by their encroachments and usurpations. But I spare long insertions, appealing to the known constitutions of both the latest Christian empires in Europe, the Greek and German, besides the French, Italian, Aragonian, English, and not least the Scottish histories: not forgetting this only by the way, that William the Norman, though a conqueror,° and not unsworn at his coronation, was compelled a second time to take oath at St Albans ere the people would be brought to yield obedience.

It being thus manifest that the power of kings and magistrates is nothing else but what is only derivative, transferred, and committed to them in trust from the people to the common good of them all, in whom the power yet remains fundamentally, and cannot be taken from them without a violation of their natural birthright; and seeing that from hence Aristotle° and the best of political writers have defined a king him who governs to the good and profit of his people, and not for his own ends, it follows from necessary causes that the titles of sovereign lord, natural lord and the like, are either arrogancies or flatteries, not admitted by emperors and kings of best note, and disliked by the church both of Jews, Isa. 26: 13,° and ancient Christians, as appears by Tertullian° and others. Although generally the people of Asia, and with them the Jews also, especially since the time they chose a king° against the advice and counsel of God, are noted by wise authors much inclinable to slavery.

Secondly, that to say, as is usual, the king hath as good right to his crown and dignity as any man to his inheritance, is to make the subject no better than the king's slave, his chattel, or his possession that may be bought and sold; and doubtless if hereditary title were sufficiently inquired, the best foundation of it would be found either but in courtesy or convenience. But suppose it to be of right hereditary, what can be more just and legal, if a subject for certain crimes be to forfeit by law from himself and posterity all his inheritance to the king, than that a king, for crimes proportional,° should forfeit all his title and inheritance to the people? Unless the people must be thought created all for him, he not for them, and they all in one body inferior to him single; which were a kind of treason against the dignity of mankind to affirm.

Thirdly, it follows that to say kings are accountable to none but God is the overturning of all law and government. For if they may refuse to give account, then all covenants made with them at coronation, all oaths are in vain and mere mockeries, all laws which they swear to keep made to no purpose; for if the king fear not God (as how many of them do not), we hold then our lives and estates by the tenure of his mere grace and mercy, as from a god, not a mortal magistrate—a position that none but court parasites or men besotted would maintain. Aristotle, therefore, whom we commonly allow for one of the best interpreters of nature and morality, writes in the fourth of his *Politics*, chap. 10, that monarchy unaccountable is the worst sort of tyranny, and least of all to be endured by free-born men.

And surely no Christian prince not drunk with high mind and prouder than those pagan Caesars that deified themselves would arrogate so unreasonably above human condition, or derogate so basely from a whole nation of men, his brethren, as if for him only subsisting, and to serve his glory, valuing them in comparison of his own brute will and pleasure no more than so many beasts, or vermin under his feet, not to be reasoned with, but to be trod on; among whom there might be found so many thousand men for wisdom, virtue, nobleness of mind, and all other respects but the fortune of his dignity, far above him. Yet some would persuade us that this absurd opinion was King David's, because in the 51st Psalm° he cries out to God, 'Against thee only have I sinned'; as if David had imagined that to murder Uriah° and adulterate his wife had been no sin against his neighbour, whenas that law of Moses was to the king expressly, Deut. 17,° not to think so highly of himself above his brethren. David, therefore, by those words could mean no other than either that the depth of his guiltiness was known to God only, or to so few as had not the will or power to question him, or that the sin against God was greater beyond compare than against Uriah. Whatever his meaning were, any wise man will see that the pathetical° words of a psalm can be no certain decision to a point that hath abundantly more certain rules to go by.

How much more rationally spake the heathen king Demophoön in a tragedy of Euripides° than these interpreters would put upon King David: 'I rule not my people by tyranny, as if they were barbarians; but am myself liable, if I do unjustly, to suffer justly.' Not unlike was the speech of Trajan,° the worthy emperor, to one whom he made general of his praetorian forces: 'Take this drawn sword', saith he, 'to use for me if I reign well; if not, to use against me.' Thus Dion relates. And not Trajan only, but Theodosius° the younger, a Christian emperor, and one of the best, caused it to be enacted as a rule undeniable and fit to be acknowledged by all kings and emperors that a prince is bound to the laws; that on the authority of law the authority of a prince depends, and to the laws ought submit. Which edict of his remains yet in the *Code of Justinian,*° *l.*° 1. *tit.* 24, as a sacred constitution to all the succeeding emperors. How then can any king in Europe maintain and write himself accountable to none but God, when emperors in their own imperial statutes have written and decreed themselves accountable to law? And indeed where such account is not feared, he° that bids a man reign over him above law may bid as well a savage beast.

It follows, lastly, that since the king or magistrate holds his authority of the people, both originally and naturally for their good in the first place, and not his own, then may the people, as oft as they shall judge it for the best, either choose him or reject him, retain him or depose him, though no tyrant, merely by the liberty and right of free-born men to be governed as seems to them best. This, though it cannot but stand with plain reason, shall be made good also by Scripture: Deut. 17: 14: 'When thou art come into the land which the Lord thy God giveth thee, and shalt say, I will set a king over me, like as all the nations about me.' These words confirm us that the right of choosing, yea of changing their own government, is by the grant of God himself in the people. And therefore when they desired a king, though then under another form of government, and though their changing displeased him, yet he that was himself their king, and rejected by them, would not be a hindrance to what they intended, further than by persuasion, but that they might do therein as they saw good, 1 Sam. 8, only he reserved to himself the nomination of who should reign over them. Neither did that exempt the king, as if he were to God only accountable, though by his especial command anointed. Therefore 'David first made a covenant with the elders of Israel, and so was by them anointed king,' 2 Sam. 5: 3; 1 Chron. 11. And Jehoiada the priest, making Jehoash king, made a covenant between him and the people, 2 Kings, 11: 17. Therefore when Rehoboam,° at his coming to the crown, rejected those conditions which the Israelites brought him, hear what they answer him: 'What portion have we in David, or inheritance in the son of Jesse? See to thine own house, David.' And for the like conditions not performed, all Israel before that time deposed Samuel;° not for his own default, but for the misgovernment of his sons.

But some will say to both these examples, it was evilly done. I answer that not the latter, because it was expressly allowed them in the law to set up a king if they pleased, and God himself joined with them in the work, though in some sort it was at that time displeasing to him, in respect of old Samuel, who had governed them uprightly. As Livy° praises the Romans who took occasion from Tarquinius, a wicked prince, to gain their liberty, which to have extorted, saith he, from Numa,° or any of the good kings before, had not been seasonable. Nor was it in the former example done unlawfully; for when Rehoboam had prepared a huge army to reduce the Israelites, he was forbidden by the prophet, 1 Kings, 12: 24: 'Thus saith the Lord, ye shall not go up, nor fight against your brethren, for this thing is from me.' He calls them their brethren, not rebels, and forbids to be proceeded against them, owning the thing himself, not by single providence, but by approbation, and that not only of the act, as in the former example, but of the fit season also; he had not otherwise forbid to molest them. And those grave and wise counsellors whom Rehoboam first advised with spake no such thing as our old grey-headed flatterers now are wont—stand upon your birthright, scorn to capitulate; you hold of God, not of them—for they knew no such matter, unless conditionally, but gave him politic counsel, as in a civil transaction.

Therefore kingdom and magistracy, whether supreme or subordinate, is without difference called 'a human ordinance', 1 Pet. 2: 13,° etc., which we are there taught is the will of God we should alike submit to, so far as for the punishment of evildoers and the encouragement of them that do well. 'Submit', saith he, 'as free men.' But to any civil power unaccountable, unquestionable and not to be resisted, no, not in wickedness and violent actions, how can we submit as free men? 'There is no power but of God', saith Paul; Rom. 13;° as much as to say, God put it into man's heart to find out that way at first for common peace and preservation, approving the exercise thereof; else° it contradicts Peter, who calls the same authority an ordinance of man. It must be also understood of lawful and just power, else we read of great power in the affairs and kingdoms of the world permitted to the devil: for saith he° to Christ, Luke 4: 6, 'All this power will I give thee, and the glory of them, for it is delivered to me, and to whomsoever I will, I give it': neither did he lie, or Christ gainsay what he affirmed; for in the thirteenth of the Revelation,° we read how the dragon gave to the beast his power, his seat and great authority: which beast so authorized most expound to be the tyrannical powers and kingdoms of the earth. Therefore St Paul in the fore-cited chapter tells us that such magistrates he means as are not a terror to the good, but to the evil; such as bear not the sword in vain, but to punish offenders and to encourage the good.

If such only be mentioned here as powers to be obeyed, and our sub-mission to them only required, then doubtless those powers that do the contrary are no powers ordained of God; and by consequence no obliga-tion laid upon us to obey or not to resist them. And it may be well observed that both these apostles, whenever they give this precept, express it in terms not concrete, but abstract,° as logicians are wont to speak; that is, they mention the ordinance, the power, the authority, before the persons that execute it; and what that power is, lest we should be deceived, they describe exactly. So that if the power be not such, or the person execute not such power, neither the one nor the other is of God, but of the devil, and by consequence to be resisted. From this exposition Chrysostom° also, on the same place, dissents not, explaining that these words were not written in behalf of a tyrant. And this is verified by David, himself a king, and likeliest to be author of the Psalm 94: 20, which saith, 'Shall the throne of iniquity have fellowship with thee?' And it were worth the knowing, since kings in these days, and that by Scripture, boast the justness of their title by holding it immediately of God,° yet cannot show the time when God ever set on the throne them or their forefathers, but only when the people chose them; why by the same reason, since God ascribes as oft to himself the casting down of princes from the throne, it should not be thought as lawful, and as much from God, when none are seen to do it but the people, and that for just causes. For if it needs must be a sin in them to depose, it may as likely be a sin to have elected. And contrary, if the people's act in election be pleaded by a king as the act of God, and the most just title to enthrone him, why may not the people's act of rejec-tion be as well pleaded by the people as the act of God, and the most just reason to depose him? So that we see the title and just right of reigning or deposing, in reference to God, is found in Scripture to be all one; visible only in the people, and depending merely upon justice and demerit.° Thus far hath been considered briefly the power of kings and magistrates; how it was and is originally the people's, and by them conferred in trust only to be employed to the common peace and bene-fit; with liberty therefore and right remaining in them to reassume it to themselves if by kings or magistrates it be abused, or to dispose of it by any alteration, as they shall judge most conducing to the public good.

We may from hence with more ease and force of argument deter-mine what a tyrant is and what the people may do against him. A tyrant, whether by wrong or by right coming to the crown, is he who, regarding neither law nor the common good, reigns only for himself and his faction: thus St Basil,° among others, defines him. And because his power is great, his will boundless and exorbitant, the fulfilling whereof is for the most part accompanied with innumerable wrongs and oppressions of the people, murders, massacres, rapes, adulteries, desolation and subversion of cities and whole provinces, look° how great a good and happiness a just king is, so great a mischief is a tyrant; as he the public father of his country, so this the common enemy. Against whom what the people lawfully may do, as against a common pest and destroyer of mankind, I suppose no man of clear judgment need go further to be guided than by the very principles of nature in him.

But because it is the vulgar folly of men to desert their own reason, and shutting their eyes, to think they see best with other men's, I shall show by such examples as ought to have most weight with us what hath been done in this case heretofore. The Greeks and Romans, as their prime authors witness, held it not only lawful, but a glorious and heroic deed, rewarded publicly with statues and garlands, to kill an infamous tyrant at any time without trial; and but reason that he who trod down all law should not be vouchsafed the benefit of law. Insomuch that Seneca the tragedian brings in Hercules,° the grand suppressor of tyrants, thus speaking:

> ———— Victima haud ulla amplior
> Potest, magisque opima mactari Jovi
> Quam rex iniquus
>
> ———— There can be slain
> No sacrifice to God more acceptable
> Than an unjust and wicked king.

But of these I name no more, lest it be objected they were heathen; and come to produce another sort of men, that had the knowledge of true religion. Among the Jews this custom of tyrant-killing was not unusual. First Ehud,° a man whom God had raised to deliver Israel from Eglon king of Moab, who had conquered and ruled over them eighteen years, being sent to him as an ambassador with a present, slew him in his own house. But he was a foreign prince, an enemy, and Ehud besides had special warrant from God. To the first I answer, it imports not whether foreign or native: for no prince so native but professes to hold by law; which when he himself overturns, breaking all the covenants and oaths that gave him title to his dignity, and were the bond and alliance between him and his people, what differs he from an outlandish° king or from an enemy?

For look how much right the king of Spain hath to govern us at all, so much right hath the king of England to govern us tyrannically. If he, though not bound to us by any league, coming from Spain in person to subdue us or to destroy us, might lawfully by the people of England either be slain in fight or put to death in captivity, what hath a native king to plead, bound by so many covenants, benefits and honours to the welfare of his people; why he through the contempt of all laws and parliaments, the only tie of our obedience to him, for his own will's sake, and a boasted prerogative unaccountable, after seven years' warring and destroying of his best subjects, overcome and yielded prisoner, should think to scape unquestionable, as a thing divine, in respect of whom so many thousand Christians destroyed should lie unaccounted for, polluting with their slaughtered carcasses all the land over, and crying for vengeance against the living that should have righted them? Who knows not that there is a mutual bond of amity and brotherhood between man and man over all the world, neither is it the English sea that can sever us from that duty and relation: a straiter bond yet there is between fellow subjects, neighbours and friends. But when any of these do one to another so as hostility could do no worse, what doth the law decree less against them than open enemies and invaders? or if the law be not present or too weak, what doth it warrant us to less than single defence or civil war? and from that time forward the law of civil defensive war differs nothing from the law of foreign hostility. Nor is it distance of place that makes enmity, but enmity that makes distance. He, therefore, that keeps peace with me, near or remote, of whatsoever nation, is to me, as far as all civil and human offices, an Englishman and a neighbour: but if an Englishman, forgetting all laws, human, civil and religious, offend against life and liberty, to him offended, and to the law in his behalf, through born in the same womb, he is no better than a Turk, a Saracen, a heathen.

This is gospel, and this was ever law among equals; how much rather than in force against any king whatever who in respect of the people is confessed inferior and not equal: to distinguish, therefore, of a tyrant by outlandish or domestic is a weak evasion. To the second,° that he was an enemy, I answer, what tyrant is not? yet Eglon by the Jews had been acknowledged as their sovereign, they had served him eighteen years, as long almost as we our William the Conqueror, in all which time he could not be so unwise a statesman but to have taken of them oaths of fealty and allegiance, by which they made themselves his proper subjects, as their homage and present sent by Ehud testified. To the third, that he had special warrant to kill Eglon in that manner, it cannot be granted, because not expressed; 'tis plain that he was raised by God to be a deliverer, and went on just principles, such as were then and ever held allowable, to deal so by a tyrant that could no otherwise be dealt with.

Neither did Samuel, though a prophet, with his own hand abstain from Agag;° a foreign enemy no doubt; but mark the reason: 'As thy sword hath made women childless'—a cause that by the sentence of law itself nullifies all relations. And as the law is between brother and brother, father and son, master and servant, wherefore not between king, or rather tyrant, and people? And whereas Jehu° had special command to slay Jehoram, a successive and hereditary tyrant, it seems not the less imitable for that; for where a thing grounded so much on natural reason hath the addition of a command from God, what does it but establish the lawfulness of such an act? Nor is it likely that God, who had so many ways of punishing the house of Ahab, would have sent a subject against his prince, if the fact in itself, as done to a tyrant, had been of bad example. And if David refused to lift his hand against the Lord's anointed,° the matter between them was not tyranny, but private enmity; and David, as a private person, had been his own revenger, not so much the people's: but when any tyrant at this day can show to be the Lord's anointed (the only mentioned reason why David withheld his hand) he may then, but not till then, presume on the same privilege.

We may pass, therefore, hence to Christian times. And first, our Saviour himself, how much he favoured tyrants, and how much intended they should be found or honoured among Christians, declares his mind not obscurely, accounting their absolute authority no better than Gentilism, yea, though they flourished it over with the splendid name of benefactors;° charging those that would be his disciples to usurp no such dominion, but that they who were to be of most authority among them should esteem themselves ministers and servants to the public, Matt. 20: 25: 'The princes of the Gentiles exercise lordship over them'; and Mark 10: 42: 'They that seem to rule', saith he, either slighting or accounting them no lawful rulers; 'but ye shall not be so, but the greatest among you shall be your servant.' And although he himself were the meekest, and came on earth to be so, yet to a tyrant we hear him not vouchsafe an humble word, but 'Tell that fox,' Luke 13.° So far we ought to be from thinking that Christ and his gospel should be made a sanctuary for tyrants from justice, to whom his law before never gave such protection. And wherefore did his mother, the Virgin Mary,° give such praise to God in her prophetic song that he had now, by the coming of Christ, cut down dynastas, or proud monarchs, from the throne, if the church, when God manifests his power in them to do so, should rather choose all misery and vassalage to serve them, and let them still sit on their potent seats to be adored for doing mischief?

Surely it is not for nothing that tyrants by a kind of natural instinct both hate and fear none more than the true church and saints of God, as the most dangerous enemies and subverters of monarchy, though indeed of tyranny; hath not this been the perpetual cry of courtiers and court prelates? whereof no likelier cause can be alleged, but that they well discerned the mind and principles of most devout and zealous men, and indeed the very discipline of church, tending to the dissolution of all tyranny. No marvel then if since the faith of Christ received, in purer or impurer times, to depose a king and put him to death for tyranny hath been accounted so just and requisite that neighbour kings have both upheld and taken part with subjects in the action. And Ludovicus Pius,° himself an emperor, and son of Charles the Great,° being made judge (du Haillan° is my author) between Milegast, king of the Vultzes, and his subjects, who had deposed him, gave his verdict for the subjects, and for him whom they had chosen in his room.° Note here that the right of electing whom they please is, by the impartial testimony of an emperor, in the people: for, said he, 'a just prince ought to be preferred before an unjust, and the end of government before the prerogative.'

And Constantinus Leo,° another emperor, in the Byzantine laws, saith 'that the end of a king is for the general good, which he not performing, is but the counterfeit of a king.' And to prove that some of our own monarchs have acknowledged that their high office exempted them not from punishment, they had the sword of St Edward borne before them by an officer who was called Earl of the Palace, even at the times of their highest pomp and solemnities, to mind them, saith Matthew Paris,° the best of our historians, 'that if they erred, the sword had power to restrain them.' And what restraint the sword comes to at length, having both edge and point, if any sceptic will doubt, let him feel. It is also affirmed from diligent search made in our ancient books of law that the peers and barons of England had a legal right to judge the king, which was the cause most likely (for it could be no slight cause) that they were called his peers, or equals. This, however, may stand immoveable, so long as man hath to deal with no better than man; that if our law judge all men to the lowest by their peers, it should, in all equity, ascend also, and judge the highest.

And so much I find both in our own and foreign story, that dukes, earls and marquisses were at first not hereditary, not empty and vain titles, but names of trust and office, and with the office ceasing; as induces me to be of opinion that every worthy man in parliament (for the word baron° imports no more) might for the public good be thought a fit peer and judge of the king, without regard had to petty caveats and circumstances, the chief impediment in high affairs, and ever stood upon most by circumstantial° men. Whence doubtless our ancestors who were not ignorant with what rights either nature or ancient constitution had endowed them, when oaths both at coronation and renewed in parliament would not serve, thought it no way illegal to depose and put to death their tyrannous kings. Insomuch that the parliament drew up a charge against Richard II, and the Commons requested to have judgment decreed against him, that the realm might not be endangered. And Peter Martyr,° a divine of foremost rank, on the third of Judges approves their doings. Sir Thomas Smith° also, a Protestant and a statesman, in his *Commonwealth of England*, putting the question whether it be lawful to rise against a tyrant, answers that the vulgar judge of it according to the event, and the learned according to the purpose of them that do it.

But far before these days, Gildas,° the most ancient of all our historians, speaking of those times wherein the Roman empire decaying quitted and relinquished what right they had by conquest to this island and resigned it all into the people's hands, testifies that the people thus reinvested with their own original right, about the year 446, both elected them kings whom they thought best (the first Christian British kings that ever reigned here since the Romans), and by the same right, when they apprehended cause, usually deposed and put them to death. This is the most fundamental and ancient tenure that any king of England can produce or pretend to, in comparison of which all other titles and pleas are but of yesterday. If any object that Gildas condemns the Britons for so doing, the answer is as ready: that he condemns them no more for so doing than he did before for choosing such; for, saith he, 'they anointed them kings not of God, but such as were more bloody than the rest.' Next, he condemns them not at all for deposing or putting them to death, but for doing it over hastily, without trial or well examining the cause, and for electing others worse in their room.°

Thus we have here both domestic and most ancient examples that the people of Britain have deposed and put to death their kings in those primitive Christian times. And to couple reason with example, if the church in all ages, primitive, Romish or Protestant, held it ever no less their duty than the power of their keys,° though without express warrant of Scripture, to bring indifferently° both king and peasant under the utmost rigour of their canons and censures ecclesiastical, even to the smiting him with a final excommunion if he persist impenitent, what hinders but that the temporal law both may and ought, though without a special text or precedent, extend with like indifference the civil sword to the cutting off, without exemption, him that capitally offends— seeing that justice and religion are from the same God, and works of justice ofttimes more acceptable? Yet because that some lately, with the tongues and arguments of malignant backsliders, have written that the proceedings now in parliament against the king are without precedent from any Protestant state or kingdom, the examples which follow shall be all Protestant, and chiefly Presbyterian.

In the year 1546 the Duke of Saxony, Landgrave of Hesse and the whole Protestant League raised open war against Charles the Fifth, their emperor, sent him a defiance, renounced all faith and allegiance toward him, and debated long in council whether they should give him so much as the title of Caesar. Sleidan° l. 17. Let all men judge what this wanted of deposing or of killing, but the power to do it.

In the year 1559 the Scots Protestants claiming promise of their queen-regent° for liberty of conscience, she answering that promises were not to be claimed of princes beyond what was commodious for them to grant, told her to her face in the parliament then at Stirling that if it were so, they renounced their obedience; and soon after betook them to arms. Buchanan° Hist. l. 16. Certainly when allegiance is renounced, that very hour the king or queen is in effect deposed.

In the year 1564 John Knox,° a most famous divine, and the reformer of Scotland to the Presbyterian discipline, at a general assembly maintained openly, in a dispute against Lethington,° the Secretary of State, that subjects might and ought to execute God's judgments upon their king; that the fact° of Jehu and others against their king having the ground of God's ordinary command to put such and such offenders to death was not extraordinary, but to be imitated of all that preferred the honour of God to the affection° of flesh and wicked princes; that kings, if they offend, have no privilege to be exempted from the punishments of law more than any other subject; so that if the king be a murderer, adulterer or idolater, he should suffer, not as a king, but as an offender; and this position he repeats again and again before them. Answerable° was the opinion of John Craig,° another learned divine, and that laws made by the tyranny of princes or the negligence of people, their posterity might abrogate and reform all things according to the original institution of commonwealths. And Knox being commanded by the nobility to write to Calvin and other learned men for their judgments in that question, refused, alleging that both himself was fully resolved in conscience, and had heard their judgments, and had the same opinion under handwriting of many the most godly and most learned that he knew in Europe; that if he should move the question to them again, what should he do but show his own forgetfulness or inconstancy? All this is far more largely in the *Ecclesiastical History of Scotland*,° *l.* 4, with many other passages to this effect all the book over, set out with diligence by Scotchmen of best repute among them at the beginning of these troubles, as if they laboured to inform us what we were to do, and what they intended upon the like occasion.

And to let the world know that the whole church and Protestant state of Scotland in those purest times of reformation were of the same belief, three years after, they met in the field Mary their lawful and hereditary queen, took her prisoner, yielding before fight, kept her in prison, and the same year° deposed her. (Buchanan, *Hist. l.* 18.)

And four years after that the Scots, in justification of their deposing Queen Mary, sent ambassadors to Queen Elizabeth, and in a written declaration alleged that they had used towards her more lenity than she deserved; that their ancestors had heretofore punished their kings by death or banishment; that the Scots were a free nation, made king whom they freely chose and with the same freedom unkinged him if they saw cause, by right of ancient laws and ceremonies yet remaining, and old customs yet among the highlanders in choosing the head of their clans or families; all which, with many other arguments, bore witness that regal power was nothing else but a mutual covenant or stipulation between king and people. (Buchanan, *Hist. l.* 20.) These were Scotchmen and Presbyterians: but what measure then have they lately offered, to think such liberty less beseeming us than themselves, presuming to put him upon us for a master whom their law scarce allows to be their own equal? If now, then, we hear them in another strain than heretofore in the purest times of their church, we may be confident it is the voice of faction speaking in them, not of truth and reformation. Which no less in England than in Scotland, by the mouths of those faithful witnesses commonly called Puritans and Nonconformists, spake as clearly for the putting down, yea, the utmost punishing of kings, as in their several treatises may be read; even from the first reign of Elizabeth to these times. Insomuch that one of them, whose name was Gibson,° foretold King James he should be rooted out and conclude his race if he persisted to uphold bishops. And that very inscription stamped upon the first coins at his coronation,° a naked sword in a hand with these words, '*Si mereor in me*', 'Against me, if I deserve', not only manifested the judgment of that state, but seemed also to presage the sentence of divine justice in this event upon his son.

In the year 1581 the states of Holland, in a general assembly at the Hague, abjured all obedience and subjection to Philip king of Spain, and in a declaration justify their so doing, for that by his tyrannous government, against faith so many times given and broken, he had lost his right to all the Belgic provinces; that therefore they deposed him, and declared it lawful to choose another in his stead. Thuan.° *l.* 74. From that time to this, no state or kingdom in the world hath equally prospered: but let them remember not to look with an evil and prejudicial eye° upon their neighbours walking by the same rule.

But what need these examples to Presbyterians, I mean to those who now of late would seem so much to abhor deposing, whenas they to all Christendom have given the latest and the liveliest example of doing it themselves? I question not the lawfulness of raising war against a tyrant in defence of religion or civil liberty; for no Protestant church, from the first Waldenses° of Lyons and Languedoc to this day, but have done it round° and maintained it lawful. But this I doubt° not to affirm, that the Presbyterians who now so much condemn deposing were the men themselves that deposed the king, and cannot with all their shifting and relapsing wash off the guiltiness from their own hands. For they themselves, by these their late doings, have made it guiltiness, and turned their own warrantable actions into rebellion.

There is nothing that so actually makes a king of England as rightful possession and supremacy in all causes both civil and ecclesiastical: and nothing that so actually makes a subject of England as those two oaths° of allegiance and supremacy observed without equivocating or any mental reservation. Out of doubt, then, when the king shall command things already constituted in church or state, obedience is the true essence of a subject, either to do, if it be lawful, or if he hold the thing unlawful, to submit to that penalty which the law imposes, so long as he intends to remain a subject. Therefore when the people, or any part of them, shall rise against the king and his authority, executing the law in anything established, civil or ecclesiastical, I do not say it is rebellion if the thing commanded, though established, be unlawful, and that they sought first all due means of redress (and no man is further bound to law); but I say it is an absolute renouncing both of supremacy and allegiance, which, in one word, is an actual and total deposing of the king, and the setting up of another supreme authority over them.

And whether the Presbyterians have not done all this and much more, they will not put me, I suppose, to reckon up a seven years'° story fresh in the memory of all men. Have they not utterly broke the oath of allegiance, rejecting the king's command and authority sent them from any part of the kingdom, whether in things lawful or unlawful? Have they not abjured the oath of supremacy by setting up the parliament without the king, supreme to all their obedience; and though their vow and covenant bound them in general to the parliament, yet sometimes° adhering to the lesser part of Lords and Commons that remained faithful, as they term it, and even of them, one while to the Commons without the Lords, another while to the Lords without the Commons? Have they not still declared their meaning, whatever their oath were, to hold them only for supreme whom they found at any time most yielding to what they petitioned? Both these oaths, which were the straightest bond of an English subject in reference to the king, being thus broke and made void, it follows undeniably that the king from that time was by them in fact absolutely deposed, and they no longer in reality to be thought his subjects, notwithstanding their fine clause° in the covenant to preserve his person, crown and dignity, set there by some dodging casuist with more craft than sincerity to mitigate the matter in case of ill success and not taken, I suppose, by any honest man but as a condition subordinate to every the least particle that might more concern religion, liberty or the public peace.

To prove it yet more plainly that they are the men who have deposed the king, I thus argue. We know that king and subject are relatives, and relatives° have no longer being than in the relation; the relation between king and subject can be no other than regal authority and subjection. Hence I infer, past their defending, that if the subject, who is one relative, take away the relation, of force he takes away also the other relative; but the Presbyterians, who were one relative, that is to say, subjects, have for this seven years taken away the relation, that is to say, the king's authority, and their subjection to it; therefore the Presbyterians for these seven years have removed and extinguished the other relative, that is to say, the king; or, to speak more in brief, have deposed him, not only by depriving him the execution of his authority, but by conferring it upon others.

If then their oaths of subjection broken, new supremacy obeyed, new oaths and covenants taken, notwithstanding frivolous evasions, have in plain terms unkinged the king much more than hath their seven years' war, not deposed him only, but outlawed him and defied him as an alien, a rebel to law and enemy to the state, it must needs be clear to any man not averse from reason that hostility and subjection are two direct and positive contraries, and can no more in one subject stand together in respect of the same king than one person at the same time can be in two remote places. Against whom therefore the subject is in act of hostility, we may be confident that to him he is in no subjection; and in whom hostility takes place of subjection (for they can by no means consist together), to him the king can be not only no king, but an enemy.

So that from hence we shall not need dispute whether they have deposed him, or what they have defaulted towards him as no king, but show manifestly how much they have done toward the killing him. Have they not levied all these wars against him, whether offensive or defensive (for defence in war equally offends, and most prudently beforehand), and given commission to slay where they knew his person could not be exempt from danger? And if chance or flight had not saved him, how often had they killed him, directing their artillery without blame or prohibition to the very place where they saw him stand? Have they not sequestered him, judged or unjudged, and converted his revenue to other uses, detaining from him, as a grand delinquent, all means of livelihood, so that for them long since he might have perished or have starved? Have they not hunted and pursued him round about the kingdom with sword and fire? Have they not formerly denied to treat° with him, and their now recanting ministers preached against him as a reprobate incurable, an enemy to God and his church marked for destruction, and therefore not to be treated with? Have they not besieged him, and to their power° forbade him water and fire, save what they shot against him to the hazard of his life? Yet while they thus assaulted and endangered it with hostile deeds, they swore in words to defend it, with his crown and dignity; not in order, as it seems now, to a firm and lasting peace, or to his repentance after all this blood; but simply, without regard, without remorse, or any comparable value of all the miseries and calamities suffered by the poor people, or to suffer hereafter, through his obstinacy or impenitence.

No understanding man can be ignorant that covenants are ever made according to the present state of persons and of things, and have ever the more general laws of nature and of reason included in them, though not expressed. If I make a voluntary covenant, as with a man to do him good, and he prove afterward a monster to me, I should conceive a disobligement. If I covenant not to hurt an enemy, in favour of him and forbearance and hope of his amendment, and he after that shall do me tenfold injury and mischief to what he had done when I so covenanted, and still be plotting what may tend to my destruction, I question not but that his after-actions release me; nor know I covenant so sacred that withholds me from demanding justice on him.

Howbeit, had not their distrust in a good cause and the fast and loose of our prevaricating divines overswayed, it had been doubtless better not to have inserted in a covenant unnecessary obligations, and words, not works, of supererogating° allegiance to their enemy; no way advantageous to themselves had the king prevailed, as to their cost many would have felt, but full of snare and distraction to our friends, useful only, as we now find, to our adversaries, who under such a latitude and shelter of ambiguous interpretation have ever since been plotting and contriving new opportunities to trouble all again. How much better had it been, and more becoming an undaunted virtue, to have declared openly and boldly whom and what power the people were to hold supreme, as on the like occasion° Protestants have done before, and many conscientious men now in these times have more than once besought the parliament to do, that they might go on upon a sure foundation, and not with a riddling covenant in their mouths, seeming to swear counter almost in the same breath allegiance and no allegiance; which doubtless had drawn off all the minds of sincere men from siding with them, had they not discerned their actions far more deposing him than their words upholding him; which words, made now the subject of cavillous interpretations, stood ever in the covenant, by judgment of the more discerning sort, an evidence of their fear, not of their fidelity.

What should I return to speak on, of those attempts for which the king himself hath often charged the Presbyterians of seeking his life, whenas, in the due estimation of things, they might without a fallacy be said to have done the deed outright? Who knows not that the king is a name of dignity and office, not of person? Who therefore kills a king must kill him while he is a king. Then they certainly, who by deposing him have long since taken from him the life of a king, his office and his dignity, they in the truest sense may be said to have killed the king: nor only by their deposing and waging war against him, which, besides the danger to his personal life, set him in the furthest opposite point from any vital function of a king, but by their holding him in prison, vanquished and yielded into their absolute and despotic power, which brought him to the lowest degradement and incapacity of the regal name. I say not by whose° matchless valour, next under God, lest the story of their ingratitude thereupon carry me from the purpose in hand, which is to convince them that they, which I repeat again, were the men who in the truest sense killed the king, not only as is proved before, but by depressing him, their king, far below the rank of a subject to the condition of a captive, without intention to restore him, as the chancellor° of Scotland in a speech told him plainly at Newcastle, unless he granted fully all their demands, which they knew he never meant.

Nor did they treat or think of treating with him till their hatred to the army that delivered them, not their love or duty to the king, joined them secretly with men sentenced so oft for reprobates in their own mouths, by whose subtle inspiring they grew mad upon a most tardy and improper treaty.° Whereas if the whole bent of their actions had not been against the king himself, but only against his evil councillors, as they feigned and published, wherefore did they not restore him all that while to the true life of a king, his office, crown, and dignity, when he was in their power, and they themselves his nearest councillors? The truth, therefore, is both that they would not and that indeed they could not without their own certain destruction, having reduced him to such a final pass as was the very death and burial of all in him that was regal, and from whence never king of England yet revived but by the new reinforcement of his own party, which was a kind of resurrection to him.

Thus having quite extinguished all that could be in him of a king, and from a total privation clad him over, like another specifical° thing, with forms and habitudes destructive to the former, they left in his person, dead as to law and all the civil right either of king or subject, the life only of a prisoner, a captive and a malefactor: whom the equal and impartial hand of justice finding was no more to spare than another ordinary man; not only made obnoxious° to the doom of law by a charge more than once drawn up against him, and his own confession to the first article at Newport,° but summoned and arraigned in the sight of God and his people, cursed and devoted° to perdition worse than any Ahab or Antiochus,° with exhortation to curse all those in the name of God that made not war against him, as bitterly as Meroz° was to be cursed, that went not out against a Canaanitish king, almost in all the sermons, prayers and fulminations that have been uttered this seven years by those cloven tongues of falsehood and dissension, who now, to the stirring up of new discord, acquit him; and against their own discipline, which they boast to be the throne and sceptre of Christ, absolve him, unconfound° him, though unconverted, unrepentant, unsensible of all their precious saints and martyrs whose blood they have so often laid upon his head. And now again with a new sovereign anointment can wash it all off, as if it were as vile and no more to be reckoned for than the blood of so many dogs in a time of pestilence: giving the most opprobrious lie to all the acted zeal that for these many years hath filled their bellies and fed them fat upon the foolish people. Ministers of sedition, not of the gospel, who, while they saw it manifestly tend to civil war and bloodshed, never ceased exasperating° the people against him; and now that they see it likely to breed new commotion, cease not to incite others against the people that have saved them from him, as if sedition were their only aim, whether against him or for him.

But God, as we have cause to trust, will put other thoughts into the people, and turn them from giving ear or heed to these mercenary noisemakers, of whose fury and false prophecies we have enough experience, and from the murmurs of new discord will incline them to hearken rather with erected minds to the voice of our supreme magistracy,° calling us to liberty and the flourishing deeds of a reformed commonwealth; with this hope, that as God was heretofore angry with the Jews who rejected him and his form of government to choose a king, so that he will bless us and be propitious to us, who reject a king to make him only our leader and supreme governor in the conformity, as near as may be, of his own ancient government; if we have at least but so much worth in us to entertain the sense of our future happiness, and the courage to receive what God vouchsafes us; wherein we have the honour to precede other nations, who are now labouring to be our followers.

For as to this question in hand, what the people by their just right may do in change of government or of governor, we see it cleared sufficiently, besides other ample authority even from the mouths of princes themselves. And surely they that shall boast, as we do, to be a free nation, and not have in themselves the power to remove or to abolish any governor supreme or subordinate, with the government itself upon urgent causes, may please their fancy with a ridiculous and painted freedom fit to cozen babies; but are indeed under tyranny and servitude, as wanting that power, which is the root and source of all liberty, to dispose and economize° in the land which God hath given them as masters of family in their own house and free inheritance. Without which natural and essential power of a free nation, though bearing high their heads, they can in due esteem be thought no better than slaves and vassals born, in the tenure and occupation of another inheriting lord, whose government, though not illegal or intolerable, hangs over them as a lordly scourge, not as a free government; and therefore to be abrogated.

How much more justly then may they fling off tyranny or tyrants; who being once deposed can be no more than private men, as subject to the reach of justice and arraignment as any other transgressors? And certainly if men, not to speak of heathen, both wise and religious, have done justice upon tyrants what way they could soonest, how much more mild and human then is it to give them fair and open trial; to teach lawless kings, and all who so much adore them, that not mortal man or his imperious will, but justice is the only true sovereign and supreme majesty upon earth? Let men cease therefore out of faction and hypocrisy to make outcries and horrid things of things so just and honourable. Though perhaps till now no Protestant state or kingdom can be alleged to have openly put to death their king, which lately some have written, and imputed to their great glory, much mistaking the matter. It is not, neither ought to be, the glory of a Protestant state never to have put their king to death; it is the glory of Protestant king never to have deserved death. And if the parliament and military council do what they do without precedent, if it appear their duty, it argues the more wisdom, virtue and magnanimity that they know themselves able to be a precedent to others, who perhaps in future ages, if they prove not too degenerate, will look up with honour, and aspire towards these exemplary and matchless deeds of their ancestors as to the highest top of their civil glory and emulation; which heretofore, in the pursuance of fame and foreign dominion, spent itself vaingloriously abroad, but henceforth may learn a better fortitude, to dare execute highest justice on them that shall by force of arms endeavour the oppressing and bereaving of religion and their liberty at home. That no unbridled potentate or tyrant, but to his sorrow, for the future may presume such high and irresponsible licence over mankind, to havoc and turn upside down whole kingdoms of men, as though they were no more in respect of his perverse will than a nation of pismires.°

As for the party called Presbyterian, of whom I believe very many to be good and faithful Christians, though misled by some of turbulent spirit, I wish them, earnestly and calmly, not to fall off from their first principles, nor to affect rigour and superiority over men not under them; not to compel unforcible things,° in religion especially, which, if not voluntary, becomes a sin; nor to assist the clamour and malicious drifts of men whom they themselves have judged to be the worst of men, the obdurate enemies of God and his church: nor to dart against the actions of their brethren, for want of other argument, those wrested laws and scriptures thrown by prelates and malignants against their own sides, which though they hurt not otherwise, yet taken up by them to the condemnation of their own doings, give scandal to all men, and discover° in themselves either extreme passion or apostasy. Let them not oppose their best friends and associates, who molest them not at all, infringe not the least of their liberties, unless they call it their liberty to bind other men's consciences, but are still seeking to live at peace with them and brotherly accord. Let them beware an old and perfect enemy,° who, though he hope by sowing discord to make them his instruments, yet cannot forbear a minute the open threatening of his destined revenge upon them when they have served his purposes. Let them fear, therefore, if they be wise, rather what they have done already than what remains to do, and be warned in time they put no confidence in princes whom they have provoked, lest they be added to the examples of those that miserably have tasted the event.°

Stories° can inform them how Christiern II, king of Denmark, not much above a hundred years past, driven out by his subjects and received again upon new oaths and conditions, broke through them all to his most bloody revenge, slaying his chief opposers when he saw his time, both them and their children, invited to a feast for that purpose. How Maximilian° dealt with those of Bruges, though by mediation of the German princes reconciled to them by solemn and public writings drawn and sealed. How the massacre at Paris° was the effect of that credulous peace which the French Protestants made with Charles IX, their king: and that the main visible cause, which to this day hath saved the Netherlands from utter ruin, was their final not believing the perfidious cruelty, which, as a constant maxim of state, hath been used by the Spanish kings on their subjects that have taken arms, and after trusted them; as no later age but can testify, heretofore in Belgia itself, and this very year in Naples.° And to conclude with one past exception, though far more ancient, David, whose sanctified prudence might be alone sufficient, not to warrant us only, but to instruct us, when once he had taken arms, never after that trusted Saul, though with tears and much relenting he twice promised° not to hurt him. These instances, few of many, might admonish them, both English and Scotch, not to let their own ends, and the driving on of a faction, betray them blindly into the snare of those enemies whose revenge looks on them as the men who first begun, fomented and carried on, beyond the cure of any sound or safe accommodation, all the evil which hath since unavoidably befallen them and their king.

I have something also to the divines, though brief to what were needful, not to be disturbers of the civil affairs, being in hands better able and more belonging to manage them, but to study harder and to attend the office of good pastors, knowing that he whose flock is least among them hath a dreadful charge, not performed by mounting twice into the chair° with a formal preachment huddled up at the odd hours of a whole lazy week, but by incessant pains and watching, in season and out of season,° from house to house, over the souls of whom they have to feed. Which if they ever well considered, how little leisure would they find to be the most pragmatical sidesmen° of every popular tumult and sedition! And all this while are to learn what the true end and reason is of the gospel which they teach, and what a world it differs from the censorious and supercilious lording over conscience. It would be good also they lived so as might persuade the people they hated covetousness, which, worse than heresy, is idolatry; hated pluralities and all kind of simony; left rambling from benefice to benefice, like ravenous wolves seeking where they may devour the biggest. Of which if some, well and warmly seated from the beginning, be not guilty, 'twere good they held not conversation° with such as are. Let them be sorry that, being called to assemble about reforming the church, they fell to progging° and soliciting the parliament, though they had renounced the name of priests, for a new settling of their tithes and oblations;° and double-lined themselves with spiritual places of commodity° beyond the possible discharge of their duty. Let them assemble in consistory° with their elders and deacons, according to ancient ecclesiastical rule, to the preserving of church discipline, each in his several charge, and not a pack of clergymen by themselves to bellycheer° in their presumptuous Sion,° or to promote designs, abuse and gull the simple laity, and stir up tumult, as the prelates did, for the maintenance of their pride and avarice.

These things if they observe, and wait with patience, no doubt but all things will go well without their importunities or exclamations; and the printed letters which they send subscribed with the ostentation of great characters° and little moment would be more considerable° than now they are. But if they be the ministers of Mammon instead of Christ, and scandalize his church with the filthy love of gain, aspiring also to sit the closest and the heaviest of all tyrants upon the conscience, and fall notoriously into the same sins whereof so lately and so loud they accused the prelates, as God rooted out those wicked ones immediately before, so will he root out them, their imitators; and to vindicate his own glory and religion will uncover their hypocrisy to the open world, and visit upon their own heads that 'Curse ye Meroz',° the very motto of their pulpits, wherewith so frequently, not as Meroz, but more like atheists, they have blasphemed the vengeance of God and traduced the zeal of his people.°

And that they be not what they go for, true ministers of the Protestant doctrine, taught by those abroad, famous and religious men who first reformed the church, or by those no less zealous who withstood corruption and the bishops here at home, branded with the name of

Puritans and Nonconformists, we shall abound with testimonies to make appear that men may yet more fully know the difference between Protestant divines and these pulpit-firebrands.

Luther, *Lib. contra Rusticos apud Sleidan,*° *l.* 5.
Is est hodie rerum status, etc. 'Such is the state of things at this day that men neither can, nor will, nor indeed ought to endure longer the domination of you princes.'
Neque vero Caesarem, etc. 'Neither is Caesar to make war as head of Christendom, Protector of the Church, Defender of the Faith, these titles being false and windy, and most kings being the greatest enemies to religion.' (*Liber De Bello contra Turcas*° *apud Sleidan, l.* 14.). What hinders then but that we may dispose or punish them?

These also are recited by Cochlaeus° in his *Miscellanies* to be the words of Luther or some other eminent divine then in Germany when the Protestants there entered into solemn covenant at Smalcaldia. *Ut ora iis obturem, etc.* 'That I may stop their mouths, the pope and emperor are not born but elected, and may also be deposed, as hath been often done.' If Luther, or whoever else, thought so, he could not stay° there, for the right of birth or succession can be no privilege in nature to let a tyrant sit irremovable over a nation free born, without transforming that nation from the nature and condition of men born free into natural, hereditary and successive slaves. Therefore he saith further, 'to displace and throw down this exactor, this Phalaris,° this Nero, is a work well pleasing to God'—namely, for being such a one; which is a moral reason. Shall then so slight a consideration as his hap to be not elective simply, but by birth, which was a mere accident, overthrow that which is moral, and make unpleasing to God that which otherwise had so well pleased him? Certainly not; for if the matter be rightly argued, election much rather than chance binds a man to content himself with what he suffers by his own bad election; though indeed neither the one nor other binds any man, much less any people, to a necessary sufferance of those wrongs and evils which they have ability and strength enough given them to remove.

Zwinglius,° *tom. 1, articul. 42.*
Quando vero perfide, etc. 'When kings reign perfidiously and against the rule of Christ they may according to the word of God be deposed.'
Mihi ergo compertum non est, etc. 'I know not how it comes to pass that kings reign by succession, unless it be with consent of the whole people.' (*Ibid.*)
Quum vero consensu, etc. 'But when by suffrage and consent of the

whole people, or the better part of them, a tyrant is deposed or put to death, God is the chief leader in that action.' (*Ibid.*)

Nunc cum tam tepidi sumus, etc. 'Now that we are so lukewarm in upholding public justice, we endure the vices of tyrants to reign nowadays with impunity. Justly therefore by them we are trod underfoot, and shall at length with them be punished. Yet ways are not wanting by which tyrants may be removed, but there wants public justice.' (*Ibid.*)

Cavete vobis O tyranni. 'Beware, ye tyrants, for now the gospel of Jesus Christ spreading far and wide will renew the lives of many to love innocence and justice, which if ye also shall do, ye shall be honoured. But if ye shall go on to rage and do violence, ye shall be trampled on by all men.' (*Ibid.*)

Romanus imperium imo quodque, etc. 'When the Roman empire or any other shall begin to oppress religion, and we negligently suffer it, we are as much guilty of religion so violated as the oppressors themselves.' (*Idem, Epist. ad Conrad. Somium.*)

Calvin on Daniel,° c. 4, v. 25.

Hodie monarchae semper in suis titulis, etc. 'Nowadays monarchs pretend always in their titles to be kings by the grace of God; but how many of them to this end only pretend it, that they may reign without control; for to what purpose is the grace of God mentioned in the title of kings but that they may acknowledge no superior? In the meanwhile God, whose name they use to support themselves, they willingly would tread under their feet. It is therefore a mere cheat when they boast to reign by the grace of God.'

Abdicant se terreni principes, etc. 'Earthly princes depose themselves while they rise against God, yea, they are unworthy to be numbered among men; rather it behoves us to spit upon their heads than to obey them.' (*on Daniel*, c. 6, v. 22.)

Bucer° on Matthew, c. 5.

Si princeps superior, etc. 'If a sovereign prince endeavour by arms to defend transgressors, to subvert those things which are taught in the word of God, they who are in authority under him ought first to dissuade him. If they prevail not, and that he now bears himself not as a prince but as an enemy, and seeks to violate privileges and rights granted to inferior magistrates and commonalities, it is the part of pious magistrates, imploring first the assistance of God, rather to try all ways and means than to betray the flock of Christ to such an enemy of God; for they also are to this end ordained, that they may defend the people of God and maintain those things which are good and just. For to have supreme power lessens not the evil committed by that power, but makes it the less tolerable by how much the more generally hurtful.' Then certainly the less tolerable, the more unpardonably to be punished.

Of Peter Martyr we have spoke before.

Paraeus° *in Rom.* 13.

Quorum est constituere magistratus, etc. 'They whose part it is to set up magistrates may restrain them also from outrageous deeds, or pull them down; but all magistrates are set up either by parliament, or by electors, or by other magistrates; they therefore who exalted them may lawfully degrade and punish them.'

Of the Scotch divines I need not mention others than the famousest among them, Knox, and his fellow labourers in the reformation of Scotland, whose large treatises on this subject defend the same opinion. To cite them sufficiently were to insert their whole books written purposely on this argument: *Knox's Appeal*° and 'To the Reader', where he promises in a postscript that the book which he intended to set forth, called *The Second Blast of the Trumpet*, should maintain more at large that the same men most justly may depose and punish him whom unadvisedly they have elected, notwithstanding birth, succession, or any oath of allegiance. Among our own divines, Cartwright° and Fenner,° two of the learnedest, may in reason satisfy us what was held by the rest, Fenner in his book of *Theology* maintaining that 'they who have power, that is to say a parliament, may either by fair means or by force depose a tyrant', whom he defines to be him that wilfully breaks all, or the principal, conditions made between him and the commonwealth (Fenner, *Sacra Theologia*, c. 13); and Cartwright in a prefixed epistle testifies his approbation of the whole book.

Gilby,° *De Obedientia*, pp. 25 and 105.

'Kings have their authority of the people, who may upon occasion reassume it to themselves.'

England's Complaint against the Canons.

'The people may kill wicked princes as monsters and cruel beasts.'

Christopher Goodman° of obedience.

'When kings or rulers become blasphemers of God, oppressors and murderers of their subjects, they ought no more to be accounted kings or lawful magistrates, but as private men to be examined, accused, condemned and punished by the law of God; and being convicted and punished by that law, it is not man's but God's doing' (c. 10, p. 139).

'By the civil laws a fool or idiot born, and so proved, shall lose the lands and inheritance whereto he is born because he is not able to use them aright. And especially ought in no case be suffered to have the government of a whole nation; but there is no such evil can come to the commonwealth by fools and idiots as doth by the rage and fury of ungodly rulers. Such, therefore, being without God ought to have no authority over God's people, who by his word requireth the contrary' (c. 11, pp. 143-4).

'No person is exempt by any law of God from this punishment, be he king, queen, or emperor, he must die the death, for God hath not placed them above others to transgress his laws as they list, but to be subject to them as well as others; and if they be subject to his laws, then to the punishment also—so much the more, as their example is more dangerous' (c. 13, p. 184).

'When magistrates cease to do their duty, the people are as it were without magistrates, yea, worse; and then God giveth the sword into the people's hand, and he himself is become immediately their head' (p. 185).

'If princes do right and keep promise with you, then do you owe to them all humble obedience; if not, ye are discharged, and your study ought to be in this case how ye may depose and punish according to the law such rebels against God and oppressors of their country' (p. 190).

This Goodman was a minister of the English church at Geneva, as Dudley Fenner was at Middleburgh, or some other place in that country. These were the pastors of those saints and confessors who, flying from the bloody persecution of Queen Mary, gathered up at length their scattered members into many congregations; whereof some in Upper, some in Lower Germany, part of them settled at Geneva, where this author having preached on this subject to the great liking of certain learned and godly men who heard him, was by them sundry times and with much instance° required to write more fully on that point. Who thereupon took it in hand, and conferring with the best learned in those parts (among whom Calvin was then living in the same city), with their special approbation he published this treatise, aiming principally, as is testified by Whittingham° in the Preface, that his brethren of England, the Protestants, might be persuaded in the truth of that doctrine concerning obedience to magistrates.

These were the true Protestant divines of England, our fathers in the faith we hold; this was their sense, who for so many years labouring under prelacy through all storms and persecutions kept religion from extinguishing, and delivered it pure to us, till there arose a covetous and ambitious generation of divines (for divines they call themselves) who, feigning on a sudden to be new converts and proselytes from episcopacy, under which they had long temporized, opened their mouths at length in show against pluralities and prelacy, but with intent to swallow them down both, gorging themselves like harpies on those simonious places and preferments of their outed predecessors as the quarry for which they hunted, not to plurality only but to multiplicity, for possessing which they had accused them, their brethren, and aspiring under another title to the same authority and usurpation over the consciences of all men.

Of this faction divers reverend and learned divines (as they are styled in the phylactery° of their own title-page) pleading the lawfulness of defensive arms against this king in a treatise called *Scripture and Reason*° seem in words to disclaim utterly the deposing of a king; but both the scripture and the reasons which they use draw consequences after them which, without their bidding, conclude it lawful. For if by Scripture, and by that especially to the Romans,° which they most insist upon, kings, doing that which is contrary to St Paul's definition of a magistrate, may be resisted, they may altogether with as much force of consequence be deposed or punished. And if by reason the unjust authority of kings 'may be forfeited in part, and his power be reassumed in part, either by the parliament or people, for the case in hazard and the present necessity', as they affirm, p. 34, there can no scripture be alleged, no imaginable reason given, that necessity continuing, as it may always, and they in all prudence and their duty may take upon them to foresee it, why in such a case they may not finally amerce° him with the loss of his kingdom, of whose amendment they have no hope. And if one wicked action persisted in against religion, laws and liberties may warrant us to thus much in part, why may not forty times as many tyrannies by him committed warrant us to proceed on restraining him, till the restraint become total? For the ways of justice are exactest proportion; if for one trespass of a king it require so much remedy or satisfaction, then for twenty more as heinous crimes it requires of him twentyfold; and so proportionably, till it come to what is utmost among men. If in these proceedings against their king they may not finish by the usual course of justice what they have begun, they could not lawfully begin at all. For this golden rule of justice and morality, as well as of arithmetic, out of three terms which they admit, will as certainly and unavoidably bring out the fourth as any problem that ever Euclid or Apollonius° made good by demonstration.

And if the parliament, being undeposable but by themselves, as is affirmed, pp. 37, 38, might for his whole life, if they saw cause, take all power, authority and the sword out of his hand, which in effect is to unmagistrate him, why might they not, being then themselves the sole magistrates in force, proceed to punish him who, being lawfully deprived of all things that define a magistrate, can be now no magistrate to be degraded lower, but an offender to be punished? Lastly, whom they may defy and meet in battle, why may they not as well prosecute by justice? For lawful war is but the execution of justice against them who refuse law. Among whom if it be lawful (as they deny not, pp. 19, 20) to slay the king himself coming in front at his own peril, wherefore may not justice do that intendedly which the chance of a defensive war might without blame have done casually, nay, purposely, if there it find him among the rest? They ask, p. 19, 'by what rule of conscience or God a state is bound to sacrifice religion, laws and liberties, rather than a prince defending such as subvert them should come in hazard of his life.' And I ask by what conscience, or divinity, or law, or reason a state is bound to leave all these sacred concernments under a perpetual hazard and extremity of danger, rather than cut off a wicked prince who sits plotting day and night to subvert them.

They tell us that the law of nature justifies any man to defend himself, even against the king in person: let them show us then why the same law may not justify much more a state or whole people to do justice upon him against whom each private man may lawfully defend himself, seeing all kind of justice done is a defence to good men, as well as a punishment to bad; and justice done upon a tyrant is no more but the necessary self-defence of a whole commonwealth. To war upon a king that his instruments may be brought to condign° punishment, and thereafter to punish them the instruments, and not to spare only, but to defend and honour him the author, is the strangest piece of justice to be called Christian, and the strangest piece of reason to be called human, that by men of reverence and learning, as their style imports them, ever yet was vented. They maintain in the third and fourth section that a judge or inferior magistrate is anointed of God, is his minister, hath the sword in his hand, is to be obeyed by St Peter's rule,° as well as the supreme, and without difference anywhere expressed: and yet will have us fight against the supreme till he remove and punish the inferior magistrate (for such were greatest delinquents) whenas by

Scripture, and by reason, there can no more authority be shown to resist the one than the other, and altogether as much to punish or depose the supreme himself as to make war upon him, till he punish or deliver up his inferior magistrates, whom in the same terms we are commanded to obey and not to resist.

Thus while they, in a cautious line or two here and there stuffed in, are only verbal against the pulling down or punishing of tyrants, all the scripture and the reason which they bring is in every leaf direct and rational, to infer it altogether as lawful as to resist them. And yet in all their sermons, as hath by others been well noted, they went much further. For divines if ye observe them have their postures and their motions no less expertly and with no less variety than they that practice feats in the artillery ground. Sometimes they seem furiously to march on, and presently march counter; by and by they stand, and then retreat; or if need be, can face about, or wheel in a whole body with that cunning and dexterity as is almost unperceivable, to wind themselves by shifting ground into places of more advantage. And providence only must be the drum, providence the word of command, that calls them from above, but always to some larger benefice, or acts them into such or such figures and promotions. At their turns and doublings no men readier, to the right, or to the left; for it is their turns which they serve chiefly; herein only singular, that with them there is no certain hand right or left but as their own commodity° thinks best to call it. But if there come a truth to be defended, which to them and their interest of this world seems not so profitable, straight these nimble motionists can find no even legs to stand upon, and are no more of use to reformation thoroughly performed, and not superficially, or to the advancement of truth (which among mortal men is always in her progress), than if on a sudden they were struck maim and crippled.

Which the better to conceal, or the more to countenance by a general conformity to their own limping, they would have Scripture, they would have reason also made to halt with them for company, and would put us off with impotent conclusions, lame and shorter than the premises.

In this posture they seem to stand with great zeal and confidence on the wall of Sion; but like Jebusites,° not like Israelites or Levites: blind also as well as lame, they discern not David from Adonibezec,° but cry him up for the Lord's anointed, whose thumbs and great toes not long before they had cut off upon their pulpit cushions. Therefore he who is our only king, the root° of David, and whose kingdom is eternal righteousness, with all those that war under him, whose happiness and final hopes are laid up in that only just and rightful kingdom (which we pray incessantly may come soon, and in so praying wish hasty ruin and destruction to all tyrants), even he our immortal king, and all that love him, must of necessity have in abomination these blind and lame defenders of Jerusalem, as the soul of David hated them, and forbid them entrance into God's house, and his own. But as to those before them, which I cited first (and with an easy search, for many more might be added) as they there stand, without more in number, being the best and chief of Protestant divines, we may follow them for faithful guides, and without doubting may receive them as witnesses abundant of what we here affirm concerning tyrants. And indeed I find it generally the clear and positive determination of them all (not prelatical, or of this late faction subprelatical), who have written on this argument that to do justice on a lawless king is to a private man unlawful; to an inferior magistrate lawful: or if they were divided in opinion, yet greater than these here alleged, or of more authority in the church, there can be none produced.

If any one shall go about by bringing other testimonies to disable these, or by bringing these against themselves in other cited passages of their books, he will not only fail to make good that false and impudent assertion of those mutinous ministers that the deposing and punishing of a king or tyrant 'is against the constant judgment of all Protestant divines', it being quite the contrary; but will prove rather what perhaps he intended not, that the judgment of divines, if it be so various and inconstant to itself, is not considerable,° or to be esteemed at all. Ere which be yielded, as I hope it never will, these ignorant assertors in their own art will have proved themselves more and more not to be Protestant divines, whose constant judgment in this point they have so audaciously belied, but rather to be a pack of hungry church-wolves, who in the steps of Simon Magus° their father, following the hot scent of double livings and pluralities, advowsons, donatives, inductions and augmentations,° though uncalled to the flock of Christ but by the mere suggestion of their bellies, like those priests of Bel, whose pranks Daniel° found out have got possession, or rather seized upon the pulpit, as the stronghold and fortress of their sedition and rebellion against the civil magistrate. Whose friendly and victorious hand having rescued them from the bishops, their insulting lords, fed them plenteously both in public and in private, raised them to be high and rich of poor and base, only suffered not their covetousness and fierce ambition (which as the pit that sent out their fellow-locusts° hath been ever bottomless and boundless) to interpose in all things and over all persons their impetuous° ignorance and importunity.

From *Second Defence of The English People*

Against the Base Anonymous Libel, Entitled

The Cry of the Royal Blood to Heaven, against the English Parricides.

BY JOHN MILTON, ENGLISHMAN

In the whole life and estate of man the first duty is to be grateful to God and mindful of his blessings, and to offer particular and solemn thanks without delay when his benefits have exceeded hope and prayer. Now, on the very threshold of my speech, I see three most weighty reasons for my discharge of this duty. First that I was born at a time in the history of my country when her citizens, with pre-eminent virtue and a nobility and steadfastness surpassing all the glory of their ancestors, invoked the Lord, followed his manifest guidance, and after accomplishing the most heroic and exemplary achievements since the foundation of the world, freed the state from grievous tyranny and the church from unworthy servitude. Secondly, that when a multitude had sprung up which in the wonted manner of a mob venomously attacked these noble achievements, and when one man° above all, swollen and complacent with his empty grammarian's conceit and the esteem of his confederates, had in a book of unparalleled baseness attacked us and wickedly assumed the defence of all tyrants, it was I and no other who was deemed equal to a foe of such repute and to the task of speaking on so great a theme, and who received from the very liberators of my country this role, which was offered spontaneously with universal consent, the task of publicly defending (if anyone ever did) the cause of the English people and thus of Liberty herself. Lastly, I thank God that in an affair so arduous and so charged with expectation, I did not disappoint the hope or the judgment of my countrymen about me, nor fail to satisfy a host of foreigners, men of learning and experience, for by God's grace I so routed my audacious foe that he fled, broken in spirit and reputation. For the last three years of his life, he did in his rage utter frequent threats, but gave us no further trouble,° save that he sought the secret help of certain rogues° and persuaded some bungling and immoderate panegyrists to repair, if they could, his fresh and unlooked-for disgrace. All this will shortly be made clear. . . .

The English people were not driven to unbridled license by scorn for the laws or desecration of them. They were not inflamed with the empty name of liberty by a false notion of virtue and glory, or senseless emulation of the ancients. It was their purity of life and their blameless character which showed them the one direct road to true liberty, and it was the most righteous defence of law and religion that of necessity gave them arms. And so, trusting completely in God, with honourable weapons, they put slavery to flight.

Although I claim for myself no share in this glory, yet it is easy to defend myself from the charge of timidity or cowardice, should such a charge be levelled. For I did not avoid the toils and dangers of military service without rendering to my fellow citizens another kind of service that was much more useful and no less perilous. In time of trial I was neither cast down in spirit nor unduly fearful of envy or death itself. Having from early youth been especially devoted to the liberal arts, with greater strength of mind than of body, I exchanged the toils of war, in which any stout trooper might outdo me, for those labours which I better understood, that with such wisdom as I owned I might add as much weight as possible to the counsels of my country and to this excellent cause, using not my lower but my higher and stronger powers. And so I concluded that if God wished those men to achieve such noble deeds, He also wished that there be other men by whom these deeds, once done, might be worthily praised and extolled, and that truth defended by arms be also defended by reason—the only defence truly appropriate to man. Hence it is that while I admire the heroes victorious in battle, I nevertheless do not complain about my own role. Indeed I congratulate myself and once again offer most fervent thanks to the heavenly bestower of gifts that such a lot has befallen me—a lot that seems much more a source of envy to others than of regret to myself. And yet, to no one, even the humblest, do I willingly compare myself, nor do I say one word about myself in arrogance, but whenever I allow my mind to dwell upon this cause, the noblest and most renowned of all, and upon the glorious task of defending the very defenders, a task assigned me by their own vote and decision,° I confess that I can scarcely restrain myself from loftier and bolder flights than are permissible in this exordium,° and from the search for a more exalted manner of expression. Indeed, in the degree that the distinguished orators of ancient times undoubtedly surpass me, both in their eloquence and in their style (especially in a foreign tongue,° which I must of necessity use, and often to my own dissatisfaction), in that same degree shall I outstrip all the orators of every age in the grandeur of my subject and my theme. This circumstance has aroused so much anticipation and notoriety that I do not now feel that I am surrounded, in the Forum or on the Rostra, by one people alone, whether Roman or Athenian, but

that, with virtually all of Europe attentive, in session, and passing judgment, I have in the *First Defence* spoken out and shall in the *Second*
speak again to the entire assembly and council of all the most influential
men, cities, and nations everywhere. I seem now to have embarked on a
journey and to be surveying from on high far-flung regions and territories across the sea, faces numberless and unknown, sentiments in
complete agreement with mine. Here the manly strength of the Germans, hostile to slavery, meets my eye; there the lively and generous
ardour of the Franks, worthy of their name; here the well-considered
courage of the Spaniards; there the serene and self-controlled magnanimity of the Italians. Wherever liberal sentiment, wherever freedom,
or wherever magnanimity either prudently conceals or openly proclaims itself, there some in silence approve, others openly cast their
votes, some make haste to applaud, others, conquered at last by the
truth, acknowledge themselves my captives.

Now, surrounded by such great throngs, from the Pillars of
Hercules° all the way to the farthest boundaries of Father Liber,° I
seem to be leading home again everywhere in the world, after a vast
space of time, Liberty herself, so long expelled and exiled. And, like
Triptolemus° of old, I seem to introduce to the nations of the earth a
product from my own country, but one far more excellent than that of
Ceres. In short, it is the renewed cultivation of freedom and civic life
that I disseminate throughout cities, kingdoms, and nations. But not
entirely unknown, nor perhaps unwelcome, shall I return if I am he°
who disposed of the contentious satellite of tyrants, hitherto deemed
unconquerable, both in the view of most men and in his own opinion.
When he with insults was attacking us and our battle array, and our
leaders looked first of all to me, I met him in single combat and plunged
into his reviling throat this pen, the weapon of his own choice. And
(unless I wish to reject outright and disparage the views and opinions of
so many intelligent readers everywhere, in no way bound or indebted to
me) I bore off the spoils of honour. . . .

But now let us come at last to this creature, whatever he is, who cries
out against us: a 'Cry' indeed I hear, not 'of the Royal Blood', as the
title boasts, but of some unknown rascal, for nowhere do I find the
crier. You there! Who are you? A man or a nobody? Surely the basest of
men—not even slaves—are without a name. Shall I then always contend with those who are nameless? . . .

Now then, hear, if you have time (it is almost a Milesian or a Baian
fable°) who he is, what his descent, and by what hope he was led, by
what bait and what enticement he was coaxed into adopting the royalist

cause. He is a certain More,° part Scot, part French (that a single race or country be not saddled with the entire disgrace of the man), a rogue and, according to the general evidence, not only of other men, but (what is most damning) of his friends, whom he changed from intimates into bitter enemies, he is faithless, treacherous, ungrateful, foul-mouthed, a consistent slanderer of men and of women, whose chastity he is wont to spare no more than their good name. To omit the more obscure events of his early life, this fellow first taught Greek at Geneva, but although he often demonstrated to his pupils the meaning of his own name Morus° in Greek, he could not unlearn the fool and the knave. Indeed, since he was conscious of the guilt of so many crimes (although not yet perhaps detected), he was all the more driven by such frenzy that he did not shrink from seeking the office of pastor in the church° and defiling it by his vicious ways. But he could not long escape the censure of the Elders. A pursuer of women, a liar, marked by many other offences, condemned for many deviations from the orthodox faith—deviations which he basely recanted and yet impiously retained after recanting—he was at last proved to be an adulterer.

He happened to have conceived a passion for a certain maidservant of his host, and although she not long afterwards married another, he did not cease to pursue her. The neighbours had often noticed that they entered all by themselves a certain summerhouse in the garden. Not quite adultery, you say. He could have done anything else in the world. Certainly. He might have talked to her, no doubt about matters horticultural, or he might have drawn from the subject of gardens (say those of Alcinous or Adonis°) certain of his lectures for this woman, who had perhaps a smattering of knowledge and a willing ear. He might now have praised the flower beds, might have wished only for some shade, were it possible merely to graft the mulberry on the fig,° whence might come forth, with utmost speed, a grove of sycamores—a very pleasant place to tread. He might then have demonstrated to this woman the method of grafting. These things and much else he could have done; who denies it? But he could not deter the Elders from branding him with censure as an adulterer and forthwith judging him unworthy of the office of pastor. The records of these and like accusations are still kept in the public library° of Geneva. In the meantime, while these charges were not publicly known, he was summoned to Holland by the Gallican church at Middleburg, through the influence of Salmasius, but to the great disgust of Spanheim,° a genuinely learned man and a blameless pastor, who had previously known him well at Geneva. More at last and with difficulty obtained letters of recommendation (as they are called) and rather cool ones at that, from the people of Geneva, solely on condition that he take his departure. Some thought it intolerable that a man of such character be honoured with the recommendation of the church; others thought anything more tolerable than the man himself.

When More arrived in Holland, he set out to call on Salmasius and at his house he cast lustful eyes on his wife's maid, whose name was Pontia, for this creature's desires always light on servant girls. Thereafter he began with the greatest persistence to cultivate Salmasius, and, as often as he could, Pontia. I do not know whether Salmasius, pleased by the fellow's adulation and courtesy, or More, thinking that he had devised a likely means of meeting Pontia more often, first broached the subject of Milton's reply to Salmasius. However it was, More undertook to defend Salmasius, and Salmasius for his part promised More the chair of theology in Middleburg.° More promised himself both this and another extra tidbit, a secret liaison with Pontia. For the sake of consulting Salmasius about his undertaking, day and night he frequented his house. And as Pyramus° was once changed into a mulberry, so now the mulberry suddenly fancied himself turned into Pyramus, the Genevan into the Babylonian. But, surpassing that young man in good fortune no less than in wickedness, More now addressed his Thisbe when he pleased, having ample opportunity beneath the very same roof. No need to seek a chink in the wall! He promised marriage. With this deluding hope, he ruined her. With this crime (I shrink from saying it, but it must be said) a minister of the holy gospel defiled even the house of his host. From the union resulted at length a marvellous and unnatural prodigy; not only the female but also the male conceived—Pontia a little More, which for a long time afterward persecuted even that persecutor of Pliny,° Salmasius; and More conceived this empty wind-egg, from which burst forth the swollen Cry of the King's Blood. At first the egg was pleasant enough for our hungry royalists in Belgium° to suck, but now, with the shell broken, they find it rotten and stinking, and they recoil from it. For More, distended by this same foetus of his, and feeling that he had deserved well of the whole Orange party, had now already, in his wicked hopes, swallowed up fresh professorial chairs, and had basely deserted his Pontia, pregnant though she now was, as being but a poor little servant girl. Complaining that she had been despised and deceived, she begged the support of the synod and the magistrates.° Thus at length the affair became public, and long provided mirth and merriment for virtually every social and convivial gathering. Hence someone, witty enough, whoever he was, composed this epigram:

> Who, Pontia, would deny that you, with child by Gallic More,
> Are mor-ally pure and More-obliging?

Only Pontia was not amused, but her complaints accomplished nothing, for the Cry of the Royal Blood had easily drowned out the cry of violated honour and the lament of the poor girl who had been seduced. Salmasius too, highly indignant that this insult and disgrace had been offered to him and his entire household, and that he had thus been made game of by his friend and supporter, so that he was once more exposed to the enemy, soon thereafter breathed his last, perhaps because this calamity as well had been added to his earlier failure in the royalist cause. But of this more later.

Meanwhile Salmasius, with a fate like that of Salmacis° (for like the name, so too the fable is apt enough), unaware that in More he had associated with himself a hermaphrodite, as fit to give birth as to beget, ignorant too of what More had begotten in his home, fondled what he had brought forth, that book in which he found himself so often called 'the great' (in his own estimation just praise, perhaps, but foolish and absurd in the opinion of others). . . .

Let us now come to the charges against me. Is there anything in my life or character which he could criticize? Nothing, certainly. What then? He does what no one but a brute and barbarian would have done—casts up to me my appearance and my blindness.

'A monster, dreadful, ugly, huge, deprived of sight.' Never did I think that I should rival the Cyclops° in appearance. But at once he corrects himself. 'Yet not huge, for there is nothing more feeble, bloodless, and pinched.' Although it ill befits a man to speak of his own appearance, yet speak I shall, since here too there is reason for me to thank God and refute liars, lest anyone think me to be perhaps a dogheaded ape or a rhinoceros, as the rabble in Spain, too credulous of their priests, believe to be true of heretics, as they call them. Ugly I have never been thought by anyone, to my knowledge, who has laid eyes on me. Whether I am handsome or not, I am less concerned. I admit that I am not tall, but my stature is closer to the medium than to the small. Yet what if it were small, as is the case with so many men of the greatest worth in both peace and war? (Although why is that stature called small which is great enough for virtue?) But neither am I especially feeble, having indeed such spirit and such strength that when my age and manner of life required it, I was not ignorant of how to handle or unsheathe a sword, nor unpractised in using it each day. Girded with my sword, as I generally was, I thought myself equal to anyone, though he was far more sturdy, and I was fearless of any injury that one man could inflict on another. Today I possess the same spirit, the same strength, but not the same eyes. And yet they have as much the appearance of being uninjured, and are as clear and bright, without a cloud, as the eyes of men who see most keenly. In this respect alone, against my will, do I deceive. In my face, than which he says there is 'nothing more bloodless', still lingers a colour exactly opposite to the bloodless and pale, so that although I am past forty, there is scarcely anyone to whom I do not seem younger by about ten years. Nor is it true that either my body or my skin is shrivelled. If I am in any way deceitful in respect to these matters, I should deserve the mockery of many thousands of my fellow-citizens, who know me by sight, and of not a few foreigners as well. But if this fellow is proved such a bold and gratuitous liar in a matter by no means calling for deceit, you will be able to draw the same conclusion as to the rest.

So much have I been forced to say about my appearance. Concerning yours, although I have heard that it is utterly despicable and the living image of the falseness and malice that dwell within you, I do not care to speak nor does anyone care to hear. Would that it were equally possible to refute this brutish adversary on the subject of my blindness, but it is not possible. Let me bear it then. Not blindness but the inability to endure blindness is a source of misery. Why should I not bear that which every man ought to prepare himself to bear with equanimity, if it befall him—that which I know may humanly befall any mortal and has indeed befallen certain men who are the most eminent and virtuous in all history? Or shall I recall those ancient bards and wise men of the most distant past, whose misfortune the gods, it is said, recompensed with far more potent gifts, and whom men treated with such respect that they preferred to blame the very gods than to impute their blindness to them as a crime? The tradition about the seer Tiresias is well known. Concerning Phineus,° Apollonius° sang as follows in the *Argonautica*:

> Nor did he fear Jupiter himself,
> Revealing truly to men the divine purpose.
> Wherefore he gave him a prolonged old age,
> But deprived him of the sweet light of his eyes.

But God himself is truth! The more veracious a man is in teaching truth to men, the more like must he be to God and the more acceptable to him. It is impious to believe that God is grudging of truth or does not wish it to be shared with men as freely as possible. Because of no offence, therefore, does it seem that this man who was godlike and eager to enlighten the human race was deprived of his eyesight, as were a great number of philosophers. Or should I mention those men of old who were renowned for statecraft and military achievements? First, Timoleon° of Corinth, who freed his own city and all Sicily, than whom no age has borne a man greater or more venerated in his state. Next, Appius Claudius,° whose vote, nobly expressed in the Senate, delivered Italy from Pyrrhus, her mortal enemy, but not himself from blindness. Thirdly, Caecilius Metellus,° the Pontifex, who, while he saved from fire not the city alone but also the Palladium, the symbol of its destiny, and its innermost mysteries, lost his own eyes, although on other occasions certainly God has given proof that he favours such remarkable piety, even among the heathen. Therefore what has befallen such a man should scarcely, I think, be regarded as an evil.

Why should I add to the list other men of later times, such as the famous Doge of Venice, Dandolo,° by far the most eminent of all, or Zizka,° the brave leader of the Bohemians and the bulwark of the orthodox faith? Why should I add theologians of the highest repute, Hieronymus Zanchius° and some others, when it is established that even Isaac° the patriarch himself—and no mortal was ever dearer to God—lived in blindness for many years, as did also (for a few years perhaps) Jacob,° his son, who was no less beloved by God. When, finally, it is perfectly certain from the divine testimony of Christ our Saviour that the man who was healed° by Him had been blind from the very womb, through no sin of his own or of his parents.

For my part, I call upon Thee, my God, who knowest my inmost mind and all my thoughts, to witness that (although I have repeatedly examined myself on this point as earnestly as I could, and have searched all the corners of my life) I am conscious of nothing, or of no deed, either recent or remote, whose wickedness could justly occasion or invite upon me this supreme misfortune. As for what I have at any time written (since the royalists think that I am now undergoing this suffering as a penance, and they accordingly rejoice), I likewise call God to witness that I have written nothing of such kind that I was not then and am not now convinced that it was right and true and pleasing to God. And I swear that my conduct was not influenced by ambition, gain, or glory, but solely by considerations of duty, honour, and devotion to my country. I did my utmost not only to free my country, but also to free the church. Hence, when the business of replying to the royal defence had been officially assigned to me, and at that same time I was afflicted at once by ill health and the virtual loss of my remaining eye, and the doctors were making learned predictions that if I should undertake this task, I would shortly lose both eyes, I was not in the least deterred by the warning. I seemed to hear, not the voice of the doctor (even that of Aesculapius,° issuing from the shrine at Epidaurus), but the sound of a certain more divine monitor within. And I thought that two lots had now been set before me by a certain command of fate: the one, blindness, the other, duty. Either I must necessarily endure the loss of my eyes, or I must abandon my most solemn duty. And there came into my mind those two fates which, the son of Thetis° relates, his mother brought back from Delphi, where she inquired concerning him:

> Two destinies lead me to the end, which is death:
> If staying here I fight around the city of Troy,
> Return is denied me, but immortal will be my fame.
> If homeward I return to my dear native land,
> Lost is fair fame, but long will be my life.

Then I reflected that many men have bought with greater evil smaller good; with death, glory. To me, on the contrary, was offered a greater good at the price of a smaller evil: that I could at the cost of blindness alone fulfil the most honourable requirement of my duty. As duty is of itself more substantial than glory, so it ought to be for every man more desirable and illustrious. I resolved therefore that I must employ this brief use of my eyes while yet I could for the greatest possible benefit to the state. You see what I chose, what I rejected, and why.

Then let those who slander the judgments of God cease to speak evil and invent empty tales about me. Let them be sure that I feel neither regret nor shame for my lot, that I stand unmoved and steady in my resolution, that I neither discern nor endure the anger of God, that in fact I know and recognize in the most momentous affairs his fatherly mercy and kindness towards me, and especially in this fact, that with his consolation strengthening my spirit I bow to his divine will, dwelling more often on what he has bestowed on me than on what he has denied. Finally, let them rest assured that I would not exchange the consciousness of my achievement for any deed of theirs, be it ever so righteous, nor would I be deprived of the recollection of my deeds, ever a source of gratitude and repose.

Finally, as to my blindness, I would rather have mine, if it be necessary, than either theirs, More, or yours. Your blindness, deeply implanted in the inmost faculties, obscures the mind, so that you may see nothing whole or real. Mine, which you make a reproach, merely deprives things of colour and superficial appearance. What is true and essential in them is not lost to my intellectual vision. How many things there are, moreover, which I have no desire to see, how many things that I should be glad not to see, how few remain that I should like to see. Nor do I feel pain at being classed with the blind, the afflicted, the suffering, and the weak (although you hold this to be wretched), since there is hope that in this way I may approach more closely the mercy and protection of the Father Almighty. There is a certain road which leads through weakness, as the apostle° teaches, to the greatest strength. May I be entirely helpless, provided that in my weakness there may arise all the more powerfully this immortal and more perfect strength; provided that in my shadows the light of the divine countenance may shine forth all the more clearly. For then I shall be at once the weakest and the strongest, at the same time blind and most keen in vision. By this infirmity may I be perfected, by this completed. So in this darkness, may I be clothed in light.

To be sure, we blind men are not the least of God's concerns, for the less able we are to perceive anything other than himself, the more mercifully and graciously does he deign to look upon us. Woe to him who mocks us, woe to him who injures us. He deserves to be cursed with a public malediction. Divine law and divine favour have rendered us not only safe from the injuries of men, but almost sacred, nor do these shadows around us seem to have been created so much by the dullness of our eyes as by the shade of angels' wings. And divine favour not infrequently is wont to lighten these shadows again, once made, by an inner and far more enduring light. To this circumstance I refer the fact that my friends now visit, esteem, and attend me more diligently even than before, and that there are some with whom I might as with true friends exchange the conversation° of Pylades [with Orestes] and Theseus [with Heracles]:

> *Orestes*: Go slowly as the rudder of my feet.
> *Pylades*: A precious care is this to me.

And elsewhere:

> *Theseus*: Give your hand to your friend and helper.
> Put your arm around my neck, and I will be your guide.

For my friends do not think that by this calamity I have been rendered altogether worthless, nor that whatever is characteristic of an honest and prudent man resides in his eyes. In fact, since the loss of my eyesight has not left me sluggish from inactivity but tireless and ready among the first to risk the greatest dangers for the sake of liberty, the chief men in the state do not desert me either, but, considering within themselves what human life is like, they gladly favour and indulge me, and grant to me rest and leisure, as to one who well deserves it. If I have any distinction, they do not remove it, if any public office, they do not take it away, if any advantage from that office, they do not diminish it, and although I am no longer as useful as I was, they think that they should reward me no less graciously. They pay me the same honour as if, according to the custom of ancient Athens, they had decreed that I take my meals in the Prytaneum.°

So long as I find in God and man such consolation for my blindness, let no one mourn for my eyes, which were lost in the cause of honour. Far be it from me either to mourn. Far be it from me to have so little spirit that I cannot easily despise the revilers of my blindness, or so little charity that I cannot even more easily pardon them. . . .

'Only one man° was found, most assuredly a great hero, whom they could oppose to Salmasius, a certain John Milton.' I did not realize that I was a hero, although you may, so far as I am concerned, be the son, perhaps, of some hero or other, since you are totally noxious.° And that I alone was found to defend the cause of the people of England, certainly I regret, if I consider the interests of the Commonwealth, but if I consider the glory involved, I am perfectly content that I have no one with whom to share it. Who I am and whence I come is uncertain, you say; so once it was uncertain who Homer was, and who Demosthenes. But in fact, I had learned to hold my peace, I had mastered the art of not writing, a lesson that Salmasius could never learn. And I carried silently in my breast that which, if I had then wished to publish it, would long since have made me as famous as I am today. But I was not greedy for fame, whose gait is slow, nor did I ever intend to publish even this, unless a fitting opportunity presented itself. It made no difference to me even if others did not realize that I knew whatever I knew, for it was not fame, but the opportune moment for each thing that I awaited. Hence it happened that I was known to a good many, long before Salmasius was known to himself. Now he is better known than the nag Andraemon.°

'Is he a man or a worm?' Indeed, I should prefer to be a worm, which even King David° confesses that he is, rather than hide in my breast your worm that dieth not. 'They say', you continue, 'that this fellow, expelled from the University of Cambridge, because of his offences, fled his disgrace and his country and travelled to Italy.' Even from this statement one can infer how truthful were your sources of information, for on this point everyone who knows me knows that both you and your informants lie most shamelessly, and I shall at once make this fact clear. If I had actually been expelled from Cambridge, why should I travel to Italy, rather than to France or Holland, where you, enveloped in so many offences, a minister of the Gospel, not only live in safety, but preach, and even defile with your unclean hands the sacred offices, to the extreme scandal of your church? But why to Italy, More? Another Saturn,° I presume, I fled to Latium that I might find a place to lurk. Yet I knew beforehand that Italy was not, as you think, a refuge or asylum for criminals, but rather the lodging-place of *humanitas* and of all the arts of civilization, and so I found it.

'Returning, he wrote his book on divorce.' I wrote nothing different from what Bucer° had written before me—and copiously—about the kingdom of Christ, nothing different from what Fagius° had written on Deuteronomy, Erasmus on the first Epistle to the Corinthians (a commentary intended for the benefit of the English people), nothing different from what many other illustrious men wrote for the common good. No one blamed them for so doing, and I fail to understand why it should be to me above all a source of reproach. One thing only could I wish, that I had not written it in the vernacular, for then I would not have met with vernacular readers, who are usually ignorant of their own good, and laugh at the misfortunes of others. But do you, vilest of men, protest about divorce, you who procured the most brutal of all divorces from Pontia, the maidservant engaged to you, after you seduced her under cover of that engagement? Moreover, she was a servant of Salmasius, an English woman it is said, warmly devoted to the royalist cause. It is beyond question that you wickedly courted her as royal property and left her as public property. Take care lest you yourself prove to have been the author of the very conversion which you profess to find so distasteful. Take care, I repeat, lest with the rule of Salmasius utterly overthrown you may yourself have converted Pontia into a 'republic'. And take care lest in this way, you, though a royalist, may be said to have founded many 'republics' in a single city, or as minister of state to have served them after their foundation by other men. These are your divorces, or, if you prefer, diversions, from which you emerge against me as a veritable Curius.°

Now you continue with your lies. 'When the conspirators were agitating the decapitation of the king, Milton wrote to them, and when they were wavering urged them to the wicked course.' But I did not write to them, nor did it rest with me to urge men who had already without me determined on precisely this course. Yet I shall describe hereafter what I did write on this subject, and I shall also speak of *Eikonoklastes*. Now since this fellow (I am uncertain whether to call him a man or the dregs of manhood), progressing from adultery with servant girls to the adulteration of all truth, has tried to render me infamous among foreigners, by piling up a whole series of lies against me, I ask that no one take it amiss or make it a source of reproach, or resent it, if I have said previously and shall say hereafter more about myself than I would wish, so that if I cannot rescue my eyes from blindness or my name from oblivion or slander, I can at least bring my life into the light out of that darkness which accompanies disgrace. And I must do this for more reasons than one. First, in order that the many good and learned men in all the neighbouring countries who are now reading my works and thinking rather well of me, may not despise me on account of this man's abuse, but may persuade themselves that I am incapable of ever disgracing honourable speech by dishonourable conduct, or free utterances by slavish deeds, and that my life, by the grace of God, has ever been far removed from all vice and crime. Next, in order that those distinguished and praiseworthy men whom I undertake to extol may know that I should consider nothing more shameful than to approach the task of praising them while myself deserving blame and censure. Finally, in order that the English people whose defence their own virtue has impelled me to undertake (whether it be my fate or my duty) may know that if I have always led a pure and honourable life, my *Defence* (whether it will be to their honour or dignity I know not) will certainly never be for them a source of shame or disgrace.

Who I am, then, and whence I come, I shall now disclose. I was born in London, of an honourable family. My father was a man of supreme integrity, my mother a woman of purest reputation, celebrated throughout the neighbourhood for her acts of charity. My father destined me in early childhood for the study of literature, for which I had so keen an appetite that from my twelfth year scarcely ever did I leave my studies for my bed before the hour of midnight. This was the first cause of injury to my eyes, whose natural weakness was augmented by frequent headaches. Since none of these defects slackened my assault upon knowledge, my father took care that I should be instructed daily both in school and under other masters at home. When I had thus become proficient in various languages and had tasted by no means superficially the sweetness of philosophy, he sent me to Cambridge, one of our two universities. There, untouched by any reproach, in the good graces of all upright men, for seven years I devoted myself to the traditional disciplines and liberal arts, until I had attained the degree of Master, as it is called, *cum laude*. Then, far from fleeing to Italy, as that filthy rascal alleges, of my own free will I returned home, to the regret of most of the fellows of the college, who bestowed on me no little honour. At my father's country place, whither he had retired to spend his declining years, I devoted myself entirely to the study of Greek and Latin writers, completely at leisure, not, however, without sometimes exchanging the country for the city, either to purchase books or to become acquainted with some new discovery in mathematics or music, in which I then took the keenest pleasure.

When I had occupied five years in this fashion, I became desirous, my mother having died, of seeing foreign parts, especially Italy, and with my father's consent I set forth, accompanied by a single attendant. On my departure Henry Wotton, a most distinguished gentleman, who had long served as King James's ambassador to the Venetians, gave single proof of his esteem for me, writing a graceful letter which contained good wishes and precepts of no little value to one going abroad. On the recommendation of others I was warmly received in Paris by the noble Thomas Scudamore,° Viscount Sligo, legate of King Charles. He on his own initiative introduced me, in company with several of his suite, to Hugo Grotius,° a most learned man (then ambassador from the Queen of Sweden to the King of France) whom I ardently desired to meet. When I set out for Italy some days thereafter, Scudamore gave me letters to English merchants along my projected route, that they might assist me as they could. Sailing from Nice, I reached Genoa, then Leghorn and Pisa, and after that Florence. In that city, which I have always admired above all others because of the elegance, not just of its tongue, but also of its wit, I lingered for about two months. There I at once became the friend of many gentlemen eminent in rank and learning, whose private academies° I frequented—a Florentine institution which deserves great praise not only for promoting humane studies but also for encouraging friendly intercourse. Time will never destroy my recollection—ever welcome and delightful—of you, Jacopo Gaddi, Carlo Dati, Frescobaldi, Coltellini, Buonmattei, Chimentelli, Francini, and many others.

From Florence I travelled to Siena and thence to Rome. When the antiquity and venerable repute of that city had detained me for almost two months and I had been graciously entertained there by Lukas Holste° and other men endowed with both learning and wit, I proceeded to Naples. Here I was introduced by a certain Eremite Friar, with whom I had made the journey from Rome, to Giovanni Battista

Manso,° Marquis of Villa, a man of high rank and influence, to whom the famous Italian poet, Torquato Tasso, dedicated his work on friendship. As long as I was there I found him a very true friend. He personally conducted me through the various quarters of the city and the Viceregal Court, and more than once came to my lodgings to call. When I was leaving he gravely apologized because even though he had especially wished to show me many more attentions, he could not do so in that city, since I was unwilling to be circumspect in regard to religion. Although I desired also to cross to Sicily and Greece, the sad tidings of civil war from England summoned me back. For I thought it base that I should travel abroad at my ease for the cultivation of my mind, while my fellow-citizens at home were fighting for liberty. As I was on the point of returning to Rome, I was warned by merchants that they had learned through letters of plots laid against me by the English Jesuits, should I return to Rome, because of the freedom with which I had spoken about religion. For I had determined within myself that in those parts I would not indeed begin a conversation about religion, but if questioned about my faith would hide nothing, whatever the consequences. And so, I none the less returned to Rome. What I was, if any man inquired, I concealed from no one. For almost two more months, in the very stronghold of the Pope, if anyone attacked the orthodox religion, I openly, as before, defended it. Thus, by the will of God, I returned again in safety to Florence, revisiting friends who were as anxious to see me as if it were my native land to which I had returned. After gladly lingering there for as many months as before (except for an excursion of a few days to Lucca) I crossed the Apennines and hastened to Venice by way of Bologna and Ferrara. When I had spent one month exploring that city and had seen to the shipping of the books which I had acquired throughout Italy, I proceeded to Geneva by way of Verona, Milan, and the Pennine Alps, and then along Lake Leman. Geneva, since it reminds me of the slanderer More, impels me once again to call God to witness that in all these places, where so much licence exists, I lived free and untouched by the slightest sin or reproach, reflecting constantly that although I might hide from the gaze of men, I could not elude the sight of God. In Geneva I conversed daily with John Diodati,° the learned professor of theology. Then by the same route as before, through France, I returned home after a year and three months, more or less, at almost the same time as Charles broke the peace and renewed the war with the Scots, which is known as the second Bishops' War.°

The royalist troops were routed in the first engagement of this war, and Charles, when he perceived that all the English, as well as the Scots, were extremely—and justly—ill-disposed towards him, soon convened Parliament, not of his own free will but compelled by disaster. I myself, seeking a place to become established, could I but find one anywhere in such upset and tumultuous times, rented a house in town, sufficiently commodious for myself and my books, and there, blissfully enough, devoted myself to my interrupted studies, willingly leaving the outcome of these events, first of all to God, and then to those whom the people had entrusted with this office. Meanwhile, as Parliament acted with vigour, the haughtiness of the bishops began to deflate. As soon as freedom of speech (at the very least) became possible, all mouths were opened against them. Some complained of the personal defects of the bishops, others of the defectiveness of the episcopal rank itself. It was wrong, they said, that their church alone should differ from all other reformed churches. It was proper for the church to be governed by the example of the brethren, but first of all by the word of God. Now, thoroughly aroused to these concerns, I perceived that men were following the true path to liberty and that from these beginnings, these first steps, they were making the most direct progress towards the liberation of all human life from slavery—provided that the discipline arising from religion should overflow into the morals and institutions of the state. Since, moreover, I had so practised myself from youth that I was above all things unable to disregard the laws of God and man, and since I had asked myself whether I should be of any future use if I now failed my country (or rather the church and so many of my brothers who were exposing themselves to danger for the sake of the Gospel) I decided, although at that time occupied with certain other matters, to devote to this conflict all my talents and all my active powers.

First, therefore, I addressed to a certain friend two books on the reformation of the English church.° Then, since two bishops° of particularly high repute were asserting their prerogatives against certain eminent ministers, and I concluded that on those subjects which I had mastered solely for love of truth and out of regard for Christian duty, I could express myself at least as well as those who were wrangling for their own profit and unjust authority, I replied to one of the bishops in two books, of which the first was entitled *Of Prelatical Episcopacy* and the second *The Reason of Church Government*, while to the other bishop I made reply in certain *Animadversions* and later in an *Apology*. I brought succour to the ministers, who were, as it was said, scarcely able to withstand the eloquence of this bishop, and from that time onward, if the bishops made any response, I took a hand. When they, having become a target for the weapons of all men, had at last fallen and troubled us no more, I directed my attention elsewhere, asking myself whether I could in any way advance the cause of true and substantial liberty, which must be sought, not without, but within, and which is best achieved, not by the sword, but by a life rightly undertaken and rightly conducted. Since, then, I observed that there are, in all, three varieties of liberty without which civilized life is scarcely possible, namely ecclesiastical liberty, domestic or personal liberty, and civil liberty, and since I had already written about the first, while I saw that the magistrates were vigorously attending to the third, I took as my province the remaining one, the second or domestic kind. This too seemed to be concerned with three problems: the nature of marriage itself, the education of the children, and finally the existence of freedom to express oneself. Hence I set forth my views on marriage, not only its proper contraction, but also, if need be, its dissolution. My explanation was in accordance with divine law, which Christ did not revoke; much less did He give approval in civil life to any other law more weighty than the law of Moses. Concerning the view which should be held on the single exception, that of fornication, I also expressed both my own opinion and that of others. Our distinguished countryman Selden° still more fully explained this point in his *Hebrew Wife*, published about two years later. For in vain does he prattle about liberty in assembly and market-place who at home endures the slavery most unworthy of man, slavery to an inferior. Concerning this matter then I published several books, at the very time when man and wife were often bitter foes, he dwelling at home with their children, she, the mother of the family, in the camp of the enemy, threatening her husband with death and disaster. Next, in one small volume, I discussed the education of children, a brief treatment, to be sure, but sufficient, as I thought, for those who devote to the subject the attention it deserves. For nothing can be more efficacious than education in moulding the minds of men to virtue (whence arises true and internal liberty), in governing the state effectively, and preserving it for the longest possible space of time.

Lastly I wrote, on the model of a genuine speech, the *Areopagitica*, concerning freedom of the press, that the judgment of truth and falsehood, what should be printed and what suppressed, ought not to be in the hands of a few men (and these mostly ignorant and of vulgar discernment) charged with the inspection of books, at whose will or whim virtually everyone is prevented from publishing aught that surpasses the understanding of the mob. Civil liberty, which was the last variety, I had not touched upon, for I saw that it was being adequately dealt with by the magistrates, nor did I write anything about the right of kings, until the king, having been declared an enemy by Parliament and vanquished in the field, was pleading his cause as a prisoner before the judges and was condemned to death. Then at last, when certain Presbyterian ministers, formerly bitter enemies of Charles, but now resentful that the Independent parties were preferred to theirs and carried more weight in Parliament, persisted in attacking the decree which Parliament had passed concerning the king (wroth, not because of the fact, but because their own faction had not performed it) and caused as much tumult as they could, even daring to assert that the doctrines of Protestants and all reformed churches shrank from such an outrageous sentence against kings, I concluded that I must openly oppose so open a lie. Not even then, however, did I write or advise anything concerning Charles, but demonstrated what was in general permissible against tyrants, adducing not a few testimonies from the foremost theologians. And I attacked, almost as if I were haranguing an assembly, the pre-eminent ignorance or insolence of these ministers, who had given promise of better things. This book° did not appear until after the death of the king, having been written to reconcile men's minds, rather than to determine anything about Charles (which was not my affair, but that of the magistrates, and which had by then been effected). This service of mine, between private walls, I freely gave, now to the church and now to the state. To me, in return, neither the one nor the other offered more than protection, but the deeds themselves undoubtedly bestowed on me a good conscience, good repute among good men, and this honourable freedom of speech. Other men gained for themselves advantages, other men secured offices at no cost to themselves. As for me, no man has ever seen me seeking office, no man has ever seen me soliciting aught through my friends, clinging with suppliant expression to the doors of Parliament, or loitering in the hallways of the lower assemblies. I kept myself at home for the most part, and from my own revenues, though often they were in large part withheld because of the civil disturbance, I endured the tax—by no means entirely just—that was laid on me and maintained my frugal way of life.

When these works had been completed and I thought that I could look forward to an abundance of leisure, I turned to the task of tracing in unbroken sequence, if I could, the history° of my country, from the earliest origins even to the present day. I had already finished four books when the kingdom of Charles was transformed into a republic, and the so-called Council of State, which was then for the first time established by the authority of Parliament, summoned me, though I was expecting no such event, and desired to employ my services, especially in connection with foreign affairs. Not long afterwards there appeared a book attributed to the king, and plainly written with great malice against Parliament. Bidden to reply to this, I opposed to the *Eikon* the *Eikonoklastes*, not, as I am falsely charged, 'insulting the departed spirit of the king', but thinking that Queen Truth should be preferred to King Charles. Indeed, since I saw that this slander would be at hand for any calumniator, in the very introduction (and as often as I could elsewhere) I averted this reproach from myself. Then Salmasius appeared. So far were they from spending a long time (as More alleges) seeking one who would reply to him, that all, of their own accord, at once named me, then present in the Council. I have given an account of myself to this extent in order to stop your mouth, More, and refute your lies, chiefly for the sake of those good men who otherwise would know me not. Do you then, I bid you, unclean More,° be silent. Hold your tongue, I say! For the more you abuse me, the more copiously will you compel me to account for my conduct. From such accounting you can gain nothing save the reproach, already most severe, of telling lies, while for me you open the door to still higher praise of my own integrity. . . .

For, my fellow countrymen, your own character is a mighty factor in the acquisition or retention of liberty. Unless your liberty is such as can neither be won nor lost by arms, but is of that kind alone which, sprung from piety, justice, temperance, in short, true virtue, has put down the deepest and most far-reaching roots in your souls, there will not be lacking one who will shortly wrench from you, even without weapons, that liberty which you boast of having sought by force of arms. Many men has war made great whom peace makes small. If, having done with war, you neglect the arts of peace, if warfare is your peace and liberty, war your only virtue, your supreme glory, you will find, believe me, that peace itself is your greatest enemy. Peace itself will be by far your hardest war, and what you thought liberty will prove to be your servitude. Unless with true and sincere devotion to God and men—not empty and verbose, but effective and fruitful devotion—you drive from your minds the superstitions that are sprung from ignorance of real and genuine religion, you will have those who will perch upon your back and shoulders as if on beasts of burden, who will sell you at public auction, though you be victors in the war, as if you were their own booty, and will reap rich reward from your ignorance and superstition. Unless you expel avarice, ambition, and luxury from your minds, yes, and extravag-

ance from your families as well, you will find at home and within that
tyrant who, you believed, was to be sought abroad and in the field—
now even more stubborn. In fact, many tyrants, impossible to endure,
will from day to day hatch out from your very vitals. Conquer them first.
This is the warfare of peace, these are its victories, hard indeed, but
bloodless, and far more noble than the gory victories of war. Unless you
be victors here as well, that enemy and tyrant whom you have just now
defeated in the field has either not been conquered at all or has been
conquered in vain. For if the ability to devise the cleverest means of
putting vast sums of money into the treasury, the power readily to equip
land and sea forces, to deal shrewdly with ambassadors from abroad,
and to contract judicious alliances and treaties has seemed to any of you
greater, wiser, and more useful to the state than to administer incorrupt
justice to the people, to help those cruelly harassed and oppressed, and
to render to every man promptly his own deserts, too late will you discover how mistaken you have been, when those great affairs have suddenly betrayed you and what now seems to you small and trifling shall
then have turned against you and become a source of ruin. Nay, the
loyalty of the armies and allies in whom you trust is fleeting, unless it be
maintained by the power of justice alone. Wealth and honours, which
most men pursue, easily change masters; they desert to the side which
excels in virtue, industry, and endurance of toil, and they abandon the
slothful. Thus nation presses upon nation, or the sounder part of a
nation overthrows the more corrupt. Thus did you drive out the royalists. If you begin to slip into the same vices, to imitate those men, to
seek the same goals, to clutch at the same vanities, you actually are
royalists yourselves, at the mercy either of the same men who up to now
have been your enemies, or of others in turn, who, depending on the
same prayers to God, the same patience, integrity, and shrewdness
which were at first your strength, will justly subdue you, who have now
become so base and slipped into royalist excess and folly. Then in
truth, as if God had become utterly disgusted with you—a horrid
state—will you seem to have passed through the fire only to perish in
the smoke. Then will you be as much despised by all men as you are
now admired and will leave behind you only this salutary lesson (which
could in the future perhaps be of assistance to others, though not to
you), how great might have been the achievements of genuine virtue
and piety, when the mere counterfeit and shadow of these qualities—
cleverly feigned, no more—could embark upon such noble undertakings and through you progress so far towards execution.

For if through your want of experience, of constancy, or of honesty such glorious deeds have issued in failure, it will yet be possible for better men to do as much hereafter, and no less must be expected of them. But no one, not even Cromwell himself, nor a whole tribe of liberating Brutuses,° if Brutus were to come to life again, either could if they would, or would if they could, free you a second time, once you had been so easily corrupted. For why should anyone then claim for you freedom to vote or the power of sending to Parliament whomever you prefer? So that each of you could elect in the cities men of his own faction, or in the country towns choose that man, however unworthy, who has entertained you more lavishly at banquets and supplied farmers and peasants with more abundant drink? Under such circumstances, not wisdom or authority, but faction and gluttony would elect to Parliament in our name either inn-keepers and hucksters of the state from city taverns or from country districts ploughboys and veritable herdsmen. Who would commit the state to men whom no one would trust with his private affairs? the treasury and revenues to men who have shamefully wasted their own substance? Who would hand over to them the public income, to steal and convert from public to private? Or how could they suddenly become legislators for the whole nation who themselves have never known what law is, what reason, what right or justice, straight or crooked, licit or illicit; who think that all power resides in violence, all grandeur in pride and arrogance; who in Parliament give priority to showing illegitimate favour to their friends and persistent hostility to their foes; who establish their relatives and friends in every section of the country to levy taxes and confiscate property—men for the most part mean and corrupt, who by bidding at their own auctions collect therefrom great sums of money, embezzle what they have collected, defraud the state, ravage the provinces, enrich themselves, and suddenly emerge into opulence and pride from the beggary and rags of yesterday? Who could endure such thieving servants, the deputies of their masters? Who could believe the masters and patrons of such thieves to be fit guardians of liberty, or think his own liberty enlarged one iota by such caretakers of the state (though the customary number of five hundred be thus elected from all the towns), since there would then be so few among the guardians and watchdogs of liberty who either knew how to enjoy, or deserved to possess, it?

Lastly (a reflection not to be neglected), men who are unworthy of liberty most often prove ungrateful to their very liberators. Who would now be willing to fight, or even encounter the smallest danger, for the liberty of such men? It is not fitting, it is not meet, for such men to be free. However loudly they shout and boast about liberty, slaves they are at home and abroad, although they know it not. When at last they do perceive it and like wild horses fretting at the bit try to shake off the yoke, driven not by the love of true liberty (to which the good man alone can rightly aspire), but by pride and base desires, even though they take arms in repeated attempts, they will accomplish naught. They can perhaps change their servitude; they cannot cast it off. This often happened even to the ancient Romans, once they had been corrupted and dissipated by luxury; still more often to the modern Romans, when after a long interval they sought under the auspices of Crescentius Nomentanus° and later under the leadership of Cola di Rienzi,° self-styled Tribune of the People, to renew the ancient glory of Rome and restore the Republic. For rest assured (that you may not be vexed, or seek to blame someone other than yourselves), rest assured, I say, that just as to be free is precisely the same as to be pious, wise, just, and temperate, careful of one's property, aloof from another's, and thus finally to be magnanimous and brave, so to be the opposite to these qualities is the same as to be a slave. And by the customary judgment and, so to speak, just retaliation of God, it happens that a nation which cannot rule and govern itself, but has delivered itself into slavery to its own lusts, is enslaved also to other masters whom it does not choose, and serves not only voluntarily but also against its will. Such is the decree of law and of nature herself, that he who cannot control himself, who through poverty of intellect or madness cannot properly administer his own affairs, should not be his own master, but like a ward be given over to the power of another. Much less should he be put in charge of the affairs of other men, or of the state. You, therefore, who wish to remain free, either be wise at the outset or recover your senses as soon as possible. If to be a slave is hard, and you do not wish it, learn to obey right reason, to master yourselves. Lastly, refrain from factions, hatreds, superstitions, injustices, lusts, and rapine against one another. Unless you do this with all your strength you cannot seem either to God or to men, or even to your recent liberators, fit to be entrusted with the liberty and guidance of the state and the power of commanding others, which you arrogate to yourselves so greedily. Then indeed, like a nation in wardship, you would rather be in need of some tutor, some brave and faithful guardian of your affairs.

As for me, whatever the issue, I have bestowed my services by no means grudgingly nor, I hope, in vain, where I judged that they would be most useful to the state. I have not borne arms° for liberty merely on my own doorstep, but have also wielded them so far afield that the reason and justification of these by no means commonplace events, having been explained and defended both at home and abroad, and having surely won the approval of all good men, are made splendidly manifest to the supreme glory of my countrymen and as an example to posterity. If the most recent deeds of my fellow countrymen should not correspond sufficiently to their earliest, let them look to it themselves. I have borne witness, I might almost say I have erected a monument° that will not soon pass away, to those deeds that were illustrious, that were glorious, that were almost beyond any praise, and if I have done nothing else, I have surely redeemed my pledge. Moreover, just as the epic poet, if he is scrupulous and disinclined to break the rules, undertakes to extol, not the whole life of the hero whom he proposes to celebrate in his verse, but usually one event of his life (the exploits of Achilles at Troy, let us say, or the return of Ulysses, or the arrival of Aeneas in Italy) and passes over the rest, so let it suffice me too, as my duty or my excuse, to have celebrated at least one heroic achievement of my countrymen. The rest I omit. Who could extol all the achievements of an entire nation? If after such brave deeds you ignobly fail, if you do aught unworthy of yourselves, be sure that posterity will speak out and pass judgment: the foundations were soundly laid, the beginnings, in fact more than the beginnings, were splendid, but posterity will look in vain, not without a certain distress, for those who were to complete the work, who were to put the pediment in place. It will be a source of grief that to such great undertakings, such great virtues, perseverance was lacking. It will seem to posterity that a mighty harvest of glory was at hand, together with the opportunity for doing the greatest deeds, but that to this opportunity men were wanting. Yet there was not wanting one who could rightly counsel, encourage, and inspire, who could honour both the noble deeds and those who had done them and make both deeds and doers illustrious with praises that will never die.

The Ready and Easy Way to Establish a Free Commonwealth

AND THE EXCELLENCE THEREOF COMPARED WITH THE INCONVENIENCES AND DANGERS OF READMITTING KINGSHIP IN THIS NATION

Et nos
Consilium dedimus Syllæ, demus populo nunc.°

Although since the writing of this treatise the face of things hath had some change, writs for new elections° have been recalled, and the members at first chosen readmitted from exclusion, yet not a little rejoicing to hear declared the resolution of those who are in power,° tending to the establishment of a free commonwealth, and to remove, if it be possible, this noxious humour of returning to bondage,° instilled of late by some deceivers, and nourished from bad principles and false apprehensions among too many of the people; I thought best not to suppress what I had written, hoping that it may now be of much more use and concernment to be freely published in the midst of our elections to a free parliament, or° their sitting to consider freely of the government, whom it behooves to have all things represented to them that may direct their judgment therein; and I never read of any state, scarce of any tyrant, grown so incurable as to refuse counsel from any in a time of public deliberation, much less to be offended. If their absolute determination be to enthrall us, before so long a Lent of servitude they may permit us a little shroving-time° first wherein to speak freely and take our leaves of liberty. And because in the former edition, through haste, many faults escaped, and many books were suddenly dispersed° ere the note to mend them could be sent, I took the opportunity from this occasion to revise and somewhat to enlarge the whole discourse, especially that part which argues for a perpetual senate. The treatise thus revised and enlarged is as follows.

The parliament of England, assisted by a great number of the people who appeared and stuck to them faithfulest in defence of religion and their civil liberties, judging kingship° by long experience a government unnecessary, burdensome and dangerous, justly and magnanimously abolished it, turning regal bondage into a free commonwealth, to the admiration and terror of our emulous neighbours. They took themselves not bound by the light of nature or religion to any former covenant,° from which the king himself, by many forfeitures of a latter date or discovery, and our own longer consideration thereon, had more and more unbound us, both to himself and his posterity; as hath been ever the justice and the prudence of all wise nations that have ejected tyranny. They covenanted 'to preserve the king's person and authority in the preservation of the true religion and our liberties'; not in his endeavouring to bring in upon our consciences a Popish religion, upon our liberties, thraldom, upon our lives, destruction, by his occasioning, if not complotting, as was after discovered, the Irish massacre, his fomenting and arming the rebellion, his covert leaguing with the rebels against us, his refusing, more than seven times, propositions most just and necessary to the true religion and our liberties tendered him by the parliament both of England and Scotland. They made not their covenant concerning him with no difference between a king and a God; or promised him, as Job° did to the Almighty, 'to trust in him though he slay us': they understood that the solemn engagement° wherein we all forswore kingship was no more a breach of the covenant than the covenant was of the protestation° before, but a faithful and prudent going on both in the words well weighed, and in the true sense of the covenant 'without respect of persons', when we could not serve two contrary masters, God and the king, or the king and that more supreme law sworn in the first place to maintain our safety and our liberty. They knew the people of England to be a free people, themselves the representers of that freedom; and although many were excluded,° and as many fled° (so they pretended) from tumults to Oxford, yet they were left a sufficient number to act in parliament, therefore not bound by any statute of preceding parliaments, but by the law of nature only, which is the only law of laws truly and properly to all mankind fundamental, the beginning and the end of all government; to which no parliament or people that will throughly reform but may and must have recourse, as they had, and must yet have in church reformation (if they throughly intend it) to evangelic rules;° not to ecclesiastical canons, though never so ancient, so ratified and established in the land by statutes which for the most part are mere positive° laws, neither natural nor moral; and so by any parliament, for just and serious considerations, without scruple to be at any time repealed.

If others of their number in these things were under force,° they were not, but under free conscience; if others were excluded by a power which they could not resist, they were not therefore to leave the helm of government in no hands, to discontinue their care of the public peace and safety, to desert the people in anarchy and confusion, no more than when so many of their members left them as made up in outward formality a more legal parliament° of three estates against them. The best affected also, and best principled of the people, stood not numbering or computing on which side appeared to them most reason, most safety, when the house divided upon main matters. What was well motioned and advised, they examined not whether fear or persuasion carried it in the vote, neither did they measure votes and counsels by the intentions° of them that voted; knowing that intentions either are but guessed at, or not soon enough known; and although good, can neither make the deed such, nor prevent the consequence from being bad. Suppose bad intentions in things otherwise well done: what was well done, was by them who so thought not the less obeyed or followed in the state; since in the church, who had not rather follow Iscariot° or Simon° the magician, though to covetous ends preaching, than Saul,° though in the uprightness of his heart persecuting the gospel?

Safer they therefore judged what they thought the better counsels, though carried on by some perhaps to bad ends, than the worse by others, though endeavoured with best intentions. And yet they were not to learn° that a greater number might be corrupt within the walls of a parliament, as well as of a city; whereof in matters of nearest concernment all men will be judges; nor easily permit that the odds of voices in their greatest council shall more endanger them by corrupt or credulous votes than the odds of enemies by open assaults; judging that most voices ought not always to prevail where main matters are in question. If others hence will pretend to disturb all counsels, what is that to them who pretend not, but are in real danger?—not they only so judging, but a great (though not the greatest) number of their chosen patriots, who might be more in weight than the others in number: there being in number little virtue, but by weight and measure wisdom working all things, and the dangers on either side they seriously thus weighed.

From the treaty,° short fruits of long labours, and seven years' war; security for twenty years, if we can hold it; reformation in the church for three years: then put to shift° again with our vanquished master. His justice, his honour, his conscience declared quite contrary to ours; which would have furnished him with many such evasions as in a book entitled *An Inquisition for Blood* ° soon after were not concealed: bishops not totally removed,° but left, as it were, in ambush, a reserve, with ordination in their sole power; their lands already sold not to be alienated,° but rented,° and the sale of them called 'sacrilege';° delinquents,° few of many brought to condign° punishment; accessories punished, the chief author° above pardon, though, after utmost resistance vanquished, not to give, but to receive laws; yet besought, treated with, and to be thanked for his gracious concessions, to be honoured, worshipped, glorified.

If this we swore° to do, with what righteousness in the sight of God, with what assurance that we bring not by such an oath the whole sea of blood-guiltiness upon our own heads? If on the other side we prefer a free government, though for the present not obtained, yet all those suggested fears and difficulties, as the event° will prove, easily overcome, we remain finally secure from the exasperated regal power, and out of snares; shall retain the best part of our liberty, which is our religion, and the civil part will be from these who defer° us much more easily recovered, being neither so subtle nor so awful as a king reinthroned. Nor were their actions less both at home and abroad than might become the hopes of a glorious rising commonwealth; nor were the expressions both of army and people, whether in their public declarations or several writings, other than such as testified a spirit in this nation no less noble and well fitted to the liberty of a commonwealth than in the ancient Greeks or Romans. Nor was the heroic cause unsuccessfully defended to all Christendom against the tongue of a famous and thought invincible adversary;° nor the constancy and fortitude that so nobly vindicated our liberty, our victory at once against two the most prevailing usurpers over mankind, superstition and tyranny, unpraised or uncelebrated in a written monument, likely to outlive detraction, as it hath hitherto convinced or silenced not a few of our detractors, especially in parts abroad.

After our liberty and religion thus prosperously fought for, gained, and many years possessed (except in those unhappy interruptions, which God hath removed), now that nothing remains but in all reason the certain hopes of a speedy and immediate settlement forever in a firm and free commonwealth for this extolled and magnified nation, regardless both of honour won, or deliverances vouchsafed from heaven, to fall back, or rather to creep back so poorly, as it seems the multitude would, to their once abjured and detested thraldom of kingship, to be ourselves the slanderers of our own just and religious deeds, though done by some to covetous and ambitious ends, yet not therefore to be stained with their infamy, or they to asperse the integrity of others; and yet these now by revolting from the conscience of deeds well done, both in church and state, to throw away and forsake, or rather to betray a just and noble cause for the mixture of bad men who have ill-managed and abused it (which had our fathers done heretofore, and on the same pretence deserted true religion, what had long ere this become of our gospel, and all Protestant reformation so much intermixed with the avarice and ambition of some reformers?) and by thus relapsing, to verify all the bitter predictions of our triumphing enemies, who will now think they wisely discerned and justly censured both us and all our actions as rash, rebellious, hypocritical and impious, not only argues a strange, degenerate contagion suddenly spread among us, fitted and prepared for new slavery, but will render us a scorn and derision to all our neighbours.

And what will they at best say of us, and of the whole English name, but scoffingly, as of that foolish builder mentioned by our Saviour,° who began to build a tower and was not able to finish it? Where is this goodly tower of a commonwealth, which the English boasted they would build to overshadow kings, and be another Rome in the west? The foundation indeed they laid gallantly, but fell into a worse confusion, not of tongues, but of factions, than those at the tower of Babel; and have left no memorial of their work behind them remaining but in the common laughter of Europe. Which must needs redound the more to our shame, if we but look on our neighbours the United Provinces,° to us inferior in all outward advantages; who notwithstanding, in the midst of greater difficulties, courageously, wisely, constantly went through with the same work, and are settled in all the happy enjoyments of a potent and flourishing republic to this day.

Besides this, if we return to kingship, and soon repent (as undoubtedly we shall when we begin to find the old encroachments coming on by little and little upon our consciences, which must necessarily proceed from king and bishop united inseparably in one interest), we may be forced perhaps to fight over again all that we have fought, and spend over again all that we have spent, but are never like to attain thus far as we are now advanced to the recovery of our freedom, never to have it in possession as we now have it, never to be vouchsafed hereafter the like mercies and signal assistances from heaven in our cause, if by our ingrateful backsliding we make these fruitless; flying now to regal concessions from his divine condescensions and gracious answers to our once importuning prayers against the tyranny which we then groaned under; making vain and viler than dirt the blood of so many thousand faithful and valiant Englishmen, who left us in this liberty, bought with their lives; losing by a strange after-game of folly all the battles we have won, together with all Scotland as to our conquest, hereby lost, which never any of our kings could conquer, all the treasure we have spent, not that corruptible treasure only, but that far more precious of all our late miraculous deliverances; treading back again with lost labour all our happy steps in the progress of reformation, and most pitifully depriving ourselves the instant fruition of that free government which we have so dearly purchased, a free commonwealth, not only held by wisest men in all ages the noblest, the manliest, the equallest,° the justest government, the most agreeable to all due liberty and proportioned equality, both human, civil and Christian, most cherishing to virtue and true religion but also (I may say it with greatest probability) plainly commended, or rather enjoined by our Saviour himself, to all Christians, not without remarkable disallowance, and the brand of Gentilism upon kingship: God in much displeasure gave a king° to the Israelites, and imputed it a sin to them that they sought one; but Christ° apparently forbids his disciples to admit of any such heathenish government: 'The kings of the Gentiles', saith he, 'exercise lordship over them', and they that 'exercise authority upon them are called benefactors: but ye shall not be so; but he that is greatest among you, let him be as the younger; and he that is chief, as he that serveth.' The occasion of these his words was the ambitious desire of Zebedee's two sons° to be exalted above their brethren in his kingdom, which they thought was to be ere long upon earth. That he speaks of civil government is manifest by the former part of the comparison, which infers the other part to be always in the same kind. And what government comes nearer to this precept of Christ than a free commonwealth; wherein they who are greatest are perpetual servants and drudges to the public at their own cost and charges, neglect their own affairs, yet are not elevated above their brethren; live soberly in their families, walk the streets as other men, may be spoken to freely, familiarly, friendly, without adoration? Whereas a king must be adored like a demigod, with a dissolute and haughty court about him, of vast expense and luxury, masques and revels, to the debauching of our prime gentry, both male and female; not in their pastimes only, but in earnest, by the loose employments of court service, which will be then thought honourable. There will be a queen also of no less charge, in most likelihood outlandish° and a Papist, besides a queen mother such already, together with both their courts and numerous train; then a royal issue, and ere long severally their sumptuous courts, to the multiplying of a servile crew, not of servants only, but of nobility and gentry, bred up then to the hopes not of public, but of court offices, to be stewards, chamberlains, ushers, grooms even of the close-stool;° and the lower their minds debased with court opinions, contrary to all virtue and reformation, the haughtier will be their pride and profuseness. We may well remember this not long since at home, or need but look at present into the French court,° where enticements and preferments daily draw away and pervert the Protestant nobility.

As to the burden of expense, to our cost we shall soon know it, for any good to us deserving to be termed no better than the vast and lavish price of our subjection and their debauchery, which we are now so greedily cheapening,° and would so fain be paying most inconsiderately to a single person; who, for anything wherein the public really needs him, will have little else to do but to bestow the eating and drinking of excessive dainties, to set a pompous face upon the superficial actings of state, to pageant himself up and down in progress among the perpetual bowings and cringings of an abject people, on either side deifying and adoring him for nothing done that can deserve it. For what can he more than another man? who, even in the expression of a late court poet,° sits only like a great cipher° set to no purpose before a long row of other significant figures. Nay, it is well and happy for the people if their king be but a cipher, being ofttimes a mischief, a pest, a scourge of the nation, and, which is worse, not to be removed, not to be controlled, much less accused or brought to punishment, without the danger of a common ruin, without the shaking and almost subversion of the whole land; whereas in a free commonwealth, any governor or chief councillor offending may be removed and punished without the least commotion.

Certainly then that people must needs be mad or strangely infatuated that build the chief hope of their common happiness or safety on a single person; who, if he happen to be good, can do no more than another man; if to be bad, hath in his hands to do more evil without check than millions of other men. The happiness of a nation must needs be firmest and certainest in a full and free council of their own electing, where no single person, but reason only, sways. And what madness is it for them who might manage nobly their own affairs themselves, sluggishly and weakly to devolve all on a single person, and, more like boys under age than men, to commit all to his patronage and disposal who neither can perform what he undertakes, and yet for undertaking it, though royally paid, will not be their servant, but their lord? How unmanly must it needs be to count such a one the breath of our nostrils, to hang all our felicity on him, all our safety, our wellbeing, for which if we were aught else but sluggards or babies, we need depend on none but God and our own counsels, our own active virtue and industry. 'Go to the ant, thou sluggard', saith Solomon;° 'consider her ways, and be wise; which having no prince, ruler, or lord, provides her meat in the summer, and gathers her food in the harvest': which evidently shows us that they who think the nation undone without a king, though they look grave or haughty, have not so much true spirit and understanding in them as a pismire;° neither are these diligent creatures hence concluded to live in lawless anarchy, or that commended; but are set the examples to imprudent and ungoverned men of a frugal and self-governing democracy or commonwealth, safer and more thriving in the joint providence and counsel of many industrious equals than under the single domination of one imperious lord.

It may be well wondered that any nation styling themselves free can suffer any man to pretend hereditary right over them as their lord whenas by acknowledging that right they conclude themselves his servants and his vassals, and so renounce their own freedom. Which how a people and their leaders especially can do who have fought so gloriously for liberty; how they can change their noble words and actions, heretofore so becoming the majesty of a free people, into the base necessity of court flatteries and prostrations, is not only strange and admirable,° but lamentable to think on. That a nation should be so valorous and courageous to win their liberty in the field, and when they have won it, should be so heartless° and unwise in their counsels as not to know how to use it, value it, what to do with it or with themselves, but after ten or twelve years' prosperous war and contestation with tyranny, basely and besottedly to run their necks again into the yoke which they have broken, and prostrate all the fruits of their victory for nought at the feet of the vanquished, besides our loss of glory, and such an example as kings or tyrants never yet had the like to boast of, will be an ignominy if it befall us that never yet befell any nation possessed of their liberty; worthy indeed themselves, whatsoever they be, to be forever slaves, but that part of the nation which consents not with them, as I persuade me of a great number, far worthier than by their means to be brought into the same bondage.

Considering these things so plain, so rational, I cannot but yet further admire on the other side how any man who hath the true princi-, ciples of justice and religion in him can presume or take upon him to be a king and lord over his brethren, whom he cannot but know, whether as men or Christians, to be for the most part every way equal or superior to himself: how he can display with such vanity and ostentation his regal splendour so supereminently above other mortal men; or, being a Christian, can assume such extraordinary honour and worship to himself, while the kingdom of Christ, our common king and lord, is hid to this world, and such gentilish imitation forbid in express words by himself to all his disciples. All Protestants hold that Christ in his church hath left no vicegerent of his power; but himself, without deputy, is the only head thereof governing it from heaven: how then can any Christian man derive his kingship from Christ, but with worse usurpation than the pope his headship over the church, since Christ not only hath not left the least shadow of a command for any such vicegerence from him in the state as the pope pretends for his in the church, but hath expressly declared that such regal dominion is from the gentiles, not from him, and hath strictly charged us not to imitate them therein?

I doubt not but all ingenuous and knowing men will readily agree with me that a free commonwealth without single person or house of lords is by far the best government, if it can be had; but we have all this while, say they, been expecting it, and cannot yet attain it. 'Tis true, indeed, when monarchy was dissolved, the form of a commonwealth should have forthwith been framed and the practice thereof immediately begun, that the people might have soon been satisfied and delighted with the decent order, ease and benefit thereof; we had been then by this time firmly rooted, past fear of commotions or mutations, and now flourishing; this care of timely settling a new government instead of the old, too much neglected, hath been our mischief. Yet the cause thereof may be ascribed with most reason to the frequent disturbances, interruptions° and dissolutions which the parliament hath had partly from the impatient or disaffected people, partly from some ambitious leaders in the army; much contrary, I believe, to the mind and approbation of the army itself and their other commanders, once undeceived, or in their own power.

Now is the opportunity, now the very season, wherein we may obtain a free commonwealth and establish it forever in the land without difficulty or much delay. Writs° are sent out for elections, and, which is worth observing, in the name not of any king, but of the keepers of our liberty, to summon a free parliament; which then only will indeed be free, and deserve the true honour of that supreme title, if they preserve us a free people. Which never parliament was more free to do, being now called not as heretofore, by the summons of a king, but by the voice of liberty. And if the people, laying aside prejudice and impatience, will seriously and calmly now consider their own good, both religious and civil, their own liberty and the only means thereof, as shall be here laid before them, and will elect their knights and burgesses° able men, and according to the just and necessary qualifications° (which, for aught I hear, remain yet in force unrepealed, as they were formerly decreed in parliament), men not addicted to a single person or house of lords, the work is done; at least the foundation firmly laid of a free commonwealth, and good part also erected of the main structure. For the ground and basis of every just and free government (since men have smarted so oft for committing all to one person) is a general council of ablest men chosen by the people to consult of public affairs from time to time for the common good. In this grand council must the sovereignty, not transferred, but delegated only, and as it were deposited, reside; with this caution, they must have the forces by sea and land committed to them for preservation of the common peace and liberty; must raise and manage the public revenue, at least with some inspectors deputed for satisfaction of the people how it is employed; must make or propose, as more expressly shall be said anon, civil laws, treat of commerce, peace or war with foreign nations; and for the carrying on some particular affairs with more secrecy and expedition, must elect, as they have already out of their own number and others, a council of state.°

And although it may seem strange at first hearing, by reason that men's minds are prepossessed with the notion of successive parliaments, I affirm that the grand or general council, being well chosen, should be perpetual: for so their business is or may be, and ofttimes urgent, the opportunity of affairs gained or lost in a moment. The day of council cannot be set as the day of a festival, but must be ready always to prevent° or answer all occasions. By this continuance they will become every way skilfullest, best provided of intelligence from abroad, best acquainted with the people at home, and the people with them. The ship of the commonwealth is always under sail; they sit at the stern, and if they steer well, what need is there to change them, it being rather dangerous? Add to this that the grand council is both foundation and main pillar of the whole state; and to move pillars and foundations not faulty cannot be safe for the building.

I see not, therefore, how we can be advantaged by successive and transitory parliaments; but that they are much likelier continually to unsettle rather than to settle a free government, to breed commotions, changes, novelties and uncertainties, to bring neglect upon present affairs and opportunities, while all minds are suspense° with expectation of a new assembly, and the assembly, for a good space, taken up with the new settling of itself. After which, if they find no great work to do, they will make it, by altering or repealing former acts, or making and multiplying new, that they may seem to see what their predecessors saw not, and not to have assembled for nothing, till all law be lost in the multitude of clashing statutes. But if the ambition of such as think themselves injured that they also partake not of the government, and are impatient till they be chosen, cannot brook the perpetuity of others chosen before them; or if it be feared that long continuance of power may corrupt sincerest men, the known expedient is, and by some lately propounded, that annually (or if the space be longer, so much perhaps the better) the third part of senators may go out according to the precedence of their election, and the like number be chosen in their places, to prevent the settling of too absolute a power if it should be perpetual: and this they call 'partial rotation'.°

But I could wish that this wheel,° or partial wheel in state, if it be possible, might be avoided, as having too much affinity with the wheel of Fortune. For it appears not how this can be done without danger and mischance of putting out a great number of the best and ablest, in whose stead new elections may bring in as many raw, unexperienced and otherwise affected, to the weakening and much altering for the worse of public transactions. Neither do I think a perpetual senate, especially chosen and entrusted by the people, much in this land to be feared, where the well-affected° either in a standing army or in a settled militia have their arms in their own hands. Safest therefore to me it seems, and of least hazard or interruption to affairs, that none of the grand council be moved, unless by death, or just conviction of some crime; for what can be expected firm or steadfast from a floating foundation? However, I forejudge not any probable expedient, any temperament° that can be found in things of this nature, so disputable on either side.

Yet lest this which I affirm be thought my single opinion, I shall add sufficient testimony. Kingship itself is therefore counted the more safe and durable because the king, and for the most part his council, is not changed during life. But a commonwealth is held immortal, and therein firmest, safest and most above fortune; for the death of a king causeth ofttimes many dangerous alterations, but the death now and then of a senator is not felt, the main body of them still continuing permanent in greatest and noblest commonwealths, and as it were eternal. Therefore among the Jews, the supreme council of seventy, called the Sanhedrin°, founded by Moses, in Athens that of Areopagus,° in Sparta that of the ancients,° in Rome the senate, consisted of members chosen for term of life; and by that means remained as it were still the same to generations. In Venice they change indeed oftener than every year some particular councils of state, as that of Six,° or such other; but the true senate, which upholds and sustains the government, is the whole aristocracy immovable. So in the United Provinces, the states-general, which are indeed but a council of state deputed° by the whole union, are not usually the same persons for above three or six years; but the states of every city, in whom the sovereignty hath been placed time out of mind, are a standing senate, without succession, and accounted chiefly in that regard the main prop of their liberty. And why they should be so in every well-ordered commonwealth, they who write of policy° give these reasons: that to make the senate successive not only impairs the dignity and lustre of the senate, but weakens the whole commonwealth, and brings it into manifest danger; while by this means the secrets of state are frequently divulged, and matters of greatest consequence committed to inexpert and novice councillors, utterly to seek° in the full and intimate knowledge of affairs past.

I know not therefore what should be peculiar in England to make successive parliaments thought safest, or convenient here more than in other nations, unless it be the fickleness which is attributed to us as we are islanders. But good education and acquisite° wisdom ought to correct the fluxible fault, if any such be, of our watery situation. It will be objected that in those places where they had perpetual senates, they had also popular remedies against their growing too imperious: as in Athens, besides Areopagus, another senate of four or five hundred; in Sparta, the Ephori; in Rome, the tribunes of the people.

But the event° tells us that these remedies either little availed the people, or brought them to such a licentious and unbridled democracy as in fine° ruined themselves with their own excessive power. So that the main reason urged why popular assemblies are to be trusted with the people's liberty, rather than a senate of principal men, because great men will be still endeavouring to enlarge their power, but the common sort will be contented to maintain their own liberty, is by experience found false; none being more immoderate and ambitious to amplify their power than such popularities, which was seen in the people of Rome, who, at first contented to have their tribunes, at length contended with the senate that one consul, then both, soon after, that the censors and praetors also should be created plebeian, and the whole empire put into their hands; adoring lastly those who most were adverse to the senate, till Marius,° by fulfilling their inordinate desires, quite lost them all the power for which they had so long been striving, and left them under the tyranny of Sulla. The balance therefore must be exactly so set as to preserve and keep up due authority on either side, as well in the senate as in the people. And this annual rotation of a senate to consist of three hundred, as is lately propounded,° requires also another popular assembly upward of a thousand, with an answerable rotation. Which, besides that it will be liable to all those inconveniences found in the aforesaid remedies, cannot but be troublesome and chargeable,° both in their motion and their session,° to the whole land, unwieldy with their own bulk, unable in so great a number to mature their consultations as they ought, if any be allotted them, and that they meet not from so many parts remote to sit a whole year lieger° in one place, only now and then to hold up a forest of fingers, or to convey each man his bean or ballot into the box, without reason shown or common deliberation; incontinent of secrets, if any be imparted to them; emulous and always jarring with the other senate.° The much better way doubtless will be, in this wavering condition of our affairs, to defer the changing or circumscribing of our senate, more than may be done with ease, till the commonwealth be thoroughly settled in peace and safety, and they themselves give us the occasion.

Military men hold it dangerous to change the form of battle in view of an enemy; neither did the people of Rome bandy with their senate while any of the Tarquins° lived, the enemies of their liberty; nor sought by creating tribunes to defend themselves against the fear of their patricians till, sixteen years after the expulsion of their kings, and in full security of their state, they had or thought they had just cause given them by the senate. Another way will be to well qualify and refine elections: not committing all to the noise and shouting° of a rude multitude, but permitting only those of them who are rightly qualified to nominate as many as they will, and out of that number others of a better breeding to choose a less number more judiciously, till after a third or fourth sifting and refining of exactest choice, they only be left chosen who are the due number, and seem by most voices° the worthiest.

To make the people fittest to choose, and the chosen fittest to govern, will be to mend our corrupt and faulty education, to teach the people faith, not without virtue, temperance, modesty, sobriety, parsimony, justice; not to admire wealth or honour; to hate turbulence and ambition; to place every one his private welfare and happiness in the public peace, liberty and safety. They shall not then need to be much mistrustful of their chosen patriots in the grand council, who will be then rightly called the true keepers of our liberty, though the most of their business will be in foreign affairs. But to prevent all mistrust, the people then will have their several ordinary assemblies (which will henceforth quite annihilate the odious power and name of committees°) in the chief towns of every county, without the trouble, charge, or time lost of summoning and assembling from far in so great a number, and so long residing from their own houses, or removing of their families, to do as much at home in their several shires, entire or subdivided, toward the securing of their liberty, as a numerous assembly of them all formed and convened on purpose with the wariest rotation. Whereof I shall speak more ere the end of this discourse; for it may be referred to time,° so we be still° going on by degrees to perfection. The people well weighing and performing these things, I suppose would have no cause to fear, though the parliament abolishing that name, as originally signifying but the parley of our Lords and Commons with their Norman king when he pleased to call them, should, with certain limitations of their power, sit perpetual, if their ends be faithful and for a free commonwealth, under the name of a grand or general council.

Till this be done, I am in doubt whether our state will be ever certainly and throughly settled; never likely till then to see an end of our troubles and continual changes, or at least never the true settlement and assurance of our liberty. The grand council being thus firmly constituted to perpetuity, and still, upon the death or default of any member, supplied and kept in full number, there can be no cause alleged why peace, justice, plentiful trade and all prosperity should not thereupon ensue throughout the whole land; with as much assurance as can be of human things that they shall so continue (if God favour us, and our wilful sins provoke him not) even to the coming of our true and rightful, and only to be expected king, only worthy as he is our only Saviour, the Messiah, the Christ, the only heir of his eternal father, the only by him anointed and ordained since the work of our redemption finished, universal Lord of all mankind.

The way propounded is plain, easy and open before us, without intricacies, without the introducement of new or obsolete forms or terms, or exotic models—ideas that would effect nothing, but with a number of new injunctions to manacle the native liberty of mankind, turning all virtue into prescription, servitude and necessity, to the great impairing and frustrating of Christian liberty. I say again, this way lies free and smooth before us; is not tangled with inconveniencies; invents no new encumbrances; requires no perilous, no injurious alteration or circumscription of men's lands and properties; secure that in this commonwealth, temporal and spiritual lords removed, no man or number of men can attain to such wealth or vast possession as will need the hedge of an agrarian law° (never successful, but the cause rather of sedition, save only where it began seasonably with first possession) to confine them from endangering our public liberty. To conclude, it can have no considerable° objection made against it that it is not practicable, lest it be said hereafter that we gave up our liberty for want of a ready way or distinct form proposed of a free commonwealth. And this facility we shall have above our next neighbouring commonwealth (if we can keep us from the fond conceit° of something like a duke of Venice, put lately into many men's heads by some one or other subtly driving on under that notion his own ambitious ends to lurch° a crown), that our liberty shall not be hampered or hovered over by any engagement to such a potent family as the house of Nassau,° of whom to stand in perpetual doubt and suspicion, but we shall live the clearest and absolutest free nation in the world.

On the contrary, if there be a king, which the inconsiderate multitude are now so mad upon, mark how far short we are like to come of all those happinesses which in a free state we shall immediately be possessed of. First, the grand council, which, as I showed before, should sit perpetually (unless their leisure give them now and then some intermissions or vacations, easily manageable by the council of state left sitting), shall be called, by the king's good will and utmost endeavour, as seldom as may be. For it is only the king's right, he will say, to call a parliament; and this he will do most commonly about his own affairs rather than the kingdom's, as will appear plainly so soon as they are called. For what will their business then be, and the chief expense of their time, but an endless tugging between petition of right and royal prerogative, especially about the negative voice,° militia, or subsidies, demanded and ofttimes extorted without reasonable cause appearing to the Commons, who are the only true representatives of the people and their liberty, but will be then mingled with a court faction; besides which, within their own walls, the sincere part of them who stand faithful to the people will again have to deal with two troublesome counterworking adversaries from without, mere creatures of the king, spiritual, and the greater part, as is likeliest of temporal lords, nothing concerned with the people's liberty.

If these prevail not in what they please, though never so much against the people's interest, the parliament shall be soon dissolved, or sit and do nothing; not suffered to remedy the least grievance or enact aught advantageous to the people. Next, the council of state shall not be chosen by the parliament, but by the king, still his own creatures, courtiers and favourites, who will be sure in all their counsels to set their master's grandeur and absolute power, in what they are able, far above the people's liberty. I deny not but that there may be such a king who may regard the common good before his own, may have no vicious favourite, may hearken only to the wisest and incorruptest of his parliament; but this rarely happens in a monarchy not elective, and it behooves not a wise nation to commit the sum of their well-being, the whole state of their safety to fortune. What need they? and how absurd would it be, whenas they themselves to whom his chief virtue will be but to hearken, may with much better management and dispatch, with much more commendation of their own worth and magnanimity, govern without a master? Can the folly be paralleled to adore and be the slaves of a single person for doing that which it is ten thousand to one whether he can or will do, and we without him might do more easily, more effectually, more laudably ourselves? Shall we never grow old enough to be wise, to make seasonable use of gravest authorities, experiences, examples? Is it such an unspeakable joy to serve, such felicity to wear a yoke? to clink our shackles, locked on by pretended law of subjection, more intolerable and hopeless to be ever shaken off than those which are knocked on by illegal injury and violence?

Aristotle, our chief instructor in the universities, lest this doctrine be thought sectarian, as the Royalist would have it thought, tells us in the third of his *Politics*° that certain men at first, for the matchless excellence of their virtue above others, or some great public benefit, were created kings by the people, in small cities and territories, and in the scarcity of others to be found like them; but when they abused their power, and governments grew larger, and the number of prudent men increased, that then the people, soon deposing their tyrants, betook them, in all civilest places, to the form of a free commonwealth. And why should we thus disparage and prejudicate° our own nation as to fear a scarcity of able and worthy men united in counsel to govern us, if we will but use diligence and impartiality to find them out and choose them, rather yoking ourselves to a single person, the natural adversary and oppressor of liberty; though good, yet far easier corruptible by the excess of his singular power and exaltation, or at best, not comparably sufficient to bear the weight of government, nor equally disposed to make us happy in the enjoyment of our liberty under him?

But admit that monarchy of itself may be convenient to some nations; yet to us who have thrown it out, received back again, it cannot but prove pernicious. For kings to come, never forgetting their former ejection, will be sure to fortify and arm themselves sufficiently for the future against all such attempts hereafter from the people, who shall be then so narrowly watched and kept so low that though they would never so fain, and at the same rate of their blood and treasure, they never shall be able to regain what they now have purchased and may enjoy, or to free themselves from any yoke imposed upon them. Nor will they dare to go about it, utterly disheartened for the future, if these their highest attempts prove unsuccessful; which will be the triumph of all tyrants hereafter over any people that shall resist oppression; and their song will then be to others, How sped the rebellious English? to our posterity, How sped the rebels, your fathers?

This is not my conjecture, but drawn from God's known denouncement against the gentilizing° Israelites, who, though they were governed in a commonwealth of God's own ordaining, he only their king, they his peculiar° people, yet affecting rather to resemble heathen, but pretending the misgovernment of Samuel's sons, no more a reason to dislike their commonwealth than the violence of Eli's sons° was imputable to that priesthood or religion, clamoured for a king. They had their longing, but with this testimony of God's wrath: 'Ye shall cry out in that day, because of your king whom ye shall have chosen, and the Lord will not hear you in that day.'° Us if he shall hear now, how much less will he hear when we cry hereafter, who once delivered by him from a king, and not without wondrous acts of his providence, insensible and unworthy of those high mercies, are returning precipitantly, if he withhold us not, back to the captivity from whence he freed us.

Yet neither shall we obtain or buy at an easy rate this new gilded yoke, which thus transports us: a new royal revenue must be found, a new episcopal; for those are individual:° both which being wholly dissipated, or bought by private persons, or assigned for service done, and especially to the army, cannot be recovered without a general detriment and confusion to men's estates, or a heavy imposition on all men's purses; benefit to none but to the worst and ignoblest sort of men, whose hope is to be either the ministers of court riot and excess, or the gainers by it. But not to speak more of losses and extraordinary levies on our estates, what will then be the revenges and offences remembered and returned, not only by the chief person, but by all his adherents; accounts and reparations that will be required, suits, indictments, inquiries, discoveries, complaints, informations, who knows against whom or how many, though perhaps neuters,° if not to utmost infliction, yet to imprisonment, fines, banishment or molestation? if not these, yet disfavour, discountenance, disregard and contempt on all but the known Royalist, or whom he favours, will be plenteous.

Nor let the new royalized Presbyterians persuade themselves that their old doings, though now recanted, will be forgotten, whatever conditions be contrived or trusted on. Will they not believe this, nor remember the pacification° how it was kept to the Scots; how other solemn promises many a time to us? Let them but now read the diabolical forerunning libels, the faces, the gestures, that now appear foremost and briskest in all public places, as the harbingers of those that are in expectation to reign over us; let them but hear the insolencies, the menaces, the insultings of our newly animated common enemies crept lately out of their holes, their hell I might say, by the language of their infernal pamphlets, the spew of every drunkard, every ribald; nameless, yet not for want of license, but for very shame of their own vile persons, not daring to name themselves, while they traduce others by name; and give us to foresee that they intend to second their wicked words, if ever they have power, with more wicked deeds.

Let our zealous backsliders forethink now with themselves how their necks yoked with these tigers of Bacchus,° these new fanatics of not the preaching but the sweating-tub,° inspired with nothing holier than the venereal pox, can draw one way under monarchy to the establishing of church discipline with these new-disgorged atheisms. Yet shall they not have the honour to yoke with these, but shall be yoked under them; these shall plough° on their backs. And do they among them who are so forward to bring in the single person think to be by him trusted or long regarded? So trusted they shall be, and so regarded, as by kings are wont reconciled enemies; neglected, and soon after discarded, if not prosecuted for old traitors; the first inciters, beginners, and more than to the third part actors,° of all that followed.

It will be found also that there must be then, as necessarily as now (for the contrary part will be still feared), a standing army; which for certain shall not be this, but of the fiercest cavaliers, of no less expense, and perhaps again under Rupert.° But let this army be sure they shall be soon disbanded, and likeliest without arrear or pay; and being disbanded, not be sure but they may as soon be questioned for being in arms against their king. The same let them fear who have contributed money, which will amount to no small number, that must then take their turn to be made delinquents and compounders.° They who past reason and recovery are devoted to kingship perhaps will answer that a greater part by far of the nation will have it so, the rest therefore must yield.

Not so much to convince these, which I little hope, as to confirm them who yield not, I reply that this greatest part° have both in reason and the trial of just battle lost the right of their election what the government shall be. Of them who have not lost that right, whether they for kingship be the greater number, who can certainly determine? Suppose they be, yet of freedom they partake all alike, one main end of government; which if the greater part value not, but will degenerately forego, is it just or reasonable that most voices against the main end of government should enslave the less number that would be free? More just it is, doubtless, if it come to force, that a less number compel a greater to retain, which can be no wrong to them, their liberty, than that a greater number, for the pleasure of their baseness, compel a less most injuriously to be their fellow-slaves. They who seek nothing but their own just liberty have always right to win it and to keep it whenever they have power, be the voices never so numerous that oppose it. And how much we above others are concerned to defend it from kingship, and from them who in pursuance thereof so perniciously would betray us and themselves to most certain misery and thraldom, will be needless to repeat.

Having thus far shown with what ease we may now obtain a free commonwealth, and by it with as much ease, all the freedom, peace, justice, plenty, that we can desire; on the other side, the difficulties, troubles, uncertainties, nay, rather impossibilities, to enjoy these things constantly under a monarch; I will now proceed to show more particularly wherein our freedom and flourishing condition will be more ample and secure to us under a free commonwealth than under kingship.

The whole freedom of man consists either in spiritual or civil liberty. As for spiritual, who can be at rest, who can enjoy anything in this world with contentment, who hath not liberty to serve God and save his own soul according to the best light which God hath planted in him to that purpose, by the reading of his revealed will and the guidance of his Holy Spirit? That this is best pleasing to God, and that the whole Protestant church allows no supreme judge or rule in matters of religion but the Scriptures, and these to be interpreted by the Scriptures themselves, which necessarily infers liberty of conscience, I have heretofore proved at large in another treatise;° and might yet further by the public declarations, confessions and admonitions of whole churches and states, obvious in all histories since the Reformation.

This liberty of conscience, which above all other things ought to be to all men dearest and most precious, no government more inclinable not to favour only, but to protect, than a free commonwealth, as being most magnanimous, most fearless and confident of its own fair proceedings. Whereas kingship, though looking big, yet indeed most pusillanimous, full of fears, full of jealousies, startled at every umbrage,° as it hath been observed of old to have ever suspected most and mistrusted them who were in most esteem for virtue and generosity of mind, so it is now known to have most in doubt and suspicion them who are most reputed to be religious. Queen Elizabeth, though herself accounted so good a Protestant, so moderate, so confident of her subjects' love, would never give way so much as to Presbyterian reformation in this land, though once and again besought, as Camden° relates; but imprisoned and persecuted the very proposers thereof, alleging it as her mind and maxim unalterable that such reformation would diminish regal authority.

What liberty of conscience can we then expect of others far worse principled from the cradle, trained up and governed by Popish and Spanish counsels, and on such depending hitherto for subsistence? Especially what can this last parliament expect, who having revived lately and published the covenant, have re-engaged themselves never to readmit episcopacy? Which no son of Charles returning but will most certainly bring back with him, if he regard the last and strictest charge of his father, 'to persevere in, not the doctrine only, but government of the Church of England, not to neglect the speedy and effectual suppressing of errors and schisms'; among which he accounted Presbytery one of the chief.

Or if, notwithstanding that charge of his father,° he submit to the covenant,° how will he keep faith to us with disobedience to him, or regard that faith given which must be founded on the breach of that last and solemnest paternal charge, and the reluctance, I may say the antipathy, which is in all kings, against Presbyterian and Independent discipline? For they hear the gospel speaking much of liberty, a word which monarchy and her bishops both fear and hate, but a free commonwealth both favours and promotes; and not the word only, but the thing itself. But let our governors beware in time, lest their hard measure to liberty of conscience be found the rock whereon they shipwreck themselves, as others have now done before them in the course wherein God was directing their steerage to a free commonwealth; and the abandoning of all those whom they call sectaries for the detected falsehood and ambition of some, be a wilful rejection of their own chief strength and interest in the freedom of all Protestant religion, under what abusive name soever calumniated.

The other part of our freedom consists in the civil rights and advancements of every person according to his merit: the enjoyment of those never more certain, and the access to these never more open, than in a free commonwealth. Both which, in my opinion, may be best and soonest obtained if every county in the land were made a kind of subordinate commonalty or commonwealth, and one chief town or more, according as the shire is in circuit,° made cities, if they be not so called already; where the nobility and chief gentry, from a proportionable compass of territory annexed to each city, may build houses or palaces befitting their quality; may bear part in the government, make their own judicial laws, or use these that are, and execute them by their own elected judicatures and judges without appeal, in all things of civil government between man and man. So they shall have justice in their own hands, law executed fully and finally in their own counties and precincts, long wished and spoken of, but never yet obtained. They shall have none then to blame but themselves if it be not well administered; and fewer laws to expect or fear from the supreme authority; or to those that shall be made of any great concernment to public liberty, they may, without much trouble in these commonalties, or in more general assemblies called to their cities from the whole territory on such occasion, declare and publish their assent or dissent by deputies within a time limited sent to the grand council; yet so as this their judgment declared shall submit to the greater number of other counties or commonalties, and not avail them to any exemption of themselves or refusal of agreement with the rest, as it may in any of the United Provinces, being sovereign within itself, ofttimes to the great disadvantage of that union.

In these employments they may, much better than they do now, exercise and fit themselves till their lot fall to be chosen into the grand council, according as their worth and merit shall be taken notice of by the people. As for controversies that shall happen between men of several counties, they may repair, as they do now, to the capital city, or any other more commodious, indifferent° place, and equal° judges. And this I find to have been practised in the old Athenian commonwealth, reputed the first and ancientest place of civility in all Greece; that they had in their several cities a peculiar,° in Athens a common government; and their right, as it befell them, to the administration of both.

They should have here also schools and academies at their own choice, wherein their children may be bred up in their own sight to all learning and noble education; not in grammar only, but in all liberal arts and exercises. This would soon spread much more knowledge and civility, yea, religion, through all parts of the land, by communicating the natural heat of government and culture more distributively to all extreme parts, which now lie numb and neglected; would soon make the whole nation more industrious, more ingenuous at home, more potent, more honourable abroad. To this a free commonwealth will easily assent (nay, the parliament hath had already some such thing in design); for of all governments a commonwealth aims most to make the people flourishing, virtuous, noble and high-spirited. Monarchs will never permit; whose aim is to make the people wealthy indeed perhaps, and well fleeced, for their own shearing, and the supply of regal prodigality; but otherwise softest, basest, viciousest, servilest, easiest to be kept under. And not only in fleece, but in mind also sheepishest; and will have all the benches of judicature annexed to the throne, as a gift of royal grace that we have justice done us, whenas nothing can be more essential to the freedom of a people than to have the administration of justice, and all public ornaments,° in their own election, and within their own bounds, without long travelling or depending on remote places to obtain their right or any civil accomplishment; so it be not supreme, but subordinate to the general power and union of the whole republic.

In which happy firmness, as in the particular above mentioned, we shall also far exceed the United Provinces by having not as they (to the retarding and distracting ofttimes of their counsels or urgentest occasions) many sovereignties united in one commonwealth, but many commonwealths under one united and intrusted sovereignty. And when we have our forces by sea and land either of a faithful army or a settled militia in our own hands, to the firm establishing of a free commonwealth, public accounts under our own inspection, general laws and taxes, with their causes in our own domestic suffrages, judicial laws, offices and ornaments at home in our own ordering and administration, all distinction of lords and commoners that may any way divide or sever the public interest removed; what can a perpetual senate have then wherein to grow corrupt, wherein to encroach upon us or usurp? Or if they do, wherein to be formidable? Yet if all this avail not to remove the fear or envy° of a perpetual sitting, it may be easily provided to change a third part of them yearly, or every two or three years, as was above mentioned; or that it be at those times in the people's choice whether they will change them or renew their power, as they shall find cause.

I have no more to say at present: few words will save us, well considered; few and easy things, now seasonably done. But if the people be so affected as to prostitute religion and liberty to the vain and groundless apprehension that nothing but kingship can restore trade, not remembering the frequent plagues and pestilences that then wasted this city, such as through God's mercy we never have felt since; and that trade flourishes nowhere more than in the free commonwealths of Italy, Germany and the Low Countries before their eyes at this day; yet if trade be grown so craving and importunate through the profuse living of tradesmen that nothing can support it but the luxurious expenses of a nation upon trifles or superfluities; so as if the people generally should betake themselves to frugality, it might prove a dangerous matter, lest tradesmen should mutiny for want of trading; and that therefore we must forego and set to sale religion, liberty, honour, safety, all concernments divine or human, to keep up trading; if, lastly, after all this light among us, the same reason shall pass for current to put our necks again under kingship as was made use of by the Jews° to return back to Egypt and to the worship of their idol queen because they falsely imagined that they then lived in more plenty and prosperity, our condition is not sound, but rotten, both in religion and all civil prudence, and will bring us soon, the way we are marching, to those calamities which attend always and unavoidably on luxury, all national judgments under foreign or domestic slavery. So far we shall be from mending our condition by monarchizing our government, whatever new conceit° now possesses us.

However, with all hazard I have ventured what I thought my duty to speak in season, and to forewarn my country in time; wherein I doubt not but there be many wise men in all places and degrees, but am sorry the effects of wisdom are so little seen among us. Many circumstances and particulars I could have added in those things whereof I have spoken; but a few main matters now put speedily in execution will suffice to recover us and set all right; and there will want at no time who are good at circumstances;° but men who set their minds on main matters and sufficiently urge them, in these most difficult times I find not many.

What I have spoken is the language of that which is not called amiss 'the good old cause': if it seem strange to any, it will not seem more strange, I hope, than convincing to backsliders. Thus much I should perhaps have said though I were sure I should have spoken only to trees and stones, and had none to cry to, but with the prophet,° 'O earth, earth, earth!' to tell the very soil itself what her perverse inhabitants are deaf to. Nay, though what I have spoke should happen (which thou suffer not, who didst create mankind free; nor thou next, who didst redeem us from being servants of men!) to be the last words of our expiring liberty. But I trust I shall have spoken persuasion to abundance of sensible and ingenuous men; to some, perhaps, whom God may raise of these stones to become children of reviving liberty; and may reclaim, though they seem now choosing them a captain back for Egypt, to bethink themselves a little, and consider whither they are rushing; to exhort this torrent also of the people not to be so impetuous, but to keep their due channel, and at length recovering and uniting their better resolutions, now that they see already how open and unbounded the insolence and rage is of our common enemies, to stay these ruinous proceedings, justly and timely fearing to what a precipice of destruction the deluge of this epidemic madness would hurry us, through the general defection of a misguided and abused multitude.

PARADISE LOST

THE VERSE

The measure is English heroic verse without rhyme, as that of Homer in Greek, and of Virgil in Latin; rhyme being no necessary adjunct or true ornament of poem or good verse, in longer works especially, but the invention of a barbarous age,° to set off wretched matter and lame metre; graced indeed since by the use of some famous modern poets, carried away by custom, but much to their own vexation, hindrance, and constraint to express many things otherwise, and for the most part worse than else they would have expressed them. Not without cause therefore some both Italian and Spanish poets of prime note have rejected rhyme both in longer and shorter works, as have also long since our best English tragedies, as a thing of itself, to all judicious ears, trivial and of no true musical delight; which consists only in apt numbers,° fit quantity of syllables, and the sense variously drawn out from one verse into another, not in the jingling sound of like endings, a fault avoided by the learned ancients both in poetry and all good oratory. This neglect then of rhyme so little is to be taken for a defect, though it may seem so perhaps to vulgar readers, that it rather is to be esteemed an example set, the first in English, of ancient liberty recovered to heroic poem from the troublesome and modern bondage of rhyming.

BOOK I

The Argument

This first book proposes, first in brief, the whole subject, man's disobedience, and the loss thereupon of Paradise wherein he was placed; then touches the prime cause of his fall, the serpent, or rather Satan in the serpent; who revolting from God, and drawing to his side many legions of angels, was by the command of God driven out of heaven with all his crew into the great deep. Which action passed over, the poem hastes into the midst of things, presenting Satan with his angels now fallen into hell, described here, not in the centre° (for heaven and earth may be supposed as yet not made, certainly not yet accursed) but in a place of utter° darkness, fitliest called Chaos: here Satan with his angels lying on the burning lake, thunderstruck and astonished, after a certain space recovers, as from confusion, calls up him who next in order and dignity lay by him; they confer of their miserable fall. Satan awakens all his legions, who lay till then in the same manner confounded; they rise, their numbers, array of battle, their chief leaders named, according to the idols known afterwards in

Canaan and the countries adjoining. To these Satan directs his speech, comforts them with hope yet of regaining heaven, but tells them lastly of a new
world and new kind of creature to be created, according to an ancient prophecy
or report in heaven; for that angels were long before this visible creation, was
the opinion of many ancient Fathers. To find out the truth of this prophecy, and
what to determine thereon he refers to a full council. What his associates thence
attempt. Pandaemonium° the palace of Satan rises, suddenly built out of the
deep: the infernal peers there sit in council.

Of man's first disobedience, and the fruit
Of that forbidden tree, whose mortal taste
Brought death into the world, and all our woe,
With loss of Eden, till one greater man°
Restore us, and regain the blissful seat,
Sing heavenly muse, that on the secret top°
Of Oreb, or of Sinai, didst inspire°
That shepherd, who first taught the chosen seed,°
In the beginning how the heavens and earth°
Rose out of chaos: or if Sion hill°   10
Delight thee more, and Siloa's brook that flowed°
Fast by the oracle of God; I thence°
Invoke thy aid to my adventurous song,
That with no middle flight intends to soar
Above the Aonian mount, while it pursues°
Things unattempted yet in prose or rhyme.
And chiefly thou O Spirit, that dost prefer
Before all temples the upright heart and pure,
Instruct me, for thou know'st; thou from the first
Wast present, and with mighty wings outspread   20
Dove-like sat'st brooding on the vast abyss°
And mad'st it pregnant: what in me is dark°
Illumine, what is low raise and support;
That to the height of this great argument°
I may assert eternal providence,
And justify the ways of God to men.
  Say first, for heaven hides nothing from thy view
Nor the deep tract of hell, say first what cause°
Moved our grand parents in that happy state,
Favoured of heaven so highly, to fall off   30
From their creator, and transgress his will
For one restraint, lords of the world besides?
Who first seduced them to that foul revolt?

The infernal serpent; he it was, whose guile
Stirred up with envy and revenge, deceived
The mother of mankind, what time his pride°
Had cast him out from heaven, with all his host
Of rebel angels, by whose aid aspiring
To set himself in glory above his peers,
He trusted to have equalled the most high,   40
If he opposed; and with ambitious aim
Against the throne and monarchy of God
Raised impious war in heaven and battle proud
With vain attempt. Him the almighty power
Hurled headlong flaming from the ethereal sky
With hideous ruin and combustion down
To bottomless perdition, there to dwell
In adamantine chains and penal fire,°
Who durst defy the omnipotent to arms.
Nine times the space that measures day and night°   50
To mortal men, he with his horrid crew
Lay vanquished, rolling in the fiery gulf
Confounded though immortal: but his doom
Reserved him to more wrath; for now the thought
Both of lost happiness and lasting pain
Torments him; round he throws his baleful eyes°
That witnessed huge affliction and dismay°
Mixed with obdurate pride and steadfast hate:
At once as far as angels' ken he views
The dismal situation waste and wild,°   60
A dungeon horrible, on all sides round
As one great furnace flamed, yet from those flames
No light, but rather darkness visible
Served only to discover sights of woe,
Regions of sorrow, doleful shades, where peace
And rest can never dwell, hope never comes°
That comes to all; but torture without end
Still urges, and a fiery deluge, fed°
With ever-burning sulphur unconsumed:
Such place eternal justice had prepared   70
For those rebellious, here their prison ordained
In utter darkness, and their portion set°
As far removed from God and light of heaven
As from the centre thrice to the utmost pole.°

O how unlike the place from whence they fell!
There the companions of his fall, o'erwhelmed
With floods and whirlwinds of tempestuous fire,
He soon discerns, and weltering by his side°
One next himself in power, and next in crime,
Long after known in Palestine, and named   80
Beelzebub. To whom the arch-enemy,°
And thence in heaven called Satan, with bold words°
Breaking the horrid silence thus began.
     If thou beest he; but O how fallen! how changed°
From him, who in the happy realms of light
Clothed with transcendent brightness didst outshine
Myriads though bright: if he whom mutual league,°
United thoughts and counsels, equal hope
And hazard in the glorious enterprise,
Joined with me once, now misery hath joined   90
In equal ruin: into what pit thou seest
From what height fallen, so much the stronger proved
He with his thunder: and till then who knew
The force of those dire arms? yet not for those,
Nor what the potent victor in his rage
Can else inflict, do I repent or change,
Though changed in outward lustre; that fixed mind
And high disdain, from sense of injured merit,
That with the mightiest raised me to contend,
And to the fierce contention brought along   100
Innumerable force of spirits armed
That durst dislike his reign, and me preferring,
His utmost power with adverse power opposed
In dubious battle on the plains of heaven,°
And shook his throne. What though the field be lost?
All is not lost; the unconquerable will,
And study of revenge, immortal hate,°
And courage never to submit or yield:
And what is else not to be overcome?
That glory never shall his wrath or might   110
Extort from me. To bow and sue for grace
With suppliant knee, and deify his power,
Who from the terror of this arm so late
Doubted his empire, that were low indeed,°
That were an ignominy and shame beneath

This downfall; since by fate the strength of gods
And this empyreal substance cannot fail,°
Since through experience of this great event
In arms not worse, in foresight much advanced,
We may with more successful hope resolve 120
To wage by force or guile eternal war
Irreconcilable, to our grand foe,
Who now triumphs, and in the excess of joy
Sole reigning holds the tyranny of heaven.
   So spake the apostate angel, though in pain,
Vaunting aloud, but racked with deep despair:
And him thus answered soon his bold compeer.
   O prince, O chief of many thronèd powers,
That led the embattled seraphim to war
Under thy conduct, and in dreadful deeds 130
Fearless, endangered heaven's perpetual king;
And put to proof his high supremacy,°
Whether upheld by strength, or chance, or fate,
Too well I see and rue the dire event,
That with sad overthrow and foul defeat
Hath lost us heaven, and all this mighty host
In horrible destruction laid thus low,
As far as gods and heavenly essences
Can perish: for the mind and spirit remains
Invincible, and vigour soon returns, 140
Though all our glory extinct, and happy state
Here swallowed up in endless misery.
But what if he our conqueror (whom I now
Of force believe almighty, since no less°
Than such could have o'erpowered such force as ours)
Have left us this our spirit and strength entire
Strongly to suffer and support our pains,
That we may so suffice his vengeful ire,°
Or do him mightier service as his thralls
By right of war, whate'er his business be 150
Here in the heart of hell to work in fire,
Or do his errands in the gloomy deep;
What can it then avail though yet we feel
Strength undiminished, or eternal being
To undergo eternal punishment?
Whereto with speedy words the arch-fiend replied.

Fallen cherub, to be weak is miserable
Doing or suffering: but of this be sure,°
To do aught good never will be our task,
But ever to do ill our sole delight,   160
As being the contrary to his high will
Whom we resist. If then his providence
Out of our evil seek to bring forth good,
Our labour must be to pervert that end,
And out of good still to find means of evil;
Which oft-times may succeed, so as perhaps
Shall grieve him, if I fail not, and disturb°
His inmost counsels from their destined aim.
But see the angry victor hath recalled
His ministers of vengeance and pursuit   170
Back to the gates of heaven: the sulphurous hail
Shot after us in storm, o'erblown hath laid°
The fiery surge, that from the precipice
Of heaven received us falling, and the thunder,
Winged with red lightning and impetuous rage,
Perhaps hath spent his shafts, and ceases now
To bellow through the vast and boundless deep.
Let us not slip the occasion, whether scorn,°
Or satiate fury yield it from our foe.
Seest thou yon dreary plain, forlorn and wild,   180
The seat of desolation, void of light,
Save what the glimmering of these livid flames
Casts pale and dreadful? Thither let us tend
From off the tossing of these fiery waves,
There rest, if any rest can harbour there,
And reassembling our afflicted powers,°
Consult how we may henceforth most offend°
Our enemy, our own loss how repair,
How overcome this dire calamity,
What reinforcement we may gain from hope,   190
If not what resolution from despair.
    Thus Satan talking to his nearest mate
With head uplift above the wave, and eyes
That sparkling blazed, his other parts besides
Prone on the flood, extended long and large
Lay floating many a rood, in bulk as huge°
As whom the fables name of monstrous size,

Titanian, or Earth-born, that warred on Jove,
Briareos or Typhon, whom the den°
By ancient Tarsus held, or that sea-beast°   200
Leviathan, which God of all his works°
Created hugest that swim the ocean stream:
Him haply slumbering on the Norway foam
The pilot of some small night-foundered skiff,
Deeming some island, oft, as seamen tell,
With fixèd anchor in his scaly rind°
Moors by his side under the lee, while night°
Invests the sea, and wishèd morn delays:°
So stretched out huge in length the arch-fiend lay
Chained on the burning lake, nor ever thence°   210
Had risen or heaved his head, but that the will
And high permission of all-ruling heaven
Left him at large to his own dark designs,
That with reiterated crimes he might
Heap on himself damnation, while he sought
Evil to others, and enraged might see
How all his malice served but to bring forth
Infinite goodness, grace and mercy shown
On man by him seduced, but on himself
Treble confusion, wrath and vengeance poured.   220
Forthwith upright he rears from off the pool
His mighty stature; on each hand the flames
Driven backward slope their pointing spires, and rolled
In billows, leave i' the midst a horrid vale.
Then with expanded wings he steers his flight
Aloft, incumbent on the dusky air°
That felt unusual weight, till on dry land
He lights, if it were land that ever burned°
With solid, as the lake with liquid fire;
And such appeared in hue, as when the force   230
Of subterranean wind transports a hill°
Torn from Pelorus, or the shattered side
Of thundering Aetna, whose combustible°
And fuelled entrails thence conceiving fire,
Sublimed with mineral fury, aid the winds,°
And leave a singèd bottom all involved
With stench and smoke: such resting found the sole
Of unblessed feet. Him followed his next mate,

Both glorying to have scaped the Stygian flood°
As gods, and by their own recovered strength,   240
Not by the sufferance of supernal power.
     Is this the region, this the soil, the clime,
Said then the lost archangel, this the seat
That we must change for heaven, this mournful gloom
For that celestial light? Be it so, since he
Who now is sovereign can dispose and bid
What shall be right: furthest from him is best
Whom reason hath equalled, force hath made supreme
Above his equals. Farewell, happy fields
Where joy forever dwells: hail horrors, hail   250
Infernal world, and thou profoundest hell
Receive thy new possessor: one who brings
A mind not to be changed by place or time.
The mind is its own place, and in itself
Can make a heaven of hell, a hell of heaven.
What matter where, if I be still the same,°
And what I should be, all but less than he
Whom thunder hath made greater? Here at least
We shall be free; the almighty hath not built
Here for his envy, will not drive us hence: 260
Here we may reign secure, and in my choice
To reign is worth ambition though in hell:
Better to reign in hell, than serve in heaven.
But wherefore let we then our faithful friends,
The associates and copartners of our loss
Lie thus astonished on the oblivious pool,°
And call them not to share with us their part
In this unhappy mansion, or once more°
With rallied arms to try what may be yet
Regained in heaven, or what more lost in hell?   270
     So Satan spake, and him Beelzebub
Thus answered. Leader of those armies bright,
Which but the omnipotent none could have foiled,
If once they hear that voice, their liveliest pledge
Of hope in fears and dangers, heard so oft
In worst extremes, and on the perilous edge°
Of battle when it raged, in all assaults
Their surest signal, they will soon resume
New courage and revive, though now they lie

Grovelling and prostrate on yon lake of fire,   280
As we erewhile, astounded and amazed,
No wonder, fallen such a pernicious height.°
   He scarce had ceased when the superior fiend
Was moving toward the shore; his ponderous shield
Ethereal temper, massy, large, and round,°
Behind him cast; the broad circumference
Hung on his shoulders like the moon, whose orb
Through optic glass the Tuscan artist views°
At evening from the top of Fesole,°
Or in Valdarno, to descry new lands,°   290
Rivers or mountains in her spotty globe.
His spear, to equal which the tallest pine
Hewn on Norwegian hills, to be the mast
Of some great admiral, were but a wand,°
He walked with to support uneasy steps
Over the burning marl, not like those steps°
On heaven's azure, and the torrid clime
Smote on him sore besides, vaulted with fire;
Natheless he so endured, till on the beach°
Of that inflamèd sea, he stood and called   300
His legions, angel forms, who lay entranced
Thick as autumnal leaves that strew the brooks
In Vallombrosa, where the Etrurian shades°
High overarched imbower; or scattered sedge°
Afloat, when with fierce winds Orion armed°
Hath vexed the Red Sea coast, whose waves o'erthrew
Busiris and his Memphian chivalry,°
While with perfidious hatred they pursued
The sojourners of Goshen, who beheld°
From the safe shore their floating carcasses   310
And broken chariot wheels, so thick bestrewn
Abject and lost lay these, covering the flood,
Under amazement of their hideous change.°
He called so loud, that all the hollow deep
Of hell resounded. Princes, potentates,
Warriors, the flower of heaven, once yours, now lost,
If such astonishment as this can seize°
Eternal spirits; or have ye chosen this place
After the toil of battle to repose
Your wearied virtue, for the ease you find°   320

To slumber here, as in the vales of heaven?
Or in this abject posture have ye sworn
To adore the conqueror? who now beholds
Cherub and seraph rolling in the flood°
With scattered arms and ensigns, till anon
His swift pursuers from heaven gates discern
The advantage, and descending tread us down
Thus drooping, or with linkèd thunderbolts
Transfix us to the bottom of this gulf.
Awake, arise, or be forever fallen.   330
    They heard, and were abashed, and up they sprung
Upon the wing, as when men wont to watch
On duty, sleeping found by whom they dread,°
Rouse and bestir themselves ere well awake.
Nor did they not perceive the evil plight
In which they were, or the fierce pains not feel;
Yet to their general's voice they soon obeyed
Innumerable. As when the potent rod
Of Amram's son in Egypt's evil day°
Waved round the coast, up called a pitchy cloud   340
Of locusts, warping on the eastern wind,°
That o'er the realm of impious Pharaoh hung
Like night, and darkened all the land of Nile:
So numberless were those bad angels seen
Hovering on wing under the cope of hell°
'Twixt upper, nether, and surrounding fires;
Till, as a signal given, the uplifted spear
Of their great sultan waving to direct
Their course, in even balance down they light
On the firm brimstone, and fill all the plain;   350
A multitude, like which the populous north
Poured never from her frozen loins, to pass
Rhene or the Danaw, when her barbarous sons°
Came like a deluge on the south, and spread
Beneath Gibralter to the Lybian sands.
Forthwith from every squadron and each band
The heads and leaders thither haste where stood
Their great commander; godlike shapes and forms
Excelling human, princely dignities,
And powers that erst in heaven sat on thrones;°   360
Though of their names in heavenly records now

Be no memorial, blotted out and razed
By their rebellion, from the books of life.°
Nor had they yet among the sons of Eve
Got them new names, till wandering o'er the earth,°
Through God's high sufferance for the trial of man,
By falsities and lies the greatest part
Of mankind they corrupted to forsake
God their creator, and the invisible
Glory of him that made them, to transform   370
Oft to the image of a brute, adorned
With gay religions full of pomp and gold,°
And devils to adore for deities:°
Then were they known to men by various names,
And various idols through the heathen world.
Say, muse, their names then known, who first, who last,°
Roused from the slumber, on that fiery couch,
At their great emperor's call, as next in worth
Came singly where he stood on the bare strand,
While the promiscuous crowd stood yet aloof?°   380
The chief were those who from the pit of hell
Roaming to seek their prey on earth, durst fix
Their seats long after next the seat of God,
Their altars by his altar, gods adored
Among the nations round, and durst abide
Jehovah thundering out of Sion, throned
Between the cherubim; yea, often placed
Within his sanctuary itself their shrines,
Abominations; and with cursèd things
His holy rites, and solemn feasts profaned,   390
And with their darkness durst affront his light.
First Moloch, horrid king besmeared with blood°
Of human sacrifice, and parents' tears,
Though for the noise of drums and timbrels loud
Their children's cries unheard, that passed through fire°
To his grim idol. Him the Ammonite°
Worshipped in Rabba and her watery plain,°
In Argob and in Basan, to the stream
Of utmost Arnon. Nor content with such°
Audacious neighbourhood, the wisest heart   400
Of Solomon he led by fraud to build
His temple right against the temple of God

On that opprobrious hill, and made his grove°
The pleasant valley of Hinnom, Tophet thence
And black Gehenna called, the type of hell.°
Next Chemos, the obscene dread of Moab's sons,°
From Aroar to Nebo, and the wild°
Of southmost Abarim; in Hesebon
And Horonaim, Seon's realm, beyond°
The flowery dale of Sibma clad with vines,   410
And Eleale to the Asphaltic Pool.°
Peor his other name, when he enticed°
Israel in Sittim, on their march from Nile,
To do him wanton rites; which cost them woe.°
Yet thence his lustful orgies he enlarged
Even to that hill of scandal, by the grove°
Of Moloch homicide, lust hard by hate;°
Till good Josiah drove them thence to hell.°
With these came they, who from the bordering flood
Of old Euphrates to the brook that parts   420
Egypt from Syrian ground, had general names°
Of Baalim and Ashtaroth, those male,°
These feminine. For spirits when they please
Can either sex assume, or both; so soft
And uncompounded is their essence pure,
Not tied or manacled with joint or limb,
Nor founded on the brittle strength of bones,
Like cumbrous flesh; but in what shape they choose°
Dilated or condensed, bright or obscure,
Can execute their airy purposes,   430
And works of love or enmity fulfil.
For those the race of Israel oft forsook
Their living strength, and unfrequented left°
His righteous altar, bowing lowly down
To bestial gods; for which their heads as low°
Bowed down in battle, sunk before the spear
Of despicable foes. With these in troop
Came Astoreth, whom the Phoenicians called
Astarte, queen of heaven, with crescent horns;°
To whose bright image nightly by the moon   440
Sidonian virgins paid their vows and songs,°
In Sion also not unsung, where stood
Her temple on the offensive mountain, built

By that uxorious king, whose heart though large,°
Beguiled by fair idolatresses, fell
To idols foul. Thammuz came next behind,
Whose annual wound in Lebanon allured
The Syrian damsels to lament his fate
In amorous ditties all a summer's day,°
While smooth Adonis from his native rock   450
Ran purple to the sea, supposed with blood°
Of Thammuz yearly wounded: the love-tale
Infected Sion's daughters with like heat,
Whose wanton passions in the sacred porch
Ezekiel saw, when by the vision led°
His eye surveyed the dark idolatries
Of alienated Judah. Next came one
Who mourned in earnest, when the captive ark
Maimed his brute image, heads and hands lopped off°
In his own temple, on the groundsel edge,°   460
Where he fell flat, and shamed his worshippers:
Dagon his name, sea monster, upward man
And downward fish: yet had his temple high
Reared in Azotus, dreaded through the coast
Of Palestine, in Gath and Ascalon
And Accaron and Gaza's frontier bounds.°
Him followed Rimmon, whose delightful seat°
Was fair Damascus, on the fertile banks
Of Abbana and Pharphar, lucid streams.
He also against the house of God was bold: 470
A leper once he lost and gained a king,°
Ahaz his sottish conqueror, whom he drew°
God's altar to disparage and displace
For one of Syrian mode, whereon to burn
His odious offerings, and adore the gods
Whom he had vanquished. After these appeared°
A crew who under names of old renown,
Osiris, Isis, Orus and their train°
With monstrous shapes and sorceries abused
Fanatic Egypt and her priests, to seek   480
Their wandering gods disguised in brutish forms
Rather than human. Nor did Israel scape
The infection when their borrowed gold composed
The calf in Oreb: and the rebel king°

Doubled that sin in Bethel and in Dan,°
Likening his maker to the grazèd ox,
Jehovah, who in one night when he passed
From Egypt marching, equalled with one stroke°
Both her first born and all her bleating gods.°
Belial came last, than whom a spirit more lewd°   490
Fell not from heaven, or more gross to love
Vice for itself: to him no temple stood
Or altar smoked; yet who more oft than he
In temples and at altars, when the priest
Turns atheist, as did Eli's sons, who filled
With lust and violence the house of God.°
In courts and palaces he also reigns
And in luxurious cities, where the noise
Of riot ascends above their loftiest towers,
And injury and outrage: and when night   500
Darkens the streets, then wander forth the sons
Of Belial, flown with insolence and wine.°
Witness the streets of Sodom, and that night
In Gibeah, when the hospitable door
Exposed a matron to avoid worse rape.°
These were the prime in order and in might;
The rest were long to tell, though far renowned,
The Ionian gods, of Javan's issue held°
Gods, yet confessed later than Heaven and Earth°
Their boasted parents; Titan Heaven's first born°   510
With his enormous brood, and birthright seized
By younger Saturn, he from mightier Jove
His own and Rhea's son like measure found;°
So Jove usurping reigned: these first in Crete
And Ida known, thence on the snowy top°
Of cold Olympus ruled the middle air
Their highest heaven; or on the Delphian cliff,
Or in Dodona, and through all the bounds°
Of Doric land; or who with Saturn old°
Fled over Adria to the Hesperian fields,   520
And o'er the Celtic roamed the utmost isles.°
All these and more came flocking; but with looks
Downcast and damp, yet such wherein appeared°
Obscure some glimpse of joy, to have found their chief
Not in despair, to have found themselves not lost

In loss itself; which on his countenance cast
Like doubtful hue: but he his wonted pride
Soon recollecting, with high words, that bore°
Semblance of worth, not substance, gently raised
Their fainting courage, and dispelled their fears. 530
Then straight commands that at the warlike sound
Of trumpets loud and clarions be upreared°
His mighty standard; that proud honour claimed
Azazel as his right, a cherub tall:°
Who forthwith from the glittering staff unfurled
The imperial ensign, which full high advanced
Shone like a meteor streaming to the wind°
With gems and golden lustre rich emblazed,°
Seraphic arms and trophies: all the while
Sonorous metal blowing martial sounds: 540
At which the universal host upsent
A shout that tore hell's concave, and beyond°
Frighted the reign of Chaos and old Night.°
All in a moment through the gloom were seen
Ten thousand banners rise into the air
With orient colours waving: with them rose°
A forest huge of spears: and thronging helms°
Appeared, and serried shields in thick array
Of depth immeasurable: anon they move
In perfect phalanx to the Dorian mode° 550
Of flutes and soft recorders; such as raised
To height of noblest temper heroes old
Arming to battle, and instead of rage
Deliberate valour breathed, firm and unmoved
With dread of death to flight or foul retreat,
Nor wanting power to mitigate and swage°
With solemn touches, troubled thoughts, and chase
Anguish and doubt and fear and sorrow and pain
From mortal or immortal minds. Thus they
Breathing united force with fixèd thought 560
Moved on in silence to soft pipes that charmed
Their painful steps o'er the burnt soil; and now
Advanced in view, they stand, a horrid front°
Of dreadful length and dazzling arms, in guise
Of warriors old with ordered spear and shield,
Awaiting what command their mighty chief

Had to impose: he through the armèd files
Darts his experienced eye, and soon traverse°
The whole battalion views, their order due,
Their visages and stature as of gods,   570
Their number last he sums. And now his heart
Distends with pride, and hardening in his strength
Glories: for never since created man,°
Met such embodied force, as named with these
Could merit more than that small infantry
Warred on by cranes: though all the Giant brood°
Of Phlegra with the heroic race were joined°
That fought at Thebes and Ilium, on each side°
Mixed with auxiliar gods; and what resounds°
In fable or romance of Uther's son°   580
Begirt with British and Armoric knights;°
And all who since, baptized or infidel
Jousted in Aspramont or Montalban,°
Damasco, or Morocco, or Trebizond,°
Or whom Bizerta sent from Afric shore°
When Charlemagne with all his peerage fell
By Fontarabia. Thus far these beyond°
Compare of mortal prowess, yet observed
Their dread commander: he above the rest
In shape and gesture proudly eminent   590
Stood like a tower; his form had yet not lost
All her original brightness, nor appeared
Less than archangel ruined, and the excess
Of glory obscured: as when the sun new risen
Looks through the horizontal misty air
Shorn of his beams, or from behind the moon
In dim eclipse disastrous twilight sheds
On half the nations, and with fear of change
Perplexes monarchs. Darkened so, yet shone°
Above them all the archangel: but his face   600
Deep scars of thunder had intrenched, and care
Sat on his faded cheek, but under brows
Of dauntless courage, and considerate pride°
Waiting revenge: cruel his eye, but cast
Signs of remorse and passion to behold
The fellows of his crime, the followers rather
(Far other once beheld in bliss) condemned

Forever now to have their lot in pain,
Millions of spirits for his fault amerced
Of heaven, and from eternal splendours flung°   610
For his revolt, yet faithful how they stood,
Their glory withered. As when heaven's fire
Hath scathed the forest oaks, or mountain pines,°
With singèd top their stately growth though bare
Stands on the blasted heath. He now prepared
To speak; whereat their doubled ranks they bend
From wing to wing, and half enclose him round°
With all his peers: attention held them mute.
Thrice he essayed, and thrice in spite of scorn,
Tears such as angels weep burst forth: at last   620
Words interwove with sighs found out their way.
    O myriads of immortal spirits, O powers
Matchless, but with almighty, and that strife
Was not inglorious, though the event was dire,°
As this place testifies, and this dire change
Hateful to utter: but what power of mind
Foreseeing or presaging, from the depth
Of knowledge past or present, could have feared,
How such united force of gods, how such
As stood like these, could ever know repulse?   630
For who can yet believe, though after loss,
That all these puissant legions, whose exile
Hath emptied heaven, shall fail to reascend
Self-raised, and repossess their native seat?
For me be witness all the host of heaven,
If counsels different, or danger shunned°
By me, have lost our hopes. But he who reigns
Monarch in heaven, till then as one secure
Sat on his throne, upheld by old repute,
Consent or custom, and his regal state   640
Put forth at full, but still his strength concealed,°
Which tempted our attempt, and wrought our fall.
Henceforth his might we know, and know our own
So as not either to provoke, or dread
New war, provoked; our better part remains
To work in close design, by fraud or guile°
What force effected not: that he no less
At length from us may find, who overcomes

By force, hath overcome but half his foe.
Space may produce new worlds; whereof so rife   650
There went a fame in heaven that he ere long°
Intended to create, and therein plant
A generation, whom his choice regard
Should favour equal to the sons of heaven:
Thither, if but to pry, shall be perhaps
Our first eruption, thither or elsewhere:°
For this infernal pit shall never hold
Celestial spirits in bondage, nor the abyss
Long under darkness cover. But these thoughts
Full counsel must mature: peace is despaired,   660
For who can think submission? War then, war
Open or understood must be resolved.

    He spake: and to confirm his words, outflew
Millions of flaming swords, drawn from the thighs
Of mighty cherubim; the sudden blaze
Far round illumined hell: highly they raged
Against the highest, and fierce with graspèd arms
Clashed on their sounding shields the din of war,
Hurling defiance toward the vault of heaven.

    There stood a hill not far whose grisly top   670
Belched fire and rolling smoke; the rest entire
Shone with a glossy scurf, undoubted sign°
That in his womb was hid metallic ore,°
The work of sulphur. Thither winged with speed°
A numerous brigade hastened. As when bands
Of pioneers with spade and pickaxe armed°
Forerun the royal camp, to trench a field,
Or cast a rampart. Mammon led them on,°
Mammon, the least erected spirit that fell
From heaven, for even in heaven his looks and thoughts   680
Were always downward bent, admiring more
The riches of heaven's pavement, trodden gold,
Than aught divine or holy else enjoyed
In vision beatific: by him first
Men also, and by his suggestion taught,
Ransacked the centre, and with impious hands°
Rifled the bowels of their mother earth
For treasures better hid. Soon had his crew
Opened into the hill a spacious wound

And digged out ribs of gold. Let none admire°   690
That riches grow in hell; that soil may best
Deserve the precious bane. And here let those
Who boast in mortal things, and wondering tell
Of Babel, and the works of Memphian kings°
Learn how their greatest monuments of fame,
And strength and art are easily outdone
By spirits reprobate, and in an hour°
What in an age they with incessant toil
And hands innumerable scarce perform.
Nigh on the plain in many cells prepared,°   700
That underneath had veins of liquid fire
Sluiced from the lake, a second multitude
With wondrous art founded the massy ore,°
Severing each kind, and scummed the bullion dross:
A third as soon had formed within the ground
A various mould, and from the boiling cells°
By strange conveyance filled each hollow nook,°
As in an organ from one blast of wind
To many a row of pipes the sound-board breathes.
Anon out of the earth a fabric huge°   710
Rose like an exhalation, with the sound°
Of dulcet symphonies and voices sweet,°
Built like a temple, where pilasters round°
Were set, and Doric pillars overlaid°
With golden architrave; nor did there want°
Cornice or frieze, with bossy sculptures graven,°
The roof was fretted gold. Not Babylon,°
Nor great Alcairo such magnificence°
Equalled in all their glories, to enshrine
Belus or Serapis their gods, or seat°   720
Their kings, when Egypt with Assyria strove
In wealth and luxury. The ascending pile
Soon fixed her stately height, and straight the doors
Opening their brazen folds discover wide°
Within her ample spaces, o'er the smooth
And level pavement: from the archèd roof
Pendent by subtle magic many a row
Of starry lamps and blazing cressets fed°
With naphtha and asphaltus yielded light°
As from a sky. The hasty multitude   730

Admiring entered, and the work some praise
And some the architect: his hand was known
In heaven by many a towered structure high,
Where sceptred angels held their residence,
And sat as princes, whom the supreme king
Exalted to such power, and gave to rule,
Each in his hierarchy, the orders bright.
Nor was his name unheard or unadored
In ancient Greece; and in Ausonian land°
Men called him Mulciber; and how he fell°   740
From heaven, they fabled, thrown by angry Jove°
Sheer o'er the crystal battlements; from morn
To noon he fell, from noon to dewy eve,
A summer's day; and with the setting sun
Dropped from the zenith like a falling star,
On Lemnos the Aegaean isle: thus they relate,
Erring; for he with this rebellious rout
Fell along before; nor aught availed him now
To have built in heaven high towers; nor did he scape
By all his engines, but was headlong sent°   750
With his industrious crew to build in hell.
Meanwhile the wingèd heralds by command
Of sovereign power, with awful ceremony
And trumpets' sound throughout the host proclaim
A solemn council forthwith to be held
At Pandaemonium, the high capital°
Of Satan and his peers: their summons called
From every band and squarèd regiment°
By place or choice the worthiest; they anon
With hundreds and with thousands trooping came   760
Attended: all access was thronged, the gates
And porches wide, but chief the spacious hall
(Though like a covered field, where champions bold
Wont ride in armed, and at the soldan's chair°
Defied the best of paynim chivalry°
To mortal combat or career with lance)°
Thick swarmed, both on the ground and in the air,
Brushed with the hiss of rustling wings. As bees
In springtime, when the sun with Taurus rides,°
Pour forth their populous youth about the hive   770
In clusters; they among fresh dews and flowers

[handwritten margin note: Vulcan / Blacksmith]

Fly to and fro, or on the smoothèd plank,
The suburb of their straw-built citadel,
New rubbed with balm, expatiate and confer°
Their state affairs. So thick the airy crowd
Swarmed and were straitened; till the signal given,
Behold a wonder! they but now who seemed
In bigness to surpass Earth's giant sons
Now less than smallest dwarfs, in narrow room
Throng numberless, like that pygmean race   780
Beyond the Indian mount, or fairy elves,
Whose midnight revels, by a forest side
Or fountain some belated peasant sees,
Or dreams he sees, while overhead the moon
Sits arbitress, and nearer to the earth°
Wheels her pale course, they on their mirth and dance
Intent, with jocund music charm his ear;
At once with joy and fear his heart rebounds.
Thus incorporeal spirits to smallest forms
Reduced their shapes immense, and were at large,   790
Though without number still amidst the hall
Of that infernal court. But far within
And in their own dimensions like themselves
The great seraphic lords and cherubim
In close recess and secret conclave sat°
A thousand demigods on golden seats,
Frequent and full. After short silence then°
And summons read, the great consult began.°

BOOK II

The Argument

The consultation begun, Satan debates whether another battle be to be
hazarded for the recovery of heaven; some advise it, others dissuade: a third
proposal is preferred, mentioned before by Satan, to search the truth of that
prophecy or tradition in heaven concerning another world, and another kind of
creature equal or not much inferior to themselves, about this time to be created:
their doubt who shall be sent on this difficult search: Satan their chief undertakes alone the voyage, is honoured and applauded. The council thus ended,
the rest betake them several ways and to several employments, as their inclina-
tions lead them, to entertain the time till Satan return. He passes on his journey
to hell gates, finds them shut, and who sat there to guard them, by whom at
length they are opened, and discover° to him the great gulf between hell and
heaven; with what difficulty he passes through, directed by Chaos, the power° of
that place, to the sight of this new world which he sought.

High on a throne of royal state, which far
Outshone the wealth of Ormuz and of Ind,°
Or where the gorgeous East with richest hand
Showers on her kings barbaric pearl and gold,
Satan exalted sat, by merit raised
To that bad eminence; and from despair
Thus high uplifted beyond hope, aspires
Beyond thus high, insatiate to pursue
Vain war with heaven, and by success untaught°
His proud imaginations thus displayed.   10

    Powers and dominions, deities of heaven,°
For since no deep within her gulf can hold
Immortal vigour, though oppressed and fallen,
I give not heaven for lost. From this descent
Celestial virtues rising, will appear°
More glorious and more dread than from no fall,
And trust themselves to fear no second fate:
Me though just right, and the fixed laws of heaven
Did first create your leader, next free choice,
With what besides, in counsel or in fight,   20
Hath been achieved of merit, yet this loss°
Thus far at least recovered, hath much more
Established in a safe unenvied throne
Yielded with full consent. The happier state
In heaven, which follows dignity, might draw
Envy from each inferior; but who here
Will envy whom the highest place exposes°
Foremost to stand against the thunderer's aim°
Your bulwark, and condemns to greatest share
Of endless pain? where there is then no good   30
For which to strive, no strife can grow up there
From faction; for none sure will claim in hell
Precedence, none, whose portion is so small
Of present pain, that with ambitious mind
Will covet more. With this advantage then
To union, and firm faith, and firm accord,
More than can be in heaven, we now return
To claim our just inheritance of old,
Surer to prosper than prosperity
Could have assured us; and by what best way,   40
Whether of open war or covert guile,

We now debate; who can advise, may speak.
            He ceased, and next him Moloch, sceptred king
Stood up, the strongest and the fiercest spirit
That fought in heaven; now fiercer by despair:
His trust was with the eternal to be deemed
Equal in strength, and rather than be less
Cared not to be at all; with that care lost
Went all his fear: of God, or hell, or worse
He recked not, and these words thereafter spake.°   50
       My sentence is for open war: of wiles,°
More unexpert, I boast not: them let those°
Contrive who need, or when they need, not now.
For while they sit contriving, shall the rest,
Millions that stand in arms, and longing wait
The signal to ascend, sit lingering here
Heaven's fugitives, and for their dwelling place
Accept this dark opprobrious den of shame,
The prison of his tyranny who reigns
By our delay? no, let us rather choose   60
Armed with hell flames and fury all at once
O'er heaven's high towers to force resistless way,
Turning our tortures into horrid arms
Against the torturer; when to meet the noise
Of his almighty engine he shall hear°
Infernal thunder, and for lightning see
Black fire and horror shot with equal rage
Among his angels; and his throne itself
Mixed with Tartarean sulphur, and strange fire,°
His own invented torments. But perhaps   70
The way seems difficult and steep to scale
With upright wing against a higher foe.
Let such bethink them, if the sleepy drench°
Of that forgetful lake benumb not still,°
That in our proper motion we ascend°
Up to our native seat: descent and fall
To us is adverse. Who but felt of late
When the fierce foe hung on our broken rear
Insulting, and pursued us through the deep,°
With what compulsion and laborious flight   80
We sunk thus low? The ascent is easy then;°
The event is feared; should we again provoke°

Our stronger, some worse way his wrath may find°
To our destruction: if there be in hell
Fear to be worse destroyed: what can be worse
Than to dwell here, driven out from bliss, condemned
In this abhorrèd deep to utter woe;
Where pain of unextinguishable fire
Must exercise us without hope of end°
The vassals of his anger, when the scourge   90
Inexorably, and the torturing hour
Calls us to penance? More destroyed than thus
We should be quite abolished and expire.
What fear we then? what doubt we to incense°
His utmost ire? which to the height enraged,
Will either quite consume us, and reduce
To nothing this essential, happier far°
Than miserable to have eternal being:
Or if our substance be indeed divine,
And cannot cease to be, we are at worst   100
On this side nothing; and by proof we feel°
Our power sufficient to disturb his heaven,
And with perpetual inroads to alarm,
Though inaccessible, his fatal throne:°
Which if not victory is yet revenge.
      He ended frowning, and his look denounced°
Desperate revenge, and battle dangerous
To less than gods. On the other side up rose
Belial, in act more graceful and humane;
A fairer person lost not heaven; he seemed   110
For dignity composed and high exploit:
But all was false and hollow; though his tongue
Dropped manna, and could make the worse appear°
The better reason, to perplex and dash
Maturest counsels: for his thoughts were low;
To vice industrious, but to nobler deeds
Timorous and slothful: yet he pleased the ear,
And with persuasive accent thus began.
      I should be much for open war, O peers,
As not behind in hate; if what was urged   120
Main reason to persuade immediate war,
Did not dissuade me most, and seem to cast
Ominous conjecture on the whole success:

When he who most excels in fact of arms,°
In what he counsels and in what excels
Mistrustful, grounds his courage on despair
And utter dissolution, as the scope°
Of all his aim, after some dire revenge.
First, what revenge? the towers of heaven are filled
With armèd watch, that render all access   130
Impregnable; oft on the bordering deep
Encamp their legions, or with obscure wing
Scout far and wide into the realm of night,
Scorning surprise. Or could we break our way
By force, and at our heels all hell should rise
With blackest insurrection, to confound
Heaven's purest light, yet our great enemy
All incorruptible would on his throne
Sit unpolluted, and the ethereal mould°
Incapable of stain would soon expel   140
Her mischief, and purge off the baser fire
Victorious. Thus repulsed, our final hope
Is flat despair: we must exasperate
The almighty victor to spend all his rage,
And that must end us, that must be our cure,
To be no more; sad cure; for who would lose,
Though full of pain, this intellectual being,
Those thoughts that wander through eternity,
To perish rather, swallowed up and lost
In the wide womb of uncreated night,   150
Devoid of sense and motion? and who knows,
Let this be good, whether our angry foe
Can give it, or will ever? how he can
Is doubtful; that he never will is sure.
Will he, so wise, let loose at once his ire,
Belike through impotence, or unaware,°
To give his enemies their wish, and end
Them in his anger, whom his anger saves
To punish endless? wherefore cease we then?
Say they who counsel war, we are decreed,   160
Reserved and destined to eternal woe;
Whatever doing, what can we suffer more,
What can we suffer worse? is this then worst,
Thus sitting, thus consulting, thus in arms?

What when we fled amain, pursued and struck°
With heaven's afflicting thunder, and besought
The deep to shelter us? this hell then seemed
A refuge from those wounds: or when we lay
Chained on the burning lake? that sure was worse.°
What if the breath that kindled those grim fires   170
Awaked should blow them into sevenfold rage
And plunge us in the flames? or from above
Should intermitted vengeance arm again
His red right hand to plague us? what if all°
Her stores were opened, and this firmament
Of hell should spout her cataracts of fire,
Impendent horrors, threatening hideous fall
One day upon our heads; while we perhaps
Designing or exhorting glorious war,
Caught in a fiery tempest shall be hurled   180
Each on his rock transfixed, the sport and prey
Of racking whirlwinds, or for ever sunk
Under yon boiling ocean, wrapped in chains;
There to converse with everlasting groans,°
Unrespited, unpitied, unreprieved,
Ages of hopeless end; this would be worse.
War therefore, open or concealed, alike
My voice dissuades; for what can force or guile
With him, or who deceive his mind, whose eye°
Views all things at one view? he from heaven's height   190
All these our motions vain, sees and derides;°
Not more almighty to resist our might
Than wise to frustrate all our plots and wiles.
Shall we then live thus vile, the race of heaven
Thus trampled, thus expelled to suffer here
Chains and these torments? better these than worse
By my advice; since fate inevitable
Subdues us, and omnipotent decree,
The victor's will. To suffer, as to do,°
Our strength is equal, nor the law unjust   200
That so ordains: this was at first resolved,
If we were wise, against so great a foe
Contending, and so doubtful what might fall.
I laugh, when those who at the spear are bold
And venturous, if that fail them, shrink and fear

What yet they know must follow, to endure
Exile, or ignominy, or bonds, or pain,
The sentence of their conqueror: this is now
Our doom; which if we can sustain and bear,
Our supreme foe in time may much remit   210
His anger, and perhaps thus far removed
Not mind us not offending, satisfied°
With what is punished; whence these raging fires
Will slacken, if his breath stir not their flames.
Our purer essence then will overcome
Their noxious vapour, or inured not feel,
Or changed at length, and to the place conformed
In temper and in nature, will receive
Familiar the fierce heat, and void of pain;
This horror will grow mild, this darkness light,°   220
Besides what hope the never-ending flight
Of future days may bring, what chance, what change
Worth waiting, since our present lot appears
For happy though but ill, for ill not worst,°
If we procure not to ourselves more woe.
    Thus Belial with words clothed in reason's garb
Counselled ignoble ease, and peaceful sloth,
Not peace: and after him thus Mammon spake.
    Either to disenthrone the king of heaven
We war, if war be best, or to regain   230
Our own right lost: him to unthrone we then
May hope when everlasting fate shall yield
To fickle chance, and Chaos judge the strife:
The former vain to hope argues as vain
The latter: for what place can be for us
Within heaven's bound, unless heaven's lord supreme
We overpower? Suppose he should relent
And publish grace to all, on promise made
Of new subjection; with what eyes could we
Stand in his presence humble, and receive   240
Strict laws imposed, to celebrate his throne
With warbled hymns, and to his godhead sing
Forced hallelujahs; while he lordly sits
Our envied sovereign, and his altar breathes
Ambrosial odours and ambrosial flowers,
Our servile offerings? This must be our task

In heaven, this our delight; how wearisome
Eternity so spent in worship paid
To whom we hate. Let us not then pursue
By force impossible, by leave obtained°   250
Unacceptable, though in heaven, our state
Of splendid vassalage, but rather seek
Our own good from ourselves, and from our own
Live to ourselves, though in this vast recess,
Free, and to none accountable, preferring
Hard liberty before the easy yoke
Of servile pomp. Our greatness will appear
Then most conspicuous, when great things of small,
Useful of hurtful, prosperous of adverse
We can create, and in what place soe'er   260
Thrive under evil, and work ease out of pain
Through labour and endurance. This deep world
Of darkness do we dread? How oft amidst
Thick clouds and dark doth heaven's all-ruling sire
Choose to reside, his glory unobscured,
And with the majesty of darkness round
Covers his throne; from whence deep thunders roar
Mustering their rage, and heaven resembles hell?
As he our darkness, cannot we his light
Imitate when we please? This desert soil   270
Wants not her hidden lustre, gems and gold;°
Nor want we skill or art, from whence to raise
Magnificence; and what can heaven show more?
Our torments also may in length of time
Become our elements, these piercing fires°
As soft as now severe, our temper changed
Into their temper; which must needs remove°
The sensible of pain. All things invite°
To peaceful counsels, and the settled state
Of order, how in safety best we may   280
Compose our present evils, with regard°
Of what we are and where, dismissing quite
All thoughts of war: ye have what I advise.
  He scarce had finished, when such murmur filled
The assembly, as when hollow rocks retain
The sound of blustering winds, which all night long
Had roused the sea, now with hoarse cadence lull

Seafaring men o'erwatched, whose bark by chance°
Or pinnace anchors in a craggy bay
After the tempest: such applause was heard   290
As Mammon ended, and his sentence pleased,°
Advising peace: for such another field
They dreaded worse than hell: so much the fear
Of thunder and the sword of Michael
Wrought still within them; and no less desire
To found this nether empire, which might rise
By policy, and long process of time,°
In emulation opposite to heaven.
Which when Beelzebub perceived, than whom,
Satan except, none higher sat, with grave   300
Aspect he rose, and in his rising seemed
A pillar of state; deep on his front engraven°
Deliberation sat and public care;
And princely counsel in his face yet shone,
Majestic though in ruin: sage he stood
With Atlantean shoulders fit to bear°
The weight of mightiest monarchies; his look
Drew audience and attention still as night
Or summer's noontide air, while thus he spake.
      Thrones and imperial powers, offspring of heaven,   310
Ethereal virtues; or these titles now°
Must we renounce, and changing style be called°
Princes of hell? for so the popular vote
Inclines, here to continue, and build up here
A growing empire; doubtless; while we dream,
And know not that the king of heaven hath doomed
This place our dungeon, not our safe retreat
Beyond his potent arm, to live exempt
From heaven's high jurisdiction, in new league
Banded against his throne, but to remain   320
In strictest bondage, though thus far removed,
Under the inevitable curb, reserved
His captive multitude: for he, be sure
In height or depth, still first and last will reign
Sole king, and of his kingdom lose no part
By our revolt, but over hell extend
His empire, and with iron sceptre rule
Us here, as with his golden those in heaven.

What sit we then projecting peace and war?°
War hath determined us, and foiled with loss   330
Irreparable; terms of peace yet none
Vouchsafed or sought; for what peace will be given
To us enslaved, but custody severe,
And stripes, and arbitrary punishment°
Inflicted? and what peace can we return,
But to our power hostility and hate,°
Untamed reluctance, and revenge though slow,°
Yet ever plotting how the conqueror least
May reap his conquest, and may least rejoice
In doing what we most in suffering feel?   340
Nor will occasion want, nor shall we need°
With dangerous expedition to invade
Heaven, whose high walls fear no assault or siege,
Or ambush from the deep. What if we find
Some easier enterprise? There is a place
(If ancient and prophetic fame in heaven
Err not), another world, the happy seat
Of some new race called Man, about this time
To be created like to us, though less
In power and excellence, but favoured more   350
Of him who rules above; so was his will
Pronounced among the gods, and by an oath,
That shook heaven's whole circumference, confirmed.
Thither let us bend all our thoughts, to learn
What creatures there inhabit, of what mould,
Or substance, how endued, and what their power,
And where their weakness, how attempted best,
By force or subtlety: though heaven be shut,
And heaven's high arbitrator sit secure°
In his own strength, this place may lie exposed   360
The utmost border of his kingdom, left
To their defence who hold it: here perhaps
Some advantageous act may be achieved
By sudden onset, either with hellfire
To waste his whole creation, or possess
All as our own, and drive as we were driven,
The puny habitants, or if not drive,°
Seduce them to our party, that their God
May prove their foe, and with repenting hand

Beelzebub's
Idea?

Abolish his own works. This would surpass   370
Common revenge, and interrupt his joy
In our confusion, and our joy upraise°
In his disturbance; when his darling sons
Hurled headlong to partake with us, shall curse
Their frail original, and faded bliss,
Faded so soon. Advise if this be worth
Attempting, or to sit in darkness here
Hatching vain empires. Thus Beelzebub
Pleaded his devilish counsel, first devised
By Satan, and in part proposed: for whence,°   380
But from the author of all ill could spring
So deep a malice, to confound the race
Of mankind in one root, and earth with hell°
To mingle and involve, done all to spite°
The great creator? But their spite still serves
His glory to augment. The bold design
Pleased highly those infernal states, and joy°
Sparkled in all their eyes; with full assent
They vote: whereat his speech he thus renews.
    Well have ye judged, well ended long debate,   390
Synod of gods, and like to what ye are,°
Great things resolved, which from the lowest deep
Will once more lift us up, in spite of fate,
Nearer our ancient seat; perhaps in view
Of those bright confines, whence with neighbouring arms
And opportune excursion we may chance
Re-enter heaven; or else in some mild zone
Dwell not unvisited of heaven's fair light
Secure, and at the brightening orient beam
Purge off this gloom; the soft delicious air,   400
To heal the scar of these corrosive fires
Shall breathe her balm. But first whom shall we send
In search of this new world, whom shall we find
Sufficient? who shall tempt with wandering feet°
The dark unbottomed infinite abyss
And through the palpable obscure find out
His uncouth way, or spread his airy flight°
Upborne with indefatigable wings
Over the vast abrupt, ere he arrive°
The happy isle; what strength, what art can then   410

Suffice, or what evasion bear him safe
Through the strict sentries and stations thick
Of angels watching round? Here he had need
All circumspection, and we now no less
Choice in our suffrage; for on whom we send,°
The weight of all and our last hope relies.

   This said, he sat; and expectation held
His look suspense, awaiting who appeared°
To second, or oppose, or undertake
The perilous attempt: but all sat mute,   420
Pondering the danger with deep thoughts; and each
In others' countenance read his own dismay
Astonished: none among the choice and prime°
Of those heaven-warring champions could be found
So hardy as to proffer or accept
Alone the dreadful voyage; till at last
Satan, whom now transcendent glory raised
Above his fellows, with monarchal pride
Conscious of highest worth, unmoved thus spake.

   O progeny of heaven, empyreal thrones,   430
With reason hath deep silence and demur
Seized us, though undismayed: long is the way
And hard, that out of hell leads up to light;°
Our prison strong, this huge convex of fire,°
Outrageous to devour, immures us round°
Ninefold, and gates of burning adamant°
Barred over us prohibit all egress.
These passed, if any pass, the void profound
Of unessential night receives him next°
Wide gaping, and with utter loss of being   440
Threatens him, plunged in that abortive gulf.°
If thence he scape into whatever world,
Or unknown region, what remains him less
Than unknown dangers and as hard escape.
But I should ill become this throne, O peers,
And this imperial sovereignty, adorned
With splendour, armed with power, if aught proposed
And judged of public moment, in the shape°
Of difficulty or danger could deter
Me from attempting. Wherefore do I assume   450
These royalties, and not refuse to reign,

Refusing to accept as great a share
Of hazard as of honour, due alike
To him who reigns, and so much to him due
Of hazard more, as he above the rest
High honoured sits? Go therefore mighty powers,
Terror of heaven, though fallen; intend at home,°
While here shall be our home, what best may ease
The present misery, and render hell
More tolerable; if there be cure or charm   460
To respite or deceive, or slack the pain
Of this ill mansion: intermit no watch°
Against a wakeful foe, while I abroad
Through all the coasts of dark destruction seek
Deliverance for us all: this enterprise
None shall partake with me. Thus saying rose
The monarch, and prevented all reply,°
Prudent, lest from his resolution raised°
Others among the chief might offer now
(Certain to be refused) what erst they feared;°   470
And so refused might in opinion stand
His rivals, winning cheap the high repute
Which he through hazard huge must earn. But they
Dreaded not more the adventure than his voice
Forbidding; and at once with him they rose;
Their rising all at once was as the sound
Of thunder heard remote. Towards him they bend
With awful reverence prone; and as a god°
Extol him equal to the highest in heaven:
Nor failed they to express how much they praised,   480
That for the general safety he despised
His own: for neither do the spirits damned
Lose all their virtue; lest bad men should boast
Their specious deeds on earth, which glory excites,
Or close ambition varnished o'er with zeal.°
Thus they their doubtful consultations dark
Ended rejoicing in their matchless chief:
As when from mountain tops the dusky clouds
Ascending, while the north wind sleeps, o'erspread
Heaven's cheerful face, the louring element°   490
Scowls o'er the darkened landscape snow, or shower;
If chance the radiant sun with farewell sweet°

Extend his evening beam, the fields revive,
The birds their notes renew, and bleating herds
Attest their joy, that hill and valley rings.°
O shame to men! Devil with devil damned
Firm concord holds, men only disagree
Of creatures rational, though under hope
Of heavenly grace: and God proclaiming peace,
Yet live in hatred, enmity, and strife   500
Among themselves, and levy cruel wars,
Wasting the earth, each other to destroy:
As if (which might induce us to accord)
Man had not hellish foes enough besides,
That day and night for his destruction wait.
      The Stygian council thus dissolved; and forth
In order came the grand infernal peers,
Midst came their mighty paramount, and seemed°
Alone the antagonist of heaven, nor less
Than hell's dread emperor with pomp supreme,   510
And Godlike imitated state; him round
A globe of fiery seraphim enclosed°
With bright emblazonry, and horrent arms.°
Then of their session ended they bid cry
With trumpets' regal sound the great result:
Toward the four winds four speedy cherubim
Put to their mouths the sounding alchemy°
By herald's voice explained: the hollow abyss
Heard far and wide, and all the host of hell
With deafening shout returned them loud acclaim.   520
Thence more at ease their minds and somewhat raised°
By false presumptuous hope, the rangèd powers
Disband, and wandering, each his several way
Pursues, as inclination or sad choice
Leads him perplexed, where he may likeliest find
Truce to his restless thoughts, and entertain
The irksome hours, till this great chief return.
Part on the plain, or in the air sublime°
Upon the wing, or in swift race contend,
As at the Olympian games or Pythian fields;°   530
Part curb their fiery steeds, or shun the goal°
With rapid wheels, or fronted brigades form.°
As when to warn proud cities war appears

Waged in the troubled sky, and armies rush
To battle in the clouds, before each van°
Prick forth the airy knights, and couch their spears°
Till thickest legions close; with feats of arms°
From either end of heaven the welkin burns.°
Others with vast Typhoean rage more fell°
Rend up both rocks and hills, and ride the air   540
In whirlwind; hell scarce holds the wild uproar.°
As when Alcides from Oechalia crowned°
With conquest, felt the envenomed robe, and tore
Through pain up by the roots Thessalian pines,
And Lichas from the top of Oeta threw°
Into the Euboic sea. Others more mild,°
Retreated in a silent valley, sing
With notes angelical to many a harp
Their own heroic deeds and hapless fall
By doom of battle; and complain that fate   550
Free virtue should enthral to force or chance.
Their song was partial, but the harmony°
(What could it less when spirits immortal sing?)
Suspended hell, and took with ravishment°
The thronging audience. In discourse more sweet
(For eloquence the soul, song charms the sense,)
Others apart sat on a hill retired,
In thoughts more elevate, and reasoned high
Of providence, foreknowledge, will and fate,
Fixed fate, free will, foreknowledge absolute,   560
And found no end, in wandering mazes lost.
Of good and evil much they argued then,
Of happiness and final misery,
Passion and apathy, and glory and shame,°
Vain wisdom all, and false philosophy:
Yet with a pleasing sorcery could charm
Pain for a while or anguish, and excite
Fallacious hope, or arm the obdurèd breast°
With stubborn patience as with triple steel.
Another part in squadrons and gross bands,°   570
On bold adventure to discover wide
That dismal world, if any clime perhaps
Might yield them easier habitation, bend
Four ways their flying march, along the banks

Of four infernal rivers that disgorge
Into the burning lake their baleful streams;
Abhorrèd Styx the flood of deadly hate,
Sad Acheron of sorrow, black and deep;
Cocytus, named of lamentation loud
Heard on the rueful stream; fierce Phlegethon   580
Whose waves of torrent fire inflame with rage.
Far off from these a slow and silent stream,
Lethe the river of oblivion rolls°
Her watery labyrinth, whereof who drinks,
Forthwith his former state and being forgets,
Forgets both joy and grief, pleasure and pain.
Beyond this flood a frozen continent
Lies dark and wild, beat with perpetual storms
Of whirlwind and dire hail, which on firm land
Thaws not, but gathers heap, and ruin seems°   590
Of ancient pile; all else deep snow and ice,°
A gulf profound as that Serbonian bog°
Betwixt Damietta and Mount Casius old,°
Where armies whole have sunk: the parching air
Burns frore, and cold performs the effect of fire.°
Thither by harpy-footed Furies haled,°
At certain revolutions all the damned°
Are brought: and feel by turns the bitter change
Of fierce extremes, extremes by change more fierce,
From beds of raging fire to starve in ice°   600
Their soft ethereal warmth, and there to pine
Immovable, infixed, and frozen round,
Periods of time, thence hurried back to fire.
They ferry over this Lethean sound°
Both to and fro, their sorrow to augment,
And wish and struggle, as they pass, to reach
The tempting stream, with one small drop to lose
In sweet forgetfulness all pain and woe,
All in one moment, and so near the brink;
But fate withstands, and to oppose the attempt   610
Medusa with gorgonian terror guards°
The ford, and of itself the water flies
All taste of living wight, as once it fled°
The lip of Tantalus. Thus roving on°
In confused march forlorn, the adventurous bands

With shuddering horror pale, and eyes aghast
Viewed first their lamentable lot, and found
No rest: through many a dark and dreary vale
They passed, and many a region dolorous,
O'er many a frozen, many a fiery alp,   620
Rocks, caves, lakes, fens, bogs, dens, and shades of death,
A universe of death, which God by curse
Created evil, for evil only good,
Where all life dies, death lives, and nature breeds,
Perverse, all monstrous, all prodigious things,°
Abominable, inutterable, and worse
Than fables yet have feigned, or fear conceived,
Gorgons and hydras, and chimeras dire.°
    Meanwhile the adversary of God and man,
Satan with thoughts inflamed of highest design,   630
Puts on swift wings, and towards the gates of hell
Explores his solitary flight; sometimes°
He scours the right hand coast, sometimes the left,
Now shaves with level wing the deep, then soars
Up to the fiery concave towering high.
As when far off at sea a fleet descried
Hangs in the clouds, by equinoctial winds
Close sailing from Bengala, or the isles°
Of Ternate and Tidore, whence merchants bring°
Their spicy drugs: they on the trading flood   640
Through the wide Ethiopian to the Cape°
Ply stemming nightly toward the pole. So seemed°
Far off the flying fiend: at last appear
Hell bounds high reaching to the horrid roof,
And thrice threefold the gates; three folds were brass,°
Three iron, three of adamantine rock,
Impenetrable, impaled with circling fire,°
Yet unconsumed. Before the gates there sat
On either side a formidable shape;
The one seemed woman to the waist, and fair,   650
But ended foul in many a scaly fold
Voluminous and vast, a serpent armed
With mortal sting: about her middle round°
A cry of hell hounds never ceasing barked°
With wide Cerberian mouths full loud, and rung°
A hideous peal: yet, when they list, would creep,°

If aught disturbed their noise, into her womb,
And kennel there, yet there still barked and howled,
Within unseen. Far less abhorred than these
Vexed Scylla bathing in the sea that parts   660
Calabria from the hoarse Trinacrian shore:°
Nor uglier follow the Night-hag, when called°
In secret, riding through the air she comes
Lured with the smell of infant blood, to dance
With Lapland witches, while the labouring moon°
Eclipses at their charms. The other shape,
If shape it might be called that shape had none
Distinguishable in member, joint, or limb,
Or substance might be called that shadow seemed,
For each seemed either; black it stood as night,   670
Fierce as ten Furies, terrible as hell,
And shook a dreadful dart; what seemed his head
The likeness of a kingly crown had on.
Satan was now at hand, and from his seat
The monster moving onward came as fast
With horrid strides, hell trembled as he strode.
The undaunted fiend what this might be admired,°
Admired, not feared; God and his son except,
Created thing nought valued he nor shunned;
And with disdainful look thus first began.   680
     Whence and what art thou, execrable shape,
That darest, though grim and terrible, advance
Thy miscreated front athwart my way
To yonder gates? through them I mean to pass,
That be assured, without leave asked of thee:
Retire, or taste thy folly, and learn by proof,°
Hell-born, not to contend with spirits of heaven.
     To whom the goblin full of wrath replied,°
Art thou that traitor angel, art thou he,
Who first broke peace in heaven and faith, till then   690
Unbroken, and in proud rebellious arms
Drew after him the third part of heaven's sons
Conjured against the highest, for which both thou°
And they outcast from God, are here condemned
To waste eternal days in woe and pain?
And reckon'st thou thyself with spirits of heaven,
Hell-doomed, and breath'st defiance here and scorn

Where I reign king, and to enrage thee more,
Thy king and lord? Back to thy punishment,
False fugitive, and to thy speed add wings,   700
Lest with a whip of scorpions I pursue
Thy lingering, or with one stroke of this dart
Strange horror seize thee, and pangs unfelt before.
  So spake the grisly terror, and in shape,
So speaking and so threatening, grew tenfold
More dreadful and deform: on the other side°
Incensed with indignation Satan stood
Unterrified, and like a comet burned,
That fires the length of Ophiuchus huge°
In the Arctic sky, and from his horrid hair°   710
Shakes pestilence and war. Each at the head°
Levelled his deadly aim; their fatal hands
No second stroke intend, and such a frown
Each cast at the other, as when two black clouds
With heaven's artillery fraught, come rattling on
Over the Caspian, then stand front to front
Hovering a space, till winds the signal blow
To join their dark encounter in midair:
So frowned the mighty combatants, that hell
Grew darker at their frown, so matched they stood;   720
For never but once more was either like
To meet so great a foe: and now great deeds
Had been achieved, whereof all hell had rung,
Had not the snaky sorceress that sat
Fast by hell gate, and kept the fatal key,
Risen, and with hideous outcry rushed between.
  O father, what intends thy hand, she cried,
Against thy only son? What fury O son,
Possesses thee to bend that mortal dart
Against thy father's head? and know'st for whom;   730
For him who sits above and laughs the while
At thee ordained his drudge, to execute
Whate'er his wrath, which he calls justice, bids,
His wrath which one day will destroy ye both.
  She spake, and at her words the hellish pest°
Forbore, then these to her Satan returned:
  So strange thy outcry, and thy words so strange
Thou interposest, that my sudden hand

Prevented spares to tell thee yet by deeds°
What it intends; till first I know of thee,   740
What thing thou art, thus double-formed, and why
In this infernal vale first met thou call'st
Me father, and that phantasm call'st my son?
I know thee not, nor ever saw till now
Sight more detestable than him and thee.
 To whom thus the portress of hell gate replied;
Hast thou forgot me then, and do I seem
Now in thine eye so foul, once deemed so fair
In heaven, when at the assembly, and in sight
Of all the seraphim with thee combined   750
In bold conspiracy against heaven's king,
All on a sudden miserable pain
Surprised thee, dim thine eyes, and dizzy swum
In darkness, while thy head flames thick and fast
Threw forth, till on the left side opening wide,
Likest to thee in shape and countenance bright,
Then shining heavenly fair, a goddess armed
Out of thy head I sprung: amazement seized°
All the host of heaven; back they recoiled afraid
At first, and called me Sin, and for a sign   760
Portentous held me; but familiar grown,°
I pleased, and with attractive graces won
The most averse, thee chiefly, who full oft
Thyself in me thy perfect image viewing
Becam'st enamoured, and such joy thou took'st
With me in secret, that my womb conceived
A growing burden. Meanwhile war arose,
And fields were fought in heaven; wherein remained
(For what could else) to our almighty foe
Clear victory, to our part loss and rout   770
Through all the empyrean: down they fell
Driven headlong from the pitch of heaven, down°
Into this deep, and in the general fall
I also; at which time this powerful key
Into my hand was given, with charge to keep
These gates for ever shut, which none can pass
Without my opening. Pensive here I sat
Alone, but long I sat not, till my womb
Pregnant by thee, and now excessive grown

Prodigious motion felt and rueful throes.   780
At last this odious offspring whom thou seest
Thine own begotten, breaking violent way
Tore through my entrails, that with fear and pain°
Distorted, all my nether shape thus grew
Transformed: but he my inbred enemy
Forth issued, brandishing his fatal dart
Made to destroy: I fled, and cried out Death;
Hell trembled at the hideous name, and sighed
From all her caves, and back resounded Death.
I fled, but he pursued (though more, it seems,   790
Inflamed with lust than rage) and swifter far,
Me overtook his mother all dismayed,
And in embraces forcible and foul
Engendering with me, of that rape begot
These yelling monsters that with ceaseless cry
Surround me, as thou sawest, hourly conceived
And hourly born, with sorrow infinite
To me, for when they list into the womb°
That bred them they return, and howl and gnaw
My bowels, their repast; then bursting forth   800
Afresh with conscious terrors vex me round,°
That rest or intermission none I find.
Before mine eyes in opposition sits
Grim Death my son and foe, who sets them on,
And me his parent would full soon devour
For want of other prey, but that he knows
His end with mine involved; and knows that I
Should prove a bitter morsel, and his bane,
Whenever that shall be; so fate pronounced.
But thou, O father, I forewarn thee, shun   810
His deadly arrow; neither vainly hope
To be invulnerable in those bright arms,
Though tempered heavenly, for that mortal dint,°
Save he who reigns above, none can resist.
      She finished, and the subtle fiend his lore°
Soon learned, now milder, and thus answered smooth.
Dear daughter, since thou claim'st me for thy sire,
And my fair son here show'st me, the dear pledge
Of dalliance had with thee in heaven, and joys
Then sweet, now sad to mention, through dire change   820

Befallen us unforeseen, unthought of, know
I come no enemy, but to set free
From out this dark and dismal house of pain,
Both him and thee, and all the heavenly host
Of spirits that in our just pretences armed°
Fell with us from on high: from them I go
This uncouth errand sole, and one for all°
Myself expose, with lonely steps to tread
The unfounded deep, and through the void immense°
To search with wandering quest a place foretold   830
Should be, and, by concurring signs, ere now
Created vast and round, a place of bliss
In the purlieus of heaven, and therein placed°
A race of upstart creatures, to supply
Perhaps our vacant room, though more removed,°
Lest heaven surcharged with potent multitude°
Might hap to move new broils: be this or aught°
Than this more secret now designed, I haste
To know, and this once known, shall soon return,
And bring ye to the place where thou and Death   840
Shall dwell at ease, and up and down unseen
Wing silently the buxom air, embalmed°
With odours; there ye shall be fed and filled
Immeasurably, all things shall be your prey.
He ceased, for both seemed highly pleased, and Death
Grinned horrible a ghastly smile, to hear
His famine should be filled, and blessed his maw°
Destined to that good hour: no less rejoiced
His mother bad, and thus bespake her sire.
    The key of this infernal pit by due,   850
And by command of heaven's all-powerful king
I keep, by him forbidden to unlock
These adamantine gates; against all force
Death ready stands to interpose his dart,
Fearless to be o'ermatched by living might.
But what owe I to his commands above
Who hates me, and hath hither thrust me down
Into this gloom of Tartarus profound,
To sit in hateful office here confined,°
Inhabitant of heaven, and heavenly-born,   860
Here in perpetual agony and pain,

With terrors and with clamours compassed round
Of mine own brood, that on my bowels feed:
Thou art my father, thou my author, thou
My being gav'st me; whom should I obey
But thee, whom follow? thou wilt bring me soon
To that new world of light and bliss, among
The gods who live at ease, where I shall reign
At thy right hand voluptuous, as beseems
Thy daughter and thy darling, without end.   870
   Thus saying, from her side the fatal key,
Sad instrument of all our woe, she took;
And towards the gate rolling her bestial train,
Forthwith the huge portcullis high updrew,°
Which but her self, not all the Stygian powers
Could once have moved; then in the keyhole turns
The intricate wards, and every bolt and bar°
Of massy iron or solid rock with ease
Unfastens: on a sudden open fly
With impetuous recoil and jarring sound   880
The infernal doors, and on their hinges grate
Harsh thunder, that the lowest bottom shook
Of Erebus. She opened, but to shut°
Excelled her power; the gates wide open stood,
That with extended wings a bannered host°
Under spread ensigns marching might pass through
With horse and chariots ranked in loose array;
So wide they stood, and like a furnace mouth
Cast forth redounding smoke and ruddy flame.°
Before their eyes in sudden view appear   890
The secrets of the hoary deep, a dark
Illimitable ocean without bound,
Without dimension, where length, breadth, and height,
And time and place are lost; where eldest Night
And Chaos, ancestors of Nature, hold
Eternal anarchy, amidst the noise
Of endless wars, and by confusion stand.
For Hot, Cold, Moist, and Dry, four champions fierce°
Strive here for mastery, and to battle bring
Their embryon atoms; they around the flag°   900
Of each his faction, in their several clans,
Light-armed or heavy, sharp, smooth, swift or slow,

Swarm populous, unnumbered as the sands
Of Barca or Cyrene's torrid soil,°
Levied to side with warring winds, and poise
Their lighter wings. To whom these most adhere,°
He rules a moment; Chaos umpire sits,
And by decision more embroils the fray
By which he reigns: next him high arbiter
Chance governs all. Into this wild abyss,   910
The womb of nature and perhaps her grave,
Of neither sea, nor shore, nor air, nor fire,
But all these in their pregnant causes mixed
Confus'dly, and which thus must ever fight,
Unless the almighty maker them ordain
His dark materials to create more worlds,
Into this wild abyss the wary fiend
Stood on the brink of hell and looked awhile,
Pondering his voyage; for no narrow frith°
He had to cross. Nor was his ear less pealed°   920
With noises loud and ruinous (to compare
Great things with small) than when Bellona storms,°
With all her battering engines bent to raze
Some capital city; or less than if this frame
Of heaven were falling, and these elements
In mutiny had from her axle torn
The steadfast earth. At last his sail-broad vans°
He spreads for flight, and in the surging smoke
Uplifted spurns the ground, thence many a league
As in a cloudy chair ascending rides°   930
Audacious, but that seat soon failing, meets
A vast vacuity: all unawares
Fluttering his pennons vain plumb down he drops°
Ten thousand fathom deep, and to this hour
Down had been falling, had not by ill chance
The strong rebuff of some tumultuous cloud
Instinct with fire and nitre hurried him°
As many miles aloft: that fury stayed,
Quenched in a boggy Syrtis, neither sea,°
Nor good dry land: nigh foundered on he fares,   940
Treading the crude consistence, half on foot,
Half flying; behoves him now both oar and sail.
As when a griffin through the wilderness°

With wingèd course o'er hill or moory dale,°
Pursues the Arimaspian, who by stealth
Had from his wakeful custody purloined
The guarded gold: so eagerly the fiend°
O'er bog or steep, through straight, rough, dense, or rare,
With head, hands, wings or feet pursues his way,
And swims or sinks, or wades, or creeps, or flies: 950
At length a universal hubbub wild
Of stunning sounds and voices all confused
Borne through the hollow dark assaults his ear
With loudest vehemence: thither he plies,
Undaunted to meet there whatever power
Or spirit of the nethermost abyss
Might in that noise reside, of whom to ask
Which way the nearest coast of darkness lies
Bordering on light; when straight behold the throne
Of Chaos, and his dark pavilion spread   960
Wide on the wasteful deep; with him enthroned°
Sat sable-vested Night, eldest of things,
The consort of his reign; and by them stood
Orcus and Ades, and the dreaded name°
Of Demogorgon; Rumour next and Chance,°
And Tumult and Confusion all embroiled,
And Discord with a thousand various mouths.
    To whom Satan turning boldly, thus. Ye powers
And spirits of this nethermost abyss,
Chaos and ancient Night, I come no spy,   970
With purpose to explore or to disturb
The secrets of your realm, but by constraint
Wandering this darksome desert, as my way
Lies through your spacious empire up to light,
Alone, and without guide, half lost, I seek
What readiest path leads where your gloomy bounds
Confine with heaven; or if some other place°
From your dominion won, the ethereal king
Possesses lately, thither to arrive
I travel this profound, direct my course;   980
Directed no mean recompense it brings
To your behoof, if I that region lost,°
All usurpation thence expelled, reduce
To her original darkness and your sway

(Which is my present journey) and once more
Erect the standard there of ancient Night;
Yours be the advantage all, mine the revenge.
    Thus Satan; and him thus the anarch old°
With faltering speech and visage incomposed°
Answered. I know thee, stranger, who thou art,   990
That mighty leading angel, who of late
Made head against heaven's king, though overthrown.
I saw and heard, for such a numerous host
Fled not in silence through the frighted deep
With ruin upon ruin, rout on rout,
Confusion worse confounded; and heaven gates
Poured out by millions her victorious bands
Pursuing. I upon my frontiers here
Keep residence; if all I can will serve,
That little which is left so to defend,   1000
Encroached on still through our intestine broils°
Weakening the sceptre of old Night: first hell
Your dungeon stretching far and wide beneath;
Now lately heaven and earth, another world
Hung o'er my realm, linked in a golden chain
To that side heaven from whence your legions fell:°
If that way be your walk, you have not far;
So much the nearer danger; go and speed;°
Havoc and spoil and ruin are my gain.
    He ceased; and Satan stayed not to reply,   1010
But glad that now his sea should find a shore,
With fresh alacrity and force renewed
Springs upward like a pyramid of fire
Into the wild expanse, and through the shock
Of fighting elements, on all sides round
Environed wins his way; harder beset
And more endangered, than when Argo passed
Through Bosphorus, betwixt the jostling rocks:°
Or when Ulysses on the larboard shunned°
Charybdis, and by the other whirlpool steered.°   1020
So he with difficulty and labour hard
Moved on, with difficulty and labour he;
But he once past, soon after when man fell,
Strange alteration! Sin and Death amain°
Following his track, such was the will of heaven,

Paved after him a broad and beaten way
Over the dark abyss, whose boiling gulf
Tamely endured a bridge of wondrous length
From hell continued reaching the utmost orb
Of this frail world; by which the spirits perverse   1030
With easy intercourse pass to and fro
To tempt or punish mortals, except whom
God and good angels guard by special grace.
But now at last the sacred influence
Of light appears, and from the walls of heaven
Shoots far into the bosom of dim night
A glimmering dawn; here nature first begins
Her farthest verge, and Chaos to retire
As from her outmost works a broken foe
With tumult less and with less hostile din,   1040
That Satan with less toil, and now with ease
Wafts on the calmer wave by dubious light
And like a weather-beaten vessel holds°
Gladly the port, though shrouds and tackle torn;°
Or in the emptier waste, resembling air,
Weighs his spread wings, at leisure to behold
Far off the empyreal heaven, extended wide
In circuit, undetermined square or round,°
With opal towers and battlements adorned
Of living sapphire, once his native seat;°   1050
And fast by hanging in a golden chain°
This pendent world, in bigness as a star°
Of smallest magnitude close by the moon.
Thither full fraught with mischievous revenge,
Accursed, and in a cursèd hour he hies.

BOOK III

The Argument

God sitting on his throne sees Satan flying towards this world, then newly
created; shows him to the Son who sat at his right hand; foretells the success of
Satan in perverting mankind; clears his own justice and wisdom from all imputation, having created man free and able enough to have withstood his tempter;
yet declares his purpose of grace towards him, in regard he fell not of his own
malice, as did Satan, but by him seduced. The Son of God renders praises to

his father for the manifestation of his gracious purpose towards man; but God again declares, that grace cannot be extended toward man without the satisfaction of divine justice; man hath offended the majesty of God by aspiring to Godhead, and therefore with all his progeny devoted to death must die, unless someone can be found sufficient to answer for his offence, and undergo his punishment. The Son of God freely offers himself a ransom for man: the Father accepts him, ordains his incarnation, pronounces his exaltation above all names in heaven and earth; commands all the angels to adore him; they obey, and hymning to their harps in full choir, celebrate the Father and the Son. Meanwhile Satan alights upon the bare convex of this world's outermost orb; where wandering he first finds a place since called the Limbo of Vanity; what persons and things fly up thither; thence comes to the gate of heaven, described ascending by stairs, and the waters above the firmament that flow about it: his passage thence to the orb of the sun; he finds there Uriel the regent of that orb, but first changes himself into the shape of a meaner angel; and pretending a zealous desire to behold the new creation and man whom God had placed here, inquires of him the place of his habitation, and is directed; alights first on Mount Niphates.

> Hail holy light, offspring of heaven first-born,
> Or of the eternal co-eternal beam
> May I express thee unblamed? since God is light,°
> And never but in unapproachèd light
> Dwelt from eternity, dwelt then in thee,
> Bright effluence of bright essence increate.°
> Or hear'st thou rather pure ethereal stream,°
> Whose fountain who shall tell? before the sun,°
> Before the heavens thou wert, and at the voice
> Of God, as with a mantle didst invest°   10
> The rising world of waters dark and deep,
> Won from the void and formless infinite.
> Thee I revisit now with bolder wing,
> Escaped the Stygian pool, though long detained
> In that obscure sojourn, while in my flight
> Through utter and through middle darkness borne
> With other notes than to the Orphean lyre
> I sung of Chaos and eternal Night,°
> Taught by the heavenly Muse to venture down°
> The dark descent, and up to reascend,   20
> Though hard and rare: thee I revisit safe,
> And feel thy sovereign vital lamp; but thou
> Revisit'st not these eyes, that roll in vain°
> To find thy piercing ray, and find no dawn;

So thick a drop serene hath quenched their orbs,
Or dim suffusion veiled. Yet not the more°
Cease I to wander where the muses haunt
Clear spring, or shady grove, or sunny hill,
Smit with the love of sacred song; but chief
Thee Sion and the flowery brooks beneath°   30
That wash thy hallowed feet, and warbling flow,
Nightly I visit: nor sometimes forget
Those other two equalled with me in fate,
So were I equalled with them in renown,°
Blind Thamyris, and blind Maeonides,°
And Tiresias and Phineus prophets old.°
Then feed on thoughts, that voluntary move°
Harmonious numbers; as the wakeful bird°
Sings darkling, and in shadiest covert hid°
Tunes her nocturnal note. Thus with the year   40
Seasons return, but not to me returns
Day, or the sweet approach of even or morn,
Or sight of vernal bloom, or summer's rose,
Or flocks, or herds, or human face divine;
But cloud instead, and ever-during dark
Surrounds me, from the cheerful ways of men
Cut off, and for the book of knowledge fair
Presented with a universal blank
Of nature's works to me expunged and razed,
And wisdom at one entrance quite shut out.   50
So much the rather thou celestial light
Shine inward, and the mind through all her powers
Irradiate, there plant eyes, all mist from thence
Purge and disperse, that I may see and tell
Of things invisible to mortal sight.
    Now had the almighty Father from above,
From the pure empyrean where he sits
High throned above all height, bent down his eye,
His own works and their works at once to view:
About him all the sanctities of heaven°   60
Stood thick as stars, and from his sight received°
Beatitude past utterance; on his right
The radiant image of his glory sat,
His only son; on earth he first beheld
Our two first parents, yet the only two

Of mankind, in the happy garden placed,
Reaping immortal fruits of joy and love,
Uninterrupted joy, unrivalled love
In blissful solitude; he then surveyed
Hell and the gulf between, and Satan there　　　　70
Coasting the wall of heaven on this side night
In the dun air sublime, and ready now°
To stoop with wearied wings, and willing feet°
On the bare outside of this world, that seemed°
Firm land embosomed without firmament,°
Uncertain which, in ocean or in air.°
Him God beholding from his prospect high,
Wherein past, present, future he beholds,
Thus to his only son foreseeing spake.

　　Only begotten Son, seest thou what rage　　　　80
Transports our adversary, whom no bounds
Prescribed, no bars of hell, nor all the chains
Heaped on him there, nor yet the main abyss
Wide interrupt can hold; so bent he seems°
On desperate revenge, that shall redound
Upon his own rebellious head. And now
Through all restraint broke loose he wings his way
Not far off heaven, in the precincts of light,
Directly towards the new created world,
And man there placed, with purpose to assay　　　　90
If him by force he can destroy, or worse,
By some false guile pervert; and shall pervert
For man will hearken to his glozing lies,°
And easily transgress the sole command,
Sole pledge of his obedience: so will fall,
He and his faithless progeny: whose fault?
Whose but his own? ingrate, he had of me
All he could have; I made him just and right,
Sufficient to have stood, though free to fall.
Such I created all the ethereal powers　　　　100
And spirits, both them who stood and them who failed;
Freely they stood who stood, and fell who fell.
Not free, what proof could they have given sincere
Of true allegiance, constant faith or love,
Where only what they needs must do, appeared,
Not what they would? what praise could they receive?°

What pleasure I from such obedience paid,
When will and reason (reason also is choice)
Useless and vain, of freedom both despoiled,
Made passive both, had served necessity,   110
Not me. They therefore as to right belonged,
So were created, nor can justly accuse
Their maker, or their making, or their fate,
As if predestination overruled
Their will, disposed by absolute decree
Or high foreknowledge; they themselves decreed
Their own revolt, not I: if I foreknew,
Foreknowledge had no influence on their fault,
Which had no less proved certain unforeknown.
So without least impulse or shadow of fate,°   120
Or aught by me immutably foreseen,
They trespass, authors to themselves in all
Both what they judge and what they choose; for so
I formed them free, and free they must remain,
Till they enthrall themselves: I else must change
Their nature, and revoke the high decree
Unchangeable, eternal, which ordained
Their freedom, they themselves ordained their fall.
The first sort by their own suggestion fell,°
Self-tempted, self-depraved: man falls deceived   130
By the other first: man therefore shall find grace,
The other none: in mercy and justice both,
Through heaven and earth, so shall my glory excel,
But mercy first and last shall brightest shine.
    Thus while God spake, ambrosial fragrance filled
All heaven, and in the blessèd spirits elect°
Sense of new joy ineffable diffused:
Beyond compare the Son of God was seen
Most glorious, in him all his father shone
Substantially expressed, and in his face°   140
Divine compassion visibly appeared,
Love without end, and without measure grace,
Which uttering thus he to his father spake.
    O Father, gracious was that word which closed
Thy sovereign sentence, that man should find grace;
For which both heaven and earth shall high extol
Thy praises, with the innumerable sound

Of hymns and sacred songs, wherewith thy throne
Encompassed shall resound thee ever blessed.
For should man finally be lost, should man 150
Thy creature late so loved, thy youngest son
Fall circumvented thus by fraud, though joined
With his own folly? that be from thee far,
That far be from thee, Father, who art judge
Of all things made, and judgest only right.
Or shall the adversary thus obtain
His end, and frustrate thine, shall he fulfil
His malice, and thy goodness bring to naught,
Or proud return though to his heavier doom,
Yet with revenge accomplished and to hell 160
Draw after him the whole race of mankind,
By him corrupted? or wilt thou thyself
Abolish thy creation, and unmake,
For him, what for thy glory thou hast made?
So should thy goodness and thy greatness both
Be questioned and blasphemed without defence.
　　To whom the great creator thus replied.
O Son, in whom my soul hath chief delight,
Son of my bosom, Son who art alone
My word, my wisdom, and effectual might,° 170
All hast thou spoken as my thoughts are, all
As my eternal purpose hath decreed:
Man shall not quite be lost, but saved who will,
Yet not of will in him, but grace in me°
Freely vouchsafed; once more I will renew
His lapsèd powers, though forfeit and enthralled°
By sin to foul exorbitant desires;°
Upheld by me, yet once more he shall stand
On even ground against his mortal foe°
By me upheld, that he may know how frail 180
His fallen condition is, and to me owe
All his deliverance, and to none but me.
Some I have chosen of peculiar grace
Elect above the rest; so is my will:
The rest shall hear me call, and oft be warned
Their sinful state, and to appease betimes
The incensèd deity, while offered grace
Invites; for I will clear their senses dark,

What may suffice, and soften stony hearts
To pray, repent, and bring obedience due.   190
To prayer, repentance, and obedience due,
Though but endeavoured with sincere intent,
Mine ear shall not be slow, mine eye not shut.
And I will place within them as a guide
My umpire conscience, whom if they will hear,
Light after light well used they shall attain,
And to the end persisting, safe arrive.
This my long sufferance and my day of grace
They who neglect and scorn, shall never taste;
But hard be hardened, blind be blinded more,   200
That they may stumble on, and deeper fall;
And none but such from mercy I exclude.
But yet all is not done; man disobeying,
Disloyal breaks his fealty, and sins°
Against the high supremacy of heaven,
Affecting godhead, and so losing all,°
To expiate his treason hath naught left,
But to destruction sacred and devote,°
He with his whole posterity must die,
Die he or justice must; unless for him   210
Some other able, and as willing, pay
The rigid satisfaction, death for death.
Say heavenly powers, where shall we find such love,
Which of ye will be mortal to redeem
Man's mortal crime, and just the unjust to save,
Dwells in all heaven charity so dear?
    He asked, but all the heavenly choir stood mute,
And silence was in heaven: on man's behalf
Patron or intercessor none appeared,°
Much less that durst upon his own head draw   220
The deadly forfeiture, and ransom set.
And now without redemption all mankind°
Must have been lost, adjudged to death and hell
By doom severe, had not the Son of God,°
In whom the fulness dwells of love divine,
His dearest mediation thus renewed.
    Father, thy word is past, man shall find grace;
And shall grace not find means, that finds her way,
The speediest of thy wingèd messengers,

To visit all thy creatures, and to all   230
Comes unprevented, unimplored, unsought,°
Happy for man, so coming; he her aid
Can never seek, once dead in sins and lost;
Atonement for himself or offering meet,°
Indebted and undone, hath none to bring:
Behold me then, me for him, life for life
I offer, on me let thine anger fall;
Account me man; I for his sake will leave
Thy bosom, and this glory next to thee
Freely put off, and for him lastly die   240
Well pleased, on me let Death wreak all his rage;
Under his gloomy power I shall not long
Lie vanquished; thou hast given me to possess
Life in myself forever, by thee I live,
Though now to Death I yield, and am his due
All that of me can die, yet that debt paid,
Thou wilt not leave me in the loathsome grave
His prey, nor suffer my unspotted soul°
Forever with corruption there to dwell;
But I shall rise victorious, and subdue   250
My vanquisher, spoiled of his vaunted spoil;°
Death his death's wound shall then receive, and stoop
Inglorious, of his mortal sting disarmed.
I through the ample air in triumph high
Shall lead hell captive maugre hell, and show°
The powers of darkness bound. Thou at the sight
Pleased, out of heaven shalt look down and smile,
While by thee raised I ruin all my foes,
Death last, and with his carcass glut the grave:
Then with the multitude of my redeemed   260
Shall enter heaven long absent, and return,
Father, to see thy face, wherein no cloud
Of anger shall remain, but peace assured,
And reconcilement; wrath shall be no more
Thenceforth, but in thy presence joy entire.
      His words here ended, but his meek aspect
Silent yet spake, and breathed immortal love
To mortal men, above which only shone
Filial obedience: as a sacrifice
Glad to be offered, he attends the will°   270

Of his great father. Admiration seized
All heaven, what this might mean, and whither tend
Wondering; but soon the almighty thus replied:
    O thou in heaven and earth the only peace
Found out for mankind under wrath, O thou
My sole complacence! well thou know'st how dear°
To me are all my works, nor man the least
Though last created, that for him I spare
Thee from my bosom and right hand, to save,
By losing thee awhile, the whole race lost.   280
Thou therefore whom thou only canst redeem,
Their nature also to thy nature join;°
And be thyself man among men on earth,
Made flesh, when time shall be, of virgin seed,
By wondrous birth: be thou in Adam's room°
The head of all mankind, though Adam's son.
As in him perish all men, so in thee
As from a second root shall be restored,
As many as are restored, without thee none.
His crime makes guilty all his sons, thy merit   290
Imputed shall absolve them who renounce°
Their own both righteous and unrighteous deeds,
And live in thee transplanted, and from thee
Receive new life. So man, as is most just,°
Shall satisfy for man, be judged and die,
And dying rise, and rising with him raise
His brethren, ransomed with his own dear life.
So heavenly love shall outdo hellish hate
Giving to death, and dying to redeem,°
So dearly to redeem what hellish hate   300
So easily destroyed, and still destroys
In those who, when they may, accept not grace.
Nor shalt thou by descending to assume°
Man's nature, lessen or degrade thine own.
Because thou hast, though throned in highest bliss
Equal to God, and equally enjoying
Godlike fruition, quitted all to save°
A world from utter loss, and hast been found
By merit more than birthright Son of God,
Found worthiest to be so by being good,   310
Far more than great or high; because in thee

Love hath abounded more than glory abounds,
Therefore thy humiliation shall exalt
With thee thy manhood also to this throne;
Here shalt thou sit incarnate, here shalt reign
Both God and man, Son both of God and man,
Anointed universal king; all power
I give thee, reign for ever, and assume
Thy merits; under thee as head supreme°
Thrones, princedoms, powers, dominions I reduce:°   320
All knees to thee shall bow, of them that bide
In heaven, or earth, or under earth in hell,
When thou attended gloriously from heaven
Shalt in the sky appear, and from thee send°
The summoning archangels to proclaim
Thy dread tribunal: forthwith from all winds°
The living, and forthwith the cited dead°
Of all past ages to the general doom°
Shall hasten, such a peal shall rouse their sleep.
Then all thy saints assembled, thou shalt judge   330
Bad men and angels, they arraigned shall sink
Beneath thy sentence; hell her numbers full,
Thenceforth shall be forever shut. Meanwhile
The world shall burn, and from her ashes spring
New heaven and earth, wherein the just shall dwell,
And after all their tribulations long
See golden days, fruitful of golden deeds,
With joy and love triumphing, and fair truth.
Then thou thy regal sceptre shalt lay by,
For regal sceptre then no more shall need,°   340
God shall be all in all. But all ye gods,°
Adore him, who to compass all this dies,
Adore the Son, and honour him as me.
    No sooner had the almighty ceased, but all
The multitude of angels with a shout
Loud as from numbers without number, sweet
As from blest voices, uttering joy, heaven rung
With jubilee, and loud hosannas filled°
The eternal regions: lowly reverent
Towards either throne they bow, and to the ground   350
With solemn adoration down they cast
Their crowns inwove with amaranth and gold,°

Immortal amaranth, a flower which once
In Paradise, fast by the tree of life°
Began to bloom, but soon for man's offence
To heaven removed where first it grew, there grows,
And flowers aloft shading the fount of life,
And where the river of bliss through midst of heaven
Rolls o'er Elysian flowers her amber stream;°
With these that never fade the spirits elect   360
Bind their resplendent locks inwreathed with beams,
Now in loose garlands thick thrown off, the bright
Pavement that like a sea of jasper shone
Impurpled with celestial roses smiled.
Then crowned again their golden harps they took,
Harps ever tuned, that glittering by their side
Like quivers hung, and with preamble sweet
Of charming symphony they introduce
Their sacred song, and waken raptures high;
No voice exempt, no voice but well could join   370
Melodious part, such concord is in heaven.
    ˋ Thee Father first they sung omnipotent,
Immutable, immortal, infinite,
Eternal king; thee author of all being,
Fountain of light, thyself invisible
Amidst the glorious brightness where thou sit'st
Throned inaccessible, but when thou shad'st°
The full blaze of thy beams, and through a cloud
Drawn round about thee like a radiant shrine,
Dark with excessive bright thy skirts appear,°   380
Yet dazzle heaven, that brightest seraphim°
Approach not, but with both wings veil their eyes.
Thee next they sang of all creation first,
Begotten Son, divine similitude,
In whose conspicuous countenance, without cloud°
Made visible, the almighty Father shines,
Whom else no creature can behold; on thee
Impressed the effulgence of his glory abides,
Transfused on thee his ample spirit rests.
He heaven of heavens and all the powers therein   390
By thee created, and by thee threw down
The aspiring dominations: thou that day°
Thy father's dreadful thunder didst not spare,

Nor stop thy flaming chariot wheels, that shook
Heaven's everlasting frame, while o'er the necks
Thou drov'st of warring angels disarrayed.
Back from pursuit thy powers with loud acclaim°
Thee only extolled, Son of thy father's might,
To execute fierce vengeance on his foes,
Not so on man; him through their malice fallen,   400
Father of mercy and grace, thou didst not doom
So strictly, but much more to pity incline:
No sooner did thy dear and only son
Perceive thee purposed not to doom frail man
So strictly, but much more to pity inclined,
He to appease thy wrath, and end the strife
Of mercy and justice in thy face discerned,
Regardless of the bliss wherein he sat
Second to thee, offered himself to die
For man's offence. O unexampled love,   410
Love nowhere to be found less than divine!
Hail, Son of God, saviour of men, thy name
Shall be the copious matter of my song
Henceforth, and never shall my harp thy praise
Forget, nor from thy father's praise disjoin.
    Thus they in heaven, above the starry sphere,
Their happy hours in joy and hymning spent.
Meanwhile upon the firm opacous globe°
Of this round world, whose first convex divides°
The luminous inferior orbs, enclosed°   420
From Chaos and the inroad of darkness old,
Satan alighted walks: a globe far off
It seemed, now seems a boundless continent
Dark, waste, and wild, under the frown of night
Starless exposed, and ever-threatening storms
Of Chaos blustering round, inclement sky;
Save on that side which from the wall of heaven
Though distant far some small reflection gains
Of glimmering air less vexed with tempest loud:
Here walked the fiend at large in spacious field.   430
As when a vulture on Imaus bred,°
Whose snowy ridge the roving Tartar bounds,
Dislodging from a region scarce of prey
To gorge the flesh of lambs or yeanling kids°

On hills where flocks are fed, flies toward the springs
Of Ganges or Hydaspes, Indian streams;°
But in his way lights on the barren plains
Of Sericana, where Chineses drive°
With sails and wind their cany wagons light:
So on this windy sea of land, the fiend   440
Walked up and down alone bent on his prey,
Alone, for other creature in this place
Living or lifeless to be found was none,
None yet, but store hereafter from the earth°
Up hither like aerial vapours flew
Of all things transitory and vain, when sin
With vanity had filled the works of men:
Both all things vain, and all who in vain things
Built their fond hopes of glory or lasting fame,°
Or happiness in this or the other life;   450
All who have their reward on earth, the fruits
Of painful superstition and blind zeal,°
Nought seeking but the praise of men, here find
Fit retribution, empty as their deeds;
All the unaccomplished works of nature's hand,
Abortive, monstrous, or unkindly mixed,°
Dissolved on earth, fleet hither, and in vain,°
Till final dissolution, wander here,
Not in the neighbouring moon, as some have dreamed;°
Those argent fields more likely habitants,°   460
Translated saints, or middle spirits hold°
Betwixt the angelical and human kind:
Hither of ill-joined sons and daughters born
First from the ancient world those Giants came°
With many a vain exploit, though then renowned:
The builders next of Babel on the plain
Of Sennaar, and still with vain design°
New Babels, had they wherewithal, would build:
Others came single; he who to be deemed
A god, leaped fondly into Aetna flames,°   470
Empedocles, and he who to enjoy°
Plato's Elysium, leaped into the sea,
Cleombrotus, and many more too long,°
Embryos and idiots, eremites and friars°
White, black and grey, with all their trumpery.°

Here pilgrims roam, that strayed so far to seek
In Golgotha him dead, who lives in heaven;°
And they who to be sure of Paradise
Dying put on the weeds of Dominic,°
Or in Franciscan think to pass disguised;   480
They pass the planets seven, and pass the fixed,°
And that crystalline sphere whose balance weighs
The trepidation talked, and that first moved;°
And now Saint Peter at heaven's wicket seems°
To wait them with his keys, and now at foot
Of heaven's ascent they lift their feet, when lo
A violent cross wind from either coast
Blows them transverse ten thousand leagues awry
Into the devious air; then might ye see°
Cowls, hoods and habits with their wearers tossed   490
And fluttered into rags, then relics, beads,°
Indulgences, dispenses, pardons, bulls,°
The sport of winds: all these upwhirled aloft
Fly o'er the backside of the world far off
Into a limbo large and broad, since called°
The Paradise of Fools, to few unknown
Long after, now unpeopled, and untrod;
All this dark globe the fiend found as he passed,
And long he wandered, till at last a gleam
Of dawning light turned thitherward in haste   500
His travelled steps; far distant he descries
Ascending by degrees magnificent
Up to the wall of heaven a structure high,
At top whereof, but far more rich appeared
The work as of a kingly palace gate
With frontispiece of diamond and gold°
Embellished, thick with sparkling orient gems°
The portal shone, inimitable on earth
By model, or by shading pencil drawn.
The stairs were such as whereon Jacob saw   510
Angels ascending and descending, bands
Of guardians bright, when he from Esau fled
To Padan-Aram in the field of Luz,°
Dreaming by night under the open sky,
And waking cried, *This is the gate of heaven.*°
Each stair mysteriously was meant, nor stood°

There always, but drawn up to heaven sometimes
Viewless, and underneath a bright sea flowed
Of jasper, or of liquid pearl, whereon
Who after came from earth, sailing arrived,   520
Wafted by angels, or flew o'er the lake
Rapt in a chariot drawn by fiery steeds.°
The stairs were then let down, whether to dare
The fiend by easy ascent, or aggravate
His sad exclusion from the doors of bliss.
Direct against which opened from beneath,
Just o'er the blissful seat of Paradise,
A passage down to the earth, a passage wide,
Wider by far than that of after-times
Over Mount Sion, and, though that were large,   530
Over the Promised Land to God so dear,
By which, to visit oft those happy tribes,
On high behests his angels to and fro
Passed frequent, and his eye with choice regard°
From Paneas the fount of Jordan's flood°
To Beersaba, where the Holy Land°
Borders on Egypt and the Arabian shore;
So wide the opening seemed, where bounds were set
To darkness, such as bound the ocean wave.
Satan from hence now on the lower stair   540
That scaled by steps of gold to heaven gate
Looks down with wonder at the sudden view
Of all this world at once. As when a scout
Through dark and desert ways with peril gone
All night; at last by break of cheerful dawn
Obtains the brow of some high-climbing hill,°
Which to his eye discovers unaware°
The goodly prospect of some foreign land
First-seen, or some renowned metropolis
With glistering spires and pinnacles adorned,   550
Which now the rising sun gilds with his beams.
Such wonder seized, though after heaven seen,°
The spirit malign, but much more envy seized
At sight of all this world beheld so fair.
Round he surveys, and well might, where he stood
So high above the circling canopy
Of night's extended shade; from eastern point

Of Libra to the fleecy star that bears°
Andromeda far off Atlantic seas°
Beyond the horizon; then from pole to pole   560
He views in breadth, and without longer pause
Down right into the world's first region throws°
His flight precipitant, and winds with ease°
Through the pure marble air his oblique way°
Amongst innumerable stars, that shone
Stars distant, but nigh hand seemed other worlds,°
Or other worlds they seemed, or happy isles,
Like those Hesperian gardens famed of old,°
Fortunate fields, and groves and flowery vales,
Thrice happy isles, but who dwelt happy there   570
He stayed not to inquire: above them all
The golden sun in splendour likest heaven
Allured his eye: thither his course he bends
Through the calm firmament; but up or down
By centre, or eccentric, hard to tell,°
Or longitude, where the great luminary°
Aloof the vulgar constellations thick,°
That from his lordly eye keep distance due,
Dispenses light from far; they as they move
Their starry dance in numbers that compute°   580
Days, months, and years, towards his all-cheering lamp
Turn swift their various motions, or are turned
By his magnetic beam, that gently warms
The universe, and to each inward part
With gentle penetration, though unseen,
Shoots invisible virtue even to the deep:°
So wondrously was set his station bright.
There lands the fiend, a spot like which perhaps
Astronomer in the sun's lucent orb
Through his glazed optic tube yet never saw.°   590
The place he found beyond expression bright,
Compared with aught on earth, metal or stone;
Not all parts like, but all alike informed
With radiant light, as glowing iron with fire;
If metal, part seemed gold, part silver clear;°
If stone, carbuncle most or chrysolite,°
Ruby or topaz, to the twelve that shone°
In Aaron's breastplate, and a stone besides°

Imagined rather oft than elsewhere seen,
That stone, or like to that which here below   600
Philosophers in vain so long have sought,°
In vain, though by their powerful art they bind
Volatile Hermes, and call up unbound°
In various shapes old Proteus from the sea,°
Drained through a limbeck to his native form.°
What wonder then if fields and regions here
Breathe forth elixir pure, and rivers run°
Potable gold, when with one virtuous touch°
The arch-chemic sun so far from us remote°
Produces with terrestrial humour mixed°   610
Here in the dark so many precious things
Of colour glorious and effect so rare?°
Here matter new to gaze the devil met
Undazzled, far and wide his eye commands,
For sight no obstacle found here, nor shade,
But all sunshine, as when his beams at noon
Culminate from the equator, as they now°
Shot upward still direct, whence no way round
Shadow from body opaque can fall, and the air,
Nowhere so clear, sharpened his visual ray   620
To objects distant far, whereby he soon
Saw within ken a glorious angel stand,°
The same whom John saw also in the sun:°
His back was turned, but not his brightness hid;
Of beaming sunny rays, a golden tiar°
Circled his head, nor less his locks behind
Illustrious on his shoulders fledge with wings°
Lay waving round; on some great charge employed
He seemed, or fixed in cogitation deep.
Glad was the spirit impure; as now in hope   630
To find who might direct his wandering flight
To Paradise the happy seat of man,
His journey's end and our beginning woe.
But first he casts to change his proper shape,°
Which else might work him danger or delay:
And now a stripling cherub he appears,
Not of the prime, yet such as in his face°
Youth smiled celestial, and to every limb
Suitable grace diffused, so well he feigned;

Under a coronet his flowing hair   640
In curls on either cheek played, wings he wore
Of many a coloured plume sprinkled with gold,
His habit fit for speed succinct, and held°
Before his decent steps a silver wand.°
He drew not nigh unheard, the angel bright,
Ere he drew nigh, his radiant visage turned,
Admonished by his ear, and straight was known
The archangel Uriel, one of the seven°
Who in God's presence, nearest to his throne
Stand ready at command, and are his eyes   650
That run through all the heavens, or down to the earth
Bear his swift errands over moist and dry,
O'er sea and land: him Satan thus accosts.
    Uriel, for thou of those seven spirits that stand
In sight of God's high throne, gloriously bright,
The first art wont his great authentic will°
Interpreter through highest heaven to bring,
Where all his sons thy embassy attend;
And here art likeliest by supreme decree
Like honour to obtain, and as his eye   660
To visit oft this new creation round;
Unspeakable desire to see, and know
All these his wondrous works, but chiefly man,
His chief delight and favour, him for whom
All these his works so wondrous he ordained,
Hath brought me from the choirs of cherubim
Alone thus wandering. Brightest seraph tell
In which of all these shining orbs hath man
His fixèd seat, or fixèd seat hath none,
But all these shining orbs his choice to dwell;   670
That I may find him, and with secret gaze,
Or open admiration him behold
On whom the great creator hath bestowed
Worlds, and on whom hath all these graces poured;
That both in him and all things, as is meet,
The universal maker we may praise;
Who justly hath driven out his rebel foes
To deepest hell, and to repair that loss
Created this new happy race of men
To serve him better: wise are all his ways.   680

   So spake the false dissembler unperceived;
For neither man nor angel can discern
Hypocrisy, the only evil that walks
Invisible, except to God alone,
By his permissive will, through heaven and earth:
And oft though wisdom wake, suspicion sleeps
At wisdom's gate, and to simplicity
Resigns her charge, while goodness thinks no ill
Where no ill seems: which now for once beguiled
Uriel, though regent of the sun, and held°   690
The sharpest sighted spirit of all in heaven;
Who to the fraudulent imposter foul
In his uprightedness answer thus returned.
Fair angel, thy desire which tends to know°
The works of God, thereby to glorify
The great work-master, leads to no excess
That reaches blame, but rather merits praise
The more it seems excess, that led thee hither
From thy empyreal mansion thus alone,°
To witness with thine eyes what some perhaps   700
Contented with report hear only in heaven:
For wonderful indeed are all his works,
Pleasant to know, and worthiest to be all
Had in remembrance always with delight;
But what created mind can comprehend
Their number, or the wisdom infinite
That brought them forth, but hid their causes deep.
I saw when at his word the formless mass,
This world's material mould, came to a heap:
Confusion heard his voice, and wild uproar   710
Stood ruled, stood vast infinitude confined;
Till at his second bidding darkness fled,°
Light shone, and order from disorder sprung:
Swift to their several quarters hasted then
The cumbrous elements, earth, flood, air, fire,
And this ethereal quintessence of heaven
Flew upward, spirited with various forms,°
That rolled orbicular, and turned to stars°
Numberless, as thou seest, and how they move;
Each had his place appointed, each his course,   720
The rest in circuit walls this universe.

Look downward on that globe whose hither side
With light from hence, though but reflected, shines;
That place is earth the seat of man, that light
His day, which else as the other hemisphere
Night would invade, but there the neighbouring moon
(So call that opposite fair star) her aid
Timely interposes, and her monthly round
Still ending, still renewing, through mid heaven;°
With borrowed light her countenance triform°   730
Hence fills and empties to enlighten the earth,°
And in her pale dominion checks the night.°
That spot to which I point is Paradise,
Adam's abode, those lofty shades his bower.
Thy way thou canst not miss, me mine requires.
   Thus said, he turned, and Satan bowing low,
As to superior spirits is wont in heaven,
Where honour due and reverence none neglects,
Took leave, and toward the coast of earth beneath,
Down from the ecliptic, sped with hoped success,°   740
Throws his steep flight in many an airy wheel,
Nor stayed, till on Niphates' top he lights.°

BOOK IV

The Argument

Satan now in prospect of Eden, and nigh the place where he must now attempt
the bold enterprise which he undertook alone against God and man, falls into
many doubts with himself, and many passions, fear, envy, and despair; but at
length confirms himself in evil, journeys on to Paradise, whose outward prospect and situation is described, overleaps the bounds, sits in the shape of a cormorant on the tree of life, as highest in the garden to look about him. The
garden described; Satan's first sight of Adam and Eve; his wonder at their
excellent form and happy state, but with resolution to work their fall; overhears
their discourse, thence gathers that the tree of knowledge was forbidden them
to eat of, under penalty of death; and thereon intends to found his temptation,
by seducing them to transgress: then leaves them awhile, to know further of
their state by some other means. Meanwhile Uriel descending on a sunbeam
warns Gabriel, who had in charge the gate of Paradise, that some evil spirit had
escaped the deep, and passed at noon by his sphere in the shape of a good angel
down to Paradise, discovered after by his furious gestures in the mount. Gabriel
promises to find him ere morning. Night coming on, Adam and Eve discourse

of going to their rest: their bower described; their evening worship. Gabriel drawing forth his bands of night-watch to walk the round of Paradise, appoints two strong angels to Adam's bower, lest the evil spirit should be there doing some harm to Adam or Eve sleeping; there they find him at the ear of Eve, tempting her in a dream, and bring him, though unwilling, to Gabriel; by whom questioned, he scornfully answers, prepares resistance, but hindered by a sign · from heaven, flies out of Paradise.

O for that warning voice, which he who saw
The Apocalypse heard cry in heaven aloud,
Then when the dragon, put to second rout,°
Came furious down to be revenged on men,
Woe to the inhabitants on earth! that now,
While time was, our first-parents had been warned°
The coming of their secret foe, and scaped,
Haply so scaped his mortal snare; for now
Satan, now first inflamed with rage, came down,
The tempter ere the accuser of mankind,   10
To wreak on innocent frail man his loss°
Of that first battle, and his flight to hell:
Yet not rejoicing in his speed, though bold,
Far off and fearless, nor with cause to boast,
Begins his dire attempt, which nigh the birth
Now rolling, boils in his tumultuous breast,
And like a devilish engine back recoils°
Upon himself; horror and doubt distract
His troubled thoughts, and from the bottom stir
The hell within him, for within him hell   20
He brings, and round about him, nor from hell
One step no more than from himself can fly
By change of place: now conscience wakes despair°
That slumbered, wakes the bitter memory
Of what he was, what is, and what must be
Worse; of worse deeds worse sufferings must ensue.
Sometimes towards Eden which now in his view
Lay pleasant, his grieved look he fixes sad,°
Sometimes towards heaven and the full-blazing sun,
Which now sat high in his meridian tower:°   30
Then much revolving, thus in sighs began.°
    O thou that with surpassing glory crowned,
Look'st from thy sole dominion like the god

Of this new world; at whose sight all the stars
Hide their diminished heads; to thee I call,
But with no friendly voice, and add thy name
O sun, to tell thee how I hate thy beams
That bring to my remembrance from what state
I fell, how glorious once above thy sphere;
Till pride and worse ambition threw me down   40
Warring in heaven against heaven's matchless king:°
Ah wherefore! he deserved no such return
From me, whom he created what I was
In that bright eminence, and with his good
Upbraided none; nor was his service hard.
What could be less than to afford him praise,
The easiest recompense, and pay him thanks,
How due! Yet all his good proved ill in me,
And wrought but malice; lifted up so high
I 'sdained subjection, and thought one step higher°   50
Would set me highest, and in a moment quit°
The debt immense of endless gratitude,
So burdensome still paying, still to owe;
Forgetful what from him I still received,°
And understood not that a grateful mind
By owing owes not, but still pays, at once°
Indebted and discharged; what burden then?
O had his powerful destiny ordained
Me some inferior angel, I had stood
Then happy; no unbounded hope had raised   60
Ambition. Yet why not? Some other power
As great might have aspired, and me though mean
Drawn to his part; but other powers as great
Fell not, but stand unshaken, from within
Or from without, to all temptations armed.
Hadst thou the same free will and power to stand?
Thou hadst: whom hast thou then or what to accuse,
But heaven's free love dealt equally to all?
Be then his love accursed, since love or hate,
To me alike, it deals eternal woe.   70
Nay cursed be thou; since against his thy will
Chose freely what it now so justly rues.
Me miserable! which way shall I fly
Infinite wrath, and infinite despair?

Which way I fly is hell; myself am hell;
And in the lowest deep a lower deep
Still threatening to devour me opens wide,
To which the hell I suffer seems a heaven.
O then at last relent: is there no place
Left for repentance, none for pardon left?   80
None left but by submission; and that word
Disdain forbids me, and my dread of shame
Among the spirits beneath, whom I seduced
With other promises and other vaunts
Than to submit, boasting I could subdue
The omnipotent. Ay me, they little know
How dearly I abide that boast so vain,°
Under what torments inwardly I groan:
While they adore me on the throne of hell,
With diadem and sceptre high advanced   90
The lower still I fall, only supreme
In misery; such joy ambition finds.
But say I could repent and could obtain
By act of grace my former state; how soon°
Would height recall high thoughts, how soon unsay
What feigned submission swore: ease would recant
Vows made in pain, as violent and void.
For never can true reconcilement grow
Where wounds of deadly hate have pierced so deep:
Which would but lead me to a worse relapse,   100
And heavier fall: so should I purchase dear
Short intermission bought with double smart.
This knows my punisher; therefore as far
From granting he, as I from begging peace:
All hope excluded thus, behold instead
Of us outcast, exiled, his new delight,
Mankind created, and for him this world.
So farewell hope, and with hope farewell fear,
Farewell remorse: all good to me is lost;
Evil be thou my good; by thee at least   110
Divided empire with heaven's king I hold
By thee, and more than half perhaps will reign;
As man ere long, and this new world shall know.
    Thus while he spake, each passion dimmed his face
Thrice changed with pale, ire, envy and despair,°

Which marred his borrowed visage, and betrayed
Him counterfeit, if any eye beheld.
For heavenly minds from such distempers foul°
Are ever clear. Whereof he soon aware,
Each perturbation smoothed with outward calm,   120
Artificer of fraud; and was the first
That practised falsehood under saintly show,
Deep malice to conceal, couched with revenge:°
Yet not enough had practised to deceive
Uriel once warned; whose eye pursued him down
The way he went, and on the Assyrian mount°
Saw him disfigured, more than could befall
Spirit of happy sort: his gestures fierce
He marked, and mad demeanour, then alone,
As he supposed, all unobserved, unseen.   130
So on he fares, and to the border comes,
Of Eden, where delicious Paradise,
Now nearer, crowns with her enclosure green,
As with a rural mound the champaign head°
Of a steep wilderness, whose hairy sides
With thicket overgrown, grotesque and wild,°
Access denied; and overhead up grew
Insuperable height of loftiest shade,
Cedar, and pine, and fir, and branching palm,
A sylvan scene, and as the ranks ascend   140
Shade above shade, a woody theatre
Of stateliest view. Yet higher than their tops
The verdurous wall of Paradise up sprung:
Which to our general sire gave prospect large
Into his nether empire neighbouring round.
And higher than that wall a circling row
Of goodliest trees loaden with fairest fruit,
Blossoms and fruits at once of golden hue
Appeared, with gay enamelled colours mixed:°
On which the sun more glad impressed his beams   150
Than in fair evening cloud, or humid bow,°
When God hath showered the earth; so lovely seemed
That landscape: and of pure now purer air°
Meets his approach, and to the heart inspires
Vernal delight and joy, able to drive
All sadness but despair: now gentle gales

Fanning their odoriferous wings dispense°
Native perfumes, and whisper whence they stole
Those balmy spoils. As when to them who sail
Beyond the Cape of Hope, and now are past°   160
Mozambique, off at sea north-east winds blow
Sabean odours from the spicy shore°
Of Araby the blest, with such delay°
Well pleased they slack their course, and many a league
Cheered with the grateful smell old Ocean smiles.°
So entertained those odorous sweets the fiend
Who came their bane, though with them better pleased°
Than Asmodeus with the fishy fume,
That drove him, though enamoured, from the spouse
Of Tobit's son, and with a vengeance sent   170
From Media post to Egypt, there fast bound.°
    Now to the ascent of that steep savage hill
Satan had journeyed on, pensive and slow;
But further way found none, so thick entwined,
As one continued brake, the undergrowth°
Of shrubs and tangling bushes had perplexed°
All path of man or beast that passed that way:
One gate there only was, and that looked east
On the other side: which when the arch-felon saw
Due entrance he disdained, and in contempt,   180
At one slight bound high overleaped all bound
Of hill or highest wall, and sheer within°
Lights on his feet. As when a prowling wolf,
Whom hunger drives to seek new haunt for prey,
Watching where shepherds pen their flocks at eve
In hurdled cotes amid the field secure,°
Leaps o'er the fence with ease into the fold:
Or as a thief bent to unhoard the cash
Of some rich burgher, whose substantial doors,
Cross-barred and bolted fast, fear no assault,   190
In at the window climbs, or o'er the tiles;
So clomb this first grand thief into God's fold:°
So since into his church lewd hirelings climb.°
Thence up he flew, and on the tree of life,
The middle tree and highest there that grew,
Sat like a cormorant; yet not true life
Thereby regained, but sat devising death

To them who lived; nor on the virtue thought°
Of that life-giving plant, but only used
For prospect, what well used had been the pledge   200
Of immortality. So little knows
Any, but God alone, to value right
The good before him, but perverts best things
To worst abuse, or to their meanest use.
Beneath him with new wonder now he views
To all delight of human sense exposed
In narrow room nature's whole wealth, yea more,
A heaven on earth, for blissful Paradise
Of God the garden was, by him in the east
Of Eden planted; Eden stretched her line   210
From Auran eastward to the royal towers°
Of great Seleucia, built by Grecian kings,°
Or where the sons of Eden long before
Dwelt in Telassar: in this pleasant soil°
His far more pleasant garden God ordained;
Out of the fertile ground he caused to grow
All trees of noblest kind for sight, smell, taste;
And all amid them stood the tree of life,
High eminent, blooming ambrosial fruit
Of vegetable gold; and next to life   220
Our death the tree of knowledge grew fast by,
Knowledge of good bought dear by knowing ill.
Southward through Eden went a river large,
Nor changed his course, but through the shaggy hill
Passed underneath engulfed, for God had thrown
That mountain as his garden mould high raised
Upon the rapid current, which through veins
Of porous earth with kindly thirst up drawn,°
Rose a fresh fountain, and with many a rill
Watered the garden; thence united fell   230
Down the steep glade, and met the nether flood,
Which from his darksome passage now appears,
And now divided into four main streams,
Runs diverse, wandering many a famous realm
And country whereof here needs no account,
But rather to tell how, if art could tell,
How from that sapphire fount the crispèd brooks,°
Rolling on orient pearl and sands of gold,

With mazy error under pendant shades°
Ran nectar, visiting each plant, and fed   240
Flowers worthy of Paradise which not nice art°
In beds and curious knots, but nature boon°
Poured forth profuse on hill and dale and plain,
Both where the morning sun first warmly smote
The open field, and where the unpierced shade
Embrowned the noontide bowers: thus was this place,
A happy rural seat of various view;
Groves whose rich trees wept odorous gums and balm,
Others whose fruit burnished with golden rind
Hung amiable, Hesperian fables true,°   250
If true, here only, and of delicious taste:
Betwixt them lawns, or level downs, and flocks
Grazing the tender herb, were interposed,
Or palmy hillock, or the flowery lap
Of some irriguous valley spread her store,°
Flowers of all hue, and without thorn the rose:
Another side, umbrageous grots and caves°
Of cool recess, o'er which the mantling vine
Lays forth her purple grape, and gently creeps
Luxuriant; meanwhile murmuring waters fall   260
Down the slope hills, dispersed, or in a lake,
That to the fringèd bank with myrtle crowned,
Her crystal mirror holds, unite their streams.
The birds their choir apply; airs, vernal airs,°
Breathing the smell of field and grove, attune
The trembling leaves, while universal Pan°
Knit with the Graces and the Hours in dance°
Led on the eternal spring. Not that fair field
Of Enna, where Proserpin' gathering flowers
Herself a fairer flower by gloomy Dis   270
Was gathered, which cost Ceres all that pain
To seek her through the world; nor that sweet grove°
Of Daphne by Orontes, and the inspired
Castalian spring, might with this Paradise°
Of Eden strive; nor that Nyseian isle
Girt with the river Triton, where old Cham,
Whom Gentiles Ammon call and Lybian Jove,
His Amalthea and her florid son°
Young Bacchus from his stepdame Rhea's eye;°

Nor where Abassin kings their issue guard,°   280
Mount Amara, though this by some supposed
True Paradise under the Ethiop line°
By Nilus' head, enclosed with shining rock,°
A whole day's journey high, but wide remote
From this Assyrian garden, where the fiend
Saw undelighted all delight, all kind
Of living creatures new to sight and strange:
Two of far nobler shape erect and tall,
Godlike erect, with native honour clad
In naked majesty seemed lords of all,   290
And worthy seemed, for in their looks divine
The image of their glorious maker shone,
Truth, wisdom, sanctitude severe and pure,
Severe but in true filial freedom placed;°
Whence true authority in men; though both°
Not equal, as their sex not equal seemed;
For contemplation he and valour formed,
For softness she and sweet attractive grace,
He for God only, she for God in him:
His fair large front and eye sublime declared°   300
Absolute rule; and hyacinthine locks°
Round from his parted forelock manly hung
Clustering, but not beneath his shoulders broad:
She as a veil down to the slender waist
Her unadornèd golden tresses wore
Dishevelled, but in wanton ringlets waved°
As the vine curls her tendrils, which implied
Subjection, but required with gentle sway,
And by her yielded, by him best received,
Yielded with coy submission, modest pride,°   310
And sweet reluctant amorous delay.
Nor those mysterious parts were then concealed,°
Then was not guilty shame, dishonest shame°
Of nature's works, honour dishonourable,
Sin-bred, how have ye troubled all mankind
With shows instead, mere shows of seeming pure,
And banished from man's life his happiest life,
Simplicity and spotless innocence.
So passed they naked on, nor shunned the sight
Of God or angel, for they thought no ill: 320

So hand in hand they passed, the loveliest pair
That ever since in love's embraces met,
Adam the goodliest man of men since born
His sons, the fairest of her daughters Eve.°
Under a tuft of shade that on a green
Stood whispering soft, by a fresh fountain side
They sat them down, and after no more toil
Of their sweet gardening labour than sufficed
To recommend cool zephyr, and made ease°
More easy, wholesome thirst and appetite   330
More grateful, to their supper fruits they fell,
Nectarine fruits which the compliant boughs°
Yielded them, sidelong as they sat recline°
On the soft downy bank damasked with flowers:
The savoury pulp they chew, and in the rind
Still as they thirsted scoop the brimming stream;
Nor gentle purpose, nor endearing smiles°
Wanted, nor youthful dalliance as beseems
Fair couple, linked in happy nuptial league,
Alone as they. About them frisking played   340
All beasts of the earth, since wild, and of all chase°
In wood or wilderness, forest or den;
Sporting the lion ramped, and in his paw°
Dandled the kid; bears, tigers, ounces, pards,°
Gambolled before them, the unwieldy elephant
To make them mirth used all his might, and wreathed
His lithe proboscis; close the serpent sly°
Insinuating, wove with Gordian twine°
His braided train, and of his fatal guile°
Gave proof unheeded; others on the grass   350
Couched, and now filled with pasture gazing sat,
Or bedward ruminating: for the sun°
Declined was hasting now with prone career°
To the Ocean Isles, and in the ascending scale°
Of heaven the stars that usher evening rose:
When Satan still in gaze, as first he stood,
Scarce thus at length failed speech recovered sad.
    O hell! what do mine eyes with grief behold,
Into our room of bliss thus high advanced°
Creatures of other mould, earth-born perhaps,   360
Not spirits, yet to heavenly spirits bright

Little inferior; whom my thoughts pursue
With wonder, and could love, so lively shines
In them divine resemblance, and such grace
The hand that formed them on their shape hath poured.
Ah gentle pair, ye little think how nigh
Your change approaches, when all these delights
Will vanish and deliver ye to woe,
More woe, the more your taste is now of joy;
Happy, but for so happy ill secured   370
Long to continue, and this high seat your heaven
Ill fenced for heaven to keep out such a foe
As now is entered; yet no purposed foe
To you whom I could pity thus forlorn
Though I unpitied: league with you I seek,
And mutual amity so strait, so close,
That I with you must dwell, or you with me
Henceforth; my dwelling haply may not please
Like this fair Paradise, your sense, yet such
Accept your maker's work; he gave it me,   380
Which I as freely give; hell shall unfold,
To entertain you two, her widest gates,
And send forth all her kings; there will be room,
Not like these narrow limits, to receive,
Your numerous offspring; if no better place,
Thank him who puts me loath to this revenge
On you who wrong me not for him who wronged.
And should I at your harmless innocence
Melt, as I do, yet public reason just,
Honour and empire with revenge enlarged,   390
By conquering this new world, compels me now
To do what else though damned I should abhor.
     So spake the fiend, and with necessity,
The tyrant's plea, excused his devilish deeds.
Then from his lofty stand on that high tree
Down he alights among the sportful herd
Of those four-footed kinds, himself now one,
Now other, as their shape served best his end
Nearer to view his prey, and unespied
To mark what of their state he more might learn   400
By word or action marked: about them round
A lion now he stalks with fiery glare,

Then as a tiger, who by chance hath spied
In some purlieu two gentle fawns at play,°
Straight couches close, then rising changes oft
His couchant watch, as one who chose his ground
Whence rushing he might surest seize them both
Gripped in each paw: when Adam first of men
To first of women Eve thus moving speech,
Turned him all ear to hear new utterance flow.°   410
Sole partner and sole part of all these joys,°
Dearer thyself than all; needs must the power
That made us, and for us this ample world
Be infinitely good, and of his good
As liberal and free as infinite,
That raised us from the dust and placed us here
In all this happiness, who at his hand
Have nothing merited, nor can perform
Aught whereof he hath need, he who requires
From us no other service than to keep   420
This one, this easy charge, of all the trees
In Paradise that bear delicious fruit
So various, not to taste that only tree
Of knowledge, planted by the tree of life,
So near grows death to life, what e'er death is,
Some dreadful thing no doubt; for well thou know'st
God hath pronounced it death to taste that tree,
The only sign of our obedience left
Among so many signs of power and rule
Conferred upon us, and dominion given   430
Over all other creatures that possess
Earth, air, and sea. Then let us not think hard
One easy prohibition, who enjoy
Free leave so large to all things else, and choice
Unlimited of manifold delights:
But let us ever praise him, and extol
His bounty, following our delightful task
To prune these growing plants, and tend these flowers,
Which were it toilsome, yet with thee were sweet.
　　　To whom thus Eve replied. O thou for whom   440
And from whom I was formed flesh of thy flesh,
And without whom am to no end, my guide
And head, what thou hast said is just and right.

For we to him indeed all praises owe,
And daily thanks, I chiefly who enjoy
So far the happier lot, enjoying thee
Pre-eminent by so much odds, while thou°
Like consort to thyself canst nowhere find.
That day I oft remember, when from sleep
I first awaked, and found myself reposed   450
Under a shade of flowers, much wondering where
And what I was, whence thither brought, and how.
Not distant far from thence a murmuring sound
Of waters issued from a cave and spread
Into a liquid plain, then stood unmoved
Pure as the expanse of heaven; I thither went
With unexperienced thought, and laid me down
On the green bank, to look into the clear
Smooth lake, that to me seemed another sky.
As I bent down to look, just opposite,   460
A shape within the watery gleam appeared
Bending to look on me, I started back,
It started back, but pleased I soon returned,
Pleased it returned as soon with answering looks
Of sympathy and love; there I had fixed
Mine eyes till now, and pined with vain desire,
Had not a voice thus warned me, What thou seest,
What there thou seest fair creature is thyself,
With thee it came and goes: but follow me,°
And I will bring thee where no shadow stays°   470
Thy coming, and thy soft embraces, he
Whose image thou art, him thou shalt enjoy
Inseparably thine, to him shalt bear
Multitudes like thyself, and thence be called
Mother of human race: what could I do,
But follow straight, invisibly thus led?
Till I espied thee, fair indeed and tall,
Under a platan, yet methought less fair,°
Less winning soft, less amiably mild,
Than that smooth watery image; back I turned,   480
Thou following cried'st aloud, Return fair Eve,
Whom fly'st thou? Whom thou fly'st, of him thou art,
His flesh, his bone; to give thee being I lent
Out of my side to thee, nearest my heart

Substantial life, to have thee by my side
Henceforth an individual solace dear;°
Part of my soul I seek thee, and thee claim
My other half: with that thy gentle hand
Seized mine, I yielded, and from that time see
How beauty is excelled by manly grace   490
And wisdom, which alone is truly fair.
    So spake our general mother, and with eyes
Of conjugal attraction unreproved,
And meek surrender, half embracing leaned
On our first father, half her swelling breast
Naked met his under the flowing gold
Of her loose tresses hid: he in delight
Both of her beauty and submissive charms
Smiled with superior love, as Jupiter
On Juno smiles, when he impregns the clouds°   500
That shed May flowers; and pressed her matron lip
With kisses pure: aside the devil turned
For envy, yet with jealous leer malign
Eyed them askance, and to himself thus plained.
    Sight hateful, sight tormenting! thus these two
Emparadised in one another's arms
The happier Eden, shall enjoy their fill
Of bliss on bliss, while I to hell am thrust,
Where neither joy nor love, but fierce desire,
Among our other torments not the least,   510
Still unfulfilled with pain of longing pines;°
Yet let me not forget what I have gained
From their own mouths; all is not theirs it seems:
One fatal tree there stands of knowledge called,
Forbidden them to taste: knowledge forbidden?
Suspicious, reasonless. Why should their Lord
Envy them that? can it be sin to know,
Can it be death? and do they only stand
By ignorance, is that their happy state,
The proof of their obedience and their faith?   520
O fair foundation laid whereon to build
Their ruin! Hence I will excite their minds
With more desire to know, and to reject
Envious commands, invented with design
To keep them low whom knowledge might exalt

Equal with gods; aspiring to be such,
They taste and die: what likelier can ensue?
But first with narrow search I must walk round
This garden, and no corner leave unspied;
A chance but chance may lead where I may meet°   530
Some wandering spirit of heaven, by fountain side,
Or in thick shade retired, from him to draw
What further would be learned. Live while ye may,
Yet happy pair; enjoy, till I return,
Short pleasures, for long woes are to succeed.
    So saying, his proud step he scornful turned,
But with sly circumspection, and began
Through wood, through waste, o'er hill, o'er dale his roam.
Meanwhile in utmost longitude, where heaven°
With earth and ocean meets, the setting sun   540
Slowly descended, and with right aspect
Against the eastern gate of Paradise°
Levelled his evening rays: it was a rock
Of alabaster, piled up to the clouds,
Conspicuous far, winding with one ascent
Accessible from earth, one entrance high;
The rest was craggy cliff, that overhung
Still as it rose, impossible to climb.°
Betwixt these rocky pillars Gabriel sat°
Chief of the angelic guards, awaiting night;   550
About him exercised heroic games
The unarmed youth of heaven, but nigh at hand
Celestial armoury, shields, helms, and spears,
Hung high with diamond flaming, and with gold.
Thither came Uriel, gliding through the even
On a sunbeam, swift as a shooting star
In autumn thwarts the night, when vapours fired°
Impress the air, and shows the mariner
From what point of his compass to beware
Impetuous winds: he thus began in haste.   560
    Gabriel, to thee thy course by lot hath given
Charge and strict watch that to this happy place
No evil thing approach or enter in;
This day at height of noon came to my sphere
A spirit, zealous, as he seemed, to know
More of the almighty's works, and chiefly man

God's latest image: I described his way°
Bent all on speed, and marked his airy gait;°
But in the mount that lies from Eden north,
Where he first lighted, soon discerned his looks   570
Alien from heaven, with passions foul obscured:
Mine eye pursued him still, but under shade
Lost sight of him; one of the banished crew
I fear, hath ventured from the deep, to raise
New troubles; him thy care must be to find.
    To whom the wingèd warrior thus returned:
Uriel, no wonder if thy perfect sight,
Amid the sun's bright circle where thou sit'st,
See far and wide: in at this gate none pass
The vigilance here placed, but such as come   580
Well known from heaven; and since meridian hour
No creature thence: if spirit of other sort,
So minded, have o'erleaped these earthy bounds
On purpose, hard thou know'st it to exclude
Spiritual substance with corporeal bar.
But if within the circuit of these walks,
In whatsoever shape he lurk, of whom
Thou tell'st, by morrow dawning I shall know.
    So promised he, and Uriel to his charge
Returned on that bright beam, whose point now raised°   590
Bore him slope downward to the sun now fallen
Beneath the Azores; whether the bright orb,
Incredible how swift, had thither rolled
Diurnal, or this less voluble earth°
By shorter flight to the east, had left him there°
Arraying with reflected purple and gold
The clouds that on his western throne attend:
Now came still evening on, and twilight grey
Had in her sober livery all things clad;
Silence accompanied, for beast and bird,°   600
They to their grassy couch, these to their nests
Were slunk, all but the wakeful nightingale;
She all night long her amorous descant sung;°
Silence was pleased: now glowed the firmament
With living sapphires: Hesperus that led°
The starry host, rode brightest, till the moon
Rising in clouded majesty, at length

Apparent queen unveiled her peerless light,°
And o'er the dark her silver mantle threw.
   When Adam thus to Eve: Fair consort, the hour   610
Of night, and all things now retired to rest
Mind us of like repose, since God hath set°
Labour and rest, as day and night to men
Successive, and the timely dew of sleep
Now falling with soft slumbrous weight inclines
Our eyelids; other creatures all day long
Rove idle unemployed, and less need rest;
Man hath his daily work of body or mind
Appointed, which declares his dignity,
And the regard of heaven on all his ways;   620
While other animals unactive range,
And of their doings God takes no account.
Tomorrow ere fresh morning streak the east
With first approach of light, we must be risen,
And at our pleasant labour, to reform
Yon flowery arbours, yonder alleys green,
Our walk at noon, with branches overgrown,
That mock our scant manuring, and require°
More hands than ours to lop their wanton growth:
Those blossoms also, and those dropping gums,   630
That lie bestrewn unsightly and unsmooth,
Ask riddance, if we mean to tread with ease;°
Meanwhile, as nature wills, night bids us rest.
   To whom thus Eve with perfect beauty adorned.
My author and disposer, what thou bid'st°
Unargued I obey; so God ordains,
God is thy law, thou mine: to know no more
Is woman's happiest knowledge and her praise.
With thee conversing I forget all time,
All seasons and their change, all please alike.°   640
Sweet is the breath of morn, her rising sweet,
With charm of earliest birds; pleasant the sun°
When first on this delightful land he spreads
His orient beams, on herb, tree, fruit, and flower,
Glistering with dew; fragrant the fertile earth
After soft showers; and sweet the coming on
Of grateful evening mild, then silent night
With this her solemn bird and this fair moon,

And these the gems of heaven, her starry train:
But neither breath of morn when she ascends   650
With charm of earliest birds, nor rising sun
On this delightful land, nor herb, fruit, flower,
Glistering with dew, nor fragrance after showers,
Nor grateful evening mild, nor silent night
With this her solemn bird, nor walk by moon,
Or glittering starlight without thee is sweet.
But wherefore all night long shine these, for whom
This glorious sight, when sleep hath shut all eyes?
　　To whom our general ancestor replied.
Daughter of God and man, accomplished Eve,   660
Those have their course to finish, round the earth,
By morrow evening, and from land to land
In order, though to nations yet unborn,
Ministering light prepared, they set and rise;
Lest total darkness should by night regain
Her old possession, and extinguish life
In nature and all things, which these soft fires
Not only enlighten, but with kindly heat
Of various influence foment and warm,°
Temper or nourish, or in part shed down   670
Their stellar virtue on all kinds that grow
On earth, made hereby apter to receive
Perfection from the sun's more potent ray.
These then, though unbeheld in deep of night,
Shine not in vain, nor think, though men were none,
That heaven would want spectators, God want praise;°
Millions of spiritual creatures walk the earth
Unseen, both when we wake, and when we sleep:
All these with ceaseless praise his works behold
Both day and night: how often from the steep   680
Of echoing hill or thicket have we heard
Celestial voices to the midnight air,
Sole, or responsive each to other's note
Singing their great creator: oft in bands
While they keep watch, or nightly rounding walk
With heavenly touch of instrumental sounds
In full harmonic number joined, their songs
Divide the night, and lift our thoughts to heaven.
　　Thus talking hand in hand alone they passed

Bower or Bliss

On to their <u>blissful</u> bower; it was a place   690
Chosen by the sovereign planter, when he framed
All things to man's delightful use; the roof
Of thickest covert was inwoven shade
Laurel and myrtle, and what higher grew
Of firm and fragrant leaf; on either side
Acanthus, and each odorous bushy shrub
Fenced up the verdant wall; each beauteous flower,
Iris all hues, roses, and jessamine°
Reared high their flourished heads between, and wrought°
Mosaic; underfoot the violet,   700
Crocus, and hyacinth with rich inlay
Broidered the ground, more coloured than with stone
Of costliest emblem: other creature here°
Beast, bird, insect, or worm durst enter none;
Such was their awe of man. In shadier bower
More sacred and sequestered, though but feigned,°
Pan or Silvanus never slept, nor nymph,°
Nor Faunus haunted. Here in close recess°
With flowers, garlands, and sweet-smelling herbs
Espousèd Eve decked first her nuptial bed,   710
And heavenly choirs the hymenean sung,°
What day the genial angel to our sire°
Brought her in naked beauty more adorned,
More lovely than Pandora, whom the gods°
Endowed with all their gifts, and O too like
In sad event, when to the unwiser son°
Of Japhet brought by Hermes, she ensnared°
Mankind with her fair looks, to be avenged
On him who had stole Jove's authentic fire.°

Thus at their shady lodge arrived, both stood,   720
Both turned, and under open sky adored
The God that made both sky, air, earth and heaven

Adam prayer

<u>Which they beheld</u>, the moon's resplendent globe
And starry pole: Thou also mad'st the night,°
Maker omnipotent, and thou the day,
Which we in our appointed work employed
Have finished happy in our mutual help
And mutual love, the crown of all our bliss
Ordained by thee, and this delicious place
For us too large, where thy abundance wants°   730

Partakers, and uncropped falls to the ground.
But thou hast promised from us two a race
To fill the earth, who shall with us extol
Thy goodness infinite, both when we wake,
And when we seek, as now, thy gift of sleep.
    This said unanimous, and other rites°
Observing none, but adoration pure
Which God likes best, into their inmost bower
Handed they went; and eased the putting off°
These troublesome disguises which we wear,   740
Straight side by side were laid, nor turned I ween
Adam from his fair spouse, nor Eve the rites
Mysterious of connubial love refused:°
Whatever hypocrites austerely talk
Of purity and place and innocence,
Defaming as impure what God declares
Pure, and commands to some, leaves free to all.°
Our maker bids increase, who bids abstain°
But our destroyer, foe to God and man?
Hail wedded love, mysterious law, true source   750
Of human offspring, sole propriety°
In Paradise of all things common else.
By thee adulterous lust was driven from men
Among the bestial herds to range, by thee
Founded in reason, loyal, just, and pure,
Relations dear, and all the charities°
Of father, son, and brother first were known.
Far be it, that I should write thee sin or blame,
Or think thee unbefitting holiest place,
Perpetual fountain of domestic sweets,   760
Whose bed is undefiled and chaste pronounced,
Present, or past, as saints and patriarchs used.
Here Love his golden shafts employs, here lights°
His constant lamp, and waves his purple wings,°
Reigns here and revels; not in the bought smile
Of harlots, loveless, joyless, unendeared,
Casual fruition, nor in court amours
Mixed dance, or wanton masque, or midnight ball,
Or serenade, which the starved lover sings°
To his proud fair, best quitted with disdain.   770
These lulled by nightingales embracing slept,

And on their naked limbs the flowery roof
Showered roses, which the morn repaired. Sleep on°
Blest pair; and O yet happiest if ye seek
No happier state, and know to know no more.
   Now had night measured with her shadowy cone
Halfway uphill this vast sublunar vault,°
And from their ivory port the cherubim°
Forth issuing at the accustomed hour stood armed
To their night watches in warlike parade,   780
When Gabriel to his next in power thus spake.
   Uzziel, half these draw off, and coast the south°
With strictest watch; these other wheel the north,
Our circuit meets full west. As flame they part
Half wheeling to the shield, half to the spear.°
From these, two strong and subtle spirits he called°
That near him stood, and gave them thus in charge.
   Ithuriel and Zephon, with winged speed°
Search through this garden, leave unsearched no nook,
But chiefly where those two fair creatures lodge,   790
Now laid perhaps asleep secure of harm.°
This evening from the sun's decline arrived
Who tells of some infernal spirit seen°
Hitherward bent (who could have thought?) escaped
The bars of hell, on errand bad no doubt:
Such where ye find, seize fast, and hither bring.
   So saying, on he led his radiant files,
Dazzling the moon; these to the bower direct
In search of whom they sought: him there they found
Squat like a toad, close at the ear of Eve;   800
Assaying by his devilish art to reach
The organs of her fancy, and with them forge
Illusions as he list, phantasms and dreams,
Or if, inspiring venom, he might taint
The animal spirits that from pure blood arise°
Like gentle breaths from rivers pure, thence raise
At least distempered, discontented thoughts,
Vain hopes, vain aims, inordinate desires
Blown up with high conceits engendering pride.°
Him thus intent Ithuriel with his spear   810
Touched lightly; for no falsehood can endure
Touch of celestial temper, but returns°

Of force to its own likeness: up he starts°
Discovered and surprised. As when a spark
Lights on a heap of nitrous powder, laid°
Fit for the tun some magazine to store°
Against a rumoured war, the smutty grain°
With sudden blaze diffused, inflames the air:
So started up in his own shape the fiend.
Back stepped those two fair angels half amazed   820
So sudden to behold the grisly king;
Yet thus, unmoved with fear, accost him soon.
    Which of those rebel spirits adjudged to hell
Com'st thou, escaped thy prison, and transformed,
Why sat'st thou like an enemy in wait
Here watching at the head of these that sleep?
    Know ye not then said Satan, filled with scorn,
Know ye not me? Ye knew me once no mate
For you, there sitting where ye durst not soar;
Not to know me argues yourselves unknown,   830
The lowest of your throng; or if ye know,
Why ask ye, and superfluous begin
Your message, like to end as much in vain?
To whom thus Zephon, answering scorn with scorn.
Think not, revolted spirit, thy shape the same,
Or undiminished brightness, to be known
As when thou stood'st in heaven upright and pure;
That glory then, when thou no more wast good,
Departed from thee, and thou resemblest now
Thy sin and place of doom obscure and foul.   840
But come, for thou, be sure, shalt give account
To him who sent us, whose charge is to keep
This place inviolable, and these from harm.
    So spake the cherub, and his grave rebuke
Severe in youthful beauty, added grace
Invincible: abashed the devil stood,
And felt how awful goodness is, and saw
Virtue in her shape how lovely, saw, and pined
His loss; but chiefly to find here observed
His lustre visibly impaired; yet seemed   850
Undaunted. If I must contend, said he,
Best with the best, the sender not the sent,
Or all at once; more glory will be won,

Or less be lost. Thy fear, said Zephon bold,
Will save us trial what the least can do
Single against thee wicked, and thence weak.
    The fiend replied not, overcome with rage;
But like a proud steed reined, went haughty on,
Champing his iron curb: to strive or fly
He held it vain; awe from above had quelled   860
His heart, not else dismayed. Now drew they nigh
The western point, where those half-rounding guards
Just met, and closing stood in squadron joined
Awaiting next command. To whom their chief
Gabriel from the front thus called aloud.
    O friends, I hear the tread of nimble feet
Hasting this way, and now by glimpse discern
Ithuriel and Zephon through the shade,
And with them comes a third of regal port,
But faded splendour wan; who by his gait   870
And fierce demeanour seems the prince of hell,
Not likely to part hence without contest;
Stand firm, for in his look defiance lours.
    He scarce had ended, when those two approached
And brief related whom they brought, where found,
How busied, in what form and posture couched.
    To whom with stern regard thus Gabriel spake.
Why hast thou, Satan, broke the bounds prescribed
To thy transgressions, and disturbed the charge°
Of others, who approve not to transgress   880
By thy example, but have power and right
To question thy bold entrance on this place;
Employed it seems to violate sleep, and those
Whose dwelling God hath planted here in bliss?
    To whom thus Satan, with contemptuous brow.
Gabriel, thou hadst in heaven the esteem of wise,°
And such I held thee; but this question asked
Puts me in doubt. Lives there who loves his pain?
Who would not, finding way, break loose from hell,
Though thither doomed? Thou wouldst thyself, no doubt,   890
And boldly venture to whatever place
Farthest from pain, where thou might'st hope to change
Torment with ease, and soonest recompense
Dole with delight, which in this place I sought;

To thee no reason, who know'st only good,
But evil hast not tried: and wilt object
His will who bound us? Let him surer bar
His iron gates, if he intends our stay
In that dark durance: thus much what was asked.°
The rest is true, they found me where they say;   900
But that implies not violence or harm.
  Thus he in scorn. The warlike angel moved,
Disdainfully half smiling thus replied.
O loss of one in heaven to judge of wise,°
Since Satan fell, whom folly overthrew,
And now returns him from his prison scaped,
Gravely in doubt whether to hold them wise
Or not, who ask what boldness brought him hither
Unlicensed from his bounds in hell prescribed;
So wise he judges it to fly from pain   910
However, and to scape his punishment.°
So judge thou still, presumptuous, till the wrath,
Which thou incurr'st by flying, meet thy flight
Sevenfold, and scourge that wisdom back to hell,
Which taught thee yet no better, that no pain
Can equal anger infinite provoked.
But wherefore thou alone? Wherefore with thee
Came not all hell broke loose? Is pain to them
Less pain, less to be fled, or thou than they
Less hardy to endure? Courageous chief,   920
The first in flight from pain, hadst thou alleged
To thy deserted host this cause of flight,
Thou surely hadst not come sole fugitive.
  To which the fiend thus answered frowning stern.
Not that I less endure, or shrink from pain,
Insulting angel, well thou know'st I stood
Thy fiercest, when in battle to thy aid
The blasting vollied thunder made all speed
And seconded thy else not dreaded spear.
But still thy words at random, as before,°   930
Argue thy inexperience what behoves
From hard assays and ill successes past
A faithful leader, not to hazard all
Through ways of danger by himself untried,
I therefore, I alone first undertook

To wing the desolate abyss, and spy
This new created world, whereof in hell
Fame is not silent, here in hope to find
Better abode, and my afflicted powers°
To settle here on earth, or in midair;   940
Though for possession put to try once more
What thou and thy gay legions dare against;°
Whose easier business were to serve their Lord
High up in heaven, with songs to hymn his throne,
And practised distances to cringe, not fight.°
    To whom the warrior angel soon replied.
To say and straight unsay, pretending first
Wise to fly pain, professing next the spy,
Argues no leader but a liar traced,°
Satan, and couldst thou faithful add? O name,   950
O sacred name of faithfulness profaned!
Faithful to whom? to thy rebellious crew?
Army of fiends, fit body to fit head;
Was this your discipline and faith engaged,
Your military obedience, to dissolve
Allegiance to the acknowledged power supreme?
And thou sly hypocrite, who now wouldst seem
Patron of liberty, who more than thou
Once fawned, and cringed, and servilely adored
Heaven's awful monarch? wherefore but in hope   960
To dispossess him, and thy self to reign?
But mark what I aread thee now, avaunt;°
Fly thither whence thou fled'st: if from this hour
Within these hallowed limits thou appear,
Back to the infernal pit I drag thee chained,
And seal thee so, as henceforth not to scorn
The facile gates of hell too slightly barred.°
    So threatened he, but Satan to no threats
Gave heed, but waxing more in rage replied.
    Then when I am thy captive talk of chains,   970
Proud limitary cherub, but ere then°
Far heavier load thyself expect to feel
From my prevailing arm, though heaven's king
Ride on thy wings, and thou with thy compeers,
Used to the yoke, draw'st his triumphant wheels
In progress through the road of heaven star-paved.°

While thus he spake, the angelic squadron bright
Turned fiery red, sharpening in moonèd horns°
Their phalanx, and began to hem him round
With ported spears, as thick as when a field°   980
Of Ceres ripe for harvest waving bends°
Her bearded grove of ears, which way the wind
Sways them; the careful ploughman doubting stands°
Lest on the threshing floor his hopeful sheaves
Prove chaff. On the other side Satan alarmed
Collecting all his might dilated stood,
Like Tenerife or Atlas unremoved:°
His stature reached the sky, and on his crest
Sat horror plumed; nor wanted in his grasp°
What seemed both spear and shield: now dreadful deeds   990
Might have ensued, nor only Paradise
In this commotion, but the starry cope
Of heaven perhaps, or all the elements
At least had gone to wrack, disturbed and torn
With violence of this conflict, had not soon
The eternal to prevent such horrid fray
Hung forth in heaven his golden scales, yet seen
Betwixt Astrea and the Scorpion sign,°
Wherein all things created first he weighed,
The pendulous round earth with balanced air   1000
In counterpoise, now ponders all events,°
Battles and realms: in these he put two weights
The sequel each of parting and of fight;
The latter quick up flew, and kicked the beam;°
Which Gabriel spying, thus bespake the fiend.
    Satan, I know thy strength, and thou know'st mine,
Neither our own but given; what folly then
To boast what arms can do, since thine no more
Than heaven permits, nor mine, though doubled now
To trample thee as mire: for proof look up,   1010
And read thy lot in yon celestial sign
Where thou art weighed, and shown how light, how weak,
If thou resist. The fiend looked up and knew°
His mounted scale aloft: nor more; but fled°
Murmuring, and with him fled the shades of night.

BOOK V

The Argument

Morning approached, Eve relates to Adam her troublesome dream; he likes it not, yet comforts her: they come forth to their day labours: their morning hymn at the door of their bower. God to render man inexcusable sends Raphael to admonish him of his obedience, of his free estate, of his enemy near at hand; who he is, and why his enemy, and whatever else may avail Adam to know. Raphael comes down to Paradise, his appearance described, his coming discerned by Adam afar off sitting at the door of his bower; he goes out to meet him, brings him to his lodge, entertains him with the choicest fruits of Paradise got together by Eve; their discourse at table: Raphael performs his message, minds Adam of his state and of his enemy; relates at Adam's request who that enemy is, and how he came to be so, beginning from his first revolt in heaven, and the occasion thereof; how he drew his legions after him to the parts of the north, and there incited them to rebel with him, persuading all but only Abdiel a seraph, who in argument dissuades and opposes him, then forsakes him.

> Now Morn her rosy steps in the eastern clime
> Advancing, sowed the earth with orient pearl,
> When Adam waked, so customed, for his sleep
> Was airy light from pure digestion bred,
> And temperate vapours bland, which the only sound
> Of leaves and fuming rills, Aurora's fan,
> Lightly dispersed, and the shrill matin song°
> Of birds on every bough; so much the more
> His wonder was to find unwakened Eve
> With tresses discomposed, and glowing cheek,   10
> As through unquiet rest: he on his side
> Leaning half-raised, with looks of cordial love°
> Hung over her enamoured, and beheld
> Beauty, which whether waking or asleep,
> Shot forth peculiar graces; then with voice°
> Mild, as when Zephyrus on Flora breathes,°
> Her hand soft touching, whispered thus. Awake
> My fairest, my espoused, my latest found,
> Heaven's last best gift, my ever new delight,
> Awake, the morning shines, and the fresh field   20
> Calls us, we lose the prime, to mark how spring°
> Our tended plants, how blows the citron grove,°
> What drops the myrrh, and what the balmy reed,°
> How nature paints her colours, how the bee

Sits on the bloom extracting liquid sweet.
    Such whispering waked her, but with startled eye
On Adam, whom embracing, thus she spake.
    O sole in whom my thoughts find all repose,
My glory, my perfection, glad I see
Thy face, and morn returned, for I this night,   30
Such night till this I never passed, have dreamed,
If dreamed, not as I oft am wont, of thee,
Works of day past, or morrow's next design,
But of offence and trouble, which my mind
Knew never till this irksome night; methought
Close at mine ear one called me forth to walk
With gentle voice, I thought it thine; it said,
Why sleep'st thou Eve? now is the pleasant time,
The cool, the silent, save where silence yields
To the night-warbling bird, that now awake   40
Tunes sweetest his love-laboured song; now reigns°
Full-orbed the moon, and with more pleasing light
Shadowy sets off the face of things; in vain,
If none regard; heaven wakes with all his eyes,
Whom to behold but thee, nature's desire,
In whose sight all things joy, with ravishment
Attracted by thy beauty still to gaze.°
I rose as at thy call, but found thee not;
To find thee I directed then my walk;
And on, methought, alone I passed through ways   50
That brought me on a sudden to the tree
Of interdicted knowledge: fair it seemed,
Much fairer to my fancy than by day:
And as I wondering looked, beside it stood
One shaped and winged like one of those from heaven
By us oft seen; his dewy locks distilled
Ambrosia; on that tree he also gazed;
And O fair plant, said he, with fruit surcharged,
Deigns none to ease thy load and taste thy sweet,
Nor God, nor man; is knowledge so despised?   60
Or envy, or what reserve forbids to taste?°
Forbid who will, none shall from me withhold
Longer thy offered good, why else set here?
This said he paused not, but with venturous arm
He plucked, he tasted; me damp horror chilled

At such bold words vouched with a deed so bold:°
But he thus overjoyed, O fruit divine,
Sweet of thy self, but much more sweet thus cropped,
Forbidden here, it seems, as only fit
For gods, yet able to make gods of men: 70
And why not gods of men, since good, the more
Communicated, more abundant grows,
The author not impaired, but honoured more?
Here, happy creature, fair angelic Eve,
Partake thou also; happy though thou art,
Happier thou mayst be, worthier canst not be:
Taste this, and be henceforth among the gods
Thyself a goddess, not to earth confined,
But sometimes in the air, as we, sometimes
Ascend to heaven, by merit thine, and see   80
What life the gods live there, and such live thou.
So saying, he drew nigh, and to me held,
Even to my mouth of that same fruit held part
Which he had plucked; the pleasant savoury smell
So quickened appetite, that I, methought,
Could not but taste. Forthwith up to the clouds
With him I flew, and underneath beheld
The earth outstretched immense, a prospect wide
And various: wondering at my flight and change
To this high exaltation; suddenly   90
My guide was gone, and I, methought, sunk down,
And fell asleep; but O how glad I waked
To find this but a dream! Thus Eve her night
Related, and thus Adam answered sad.
    Best image of my self and dearer half,
The trouble of thy thoughts this night in sleep
Affects me equally; nor can I like
This uncouth dream, of evil sprung I fear;°
Yet evil whence? in thee can harbour none,
Created pure. But know that in the soul   100
Are many lesser faculties that serve
Reason as chief; among these fancy next°
Her office holds; of all external things,
Which the five watchful senses represent,
She forms imaginations, airy shapes,
Which reason joining or disjoining, frames

All what we affirm or what deny, and call
Our knowledge or opinion; then retires
Into her private cell when nature rests.°
Oft in her absence mimic fancy wakes   110
To imitate her; but misjoining shapes,
Wild work produces oft, and most in dreams,
Ill matching words and deeds long past or late.
Some such resemblances methinks I find
Of our last evening's talk, in this thy dream,
But with addition strange; yet be not sad.
Evil into the mind of god or man
May come and go, so unapproved, and leave
No spot or blame behind: which gives me hope
That what in sleep thou didst abhor to dream,   120
Waking thou never wilt consent to do.
Be not disheartened then, nor cloud those looks
That wont to be more cheerful and serene
Than when fair morning first smiles on the world,
And let us to our fresh employments rise
Among the groves, the fountains, and the flowers
That open now their choicest bosomed smells°
Reserved from night, and kept for thee in store.
      So cheered he his fair spouse, and she was cheered,
But silently a gentle tear let fall   130
From either eye, and wiped them with her hair;
Two other precious drops that ready stood,
Each in their crystal sluice, he ere they fell
Kissed as the gracious signs of sweet remorse
And pious awe, that feared to have offended.
      So all was cleared, and to the field they haste.
But first from under shady arborous roof,
Soon as they forth were come to open sight
Of day-spring, and the sun, who scarce up risen
With wheels yet hovering o'er the ocean brim,   140
Shot parallel to the earth his dewy ray,
Discovering in wide landscape all the east
Of Paradise and Eden's happy plains,
Lowly they bowed adoring, and began
Their orisons, each morning duly paid°
In various style, for neither various style°
Nor holy rapture wanted they to praise

Their maker, in fit strains pronounced or sung°
Unmeditated, such prompt eloquence
Flowed from their lips, in prose or numerous verse,°   150
More tuneable than needed lute or harp°
To add more sweetness, and they thus began.
　　These are thy glorious works, parent of good,
Almighty, thine this universal frame,
Thus wondrous fair; thyself how wondrous then!
Unspeakable, who sit'st above these heavens
To us invisible or dimly seen
In these thy lowest works, yet these declare
Thy goodness beyond thought, and power divine:
Speak ye who best can tell, ye sons of light,   160
Angels, for ye behold him, and with songs
And choral symphonies, day without night,
Circle his throne rejoicing, ye in heaven,
On earth join all ye creatures to extol
Him first, him last, him midst, and without end.
Fairest of stars, last in the train of night,°
If better thou belong not to the dawn,
Sure pledge of day, that crown'st the smiling morn
With thy bright circlet, praise him in thy sphere
While day arises, that sweet hour of prime.   170
Thou sun, of this great world both eye and soul,
Acknowledge him thy greater, sound his praise
In thy eternal course, both when thou climb'st,
And when high noon hast gained, and when thou fall'st.
Moon, that now meet'st the orient sun, now fly'st
With the fixed stars, fixed in their orb that flies,°
And ye five other wandering fires that move°
In mystic dance not without song, resound°
His praise, who out of darkness called up light.
Air, and ye elements the eldest birth   180
Of nature's womb, that in quaternion run°
Perpetual circle, multiform; and mix
And nourish all things, let your ceaseless change
Vary to our great maker still new praise.
Ye mists and exhalations that now rise°
From hill or steaming lake, dusky or grey,
Till the sun paint your fleecy skirts with gold,
In honour to the world's great author rise,

Whether to deck with clouds the uncoloured sky,
Or wet the thirsty earth with falling showers,   190
Rising or falling still advance his praise.°
His praise ye winds, that from four quarters blow,
Breathe soft or loud; and wave your tops, ye pines,
With every plant, in sign of worship wave.
Fountains and ye, that warble, as ye flow,
Melodious murmurs, warbling tune his praise.
Join voices all ye living souls, ye birds,
That singing up to heaven gate ascend,
Bear on your wings and in your notes his praise;
Ye that in waters glide, and ye that walk   200
The earth, and stately tread, or lowly creep;
Witness if I be silent, morn or even,
To hill, or valley, fountain, or fresh shade
Made vocal by my song, and taught his praise.
Hail universal Lord, be bounteous still
To give us only good; and if the night
Have gathered aught of evil or concealed,
Disperse it, as now light dispels the dark.
    So prayed they innocent, and to their thoughts
Firm peace recovered soon and wonted calm.   210
On to their morning's rural work they haste
Among sweet dews and flowers; where any row
Of fruit trees over-woody reached too far
Their pampered boughs, and needed hands to check
Fruitless embraces: or they led the vine
To wed her elm; she spoused about him twines
Her marriageable arms, and with her brings
Her dower the adopted clusters, to adorn
His barren leaves. Them thus employed beheld
With pity heaven's high king, and to him called   220
Raphael, the sociable spirit, that deigned
To travel with Tobias, and secured
His marriage with the seven-times-wedded maid.°
    Raphael, said he, thou hear'st what stir on earth
Satan from hell scaped through the darksome gulf
Hath raised in Paradise, and how disturbed
This night the human pair, how he designs
In them at once to ruin all mankind.
Go therefore, half this day as friend with friend

Converse with Adam, in what bower or shade   230
Thou find'st him from the heat of noon retired,
To respite his day-labour with repast,
Or with repose; and such discourse bring on,
As may advise him of his happy state,
Happiness in his power left free to will,
Left to his own free will, his will though free,
Yet mutable; whence warn him to beware
He swerve not too secure: tell him withal°
His danger, and from whom, what enemy
Late fallen himself from heaven, is plotting now   240
The fall of others from like state of bliss;
By violence, no, for that shall be withstood,
But by deceit and lies; this let him know,
Lest wilfully transgressing he pretend
Surprisal, unadmonished, unforewarned.
    So spake the eternal Father, and fulfilled
All justice: nor delayed the wingèd saint
After his charge received; but from among
Thousand celestial ardours, where he stood°
Veiled with his gorgeous wings, up springing light   250
Flew through the midst of heaven; the angelic choirs
On each hand parting, to his speed gave way
Through all the empyreal road; till at the gate
Of heaven arrived, the gate self-opened wide
On golden hinges turning, as by work
Divine the sovereign architect had framed.
From hence, no cloud, or, to obstruct his sight,
Star interposed, however small he sees,
Not unconform to other shining globes,°
Earth and the garden of God, with cedars crowned   260
Above all hills. As when by night the glass
Of Galileo, less assured, observes
Imagined lands and regions in the moon:
Or pilot from amidst the Cyclades°
Delos or Samos first appearing kens°
A cloudy spot. Down thither prone in flight°
He speeds, and through the vast ethereal sky
Sails between worlds and worlds, with steady wing
Now on the polar winds, then with quick fan°
Winnows the buxom air; till within soar°   270

Of towering eagles, to all the fowls he seems
A phoenix, gazed by all, as that sole bird
When to enshrine his relics in the sun's
Bright temple, to Egyptian Thebes he flies.°
At once on the eastern cliff of Paradise
He lights, and to his proper shape returns
A seraph winged; six wings he wore, to shade
His lineaments divine; the pair that clad
Each shoulder broad, came mantling o'er his breast
With regal ornament; the middle pair   280
Girt like a starry zone his waist, and round°
Skirted his loins and thighs with downy gold
And colours dipped in heaven; the third his feet
Shadowed from either heel with feathered mail
Sky-tinctured grain. Like Maia's son he stood,°
And shook his plumes, that heavenly fragrance filled
The circuit wide. Straight knew him all the bands
Of angels under watch; and to his state,°
And to his message high in honour rise;°
For on some message high they guessed him bound.   290
Their glittering tents he passed, and now is come
Into the blissful field, through groves of myrrh,
And flowering odours, cassia, nard, and balm;°
A wilderness of sweets; for nature here
Wantoned as in her prime, and played at will°
Her virgin fancies, pouring forth more sweet,
Wild above rule or art; enormous bliss.°
Him through the spicy forest onward come
Adam discerned, as in the door he sat
Of his cool bower, while now the mounted sun   300
Shot down direct his fervid rays to warm
Earth's inmost womb, more warmth than Adam needs;
And Eve within, due at her hour prepared
For dinner savoury fruits, of taste to please
True appetite, and not disrelish thirst
Of nectarous draughts between, from milky stream,°
Berry or grape: to whom thus Adam called.
     Haste hither Eve, and worth thy sight behold
Eastward among those trees, what glorious shape
Comes this way moving; seems another morn   310
Risen on mid-noon; some great behest from heaven

To us perhaps he brings, and will vouchsafe
This day to be our guest. But go with speed,
And what thy stores contain, bring forth and pour
Abundance, fit to honour and receive
Our heavenly stranger; well we may afford
Our givers their own gifts, and large bestow
From large bestowed, where nature multiplies
Her fertile growth, and by disburdening grows
More fruitful, which instructs us not to spare.   320
  To whom thus Eve. Adam, earth's hallowed mould,
Of God inspired, small store will serve, where store,
All seasons, ripe for use hangs on the stalk;
Save what by frugal storing firmness gains°
To nourish, and superfluous moist consumes:
But I will haste and from each bough and brake,
Each plant and juiciest gourd will pluck such choice
To entertain our angel guest, as he
Beholding shall confess that here on earth
God hath dispensed his bounties as in heaven.   330
  So saying, with dispatchful looks in haste
She turns, on hospitable thoughts intent
What choice to choose for delicacy best,
What order, so contrived as not to mix
Tastes, not well joined, inelegant, but bring
Taste after taste upheld with kindliest change,°
Bestirs her then, and from each tender stalk
Whatever Earth all-bearing mother yields
In India east or west, or middle shore°
In Pontus or the Punic coast, or where°   340
Alcinous reigned, fruit of all kinds, in coat,°
Rough, or smooth rind, or bearded husk, or shell
She gathers, tribute large, and on the board
Heaps with unsparing hand; for drink the grape
She crushes, inoffensive must, and meads°
From many a berry, and from sweet kernels pressed
She tempers dulcet creams, nor these to hold°
Wants her fit vessels pure, then strews the ground°
With rose and odours from the shrub unfumed.°
Meanwhile our primitive great sire, to meet   350
His godlike guest, walks forth, without more train
Accompanied than with his own complete

Perfections, in himself was all his state,
More solemn than the tedious pomp that waits
On princes, when their rich retinue long
Of horses led, and grooms besmeared with gold
Dazzles the crowd, and sets them all agape.
Nearer his presence Adam though not awed,
Yet with submiss approach and reverence meek,°
As to a superior nature, bowing low,   360
    Thus said. Native of heaven, for other place
None can than heaven such glorious shape contain;
Since by descending from the thrones above,
Those happy places thou hast deigned awhile
To want, and honour these, vouchsafe with us°
Two only, who yet by sovereign gift possess
This spacious ground, in yonder shady bower
To rest, and what the garden choicest bears
To sit and taste, till this meridian heat°
Be over, and the sun more cool decline.   370
    Whom thus the angelic virtue answered mild.°
Adam, I therefore came, nor art thou such
Created, or such place hast here to dwell,
As may not oft invite, though spirits of heaven
To visit thee; lead on then where thy bower
O'ershades; for these mid-hours, till evening rise
I have at will. So to the sylvan lodge
They came, that like Pomona's arbour smiled°
With flowerets decked and fragrant smells; but Eve
Undecked, save with herself more lovely fair   380
Than wood-nymph, or the fairest goddess feigned
Of three that in Mount Ida naked strove,°
Stood to entertain her guest from heaven; no veil
She needed, virtue-proof, no thought infirm°
Altered her cheek. On whom the angel Hail
Bestowed, the holy salutation used
Long after to blest Mary, second Eve.
    Hail mother of mankind, whose fruitful womb
Shall fill the world more numerous with thy sons
Than with these various fruits the trees of God   390
Have heaped this table. Raised of grassy turf
Their table was, and mossy seats had round,
And on her ample square from side to side

All autumn piled, though spring and autumn here
Danced hand in hand. Awhile discourse they hold;°
No fear lest dinner cool; when thus began°
Our author. Heavenly stranger, please to taste°
These bounties which our nourisher, from whom
All perfect good unmeasured out, descends,
To us for food and for delight hath caused   400
The earth to yield; unsavoury food perhaps
To spiritual natures; only this I know,
That one celestial Father gives to all.
     To whom the angel. Therefore what he gives
(Whose praise be ever sung) to man in part
Spiritual, may of purest spirits be found°
No ingrateful food: and food alike those pure°
Intelligential substances require,°
As doth your rational; and both contain°
Within them every lower faculty   410
Of sense, whereby they hear, see, smell, touch, taste,
Tasting concoct, digest, assimilate,°
And corporeal to incorporeal turn.
For know, whatever was created, needs
To be sustained and fed; of elements
The grosser feeds the purer, earth the sea,
Earth and the sea feed air, the air those fires
Ethereal, and as lowest first the moon;°
Whence in her visage round those spots, unpurged
Vapours not yet into her substance turned.°   420
Nor doth the moon no nourishment exhale
From her moist continent to higher orbs.
The sun that light imparts to all, receives
From all his alimental recompense
In humid exhalations, and at even
Sups with the ocean: though in heaven the trees
Of life ambrosial fruitage bear, and vines
Yield nectar, though from off the boughs each morn
We brush mellifluous dews, and find the ground°
Covered with pearly grain: yet God hath here   430
Varied his bounty so with new delights,
As may compare with heaven; and to taste
Think not I shall be nice. So down they sat,°
And to their viands fell, nor seemingly

The angel, nor in mist, the common gloss
Of theologians, but with keen despatch°
Of real hunger, and concoctive heat°
To transubstantiate; what redounds, transpires°
Through spirits with ease; nor wonder; if by fire
Of sooty coal the empiric alchemist°   440
Can turn, or holds it possible to turn
Metals of drossiest ore to perfect gold
As from the mine. Meanwhile at table Eve
Ministered naked, and their flowing cups
With pleasant liquors crowned: O innocence°
Deserving Paradise! if ever, then,
Then had the sons of God excuse to have been
Enamoured at that sight; but in those hearts
Love unlibidinous reigned, nor jealousy
Was understood, the injured lover's hell.   450
     Thus when with meats and drinks they had sufficed,
Not burdened nature, sudden mind arose
In Adam, not to let the occasion pass
Given him by this great conference to know
Of things above his world, and of their being
Who dwell in heaven, whose excellence he saw
Transcend his own so far, whose radiant forms
Divine effulgence, whose high power so far
Exceeded human, and his wary speech
Thus to the empyreal minister he framed.   460
     Inhabitant with God, now know I well
Thy favour, in this honour done to man,
Under whose lowly roof thou hast vouchsafed
To enter, and these earthly fruits to taste,
Food not of angels, yet accepted so,
As that more willingly thou couldst not seem
At heaven's high feasts to have fed: yet what compare?°
     To whom the winged hierarch replied.°
O Adam, one almighty is, from whom
All things proceed, and up to him return,   470
If not depraved from good, created all
Such to perfection, one first matter all,°
Indued with various forms, various degrees
Of substance, and in things that live, of life;
But more refined, more spiritous, and pure,

As nearer to him placed or nearer tending
Each in their several active spheres assigned,
Till body up to spirit work, in bounds
Proportioned to each kind. So from the root°
Springs lighter the green stalk, from thence the leaves   480
More airy, last the bright consummate flower°
Spirits odorous breathes: flowers and their fruit
Man's nourishment, by gradual scale sublimed°
To vital spirits aspire, to animal,
To intellectual, give both life and sense,°
Fancy and understanding, whence the soul
Reason receives, and reason is her being,
Discursive, or intuitive; discourse°
Is oftest yours, the latter most is ours,
Differing but in degree, of kind the same.   490
Wonder not then, what God for you saw good
If I refuse not, but convert, as you,
To proper substance; time may come when men°
With angels may participate, and find
No inconvenient diet, nor too light fare:
And from these corporal nutriments perhaps
Your bodies may at last turn all to spirit,
Improved by tract of time, and winged ascend°
Ethereal, as we, or may at choice
Here or in heavenly paradises dwell;   500
If ye be found obedient, and retain
Unalterably firm his love entire
Whose progeny you are. Meanwhile enjoy
Your fill what happiness this happy state
Can comprehend, incapable of more.
    To whom the patriarch of mankind replied,
O favourable spirit, propitious guest,
Well hast thou taught the way that might direct
Our knowledge, and the scale of nature set
From centre to circumference, whereon   510
In contemplation of created things
By steps we may ascend to God. But say,
What meant that caution joined, *If ye be found
Obedient?* Can we want obedience then°
To him, or possibly his love desert
Who formed us from the dust, and placed us here

Full to the utmost measure of what bliss
Human desires can seek or apprehend?
    To whom the angel. Son of heaven and earth,
Attend: that thou art happy, owe to God;   520
That thou continuest such, owe to thyself,
That is, to thy obedience; therein stand.
This was that caution given thee; be advised.
God made thee perfect, not immutable;
And good he made thee, but to persevere
He left it in thy power, ordained thy will
By nature free, not overruled by fate
Inextricable, or strict necessity;
Our voluntary service he requires,
Not our necessitated, such with him   530
Finds no acceptance, nor can find, for how
Can hearts, not free, be tried whether they serve
Willing or no, who will but what they must
By destiny, and can no other choose?
Myself and all the angelic host that stand
In sight of God enthroned, our happy state
Hold, as you yours, while our obedience holds;
On other surety none; freely we serve,
Because we freely love, as in our will
To love or not; in this we stand or fall: 540
And some are fallen, to disobedience fallen,
And so from heaven to deepest hell; O fall
From what high state of bliss into what woe!
    To whom our great progenitor. Thy words
Attentive, and with more delighted ear,
Divine instructor, I have heard, than when
Cherubic songs by night from neighbouring hills
Aerial music send: nor knew I not
To be both will and deed created free;
Yet that we never shall forget to love   550
Our maker, and obey him whose command
Single, is yet so just, my constant thoughts
Assured me, and still assure: though what thou tell'st
Hath passed in heaven, some doubt within me move,
But more desire to hear, if thou consent,
The full relation, which must needs be strange,
Worthy of sacred silence to be heard;°

And we have yet large day, for scarce the sun
Hath finished half his journey, and scarce begins
His other half in the great zone of heaven.   560
   Thus Adam made request, and Raphael
After short pause assenting, thus began.
   High matter thou enjoin'st me, O prime of men,
Sad task and hard, for how shall I relate
To human sense the invisible exploits
Of warring spirits; how without remorse°
The ruin of so many glorious once
And perfect while they stood; how last unfold
The secrets of another world, perhaps
Not lawful to reveal? Yet for thy good   570
This is dispensed, and what surmounts the reach
Of human sense, I shall delineate so,
By likening spiritual to corporal forms,
As may express them best, though what if earth
Be but the shadow of heaven, and things therein
Each to other like, more than on earth is thought?°
   As yet this world was not, and Chaos wild
Reigned where these heavens now roll, where earth now rests
Upon her centre poised, when on a day
(For time, though in eternity, applied   580
To motion, measures all things durable°
By present, past, and future) on such day
As heaven's great year brings forth, the empyreal host°
Of angels by imperial summons called,
Innumerable before the almighty's throne
Forthwith from all the ends of heaven appeared
Under their hierarchs in orders bright:
Ten thousand thousand ensigns high advanced,
Standards, and gonfalons twixt van and rear°
Stream in the air, and for distinction serve   590
Of hierarchies, of orders, and degrees;
Or in their glittering tissues bear emblazed
Holy memorials, acts of zeal and love°
Recorded eminent. Thus when in orbs
Of circuit inexpressible they stood,
Orb within orb, the Father infinite,
By whom in bliss embosomed sat the Son,
Amidst as from a flaming mount, whose top

Brightness had made invisible, thus spake.

   Hear all ye angels, progeny of light,   600
Thrones, dominations, princedoms, virtues, powers,
Hear my decree, which unrevoked shall stand.
This day I have begot whom I declare
My only son, and on this holy hill°
Him have anointed, whom ye now behold
At my right hand; your head I him appoint;
And by myself have sworn to him shall bow
All knees in heaven, and shall confess him Lord:
Under his great vicegerent reign abide°
United as one individual soul°   610
Forever happy: him who disobeys
Me disobeys, breaks union, and that day
Cast out from God and blessèd vision, falls
Into utter darkness, deep engulfed, his place
Ordained without redemption, without end.
   So spake the omnipotent, and with his words
All seemed well pleased, all seemed, but were not all.
That day, as other solemn days, they spent
In song and dance about the sacred hill,
Mystical dance, which yonder starry sphere   620
Of planets and of fixed in all her wheels
Resembles nearest, mazes intricate,
Eccentric intervolved, yet regular°
Then most, when most irregular they seem,
And in their motions harmony divine
So smooths her charming tones, that God's own ear
Listens delighted. Evening now approached
(For we have also our evening and our morn,
We ours for change delectable, not need)
Forthwith from dance to sweet repast they turn   630
Desirous; all in circles as they stood,
Tables are set, and on a sudden piled
With angels' food, and rubied nectar flows
In pearl, in diamond, and massy gold,
Fruit of delicious vines, the growth of heaven.
On flowers reposed, and with fresh flowerets crowned,
They eat, they drink, and in communion sweet
Quaff immortality and joy, secure
Of surfeit where full measure only bounds

Excess, before the all bounteous king, who showered°   640
With copious hand, rejoicing in their joy.
Now when ambrosial night with clouds exhaled
From that high mount of God, whence light and shade
Spring both, the face of brightest heaven had changed
To grateful twilight (for night comes not there
In darker veil) and roseate dews disposed°
All but the unsleeping eyes of God to rest,
Wide over all the plain, and wider far
Than all this globous earth in plain outspread,
(Such are the courts of God) the angelic throng   650
Dispersed in bands and files their camp extend
By living streams among the trees of life,
Pavilions numberless, and sudden reared,
Celestial tabernacles, where they slept
Fanned with cool winds, save those who in their course
Melodious hymns about the sovereign throne
Alternate all night long: but not so waked
Satan, so call him now, his former name°
Is heard no more in heaven; he of the first,
If not the first archangel, great in power,   660
In favour and pre-eminence, yet fraught
With envy against the Son of God, that day
Honoured by his great father, and proclaimed
Messiah king anointed, could not bear°
Through pride that sight, and thought himself impaired.°
Deep malice thence conceiving and disdain,
Soon as midnight brought on the dusky hour
Friendliest to sleep and silence, he resolved
With all his legions to dislodge, and leave°
Unworshipped, unobeyed the throne supreme   670
Contemptuous, and his next subordinate°
Awakening, thus to him in secret spake.
     Sleep'st thou companion dear, what sleep can close
Thy eyelids? and rememb'rest what decree
Of yesterday, so late hath passed the lips
Of heaven's almighty. Thou to me thy thoughts
Wast wont, I mine to thee was wont to impart;
Both waking we were one; how then can now
Thy sleep dissent? new laws thou seest imposed;
New laws from him who reigns, new minds may raise   680

In us who serve, new counsels, to debate
What doubtful may ensue, more in this place
To utter is not safe. Assemble thou
Of all those myriads which we lead the chief;
Tell them that by command, ere yet dim night
Her shadowy cloud withdraws, I am to haste,
And all who under me their banners wave,
Homeward with flying march where we possess
The quarters of the north, there to prepare
Fit entertainment to receive our king   690
The great Messiah, and his new commands,
Who speedily through all the hierarchies
Intends to pass triumphant, and give laws.
　So spake the false archangel, and infused
Bad influence into the unwary breast
Of his associate; he together calls,
Or several one by one, the regent powers,°
Under him regent, tells, as he was taught,
That the most high commanding, now ere night,
Now ere dim night had disencumbered heaven,   700
The great hierarchal standard was to move;
Tells the suggested cause, and casts between
Ambiguous words and jealousies, to sound
Or taint integrity; but all obeyed
The wonted signal, and superior voice
Of their great potentate; for great indeed
His name, and high was his degree in heaven;
His countenance, as the morning star that guides°
The starry flock, allured them, and with lies
Drew after him the third part of heaven's host: 710
Meanwhile the eternal eye, whose sight discerns
Abstrusest thoughts, from forth his holy mount°
And from within the golden lamps that burn
Nightly before him, saw without their light
Rebellion rising, saw in whom, how spread
Among the sons of morn, what multitudes
Were banded to oppose his high decree;
And smiling to his only son thus said.
　Son, thou in whom my glory I behold
In full resplendence, heir of all my might,   720
Nearly it now concerns us to be sure°

Of our omnipotence, and with what arms
We mean to hold what anciently we claim
Of deity or empire, such a foe
Is rising, who intends to erect his throne
Equal to ours, throughout the spacious north;
Nor so content, hath in his thought to try
In battle, what our power is, or our right.
Let us advise, and to this hazard draw°
With speed what force is left, and all employ   730
In our defence, lest unawares we lose
This our high place, our sanctuary, our hill.
    To whom the Son with calm aspect and clear
Lightning divine, ineffable, serene,
Made answer. Mighty Father, thou thy foes
Justly hast in derision, and secure°
Laugh'st at their vain designs and tumults vain,
Matter to me of glory, whom their hate
Illustrates, when they see all regal power°
Given me to quell their pride, and in event°   740
Know whether I be dextrous to subdue°
Thy rebels, or be found the worst in heaven.
    So spake the Son, but Satan with his powers
Far was advanced on wingèd speed, an host
Innumerable as the stars of night,
Or stars of morning, dewdrops, which the sun
Impearls on every leaf and every flower.
Regions they passed, the mighty regencies ·
Of seraphim and potentates and thrones°
In their triple degrees, regions to which°   750
All thy dominion, Adam, is no more
Than what this garden is to all the earth,
And all the sea, from one entire globose
Stretched into longitude; which having passed°
At length into the limits of the north
They came, and Satan to his royal seat
High on a hill, far blazing, as a mount
Raised on a mount, with pyramids and towers
From diamond quarries hewn, and rocks of gold,
The palace of great Lucifer, (so call   760
That structure in the dialect of men
Interpreted) which not long after, he

Affecting all equality with God,°
In imitation of that mount whereon
Messiah was declared in sight of heaven,
The Mountain of the Congregation called;°
For thither he assembled all his train,
Pretending so commanded to consult
About the great reception of their king,
Thither to come, and with calumnious art   770
Of counterfeited truth thus held their ears.

SATAN

　　Thrones, dominations, princedoms, virtues, powers,
If these magnific titles yet remain
Not merely titular, since by decree
Another now hath to himself engrossed
All power, and us eclipsed under the name
Of king anointed, for whom all this haste
Of midnight march, and hurried meeting here,
This only to consult how we may best
With what may be devised of honours new   780
Receive him coming to receive from us
Knee-tribute yet unpaid, prostration vile,
Too much to one, but double how endured,
To one and to his image now proclaimed?
But what if better counsels might erect
Our minds and teach us to cast off this yoke?
Will ye submit your necks, and choose to bend
The supple knee? Ye will not, if I trust°
To know ye right, or if ye know yourselves
Natives and sons of heaven possessed before   790
By none, and if not equal all, yet free,
Equally free; for orders and degrees
Jar not with liberty, but well consist.°
Who can in reason then or right assume
Monarchy over such as live by right
His equals, if in power and splendour less,
In freedom equal? or can introduce
Law and edict on us, who without law
Err not, much less for this to be our lord,
And look for adoration to the abuse   800
Of those imperial titles which assert
Our being ordained to govern, not to serve?
　　Thus far his bold discourse without control

Had audience, when among the seraphim
Abdiel, than whom none with more zeal adored°
The Deity, and divine commands obeyed,
Stood up, and in a flame of zeal severe
The current of his fury thus opposed.
   O argument blasphemous, false and proud!
Words which no ear ever to hear in heaven   810
Expected, least of all from thee, ingrate
In place thyself so high above thy peers.
Canst thou with impious obloquy condemn
The just decree of God, pronounced and sworn,
That to his only son by right endued
With regal sceptre, every soul in heaven
Shall bend the knee, and in that honour due
Confess him rightful king? Unjust thou say'st
Flatly unjust, to bind with laws the free,
And equal over equals to let reign,   820
One over all with unsucceeded power.°
Shalt thou give law to God, shalt thou dispute
With him the points of liberty, who made
Thee what thou art, and formed the powers of heaven
Such as he pleased, and circumscribed their being?
Yet by experience taught we know how good,
And of our good, and of our dignity
How provident he is, how far from thought
To make us less, bent rather to exalt
Our happy state under one head more near   830
United. But to grant it thee unjust,
That equal over equals monarch reign:
Thyself though great and glorious dost thou count,
Or all angelic nature joined in one,
Equal to him begotten son, by whom
As by his word the mighty Father made
All things, even thee, and all the spirits of heaven
By him created in their bright degrees,
Crowned them with glory, and to their glory named
Thrones, dominations, princedoms, virtues, powers,   840
Essential powers, nor by his reign obscured,
But more illustrious made, since he the head
One of our number thus reduced becomes,
His laws our laws, all honour to him done

Returns our own. Cease then this impious rage,
And tempt not these; but hasten to appease
The incensèd Father, and the incensèd Son,
While pardon may be found in time besought.
    So spake the fervent angel, but his zeal
None seconded, as out of season judged,   850
Or singular and rash, whereat rejoiced
The apostate, and more haughty thus replied.
That we were formed then say'st thou? and the work
Of secondary hands, by task transferred
From Father to his son? strange point and new!
Doctrine which we would know whence learned: who saw
When this creation was? rememb'rest thou
Thy making, while the maker gave thee being?
We know no time when we were not as now;
Know none before us, self-begot, self-raised   860
By our own quickening power, when fatal course°
Had circled his full orb, the birth mature
Of this our native heaven, ethereal sons.
Our puissance is our own, our own right hand
Shall teach us highest deeds, by proof to try
Who is our equal: then thou shalt behold
Whether by supplication we intend
Address, and to begirt the almighty throne
Beseeching or besieging. This report,
These tidings carry to the anointed king;   870
And fly, ere evil intercept thy flight.
    He said, and as the sound of waters deep
Hoarse murmur echoed to his words applause
Through the infinite host, nor less for that
The flaming seraph fearless, though alone
Encompassed round with foes, thus answered bold.
    O alienate from God, O spirit accursed,
Forsaken of all good; I see thy fall
Determined, and thy hapless crew involved
In this perfidious fraud, contagion spread   880
Both of thy crime and punishment: henceforth
No more be troubled how to quit the yoke
Of God's Messiah; those indulgent laws
Will not be now vouchsafed, other decrees
Against thee are gone forth without recall;

That golden sceptre which thou didst reject
Is now an iron rod to bruise and break
Thy disobedience. Well thou didst advise,
Yet not for thy advice or threats I fly
.These wicked tents devoted, lest the wrath°　　　　890
Impendent, raging into sudden flame
Distinguish not: for soon expect to feel
His thunder on thy head, devouring fire.
Then who created thee lamenting learn,
When who can uncreate thee thou shalt know.
　So spake the seraph Abdiel faithful found,
Among the faithless, faithful only he;
　Among innumerable false, unmoved,
　Unshaken, unseduced, unterrified
　His loyalty he kept, his love, his zeal;　　　　900
Nor number, nor example with him wrought°
To swerve from truth, or change his constant mind
Though single. From amidst them forth he passed,
Long way through hostile scorn, which he sustained
Superior, nor of violence feared aught;
And with retorted scorn his back he turned°
On those proud towers to swift destruction doomed.

BOOK VI

The Argument

Raphael continues to relate how Michael and Gabriel were sent forth to battle against Satan and his angels. The first fight described: Satan and his powers retire under night: he calls a council, invents devilish engines, which in the second day's fight put Michael and his angels to some disorder; but they at length pulling up mountains overwhelmed both the force and machines of Satan: yet the tumult not so ending, God on the third day sends Messiah his son, for whom he had reserved the glory of that victory: he in the power of his father coming to the place, and causing all his legions to stand still on either side, with his chariot and thunder driving into the midst of his enemies, pursues them unable to resist towards the wall of heaven; which opening, they leap down with horror and confusion into the place of punishment prepared for them in the deep: Messiah returns with triumph to his father.

All night the dreadless angel unpursued
Through heaven's wide champaign held his way, till Morn,°

Waked by the circling Hours, with rosy hand°
Unbarred the gates of light. There is a cave
Within the mount of God, fast by his throne,°
Where light and darkness in perpetual round
Lodge and dislodge by turns, which makes through heaven
Grateful vicissitude, like day and night;°
Light issues forth, and at the other door
Obsequious darkness enters, till her hour°   10
To veil the heaven, though darkness there might well
Seem twilight here; and now went forth the morn
Such as in highest heaven, arrayed in gold
Empyreal, from before her vanished night,
Shot through with orient beams: when all the plain
Covered with thick embattled squadrons bright,°
Chariots and flaming arms, and fiery steeds
Reflecting blaze on blaze, first met his view:
War he perceived, war in procinct, and found°
Already known what he for news had thought   20
To have reported: gladly then he mixed
Among those friendly powers who him received
With joy and acclamations loud, that one
That of so many myriads fallen, yet one
Returned not lost: on to the sacred hill
They led him high applauded, and present
Before the seat supreme; from whence a voice
From midst a golden cloud thus mild was heard.
   Servant of God, well done, well hast thou fought°
The better fight, who single hast maintained   30
Against revolted multitudes the cause
Of truth, in word mightier than they in arms;
And for the testimony of truth has borne
Universal reproach, far worse to bear
Than violence: for this was all thy care
To stand approved in sight of God, though worlds
Judged thee perverse: the easier conquest now
Remains thee, aided by this host of friends,
Back on thy foes more glorious to return
Than scorned thou didst depart, and to subdue   40
By force, who reason for their law refuse,
Right reason for their law, and for their king
Messiah, who by right of merit reigns.

Go Michael of celestial armies prince,
And thou in military prowess next
Gabriel, lead forth to battle these my sons
Invincible, lead forth my armèd saints
By thousands and by millions ranged for fight;
Equal in number to that godless crew
Rebellious, them with fire and hostile arms   50
Fearless assault, and to the brow of heaven
Pursuing drive them out from God and bliss,
Into their place of punishment, the gulf
Of Tartarus, which ready opens wide
His fiery chaos to receive their fall.

So spake the sovereign voice, and clouds began
To darken all the hill, and smoke to roll
In dusky wreaths, reluctant flames, the sign°
Of wrath awaked: nor with less dread the loud
Ethereal trumpet from on high gan blow: 60
At which command the powers militant,
That stood for heaven, in mighty quadrate joined°
Of union irresistible, moved on
In silence their bright legions, to the sound
Of instrumental harmony that breathed
Heroic ardour to adventurous deeds
Under their godlike leaders, in the cause
Of God and his Messiah. On they move
Indissolubly firm; nor obvious hill,°
Nor straitening vale, nor wood, nor stream divides°   70
Their perfect ranks; for high above the ground
Their march was, and the passive air upbore
Their nimble tread, as when the total kind
Of birds in orderly array on wing
Came summoned over Eden to receive
Their names of thee; so over many a tract
Of heaven they marched, and many a province wide
Tenfold the length of this terrene: at last°
Far in th' horizon to the north appeared
From skirt to skirt a fiery region, stretched°   80
In battailous aspect, and nearer view
Bristled with upright beams innumerable
Of rigid spears, and helmets thronged, and shields
Various, with boastful argument portrayed,°

The banded powers of Satan hasting on
With furious expedition; for they weened°
That selfsame day by fight, or by surprise
To win the mount of God, and on his throne
To set the envier of his state, the proud
Aspirer, but their thoughts proved fond and vain°   90
In the mid-way: though strange to us it seemed
At first, that angel should with angel war,
And in fierce hosting meet, who wont to meet°
So oft in festivals of joy and love
Unanimous, as sons of one great sire
Hymning the eternal Father: but the shout
Of battle now began, and rushing sound
Of onset ended soon each milder thought.
High in the midst exalted as a god
The apostate in his sun-bright chariot sat   100
Idol of majesty divine, enclosed
With flaming cherubim, and golden shields;
Then lighted from his gorgeous throne, for now
'Twixt host and host but narrow space was left,
A dreadful interval, and front to front
Presented stood in terrible array
Of hideous length: before the cloudy van,°
On the rough edge of battle ere it joined,
Satan with vast and haughty strides advanced,
Came towering, armed in adamant and gold;°   110
Abdiel that sight endured not, where he stood
Among the mightiest, bent on highest deeds,
And thus his own undaunted heart explores.
      O heaven! that such resemblance of the highest
Should yet remain, where faith and realty°
Remain not; wherefore should not strength and might
There fail where virtue fails, or weakest prove
Where boldest; though to sight unconquerable?°
His puissance, trusting in the almighty's aid,
I mean to try, whose reason I have tried°   120
Unsound and false; nor is it aught but just,
That he who in debate of truth hath won,
Should win in arms, in both disputes alike
Victor; though brutish that contest and foul,
When reason hath to deal with force, yet so

Most reason is that reason overcome.°
   So pondering, and from his armèd peers
Forth stepping opposite, halfway he met
His daring foe, at this prevention more°
Incensed, and thus securely him defied.°   130
   Proud, art thou met? Thy hope was to have reached
The height of thy aspiring unopposed,
The throne of God unguarded, and his side
Abandoned at the terror of thy power
Or potent tongue; fool, not to think how vain
Against the omnipotent to rise in arms;
Who out of smallest things could without end
Have raised incessant armies to defeat
Thy folly; or with solitary hand
Reaching beyond all limit at one blow   140
Unaided could have finished thee, and whelmed°
Thy legions under darkness; but thou seest
All are not of thy train; there be who faith°
Prefer, and piety to God, though then
To thee not visible, when I alone
Seemed in thy world erroneous to dissent
From all: my sect thou seest, now learn too late°
How few sometimes may know, when thousands err.
   Whom the grand foe with scornful eye askance
Thus answered. Ill for thee, but in wished hour   150
Of my revenge, first sought for thou return'st
From flight, seditious angel, to receive
Thy merited reward, the first assay°
Of this right hand provoked, since first that tongue
Inspired with contradiction durst oppose
A third part of the gods, in synod met°
Their deities to assert, who while they feel
Vigour divine within them, can allow
Omnipotence to none. But well thou com'st
Before thy fellows, ambitious to win   160
From me some plume, that thy success may show°
Destruction to the rest: this pause between°
(Unanswered lest thou boast) to let thee know;°
At first I thought that liberty and heaven
To heavenly souls had been all one; but now
I see that most through sloth had rather serve,

Ministering spirits, trained up in feast and song;
Such hast thou armed, the minstrelsy of heaven,°
Servility with freedom to contend,
As both their deeds compared this day shall prove.   170
    To whom in brief thus Abdiel stern replied.
Apostate, still thou err'st, nor end wilt find
Of erring, from the path of truth remote:
Unjustly thou deprav'st it with the name°
Of servitude to serve whom God ordains,
Or nature; God and nature bid the same,
When he who rules is worthiest, and excels
Them whom he governs. This is servitude,
To serve the unwise, or him who hath rebelled
Against his worthier, as thine now serve thee,   180
Thyself not free, but to thyself enthralled;
Yet lewdly dar'st our ministering upbraid.°
Reign thou in hell thy kingdom, let me serve
In heaven God ever blessed, and his divine
Behests obey, worthiest to be obeyed;
Yet chains in hell, not realms expect: meanwhile
From me returned, as erst thou saidst, from flight,
This greeting on thy impious crest receive.
    So saying, a noble stroke he lifted high,
Which hung not, but so swift with tempest fell   190
On the proud crest of Satan, that no sight,
Nor motion of swift thought, less could his shield
Such ruin intercept: ten paces huge
He back recoiled; the tenth on bended knee
His massy spear upstayed; as if on earth
Winds underground or waters forcing way
Sidelong, had pushed a mountain from his seat
Half sunk with all his pines. Amazement seized
The rebel thrones, but greater rage to see
Thus foiled their mightiest, ours joy filled, and shout,   200
Presage of victory and fierce desire
Of battle: whereat Michael bid sound
The archangel trumpet; through the vast of heaven
It sounded, and the faithful armies rung
Hosanna to the highest: nor stood at gaze
The adverse legions, nor less hideous joined
The horrid shock: now storming fury rose,

And clamour such as heard in heaven till now
Was never, arms on armour clashing brayed
Horrible discord, and the madding wheels°   210
Of brazen chariots raged; dire was the noise
Of conflict; overhead the dismal hiss
Of fiery darts in flaming volleys flew,
And flying vaulted either host with fire.
So under fiery cope together rushed°
Both battles main, with ruinous assault°
And inextinguishable rage; all heaven
Resounded, and had earth been then, all earth
Had to her centre shook. What wonder? when
Millions of fierce encountering angels fought   220
On either side, the least of whom could wield
These elements, and arm him with the force
Of all their regions: how much more of power
Army against army numberless to raise
Dreadful combustion warring, and disturb,°
Though not destroy, their happy native seat;
Had not the eternal king omnipotent
From his stronghold of heaven high overruled
And limited their might; though numbered such°
As each divided legion might have seemed   230
A numerous host, in strength each armèd hand
A legion; led in fight, yet leader seemed
Each warrior single as in chief, expert°
When to advance, or stand, or turn the sway
Of battle, open when, and when to close
The ridges of grim war; no thought of flight,
None of retreat, no unbecoming deed
That argued fear; each on himself relied,
As only in his arm the moment lay°
Of victory; deeds of eternal fame   240
Were done, but infinite: for wide was spread
That war and various; sometimes on firm ground
A standing fight, then soaring on main wing°
Tormented all the air; all air seemed then
Conflicting fire: long time in even scale
The battle hung; till Satan, who that day
Prodigious power had shown, and met in arms
No equal, ranging through the dire attack

Of fighting seraphim confused, at length
Saw where the sword of Michael smote, and felled   250
Squadrons at once, with huge two-handed sway°
Brandished aloft the horrid edge came down
Wide wasting; such destruction to withstand
He hasted, and opposed the rocky orb
Of tenfold adamant, his ample shield
A vast circumference: at his approach
The great archangel from his warlike toil
Surceased, and glad as hoping here to end
Intestine war in heaven, the arch foe subdued°
Or captive dragged in chains, with hostile frown   260
And visage all inflamed first thus began.
　　Author of evil, unknown till thy revolt,
Unnamed in heaven, now plenteous, as thou seest
These acts of hateful strife, hateful to all,
Though heaviest by just measure on thyself
And thy adherents: how hast thou disturbed
Heaven's blessèd peace, and into nature brought
Misery, uncreated till the crime
Of thy rebellion? how hast thou instilled
Thy malice into thousands, once upright   270
And faithful, now proved false. But think not here
To trouble holy rest; heaven casts thee out
From all her confines. Heaven the seat of bliss
Brooks not the works of violence and war.
Hence then, and evil go with thee along
Thy offspring, to the place of evil, hell,
Thou and thy wicked crew; there mingle broils,
Ere this avenging sword begin thy doom,
Or some more sudden vengeance wingèd from God
Precipitate thee with augmented pain.   280
　　So spake the prince of angels; to whom thus
The adversary. Nor think thou with wind
Of airy threats to awe whom yet with deeds
Thou canst not. Hast thou turned the least of these
To flight, or if to fall, but that they rise
Unvanquished, easier to transact with me
That thou shouldst hope, imperious, and with threats
To chase me hence? err not that so shall end°
The strife which thou call'st evil, but we style

The strife of glory: which we mean to win,   290
Or turn this heaven itself into the hell
Thou fablest, here however to dwell free,
If not to reign: meanwhile thy utmost force,
And join him named Almighty to thy aid,
I fly not, but have sought thee far and nigh.

  They ended parle, and both addressed for fight°
Unspeakable; for who, though with the tongue
Of angels, can relate, or to what things
Liken on earth conspicuous, that may lift
Human imagination to such height   300
Of godlike power: for likest gods they seemed,
Stood they or moved, in stature, motion, arms
Fit to decide the empire of great heaven.
Now waved their fiery swords, and in the air
Made horrid circles; two broad suns their shields
Blazed opposite, while expectation stood
In horror; from each hand with speed retired
Where erst was thickest fight, the angelic throng,°
And left large field, unsafe within the wind
Of such commotion, such as to set forth   310
Great things by small, if nature's concord broke,
Among the constellations war were sprung,
Two planets rushing from aspect malign°
Of fiercest opposition in mid sky,
Should combat, and their jarring spheres confound.
Together both with next to almighty arm,
Uplifted imminent one stroke they aimed
That might determine, and not need repeat,°
As not of power, at once; nor odds appeared°
In might or swift prevention; but the sword°   320
Of Michael from the armoury of God
Was given him tempered so, that neither keen
Nor solid might resist that edge: it met
The sword of Satan with steep force to smite
Descending, and in half cut sheer, nor stayed,
But with swift wheel reverse, deep entering sheared
All his right side; then Satan first knew pain,
And writhed him to and fro convolved; so sore
The griding sword with discontinuous wound°
Passed through him, but the ethereal substance closed   330

Not long divisible, and from the gash
A stream of nectarous humour issuing flowed°
Sanguine, such as celestial spirits may bleed,°
And all his armour stained erewhile so bright.
Forthwith on all sides to his aid was run
By angels many and strong, who interposed
Defence, while others bore him on their shields
Back to his chariot; where it stood retired
From off the files of war; there they him laid
Gnashing for anguish and despite and shame   340
To find himself not matchless, and his pride
Humbled by such rebuke, so far beneath
His confidence to equal God in power.
Yet soon he healed; for spirits that live throughout
Vital in every part, not as frail man
In entrails, heart or head, liver or reins,°
Cannot but by annihilating die;
Nor in their liquid texture mortal wound
Receive, no more than can the fluid air:
All heart they live, all head, all eye, all ear,   350
All intellect, all sense, and as they please,
They limb themselves, and colour, shape or size
Assume, as likes them best, condense or rare.°
    Meanwhile in other parts like deeds deserved
Memorial, where the might of Gabriel fought,
And with fierce ensigns pierced the deep array
Of Moloch furious king, who him defied,
And at his chariot wheels to drag him bound
Threatened, nor from the holy one of heaven
Refrained his tongue blasphemous; but anon   360
Down cloven to the waist, with shattered arms
And uncouth pain fled bellowing. On each wing°
Uriel and Raphael his vaunting foe,°
Though huge, and in a rock of diamond armed,
Vanquished Adramelec, and Asmadai,°
Two potent thrones, that to be less than gods
Disdained, but meaner thoughts learned in their flight,
Mangled with ghastly wounds through plate and mail,
Nor stood unmindful Abdiel to annoy°
The atheist crew, but with redoubled blow°   370
Ariel and Arioch, and the violence°

Of Ramiel scorched and blasted overthrew.°
I might relate of thousands, and their names
Eternize here on earth; but those elect
Angels contented with their fame in heaven
Seek not the praise of men: the other sort
In might though wondrous and in acts of war,
Nor of renown less eager, yet by doom
Cancelled from heaven and sacred memory,
Nameless in dark oblivion let them dwell.   380
For strength from truth divided and from just,
Illaudable, naught merits but dispraise°
And ignominy, yet to glory aspires
Vainglorious, and through infamy seeks fame:
Therefore eternal silence be their doom.
   And now their mightiest quelled, the battle swerved,
With many an inroad gored; deformèd rout
Entered, and foul disorder; all the ground
With shivered armour strewn, and on a heap
Chariot and charioteer lay overturned   390
And fiery foaming steeds; what stood, recoiled
O'er-wearied, through the faint Satanic host
Defensive scarce, or with pale fear surprised,°
Then first with fear surprised and sense of pain
Fled ignominious, to such evil brought
By sin of disobedience, till that hour
Not liable to fear or flight or pain.
Far otherwise the inviolable saints
In cubic phalanx firm advanced entire,
Invulnerable, impenetrably armed: 400
Such high advantages their innocence
Gave them above their foes, not to have sinned,
Not to have disobeyed; in fight they stood
Unwearied, unobnoxious to be pained°
By wound, though from their place by violence moved.
   Now night her course began, and over heaven
Inducing darkness, grateful truce imposed,
And silence on the odious din of war:
Under her cloudy covert both retired,
Victor and vanquished: on the foughten field°   410
Michael and his angels prevalent°
Encamping, placed in guard their watches round,

Cherubic waving fires: on the other part
Satan with his rebellious disappeared,
Far in the dark dislodged, and void of rest,
His potentates to council called by night;
And in the midst thus undismayed began.

  O now in danger tried, now known in arms
Not to be overpowered, companions dear,
Found worthy not of liberty alone,   420
Too mean pretence, but what we more affect,°
Honour, dominion, glory, and renown,
Who have sustained one day in doubtful fight
(And if one day, why not eternal days?)
What heaven's lord had powerfullest to send
Against us from about his throne, and judged
Sufficient to subdue us to his will,
But proves not so: then fallible, it seems,
Of future we may deem him, though till now°
Omniscient thought. True is, less firmly armed,   430
Some disadvantage we endured and pain,
Till now not known, but known as soon contemned,
Since now we find this our empyreal form
Incapable of mortal injury
Imperishable, and though pierced with wound,
Soon closing, and by native vigour healed.
Of evil then so small as easy think
The remedy; perhaps more valid arms,
Weapons more violent, when next we meet,
May serve to better us, and worse our foes,   440
Or equal what between us made the odds,
In nature none: if other hidden cause
Left them superior, while we can preserve
Unhurt our minds, and understanding sound,
Due search and consultation will disclose.

  He sat; and in the assembly next upstood
Nisroch, of principalities the prime;°
As one he stood escaped from cruel fight,
Sore toiled, his riven arms to havoc hewn,
And cloudy in aspect thus answering spake.   450
Deliverer from new lords, leader to free
Enjoyment of our right as gods; yet hard
For gods, and too unequal work we find

Against unequal arms to fight in pain,
Against unpained, impassive; from which evil°
Ruin must needs ensue; for what avails
Valour or strength, though matchless, quelled with pain
Which all subdues, and makes remiss the hands°
Of mightiest. Sense of pleasure we may well
Spare out of life perhaps, and not repine,   460
But live content, which is the calmest life:
But pain is perfect misery, the worst
Of evils, and excessive, overturns
All patience. He who therefore can invent
With what more forcible we may offend°
Our yet unwounded enemies, or arm
Ourselves with like defence, to me deserves
No less than for deliverance what we owe.
    Whereto with look composed Satan replied.
Not uninvented that, which thou aright   470
Believ'st so main to our success, I bring;
Which of us who beholds the bright surface
Of this ethereous mould whereon we stand,
This continent of spacious heaven, adorned
With plant, fruit, flower ambrosial, gems and gold,
Whose eye so superficially surveys
These things, as not to mind from whence they grow°
Deep underground, materials dark and crude,
Of spiritous and fiery spume, till touched
With heaven's ray, and tempered they shoot forth   480
So beauteous, opening to the ambient light.
These in their dark nativity the deep
Shall yield us pregnant with infernal flame,
Which into hollow engines long and round
Thick-rammed, at the other bore with touch of fire°
Dilated and infuriate shall send forth
From far with thundering noise among our foes
Such implements of mischief as shall dash
To pieces, and o'erwhelm whatever stands
Adverse, that they shall fear we have disarmed   490
The thunderer of his only dreaded bolt.
Nor long shall be our labour, yet ere dawn,
Effect shall end our wish. Meanwhile revive;
Abandon fear; to strength and counsel joined

Think nothing hard, much less to be despaired.
He ended, and his words their drooping cheer°
Enlightened, and their languished hope revived.
The invention all admired, and each, how he
To be the inventor missed, so easy it seemed
Once found, which yet unfound most would have thought   500
Impossible: yet haply of thy race
In future days, if malice should abound,
Someone intent on mischief, or inspired
With devilish machination might devise
Like instrument to plague the sons of men
For sin, on war and mutual slaughter bent.
Forthwith from council to the work they flew,
None arguing stood, innumerable hands
Were ready, in a moment up they turned
Wide the celestial soil, and saw beneath   510
The originals of nature in their crude°
Conception; sulphurous and nitrous foam
They found, they mingled, and with subtle art,
Concocted and adusted they reduced°
To blackest grain, and into store conveyed:
Part hidden veins digged up (nor hath this earth
Entrails unlike) of mineral and stone,
Whereof to found their engines and their balls°
Of missive ruin; part incentive reed°
Provide, pernicious with one touch to fire.°   520
So all ere day-spring, under conscious night°
Secret they finished, and in order set,
With silent circumspection unespied.
Now when fair morn orient in heaven appeared°
Up rose the victor angels, and to arms
The matin trumpet sung: in arms they stood
Of golden panoply, refulgent host,
Soon banded; others from the dawning hills
Looked round, and scouts each coast light-ar|mèd scour,
Each quarter, to descry the distant foe,   530
Where lodged, or whither fled, or if for fight,
In motion or in halt: him soon they met
Under spread ensigns moving nigh, in slow
But firm battalion; back with speediest sail
Zophiel, of cherubim the swiftest wing,°

Came flying, and in midair aloud thus cried.
Arm, warriors, arm for fight, the foe at hand,
Whom fled we thought, will save us long pursuit
This day, fear not his flight; so thick a cloud
He comes, and settled in his face I see   540
Sad resolution and secure: let each°
His adamantine coat gird well, and each
Fit well his helm, gripe fast his orbèd shield,
Borne even or high, for this day will pour down,
If I conjecture aught, no drizzling shower,
But rattling storm of arrows barbed with fire.
So warned he them aware themselves, and soon
In order, quit of all impediment;
Instant without disturb they took alarm,°
And onward move embattled; when behold   550
Not distant far with heavy pace the foe
Approaching gross and huge; in hollow cube
Training his devilish enginery, impaled°
On every side with shadowing squadrons deep,
To hide the fraud. At interview both stood°
Awhile, but suddenly at head appeared
Satan: and thus was heard commanding loud.
   Vanguard, to right and left the front unfold;
That all may see who hate us, how we seek
Peace and composure, and with open breast°   560
Stand ready to receive them, if they like
Our overture, and turn not back perverse;
But that I doubt, however witness heaven,
Heaven witness thou anon, while we discharge
Freely our part; ye who appointed stand
Do as you have in charge, and briefly touch
What we propound, and loud that all may hear.
   So scoffing in ambiguous words, he scarce°
Had ended; when to right and left the front
Divided, and to either flank retired.   570
Which to our eyes discovered new and strange,°
A triple mounted row of pillars laid
On wheels (for like to pillars most they seemed
Or hollowed bodies made of oak or fir,
With branches lopped, in wood or mountain felled)
Brass, iron, stony mould, had not their mouths°

With hideous orifice gapèd on us wide,
Portending hollow truce; at each behind°
A seraph stood, and in his hand a reed
Stood waving tipped with fire; while we suspense,°   580
Collected stood within our thoughts amused,°
Not long, for sudden all at once their reeds
Put forth, and to a narrow vent applied
With nicest touch. Immediate in a flame,
But soon obscured with smoke, all heaven appeared,
From those deep throated engines belched, whose roar
Embowelled with outrageous noise the air,
And all her entrails tore, disgorging foul
Their devilish glut, chained thunderbolts and hail°
Of iron globes, which on the victor host   590
Levelled, with such impetuous fury smote,
That whom they hit, none on their feet might stand,
Though standing else as rocks, but down they fell
By thousands, angel on archangel rolled;
The sooner for their arms, unarmed they might
Have easily as spirits evaded swift
By quick contraction or remove; but now°
Foul dissipation followed and forced rout;°
Nor served it to relax their serried files.
What should they do? If on they rushed, repulse   600
Repeated, and indecent overthrow°
Doubled, would render them yet more despised,
And to their foes a laughter; for in view
Stood ranked of seraphim another row
In posture to displode their second tire°
Of thunder: back defeated to return
They worse abhorred. Satan beheld their plight,
And to his mates thus in derision called.
    O friends, why come not on these victors proud?
Erewhile they fierce were coming, and when we,   610
To entertain them fair with open front
And breast, (what could we more?) propounded terms
Of composition, straight they changed their minds,
Flew off, and into strange vagaries fell,
As they would dance, yet for a dance they seemed
Somewhat extravagant and wild, perhaps
For joy of offered peace: but I suppose

If our proposals once again were heard
We should compel them to a quick result.
　　To whom thus Belial in like gamesome mood,   620
Leader, the terms we sent were terms of weight,
Of hard contents, and full of force urged home,
Such as we might perceive amused them all,°
And stumbled many; who receives them right,°
Had need from head to foot well understand;°
Not understood, this gift they have besides,
They show us when our foes walk not upright.
　　So they among themselves in pleasant vein
Stood scoffing, heightened in their thoughts beyond
All doubt of victory, eternal might   630
To match with their inventions they presumed
So easy, and of his thunder made a scorn,
And all his host derided, while they stood
Awhile in trouble; but they stood not long,
Rage prompted them at length, and found them arms
Against such hellish mischief fit to oppose.
Forthwith (behold the excellence, the power
Which God hath in his mighty angels placed)
Their arms away they threw, and to the hills
(For earth hath this variety from heaven   640
Of pleasure situate in hill and dale)
Light as the lightning glimpse they ran, they flew,
From their foundations loosening to and fro
They plucked the seated hills with all their load,°
Rocks, waters, woods, and by the shaggy tops
Up lifting bore them in their hands: amaze,
Be sure, and terror seized the rebel host,
When coming towards them so dread they saw
The bottom of the mountains upward turned,
Till on those cursèd engines' triple-row   650
They saw them whelmed, and all their confidence
Under the weight of mountains buried deep,
Themselves invaded next, and on their heads
Main promontories flung, which in the air°
Came shadowing, and oppressed whole legions armed,
Their armour helped their harm, crushed in and bruised
Into their substance pent, which wrought them pain
Implacable, and many a dolorous groan,

Long struggling underneath, ere they could wind
Out of such prison, though spirits of purest light, 660
Purest at first, now gross by sinning grown.
The rest in imitation to like arms
Betook them, and the neighbouring hills uptore;
So hills amid the air encountered hills
Hurled to and fro with jaculation dire,°
That underground they fought in dismal shade;
Infernal noise; war seemed a civil game
To this uproar; horrid confusion heaped°
Upon confusion rose: and now all heaven
Had gone to wrack, with ruin overspread, 670
Had not the almighty Father where he sits
Shrined in his sanctuary of heaven secure,
Consulting on the sum of things, foreseen°
This tumult, and permitted all, advised:°
That his great purpose he might so fulfil,
To honour his anointed son avenged
Upon his enemies, and to declare
All power on him transferred: whence to his son
The assessor of his throne he thus began.°
   Effulgence of my glory, Son beloved, 680
Son in whose face invisible is beheld
Visibly, what by deity I am,
And in whose hand what by decree I do,
Second omnipotence, two days are past,
Two days, as we compute the days of heaven,
Since Michael and his powers went forth to tame
These disobedient; sore hath been their fight,
As likeliest was, when two such foes met armed;
For to themselves I left them, and thou know'st,
Equal in their creation they were formed, 690
Save what sin hath impaired, which yet hath wrought
Insensibly, for I suspend their doom;°
Whence in perpetual fight they needs must last
Endless, and no solution will be found:
War wearied hath performed what war can do,
And to disordered rage let loose the reins,
With mountains as with weapons armed, which makes
Wild work in heaven, and dangerous to the main.°
Two days are therefore past, the third is thine;

For thee I have ordained it, and thus far   700
Have suffered, that the glory may be thine°
Of ending this great war, since none but thou
Can end it. Into thee such virtue and grace
Immense I have transfused, that all may know
In heaven and hell thy power above compare,
And this perverse commotion governed thus,
To manifest thee worthiest to be heir
Of all things, to be heir and to be king
By sacred unction, thy deservèd right.°
Go then thou mightiest in thy father's might,   710
Ascend my chariot, guide the rapid wheels
That shake heaven's basis, bring forth all my war,
My bow and thunder, my almighty arms
Gird on, and sword upon thy puissant thigh;
Pursue these sons of darkness, drive them out
From all heaven's bounds into the utter deep:
There let them learn, as likes them, to despise
God and Messiah his anointed king.
    He said, and on his son with rays direct
Shone full, he all his father full expressed   720
Ineffably into his face received,
And thus the filial Godhead answering spake.
    O Father, O supreme of heavenly thrones,
First, highest, holiest, best, thou always seek'st
To glorify thy son, I always thee,
As is most just; this I my glory account,
My exaltation, and my whole delight,
That thou in me well pleased, declar'st thy will
Fulfilled, which to fulfil is all my bliss.
Sceptre and power, thy giving, I assume,   730
And gladlier shall resign, when in the end
Thou shalt be all in all, and I in thee
Forever, and in me all whom thou lov'st:
But whom thou hat'st, I hate, and can put on
Thy terrors, as I put thy mildness on,
Image of thee in all things; and shall soon,
Armed with thy might, rid heaven of these rebelled,
To their prepared ill mansion driven down
To chains of darkness, and the undying worm,
That from thy just obedience could revolt,   740

Whom to obey is happiness entire.
Then shall thy saints unmixed, and from the impure
Far separate, circling thy holy mount
Unfeignèd hallelujahs to thee sing,
Hymns of high praise, and I among them chief.
So said, he o'er his sceptre bowing, rose
From the right hand of glory where he sat,
And the third sacred morn began to shine
Dawning through heaven: forth rushed with whirlwind sound
The chariot of paternal deity,   750
Flashing thick flames, wheel within wheel undrawn,
Itself instinct with spirit, but convoyed°
By four cherubic shapes, four faces each
Had wondrous, as with stars their bodies all
And wings were set with eyes, with eyes the wheels
Of beryl, and careering fires between;
Over their heads a crystal firmament,
Whereon a sapphire throne, inlaid with pure
Amber, and colours of the showery arch.°
He in celestial panoply all armed   760
Of radiant urim, work divinely wrought,°
Ascended, at his right hand Victory
Sat, eagle-winged, beside him hung his bow
And quiver with three-bolted thunder stored,
And from about him fierce effusion rolled
Of smoke and bickering flame, and sparkles dire;°
Attended with ten thousand thousand saints,
He onward came, far off his coming shone,
And twenty thousand (I their number heard)
Chariots of God, half on each hand were seen: 770
He on the wings of cherub rode sublime°
On the crystalline sky, in sapphire throned.
Illustrious far and wide, but by his own°
First seen, them unexpected joy surprised,
When the great ensign of Messiah blazed
Aloft by angels borne, his sign in heaven:
Under whose conduct Michael soon reduced°
His army, circumfused on either wing,°
Under their head embodied all in one.°
Before him power divine his way prepared;   780
At his command the uprooted hills retired

Each to his place, they heard his voice and went
Obsequious, heaven his wonted face renewed,°
And with fresh flowerets hill and valley smiled.
This saw his hapless foes but stood obdured,°
And to rebellious fight rallied their powers
Insensate, hope conceiving from despair.°
In heavenly spirits could such perverseness dwell?°
But to convince the proud what signs avail,
Or wonders move the obdurate to relent?   790
They hardened more by what might most reclaim,
Grieving to see his glory, at the sight
Took envy, and aspiring to his height,°
Stood re-embattled fierce, by force or fraud
Weening to prosper, and at length prevail
Against God and Messiah, or to fall
In universal ruin last, and now
To final battle drew, disdaining flight,
Or faint retreat; when the great Son of God
To all his host on either hand thus spake.   800
    Stand still in bright array ye saints, here stand
Ye angels armed, this day from battle rest;
Faithful hath been your warfare, and of God
Accepted, fearless in his righteous cause,
And as ye have received, so have ye done
Invincibly; but of this cursèd crew
The punishment to other hand belongs,
Vengeance is his, or whose he sole appoints;
Number to this day's work is not ordained
Nor multitude, stand only and behold°   810
God's indignation on these godless poured
By me, not you but me they have despised,
Yet envied; against me is all their rage,
Because the Father, to whom in heaven supreme
Kingdom and power and glory appertains,
Hath honoured me according to his will.
Therefore to me their doom he hath assigned;
That they may have their wish, to try with me
In battle which the stronger proves, they all,
Or I alone against them, since by strength   820
They measure all, of other excellence
Not emulous, nor care who them excels;

Nor other strife with them do I vouchsafe.°
    So spake the Son, and into terror changed
His countenance too severe to be beheld
And full of wrath bent on his enemies.
At once the four spread out their starry wings°
With dreadful shade contiguous, and the orbs
Of his fierce chariot rolled, as with the sound
Of torrent floods, or of a numerous host.   830
He on his impious foes right onward drove,
Gloomy as night; under his burning wheels
The steadfast empyrean shook throughout,
All but the throne itself of God. Full soon
Among them he arrived; in his right hand
Grasping ten thousand thunders, which he sent°
Before him, such as in their souls infixed
Plagues; they astonished all resistance lost,°
All courage; down their idle weapons dropped;
O'er shields and helms, and helmèd heads he rode   840
Of thrones and mighty seraphim prostrate,
That wished the mountains now might be again
Thrown on them as a shelter from his ire.
Nor less on either side tempestuous fell
His arrows, from the fourfold-visaged four,°
Distinct with eyes, and from the living wheels°
Distinct alike with multitude of eyes;
One spirit in them ruled, and every eye
Glared lightning, and shot forth pernicious fire°
Among the accursed, that withered all their strength,   850
And of their wonted vigour left them drained,
Exhausted, spiritless, afflicted, fallen.
Yet half his strength he put not forth, but checked
His thunder in mid-volley, for he meant
Not to destroy, but root them out of heaven:
The overthrown he raised, and as a herd
Of goats or timorous flock together thronged
Drove them before him thunderstruck, pursued
With terrors and with furies to the bounds
And crystal wall of heaven, which opening wide,   860
Rolled inward, and a spacious gap disclosed
Into the wasteful deep; the monstrous sight°
Struck them with horror backward, but far worse

Urged them behind; headlong themselves they threw
Down from the verge of heaven, eternal wrath
Burnt after them to the bottomless pit.
 Hell heard the unsufferable noise, hell saw
Heaven ruining from heaven and would have fled
Affrighted; but strict fate had cast too deep
Her dark foundations, and too fast had bound.   870
Nine days they fell; confounded Chaos roared,
And felt tenfold confusion in their fall
Through his wild anarchy, so huge a rout
Encumbered him with ruin: hell at last
Yawning received them whole, and on them closed,
Hell their fit habitation fraught with fire
Unquenchable, the house of woe and pain.
Disburdened heaven rejoiced, and soon repaired
Her mural breach, returning whence it rolled.
Sole victor from the expulsion of his foes   880
Messiah his triumphal chariot turned:
To meet him all his saints, who silent stood
Eyewitnesses of his almighty acts,
With jubilee advanced; and as they went,
Shaded with branching palm, each order bright,
Sung triumph, and him sung victorious king,
Son, heir, and Lord, to him dominion given,
Worthiest to reign: he celebrated rode
Triumphant through mid-heaven, into the courts
And temple of his mighty father throned   890
On high: who into glory him received,
Where now he sits at the right hand of bliss.
 Thus measuring things in heaven by things on earth
At thy request, and that thou mayst beware
By what is past, to thee I have revealed
What might have else to human race been hid;
The discord which befell, and war in heaven
Among the angelic powers, and the deep fall
Of those too high aspiring, who rebelled
With Satan, he who envies now thy state,   900
Who now is plotting how he may seduce
Thee also from obedience, that with him
Bereaved of happiness thou mayst partake
His punishment, eternal misery;

Which would be all his solace and revenge,
As a despite done against the most high,
Thee once to gain companion of his woe.
But listen not to his temptations, warn
Thy weaker; let it profit thee to have heard°
By terrible example the reward   910
Of disobedience; firm they might have stood,
Yet fell; remember, and fear to transgress.

BOOK VII

The Argument

Raphael at the request of Adam relates how and wherefore this world was first
created; that God, after the expelling of Satan and his angels out of heaven,
declared his pleasure to create another world and other creatures to dwell
therein; sends his son with glory and attendance of angels to perform the work
of creation in six days: the angels celebrate with hymns the performance
thereof, and his re-ascension into heaven.

Descend from heaven Urania, by that name°
If rightly thou art called, whose voice divine
Following, above the Olympian hill I soar,°
Above the flight of Pegasean wing.°
The meaning, not the name I call: for thou
Nor of the muses nine, nor on the top
Of old Olympus dwell'st, but heavenly born,
Before the hills appeared, or fountain flowed,
Thou with eternal wisdom didst converse,°
Wisdom thy sister, and with her didst play   10
In presence of the almighty Father, pleased
With thy celestial song. Up led by thee
Into the heaven of heavens I have presumed,
An earthly guest, and drawn empyreal air,
Thy tempering; with like safety guided down°
Return me to my native element:
Lest from this flying steed unreined, (as once
Bellerophon, though from a lower clime)°
Dismounted, on the Aleian field I fall°
Erroneous there to wander and forlorn.°   20
Half yet remains unsung, but narrower bound
Within the visible diurnal sphere;°

Standing on earth, not rapt above the pole,°
More safe I sing with mortal voice, unchanged
To hoarse or mute, though fallen on evil days,
On evil days though fallen, and evil tongues;°
In darkness, and with dangers compassed round,°
And solitude; yet not alone, while thou
Visit'st my slumbers nightly, or when morn
Purples the east: still govern thou my song,   30
Urania, and fit audience find, though few.
But drive far off the barbarous dissonance
Of Bacchus and his revellers, the race°
Of that wild rout that tore the Thracian bard
In Rhodope, where woods and rocks had ears°
To rapture, till the savage clamour drowned°
Both harp and voice; nor could the muse defend°
Her son. So fail not thou, who thee implores:°
For thou art heavenly, she an empty dream.
    Say goddess, what ensued when Raphael,   40
The affable archangel, had forewarned
Adam by dire example to beware
Apostasy, by what befell in heaven
To those apostates, lest the like befall
In Paradise to Adam or his race,
Charged not to touch the interdicted tree,
If they transgress, and slight that sole command,
So easily obeyed amid the choice
Of all tastes else to please their appetite,
Though wandering. He with his consorted Eve°   50
The story heard attentive, and was filled
With admiration, and deep muse to hear°
Of things so high and strange, things to their thought
So unimaginable as hate in heaven,
And war so near the peace of God in bliss
With such confusion: but the evil soon
Driven back redounded as a flood on those
From whom it sprung, impossible to mix
With blessedness. Whence Adam soon repealed°
The doubts that in his heart arose: and now   60
Led on, yet sinless, with desire to know
What nearer might concern him, how this world
Of heaven and earth conspicuous first began,°

When, and whereof created, for what cause,
What within Eden or without was done
Before his memory, as one whose drought
Yet scarce allayed still eyes the current stream,°
Whose liquid murmur heard new thirst excites,
Proceeded thus to ask his heavenly guest.

  Great things, and full of wonder in our ears,   70
Far differing from this world, thou hast revealed
Divine interpreter, by favour sent
Down from the empyrean to forewarn
Us timely of what might else have been our loss,
Unknown, which human knowledge could not reach:
For which to the infinitely good we owe
Immortal thanks, and his admonishment
Receive with solemn purpose to observe
Immutably his sovereign will, the end
Of what we are. But since thou hast vouchsafed   80
Gently for our instruction to impart
Things above earthly thought, which yet concerned
Our knowing, as to highest wisdom seemed,
Deign to descend now lower, and relate
What may no less perhaps avail us known,
How first began this heaven which we behold
Distant so high, with moving fires adorned
Innumerable, and this which yields or fills
All space, the ambient air wide interfused
Embracing round this florid earth, what cause°   90
Moved the creator in his holy rest
Through all eternity so late to build
In chaos, and the work begun, how soon
Absolved, if unforbid thou mayst unfold°
What we, not to explore the secrets ask
Of his eternal empire, but the more
To magnify his works, the more we know.
And the great light of day yet wants to run
Much of his race though steep, suspense in heaven°
Held by thy voice, thy potent voice he hears,   100
And longer will delay to hear thee tell
His generation, and the rising birth°
Of nature from the unapparent deep:°
Or if the star of evening and the moon

Haste to thy audience, night with her will bring
Silence, and sleep listening to thee will watch,°
Or we can bid his absence, till thy song
End, and dismiss thee ere the morning shine.
Thus Adam his illustrious guest besought:
And thus the godlike angel answered mild.   110
This also thy request with caution asked
Obtain: though to recount almighty works
What words or tongue of seraph can suffice,
Or heart of man suffice to comprehend?
Yet what thou canst attain, which best may serve
To glorify the maker, and infer°
Thee also happier, shall not be withheld
Thy hearing, such commission from above
I have received, to answer thy desire
Of knowledge within bounds; beyond abstain   120
To ask, nor let thine own inventions hope°
Things not revealed, which the invisible king,
Only omniscient, hath suppressed in night,
To none communicable in earth or heaven:
Enough is left besides to search and know.
But knowledge is as food, and needs no less
Her temperance over appetite, to know
In measure what the mind may well contain,
Oppresses else with surfeit, and soon turns
Wisdom to folly, as nourishment to wind.   130
     Know then, that after Lucifer from heaven
(So call him, brighter once amidst the host°
Of angels, than that star the stars among)°
Fell with his flaming legions through the deep
Into his place, and the great Son returned
Victorious with his saints, the omnipotent
Eternal Father from his throne beheld
Their multitude, and to his son thus spake.
     At least our envious foe hath failed, who thought
All like himself rebellious, by whose aid   140
This inaccessible high strength, the seat
Of deity supreme, us dispossessed,°
He trusted to have seized, and into fraud°
Drew many, whom their place knows here no more;
Yet far the greater part have kept, I see,

Their station, heaven yet populous retains
Number sufficient to possess her realms
Though wide, and this high temple to frequent
With ministeries due and solemn rites:
But lest his heart exalt him in the harm   150
Already done, to have dispeopled heaven
My damage fondly deemed, I can repair°
That detriment, if such it be to lose
Self-lost, and in a moment will create
Another world, out of one man a race
Of men innumerable, there to dwell,
Not here, till by degrees of merit raised
They open to themselves at length the way
Up hither, under long obedience tried,
And earth be changed to heaven, and heaven to earth,   160
One kingdom, joy and union without end.
Meanwhile inhabit lax, ye powers of heaven,°
And thou my word, begotten Son, by thee
This I perform, speak thou, and be it done:
My overshadowing spirit and might with thee
I send along, ride forth, and bid the deep
Within appointed bounds be heaven and earth,
Boundless the deep, because I am who fill
Infinitude, nor vacuous the space.
Though I uncircumscribed myself retire,   170
And put not forth my goodness, which is free
To act or not, necessity and chance
Approach not me, and what I will is fate.
    So spake the almighty, and to what he spake
His word, the filial Godhead, gave effect.
Immediate are the acts of God, more swift
Than time or motion, but to human ears
Cannot without process of speech be told,
So told as earthly notion can receive.°
Great triumph and rejoicing was in heaven   180
When such was heard declared the almighty's will;
Glory they sung to the most high, good will
To future men, and in their dwellings peace:
Glory to him whose just avenging ire
Had driven out the ungodly from his sight
And th' habitations of the just; to him

Glory and praise, whose wisdom had ordained
Good out of evil to create, instead
Of spirits malign a better race to bring
Into their vacant room, and thence diffuse   190
His good to worlds and ages infinite.
So sang the hierarchies: meanwhile the Son
On his great expedition now appeared,
Girt with omnipotence, with radiance crowned
Of majesty divine, sapience and love
Immense, and all his father in him shone.
About his chariot numberless were poured
Cherub and seraph, potentates and thrones,
And virtues, wingèd spirits, and chariots winged,
From the armoury of God, where stand of old   200
Myriads between two brazen mountains lodged
Against a solemn day, harnessed at hand,
Celestial equipage; and now came forth
Spontaneous, for within them spirit lived,
Attendant on their Lord: heaven opened wide
Her ever during gates, harmonious sound
On golden hinges moving, to let forth
The king of glory in his powerful word
And spirit coming to create new worlds.
On heavenly ground they stood, and from the shore   210
They viewed the vast immeasurable abyss
Outrageous as a sea, dark, wasteful, wild,°
Up from the bottom turned by furious winds
And surging waves, as mountains to assault
Heaven's height, and with the centre mix the pole.
    Silence, ye troubled waves, and thou deep, peace,
Said then the omnific word, your discord end:°
    Nor stayed, but on the wings of cherubim
Uplifted, in paternal glory rode
Far into chaos, and the world unborn;   220
For chaos heard his voice: him all his train
Followed in bright procession to behold
Creation, and the wonders of his might.
Then stayed the fervid wheels, and in his hand°
He took the golden compasses, prepared
In God's eternal store, to circumscribe
This universe, and all created things:

One foot he centred, and the other turned
Round through the vast profundity obscure,
And said, Thus far extend, thus far thy bounds,   230
This be thy just circumference, O world.
Thus God the heaven created, thus the earth,
Matter unformed and void: darkness profound
Covered the abyss: but on the watery calm
His brooding wings the spirit of God outspread,
And vital virtue infused, and vital warmth°
Throughout the fluid mass, but downward purged
The black tartareous cold infernal dregs°
Adverse to life: then founded, then conglobed°
Like things to like, the rest to several place   240
Disparted, and between spun out the air,
And earth self balanced on her centre hung.
    Let there be light, said God, and forthwith light°
Ethereal, first of things, quintessence pure
Sprung from the deep, and from her native east
To journey through the airy gloom began,
Sphered in a radiant cloud, for yet the sun
Was not; she in a cloudy tabernacle
Sojourned the while. God saw the light was good;
And light from darkness by the hemisphere   250
Divided: light the day, and darkness night
He named. Thus was the first day even and morn:
Nor passed uncelebrated, nor unsung
By the celestial choirs, when orient light
Exhaling first from darkness they beheld;
Birth day of heaven and earth; with joy and shout
The hollow universal orb they filled,
And touched their golden harps, and hymning praised
God and his works, creator him they sung,
Both when first evening was, and when first morn.   260
    Again, God said, Let there be firmament
Amid the waters, and let it divide
The waters from the waters: and God made
The firmament, expanse of liquid, pure,
Transparent, elemental air, diffused
In circuit to the uttermost convex
Of this great round: partition firm and sure,
The waters underneath from those above

Dividing: for as earth, so he the world
Built on circumfluous waters calm, in wide   270
Crystalline ocean, and the loud misrule
Of Chaos far removed, lest fierce extremes
Contiguous might distemper the whole frame:°
And Heaven he named the firmament: so even
And morning chorus sung the second day.
   The earth was formed, but in the womb as yet
Of waters, embryon immature involved,°
Appeared not: over all the face of earth
Main ocean flowed, not idle, but with warm°
Prolific humour softening all her globe,°   280
Fermented the great mother to conceive,
Satiate with genial moisture, when God said°
Be gathered now ye waters under heaven
Into one place, and let dry land appear.
Immediately the mountains huge appear
Emergent, and their broad bare backs upheave
Into the clouds, their tops ascend the sky:
So high as heaved the tumid hills, so low°
Down sunk a hollow bottom broad and deep,
Capacious bed of waters: thither they   290
Hasted with glad precipitance, uprolled
As drops on dust conglobing from the dry;°
Part rise in crystal wall, or ridge direct,
For haste; such flight the great command impressed
On the swift floods: as armies at the call
Of trumpet (for of armies thou hast heard)
Troop to their standard, so the watery throng,
Wave rolling after wave, where way they found,
If steep, with torrent rapture, if through plain,°
Soft ebbing; nor withstood them rock or hill,   300
But they, or underground, or circuit wide
With serpent error wandering, found their way,°
And on the washy ooze deep channels wore;
Easy, ere God had bid the ground be dry,
All but within those banks, where rivers now
Stream, and perpetual draw their humid train.
The dry land, earth, and the great receptacle
Of congregated waters he called seas:
And saw that it was good, and said, Let the earth

Put forth the verdant grass, herb yielding seed,   310
And fruit tree yielding fruit after her kind;
Whose seed is in herself upon the earth.°
He scarce had said, when the bare earth, till then
Desert and bare, unsightly, unadorned,
Brought forth the tender grass whose verdure clad
Her universal face with pleasant green,
Then herbs of every leaf, that sudden flowered
Opening their various colours, and made gay
Her bosom smelling sweet: and these scarce blown,
Forth flourished thick the clustering vine, forth crept   320
The swelling gourd, up stood the corny reed°
Embattled in her field: and the humble shrub,°
And bush with frizzled hair implicit: last°
Rose as in dance the stately trees, and spread
Their branches hung with copious fruit; or gemmed°
Their blossoms: with high woods the hills were crowned,
With tufts the valleys and each fountain side,
With borders long the rivers. That earth now
Seemed like to heaven, a seat where gods might dwell,
Or wander with delight, and love to haunt   330
Her sacred shades: though God had yet not rained
Upon the earth, and man to till the ground
None was, but from the earth a dewy mist
Went up and watered all the ground, and each
Plant of the field, which ere it was in the earth
God made, and every herb, before it grew
On the green stem; God saw that it was good.
So even and morn recorded the third day.
    Again the almighty spake: Let there be lights°
High in the expanse of heaven to divide   340
The day from night; and let them be for signs,
For seasons, and for days, and circling years,
And let them be for lights as I ordain
Their office in the firmament of heaven
To give light on the earth; and it was so.
And God made two great lights, great for their use
To man, the greater to have rule by day,
The less by night altern: and made the stars,°
And set them in the firmament of heaven
To illuminate the earth, and rule the day   350

In their vicissitude, and rule the night,°
And light from darkness to divide. God saw,
Surveying his great work, that it was good:
For of celestial bodies first the sun
A mighty sphere he framed, unlightsome first,
Though of ethereal mould: then formed the moon
Globose, and every magnitude of stars,
And sowed with stars the heaven thick as a field:
Of light by far the greater part he took,
Transplanted from her cloudy shrine, and placed°   360
In the sun's orb, made porous to receive
And drink the liquid light, firm to retain
Her gathered beams, great palace now of light.
Hither as to their fountain other stars
Repairing, in their golden urns draw light,
And hence the morning planet gilds her horns;°
By tincture or reflection they augment°
Their small peculiar, though from human sight°
So far remote, with diminution seen.
First in his east the glorious lamp was seen,   370
Regent of day, and all th' horizon round
Invested with bright rays, jocund to run
His longitude through heaven's high road: the grey
Dawn, and the Pleiades before him danced°
Shedding sweet influence: less bright the moon,
But opposite in levelled west was set
His mirror, with full face borrowing her light°
From him, for other light she needed none
In that aspect, and still that distance keeps
Till night, then in the east her turn she shines,   380
Revolved on heaven's great axle, and her reign
With thousand lesser lights dividual holds,°
With thousand thousand stars, that then appeared
Spangling the hemisphere: then first adorned
With their bright luminaries that set and rose,
Glad evening and glad morn crowned the fourth day.
  And God said, Let the waters generate
Reptile with spawn abundant, living soul:
And let fowl fly above the earth, with wings
Displayed on the open firmament of heaven.   390
And God created the great whales, and each

Soul living, each that crept, which plenteously
The waters generated by their kinds,
And every bird of wing after his kind;
And saw that it was good, and blessed them, saying,
Be fruitful, multiply, and in the seas
And lakes and running streams the waters fill;
And let the fowl be multiplied on the earth.°
Forthwith the sounds and seas, each creek and bay
With fry innumerable swarm, and shoals   400
Of fish that with their fins and shining scales
Glide under the green wave, in schools that oft
Bank the mid-sea: part single or with mate°
Graze the seaweed their pasture, and through groves
Of coral stray, or sporting with quick glance
Show to the sun their waved coats dropped with gold,°
Or in their pearly shells at ease, attend°
Moist nutriment, or under rocks their food
In jointed armour watch: on smooth the seal,°
And bended dolphins play: part huge of bulk   410
Wallowing unwieldy, enormous in their gait
Tempest the ocean: there leviathan°
Hugest of living creatures, on the deep
Stretched like a promontory sleeps or swims,
And seems a moving land, and at his gills°
Draws in, and at his trunk spouts out a sea.
Meanwhile the tepid caves, and fens and shores
Their brood as numerous hatch, from the egg that soon
Bursting with kindly rupture forth disclosed°
Their callow young, but feathered soon and fledge°   420
They summed their pens, and soaring the air sublime°
With clang despised the ground, under a cloud°
In prospect; there the eagle and the stork°
On cliffs and cedar tops their eyries build:
Part loosely wing the region, part more wise
In common, ranged in figure wedge their way,°
Intelligent of seasons, and set forth°
Their airy caravan high over seas
Flying, and over lands with mutual wing
Easing their flight; so steers the prudent crane   430
Her annual voyage, borne on winds; the air
Floats, as they pass, fanned with unnumbered plumes:°

From branch to branch the smaller birds with song
Solaced the woods, and spread their painted wings
Till even, nor then the solemn nightingale
Ceased warbling, but all night tuned her soft lays:
Others on silver lakes and rivers bathed
Their downy breast: the swan with archèd neck
Between her white wings mantling proudly, rows°
Her state with oary feet: yet oft they quit°   440
The dank, and rising on stiff pennons, tower°
The mid aerial sky: others on ground
Walked firm; the crested cock whose clarion sounds
The silent hours, and the other whose gay train°
Adorns him, coloured with the florid hue
Of rainbows and starry eyes. The waters thus
With fish replenished, and the air with fowl,
Evening and morn solemnized the fifth day.

The sixth, and of creation last arose
With evening harps and matin, when God said,   450
Let the earth bring forth soul living in her kind,°
Cattle and creeping things, and beast of the earth,
Each in their kind. The earth obeyed, and straight
Opening her fertile womb teemed at a birth°
Innumerous living creatures, perfect forms,°
Limbed and full grown: out of the ground up rose
As from his lair the wild beast where he wons°
In forest wild, in thicket, brake, or den;
Among the trees in pairs they rose, they walked:
The cattle in the fields and meadows green: 460
Those rare and solitary, these in flocks
Pasturing at once, and in broad herds upsprung.
The grassy clods now calved, now half appeared°
The tawny lion, pawing to get free
His hinder parts, then springs as broke from bonds,
And rampant shakes his brinded mane; the ounce,°
The leopard, and the tiger, as the mole
Rising, the crumbled earth above them threw
In hillocks; the swift stag from underground
Bore up his branching head: scarce from his mould   470
Behemoth biggest born of earth upheaved°
His vastness: fleeced the flocks and bleating rose,
As plants: ambiguous between sea and land°

The river horse and scaly crocodile.°
At once came forth whatever creeps the ground,
Insect or worm; those waved their limber fans
For wings, and smallest lineaments exact
In all the liveries decked of summer's pride
With spots of gold and purple, azure and green:
These as a line their long dimension drew,   480
Streaking the ground with sinuous trace; not all
Minims of nature; some of serpent kind°
Wondrous in length and corpulence involved°
Their snaky folds, and added wings. First crept°
The parsimonious emmet, provident°
Of future, in small room large heart enclosed,
Pattern of just equality perhaps
Hereafter, joined in her popular tribes
Of commonalty: swarming next appeared°
The female bee that feeds her husband drone   490
Deliciously, and builds her waxen cells
With honey stored: the rest are numberless,
And thou their natures know'st, and gav'st them names,
Needless to thee repeated; nor unknown
The serpent subtlest beast of all the field,
Of huge extent sometimes, with brazen eyes
And hairy mane terrific, though to thee°
Not noxious, but obedient at thy call.
Now heaven in all her glory shone, and rolled
Her motions, as the great first mover's hand   500
First wheeled their course; earth in her rich attire
Consummate lovely smiled; air, water, earth,°
By fowl, fish, beast, was flown, was swum, was walked
Frequent; and of the sixth day yet remained;°
There wanted yet the masterwork, the end°
Of all yet done; a creature who not prone
And brute as other creatures, but endued
With sanctity of reason, might erect
His stature, and upright with front serene°
Govern the rest, self-knowing, and from thence   510
Magnanimous to correspond with heaven,°
But grateful to acknowledge whence his good
Descends, thither with heart and voice and eyes
Directed in devotion, to adore

And worship God supreme, who made him chief
Of all his works: therefore the omnipotent
Eternal Father (for where is not he
Present) thus to his son audibly spake.
    Let us make now man in our image, man
In our similitude, and let them rule   520
Over the fish and fowl of sea and air,
Beast of the field, and over all the earth,
And every creeping thing that creeps the ground.
This said, he formed thee, Adam, thee O man
Dust of the ground, and in thy nostrils breathed
The breath of life; in his own image he
Created thee, in the image of God
Express, and thou becam'st a living soul.°
Male he created thee, but thy consort
Female for race; then blessed mankind, and said,   530
Be fruitful, multiply, and fill the earth,
Subdue it, and throughout dominion hold
Over fish of the sea, and fowl of the air,
And every living thing that moves on the earth.°
Wherever thus created, for no place
Is yet distinct by name, thence, as thou know'st
He brought thee into this delicious grove,
This garden, planted with the trees of God,
Delectable both to behold and taste;
And freely all their pleasant fruit for food   540
Gave thee, all sorts are here that all the earth yields,
Variety without end; but of the tree
Which tasted works knowledge of good and evil,
Thou mayst not; in the day thou eat'st, thou diest;°
Death is the penalty imposed, beware,
And govern well thy appetite, lest Sin
Surprise thee, and her black attendant Death.
Here finished he, and all that he had made
Viewed, and behold all was entirely good;
So even and morn accomplished the sixth day: 550
Yet not till the creator from his work
Desisting, though unwearied, up returned
Up to the heaven of heavens his high abode,°
Thence to behold this new created world
The addition of his empire, how it showed

In prospect from his throne, how good how fair,
Answering his great idea. Up he rode°
Followed with acclamation and the sound
Symphonious of ten thousand harps that tuned°
Angelic harmonies: the earth, the air   560
Resounded, (thou remember'st, for thou heard'st)
The heavens and all the constellations rung,
The planets in their station listening stood,
While the bright pomp ascended jubilant.°
Open, ye everlasting gates, they sung,
Open, ye heavens, your living doors; let in
The great creator from his work returned
Magnificent, his six days' work, a world;
Open, and henceforth oft; for God will deign
To visit oft the dwellings of just men   570
Delighted, and with frequent intercourse
Thither will send his wingèd messengers
On errands of supernal grace. So sung
The glorious train ascending: he through heaven,
That opened wide her blazing portals, led
To God's eternal house direct the way,
A broad and ample road, whose dust is gold
And pavement stars, as stars to thee appear,
.Seen in the galaxy, that Milky Way
Which nightly as a circling zone thou seest   580
Powdered with stars. And now on earth the seventh
Evening arose in Eden, for the sun
Was set, and twilight from the east came on,
Forerunning night; when at the holy mount
Of heaven's high-seated top, the imperial throne
Of Godhead, fixed for ever firm and sure,
The filial power arrived, and sat him down
With his great father, for he also went
Invisible, yet stayed (such privilege
Hath omnipresence) and the work ordained,   590
Author and end of all things, and from work
Now resting, blessed and hallowed the seventh day,
As resting on that day from all his work,
But not in silence holy kept; the harp
Had work and rested not, the solemn pipe,
And dulcimer, all organs of sweet stop,

All sounds on fret by string or golden wire°
Tempered soft tunings; intermixed with voice
Choral or unison: of incense clouds
Fuming from golden censers hid the mount.   600
Creation and the six days' acts they sung,
Great are thy works, Jehovah, infinite
Thy power; what thought can measure thee or tongue
Relate thee; greater now in thy return
Than from the giant angels; thee that day°
Thy thunders magnified; but to create
Is greater than created to destroy.
Who can impair thee, mighty king, or bound
Thy empire? Easily the proud attempt
Of spirits apostate and their counsels vain   610
Thou hast repelled, while impiously they thought
Thee to diminish, and from thee withdraw
The number of thy worshippers. Who seeks
To lessen thee, against his purpose serves
To manifest the more thy might: his evil
Thou usest, and from thence creat'st more good.
Witness this new-made world, another heaven
From heaven gate not far, founded in view
On the clear hyaline, the glassy sea;°
Of amplitude almost immense, with stars°   620
Numerous, and every star perhaps a world
Of destined habitation; but thou know'st
Their seasons: among these the seat of men,
Earth with her nether ocean circumfused,
Their pleasant dwelling place. Thrice happy men,
And sons of men, whom God hath thus advanced,
Created in his image, there to dwell
And worship him, and in reward to rule
Over his works, on earth, in sea, or air,
And multiply a race of worshippers   630
Holy and just: thrice happy if they know
Their happiness, and persevere upright.
    So sung they, and the empyrean rung,
With hallelujahs: thus was Sabbath kept.
And thy request think now fulfilled, that asked
How first this world and face of things began,°
And what before thy memory was done

From the beginning, that posterity
Informed by thee might know; if else thou seek'st
Aught, not surpassing human measure, say.   640

BOOK VIII

The Argument

Adam inquires concerning celestial motions, is doubtfully answered, and exhorted to search rather things more worthy of knowledge: Adam assents, and still desirous to detain Raphael, relates to him what he remembered since his own creation, his placing in Paradise, his talk with God concerning solitude and fit society, his first meeting and nuptials with Eve, his discourse with the angel thereupon; who after admonitions repeated departs.

The angel ended, and in Adam's ear
So charming left his voice, that he awhile°
Thought him still speaking, still stood fixed to hear;
Then as new waked thus gratefully replied.°
What thanks sufficient, or what recompense
Equal have I to render thee, divine
Historian, who thus largely hast allayed
The thirst I had of knowledge, and vouchsafed
This friendly condescension to relate°
Things else by me unsearchable, now heard   10
With wonder, but delight, and, as is due,
With glory attributed to the high
Creator; something yet of doubt remains,
Which only thy solution can resolve.
When I behold this goodly frame, this world
Of heaven and earth consisting, and compute
Their magnitudes, this earth a spot, a grain,
An atom, with the firmament compared
And all her numbered stars, that seem to roll
Spaces incomprehensible (for such   20
Their distance argues and their swift return
Diurnal) merely to officiate light°
Round this opacous earth, this punctual spot,°
Once day and night; in all their vast survey
Useless besides, reasoning I oft admire,°
How nature wise and frugal could commit
Such disproportions, with superfluous hand

So many nobler bodies to create,
Greater so manifold to this one use,
For aught appears, and on their orbs impose   30
Such restless revolution day by day
Repeated, while the sedentary earth,°
That better might with far less compass move,
Served by more noble than herself, attains
Her end without least motion, and receives
As tribute such a sumless journey brought°
Of incorporeal speed, her warmth and light;°
Speed, to describe whose swiftness number fails.
   So spake our sire, and by his countenance seemed
Entering on studious thoughts abstruse, which Eve   40
Perceiving where she sat retired in sight,
With lowliness majestic from her seat,
And grace that won who saw to wish her stay,
Rose, and went forth among her fruits and flowers,
To visit how they prospered, bud and bloom,°
Her nursery; they at her coming sprung°
And touched by her fair tendance gladlier grew.°
Yet went she not, as not with such discourse
Delighted, or not capable her ear
Of what was high: such pleasure she reserved,   50
Adam relating, she sole auditress;
Her husband the relater she preferred
Before the angel, and of him to ask
Chose rather; he, she knew would intermix
Grateful digressions, and solve high dispute
With conjugal caresses, from his lip
Not words alone pleased her. O when meet now
Such pairs, in love and mutual honour joined?
With goddess-like demeanour forth she went;
Not unattended, for on her as queen   60
A pomp of winning graces waited still,°
And from about her shot darts of desire
Into all eyes to wish her still in sight.
And Raphael now to Adam's doubt proposed
Benevolent and facile thus replied.°
   To ask or search I blame thee not, for heaven
Is as the book of God before thee set,
Wherein to read his wondrous works, and learn

His seasons, hours, or days, or months, or years:
This to attain, whether heaven move or earth,   70
Imports not, if thou reckon right, the rest
From man or angel the great architect
Did wisely to conceal, and not divulge
His secrets to be scanned by them who ought
Rather admire; or if they list to try
Conjecture, he his fabric of the heavens
Hath left to their disputes, perhaps to move
His laughter at their quaint opinions wide°
Hereafter, when they come to model heaven
And calculate the stars, how they will wield   80
The mighty frame, how build, unbuild, contrive
To save appearances, how gird the sphere°
With centric and eccentric scribbled o'er,°
Cycle and epicycle, orb in orb:°
Already by thy reasoning this I guess,
Who art to lead thy offspring, and supposest
That bodies bright and greater should not serve
The less not bright, nor heaven such journeys run,
Earth sitting still, when she alone receives
The benefit: consider first, that great   90
Or bright infers not excellence: the earth°
Though, in comparison of heaven, so small,
Nor glistering, may of solid good contain
More plenty than the sun that barren shines,
Whose virtue on itself works no effect,
But in the fruitful earth; there first received
His beams, unactive else, their vigour find.
Yet not to earth are those bright luminaries
Officious, but to thee earth's habitant.°
And for the heaven's wide circuit, let it speak   100
The maker's high magnificence, who built
So spacious, and his line stretched out so far;
That man may know he dwells not in his own;
An edifice too large for him to fill,
Lodged in a small partition, and the rest
Ordained for uses to his Lord best known.
The swiftness of those circles attribute,
Though numberless, to his omnipotence,
That to corporeal substances could add

Speed almost spiritual; me thou think'st not slow,   110
Who since the morning hour set out from heaven
Where God resides, and ere midday arrived
In Eden, distance inexpressible
By numbers that have name. But this I urge,
Admitting motion in the heavens, to show
Invalid that which thee to doubt it moved;
Not that I so affirm, though so it seem
To thee who hast thy dwelling here on earth.
God to remove his ways from human sense,
Placed heaven from earth so far, that earthly sight,   120
If it presume, might err in things too high,
And no advantage gain. What if the sun
Be centre to the world, and other stars
By his attractive virtue and their own°
Incited, dance about him various rounds?
Their wandering course now high, now low, then hid,°
Progressive, retrograde, or standing still,
In six thou seest, and what if seventh to these
The planet earth, so steadfast though she seem,
Insensibly three different motions move?°   130
Which else to several spheres thou must ascribe,
Moved contrary with thwart obliquities,°
Or save the sun his labour, and that swift
Nocturnal and diurnal rhomb supposed,°
Invisible else above all stars, the wheel
Of day and night; which needs not thy belief,
If earth industrious of her self fetch day
Travelling east, and with her part averse
From the sun's beam meet night, her other part
Still luminous by his ray. What if that light   140
Sent from her through the wide transpicuous air,°
To the terrestrial moon be as a star°
Enlightening her by day, as she by night
This earth? reciprocal, if land be there,
Fields and inhabitants: her spots thou seest
As clouds, and clouds may rain, and rain produce
Fruits in her softened soil, for some to eat
Allotted there; and other suns perhaps
With their attendant moons thou wilt descry
Communicating male and female light,°   150

Which two great sexes animate the world,
Stored in each orb perhaps with some that live.
For such vast room in nature unpossessed
By living soul, desert and desolate,
Only to shine, yet scarce to contribute
Each orb a glimpse of light, conveyed so far
Down to this habitable, which returns
Light back to them, is obvious to dispute.°
But whether thus these things, or whether not,
Whether the sun predominant in heaven   160
Rise on the earth, or earth rise on the sun,
He from the east his flaming road begin,
Or she from west her silent course advance
With inoffensive pace that spinning sleeps°
On her soft axle, while she paces even,
And bears thee soft with the smooth air along,
Solicit not thy thoughts with matters hid,°
Leave them to God above, him serve and fear;
Of other creatures, as him pleases best,
Wherever placed, let him dispose: joy thou   170
In what he gives to thee, this Paradise
And thy fair Eve; heaven is for thee too high
To know what passes there; be lowly wise:
Think only what concerns thee and thy being;
Dream not of other worlds, what creatures there
Live, in what state, condition or degree,
Contented that thus far hath been revealed
Not of earth only but of highest heaven.
    To whom thus Adam cleared of doubt, replied.
How fully hast thou satisfied me, pure   180
Intelligence of heaven, angel serene,°
And freed from intricacies, taught to live,
The easiest way, nor with perplexing thoughts
To interrupt the sweet of life, from which
God hath bid dwell far off all anxious cares,
And not molest us, unless we our selves
Seek them with wandering thoughts, and notions vain.
But apt the mind or fancy is to rove
Unchecked, and of her roving is no end;
Till warned, or by experience taught, she learn,   190
That not to know at large of things remote

From use, obscure and subtle, but to know
That which before us lies in daily life,
Is the prime wisdom, what is more, is fume,°
Or emptiness, or fond impertinence,°
And renders us in things that most concern
Unpractised, unprepared, and still to seek.°
Therefore from this high pitch let us descend
A lower flight, and speak of things at hand
Useful, whence haply mention may arise   200
Of something not unseasonable to ask
By sufferance, and thy wónted favour deigned.
Thee I have heard relating what was done
Ere my remembrance: now hear me relate
My story, which perhaps thou hast not heard;
And day is yet not spent; till then thou seest
How subtly to detain thee I devise,
Inviting thee to hear while I relate,
Fond, were it not in hope of thy reply:
For while I sit with thee, I seem in heaven,   210
And sweeter thy discourse is to my ear
Than fruits of palm-tree pleasantest to thirst
And hunger both, from labour, at the hour
Of sweet repast; they satiate, and soon fill,
Though pleasant, but thy words with grace divine
Imbued, bring to their sweetness no satiety.
     To whom thus Raphael answered heavenly meek.
Nor are thy lips ungraceful, sire of men,
Nor tongue ineloquent; for God on thee
Abundantly his gifts hath also poured   220
Inward and outward both, his image fair:
Speaking or mute all comeliness and grace
Attends thee, and each word, each motion forms.
Nor less think we in heaven of thee on earth
Than of our fellow servant, and inquire
Gladly into the ways of God with man:
For God we see hath honoured thee, and set
On man his equal love: say therefore on;
For I that day was absent, as befell,
Bound on a voyage uncouth and obscure,°   230
Far on excursion toward the gates of hell;
Squared in full legion (such command we had)

To see that none thence issued forth a spy,
Or enemy, while God was in his work,
Lest he incensed at such eruption bold,
Destruction with creation might have mixed.
Not that they durst without his leave attempt,
But us he sends upon his high behests
For state, as sovereign king, and to inure°
Our prompt obedience. Fast we found, fast shut   240
The dismal gates, and barricadoed strong;
But long ere our approaching heard within
Noise, other than the sound of dance or song,
Torment, and loud lament, and furious rage.
Glad we returned up to the coasts of light
Ere Sabbath evening: so we had in charge.
But thy relation now; for I attend,°
Pleased with thy words no less than thou with mine.
    So spake the godlike power, and thus our sire.
For man to tell how human life began   250
Is hard; for who himself beginning knew?
Desire with thee still longer to converse
Induced me. As new waked from soundest sleep
Soft on the flowery herb I found me laid
In balmy sweat, which with his beams the sun
Soon dried, and on the reeking moisture fed.°
Straight toward heaven my wondering eyes I turned,
And gazed awhile the ample sky, till raised
By quick instinctive motion up I sprung,
As thitherward endeavouring, and upright   260
Stood on my feet; about me round I saw
Hill, dale, and shady woods, and sunny plains,
And liquid lapse of murmuring streams; by these,°
Creatures that lived, and moved, and walked, or flew,
Birds on the branches warbling; all things smiled,
With fragrance and with joy my heart o'erflowed.
My self I then perused, and limb by limb
Surveyed, and sometimes went, and sometimes ran°
With supple joints, and lively vigour led:
But who I was, or where, or from what cause,   270
Knew not; to speak I tried, and forthwith spake,
My tongue obeyed and readily could name
Whate'er I saw. Thou sun, said I, fair light,

And thou enlightened earth, so fresh and gay,
Ye hills and dales, ye rivers, woods, and plains,
And ye that live and move, fair creatures, tell,
Tell, if ye saw, how came I thus, how here?
Not of myself; by some great maker then,
In goodness and in power pre-eminent;
Tell me, how may I know him, how adore,   280
From whom I have that thus I move and live,
And feel that I am happier than I know.
While thus I called, and strayed I knew not whither,
From where I first drew air, and first beheld
This happy light, when answer none returned,
On a green shady bank profuse of flowers
Pensive I sat me down; there gentle sleep
First found me, and with soft oppression seized
My drowsèd sense, untroubled, though I thought
I then was passing to my former state   290
Insensible, and forthwith to dissolve:
When suddenly stood at my head a dream,
Whose inward apparition gently moved
My fancy to believe I yet had being,
And lived: one came, methought, of shape divine,
And said, Thy mansion wants thee, Adam, rise,°
First man, of men innumerable ordained
First father, called by thee I come thy guide
To the garden of bliss, thy seat prepared.°
So saying, by the hand he took me raised,   300
And over fields and waters, as in air
Smooth sliding without step, last led me up
A woody mountain; whose high top was plain,
A circuit wide, enclosed, with goodliest trees
Planted, with walks, and bowers, that what I saw
Of earth before scarce pleasant seemed. Each tree
Loaden with fairest fruit that hung to the eye
Tempting, stirred in me sudden appetite
To pluck and eat; whereat I waked, and found
Before mine eyes all real, as the dream   310
Had lively shadowed: here had new begun
My wandering, had not he who was my guide
Up hither, from among the trees appeared
Presence divine. Rejoicing, but with awe

In adoration at his feet I fell
Submiss: he reared me, and Whom thou sought'st I am,°
Said mildly, Author of all this thou seest
Above, or round about thee or beneath.
This Paradise I give thee, count it thine
To till and keep, and of the fruit to eat: 320
Of every tree that in the garden grows
Eat freely with glad heart; fear here no dearth:
But of the tree whose operation brings
Knowledge of good and ill, which I have set
The pledge of thy obedience and thy faith,
Amid the garden by the tree of life,
Remember what I warn thee, shun to taste,
And shun the bitter consequence: for know,
The day thou eat'st thereof, my sole command
Transgressed, inevitably thou shalt die;°   330
From that day mortal, and this happy state
Shalt lose, expelled from hence into a world
Of woe and sorrow. Sternly he pronounced
The rigid interdiction, which resounds
Yet dreadful in mine ear, though in my choice
Not to incur; but soon his clear aspect
Returned and gracious purpose thus renewed.°
Not only these fair bounds, but all the earth
To thee and to thy race I give; as lords
Possess it, and all things that therein live,   340
Or live in sea, or air, beast, fish, and fowl.
In sign whereof each bird and beast behold
After their kinds; I bring them to receive
From thee their names, and pay thee fealty
With low subjection; understand the same
Of fish within their watery residence,
Not hither summoned, since they cannot change
Their element to draw the thinner air.
As thus he spake, each bird and beast behold
Approaching two and two, these cowering low   350
With blandishment, each bird stooped on his wing.
I named them, as they passed, and understood
Their nature, with such knowledge God endued
My sudden apprehension: but in these
I found not what methought I wanted still;

And to the heavenly vision thus presumed.
　O by what name, for thou above all these,
Above mankind, or aught than mankind higher,
Surpassest far my naming, how may I
Adore thee, author of this universe,　　　　　　　　　360
And all this good to man, for whose well being
So amply, and with hands so liberal
Thou hast provided all things: but with me
I see not who partakes. In solitude
What happiness, who can enjoy alone,
Or all enjoying, what contentment find?
Thus I presumptuous; and the vision bright,
As with a smile more brightened, thus replied.
　What call'st thou solitude, is not the earth
With various living creatures, and the air　　　　　370
Replenished, and all these at thy command°
To come and play before thee, know'st thou not
Their language and their ways, they also know,
And reason not contemptibly; with these
Find pastime, and bear rule; thy realm is large.
So spake the universal Lord, and seemed
So ordering. I with leave of speech implored,
And humble deprecation thus replied.
　Let not my words offend thee, heavenly power,
My maker, be propitious while I speak.　　　　　380
Hast thou not made me here thy substitute,
And these inferior far beneath me set?
Among unequals what society
Can sort, what harmony or true delight?
Which must be mutual, in proportion due
Given and received; but in disparity
The one intense, the other still remiss°
Cannot well suit with either, but soon prove
Tedious alike: of fellowship I speak
Such as I seek, fit to participate　　　　　　　　　390
All rational delight, wherein the brute
Cannot be human consort; they rejoice
Each with their kind, lion with lioness;
So fitly them in pairs thou hast combined;
Much less can bird with beast, or fish with fowl
So well converse, nor with the ox the ape;°

Worse then can man with beast, and least of all.
Whereto the almighty answered, not displeased.
A nice and subtle happiness I see°
Thou to thy self proposest, in the choice   400
Of thy associates, Adam, and wilt taste
No pleasure, though in pleasure, solitary.°
What think'st thou then of me, and this my state,
Seem I to thee sufficiently possessed
Of happiness, or not? who am alone
From all eternity, for none I know
Second to me or like, equal much less.
How have I then with whom to hold converse
Save with the creatures which I made, and those
To me inferior, infinite descents   410
Beneath what other creatures are to thee?
    He ceased, I lowly answered. To attain
The height and depth of thy eternal ways
All human thoughts come short, supreme of things;
Thou in thyself art perfect, and in thee
Is no deficience found; not so is man,
But in degree, the cause of his desire
By conversation with his like to help,
Or solace his defects. No need that thou
Shouldst propagate, already infinite;   420
And through all numbers absolute, though one;°
But man by number is to manifest
His single imperfection, and beget°
Like of his like, his image multiplied,
In unity defective, which requires°
Collateral love, and dearest amity.
Thou in thy secrecy although alone,
Best with thy self accompanied, seek'st not
Social communication, yet so pleased,
Canst raise thy creature to what height thou wilt   430
Of union or communion, deified;
I by conversing cannot these erect°
From prone, nor in their ways complacence find.°
Thus I emboldened spake, and freedom used
Permissive, and acceptance found, which gained°
This answer from the gracious voice divine.
    Thus far to try thee, Adam, I was pleased,

And find thee knowing not of beasts alone,
Which thou hast rightly named, but of thyself,
Expressing well the spirit within thee free,   440
My image, not imparted to the brute,
Whose fellowship therefore unmeet for thee
Good reason was thou freely shouldst dislike,
And be so minded still; I, ere thou spak'st,
Knew it not good for man to be alone,
And no such company as then thou saw'st
Intended thee, for trial only brought,
To see how thou couldst judge of fit and meet:
What next I bring shall please thee, be assured,
Thy likeness, thy fit help, thy other self,   450
Thy wish exactly to thy heart's desire.
      He ended, or I heard no more, for now
My earthly by his heavenly overpowered,°
Which it had long stood under, strained to the height
In that celestial colloquy sublime,
As with an object that excels the sense,
Dazzled and spent, sunk down, and sought repair
Of sleep, which instantly fell on me, called
By nature as in aid, and closed mine eyes.
Mine eyes he closed, but open left the cell   460
Of fancy my internal sight, by which
Abstract as in a trance methought I saw,°
Though sleeping, where I lay, and saw the shape
Still glorious before whom awake I stood;
Who stooping opened my left side, and took
From thence a rib, with cordial spirits warm,°
And life-blood streaming fresh; wide was the wound,
But suddenly with flesh filled up and healed:
The rib he formed and fashioned with his hands;
Under his forming hands a creature grew,   470
Manlike, but different sex, so lovely fair,
That what seemed fair in all the world, seemed now
Mean, or in her summed up, in her contained
And in her looks, which from that time infused
Sweetness into my heart, unfelt before,
And into all things from her air inspired°
The spirit of love and amorous delight.
She disappeared, and left me dark, I waked

To find her, or forever to deplore
Her loss, and other pleasures all abjure: 480
When out of hope, behold her, not far off,°
Such as I saw her in my dream, adorned
With what all earth or heaven could bestow
To make her amiable: on she came,
Led by her heavenly maker, though unseen,
And guided by his voice, nor uninformed
Of nuptial sanctity and marriage rites:
Grace was in all her steps, heaven in her eye,
In every gesture dignity and love.
I overjoyed could not forbear aloud.°   490
    This turn hath made amends; thou hast fulfilled
Thy words, creator bounteous and benign,
Giver of all things fair, but fairest this
Of all thy gifts, nor enviest. I now see°
Bone of my bone, flesh of my flesh, myself
Before me; woman is her name, of man
Extracted; for this cause he shall forego
Father and mother, and to his wife adhere;
And they shall be one flesh, one heart, one soul.°
    She heard me thus, and though divinely brought,   500
Yet innocence and virgin modesty,
Her virtue and the conscience of her worth,°
That would be wooed, and not unsought be won,
Not obvious, not obtrusive, but retired,°
The more desirable, or to say all,
Nature herself, though pure of sinful thought,
Wrought in her so, that seeing me, she turned;
I followed her, she what was honour knew,
And with obsequious majesty approved°
My pleaded reason. To the nuptial bower   510
I led her blushing like the morn: all heaven,
And happy constellations on that hour
Shed their selectest influence; the earth
Gave sign of gratulation, and each hill;°
Joyous the birds; fresh gales and gentle airs
Whispered it to the woods, and from their wings°
Flung rose, flung odours from the spicy shrub,
Disporting, till the amorous bird of night°
Sung spousal, and bid haste the evening star

On his hilltop, to light the bridal lamp.   520
Thus I have told thee all my state, and brought
My story to the sum of earthly bliss
Which I enjoy, and must confess to find
In all things else delight indeed, but such
As used or not, works in the mind no change,
Nor vehement desire, these delicacies°
I mean of taste, sight, smell, herbs, fruits, and flowers,
Walks, and the melody of birds; but here
Far otherwise, transported I behold,°
Transported touch; here passion first I felt,   530
Commotion strange, in all enjoyments else
Superior and unmoved, here only weak
Against the charm of beauty's powerful glance.°
Or nature failed in me, and left some part
Not proof enough such object to sustain,°
Or from my side subducting, took perhaps°
More than enough; at least on her bestowed
Too much of ornament, in outward show
Elaborate, of inward less exact.°
For well I understand in the prime end   540
Of nature her the inferior, in the mind
And inward faculties, which most excel,
In outward also her resembling less
His image who made both, and less expressing
The character of that dominion given
O'er other creatures; yet when I approach
Her loveliness, so absolute she seems
And in her self complete, so well to know
Her own, that what she wills to do or say,
Seems wisest, virtuousest, discreetest, best;°   550
All higher knowledge in her presence falls
Degraded, wisdom in discourse with her
Loses discountenanced, and like folly shows;
Authority and reason on her wait,
As one intended first, not after made
Occasionally; and to consummate all,°
Greatness of mind and nobleness their seat
Build in her loveliest, and create an awe
About her, as a guard angelic placed.
To whom the angel with contracted brow.   560

Accuse not nature, she hath done her part;
Do thou but thine, and be not diffident°
Of wisdom, she deserts thee not, if thou
Dismiss not her, when most thou need'st her nigh,
By attributing overmuch to things
Less excellent, as thou thy self perceiv'st.
For what admir'st thou, what transports thee so,
An outside? fair no doubt, and worthy well
Thy cherishing, thy honouring, and thy love,
Not thy subjection: weigh with her thyself;   570
Then value: ofttimes nothing profits more
Than self esteem, grounded on just and right
Well managed; of that skill the more thou know'st,
The more she will acknowledge thee her head,
And to realities yield all her shows:
Made so adorn for thy delight the more,°
So awful, that with honour thou mayst love°
Thy mate, who sees when thou art seen least wise.
But if the sense of touch whereby mankind
Is propagated seem such dear delight   580
Beyond all other, think the same vouchsafed
To cattle and each beast; which would not be
To them made common and divulged, if aught
Therein enjoyed were worthy to subdue
The soul of man, or passion in him move.
What higher in her society thou find'st
Attractive, human, rational, love still;
In loving thou dost well, in passion not,
Wherein true love consists not; love refines
The thoughts, and heart enlarges, hath his seat   590
In reason, and is judicious, is the scale
By which to heavenly love thou mayst ascend,
Not sunk in carnal pleasure, for which cause
Among the beasts no mate for thee was found.
    To whom thus half abashed Adam replied.
Neither her outside formed so fair, nor aught
In procreation common to all kinds
(Though higher of the genial bed by far,°
And with mysterious reverence I deem)
So much delights me as those graceful acts,   600
Those thousand decencies that daily flow

From all her words and actions mixed with love
And sweet compliance, which declare unfeigned
Union of mind, or in us both one soul;
Harmony to behold in wedded pair
More grateful than harmonious sound to the ear.
Yet these subject not; I to thee disclose°
What inward thence I feel, not therefore foiled,°
Who meet with various objects, from the sense
Variously representing; yet still free°   610
Approve the best, and follow what I approve.
To love thou blam'st me not, for love thou say'st
Leads up to heaven, is both the way and guide;
Bear with me then, if lawful what I ask;
Love not the heavenly spirits, and how their love
Express they, by looks only, or do they mix
Irradiance, virtual or immediate touch?°
    To whom the angel with a smile that glowed
Celestial rosy red, love's proper hue,
Answered. Let it suffice thee that thou know'st   620
Us happy, and without love no happiness.
Whatever pure thou in the body enjoy'st
(And pure thou wert created) we enjoy
In eminence, and obstacle find none°
Of membrane, joint, or limb, exclusive bars:
Easier than air with air, if spirits embrace,
Total they mix, union of pure with pure
Desiring; nor restrained conveyance need°
As flesh to mix with flesh, or soul with soul.
But I can now no more; the parting sun   630
Beyond the earth's green cape and verdant isles°
Hesperian sets, my signal to depart.°
Be strong, live happy, and love, but first of all
Him whom to love is to obey, and keep
His great command; take heed lest passion sway
Thy judgment to do aught, which else free will
Would not admit; thine and of all thy sons
The weal or woe in thee is placed; beware.
I in thy persevering shall rejoice,
And all the blessed: stand fast; to stand or fall   640
Free in thine own arbitrament it lies.
Perfect within, no outward aid require;

And all temptation to transgress repel.
   So saying, he arose; whom Adam thus
Followed with benediction. Since to part,
Go heavenly guest, ethereal messenger,
Sent from whose sovereign goodness I adore.
Gentle to me and affable hath been
Thy condescension, and shall be honoured ever
With grateful memory: thou to mankind   650
Be good and friendly still, and oft return.
   So parted they, the angel up to heaven
From the thick shade, and Adam to his bower.

BOOK IX

The Argument

Satan having compassed the earth, with meditated guile returns as a mist by night into Paradise, enters into the serpent sleeping. Adam and Eve in the morning go forth to their labours, which Eve proposes to divide in several places, each labouring apart: Adam consents not, alleging the danger, lest that enemy, of whom they were forewarned, should attempt her found alone: Eve loath to be thought not circumspect or firm enough, urges her going apart, the rather desirous to make trial of her strength; Adam at last yields: the serpent finds her alone; his subtle approach, first gazing, then speaking, with much flattery extolling Eve above all other creatures. Eve wondering to hear the serpent speak, asks how he attained to human speech and such understanding not till now; the serpent answers, that by tasting of a certain tree in the garden he attained both to speech and reason, till then void of both: Eve requires him to bring her to that tree, and finds it to be the tree of knowledge forbidden: the serpent now grown bolder, with many wiles and arguments induces her at length to eat; she pleased with the taste deliberates awhile whether to impart thereof to Adam or not, at last brings him of the fruit, relates what persuaded her to eat thereof: Adam at first amazed, but perceiving her lost, resolves through vehemence of love to perish with her; and extenuating the trespass eats also of the fruit: the effects thereof in them both; they seek to cover their nakedness; then fall to variance and accusation of one another.

   No more of talk where God or angel guest
With man, as with his friend, familiar used°
To sit indulgent, and with him partake
Rural repast, permitting him the while
Venial discourse unblamed: I now must change°
Those notes to tragic; foul distrust, and breach

Disloyal on the part of man, revolt,
And disobedience: on the part of heaven
Now alienated, distance and distaste,
Anger and just rebuke, and judgment given,   10
That brought into this world a world of woe,
Sin and her shadow Death, and Misery
Death's harbinger: sad task, yet argument°
Not less but more heroic than the wrath
Of stern Achilles on his foe pursued°
Thrice fugitive about Troy wall; or rage°
Of Turnus for Lavinia disespoused,°
Or Neptune's ire or Juno's, that so long
Perplexed the Greek and Cytherea's son;°
If answerable style I can obtain°   20
Of my celestial patroness, who deigns°
Her nightly visitation unimplored,
And dictates to me slumbering, or inspires
Easy my unpremeditated verse:
Since first this subject for heroic song
Pleased me long choosing, and beginning late;°
Not sedulous by nature to indite°
Wars, hitherto the only argument°
Heroic deemed, chief mastery to dissect°
With long and tedious havoc fabled knights   30
In battles feigned; the better fortitude°
Of patience and heroic martyrdom
Unsung; or to describe races and games,
Or tilting furniture, emblazoned shields,°
Impresas quaint, caparisons and steeds;°
Bases and tinsel trappings, gorgeous knights°
At joust and tournament; then marshalled feast
Served up in hall with sewers, and seneschals;°
The skill of artifice or office mean,
Not that which justly gives heroic name   40
To person or to poem. Me of these
Nor skilled nor studious, higher argument
Remains, sufficient of itself to raise
That name, unless an age too late, or cold°
Climate, or years damp my intended wing°
Depressed, and much they may, if all be mine,
Not hers who brings it nightly to my ear.

The sun was sunk, and after him the star
Of Hesperus, whose office is to bring°
Twilight upon the earth, short arbiter   50
Twixt day and night, and now from end to end
Night's hemisphere had veiled the horizon round:
When Satan who late fled before the threats
Of Gabriel out of Eden, now improved°
In meditated fraud and malice, bent
On man's destruction, maugre what might hap°
Of heavier on himself, fearless returned.
By night he fled, and at midnight returned
From compassing the earth, cautious of day,
Since Uriel regent of the sun descried   60
His entrance, and forewarned the cherubim
That kept their watch; thence full of anguish driven,
The space of seven continued nights he rode
With darkness, thrice the equinoctial line
He circled, four times crossed the car of Night°
From pole to pole, traversing each colure;°
On the eighth returned, and on the coast averse
From entrance or cherubic watch, by stealth
Found unsuspected way. There was a place,
Now not, though sin, not time, first wrought the change,   70
Where Tigris at the foot of Paradise
Into a gulf shot underground, till part
Rose up a fountain by the tree of life;
In with the river sunk, and with it rose
Satan involved in rising mist, then sought
Where to lie hid; sea he had searched and land
From Eden over Pontus, and the pool°
Maeotis, up beyond the river Ob;°
Downward as far antarctic; and in length
West from Orontes to the ocean barred°   80
At Darien, thence to the land where flows°
Ganges and Indus: thus the orb he roamed
With narrow search; and with inspection deep
Considered every creature, which of all
Most opportune might serve his wiles, and found
The serpent subtlest beast of all the field.
Him after long debate, irresolute
Of thoughts revolved, his final sentence chose

Fit vessel, fittest imp of fraud, in whom
To enter, and his dark suggestions hide°   90
From sharpest sight: for in the wily snake,
Whatever sleights none would suspicious mark,
As from his wit and native subtlety
Proceeding, which in other beasts observed
Doubt might beget of diabolic power°
Active within beyond the sense of brute.
Thus he resolved, but first from inward grief
His bursting passion into plaints thus poured:
    O earth, how like to heaven, if not preferred
More justly, seat worthier of gods, as built   100
With second thoughts, reforming what was old!
For what god after better worse would build?
Terrestrial heaven, danced round by other heavens
That shine, yet bear their bright officious lamps,°
Light above light, for thee alone, as seems,
In thee concentring all their precious beams
Of sacred influence: as God in heaven
Is centre, yet extends to all, so thou
Centring receiv'st from all those orbs; in thee,
Not in themselves, all their known virtue appears   110
Productive in herb, plant, and nobler birth
Of creatures animate with gradual life°
Of growth, sense, reason, all summed up in man.
With what delight could I have walked thee round,
If I could joy in aught, sweet interchange
Of hill, and valley, rivers, woods and plains,
Now land, now sea, and shores with forest crowned,
Rocks, dens, and caves; but I in none of these
Find place or refuge; and the more I see
Pleasures about me, so much more I feel   120
Torment within me, as from the hateful siege°
Of contraries; all good to me becomes
Bane, and in heaven much worse would by my state,
But neither here seek I, no nor in heaven
To dwell, unless by mastering heaven's supreme;
Nor hope to be myself less miserable
By what I seek, but others to make such
As I, though thereby worse to me redound:
For only in destroying I find ease

To my relentless thoughts; and him destroyed,   130
Or won to what may work his utter loss,
For whom all this was made, all this will soon
Follow, as to him linked in weal or woe,
In woe then; that destruction wide may range:
To me shall be the glory sole among
The infernal powers, in one day to have marred
What he almighty styled, six nights and days
Continued making, and who knows how long
Before had been contriving, though perhaps
Not longer than since I in one night freed   140
From servitude inglorious well-nigh half
The angelic name, and thinner left the throng
Of his adorers: he to be avenged
And to repair his numbers thus impaired,
Whether such virtue spent of old now failed°
More angels to create, if they at least
Are his created, or to spite us more,°
Determined to advance into our room°
A creature formed of earth, and him endow,
Exalted from so base original,°   150
With heavenly spoils, our spoils: what he decreed
He effected; man he made, and for him built
Magnificent this world, and earth his seat,
Him lord pronounced, and, O indignity!
Subjected to his service angel wings,
And flaming ministers to watch and tend
Their earthy charge: of these the vigilance
I dread, and to elude, thus wrapped in mist
Of midnight vapour glide obscure, and pry
In every bush and brake, where hap may find   160
The serpent sleeping, in whose mazy folds
To hide me, and the dark intent I bring.
O foul descent! that I who erst contended
With gods to sit the highest, am now constrained
Into a beast, and mixed with bestial slime,
This essence to incarnate and imbrute,
That to the height of deity aspired;
But what will not ambition and revenge
Descend to? Who aspires must down as low
As high he soared, obnoxious first or last   170

To basest things. Revenge, at first though sweet,°
Bitter ere long back on itself recoils;
Let it; I reck not, so it light well aimed,°
Since higher I fall short, on him who next°
Provokes my envy, this new favourite
Of heaven, this man of clay, son of despite,
Whom us the more to spite his maker raised
From dust: spite then with spite is best repaid.
　　So saying, through each thicket dank or dry,
Like a black mist low creeping, he held on   180
His midnight search, where soonest he might find
The serpent: him fast sleeping soon he found
In labyrinth of many a round self-rolled,
His head the midst, well stored with subtle wiles:
Not yet in horrid shade or dismal den,
Nor nocent yet, but on the grassy herb°
Fearless unfeared he slept: in at his mouth
The devil entered, and his brutal sense,°
In heart or head, possessing soon inspired
With act intelligential; but his sleep   190
Disturbed not, waiting close the approach of morn.°
Now whenas sacred light began to dawn
In Eden on the humid flowers, that breathed
Their morning incense, when all things that breathe,
From the earth's great altar send up silent praise
To the creator, and his nostrils fill
With grateful smell, forth came the human pair°
And joined their vocal worship to the choir
Of creatures wanting voice, that done, partake°
The season, prime for sweetest scents and airs: 200
Then commune how that day they best may ply
Their growing work: for much their work outgrew
The hands' dispatch of two, gardening so wide.
And Eve first to her husband thus began.
　　Adam, well may we labour still to dress
This garden, still to tend plant, herb and flower,
Our pleasant task enjoined, but till more hands
Aid us, the work under our labour grows,
Luxurious by restraint; what we by day°
Lop overgrown, or prune, or prop, or bind,   210
One night or two with wanton growth derides°

Tending to wild. Thou therefore now advise
Or hear what to my mind first thoughts present,
Let us divide our labours, thou where choice
Leads thee, or where most needs, whether to wind
The woodbine round this arbour, or direct
The clasping ivy where to climb, while I
In yonder spring of roses intermixed°
With myrtle, find what to redress till noon:°
For while so near each other thus all day   220
Our task we choose, what wonder if so near
Looks intervene and smiles, or object new
Casual discourse draw on, which intermits
Our day's work brought to little, though begun
Early, and the hour of supper comes unearned.
    To whom mild answer Adam thus returned.
Sole Eve, associate sole, to me beyond
Compare above all living creatures dear,
Well hast thou motioned, well thy thoughts employed°
How we might best fulfil the work which here   230
God hath assigned us, nor of me shalt pass
Unpraised: for nothing lovelier can be found
In woman, than to study household good,
And good works in her husband to promote.
Yet not so strictly hath our Lord imposed
Labour, as to debar us when we need
Refreshment, whether food, or talk between,
Food of the mind, or this sweet intercourse
Of looks and smiles, for smiles from reason flow,
To brute denied, and are of love the food,   240
Love not the lowest end of human life.
For not to irksome toil, but to delight
He made us, and delight to reason joined.
These paths and bowers doubt not but our joint hands
Will keep from wilderness with ease, as wide
As we need walk, till younger hands ere long
Assist us: but if much converse perhaps
Thee satiate, to short absence I could yield.
For solitude sometimes is best society,
And short retirement urges sweet return.   250
But other doubt possesses me, lest harm
Befall thee severed from me; for thou know'st

What hath been warned us, what malicious foe
Envying our happiness, and of his own
Despairing, seeks to work us woe and shame
By sly assault; and somewhere nigh at hand
Watches, no doubt, with greedy hope to find
His wish and best advantage, us asunder,
Hopeless to circumvent us joined, where each
To other speedy aid might lend at need;   260
Whether his first design be to withdraw
Our fealty from God, or to disturb
Conjugal love, than which perhaps no bliss
Enjoyed by us excites his envy more;
Or this, or worse, leave not the faithful side°
That gave thee being, still shades thee and protects.
The wife, where danger or dishonour lurks,
Safest and seemliest by her husband stays,
Who guards her, or with her the worst endures.
        To whom the virgin majesty of Eve,°   270
As one who loves, and some unkindness meets,
With sweet austere composure thus replied.
        Offspring of heaven and earth, and all earth's lord,
That such an enemy we have, who seeks
Our ruin, both by thee informed I learn,
And from the parting angel overheard
As in a shady nook I stood behind,
Just then returned at shut of evening flowers.
But that thou shouldst my firmness therefore doubt
To God or thee, because we have a foe   280
May tempt it, I expected not to hear.
His violence thou fear'st not, being such,
As we, not capable of death or pain,
Can either not receive, or can repel.
His fraud is then thy fear, which plain infers
Thy equal fear that my firm faith and love
Can by his fraud be shaken or seduced;
Thoughts, which how found they harbour in thy breast
Adam, misthought of her to thee so dear?
        To whom with healing words Adam replied.   290
Daughter of God and man, immortal Eve,
For such thou art, from sin and blame entire:°
Not diffident of thee do I dissuade

Thy absence from my sight, but to avoid
The attempt itself, intended by our foe.
For he who tempts, though in vain, at least asperses°
The tempted with dishonour foul, supposed
Not incorruptible of faith, not proof
Against temptation: thou thyself with scorn
And anger wouldst resent the offered wrong,   300
Though ineffectual found: misdeem not then,
If such affront I labour to avert
From thee alone, which on us both at once
The enemy, though bold, will hardly dare,
Or daring, first on me the assault shall light.
Nor thou his malice and false guile contemn;
Subtle he needs must be, who could seduce
Angels, nor think superfluous others' aid.
I from the influence of thy looks receive
Access in every virtue, in thy sight°   310
More wise, more watchful, stronger, if need were
Of outward strength; while shame, thou looking on,
Shame to be overcome or over-reached
Would utmost vigour raise, and raised unite.
Why shouldst not thou like sense within thee feel
When I am present, and thy trial choose
With me, best witness of thy virtue tried.
    So spake domestic Adam in his care
And matrimonial love; but Eve, who thought
Less attributed to her faith sincere,   320
Thus her reply with accent sweet renewed.
    If this be our condition, thus to dwell
In narrow circuit straitened by a foe,
Subtle or violent, we not endued
Single with like defence, wherever met,
How are we happy, still in fear of harm?°
But harm precedes not sin: only our foe
Tempting affronts us with his foul esteem
Of our integrity: his foul esteem
Sticks no dishonour on our front, but turns°   330
Foul on himself; then wherefore shunned or feared
By us? who rather double honour gain
From his surmise proved false, find peace within,
Favour from heaven, our witness from the event.°

And what is faith, love, virtue unassayed
Alone, without exterior help sustained?
Let us not then suspect our happy state
Left so imperfect by the maker wise,
As not secure to single or combined.
Frail is our happiness, if this be so,   340
And Eden were no Eden thus exposed.
    To whom thus Adam fervently replied.
O woman, best are all things as the will
Of God ordained them, his creating hand
Nothing imperfect or deficient left
Of all that he created, much less man,
Or aught that might his happy state secure,
Secure from outward force; within himself
The danger lies, yet lies within his power:
Against his will he can receive no harm.   350
But God left free the will, for what obeys
Reason, is free, and reason he made right,
But bid her well beware, and still erect,°
Lest by some fair-appearing good surprised
She dictate false, and misinform the will
To do what God expressly hath forbid.
Not then mistrust, but tender love enjoins,
That I should mind thee oft, and mind thou me.°
Firm we subsist, yet possible to swerve,
Since reason not impossibly may meet   360
Some specious object by the foe suborned,°
And fall into deception unaware,
Not keeping strictest watch, as she was warned.
Seek not temptation then, which to avoid
Were better, and most likely if from me
Thou sever not: trial will come unsought.
Wouldst thou approve thy constancy, approve°
First thy obedience; the other who can know,
Not seeing thee attempted, who attest?
But if thou think, trial unsought may find   370
Us both securer than thus warned thou seem'st,°
Go; for thy stay, not free, absents thee more;
Go in thy native innocence, rely
On what thou hast of virtue, summon all,
For God towards thee hath done his part, do thine.

So spake the patriarch of mankind, but Eve
Persisted, yet submiss, though last, replied.
 With thy permission then, and thus forewarned
Chiefly by what thy own last reasoning words
Touched only, that our trial, when least sought,   380
May find us both perhaps far less prepared,
The willinger I go, nor much expect
A foe so proud will first the weaker seek;
So bent, the more shall shame him his repulse.
 Thus saying, from her husband's hand her hand
Soft she withdrew, and like a wood-nymph light
Oread or dryad, or of Delia's train,°
Betook her to the groves, but Delia's self
In gait surpassed and goddess-like deport,
Though not as she with bow and quiver armed,°   390
But with such gardening tools as art yet rude,
Guiltless of fire had formed, or angels brought.°
To Pales, or Pomona thus adorned,°
Likeliest she seemed, Pomona when she fled
Vertumnus, or to Ceres in her prime,°
Yet virgin of Proserpina from Jove.°
Her long with ardent look his eye pursued
Delighted, but desiring more her stay.
Oft he to her his charge of quick return
Repeated, she to him as oft engaged   400
To be returned by noon amid the bower,
And all things in best order to invite
Noontide repast, or afternoon's repose.
O much deceived, much failing, hapless Eve,
Of thy presumed return! event perverse!°
Thou never from that hour in Paradise
Found'st either sweet repast, or sound repose;
Such ambush hid among sweet flowers and shades
Waited with hellish rancour imminent
To intercept thy way, or send thee back   410
Despoiled of innocence, of faith, of bliss.
For now, and since first break of dawn the fiend,
Mere serpent in appearance, forth was come,°
And on his quest, where likeliest he might find
The only two of mankind, but in them
The whole included race, his purposed prey.

In bower and field he sought, where any tuft
Of grove or garden-plot more pleasant lay,
Their tendance or plantation for delight,°
By fountain or by shady rivulet   420
He sought them both, but wished his hap might find
Eve separate, he wished, but not with hope
Of what so seldom chanced, when to his wish,
Beyond his hope, Eve separate he spies,
Veiled in a cloud of fragrance, where she stood,
Half spied, so thick the roses bushing round
About her glowed, oft stooping to support
Each flower of slender stalk, whose head though gay
Carnation, purple, azure, or specked with gold,
Hung drooping unsustained, them she upstays   430
Gently with myrtle band, mindless the while,°
Herself, though fairest unsupported flower,
From her best prop so far, and storm so nigh.
Nearer he drew, and many a walk traversed
Of stateliest covert, cedar, pine, or palm,
Then voluble and bold, now hid, now seen°
Among thick-woven arborets and flowers°
Embordered on each bank, the hand of Eve:°
Spot more delicious than those gardens feigned
Or of revived Adonis, or renowned°   440
Alcinous, host of old Laertes' son,°
Or that, not mystic, where the sapient king°
Held dalliance with his fair Egyptian spouse.°
Much he the place admired, the person more.
As one who long in populous city pent,
Where houses thick and sewers annoy the air,
Forth issuing on a summer's morn to breathe
Among the pleasant villages and farms
Adjoined, from each thing met conceives delight,
The smell of grain, or tedded grass, or kine,°   450
Or dairy, each rural sight, each rural sound;
If chance with nymph-like step fair virgin pass,
What pleasing seemed, for her now pleases more,°
She most, and in her look sums all delight.
Such pleasure took the serpent to behold
This flowery plat, the sweet recess of Eve°
Thus early, thus alone; her heavenly form

Angelic, but more soft, and feminine,
Her graceful innocence, her every air
Of gesture or least action overawed   460
His malice, and with rapine sweet bereaved
His fierceness of the fierce intent it brought:
That space the evil one abstracted stood
From his own evil, and for the time remained
Stupidly good, of enmity disarmed,
Of guile, of hate, of envy, of revenge;
But the hot hell that always in him burns,
Though in mid-heaven, soon ended his delight,
And tortures him now more, the more he sees
Of pleasure not for him ordained: then soon   470
Fierce hate he recollects, and all his thoughts
Of mischief, gratulating, thus excites.°
    Thoughts, whither have ye led me, with what sweet
Compulsion thus transported to forget
What hither brought us, hate, not love, nor hope
Of Paradise for hell, hope here to taste°
Of pleasure, but all pleasure to destroy,
Save what is in destroying, other joy
To me is lost. Then let me not let pass
Occasion which now smiles, behold alone   480
The woman, opportune to all attempts,°
Her husband, for I view far round, not nigh,
Whose higher intellectual more I shun,°
And strength, of courage haughty, and of limb°
Heroic built, though of terrestrial mould,
Foe not informidable, exempt from wound,
I not; so much hath hell debased, and pain
Enfeebled me, to what I was in heaven.°
She fair, divinely fair, fit love for gods,
Not terrible, though terror be in love   490
And beauty, not approached by stronger hate,
Hate stronger, under show of love well feigned,
The way which to her ruin now I tend.
    So spake the enemy of mankind, enclosed
In serpent, inmate bad, and toward Eve
Addressed his way, not with indented wave,
Prone on the ground, as since, but on his rear,
Circular base of rising folds, that towered

Fold above fold a surging maze, his head
Crested aloft, and carbuncle his eyes;°   500
With burnished neck of verdant gold, erect
Amidst his circling spires, that on the grass°
Floated redundant: pleasing was his shape,°
And lovely, never since of serpent kind
Lovelier, not those that in Illyria changed
Hermione and Cadmus, or the god°
In Epidaurus; nor to which transformed°
Ammonian Jove, or Capitoline was seen,
He with Olympias, this with her who bore
Scipio the height of Rome. With tract oblique°   510
At first, as one who sought access, but feared
To interrupt, sidelong he works his way.
As when a ship by skilful steersman wrought
Nigh river's mouth or foreland, where the wind
Veers oft, as oft so steers, and shifts her sail;
So varied he, and of his tortuous train
Curled many a wanton wreath in sight of Eve,
To lure her eye; she busied heard the sound
Of rustling leaves, but minded not, as used
To such disport before her through the field,   520
From every beast, more duteous at her call,
Than at Circean call the herd disguised.°
He bolder now, uncalled before her stood;
But as in gaze admiring: oft he bowed
His turret crest, and sleek enamelled neck,
Fawning, and licked the ground whereon she trod.
His gentle dumb expression turned at length
The eye of Eve to mark his play; he glad
Of her attention gained, with serpent tongue
Organic, or impulse of vocal air,°   530
His fraudulent temptation thus began.
    Wonder not, sovereign mistress, if perhaps
Thou canst, who art sole wonder, much less arm
Thy looks, the heaven of mildness, with disdain,
Displeased that I approach thee thus, and gaze
Insatiate, I thus single, nor have feared
Thy awful brow, more awful thus retired.
Fairest resemblance of thy maker fair,
Thee all things living gaze on, all things thine

By gift, and thy celestial beauty adore   540
With ravishment beheld, there best beheld
Where universally admired; but here
In this enclosure wild, these beasts among,
Beholders rude, and shallow to discern
Half what in thee is fair, one man except,
Who sees thee? (and what is one?) who shouldst be seen
A goddess among gods, adored and served
By angels numberless, thy daily train.
    So glozed the tempter, and his proem tuned;°
Into the heart of Eve his words made way,   550
Though at the voice much marvelling; at length
Not unamazed she thus in answer spake.
What may this mean? Language of man pronounced
By tongue of brute, and human sense expressed?
The first at least of these I thought denied
To beasts, whom God on their creation-day
Created mute to all articulate sound;
The latter I demur, for in their looks°
Much reason, and in their actions oft appears.
Thee, serpent, subtlest beast of all the field   560
I knew, but not with human voice endued;
Redouble then this miracle, and say,
How cam'st thou speakable of mute, and how
To me so friendly grown above the rest
Of brutal kind, that daily are in sight?
Say, for such wonder claims attention due.
    To whom the guileful tempter thus replied.
Empress of this fair world, resplendent Eve,
Easy to me it is to tell thee all
What thou command'st, and right thou shouldst be obeyed: 570
I was at first as other beasts that graze
The trodden herb, of abject thoughts and low,
As was my food, nor aught but food discerned
Or sex, and apprehended nothing high:
Till on a day roving the field, I chanced
A goodly tree far distant to behold
Loaden with fruit of fairest colours mixed,
Ruddy and gold: I nearer drew to gaze;
When from the boughs a savoury odour blown,
Grateful to appetite, more pleased my sense°   580

Than smell of sweetest fennel, or the teats°
Of ewe or goat dropping with milk at even,
Unsucked of lamb or kid, that tend their play.
To satisfy the sharp desire I had
Of tasting those fair apples, I resolved
Not to defer; hunger and thirst at once,°
Powerful persuaders, quickened at the scent
Of that alluring fruit, urged me so keen.
About the mossy trunk I wound me soon,
For high from ground the branches would require   590
Thy utmost reach or Adam's: round the tree
All other beasts that saw, with like desire
Longing and envying stood, but could not reach.
Amid the tree now got, where plenty hung
Tempting so nigh, to pluck and eat my fill
I spared not, for such pleasure till that hour
At feed or fountain never had I found.
Sated at length, ere long I might perceive
Strange alteration in me, to degree
Of reason in my inward powers, and speech   600
Wanted not long, though to this shape retained.°
Thenceforth to speculations high or deep
I turned my thoughts, and with capacious mind
Considered all things visible in heaven,
Or earth, or middle, all things fair and good;°
But all that fair and good in thy divine
Semblance, and in thy beauty's heavenly ray
United I beheld; no fair to thine
Equivalent or second, which compelled
Me thus, though importune perhaps, to come   610
And gaze, and worship thee of right declared
Sovereign of creatures, universal dame.
     So talked the spirited sly snake; and Eve
Yet more amazed unwary thus replied.
     Serpent, thy overpraising leaves in doubt
The virtue of that fruit, in thee first proved:°
But say, where grows the tree, from hence how far?
For many are the trees of God that grow
In Paradise, and various, yet unknown
To us, in such abundance lies our choice,   620
As leaves a greater store of fruit untouched,

Still hanging incorruptible, till men
Grow up to their provision, and more hands°
Help to disburden nature of her birth.°
    To whom the wily adder, blithe and glad.
Empress, the way is ready, and not long,
Beyond a row of myrtles, on a flat,
Fast by a fountain, one small thicket past
Of blowing myrrh and balm; if thou accept°
My conduct, I can bring thee thither soon.   630
    Lead then, said Eve. He leading swiftly rolled
In tangles, and made intricate seem straight,
To mischief swift. Hope elevates, and joy
Brightens his crest, as when a wandering fire,
Compact of unctuous vapour, which the night°
Condenses, and the cold environs round,
Kindled through agitation to a flame,
Which oft, they say, some evil spirit attends
Hovering and blazing with delusive light,
Misleads the amazed night-wanderer from his way   640
To bogs and mires, and oft through pond or pool,
There swallowed up and lost, from succour far.
So glistered the dire snake, and into fraud
Led Eve our credulous mother, to the tree
Of prohibition, root of all our woe;
Which when she saw, thus to her guide she spake.
    Serpent, we might have spared our coming hither,
Fruitless to me, though fruit be here to excess,
The credit of whose virtue rest with thee,
Wondrous indeed, if cause of such effects.   650
But of this tree we may not taste nor touch;
God so commanded, and left that command
Sole daughter of his voice; the rest, we live
Law to our selves, our reason is our law.
    To whom the tempter guilefully replied.
Indeed? hath God then said that of the fruit
Of all these garden trees ye shall not eat,
Yet lords declared of all in earth or air?
    To whom thus Eve yet sinless. Of the fruit
Of each tree in the garden we may eat,   660
But of the fruit of this fair tree amidst
The garden, God hath said, Ye shall not eat

Thereof, nor shall ye touch it, lest ye die.
　　She scarce had said, though brief, when now more bold
The tempter, but with show of zeal and love
To man, and indignation at his wrong,
New part puts on, and as to passion moved,
Fluctuates disturbed, yet comely and in act°
Raised, as of some great matter to begin.
As when of old some orator renowned　　　　　　　　　670
In Athens or free Rome, where eloquence
Flourished, since mute, to some great cause addressed,
Stood in himself collected, while each part,
Motion, each act won audience ere the tongue,
Sometimes in height began, as no delay
Of preface brooking through his zeal of right.°
So standing, moving, or to height upgrown
The tempter all impassioned thus began.
　　O sacred, wise, and wisdom-giving plant,
Mother of science, now I feel thy power°　　　　　　680
Within me clear, not only to discern
Things in their causes, but to trace the ways
Of highest agents, deemed however wise.
Queen of this universe, do not believe
Those rigid threats of death; ye shall not die:
How should ye? by the fruit? it gives you life
To knowledge: by the threatener? look on me,°
Me who have touched and tasted, yet both live,
And life more perfect have attained than fate
Meant me, by venturing higher than my lot.　　　　690
Shall that be shut to man, which to the beast
Is open? or will God incense his ire
For such a petty trespass, and not praise
Rather your dauntless virtue, whom the pain
Of death denounced, whatever thing death be,°
Deterred not from achieving what might lead
To happier life, knowledge of good and evil;
Of good, how just? of evil, if what is evil
Be real, why not known, since easier shunned?
God therefore cannot hurt ye, and be just;　　　　　700
Not just, not God; not feared then, nor obeyed:
Your fear itself of death removes the fear.
Why then was this forbid? Why but to awe,

Why but to keep ye low and ignorant,
His worshipper; he knows that in the day
Ye eat thereof, your eyes that seem so clear,
Yet are but dim, shall perfectly be then
Opened and cleared, and ye shall be as gods,
Knowing both good and evil as they know.
That ye should be as gods, since I as man,   710
Internal man, is but proportion meet,
I of brute human, ye of human gods.
So ye shall die perhaps, by putting off
Human, to put on gods, death to be wished,
Though threatened, which no worse than this can bring.
And what are gods that man may not become
As they, participating godlike food?°
The gods are first, and that advantage use
On our belief, that all from them proceeds;
I question it, for this fair earth I see,   720
Warmed by the sun, producing every kind,
Them nothing: if they all things, who enclosed°
Knowledge of good and evil in this tree,
That whoso eats thereof, forthwith attains
Wisdom without their leave? and wherein lies
The offence, that man should thus attain to know?
What can your knowledge hurt him, or this tree
Impart against his will if all be his?
Or is it envy, and can envy dwell
In heavenly breasts? these, these and many more   730
Causes import your need of this fair fruit.
Goddess humane, reach then, and freely taste.°
    He ended, and his words replete with guile
Into her heart too easy entrance won:
Fixed on the fruit she gazed, which to behold
Might tempt alone, and in her ears the sound
Yet rung of his persuasive words, impregned°
With reason, to her seeming, and with truth;
Meanwhile the hour of noon drew on, and waked
An eager appetite, raised by the smell   740
So savoury of that fruit, which with desire,
Inclinable now grown to touch or taste,°
Solicited her longing eye; yet first
Pausing a while, thus to her self she mused.

Great are thy virtues, doubtless, best of fruits,
Though kept from man, and worthy to be admired,
Whose taste, too long forborne, at first assay
Gave elocution to the mute, and taught
The tongue not made for speech to speak thy praise:
Thy praise he also who forbids thy use,   750
Conceals not from us, naming thee the tree
Of knowledge, knowledge both of good and evil;
Forbids us then to taste, but his forbidding
Commends thee more, while it infers the good°
By thee communicated, and our want:
For good unknown, sure is not had, or had
And yet unknown, is as not had at all.
In plain then, what forbids he but to know,°
Forbids us good, forbids us to be wise?
Such prohibitions bind not. But if death   760
Bind us with after-bands, what profits then
Our inward freedom? In the day we eat
Of this fair fruit, our doom is, we shall die.
How dies the serpent? he hath eaten and lives,
And knows, and speaks, and reasons, and discerns,
Irrational till then. For us alone
Was death invented? or to us denied
This intellectual food, for beasts reserved?
For beasts it seems: yet that one beast which first
Hath tasted, envies not, but brings with joy   770
The good befallen him, author unsuspect,°
Friendly to man, far from deceit or guile.
What fear I then, rather what know to fear
Under this ignorance of good and evil,
Of God or death, of law or penalty?
Here grows the cure of all, this fruit divine,
Fair to the eye, inviting to the taste,
Of virtue to make wise: what hinders then
To reach, and feed at once both body and mind?
    So saying, her rash hand in evil hour   780
Forth reaching to the fruit, she plucked, she ate:
Earth felt the wound, and nature from her seat
Sighing through all her works gave signs of woe,
That all was lost. Back to the thicket slunk
The guilty serpent, and well might, for Eve

Intent now wholly on her taste, naught else
Regarded, such delight till then, as seemed,
In fruit she never tasted, whether true
Or fancied so, through expectation high
Of knowledge, nor was godhead from her thought.   790
Greedily she engorged without restraint,
And knew not eating death: satiate at length,
And heightened as with wine, jocund and boon,°
Thus to herself she pleasingly began.
   O sovereign, virtuous, precious of all trees
In Paradise, of operation blessed
To sapience, hitherto obscured, infamed,°
And thy fair fruit let hang, as to no end
Created; but henceforth my early care,
Not without song, each morning, and due praise   800
Shall tend thee, and the fertile burden ease
Of thy full branches offered free to all;
Till dieted by thee I grow mature
In knowledge, as the gods who all things know;
Though others envy what they cannot give;
For had the gift been theirs, it had not here
Thus grown. Experience, next to thee I owe,
Best guide; not following thee, I had remained
In ignorance, thou open'st wisdom's way,
And giv'st access, though secret she retire.   810
And I perhaps am secret; heaven is high,
High and remote to see from thence distinct
Each thing on earth; and other care perhaps
May have diverted from continual watch
Our great forbidder, safe with all his spies
About him. But to Adam in what sort
Shall I appear? shall I to him make known
As yet my change, and give him to partake
Full happiness with me, or rather not,
But keep the odds of knowledge in my power   820
Without copartner? so to add what wants°
In female sex, the more to draw his love,
And render me more equal, and perhaps,
A thing not undesirable, sometime
Superior; for inferior who is free?
This may be well: but what if God have seen,

And death ensue? then I shall be no more,
And Adam wedded to another Eve,
Shall live with her enjoying, I extinct;
A death to think. Confirmed then I resolve,   830
Adam shall share with me in bliss or woe:
So dear I love him, that with him all deaths
I could endure, without him live no life.

   So saying, from the tree her step she turned,
But first low reverence done, as to the power
That dwelt within, whose presence had infused
Into the plant sciential sap, derived°
From nectar, drink of gods. Adam the while
Waiting desirous her return, had wove
Of choicest flowers a garland to adorn   840
Her tresses, and her rural labours crown,
As reapers oft are wont their harvest queen.
Great joy he promised to his thoughts, and new
Solace in her return, so long delayed;
Yet oft his heart, divine of something ill,°
Misgave him; he the faltering measure felt;°
And forth to meet her went, the way she took
That morn when first they parted; by the tree
Of knowledge he must pass, there he her met,
Scarce from the tree returning; in her hand   850
A bough of fairest fruit that downy smiled,
New gathered, and ambrosial smell diffused.
To him she hasted, in her face excuse
Came prologue, and apology to prompt,
Which with bland words at will she thus addressed.

   Hast thou not wondered, Adam, at my stay?
Thee I have missed, and thought it long, deprived
Thy presence, agony of love till now
Not felt, nor shall be twice, for never more
Mean I to try, what rash untried I sought,   860
The pain of absence from thy sight. But strange
Hath been the cause, and wonderful to hear:
This tree is not as we are told, a tree
Of danger tasted, nor to evil unknown
Opening the way, but of divine effect
To open eyes, and make them gods who taste;
And hath been tasted such: the serpent wise,

Or not restrained as we, or not obeying,
Hath eaten of the fruit, and is become,
Not dead, as we are threatened, but thenceforth   870
Endued with human voice and human sense,
Reasoning to admiration, and with me
Persuasively hath so prevailed, that I
Have also tasted, and have also found
The effects to correspond, opener mine eyes,
Dim erst, dilated spirits, ampler heart,°
And growing up to godhead; which for thee
Chiefly I sought, without thee can despise.
For bliss, as thou hast part, to me is bliss,
Tedious, unshared with thee, and odious soon.   880
Thou therefore also taste, that equal lot
May join us, equal joy, as equal love;
Lest thou not tasting, different degree
Disjoin us, and I then too late renounce
Deity for thee, when fate will not permit.
    Thus Eve with countenance blithe her story told;
But in her cheek distemper flushing glowed.°
On the other side, Adam, soon as he heard
The fatal trespass done by Eve, amazed,
Astonied stood and blank, while horror chill°   890
Ran through his veins, and all his joints relaxed;
From his slack hand the garland wreathed for Eve
Down dropped, and all the faded roses shed:
Speechless he stood and pale, till thus at length
First to himself he inward silence broke.
    O fairest of creation, last and best
Of all God's works, creature in whom excelled
Whatever can to sight or thought be formed,
Holy, divine, good, amiable or sweet!
How art thou lost, how on a sudden lost,   900
Defaced, deflowered, and now to death devote?°
Rather how hast thou yielded to transgress
The strict forbiddance, how to violate
The sacred fruit forbidden! some cursed fraud
Of enemy hath beguiled thee, yet unknown,
And me with thee hath ruined, for with thee
Certain my resolution is to die;
How can I live without thee, how forgo

Thy sweet converse and love so dearly joined,
To live again in these wild woods forlorn?   910
Should God create another Eve, and I
Another rib afford, yet loss of thee
Would never from my heart; no no, I feel
The link of nature draw me: flesh of flesh,
Bone of my bone thou art, and from thy state
Mine never shall be parted, bliss or woe.

So having said, as one from sad dismay
Recomforted, and after thoughts disturbed
Submitting to what seemed remediless,
Thus in calm mood his words to Eve he turned.   920
Bold deed thou hast presumed, adventurous Eve,
And peril great provoked, who thus hath dared
Had it been only coveting to eye
That sacred fruit, sacred to abstinence,
Much more to taste it under ban to touch.
But past who can recall, or done undo?
Not God omnipotent, nor fate, yet so
Perhaps thou shalt not die, perhaps the fact°
Is not so heinous now, foretasted fruit,
Profaned first by the serpent, by him first   930
Made common and unhallowed ere our taste;
Nor yet on him found deadly, he yet lives,
Lives, as thou saidst, and gains to live as man
Higher degree of life, inducement strong
To us, as likely tasting to attain
Proportional ascent, which cannot be
But to be gods, or angels demigods.
Nor can I think that God, creator wise,
Though threatening, will in earnest so destroy
Us his prime creatures, dignified so high,   940
Set over all his works, which in our fall,
For us created, needs with us must fail,
Dependent made; so God shall uncreate,
Be frustrate, do, undo, and labour lose,
Not well conceived of God, who though his power
Creation could repeat, yet would be loath
Us to abolish, lest the adversary
Triumph and say, Fickle their state whom God
Most favours, who can please him long; me first

He ruined, now mankind; whom will he next?   950
Matter of scorn, not to be given the foe,°
However I with thee have fixed my lot,
Certain to undergo like doom, if death°
Consort with thee, death is to me as life;
So forcible within my heart I feel
The bond of nature draw me to my own,
My own in thee, for what thou art is mine;
Our state cannot be severed, we are one,
One flesh; to lose thee were to lose my self.
  So Adam, and thus Eve to him replied.   960
O glorious trial of exceeding love,
Illustrious evidence, example high!
Engaging me to emulate, but short
Of thy perfection, how shall I attain,
Adam, from whose dear side I boast me sprung,
And gladly of our union hear thee speak,
One heart, one soul in both; whereof good proof
This day affords, declaring thee resolved,
Rather than death or aught than death more dread
Shall separate us, linked in love so dear,   970
To undergo with me one guilt, one crime,
If any be, of tasting this fair fruit,
Whose virtue, for of good still good proceeds,
Direct, or by occasion hath presented
This happy trial of thy love, which else
So eminently never had been known.
Were it I thought death menaced would ensue
This my attempt, I would sustain alone
The worst, and not persuade thee rather die
Deserted, than oblige thee with a fact°   980
Pernicious to thy peace, chiefly assured
Remarkably so late of thy so true,
So faithful love unequalled; but I feel
Far otherwise the event, not death, but life°
Augmented, opened eyes, new hopes, new joys,
Taste so divine, that what of sweet before
Hath touched my sense, flat seems to this, and harsh.°
On my experience, Adam, freely taste,
And fear of death deliver to the winds.
  So saying, she embraced him, and for joy   990

Tenderly wept, much won that he his love
Had so ennobled, as of choice to incur
Divine displeasure for her sake, or death.
In recompense (for such compliance bad
Such recompense best merits) from the bough
She gave him of that fair enticing fruit
With liberal hand: he scrupled not to eat
Against his better knowledge, not deceived,
But fondly overcome with female charm.°
Earth trembled from her entrails, as again   1000
In pangs, and nature gave a second groan,
Sky loured and muttering thunder, some sad drops
Wept at completing of the mortal sin
Original; while Adam took no thought,
Eating his fill, nor Eve to iterate
Her former trespass feared, the more to soothe
Him with her loved society, that now
As with new wine intoxicated both
They swim in mirth, and fancy that they feel
Divinity within them breeding wings   1010
Wherewith to scorn the earth: but that false fruit
Far other operation first displayed,
Carnal desire inflaming, he on Eve
Began to cast lascivious eyes, she him
As wantonly repaid; in lust they burn:
Till Adam thus gan Eve to dalliance move.°
    Eve, now I see thou art exact of taste,
And elegant, of sapience no small part,°
Since to each meaning savour we apply,°
And palate call judicious; I the praise   1020
Yield thee, so well this day thou hast purveyed.
Much pleasure we have lost, while we abstained
From this delightful fruit, nor known till now
True relish, tasting; if such pleasure be
In things to us forbidden, it might be wished,
For this one tree had been forbidden ten.
But come, so well refreshed, now let us play,
As meet is, after such delicious fare;°
For never did thy beauty since the day
I saw thee first and wedded thee, adorned   1030
With all perfections, so inflame my sense

With ardour to enjoy thee, fairer now
Than ever, bounty of this virtuous tree.
   So said he, and forbore not glance or toy°
Of amorous intent, well understood
Of Eve, whose eye darted contagious fire.
Her hand he seized, and to a shady bank,
Thick overhead with verdant roof embowered
He led her nothing loath; flowers were the couch,
Pansies, and violets, and asphodel,   1040
And hyacinth, earth's freshest softest lap.
There they their fill of love and love's disport
Took largely, of their mutual guilt the seal,
The solace of their sin, till dewy sleep
Oppressed them, wearied with their amorous play.
Soon as the force of that fallacious fruit,
That with exhilarating vapour bland°
About their spirits had played, and inmost powers
Made err, was now exhaled, and grosser sleep
Bred of unkindly fumes, with conscious dreams°   1050
Encumbered, now had left them, up they rose
As from unrest, and each the other viewing,
Soon found their eyes how opened, and their minds
How darkened; innocence, that as a veil
Had shadowed them from knowing ill, was gone,
Just confidence, and native righteousness
And honour from about them, naked left
To guilty shame he covered, but his robe
Uncovered more, so rose the Danite strong°
Herculean Samson from the harlot-lap   1060
Of Philistean Dalilah, and waked°
Shorn of his strength, they destitute and bare°
Of all their virtue: silent, and in face
Confounded long they sat, as stricken mute,
Till Adam, though not less than Eve abashed,
At length gave utterance to these words constrained.
   O Eve, in evil hour thou didst give ear
To that false worm, of whomsoever taught
To counterfeit man's voice, true in our fall,
False in our promised rising; since our eyes   1070
Opened we find indeed, and find we know
Both good and evil, good lost, and evil got,

Bad fruit of knowledge, if this be to know,
Which leaves us naked thus, of honour void,
Of innocence, of faith, of purity,
Our wonted ornaments now soiled and stained,
And in our faces evident the signs
Of foul concupiscence; whence evil store;°
Even shame, the last of evils; of the first
Be sure then. How shall I behold the face   1080
Henceforth of God or angel, erst with joy°
And rapture so oft beheld? those heavenly shapes
Will dazzle now this earthly, with their blaze
Insufferably bright. O might I here
In solitude live savage, in some glade
Obscured, where highest woods impenetrable
To star or sunlight, spread their umbrage broad
And brown as evening: cover me ye pines,
Ye cedars, with innumerable boughs
Hide me, where I may never see them more.   1090
But let us now, as in bad plight, devise
What best may for the present serve to hide
The parts of each from other, that seem most
To shame obnoxious, and unseemliest seen,°
Some tree whose broad smooth leaves together sewed,
And girded on our loins, may cover round
Those middle parts, that this newcomer, shame,
There sit not, and reproach us as unclean.
    So counselled he, and both together went
Into the thickest wood, there soon they chose   1100
The fig-tree, not that kind for fruit renowned,°
But such as at this day to Indians known
In Malabar or Deccan spreads her arms
Branching so broad and long, that in the ground
The bended twigs take root, and daughters grow
About the mother tree, a pillared shade
High overarched, and echoing walks between;
There oft the Indian herdsman shunning heat
Shelters in cool, and tends his pasturing herds
At loopholes cut through thickest shade: those leaves   1110
They gathered, broad as Amazonian targe,°
And with what skill they had, together sewed,
To gird their waist, vain covering if to hide

Their guilt and dreaded shame; O how unlike
To that first naked glory. Such of late
Columbus found the American so girt
With feathered cincture, naked else and wild
Among the trees on isles and woody shores.
Thus fenced, and as they thought, their shame in part
Covered, but not at rest or ease of mind,   1120
They sat them down to weep, nor only tears
Rained at their eyes, but high winds worse within
Began to rise, high passions, anger, hate,
Mistrust, suspicion, discord, and shook sore
Their inward state of mind, calm region once
And full of peace, now tossed and turbulent:
For understanding ruled not, and the will
Heard not her lore, both in subjection now
To sensual appetite, who from beneath
Usurping over sovereign reason claimed   1130
Superior sway: from thus distempered breast,
Adam, estranged in look and altered style,
Speech intermitted thus to Eve renewed.
    Would thou hadst hearkened to my words, and stayed
With me, as I besought thee, when that strange
Desire of wandering this unhappy morn,
I know not whence possessed thee; we had then
Remained still happy, not as now, despoiled
Of all our good, shamed, naked, miserable.
Let none henceforth seek needless cause to approve°   1140
The faith they owe; when earnestly they seek°
Such proof, conclude, they then begin to fail.
    To whom soon moved with touch of blame thus Eve.
What words have passed thy lips, Adam severe,
Imput'st thou that to my default, or will
Of wandering, as thou call'st it, which who knows
But might as ill have happened thou being by,
Or to thy self perhaps: hadst thou been there,
Or here the attempt, thou couldst not have discerned
Fraud in the serpent, speaking as he spake;   1150
No ground of enmity between us known,
Why he should mean me ill, or seek to harm.
Was I to have never parted from thy side?
As good have grown there still a lifeless rib.

Being as I am, why didst not thou the head
Command me absolutely not to go,
Going into such danger as thou saidst?
Too facile then thou didst not much gainsay,
Nay didst permit, approve, and fair dismiss.
Hadst thou been firm and fixed in thy dissent,   1160
Neither had I transgressed, nor thou with me.
     To whom then first incensed Adam replied,
Is this the love, is this the recompense
Of mine to thee, ingrateful Eve, expressed
Immutable when thou wert lost, not I,°
Who might have lived and joyed immortal bliss,
Yet willingly chose rather death with thee:
And am I now upbraided, as the cause
Of thy transgressing? not enough severe,
It seems, in thy restraint: what could I more?   1170
I warned thee, I admonished thee, foretold
The danger, and the lurking enemy
That lay in wait; beyond this had been force,
And force upon free will hath here no place.
But confidence then bore thee on, secure°
Either to meet no danger, or to find
Matter of glorious trial; and perhaps
I also erred in overmuch admiring
What seemed in thee so perfect, that I thought
No evil durst attempt thee, but I rue   1180
That error now, which is become my crime,
And thou the accuser. Thus it shall befall
Him who to worth in women overtrusting
Lets her will rule; restraint she will not brook,
And left to herself, if evil thence ensue,
She first his weak indulgence will accuse.
     Thus they in mutual accusation spent
The fruitless hours, but neither self-condemning,
And of their vain contest appeared no end.

BOOK X

The Argument

Man's transgression known, the guardian angels forsake Paradise, and return
up to heaven to approve their vigilance, and are approved, God declaring that

the entrance of Satan could not be by them prevented. He sends his son to judge the transgressors, who descends and gives sentence accordingly; then in pity clothes them both, and re-ascends. Sin and Death sitting till then at the gates of hell, by wondrous sympathy feeling the success of Satan in this new world, and the sin by man there committed, resolve to sit no longer confined in hell, but to follow Satan their sire up to the place of man: to make the way easier from hell to this world to and fro, they pave a broad highway or bridge over Chaos, according to the track that Satan first made; then preparing for earth, they meet him proud of his success returning to hell; their mutual gratulation. Satan arrives at Pandaemonium, in full assembly relates with boasting his success against man; instead of applause is entertained with a general hiss by all his audience, transformed with himself also suddenly into serpents, according to his doom given in Paradise; then deluded with a show of the forbidden tree springing up before them, they greedily reaching to take of the fruit, chew dust and bitter ashes. The proceedings of Sin and Death; God foretells the final victory of his son over them, and the renewing of all things; but for the present commands his angels to make several alterations in the heavens and elements. Adam more and more perceiving his fallen condition heavily bewails, rejects the condolement of Eve; she persists and at length appeases him: then to evade the curse likely to fall on their offspring, proposes to Adam violent ways which he approves not, but conceiving better hope, puts her in mind of the late promise made them, that her seed should be revenged on the serpent, and exhorts her with him to seek peace of the offended Deity, by repentance and supplication.

> Meanwhile the heinous and despiteful act
> Of Satan done in Paradise, and how
> He in the serpent, had perverted Eve,
> Her husband she, to taste the fatal fruit,
> Was known in heaven; for what can scape the eye
> Of God all-seeing, or deceive his heart
> Omniscient, who in all things wise and just,
> Hindered not Satan to attempt the mind
> Of man, with strength entire, and free will armed,
> Complete to have discovered and repulsed°   10
> Whatever wiles of foe or seeming friend.
> For still they knew, and ought to have still remembered°
> The high injunction not to taste that fruit,
> Whoever tempted; which they not obeying,
> Incurred, what could they less, the penalty,
> And manifold in sin, deserved to fall.
> Up into heaven from Paradise in haste
> The angelic guards ascended, mute and sad
> For man, for of his state by this they knew,°

Much wondering how the subtle fiend had stolen   20
Entrance unseen. Soon as the unwelcome news
From earth arrived at heaven gate, displeased
All were who heard, dim sadness did not spare
That time celestial visages, yet mixed
With pity, violated not their bliss.
About the new-arrived, in multitudes
The ethereal people ran, to hear and know
How all befell: they towards the throne supreme
Accountable made haste to make appear°
With righteous plea, their utmost vigilance,   30
And easily approved; when the most high°
Eternal Father from his secret cloud,
Amidst in thunder uttered thus his voice.
  Assembled angels, and ye powers returned
From unsuccessful charge, be not dismayed,
Nor troubled at these tidings from the earth,
Which your sincerest care could not prevent,
Foretold so lately what would come to pass,
When first this tempter crossed the gulf from hell.
I told ye then he should prevail and speed°   40
On his bad errand, man should be seduced
And flattered out of all, believing lies
Against his maker; no decree of mine
Concurring to necessitate his fall,
Or touch with lightest moment of impulse
His free will, to her own inclining left
In even scale. But fallen he is, and now
What rests but that the mortal sentence pass°
On his transgression, death denounced that day,°
Which he presumes already vain and void,   50
Because not yet inflicted, as he feared,
By some immediate stroke; but soon shall find
Forbearance no acquittance ere day end.°
Justice shall not return as bounty scorned.°
But whom send I to judge them? whom but thee
Vicegerent Son, to thee I have transferred
All judgment, whether in heaven, or earth, or hell.
Easy it might be seen that I intend
Mercy colleague with justice, sending thee
Man's friend, his mediator, his designed   60

Both ransom and redeemer voluntary,
And destined man himself to judge man fallen.
    So spake the Father, and unfolding bright
Toward the right hand his glory, on the Son
Blazed forth unclouded deity; he full
Resplendent all his father manifest
Expressed, and thus divinely answered mild.
    Father eternal, thine is to decree,
Mine both in heaven and earth to do thy will
Supreme, that thou in me thy son beloved   70
Mayst ever rest well pleased. I go to judge
On earth these thy transgressors, but thou know'st,
Whoever judged, the worst on me must light,
When time shall be, for so I undertook
Before thee; and not repenting, this obtain
Of right, that I may mitigate their doom
On me derived, yet I shall temper so°
Justice with mercy, as may illustrate most°
Them fully satisfied, and thee appease.°
Attendance none shall need, nor train, where none°   80
Are to behold the judgment, but the judged,
Those two; the third best absent is condemned,°
Convict by flight, and rebel to all law°
Conviction to the serpent none belongs.°
    Thus saying, from his radiant seat he rose
Of high collateral glory: him thrones and powers,
Princedoms, and dominations ministrant
Accompanied to heaven gate, from whence
Eden and all the coast in prospect lay.
Down he descended straight; the speed of gods   90
Time counts not, though with swiftest minutes winged.
Now was the sun in western cadence low°
From noon, and gentle airs due at their hour
To fan the earth now waked, and usher in
The evening cool when he from wrath more cool
Came the mild judge and intercessor both
To sentence man: the voice of God they heard°
Now walking in the garden, by soft winds
Brought to their ears, while day declined, they heard,
And from his presence hid themselves among   100
The thickest trees, both man and wife, till God

Approaching, thus to Adam called aloud.
Where art thou Adam, wont with joy to meet
My coming seen far off? I miss thee here,
Not pleased, thus entertained with solitude,
Where obvious duty erewhile appeared unsought:
Or come I less conspicuous, or what change
Absents thee, or what chance detains? Come forth.
He came, and with him Eve, more loath, though first
To offend, discountenanced both, and discomposed;   110
Love was not in their looks, either to God
Or to each other, but apparent guilt,
And shame, and perturbation, and despair,
Anger, and obstinacy, and hate, and guile.
Whence Adam faltering long, thus answered brief.
    I heard thee in the garden, and of thy voice
Afraid, being naked, hid myself. To whom
The gracious judge without revile replied.°
    My voice thou oft hast heard, and hast not feared,
But still rejoiced, how is it now become   120
So dreadful to thee? that thou art naked, who
Hath told thee? hast thou eaten of the tree
Whereof I gave thee charge thou shouldst not eat?
    To whom thus Adam sore beset replied.
O heaven! in evil strait this day I stand
Before my judge, either to undergo
My self the total crime, or to accuse
My other self, the partner of my life;
Whose failing, while her faith to me remains,
I should conceal, and not expose to blame   130
By my complaint; but strict necessity
Subdues me, and calamitous constraint
Lest on my head both sin and punishment,
However insupportable, be all
Devolved; though should I hold my peace, yet thou
Wouldst easily detect what I conceal.
This woman whom thou mad'st to be my help,
And gav'st me as thy perfect gift, so good,
So fit, so acceptable, so divine,
That from her hand I could suspect no ill,   140
And what she did, whatever in itself,
Her doing seemed to justify the deed;

She gave me of the tree, and I did eat.
    To whom the sovereign presence thus replied.
Was she thy God, that her thou didst obey
Before his voice, or was she made thy guide,
Superior, or but equal, that to her
Thou didst resign thy manhood, and the place
Wherein God set thee above her made of thee,
And for thee, whose perfection far excelled   150
Hers in all real dignity: adorned
She was indeed, and lovely to attract
Thy love, not thy subjection, and her gifts
Were such as under government well seemed,
Unseemly to bear rule, which was thy part
And person, hadst thou known thyself aright.°
    So having said, he thus to Eve in few:°
Say woman, what is this which thou hast done?
    To whom sad Eve with shame nigh overwhelmed,
Confessing soon, yet not before her judge   160
Bold or loquacious, thus abashed replied.
    The serpent me beguiled and I did eat.
    Which when the Lord God heard, without delay
To judgment he proceeded on the accused
Serpent though brute, unable to transfer
The guilt on him who made him instrument
Of mischief, and polluted from the end°
Of his creation; justly then accursed,
As vitiated in nature: more to know
Concerned not man (since he no further knew)   170
Nor altered his offence; yet God at last
To Satan first in sin his doom applied,
Though in mysterious terms, judged as then best:
And on the serpent thus his curse let fall.
    Because thou hast done this, thou art accursed
Above all cattle, each beast of the field;
Upon thy belly grovelling thou shalt go,
And dust shalt eat all the days of thy life.
Between thee and the woman I will put
Enmity, and between thine and her seed;   180
Her seed shall bruise thy head, thou bruise his heel.
    So spake this oracle, then verified
When Jesus son of Mary second Eve,

Saw Satan fall like lightning down from heaven,°
Prince of the air; then rising from his grave
Spoiled principalities and powers, triumphed
In open show, and with ascension bright°
Captivity led captive through the air,°
The realm itself of Satan long usurped,
Whom he shall tread at last under our feet;   190
Even he who now foretold his fatal bruise,
And to the woman thus his sentence turned.
    Thy sorrow I will greatly multiply
By thy conception; children thou shalt bring
In sorrow forth, and to thy husband's will
Thine shall submit, he over thee shall rule.
    On Adam last thus judgment he pronounced.
Because thou hast hearkened to the voice of thy wife,
And eaten of the tree concerning which
I charged thee, saying: Thou shalt not eat thereof,   200
Cursed is the ground for thy sake, thou in sorrow
Shalt eat thereof all the days of thy life;
Thorns also and thistles it shall bring thee forth
Unbid, and thou shalt eat the herb of the field,
In the sweat of thy face shalt thou eat bread,
Till thou return unto the ground, for thou
Out of the ground wast taken, know thy birth,
For dust thou art, and shalt to dust return.°
    So judged he man, both judge and saviour sent,
And the instant stroke of death denounced that day°   210
Removed far off; then pitying how they stood
Before him naked to the air, that now
Must suffer change, disdained not to begin
Thenceforth the form of servant to assume,
As when he washed his servants' feet so now°
As father of his family he clad
Their nakedness with skins of beasts, or slain,
Or as the snake with youthful coat repaid;°
And thought not much to clothe his enemies:
Nor he their outward only with the skins   220
Of beasts, but inward nakedness, much more
Opprobrious, with his robe of righteousness,
Arraying covered from his father's sight.
To him with swift ascent he up returned,

Into his blissful bosom reassumed
In glory as of old, to him appeased
All, though all-knowing, what had passed with man
Recounted, mixing intercession sweet.
Meanwhile ere thus was sinned and judged on earth,
Within the gates of hell sat Sin and Death,   230
In counterview within the gates, that now°
Stood open wide, belching outrageous flame
Far into Chaos, since the fiend passed through,
Sin opening, who thus now to Death began.
    O son, why sit we here each other viewing
Idly, while Satan our great author thrives
In other worlds, and happier seat provides
For us his offspring dear? It cannot be
But that success attends him; if mishap,
Ere this he had returned, with fury driven   240
By his avengers, since no place like this
Can fit his punishment, or their revenge.°
Methinks I feel new strength within me rise,
Wings growing, and dominion given me large
Beyond this deep; whatever draws me on,
Or sympathy, or some connatural force°
Powerful at greatest distance to unite
With secret amity things of like kind
By secretest conveyance. Thou my shade°
Inseparable must with me along: 250
For Death from Sin no power can separate.
But lest the difficulty of passing back
Stay his return perhaps over this gulf
Impassable, impervious, let us try
Adventurous work, yet to thy power and mine
Not unagreeable, to found a path
Over this main from hell to that new world°
Where Satan now prevails, a monument
Of merit high to all the infernal host,
Easing their passage hence, for intercourse,°   260
Or transmigration, as their lot shall lead.°
Nor can I miss the way, so strongly drawn
By this new-felt attraction and instinct.
    Whom thus the meagre shadow answered soon.
Go whither fate and inclination strong

Leads thee, I shall not lag behind, nor err
The way, thou leading, such a scent I draw
Of carnage, prey innumerable, and taste
The savour of death from all things there that live:
Nor shall I to the work thou enterprisest   270
Be wanting, but afford thee equal aid.
    So saying, with delight he snuffed the smell°
Of mortal change on earth. As when a flock
Of ravenous fowl, though many a league remote,
Against the day of battle, to a field,°
Where armies lie encamped, come flying, lured
With scent of living carcasses designed°
For death, the following day, in bloody fight.
So scented the grim feature, and upturned°
His nostril wide into the murky air,   280
Sagacious of his quarry from so far.°
Then both from out hell gates into the waste
Wide anarchy of Chaos damp and dark
Flew diverse, and with power (their power was great)°
Hovering upon the waters; what they met
Solid or slimy, as in raging sea
Tossed up and down, together crowded drove
From each side shoaling towards the mouth of hell.°
As when two polar winds blowing adverse
Upon the Cronian sea, together drive°   290
Mountains of ice, that stop the imagined way°
Beyond Petsora eastward, to the rich°
Cathayan coast. The aggregated soil
Death with his mace petrific, cold and dry,°
As with a trident smote, and fixed as firm°
As Delos floating once; the rest his look°
Bound with Gorgonian rigor not to move,°
And with asphaltic slime; broad as the gate,°
Deep to the roots of hell the gathered beach
They fastened, and the mole immense wrought on°   300
Over the foaming deep high arched, a bridge
Of length prodigious joining to the wall°
Immovable of this now fenceless world°
Forfeit to Death; from hence a passage broad,
Smooth, easy, inoffensive down to hell.°
So, if great things to small may be compared,

Xerxes, the liberty of Greece to yoke,
From Susa his Memnonian palace high°
Came to the sea, and over Hellespont°
Bridging his way, Europe with Asia joined,   310
And scourged with many a stroke the indignant waves.°
Now had they brought the work by wondrous art
Pontifical, a ridge of pendent rock°
Over the vexed abyss, following the track°
Of Satan, to the selfsame place where he
First lighted from his wing, and landed safe
From out of Chaos to the outside bare
Of this round world: with pins of adamant°
And chains they made all fast, too fast they made
And durable; and now in little space   320
The confines met of empyrean heaven°
And of this world, and on the left hand hell
With long reach interposed; three several ways
In sight, to each of these three places led.
And now their way to earth they had descried,
To Paradise first tending, when behold
Satan in likeness of an angel bright
Betwixt the Centaur and the Scorpion steering°
His zenith, while the sun in Aries rose:
Disguised he came, but those his children dear   330
Their parent soon discerned, though in disguise.
He after Eve seduced, unminded slunk°
Into the wood fast by, and changing shape
To observe the sequel, saw his guileful act
By Eve, though all unweeting, seconded
Upon her husband, saw their shame that sought
Vain covertures; but when he saw descend
The Son of God to judge them terrified
He fled, not hoping to escape, but shun
The present, fearing guilty what his wrath   340
Might suddenly inflict; that past, returned
By night, and listening where the hapless pair
Sat in their sad discourse, and various plaint,
Thence gathered his own doom, which understood
Not instant, but of future time. With joy
And tidings fraught, to hell he now returned,
And at the brink of Chaos, near the foot

Of this new wondrous pontifice, unhoped°
Met who to meet him came, his offspring dear.
Great joy was at their meeting, and at sight   350
Of that stupendous bridge his joy increased.
Long he admiring stood, till Sin, his fair
Enchanting daughter, thus the silence broke.
    O parent, these are thy magnific deeds,
Thy trophies, which thou view'st as not thine own,
Thou art their author and prime architect:
For I no sooner in my heart divined,
My heart, which by a secret harmony
Still moves with thine, joined in connection sweet,
That thou on earth hadst prospered, which thy looks   360
Now also evidence, but straight I felt
Though distant from thee worlds between, yet felt
That I must after thee with this thy son;
Such fatal consequence unites us three:
Hell could no longer hold us in her bounds,
Nor this unvoyageable gulf obscure
Detain from following thy illustrious track.
Thou hast achieved our liberty, confined
Within hell gates till now, thou us empowered
To fortify thus far, and overlay°   370
With this portentous bridge the dark abyss.°
Thine now is all this world, thy virtue hath won°
What thy hands builded not, thy wisdom gained
With odds what war hath lost, and fully avenged°
Our foil in heaven; here thou shalt monarch reign,°
There didst not; there let him still victor sway,
As battle hath adjudged, from this new world
Retiring, by his own doom alienated,°
And henceforth monarchy with thee divide
Of all things parted by the empyreal bounds,   380
His quadrature, from thy orbicular world,°
Or try thee now more dangerous to his throne.°
    Whom thus the prince of darkness answered glad.
Fair daughter, and thou son and grandchild both,°
High proof ye now have given to be the race
Of Satan (for I glory in the name,
Antagonist of heaven's almighty king)°
Amply have merited of me, of all

The infernal empire, that so near heaven's door
Triumphal with triumphal act have met,   390
Mine with this glorious work, and made one realm
Hell and this world, one realm, one continent
Of easy thoroughfare. Therefore while I
Descend through darkness, on your road with ease
To my associate powers, them to acquaint
With these successes, and with them rejoice,
You two this way, among these numerous orbs
All yours, right down to Paradise descend;
There dwell and reign in bliss, thence on the earth
Dominion exercise and in the air,   400
Chiefly on man, sole lord of all declared,
Him first make sure your thrall, and lastly kill.
My substitutes I send ye, and create
Plenipotent on earth, of matchless might°
Issuing from me: on your joint vigour now
My hold of this new kingdom all depends,
Through Sin to Death exposed by my exploit.
If your joint power prevails, the affairs of hell
No detriment need fear, go and be strong.
    So saying he dismissed them, they with speed   410
Their course through thickest constellations held
Spreading their bane; the blasted stars looked wan,
And planets, planet-struck, real eclipse°
Then suffered. The other way Satan went down
The causeway to hell gate; on either side
Disparted Chaos over-built exclaimed,
And with rebounding surge the bars assailed,
That scorned his indignation: through the gate,°
Wide open and unguarded, Satan passed,
And all about found desolate; for those   420
Appointed to sit there, had left their charge,
Flown to the upper world; the rest were all
Far to the inland retired, about the walls
Of Pandaemonium, city and proud seat
Of Lucifer, so by allusion called,
Of that bright star to Satan paragoned.°
There kept their watch the legions, while the grand
In council sat, solicitous what chance°
Might intercept their emperor sent, so he

Departing gave command, and they observed.   430
As when the Tartar from his Russian foe
By Astrakhan over the snowy plains°
Retires, or Bactrian sophy from the horns°
Of Turkish crescent, leaves all waste beyond°
The realm of Aladule, in his retreat°
To Tauris or Casbeen. So these the late°
Heaven-banished host, left desert utmost hell°
Many a dark league, reduced in careful watch°
Round their metropolis, and now expecting
Each hour their great adventurer from the search   440
Of foreign worlds: he through the midst unmarked,
In show plebeian angel militant°
Of lowest order, passed; and from the door
Of that Plutonian hall, invisible°
Ascended his high throne, which under state°
Of richest texture spread, at the upper end
Was placed in regal lustre. Down awhile
He sat, and round about him saw unseen:
At last as from a cloud his fulgent head°
And shape star-bright appeared, or brighter, clad   450
With what permissive glory since his fall
Was left him, or false glitter: all amazed
At that so sudden blaze the Stygian throng
Bent their aspect, and whom they wished beheld,
Their mighty chief returned: loud was the acclaim:
Forth rushed in haste the great consulting peers,
Raised from their dark divan, and with like joy°
Congratulant approached him, who with hand
Silence, and with these words attention won.
    Thrones, dominations, princedoms, virtues, powers,   460
For in possession such, not only of right,
I call ye and declare ye now, returned
Successful beyond hope, to lead ye forth
Triumphant out of this infernal pit
Abominable, accursed, the house of woe,
And dungeon of our tyrant: now possess,
As lords, a spacious world, to our native heaven
Little inferior, by my adventure hard
With peril great achieved. Long were to tell
What I have done, what suffered, with what pain   470

Voyaged the unreal, vast, unbounded deep
Of horrible confusion, over which
By Sin and Death a broad way now is paved
To expedite your glorious march; but I
Toiled out my uncouth passage, forced to ride°
The untractable abyss, plunged in the womb
Of unoriginal Night and Chaos wild,°
That jealous of their secrets fiercely opposed°
My journey strange, with clamorous uproar
Protesting fate supreme; thence how I found   480
The new created world, which fame in heaven°
Long had foretold, a fabric wonderful
Of absolute perfection, therein man
Placed in a paradise, by our exile
Made happy: him by fraud I have seduced
From his creator, and the more to increase
Your wonder, with an apple; he thereat
Offended, worth your laughter, hath given up
Both his belovèd man and all his world,
To Sin and Death a prey, and so to us,   490
Without our hazard, labour, or alarm,
To range in, and to dwell, and over man
To rule, as over all he should have ruled.
True is, me also he hath judged, or rather
Me not, but the brute serpent in whose shape
Man I deceived: that which to me belongs,
Is enmity, which he will put between
Me and mankind; I am to bruise his heel;
His seed, when is not set, shall bruise my head:°
A world who would not purchase with a bruise,   500
Or much more grievous pain? Ye have the account
Of my performance: what remains, ye gods,
But up and enter now into full bliss.
    So having said, a while he stood, expecting
Their universal shout and high applause
To fill his ear, when contrary he hears
On all sides, from innumerable tongues
A dismal universal hiss, the sound
Of public scorn; he wondered, but not long
Had leisure, wondering at himself now more;   510
His visage drawn he felt to sharp and spare,

His arms clung to his ribs, his legs entwining
Each other, till supplanted down he fell°
A monstrous serpent on his belly prone,
Reluctant, but in vain, a greater power°
Now ruled him, punished in the shape he sinned,
According to his doom: he would have spoke,°
But hiss for hiss returned with forkèd tongue
To forkèd tongue, for now were all transformed
Alike, to serpents all as accessories   520
To his bold riot: dreadful was the din°
Of hissing through the hall, thick swarming now
With complicated monsters head and tail,°
Scorpion and asp, and amphisbaena dire,°
Cerastes horned, hydrus, and ellops drear,°
And dipsas (not so thick swarmed once the soil°
Bedropped with blood of Gorgon, or the isle°
Ophiusa) but still greatest he the midst,°
Now dragon grown, larger than whom the sun°
Engendered in the Pythian vale on slime,   530
Huge Python, and his power no less he seemed°
Above the rest still to retain; they all
Him followed issuing forth to the open field,
Where all yet left of that revolted rout
Heaven-fallen, in station stood or just array,°
Sublime with expectation when to see°
In triumph issuing forth their glorious chief;
They saw, but other sight instead, a crowd
Of ugly serpents; horror on them fell,
And horrid sympathy; for what they saw,   540
They felt themselves now changing; down their arms,
Down fell both spear and shield, down they as fast,
And the dire hiss renewed, and the dire form
Catched by contagion, like in punishment,
As in their crime. Thus was the applause they meant,
Turned to exploding hiss, triumph to shame°
Cast on themselves from their own mouths. There stood
A grove hard by, sprung up with this their change,
His will who reigns above, to aggravate
Their penance, laden with fair fruit, like that   550
Which grew in Paradise, the bait of Eve
Used by the tempter: on that prospect strange

Their earnest eyes they fixed, imagining
For one forbidden tree a multitude
Now risen, to work them further woe or shame;
Yet parched with scalding thirst and hunger fierce,
Though to delude them sent, could not abstain,
But on they rolled in heaps, and up the trees
Climbing, sat thicker than the snaky locks
That curled Megaera: greedily they plucked°   560
The fruitage fair to sight, like that which grew
Near that bituminous lake where Sodom flamed;
This more delusive, not the touch, but taste
Deceived; they fondly thinking to allay
Their appetite with gust, instead of fruit°
Chewed bitter ashes, which the offended taste
With spattering noise rejected: oft they assayed,
Hunger and thirst constraining, drugged as oft,°
With hatefulest disrelish writhed their jaws
With soot and cinders filled; so oft they fell   570
Into the same illusion, not as man
Whom they triumphed once lapsed. Thus were they plagued°
And worn with famine, long and ceaseless hiss,
Till their lost shape, permitted, they resumed,
Yearly enjoined, some say, to undergo
This annual humbling certain numbered days,
To dash their pride, and joy for man seduced.
However some tradition they dispersed
Among the heathen of their purchase got,°
And fabled how the serpent, whom they called   580
Ophion with Eurynome, the wide-°
Encroaching Eve perhaps, had first the rule
Of high Olympus, thence by Saturn driven
And Ops, ere yet Dictaean Jove was born.°
Meanwhile in Paradise the hellish pair
Too soon arrived, Sin there in power before,°
Once actual, now in body, and to dwell°
Habitual habitant; behind her Death
Close following pace for pace, not mounted yet
On his pale horse; to whom Sin thus began.°   590
    Second of Satan sprung, all-conquering Death,
What think'st thou of our empire now, though earned
With travail difficult, not better far

Than still at hell's dark threshold to have sat watch,
Unnamed, undreaded, and thy self half starved?
    Whom thus the Sin-born monster answered soon.
To me, who with eternal famine pine,
Alike is hell, or Paradise, or heaven,
There best, where most with ravin I may meet;°
Which here, though plenteous, all too little seems   600
To stuff this maw, this vast unhide-bound corpse.°
    To whom the incestuous mother thus replied.
Thou therefore on these herbs, and fruits, and flowers
Feed first, on each beast next, and fish, and fowl,
No homely morsels, and whatever thing
The scythe of time mows down, devour unspared,
Till I in man residing through the race,
His thoughts, his looks, words, actions all infect,
And season him thy last and sweetest prey.
    This said, they both betook them several ways,   610
Both to destroy, or unimmortal make
All kinds, and for destruction to mature
Sooner or later; which the almighty seeing,
From his transcendent seat the saints among,
To those bright orders uttered thus his voice.
    See with what heat these dogs of hell advance
To waste and havoc yonder world, which I
So fair and good created, and had still
Kept in that state, had not the folly of man
Let in these wasteful furies, who impute   620
Folly to me, so doth the prince of hell
And his adherents, that with so much ease
I suffer them to enter and possess
A place so heavenly, and conniving seem°
To gratify my scornful enemies,
That laugh, as if transported with some fit
Of passion, I to them had quitted all,°
At random yielded up to their misrule;
And know not that I called and drew them thither
My hell-hounds, to lick up the draff and filth°   630
Which man's polluting sin with taint hath shed
On what was pure, till crammed and gorged, nigh burst
With sucked and glutted offal, at one sling
Of thy victorious arm, well-pleasing Son,

Both Sin, and Death, and yawning grave at last
Through Chaos hurled, obstruct the mouth of hell
Forever, and seal up his ravenous jaws.
Then heaven and earth renewed shall be made pure
To sanctity that shall receive no stain:
Till then the curse pronounced on both precedes.°   640
    He ended, and the heavenly audience loud
Sung hallelujah, as the sound of seas,
Through multitude that sung: Just are thy ways,
Righteous are thy decrees on all thy works;
Who can extenuate thee? Next, to the Son,°
Destined restorer of mankind, by whom
New heaven and earth shall to the ages rise,
Or down from heaven descend. Such was their song,
While the creator calling forth by name
His mighty angels gave them several charge,   650
As sorted best with present things. The sun°
Had first his precept so to move, so shine,
As might affect the earth with cold and heat
Scarce tolerable, and from the north to call
Decrepit winter, from the south to bring
Solstitial summer's heat. To the blank moon°
Her office they prescribed, to the other five°
Their planetary motions and aspects°
In sextile, square, and trine, and opposite,
Of noxious efficacy, and when to join°   660
In synod unbenign, and taught the fixed°
Their influence malignant when to shower,
Which of them rising with the sun, or falling,
Should prove tempestuous: to the winds they set
Their corners, when with bluster to confound°
Sea, air, and shore, the thunder when to roll
With terror through the dark aerial hall.
Some say he bid his angels turn askance
The poles of earth twice ten degrees and more
From the sun's axle; they with labour pushed   670
Oblique the centric globe: some say the sun°
Was bid turn reins from the equinoctial road°
Like distant breadth to Taurus with the Seven°
Atlantic Sisters, and the Spartan Twins°
Up to the tropic Crab; thence down amain°

By Leo and the Virgin and the Scales,°
As deep as Capricorn, to bring in change
Of seasons to each clime; else had the spring
Perpetual smiled on earth with vernant flowers,°
Equal in days and nights, except to those°   680
Beyond the polar circles; to them day
Had unbenighted shone, while the low sun
To recompense his distance, in their sight
Had rounded still the horizon, and not known
Or east or west, which had forbid the snow
From cold Estotiland, and south as far°
Beneath Magellan. At that tasted fruit°
The sun, as from Thyestean banquet, turned
His course intended; else how had the world°
Inhabited, though sinless, more than now,   690
Avoided pinching cold and scorching heat?
These changes in the heavens, though slow, produced
Like change on sea and land, sideral blast,°
Vapour, and mist, and exhalation hot,
Corrupt and pestilent: now from the north
Of Norumbega, and the Samoed shore°
Bursting their brazen dungeon, armed with ice
And snow and hail and stormy gust and flaw,°
Boreas, and Caecias and Argestes loud°
And Thrascias rend the woods and seas upturn;   700
With adverse blast upturns them from the south
Notus and Afer black with thunderous clouds
From Serraliona; thwart of these as fierce°
Forth rush the levant and the ponent winds°
Eurus and Zephyr, with their lateral noise,
Sirocco, and Libecchio, thus began°
Outrage from lifeless things; but Discord first
Daughter of Sin, among the irrational,
Death introduced through fierce antipathy:
Beast now with beast gan war, and fowl with fowl,   710
And fish with fish; to graze the herb all leaving,
Devoured each other; nor stood much in awe
Of man but fled him, or with countenance grim
Glared on him passing: these were from without
The growing miscries, which Adam saw
Already in part, though hid in gloomiest shade,

To sorrow abandoned, but worse felt within,
And in a troubled sea of passion tossed,
Thus to disburden sought with sad complaint.
   O miserable of happy! is this the end   720
Of this new glorious world, and me so late
The glory of that glory, who now become
Accursed of blessed, hide me from the face
Of God, whom to behold was then my height
Of happiness: yet well, if here would end
The misery, I deserved it, and would bear
My own deservings; but this will not serve;
All that I eat or drink, or shall beget,
Is propagated curse. O voice once heard°
Delightfully, *Increase and multiply*,   730
Now death to hear! for what can I increase
Or multiply, but curses on my head?
Who of all ages to succeed, but feeling
The evil on him brought by me, will curse
My head, Ill fare our ancestor impure,
For this we may thank Adam; but his thanks
Shall be the execration; so besides
Mine own that bide upon me, all from me°
Shall with a fierce reflux on me redound,
On me as on their natural centre light   740
Heavy, though in their place. O fleeting joys
Of Paradise, dear bought with lasting woes!
Did I request thee, maker, from my clay
To mould me man, did I solicit thee
From darkness to promote me, or here place
In this delicious garden? as my will
Concurred not to my being, it were but right
And equal to reduce me to my dust,°
Desirous to resign, and render back
All I received, unable to perform   750
Thy terms too hard, by which I was to hold
The good I sought not. To the loss of that,
Sufficient penalty, why hast thou added
The sense of endless woes? inexplicable
Thy justice seems; yet to say truth, too late,
I thus contest; then should have been refused
Those terms whatever, when they were proposed:

Thou didst accept them; wilt thou enjoy the good,
Then cavil the conditions? and though God
Made thee without thy leave, what if thy son   760
Prove disobedient, and reproved, retort,
Wherefore didst thou beget me? I sought it not:
Wouldst thou admit for his contempt of thee
That proud excuse? yet him not thy election,°
But natural necessity begot.
God made thee of choice his own, and of his own°
To serve him, thy reward was of his grace,
Thy punishment then justly is at his will.
Be it so, for I submit, his doom is fair,
That dust I am, and shall to dust return: 770
O welcome hour whenever! why delays
His hand to execute what his decree
Fixed on this day? why do I overlive,
Why am I mocked with death, and lengthened out
To deathless pain? how gladly would I meet
Mortality my sentence, and be earth
Insensible, how glad would lay me down
As in my mother's lap? there I should rest
And sleep secure; his dreadful voice no more
Would thunder in my ears, no fear of worse   780
To me and to my offspring would torment me
With cruel expectation. Yet one doubt
Pursues me still, lest all I cannot die,°
Lest that pure breath of life, the spirit of man
Which God inspired, cannot together perish
With this corporeal clod; then in the grave,
Or in some other dismal place who knows
But I shall die a living death? O thought
Horrid, if true! yet why? it was but breath
Of life that sinned; what dies but what had life   790
And sin? the body properly hath neither.
All of me then shall die: let this appease
The doubt, since human reach no further knows.
For though the Lord of all be infinite,
Is his wrath also? be it, man is not so,°
But mortal doomed. How can he exercise
Wrath without end on man whom death must end?
Can he make deathless death? that were to make

Strange contradiction, which to God himself
Impossible is held, as argument   800
Of weakness, not of power. Will he draw out,
For anger's sake, finite to infinite
In punished man, to satisfy his rigour
Satisfied never; that were to extend
His sentence beyond dust and nature's law,
By which all causes else according still
To the reception of their matter act,
Not to the extent of their own sphere. But say°
That death be not one stroke, as I supposed,
Bereaving sense, but endless misery   810
From this day onward, which I feel begun
Both in me, and without me, and so last
To perpetuity; ay me, that fear
Comes thundering back with dreadful revolution
On my defenceless head; both death and I
Am found eternal, and incorporate both,°
Nor I on my part single, in me all°
Posterity stands cursed: fair patrimony
That I must leave ye, sons; O were I able
To waste it all my self, and leave ye none!   820
So disinherited how would ye bless
Me now your curse! Ah, why should all mankind
For one man's fault thus guiltless be condemned,
If guiltless? But from me what can proceed,
But all corrupt, both mind and will depraved,
Not to do only, but to will the same
With me? how can they then acquitted stand
In sight of God? Him after all disputes
Forced I absolve: all my evasions vain,
And reasonings, though through mazes, lead me still   830
But to my own conviction: first and last
On me, me only, as the source and spring
Of all corruption, all the blame lights due;
So might the wrath. Fond wish! couldst thou support°
That burden heavier than the earth to bear,
Than all the world much heavier, though divided
With that bad woman? Thus what thou desir'st
And what thou fear'st, alike destroys all hope
Of refuge, and concludes thee miserable

Beyond all past example and future,   840
To Satan only like both crime and doom.
O conscience, into what abyss of fears
And horrors hast thou driven me; out of which
I find no way, from deep to deeper plunged!
   Thus Adam to himself lamented loud
Through the still night, not now, as ere man fell,
Wholesome and cool, and mild, but with black air
Accompanied, with damps and dreadful gloom,
Which to his evil conscience represented
All things with double terror: on the ground   850
Outstretched he lay, on the cold ground, and oft
Cursed his creation, death as oft accused
Of tardy execution, since denounced°
The day of his offence. Why comes not death,
Said he, with one thrice acceptable stroke
To end me? Shall truth fail to keep her word,
Justice divine not hasten to be just?
But death comes not at call, justice divine
Mends not her slowest pace for prayers or cries.
O woods, O fountains, hillocks, dales and bowers,   860
With other echo late I taught your shades
To answer, and resound far other song.
Whom thus afflicted when sad Eve beheld,
Desolate where she sat, approaching nigh
Soft words to his fierce passion she assayed:
But her with stern regard he thus repelled.
   Out of my sight, thou serpent, that name best°
Befits thee with him leagued, thyself as false
And hateful; nothing wants, but that thy shape,°
Like his, and colour serpentine may show   870
Thy inward fraud, to warn all creatures from thee
Henceforth; lest that too heavenly form, pretended
To hellish falsehood, snare them. But for thee°
I had persisted happy, had not thy pride
And wand'ring vanity, when least was safe,
Rejected my forewarning, and disdained
Not to be trusted, longing to be seen
Though by the devil himself, him overweening
To over-reach, but with the serpent meeting°
Fooled and beguiled, by him thou, I by thee,   880

To trust thee from my side, imagined wise,
Constant, mature, proof against all assaults,
And understood not all was but a show
Rather than solid virtue, all but a rib
Crooked by nature, bent, as now appears,
More to the part sinister from me drawn,°
Well if thrown out, as supernumerary
To my just number found. O why did God,°
Creator wise, that peopled highest heaven
With spirits masculine, create at last   890
This novelty on earth, this fair defect
Of nature, and not fill the world at once
With men as angels without feminine,
Or find some other way to generate
Mankind? this mischief had not then befallen,
And more that shall befall, innumerable
Disturbances on earth through female snares,
And strait conjunction with this sex: for either°
He never shall find out fit mate, but such
As some misfortune brings him, or mistake,   900
Or whom he wishes most shall seldom gain
Through her perverseness, but shall see her gained
By a far worse, or if she love, withheld
By parents, or his happiest choice too late
Shall meet, already linked and wedlock-bound
To a fell adversary, his hate or shame:
Which infinite calamity shall cause
To human life, and household peace confound.
    He added not, and from her turned, but Eve
Not so repulsed, with tears that ceased not flowing,   910
And tresses all disordered, at his feet
Fell humble, and embracing them, besought
His peace, and thus proceeded in her plaint.
    Forsake me not thus, Adam, witness heaven
What love sincere, and reverence in my heart
I bear thee, and unweeting have offended,
Unhappily deceived; thy suppliant
I beg, and clasp thy knees; bereave me not,
Whereon I live, thy gentle looks, thy aid,
Thy counsel in this uttermost distress,   920
My only strength and stay: forlorn of thee,

Whither shall I betake me, where subsist?
While yet we live, scarce one short hour perhaps,
Between us two let there be peace, both joining,
As joined in injuries, one enmity
Against a foe by doom express assigned us,°
That cruel serpent: on me exercise not
Thy hatred for this misery befallen,
On me already lost, me than thyself
More miserable; both have sinned, but thou   930
Against God only, I against God and thee,
And to the place of judgment will return,
There with my cries importune heaven, that all
The sentence from thy head removed may light
On me, sole cause to thee of all this woe,
Me me only just object of his ire.
    She ended weeping, and her lowly plight,
Immovable till peace obtained from fault
Acknowledged and deplored, in Adam wrought
Commiseration; soon his heart relented   940
Towards her, his life so late and sole delight,
Now at his feet submissive in distress,
Creature so fair his reconcilement seeking,
His counsel whom she had displeased, his aid;
As one disarmed, his anger all he lost,
And thus with peaceful words upraised her soon.
    Unwary, and too desirous, as before,
So now of what thou know'st not, who desir'st
The punishment all on thyself; alas,
Bear thine own first, ill able to sustain   950
His full wrath whose thou feel'st as yet least part,
And my displeasure bear'st so ill. If prayers
Could alter high decrees, I to that place
Would speed before thee, and be louder heard,
That on my head all might be visited,
Thy frailty and infirmer sex forgiven,
To me committed and by me exposed.
But rise, let us no more contend, nor blame
Each other, blamed enough elsewhere, but strive
In offices of love, how we may lighten   960
Each other's burden in our share of woe;
Since this day's death denounced, if aught I see,

Will prove no sudden, but a slow-paced evil,
A long day's dying to augment our pain,
And to our seed (O hapless seed!) derived.°
    To whom thus Eve, recovering heart, replied.
Adam, by sad experiment I know
How little weight my words with thee can find,
Found so erroneous, thence by just event
Found so unfortunate; nevertheless,   970
Restored by thee, vile as I am, to place
Of new acceptance, hopeful to regain
Thy love, the sole contentment of my heart
Living or dying, from thee I will not hide
What thoughts in my unquiet breast are risen,
Tending to some relief of our extremes,
Or end, though sharp and sad, yet tolerable,
As in our evils, and of easier choice.°
If care of our descent perplex us most,°
Which must be born to certain woe, devoured   980
By death at last, and miserable it is
To be to others cause of misery,
Our own begotten, and of our loins to bring
Into this cursèd world a woeful race,
That after wretched life must be at last
Food for so foul a monster, in thy power
It lies, yet ere conception to prevent
The race unblest, to being yet unbegot.
Childless thou art, childless remain: so death°
Shall be deceived his glut, and with us two°   990
Be forced to satisfy his ravenous maw.
But if thou judge it hard and difficult,
Conversing, looking, loving, to abstain°
From love's due rights, nuptial embraces sweet,
And with desire to languish without hope,
Before the present object languishing°
With like desire, which would be misery
And torment less than none of what we dread,
Then both ourselves and seed at once to free
From what we fear for both, let us make short,°   1000
Let us seek death, or he not found, supply
With our own hands his office on ourselves;
Why stand we longer shivering under fears,

That show no end but death, and have the power,
Of many ways to die the shortest choosing,
Destruction with destruction to destroy.
   She ended here, or vehement despair
Broke off the rest; so much of death her thoughts
Had entertained, as dyed her cheeks with pale.
But Adam with such counsel nothing swayed,   1010
To better hopes his more attentive mind
Labouring had raised, and thus to Eve replied.
   Eve, thy contempt of life and pleasures seems
To argue in thee something more sublime
And excellent than what thy mind contemns;
But self-destruction therefore sought, refutes
That excellence thought in thee, and implies,
Not thy contempt, but anguish and regret
For loss of life and pleasure overloved.
Or if thou covet death, as utmost end   1020
Of misery, so thinking to evade
The penalty pronounced, doubt not but God
Hath wiselier armed his vengeful ire than so
To be forestalled; much more I fear lest death
So snatched will not exempt us from the pain
We are by doom to pay; rather such acts
Of contumacy will provoke the highest°
To make death in us live: then let us seek
Some safer resolution, which methinks
I have in view, calling to mind with heed   1030
Part of our sentence, that thy seed shall bruise
The serpent's head; piteous amends, unless
Be meant, whom I conjecture, our grand foe
Satan, who in the serpent hath contrived
Against us this deceit: to crush his head
Would be revenge indeed; which will be lost
By death brought on ourselves, or childless days
Resolved, as thou proposest; so our foe
Shall scape his punishment ordained, and we
Instead shall double ours upon our heads.   1040
No more be mentioned then of violence
Against ourselves, and wilful barrenness,
That cuts us off from hope, and savours only
Rancour and pride, impatience and despite,

Reluctance against God and his just yoke°
Laid on our necks. Remember with what mild
And gracious temper he both heard and judged
Without wrath or reviling; we expected
Immediate dissolution, which we thought
Was meant by death that day, when lo, to thee   1050
Pains only in child-bearing were foretold,
And bringing forth, soon recompensed with joy,
Fruit of thy womb: on me the curse aslope°
Glanced on the ground, with labour I must earn
My bread; what harm? Idleness had been worse;
My labour will sustain me; and lest cold
Or heat should injure us, his timely care
Hath unbesought provided, and his hands
Clothed us unworthy, pitying while he judged;
How much more, if we pray him, will his ear   1060
Be open, and his heart to pity incline,
And teach us further by what means to shun
The inclement seasons, rain, ice, hail and snow,
Which now the sky with various face begins
To show us in this mountain, while the winds
Blow moist and keen, shattering the graceful locks
Of these fair spreading trees; which bids us seek
Some better shroud, some better warmth to cherish°
Our limbs benumbed, ere this diurnal star°
Leave cold the night, how we his gathered beams°   1070
Reflected, may with matter sere foment,°
Or by collision of two bodies grind
The air attrite to fire, as late the clouds°
Jostling or pushed with winds rude in their shock
Tine the slant lightning, whose thwart flame driven down°
Kindles the gummy bark of fir or pine,
And sends a comfortable heat from far,
Which might supply the sun: such fire to use°
And what may else be remedy or cure
To evils which our own misdeeds have wrought,   1080
He will instruct us praying, and of grace
Beseeching him, so as we need not fear°
To pass commodiously this life, sustained
By him with many comforts, till we end
In dust, our final rest and native home.

What better can we do, than to the place
Repairing where he judged us, prostrate fall
Before him reverent, and there confess
Humbly our faults, and pardon beg, with tears
Watering the ground, and with our sighs the air   1090
Frequenting, sent from hearts contrite, in sign°
Of sorrow unfeigned, and humiliation meek.
Undoubtedly he will relent and turn
From his displeasure; in whose look serene,
When angry most he seemed and most severe,
What else but favour, grace, and mercy shone?
    So spake our father penitent, nor Eve
Felt less remorse: they forthwith to the place
Repairing where he judged them prostrate fell
Before him reverent, and both confessed   1100
Humbly their faults, and pardon begged, with tears
Watering the ground, and with their sighs the air
Frequenting, sent from hearts contrite, in sign
Of sorrow unfeigned, and humiliation meek.

BOOK XI

The Argument

The Son of God presents to his father the prayers of our first parents now
repenting, and intercedes for them: God accepts them, but declares that they
must no longer abide in Paradise; sends Michael with a band of cherubim to
dispossess them; but first to reveal to Adam future things: Michael's coming
down. Adam shows to Eve certain ominous signs; he discerns Michael's
approach, goes out to meet him: the angel denounces their departure. Eve's
lamentation. Adam pleads, but submits: the angel leads him up to a high hill,
sets before him in vision what shall happen till the flood.

Thus they in lowliest plight repentant stood
Praying, for from the mercy-seat above
Prevenient grace descending had removed°
The stony from their hearts, and made new flesh
Regenerate grow instead, that sighs now breathed
Unutterable, which the spirit of prayer
Inspired, and winged for heaven with speedier flight
Than loudest oratory: yet their port
Not of mean suitors, nor important less

Seemed their petition, than when the ancient pair   10
In fables old, less ancient yet than these,
Deucalion and chaste Pyrrha to restore
The race of mankind drowned, before the shrine
Of Themis stood devout. To heaven their prayers°
Flew up, nor missed the way, by envious winds
Blown vagabond or frustrate: in they passed
Dimensionless through heavenly doors; then clad°
With incense, where the golden altar fumed,
By their great intercessor, came in sight
Before the Father's throne: them the glad Son   20
Presenting, thus to intercede began.
  See Father, what first fruits on earth are sprung
From thy implanted grace in man, these sighs
And prayers, which in this golden censer, mixed
With incense, I thy priest before thee bring,
Fruits of more pleasing savour from thy seed
Sown with contrition in his heart, than those
Which his own hand manuring all the trees°
Of Paradise could have produced, ere fallen
From innocence. Now therefore bend thine ear   30
To supplication, hear his sighs though mute;
Unskilful with what words to pray, let me
Interpret for him, me his advocate
And propitiation, all his works on me
Good or not good engraft, my merit those
Shall perfect, and for these my death shall pay.
Accept me, and in me from these receive
The smell of peace toward mankind, let him live°
Before thee reconciled, at least his days
Numbered, though sad, till death, his doom (which I   40
To mitigate thus plead, not to reverse)
To better life shall yield him, where with me
All my redeemed may dwell in joy and bliss,
Made one with me as I with thee am one.
  To whom the Father, without cloud, serene.
All thy request for man, accepted Son,
Obtain, all thy request was my decree:
But longer in that Paradise to dwell,
The law I gave to nature him forbids:
Those pure immortal elements that know   50

No gross, no unharmonious mixture foul,
Eject him tainted now, and purge him off
As a distemper, gross to air as gross,°
And mortal food, as may dispose him best
For dissolution wrought by sin, that first
Distempered all things, and of incorrupt
Corrupted. I at first with two fair gifts
Created him endowed, with happiness
And immortality: that fondly lost,°
This other served but to eternize woe;   60
Till I provided death; so death becomes
His final remedy, and after life
Tried in sharp tribulation, and refined
By faith and faithful works, to second life,
Waked in the renovation of the just,
Resigns him up with heaven and earth renewed.
But let us call to synod all the blessed°
Through heaven's wide bounds; from them I will not hide
My judgments, how with mankind I proceed,
As how with peccant angels late they saw;°   70
And in their state, though firm, stood more confirmed.
      He ended, and the Son gave signal high
To the bright minister that watched, he blew
His trumpet, heard in Oreb since perhaps°
When God descended, and perhaps once more
To sound at general doom. The angelic blast°
Filled all the regions: from their blissful bowers
Of armarantine shade, fountain or spring,°
By the waters of life, where'er they sat
In fellowships of joy: the sons of light   80
Hasted, resorting to the summons high,
And took their seats; till from his throne supreme
The almighty thus pronounced his sovereign will.
      O sons, like one of us man is become
To know both good and evil, since his taste
Of that defended fruit; but let him boast°
His knowledge of good lost, and evil got,
Happier, had it sufficed him to have known
Good by itself, and evil not at all.
He sorrows now, repents, and prays contrite,   90
My motions in him, longer than they move,°

His heart I know, how variable and vain
Self-left. Lest therefore his now bolder hand°
Reach also of the tree of life, and eat,
And live forever, dream at least to live
Forever, to remove him I decree,
And send him from the garden forth to till
The ground whence he was taken, fitter soil.
   Michael, this my behest have thou in charge,
Take to thee from among the cherubim   100
Thy choice of flaming warriors, lest the fiend
Or in behalf of man, or to invade
Vacant possession some new trouble raise:°
Haste thee, and from the Paradise of God
Without remorse drive out the sinful pair,
From hallowed ground the unholy, and denounce°
To them and to their progeny from thence
Perpetual banishment. Yet lest they faint
At the sad sentence rigorously urged,
For I behold them softened and with tears   110
Bewailing their excess, all terror hide.°
If patiently thy bidding they obey,
Dismiss them not disconsolate; reveal
To Adam what shall come in future days,
As I shall thee enlighten, intermix
My covenant in the woman's seed renewed;
So send them forth, though sorrowing, yet in peace:
And on the east side of the garden place,
Where entrance up from Eden easiest climbs,
Cherubic watch, and of a sword the flame   120
Wide waving, all approach far off to fright,
And guard all passage to the tree of life:
Lest Paradise a receptacle prove
To spirits foul, and all my trees their prey,
With whose stolen fruit man once more to delude.
   He ceased; and the archangelic power prepared
For swift descent, with him the cohort bright
Of watchful cherubim; four faces each
Had, like a double Janus, all their shape°
Spangled with eyes more numerous than those   130
Of Argus, and more wakeful than to drowse,°
Charmed with Arcadian pipe, the pastoral reed

Of Hermes, or his opiate rod. Meanwhile
To resalute the world with sacred light
Leucothea waked, and with fresh dews embalmed°
The earth, when Adam and first matron Eve
Had ended now their orisons, and found
Strength added from above, new hope to spring
Out of despair, joy, but with fear yet linked;
Which thus to Eve his welcome words renewed.   140
    Eve, easily may faith admit, that all
The good which we enjoy, from heaven descends;
But that from us aught should ascend to heaven
So prevalent as to concern the mind°
Of God high-blessed, or to incline his will,
Hard to belief may seem; yet this will prayer,
Or one short sigh of human breath, upborne
Even to the seat of God. For since I sought
By prayer the offended Deity to appease,
Kneeled and before him humbled all my heart,   150
Methought I saw him placable and mild,
Bending his ear; persuasion in me grew
That I was heard with favour; peace returned
Home to my breast, and to my memory
His promise, that thy seed shall bruise our foe;
Which then not minded in dismay, yet now
Assures me that the bitterness of death
Is past, and we shall live. Whence hail to thee,
Eve rightly called, mother of all mankind,
Mother of all things living, since by thee°   160
Man is to live, and all things live for man.
    To whom thus Eve with sad demeanour meek.
Ill worthy I such title should belong
To me transgressor, who for thee ordained
A help, became thy snare; to me reproach
Rather belongs, distrust and all dispraise:
But infinite in pardon was my judge,
That I who first brought death on all, am graced
The source of life; next favourable thou,
Who highly thus to entitle me vouchsaf'st,   170
Far other name deserving. But the field
To labour calls us now with sweat imposed,
Though after sleepless night; for see the morn,

All unconcerned with our unrest, begins
Her rosy progress smiling; let us forth,
I never from thy side henceforth to stray,
Where'er our day's work lies, though now enjoined
Laborious, till day droop; while here we dwell,
What can be toilsome in these pleasant walks?
Here let us live, though in fallen state, content.   180
    So spake, so wished much-humbled Eve, but fate
Subscribed not; nature first gave signs, impressed
On bird, beast, air, air suddenly eclipsed
After short blush of morn; nigh in her sight
The bird of Jove, stooped from his airy tower,°
Two birds of gayest plume before him drove:
Down from a hill the beast that reigns in woods,°
First hunter then, pursued a gentle brace,°
Goodliest of all the forest, hart and hind;
Direct to the eastern gate was bent their flight.   190
Adam observed, and with his eye the chase
Pursuing, not unmoved to Eve thus spake.
    O Eve, some further change awaits us nigh,
Which heaven by these mute signs in nature shows
Forerunners of his purpose, or to warn
Us haply too secure of our discharge°
From penalty, because from death released
Some days; how long, and what till then our life,
Who knows, or more than this, that we are dust,
And thither must return and be no more.   200
Why else this double object in our sight
Of flight pursued in the air and o'er the ground
One way the self-same hour? why in the east
Darkness ere day's mid-course, and morning light
More orient in yon western cloud that draws°
O'er the blue firmament a radiant white,
And slow descends, with something heavenly fraught.
    He erred not, for by this the heavenly bands°
Down from a sky of jasper lighted now°
In Paradise, and on a hill made alt,°   210
A glorious apparition, had not doubt
And carnal fear that day dimmed Adam's eye.°
Not that more glorious, when the angels met
Jacob in Mahanaim, where he saw°

The field pavilioned with his guardians bright;
Nor that which on the flaming mount appeared
In Dothan, covered with a camp of fire,°
Against the Syrian king, who to surprise
One man, assassin-like had levied war,
War unproclaimed. The princely hierarch°   220
In their bright stand, there left his powers to seize°
Possession of the garden; he alone,
To find where Adam sheltered, took his way,
Not unperceived of Adam, who to Eve,
While the great visitant approached, thus spake.
    Eve, now expect great tidings, which perhaps
Of us will soon determine, or impose
New laws to be observed; for I descry
From yonder blazing cloud that veils the hill
One of the heavenly host, and by his gait   230
None of the meanest, some great potentate
Or of the thrones above, such majesty
Invests him coming; yet not terrible,
That I should fear, nor sociably mild,
As Raphael, that I should much confide,
But solemn and sublime, whom not to offend,
With reverence I must meet, and thou retire.
He ended; and the archangel soon drew nigh,
Not in his shape celestial, but as man
Clad to meet man; over his lucid arms°   240
A military vest of purple flowed
Livelier than Meliboean, or the grain°
Of Sarra, worn by kings and heroes old°
In time of truce; Iris had dipped the woof;°
His starry helm unbuckled showed him prime
In manhood where youth ended; by his side
As in a glistering zodiac hung the sword,°
Satan's dire dread, and in his hand the spear.
Adam bowed low, he kingly from his state
Inclined not, but his coming thus declared.   250
    Adam, heaven's high behest no preface needs:
Sufficient that thy prayers are heard, and death,
Then due by sentence when thou didst transgress,
Defeated of his seizure many days
Given thee of grace, wherein thou mayst repent,

And one bad act with many deeds well done
Mayst cover: well may then thy Lord appeased
Redeem thee quite from Death's rapacious claim;
But longer in this Paradise to dwell
Permits not; to remove thee I am come,   260
And send thee from the garden forth to till
The ground whence thou wast taken, fitter soil.
   He added not, for Adam at the news
Heart-struck with chilling gripe of sorrow stood,°
That all his senses bound; Eve, who unseen
Yet all had heard, with audible lament
Discovered soon the place of her retire.°
   O unexpected stroke, worse than of death!
Must I thus leave thee Paradise? thus leave
Thee native soil, these happy walks and shades,   270
Fit haunt of gods? where I had hope to spend,
Quiet though sad, the respite of that day°
That must be mortal to us both. O flowers,
That never will in other climate grow,
My early visitation, and my last
At even, which I bred up with tender hand
From the first opening bud, and gave ye names,
Who now shall rear ye to the sun, or rank
Your tribes, and water from the ambrosial fount?
Thee lastly nuptial bower, by me adorned   280
With what to sight or smell was sweet; from thee
How shall I part, and whither wander down
Into a lower world, to this obscure°
And wild, how shall we breathe in other air
Less pure, accustomed to immortal fruits?
   Whom thus the angel interrupted mild.
Lament not Eve, but patiently resign
What justly thou hast lost; nor set thy heart,
Thus over-fond, on that which is not thine;
Thy going is not lonely, with thee goes   290
Thy husband, him to follow thou art bound;
Where he abides, think there thy native soil.
   Adam by this from the cold sudden damp°
Recovering, and his scattered spirits returned,
To Michael thus his humble words addressed.
   Celestial, whether among the thrones, or named

Of them the highest, for such of shape may seem
Prince above princes, gently hast thou told
Thy message, which might else in telling wound,
And in performing end us; what besides   300
Of sorrow and dejection and despair
Our frailty can sustain, thy tidings bring,
Departure from this happy place, our sweet
Recess, and only consolation left
Familiar to our eyes, all places else
Inhospitable appear and desolate,
Nor knowing us nor known: and if by prayer
Incessant I could hope to change the will
Of him who all things can, I would not cease
To weary him with my assiduous cries: 310
But prayer against his absolute decree
No more avails than breath against the wind,
Blown stifling back on him that breathes it forth:
Therefore to his great bidding I submit.
This most afflicts me, that departing hence,
As from his face I shall be hid, deprived
His blessèd countenance; here I could frequent,
With worship, place by place where he vouchsafed
Presence divine, and to my sons relate;
On this mount he appeared, under this tree   320
Stood visible, among these pines his voice
I heard, here with him at this fountain talked:
So many grateful altars I would rear
Of grassy turf, and pile up every stone
Of lustre from the brook, in memory,
Or monument to ages, and thereon
Offer sweet smelling gums and fruits and flowers:
In yonder nether world where shall I seek
His bright appearances, or footstep trace?
For though I fled him angry, yet recalled   330
To life prolonged and promised race, I now
Gladly behold though but his utmost skirts
Of glory, and far off his steps adore.
      To whom thus Michael with regard benign.
Adam, thou know'st heaven his, and all the earth,
Not this rock only; his omnipresence fills
Land, sea, and air, and every kind that lives,

Fomented by his virtual power and warmed:°
All the earth he gave thee to possess and rule,
No despicable gift; surmise not then   340
His presence to these narrow bounds confined
Of Paradise or Eden: this had been
Perhaps thy capital seat, frcm whence had spread
All generations, and had hither come
From all the ends of the earth, to celebrate
And reverence thee their great progenitor.
But this pre-eminence thou hast lost, brought down
To dwell on even ground now with thy sons:
Yet doubt not but in valley and in plain
God is as here, and will be found alike   350
Present, and of his presençe many a sign
Still following thee, still compassing thee round
With goodness and paternal love, his face
Express, and of his steps the track divine.
Which that thou mayst believe, and be confirmed
Ere thou from hence depart, know I am sent
To show thee what shall come in future days
To thee and to thy offspring; good with bad
Expect to hear, supernal grace contending°
With sinfulness of men; thereby to learn   360
True patience, and to temper joy with fear
And pious sorrow, equally inured
By moderation either state to bear,
Prosperous or adverse: so shalt thou lead
Safest thy life, and best prepared endure
Thy mortal passage when it comes. Ascend
This hill; let Eve (for I have drenched her eyes)
Here sleep below while thou to foresight wak'st,
As once thou slept'st, while she to life was formed.
    To whom thus Adam gratefully replied.   370
Ascend, I follow thee, safe guide, the path
Thou lead'st me, and to the hand of heaven submit,
However chastening, to the evil turn
My obvious breast, arming to overcome°
By suffering, and earn rest from labour won,
If so I may attain. So both ascend
In the visions of God: it was a hill
Of Paradise the highest, from whose top

The hemisphere of earth in clearest ken°
Stretched out to the amplest reach of prospect lay.   380
Not higher that hill nor wider looking round,
Whereon for different cause the tempter set
Our second Adam in the wilderness,
To show him all earth's kingdoms and their glory.°
His eye might there command wherever stood
City of old or modern fame, the seat
Of mightiest empire, from the destined walls
Of Cambalu, seat of Cathayan khan°
And Samarkand by Oxus, Temir's throne,°
To Paquin of Sinaean kings, and thence°   390
To Agra and Lahore of great mogul°
Down to the golden Chersonese, or where°
The Persian in Ecbatan sat, or since°
In Hispahan, or where the Russian czar°
In Moscow, or the sultan in Bizance,°
Turkestan-born; nor could his eye not ken
The empire of Negus to his utmost port°
Ercoco and the less maritime kings°
Mombasa, and Quiloa, and Melind,°
And Sofala thought Ophir, to the realm°   400
Of Congo, and Angola farthest south;
Or thence from Niger flood to Atlas mount
The kingdoms of Almansor, Fez and Sus,°
Morocco and Algiers, and Tremisen;°
On Europe thence, and where Rome was to sway
The world: in spirit perhaps he also saw°
Rich Mexico the seat of Montezume,
And Cuzco in Peru, the richer seat
Of Atabalipa, and yet unspoiled°
Guiana, whose great city Geryon's sons°   410
Call El Dorado: but to nobler sights
Michael from Adam's eyes the film removed
Which that false fruit that promised clearer sight
Had bred; then purged with euphrasy and rue°
The visual nerve, for he had much to see;
And from the well of life three drops instilled.
So deep the power of these ingredients pierced,
Even to the inmost seat of mental sight,
That Adam now enforced to close his eyes,

Sunk down and all his spirits became entranced: 420
But him the gentle angel by the hand
Soon raised, and his attention thus recalled.
 Adam, now ope thine eyes, and first behold
The effects which thy original crime hath wrought
In some to spring from thee, who never touched
The excepted tree, nor with the snake conspired,°
Nor sinned thy sin, yet from that sin derive
Corruption to bring forth more violent deeds.
 His eyes he opened, and beheld a field,°
Part arable and tilth, whereon were sheaves° 430
New reaped, the other part sheep-walks and folds;
I' the midst an altar as the landmark stood
Rustic, of grassy sward; thither anon
A sweaty reaper from his tillage brought
First fruits, the green ear, and the yellow sheaf,
Unculled, as came to hand; a shepherd next°
More meek came with the firstlings of his flock
Choicest and best; then sacrificing, laid
The innards and their fat, with incense strewed,
On the cleft wood, and all due rites performed. 440
His offering soon propitious fire from heaven
Consumed with nimble glance, and grateful steam;°
The other's not, for his was not sincere;
Whereat he inly raged, and as they talked,
Smote him into the midriff with a stone
That beat out life; he fell, and deadly pale
Groaned out his soul with gushing blood effused.
Much at that sight was Adam in his heart
Dismayed, and thus in haste to the angel cried.
 O teacher, some great mischief hath befallen 450
To that meek man, who well had sacrificed;
Is piety thus and pure devotion paid?
 To whom Michael thus, he also moved, replied.
These two are brethren, Adam, and to come
Out of thy loins; the unjust the just hath slain,
For envy that his brother's offering found
From heaven acceptance; but the bloody fact°
Will be avenged, and the other's faith approved
Lose no reward, though here thou see him die,
Rolling in dust and gore. To which our sire. 460

Alas, both for the deed and for the cause!
But have I now seen death? Is this the way
I must return to native dust? O sight
Of terror, foul and ugly to behold,
Horrid to think, how horrible to feel!
    To whom thus Michael. Death thou hast seen
In his first shape on man; but many shapes
Of death, and many are the ways that lead
To his grim cave, all dismal; yet to sense
More terrible at the entrance than within.   470
Some, as thou saw'st, by violent stroke shall die,
By fire, flood, famine, by intemperance more
In meats and drinks, which on the earth shall bring
Diseases dire, of which a monstrous crew
Before thee shall appear; that thou mayst know
What misery the inabstinence of Eve
Shall bring on men. Immediately a place
Before his eyes appeared, sad, noisome, dark,
A lazar-house it seemed, wherein were laid°
Numbers of all diseased, all maladies   480
Of ghastly spasm, or racking torture, qualms°
Of heart-sick agony, all feverous kinds,
Convulsions, epilepsies, fierce catarrhs,
Intestine stone and ulcer, colic pangs,
Demoniac frenzy, moping melancholy
And moon-struck madness, pining atrophy,
Marasmus, and wide-wasting pestilence,°
Dropsies, and asthmas, and joint-racking rheums.
Dire was the tossing, deep the groans, despair
Tended the sick busiest from couch to couch;   490
And over them triumphant Death his dart
Shook, but delayed to strike, though oft invoked
With vows, as their chief good, and final hope.
Sight so deform what heart of rock could long
Dry-eyed behold? Adam could not, but wept,
Though not of woman born; compassion quelled°
His best of man, and gave him up to tears
A space, till firmer thoughts restrained excess,
And scarce recovering words his plaint renewed.
    O miserable mankind, to what fall   500
Degraded, to what wretched state reserved!

Better end here unborn. Why is life given
To be thus wrested from us? rather why
Obtruded on us thus? who if we knew
What we receive, would either not accept
Life offered, or soon beg to lay it down,
Glad to be so dismissed in peace. Can thus
The image of God in man created once
So goodly and erect, though faulty since,
To such unsightly sufferings be debased   510
Under inhuman pains? Why should not man,
Retaining still divine similitude
In part, from such deformities be free,
And for his maker's image sake exempt?
       Their maker's image, answered Michael, then
Forsook them, when themselves they vilified
To serve ungoverned appetite, and took
His image whom they served, a brutish vice,
Inductive mainly to the sin of Eve.°
Therefore so abject is their punishment,   520
Disfiguring not God's likeness, but their own,
Or if his likeness, by themselves defaced
While they pervert pure nature's healthful rules
To loathsome sickness, worthily, since they
God's image did not reverence in themselves.
       I yield it just, said Adam, and submit.
But is there yet no other way, besides
These painful passages, how we may come
To death, and mix with our connatural dust?
       There is, said Michael, if thou well observe   530
The rule of not too much, by temperance taught
In what thou eat'st and drink'st, seeking from thence
Due nourishment, not gluttonous delight,
Till many years over thy head return:
So mayst thou live, till like ripe fruit thou drop
Into thy mother's lap, or be with ease
Gathered, not harshly plucked, for death mature:
This is old age; but then thou must outlive
Thy youth, thy strength, thy beauty, which will change
To withered weak and grey; thy senses then   540
Obtuse, all taste of pleasure must forego,°
To what thou hast, and for the air of youth

Hopeful and cheerful, in thy blood will reign
A melancholy damp of cold and dry°
To weigh thy spirits down, and last consume
The balm of life. To whom our ancestor.
　Henceforth I fly not death, nor would prolong
Life much, bent rather how I may be quit
Fairest and easiest of this cumbrous charge,
Which I must keep till my appointed day   550
Of rendering up, and patiently attend
My dissolution. Michael replied,°
　Nor love thy life, nor hate; but what thou liv'st
Live well, how long or short permit to heaven:
And now prepare thee for another sight.
　He looked and saw a spacious plain, whereon°
Were tents of various hue; by some were herds
Of cattle grazing: others, whence the sound
Of instruments that made melodious chime
Was heard, of harp and organ; and who moved   560
Their stops and chords was seen: his volant touch°
Instinct through all proportions low and high°
Fled and pursued transverse the resonant fugue.°
In other part stood one who at the forge°
Labouring, two massy clods of iron and brass
Had melted (whether found where casual fire°
Had wasted woods on mountain or in vale,
Down to the veins of earth, thence gliding hot
To some cave's mouth, or whether washed by stream
From undergound) the liquid ore he drained   570
Into fit moulds prepared; from which he formed
First his own tools; then, what might else be wrought
Fusile or graven in metal. After these,°
But on the hither side a different sort°
From the high neighbouring hills, which was their seat,
Down to the plain descended: by their guise
Just men they seemed, and all their study bent
To worship God aright, and know his works
Not hid, nor those things last which might preserve
Freedom and peace to men: they on the plain   580
Long had not walked, when from the tents behold
A bevy of fair women, richly gay
In gems and wanton dress; to the harp they sung

Soft amorous ditties, and in dance came on:
The men though grave, eyed them, and let their eyes
Rove without rein, till in the amorous net
Fast caught, they liked, and each his liking chose;
And now of love they treat till the evening star°
Love's harbinger appeared; then all in heat
They light the nuptial torch, and bid invoke   590
Hymen, then first to marriage rites invoked;°
With feast and music all the tents resound.
Such happy interview and fair event
Of love and youth not lost, songs, garlands, flowers,
And charming symphonies attached the heart°
Of Adam, soon inclined to admit delight,
The bent of nature; which he thus expressed.
    True opener of mine eyes, prime angel blessed,
Much better seems this vision, and more hope
Of peaceful days portends, than those two past;   600
Those were of hate and death, or pain much worse,
Here nature seems fulfilled in all her ends.
    To whom thus Michael. Judge not what is best
By pleasure, though to nature seeming meet,
Created, as thou art, to nobler end
Holy and pure, conformity divine.
Those tents thou saw'st so pleasant, were the tents
Of wickedness, wherein shall dwell his race
Who slew his brother; studious they appear
Of arts that polish life, inventors rare,   610
Unmindful of their maker, though his Spirit
Taught them, but they his gifts acknowledged none.
Yet they a beauteous offspring shall beget;
For that fair female troop thou saw'st, that seemed
Of goddesses, so blithe, so smooth, so gay,
Yet empty of all good wherein consists
Woman's domestic honour and chief praise;
Bred only and completed to the taste
Of lustful appetance, to sing, to dance,°
To dress, and troll the tongue, and roll the eye.°   620
To these that sober race of men, whose lives
Religious titled them the sons of God,
Shall yield up all their virtue, all their fame
Ignobly, to the trains and to the smiles°

Of these fair atheists, and now swim in joy,
(Erelong to swim at large) and laugh; for which
The world erelong a world of tears must weep.
    To whom thus Adam of short joy bereft.
O pity and shame, that they who to live well
Entered so fair, should turn aside to tread   630
Paths indirect, or in the mid-way faint!
But still I see the tenor of man's woe
Holds on the same, from woman to begin.
    From man's effeminate slackness it begins,
Said the angel, who should better hold his place
By wisdom, and superior gifts received.
But now prepare thee for another scene.
    He looked and saw wide territory spread°
Before him, towns, and rural works between,
Cities of men with lofty gates and towers,   640
Concourse in arms, fierce faces threatening war,°
Giants of mighty bone, and bold emprise;°
Part wield their arms, part curb the foaming steed,
Single or in array of battle ranged
Both horse and foot, nor idly mustering stood;
One way a band select from forage drives
A herd of beeves, fair oxen and fair kine°
From a fat meadow ground; or fleecy flock,
Ewes and their bleating lambs over the plain,
Their booty; scarce with life the shepherds fly,   650
But call in aid, which makes a bloody fray;
With cruel tournament the squadrons join;
Where cattle pastured late, now scattered lies
With carcasses and arms the ensanguined field°
Deserted: others to a city strong
Lay siege, encamped; by battery, scale, and mine,°
Assaulting; others from the wall defend
With dart and javelin, stones and sulphurous fire;
On each hand slaughter and gigantic deeds.
In other part the sceptred heralds call   660
To council in the city gates: anon
Grey-headed men and grave, with warriors mixed,
Assemble, and harangues are heard, but soon
In factious opposition, till at last
Of middle age one rising, eminent°

In wise deport, spake much of right and wrong,
Of justice, of religion, truth and peace,
And judgment from above: him old and young
Exploded and had seized with violent hands,°
Had not a cloud descending snatched him thence   670
Unseen amid the throng: so violence
Proceeded, and oppression, and sword-law
Through all the plain, and refuge none was found.
Adam was all in tears, and to his guide
Lamenting turned full sad; O what are these,
Death's ministers, not men, who thus deal death
Inhumanly to men, and multiply
Ten thousandfold the sin of him who slew
His brother; for of whom such massacre
Make they but of their brethren, men of men?   680
But who was that just man, whom had not heaven
Rescued, had in his righteousness been lost?
    To whom thus Michael. These are the product
Of those ill-mated marriages thou saw'st:
Where good with bad were matched, who of themselves
Abhor to join; and by imprudence mixed,
Produce prodigious births of body or mind.
Such were these giants, men of high renown;
For in those days might only shall be admired,
And valour and heroic virtue called;   690
To overcome in battle, and subdue
Nations, and bring home spoils with infinite
Manslaughter, shall be held the highest pitch
Of human glory, and for glory done
Of triumph, to be styled great conquerors,
Patrons of mankind, gods, and sons of gods,
Destroyers rightlier called and plagues of men.
Thus fame shall be achieved, renown on earth,
And what most merits fame in silence hid.
But he the seventh from thee, whom thou beheld'st°   700
The only righteous in a world perverse,
And therefore hated, therefore so beset
With foes for daring single to be just,
And utter odious truth, that God would come
To judge them with his saints: him the most high
Rapt in a balmy cloud with wingèd steeds

Did, as thou saw'st, receive, to walk with God
High in salvation and the climes of bliss,
Exempt from death; to show thee what reward
Awaits the good, the rest what punishment;   710
Which now direct thine eyes and soon behold.
  He looked, and saw the face of things quite changed,
The brazen throat of war had ceased to roar,
All now was turned to jollity and game,
To luxury and riot, feast and dance,°
Marrying or prostituting, as befell,
Rape or adultery, where passing fair°
Allured them; thence from cups to civil broils.
At length a reverend sire among them came,°
And of their doings great dislike declared,   720
And testified against their ways; he oft
Frequented their assemblies, whereso met,
Triumphs or festivals, and to them preached
Conversion and repentance, as to souls
In prison under judgments imminent:
But all in vain: which when he saw, he ceased
Contending, and removed his tents far off;
Then from the mountain hewing timber tall,
Began to build a vessel of huge bulk,
Measured by cubit, length, and breadth, and height,   730
Smeared round with pitch, and in the side a door°
Contrived, and of provisions laid in large
For man and beast: when lo a wonder strange!
Of every beast, and bird, and insect small
Came sevens, and pairs, and entered in, as taught°
Their order: last the sire, and his three sons
With their four wives; and God made fast the door.
Meanwhile the south wind rose, and with black wings
Wide hovering, all the clouds together drove
From under heaven; the hills to their supply   740
Vapour, and exhalation dusk and moist,°
Sent up amain; and now the thickened sky°
Like a dark ceiling stood; down rushed the rain
Impetuous, and continued till the earth
No more was seen; the floating vessel swum
Uplifted; and sccure with beakèd prow
Rode tilting o'er the waves, all dwellings else

Flood overwhelmed, and them with all their pomp
Deep under water rolled; sea covered sea,
Sea without shore; and in their palaces   750
Where luxury late reigned, sea monsters whelped
And stabled; of mankind, so numerous late,
All left, in one small bottom swum embarked.°
How didst thou grieve then, Adam, to behold
The end of all thy offspring, end so sad,
Depopulation; thee another flood,
Of tears and sorrow a flood thee also drowned,
And sunk thee as thy sons; till gently reared
By the angel, on thy feet thou stood'st at last,
Though comfortless, as when a father mourns   760
His children, all in view destroyed at once;
And scarce to the angel utter'd'st thus thy plaint.
    O visions ill foreseen! better had I
Lived ignorant of future, so had borne
My part of evil only, each day's lot
Enough to bear; those now, that were dispensed
The burden of many ages, on me light
At once, by my foreknowledge gaining birth
Abortive, to torment me ere their being,
With thought that they must be. Let no man seek   770
Henceforth to be foretold what shall befall
Him or his children, evil he may be sure,
Which neither his foreknowing can prevent,
And he the future evil shall no less
In apprehension than in substance feel
Grievous to bear: but that care now is past,
Man is not whom to warn: those few escaped°
Famine and anguish will at last consume
Wand'ring that wat'ry desert: I had hope
When violence was ceased, and war on earth,   780
All would have then gone well, peace would have crowned
With length of happy days the race of man;
But I was far deceived; for now I see
Peace to corrupt no less than war to waste.
How comes it thus? unfold, celestial guide,
And whether here the race of man will end.
To whom thus Michael. Those whom last thou saw'st
In triumph and luxurious wealth, are they

First seen in acts of prowess eminent
And great exploits, but of true virtue void;   790
Who having spilled much blood, and done much waste
Subduing nations, and achieved thereby
Fame in the world, high titles, and rich prey,
Shall change their course to pleasure, ease, and sloth,
Surfeit, and lust, till wantonness and pride
Raise out of friendship hostile deeds in peace.
The conquered also, and enslaved by war
Shall with their freedom lost all virtue lose
And fear of God, from whom their piety feigned
In sharp contest of battle found no aid   800
Against invaders; therefore cooled in zeal
Thenceforth shall practise how to live secure,
Worldly or dissolute, on what their lords
Shall leave them to enjoy; for the earth shall bear
More than enough, that temperance may be tried:°
So all shall turn degenerate, all depraved,
Justice and temperance, truth and faith forgot;
One man except, the only son of light
In a dark age, against example good,
Against allurement, custom, and a world   810
Offended; fearless of reproach and scorn,
Or violence, he of their wicked ways
Shall them admonish, and before them set
The paths of righteousness, how much more safe,
And full of peace, denouncing wrath to come°
On their impenitence; and shall return
Of them derided, but of God observed
The one just man alive; by his command
Shall build a wondrous ark, as thou beheld'st
To save himself and household from amidst   820
A world devote to universal rack.°
No sooner he with them of man and beast
Select for life shall in the ark be lodged,
And sheltered round, but all the cataracts
Of heaven set open on the earth shall pour
Rain day and night, all fountains of the deep
Broke up, shall heave the ocean to usurp
Beyond all bounds, till inundation rise
Above the highest hills: then shall this mount

Of Paradise by might of waves be moved 830
Out of his place, pushed by the hornèd flood,°
With all his verdure spoiled, and trees adrift
Down the great river to the opening gulf,
And there take root an island salt and bare,
The haunt of seals and orcs, and seamews' clang.°
To teach thee that God attributes to place
No sanctity, if none be thither brought
By men who there frequent, or therein dwell.
And now what further shall ensue, behold.
　He looked, and saw the ark hull on the flood,° 840
Which now abated, for the clouds were fled,
Driven by a keen north wind, that blowing dry
Wrinkled the face of deluge, as decayed;
And the clear sun on his wide watery glass
Gazed hot, and of the fresh wave largely drew,
As after thirst, which made their flowing shrink
From standing lake to tripping ebb, that stole°
With soft foot towards the deep, who now had stopped
His sluices, as the heaven his windows shut.
The ark no more now floats, but seems on ground 850
Fast on the top of some high mountain fixed.
And now the tops of hills as rocks appear;
With clamour thence the rapid currents drive
Towards the retreating sea their furious tide.
Forthwith from out the ark a raven flies,
And after him, the surer messenger,
A dove sent forth once and again to spy
Green tree or ground whereon his foot may light;
The second time returning, in his bill
An olive leaf he brings, pacific sign: 860
Anon dry ground appears, and from his ark
The ancient sire descends with all his train;
Then with uplifted hands, and eyes devout,
Grateful to heaven, over his head beholds
A dewy cloud, and in the cloud a bow
Conspicuous with three listed colours gay,°
Betok'ning peace from God, and cov'nant new.
Whereat the heart of Adam erst so sad
Greatly rejoiced, and thus his joy broke forth.
　O thou who future things canst represent 870

As present, heavenly instructor, I revive
At this last sight, assured that man shall live
With all the creatures, and their seed preserve.
Far less I now lament for one whole world
Of wicked sons destroyed, than I rejoice
For one man found so perfect and so just,
That God vouchsafes to raise another world
From him, and all his anger to forget.
But say, what mean those coloured streaks in heaven,
Distended as the brow of God appeased,°   880
Or serve they as a flowery verge to bind
The fluid skirts of that same watery cloud,
Lest it again dissolve and shower the earth?
   To whom the archangel. Dextrously thou aim'st;
So willingly doth God remit his ire,
Though late repenting him of man depraved,
Grieved at his heart, when looking down he saw°
The whole earth filled with violence, and all flesh
Corrupting each their way; yet those removed,
Such grace shall one just man find in his sight,   890
That he relents, not to blot out mankind,
And makes a covenant never to destroy
The earth again by flood, nor let the sea
Surpass his bounds, nor rain to drown the world
With man therein or beast; but when he brings
Over the earth a cloud, will therein set
His triple-coloured bow, whereon to look
And call to mind his covenant: day and night,
Seed time and harvest, heat and hoary frost
Shall hold their course, till fire purge all things new,   900
Both heaven and earth, wherein the just shall dwell.

BOOK XII

The Argument

The angel Michael continues from the flood to relate what shall succeed; then, in the mention of Abraham, comes by degrees to explain, who that seed of the woman shall be, which was promised Adam and Eve in the Fall; his incarnation, death, resurrection, and ascension; the state of the church till his second coming. Adam greatly satisfied and recomforted by these relations and promises

descends the hill with Michael; wakens Eve, who all this while had slept, but
with gentle dreams composed to quietness of mind and submission. Michael in
either hand leads them out of Paradise, the fiery sword waving behind them,
and the cherubim taking their stations to guard the place.

As one who in his journey bates at noon,°
Though bent on speed, so here the archangel paused
Betwixt the world destroyed and world restored,
If Adam aught perhaps might interpose;
Then with transition sweet new speech resumes.°
    Thus thou hast seen one world begin and end;
And man as from a second stock proceed.
Much thou hast yet to see, but I perceive
Thy mortal sight to fail; objects divine
Must needs impair and weary human sense: 10
Henceforth what is to come I will relate,
Thou therefore give due audience, and attend.
This second source of men, while yet but few,
And while the dread of judgment past remains
Fresh in their minds, fearing the Deity,
With some regard to what is just and right
Shall lead their lives, and multiply apace,
Labouring the soil, and reaping plenteous crop,
Corn wine and oil; and from the herd or flock,
Oft sacrificing bullock, lamb, or kid,   20
With large wine-offerings poured, and sacred feast,
Shall spend their days in joy unblamed, and dwell
Long time in peace by families and tribes
Under paternal rule; till one shall rise°
Of proud ambitious heart, who not content
With fair equality, fraternal state,
Will arrogate dominion undeserved
Over his brethren, and quite dispossess
Concord and law of nature from the earth,
Hunting (and men not beasts shall be his game)   30
With war and hostile snare such as refuse
Subjection to his empire tyrannous:
A mighty hunter thence he shall be styled
Before the Lord, as in despite of heaven,
Or from heaven claiming second sovereignty;
And from rebellion shall derive his name,°

Though of rebellion others he accuse.
He with a crew, whom like ambition joins
With him or under him to tyrannize,
Marching from Eden towards the west, shall find   40
The plain, wherein a black bituminous gurge°
Boils out from underground, the mouth of hell;
Of brick, and of that stuff they cast to build°
A city and tower, whose top may reach to heaven;
And get themselves a name, lest far dispersed
In foreign lands their memory be lost
Regardless whether good or evil fame.
But God who oft descends to visit men
Unseen, and through their habitations walks
To mark their doings, them beholding soon,   50
Comes down to see their city, ere the tower
Obstruct heaven towers, and in derision sets
Upon their tongues a various spirit to rase°
Quite out their native language, and instead
To sow a jangling noise of words unknown:
Forthwith a hideous gabble rises loud
Among the builders; each to other calls
Not understood, till hoarse, and all in rage,
As mocked they storm; great laughter was in heaven
And looking down, to see the hubbub strange   60
And hear the din; thus was the building left
Ridiculous, and the work Confusion named.°
     Whereto thus Adam fatherly displeased.
O execrable son so to aspire
Above his brethren, to himself assuming
Authority usurped, from God not given:
He gave us only over beast, fish, fowl
Dominion absolute; that right we hold
By his donation; but man over men
He made not lord; such title to himself   70
Reserving, human left from human free.
But this usurper his encroachment proud
Stays not on man; to God his tower intends
Siege and defiance: wretched man! what food
Will he convey up thither to sustain
Himself and his rash army, where thin air
Above the clouds will pine his entrails gross,

And famish him of breath, if not of bread?
  To whom thus Michael. Justly thou abhorr'st
That son, who on the quiet state of men   80
Such trouble brought, affecting to subdue°
Rational liberty; yet know withal,
Since thy original lapse, true liberty
Is lost, which always with right reason dwells°
Twinned, and from her hath no dividual being:°
Reason in man obscured, or not obeyed,
Immediately inordinate desires
And upstart passions catch the government
From reason, and to servitude reduce
Man till then free. Therefore since he permits   90
Within himself unworthy powers to reign
Over free reason, God in judgment just
Subjects him from without to violent lords;
Who oft as undeservedly enthral
His outward freedom: tyranny must be,
Though to the tyrant thereby no excuse.
Yet sometimes nations will decline so low
From virtue, which is reason, that no wrong,
But justice, and some fatal curse annexed
Deprives them of their outward liberty,   100
Their inward lost: witness the irreverent son,
Of him who built the ark, who for the shame
Done to his father, heard this heavy curse,
Servant of servants, on his vicious race.°
Thus will this latter, as the former world,
Still tend from bad to worse, till God at last
Wearied with their iniquities, withdraw
His presence from among them, and avert
His holy eyes; resolving from thenceforth
To leave them to their own polluted ways;   110
And one peculiar nation to select°
From all the rest, of whom to be invoked,
A nation from one faithful man to spring:
Him on this side Euphrates yet residing,°
Bred up in idol worship; O that men
(Canst thou believe?) should be so stupid grown,
While yet the patriarch lived, who scaped the flood,°
As to forsake the living God, and fall

To worship their own work in wood and stone
For gods! yet him God the most high vouchsafes   120
To call by vision from his father's house,
His kindred and false gods, into a land
Which he will show him, and from him will raise
A mighty nation, and upon him shower
His benediction so, that in his seed
All nations shall be blest; he straight obeys,
Not knowing to what land, yet firm believes:
I see him, but thou canst not, with what faith
He leaves his gods, his friends, and native soil
Ur of Chaldaea, passing now the ford°   130
To Haran, after him a cumbrous train°
Of herds and flocks, and numerous servitude;°
Not wand'ring poor, but trusting all his wealth
With God, who called him, in a land unknown.
Canaan he now attains, I see his tents
Pitched about Sechem, and the neighbouring plain°
Of Moreh; there by promise he receives
Gift to his progeny of all that land;
From Hamath northward to the desert south°
(Things by their names I call, though yet unnamed)   140
From Hermon east to the great western sea,°
Mount Hermon, yonder sea, each place behold
In prospect, as I point them; on the shore
Mount Carmel; here the double-founted stream
Jordan, true limit eastward; but his sons°
Shall dwell to Senir, that long ridge of hills.°
This ponder, that all nations of the earth
Shall in his seed be blessèd; by that seed
Is meant thy great deliverer, who shall bruise
The serpent's head; whereof to thee anon   150
Plainlier shall be revealed. This patriarch blessed,
Whom faithful Abraham due time shall call,
A son, and of his son a grandchild leaves,°
Like him in faith, in wisdom, and renown;
The grandchild with twelve sons increased, departs
From Canaan, to a land hereafter called
Egypt, divided by the river Nile;
See where it flows, disgorging at seven mouths
Into the sea: to sojourn in that land

He comes invited by a younger son°   160
In time of dearth, a son whose worthy deeds
Raise him to be the second in that realm
Of Pharaoh: there he dies, and leaves his race
Growing into a nation, and now grown
Suspected to a sequent king, who seeks°
To stop their overgrowth, as inmate guests
Too numerous; whence of guests he makes them slaves
Inhospitably, and kills their infant males:
Till by two brethren (those two brethren call
Moses and Aaron) sent from God to claim   170
His people from enthralment, they return
With glory and spoil back to their promised land.
But first the lawless tyrant, who denies°
To know their God, or message to regard,
Must be compelled by signs and judgments dire;
To blood unshed the rivers must be turned,°
Frogs, lice and flies must all his palace fill
With loathed intrusion, and fill all the land;
His cattle must of rot and murrain die,
Botches and blains must all his flesh emboss,°   180
And all his people; thunder mixed with hail,
Hail mixed with fire must rend the Egyptian sky
And wheel on the earth, devouring where it rolls;
What it devours not, herb, or fruit, or grain,
A darksome cloud of locusts swarming down
Must eat, and on the ground leave nothing green:
Darkness must overshadow all his bounds,
Palpable darkness, and blot out three days;
Last with one midnight stroke all the first-born
Of Egypt must lie dead. Thus with ten wounds   190
The river dragon tamed at length submits°
To let his sojourners depart, and oft
Humbles his stubborn heart, but still as ice
More hardened after thaw, till in his rage
Pursuing whom he late dismissed, the sea
Swallows him with his host, but them lets pass
As on dry land between two crystal walls,
Awed by the rod of Moses so to stand
Divided, till his rescued gain their shore:
Such wondrous power God to his saint will lend,°   200

Though present in his angel, who shall go
Before them in a cloud, and pillar of fire,
By day a cloud, by night a pillar of fire,°
To guide them in their journey, and remove
Behind them, while the obdurate king pursues:
All night he will pursue, but his approach
Darkness defends between till morning watch;°
Then through the fiery pillar and the cloud
God looking forth will trouble all his host
And craze their chariot wheels: when by command°   210
Moses once more his potent rod extends
Over the sea; the sea his rod obeys;
On their embattled ranks the waves return,
And overwhelm their war: the race elect°
Safe towards Canaan from the shore advance
Through the wild desert, not the readiest way,
Lest entering on the Canaanite alarmed
War terrify them inexpert, and fear
Return them back to Egypt, choosing rather°
Inglorious life with servitude; for life   220
To noble and ignoble is more sweet
Untrained in arms, where rashness leads not on.
This also shall they gain by their delay
In the wide wilderness, there they shall found
Their government, and their great senate choose°
Through the twelve tribes, to rule by laws ordained:
God from the mount of Sinai, whose grey top
Shall tremble, he descending, will himself
In thunder lightning and loud trumpets' sound
Ordain them laws; part such as appertain   230
To civil justice, part religious rites
Of sacrifice, informing them, by types
And shadows, of that destined seed to bruise
The serpent, by what means he shall achieve
Mankind's deliverance. But the voice of God
To mortal ear is dreadful; they beseech
That Moses might report to them his will,
And terror cease; he grants what they besought°
Instructed that to God is no access
Without mediator, whose high office now   240
Moses in figure bears, to introduce°

One greater, of whose day he shall foretell,
And all the prophets in their age the times
Of great Messiah shall sing. Thus laws and rites
Established, such delight hath God in men
Obedient to his will, that he vouchsafes
Among them to set up his tabernacle,°
The holy one with mortal men to dwell:
By his prescript a sanctuary is framed
Of cedar, overlaid with gold, therein   250
An ark, and in the ark his testimony,
The records of his covenant, over these
A mercy-seat of gold between the wings°
Of two bright cherubim, before him burn
Seven lamps as in a zodiac representing
The heavenly fires; over the tent a cloud
Shall rest by day, a fiery gleam by night,
Save when they journey, and at length they come,
Conducted by his angel to the land
Promised to Abraham and his seed: the rest   260
Were long to tell, how many battles fought,
How many kings destroyed, and kingdoms won,
Or how the sun shall in mid heaven stand still
A day entire, and night's due course adjourn,°
Man's voice commanding, sun in Gibeon stand,°
And thou moon in the vale of Aialon,°
Till Israel overcome; so call the third°
From Abraham, son of Isaac, and from him
His whole descent, who thus shall Canaan win.

    Here Adam interposed. O sent from heaven,   270
Enlightener of my darkness, gracious things
Thou hast revealed, those chiefly which concern
Just Abraham and his seed: now first I find
Mine eyes true opening, and my heart much eased,
Erewhile perplexed with thoughts what would become
Of me and all mankind; but now I see
His day, in whom all nations shall be blessed,
Favour unmerited by me, who sought
Forbidden knowledge by forbidden means.
This yet I apprehend not, why to those   280
Among whom God will deign to dwell on earth
So many and so various laws are given;

So many laws argue so many sins
Among them; how can God with such reside?
   To whom thus Michael. Doubt not but that sin
Will reign among them, as of thee begot;
And therefore was law given them to evince°
Their natural pravity, by stirring up°
Sin against law to fight: that when they see
Law can discover sin, but not remove,   290
Save by those shadowy expiations weak,
The blood of bulls and goats, they may conclude
Some blood more precious must be paid for man,
Just for unjust, that in such righteousness
To them by faith imputed, they may find°
Justification towards God, and peace
Of conscience, which the law by ceremonies
Cannot appease, nor man the moral part
Perform, and not performing cannot live.
So law appears imperfect, and but given   300
With purpose to resign them in full time°
Up to a better covenant, disciplined
From shadowy types to truth, from flesh to spirit,°
From imposition of strict laws, to free
Acceptance of large grace, from servile fear
To filial, works of law to works of faith.
And therefore shall not Moses, though of God
Highly beloved, being but the minister
Of law, his people into Canaan lead;
But Joshua whom the gentiles Jesus call,   310
His name and office bearing, who shall quell
The adversary serpent, and bring back
Through the world's wilderness long wandered man
Safe to eternal paradise of rest.°
Meanwhile they in their earthly Canaan placed
Long time shall dwell and prosper, but when sins°
National interrupt their public peace,
Provoking God to raise them enemies:
From whom as oft he saves them penitent
By judges first, then under kings; of whom   320
The second, both for piety renowned
And puissant deeds, a promise shall receive
Irrevocable, that his regal throne

Forever shall endure; the like shall sing
All prophecy, that of the royal stock
Of David (so I name this king) shall rise
A son, the woman's seed to thee foretold,°
Foretold to Abraham, as in whom shall trust
All nations, and to kings foretold, of kings
The last, for of his reign shall be no end.   330
But first a long succession must ensue,
And his next son for wealth and wisdom famed,°
The clouded ark of God till then in tents
Wandering, shall in a glorious temple enshrine.
Such follow him, as shall be registered
Part good, part bad, of bad the longer scroll,
Whose foul idolatries, and other faults
Heaped to the popular sum, will so incense°
God, as to leave them, and expose their land,
Their city, his temple, and his holy ark   340
With all his sacred things, a scorn and prey
To that proud city, whose high walls thou saw'st
Left in confusion, Babylon thence called.
There in captivity he lets them dwell
The space of seventy years, then brings them back,
Remembering mercy, and his covenant sworn
To David, stablished as the days of heaven.
Returned from Babylon by leave of kings
Their lords, whom God disposed, the house of God
They first re-edify, and for a while°   350
In mean estate live moderate, till grown°
In wealth and multitude, factious they grow;
But first among the priests dissension springs,
Men who attend the altar, and should most
Endeavour peace: their strife pollution brings
Upon the temple itself: at last they seize
The sceptre, and regard not David's sons,°
Then lose it to a stranger, that the true°
Anointed king Messiah might be born
Barred of his right; yet at his birth a star   360
Unseen before in heaven proclaims him come,
And guides the eastern sages, who inquire
His place, to offer incense, myrrh, and gold;
His place of birth a solemn angel tells

To simple shepherds, keeping watch by night;
They gladly thither haste, and by a choir
Of squadroned angels hear his carol sung.
A virgin is his mother, but his sire
The power of the most high; he shall ascend
The throne hereditary, and bound his reign   370
With earth's wide bounds, his glory with the heavens.
     He ceased, discerning Adam with such joy
Surcharged, as had like grief been dewed in tears,°
Without the vent of words, which these he breathed.
     O prophet of glad tidings, finisher
Of utmost hope! now clear I understand°
What oft my steadiest thoughts have searched in vain,
Why our great expectation should be called
The seed of woman: virgin mother, hail,
High in the love of heaven, yet from my loins   380
Thou shalt proceed, and from thy womb the Son
Of God most high; so God with man unites.
Needs must the serpent now his capital bruise°
Expect with mortal pain: say where and when
Their fight, what stroke shall bruise the victor's heel.
     To whom thus Michael. Dream not of their fight,
As of a duel, or the local wounds
Of head or heel: not therefore joins the Son
Manhood to Godhead, with more strength to foil
Thy enemy; nor so is overcome   390
Satan, whose fall from heaven, a deadlier bruise,
Disabled not to give thee thy death's wound:
Which he, who comes thy saviour, shall recure,°
Not by destroying Satan, but his works
In thee and in thy seed: nor can this be,
But by fulfilling that which thou didst want,°
Obedience to the law of God, imposed
On penalty of death, and suffering death,
The penalty to thy transgression due,
And due to theirs which out of thine will grow: 400
So only can high justice rest apaid.°
The law of God exact he shall fulfil
Both by obedience and by love, though love
Alone fulfil the law; thy punishment
He shall endure by coming in the flesh

To a reproachful life and cursèd death,
Proclaiming life to all who shall believe
In his redemption, and that his obedience
Imputed becomes theirs by faith, his merits°
To save them, not their own, though legal works.°   410
For this he shall live hated, be blasphemed,
Seized on by force, judged, and to death condemned
A shameful and accurst, nailed to the cross
By his own nation, slain for bringing life;
But to the cross he nails thy enemies,
The law that is against thee, and the sins
Of all mankind, with him there crucified,
Never to hurt them more who rightly trust
In this his satisfaction; so he dies,°
But soon revives, Death over him no power   420
Shall long usurp; ere the third dawning light
Return, the stars of morn shall see him rise
Out of his grave, fresh as the dawning light,
Thy ransom paid, which man from death redeems,
His death for man, as many as offered life
Neglect not, and the benefit embrace
By faith not void of works: this Godlike act
Annuls thy doom, the death thou shouldst have died,
In sin forever lost from life; this act
Shall bruise the head of Satan, crush his strength   430
Defeating Sin and Death, his two main arms,
And fix far deeper in his head their stings
Than temporal death shall bruise the victor's heel,°
Or theirs whom he redeems, a death like sleep,
A gentle wafting to immortal life.
Nor after resurrection shall he stay
Longer on earth than certain times to appear
To his disciples, men who in his life
Still followed him; to them shall leave in charge°
To teach all nations what of him they learned   440
And his salvation, them who shall believe
Baptising in the profluent stream, the sign°
Of washing them from guilt of sin to life
Pure, and in mind prepared, if so befall,
For death, like that which the redeemer died.
All nations they shall teach; for from that day

Not only to the sons of Abraham's loins
Salvation shall be preached, but to the sons
Of Abraham's faith wherever through the world;
So in his seed all nations shall be blessed.   450
Then to the heaven of heavens he shall ascend
With victory, triumphing through the air
Over his foes and thine; there shall surprise
The serpent, prince of air, and drag in chains
Through all his realm, and there confounded leave;
Then enter into glory, and resume
His seat at God's right hand, exalted high
Above all names in heaven; and thence shall come,
When this world's dissolution shall be ripe,
With glory and power to judge both quick and dead,°   460
To judge the unfaithful dead, but to reward
His faithful, and receive them into bliss,
Whether in heaven or earth, for then the earth
Shall all be paradise, far happier place
Than this of Eden, and far happier days.
    So spake the archangel Michael, then paused,
As at the world's great period; and our sire°
Replete with joy and wonder thus replied.
    O goodness infinite, goodness immense!°
That all this good of evil shall produce,   470
And evil turn to good; more wonderful
Than that which by creation first brought forth
Light out of darkness! full of doubt I stand,
Whether I should repent me now of sin
By me done and occasioned, or rejoice
Much more, that much more good thereof shall spring,
To God more glory, more good will to men
From God, and over wrath grace shall abound.
But say, if our deliverer up to heaven
Must reascend, what will betide the few   480
His faithful, left among the unfaithful herd,
The enemies of truth; who then shall guide
His people, who defend? will they not deal
Worse with his followers than with him they dealt?
    Be sure they will, said the angel; but from heaven
He to his own a comforter will send,°
The promise of the Father, who shall dwell

His spirit within them, and the law of faith
Working through love, upon their hearts shall write,
To guide them in all truth, and also arm   490
With spiritual armour, able to resist
Satan's assaults, and quench his fiery darts,
What man can do against them, not afraid,
Though to the death, against such cruelties
With inward consolations recompensed,
And oft supported so as shall amaze
Their proudest persecutors: for the spirit
Poured first on his apostles, whom he sends
To evangelize the nations, then on all
Baptized, shall them with wondrous gifts endue   500
To speak all tongues, and do all miracles,
As did their Lord before them. Thus they win
Great numbers of each nation to receive
With joy the tidings brought from heaven: at length
Their ministry performed, and race well run,
Their doctrine and their story written left,
They die; but in their room, as they forewarn,°
Wolves shall succeed for teachers, grievous wolves,°
Who all the sacred mysteries of heaven
To their own vile advantages shall turn   510
Of lucre and ambition, and the truth
With superstitions and traditions taint,
Left only in those written records pure,
Though not but by the spirit understood.
Then shall they seek to avail themselves of names,
Places and titles, and with these to join
Secular power, though feigning still to act
By spiritual, to themselves appropriating
The spirit of God, promised alike and given
To all believers; and from that pretence,   520
Spiritual laws by carnal power shall force
On every conscience; laws which none shall find
Left them enrolled, or what the spirit within°
Shall on the heart engrave. What will they then
But force the spirit of grace itself, and bind
His consort liberty; what, but unbuild
His living temples, built by faith to stand,
Their own faith not another's: for on earth

Who against faith and conscience can be heard
Infallible? yet many will presume: 530
Whence heavy persecution shall arise
On all who in the worship persevere
Of spirit and truth; the rest, far greater part,
Will deem in outward rites and specious forms
Religion satisfied; truth shall retire
Bestuck with slanderous darts, and works of faith
Rarely be found: so shall the world go on,
To good malignant, to bad men benign,
Under her own weight groaning till the day
Appear of respiration to the just,°   540
And vengeance to the wicked, at return
Of him so lately promised to thy aid
The woman's seed, obscurely then foretold,
Now amplier known thy saviour and thy Lord,
Last in the clouds from heaven to be revealed
In glory of the Father, to dissolve°
Satan with his perverted world, then raise
From the conflagrant mass, purged and refined,
New heavens, new earth, ages of endless date
Founded in righteousness and peace and love   550
To bring forth fruits joy and eternal bliss.
    He ended; and thus Adam last replied.
How soon hath thy prediction, seer blessed,
Measured this transient world, the race of time,
Till time stand fixed: beyond is all abyss,
Eternity, whose end no eye can reach.
Greatly instructed I shall hence depart,
Greatly in peace of thought, and have my fill
Of knowledge, what this vessel can contain;
Beyond which was my folly to aspire.   560
Henceforth I learn, that to obey is best,
And love with fear the only God, to walk
As in presence, ever to observe
His providence, and on him sole depend,
Merciful over all his works, with good
Still overcoming evil, and by small
Accomplishing great things, by things deemed weak
Subverting worldly strong, and worldly wise
By simply meek; that suffering for truth's sake

Is fortitude to highest victory,   570
And to the faithful death the gate of life;
Taught this by his example whom I now
Acknowledge my redeemer ever blessed.
    To whom thus also the angel last replied:
This having learned, thou hast attained the sum
Of wisdom; hope no higher, though all the stars
Thou knew'st by name, and all the ethereal powers,
All secrets of the deep, all nature's works,
Or works of God in heaven, air, earth, or sea,
And all the riches of this world enjoyed'st,   580
And all the rule, one empire; only add
Deeds to thy knowledge answerable, add faith,
Add virtue, patience, temperance, add love,
By name to come called Charity, the soul
Of all the rest: then wilt thou not be loath
To leave this Paradise, but shalt possess
A paradise within thee, happier far.
Let us descend now therefore from this top
Of speculation; for the hour precise°
Exacts our parting hence; and see the guards,   590
By me encamped on yonder hill, expect
Their motion, at whose front a flaming sword,°
In signal of remove, waves fiercely round;
We may no longer stay: go, waken Eve;
Her also I with gentle dreams have calmed
Portending good, and all her spirits composed
To meek submission: thou at season fit
Let her with thee partake what thou hast heard,
Chiefly what may concern her faith to know,
The great deliverance by her seed to come   600
(For by the woman's seed) on all mankind.
That ye may live, which will be many days,
Both in one faith unanimous though sad,
With cause for evils past, yet much more cheered
With meditation on the happy end.
    He ended, and they both descend the hill;
Descended, Adam to the bower where Eve
Lay sleeping ran before, but found her waked;
And thus with words not sad she him received.
    Whence thou return'st, and whither went'st, I know;   610

For God is also in sleep, and dreams advise,
Which he hath sent propitious, some great good
Presaging, since with sorrow and heart's distress
Wearied I fell asleep: but now lead on;
In me is no delay; with thee to go,
Is to stay here; without thee here to stay,
Is to go hence unwilling; thou to me
Art all things under heaven, all places thou,
Who for my wilful crime art banished hence.
This further consolation yet secure   620
I carry hence; though all by me is lost,
Such favour I unworthy am vouchsafed,
By me the promised seed shall all restore.
   So spake our mother Eve, and Adam heard
Well pleased, but answered not; for now too nigh
The archangel stood, and from the other hill
To their fixed station, all in bright array
The cherubim descended; on the ground
Gliding meteorous, as evening mist°
Risen from a river o'er the marish glides,°   630
And gathers ground fast at the labourer's heel
Homeward returning. High in front advanced,
The brandished sword of God before them blazed
Fierce as a comet; which with torrid heat,
And vapour as the Lybian air adust,°
Began to parch that temperate clime; whereat
In either hand the hastening angel caught
Our lingering parents, and to the eastern gate
Led them direct, and down the cliff as fast
To the subjected plain; then disappeared.°   640
They looking back, all the eastern side beheld
Of Paradise, so late their happy seat,
Waved over by that flaming brand, the gate
With dreadful faces thronged and fiery arms:
Some natural tears they dropped, but wiped them soon;
The world was all before them, where to choose
Their place of rest, and providence their guide:
They hand in hand with wandering steps and slow,
Through Eden took their solitary way.

PARADISE REGAINED

THE FIRST BOOK

I who erewhile the happy garden sung,°
By one man's disobedience lost, now sing
Recovered Paradise to all mankind,
By one man's firm obedience fully tried°
Through all temptation, and the tempter foiled
In all his wiles, defeated and repulsed,
And Eden raised in the waste wilderness.°
    Thou spirit who led'st this glorious eremite°
Into the desert, his victorious field
Against the spiritual foe, and brought'st him thence   10
By proof the undoubted Son of God, inspire,°
As thou art wont, my prompted song else mute,
And bear through height or depth of nature's bounds
With prosperous wing full summed to tell of deeds°
Above heroic, though in secret done,
And unrecorded left through many an age,°
Worthy t' have not remained so long unsung.
    Now had the great proclaimer with a voice°
More awful than the sound of trumpet, cried
Repentance, and heaven's kingdom nigh at hand   20
To all baptized: to his great baptism flocked
With awe the regions round, and with them came
From Nazareth the son of Joseph deemed
To the flood Jordan, came as then obscure,°
Unmarked, unknown; but him the Baptist soon
Descried, divinely warned, and witness bore
As to his worthier, and would have resigned°
To him his heavenly office, nor was long
His witness unconfirmed: on him baptized
Heaven opened, and in likeness of a dove   30
The Spirit descended, while the Father's voice
From heaven pronounced him his beloved son.
That heard the adversary, who roving still°

About the world, at that assembly famed
Would not be last, and with the voice divine
Nigh thunder-struck, the exalted man, to whom
Such high attest was given, awhile surveyed
With wonder, then with envy fraught and rage
Flies to his place, nor rests, but in midair
To council summons all his mighty peers,   40
Within thick clouds and dark tenfold involved,
A gloomy consistory; and them amidst°
With looks aghast and sad he thus bespake.
      O ancient powers of air and this wide world,
For much more willingly I mention air,
This our old conquest, than remember hell
Our hated habitation; well ye know
How many ages, as the years of men,°
This universe we have possessed, and ruled
In manner at our will the affairs of earth,°   50
Since Adam and his facile consort Eve°
Lost Paradise deceived by me, though since
With dread attending when that fatal wound°
Shall be inflicted by the seed of Eve°
Upon my head, long the decrees of heaven
Delay, for longest time to him is short;°
And now too soon for us the circling hours
This dreaded time have compassed, wherein we
Must bide the stroke of that long-threatened wound,
At least if so we can, and by the head   60
Broken be not intended all our power
To be infringed, our freedom and our being°
In this fair empire won of earth and air;
For this ill news I bring, the woman's seed
Destined to this, is late of woman born,°
His birth to our just fear gave no small cause,
But his growth now to youth's full flower, displaying
All virtue, grace and wisdom to achieve
Things highest, greatest, multiplies my fear.
Before him a great prophet, to proclaim   70
His coming, is sent harbinger, who all
Invites, and in the consecrated stream
Pretends to wash off sin, and fit them so°
Purified to receive him pure, or rather

To do him honour as their king; all come,
And he himself among them was baptized,
Not thence to be more pure, but to receive
The testimony of heaven, that who he is
Thenceforth the nations may not doubt; I saw
The prophet do him reverence, on him rising   80
Out of the water, heaven above the clouds
Unfold her crystal doors, thence on his head
A perfect dove descend, whate'er it meant,°
And out of heaven the sovereign voice I heard,
This is my son beloved, in him am pleased.
His mother then is mortal, but his sire,
He who obtains the monarchy of heaven,°
And what will he not do to advance his son?
His first-begot we know, and sore have felt,°
When his fierce thunder drove us to the deep;   90
Who this is we must learn, for man he seems
In all his lineaments, though in his face
The glimpses of his father's glory shine.
Ye see our danger on the utmost edge
Of hazard, which admits no long debate,°
But must with something sudden be opposed,
Not force, but well-couched fraud, well-woven snares,°
Ere in the head of nations he appear
Their king, their leader, and supreme on earth.
I, when no other durst, sole undertook°   100
The dismal expedition to find out
And ruin Adam, and the exploit performed
Successfully; a calmer voyage now
Will waft me; and the way found prosperous once
Induces best to hope of like success.
　　He ended, and his words impression left
Of much amazement to the infernal crew,°
Distracted and surprised with deep dismay
At these sad tidings; but no time was then°
For long indulgence to their fears or grief: 110
Unanimous they all commit the care
And management of this main enterprise°
To him their great dictator, whose attempt°
At first against mankind so well had thrived
In Adam's overthrow, and led their march

From hell's deep-vaulted den to dwell in light,
Regents and potentates, and kings, yea gods
Of many a pleasant realm and province wide.
So to the coast of Jordan he directs°
His easy steps; girded with snaky wiles,   120
Where he might likeliest find this new-declared,
This man of men, attested Son of God,
Temptation and all guile on him to try;
So to subvert whom he suspected raised
To end his reign on earth so long enjoyed:
But contrary unweeting he fulfilled
The purposed counsel pre-ordained and fixed
Of the most high, who in full frequence bright°
Of angels, thus to Gabriel smiling spake.°

    Gabriel this day by proof thou shalt behold,   130
Thou and all angels conversant on earth
With man or men's affairs, how I begin
To verify that solemn message late,
On which I sent thee to the virgin pure
In Galilee, that she should bear a son
Great in renown, and called the Son of God;
Then told'st her doubting how these things could be
To her a virgin, that on her should come
The Holy Ghost, and the power of the highest
O'ershadow her: this man born and now upgrown,   140
To show him worthy of his birth divine
And high prediction, henceforth I expose
To Satan; let him tempt and now assay
His utmost subtlety, because he boasts
And vaunts of his great cunning to the throng
Of his apostasy; he might have learned°
Less overweening, since he failed in Job,°
Whose constant perseverance overcame
Whate'er his cruel malice could invent.
He now shall know I can produce a man   150
Of female seed, far abler to resist
All his solicitations, and at length
All his vast force, and drive him back to hell,
Winning by conquest what the first man lost
By fallacy surprised. But first I mean°
To exercise him in the wilderness,°

There he shall first lay down the rudiments
Of his great warfare, ere I send him forth
To conquer Sin and Death the two grand foes,°
By humiliation and strong sufferance: 160
His weakness shall o'ercome Satanic strength°
And all the world, and mass of sinful flesh;
That all the angels and ethereal powers,
They now, and men hereafter may discern,
From what consummate virtue I have chose
This perfect man, by merit called my son,°
To earn salvation for the sons of men.
    So spake the eternal Father, and all heaven
Admiring stood a space; then into hymns
Burst forth, and in celestial measures moved,   170
Circling the throne and singing, while the hand°
Sung with the voice, and this the argument.°
    Victory and triumph to the Son of God
Now ent'ring his great duel, not of arms,
But to vanquish by wisdom hellish wiles.
The Father knows the Son; therefore secure°
Ventures his filial virtue, though untried,
Against whate'er may tempt, whate'er seduce,
Allure, or terrify, or undermine.
Be frustrate all ye stratagems of hell,°   180
And devilish machinations come to nought.
    So they in heaven their odes and vigils tuned:°
Meanwhile the Son of God, who yet some days
Lodged in Bethabara where John baptized,°
Musing and much revolving in his breast,
How best the mighty work he might begin
Of saviour to mankind, and which way first
Publish his godlike office now mature,°
One day forth walked alone, the spirit leading,
And his deep thoughts, the better to converse   190
With solitude, till far from track of men,°
Thought following thought, and step by step led on,
He entered now the bordering desert wild,
And with dark shades and rocks environed round,
His holy meditations thus pursued.
    O what a multitude of thoughts at once
Awakened in me swarm, while I consider°

What from within I feel myself, and hear
What from without comes often to my ears,
Ill sorting with my present state compared.°   200
When I was yet a child, no childish play°
To me was pleasing, all my mind was set
Serious to learn and know, and thence to do°
What might be public good; myself I thought
Born to that end, born to promote all truth,°
All righteous things: therefore above my years,
The law of God I read, and found it sweet,
Made it my whole delight, and in it grew
To such perfection, that ere yet my age
Had measured twice six years, at our great feast°   210
I went into the Temple, there to hear
The teachers of our law, and to propose
What might improve my knowledge or their own;
And was admired by all, yet this not all°
To which my spirit aspired, victorious deeds
Flamed in my heart, heroic acts, one while
To rescue Israel from the Roman yoke,
Then to subdue and quell o'er all the earth
Brute violence and proud tyrannic power,
Till truth were freed, and equity restored: 220
Yet held it more humane, more heavenly first
By winning words to conquer willing hearts,
And make persuasion do the work of fear;
At least to try, and teach the erring soul°
Not wilfully misdoing, but unware
Misled; the stubborn only to subdue.
These growing thoughts my mother soon perceiving
By words at times cast forth inly rejoiced,
And said to me apart, High are thy thoughts
O son, but nourish them and let them soar   230
To what height sacred virtue and true worth
Can raise them, though above example high;
By matchless deeds express thy matchless sire.°
For know, thou art no son of mortal man,
Though men esteem thee low of parentage,
Thy father is the eternal King, who rules
All heaven and earth, angels and sons of men;
A messenger from God foretold thy birth°

Conceived in me a virgin, he foretold
Thou shouldst be great and sit on David's throne,   240
And of thy kingdom there should be no end.
At thy nativity a glorious choir
Of angels in the fields of Bethlehem sung
To shepherds watching at their folds by night,
And told them the Messiah now was born,
Where they might see him, and to thee they came;
Directed to the manger where thou lay'st,
For in the inn was left no better room:
A star, not seen before in heaven appearing
Guided the wise men thither from the east,   250
To honour thee with incense, myrrh, and gold,
By whose bright course led on they found the place,
Affirming it thy star new graven in heaven,°
By which they knew thee King of Israel born.
Just Simeon and prophetic Anna, warned°
By vision, found thee in the Temple, and spake
Before the altar and the vested priest,
Like things of thee to all that present stood.
This having heard, straight I again revolved°
The law and prophets, searching what was writ   260
Concerning the Messiah, to our scribes
Known partly, and soon found of whom they spake
I am; this chiefly, that my way must lie
Through many a hard assay even to the death,°
Ere I the promised kingdom can attain,
Or work redemption for mankind, whose sins'
Full weight must be transferred upon my head.
Yet neither thus disheartened or dismayed,
The time prefixed I waited, when behold
The Baptist (of whose birth I oft had heard,   270
Not knew by sight), now come, who was to come
Before Messiah and his way prepare.
I as all others to his baptism came,
Which I believed was from above; but he
Straight knew me, and with loudest voice proclaimed
Me him (for it was shown him so from heaven)
Me him whose harbinger he was; and first
Refused on me his baptism to confer,
As much his greater, and was hardly won;°

But as I rose out of the laving stream,   280
Heaven opened her eternal doors, from whence
The Spirit descended on me like a dove,
And last the sum of all, my father's voice,°
Audibly heard from heaven, pronounced me his,
Me his beloved son, in whom alone
He was well pleased; by which I knew the time
Now full, that I no more should live obscure,
But openly begin, as best becomes
The authority which I derived from heaven.
And now by some strong motion I am led°   290
Into this wilderness, to what intent
I learn not yet, perhaps I need not know;°
For what concerns my knowledge God reveals.
    So spake our morning star, then in his rise,°
And looking round on every side beheld
A pathless desert, dusk with horrid shades;°
The way he came not having marked, return
Was difficult, by human steps untrod;
And he still on was led, but with such thoughts
Accompanied of things past and to come   300
Lodged in his breast, as well might recommend
Such solitude before choicest society.°
Full forty days he passed, whether on hill°
Sometimes, anon in shady vale, each night
Under the covert of some ancient oak,°
Or cedar, to defend him from the dew,
Or harboured in one cave, is not revealed;
Nor tasted human food, nor hunger felt
Till those days ended, hungered then at last
Among wild beasts: they at his sight grew mild,°   310
Nor sleeping him nor waking harmed, his walk
The fiery serpent fled, and noxious worm,°
The lion and fierce tiger glared aloof.
But now an agèd man in rural weeds,°
Following, as seemed, the quest of some stray ewe,
Or withered sticks to gather; which might serve
Against a winter's day when winds blow keen,
To warm him wet returned from field at eve,
He saw approach, who first with curious eye°
Perused him, then with words thus uttered spake.   320

Sir, what ill chance hath brought thee to this place
So far from path or road of men, who pass
In troop or caravan, for single none
Durst ever, who returned, and dropped not here
His carcase, pined with hunger and with drouth?°
I ask the rather, and the more admire,°
For that to me thou seem'st the man, whom late
Our new baptizing prophet at the ford
Of Jordan honoured so, and called thee Son
Of God; I saw and heard, for we sometimes   330
Who dwell this wild, constrained by want, come forth
To town or village nigh (nighest is far)
Where aught we hear, and curious are to hear,
What happens new; fame also finds us out.°
    To whom the Son of God. Who brought me hither
Will bring me hence, no other guide I seek.
    By miracle he may, replied the swain,
What other way I see not, for we here
Live on tough roots and stubs, to thirst inured°
More than the camel, and to drink go far,   340
Men to much misery and hardship born;
But if thou be the Son of God, command
That out of these hard stones be made thee bread;
So shalt thou save thyself and us relieve
With food, whereof we wretched seldom taste.
    He ended, and the Son of God replied.
Think'st thou such force in bread? is it not written
(For I discern thee other than thou seem'st)
Man lives not by bread only, but each word°
Proceeding from the mouth of God; who fed   350
Our fathers here with manna; in the mount
Moses was forty days, nor ate nor drank,°
And forty days Elijah without food°
Wandered this barren waste, the same I now:
Why dost thou then suggest to me distrust,
Knowing who I am, as I know who thou art?
    Whom thus answered the arch-fiend now undisguised.
'Tis true, I am that spirit unfortunate,
Who leagued with millions more in rash revolt
Kept not my happy station, but was driven   360
With them from bliss to the bottomless deep,

Yet to that hideous place not so confined
By rigour unconniving, but that oft°
Leaving my dolorous prison I enjoy
Large liberty to round this globe of earth,°
Or range in the air, nor from the heaven of heavens
Hath he excluded my resort sometimes.
I came among the sons of God, when he°
Gave up into my hands Uzzean Job°
To prove him, and illustrate his high worth;°   370
And when to all his angels he proposed
To draw the proud King Ahab into fraud°
That he might fall in Ramoth, they demurring,°
I undertook that office, and the tongues
Of all his flattering prophets glibbed with lies°
To his destruction, as I had in charge.
For what he bids I do; though I have lost
Much lustre of my native brightness, lost
To be beloved of God, I have not lost
To love, at least contemplate and admire   380
What I see excellent in good, or fair,
Or virtuous, I should so have lost all sense.
What can be then less in me than desire°
To see thee and approach thee, whom I know
Declared the Son of God, to hear attent°
Thy wisdom, and behold thy godlike deeds?
Men generally think me much a foe
To all mankind: why should I? they to me
Never did wrong or violence, by them
I lost not what I lost, rather by them   390
I gained what I have gained, and with them dwell
Copartner in these regions of the world,
If not disposer; lend them oft my aid,
Oft my advice by presages and signs,
And answers, oracles, portents and dreams,
Whereby they may direct their future life.
Envy they say excites me, thus to gain
Companions of my misery and woe.
At first it may be; but long since with woe
Nearer acquainted, now I feel by proof,°   400
That fellowship in pain divides not smart,°
Nor lightens aught each man's peculiar load.

Small consolation then, were man adjoined:
This wounds me most (what can it less) that man,
Man fall'n shall be restored, I never more.
　　To whom our saviour sternly thus replied.
Deservedly thou griev'st, composed of lies
From the beginning, and in lies wilt end;
Who boast'st release from hell, and leave to come
Into the heaven of heavens; thou com'st indeed,　　410
As a poor miserable captive thrall
Comes to the place where he before had sat
Among the prime in splendour, now deposed,°
Ejected, emptied, gazed, unpitied, shunned,°
A spectacle of ruin or of scorn
To all the host of heaven; the happy place
Imparts to thee no happiness, no joy,
Rather inflames thy torment, representing
Lost bliss, to thee no more communicable,
So never more in hell than when in heaven.　　420
But thou art serviceable to heaven's king.
Wilt thou impute to obedience what thy fear
Extorts, or pleasure to do ill excites?
What but thy malice moved thee to misdeem
Of righteous Job, then cruelly to afflict him
With all inflictions, but his patience won?
The other service was thy chosen task,
To be a liar in four hundred mouths;°
For lying is thy sustenance, thy food.
Yet thou pretend'st to truth; all oracles　　430
By thee are given, and what confessed more true
Among the nations? that hath been thy craft,
By mixing somewhat true to vent more lies.
But what have been thy answers, what but dark
Ambiguous and with double sense deluding,°
Which they who asked have seldom understood,
And not well understood as good not known?
Who ever by consulting at thy shrine
Returned the wiser, or the more instruct°
To fly or follow what concerned him most,　　440
And run not sooner to his fatal snare?
For God hath justly given the nations up
To thy delusions; justly, since they fell

Idolatrous, but when his purpose is
Among them to declare his providence
To thee not known, whence hast thou then thy truth,
But from him or his angels president°
In every province, who themselves disdaining
To approach thy temples, give thee in command
What to the smallest tittle thou shalt say   450
To thy adorers; thou with trembling fear,
Or like a fawning parasite obey'st;
Then to thyself ascrib'st the truth foretold.
But this thy glory shall be soon retrenched;°
No more shalt thou by oracling abuse
The Gentiles; henceforth oracles are ceased,°
And thou no more with pomp and sacrifice
Shalt be inquired at Delphos or elsewhere,°
At least in vain, for they shall find thee mute.
God hath now sent his living oracle°   460
Into the world, to teach his final will,
And sends his spirit of truth henceforth to dwell
In pious hearts, an inward oracle
To all truth requisite for men to know.
     So spake our saviour; but the subtle fiend,
Though inly stung with anger and disdain,
Dissembled, and this answer smooth returned.
     Sharply thou hast insisted on rebuke,
And urged me hard with doings, which not will
But misery hath wrested from me; where   470
Easily canst thou find one miserable,
And not enforced ofttimes to part from truth;
If it may stand him more in stead to lie,
Say and unsay, feign, flatter, or abjure?
But thou art placed above me, thou art Lord;
From thee I can and must submiss endure°
Check or reproof, and glad to scape so quit.°
Hard are the ways of truth, and rough to walk,
Smooth on the tongue discoursed, pleasing to the ear,
And tuneable as sylvan pipe or song;°   480
What wonder then if I delight to hear
Her dictates from thy mouth? most men admire
Virtue, who follow not her lore: permit me
To hear thee when I come (since no man comes)

And talk at least, though I despair to attain.
Thy father, who is holy, wise and pure,
Suffers the hypocrite or atheous priest°
To tread his sacred courts, and minister
About his altar, handling holy things,
Praying or vowing, and vouchsafed his voice   490
To Balaam reprobate, a prophet yet°
Inspired; disdain not such access to me.

   To whom our saviour with unaltered brow.
Thy coming hither, though I know thy scope,°
I bid not or forbid; do as thou find'st
Permission from above; thou canst not more.

   He added not; and Satan bowing low
His grey dissimulation, disappeared
Into thin air diffused: for now began°
Night with her sullen wing to double-shade°   500
The desert, fowls in their clay nests were couched;
And now wild beasts came forth the woods to roam.

THE SECOND BOOK

   Meanwhile the new-baptized, who yet remained
At Jordan with the Baptist, and had seen
Him whom they heard so late expressly called
Jesus Messiah Son of God declared,
And on that high authority had believed,
And with him talked, and with him lodged, I mean
Andrew and Simon, famous after known°
With others though in holy writ not named,
Now missing him their joy so lately found,
So lately found, and so abruptly gone,   10
Began to doubt, and doubted many days,°
And as the days increased, increased their doubt:
Sometimes they thought he might be only shown,
And for a time caught up to God, as once°
Moses was in the mount, and missing long;°
And the great Thisbite who on fiery wheels°
Rode up to heaven, yet once again to come.
Therefore as those young prophets then with care
Sought lost Elijah, so in each place these°

Nigh to Bethabara, in Jericho
The city of palms, Aenon, and Salem old,°
Machaerus and each town or city walled°
On this side the broad lake Genezaret,°
Or in Perea, but returned in vain.
Then on the bank of Jordan, by a creek:
Where winds with reeds, and osiers whisp'ring play
Plain fishermen, no greater men them call,°
Close in a cottage low together got
Their unexpected loss and plaints outbreathed.
    Alas, from what high hope to what relapse   30
Unlooked for are we fallen, our eyes beheld
Messiah certainly now come, so long
Expected of our fathers; we have heard
His words, his wisdom full of grace and truth,°
Now, now, for sure, deliverance is at hand,
The kingdom shall to Israel be restored:
Thus we rejoiced, but soon our joy is turned
Into perplexity and new amaze:°
For whither is he gone, what accident
Hath rapt him from us? will he now retire°   40
After appearance, and again prolong
Our expectation? God of Israel,
Send thy Messiah forth, the time is come;
Behold the kings of the earth how they oppress°
Thy chosen, to what height their power unjust
They have exalted, and behind them cast
All fear of thee, arise and vindicate
Thy glory, free thy people from their yoke,
But let us wait; thus far he hath performed,
Sent his anointed, and to us revealed him,   50
By his great prophet, pointed at and shown,
In public, and with him we have conversed;
Let us be glad of this, and all our fears
Lay on his providence; he will not fail
Nor will withdraw him now, nor will recall,
Mock us with his blessed sight, then snatch him hence,
Soon we shall see our hope, our joy return.
    Thus they out of their plaints new hope resume
To find whom at the first they found unsought:
But to his mother Mary, when she saw   60

Others returned from baptism, not her son,
Nor left at Jordan, tidings of him none;
Within her breast, though calm; her breast though pure,
Motherly cares and fears got head, and raised
Some troubled thoughts, which she in sighs thus clad.
  O what avails me now that honour high°
To have conceived of God, or that salute
Hail highly favoured, among women blessed;°
While I to sorrows am no less advanced,
And fears as eminent, above the lot   70
Of other women, by the birth I bore,
In such a season born when scarce a shed
Could be obtained to shelter him or me
From the bleak air; a stable was our warmth,
A manger his; yet soon enforced to fly
Thence into Egypt, till the murderous king°
Were dead, who sought his life, and missing filled
With infant blood the streets of Bethlehem;
From Egypt home returned, in Nazareth
Hath been our dwelling many years, his life   80
Private, unactive, calm, contemplative,
Little suspicious to any king; but now
Full grown to man, acknowledged, as I hear,
By John the Baptist, and in public shown,
Son owned from heaven by his father's voice;
I looked for some great change; to honour? no,
But trouble, as old Simeon plain foretold,°
That to the fall and rising he should be
Of many in Israel, and to a sign
Spoken against, that through my very soul   90
A sword shall pierce, this is my favoured lot,
My exaltation to afflictions high;
Afflicted I may be, it seems, and blessed;
I will not argue that, nor will repine.°
But where delays he now? some great intent
Conceals him: when twelve years he scarce had seen,
I lost him, but so found, as well I saw
He could not lose himself; but went about
His father's business; what he meant I mused,°
Since understand; much more his absence now   100
Thus long to some great purpose he obscures.°

But I to wait with patience am inured;
My heart hath been a storehouse long of things
And sayings laid up, portending strange events.
  Thus Mary pondering oft, and oft to mind
Recalling what remarkably had passed°
Since first her salutation heard, with thoughts
Meekly composed awaited the fulfilling:
The while her son tracing the desert wild,°
Sole but with holiest meditations fed,   110
Into himself descended, and at once
All his great work to come before him set;
How to begin, how to accomplish best
His end of being on earth, and mission high:
For Satan with sly preface to return°
Had left him vacant, and with speed was gone°
Up to the middle region of thick air,
Where all his potentates in council sat;
There without sign of boast, or sign of joy,
Solicitous and blank he thus began.°   120
  Princes, heaven's ancient sons, ethereal thrones,
Demonian spirits now, from the element
Each of his reign allotted, rightlier called,
Powers of fire, air, water, and earth beneath,°
So may we hold our place and these mild seats
Without new trouble; such an enemy
Is risen to invade us, who no less
Threatens than our expulsion down to hell;
I, as I undertook, and with the vote
Consenting in full frequence was empowered,°   130
Have found him, viewed him, tasted him, but find°
Far other labour to be undergone
Than when I dealt with Adam first of men,
Though Adam by his wife's allurement fell,
However to this man inferior far,
If he be man by mother's side at least,
With more than human gifts from heaven adorned,
Perfections absolute, graces divine,
And amplitude of mind to greatest deeds.°
Therefore I am returned, lest confidence   140
Of my success with Eve in Paradise
Deceive ye to persuasion over-sure

Of like succeeding here; I summon all
Rather to be in readiness, with hand
Or counsel to assist; lest I who erst
Thought none my equal, now be overmatched.
    So spake the old serpent doubting, and from all°
With clamour was assured their utmost aid
At his command; when from amidst them rose
Belial the dissolutest spirit that fell,°   150
The sensualest, and after Asmodai°
The fleshliest incubus, and thus advised.°
    Set women in his eye and in his walk,°
Among daughters of men the fairest found;
Many are in each region passing fair
As the noon sky; more like to goddesses
Than mortal creatures, graceful and discreet,
Expert in amorous arts, enchanting tongues
Persuasive, virgin majesty with mild
And sweet allayed, yet terrible to approach,   160
Skilled to retire, and in retiring draw
Hearts after them tangled in amorous nets.
Such object hath the power to soften and tame
Severest temper, smooth the rugged'st brow,°
Enerve, and with voluptuous hope dissolve,°
Draw out with credulous desire, and lead
At will the manliest, resolutest breast,
As the magnetic hardest iron draws.°
Women, when nothing else, beguiled the heart
Of wisest Solomon, and made him build,°   170
And made him bow to the gods of his wives.
    To whom quick answer Satan thus returned.
Belial, in much uneven scale thou weigh'st
All others by thyself; because of old
Thou thyself dot'st on womankind, admiring
Their shape, their colour, and attractive grace,
None are, thou think'st, but taken with such toys.
Before the flood thou with thy lusty crew,
False titled Sons of God, roaming the earth
Cast wanton eyes on the daughters of men,   180
And coupled with them, and begot a race.°
Have we not seen, or by relation heard,
In courts and regal chambers how thou lurk'st,

In wood or grove by mossy fountain-side,
In valley or green meadow to waylay
Some beauty rare, Calisto, Clymene,
Daphne, or Semele, Antiopa,
Or Amymone, Syrinx, many more°
Too long, then lay'st thy scapes on names adored,°
Apollo, Neptune, Jupiter, or Pan,   190
Satyr, or faun, or sylvan? But these haunts°
Delight not all; among the sons of men
How many have with a smile made small account
Of beauty and her lures, easily scorned
All her assaults, on worthier things intent?
Remember that Pellean conqueror,°
A youth, how all the beauties of the East
He slightly viewed, and slightly overpassed;°
How he surnamed of Africa dismissed°
In his prime youth the fair Iberian maid.   200
For Solomon he lived at ease, and full°
Of honour, wealth, high fare, aimed not beyond
Higher design than to enjoy his state;
Thence to the bait of women lay exposed;
But he whom we attempt is wiser far°
Than Solomon, of more exalted mind,
Made and set wholly on the accomplishment
Of greatest things; what woman will you find,
Though of this age the wonder and the fame,
On whom his leisure will vouchsafe an eye   210
Of fond desire? or should she confident,°
As sitting queen adored on beauty's throne,
Descend with all her winning charms begirt
To enamour, as the zone of Venus once°
Wrought that effect on Jove, so fables tell;
How would one look from his majestic brow
Seated as on the top of virtue's hill,
Discount'nance her despised, and put to rout
All her array; her female pride deject,°
Or turn to reverent awe! for beauty stands   220
In the admiration only of weak minds
Led captive; cease to admire, and all her plumes
Fall flat and shrink into a trivial toy,
At every sudden slighting quite abashed:

Therefore with manlier objects we must try
His constancy, with such as have more show
Of worth, of honour, glory, and popular praise;
Rocks whereon greatest men have oftest wrecked;
Or that which only seems to satisfy
Lawful desires of nature, not beyond;   230
And now I know he hungers where no food
Is to be found, in the wide wilderness;
The rest commit to me, I shall let pass
No advantage, and his strength as oft assay.

   He ceased, and heard their grant in loud acclaim;
Then forthwith to him takes a chosen band
Of spirits likest to himself in guile
To be at hand, and at his beck appear,
If cause were to unfold some active scene
Of various persons each to know his part;   240
Then to the desert takes with these his flight;
Where still from shade to shade the Son of God°
After forty days' fasting had remained,
Now hung'ring first, and to himself thus said.

   Where will this end? four times ten days I have passed
Wand'ring this woody maze, and human food
Nor tasted, nor had appetite; that fast
To virtue I impute not, or count part
Of what I suffer here; if nature need not,
Or God support nature without repast   250
Though needing, what praise is it to endure?
But now I feel I hunger, which declares,
Nature hath need of what she asks; yet God
Can satisfy that need some other way,
Though hunger still remain: so it remain°
Without this body's wasting, I content me,
And from the sting of famine fear no harm,
Nor mind it, fed with better thoughts that feed
Me hung'ring more to do my father's will.°

   It was the hour of night, when thus the Son   260
Communed in silent walk, then laid him down
Under the hospitable covert nigh
Of trees thick interwoven; there he slept,
And dreamed, as appetite is wont to dream,
Of meats and drinks, nature's refreshment sweet;

Him thought, he by the brook of Cherith stood°
And saw the ravens with their horny beaks
Food to Elijah bringing even and morn,
Though ravenous, taught to abstain from what they brought:
He saw the prophet also how he fled   270
Into the desert, and how there he slept
Under a juniper; then how awaked,
He found his supper on the coals prepared,
And by the angel was bid rise and eat,
And eat the second time after repose,
The strength whereof sufficed him forty days;
Sometimes that with Elijah he partook,
Or as a guest with Daniel at his pulse.°
Thus wore out night, and now the herald lark
Left his ground-nest, high towering to descry   280
The morn's approach, and greet her with his song:
As lightly from his grassy couch uprose
Our saviour, and found all was but a dream,
Fasting he went to sleep, and fasting waked.
Up to a hill anon his steps he reared,
From whose high top to ken the prospect round,
If cottage were in view, sheep-cote or herd;
But cottage, herd or sheep-cote none he saw,
Only in a bottom saw a pleasant grove,°
With chant of tuneful birds resounding loud;   290
Thither he bent his way, determined there
To rest at noon, and entered soon the shade°
High-roofed and walks beneath, and alleys brown°
That opened in the midst a woody scene,
Nature's own work it seemed (nature taught art)
And to a superstitious eye the haunt
Of wood-gods and wood-nymphs; he viewed it round,
When suddenly a man before him stood,
Not rustic as before, but seemlier clad,
As one in city, or court, or palace bred,   300
And with fair speech these words to him addressed.
    With granted leave officious I return,°
But much more wonder that the Son of God
In this wild solitude so long should bide
Of all things destitute, and well I know,
Not without hunger. Others of some note,

As story tells, have trod this wilderness;
The fugitive bondwoman with her son
Outcast Nebaioth, yet found he relief
By a providing angel; all the race°   310
Of Israel here had famished, had not God
Rained from heaven manna, and that prophet bold°
Native of Thebez wandering here was fed
Twice by a voice inviting him to eat.
Of thee these forty days none hath regard,
Forty and more deserted here indeed.
   To whom thus Jesus; What conclud'st thou hence?
They all had need, I as thou seest have none.
   How hast thou hunger then? Satan replied,
Tell me if food were now before thee set,   320
Wouldst thou not eat? thereafter as I like
The giver, answered Jesus. Why should that
Cause thy refusal, said the subtle fiend,
Hast thou not right to all created things,
Owe not all creatures by just right to thee
Duty and service, nor to stay till bid,
But tender all their power? nor mention I
Meats by the law unclean, or offered first°
To idols, those young Daniel could refuse;°
Nor proffered by an enemy, though who   330
Would scruple that, with want oppressed? behold
Nature ashamed, or better to express,
Troubled that thou shouldst hunger, hath purveyed
From all the elements her choicest store
To treat thee as beseems, and as her Lord
With honour, only deign to sit and eat.
   He spake no dream, for as his words had end,°
Our saviour lifting up his eyes, beheld
In ample space under the broadest shade
A table richly spread, in regal mode,   340
With dishes piled, and meats of noblest sort
And savour, beasts of chase, or fowl of game,
In pastry built, or from the spit, or boiled,°
Grisamber-steamed; all fish from sea or shore,°
Freshet, or purling brook, of shell or fin,°
And exquisitest name, for which was drained
Pontus and Lucrine bay, and Afric coast.°

Alas how simple, to these cates compared,°
Was that crude apple that diverted Eve!°
And at a stately sideboard by the wine   350
That fragrant smell diffused, in order stood
Tall stripling youths rich-clad, of fairer hue
Than Ganymede or Hylas, distant more°
Under the trees now tripped, now solemn stood
Nymphs of Diana's train, and Naiades°
With fruits and flowers from Amalthea's horn,°
And ladies of the Hesperides, that seemed°
Fairer than feigned of old, or fabled since
Of fairy damsels met in forest wide
By knights of Logres, or of Lyonesse,°   360
Lancelot or Pelleas, or Pellenore,°
And all the while harmonious airs were heard
Of chiming strings, or charming pipes and winds
Of gentlest gale Arabian odours fanned°
From their soft wings, and Flora's earliest smells.°
Such was the splendour, and the tempter now
His invitation earnestly renewed.
     What doubts the Son of God to sit and eat?°
These are not fruits forbidden, no interdict
Defends the touching of these viands pure,°   370
Their taste no knowledge works, at least of evil,°
But life preserves, destroys life's enemy,
Hunger, with sweet restorative delight.
All these are spirits of air, and woods, and springs,
Thy gentle ministers, who come to pay
Thee homage, and acknowledge thee their Lord:
What doubt'st thou Son of God? Sit down and eat.
     To whom thus Jesus temperately replied:
Said'st thou not that to all things I had right?
And who withholds my power that right to use?   380
Shall I receive by gift what of my own,
When and where likes me best, I can command?°
I can at will, doubt not, as soon as thou,
Command a table in this wilderness,°
And call swift flights of angels ministrant
Arrayed in glory on my cup to attend:°
Why shouldst thou then obtrude this diligence,°
In vain, where no acceptance it can find,

And with my hunger what hast thou to do?
Thy pompous delicacies I contemn,   390
And count thy specious gifts no gifts but guiles.
   To whom thus answered Satan malcontent:
That I have also power to give thou seest,
If of that power I bring thee voluntary
What I might have bestowed on whom I pleased,
And rather opportunely in this place
Chose to impart to thy apparent need,
Why shouldst thou not accept it? but I see
What I can do or offer is suspect;
Of these things others quickly will dispose   400
Whose pains have earned the far-fet spoil. With that°
Both table and provision vanished quite
With sound of harpies' wings, and talons heard;°
Only th' importune tempter still remained,°
And with these words his temptation pursued.
   By hunger, that each other creature tames,
Thou art not to be harmed, therefore not moved;
Thy temperance invincible besides,°
For no allurement yields to appetite,
And all thy heart is set on high designs,   410
High actions; but wherewith to be achieved?
Great acts require great means of enterprise,
Thou art unknown, unfriended, low of birth,
A carpenter thy father known, thyself
Bred up in poverty and straits at home;
Lost in a desert here and hunger-bit:
Which way or from what hope dost thou aspire
To greatness? whence authority deriv'st,
What followers, what retinue canst thou gain,
Or at thy heels the dizzy multitude,   420
Longer than thou canst feed them on thy cost?
Money brings honour, friends, conquest, and realms;°
What raised Antipater the Edomite,°
And his son Herod placed on Judah's throne;
(Thy throne) but gold that got him puissant friends?
Therefore, if at great things thou wouldst arrive,
Get riches first, get wealth, and treasure heap,
Not difficult, if thou hearken to me,
Riches are mine, fortune is in my hand;

They whom I favour thrive in wealth amain,   430
While virtue, valour, wisdom sit in want.
   To whom thus Jesus patiently replied;
Yet wealth without these three is impotent,
To gain dominion or to keep it gained.
Witness those ancient empires of the earth,
In height of all their flowing wealth dissolved:
But men endued with these have oft attained
In lowest poverty to highest deeds;
Gideon and Jephtha, and the shepherd lad,°
Whose offspring on the throne of Judah sat   440
So many ages, and shall yet regain
That seat, and reign in Israel without end.
Among the heathen (for throughout the world
To me is not unknown what hath been done
Worthy of memorial) canst thou not remember
Quintius, Fabricius, Curius, Regulus?°
For I esteem those names of men so poor
Who could do mighty things, and could contemn
Riches though offered from the hand of kings.
And what in me seems wanting, but that I   450
May also in this poverty as soon
Accomplish what they did, perhaps and more?
Extol not riches then, the toil of fools,°
The wise man's cumbrance if not snare, more apt
To slacken virtue, and abate her edge,
Than prompt her to do aught may merit praise.°
What if with like aversion I reject
Riches and realms; yet not for that a crown,°
Golden in show, is but a wreath of thorns,
Brings dangers, troubles, cares, and sleepless nights   460
To him who wears the regal diadem,
When on his shoulders each man's burden lies;
For therein stands the office of a king,
His honour, virtue, merit, and chief praise,
That for the public all this weight he bears.
Yet he who reigns within himself, and rules°
Passions, desires, and fears, is more a king;
Which every wise and virtuous man attains:
And who attains not, ill aspires to rule
Cities of men, or headstrong multitudes,   470

Subject himself to anarchy within,
Or lawless passions in him which he serves.
But to guide nations in the way of truth
By saving doctrine, and from error lead
To know, and, knowing worship God aright,
Is yet more kingly, this attracts the soul,
Governs the inner man, the nobler part,
That other o'er the body only reigns,
And oft by force, which to a generous mind
So reigning can be no sincere delight.   480
Besides to give a kingdom hath been thought
Greater and nobler done, and to lay down°
Far more magnanimous, than to assume.
Riches are needless then, both for themselves,
And for thy reason why they should be sought,
To gain a sceptre, oftest better missed.

THE THIRD BOOK

So spake the Son of God, and Satan stood
Awhile as mute confounded what to say,
What to reply, confuted and convinced
Of his weak arguing, and fallacious drift;
At length collecting all his serpent wiles,
With soothing words renewed, him thus accosts.
I see thou know'st what is of use to know,
What best to say canst say, to do canst do;
Thy actions to thy words accord, thy words
To thy large heart give utterance due, thy heart   10
Contains of good, wise, just, the perfect shape.
Should kings and nations from thy mouth consult,
Thy counsel would be as the oracle
Urim and Thummim, those oraculous gems°
On Aaron's breast: or tongue of seers old
Infallible; or wert thou sought to deeds°
That might require the array of war, thy skill
Of conduct would be such, that all the world
Could not sustain thy prowess, or subsist°
In battle, though against thy few in arms.   20
These godlike virtues wherefore dost thou hide?

Affecting private life, or more obscure
In savage wilderness, wherefore deprive
All earth her wonder at thy acts, thyself
The fame and glory, glory the reward
That sole excites to high attempts the flame
Of most erected spirits, most tempered pure°
Ethereal, who all pleasures else despise,°
All treasures and all gain esteem as dross,
And dignities and powers all but the highest?   30
Thy years are ripe, and over-ripe, the son°
Of Macedonian Philip had ere these
Won Asia and the throne of Cyrus held°
At his dispose, young Scipio had brought down
The Carthaginian pride, young Pompey quelled
The Pontic king and in triumph had rode.°
Yet years, and to ripe years judgment mature,°
Quench not the thirst of glory, but augment.
Great Julius, whom now all the world admires
The more he grew in years, the more inflamed   40
With glory, wept that he had lived so long°
Inglorious: but thou yet art not too late.
    To whom our saviour calmly thus replied.
Thou neither dost persuade me to seek wealth
For empire's sake, nor empire to affect
For glory's sake by all thy argument.
For what is glory but the blaze of fame,°
The people's praise, if always praise unmixed?
And what the people but a herd confused,
A miscellaneous rabble, who extol   50
Things vulgar, and well weighed, scarce worth the praise,°
They praise and they admire they know not what;
And know not whom, but as one leads the other;
And what delight to be by such extolled,
To live upon their tongues and be their talk,
Of whom to be dispraised were no small praise?
His lot who dares be singularly good.
The intelligent among them and the wise
Are few, and glory scarce of few is raised.
This is true glory and renown, when God,   60
Looking on the earth, with approbation marks
The just man, and divulges him through heaven°

To all his angels, who with true applause
Recount his praises; thus he did to Job,
When to extend his fame through heaven and earth,
As thou to thy reproach may'st well remember,
He asked thee, Hast thou seen my servant Job?°
Famous he was in heaven, on earth less known;
Where glory is false glory, attributed
To things not glorious, men not worthy of fame.   70
They err who count it glorious to subdue
By conquest far and wide, to overrun
Large countries, and in field great battles win,
Great cities by assault: what do these worthies,
But rob and spoil, burn, slaughter, and enslave
Peaceable nations, neighbouring, or remote,
Made captive, yet deserving freedom more
Than those their conquerors, who leave behind
Nothing but ruin wheresoe'er they rove,
And all the flourishing works of peace destroy,   80
Then swell with pride, and must be titled gods,
Great benefactors of mankind, deliverers,
Worshipped with temple, priest, and sacrifice;
One is the son of Jove, of Mars the other,°
Till conqueror Death discover them scarce men,
Rolling in brutish vices, and deformed,°
Violent or shameful death their due reward.
But if there be in glory aught of good,
It may by means far different be attained
Without ambition, war, or violence;   90
By deeds of peace, by wisdom eminent,
By patience, temperance; I mention still
Him whom thy wrongs with saintly patience borne,
Made famous in a land and times obscure;
Who names not now with honour patient Job?
Poor Socrates (who next more memorable?)
By what he taught and suffered for so doing,
For truth's sake suffering death unjust, lives now°
Equal in fame to proudest conquerors.
Yet if for fame and glory aught be done,   100
Aught suffered; if young African for fame°
His wasted country freed from Punic rage,
The deed becomes unpraised, the man at least,

And loses, though but verbal, his reward.
Shall I seek glory then, as vain men seek
Oft not deserved? I seek not mine, but his°
Who sent me, and thereby witness whence I am.
　　To whom the tempter murmuring thus replied.
Think not so slight of glory; therein least
Resembling thy great father: he seeks glory,°　　　　　110
And for his glory all things made, all things
Orders and governs, nor content in heaven
By all his angels glorified, requires
Glory from men, from all men good or bad,
Wise or unwise, no difference, no exemption;
Above all sacrifice, or hallowed gift
Glory he requires, and glory he receives
Promiscuous from all nations, Jew, or Greek,°
Or barbarous, nor exception hath declared;°
From us his foes pronounced glory he exacts.　　　　　120
　　To whom our saviour fervently replied.
And reason; since his word all things produced,
Though chiefly not for glory as prime end,
But to show forth his goodness, and impart
His good communicable to every soul
Freely; of whom what could he less expect
Than glory and benediction, that is thanks,
The slightest, easiest, readiest recompense
From them who could return him nothing else,
And not returning that would likeliest render　　　　　130
Contempt instead, dishonour, obloquy?
Hard recompense, unsuitable return
For so much good, so much beneficence.
But why should man seek glory? who of his own
Hath nothing, and to whom nothing belongs
But condemnation, ignominy, and shame?
Who for so many benefits received
Turned recreant to God, ingrate and false,°
And so of all true good himself despoiled,
Yet, sacrilegious, to himself would take　　　　　140
That which to God alone of right belongs;
Yet so much bounty is in God, such grace,
That who advance his glory, not their own,
Them he himself to glory will advance.

So spake the Son of God; and here again
Satan had not to answer, but stood struck°
With guilt of his own sin, for he himself
Insatiable of glory had lost all,
Yet of another plea bethought him soon.
Of glory as thou wilt, said he, so deem,   150
Worth or not worth the seeking, let it pass:
But to a kingdom thou art born, ordained
To sit upon thy father David's throne; °
By mother's side thy father, though thy right°
Be now in powerful hands, that will not part
Easily from possession won with arms;
Judaea now and all the promised land
Reduced a province under Roman yoke,
Obeys Tiberius; nor is always ruled
With temperate sway; oft have they violated   160
The Temple, oft the law with foul affronts,°
Abominations rather, as did once
Antiochus: and think'st thou to regain°
Thy right by sitting still or thus retiring?
So did not Maccabeus: he indeed
Retired unto the desert, but with arms;
And o'er a mighty king so oft prevailed,°
That by strong hand his family obtained,
Though priests, the crown, and David's throne usurped,
With Modin and her suburbs once content.°   170
If kingdom move thee not, let move thee zeal,
And duty; zeal and duty are not slow;
But on occasion's forelock watchful wait.°
They themselves rather are occasion best,
Zeal of thy father's house, duty to free
Thy country from her heathen servitude;
So shalt thou best fulfil, best verify
The prophets old, who sung thy endless reign,
The happier reign the sooner it begins,
Reign then; what canst thou better do the while?   180
   To whom our saviour answer thus returned.
All things are best fulfilled in their due time,°
And time there is for all things, truth hath said:°
If of my reign prophetic writ hath told,
That it shall never end, so when begin°

The Father in his purpose hath decreed,
He in whose hand all times and seasons roll.
What if he hath decreed that I shall first
Be tried in humble state, and things adverse,
By tribulations, injuries, insults,   190
Contempts, and scorns, and snares, and violence,
Suffering, abstaining, quietly expecting
Without distrust or doubt, that he may know
What I can suffer, how obey? who best
Can suffer, best can do; best reign, who first
Well hath obeyed; just trial ere I merit
My exaltation without change or end.
But what concerns it thee when I begin
My everlasting kingdom, why art thou
Solicitous, what moves thy inquisition?   200
Know'st thou not that my rising is thy fall,
And my promotion will be thy destruction?
    To whom the tempter inly racked replied.
Let that come when it comes; all hope is lost
Of my reception into grace; what worse?
For where no hope is left, is left no fear;
If there be worse, the expectation more
Of worse torments me than the feeling can.
I would be at the worst; worst is my port,
My harbour and my ultimate repose,   210
The end I would attain, my final good.
My error was my error, and my crime
My crime; whatever for itself condemned,°
And will alike be punished; whether thou
Reign or reign not; though to that gentle brow
Willingly I could fly, and hope thy reign,
From that placid aspect and meek regard,
Rather than aggravate my evil state,
Would stand between me and thy father's ire
(Whose ire I dread more than the fire of hell),   220
A shelter and a kind of shading cool
Interposition, as a summer's cloud.
If I then to the worst that can be haste,
Why move thy feet so slow to what is best,
Happiest both to thyself and all the world,
That thou who worthiest art shouldst be their king?

Perhaps thou linger'st in deep thoughts detained
Of the enterprise so hazardous and high;
No wonder, for though in thee be united
What of perfection can in man be found,   230
Or human nature can receive, consider
Thy life hath yet been private, most part spent
At home, scarce viewed the Galilean towns,
And once a year Jerusalem, few days'
Short sojourn; and what thence couldst thou observe?
The world thou hast not seen, much less her glory,
Empires, and monarchs, and their radiant courts,
Best school of best experience, quickest in sight
In all things that to greatest actions lead.
The wisest, unexperienced, will be ever   240
Timorous and loath, with novice modesty
(As he who seeking asses found a kingdom),°
Irresolute, unhardy, unadvent'rous:
But I will bring thee where thou soon shalt quit
Those rudiments, and see before thine eyes
The monarchies of the earth, their pomp and state,°
Sufficient introduction to inform°
Thee, of thyself so apt, in regal arts,
And regal mysteries; that thou may'st know°
How best their opposition to withstand.°   250
    With that (such power was given him then) he took
The Son of God up to a mountain high.°
It was a mountain at whose verdant feet
A spacious plain outstretched in circuit wide
Lay pleasant; from his side two rivers flowed,°
Th' one winding, the other straight, and left between
Fair champaign with less rivers interveined,°
Then meeting joined their tribute to the sea:
Fertile of corn the glebe, of oil and wine,°
With herds the pastures thronged, with flocks the hills,   260
Huge cities and high-towered, that well might seem
The seats of mightiest monarchs, and so large
The prospect was, that here and there was room
For barren desert fountainless and dry.
To this high mountain-top the tempter brought
Our saviour, and new train of words began.
    Well have we speeded, and o'er hill and dale,

Forest and field, and flood, temples and towers
Cut shorter many a league; here thou behold'st°
Assyria and her empire's ancient bounds,   270
Araxes and the Caspain lake, thence on°
As far as Indus east, Euphrates west,
And oft beyond; to south the Persian bay,
And inaccessible the Arabian drouth:°
Here Nineveh, of length within her wall°
Several days' journey, built by Ninus old,°
Of that first golden monarchy the seat,
And seat of Salmanassar, whose success°
Israel in long captivity still mourns;
There Babylon the wonder of all tongues,   280
As ancient, but rebuilt by him who twice°
Judah and all thy father David's house
Led captive, and Jerusalem laid waste,
Till Cyrus set them free; Persepolis,°
His city there thou seest, and Bactra there;
Ecbatana her structure vast there shows,
And Hecatompylos her hundred gates,
There Susa by Choaspes, amber stream,°
The drink of none but kings; of later fame
Built by Emathian, or by Parthian hands,°   290
The great Seleucia, Nisibis, and there
Artaxata, Teredon, Ctesiphon,
Turning with easy eye thou may'st behold.
All these the Parthian, now some ages past,
By great Arsaces led, who founded first°
That empire, under his dominion holds
From the luxurious kings of Antioch won.
And just in time thou com'st to have a view
Of his great power; for now the Parthian king
In Ctesiphon hath gathered all his host   300
Against the Scythian, whose incursions wild°
Have wasted Sogdiana; to her aid°
He marches now in haste; see, though from far,
His thousands, in what martial equipage
They issue forth, steel bows, and shafts their arms
Of equal dread in flight, or in pursuit;
All horsemen, in which fight they most excel;
See how in warlike muster they appear,

In rhombs and wedges, and half-moons, and wings.°
    He looked and saw what numbers numberless°   310
The city gates outpoured, light-armèd troops
In coats of mail and military pride;
In mail their horses clad, yet fleet and strong,
Prancing their riders bore, the flower and choice
Of many provinces from bound to bound;
From Arachosia, from Candaor east,
And Margiana to the Hyrcanian cliffs
Of Caucasus, and dark Iberian dales,
From Atropatia and the neighbouring plains
Of Adiabene, Media, and the south   320
Of Susiana to Balsara's haven.°
He saw them in their forms of battle ranged,
How quick they wheeled, and flying behind them shot
Sharp sleet of arrowy showers against the face
Of their pursuers, and overcame by flight;
The field all iron cast a gleaming brown,
Nor wanted clouds of foot, nor on each horn,°
Cuirassiers all in steel for standing fight;°
Chariots or elephants endorsed with towers°
Of archers, nor of labouring pioneers°   330
A multitude with spades and axes armed
To lay hills plain, fell woods, or valleys fill,
Or where plain was raise hill, or overlay
With bridges rivers proud, as with a yoke;
Mules after these, camels and dromedaries,
And wagons fraught with utensils of war.
Such forces met not, nor so wide a camp,
When Agrican with all his northern powers
Besieged Albracca, as romances tell;
The city of Gallaphrone, from thence to win   340
The fairest of her sex Angelica
His daughter, sought by many prowest knights,°
Both paynim, and the peers of Charlemagne.°
Such and so numerous was their chivalry;°
At sight whereof the fiend yet more presumed,
And to our saviour thus his words renewed.
    That thou mayst know I seek not to engage
Thy virtue, and not every way secure
On no slight grounds thy safety; hear, and mark°

To what end I have brought thee hither and shown   350
All this fair sight; thy kingdom though foretold
By prophet or by angel, unless thou
Endeavour, as thy father David did,°
Thou never shalt obtain; prediction still
In all things, and all men, supposes means,
Without means used, what it predicts revokes.
But say thou wert possessed of David's throne
By free consent of all, none opposite,°
Samaritan or Jew; how couldst thou hope
Long to enjoy it quiet and secure,   360
Between two such enclosing enemies
Roman and Parthian? therefore one of these
Thou must make sure thy own, the Parthian first
By my advice, as nearer and of late
Found able by invasion to annoy°
Thy country, and captive lead away her kings
Antigonus, and old Hyrcanus bound,°
Maugre the Roman: it shall be my task°
To render thee the Parthian at dispose;°
Choose which thou wilt by conquest or by league.   370
By him thou shalt regain, without him not,
That which alone can truly reinstall thee
In David's royal seat, his true successor,
Deliverance of thy brethren, those ten tribes°
Whose offspring in his territory yet serve
In Habor, and among the Medes dispersed,°
Ten sons of Jacob, two of Joseph lost°
Thus long from Israel; serving as of old
Their fathers in the land of Egypt served,
This offer sets before thee to deliver.   380
These if from servitude thou shalt restore
To their inheritance, then, nor till then,
Thou on the throne of David in full glory,
From Egypt to Euphrates and beyond°
Shalt reign, and Rome or Caesar not need fear.
    To whom our saviour answered thus unmoved.
Much ostentation vain of fleshly arm,
And fragile arms, much instrument of war
Long in preparing, soon to nothing brought,
Before mine eyes thou hast set; and in my ear   390

Vented much policy, and projects deep°
Of enemies, of aids, battles and leagues,
Plausible to the world, to me worth naught.
Means I must use thou say'st, prediction else
Will unpredict and fail me of the throne:
My time I told thee (and that time for thee
Were better farthest off) is not yet come;
When that comes think not thou to find me slack
On my part aught endeavouring, or to need
Thy politic maxims, or that cumbersome   400
Luggage of war there shown me, argument
Of human weakness rather than of strength.
My brethren, as thou call'st them; those ten tribes
I must deliver, if I mean to reign
David's true heir, and his full sceptre sway
To just extent over all Israel's sons;
But whence to thee this zeal, where was it then
For Israel, or for David, or his throne,
When thou stood'st up his tempter to the pride
Of numb'ring Israel, which cost the lives°   410
Of threescore and ten thousand Israelites
By three days' pestilence? such was thy zeal
To Israel then, the same that now to me.
As for those captive tribes, themselves were they
Who wrought their own captivity, fell off°
From God to worship calves, the deities°
Of Egypt, Baal next and Ashtaroth,°
And all the idolatries of heathen round,
Besides their other worse than heathenish crimes;
Nor in the land of their captivity   420
Humbled themselves, or penitent besought
The God of their forefathers; but so died
Impenitent, and left a race behind
Like to themselves, distinguishable scarce
From Gentiles, but by circumcision vain,
And God with idols in their worship joined.
Should I of these the liberty regard,
Who freed, as to their ancient patrimony,
Unhumbled, unrepentant, unreformed,
Headlong would follow; and to their gods perhaps° 430
Of Bethel and of Dan? no, let them serve

Their enemies, who serve idols with God.
Yet he at length, time to himself best known,
Rememb'ring Abraham by some wondrous call
May bring them back repentant and sincere,
And at their passing cleave the Assyrian flood,
While to their native land with joy they haste,
As the Red Sea and Jordan once he cleft,°
When to the promised land their fathers passed;
To his due time and providence I leave them.   440
    So spake Israel's true king, and to the fiend
Made answer meet, that made void all his wiles.
So fares it when with truth falsehood contends.

THE FOURTH BOOK

Perplexed and troubled at his bad success°
The tempter stood, nor had what to reply,
Discovered in his fraud, thrown from his hope,
So oft, and the persuasive rhetoric
That sleeked his tongue, and won so much on Eve,°
So little here, nay lost; but Eve was Eve,
This far his over-match, who self-deceived°
And rash, beforehand had no better weighed
The strength he was to cope with, or his own:
But as a man who had been matchless held   10
In cunning, over-reached where least he thought,
To salve his credit, and for very spite
Still will be tempting him who foils him still,
And never cease, though to his shame the more;
Or as a swarm of flies in vintage-time,
About the wine-press where sweet must is poured,°
Beat off, returns as oft with humming sound;
Or surging waves against a solid rock,°
Though all to shivers dashed, the assault renew,°
Vain battery, and in froth or bubbles end;   20
So Satan, whom repulse upon repulse
Met ever; and to shameful silence brought,
Yet gives not o'er though desperate of success,
And his vain importunity pursues.
He brought our saviour to the western side

Of that high mountain, whence he might behold
Another plain, long but in breadth not wide;
Washed by the southern sea, and on the north
To equal length backed with a ridge of hills
That screened the fruits of the earth and seats of men   30
From cold septentrion blasts, thence in the midst
Divided by a river, of whose banks
On each side an imperial city stood,°
With towers and temples proudly elevate
On seven small hills, with palaces adorned,
Porches and theatres, baths, aqueducts,°
Statues and trophies, and triumphal arcs,°
Gardens and groves presented to his eyes,
Above the height of mountains interposed.
By what strange parallax or optic skill°   40
Of vision multiplied through air, or glass
Of telescope, were curious to inquire:°
And now the tempter thus his silence broke.
    The city which thou seest no other deem
Than great and glorious Rome, queen of the earth
So far renowned, and with the spoils enriched
Of nations; there the Capitol thou seest
Above the rest lifting his stately head
On the Tarpeian rock, her citadel°
Impregnable, and there Mount Palatine°   50
The imperial palace, compass huge, and high
The structure, skill of noblest architects,
With gilded battlements, conspicuous far,
Turrets and terraces, and glittering spires.
Many a fair edifice besides, more like
Houses of gods (so well I have disposed
My airy microscope) thou mayst behold
Outside and inside both, pillars and roofs
Carved work, the hand of famed artificers°
In cedar, marble, ivory or gold.   60
Thence to the gates cast round thine eye, and see
What conflux issuing forth, or entering in,
Praetors, proconsuls to their provinces°
Hasting or on return, in robes of state;
Lictors and rods the ensigns of their power,°
Legions and cohorts, turms of horse and wings:°

Or embassies from regions far remote
In various habits on the Appian road,°
Or on the Aemilian, some from farthest south,°
Syene, and where the shadow both way falls,°   70
Meroe Nilotic isle, and more to west,°
The realm of Bocchus to the Blackmoor sea;°
From the Asian kings and Parthian among these,
From India and the golden Chersoness,°
And utmost Indian isle Taprobane,°
Dusk faces with white silken turbans wreathed:
From Gallia, Gades, and the British west,°
Germans and Scythians, and Sarmatians north°
Beyond Danubius to the Tauric pool.°
All nations now to Rome obedience pay,   80
To Rome's great emperor, whose wide domain
In ample territory, wealth and power,
Civility of manners, arts, and arms,
And long renown thou justly mayst prefer
Before the Parthian; these two thrones except,
The rest are barbarous, and scarce worth the sight,
Shared among petty kings too far removed;
These having shown thee, I have shown thee all
The kingdoms of the world, and all their glory.
This emperor hath no son, and now is old,°   90
Old, and lascivious, and from Rome retired
To Capreae an island small but strong
On the Campanian shore, with purpose there
His horrid lusts in private to enjoy,
Committing to a wicked favourite°
All public cares, and yet of him suspicious,
Hated of all, and hating; with what ease
Endued with regal virtues as thou art,
Appearing, and beginning noble deeds,
Might'st thou expel this monster from his throne   100
Now made a sty, and in his place ascending
A victor people free from servile yoke!
And with my help thou mayst; to me the power°
Is given, and by that right I give it thee.
Aim therefore at no less than all the world,
Aim at the highest, without the highest attained
Will be for thee no sitting, or not long

On David's throne, be prophesied what will.°
    To whom the Son of God unmoved replied.
Nor doth this grandeur and majestic show   110
Of luxury, though called magnificence,
More than of arms before, allure mine eye,
Much less my mind; though thou should'st add to tell
Their sumptuous gluttonies, and gorgeous feasts
On citron tables or Atlantic stone°
(For I have also heard, perhaps have read),
Their wines of Setia, Cales, and Falerne,°
Chios and Crete, and how they quaff in gold,
Crystal and myrrhine cups embossed with gems°
And studs of pearl, to me should'st tell who thirst   120
And hunger still: then embassies thou show'st
From nations far and nigh; what honour that,
But tedious waste of time to sit and hear
So many hollow compliments and lies,
Outlandish flatteries? then proceed'st to talk
Of the emperor, how easily subdued,
How gloriously; I shall, thou say'st, expel
A brutish monster: what if I withal
Expel a devil who first made him such?
Let his tormentor conscience find him out,   130
For him I was not sent, nor yet to free
That people victor once, now vile and base,°
Deservedly made vassal, who once just,
Frugal, and mild, and temperate, conquered well,
But govern ill the nations under yoke,
Peeling their provinces, exhausted all°
By lust and rapine; first ambitious grown
Of triumph that insulting vanity;°
Then cruel, by their sports to blood inured°
Of fighting beasts, and men to beasts exposed,   140
Luxurious by their wealth, and greedier still,
And from the daily scene effeminate.°
What wise and valiant man would seek to free
These thus degenerate, by themselves enslaved,
Or could of inward slaves make outward free?
Know therefore when my season comes to sit
On David's throne, it shall be like a tree°
Spreading and overshadowing all the earth,

Or as a stone that shall to pieces dash°
All monarchies besides throughout the world,   150
And of my kingdom there shall be no end:°
Means there shall be to this, but what the means,
Is not for thee to know, nor me to tell.
   To whom the tempter impudent replied.
I see all offers made by me how slight
Thou valu'st, because offered, and reject'st:
Nothing will please the difficult and nice,°
Or nothing more than still to contradict:°
On the other side know also thou, that I
On what I offer set as high esteem,   160
Nor what I part with mean to give for naught;
All these which in a moment thou behold'st,
The kingdoms of the world to thee I give;
For given to me, I give to whom I please,
No trifle; yet with this reserve, not else,
On this condition, if thou wilt fall down,
And worship me as thy superior lord,
Easily done, and hold them all of me;
For what can less so great a gift deserve?
   Whom thus our saviour answered with disdain.   170
I never liked thy talk, thy offers less,
Now both abhor, since thou hast dared to utter
The abominable terms, impious condition;
But I endure the time, till which expired,
Thou hast permission on me. It is written
The first of all commandments, Thou shalt worship°
The Lord thy God, and only him shalt serve;
And dar'st thou to the Son of God propound
To worship thee accursed, now more accursed
For this attempt bolder than that on Eve,   180
And more blasphemous? which expect to rue.
The kingdoms of the world to thee were given,
Permitted rather, and by thee usurped,
Other donation none thou canst produce:°
If given, by whom but by the King of kings,
God over all supreme? if given to thee,
By thee how fairly is the giver now
Repaid! But gratitude in thee is lost
Long since. Wert thou so void of fear or shame,

As offer them to me the Son of God, 190
To me my own, on such abhorrèd pact,
That I fall down and worship thee as God?
Get thee behind me; plain thou now appear'st°
That evil one, Satan forever damned.
　To whom the fiend with fear abashed replied.
Be not so sore offended, Son of God;
Though sons of God both angels are and men,°
If I to try whether in higher sort
Than these thou bear'st that title, have proposed
What both from men and angels I receive, 200
Tetrarchs of fire, air, flood, and on the earth°
Nations besides from all the quartered winds,
God of this world invoked and world beneath;
Who then thou art, whose coming is foretold
To me so fatal, me it most concerns.
The trial hath endamaged thee no way,
Rather more honour left and more esteem;
Me naught advantaged, missing what I aimed.
Therefore let pass, as they are transitory,
The kingdoms of this world; I shall no more 210
Advise thee, gain them as thou canst, or not.
And thou thyself seem'st otherwise inclined
Than to a worldly crown, addicted more
To contemplation and profound dispute,
As by that early action may be judged,
When slipping from thy mother's eye thou went'st
Alone into the Temple; there wast found
Amongst the gravest rabbis disputant
On points and questions fitting Moses' chair,°
Teaching not taught; the childhood shows the man, 220
As morning shows the day. Be famous then
By wisdom; as thy empire must extend,
So let extend thy mind o'er all the world,
In knowledge, all things in it comprehend,
All knowledge is not couched in Moses' law,
The Pentateuch or what the prophets wrote,°
The Gentiles also know, and write, and teach
To admiration, led by nature's light;°
And with the Gentiles much thou must converse,
Ruling them by persuasion as thou mean'st, 230

Without their learning how wilt thou with them,
Or they with thee hold conversation meet?°
How wilt thou reason with them, how refute
Their idolisms, traditions, paradoxes?°
Error by his own arms is best evinced.°
Look once more ere we leave this specular mount°
Westward, much nearer by south-west, behold
Where on the Aegean shore a city stands
Built nobly, pure the air, and light the soil,
Athens the eye of Greece, mother of arts°   240
And eloquence, native to famous wits
Or hospitable, in her sweet recess,°
City or suburban, studious walks and shades;°
See there the olive-grove of Academe,°
Plato's retirement, where the Attic bird°
Trills her thick-warbled notes the summer long,
There flowery hill Hymettus with the sound°
Of bees' industrious murmur oft invites
To studious musing; there Ilissus rolls°
His whispering stream; within the walls then view   250
The schools of ancient sages; his who bred
Great Alexander to subdue the world,°
Lyceum there, and painted Stoa next:°
There thou shalt hear and learn the secret power
Of harmony in tones and numbers hit°
By voice or hand, and various-measured verse,
Aeolian charms and Dorian lyric odes,°
And his who gave them breath, but higher sung,
Blind Melesigenes thence Homer called,°
Whose poem Phoebus challenged for his own.°   260
Thence what the lofty grave tragedians taught
In chorus or iambic, teachers best°
Of moral prudence, with delight received
In brief sententious precepts, while they treat°
Of fate, and chance, and change in human life;
High actions, and high passions best describing:
Thence to the famous orators repair,
Those ancient, whose resistless eloquence°
Wielded at will that fierce democracy,°
Shook the Arsenal and fulmined over Greece,°   270
To Macedon, and Artaxerxes' throne;°

To sage philosophy next lend thine ear,
From heaven descended to the low-roofed house
Of Socrates, see there his tenement,°
Whom well inspired the oracle pronounced
Wisest of men; from whose mouth issued forth°
Mellifluous streams that watered all the schools°
Of Academics old and new, with those
Surnamed Peripatetics, and the sect
Epicurean, and the Stoic severe;   280
These here revolve, or, as thou lik'st, at home,°
Till time mature thee to a kingdom's weight;
These rules will render thee a king complete
Within thyself, much more with empire joined.
　　To whom our saviour sagely thus replied.
Think not but that I know these things, or think
I know them not; not therefore am I short
Of knowing what I ought: he who receives
Light from above, from the fountain of light,
No other doctrine needs, though granted true;   290
But these are false, or little else but dreams,
Conjectures, fancies, built on nothing firm.
The first and wisest of them all professed
To know this only, that he nothing knew;
The next to fabling fell and smooth conceits,°
A third sort doubted all things, though plain sense;°
Others in virtue placed felicity,
But virtue joined with riches and long life,°
In corporal pleasure he, and careless ease,°
The Stoic last in philosophic pride,   300
By him called virtue; and his virtuous man,
Wise, perfect in himself, and all possessing,
Equal to God, oft shames not to prefer,°
As fearing God nor man, contemning all
Wealth, pleasure, pain or torment, death and life,
Which when he lists, he leaves, or boasts he can,°
For all his tedious talk is but vain boast,
Or subtle shifts conviction to evade.
Alas what can they teach, and not mislead;
Ignorant of themselves, of God much more,   310
And how the world began, and how man fell
Degraded by himself, on grace depending?

Much of the soul they talk, but all awry,
And in themselves seek virtue, and to themselves
All glory arrogate, to God give none,
Rather accuse him under usual names,
Fortune and fate, as one regardless quite
Of mortal things. Who therefore seeks in these°
True wisdom, finds her not, or by delusion
Far worse, her false resemblance only meets,   320
An empty cloud. However many books
Wise men have said are wearisome; who reads°
Incessantly, and to his reading brings not
A spirit and judgment equal or superior
(And what he brings, what needs he elsewhere seek),°
Uncertain and unsettled still remains,
Deep-versed in books and shallow in himself,
Crude or intoxicate, collecting toys,°
And trifles for choice matters, worth a sponge;°
As children gathering pebbles on the shore.   330
Or if I would delight my private hours
With music or with poem, where so soon
As in our native language can I find
That solace? All our Law and story strewed°
With hymns, our psalms with artful terms inscribed,°
Our Hebrew songs and harps in Babylon,
That pleased so well our victor's ear, declare°
That rather Greece from us these arts derived;
Ill imitated, while they loudest sing
The vices of their deities, and their own   340
In fable, hymn, or song, so personating
Their gods ridiculous, and themselves past shame.
Remove their swelling epithets thick laid°
As varnish on a harlot's cheek, the rest,°
Thin sown with aught of profit or delight,
Will far be found unworthy to compare
With Sion's songs, to all true tastes excelling,
Where God is praised aright, and godlike men,
The holiest of holies, and his saints;
Such are from God inspired, not such from thee;   350
Unless where moral virtue is expressed°
By light of nature not in all quite lost.
Their orators thou then extoll'st, as those

The top of eloquence, statists indeed,°
And lovers of their country, as may seem;
But herein to our prophets far beneath,
As men divinely taught, and better teaching
The solid rules of civil government
In their majestic unaffected style
Than all the oratory of Greece and Rome.   360
In them is plainest taught, and easiest learnt,
What makes a nation happy, and keeps it so,
What ruins kingdoms, and lays cities flat;
These only with our law best form a king.
    So spake the Son of God; but Satan now
Quite at a loss, for all his darts were spent,
Thus to our saviour with stern brow replied.
    Since neither wealth, nor honour, arms nor arts,
Kingdom nor empire pleases thee, nor aught
By me proposed in life contemplative,   370
Or active, tended on by glory, or fame,
What dost thou in this world? the wilderness
For thee is fittest place, I found thee there,
And thither will return thee, yet remember
What I foretell thee, soon thou shalt have cause
To wish thou never hadst rejected thus
Nicely or cautiously my offered aid,°
Which would have set thee in short time with ease
On David's throne; or throne of all the world,
Now at full age, fulness of time, thy season,°   380
When prophecies of thee are best fulfilled.
Now contrary, if I read aught in heaven,
Or heaven write aught of fate, by what the stars
Voluminous, or single characters,
In their conjunction met, give me to spell,°
Sorrows, and labours, opposition, hate,
Attends thee, scorns, reproaches, injuries,
Violence and stripes, and lastly cruel death,°
A kingdom they portend thee, but what kingdom,
Real or allegoric I discern not,   390
Nor when, eternal sure, as without end,
Without beginning; for no date prefixed
Directs me in the starry rubric set.°
    So saying he took (for still he knew his power

Not yet expired) and to the wilderness
Brought back the Son of God, and left him there,
Feigning to disappear. Darkness now rose,
As daylight sunk, and brought in louring night
Her shadowy offspring unsubstantial both,
Privation mere of light and absent day.°   400
Our saviour meek and with untroubled mind
After his airy jaunt, though hurried sore,°
Hungry and cold betook him to his rest,
Wherever, under some concourse of shades
Whose branching arms thick intertwined might shield
From dews and damps of night his sheltered head,
But sheltered slept in vain, for at his head°
The tempter watched, and soon with ugly dreams
Disturbed his sleep; and either tropic now°
'Gan thunder, and both ends of heaven, the clouds   410
From many a horrid rift abortive poured°
Fierce rain with lightning mixed, water with fire
In ruin reconciled: nor slept the winds°
Within their stony caves, but rushed abroad
From the four hinges of the world, and fell°
On the vexed wilderness, whose tallest pines,
Though rooted deep as high, and sturdiest oaks
Bowed their stiff necks, loaden with stormy blasts,
Or torn up sheer: ill wast thou shrouded then,
O patient Son of God, yet only stood'st°   420
Unshaken; nor yet stayed the terror there,°
Infernal ghosts, and hellish furies, round
Environed thee, some howled, some yelled, some shrieked,
Some bent at thee their fiery darts, while thou
Sat'st unappalled in calm and sinless peace.
Thus passed the night so foul till morning fair
Came forth with pilgrim steps in amice grey;°
Who with her radiant finger stilled the roar°
Of thunder, chased the clouds, and laid the winds, .
And grisly spectres, which the fiend had raised   430
To tempt the Son of God with terrors dire.
And now the sun with more effectual beams
Had cheered the face of earth, and dried the wet
From drooping plant, or dropping tree; the birds
Who all things now behold more fresh and green,

After a night of storm so ruinous,
Cleared up their choicest notes in bush and spray°
To gratulate the sweet return of morn;°
Nor yet amidst this joy and brightest morn
Was absent, after all his mischief done,   440
The Prince of Darkness, glad would also seem
Of this fair change, and to our saviour came,
Yet with no new device, they all were spent,
Rather by this his last affront resolved,
Desperate of better course, to vent his rage,
And mad despite to be so oft repelled.
Him walking on a sunny hill he found,
Backed on the north and west by a thick wood,
Out of the wood he starts in wonted shape;°
And in a careless mood thus to him said.°   450
    Fair morning yet betides thee Son of God,
After a dismal night; I heard the rack°
As earth and sky would mingle; but myself
Was distant; and these flaws, though mortals fear them°
As dangerous to the pillared frame of heaven,
Or to the earth's dark basis underneath,
Are to the main as inconsiderable,°
And harmless, if not wholesome, as a sneeze°
To man's less universe, and soon are gone;
Yet as being oft-times noxious where they light   460
On man, beast, plant, wasteful and turbulent,
Like turbulencies in the affairs of men,
Over whose heads they roar, and seem to point,
They oft fore-signify and threaten ill:
This tempest at this desert most was bent;
Of men at thee, for only thou here dwell'st.
Did I not tell thee, if thou didst reject
The perfect season offered with my aid
To win thy destined seat, but wilt prolong
All to the push of fate, pursue thy way   470
Of gaining David's throne no man knows when,
For both the when and how is nowhere told,
Thou shalt be what thou art ordained, no doubt;
For angels have proclaimed it, but concealing
The time and means: each act is rightliest done,
Not when it must, but when it may be best.

If thou observe not this, be sure to find,
What I foretold thee, many a hard assay
Of dangers, and adversities and pains,
Ere thou of Israel's sceptre get fast hold;   480
Whereof this ominous night that closed thee round,
So many terrors, voices, prodigies
May warn thee, as a sure foregoing sign.
    So talked he, while the Son of God went on
And stayed not, but in brief him answered thus.
    Me worse than wet thou find'st not; other harm
Those terrors which thou speak'st of, did me none;
I never feared they could, though noising loud
And threat'ning nigh; what they can do as signs
Betokening, or ill boding, I contemn   490
As false portents, not sent from God, but thee;
Who knowing I shall reign past thy preventing,
Obtrud'st thy offered aid, that I accepting
At least might seem to hold all power of thee,
Ambitious spirit, and would'st be thought my God,
And storm'st refused, thinking to terrify
Me to thy will; desist, thou art discerned
And toil'st in vain, nor me in vain molest.
    To whom the fiend now swoll'n with rage replied:
Then hear, O Son of David, virgin-born;   500
For Son of God to me is yet in doubt,
Of the Messiah I have heard foretold
By all the prophets; of thy birth at length
Announced by Gabriel with the first I knew,
And of the angelic song in Bethlehem field,
On thy birth-night, that sung thee saviour born.
From that time seldom have I ceased to eye
Thy infancy, thy childhood, and thy youth,
Thy manhood last, though yet in private bred;
Till at the ford of Jordan whither all   510
Flocked to the Baptist, I among the rest,
Though not to be baptized, by voice from heaven
Heard thee pronounced the Son of God beloved.
Thenceforth I thought thee worth my nearer view
And narrower scrutiny, that I might learn
In what degree or meaning thou art called
The Son of God, which bears no single sense;

The son of God I also am, or was,
And if I was, I am; relation stands;
All men are sons of God; yet thee I thought   520
In some respect far higher so declared.
Therefore I watched thy footsteps from that hour,
And followed thee still on to this waste wild;
Where by all best conjectures I collect°
Thou art to be my fatal enemy.°
Good reason then, if I beforehand seek
To understand my adversary, who
And what he is; his wisdom, power, intent,
By parle, or composition, truce, or league°
To win him, or win from him what I can.   530
And opportunity I here have had
To try thee, sift thee, and confess have found thee°
Proof against all temptation as a rock
Of adamant, and as a centre, firm°
To the utmost of mere man both wise and good,
Not more; for honours, riches, kingdoms, glory
Have been before contemned, and may again:
Therefore to know what more thou art than man,
Worth naming Son of God by voice from heaven,
Another method I must now begin.   540
     So saying he caught him up, and without wing
Of hippogriff bore through the air sublime°
Over the wilderness and o'er the plain;
Till underneath them fair Jerusalem,
The holy city lifted high her towers,
And higher yet the glorious Temple reared
Her pile, far off appearing like a mount°
Of alabaster, topped with golden spires:°
There on the highest pinnacle he set°
The Son of God; and added thus in scorn: 550
     There stand, if thou wilt stand; to stand upright
Will ask thee skill; I to thy father's house
Have brought thee, and highest placed, highest is best,
Now show thy progeny; if not to stand,°
Cast thyself down; safely if Son of God:
For it is written, He will give command°
Concerning thee to his angels, in their hands
They shall uplift thee, lest at any time

Thou chance to dash thy foot against a stone.
    To whom thus Jesus: Also it is written,°   560
Tempt not the Lord thy God, he said and stood.
But Satan smitten with amazement fell
As when Earth's son Antaeus (to compare°
Small things with greatest) in Irassa strove°
With Jove's Alcides, and oft foiled still rose,°
Receiving from his mother Earth new strength,
Fresh from his fall, and fiercer grapple joined,
Throttled at length in the air, expired and fell;
So after many a foil the tempter proud,
Renewing fresh assaults, amidst his pride   570
Fell whence he stood to see his victor fall.
And as that Theban monster that proposed°
Her riddle, and him, who solved it not, devoured;
That once found out and solved, for grief and spite
Cast herself headlong from the Ismenian steep,
So struck with dread and anguish fell the fiend,
And to his crew, that sat consulting, brought
Joyless triumphals of his hoped success,°
Ruin, and desperation, and dismay,
Who durst so proudly tempt the Son of God.   580
So Satan fell and straight a fiery globe°
Of angels on full sail of wing flew nigh,
Who on their plumy vans received him soft°
From his uneasy station, and upbore
As on a floating couch through the blithe air,°
Then in a flowery valley set him down
On a green bank, and set before him spread
A table of celestial food, divine,
Ambrosial, fruits fetched from the tree of life,°
And from the fount of life ambrosial drink,°   590
That soon refreshed him wearied, and repaired
What hunger, if aught hunger had impaired,
Or thirst, and as he fed, angelic choirs
Sung heavenly anthems of his victory
Over temptation, and the tempter proud.
    True image of the Father whether throned
In the bosom of bliss, and light of light°
Conceiving, or remote from heaven, enshrined°
In fleshly tabernacle, and human form,

Wandering the wilderness, whatever place,°   600
Habit, or state, or motion, still expressing
The Son of God, with godlike force endued
Against the attempter of thy father's throne,
And thief of Paradise; him long of old
Thou didst debel, and down from heaven cast°
With all his army, now thou hast avenged
Supplanted Adam, and, by vanquishing°
Temptation, hast regained lost Paradise,
And frustrated the conquest fraudulent:
He never more henceforth will dare set foot   610
In Paradise to tempt; his snares are broke:
For though that seat of earthly bliss be failed,°
A fairer Paradise is founded now
For Adam and his chosen sons, whom thou
A saviour art come down to reinstall.
Where they shall dwell secure, when time shall be
Of tempter and temptation without fear.
But thou, infernal serpent, shalt not long
Rule in the clouds; like an autumnal star
Or lightning thou shalt fall from heaven trod down   620
Under his feet: for proof, ere this thou feel'st°
Thy wound, yet not thy last and deadliest wound°
By this repulse received, and hold'st in hell
No triumph; in all her gates Abaddon rues°
Thy bold attempt; hereafter learn with awe
To dread the Son of God: he all unarmed
Shall chase thee with the terror of his voice
From thy demoniac holds, possession foul,°
Thee and thy legions, yelling they shall fly,
And beg to hide them in a herd of swine,   630
Lest he command them down into the deep°
Bound, and to torment sent before their time.
Hail Son of the most high, heir of both worlds,
Queller of Satan, on thy glorious work
Now enter, and begin to save mankind.

    Thus they the Son of God our saviour meek
Sung victor, and from heavenly feast refreshed
Brought on his way with joy; he unobserved
Home to his mother's house private returned.

SAMSON AGONISTES

OF THAT SORT OF DRAMATIC POEM
WHICH IS CALLED TRAGEDY

Tragedy, as it was anciently composed, hath been ever held the gravest, moralest, and most profitable of all other poems: therefore said by Aristotle° to be of power by raising pity and fear, or terror, to purge the mind of those and such-like passions, that is to temper and reduce them to just measure with a kind of delight, stirred up by reading or seeing those passions well imitated. Nor is nature wanting in her own effects to make good his assertion: for so in physic things of melancholic hue and quality are used against melancholy, sour against sour, salt to remove salt humours. Hence philosophers and other gravest writers, as Cicero, Plutarch and others, frequently cite out of tragic poets, both to adorn and illustrate their discourse. The Apostle Paul himself thought it not unworthy to insert a verse of Euripides° into the text of Holy Scripture, 1 Cor. xv. 33, and Paraeus° commenting on the *Revelation*, divides the whole book as a tragedy, into acts distinguished each by a chorus of heavenly harpings and song between. Heretofore men in highest dignity have laboured not a little to be thought able to compose a tragedy. Of that honour Dionysius the elder° was no less ambitious, than before of his attaining to the tyranny. Augustus Caesar° also had begun his *Ajax*, but unable to please his own judgement with what he had begun, left it unfinished. Seneca° the philosopher is by some thought the author of those tragedies (at least the best of them) that go under that name. Gregory Nazianzen° a Father of the church, thought it not unbeseeming the sanctity of his person to write a tragedy, which he entitled, *Christ Suffering*. This is mentioned to vindicate tragedy from the small esteem, or rather infamy, which in the account of many it undergoes at this day with other common interludes; happening through the poet's error of intermixing comic stuff with tragic sadness° and gravity;° or introducing trivial and vulgar persons, which by all judicious hath been counted absurd; and brought in without discretion, corruptly to gratify the people. And though ancient tragedy use no prologue,° yet using sometimes, in case of self-defence, or explanation, that which Martial calls an epistle;° in behalf of this tragedy coming forth after the ancient manner, much different from what among us passes for best, thus much beforehand may be epistled; that chorus is here introduced after the Greek manner, not ancient only but modern, and still in use among the Italians. In the modelling therefore of this poem, with good reason, the ancients and Italians are rather followed, as of much more authority and fame. The measure of verse used in the chorus is of all sorts, called by the Greeks monostrophic, or rather *apolelymenon*,° without regard had to strophe, antistrophe or epode, which were a kind of stanzas framed only for the music, then used with the chorus that sung; not essential to the poem, and therefore not material; or being divided into stanzas or pauses, they may be called *alleostropha*.° Division into act and scene referring chiefly to the stage (to which this work never was intended) is here omitted. It suffices if the whole drama be found not produced beyond the fifth act.°

Of the style and uniformity, and that commonly called the plot, whether intricate or explicit,° which is nothing indeed but such economy, or disposition of the fable as may stand best with verisimilitude and decorum; they only will best judge who are not unacquainted with Aeschylus, Sophocles, and Euripides, the three tragic poets unequalled yet by any, and the best rule to all who endeavour to write tragedy. The circumscription of time wherein the whole drama begins and ends, is according to ancient rule,° and best example, within the space of twenty-four hours.

THE ARGUMENT

Samson made captive, blind, and now in the prison at Gaza, there to labour as in a common workhouse, on a festival day, in the general cessation from labour, comes forth into the open air, to a place nigh, somewhat retired there to sit a while and bemoan his condition. Where he happens at length to be visited by certain friends and equals of his tribe, which make the Chorus, who seek to comfort him what they can; then by his old father Manoa,° who endeavours the like, and withal tells him his purpose to procure his liberty by ransom; lastly, that this feast was proclaimed by the Philistines as a day of thanksgiving for their deliverance from the hands of Samson, which yet more troubles him. Manoa then departs to prosecute his endeavour with the Philistian lords for Samson's redemption; who in the meanwhile is visited by other persons; and lastly by a public officer to require his coming to the feast before the lords and people, to play or show his strength in their presence; he at first refuses, dismissing the public officer with absolute denial to come; at length persuaded inwardly that this was from God, he yields to go along with him, who came now the second time with great threatenings to fetch him; the Chorus yet remaining on the place, Manoa returns full of joyful hope, to procure ere long his son's deliverance: in the midst of which discourse an Hebrew comes in haste confusedly at first; and afterward more distinctly relating the catastrophe,° what Samson had done to the Philistines, and by accident° to himself; wherewith the tragedy ends.

THE PERSONS

Samson
Manoa, the father of Samson
Dalila his wife
Harapha of Gath
Public Officer
Messenger
Chorus of Danites

The Scene before the Prison in Gaza

Sam. A little onward lend thy guiding hand
To these dark steps, a little further on;
For yonder bank hath choice of sun or shade,
There I am wont to sit, when any chance
Relieves me from my task of servile toil,
Daily in the common prison else enjoined me,°
Where I a prisoner chained, scarce freely draw
The air imprisoned also, close and damp,
Unwholesome draught: but here I feel amends,
The breath of heaven fresh blowing, pure and sweet,   10
With day-spring born; here leave me to respire.°
This day a solemn feast the people hold
To Dagon their sea-idol, and forbid°
Laborious works, unwillingly this rest
Their superstition yields me; hence with leave
Retiring from the popular noise, I seek°
This unfrequented place to find some ease,
Ease to the body some, none to the mind
From restless thoughts, that like a deadly swarm
Of hornets armed, no sooner found alone,°   20
But rush upon me thronging, and present
Times past, what once I was, and what am now.
O wherefore was my birth from heaven foretold
Twice by an angel, who at last in sight°
Of both my parents all in flames ascended
From off the altar, where an offering burned,
As in a fiery column charioting°
His godlike presence, and from some great act
Or benefit revealed to Abraham's race?
Why was my breeding ordered and prescribed   30
As of a person separate to God,°
Designed for great exploits; if I must die
Betrayed, captived, and both my eyes put out,
Made of my enemies the scorn and gaze;°
To grind in brazen fetters under task
With this heaven-gifted strength? O glorious strength
Put to the labour of a beast, debased
Lower than bond-slave! Promise was that I°
Should Israel from Philistian yoke deliver;
Ask for this great deliverer now, and find him   40

Eyeless in Gaza at the mill with slaves,
Himself in bonds under Philistian yoke;
Yet stay, let me not rashly call in doubt
Divine prediction; what if all foretold
Had been fulfilled but through mine own default,
Whom have I to complain of but myself?
Who this high gift of strength committed to me,
In what part lodged, how easily bereft me,
Under the seal of silence could not keep,
But weakly to a woman must reveal it,   50
O'ercome with importunity and tears.°
O impotence of mind, in body strong!
But what is strength without a double share
Of wisdom, vast, unwieldy, burdensome,
Proudly secure, yet liable to fall°
By weakest subtleties, not made to rule,
But to subserve where wisdom bears command.
God, when he gave me strength, to show withal
How slight the gift was, hung it in my hair.
But peace, I must not quarrel with the will   60
Of highest dispensation, which herein
Haply had ends above my reach to know:
Suffices that to me strength is my bane,°
And proves the source of all my miseries;
So many, and so huge, that each apart
Would ask a life to wail, but chief of all,°
O loss of sight, of thee I most complain!
Blind among enemies, O worse than chains,
Dungeon, or beggary, or decrepit age!
Light the prime work of God to me is extinct,°   70
And all her various objects of delight
Annulled, which might in part my grief have eased,
Inferior to the vilest now become
Of man or worm; the vilest here excel me,
They creep, yet see, I dark in light exposed
To daily fraud, contempt, abuse and wrong,
Within doors, or without, still as a fool,°
In power of others, never in my own;
Scarce half I seem to live, dead more than half.
O dark, dark, dark, amid the blaze of noon,   80
Irrecoverably dark, total eclipse

Without all hope of day!
O first-created beam, and thou great word,
Let there be light, and light was over all;
Why am I thus bereaved thy prime decree?
The sun to me is dark
And silent as the moon,°
When she deserts the night
Hid in her vacant interlunar cave.°
Since light so necessary is to life,   90
And almost life itself, if it be true
That light is in the soul,
She all in every part; why was the sight°
To such a tender ball as the eye confined?
So obvious and so easy to be quenched,°
And not as feeling through all parts diffused,
That she might look at will through every pore?
Then had I not been thus exiled from light;
As in the land of darkness yet in light,
To live a life half dead, a living death,   100
And buried; but O yet more miserable!
Myself, my sepulchre, a moving grave,
Buried, yet not exempt
By privilege of death and burial
From worst of other evils, pains and wrongs,
But made hereby obnoxious more°
To all the miseries of life,
Life in captivity
Among inhuman foes.
But who are these? for with joint pace I hear   110
The tread of many feet steering this way;
Perhaps my enemies who come to stare
At my affliction, and perhaps to insult,
Their daily practice to afflict me more.
Chor. This, this is he; softly awhile,
Let us not break in upon him;
O change beyond report, thought, or belief!
See how he lies at random, carelessly diffused,°
With languished head unpropped,
As one past hope, abandoned,   120
And by himself given over;
In slavish habit, ill-fitted weeds°

O'er-worn and soiled;
Or do my eyes misrepresent? Can this be he,
That heroic, that renowned,
Irresistible Samson? whom unarmed
No strength of man, or fiercest wild beast could withstand;
Who tore the lion, as the lion tears the kid,°
Ran on embattled armies clad in iron,°
And weaponless himself,   130
Made arms ridiculous, useless the forgery°
Of brazen shield and spear, the hammered cuirass,°
Chalybean-tempered steel, and frock of mail°
Adamantean proof;°
But safest he who stood aloof,
When insupportably his foot advanced,°
In scorn of their proud arms and warlike tools,
Spurned them to death by troops. The bold Ascalonite°
Fled from his lion ramp, old warriors turned°
Their plated backs under his heel;°   140
Or grovelling soiled their crested helmets in the dust.
Then with what trivial weapon came to hand,
The jaw of a dead ass, his sword of bone,°
A thousand foreskins fell, the flower of Palestine°
In Ramath-lehi famous to this day:°
Then by main force pulled up, and on his shoulders bore
The gates of Azza; post, and massy bar°
Up to the hill by Hebron, seat of giants old,°
No journey of a sabbath-day, and loaded so;°
Like whom the Gentiles feign to bear up heaven.°   150
Which shall I first bewail,
Thy bondage or lost sight,
Prison within prison
Inseparably dark?
Thou art become (O worst imprisonment!)
The dungeon of thyself; thy soul
(Which men enjoying sight oft without cause complain)
Imprisoned now indeed,
In real darkness of the body dwells,
Shut up from outward light   160
To incorporate with gloomy night;°
For inward light alas
Puts forth no visual beam.°

O mirror of our fickle state,
Since man on earth unparalleled!°
The rarer thy example stands,
By how much from the top of wondrous glory,
Strongest of mortal men,
To lowest pitch of abject fortune thou art fallen.
For him I reckon not in high estate°   170
Whom long descent of birth
Or the sphere of fortune raises;
But thee whose strength, while virtue was her mate,
Might have subdued the earth,
Universally crowned with highest praises.
Sam. I hear the sound of words, their sense the air
Dissolves unjointed ere it reach my ear.
Chor. He speaks, let us draw nigh. Matchless in might,
The glory late of Israel, now the grief;
We come thy friends and neighbours not unknown   180
From Eshtaol and Zora's fruitful vale°
To visit or bewail thee, or if better,
Counsel or consolation we may bring,
Salve to thy sores, apt words have power to suage
The tumours of a troubled mind,°
And are as balm to festered wounds.
Sam. Your coming, friends, revives me, for I learn
Now of my own experience, not by talk,
How counterfeit a coin they are who friends
Bear in their superscription (of the most°   190
I would be understood), in prosperous days°
They swarm, but in adverse withdraw their head
Not to be found, though sought. Ye see, O friends,
How many evils have enclosed me round;
Yet that which was the worst now least afflicts me,
Blindness, for had I sight, confused with shame,
How could I once look up, or heave the head,
Who like a foolish pilot have shipwrecked,
My vessel trusted to me from above,
Gloriously rigged; and for a word, a tear,   200
Fool, have divulged the secret gift of God
To a deceitful woman: tell me friends,
Am I not sung and proverbed for a fool
In every street, do they not say, how well

Are come upon him his deserts? yet why?
Immeasurable strength they might behold
In me, of wisdom nothing more than mean;°
This with the other should, at least, have paired,°
These two proportioned ill drove me transverse.°
Chor. Tax not divine disposal, wisest men°   210
Have erred, and by bad women been deceived;
And shall again, pretend they ne'er so wise.°
Deject not then so overmuch thyself,
Who hast of sorrow thy full load besides;
Yet truth to say, I oft have heard men wonder
Why thou shouldst wed Philistian women rather
Than of thine own tribe fairer, or as fair,
At least of thy own nation, and as noble.
Sam. The first I saw at Timna, and she pleased°
Me, not my parents, that I sought to wed,   220
The daughter of an infidel: they knew not
That what I motioned was of God; I knew
From intimate impulse, and therefore urged°
The marriage on; that by occasion hence
I might begin Israel's deliverance,
The work to which I was divinely called;
She proving false, the next I took to wife
(O that I never had! fond wish too late)°
Was in the vale of Sorec, Dalila,°
That specious monster, my accomplished snare.°   230
I thought it lawful from my former act,
And the same end; still watching to oppress
Israel's oppressors: of what now I suffer
She was not the prime cause, but I myself,
Who vanquished with a peal of words (O weakness!)°
Gave up my fort of silence to a woman.
Chor. In seeking just occasion to provoke
The Philistine, thy country's enemy,
Thou never wast remiss, I bear thee witness:
Yet Israel still serves with all his sons.   240
Sam. That fault I take not on me, but transfer
On Israel's governors, and heads of tribes,
Who seeing those great acts which God had done
Singly by me against their conquerors
Acknowledged not, or not at all considered

Deliverance offered: I on the other side
Used no ambition to commend my deeds,°
The deeds themselves, though mute, spoke loud the doer;
But they persisted deaf, and would not seem
To count them things worth notice, till at length   250
Their lords the Philistines with gathered powers
Entered Judea seeking me, who then
Safe to the rock of Etham was retired,°
Not flying, but forecasting in what place°
To set upon them, what advantaged best;
Meanwhile the men of Judah to prevent
The harass of their land, beset me round;
I willingly on some conditions came°
Into their hands, and they as gladly yield me
To the uncircumcised a welcome prey,   260
Bound with two cords; but cords to me were threads
Touched with the flame: on their whole host I flew
Unarmed, and with a trivial weapon felled°
Their choicest youth; they only lived who fled.
Had Judah that day joined, or one whole tribe,
They had by this possessed the towers of Gath,°
And lorded over them whom now they serve;
But what more oft in nations grown corrupt,
And by their vices brought to servitude,
Than to love bondage more than liberty,   270
Bondage with ease than strenuous liberty;
And to despise, or envy, or suspect
Whom God hath of his special favour raised
As their deliverer; if he aught begin,
How frequent to desert him, and at last°
To heap ingratitude on worthiest deeds?
Chor. Thy words to my remembrance bring
How Succoth and the fort of Penuel°
Their great deliverer contemned,
The matchless Gideon in pursuit   280
Of Madian and her vanquished kings;
And how ingrateful Ephraim°
Had dealt with Jephtha, who by argument,
Not worse than by his shield and spear
Defended Israel from the Ammonite,
Had not his prowess quelled their pride

In that sore battle when so many died
Without reprieve adjudged to death,
For want of well pronouncing *shibboleth*.
Sam. Of such examples add me to the roll,   290
Me easily indeed mine may neglect,°
But God's proposed deliverance not so.
Chor. Just are the ways of God,
And justifiable to men;
Unless there be who think not God at all,°
If any be, they walk obscure;
For of such doctrine never was there school,
But the heart of the fool,°
And no man therein doctor but himself.°
    Yet more there be who doubt his ways not just,°   300
As to his own edicts, found contradicting,
Then give the reins to wandering thought,
Regardless of his glory's diminution;
Till by their own perplexities involved
They ravel more, still less resolved,°
But never find self-satisfing solution.
    As if they would confine the interminable,°
And tie him to his own prescript,
Who made our laws to bind us, not himself,
And hath full right to exempt   310
Whom so it pleases him by choice
From national obstriction, without taint°
Of sin, or legal debt;°
For with his own laws he can best dispense.
    He would not else who never wanted means,
Nor in respect of the enemy just cause
To set his people free,
Have prompted this heroic Nazarite,
Against his vow of strictest purity,
To seek in marriage that fallacious bride,°   320
Unclean, unchaste.
    Down reason then, at least vain reasonings down,
Though reason here aver
That moral verdict quits her of unclean:°
Unchaste was subsequent, her stain not his.
    But see here comes thy reverend sire
With careful step, locks white as down,°

Old Manoa: advise
Forthwith how thou ought'st to receive him.
Sam. Ay me, another inward grief awaked,   330
With mention of that name renews the assault.
Man. Brethren and men of Dan, for such ye seem,
Though in this uncouth place; if old respect,°
As I suppose, towards your once gloried friend,
My son now captive, hither hath informed°
Your younger feet, while mine cast back with age
Came lagging after; say if he be here.
Chor. As signal now in low dejected state,°
As erst in highest, behold him where he lies.
Man. O miserable change! is this the man,   340
That invincible Samson, far renowned,
The dread of Israel's foes, who with a strength
Equivalent to angel's walked their streets,
None offering fight; who single combatant
Duelled their armies ranked in proud array,
Himself an army, now unequal match
To save himself against a coward armed
At one spear's length. O ever-failing trust
In mortal strength! and O what not in man
Deceivable and vain! Nay what thing good   350
Prayed for, but often proves our woe, our bane?
I prayed for children, and thought barrenness°
In wedlock a reproach; I gained a son,
And such a son as all men hailed me happy;
Who would be now a father in my stead?
O wherefore did God grant me my request,
And as a blessing with such pomp adorned?
Why are his gifts desirable, to tempt
Our earnest prayers, then given with solemn hand
As graces, draw a scorpion's tail behind?°   360
For this did the angel twice descend? for this
Ordained thy nurture holy, as of a plant;
Select, and sacred, glorious for awhile,
The miracle of men: then in an hour
Ensnared, assaulted, overcome, led bound,
Thy foes' derision, captive, poor, and blind
Into a dungeon thrust, to work with slaves?
Alas methinks whom God hath chosen once

To worthiest deeds, if he through frailty err,
He should not so o'erwhelm, and as a thrall   370
Subject him to so foul indignities,
Be it but for honour's sake of former deeds.
Sam. Appoint not heavenly disposition, father,°
Nothing of all these evils hath befall'n me
But justly; I myself have brought them on,
Sole author I, sole cause: if aught seem vile,
As vile hath been my folly, who have profaned°
The mystery of God given me under pledge
Of vow, and have betrayed it to a woman,
A Canaanite, my faithless enemy.   380
This well I knew, nor was at all surprised,
But warned by oft experience: did not she
Of Timna first betray me, and reveal
The secret wrested from me in her height°
Of nuptial love professed, carrying it straight
To them who had corrupted her, my spies,
And rivals? In this other was there found
More faith? who also in her prime of love,
Spousal embraces, vitiated with gold,°
Though offered only, by the scent conceived   390
Her spurious first-born; treason against me?°
Thrice she assayed with flattering prayers and sighs,
And amorous reproaches to win from me
My capital secret, in what part my strength°
Lay stored, in what part summed, that she might know:°
Thrice I deluded her, and turned to sport
Her importunity, each time perceiving
How openly, and with what impudence
She purposed to betray me, and (which was worse
Than undissembled hate) with what contempt   400
She sought to make me traitor to myself;
Yet the fourth time, when mustering all her wiles,
With blandished parleys, feminine assaults,
Tongue-batteries, she surceased not day nor night
To storm me over-watched, and wearied out.°
At times when men seek most repose and rest,
I yielded, and unlocked her all my heart,
Who with a grain of manhood well resolved
Might easily have shook off all her snares:

But foul effeminacy held me yoked 410
Her bond-slave; O indignity, O blot
To honour and religion! servile mind
Rewarded well with servile punishment!
The base degree to which I now am fall'n,
These rags, this grinding, is not yet so base
As was my former servitude, ignoble,
Unmanly, ignominious, infamous,
True slavery, and that blindness worse than this,
That saw not how degenerately I served.
Man. I cannot praise thy marriage-choices, son, 420
Rather approved them not; but thou didst plead
Divine impulsion prompting how thou might'st
Find some occasion to infest our foes.°
I state not that; this I am sure; our foes°
Found soon occasion thereby to make thee
Their captive, and their triumph; thou the sooner
Temptation found'st, or over-potent charms
To violate the sacred trust of silence
Deposited within thee; which to have kept
Tacit, was in thy power; true; and thou bear'st° 430
Enough, and more the burden of that fault;
Bitterly hast thou paid, and still art paying
That rigid score. A worse thing yet remains,°
This day the Philistines a popular feast°
Here celebrate in Gaza, and proclaim
Great pomp, and sacrifice, and praises loud
To Dagon, as their god who hath delivered
Thee Samson bound and blind into their hands,
Them out of thine, who slew'st them many a slain.°
So Dagon shall be magnified, and God, 440
Besides whom is no god, compared with idols,
Disglorified, blasphemed, and had in scorn
By the idolatrous rout amidst their wine;
Which to have come to pass by means of thee,
Samson, of all thy sufferings think the heaviest,
Of all reproach the most with shame that ever
Could have befall'n thee and thy father's house.
Sam. Father, I do acknowledge and confess
That I this honour, I this pomp have brought
To Dagon, and advanced his praises high 450

Among the heathen round; to God have brought
Dishonour, obloquy, and oped the mouths
Of idolists, and atheists; have brought scandal
To Israel, diffidence of God, and doubt°
In feeble hearts, propense enough before°
To waver, or fall off and join with idols;
Which is my chief affliction, shame and sorrow,
The anguish of my soul, that suffers not
Mine eye to harbour sleep, or thoughts to rest.
This only hope relieves me, that the strife   460
With me hath end; all the contest is now
'Twixt God and Dagon; Dagon hath presumed,
Me overthrown, to enter lists with God,
His deity comparing and preferring
Before the God of Abraham. He, be sure,
Will not connive, or linger, thus provoked,°
But will arise and his great name assert:
Dagon must stoop, and shall ere long receive
Such a discomfit, as shall quite despoil him°
Of all these boasted trophies won on me,   470
And with confusion blank his worshippers.°
Man. With cause this hope relieves thee, and these words
I as a prophecy receive: for God,
Nothing more certain, will not long defer
To vindicate the glory of his name
Against all competition, nor will long
Endure it, doubtful whether God be Lord,
Or Dagon. But for thee what shall be done?
Thou must not in the meanwhile here forgot
Lie in this miserable loathsome plight   480
Neglected. I already have made way
To some Philistian lords, with whom to treat
About thy ransom: well they may by this°
Have satisfied their utmost of revenge
By pains and slaveries, worse than death inflicted
On thee, who now no more canst do them harm.
Sam. Spare that proposal, father, spare the trouble
Of that solicitation; let me here,
As I deserve, pay on my punishment;
And expiate, if possible, my crime,   490
Shameful garrulity. To have revealed

Secrets of men, the secrets of a friend,
How heinous had the fact been, how deserving°
Contempt, and scorn of all, to be excluded
All friendship, and avoided as a blab,
The mark of fool set on his front!°
But I God's counsel have not kept, his holy secret
Presumptuously have published, impiously,
Weakly at least, and shamefully: a sin
That Gentiles in their parables condemn   500
To their abyss and horrid pains confined.°
Man. Be penitent and for thy fault contrite,
But act not in thy own affliction, son,
Repent the sin, but if the punishment
Thou canst avoid, self-preservation bids;
Or the execution leave to high disposal,
And let another hand, not thine, exact
Thy penal forfeit from thyself; perhaps
God will relent, and quit thee all his debt;°
Who evermore approves and more accepts   510
(Best pleased with humble and filial submission)
Him who imploring mercy sues for life,
Than who self-rigorous chooses death as due;
Which argues over-just, and self-displeased°
For self-offence, more than for God offended.°
Reject not then what offered means, who knows°
But God hath set before us, to return thee
Home to thy country and his sacred house,
Where thou may'st bring thy off'rings, to avert
His further ire, with prayers and vows renewed.   520
Sam. His pardon I implore; but as for life,
To what end should I seek it? when in strength
All mortals I excelled, and great in hopes
With youthful courage and magnanimous thoughts
Of birth from heaven foretold and high exploits,
Full of divine instinct, after some proof°
Of acts indeed heroic, far beyond
The sons of Anak, famous now and blazed,°
Fearless of danger, like a petty god
I walked about admired of all and dreaded   530
On hostile ground, none daring my affront.
Then swoll'n with pride into the snare I fell

Of fair fallacious looks, venereal trains,°
Softened with pleasure and voluptuous life;
At length to lay my head and hallowed pledge°
Of all my strength in the lascivious lap
Of a deceitful concubine who shore me°
Like a tame wether, all my precious fleece,°
Then turned me out ridiculous, despoiled,
Shaven, and disarmed among my enemies.   540
Chor. Desire of wine and all delicious drinks,°
Which many a famous warrior overturns,
Thou couldst repress, nor did the dancing ruby
Sparkling, out-poured, the flavour, or the smell,
Or taste that cheers the heart of gods and men,
Allure thee from the cool crystalline stream.
Sam. Wherever fountain or fresh current flowed
Against the eastern ray, translucent, pure
With touch ethereal of heaven's fiery rod°
I drank, from the clear milky juice allaying°   550
Thirst, and refreshed; nor envied them the grape
Whose heads that turbulent liquor fills with fumes.
Chor. O madness, to think use of strongest wines
And strongest drinks our chief support of health,
When God with these forbidden made choice to rear
His mighty champion, strong above compare,
Whose drink was only from the liquid brook.°
Sam. But what availed this temperance, not complete
Against another object more enticing?
What boots it at one gate to make defence,°   560
And at another to let in the foe
Effeminately vanquished? by which means,
Now blind, disheartened, shamed, dishonoured, quelled,
To what can I be useful, wherein serve
My nation, and the work from heaven imposed,
But to sit idle on the household hearth,
A burdenous drone; to visitants a gaze,°
Or pitied object, these redundant locks°
Robustious to no purpose clustering down,°
Vain monument of strength; till length of years   570
And sedentary numbness craze my limbs°
To a contemptible old age obscure.
Here rather let me drudge and earn my bread,

Till vermin or the draff of servile food°
Consume me, and oft-invocated death
Hasten the welcome end of all my pains.
Man. Wilt thou then serve the Philistines with that gift
Which was expressly given thee to annoy them?°
Better at home lie bed-rid, not only idle,
Inglorious, unemployed, with age outworn.   580
But God who caused a fountain at thy prayer°
From the dry ground to spring, thy thirst to allay
After the brunt of battle, can as easy
Cause light again within thy eyes to spring,
Wherewith to serve him better than thou hast;
And I persuade me so; why else this strength
Miraculous yet remaining in those locks?
His might continues in thee not for naught,
Nor shall his wondrous gifts be frustrate thus.
Sam. All otherwise to me my thoughts portend,   590
That these dark orbs no more shall treat with light,°
Nor the other light of life continue long,
But yield to double darkness nigh at hand:
So much I feel my genial spirits droop,°
My hopes all flat, nature within me seems
In all her functions weary of herself;
My race of glory run, and race of shame,
And I shall shortly be with them that rest.
Man. Believe not these suggestions, which proceed
From anguish of the mind and humours black,°   600
That mingle with thy fancy. I however°
Must not omit a father's timely care
To prosecute the means of thy deliverance°
By ransom or how else: meanwhile be calm,°
And healing words from these thy friends admit.
Sam. O that torment should not be confined
To the body's wounds and sores
With maladies innumerable
In heart, head, breast, and reins;°
But must secret passage find   610
To the inmost mind,
There exercise all his fierce accidents,°
And on her purest spirits prey,
As on entrails, joints, and limbs,

With answerable pains, but more intense,°
Though void of corporal sense.
  My griefs not only pain me
As a lingering disease,
But finding no redress, ferment and rage,
Nor less than wounds immedicable   620
Rankle, and fester, and gangrene,
To black mortification.°
Thoughts my tormentors armed with deadly stings
Mangle my apprehensive tenderest parts,°
Exasperate, exulcerate, and raise°
Dire inflammation which no cooling herb
Or med'cinal liquor can assuage,
Nor breath of vernal air from snowy alp.°
Sleep hath forsook and given me o'er
To death's benumbing opium as my only cure.   630
Thence faintings, swoonings of despair,
And sense of heaven's desertion.
  I was his nursling once and choice delight,
His destined from the womb,
Promised by heavenly message twice descending.°
Under his special eye
Abstemious I grew up and thrived amain;
He led me on to mightiest deeds
Above the nerve of mortal arm°
Against the uncircumcised, our enemies.   640
But now hath cast me off as never known,
And to those cruel enemies,
Whom I by his appointment had provoked,
Left me all helpless with the irreparable loss
Of sight, reserved alive to be repeated°
The subject of their cruelty, or scorn.
Nor am I in the list of them that hope;
Hopeless are all my evils, all remediless;
This one prayer yet remains, might I be heard,
No long petition, speedy death,   650
The close of all my miseries, and the balm.
Chor. Many are the sayings of the wise
In ancient and in modern books enrolled;
Extolling patience as the truest fortitude;
And to the bearing well of all calamities,

All chances incident to man's frail life
Consolatories writ°
With studied argument, and much persuasion sought
Lenient of grief and anxious thought,°
But with the afflicted in his pangs their sound   660
Little prevails, or rather seems a tune,
Harsh, and of dissonant mood from his complaint,
Unless he feel within
Some source of consolation from above;
Secret refreshings, that repair his strength,
And fainting spirits uphold.
   God of our fathers, what is man!
That thou towards him with hand so various,
O might I say contrarious,
Temper'st thy providence through his short course,   670
Not evenly, as thou rul'st
The angelic orders and inferior creatures mute,
Irrational and brute.
Nor do I name of men the common rout,
That wand'ring loose about
Grow up and perish, as the summer fly,
Heads without name no more remembered,°
But such as thou hast solemnly elected,
With gifts and graces eminently adorned
To some great work, thy glory,   680
And people's safety, which in part they effect:
Yet toward these thus dignified, thou oft
Amidst their height of noon,
Changest thy countenance, and thy hand with no regard
Of highest favours past
From thee on them, or them to thee of service.
   Nor only dost degrade them, or remit°
To life obscured, which were a fair dismission,°
But throw'st them lower than thou didst exalt them high,
Unseemly falls in human eye,   690
Too grievous for the trespass or omission,
Oft leav'st them to the hostile sword
Of heathen and profane, their carcases
To dogs and fowls a prey, or else captived:
Or to the unjust tribunals, under change of times,
And condemnation of the ingrateful multitude.

If these they scape, perhaps in poverty
With sickness and disease thou bow'st them down,
Painful diseases and deformed,
In crude old age;°   700
Though not disordinate, yet causeless suffering°
The punishment of dissolute days, in fine,°
Just or unjust, alike seem miserable,
For oft alike, both come to evil end.
    So deal not with this once thy glorious champion,
The image of thy strength, and mighty minister.°
What do I beg? how hast thou dealt already?
Behold him in this state calamitous, and turn
His labours, for thou canst, to peaceful end.
    But who is this, what thing of sea or land?   710
Female of sex it seems,
That so bedecked, ornate, and gay,
Comes this way sailing
Like a stately ship
Of Tarsus, bound for th' isles°
Of Javan or Gadire°
With all her bravery on, and tackle trim,°
Sails filled, and streamers waving,
Courted by all the winds that hold them play,°
An amber scent of odorous perfume°   720
Her harbinger, a damsel train behind;
Some rich Philistian matron she may seem,
And now at nearer view, no other certain
Than Dalila thy wife.
Sam. My wife, my traitress, let her not come near me.
Chor. Yet on she moves, now stands and eyes thee fixed,
About t' have spoke, but now, with head declined
Like a fair flower surcharged with dew, she weeps
And words addressed seem into tears dissolved,
Wetting the borders of her silken veil: 730
But now again she makes address to speak.°
Dal. With doubtful feet and wavering resolution
I came, still dreading thy displeasure, Samson,
Which to have merited, without excuse,
I cannot but acknowledge; yet if tears
May expiate (though the fact more evil drew°
In the perverse event than I foresaw)°

My penance hath not slackened, though my pardon
No way assured. But conjugal affection
Prevailing over fear, and timorous doubt   740
Hath led me on desirous to behold
Once more thy face, and know of thy estate.
If aught in my ability may serve
To lighten what thou suffer'st, and appease
Thy mind with what amends is in my power,
Though late, yet in some part to recompense
My rash but more unfortunate misdeed.
Sam. Out, out hyena; these are thy wonted arts,°
And arts of every woman false like thee,
To break all faith, all vows, deceive, betray,   750
Then as repentant to submit, beseech,
And reconcilement move with feigned remorse,°
Confess, and promise wonders in her change,
Not truly penitent, but chief to try
Her husband, how far urged his patience bears,
His virtue or weakness which way to assail:
Then with more cautious and instructed skill
Again transgresses, and again submits;
That wisest and best men full oft beguiled
With goodness principled not to reject   760
The penitent, but ever to forgive,
Are drawn to wear out miserable days,
Entangled with a poisonous bosom snake,
If not by quick destruction soon cut off
As I be thee, to ages an example.
Dal. Yet hear me Samson; not that I endeavour
To lessen or extenuate my offence,
But that on the other side, if it be weighed
By itself, with aggravations not surcharged,°
Or else with just allowance counterpoised,   770
I may, if possible, thy pardon find
The easier towards me, or thy hatred less.
First granting, as I do, it was a weakness
In me, but incident to all our sex,
Curiosity, inquisitive, importune°
Of secrets, then with like infirmity
To publish them, both common female faults:
Was it not weakness also to make known

For importunity, that is for naught,
Wherein consisted all thy strength and safety?   780
To what I did thou show'dst me first the way.
But I to enemies revealed, and should not.
Nor shouldst thou have trusted that to woman's frailty:
Ere I to thee, thou to thyself wast cruel.
Let weakness then with weakness come to parle°
So near related, or the same of kind,°
Thine forgive mine; that men may censure thine
The gentler, if severely thou exact not
More strength from me, than in thyself was found.
And what if love, which thou interpret'st hate,   790
The jealousy of love, powerful of sway
In human hearts, nor less in mine towards thee,
Caused what I did? I saw thee mutable
Of fancy, feared lest one day thou wouldst leave me°
As her at Timna, sought by all means therefore
How to endear, and hold thee to me firmest:
No better way I saw than by importuning
To learn thy secrets, get into my power
Thy key of strength and safety: thou wilt say,
Why then revealed? I was assured by those   800
Who tempted me, that nothing was designed
Against thee but safe custody, and hold:°
That made for me; I knew that liberty°
Would draw thee forth to perilous enterprises,
While I at home sat full of cares and fears
Wailing thy absence in my widowed bed;
Here I should still enjoy thee day and night
Mine and love's prisoner, not the Philistines',
Whole to myself, unhazarded abroad,
Fearless at home of partners in my love.   810
These reasons in love's law have passed for good,
Though fond and reasonless to some perhaps;°
And love hath oft, well meaning, wrought much woe,
Yet always pity or pardon hath obtained.
Be not unlike all others, not austere
As thou art strong, inflexible as steel.
If thou in strength all mortals dost exceed,
In uncompassionate anger do not so.
Sam. How cunningly the sorceress displays

Her own transgressions, to upbraid me mine! 820
That malice not repentance brought thee hither,
By this appears: I gave, thou say'st, the example,
I led the way; bitter reproach, but true,
I to myself was false ere thou to me,
Such pardon therefore as I give my folly,
Take to thy wicked deed: which when thou seest°
Impartial, self-severe, inexorable,
Thou wilt renounce thy seeking, and much rather
Confess it feigned, weakness is thy excuse,
And I believe it, weakness to resist 830
Philistian gold: if weakness may excuse,
What murderer, what traitor, parricide,
Incestuous, sacrilegious, but may plead it?
All wickedness is weakness: that plea therefore
With God or man will gain thee no remission.
But love constrained thee; call it furious rage
To satisfy thy lust: love seeks to have love;
My love how couldst thou hope, who took'st the way
To raise in me inexpiable hate,
Knowing, as needs I must, by thee betrayed? 840
In vain thou striv'st to cover shame with shame,
Or by evasions thy crime uncover'st more.
Dal. Since thou determin'st weakness for no plea
In man or woman, though to thy own condemning,
Hear what assaults I had, what snares besides,
What sieges girt me round, ere I consented;
Which might have awed the best-resolved of men,°
The constantest to have yielded without blame.
It was not gold, as to my charge thou lay'st,
That wrought with me; thou know'st the magistrates 850
And princes of my country came in person,
Solicited, commanded, threatened, urged,
Adjured by all the bonds of civil duty
And of religion, pressed how just it was,
How honourable, how glorious to entrap
A common enemy, who had destroyed
Such numbers of our nation: and the priest
Was not behind, but ever at my ear,
Preaching how meritorious with the gods
It would be to ensnare an irreligious 860

Dishonourer of Dagon: what had I
To oppose against such powerful arguments?
Only my love of thee held long debate;
And combated in silence all these reasons
With hard contest: at length that grounded maxim°
So rife and celebrated in the mouths
Of wisest men; that to the public good
Private respects must yielα; with grave authority
Took full possession of me and prevailed;
Virtue, as I thought, truth, duty so enjoining.   870
Sam. I thought where all thy circling wiles would end;
In feigned religion, smooth hypocrisy.
But had thy love, still odiously pretended,
Been, as it ought, sincere, it would have taught thee
Far other reasonings, brought forth other deeds.
I before all the daughters of my tribe
And of my nation chose thee from among
My enemies, loved thee, as too well thou knew'st,
Too well, unbosomed all my secrets to thee,
Not out of levity, but overpowered   880
By thy request, who could deny thee nothing;
Yet now am judged an enemy. Why then
Didst thou at first receive me for thy husband?
Then, as since then, thy country's foe professed:
Being once a wife, for me thou wast to leave
Parents and country; nor was I their subject,
Nor under their protection but my own,
Thou mine, not theirs: if aught against my life
Thy country sought of thee, it sought unjustly,
Against the law of nature, law of nations,   890
No more thy country, but an impious crew
Of men conspiring to uphold their state
By worse than hostile deeds, violating the ends
For which our country is a name so dear;
Not therefore to be obeyed. But zeal moved thee;
To please thy gods thou didst it; gods unable
To acquit themselves and prosecute their foes°
But by ungodly deeds, the contradiction
Of their own deity, gods cannot be:
Less therefore to be pleased, obeyed, or feared,   900
These false pretexts and varnished colours failing,°

Bare in thy guilt how foul must thou appear!
Dal. In argument with men a woman ever
Goes by the worse, whatever be her cause.
Sam. For want of words no doubt, or lack of breath,
Witness when I was worried with thy peals.°
Dal. I was a fool, too rash, and quite mistaken
In what I thought would have succeeded best.
Let me obtain forgiveness of thee, Samson,
Afford me place to show what recompense°   910
Towards thee I intend for what I have misdone,
Misguided; only what remains past cure
Bear not too sensibly, nor still insist°
To afflict thyself in vain: though sight be lost,
Life yet hath many solaces, enjoyed
Where other senses want not their delights°
At home in leisure and domestic ease,
Exempt from many a care and chance to which
Eyesight exposes daily men abroad.
I to the lords will intercede, not doubting   920
Their favourable ear, that I may fetch thee
From forth this loathsome prison-house, to abide
With me, where my redoubled love and care
With nursing diligence, to me glad office,
May ever tend about thee to old age
With all things grateful cheered, and so supplied,°
That what by me thou hast lost thou least shalt miss.
Sam. No, no, of my condition take no care;
It fits not; thou and I long since are twain;
Nor think me so unwary or accursed   930
To bring my feet again into the snare
Where once I have been caught; I know thy trains
Though dearly to my cost, thy gins, and toils;°
Thy fair enchanted cup, and warbling charms°
No more on me have power, their force is nulled,
So much of adder's wisdom I have learnt°
To fence my ear against thy sorceries.
If in my flower of youth and strength, when all men
Loved, honoured, feared me, thou alone could hate me
Thy husband, slight me, sell me, and forgo me;   940
How wouldst thou use me now, blind, and thereby
Deceivable, in most things as a child

Helpless, thence easily contemned, and scorned,
And last neglected? How wouldst thou insult°
When I must live uxorious to thy will
In perfect thraldom, how again betray me,
Bearing my words and doings to the lords
To gloss upon, and censuring, frown or smile?°
This jail I count the house of liberty
To thine whose doors my feet shall never enter.° 950
Dal. Let me approach at least, and touch thy hand.
Sam. Not for thy life, lest fierce remembrance wake
My sudden rage to tear thee joint by joint.
At distance I forgive thee, go with that;
Bewail thy falsehood, and the pious works
It hath brought forth to make thee memorable
Among illustrious women, faithful wives:
Cherish thy hastened widowhood with the gold
Of matrimonial treason: so farewell.
Dal. I see thou art implacable, more deaf 960
To prayers than winds and seas, yet winds to seas
Are reconciled at length, and sea to shore:
Thy anger, unappeasable, still rages,
Eternal tempest never to be calmed.
Why do I humble thus myself, and suing
For peace, reap nothing but repulse and hate?
Bid go with evil omen and the brand°
Of infamy upon my name denounced?°
To mix with thy concernments I desist°
Henceforth, nor too much disapprove my own. 970
Fame if not double-faced is double-mouthed,
And with contrary blast proclaims most deeds,°
On both his wings, one black, the other white,°
Bears greatest names in his wild airy flight.
My name perhaps among the circumcised°
In Dan, in Judah, and the bordering tribes,
To all posterity may stand defamed,
With malediction mentioned, and the blot
Of falsehood most unconjugal traduced.
But in my country where I most desire, 980
In Ecron, Gaza, Asdod, and in Gath°
I shall be named among the famousest
Of women, sung at solemn festivals,

Living and dead recorded, who to save
Her country from a fierce destroyer, chose
Above the faith of wedlock-bands, my tomb
With odours visited and annual flowers.°
Not less renowned than in Mount Ephraim,
Jael, who with inhospitable guile
Smote Sisera sleeping through the temples nailed.°   990
Nor shall I count it heinous to enjoy
The public marks of honour and reward
Conferred upon me, for the piety
Which to my country I was judged to have shown.
At this whoever envies or repines
I leave him to his lot, and like my own.
Chor. She's gone, a manifest serpent by her sting
Discovered in the end, till now concealed.
Sam. So let her go, God sent her to debase me,
And aggravate my folly who committed°   1000
To such a viper his most sacred trust
Of secrecy, my safety, and my life.
Chor. Yet beauty, though injurious, hath strange power,
After offence returning, to regain
Love once possessed, nor can be easily
Repulsed, without much inward passion felt
And secret sting of amorous remorse.
Sam. Love-quarrels oft in pleasing concord end,
Not wedlock-treachery endangering life.
Chor. It is not virtue, wisdom, valour, wit,   1010
Strength, comeliness of shape, or amplest merit
That woman's love can win or long inherit;°
But what it is, hard is to say,
Harder to hit
(Which way soever men refer it),
Much like thy riddle, Samson, in one day°
Or seven, though one should musing sit;
    If any of these or all, the Timnian bride°
Had not so soon preferred
Thy paranymph, worthless to thee compared,°   1020
Successor in thy bed,
Nor both so loosely disallied°
Their nuptials, nor this last so treacherously
Had shorn the fatal harvest of thy head.

Is it for that such outward ornament°
Was lavished on their sex, that inward gifts
Were left for haste unfinished, judgment scant,
Capacity not raised to apprehend
Or value what is best
In choice, but oftest to affect the wrong?   1030
Or was too much of self-love mixed,
Of constancy no root infixed,
That either they love nothing, or not long?
     Whate'er it be, to wisest men and best
Seeming at first all heavenly under virgin veil,
Soft, modest, meek, demure,
Once joined, the contrary she proves, a thorn°
Intestine, far within defensive arms°
A cleaving mischief, in his way to virtue°
Adverse and turbulent, or by her charms   1040
Draws him awry enslaved
With dotage, and his sense depraved
To folly and shameful deeds which ruin ends.
What pilot so expert but needs must wreck
Embarked with such a steers-mate at the helm?
     Favoured of heaven who finds
One virtuous rarely found,
That in domestic good combines:°
Happy that house! his way to peace is smooth:
But virtue which breaks through all opposition,   1050
And all temptation can remove,
Most shines and most is acceptable above.
     Therefore God's universal law
Gave to the man despotic power
Over his female in due awe,
Nor from that right to part an hour,
Smile she or lour:
So shall he least confusion draw°
On his whole life, not swayed
By female usurpation, nor dismayed.   1060
     But had we best retire, I see a storm?
Sam. Fair days have oft contracted wind and rain.°
Chor. But this another kind of tempest brings.
Sam. Be less abstruse, my riddling days are past.
Chor. Look now for no enchanting voice, nor fear

The bait of honeyed words; a rougher tongue
Draws hitherward, I know him by his stride,
The giant Harapha of Gath, his look°
Haughty as is his pile high-built and proud.°
Comes he in peace? what wind hath blown him hither   1070
I less conjecture than when first I saw
The sumptuous Dalila floating this way:
His habit carries peace, his brow defiance.°
Sam. Or peace or not, alike to me he comes.
Chor. His fraught we soon shall know, he now arrives.°
Har. I come not Samson, to condole thy chance,°
As these perhaps, yet wish it had not been,
Though for no friendly intent. I am of Gath,
Men call me Harapha, of stock renowned
As Og or Anak and the Emims old°   1080
That Kiriathaim held, thou know'st me now°
If thou at all art known. Much I have heard°
Of thy prodigious might and feats performed
Incredible to me, in this displeased,
That I was never present on the place
Of those encounters, where we might have tried
Each other's force in camp or listed field:°
And now am come to see of whom such noise
Hath walked about, and each limb to survey,°
If thy appearance answer loud report.   1090
Sam. The way to know were not to see but taste.
Har. Dost thou already single me? I thought°
Gyves and the mill had tamed thee. O that fortune
Had brought me to the field where thou art famed
To have wrought such wonders with an ass's jaw;
I should have forced thee soon wish other arms,
Or left thy carcase where the ass lay thrown:
So had the glory of prowess been recovered
To Palestine, won by a Philistine
From the unforeskinned race, of whom thou bear'st   1100
The highest name for valiant acts, that honour
Certain to have won by mortal duel from thee,
I lose, prevented by thy eyes put out.
Sam. Boast not of what thou wouldst have done, but do
What then thou wouldst, thou seest it in thy hand.°
Har. To combat with a blind man I disdain,

And thou hast need much washing to be touched.
Sam. Such usage as your honourable lords
Afford me assassinated and betrayed,°
Who durst not with their whole united powers   1110
In fight withstand me single and unarmed,
Nor in the house with chamber ambushes
Close-banded durst attack me, no not sleeping,°
Till they had hired a woman with their gold
Breaking her marriage faith to circumvent me.
Therefore without feigned shifts let be assigned
Some narrow place enclosed, where sight may give thee,
Or rather flight, no great advantage on me;
Then put on all thy gorgeous arms, thy helmet
And brigandine of brass, thy broad habergeon,°   1120
Vantbrace and greaves, and gauntlet, add thy spear°
A weaver's beam, and seven-times-folded shield,°
I only with an oaken staff will meet thee,
And raise such outcries on thy clattered iron,
Which long shall not withhold me from thy head,
That in a little time while breath remains thee,
Thou oft shalt wish thyself at Gath to boast
Again in safety what thou wouldst have done
To Samson, but shalt never see Gath more.
Har. Thou durst not thus disparage glorious arms   1130
Which greatest heroes have in battle worn,
Their ornament and safety, had not spells
And black enchantments, some magician's art
Armed thee or charmed thee strong, which thou from heaven
Feign'dst at thy birth was given thee in thy hair,
Where strength can least abide, though all thy hairs
Were bristles ranged like those that ridge the back
Of chafed wild boars or ruffled porcupines.°
Sam. I know no spells, use no forbidden arts;
My trust is in the living God who gave me   1140
At my nativity this strength, diffused
No less through all my sinews, joints and bones,
Than thine, while I preserved these locks unshorn,
The pledge of my unviolated vow.
For proof hereof, if Dagon be thy god,
Go to his temple, invocate his aid
With solemnest devotion, spread before him°

How highly it concerns his glory now
To frustrate and dissolve these magic spells,
Which I to be the power of Israel's God   1150
Avow, and challenge Dagon to the test,
Offering to combat thee his champion bold,
With the utmost of his godhead seconded:
Then thou shalt see, or rather to thy sorrow
Soon feel, whose God is strongest, thine or mine.
Har. Presume not on thy God, whate'er he be,
Thee he regards not, owns not, hath cut off
Quite from his people, and delivered up
Into thy enemies' hand, permitted them
To put out both thine eyes, and fettered send thee   1160
Into the common prison, there to grind
Among the slaves and asses thy comrades,
As good for nothing else, no better service
With those thy boisterous locks, no worthy match°
For valour to assail, nor by the sword
Of noble warrior, so to stain his honour,
But by the barber's razor best subdued.
Sam. All these indignities, for such they are
From thine, these evils I deserve and more,°
Acknowledge them from God inflicted on me   1170
Justly, yet despair not of his final pardon
Whose ear is ever open; and his eye
Gracious to readmit the suppliant;
In confidence whereof I once again
Defy thee to the trial of mortal fight,
By combat to decide whose god is God,
Thine or whom I with Israel's sons adore.
Har. Fair honour that thou dost thy God, in trusting
He will accept thee to defend his cause,
A murderer, a revolter, and a robber.   1180
Sam. Tongue-doughty giant, how dost thou prove me these?
Har. Is not thy nation subject to our lords?
Their magistrates confessed it, when they took thee
As a league-breaker and delivered bound
Into our hands: for hadst thou not committed°
Notorious murder on those thirty men
At Ascalon, who never did thee harm,
Then like a robber stripp'dst them of their robes?°

The Philistines, when thou hadst broke the league,
Went up with armèd powers thee only seeking,   1190
To others did no violence nor spoil.
Sam. Among the daughters of the Philistines
I chose a wife, which argued me no foe;
And in your city held my nuptial feast:
But your ill-meaning politician lords,
Under pretence of bridal friends and guests,
Appointed to await me thirty spies,°
Who threatening cruel death constrained the bride
To wring from me and tell to them my secret,
That solved the riddle which I had proposed.   1200
When I perceived all set on enmity,
As on my enemies, wherever chanced,
I used hostility, and took their spoil°
To pay my underminers in their coin.°
My nation was subjected to your lords.
It was the force of conquest; force with force
Is well ejected when the conquered can.
But I a private person, whom my country
As a league-breaker gave up bound, presumed
Single rebellion and did hostile acts.   1210
I was no private but a person raised
With strength sufficient and command from heaven
To free my country; if their servile minds
Me their deliverer sent would not receive,
But to their masters gave me up for nought,
The unworthier they; whence to this day they serve.
I was to do my part from heaven assigned,
And had performed it if my known offence
Had not disabled me, not all your force:
These shifts refuted, answer thy appellant°   1220
Though by his blindness maimed for high attempts,°
Who now defies thee thrice to single fight,
As a petty enterprise of small enforce.°
Har. With thee a man condemned, a slave enrolled,
Due by the law to capital punishment?
To fight with thee no man of arms will deign.
Sam. Cam'st thou for this, vain boaster, to survey me,
To descant on my strength, and give thy verdict?
Come nearer, part not hence so slight informed;

But take good heed my hand survey not thee. 1230
Har. O Baal-zebub! can my ears unused°
Hear these dishonours, and not render death?
Sam. No man withholds thee, nothing from thy hand
Fear I incurable; bring up thy van,°
My heels are fettered, but my fist is free.
Har. This insolence other kind of answer fits.
Sam. Go baffled coward, lest I run upon thee,°
Though in these chains, bulk without spirit vast,°
And with one buffet lay thy structure low,
Or swing thee in the air, then dash thee down 1240
To the hazard of thy brains and shattered sides.
Har. By Astaroth ere long thou shalt lament°
These braveries in irons loaden on thee.°
Chor. His giantship is gone somewhat crestfall'n,
Stalking with less unconscionable strides,°
And lower looks, but in a sultry chafe.
Sam. I dread him not, nor all his giant-brood,
Though fame divulge him father of five sons°
All of gigantic size, Goliah chief.°
Chor. He will directly to the lords, I fear, 1250
And with malicious counsel stir them up
Some way or other yet further to afflict thee.
Sam. He must allege some cause, and offered fight
Will not dare mention, lest a question rise
Whether he durst accept the offer or not,
And that he durst not plain enough appeared.
Much more affliction than already felt
They cannot well impose, nor I sustain;
If they intend advantage of my labours,
The work of many hands, which earns my keeping 1260
With no small profit daily to my owners.
But come what will, my deadliest foe will prove
My speediest friend, by death to rid me hence,
The worst that he can give, to me the best.
Yet so it may fall out, because their end
Is hate, not help to me, it may with mine
Draw their own ruin who attempt the deed.
Chor. O how comely it is and how reviving
To the spirits of just men long oppressed!
When God into the hands of their deliverer 1270

Puts invincible might
To quell the mighty of the earth, the oppressor,
The brute and boisterous force of violent men
Hardy and industrious to support
Tyrannic power, but raging to pursue
The righteous and all such as honour truth;
He all their ammunition°
And feats of war defeats
With plain heroic magnitude of mind
And celestial vigour armed,   1280
Their armouries and magazines contemns,
Renders them useless, while
With wingèd expedition°
Swift as the lightning glance he executes
His errand on the wicked, who surprised
Lose their defence distracted and amazed.
    But patience is more oft the exercise°
Of saints, the trial of their fortitude,°
Making them each his own deliverer,
And victor over all   1290
That tyranny or fortune can inflict,
Either of these is in thy lot,
Samson, with might endued
Above the sons of men; but sight bereaved
May chance to number thee with those
Whom patience finally must crown.
This idol's day hath been to thee no day of rest,
    Labouring thy mind
More than the working day thy hands,
And yet perhaps more trouble is behind.°   1300
For I descry this way
Some other tending, in his hand
A sceptre or quaint staff he bears,°
Comes on amain, speed in his look.
By his habit I discern him now°
A public officer, and now at hand.
His message will be short and voluble.°
Off. Hebrews, the prisoner Samson here I seek.
Chor. His manacles remark him, there he sits.°
Off. Samson, to thee our lords thus bid me say;   1310
This day to Dagon is a solemn feast,

With sacrifices, triumph, pomp, and games;
Thy strength they know surpassing human rate,
And now some public proof thereof require
To honour this great feast, and great assembly;
Rise therefore with all speed and come along,
Where I will see thee heartened and fresh clad°
To appear as fits before the illustrious lords.
Sam. Thou know'st I am an Hebrew, therefore tell them,
Our law forbids at their religious rites°   1320
My presence; for that cause I cannot come.
Off. This answer, be assured, will not content them.
Sam. Have they not sword-players, and every sort
Of gymnic artists, wrestlers, riders, runners,
Jugglers and dancers, antics, mummers, mimics,°
But they must pick me out with shackles tired,
And over-laboured at their public mill,
To make them sport with blind activity?
Do they not seek occasion of new quarrels
On my refusal to distress me more,   1330
Or make a game of my calamities?
Return the way thou cam'st, I will not come.
Off. Regard thyself, this will offend them highly.°
Sam. Myself? my conscience and internal peace.
Can they think me so broken, so debased
With corporal servitude, that my mind ever
Will condescend to such absurd commands?
Although their drudge, to be their fool or jester,
And in my midst of sorrow and heart-grief
To show them feats, and play before their god,   1340
The worst of all indignities, yet on me
Joined with extreme contempt? I will not come.°
Off. My message was imposed on me with speed,
Brooks no delay: is this thy resolution?°
Sam. So take it with what speed thy message needs.
Off. I am sorry what this stoutness will produce.°
Sam. Perhaps thou shalt have cause to sorrow indeed.
Chor. Consider, Samson; matters now are strained
Up to the height, whether to hold or break;
He's gone, and who knows how he may report   1350
Thy words by adding fuel to the flame?
Expect another message more imperious,

More lordly thundering than thou well wilt bear.
Sam. Shall I abuse this consecrated gift
Of strength, again returning with my hair
After my great transgression, so requite
Favour renewed, and add a greater sin
By prostituting holy things to idols;
A Nazarite in place abominable
Vaunting my strength in honour to their Dagon?   1360
Besides, how vile, contemptible, ridiculous,
What act more execrably unclean, profane?
Chor. Yet with this strength thou serv'st the Philistines,
Idolatrous, uncircumcised, unclean.
Sam. Not in their idol-worship, but by labour
Honest and lawful to deserve my food
Of those who have me in their civil power.
Chor. Where the heart joins not, outward acts defile not.
Sam. Where outward force constrains, the sentence holds°
But who constrains me to the temple of Dagon,   1370
Not dragging? the Philistian lords command,
Commands are no constraints. If I obey them,
I do it freely; venturing to displease
God for the fear of man, and man prefer,
Set God behind: which in his jealousy°
Shall never, unrepented, find forgiveness.
Yet that he may dispense with me or thee
Present in temples at idolatrous rites°
For some important cause, thou need'st not doubt.
Chor. How thou wilt here come off surmounts my reach.°   1380
Sam. Be of good courage, I begin to feel
Some rousing motions in me which dispose
To something extraordinary my thoughts.
I with this messenger will go along,
Nothing to do, be sure, that may dishonour
Our law, or stain my vow of Nazarite.
If there be aught of presage in the mind,
This day will be remarkable in my life
By some great act, or of my days the last.
Chor. In time thou hast resolved, the man returns.   1390
Off. Samson, this second message from our lords
To thee I am bid say. Art thou our slave,
Our captive, at the public mill our drudge,

And dar'st thou at our sending and command
Dispute thy coming? come without delay;
Or we shall find such engines to assail
And hamper thee, as thou shalt come of force,
Though thou wert firmlier fastened than a rock.
Sam. I could be well content to try their art,°
Which to no few of them would prove pernicious.   1400
Yet knowing their advantages to many,
Because they shall not trail me through their streets°
Like a wild beast, I am content to go.
Masters' commands come with a power resistless
To such as owe them absolute subjection;
And for a life who will not change his purpose?
(So mutable are all the ways of men)
Yet this be sure, in nothing to comply
Scandalous or forbidden in our law.
Off. I praise thy resolution, doff these links: 1410
By this compliance thou wilt win the lords
To favour, and perhaps to set thee free.
Sam. Brethren farewell, your company along
I will not wish, lest it perhaps offend them
To see me girt with friends; and how the sight
Of me as of a common enemy,
So dreaded once, may now exasperate them
I know not. Lords are lordliest in their wine;
And the well-feasted priest then soonest fired
With zeal, if aught religion seem concerned:°   1420
No less the people on their holydays
Impetuous, insolent, unquenchable;
Happen what may, of me expect to hear
Nothing dishonourable, impure, unworthy
Our God, our law, my nation, or myself,
The last of me or no I cannot warrant.
Chor. Go, and the holy one
Of Israel be thy guide
To what may serve his glory best, and spread his name
Great among the heathen round: 1430
Send thee the angel of thy birth, to stand
Fast by thy side, who from thy father's field
Rode up in flames after his message told°
Of thy conception, and be now a shield

Of fire; that spirit that first rushed on thee
In the camp of Dan
Be efficacious in thee now at need.
For never was from heaven imparted
Measure of strength so great to mortal seed,
As in thy wondrous actions hath been seen.   1440
But wherefore comes old Manoa in such haste
With youthful steps? much livelier than erewhile
He seems: supposing here to find his son,
Or of him bringing to us some glad news?
Man. Peace with you brethren; my inducement hither
Was not at present here to find my son,
By order of the lords new parted hence
To come and play before them at their feast.
I heard all as I came, the city rings
And numbers thither flock, I had no will,°   1450
Lest I should see him forced to things unseemly.
But that which moved my coming now, was chiefly
To give ye part with me what hope I have°
With good success to work his liberty.°
Chor. That hope would much rejoice us to partake
With thee; say reverend sire, we thirst to hear.
Man. I have attempted one by one the lords°
Either at home, or through the high street passing,
With supplication prone and father's tears°
To accept of ransom for my son their prisoner,   1460
Some much averse I found and wondrous harsh,
Contemptuous, proud, set on revenge and spite;
That part most reverenced Dagon and his priests,
Others more moderate seeming, but their aim
Private reward, for which both god and state
They easily would set to sale, a third
More generous far and civil, who confessed
They had enough revenged, having reduced
Their foe to misery beneath their fears,
The rest was magnanimity to remit,°   1470
If some convenient ransom were proposed.
What noise or shout was that? it tore the sky.
Chor. Doubtless the people shouting to behold
Their once great dread, captive, and blind before them,
Or at some proof of strength before them shown.

Man. His ransom, if my whole inheritance
May compass it, shall willingly be paid
And numbered down: much rather I shall choose°
To live the poorest in my tribe, than richest,
And he in that calamitous prison left.   1480
No, I am fixed not to part hence without him.
For his redemption all my patrimony,
If need be, I am ready to forgo
And quit: not wanting him, I shall want nothing.°
Chor. Fathers are wont to lay up for their sons,
Thou for thy son art bent to lay out all;
Sons wont to nurse their parents in old age,
Thou in old age car'st how to nurse thy son,
Made older than thy age through eyesight lost.
Man. It shall be my delight to tend his eyes,   1490
And view him sitting in the house, ennobled
With all those high exploits by him achieved,
And on his shoulders waving down those locks,
That of a nation armed the strength contained:
And I persuade me God had not permitted
His strength again to grown up with his hair
Garrisoned round about him like a camp
Of faithful soldiery, were not his purpose
To use him further yet in some great service,
Not to sit idle with so great a gift   1500
Useless, and thence ridiculous about him.
And since his strength with eyesight was not lost,
God will restore him eyesight to his strength.°
Chor. Thy hopes are not ill founded nor seem vain
Of his delivery, and thy joy thereon
Conceived, agreeable to a father's love,
In both which we, as next participate.°
Man. I know your friendly minds and—O what noise!
Mercy of heaven what hideous noise was that!
Horribly loud unlike the former shout.   1510
Chor. Noise call you it or universal groan
As if the whole inhabitation perished,
Blood, death, and deathful deeds are in that noise,
Ruin, destruction at the utmost point.
Man. Of ruin indeed methought I heard the noise,°
O it continues, they have slain my son.

Chor. Thy son is rather slaying them, that outcry
From slaughter of one foe could not ascend.
Man. Some dismal accident it needs must be;
What shall we do, stay here or run and see?   1520
Chor. Best keep together here, lest running thither
We unawares run into danger's mouth.
This evil on the Philistines is fall'n,
From whom could else a general cry be heard?
The sufferers then will scarce molest us here,
From other hands we need not much to fear.
What if his eyesight (for to Israel's God
Nothing is hard) by miracle restored,
He now be dealing dole among his foes,°
And over heaps of slaughtered walk his way?   1530
Man. That were a joy presumptuous to be thought.
Chor. Yet God hath wrought things as incredible
For his people of old; what hinders now?
Man. He can I know, but doubt to think he will;
Yet hope would fain subscribe, and tempts belief.°
A little stay will bring some notice hither.°
Chor. Of good or bad so great, of bad the sooner;
For evil news rides post, while good news baits.°
And to our wish I see one hither speeding,°
An Hebrew, as I guess, and of our tribe.   1540
Messenger. O whither shall I run, or which way fly
The sight of this so horrid spectacle
Which erst my eyes beheld and yet behold;°
For dire imagination still pursues me.
But providence or instinct of nature seems,
Or reason though disturbed, and scarce consulted
To have guided me aright, I know not how,
To thee first reverend Manoa, and to these
My countrymen, whom here I knew remaining,
As at some distance from the place of horror,   1550
So in the sad event too much concerned.
Man. The accident was loud, and here before thee°
With rueful cry, yet what it was we hear not,
No preface needs, thou seest we long to know.
Mess. It would burst forth, but I recover breath
And sense distract, to know well what I utter.
Man. Tell us the sum, the circumstance defer.

Mess. Gaza yet stands, but all her sons are fall'n,
All in a moment overwhelmed and fall'n.
Man. Sad, but thou know'st to Israelites not saddest   1560
The desolation of a hostile city.
Mess. Feed on that first, there may in grief be surfeit.
Man. Relate by whom.
Mess.   By Samson.
Man.   That still lessens
The sorrow, and converts it nigh to joy.
Mess. Ah Manoa I refrain, too suddenly
To utter what will come at last too soon;
Lest evil tidings with too rude irruption°
Hitting thy aged ear should pierce too deep.
Man. Suspense in news is torture, speak them out.
Mess. Then take the worst in brief, Samson is dead.   1570
Man. The worst indeed, O all my hope's defeated
To free him hence! but death who sets all free
Hath paid his ransom now and full discharge.
What windy joy this day had I conceived°
Hopeful of his delivery, which now proves
Abortive as the first-born bloom of spring
Nipped with the lagging rear of winter's frost.
Yet ere I give the reins to grief, say first,
How died he? death to life is crown or shame.
All by him fell thou say'st, by whom fell he,   1580
What glorious hand gave Samson his death's wound?
Mess. Unwounded of his enemies he fell
Man. Wearied with slaughter then or how? explain.
Mess. By his own hands.
Man.   Self-violence? what cause
Brought him so soon at variance with himself°
Among his foes?
Mess.   Inevitable cause
At once both to destroy and be destroyed;
The edifice where all were met to see him
Upon their heads and on his own he pulled.
Man. O lastly over-strong against thyself!   1590
A dreadful way thou took'st to thy revenge.
More than enough we know; but while things yet
Are in confusion, give us if thou canst,
Eye-witness of what first or last was done,

Relation more particular and distinct.
Mess. Occasions drew me early to this city,°
And as the gates I entered with sunrise,
The morning trumpets festival proclaimed
Through each high street: little I had dispatched°
When all abroad was rumoured that this day   1600
Samson should be brought forth to show the people
Proof of his mighty strength in feats and games;
I sorrowed at his captive state, but minded°
Not to be absent at that spectacle.
The building was a spacious theatre,°
Half round on two main pillars vaulted high,
With seats where all the lords and each degree
Of sort, might sit in order to behold,°
The other side was open, where the throng
On banks and scaffolds under sky might stand;°   1610
I among these aloof obscurely stood.
The feast and noon grew high, and sacrifice
Had filled their hearts with mirth, high cheer, and wine,
When to their sports they turned. Immediately
Was Samson as a public servant brought,
In their state livery clad; before him pipes
And timbrels, on each side went armèd guards,
Both horse and foot before him and behind
Archers, and slingers, cataphracts and spears.°
At sight of him the people with a shout   1620
Rifted the air clamouring their god with praise,
Who had made their dreadful enemy their thrall.
He patient but undaunted where they led him,
Came to the place, and what was set before him
Which without help of eye might be assayed,
To heave, pull, draw, or break, he still performed
All with incredible, stupendious force,°
None daring to appear antagonist.
At length for intermission sake they led him
Between the pillars; he his guide requested°   1630
(For so from such as nearer stood we heard)
As over-tired to let him lean awhile
With both his arms on those two massy pillars
That to the archèd roof gave main support.
He unsuspicious led him; which when Samson

Felt in his arms, with head a while inclined,
And eyes fast fixed he stood, as one who prayed,
Or some great matter in his mind revolved.
At last with head erect thus cried aloud,
Hitherto, lords, what your commands imposed   1640
I have performed, as reason was, obeying,
Not without wonder or delight beheld.
Now of my own accord such other trial
I mean to show you of my strength, yet greater;
As with amaze shall strike all who behold.
This uttered, straining all his nerves he bowed,°
As with the force of winds and waters pent,
When mountains tremble, those two massy pillars°
With horrible convulsion to and fro,
He tugged, he shook, till down they came and drew   1650
The whole roof after them, with burst of thunder
Upon the heads of all who sat beneath,
Lords, ladies, captains, counsellors, or priests,
Their choice nobility and flower, not only
Of this but each Philistian city round
Met from all parts to solemnize this feast.
Samson with these immixed, inevitably
Pulled down the same destruction on himself;
The vulgar only scaped who stood without.°
Chor. O dearly-bought revenge, yet glorious!   1660
Living or dying thou hast fulfilled
The work for which thou wast foretold
To Israel, and now li'st victorious
Among thy slain self-killed
Not willingly, but tangled in the fold,
Of dire necessity, whose law in death conjoined
Thee with thy slaughtered foes in number more
Than all thy life had slain before.
Semichor. While their hearts were jocund and sublime,°
Drunk with idolatry, drunk with wine,   1670
And fat regorged of bulls and goats,°
Chanting their idol, and preferring
Before our living dread who dwells
In Silo his bright sanctuary:°
Among them he a spirit of frenzy sent,
Who hurt their minds,

And urged them on with mad desire
To call in haste for their destroyer;
They only set on sport and play
Unweetingly importuned   1680
Their own destruction to come speedy upon them.
So fond are mortal men°
Fall'n into wrath divine,
As their own ruin on themselves to invite,
Insensate left, or to sense reprobate,°
And with blindness internal struck.
Semichor. But he though blind of sight,
Despised and thought extinguished quite,
With inward eyes illuminated
His fiery virtue roused   1690
From under ashes into sudden flame,
And as an evening dragon came,°
Assailant on the perchèd roosts,
And nests in order ranged
Of tame villatic fowl; but as an eagle°
His cloudless thunder bolted on their heads.
So virtue given for lost,
Depressed, and overthrown, as seemed,
Like that self-begotten bird°
In the Arabian woods embossed,°   1700
That no second knows nor third,°
And lay erewhile a holocaust,°
From out her ashy womb now teemed,°
Revives, reflourishes, then vigorous most
When most unactive deemed,
And though her body die, her fame survives,
A secular bird ages of lives.°
Man. Come, come, no time for lamentation now,
Nor much more cause, Samson hath quit himself°
Like Samson, and heroically hath finished   1710
A life heroic, on his enemies
Fully revenged, hath left them years of mourning,
And lamentation to the sons of Caphtor°
Through all Philistian bounds. To Israel
Honour hath left, and freedom, let but them°
Find courage to lay hold on this occasion,
To himself and father's house eternal fame;

And which is best and happiest yet, all this
With God not parted from him, as was feared,
But favouring and assisting to the end.   1720
Nothing is here for tears, nothing to wail
Or knock the breast, no weakness, no contempt,
Dispraise, or blame, nothing but well and fair,
And what may quiet us in a death so noble.
Let us go find the body where it lies
Soaked in his enemies' blood, and from the stream
With lavers pure, and cleansing herbs wash off°
The clotted gore. I with what speed the while°
(Gaza is not in plight to say us nay)°
Will send for all my kindred, all my friends   1730
To fetch him hence and solemnly attend
With silent obsequy and funeral train
Home to his father's house: there will I build him
A monument, and plant it round with shade
Of laurel ever green, and branching palm,
With all his trophies hung, and acts enrolled
In copious legend, or sweet lyric song.°
Thither shall all the valiant youth resort,
And from his memory inflame their breasts
To matchless valour, and adventures high: 1740
The virgins also shall on feastful days
Visit his tomb with flowers, only bewailing
His lot unfortunate in nuptial choice,
From whence captivity and loss of eyes.
Chor. All is best, though we oft doubt,
What the unsearchable dispose°
Of highest wisdom brings about,
And ever best found in the close.
Oft he seems to hide his face,
But unexpectedly returns   1750
And to his faithful champion hath in place°
Bore witness gloriously; whence Gaza mourns
And all that band them to resist°
His uncontrollable intent,
His servants he with new acquist°
Of true experience from this great event
With peace and consolation hath dismissed,
And calm of mind all passion spent.

FAMILIAR LETTERS 1674

To Charles Diodati, 1637

I see now why you wish me so many healths, when my other friends in their letters usually manage to wish me only one: you evidently want me to know that to those mere wishes which were all that you yourself could formerly and others can still offer, there are just now added to your art° as well, and the whole mass as it were of medical power. For you bid me be well six hundred times, as well as I wish to be, and so on. Certainly you must have recently been made Health's very steward, you so squander the whole store of salubrity; or rather Health herself must doubtless now be your parasite, you so act the king and order her to obey. And so I congratulate you and must thank you on two scores, both for your friendship and for your excellent skill. Indeed, since we had agreed upon it, I long expected letters from you; but though I had not yet received any, I did not, believe me, allow my old affection towards you to cool because of such a trifle. On the contrary, I had already suspected that you would use that very same excuse for tardiness which you have used at the beginning of your letter, and rightly so, considering the intimacy of our friendship. For I do not wish true friendship to be weighed by letters and salutations, which may all be false but on either hand to rest and sustain itself upon the deep roots of the soul, and, begun with sincere and blameless motives, even though mutual courtesies cease, to be free for life from suspicion and blame. For fostering such a friendship there is need not so much for writing as for a living remembrance of virtues on both sides. Even if you had not written, that obligation would not necessarily remain unfulfilled. Your worth writes to me instead and inscribes real letters on my inmost consciousness; your candor of character writes, and your love of right; your genius writes too (by no means an ordinary one) and further recommends you to me. Therefore do not try to terrorize me, now that you hold that tyrannical citadel of medicine, as if you would take back your six hundred healths, withdrawing them little by little, to the last one, should I by chance desert friendship, which God forbid. And so remove that terrible battery which you seem to have trained on me, forbidding me to be sick without your permission. For lest you threaten too much, know that I cannot help loving people like you. For though I do not know what else God may have decreed for me, this certainly is true: He has instilled into me, if into anyone, a vehement love of the beautiful. Not so diligently is Ceres,° according to the fables, said to have sought her daughter Proserpina, as I seek for this idea of the beautiful, as if for some glorious image, throughout all the shapes and forms of things ('for many are the shapes of things divine');° day and night I search and follow its lead eagerly as if by certain clear traces. Whence it happens that if I find anywhere one who, despising the warped judgment of the public, dares to feel and speak and be that which the greatest wisdom throughout all ages has taught to be best, I shall cling to him immediately from a kind of necessity. But if I, whether by nature or by my fate, am so equipped that I can by no effort and labour of mine rise to such glory and height of fame, still, I think that neither men nor Gods forbid me to reverence and honour those who have attained that glory or who are successfully aspiring to it. But now I know you wish your curiosity satisfied. You make many anxious inquiries, even about what I am thinking. Listen, Diodati, but in secret, lest I blush; and let me talk to you grandiloquently for a while. You ask what I am thinking of? So help me God, an immortality of fame. What am I doing? Growing my wings and practising flight. But my Pegasus° still raises himself on very tender wings. Let me be wise on my humble level. I shall now tell you seriously what I am planning: to move into some one of the Inns of Court,° wherever there is a pleasant and shady walk; for that dwelling will be more satisfactory, both for companionship, if I wish to remain at home, and as a more suitable headquarters, if I choose to venture forth. Where I am now, as you know, I live in obscurity and cramped quarters. You shall also hear about my studies. By continued reading I have brought the affairs of the Greeks to the time when they ceased to be Greeks. I have been occupied for a long time by the obscure history of the Italians under the Longobards, Franks, and Germans, to the time when liberty was granted them by Rudolph, King of Germany. From there it will be better to read separately about what each state did by its own effort. But what about you? How long will you act the son of the family and devote yourself to domestic matters, forgetting urban companionships? For unless this stepmotherly warfare° be more hazardous than either the Dacian or Sarmatian,° you must certainly hurry, and at least make your winter quarters with us. Meanwhile, if you conveniently can, please send me

Giustiniani, historian of the Veneti.° On my word I shall see either that he is well cared for until your arrival, or, if you prefer, that he is returned to you shortly. Farewell.

London, Septemb. [November?] 23. 1637.

To Benedetto Buonmattei, 1638

Since you are preparing new Institutes of your native tongue, Benedetto Buonmattei, to which you are about to give the finishing touch, you are both beginning a journey to fame shared by some of the highest intellects, and you have aroused, I see, a hope and an opinion among your fellow citizens that by your own effort you will easily bring either light, or richness, or at least polish and order to previous works. By what an extraordinary debt you will have bound your countrymen they will indeed be ungrateful if they themselves do not perceive. Whoever in a state knows how to form the manners of men wisely, to rule them at home and at war with excellent precepts, him before others do I think especially worthy of all honour. Next to him, however, is the one who tries to fix by precepts and rules the order and pattern of writing and speaking received from a good age of the nation, and in a sense to enclose it within a wall; indeed, in order that no one may overstep it, it ought to be secured by a law all but Romulean.° For if we wish to compare the usefulness of the two men, the one alone is able to effect an upright and holy society of citizens; the other alone can make it truly noble, and splendid, and brilliant, which is the next thing to be wished. The one provides, I believe, a noble ferocity and intrepid strategy against an enemy invading the boundaries; the other, with a learned censorship of ears and a light-armed guard of good authors, undertakes to overcome and drive out barbarism, that filthy civil enemy of character which attacks the spirits of men. Nor is it to be thought unimportant what speech people have, whether pure or corrupted, or how correct their daily use of it, a matter which more than once involved the welfare of Athens.° Nay more, though it is the opinion of Plato° that grave actions and mutations in the republic are portended by changed custom and style in dressing, I should rather believe that the downfall of that city, and its consequent meanness of affairs, might follow blemish and error in speech. For when speech is partly awkward and pedantic, partly inaccurate and badly pronounced, what does it say but that the souls of the people are slothful and gaping and already prepared for any servility? On the other hand, not once have we heard of an empire or state not flourishing at least moderately as long as it continued to have pride in its language, and to cultivate it. Therefore, Benedetto, you see clearly that if you would be sure of winning the pleasant and substantial gratitude of your fellow citizens, you need only proceed earnestly to do this service for your republic. I say these things not because I think you are ignorant of any of them, but because I persuade myself that you are much more intent on what you may do for your country than on what it will, in good right, owe to you. I will now speak of foreigners, for obliging whom, if you want to do that, there is certainly ample occasion. For anyone among them who is by chance more flourishing in wit than the rest, or in pleasing and elegant manners, has the Etruscan tongue° among his chief delights, yea rather considers it a solid part of his learning, especially if he has imbibed Greek and Latin either not at all or in moderate tincture. Certainly I, who have not merely wet my lips in these languages but have drunk deeper drafts—as much as anyone of my years, am nevertheless glad to go for a feast to Dante and Petrarch, and to a good many of your other authors. Neither Attic Athens with her bright and clear Ilissus nor old Rome with her bank of the Tiber can hold me so firmly that I do not love to visit often your Arno and those hills of Fiesole.° See now, I pray, whether there was not some providential design which sent you, as your latest guest from the ocean for these few days, me, such a lover of your nation that no other, I think, is a greater. You may, for this reason, be better able to remember what I have been at such pains to request of you: that you would be willing to add to your work, already begun and in large part completed, a little something on right pronunciation—as much as the work itself will bear, for the sake of us foreigners. For the intention of all previous authorities on your speech seems to have been to satisfy their own people, caring nothing about us. Although in my judgment they would have provided more surely for their own fame and the glory of the Italian speech if they had presented their precepts as if it were the business of all mortals to acquire the language, still, as far as they are concerned, you Italians might seem to have wished to be wise only within the boundary of the Alps. Therefore the praise heretofore tasted by none will be all yours and has kept itself intact and whole for you until this time. And another honor will be no less yours if, in such a crowd of writers, you do not find it too burdensome to discuss fully each one who, after those well-known authors in the Florentine tongue, will be able justly to place himself among the next best: who is distinguished in tragedy, who in comedy gay and light, who in epistles or dialogues witty or grave, who in history noble; and thus it will not be difficult for the willing and studious to select the better of them; and there will be, whenever he wishes to wander more widely afield, a place where he may fix his foot with assurance. In this matter you will have, among the ancients, Cicero and Fabius° to imitate; whether any of your own age, however, I do not know. And though (unless my memory fails me) it seems to me that you have already granted my request whenever we mention the matter—such is your courtesy and good disposition, I am unwilling to regard that as an excuse for not making the same request carefully and, so to speak, elegantly. For although your own worth and sincerity award the lowest value and honour to your own works, I hope that my opinion, and their real dignity, may fix the true and accurate value upon them; also it is only fair everywhere that the more easily one grants a request, the less there ought to be lacking in the reward of his compliance. Finally, if you should wonder why, on this subject, I use Latin rather than your tongue, I do it for this reason, that you may understand that I wish that tongue clarified for me by your precepts, and to confess my awkwardness and ignorance plainly in Latin. By this method I have hoped to prevail the better with you; and I have also believed that if I brought with me as helper in her daughter's cause that grey and venerable mother from Latium,° you could deny nothing to her authority and reverence, her majesty august through so many ages. Farewell.

Florence, Septemb. 10. 1638.

To Leonard Philaras, Athenian

Since I have been from boyhood a worshipper of all things Greek and of your Athens first and foremost, I have always been most firmly convinced that this city would someday nobly recompense my goodwill towards her. Nor has the ancient spirit of your noble country belied my prophecy, but has given me you, both an Attic brother and a very loving one: it was you who addressed me most kindly by letter, though far distant and knowing me only by my writings; and afterwards, arriving unexpectedly in London, you continued that kindness by going to see one who could not see, even in that misfortune which has made me more respectable to none, more despicable perhaps to many.° And so, since you tell me that I should not give up all hope of regaining my sight, that you have a friend and intimate in the Paris physician Thévenot (especially outstanding as an occulist), whom you will consult about my eyes if only I send you the means by which he can diagnose the causes and symptoms of the disease, I shall do what you urge, that I may not seem to refuse aid whencesoever offered, perhaps divinely.

It is ten years, I think, more or less, since I noticed my sight becoming weak and growing dim, and at the same time my spleen and all my viscera burdened and shaken with flatulence. And even in the morning, if I began as usual to read, I noticed that my eyes felt immediate pain deep within and turned from reading, though later refreshed after moderate bodily exercise; as often as I looked at a lamp, a sort of rainbow seemed to obscure it. Soon a mist appearing in the left part of the left eye (for that eye became clouded some years before the other) removed from my sight everything on that side. Objects further forward too seemed smaller, if I chanced to close my right eye. The other eye also failing slowly and gradually over a period of almost three years, some months before my sight was completely destroyed, everything which I distinguished when I myself was still seemed to swim, now to the right, now to the left. Certain permanent vapors seem to have settled upon my entire forehead and temples, which press and oppress my eyes with a sort of sleepy heaviness, especially from mealtime to evening, so that I often think of the Salmydessian seer Phineus in the *Argonauts*,°

> All round him then there grew
> A purple thickness; and he thought the earth
> Whirling beneath his feet, and so he sank,
> Speechless at length, into a feeble sleep.

But I must not omit that, while considerable sight still remained, when I would first go to bed and lie on one side or the other, abundant light would dart from my closed eyes; then, as sight daily diminished, colours proportionately darker would burst forth with violence and a sort of crash from within; but now, pure black, marked as if with extinguished or ashy light, and as if interwoven with it, pours forth. Yet the mist which always hovers before my eyes both night and day seems always to be approaching white rather than black; and upon the eyes turning, it admits a minute quantity of light as if through a crack.

Although some glimmer of hope too may radiate from that physician, I prepare and resign myself as if the case were quite incurable; and I often reflect that since many days of darkness are destined to everyone, as the wise man° warns, mine thus far, by the signal kindness of Providence, between leisure and study, and the voices and visits of friends, are much more mild than those lethal ones. But if, as it is written,° man shall not live by bread alone, but by every word that proceedeth out of the mouth of God, why should one not likewise find comfort in believing that he cannot see by the eyes alone, but by the guidance and wisdom of God. Indeed while He himself looks out for me and provides for me, which He does, and takes me as if by the hand and leads me throughout life, surely, since it has pleased Him, I shall be pleased to grant my eyes a holiday.

And you, my Philaras, whatever happens, I bid you farewell with a spirit no less stout and bold than if I were Lynceus.°

Westminster, September 28, 1654.

From *Christian Doctrine*

To All the Churches of Christ and to All in any part of the world who profess the Christian Faith, Peace, Knowledge of the Truth, and Eternal Salvation in God the Father and in our Lord Jesus Christ.

The process of restoring religion to something of its pure original state, after it had been defiled with impurities for more than thirteen hundred years, dates from the beginning of the last century. Since that time many theological systems have been propounded, aiming at further purification, and providing sometimes brief, sometimes more lengthy and methodical expositions of almost all the chief points of Christian doctrine. This being so, I think I should explain straight away why, if any work has yet been published on this subject which is as exhaustive as possible, I have been dissatisfied with it, and why, on the other hand, if all previous writers have failed in this attempt, I have not been discouraged from making the same attempt myself.

If I were to say that I had focused my studies principally upon Christian doctrine because nothing else can so effectually wipe away those two repulsive afflictions, tyranny and superstition, from human life and the human mind, I should show that I had been concerned not for religion but for life's well-being.

But in fact I decided not to depend upon the belief or judgment of others in religious questions for this reason: God has revealed the way of eternal salvation only to the individual faith of each man, and demands of us that any man who wishes to be saved should work out his beliefs for himself. So I made up my mind to puzzle out a religious creed for myself by my own exertions, and to acquaint myself with it thoroughly. In this the only authority I accepted was God's self-revelation, and accordingly I read and pondered the Holy Scriptures themselves with all possible diligence, never sparing myself in any way.

I shall mention those methods that proved profitable for me, in case desire for similar profit should, perhaps, lead someone else to start out upon the same path in the future. I began by devoting myself when I was a boy to an earnest study of the Old and New Testaments in their original languages, and then proceeded to go carefully through some of the shorter systems of theologians. I also started, following the example of these writers, to list under general headings all passages from the scriptures which suggested themselves for quotation, so that I might have them ready at hand when necessary. At length, gaining confidence, I transferred my attention to more diffuse volumes of divinity, and to the conflicting arguments in controversies over certain heads of faith. But, to be frank, I was very sorry to find, in these works, that the authors frequently evaded an opponent's point in a thoroughly dishonest way, or countered it, in appearance rather than in reality, by an affected display of logical ingenuity or by constant linguistic quibbles. Such writers, moreover, often defended their prejudices tooth and nail, though with more fervour than force, by misinterpretations of biblical texts or by the false conclusions which they wrung from these. Hence, they sometimes violently attacked the truth as error and heresy, while calling error and heresy truth and upholding them not upon the authority of the Bible but as a result of habit and partisanship.

So I considered that I could not properly entrust either my creed or my hope of salvation to such guides. But I still thought that it was absolutely necessary to possess a systematic exposition of Christian teaching, or at any rate a written investigation of it, which could assist my faith or my memory or both. It seemed, then, safest and most advisable for me to make a fresh start and compile for myself, by my own exertion and long hours of study, some work of this kind which might be always at hand. I should derive this from the word of God and from that alone, and should be scrupulously faithful to the text, for to do otherwise would be merely to cheat myself. After I had painstakingly persevered in this work for several years, I saw that the citadel of reformed religion was adequately fortified against the Papists. Through neglect, however, it was open to attack in many other places where defences and defenders were alike wanting to make it safe. In religion as in other things, I discerned, God offers all his rewards not to those who are thoughtless and credulous, but to those who labour constantly and seek tirelessly after truth. Thus I concluded that there was more than I realized which still needed to be measured with greater strictness against the yardstick of the Bible, and reformed with greater care. I pursued my studies, and so far satisfied myself that eventually I had no doubt about my ability to distinguish correctly in religion between matters of faith and matters of opinion. It was, furthermore, my greatest comfort that I had constructed, with God's help, a powerful support for my faith, or rather that I had laid up provision for the future in that I should not thenceforth be unprepared or hesitant when I needed to give an account of my beliefs.

God is my witness that it is with feelings of universal brotherhood and good will that I make this account public. By so doing I am sharing, and that most willingly, my dearest and best possession with as many people as possible. I hope, then, that all my readers will be sympathetic, and will avoid prejudice and malice, even though they see at once that many of the views I have published are at odds with certain conventional opinions. I implore all friends of truth not to start shouting that the church is being thrown into confusion by free discussion and inquiry. These are allowed in academic circles, and should certainly be denied to no believer. For we are ordered to find out the truth about all things, and the daily increase of the light of truth fills the church much rather with brightness and strength than with confusion. I do not see how anyone should be able or is able to throw the church into confusion by searching after truth, any more than the heathen were thrown into confusion when the gospel was first preached. For assuredly I do not urge or enforce anything upon my own authority. On the contrary, I advise every reader, and set him an example by doing the same myself, to withhold his consent from those opinions about which he does not feel fully convinced, until the evidence of the Bible convinces him and induces his reason to assent and to believe. I do not seek to conceal any part of my meaning. Indeed I address myself with much more confidence to learned than to untutored readers or, if the very learned are not always the best judges and critics of such matters, at any rate to mature, strong-minded men who thoroughly understand the teaching of the gospel. Most authors who have dealt with this subject at the greatest length in the past have been in the habit of filling their pages almost entirely with expositions of their own ideas. They have relegated to the margin, with brief reference to chapter and verse, the scriptural texts upon which all that they teach is utterly dependent. I, on the other hand, have striven to cram my pages even to overflowing, with quotations drawn from all parts of the Bible and to leave as little space as possible for my own words, even when they arise from the putting together of actual scriptural texts.

I intend also to make people understand how much it is in the interests of the Christian religion that men should be free not only to sift
and winnow any doctrine, but also openly to give their opinions of it and
even to write about it, according to what each believes. This I aim to
achieve not only by virtue of the intrinsic soundness and power of the
arguments, new or old, which my readers will find me bringing forward, but much more by virtue of the authority of the Bible, upon very
frequent citations of which these arguments are based. Without this
freedom to which I refer, there is no religion and no gospel. Violence
alone prevails; and it is disgraceful and disgusting that the Christian
religion should be supported by violence. Without this freedom, we are
still enslaved: not, as once, by the law of God but, what is vilest of all, by
human law, or rather, to be more exact, by an inhuman tyranny. There
are some irrational bigots who, by a perversion of justice, condemn
anything they consider inconsistent with conventional beliefs and give it
an invidious title—'heretic' or 'heresy'—without consulting the evidence of the Bible upon the point. To their way of thinking, by branding
anyone out of hand with this hateful name, they silence him with one
word and need take no further trouble. They imagine that they have
struck their opponent to the ground as with a single blow, by the impact
of the name heretic alone. I do not expect that my unprejudiced and
intelligent readers will behave in this way: such conduct would be
utterly unworthy of them. But to these bigots I retort that, in apostolic
times, before the New Testament was written, the word heresy, whenever it was used as an accusation, was applied only to something which
contradicted the teaching of the apostles as it passed from mouth to
mouth. Heretics were then, according to Rom. 16: 17, 18, only those
people who *caused divisions of opinion and offences contrary to the teaching
of the apostles: serving not our Lord Jesus Christ but their own belly*. On the
same grounds I hold that, since the compilation of the New Testament,
nothing can correctly be called heresy unless it contradicts that. For my
own part, I devote my attention to the Holy Scriptures alone. I follow
no other heresy or sect. I had not even studied any of the so-called
heretical writers, when the blunders of those who are styled orthodox,
and their unthinking distortions of the sense of scripture, first taught
me to agree with their opponents whenever these agreed with the Bible.
If this is heresy, I confess, as does Paul in Acts 24: 14, that *following the
way which is called heresy I worship the God of my fathers, believing all things
that are written in the law and the prophets* and, I add, whatever is written
in the New Testament as well. In common with the whole Protestant
Church I refuse to recognize any other arbiters of or any other supreme

authorities for Christian belief, or any faith not independently arrived at but 'implicit', as it is termed. For the rest, brethren, cherish the truth with love for your fellow men. Assess this work as God's spirit shall direct you. Do not accept or reject what I say unless you are absolutely convinced by the clear evidence of the Bible. Lastly, live in the spirit of our Lord Saviour Jesus Christ, and so I bid your farewell.

J.M.

[*Anthropomorphism*]

God attributes to himself again and again a human shape and form, why should we be afraid of assigning to him something he assigns to himself, provided we believe that what is imperfect and weak in us is, when ascribed to God, utterly perfect and utterly beautiful? We may be certain that God's majesty and glory were so dear to him that he could never say anything about himself which was lower or meaner than his real nature, nor would he ever ascribe to himself any property if he did not wish us to ascribe it to him. Let there be no question about it: they understand best what God is like who adjust their understanding to the word of God, for he has adjusted his word to our understanding, and has shown what kind of an idea of him he wishes us to have. In short, God either is or is not really like he says he is. If he really is like this, why should we think otherwise? If he is not really like this, on what authority do we contradict God? If, at any rate, he wants us to imagine him in this way, why does our imagination go off on some other tack? Why does our imagination shy away from a notion of God which he himself does not hesitate to promulgate in unambiguous terms? For God in his goodness has revealed to us in ample quantity those things which we need to understand about him for our salvation: Deut. 29: 29: *hidden things are in the power of Jehovah, but the things which are revealed are revealed to us that we may do them.* We do not imply by this argument that God, in all his parts and members, is of human form, but that, so far as it concerns us to know, he has that form which he attributes to himself in Holy Writ. God, then, has disclosed just such an idea of himself to our understanding as he wishes us to possess. If we form some other idea of him, we are not acting according to his will, but are frustrating him of his purpose, as if, indeed, we wished to show that our concept of God was not too debased, but that his concept of us was.

(i.2)

[*Foreknowledge*]

To sum up these numerous arguments in a few words, this is briefly how the matter stands, looked at from a thoroughly reasonable angle. By virtue of his wisdom God decreed the creation of angels and men as beings gifted with reason and thus with free will. At the same time he foresaw the direction in which they would tend when they used this absolutely unimpaired freedom. What then? Shall we say that God's providence or foreknowledge imposes any necessity upon them? Certainly not: no more than if some human being possessed the same foresight. For an occurrence foreseen with absolute certainty by a human being will no less certainly take place than one foretold by God. For example, Elisha foresaw what evils King Hazael would bring upon the Israelites in a few years' time: 2 Kings 8: 12. But no one would claim that these happened inevitably as a result of Elisha's foreknowledge: for these events, no less than any others, clearly arose from man's will, which is always free. Similarly, nothing happens because God has foreseen it, but rather he has foreseen each event because each is the result of particular causes which, by his decree, work quite freely and with which he is thoroughly familiar. So the outcome does not rest with God who foresees it, but only with the man whose action God foresees.

(i.3)

[*The Trinity*]

I am now going to talk about the Son of God and the Holy Spirit, and I do not think I should broach such a difficult subject without some fresh preliminary remarks. The Roman Church demands implicit obedience on all points of faith. If I professed myself a member of it, I should be so indoctrinated, or at any rate so besotted by habit, that I should yield to its authority and to its mere decree even if it were to assert that the doctrine of the Trinity, as accepted at present, could not be proved from any passage of scripture. As it happens, however, I am one of those who recognize God's word alone as the rule of faith; so I shall state quite openly what seems to me much more clearly deducible from the text of scripture than the currently accepted doctrine. I do not see how anyone who calls himself a Protestant or a member of the Reformed Church, and who acknowledges the same rule of faith as myself, could be offended with me for this, especially as I am not trying to browbeat anyone, but am merely pointing out what I consider the more credible doctrine. This one thing I beg of my reader: that he will weigh each statement and evaluate it with a mind innocent of prejudice and eager only for the truth. For I take it upon myself to refute, whenever necessary, not scriptural authority, which is inviolable, but human interpretations. That is my right, and indeed my duty as a human being. Of course, if my opponents could show that the doctrine they defend was revealed to them by a voice from heaven, he would be an impious wretch who dared to raise so much as a murmur against it, let alone a sustained protest. But in fact they can lay claim to nothing more than human powers and that spiritual illumination which is common to all men. What is more just, then, than that they should allow someone else to play his part in the business of research and discussion: someone else who is hunting the same truth, following the same track, and using the same methods as they, and who is equally anxious to benefit his fellow men? Now, relying on God's help, let us come to grips with the subject itself.

(i.5)

[The Son]

[God] was in a real sense Father of the Son, whom he made of his own substance. It does not follow, however, that the Son is of the same essence as the Father. Indeed, if he were, it would be quite incorrect to call him Son. For a real son is not of the same age as his father, still less of the same numerical essence: otherwise father and son would be one person. This particular Father begot his Son not from any natural necessity but of his own free will: a method more excellent and more in keeping with paternal dignity, especially as this Father is God. For it has already been demonstrated from the text of scripture that God always acts with absolute freedom, working out his own purpose and volition. Therefore he must have begotten his Son with absolute freedom.

God could certainly have refrained from the act of generation and yet remained true to his own essence, for he stands in no need of propagation. So generation has nothing to do with the essence of deity. And if a thing has nothing to do with his essence or nature, he does not do it from natural necessity like a natural agent. Moreover, if natural necessity was the deciding factor, then God violated his own essence by begetting, through the force of nature, an equal. He could no more do this than deny himself. Therefore he could not have begotten the Son except of his own free will and as a result of his own decree.

So God begot the Son as a result of his own decree. Therefore it took place within the bounds of time, for the decree itself must have preceded its execution.

(i.5)

[The Holy Spirit]

Although the scriptures do not tell us explicitly who or what the Holy Spirit is, we need not be completely ignorant about it, as this much may be understood from the texts quoted above. The Holy Spirit, since he is a minister of God, and therefore a creature, was created, that is, produced, from the substance of God, not by natural necessity, but by the free will of the agent, maybe before the foundations of the world were laid, but after the Son, to whom he is far inferior, was made. You will say that this does not really distinguish the Holy Spirit from the Son. I reply that, in the same way, the expressions *to go forth from* and *to go out from* and *to proceed from the Father*, which are all the same in the Greek, do not distinguish the Son from the Holy Spirit, since they are used about both and signify the mission not the nature of each. There is sufficient reason for placing the name and also the nature of the Son above that of the Holy Spirit, when discussing matters relative to the Deity, in that the brightness of God's glory and the image of his divine subsistence are said to have been impressed on the Son but not on the Holy Spirit.

(i.6)

[Creation Is Not Ex Nihilo]

It is clear, then, that the world was made out of some sort of matter. For since 'action' and 'passivity' are relative terms, and since no agent can act externally unless there is something, and something material, which can be acted upon, it is apparent that God could not have created this world out of nothing. *Could* not, that is, not because of any defect of power or omnipotence on his part, but because it was necessary that something should have existed previously, so that it could be acted upon by his supremely powerful active efficacy. Since, then, both the Holy Scriptures and reason itself suggest that all these things were made not out of nothing but out of matter, matter must either have always existed, independently of God, or else originated from God at some point in time. That matter should have always existed independently of God is inconceivable. In the first place, it is only a passive principle, dependent upon God and subservient to him; and, in the second place, there is no inherent force or efficacy in time or eternity, any more than there is in the concept of number. But if matter did not exist from eternity, it is not very easy to see where it originally came from. There remains only this solution, especially if we allow ourselves to be guided by scripture, namely, that all things came from God. Rom. 11: 36: *from him and through him and in him are all things*; 1 Cor. 8: 6: *one God, the Father, from whom all things are,—from*, as the Greek reads in both cases. Heb. 2: 11: *for both he who sanctifies and he who is sanctified, are all from one.*

(i.7)

[*The Death of the Soul*]

The death of the body, as it is called, is the loss or extinction of life. For the separation of body and soul, which is the usual definition of death, cannot possibly be death at all. What part of man dies when this separation takes place? The soul? Even those who adhere to the usual definition deny that. The body? But how can that be said to die which never had any life of its own? This separation, then, cannot be called the death of man.

This gives rise to a very important question which, because of the prejudice of theologians, has usually been dismissed out of hand, instead of receiving proper and careful examination. Does the whole man die, or only the body? It is a question which can be debated without detriment to faith or devotion, whichever side we may be on. So I shall put forward quite unreservedly the doctrine which seems to me to be instilled by virtually innumerable passages of scripture. I assume that no one thinks you should look for truth among philosophers and schoolmen rather than in the Bible!

Man is always said to be made up of body, spirit and soul, whatever we may think about where one starts and the other leaves off. So I will first prove that the whole man dies, and then that each separate part dies.

(i.13)

[*The Death of Christ*]

For if Christ really died, then both his soul and his body died, as I have proved above, on the same day. As for his divine nature, it is more questionable whether that also succumbed to death. A lot of passages in the Bible make his divine nature succumb to death along with his human nature, and they seem to do so too clearly for it to be explained away as mere idiomatic parallelism, Rom. 10: 9: *if you will confess the Lord Jesus with your mouth, and will believe in your heart that God has raised him from the dead, you will be saved.* The man whom we ought to confess with our mouths is the same as the man whom God has raised from the dead. But we ought to confess *the Lord Jesus,* that is, the whole person of Jesus: therefore God raised the whole person of the Lord Jesus from the dead. 1 Cor. 2: 8: *if they had known, they would not have crucified the Lord of glory;* Gal. 1. 1: *not by men, nor through man, but through Jesus Christ and God the Father who raised him from the dead.* God, therefore raised not only Christ as man but the whole Christ, and it was through Christ not as man but as θεάνθρωπος that Paul was sent. Philipp. 2: 6–8: *he was in the form of God he emptied himself, and took the form of a servant; he humbled himself, and was made obedient right up to his death;* 1 John 3: 16: *through this we know God's love, because he laid down his life for us;* Rev. 1: 17, 18: *I am the first and the last, and I am alive and was dead,* also 2: 8. It is only Christ's speech to the thief, *today you will be with me in paradise,* which makes one hesitate, and it is a speech which has, for other reasons, worried some of the most learned commentators. I am less troubled by that terseness of expression in 1 Pet. 3: 18: *put to death in the flesh, but given life in the spirit.* Because here, if the antithesis holds, what we are being told is in which part he was put to death and in which part he was given life. And no part could be given life unless it were first dead. On the other hand, if *the spirit* is here intended to represent the cause of life, there are far less obscure passages which show us that this must be understood to mean the spirit of God the Father. Of course, the fact that Christ became a sacrifice both in his divine and in his human nature, is questioned by no one. It is moreover, necessary for the whole of a sacrifice to be killed. So it follows that Christ, the sacrificial lamb, was totally killed.

(i.16)

[*The Interpretation of Scripture*]

Every believer is entitled to interpret the scriptures; and by that I mean interpret them for himself. He has the spirit, who guides truth, and he has the mind of Christ. Indeed, no one else can usefully interpret them for him, unless that person's interpretation coincides with the one he makes for himself and his own conscience. . . . Whoever God has appointed as apostle or prophet or evangelist or pastor or teacher, is entitled to interpret the scriptures for others in public, 1 Cor. 12: 8, 9;

Eph. 4: 11–13: in other words, anyone endowed with the gift of teaching, *every teacher of the law who has been instructed in readiness for the kingdom of heaven*, Matt. 13: 52. . . .

No visible church, then, let alone any magistrate, has the right to impose its own interpretations upon the consciences of men as matters of legal obligation, thus demanding implicit faith. . . .

We have, particularly under the gospel, a double scripture. There is the external scripture of the written word and the internal scripture of the Holy Spirit which he, according to God's promise, has engraved upon the hearts of believers, and which is certainly not to be neglected. . . .

Nowadays the external authority for our faith, in other words, the scriptures, is of very considerable importance and, generally speaking, it is the authority of which we first have experience. The pre-eminent and supreme authority, however, is the authority of the Spirit, which is internal, and the individual possession of each man. . . .

Each believer is ruled by the Spirit of God. So if anyone imposes any kind of sanction or dogma upon believers against their will, whether he acts in the name of the church or of a Christian magistrate, he is placing a yoke not only upon man but upon the Holy Spirit itself.

(i.30)

NOTES

ABBREVIATIONS

Aen.	[Virgil] *Aeneid*
Apol.	*Apology for Smectymnuus*
Areo.	*Areopagitica*
CD	*Christian Doctrine*
DDD	*Doctrine and Discipline of Divorce*
ELH	*Journal of English Literary History*
FQ	[Spenser] *Faerie Queene*
Il.	[Homer] *Iliad*
Met.	[Ovid] *Metamorphoses*
MP	*Modern Philology*
OED	*Oxford English Dictionary*
Od.	[Homer] *Odyssey*
PL	*Paradise Lost*
PR	*Paradise Regained*
REW	*Ready and Easy Way*
RCG	*Reason of Church Government*
SA	*Samson Agonistes*
TKM	*Tenure of Kings and Magistrates*

1 *Letter to a Friend (?1633).* Neither the recipient nor the date of this letter is known (Parker conjectures Thomas Young, Milton's tutor, as the possible addressee and dates it 1633). It survives in two holograph drafts in the Trinity MS, neither of them final copies of the letter, both full of second thoughts and crossings out. It is possible that the letter was never sent. It was not published during Milton's lifetime. We print it first since it reveals Milton struggling with questions about his vocation and sending a copy of Sonnet 7 ('How soon hath time') as a token of his commitment to poetry.

a good watchman. Alluding to John 9. Jesus sees a blind man and assures his disciples that blindness is not a sign of sinfulness (9: 1–3). He then continues: 'I must work the works of him that sent me, while it is day: the night cometh, when no man can work' (9: 4). Then he anoints the eyes of the blind man who, upon washing in the pool at Siloam, regains his sight (9: 5–7). Cf. *PL*, i. 11, 'Siloa's brook'.

set apology. Formal defence of his lack of progress.

Endymion. Granted by Jupiter the desire to be young and to sleep as much as he desired, Endymion was seen sleeping naked on Mount Latmos by Diana, who fell in love and slept with him; the fable was treated as an allegory about astronomical knowledge, since Diana is goddess of the moon.

fond. Foolish.

fledge. Lit. 'provided with new feathers for wings'.

1 *regardless.* Unregarded.

curiosity. The search for useless knowledge.

as well those. i.e. the desire for immortal fame inflames both those who are destined to succeed and those who are not.

2 *presently.* Immediately.

the inferior bent. i.e. the desire for learning is viewed as simply natural.

gospel . . . talent. Alluding to the parable of the talents (Matt. 25: 14–30), in which the servant who buries the talent (coin) given him by the master is severely reprimanded for his unprofitableness; see Sonnet 19, 'When I consider how my light is spent' and *RCG* (and notes) for further allusions to this parable.

master of the vineyard. Alluding to the parable (Matt. 20: 1–16) in which the workers last called to the vineyard are more welcome into the kingdom of heaven than those who were called first and laboured longest.

stream-head copious. A fountainhead of material for further exposition (as in a sermon or rhetorical performance).

Nilus. The Nile flows upstream, thus ebbing and flowing at once.

period. Conclusion, complete syntactic unit.

POEMS (1645)

3 *On the Morning of Christ's Nativity.* The poem stands first both in 1645 and 1673; it is dated 1629 in a headnote in 1645, and Milton says in Elegy VI, addressed to Diodati, that he is in the process of composing it (see ll. 79 ff.). This is the only poem in the 1645 volume that Milton can be shown to have revised for the 1673 edition; we therefore print the revised text (1645 readings are indicated in the notes).

l. 5. *holy sages.* Old Testament prophets of redemption, but perhaps also Virgil, who predicts the birth of a peace-bearing child in Eclogues, iv.

l. 6. *forfeit.* Crime, transgression.   *release.* Cancel, grant remission of.

l. 8. *unsufferable.* Unendurable (because 'going beyond all natural limits' [*OED*]).

l. 10. *wont.* Was accustomed.

l. 11. *the midst . . . unity.* As the middle figure of the Trinity.

l. 14. *mortal clay.* Flesh; in Gen. 2: 7, Adam is created from dust; cf. l. 138 below.

l. 15. *muse.* Usually identified as Urania, muse of astronomy and hence of heavenly matters, as Christianized by Du Bartas in *Divine Weeks.* See *PL*, i. 6.   *vein.* Poetic genius.

l. 16. *Afford.* Furnish.

l. 19. *sun's team.* Horses of Apollo's chariot.

3 l. 21. *spangled host.* The stars, although the imagery is also applied to the angelic orders; cf. ll. 112–14, 243 below.

l. 23. *wizards.* Wise men, the Magi.

l. 24. *prevent.* Come before (Lat. *praevenire*), anticipate (and, by implication, delay; cf. l. 239 below).

4 l. 28. *From out his secret altar* . . . The syntax is inverted; he asks to be touched with hallowed fire drawn from the secret altar (as Isaiah had been, Isa. 6: 6–7). *secret.* Set apart.

l. 36. *wanton.* Play amorously, heedlessly, idly.

l. 39. *guilty.* Nature is guilty because corrupted by the Fall: see *PL*, x. 649 ff. *front.* Face, demeanour.

ll. 39–42. *To hide . . . throw.* Cf. Rev. 3: 18.

l. 41. *Pollute.* Polluted.

l. 45. *cease.* Commonly used transitively in the seventeenth century.

l. 47. *olive green.* Olive branches were emblematic of peace.

l. 48. *turning sphere.* In the Ptolemaic scheme of the universe, the outermost of the hollow spheres that revolved around the earth bearing the heavenly bodies (cf. ll. 75, 102 below); a stage machine of the sort used in court masques may also be implied (cf. ll. 141–8 below).

l. 50. *turtle wing.* Wing of the turtledove.

l. 51. *myrtle.* An attribute of Venus.

5 l. 56. *hookèd.* Armed with hooks, as in Spenser's description of the Souldan's chariot, *FQ*, v. xxviii. 5.

l. 59. *awful.* Filled with awe.

l. 64. *whist.* Hushed.

l. 68. *birds of calm.* Halcyons, or kingfishers: the sea was said to remain calm during their winter nesting period. *brooding.* Nesting. *charmèd.* Under a spell.

l. 71. *influence.* Forces emanating from the stars and planets and affecting mankind.

l. 73. *For all.* Despite, notwithstanding.

l. 74. *Lucifer.* The morning star (Hesperus, Venus) as well as the devil; cf. Isa. 14: 12 and l. 119 below.

l. 78. *room.* Space.

ll. 79–84. *The sun . . . bear.* For the metaphor, cf. Spenser, *Shepheardes Calender*, 'Aprill', ll. 73–81.

l. 81. *As.* As if.

l. 84. *axle-tree.* Axle of the sun's chariot.

l. 86. *Or ere.* Both words mean before; the doubling is for emphasis.

6 l. 89. *Pan.* God of nature, patron of shepherds; Pan is glossed as Christ in Spenser's *Shepheardes Calender*, 'May'.

l. 90. *kindly.* Both according to his nature and lovingly.

l .92. *silly.* Simple, rustic.

l. 95. *strook.* Struck; the form was still in use in the seventeenth century.

l. 100. *close.* Conclusion of a musical phrase, cadence.

ll. 102–3. *round . . . seat.* The sphere of the moon.   *Cynthia.* Diana, the moon goddess (from her birthplace on Mount Cynthus).

l. 104. *won.* Rescued, delivered.

ll. 112–13. *cherubim . . . seraphim.* Lower and higher orders of angels respectively.

l. 116. *unexpressive.* Inexpressible, indescribable.

6–7 ll. 117–21. *Such music . . . set.* Cf. Job 38: 4, 7.

7 l. 122. *on hinges.* On its axis; cf. Spenser, *FQ*, 1. 11. 21. 8.

l. 124. *welt'ring.* Surging.

ll. 125–7. *Ring out . . . so.* The lines allude to the Pythagorean idea that the turning spheres make a music inaudible to human ears; this was the topic of Milton's second *Prolusion*.

l. 130. *base of heaven.* Earth, invoked (with a play on 'bass') to join in the heavenly harmony.   *organ.* the instrument used to play the ground bass in a musical composition; also, since it was thought of as the universal instrument, an image for the universe as a musical structure.

l. 131. *ninefold.* The number of both the spheres and the angelic orders.

l. 132. *Make up full consort to.* Complete the harmony of.   *consort.* 'The accord or harmony of several instruments or voices playing or singing in tune' (*OED*).

l. 135. *Time will run back.* Cf. the return to the golden age prophesied in Virgil, *Eclogues*, iv.

l. 136. *speckled.* Blemished, opposite of immaculate.

l. 140. *mansions.* Dwelling places (not necessarily buildings).

l. 141. *Justice.* The return of the goddess of justice, Astraea, is announced in Virgil, *Eclogues*, 4.

ll. 143–4. *Orbed . . . between.* In 1645, these lines read: 'Th' enameld *Arras* of the Rainbow wearing, / And Mercy set between.'

l. 146. *tissued.* As if made of a cloth interwoven with gold or silver.

l. 147. *as.* As if.

8 l. 155. *ychained.* Spenserian archaism.

ll. 157–64. *With such . . . throne.* Exod. 19: 16–20 describes the effects of the delivery of the law to Moses on Mount Sinai; Matt. 24: 29–31 predicts similar events at Christ's second coming.

8 l. 163. *session.* Three syllables.

l. 168. *the old dragon.* 'The dragon, that old serpent, which is the Devil' (Rev. 20: 2).

l. 172. *Swinges.* Lashes.

l. 173. *The oracles are dumb.* The pagan oracles were said to have ceased functioning after the advent of Christ; cf. *PR*, i. 393–464.

l. 178. *Delphos.* Delphi, site of Apollo's oracle, was generally called Delphos in the period, though the two places were not confused.

9 l. 186. *genius.* The *genius loci*, guardian spirit of a place; cf. *Lycidas*, l. 183.

l. 191. *lars.* Roman tutelary deities of home and family.　　*lemures.* Roman spirits of the dead.

l. 194. *flamens.* Roman priests.　　*quaint.* Strange, curious.

l. 196. *peculiar.* Particular.

l. 197. *Peor, and Baalim.* The Canaanite sun god Baal was worshipped at Peor as Baal-Peor (see Ps. 106: 28 and *PL*, i. 412, 421–3); Baalim is a plural designating various other manifestations of the god.

l. 199. *twice battered god.* Dagon, the Philistine god whose idol was twice thrown down in 1 Sam. 5: 3–4 and whose followers were defeated by Samson, who destroys his temple in Judg. 16: 23–30.

l. 200. *Ashtaroth.* A plural form of the Syrian goddess of the moon and fertility (also called Astarte), paired with Baalim in *PL*, i. 421–3 and described in *PL*, i. 437–46.

l. 203. *Libyc Hammon.* Ammon, Lybian (and Egyptian) god represented as a horned ram.

l. 204. *Tyrian.* Phoenician (from Tyre, the capital).　　*Thammuz.* Lover of Astarte, the Phoenician version of Adonis. His death was celebrated annually.

l. 205. *Moloch.* An Ammonite god (the name literally means king) whose rites included child sacrifice to a calf-headed brass idol filled with fire; cf. *PL*, i. 392–9.

l. 211. *brutish.* In animal form.

l. 212. *Isis.* Egyptian moon goddess.　　*Orus.* Horus, offspring of Isis and her brother Osiris.　　*Anubis.* Dog-headed offspring of Osiris and Nepthys, also his sister.

10 ll. 213–20. *Nor is . . . ark.* See Plutarch's account in *Isis and Osiris* (in his *Moralia*); at Memphis, Osiris was worshipped as the bull Apis.

l. 218. *Shroud.* Both a place of shelter and a winding cloth.

l. 223. *eyn.* Eyes; not an archaic usage.

l. 226. *Typhon.* Both an Egyptian god and a monster from Greek mythology.

ll. 227–8. *Our babe . . . crew.* As Hercules in his infancy strangled two snakes.

10 l. 231. *Pillows.* Earliest use of the verb recorded in *OED.*   *orient.* Eastern, hence the source of light.

l. 236. *night-steeds.* Horses of the chariot of Night.

l. 239. *Time is.* It is time.   *tedious.* Wearisome; also dilatory, slow.

l. 240. *teemèd.* Born.

l. 244. *harnessed.* Armoured.

A Paraphrase on Psalm 114

l. 1. *Terah's faithful son.* Abraham; Terah was an idol-worshipper.

11 l. 3. *Pharian.* Egyptian (from the island of Pharos, near Alexandria).

l. 10. *foil.* Defeat.

Psalm 136. At ll. 10, 13, 17, 21, and 25, *1673* prints 'Who' where *1645* has 'That'.

l. 3. *ay.* Ever.

l. 19. *painted.* 'Adorned with bright or varied colouring' (*OED*).   *state.* Majesty.

12 l. 41. *fell.* Fierce, cruel.

l. 46. *Erythraean main.* The Red Sea (from Gk. *erythros*, red).

l. 65. *Seon.* Amorite king, whose defeat is recounted in Num. 21: 21–4.

l. 69. *Og.* King of Bashan, a descendant of giants (see Josh. 13: 12), and linked with Seon in Deut. 31: 4.

13 l. 73. *Israel.* Jacob.

The Passion. Date: *c.*1630.

l. 1. *Erewhile.* Formerly.

l. 4. *My . . . sing.* The 'Nativity Ode' was composed for Christmas 1629.   *divide.* Run embellishments on a basic musical theme; perhaps divide into two choirs.

14 ll. 13–14. *Most perfect hero . . . labours.* Analogizing Christ's deeds to the labours of Hercules.   *wight.* Creature.

l. 15. *priest.* Christ is frequently referred to as the high priest (see e.g. Heb. 2: 17), and like the high priest he was anointed before the last supper (see Matt. 26: 7).

l. 17. *tabernacle.* Body; the body of Christ replaces the tabernacle in which the Jewish law was kept.

l. 18. *front.* Forehead.

l. 22. *latter.* *1673* reads 'latest'.

l. 23. *Phoebus.* Apollo, god of poetry.

14 l. 26. *Cremona's trump.* The *Christiad* (1535) by Marco Girolamo Vida of Cremona, a Latin epic on the life of Christ.

l. 28. *still.* Quiet.

l. 30. *pole.* Sky.

ll. 34–5. *The leaves . . . white.* Some seventeenth-century funeral poems were printed in white letters on black paper.

ll. 36–9. *See . . . Salem stood.* Beside the river Chebar, the prophet Ezekiel had a vision of wheels that became angels; see Ezek. 1.   *Salem* Jerusalem.

15 l. 43. *rock.* The holy sepulchre.

l. 46. *score.* Incise.

l. 47. *lively.* Vividly.

l. 49. *characters.* Letters.

l. 50. *viewless.* Invisible.

l. 56. *got.* Begot.

On Time. A subtitle, 'To be set on a clock case', appears, crossed out, in the Trinity MS of the poem. There is no evidence for a date of composition; usually dated 1633.

ll. 2–3. *leaden-stepping . . . plummet's pace.* The plummet is the weight, often made of lead, whose slow descent moves a clock.

l. 4. *womb.* The word was used of the stomach and bowels, as well as of the uterus.

l. 9. *whenas.* When.

l. 12. *individual.* Indivisible, i.e. everlasting, and also, as proper to each soul.

l. 18. *happy-making sight.* Beatific vision.

16 l. 20. *quit.* Having been left behind.

Upon the Circumcision. Usually dated 1633. Christ's circumcision is recorded by Luke (2: 21); its theological meaning is a frequent subject in Paul's epistles (e.g. Rom. 2: 25–9, 3: 30–1, 4: 9–16).

l. 1. *powers.* One of the orders of angels; see *PL*, ii. 11.

l. 2. *erst.* Formerly, i.e. at Christ's birth.

l. 10. *heraldry.* Pomp and ceremony.   *whilere.* A while ago.

l. 17. *doom.* Judgment.

l. 19. *secret.* Hidden from observation. 'removed from the resort of men' (*OED*).

l. 21. *cov'nant.* The Mosaic law.   *still.* Continually, yet.

l. 27. *heart.* As at the crucifixion (see John 19: 34).

17 *At a Solemn Music.* Like *On Time* and *Upon the Circumcision*, with which it forms a logical group, usually dated 1633.

l. 1. *sirens.* Plato imagined (*Republic.* x. 616–17) that the celestial spheres were moved by sirens who produced the music of the spheres.   *pledges.* Earthly music; the 'voice and verse' of l. 2, are conceived as both offspring and anticipatory assurances of heavenly harmony.

l. 2. *Sphere-born.* MSS have 'sphere-borne', suggesting sirens conveyed by or on the spheres.

l. 5. *fantasy.* Imagination, the image-making capacity.

l. 6. *concent.* Harmony. *1645* reads 'content'; but MSS read 'concent', and a copy of *1645* (now in the Bodleian Library) has been so corrected, possibly in Milton's hand.

l. 7. *Ay.* Ever.   *sapphire-coloured throne.* Cf. Ezek. 1: 26.

l. 14. *victorious palms.* Cf. Rev. 7: 9.

l. 17. *That.* So that.

l. 23. *diapason.* The harmonic interval of an octave; perfect concord.

l. 27. *consort.* A group of musicians (here angels), but also musical harmony, or a marriage partner.

An Epitaph on the Marchioness of Winchester. Jane, Marchioness of Winchester, daughter of Thomas, Viscount Savage, and wife of John Paulet, fifth Marquis of Winchester, died 15 April 1631, of an infection after delivering a stillborn child; she was 23. She was also eulogized by Jonson and Davenant. No evidence of Milton's relationship with this Catholic, and subsequently Royalist, family survives; through her kinsman Henry Rich, Chancellor of the University, she was connected to Cambridge, and ll. 53ff. have been supposed to indicate that Milton's poem was to have been part of a volume of Cambridge tributes.

l. 1. *marble.* Tomb.

l. 3. *earl's heir.* Through her mother Elizabeth, the daughter of Thomas Darcy, Earl Rivers.

18 l. 8. *told.* Numbered, counted.

l. 16. *Quickly . . . lover.* She married John Paulet in 1622, when she was 14.

l. 17. *virgin choir.* Bridesmaids.

l. 18. *The god.* Hymen, Roman god of marriage; his ill-lit flame and cypress crown have ominous and funereal associations.

l. 23. *matrons.* The word was also used of midwives.

l. 24. *greet her of.* Congratulate her on.   *son.* Charles, later sixth Marquis and Duke of Bolton, b. 1629.

l. 26. *Lucina.* Roman goddess of childbirth.

l. 27. *blame.* Fault.

18 l. 28. *Atropos.* One of the three Fates; she cuts the threads of life.

l. 35. *slip.* Cutting, shoot.

l. 37. *carnation.* Either the flower or its flesh-pink colour.   *train.* Attendants, retinue.

19 l. 49. *travail.* Labour.

l. 50. *seize.* Take possession of.

l. 56. *Helicon.* A mountain in Boeotia with a grove sacred to the muses, and the Hippocrene and Aganippe streams, sources of poetic inspiration.

l. 57. *bays.* Bay leaves, emblematic of poetic fame.

l. 59. *Came.* The river Cam, which runs through Cambridge; compare *Lycidas*, ll. 103 ff.

l. 63. *Syrian shepherdess.* Rachel; for her barrenness see Gen. 30: 22–4; for her death giving birth to Benjamin see Gen. 35: 16–20. For Joseph's fourteen-year service see Gen. 29: 18–28.

l. 66. *him.* Jacob, who had been Rachel's servant and subsequently married her.

Song. On May Morning. Dated variously between 1629 and 1631.

l. 1. *morning star.* Venus, also called Lucifer ('light-bringer').

20 *On Shakespeare.* Milton's first published poem; it appeared anonymously in the second folio (1632) of Shakespeare's plays.

l. 4. *ypointing.* Imitating Spenser, but inaccurately: the Middle English prefix 'y-' was used before a past participle, not before a present participle.

l. 10. *easy numbers.* In the prefatory epistle to the first Shakespeare folio (1623), Heminge and Condell remark: 'His mind and hand went together; and what he thought, he uttered with that easiness, that we have scarce received from him a blot in his papers.' Numbers are metrical periods, hence lines, verses.

ll. 10–14. *Thy . . . conceiving.* 'Because each reader's heart bears the impress of your wisdom, your powers replace our own; so that, being merely the material on which your thought is carved, we become your monument'. For the metaphor, compare *Il Penseroso*, ll. 40–2.

l. 11. *unvalued.* Invaluable.

l. 12. *Delphic.* Delphi was the site of the oracle of Apollo, god of poetry.

On the University Carrier

l. 1. *Hobson.* Thomas Hobson died 1 January 1631 at the age of 86, having carried mail and occasional passengers between Cambridge and London for some sixty years.   *girt.* Girth; also a belt used to harness the saddle and other articles to the back of a horse.

l. 5. *'Twas.* He was.   *shifter.* Trickster, dodger.

l. 8. *Bull.* Bull Inn, Bishopsgate, Hobson's London terminus.

20 l. 11. *lately.* The plague interrupted mail service in 1630.

l. 13. *ta'en . . . inn.* Taken a room at his last inn.

l. 14. *chamberlain.* The attendant at an inn in charge of the bedchambers.

21 *Another on the Same.* A version of this poem was first printed in *A Banquet of Jests* (1640).

ll. 3–4. *hung . . . trot.* i.e. his fate was in suspense as long as he was in motion.

l. 5. *sphere-metal.* The immutable substance of the heavenly spheres.

l. 6. *at stay.* At a stop.

l. 7. *Time numbers motion.* Time is the measure of motion (Cf. Aristotle, *Physics*, IV. xii. 221b).

l. 9. *engine.* Machine, here a clock.

l. 10. *principles.* Source of motion, force.

l. 12. *breathing.* Breathing space, rest.

l. 14. *vacation . . . term.* Freedom from business, limit or end; with puns on the words as used in the university calendar.

l. 16. *quickened.* Brought to life.

l. 18. *fetched.* Restored to consciousness (*OED*), with a play on 'fetch and carry'.

l. 19. *cross.* Opposing.

l. 20. *bearers.* Both pallbearers and letter carriers.

l. 22. *heaviness.* Grief.

l. 26. *As.* As if.   *cried . . . weight.* As prisoners who were pressed to death often did, to speed the end of the torture.

ll. 29–30. *Obedient . . . reciprocal.* i.e. he went back and forth like the tides.

l. 32. *wain.* Wagon, with a pun on 'wane'.

l. 34. *superscription.* (1) Address on a letter; (2) epitaph.

22 *L'Allegro.* 'The Happy Man'. As with its companion poem, *Il Penseroso*, 'The Melancholy Man', the title designates a personification or abstraction for the state of mind invoked in the poem. Usually dated *c.*1631.

l. 1. *Melancholy.* As a physiological condition caused by an excess of black bile, melancholy was associated with depression as well as genius. See R. Klibansky, E. Panofsky, and F. Saxl, *Saturn and Melancholy*; and Burton's *Anatomy of Melancholy*, the most compendious seventeenth-century treatment.

ll. 2–3. *Of Cerberus . . . forlorn.* The genealogy is invented. *Cerberus* was the three-headed hound, guardian of hell; the name means heart-devouring in Greek (cf. l. 135, below). Virgil depicts Cerberus in a cave overlooking the river Styx in *Aen.*, vi. 417–18.

22 l. 5. *uncouth*. Unknown, desolate, wild.   *cell*. Technically, a single-room dwelling; by the seventeenth century, poetic usage for a humble cottage (not applied to prisons until the eighteenth century).

l. 10. *Cimmerian desert*. The Homeric land of the Cimmerians was a place of perpetual night in *Od*., xi. 13–19.

l. 12. *yclept*. Named; a Spenserian archaism.   *Euphrosyne*. (Mirth) with Aglaia (Brightness) and Thalia (Bloom), one of the three graces, usually associated with Venus (although not always as her offspring), and implying love, beauty, and generosity.

l. 17. *some sager*. No source has been identified for this alternative genealogy.

l. 19. *Zephyr . . . Aurora*. The west wind and the dawn.

l. 24. *buxom, blithe, and debonair*. Three characteristics of Mirth with much semantic overlap; buxom suggests pliability; blithe, kindliness as well as good-humour; debonair, affability.

l. 27. *Quips*. Witty remarks.   *cranks*. Verbal tricks.   *wanton wiles*. Unrestrained, playful tricks.

l. 28. *becks*. Beckonings, 'come-ons'.

l. 29. *Hebe*. Goddess of youth.

l. 34. *fantastic*. Fanciful, elaborately conceived, perhaps alluding to dances in masques that executed complicated designs bearing philosophical meanings, as in Jonson's *Pleasure Reconciled to Virtue*.

22–3 ll. 37–40. *And if . . . pleasures free*. Echoing Marlowe, 'The Passionate Shepherd to his Love', ll. 19–20; cf. ll. 151–2 below, and *Il Penseroso*, ll. 175–6.

23 l. 39. *her*. Liberty.

l. 40. *unreprovèd*. Unreprovable, blameless.

l. 41. *the lark*. Traditionally the first bird to sing in the morning; cf. *PR*, ii. 279–81.

ll. 45–6. *to come . . . good morrow*. Editorial opinion has been divided over whether it is L'Allegro who comes to his window and bids good morrow to the day, or the lark who bids good morrow to L'Allegro; most critics favour the former interpretation, which accords most easily with the syntax.

l. 49. *the cock*. The crowing of the rooster signals dawn. Cf. l. 114 below.

l. 50. *Scatters the rear*. The image is of a retreating army.

l. 51. *stack*. Haystack.

l. 55. *hoar*. Grey, either with frost or mist.

l. 60. *state*. Stately march, as of a monarch.

l. 62. *dight*. Clothed.

l. 67. *tells his tale*. Counts the number of his flock and/or recounts his story.

l. 71. *fallows*. Unploughed, fallow land.

23 l. 75. *trim.* Neat.   *pied.* Variegated.

24 l. 80. *cynosure.* Centre of attraction (the name of the constellation otherwise called Ursa Minor, containing the North Star).

ll. 83–8. *Where Corydon . . . sheaves.* The pastoral names here appear in Virgil's *Eclogues*, and in countless Renaissance poems.

l. 85 *herbs.* Vegetables.   *messes.* Food.

l. 91. *secure.* Free from care (from L it. *sine cura*).

l. 92. *upland.* On the hills, above the meadows.

l. 94. *rebecks.* Three-stringed instruments, like fiddles.

l. 98. *sunshine.* Sunny.

l. 102. *Mab.* Queen of the fairies, as in *Romeo and Juliet*, i. iv. 54 ff. *junkets.* Cream-cheeses, or other forms of cream.

l. 104. *And he . . . led.* In 1673, the line read: 'And by the friar's lantern led'; the friar's lantern is the will-o'-the-wisp.

l. 105 *drudging goblin.* Robin Goodfellow, a folklore figure noted for both household help and mischievous pranks, and propitiated with offerings of cream; he is Shakespeare's Puck (called a 'hobgoblin' in *A Midsummer Night's Dream*, ii. i. 40) and the presenter in Jonson's masque *Love Restored*.

l. 110. *lubber.* Loutish.

l. 111. *chimney.* Fireplace.

l. 113. *crop-full.* Totally satiated.   *flings.* Rushes.

l. 120. *weeds.* Clothing, here the costumes appropriate to these courtly celebrations.

25 l. 121. *store of.* Many.

l. 122. *influence.* The eyes are imagined as stars with their supposed power to affect destiny; cf. 'Nativity Ode', l. 71.

l. 125. *Hymen.* Roman god of marriage, with his usual attributes of saffron-coloured robe and torch.

l. 126. *taper clear.* If the torch burned without smoke, the omens for the marriage were propitious. Cf. 'Epistle on the Marchioness of Winchester', l. 18.

l. 132. *sock.* The slipper worn by the Greek comic actor, as opposed to the tragic actor's buskin; here, a synedoche for comedy.

l. 133. *fancy.* Imagination, fantasy; cf. *Il Penseroso*, l. 6.

l. 136. *Lydian.* Greek musical mode associated in Plato, *Republic*, iii. 398e, primarily with laxness, conviviality, 'softness and sloth' (but also with 'dirges and lamentations').

l. 137. *Married.* Cf. the similar overlap with musical terms in 'At a Solemn Music', ll. 2, 27. See Leo Spitzer, *Classical and Christian Ideas of World Harmony*.

25 l. 138. *meeting.* Responsive, outgoing.

l. 139. *bout.* 'A roundabout way' (*OED*).

ll. 145–50. *That Orpheus' . . . Eurydice.* The story of Orpheus and Eurydice is in Ovid, *Met.*, 10 and 11, and in Virgil, *Georgics*, iv. 453–527. Orpheus, the archetypal poet, attempts to regain his wife Eurydice, who has been killed by a serpent; Pluto, the god of hell, grants his wish, but on condition that Orpheus not look back at Eurydice; he does, and loses her again. Ultimately, he is decapitated by the frenzied maenads. Virgil ends the story with the wailing of the severed head; Ovid reunites the couple in Elysium.

l. 145. *Orpheus' self.* Orpheus himself.

l. 149. *quite.* Entirely.

Il Penseroso

l. 3. *bestead.* Avail.

l. 4. *toys.* Idle thoughts.

26 l. 6. *fond.* Foolish.   *shapes.* The images of fancy, or imagination.

l. 10. *pensioners.* Military attendants.   *Morpheus.* God of dreams. *train.* Entourage.

ll. 13–16. *Whose saintly . . . hue.* Cf. *PL*, iii. 377–80.

l. 14. *hit.* Suit.

l. 18. *Memnon's sister.* Memnon was an Ethiopian (hence black) king who fought on the Trojan side and was killed by Achilles; in *Od.*, xi. 522 he is a paradigm of manly beauty. His sister Himera (or Hemera) is mentioned in later redactions of the Troy story, e.g. by Dictys Cretensis, Guido de Columnis, and John Lydgate.

l. 19. *starred Ethiop queen.* Cassiopeia, wife of the Ethiopian king Cepheus, and mother of Andromeda; boasting of her beauty (or in some accounts, of her daughter's) offended the gods and provoked her metamorphosis into the constellation that bears her name.

l. 23. *Vesta.* Goddess of the hearth and the chaste daughter of Saturn. The story of the genesis of Melancholy is Milton's invention.

l. 24. *solitary Saturn.* As patron of melancholics (those with a saturnine temperament), the god was represented as unsociable.

ll. 29–30. *Ida's . . . Jove.* In the Golden Age, Saturn ruled the world from atop Mount Ida, in Crete. Jove was born there, and subsequently overthrew and expelled his father.

l. 31. *nun.* 'A priestess or votaress of some pagan deity' (*OED*).

l. 33. *grain.* Dye.

l. 35. *cypress lawn.* Fine black linen.

l. 39. *commercing.* Conversing, communicating.

ll. 40–2. *Thy rapt . . . till.* Cf. 'On Shakespeare', ll. 13–14.

26 l. 43. *sad.* Both melancholy and serious, grave; cf. l. 103 below. *leaden.* Saturn was associated with lead.

l. 44. *fast.* Fixedly.

27 l. 48. *Ay.* Always.

l. 53. *fiery-wheelèd throne.* Perhaps alluding to Ezekiel's vision; cf. 'The Passion', ll. 36–9.

l. 55. *hist.* Summon silently.

l. 56. *Philomel.* The nightingale; her rape and transformation are recounted in *Met.*, vi.

l. 59. *Cynthia.* Goddess of the moon, similarly represented with a dragon-drawn chariot in Marlowe's *Hero and Leander*, l. 107 ff., though the dragons more usually conveyed the underworld goddess Hecate through the skies.

l. 68. *noon.* Apogee.

l. 73. *plat.* Plot, patch.

l. 76. *sullen.* The word also meant solemn.

l. 77. *air.* Weather, climate.

l. 78. *still removèd place.* Either an equally remote place, or a remote quiet place.

l. 83. *bellman.* Watchman.   *charm.* Both song (Lat. *carmen*) and spell (OE *cierm*).

28 l. 87. *Bear.* Ursa Major, visible until daybreak.

l. 88. *With . . . Hermes.* With the works of Hermes Trismegistus, supposed author of the *Corpus Hermeticum*, a series of mystical writings, for the most part composed in Alexandria in the second and third centuries; they were the first neoplatonic texts translated into Latin by Ficino in 1463, and were regarded as the founding texts for Renaissance Neoplatonism. See Edgar Wind, *Pagan Mysteries in the Renaissance.*

ll. 88–9. *unsphere . . . Plato.* Plato's spirit is presumed to occupy its own heavenly sphere, from which the mystical practitioner attempts to summon it.

l. 92. *mansion.* Dwelling (not necessarily a building).   *fleshly nook.* mortal place; *nook* means here a remote part of the world.

l. 93. *daemons.* Daemons, sublunary spirits, here assigned control of the four elements. Cf. *PR*, ii. 122–4.

ll. 95–6. *Whose . . . element.* i.e. the daemons control the mystical correspondence and harmony between the elements and the heavens.   *consent.* Sympathy, harmony.

l. 98. *pall.* Mantle of the Greek tragic actor.

l. 99. *Thebes.* Where Oedipus ruled.   *Pelops' line.* The house of Agamemnon, Pelops' grandson.

28 l. 102. *buskined.* Tragic (lit. wearing the buskin or high boot of the Greek tragic actor).

l. 104. *Musaeus.* Mythical poet, sometimes described as the son of Orpheus and a priest of Demeter, and hence as the founder of religious poetry; the late classical poem on Hero and Leander from which Marlowe's poem derives was until the early seventeenth century generally ascribed to him.

ll. 105–8. *Orpheus . . . seek.* See *L'Allegro,* ll. 145–50.

l. 109 ff. *him . . . half-told.* Chaucer, in the uncompleted *Squire's Tale,* continued by Spenser in *FQ,* iv; the relationship between those texts is discussed in Jonathan Goldberg, *Endlesse Worke: Spenser and the Structures of Discourse.*

l. 113. *virtuous.* Magical.

l. 121. *career.* Course; 'pale' because moonlit.

l. 122. *civil-suited.* Soberly attired.   *Morn.* Ovid's Aurora, who seduced Cephalus ('the Attic boy', l. 124); see *Met.,* vii. 690–865. Milton also alludes to the story in the Latin Elegy V, 'On the Coming of Spring', ll. 51–2.

l. 123. *tricked and frounced.* Adorned and curled.

l. 125. *kerchiefed.* Covered as with a shawl.

l. 127. *still.* Gentle.

29 l. 134. *Sylvan.* Sylvanus, the Roman woodland deity.

l. 145. *consort.* Harmony.

l. 154. *genius.* The spirit of the place (*genius loci*).

l. 155. *due.* Proper, dutiful.

l. 156. *pale.* Enclosure.

l. 157. *embowèd.* Vaulted, as a cathedral.

l. 158. *antic.* Fantastic, quaint; many editors modernize to 'antique'. *massy proof.* Massive strength.

l. 159. *storied.* Pictorial, stained-glass.   *dight.* Decorated.

30 l. 170. *spell.* Decipher, with an overtone of its magical sense.

ll. 175–6. *These pleasures . . . live.* See *L'Allegro* ll. 37–40, 151–2.

Sonnet 1 ('*O nightingale*'). This, the following Sonnets 2 to 6, and the Canzone '*Ridonsi donne . . .*' are associated by theme and style, and dated *c.*1628–30.

l. 4. *hours.* Horae, the deities whose dance led the months and seasons, and determined the course of the year.

ll. 6–7. *First . . . love.* It was considered lucky to hear the nightingale before the cuckoo, which was associated with cuckoldry.

l. 6. *shallow.* Shrill, thin.

l. 9. *timely.* Early, promptly.   *bird of hate.* Cuckoo.

30 *Sonnet 2* (*'Donna leggiadra'*)

31 ll. 1–2. *name . . . valley* [*nome . . . val*]. Both the region and the lady are called Emilia.

l. 2. *famous ford* [*nobil varco*]. Where Caesar crossed the Rubicon, which also runs through Emilia.

Sonnet 3 (*'Qual in colle aspro'*)

l. 10. *Arno*. The river of Florence as a figure for the Tuscan language, as the Thames represents English. Cf. a similar trope in 'Canzone', ll. 7 ff.

32 *Sonnet 4* (*'Diodati, e te'l dirò'*). Charles Diodati, to whom Milton also addressed his first and sixth Latin elegies and several letters, and whose death is commemorated in *Epitaphium Damonis*, was his closest friend from their schooldays at St Paul's in the 1620s until Diodati's death in 1638.

33 l. 6. *rare pattern* [*nuova idea*]. i.e. a Platonic idea.

l. 14. *sealing . . . wax* [*incerar . . . orecchi*]. As Odysseus had his men do in order not to hear the song of the Sirens, *Od.*, xii.

Sonnet 5 (*'Per certo i bei vostr'occhi'*)

l. 6. *that side* (*quel lato*). i.e. where his heart is.

34 *Sonnet 6* (*'Giovane piano'*)

l. 8. *adamant* (*diamante*). Legendary substance of impenetrable hardness.

Sonnet 7 (*'How soon hath time'*). Date: either 9 Dec. 1631, Milton's twenty-third birthday, or 9 Dec. 1632, when he ceased being twenty-three (see l. 2).

l. 3. *full career*. Swift course.

l. 5. *deceive*. Misrepresent.

l. 8. *timely-happy*. Seasonable, perhaps precocious.

35 l. 9. *it*. If there is a definite antecedent, this refers to 'inward ripeness'; there are similar difficulties with 'it' at l. 13 below.

l. 10. *still*. Always.   *even*. Equal, appropriate.

Sonnet 8 (*'Captain or colonel, or knight in arms'*). In the Trinity MS, a sub-title, 'on his door when the City expected an assault', has been crossed out and replaced with a substitute in Milton's hand, 'When the assault was intended to the City'. In Oct. 1642, the king's forces approached London.

l. 1. *colonel*. Three syllables, usually pronounced coronel.

l. 3. *If . . . thee*. In 1673, the passage reads 'If deed of honour did thee ever'.

l. 5. *charms*. Both spells (OE *cierm*) and songs (Lat. *carmen*).

l. 10. *Emathian conqueror*. Emathia is a district in Macedon; the conqueror is Alexander the Great. Pliny tells the story of how he spared Pindar's house in Thebes; it also appears in the gloss to 'October' in Spenser's *Shepheardes Calender*.

35 l. *13. Electra's poet.* Euripides. Plutarch reports in his *Life of Lysander* (15) that Athens was spared when one of Lysander's generals pleaded for the city by reciting a chorus from *Electra.*

Sonnet 9 ('Lady, that in the prime'). The subject's identity is unknown; *c.*1642–5.

l. *1. prime . . . youth.* 'The "springtime" of human life; the time of early manhood or womanhood, from about 21 to 28 years of age' (*OED*).

l. *2. the broad way.* Cf. Matt. 7: 13.

l. *5. Mary.* Jesus praises Mary, the sister of Martha, for choosing 'that good part, which shall not be taken away from her' (Luke 10: 42) by attending to him rather than to household chores.   *Ruth.* Ruth abandoned her home in Moab to live with Naomi, her Hebrew mother-in-law (Ruth 1: 16).

l. *6. overween.* Are presumptuous.

l. *7. fret their spleen.* 'Fret' = irritate, aggravate; the spleen was considered the seat of ill temper or melancholy.

ll. *9–14. Thy care . . . pure.* Alluding to one of the parables of the kingdom in Matt. 25: 1–13, of the wise and foolish virgins, half of whom kept their lamps burning in readiness for the midnight return of the bridegroom summoning them to the marriage feast.

36 *Sonnet 10 ('Daughter to that good earl').* Titled in the Trinity MS, 'To the Lady Margaret Ley'; she was the daughter of James Ley (1550–1629), the Lord Chief Justice who presided over the trial of Francis Bacon; he was briefly Lord High Treasurer and Lord President of the Council under Charles I, who created him Earl of Marlborough in 1626. Lady Margaret married John Hobson in Dec. 1641 and was for a time Milton's neighbour; Edward Phillips reports the intimacy between the two families in the 1640s.

l. *5. sad breaking of that parliament.* On 10 Mar. 1629, Charles I dissolved a hostile parliament, but members held the speaker in his chair while they passed three resolutions condemning the king's policies. The earl died four days later.

l. *6. dishonest.* From Lat. *inhonestus*, inglorious.

l. *7. Chaeronea.* Where Philip of Macedon destroyed the armies of Athens and Thebes, and thereby Greek liberty, in 338 BC.

l. *8. old man eloquent.* Isocrates, who starved himself to death on hearing the news.

l. *9. later . . . than.* Born too late.

Arcades. The title refers to the inhabitants of Arcadia; the dates of composition and performance are uncertain: Parker has proposed 1629–30, French 1631, Carey 1633. The statement on the title-page of *1645* that 'The Songs were set in Music by Mr Henry Lawes' may be taken to apply to this as well as to *Comus*; Lawes was acquainted with Milton and may have been instrumental in arranging the commission for the young poet, as he may also have been in the case of Milton's later masque, composed for the same family. The Dowager Countess of Derby (1559–1636) was born Alice Spencer; she owed her title to her first husband, Ferdinando Stanley, Lord Strange (d. 1594). Spenser dedicated poems to her and her sisters and alludes to them (and their supposed family connection with him) in *Colin Clout's Come Home Again*, ll. 536–9. She subsequently married Sir Thomas Egerton, later Lord Ellesmere (d. 1617), and her daughter married his son Sir John, later Earl of Bridgewater, patron of *Comus* and, presumably, of this entertainment as well. She performed in Jacobean masques at court (e.g., Jonson's *Masque of Beauty*), and a 1607 masque in her honour by Marston survives. The estate at Harefield, about thirty miles from London, was acquired by Egerton in 1601; Queen Elizabeth I visited it in 1602 and the entertainment for that occasion has similarities to this one. Milton may also have used Ben Jonson's *Althorpe Entertainment*, which he would certainly have known, as a model.

36 [stage direction] *seat of state*. Chair for the principal spectator, here the Countess of Derby.

l. 9. *erst*. Formerly, as in previous poetic celebrations of the Countess, such as those by Spenser and Sir John Davies.

37 l. 20. *Latona*. Mother of Diana and Apollo.

l. 21. *Cybele*. Phrygian goddess identified with Rhea or Ops, wife of Saturn and mother of Jove, Juno, and others, 'towered' because she was represented with a turreted crown.

l. 23. *give her odds*. Compete with her.

[stage direction] *Genius*. The spirit of the place (*genius loci*).

l. 26. *gentle*. Noble.

l. 30. *Alpheus*. Arcadian river god who pursued the water nymph Arethusa to Sicily, where their streams joined in a fountain; see *Met*., v. 572–641. Cf. *Lycidas*, ll. 85–6, 132.   *secret sluice*. Hidden channel.

l. 32. *breathing*. Both emitting odour and living.

l. 33. *buskined*. High booted.

l. 44. *lot*. Destiny.   *power*. Tutelary deity.

l. 47. *quaint*. Intricate or ingenious.   *wanton*. Free, playful (with no pejorative implications).   *wove*. Woven.

l. 49. *noisome*. Noxious.   *blasting*. Withering.

l. 51. *thwarting thunder blue*. The lightning bolt cutting across the sky (or at cross-purposes to those of the Genius); 'blue' = harmful, dangerous, 'the colour of plagues and things hurtful' (*OED*).

38 l. 52. *dire-looking planet*. Saturn, the planet of evil aspect.

l. 53. *worm . . . venom*. The cankerworm, 'a caterpillar that destroys buds and leaves' (*OED*).

l. 54. *fetch my round*. Make my rounds.

38 l. 59. *Number my ranks.* Counts my rows (of plants), as if in military formation.

l. 60. *murmurs.* Muttered incantations (cf. *Comus*, l. 525).

l. 63. *celestial sirens' harmony.* The music of the spheres. The entire passage is indebted to Plato, *Republic*, x. 616–17, which describes the concentric spheres placed on 'the spindle turned on the knees of Necessity', each sphere having its own singing siren; cf. 'Nativity Ode' ll. 125–7.

l. 64. *nine . . . spheres.* There are eight spheres in Plato, nine in later versions of the Ptolemaic system.

l. 65. *those . . . shears.* The Fates (Lachesis, Clotho, and Atropos), daughters of Necessity, who are represented as spinning, weaving and cutting the threads of life. Plato depicts them singing what has been, what is, and what will be.

l. 66. *adamantine.* Of indestructible steel.

ll. 72–3. *none . . . ear.* According to Pythagorean doctrine, our corporeality makes it impossible for us to hear the celestial music. Cf. *Il Penseroso*, ll. 46–8, and *Merchant of Venice*, v. i. 63–5.

l. 74. *blaze.* Proclaim, blazon.

l. 81. *toward . . . state.* The masquers make the move customary at the conclusion of masques, to compliment the Countess enthroned on the seat of state set in the hall opposite the stage.

l. 82. *stem.* Stock.

l. 87. *warbled.* Melodiously sounding.

39 l. 97. *Ladon.* Arcadian river, tributary of the Alpheus.

l. 98. *Lycaeus or Cyllene.* Arcadian mountains, as are Erymanth, l. 100, and Maenalus, l. 102 below.

l. 106. *Syrinx . . . Pan's.* Pan (associated with both Cyllene, where he was born, and Lycaeus, where he lived) pursued the nymph Syrinx as she was returning from Lycaeus; as he reached her at the River Ladon she became a reed: see *Met.*, i. 689–712.

Lycidas. The name Milton assigns his 'learned friend' Edward King is a commonplace one in classical and Renaissance pastorals. King (1612–37) entered Christ's College, Cambridge, in 1626 at the age of 14; he and Milton had the same tutor, William Chappell. In 1630, upon receiving his BA, King was made a Fellow of Christ's at the instigation of King Charles I; the appointment was due largely to politics and family connections rather than scholastic excellence, though some Latin poems of King's ('wholly undistinguished' according to Douglas Bush in the *Variorum*) are extant. In Aug. 1637, as he was on his way to Dublin for the long vacation, King was drowned in a shipwreck near the coast of Wales; his body was not recovered. The Trinity MS of *Lycidas* is dated Nov. 1637, three months after King's death; the poem was first published in a commemorative volume, *Justa Edouardo King naufrago* (1638), as the last poem in a final section of English elegies entitled *Obsequies to the memorie of Mr Edward King, Anno Dom, 1638*, and is signed J.M.

39 l. 1. *laurels*. Sacred to Apollo and traditional crown of poets.

l. 2. *myrtles*. Sacred to Venus and hence emblematic of love poetry. *ivy*. sacred to Bacchus, patron of ecstatic poetry. At his investiture as Poet Laureate in 1341, Petrarch was crowned with these three plants.   *never sere*. All three plants are evergreen.

l. 3. *crude*. Unripe (Lat. *crudus*).

l. 4. *rude*. Unskilled.

l. 5. *Shatter*. Originally a variant form of scatter, hence both destroy and fling about.

l. 6. *dear*. Both severe and precious.

l. 10. *Who . . . Lycidas?* Cf. Virgil, *Eclogues*, x. 3: '*neget quis carmina Gallo?*', 'Who would not sing for Gallus?'.

l. 11. *to sing*. How to sing.

l. 13. *welter*. Roll or toss about.

40 l. 14. *meed*. Honour, something merited.   *melodious tear*. Elegy; the metaphor was a common one (cf., e.g., Spenser's title *The Teares of the Muses*).

ll. 15–17. *Begin then . . . string*. Cf. Virgil, *Eclogues*, iv. 1: '*Sicilides Musae, paulo maiora canamus*', 'Sicilian Muses, let us sing a somewhat loftier strain.' The muses are invoked from one of their sacred fountains, either Aganippe on Mount Helicon, where there was a shrine to Jove, or the Pierian spring on Mount Olympus, their birthplace.

l. 17. *somewhat loudly*. As in Virgil's 'somewhat loftier', an allusion to pastoral constraints upon a higher poetic mode.

l. 18. *coy*. Modest, reserved.

l. 19. *muse*. Poet (one inspired by the muse), and hence male in l. 21; earlier examples of the trope are rare, but see Chapman's use of it in his *Odyssey*, viii. 499–500.

l. 20. *lucky*. Well-omened; 'felicitous' has also been suggested.

l. 21. *he*. Refers to muse, l. 19 above.

l. 25. *lawns*. Untilled, grass-covered land; cf. *L'Allegro*, l. 71.

l. 28. *What time*. A Latinism (*quo tempore*): at what time, when.   *winds*. Blows.

l. 29. *Battening*. Feeding, fattening.   *dews*. Grass with the dew still on it; Virgil (*Eclogues*, viii, 14–15) mentions the flocks' preference for grass on which the dew remains.

l. 30. *the star*. Venus as Hesperus, the evening star.

l. 31. *westering*. Moving westward.

40 l. 33. *Tempered.* Attuned.　　　*oaten flute.* The traditional pastoral wind instrument, made of oat reeds.

l. 36. *Damaetas.* A conventional pastoral name; commentators have attempted to identify him with a particular Cambridge figure, e.g. William Chappell, Milton's and King's Cambridge tutor.

l. 40. *gadding.* Straggling.

l. 46. *taint-worm.* The modern term is 'husk', an intestinal parasite fatal to newly weaned calves (see F. W. Bateson, *English Poetry* [1950], 159).

l. 48. *whitethorn.* Hawthorn.

l. 51. *Closed . . . head.* Introducing the comparison of Lycidas with Orpheus (see ll. 58–63 below), decapitated by the maenads when his songs offended them (*Met.*, xi. 1–66; Virgil, *Georgics*, iv. 453–527). For Orpheus, cf. *L'Allegro*, ll. 145–50, *Il Penseroso*, ll. 103–8, and *PL*, vi. 33–8.

ll. 52–4. *the steep . . . Mona high.* In tracing King's sea route, which was from Chester to Dublin, Milton depends upon, and partly misinterprets, a number of contemporary authorities including William Camden's *Britannia*, Ortelius' *Theatrum Orbis Terrarum*, and John Selden's annotations to Drayton's *Polyolbion*, from which he learned (incorrectly) that the mountainous island Bardsey (the bard's island) was an ancient Druid burial ground—it was in fact a Christian site—and that the authentically Druidic island of Mona (Anglesey), with its wooded hills, was adjacent—it is in fact forty miles away.

41 l. 55. *Deva . . . stream.* The river Dee, on which Chester stands, said to have magical properties; cf. Spenser, *FQ*, IV. xi. 39.

l. 56. *fondly.* Foolishly.

l. 58. *the muse.* Calliope.

l. 61. *rout.* Disorderly crowd, here the maenads.

ll. 62–3. *His gory . . . shore.* Orpheus was torn to bits by the enraged women, and his head was thrown into the river Hebrus and eventually washed up on the island of Lesbos. The story is in Ovid, *Met.*, xi. 1–66, and in Virgil, *Georgics*, iv. 517–27.

l. 64. *boots.* Avails.

l. 65. *tend.* Attend to.

l. 68. *Amaryllis.* A conventional pastoral figure, notably in Virgil, where the woods resound the name (*Eclogues*, i. 4–5), and where Corydon considers whether it would not have been better to suffer her rage rather than the scorn of his beloved Alexis (*Eclogues*, ii. 14–15).

l. 69. *Neaera.* The name appears in Virgil, *Eclogues*, iii. 3, and as the name of the poet's mistress in numerous classical and Renaissance pastorals.

ll. 70–3. *Fame . . . find.* Cf. Spenser, *Teares of the Muses*, ll. 444–54.　　　*clear* [l. 70]. Noble (Lat. *clarus*); blameless.

l. 73. *guerdon.* Reward.

l. 75. *Fury.* Atropos, the Fate who cuts the thread of life.

41 l. 77. *Phoebus.* Apollo, god of poetry, who similarly touches the poet's ear in Virgil, *Eclogues*, vi. 3–5, restraining him from epic and enjoining him to feed his sheep and sing.

l. 79. *glistering foil.* The glittering leaf of metal used to set off a jewel and enhance its lustre.

l. 85. *Arethuse.* Sicilian river, whose nymph was wooed and pursued by Alpheus (see l. 132, below); associated with Theocritean pastoral. Cf. 'Arcades', ll. 30–1.

l. 86. *Mincius.* The river of Mantua, Virgil's birthplace; *Georgics*, iii. 14–15, describes its slow winding and reed-fringed banks.

l. 87. *mood.* Musical mode.

l. 88. *oat.* The oaten flute of l. 33.

l. 89. *herald.* Triton.

l. 90. *plea.* Triton is conceived either as gathering evidence for Neptune's court, or as exonerating Neptune, who is on trial.

l. 91. *felon.* Savage, wild, criminal.

42 l. 96. *Hippotades.* Aeolus (son of Hippotas), god of winds, who keeps them in a cave (the dungeon of l. 97, below).

l. 99. *Panope.* One of the fifty sea nymphs (nereids) born to the sea deities Nereus and Doris.

l. 101. *eclipse.* Portent of disaster.

l. 103. *Camus.* The river Cam (cf. 'Winchester', l. 59) imagined as a classical river god.

l. 104. *hairy.* Here, alluding to the river reeds; Milton associates the hairy mantle with studiousness: cf. *Il Penseroso*, l. 169.

l. 105. *Inwrought.* Inscribed or embroidered (in the Trinity MS Milton first wrote 'scrawled o'er').

l. 106. *sanguine flower.* The hyacinth, inscribed AI AI by Apollo to record his grief for his dead and metamorphosed beloved, Hyacinthus (*Met.*, x. 214–15).

l. 107. *pledge.* A person acting as a surety for another, thus, figuratively, Lycidas as token of Cambridge's care (as a child is token of its parents' love), and as promise of futurity.

l. 109. *the pilot.* St Peter, the founder of the Church; the keys in l. 110 are his usual attribute, deriving from Matt. 16: 18–28. Peter was a fisherman on Lake Galilee when Christ called him (see Luke 5: 3–11); when Christ walks on Lake Galilee (in Matt. 14: 25–31; cf. l. 173, below), he rebukes Peter for lacking faith. In his final appearance to Peter, Christ commands him to 'feed my lambs' (John 21: 15); cf. ll. 114–25, below.

l. 111. *amain.* Forcefully.

l. 112. *mitred.* Wearing the mitre, the bishop's ceremonial head-dress.

42 ll. 114–31. *How well . . . no more.* Among the numerous biblical passages describing the offices and abuses of the shepherd, see especially Ezek. 34, which condemns shepherds who 'feed themselves' but 'feed not the flock', and promises retribution; and the parable of the good shepherd (John 10).

l. 114. *Enow.* Enough.

l. 119. *Blind mouths.* i.e. pure gluttony. Ruskin comments in *Sesame and Lilies*: 'A "Bishop" means "a person who sees." A "Pastor" means one who feeds. The most unbishoply character . . . is therefore to be blind. The most unpastoral is, instead of feeding, to want to be fed,—to be a mouth'.

l. 122. *What recks it them?* What do they care?   *They are sped.* They succeed and thrive; they are promoted or furthered; also, they are dispatched, destroyed.

l. 123. *list.* Choose, please.

l. 124. *scrannel.* Thin, meagre, harsh; first usage recorded in *OED* of what is probably a dialect word.

l. 126. *draw.* Inhale, breathe.

l. 128. *wolf.* Regularly identified with Catholicism in Renaissance Protestant rhetoric.   *privy.* secret, hidden.

ll. 130–1. *But that . . . no more.* These lines have occasioned extensive commentary. A 'two-handed engine' is a sword so large that wielding it requires two hands; Michael similarly wields a sword 'with two-handed sway' (*PL*, vi. 251), and Peter's power here seems to extend to the threat of ultimate judgment.   *engine.* Machine or instrument (of war).

l. 132. *Alpheus.* See l. 85 n., above.

l. 135. *bells.* Bell-shaped flowers.

l. 136. *use.* Frequent, habitually resort.

43 l. 137. *wanton.* Unrestrained.

l. 138. *swart star.* Sirius, the dog star, associated with summer heat, and hence black (swart), alluding to the effect of heat.

l. 142. *rathe.* Early blooming.

l. 143. *crow-toe.* Variously identified as the hyacinth, wild hyacinth, and buttercup.   *jessamine.* Jasmine.

l. 144. *pink.* Dianthus.   *freaked.* Striped, variegated.

l. 157. *whelming.* Overthrowing violently, submerging, sinking. *1638* reads 'humming'.

l. 159. *moist vows.* Tearful prayers (Lat. *votum*).

l. 160. *Bellerus.* Bellerium was the Latin name of Land's End, the southwest tip of England; Milton apparently invented Bellerus from the place-name. (The name in the Trinity MS was originally Corineus, a legendary Cornish king).

43 l. 161. *vision . . . mount.* Camden reports that on St Michael's Mount, off the Cornish coast near Land's End, the archangel himself appeared in a vision to the monks. He is conceived as keeping guard against the Spanish Catholic threat implied in l. 162.

l. 162. *Namancos and Bayona's hold.* A district (properly Nemancos) and fortress town ('hold') in north-western Spain, facing Cornwall.

l. 163. *Look homeward.* The injunction is, presumably, to St Michael, either to return his gaze from distant Spain to England and its tragic loss immediately northward, or, perhaps to heaven; some commentators, however, have felt that the grammar of ll. 154 ff. requires 'angel' to refer back to 'thou' (at ll. 157, 159), i.e. Lycidas, who is being asked to look to his heavenly (or perhaps to his earthly) home.

l. 164. *waft.* 'Convey safely by water' (*OED*), as the poet Arion was rescued by dolphins charmed with his songs.

l. 168. *day-star.* The sun, or conceivably Lucifer, the morning star.

l. 170. *tricks.* Adorns, or trims.

l. 176. *unexpressive.* Inexpressible, indescribable; perhaps, too, inapprehensible.   *nuptial song.* Combining the song of the 144,000 virgins in Rev. 14: 1–5 and the song for the mystic marriage with the lamb in Rev. 19: 6–9.

44 l. 183. *genius.* The spirit of the place (*genius loci*), the guardian.

l. 184. *In . . . recompense.* As your reward.

l. 186. *uncouth.* Unknown, untutored, rustic.

l. 188. *tender stops.* Frail, responsive holes in the reed pipe.   *quills.* Reeds.

l. 189. *Doric.* The dialect of Theocritus, Bion, and Moschus; hence 'pastoral'.

l. 192. *twitched.* Pulled around his shoulders.

A Masque . . . Presented at Ludlow Castle ['*Comus*']. Milton's masque was commissioned as an entertainment for the Earl of Bridgewater and his family at Ludlow Castle in Herefordshire. It was performed on 29 Sept. 1634. The earl had recently been appointed Lord Lieutenant of Wales and President of the Council; the masque is often said to celebrate his investiture, which, however, took place several months earlier. His three children were among the principal performers: Lady Alice Egerton, aged 15, played the Lady, and her brothers John, Viscount Brackley, aged 11, and Thomas Egerton, aged 9, played the two brothers. The children's music master, Henry Lawes, composed the music for the masque, and took the role of the Attendant Spirit. Lawes was acquainted with Milton and may have been instrumental in arranging the commission for him to write the text; Milton had already contributed verses to *Arcades*, an entertainment for Bridgewater's mother-in-law the Dowager Countess of Derby, the music for which is presumed to have been by Lawes as well. The Bridgewater children had twice performed in masques at the court at Whitehall. In 1632 they appeared in Aurelian Townshend's and Inigo Jones's *Tempe Restored*, which is about Circe and the transformation of men into animals and has strong affinities with Milton's masque; and in 1634 the two boys served as torchbearers in the most splendid of the Caroline court productions, Thomas Carew's and Jones's *Coelum Britannicum*. Milton's masque is deeply imbued with a sense of the genre, but it differs significantly from masques intended for the court. Courtiers never took speaking roles in royal masques; to do so would have constituted a violation of aristocratic decorum—the fact that the Bridgewater children spoke, and at length, reveals just how intimate a family affair this entertainment was. The text survives in several stages of composition. Milton, moving towards publication, turned his masque increasingly away from family intimacy and towards philosophical reasoning and Neoplatonic symbolism, adding about one hundred lines in the process. The version closest to the one prepared for the original performance is preserved in the Trinity College MS at Cambridge, which also includes corrections and revisions; other versions are in the Bridgewater MS (the family's own copy), the first printed edition, issued anonymously in 1637, and the final, much revised text included in Milton's 1645 *Poems* (our text here); the 1673 text differs significantly from that of 1645 in only one passage, at ll. 166–9. (A detailed study of the versions before 1645 is in S. E. Sprott, ed., John Milton, *A Maske: The Earlier Versions* [1973].) The title *Comus* was given to the work in the eighteenth century, when an operatic version was prepared by John Dalton, with music by Thomas Arne.

44 [stage direction] *discovers.* Reveals.   *Attendant Spirit.* In the manuscripts, 'a guardian spirit or daemon'. 'Daemon' transliterates the Greek term for a tutelary deity or genius, in Christian terms a guardian angel.

45 l. 2. *mansion.* Dwelling (not necessarily a building); also an astrological term for one of the 28 divisions of the ecliptic.

l. 3. *ensphered.* In the sphere of heaven.

l. 7. *pestered.* Crowded, encumbered.   *pinfold.* Lit. a cattle pen; hence 'a place of confinement, a pen, a trap' (*OED*).

l. 11. *enthroned . . . seats.* As in *PL*, Milton conceives the classical gods as versions of the angels.

l. 16. *ambrosial.* Divine (lit. pertaining to the immortals).   *weeds.* Garments.

l. 17. *sin-worn mould.* Earth worn out with sin.

l. 19. *salt flood.* Ocean.

l. 20. *Took . . . Jove.* After the victory of the Olympian gods over the Titans, Jove and his brothers Neptune and Pluto (in Greek Zeus, Poseidon, and Hades) drew lots to divide the universe among themselves. Jove drew the heavens, Neptune the waters and islands, Pluto (the 'nether Jove') the underworld. See *Il.*, xv. 187–93.

45 l. 24. *to grace . . . gods.* To show favour to the lesser gods (those of rivers and islands) who pay him tribute.

l. 25. *several.* Various.

l. 28. *main.* Ocean.

l. 29. *quarters.* Gives as their dwelling.   *blue-haired deities.* The tritons, Neptune's children, represented as blue-haired in Jonson's *Masque of Blackness* (1605; pub. 1608). Ovid, whom Jonson cites as his source, describes them as entirely blue (*caeruleum*) in *Met.*, i. 333.

ll. 30–1. *tract . . . peer.* As Lord Lieutenant, the Earl of Bridgewater had administrative responsibility for the Welsh counties in the west of England.   *mickle.* Great; archaic, and Spenserian, usage.

l. 32. *tempered awe.* Temperately used authority. 'Awe' = 'power to inspire fear or reverence' (*OED*).

l. 33. *nation.* Wales.

l. 35. *state.* Combining the senses of throne and high rank.

l. 37. *perplexed.* Intricate, entangled.   *drear wood.* Recalling the '*selva oscura*' of Dante's *Inferno*, l. 2, and the opening of Book 1 of Spenser's *Faerie Queene.*

l. 38. *horror.* With an overtone of its Latin meaning, 'bristling'.

46 l. 46. *Bacchus.* The Greek Dionysus, god of wine, theatre, and ecstatic poetry.

l. 48. *After . . . transformed.* The seventh Homeric Hymn *To Dionysus*, elaborated by Ovid, *Met.*, iii. 650–91, tells how the god was captured by Italian ('Tuscan') pirates, but he turned them into dolphins and their ship into a grape arbour. (The syntax is Latin.)   *transformed.* Had been transformed.

l. 49. *Tyrrhene shore.* The Italian coast north of Sicily, opposite Sardinia and Corsica.   *listed.* Wished.

l. 50. *Circe's island.* Aeaea (*Od.*, x. 135); Homer is vague about its location.

l. 51. *The daughter of the Sun.* Circe's father was Helios, the sun god.

ll. 51–3. *Whose . . . swine.* The account of Circe's transformation of Odysseus' men into swine is in *Od.*, x. 238. It is also the subject of William Browne's *Inner Temple Masque* (1615), which Milton certainly knew, and of Aurelian Townshend's and Inigo Jones's masque *Tempe Restored*, performed at court in 1632, and in which the three Bridgewater children danced.

l. 58. *Comus.* The name is a Latinization of the Greek *komos*, meaning 'revelry', and cognate with 'comedy'. In Philostratus' *Icones* (or *Imagines*, l. 2), he is described as a charming and graceful youth crowned with roses and sleepy from wine, presiding over a wedding celebration. In Jonson's masque *Pleasure Reconciled to Virtue* (1618), he is presented as a gross belly-god and his revelry as a danger to the pursuit of virtue. The story of his birth is original with Milton.

46 l. 59. *frolic of.* Merry in.

l. 60. *Celtic, and Iberian.* French and Spanish.

l. 65. *orient.* Shining.

l. 66. *drought of Phoebus.* Thirst caused by the hot sun.

l. 67. *fond.* Foolish.

ll. 69–70. *changed . . . form.* In Renaissance moralizations of the Circe story, her victims were transformed not into swine but into whatever animal most truly expressed their inner bestial natures. The metamorphosis was dramatized in Townshend's and Jones's 1632 masque *Tempe Restored*, with the Bridgewater children as participants, and Jones's costume designs for Circe's animal-headed followers survive (see ll. 51–3).

l. 71. *ounce.* Lynx.

l. 73. *perfect is their misery.* Complete is their depravity.

l. 79. *advent'rous.* Hazardous.

47 l. 83. *Iris' woof.* The rainbow.

l. 84. *weeds.* Garments.   *swain.* The word had a wide variety of meanings, of which the relevant ones here are young man, rustic, attendant, shepherd.

ll. 86–8. *soft pipe . . . waving woods.* The role was played by the musician and composer Henry Lawes; the swain's control over nature analogizes him to the arch-musician Orpheus.

l. 87. *knows to.* Knows how to.

l. 88. *nor of less faith.* No less trustworthy (than musically talented).

l. 90. *present.* Immediate.

l. 92. *viewless.* Invisible.

l. 93. *The star . . . fold.* The appearance of Venus (or Hesperus) as the evening star is the signal for the shepherd to lead his flock to the sheepfold.

l. 95. *gilded car of day.* Sun's chariot.

l. 96. *allay.* Cool down.

l. 97. *steep.* Flowing precipitously.

l. 98. *slope.* Sloping, setting.

l. 99. *pole.* Sky.

l. 110. *saws.* Sententious wisdom.

ll. 112–14. *starry choir . . . years.* The cosmological dance was a commonplace; see e.g. Sir John Davies' *Orchestra, a Poem of Dancing*, stanzas 26 ff.

l. 112. *choir.* 'A band of dancers, or of dancers and singers' (*OED*).

l. 115. *sounds.* Straits, inlets.

l. 116. *morris.* Morris-dance, a lively group dance.

l. 117. *shelves.* Banks.

48 l. 121. *wakes*. Nocturnal revels.

l. 123. *prove*. Experience.

l. 129. *Cotytto*. A Thracian earth goddess whose cult spread throughout Greece and Rome. Her orgiastic rites were attacked by Juvenal (*Satires*, ii. 91–2) and satirized by Horace (*Epodes*, xiv. 56–7).

l. 131. *dragon womb*. Dragons were associated with Hecate, queen of the underworld (see l. 135).

l. 132. *Stygian*. Hellish (from the River Styx, which flows through the underworld).

l. 134. *ebon*. Black.

l. 137. *dues*. Rites.

l. 139. *nice*. Relevant senses are ignorant, tender, delicate, coy, shy, over-modest, and over-fastidious.   *steep*. Mountain.

l. 140. *cabined loophole*. Small window; *cabined* = confined, *loophole* = a hole to peer through.

l. 141. *descry*. Reveal.

l. 142. *solemnity*. Ceremonies.

l. 144. *round*. Circular dance.

[stage direction] *Measure*. The term denoted any rhythmical performance; here, both the dance and the music.

l. 147. *shrouds*. Hiding places.

l. 151. *trains*. Lit. the bait for luring wild animals into a trap.

l. 154. *dazzling spells*. The Trinity MS reads 'powdered spells', suggesting that Comus here threw some sparkling powder, the 'magic dust' of l. 165, into the air.   *spongy*. Absorbent, receptive.

l. 155. *blear*. Dimming or confusing the sight.

l. 156. *presentments*. Images, displays.

l. 157. *quaint habits*. Strange garments.

49 l. 161. *glozing*. Flattering.

l. 163. *Wind me*. Insinuate myself; but, taken with *hug* (l. 164), including overtones of a constrictor snake.

l. 165. *virtue*. Power.

ll. 166–9. *I shall . . . here*. In the 1673 text, this passage reads as follows:

> I shall appear some harmless villager
> And hearken, if I may, her business here.
> But here she comes, I fairly step aside.

In the list of errata, l. 167 is changed to 'And hearken, if I may her business hear'. There has been much inconclusive debate over whether these changes represent Milton's revision, that of an editor, a printer's error, or some combination of these. Since in almost every instance of divergence the 1645 text is more authoritative than that of 1673, the former has been followed here; but there are arguments in favour of the later reading, and both have been used in responsible editions.

49 l. 168. *fairly.* Quietly.

l. 174. *loose.* Unrestrained, wanton.   *unlettered hinds.* Uneducated farm labourers.

l. 175. *teeming.* Fertile, breeding.

l. 176. *Pan.* God of nature, patron of shepherds, and especially associated with licentious sexuality.

l. 178. *swilled.* Drunken; *OED*'s only citation for the adjective, but 'swilled with drink' [= drunk to excess] was in common usage.

l. 179. *wassailers.* Revellers.

l. 180. *inform.* Direct.   *unacquainted.* Unfamiliar (with the way).

l. 188. *Even.* Evening.

l. 189. *sad votarist.* Solemn pilgrim.   *in palmer's weed.* Dressed like a palmer, a pilgrim who carried a palm branch in token of his visit to the Holy Land.

l. 190. *Phoebus' wain.* The chariot of the sun.

l. 193. *engaged.* Committed.

50 l. 197. *dark lantern.* 'A lantern with a slide or arrangement by which the light can be concealed' (*OED*).

l. 203. *rife.* Abundant, strong, loud-sounding.   *perfect.* Absolutely distinct.

l. 204. *single.* Total.

l. 210. *astound.* Stun, stupefy.

l. 212. *siding.* Supporting (taking one's side).

l. 215. *Chastity.* The Lady invokes as the third of the triad the classical Chastity, the virtue of adherence to the highest Reason, rather than the expected Christian Charity, divine or holy love.

l. 230. *Echo.* A nymph who was so talkative that Juno commanded her to speak only when spoken to, and then to repeat only what she heard. She fell in love with Narcissus, who spurned her, and whom Venus punished by making him fall in love with his own image in a pool. Echo pined away with grief until only her voice remained. The story is in *Met.*, iii. 351–401. Echo songs, in which the refrain repeats the end of the line preceding it, were common; and the invocation of the nymph leads one to expect a refrain which never comes.

l. 231. *airy shell.* The sphere of the sky.

l. 232. *Meander.* A river in Phrygia to which Echo wandered in her despair.

50 l. 234. *love-lorn nightingale.* Philomela, raped and mutilated by her brother-in-law Tereus, was transformed into the nightingale, who sings nightly of the grief of love (*Met.*, vi. 440 ff.).

51 l. 241. *parley.* Speech, alluding to her notorious loquacity.　　*sphere.* The sky, the 'airy shell' of l. 231.

l. 244. *mould.* Clay.

l. 247. *air.* Both song and atmosphere.

l. 248. *his.* Its, the 'something holy' of l. 246.

l. 251. *fall.* Cadence.

l. 253. *Sirens.* In *Od.*, xii. 39–72, beautiful sea nymphs who drew sailors to their destruction by the power of their songs.

l. 254. *Naiades.* Nymphs of streams and springs.

l. 257. *Scylla.* A nymph who was changed by Circe (or in some versions of the story by Amphitrite), her rival in love, into a monster with ferocious dogs sprouting from her lower body. She ultimately became a dangerous rock off the Sicilian coast (see *Met.*, xiv. 8–74).

l. 259. *fell.* Cruel, savage.　　*Charybdis.* A violent whirlpool opposite Scylla.

l. 262. *home-felt.* Heartfelt, apparently a Miltonic coinage.

l. 265. *Hail foreign wonder.* Echoing Ferdinand on his first sight of Miranda, 'O you wonder!' (*Tempest*, I. ii. 427).

l. 267. *Unless the goddess.* i.e. unless you are she; the suggestion recalls Aeneas' reaction to seeing Venus after the Trojan shipwreck, '*O dea certe*' (*Aen.*, i. 328), and Ferdinand's response to his first sight of Miranda, 'Most sure the goddess / On whom these airs attend' (*Tempest*, I. ii. 422–3).

l. 268. *Sylvan.* Sylvanus, god of woods.

l. 273. *shift.* Expedient.

52 ll. 277–90. *What chance . . . lips.* Milton uses the classical *stichomythia*, dialogue in alternating lines of verse, common both in ancient Greek and Italian neo-classic drama.

l. 286. *hit.* Guess.

l. 287. *Imports their loss.* Does their loss matter?

l. 290. *Hebe.* Lit. 'youth', the daughter of Zeus and Hera, and cupbearer to the gods.

ll. 291–2. *what time . . . came.* i.e. at evening, when the oxen were unyoked. The diction of 'what time' is latinate, though the expression was in use in English.　　*traces.* Harness.

l. 293. *swinked.* Wearied with toil (from *swink*, labour, but the normal past participle is *swonk*; *swinked* is apparently Milton's invention).　　*hedger.* Workman in charge of maintaining hedges and fences.

l. 294. *mantling.* Enveloping, covering.

52 l. 297. *port.* Bearing.

l. 298. *fairy.* Milton's spelling, faëry, seems to preserve the Spenserian trisyllabic pronunciation, though both this and l. 436, the only places the word appears, require disyllables. The diaeresis is a feature only of the printed texts, not of the manuscripts. In any case, the creatures described in ll. 299–301 have more to do with the fairies of *A Midsummer Night's Dream* than with Spenser's knights, dragons, and enchanters.

l. 299. *element.* The word was used both for the sky and the air.

l. 301. *plighted.* Pleated.

l. 312. *Dingle.* Woodland hollow.

l. 313. *bosky bourn.* Stream bordered by shrubs.

l. 315. *attendance.* Companions (those who attend you).

53 l. 316. *shroud.* Sheltered (past participle of *shroud*, to take shelter).

l. 318. *thatched pallet.* Nest of straw.

l. 325. *it.* Courtesy, which derives from 'court'.

l. 326. *yet.* Both 'still' and 'nevertheless'.

l. 329. *square.* Adjust, adapt.

l. 332. *wont'st.* Are used to. *benison.* Blessing.

l. 334. *disinherit.* Dispossess.

l. 335. *shades.* Shadows.

l. 338. *rush-candle.* A candle made by dipping a rush in tallow or oil, which gave a very weak light. *wicker hole.* Window filled with wicker-work (instead of glass, hence implying a very poor dwelling).

l. 340. *rule.* Ray, beam.

ll. 341–2. *star . . . Cynosure.* North Star: the Cynosure is the constellation Ursa Minor, the little bear, which has the North Star in its tail; it is *Tyrian* because the Tyrians, or Phoenicians (from their capital Tyre), used it to steer by, unlike the Greeks, who steered by Ursa Major; it is the *star of Arcady* because the Arcadian prince Arcas was transformed by Zeus into Ursa Minor when he was about to kill his mother Callisto, who had been metamorphosed into a bear, and who thereupon became the constellation Ursa Major. The story is in *Met.*, ii. 401–507.

l. 344. *folded.* i.e. in their sheepfolds. *wattled cotes.* Sheds constructed of woven twigs.

l. 345. *pastoral . . . stops.* The shepherd's pipe, traditionally made of oat stalks; the *stops* are the finger holes.

l. 349. *innumerous.* Innumerable.

54 l. 359. *over-exquisite.* Over-elaborate or unreasonably precise.

l. 360. *cast.* Forecast.

l. 361. *so.* As they have been predicted.

54 l. 362. *forestall.* Anticipate; 'think of, deal with, or introduce before the appropriate time; "to meet [misfortune, etc.] halfway" ' (*OED*).

l. 366. *to seek.* Lacking, at a loss.

l. 367. *unprincipled in.* Ignorant of the principles of.

l. 368. *bosoms.* Embraces, holds in its bosom.

l. 369. *single.* Mere.

l. 372. *misbecoming.* Unbecoming.

l. 375. *flat.* Including the sense of lifeless, dull.

l. 376. *seeks.* Resorts.

l. 378. *plumes.* Dresses or preens (antedating *OED*'s earliest citations for the former sense, 1707, and for the latter, 1821).

l. 379. *resort.* 'Concourse or assemblage of people' (*OED*).

l. 380. *all to-.* Utterly; both words are intensives.

l. 382. *centre.* Of the earth (hence as far as possible from daylight).

l. 386. *affects.* Prefers.

l. 387. *cell.* Technically, a single-chamber dwelling, often with monastic implications; by the late sixteenth century used poetically for 'a small and humble dwelling, a cottage' (*OED*). Not applied to prisons until the eighteenth century.

l. 388. *haunt.* Companionship, society.

l. 390. *weeds.* Clothing.

l. 391. *beads.* Rosary.   *maple dish.* Wooden bowl.

55 l. 393. *Hesperian tree.* The tree, which bore golden apples, was a wedding gift from the earth goddess Ge to Hera when she married Zeus. Hera planted it in the garden of the Hesperides, daughters of the evening star Hesperus, and set the dragon Ladon to guard it. Stealing the golden apples was one of the labours of Hercules. In some versions, he succeeded by persuading Atlas, the brother of Hesperus, to bring him the apples; in others, he killed the dragon and took the fruit himself.

l. 395. *unenchanted eye.* Hercules used charms to put the dragon to sleep.

l. 397. *Incontinence.* Specifically, in the seventeenth century, uncontrolled sexual passion.

l. 398. *unsunned.* Hidden.

l. 401. *wink on.* Wink at, overlook.

l. 404. *Of . . . not.* 'It is not night or loneliness that worry me.'

l. 407. *unowned.* Lost; *OED*'s only example of the word in this sense.

l. 408. *Infer, as if.* Imply that.

l. 410. *equal . . . fear.* The metaphor is of a balance weighing hope against fear.

l. 411. *arbitrate the event.* Decide the outcome.

55   l. 413. *squint.* Not looking straight.

    l. 420. *chastity.* See l. 215.

    l. 422. *quivered nymph.* On the model of the chaste Diana, goddess of the hunt (see l. 441).

    l. 423. *trace.* Travel through.   *unharboured.* Without shelter.

    l. 426. *mountaineer.* Mountain dweller.

    l. 428. *very desolation.* Utter desolation, desolation itself.

    l. 429. *shagged.* Shaggy.

    l. 430. *unblenched.* Unflinching.

    l. 431. *Be it.* So long as it is.

56   l. 433. *fire.* The will-o'-the-wisp.   *moorish.* Marshy.

    l. 434. *Blue.* 'The colour of plagues and things hurtful' (*OED*).   *stubborn unlaid ghost.* Ghost that refuses to remain buried.

    l. 435. *curfew.* The evening bell, rung at nine o'clock in Milton's time, originally as a signal to extinguish all household fires (the word derives from *couvre feu*), but by the sixteenth century merely marking the hour. Spirits were free to walk either then or at midnight, and to continue till the first cock-crow.

    l. 436. *swart . . . mine.* Black underground fairy; cf. the underground demons in *Il Penseroso*, ll. 93–4.

    l. 439. *old schools.* Philosophical academies.

    l. 443. *brinded.* Tawny and streaked or spotted.

    l. 444. *pard.* The word was used for both the panther and leopard.

    l. 445. *bolt.* Arrow.

    ll. 447–8. *What . . . wore.* Minerva carried on her shield the snake-haired head of the Gorgon Medusa, which turned those who looked at it to stone.

    ll. 459–63. *Till oft . . . immortal.* In *PL*, v. 497–503, Raphael similarly offers Adam the hope that his body may ultimately be refined into pure spirit.

    l. 459. *oft converse.* Frequent conversation.

56–7 ll. 465–75. *But most . . . state.* The argument follows that of Socrates in the *Phaedo*, 81: virtuous souls rejoice in their liberation from the body at death, but the souls of carnal and worldly people fear the realms of the spirit and are dragged back to this world, where they haunt their graves and are visible as ghosts.

    l. 468. *Embodies, and imbrutes.* Becomes physical and bestial.

57   l. 479. *nectared.* Both deliciously sweet and heavenly; nectar was the food of the gods.

    l. 480. *crude.* Indigestible.

    l. 483. *night-foundered.* Submerged in night.

    l. 491. *iron stakes.* i.e. their weapons, swords or daggers.

57 l. 494. *Thyrsis.* A singer-shepherd in Theocritus' *Idyll* 1 and Virgil's *Eclogue* 7, hence alluding again to Lawes (see ll. 86–8).

57–8 ll. 495–512. *The huddling . . . shew.* As Lawes appears in the guise of Thyrsis, the shift to couplets recalls the language of the pastoral eclogue, with its poetic debates, and of such pastoral dramas as Fletcher's *Faithful Shepherdess* and Jonson's *Sad Shepherd.*

57 l. 495. *huddling.* Pressing together.   *Madrigal.* Technically a part song for three or more voices, but here simply music. Milton may be thinking of the word's presumed derivation, from Latin *mandra,* sheepfold, and associating it therefore specifically with pastoral music.

l. 501. *next.* Closest, dearest.

l. 502. *toy.* Trifle.

l. 506. *To.* Compared with.

58 l. 509. *sadly.* In earnest.

l. 511. *me unhappy.* Imitating the Latin *me miserum;* cf. Satan's 'Me miserable!', *PL,* iv. 73.

l. 513. *fabulous.* Mere fables.

l. 517. *chimeras.* The chimera was a composite monster with three heads of lion, goat, and dragon; see Hesiod, *Theogeny,* 319–25.

l. 520. *navel.* Centre.

l. 530. *Charactered.* Lit. engraved or imprinted, continuing the coining metaphor.

l. 531. *hard.* Close.   *crofts.* Enclosed fields.

l. 532. *brow.* Form the brow of, overlook.

l. 534. *stabled.* The word apparently meant simply 'in their lairs' for Milton; cf. *PL,* ix. 748, where sea-monsters are described as 'stabled'.

l. 535 *Hecate.* Queen of the underworld, patroness of sorcerers (see l. 135).

l. 539. *unweeting.* Not knowing, or unwittingly.

l. 542. *knot-grass.* A common weed with intricately branched creeping stems and pink flowers (*polygonum aviculare*).

l. 545. *flaunting.* 'Waving gaily or proudly like a plume or banner' (*OED*).

l. 546. *melancholy.* The serious mood associated with artistic composition: see *Il Penseroso,* ll. 11 ff.

l. 547. *meditate.* Exercise, with an echo of Virgil's '*musam meditari*' (*Eclogues,* i. 2), to occupy oneself with song or poetry.

l. 548. *close.* Cadence.

59 l. 551. *listened them.* 'Listen' was regularly used transitively until the nineteenth century.

l. 553. *drowsy frighted.* The reading of all the early printed editions. The Trinity MS, followed by many editors, reads 'drowsie-flighted'.

59 l. 558. *took . . . ware.* Captured before she knew it.

ll. 559–60. *never . . . displaced.* (1) [Silence was willing to be] annihilated if such music could always replace her; (2) [Silence was willing to] cease being silent if she could be superseded in this way.

l. 585. *period.* Sentence, or full stop (hence, 'not even a punctuation mark . . . ').

60 l. 599. *stubble.* The short stalks of grain left after reaping, i.e. not a solid foundation.

l. 604. *sooty.* Black.   *Acheron.* Hell: Acheron was one of the four rivers of the underworld.

l. 605. *Harpies and hydras.* The harpies, who attacked Aeneas and his men and destroyed their food (*Aen.*, iii. 225–8), had the faces of women and the bodies and talons of birds; the hydra was a many-headed poisonous serpent killed by Hercules.

l. 606. *Ind.* India.

l. 607. *purchase.* Prey or plunder; the word literally means the pursuit of game in hunting.

l. 608. *curls.* Curled hair, an attribute of Bacchus, was considered a sign of licentiousness or effeminacy.

l. 610. *emprise.* Chivalric enterprise.

l. 611. *stead.* Service.

l. 617. *shifts.* Expedients.

l. 618. *surprisal.* Being surprised.

ll. 619–21. *shepherd . . . herb.* A number of commentators since the nineteenth century have seen autobiographical allusions in this passage. The shepherd lad has been identified by some as Milton's close friend Charles Diodati (whose death in 1638 Milton was to commemorate in *Epitaphium Damonis*), though other critics have argued that Milton is referring to himself, or to another friend. There are, needless to say, no grounds for such speculation, but it has significantly influenced the critical history of *A Masque*.

l. 620. *Of small regard to see to.* Unimpressive in appearance.

l. 621. *virtuous.* Potent, capable of producing great effects.

l. 626. *scrip.* 'A small bag, especially one carried by . . . a shepherd' (*OED*).

61 l. 627. *simples.* Medicinal herbs.

l. 635. *clouted shoon.* Either patched shoes, or shoes with clouted soles, studded with broad-headed nails.

ll. 636–7. *moly . . . gave.* In *Od.*, x. 287–303, Hermes gives Odysseus the magic herb moly, with a white flower and a black root, to protect him against the charms of Circe. Moly was often allegorized in the Renaissance as temperance or prudence.

61 l. 638. *haemony.* Various derivations for the name have been proposed, from Haemonia, or Thessaly, traditionally the home of witchcraft, or from the Greek *haimon*, skilful, or from *haimonios*, blood-red (suggesting Christ's redemptive blood).

l. 646. *lime-twigs.* Traps; lit. twigs smeared with the sticky substance bird-lime, used for catching birds.

l. 647. *came off.* Got away.

l. 651. *brandished blade.* Following Hermes' instructions to Odysseus that he must approach Circe with his sword drawn (*Od.*, x. 294–5).

l. 655. *sons of Vulcan.* The underground spirits that cause volcanoes to erupt. Vulcan was god of fire, and kept the forges of the gods. In *PL*, Milton identifies him with Mammon (i. 740).

l. 657. *apace.* Quickly.

[stage direction] *puts . . . about.* Pushes away and begins.

l. 660. *nerves.* Muscles.

ll. 661–2. *Daphne . . . Apollo.* Daphne was a chaste nymph pursued by Apollo. As he was about to catch her, the gods answered her prayers and transformed her into a laurel; see *Met.*, i. 547–52.

62 l. 664. *corporal rind.* Bodily shell; *rind* = the skin of a person or animal (still in use in 'bacon rind').

l. 669. *fancy.* Imagination in the sense of fantasy (of which it is originally a variant spelling); often applied to love.

l. 672. *cordial julep.* Restorative drink; both words had medicinal overtones.

l. 673. *his.* Its.

l. 674. *balm.* Specifically, balsam, an aromatic resin 'much prized for its fragrance and medicinal properties' (*OED*), and more generally any fragrant and healing substance or agency.

ll. 675–6. *nepenthes . . . Helena.* Returning from Troy, Menelaus and Helen stopped in Egypt, where they were hospitably received by Thone and his wife Polydamna. Polydamna gave Helen the drug *nepenthes*, which could banish grief from the mind, and she administered it to Menelaus (*Od.*, iv. 219–32). *Jove-born Helena.* Helen was the child of Jove by Leda.

l. 685. *unexempt condition.* Condition to which there can be no exceptions.

l. 688. *That have.* You who have.

l. 694. *aspects.* Both faces and looks.

l. 698. *vizored.* Masked.   *forgery.* Deception.

l. 700. *lickerish.* Tempting, delicious, lecherous.

63 l. 707. *budge doctors.* Stodgy or pompous teachers (probably alluding to the lambswool fur, called *budge*, that trimmed academic gowns.   *Stoic.* The philosophical school that advocated renunciation of wordly things.

fur. Academic discipline (alluding again to the trimming of university gowns).

63 l. 708. *Cynic tub.* The Cynics counselled a life of poverty and renunciation of pleasure; in pursuit of these ideals Diogenes made a tub his home.

l. 714. *curious.* Fastidious, difficult to satisfy.

l. 716. *shops.* Workshops.

l. 719. *hutched.* Stored.

l. 720. *store.* Furnish.

l. 721. *pet.* Ill-humoured fit.   *pulse.* Legume seeds; beans, peas, lentils, etc., typifying the simplest foods.

l. 722. *frieze.* Rough wool.

l. 730. *cumbered.* Overwhelmed, blocked up.

l. 733. *the forehead of the deep.* That part of the earth's core nearest the surface. 'Deep' usually signified the ocean, but could mean the depths of the earth as well, and diamonds come from the earth not the sea. The Trinity MS reads 'Would so bestud the centre with their starlight'.

l. 737. *coy.* Shy.

ll. 737–8. *cozened / With.* Deceived by.

l. 740. *current.* In circulation, as currency.

64 l. 745. *brag.* Display, with an overtone of boastfulness.

l. 750. *sorry grain.* Poor colour.   *ply.* Work at.

l. 751. *tease.* Comb out, for spinning.

l. 752. *vermeil.* Scarlet.

l. 759. *pranked.* Dressed up.

l. 760. *bolt.* Sift, as in running flour through a sieve (thereby separating the attractive from the unattractive arguments, letting only the 'refined' ones appear).

l. 769. *beseeming.* Befitting.

l. 770. *lewdly.* Wickedly, with an overtone of lasciviously.

l. 774. *no whit.* Not a bit.

l. 775. *the giver.* God, not Nature (see 'His', l. 776).

l. 782. *sun-clad.* Radiant.

65 l. 785. *high mystery.* Holy doctrine.

l. 791. *fence.* Fencing skill.

l. 793. *uncontrollèd.* Uncontrollable.

l. 794. *rapt.* Enraptured.

l. 797. *brute . . . shake.* Alluding to Horace's *'bruta tellus . . . concutitur'*, the brute earth was shaken so violently by a thunderbolt that the existence of the gods seemed to be confirmed (*Odes*, I. xxxiv. 9–12).   *nerves.* Strength, energy.

65 l. 803. *Dips me.* Suffuses me with moisture, the first recorded use of dip in this sense.

l. 804. *Speaks . . . chains.* i.e. has a voice of thunder and pronounces a sentence of chains.   *Erebus.* Primeval darkness, the son of Chaos, according to Hesiod; here used for the underworld.

l. 805. *Saturn's crew.* The giants and Titans: with Saturn (the Greek Cronos) they made war on Saturn's son Jove (or Zeus), who defeated them and imprisoned them in the underworld.

l. 806. *try her.* Test her strength.

l. 808. *canon laws.* Fundamental principles; but the use is ironic, since the term literally means the laws of the church as established by an ecclesiastical council.

l. 809. *suffer.* Permit.

ll. 809–10. *lees . . . blood.* The melancholic humour, the part of blood associated with the element earth, was conceived to precipitate as sediment, causing depression or madness.

l. 811. *straight.* Immediately.

l. 816. *reversed.* Turned backwards or upside down; Circe's charms were similarly undone by reversing her wand (*Met.*, xiv. 300).

l. 817. *backward . . . power.* i.e. his spells can only be undone by reciting them backwards.

66 l. 822. *Meliboeus.* In Virgil's *Eclogues* 1 and 7, an old shepherd/poet; the name was often used as the type of the wise shepherd in Renaissance pastorals. Since the Sabrina story (ll. 824 ff.) derives most directly from *FQ*, commentators have usually identified Meliboeus with Spenser.

l. 823. *soothest.* Wisest.

l. 825. *with . . . sways.* With watery power controls: a *curb* is the leash or reins used to control an animal.

ll. 826–31. *Sabrina . . . flood.* Sabrina is the Latin name of the River Severn. Milton's immediate source for the story of the death of the girl who became the tutelary nymph of the river is in *FQ*, II. x. 17–19; the account ultimately derives from Geoffrey of Monmouth's *Historia Regum Britanniae.* Sabrina was the illegitimate child of King Locrine by his beloved mistress Estrildis; both she and Sabrina were drowned on the orders of Locrine's queen Gwendolen after she had defeated and killed her husband in battle. In Geoffrey, the story is about thwarted love and destructive jealousy; sixteenth-century versions, of which there are several, generally stress Sabrina's innocence and the pathos of her situation.

l. 827. *Whilom.* Formerly (i.e. before she became a nymph); a Spenserian archaism.

l. 828. *Brute.* Brutus, great-grandson of Aeneas and legendary founder of Britain.

l. 831. *Commended.* Entrusted.   *flood.* River.

66 l. 832. *stayed.* Hindered.

l. 835. *Nereus.* A sea-god, the 'old man of the sea' in Homer (*Il.*, xviii. 141), and, unlike the other sea deities Neptune and Proteus, wise and generous.

l. 836. *lank.* Drooping, languid (*OED* 3, citing only this passage).

l. 837. *his daughters.* The Nereids, recalling Spenser's account of the wounded Marinell cured by the Nereids with 'sovereign balm and nectar good', *FQ*, III. iv. 40.

l. 838. *nectared lavers.* Perfumed basins.   *asphodel.* Immortal flower found in the Elysian Fields.

l. 839. *porch and inlet.* Both mean entrance; a distinction between outer and inner openings seems to be intended.

l. 840. *ambrosial.* Heavenly, hence restorative.

l. 841. *quick.* Both swift and living.   *immortal change.* Change to an immortal.

l. 845. *urchin blasts.* Wounds or illnesses caused by goblins: an urchin is a hedgehog, and goblins were called urchins because they were said to assume that shape.

l. 846. *shrewd.* Malignant, mischievous.

l. 849. *lays.* Songs.

l. 852. *the old swain.* Meliboeus (see l. 822).

l. 858. *adjuring.* Entreating (*OED*, citing only this passage, suggests 'exorcising').

67 l. 863. *amber-dropping hair.* (1) Flowing hair the colour of amber; (2) hair perfumed with ambergris.

l. 864. *honour's.* Chastity's

l. 865. *lake.* The word could mean a running stream, but Milton may be thinking of Virgil, who refers to the Tiber as a lake (*lacus*) in *Aen.*, viii. 74.

l. 868. *Oceanus.* One of the Titans, father of the rivers and in Homer the progenitor of the Olympian gods (*Il.*, xiv. 201 ff.).

l. 869. *earth-shaking.* Homer's standard epithet for Neptune.

l. 870. *Tethys.* Wife of Oceanus.

l. 871. *Nereus.* See l. 835.

l. 872. *Carpathian wizard's hook.* Proteus could change his shape, lived, according to Virgil, in the Carpathian sea, was a *vates*, or seer, and, with his shepherd's crook, herded Neptune's flocks of sea-lions (*Georgics*, iv. 387–95).

l. 873. *Triton.* Neptune's herald (see *Lycidas*, l. 89), who plays a conch shell. *winding.* Both played like a trumpet and twisted.

l. 874. *Glaucus.* Boeotian fisherman transformed into a sea god by eating a magic herb, which also endowed him with the power of prophecy (see *Met.*, xiii. 904–68).

67 l. 875. *Leucothea.* Lit. 'white goddess', the sea deity into whom Neptune transformed Ino, aunt of Dionysus/Bacchus (and his foster mother after the death of his mother Semele), to save her from the wrath of Juno. She is generous to mortals, and gave Odysseus her magic scarf to keep him from drowning (*Od.*, v. 333 ff.).

l. 876. *her son.* Melicertes, transformed with Ino into the sea god Palaemon, the Roman Portunus, guardian of ports and harbours (*Met.*, iv. 416–542).

l. 877. *Thetis.* A Nereid, the mother of Achilles.   *tinsel-slippered feet.* Homer calls Thetis 'silver-footed'; *tinsel* (lit. 'sparkling') was originally cloth made with silver or gold threads; subsequently any glittering cloth or decoration, usually with disparaging connotations.

l. 878. *Sirens.* Sea creatures whose singing was irresistible; but unlike the other sea creatures invoked, these are not beneficent, and Milton has already alluded to their dangerous attractions and their association with Circe and Comus (l. 253). Odysseus did, however, through wisdom and cunning, hear their songs and escape unharmed (*Od.*, xii. 165–200).

l. 879. *Parthenope.* One of the Sirens. According to post-Homeric legend, after the escape of Odysseus the Sirens drowned themselves, and Parthenope was washed up on the shore near Naples. A tomb was erected for her and the city originally bore her name.

l. 880. *Ligea.* Another Siren, according to Eustathius' commentary on Homer, and a river nymph with '*caesariem . . . nitidam*' (lustrous hair) in Virgil (*Georgics*, iv. 336).

l. 884. *wily.* Cunning, artful—apparently not used pejoratively here.

l. 892. *sliding.* Gliding.   *stays.* Stops.

l. 893. *azurn.* Azure, Milton's coinage, probably following the Italian *azzurino*; cf. '*cedarn*', l. 990.

68 l. 896. *fleet.* Swift.

l. 904. *charmèd band.* Magic bonds.

l. 907. *unblessed.* Unholy, wicked.

l. 913. *of precious cure.* Valuable for healing.

l. 917. *glutinous heat.* Heat sufficient to make the gums like glue.

l. 921. *Amphitrite.* A nereid, the wife of Neptune.

l. 923. *Anchises.* Father of Aeneas, hence ancestor of Locrine and Sabrina.

l. 924. *brimmèd.* Brimming.

l. 926. *petty.* Little.

l. 928. *singèd.* Scorching.

l. 930. *torrent.* Torrential (*OED* B; recorded as an adjective only in Milton before the nineteenth century).

l. 933. *beryl.* General name for a group of greenish and blue-green precious and semi-precious stones, including the emerald and aquamarine.

69 l. 941. *device.* Trick.

l. 942. *waste.* Superfluous.

l. 949. *gratulate.* Welcome.

l. 959. *sunshine.* Sunny.

l. 960. *duck or nod.* Curtsy or bow, the graces of courtly dances.

l. 961. *trippings.* Dances.

l. 962. *Of.* By.   *court guise.* Courtly style or behaviour.

l. 963. *Mercury . . . devise.* Hermes / Mercury was the inventor of the lyre, but there is no classical source crediting him with the invention of dancing. However, Milton may be thinking of the masque tradition: Mercury introduces the final dances of Jonson's *Pleasure Reconciled to Virtue*, and in Jonson's *Pan's Anniversary* (1621), Hermes is cited as the archetype choreographer, exceeded only by Pan (ll. 176–8).

l. 964. *mincing.* Dainty, elegant (apparently not pejorative). The word also 'was a dancing term that meant doubling the time to make twice as many steps to a musical measure' (J. Demaray, *Milton and the Masque Tradition* [1968], 119).   *Dryades.* Wood nymphs.

l. 965. *lawns . . . leas.* Glades . . . meadows.

70 l. 970. *timely.* Early.

l. 971. *patience.* Lit. 'endurance of suffering'.   *truth.* Constancy, fidelity.

l. 972. *assays.* Trials.

l. 980. *liquid.* Clear, bright.

ll. 981–3. *gardens . . . tree.* See l. 393.

l. 984. *crispèd.* A poetic word 'applied to trees: sense uncertain' (*OED* 4, citing only Milton and Herrick). The word generally means curled, crinkled, or puckered.

l. 985. *spruce.* Lively.

l. 986. *Graces . . . Hours.* Or Charites and Horae, goddesses respectively of natural beauty and of the seasons (see *PL*, iv. 267).

l. 988. *That.* So that.

l. 989. *west winds.* Zephyrs, gentle breezes.   *musky.* Fragrant.

l. 990. *cedarn alleys.* Walks between rows of cedars; *cedarn* is apparently Milton's coinage (cf. *azurn*, l. 893).

l. 991. *Nard, . . . cassia.* Aromatic plants: nard, or spikenard, is a root, cassia a bark.

l. 992. *Iris.* Goddess of the rainbow.

l. 993. *that blow.* Where bloom.

l. 995. *purfled.* Multi-coloured.

70 l. 996. *Elysian.* Heavenly; from Elysium, in classical myth the fields where the spirits of the blessed live after death.

l. 997. *List.* Hearken.   *true.* 'Of the right kind' (*OED*), i.e. capable of apprehending spiritual things.

l. 999. *Adonis.* Lover of Venus, killed by a boar and restored to immortal life in the Garden of Adonis. See *PL*, ix. 439–40.

l. 1000. *Waxing.* Growing.

l. 1002. *Assyrian queen.* Venus, or Aphrodite, first worshipped, according to Pausanias, in Assyria (*Description of Greece*, 1. xiv. 6).

l. 1004. *advanced.* Raised high.

ll. 1004–8. *Cupid . . . bride.* The story is in Apuleius' *Golden Ass*; 4.28–6.24; Psyche was a mortal woman so beautiful that Venus, envious of her, sent Cupid to maker her fall in love with someone loathsome, but Cupid fell in love with her instead. He visited her only in the dark at night, and forbade her to see him. Her sisters convinced her that her lover was a monster, and one night as he slept beside her she lit a candle to look at him, and, overcome with his beauty, let some wax drop on him, waking him. For her disobedience she was punished with many trials and wanderings, but Jove finally relented and allowed her to marry Cupid and live with him in heaven. Spenser places the lovers in the Garden of Adonis (*FQ*, III. vi. 49–50).

71 ll. 1010–11. *Two . . . Joy.* In Apuleius, their child is Voluptas; in Spenser, Pleasure.

l. 1015. *bowed welkin.* Arch of the sky.

l. 1017. *corners.* Farthest extremities (on the analogy of 'the four corners of the earth'); but Milton may also be taking the word in its etymological sense of horns, from Latin *cornu.*

l. 1021. *Higher . . . chime.* Above the music of the spheres, hence to the highest heaven.

ENGLISH POEMS ADDED IN 1673

We print all the English poems added in 1673, except for paraphrases of Psalms 1–8 and 80–8, which conclude the volume.

73 *On the Death of a Fair Infant Dying of a Cough.* Milton dates the poem 'Anno aetatis 17' (i.e. between Dec. 1625 and Dec. 1626); his nephew, Edward Phillips, identifies the 'infant' as the daughter of Milton's sister Anne (this child would have been a sister of Phillips's who died before he was born). William Riley Parker's search through parish records has identified a daughter of Anne Phillips also named Anne (12 Jan. 1626–22 Jan. 1628) as the only possible subject of the poem, and has therefore argued for a 1628 date for its composition, a view supported by the argument of E. S. LeComte, who demonstrates in *Milton's Unchanging Mind* that Milton frequently predated poems in order to establish an image of precocity.

l. 1. *blown.* In bloom.

73 l. 2. *primrose*. Cf. *Lycidas*, l. 142.   *timelessly*. Unseasonably, not in due time.

l. 6. *envermeil*. Tinge with vermilion.

ll. 6–7. *thought to kiss / But killed*. Cf. Shakespeare, *Venus and Adonis*, l. 1110.

l. 8. *Aquilo*. Or Boreas, the north wind, who resorted to force when the Athenian princess Orithyia resisted his advances; see Ovid. *Met.*, vi. 682–713.

l. 9. *boisterous*. Violent.

l. 13. *eld*. Old age.

l. 16. *middle empire*. The atmospheric region between the sun and earth; Satan's realm in *PR*.

l. 18. *care*. Anxiety.

l. 19. *chair*. The car of l. 15, a flying chariot, perhaps imagined as stage machinery; cf. ll. 55–6, below.

l. 20. *cold-kind*. Both cold in nature, and chilling to death when his intentions were kind.

l. 23. *Apollo*. The god accidentally killed his lover Hyacinthus; see Ovid, *Met.*, x. 162–219, and cf. *Lycidas*, l. 106.

74 l. 25. *Eurotas*. The river on which Sparta was built.

l. 30. *corse*. Corpse.

l. 39. *first-moving sphere*. The Primum Mobile, the outer limit and source of motion of the Ptolemaic universe.

l. 40. *Elysian fields*. A paradise for the dead, in Plato and Homer located beyond the earth's limits, and in hell by Ovid and Virgil.

l. 41. *wight*. Creature.

ll. 43–4. *ruined . . . Olympus*. Damaged heavens (presumably alluding to the war between the Titans and the Olympian gods).

l. 45. *in . . . behoof*. For nature's advantage.

l. 47. *Earth's sons*. The giants, brothers of the Titans, who drove the gods from heaven and chased them into Egypt (cf. *Naturam non Pati Senium*, ll. 20–2; the story is in Ovid, *Met.*, v. 321–31).

l. 48. *sheeny*. Shining.

l. 50. *just maid*. Astraea, goddess of justice, the last of the gods to flee the earth at the close of the iron age (see Ovid, *Met.*, i. 149–50).

l. 53. *that . . . youth*. The line is short a foot, apparently a printer's error resulting in the omission of the identity of the figure. The various emendations include 'Mercy [or Virtue] that sweet smiling youth', and 'that sweet Peace, in smiling youth', which has the advantage of keeping the figure female.

75 l. 57. *golden-wingèd host*. The angels.

l. 58. *weed*. Clothing; here, flesh.

l. 59. *prefixèd*. Predetermined.

75 l. 66. *his.* Commentators have suggested Death or God as possible referents for this indeterminate pronoun.

l. 68. *pestilence.* May allude to the plague that broke out in London in 1625–6, although a more general biblical sense of penalty for sin is also possible.

ll. 74–5. *Think . . . lent.* Cf. Jonson, 'On my first Son'.

l. 76. *offspring.* Some commentators see in this an allusion to the next Phillips child (Elizabeth, b. Apr. 1628, d. Feb. 1631); others find a more general reference to spiritual life (cf. Acts 17: 28, 'for in him we live, and move, and have our being . . . for we are also his offspring').

At a Vacation Exercise. Milton had been chosen to preside over the festivities marking the beginning of the Cambridge long vacation in July 1628, at which this poetic oration was originally delivered. It was preceded by a Latin oratorical performance (*Oratio in feriis aestivis collegii;* the sixth of Milton's prolusions)—the inclusion of English verses in such a ceremony was Milton's innovation. The poem's placement after *On the Death of a Fair Infant* is indicated in the errata slip to 1673; as printed, it appears after *The Fifth Ode of Horace.*

l. 8. *latter task.* i.e. this English poem, in contrast with the preceding Latin oration.

76 l. 12. *thither.* i.e. into the preceding Latin.

l. 18. *wardrobe.* Implying the metaphor of style as a garment, developed in the following lines, with their critique of poetic fashions.

l. 19. *toys.* Conceits, fancies.   *trimming slight.* Trivial ornamentation.

l. 21. *gayest.* Finest, brightest.

l. 27. *suspect.* Suspicion.

l. 32. *fancy.* Imagination.

l. 33. *deep transported mind.* Cf. *Il Penseroso,* ll. 85–96; 'deep' translates Lat. *altus.*

l. 34. *wheeling poles.* The axes that turn the Ptolemaic spheres; the unmoving Empyreum above was the heaven of the gods.

l. 36. *thunderous throne.* The throne of Jove, the thunderer.

l. 37. *unshorn.* A standard classical epithet for Apollo, alluding to his long golden hair.

l. 38. *wires.* Strings (of the harp or lyre).   *Hebe.* Cupbearer of the gods and goddess of youth, the daughter of Zeus (Jove).

l. 40. *watchful fire.* The light of the stars was assumed in the Ptolemaic universe to be derived from the eternal (and thus, by analogy, always watchful) element of fire.

l. 42. *lofts.* Upper regions (*loft* originally meant the sky).

76 l. 48. *Demodocus.* The bard at the court of King Alcinous, whose songs moved Odysseus to tears (*Od.*, viii. 487–543).

77 ll. 51–2. *held . . . captivity.* Cf. *L'Allegro*, ll. 143–4.

l. 54. *another way.* A return to the Aristotelian argument of the prolusion, which now provides the direction ('bent', l. 56, below).

l. 56. *predicament.* Aristotle posited ten categories, called in scholastic logic predicaments (i.e., what can be predicated of any substance) which provided rules (the 'canons' in the stage direction below) for defining the nature of a substance.

l. 58. *room.* Office; his role as 'father' of the festivities, resigned once the part has been played. Here, he plays the part of Ens (Being); his 'sons', other students, play the ten Aristotelian categories, Substance and its nine accidents, or attributes ('canons'): Quantity, Quality, Relation, Place, Time, Position, Possession, Action, Passion (or Passivity).

l. 65. *still.* Always.

l. 66. *invisible.* Substance is invisible because it is an abstract form and only manifest through its accidental attributes of quantity, quality, etc.

l. 69. *Sibyl.* Prophetess.

l. 71. *prospective glass.* A mirror (or crystal ball) in which the future is seen.

l. 74. *subject . . . accident.* Playing on their technical senses in logic, in which substance is the subject of its accidents.

78 l. 90. *Gordian knot.* The enigma of the paradoxical relationships between substance and accident, alluding to the complex knot tied by Gordius, which could not be untied but which Alexander the Great cut. The following prose speeches do not survive.

l. 91. *Rivers.* A parody of poetic catalogues of rivers, e.g. in Spenser's marriage of the Thames and Medway (*FQ*, iv. 10) and throughout Drayton's *Poly-Olbion*. But also, George and Nizell Rivers were fellow students of Milton's, and as the stage direction indicates, one of them is playing the part of Relation.

l. 92. *utmost Tweed.* The border between England and Scotland.   *gulfy.* Full of eddies.

l. 95. *sullen.* Sluggish; possibly also alluding to Drayton's story of the nymph of the River Mole, whose parents forbade her marriage with the Thames, and whom she therefore secretly joins underground (*Poly-Olbion*, xvii. 49–64).

l. 96. *maiden's death.* Sabrina committed suicide in the Severn; see *Comus*, ll. 823–31.

l. 98. *coaly . . . Dee.* The Tyne flows by Newcastle, proverbial for its coal. On the Dee, cf. *Lycidas*, l. 55 n.

l. 99. *Humber . . . name.* Humber was said to have been the name of a Scythian invader who drowned in the river.

78 *Sonnet 11* ('A book was writ of late'). In the Trinity MS, Sonnet 11 follows Sonnet 12. The MS subtitle, 'On the Detraction Which Followed Upon My Writing Certain Treatises', refers to the four divorce tracts, *Doctrine and Discipline of Divorce* (1643, 1644), *Judgment of Martin Bucer* (1644), *Tetrachordon*, and *Colasterion* (both 1645). The sonnet would thus date from late 1645 or early 1646.

l. 1. Tetrachordon. Lit. a four-note scale, or a musical instrument with four strings; here, the four places in scripture relevant to the question of divorce (Gen. 1: 27–8, 2: 18, 23–;; Deut. 24: 1–2; Matt. 5: 31–2, 19: 3–11; 1 Cor. 7: 10–16) 'harmonized' to present the argument for divorce on the basis of incompatibility.

l. 4. *Numbering.* Either determining the number of, or comprising (as its readers).

l. 5. *stall-reader.* Who reads the book at the bookstall, and has not purchased it.

ll. 6–7. *in file . . . false.* Stand in a row misreading.

ll. 7–8. *Mile-End Green.* Located a mile beyond Aldgate, the eastern end of London.

ll. 8–9. *Gordon . . . Galasp.* Rough Scottish names (Colkitto is a nickname, 'lefty Colin', and Galasp seems to be a version of Gillespie). They have been identified, at least plausibly, as three Royalist followers of the Marquis of Montrose and a leader of the Westminster Assembly; but more broadly, Milton's allusion would be both to the general assimilation of the Scots in England after the Stuarts ascended the throne, and to the more immediate ubiquitousness of Scottish Presbyterians.

l. 10. *rugged.* Harsh; the manuscript originally read 'barbarous'.

l. 11. *Quintilian.* Late first-century author of an important treatise on rhetoric, *The Institutes,* which has a section (I. v. 8) condemning the importation of foreign words into Latin.

l. 12. *Sir John Cheke.* Mid-sixteenth-century English humanist, first Professor of Greek at Cambridge, and tutor of Edward VI.

79 *Sonnet 12. On the Same* ('I did but prompt the age'). Date: see Sonnet 11.

l. 1. *clogs.* Prisoners' restraints.

l. 2. *ancient liberty.* This implies not only the laws in scripture, but also those inscribed internally and naturally, reason and the promptings of nature, the Christian liberty central to Milton's thought.

l. 4. *owls.* Considered stupid birds in Renaissance birdlore.   *cuckoos.* Noisy birds associated with cuckoldry.

ll. 5–7. *hinds . . . fee.* Latona, or Leto, transformed two peasants ('hinds') into frogs when they refused to give her a drink for her infants, Apollo and Diana, who were destined to control ('hold in fee') the sun and moon. The story is in Ovid, *Met.*, vi. 317–81.

l. 8. *casting pearl to hogs.* Alluding to Matt. 7: 6.

79 l. 10. *truth . . . free.* Cf. John 8: 32.

l. 13. *mark.* Target.

l. 14. *For.* Despite.

Sonnet 13. To Mr H. Lawes ('Harry whose tuneful'). The poem first appeared in *Choice Psalms* (1648) by Henry and William Lawes; the volume was dedicated to King Charles and commemorated William Lawes, who had died in his cause. Henry Lawes wrote the music for *Comus* and played the part of the Attendant Spirit; he may also have collaborated on *Arcades.* There are three drafts of this poem in the Trinity MS.

ll. 2–3. *span . . . accent.* Give words their proper measure of length and stress.   *scan.* Count.

l. 4. *Midas' ears.* Midas was punished with the ears of an ass for preferring Pan's music to Apollo's (see *Met.*, xi. 146–93).   *committing.* Joining together (*OED* 7), joining in conflict (*OED* 9); the Trinity MS originally read 'misjoyning'.   *short and long.* Syllables or notes; the metrical values of words and music.

l. 8. *humour.* Fit, suit.

l. 10. *Phoebus.* Apollo, as god of music.

l. 11. *story.* According to a marginal note in *Choice Psalms*, this alludes to 'The story of Ariadne set by him in music': Lawes' setting of William Cartwright's *Complaint of Ariadne* appears in Lawes' *Ayres and Dialogues* (1653).

ll. 12–13. *Dante . . . Casella.* Dante's meeting with the musician Casella is described in *Purgatorio*, ii. 76–117; Casella sings his setting of one of Dante's *canzoni.*

80 *Sonnet 14* ('When faith and love which parted from thee never'). There are three MSS of this poem; one in Milton's hand is titled 'On the religious memory of Mrs Catharine Thomason my Christian friend deceased 16 December 1646'. She was the wife of George Thomason, a London bookseller; both she and her husband were collectors of contemporary pamphlets (the present Thomason Collection in the British Library contains over 22,000 items from 1640 to 60, including several works by Milton inscribed as gifts of the author). The date of her death appears to be an error; parish records indicate she was buried at St. Dunstan's in the West on 12 Dec. 1646, and Milton's date may be intended as the date of the poem's composition.

l. 4. *from life.* i.e. from eternal life.

l. 8. *Followed thee.* Cf. Rev. 14: 13.

Sonnet 15. On the Late Massacre in Piedmont. On 24 Apr. 1655, the Duke of Savoy's troops slaughtered the Vaudois, or Waldensians, a Protestant sect regarded by contemporaries as the repository of primitive Christianity (modern historians find their origins in the twelfth-century followers of

Valdes of Lyons, founder of a mendicant order). They had been granted limited rights in Savoy and, on the pretext that they had settled in territory forbidden them, were massacred. Cromwell issued a protest composed by Milton in May 1655. Later that summer the remaining Waldensian forces were able to defeat their persecutors and to secure their rights.

80 l. 1. *Avenge.* Cf. Rev. 6: 10.   *bones.* Cf. Ps. 141: 7.

l. 4. *stocks and stones.* Idols made of wood and stone.

l. 5. *thy book.* The book of God's judgments, recording those who are to have eternal life; see, e.g., Exod. 32: 32–3, and Rev., *passim.*

l. 10. *martyred blood . . . sow.* Recalling Tertullian's famous dictum 'The blood of the martyrs is the seed of the Church' (*Patrologia Latina*, i.535), as well as the parable of the sower (Matt. 13), and the myth of Cadmus, who sowed the teeth of a serpent from which armed men arose.

l. 12. *triple Tyrant.* The pope; his tiara is composed of a triple crown.

l. 14. *Babylonian woe.* Babylon was the place of Jewish exile, the city of reprobation throughout Revelation, and was often identified by Protestants with papal Rome.

81 *Sonnet 16* ('When I consider how my light is spent'). The date of this poem has occasioned much debate. Assuming that the order of the sonnets in the 1673 edition is chronological, its placement appears to date it after 1655; yet many readers have felt that the attitudes expressed would seem more appropriate to the onslaught of blindness in 1652. Neither date fits well with the second line of the sonnet, 'Ere half my days . . .': Milton was 44 in 1652. The usual subtitle, 'On his blindness', is an eighteenth-century addition.

l. 1. *When I consider.* The opening phrase of Shakespeare, Sonnet 15. Connections between the two poems are suggested in Jonathan Goldberg, *Voice Terminal Echo.*

l. 2. *Ere half my days.* If the biblical allotment of 70 years is meant, the poem would date from before 1643. Commentators have stretched their ingenuity to explain the figure—e.g., arguing that Milton is thinking of half his father's lifespan (84 years), or half his working days. In *Milton's Unchanging Mind*, E. S. LeComte convincingly relates the line to Milton's habitual misdating of his work as a way of presenting an image of precocity, and of forestalling the major work he felt was required of him.

ll. 3–6. *talent . . . chide.* Punning on the double sense of 'talent', ability, and the valuable coin of the ancient world. Milton alludes here to the parable of the talents (Matt. 25: 14–30), as he does also in the letter to a friend enclosing a copy of Sonnet 7 (see p. 1), and in the prefatory autobiographical section of the second part of *RCG* (p. 165).

l. 7. *day-labour.* Cf. John 9: 4 and the parable of the bridegroom (Matt. 25: 1–13) that immediately precedes the parable of the talents.

l. 8. *fondly.* Foolishly.   *prevent.* Forestall, preclude.

81 l. 11. *yoke.* Cf. Matt. 11: 30.

l. 12. *Thousands.* The angels.

Sonnet 17 ('Lawrence of virtuous father/virtuous son'). Edward Lawrence (1633–57) was the elder son of Henry Lawrence, who became President of Cromwell's Council of State in 1654; his studious and literary son became a Member of Parliament in the last year of his life. Commentators have remarked on the Horatian quality of the poem. Generally dated *c.*1655, though as Carey points out, 'The sonnet could have been written during any winter from 1651–2 to 1656–7.'

l. 4. *waste.* Spend, pass; not necessarily pejorative.

l. 6. *Favonius.* The west wind.

l. 8. *lily . . . spun.* Cf. Matt. 6: 28–9.

l. 9. *neat.* Elegant, tasteful, not excessive.

l. 10. *Of Attic taste.* As would have pleased the Athenians, with their refined food and conversation.

l. 12. *Tuscan air.* Italian music.

ll. 13–14. *spare/To interpose.* Ambiguous—either refrain from or find time for; see the incisive discussion of this crux in S. Fish, *Is There a Text in this Class?*

82 *Sonnet 18* ('Cyriack whose grandsire on the royal bench'). Cyriack Skinner (1627–1700), was the grandson of Sir Edward Coke (1552–1634), Chief Justice of the Common Pleas and, from 1613 to 16, of the King's Bench, the most important legal mind of his time, especially as an advocate of the privileges of Parliament. Skinner may have been a student of Milton's, and is the likely author of an anonymous early life; he became an intimate friend. His interests were wide-ranging, including politics (particularly foreign affairs), mathematics and science. Written *c.*1655.

l. 2. *Themis.* Goddess of justice.

l. 3. *volumes.* Among Coke's books are *The Institutes of the Law of England.*

l. 4. *others.* Other judges.

l. 5. *resolve . . .* The verb is an imperative addressed to Skinner; the syntax is, 'resolve with me to drench deep thoughts in mirth.' For the sentiment, compare Ben Jonson, 'Inviting a Friend to Supper' (Epigram 101).

l. 8. *Swede . . . French.* Skinner's interest in international politics is exemplified by reference to Charles X of Sweden's recent attack on Poland, and Cromwell's negotiations with Cardinal Mazarin, resulting in the Treaty of Westminster. Cf. Horace, *Odes,* II. xi. 1–6, in which the poet urges his friend to remember that youth is fleeting, and to forget the foreign adventures of 'the warlike Cantabrian . . . and the Scythian'.

l. 9. *betimes.* Early.

l. 11. *a time ordains.* Cf. Eccles. 3: 1.

82 *Sonnet 19* ('Methought I saw my late espousèd saint'). Commentators have debated the identity of the 'late espousèd saint'. Readers who insist on the literalness of the allusions to childbirth in ll. 5–6 opt for Milton's first wife Mary Powell, who died in childbirth in 1652; however, Katherine Woodcock, Milton's second wife, who died of a fever in Feb. 1658, several months after delivering a child, would nevertheless have lived long enough to fulfil the prescribed period of purification alluded to in the poem. The reference to ritual purification in fact can be used to support either identification—it was *Mary* who brought Jesus to the temple 'when the days of her purification according to the law of Moses were accomplished' (Luke 2: 22): On the other hand, 'pure' (l. 9) is linked etymologically to the name Katherine by way of Gk. *katharos*, pure, and the purification in the poem is in any case being used as a simile: the woman is dressed in white *like* one who had been purified. Similar difficulties attend the question of whether the wife that he hopes to see again is a wife he ever, literally, saw—Milton was blind by the time he married Katherine Woodcock; on the other hand, the fact that the figure's face is veiled may imply that he has not in fact seen her. In the light of such ambiguous evidence, it might be worth entertaining the possibility that Milton is thinking of both his marriages in the poem.

l. 1. *late*. Both recently (modifying 'espousèd'), and deceased.

l. 2. *Alcestis*. The wife of Admetus; she sacrificed her life to save her husband from death, and was rescued from the grave by Hercules ('Jove's great son', l. 3, below). The story is the subject of Euripides' *Alcestis*.

l. 5. *as whom*. As one whom.

l. 6. *Purification . . . law*. Rules for purification after childbirth are detailed in Lev. 12. Cleansing (the 'washing' of l. 5) occurred one week after the birth of a son, two weeks after the birth of a daughter; purification after another 33 or 66 days respectively. During that period, the woman could not enter the temple.

l. 9. *vested . . . white*. Cf. Rev. 7: 14. and 19: 8.

l. 10. *veiled*. Alcestis also returns veiled from the grave.

l. 13. *to embrace me*. Similar failed embraces can be found in *Od*., xi. 204–9 (Odysseus' attempt to embrace his mother's shade), *Aen*., ii. 789–95 (Aeneas and his dead wife Creusa), *Aen*., vi. 700–2 (Aeneas and Anchises), *Purgatorio*, ii. 80–1 (Dante and Casella; compare Sonnet 13, above); see also *PL*, viii. 478–80. Aeneas implores Dido's shade not to flee, though he does not attempt to take hold of her (*Aen*., vi. 465–9). Perhaps the closest analogue (a dream vision, a single attempt at an embrace) is that of Achilles and the ghost of Patroclus (*Il*., xxiii. 99–107).

83 *The Fifth Ode of Horace, Lib. I*. Although placed after the sonnets in the 1673 edition, this is considered an early work by most commentators, who also assume that an errata slip moving the *Vac. Ex.* forward was meant to apply to this as well.

l. 1. *odours*. Perfumes.

83 l. 8. *admire.* Wonder at.

l. 9. *credulous, all gold.* Foolishly believing that you are all gold, i.e. true and beautiful.

ll. 10–11. *vacant . . . thee.* Hopes that you are unoccupied (with other suitors).

ll. 13–14. *Me . . . Picture.* He has hung a votive image ('vowed picture') on the wall of the temple of Neptune; his clothing ('weeds') are a tribute for having survived the shipwreck (of love for Pyrrha).

On the New Forcers of Conscience under the Long Parliament. Episcopacy was abolished in 1643, and after long and acrimonious debate the ordinances establishing Presbyterianism were finally formulated in 1646. Usually dated 1646.

l. 1. *prelate lord.* Bishops were 'lords spiritual'.

l. 3. *plurality.* Holding more than one benefice, an episcopal abuse that was continued by the Presbyterians.

l. 5. *adjure.* Charge, bind (as to an oath): the Presbyterians demanded the enforcement of conformity to the reformed Church.

l. 7. *classic hierarchy.* The division of parishes into classes (presbyteries), which were below the synod and national assembly in the Church hierarchy.

l. 8. *A. S.* Adam Stewart, a Scottish divine who replied to the Independent position.   *Rutherford.* Samuel Rutherford, a Scottish member of the Westminster Assembly, whose *Divine Right of Church-Government* (1646) argued against toleration.

l. 10. *Paul.* St Paul, from whom Milton derived the concept of liberty of conscience against which Rutherford argued in his 1649 *Free Disputation Against pretended Liberty of Conscience.*

84 l. 12. *Edwards.* Thomas Edwards, who attacked Milton's views on divorce in *Gangrena . . . a Catalogue of . . . Heresies* (1646).   *Scotch What-d'ye-call.* Cf. the generic Scots names in Sonnet 11; here, although editors have proposed various particular members of the Assembly, a general allusion to Scottish presbyters seems more likely to be intended—'any old Scot'.

l. 14. *packing.* Manipulation by packing the meetings of the assembly in order to outnumber the dissenters.   *Trent.* The Council of Trent.

l. 17. *phylacteries.* Small leather case containing texts from Exod. and Deut. worn by Jews in prayer; here, as an outward and hypocritical display. *balk your ears.* Stop short of clipping your ears. The MS reads 'Cropp yee as close as marginall P_____'s ears', alluding to the punishment of William Prynne, a Presbyterian who lost his ears for writing *Histriomastix* (1632), an attack on the stage that was read as an attack on the monarchy; in the 1640s, Prynne was no friend to toleration of sects.

84 l. 19. *they*. Parliament.   *charge*. Indictment.

l. 20. *old Priest*. Etymologically, 'priest' is a contracted form of 'presbyter'.

UNCOLLECTED ENGLISH POEMS

85 *On the Lord General Fairfax* ('Fairfax, whose name in arms through Europe rings'). First printed in *Letters of State* (1694), ed. Edward Phillips. The Trinity MS in Milton's hand (our text here) titles it 'On the Lord General Fairfax at the siege of Colchester'; the siege occurred in the summer of 1648. Sir Thomas Fairfax was commander-in-chief of the New Model Army.

l. 1. *rings*. Resounds.

l. 5. *virtue*. Retaining the sense of Lat. *virtus*, physical strength, courage, manliness; Phillips's 1694 version reads 'valour'.

l. 6. *Victory*. Besides Colchester, Fairfax's victories included the battles of Marston Moor and Naseby, decisive events in the war.

l. 7. *hydra*. A mythical beast with many heads; when one head was cut off, two sprouted as replacements. Hercules slew it (see *Met.*, ix. 64–74). *false north*. The Scots, who broke the Solemn League and Covenant, and sent troops in support of Charles I in 1648.

l. 8. *imp*. Graft new feathers on. Although the hydra was not usually depicted as winged, its sister the sphinx was, as were other offspring of its mother, the monstrous Echidna, half woman, half snake.

l. 9. *a nobler task*. Fairfax, in fact, did not serve in the government. After Charles I was executed he resigned his position and retired to his estate at Nun Appleton; Marvell's *Upon Appleton House* celebrates that part of his career.

To the Lord General Cromwell ('Cromwell, our chief of men'). Like the preceding sonnet to Fairfax, this poem first appeared in *Letters of State* (1694). In the Trinity MS (our text here) it is titled, in the hand of a scribe, 'To the Lord General Cromwell May 1652 / On the proposals of certain ministers at the Committee for Propagation of the Gospel'. The Committee's business included regulating worship and promulgating basic tenets of belief; Cromwell was a member of the Committee along with the other Independent ministers who championed a nationally supported church with limited toleration for dissent.

l. 1. *through a cloud*. Cf. the similar image in Marvell's 'Horatian Ode', ll. 13 ff.

l. 4. *peace and truth*. M. Y. Hughes points out that the phrase appeared on a coin struck in celebration of Cromwell's victories; the words were also used to summarize the aims of the Solemn League and Covenant (1643).

ll. 5–6. *on the neck . . . pursued*. Cromwell overcame 'crowned fortune' by defeating not only Charles I, but also Charles II, crowned in Scotland in 1651 and defeated at Worcester in that year (see l. 9, below). Of that victory, Cromwell said, 'the dimensions of this mercy are above my thoughts.

85 It is, for aught I know, a crowning mercy.'   *reared . . . trophies.*
Erected memorials to God's triumph.

l. 7. *Darwen.* The river in Lancashire near which the battle of Preston
(Aug. 1648) was fought against the Scots.   *imbrued.* Stained with
blood.

l. 8. *Dunbar.* Where Cromwell won a decisive victory over the Scots (Sept.
1650).

l. 9. *laureate wreath.* The laurel crown of victory.

l. 10. *peace . . . victories.* The sentiment goes back at least as far as Cicero,
De officiis, l. xxii. 74, in which the achievements of peace are extolled over
victories in war; Sir William Davenant's and Inigo Jones's 1640 court
masque *Salmacida Spolia* made a similar plea to its Royalist audience; Marvell's *Horatian Ode* ends on the same note, as does the section praising
Cromwell in Milton's *Second Defence.*

ll. 11–12. *foes . . . chains.* Alluding to those ministers who petitioned
Parliament in 1652 to enforce conformity to a state-controlled Church.

l. 14. *hireling.* Under the proposals of 1652, the clergy were to be paid by
the government. Cf. John 10: 13–14; Matt. 7: 15; *Lycidas,* ll. 113–22.
maw. Belly, mouth, appetite.

86 *To Sir Henry Vane the Younger* ('Vane, young in years, but in sage counsel
old'). The title is from the Trinity MS (our text here), where the poem is in
a scribe's hand. Vane had been Governor of Massachusetts (1635–7),
Treasurer of the Navy (1639), and was a member of the Council of State
concerned with foreign affairs in 1652 when the poem was written. He was
executed in 1662 after the restoration of Charles II. The poem was first
published in George Sikes, *The Life and Death of Sir Henry Vane* (1662),
introduced as follows: 'The character of this deceased statesman . . . I
shall exhibit to you in a paper of verses, composed by a learned gentleman,
and sent him, July 3, 1652.'

l. 1. *young in years.* Vane was born in 1613, and was therefore almost 40. He
was called 'the Younger' because his father, with the same name, was still
alive. On the trope of the *puer senex* (the youth as sage), see E. R. Curtius,
European Literature in the Latin Middle Ages.

l. 3. *gowns.* Roman senatorial togas.

l. 4. *Epirot . . . African.* Pyrrhus, King of Epirus, and Hannibal; both
invaded Italy and were defeated.

ll. 5–6. *unfold . . . spelled.* Uncover designs not easily deciphered
hollow. Untrustworthy; punning, most commentators contend, on Holland,
with whom Vane had urged an alliance, and against whom, when negotiations failed, he prepared the navy, suspecting their peace envoys.

l. 8. *nerves.* Sinews.   *iron and gold.* Milton had noted in his commonplace book Machiavelli's dictum (*Discorsi,* ii. 10) that arms, not money, are
the sinews ('*il nervo*') of war.

86 l. 9. *equipage.* War machinery.

l. 12. *either sword.* Of 'spiritual power and civil', l. 9, above.

To Mr Cyriack Skinner Upon his Blindness ('Cyriack, this three years day these eyes'). For Skinner, see headnote to Sonnet 18, above. The poem was first published in Phillips's *Letters of State* (1694), titled 'To Mr Cyriack Skinner Upon his Blindness'. Our text is that of the Trinity MS, where the poem is probably in Skinner's hand. Date: 1655 (see ll. 1–3).

l. 1. *three years' day.* Milton became totally blind in 1651–2. (For his account of the course of his disease, see his letter to Leonard Philaras, pp. 721–3.)   *clear.* In the *Second Defence*, Milton remarks that his eyes gave no outward sign of blindness. See p. 314.

l. 3. *light.* The 1694 text reads 'sight'.

ll. 4–6. *Nor . . . woman.* Cf. descriptions of his blindness in *PL*, iii. 22–55.

l. 8. *bear up.* Including the nautical meaning of sailing with the wind.

l. 10. *conscience.* Including the sense of 'consciousness'.   *overplied.* overworked; the nautical sense is steering against the wind.

l. 13. *mask.* Perhaps in the theatrical sense (masque), especially for its royalist associations and its extravagant and ephemeral quality; also masquerade, false show, disguise.

LATIN POEMS

Milton's 1645 volume was divided into English and Latin poems (including two in Greek), the latter section with a separate title page, *Joannis Miltoni Londinensis Poemata*, and further subdivided into a first book of poems written in elegiac verse (*Elegiarum Liber primus*), which we include in its entirety, epigrams, which we omit, and a miscellany (*Sylvarum Liber*), from which we include selections. The 1673 edition added three Latin and Greek poems to those printed in 1645; two Latin epigrams attacking Salmacius appeared in two of Milton's prose tracts, and two early Latin poems were discovered in Milton's commonplace book and printed in 1874: from among these, we have selected two poems. The standard modern edition is *The Latin Poems of John Milton*, ed. Walter MacKellar (1930), whose translations (with some minor revisions) we use by kind permission of the Cornell University Press; the two additional poems are translated by Stephen Orgel. Notes are keyed to the translations.

89 *Elegy 1. To Charles Diodati.* The poem is cast as a letter to Milton's friend Charles Diodati (see Sonnet 4), who was in Chester at the time. It was written from London in 1626, during a short period of rustication (a temporary dismissal from Cambridge), for reasons which are not known, but which appear to have stemmed from a dispute between Milton and his tutor, William Chappell.

l. 4. *Vergivian sea.* The Irish sea.

l. 14. *cult of Phoebus.* Poets.

ll. 21–2. *bard . . . Tomis.* Ovid, exiled to Tomis, on the Black Sea.

89 ll. 27 ff. *theatre.* The theatrical references, including the stock characters of Roman comedy and the ancestral houses of Greek and Senecan tragic heroes, suggest classical rather than contemporary dramas.

ll. 37–8. *raging Tragedy.* Alluding to Ovid's description in *Amores*, III. i. 11–13.

91 l. 45. *house of Pelops.* The family of Atreus and Agamemnon, son and grandson of Pelops.   *Ilus.* Founder of Troy (Ilium).

l. 46. *Creon.* Successor to Oedipus; he appears in all three of Sophocles' dramas about the house of Oedipus.

l. 57. *twice-living Pelops.* Pelops is 'twice-living' because, after having been dismembered by his father Tantalus, and served up to the gods in a stew, they restored him to life; his shoulder, however, had been eaten, and they fashioned one of ivory as a replacement (see Ovid, *Met.*, vi. 407–11).

l. 62. *your flower, O Adonis.* The anemone, which Venus created from the blood of her slain lover, Adonis (see *Met.*, x. 735–9). The hyacinth, alluded to in l. 61 above, has a similar history, Hyacinthus having been the lover of Apollo (see *Met.*, x. 214–16 and *Lycidas*, 105–7).

l. 63. *heroines . . . lauded.* In Ovid's *Heroides.*

l. 65. *Achaemenian.* Persian, after the progenitor of the Persian kings, Achaemenes.

l. 66. *Susa . . . Nineveh.* Susa was the Persian capital, founded by Tithonus, the father of Memnon, the first Persian king; it is not clear why Milton associates Memnon with the Assyrian city of Nineveh.

l. 69. *Tarpeian muse.* The poet Ovid, 'Tarpeian' from the location of his home, near the Tarpeian rock beside the Capitoline hill in Rome. *Pompey's porch.* The porch of the theatre of Pompey, a fashionable meeting-place in ancient Rome.

l. 70. *Ausonian.* Italian.

l. 73. *Dardanian colonists.* Dardanus, son of Jupiter, was the ancestor of the Trojan kings; hence, the descendants of Brutus, grandson of Aeneas, and his Trojan companions, legendary founders of Britain.

93 l. 78. *Endymion's goddess.* Diana, who fell in love with the shepherd youth Endymion.

ll. 83–4. *Cnidus . . . Cyprus.* Locations of shrines of Venus; Simois, the river of Troy, flows from Mount Ida, site of the Judgment of Paris, where the Trojan prince preferred Venus to Juno and Minerva and awarded her the prize that precipitated the Trojan War.

l. 85. *blind boy.* Cupid.

l. 88. *moly.* the substance Hermes gave Odysseus to protect him from being transformed into an animal by the sorceress Circe (see *Od.*, x and *Met.*, xiv).

l. 92. *alternate measures.* The elegiac metre is composed in alternating hexameters and pentameters.

93 *Elegy 2. On the Death of the Cambridge University Beadle.* Richard Ridding, the Beadle of Cambridge University, died in 1626.

l. 1. *staff.* Sign of the beadle's office, carried in academic processions.

l. 2. *Palladian band.* Devotees of Pallas Athena, goddess of wisdom; the Cambridge scholars whom Ridding summoned.

ll. 5–6. *plumes . . . Jove.* Jove ravished Leda in the shape of a swan.

l. 7. *Haemonian potion.* Magic drugs used by Medea to restore Aeson to youth (see *Met.*, vii. 251–93); *Haemonia* = Thrace, notorious for its association with witchcraft. See *Comus*, ll. 636–40.

ll. 9–10. *Coronides . . . Styx.* Aesculapius, god of medicine (son of Coronis, hence 'Coronides'), at the urging of Diana restored Hippolytus to life.

l. 13. *Cyllenius . . . halls.* Hermes (born on Mount Cyllene in Arcadia), whom Zeus dispatched to Priam (see *Il.*, xxiv. 337 ff.).

l. 15. *Eurybates.* Herald of Agamemnon ('son of Atreus', l. 16), sent to negotiate with Achilles (see *Il.*, i. 320 ff.).

l. 17. *great queen.* Death.   *Avernus.* The underworld, from Lake Avernus, near Naples, one of the entrances to hell.

95 *Elegy 3. On the Death of the Bishop of Winchester.* Lancelot Andrewes, Bishop of Winchester, died in Sept. 1626; one of the translators of the King James Bible, he was an eminent Anglican divine.

l. 4. *Libitina.* Roman goddess of corpses; the name in Horace is synonymous with death.

ll. 9–10. *duke . . . brother.* No entirely satisfactory candidates have been proposed. Editors since the eighteenth century have identified the figures as Christian, Duke of Brunswick (d. 1626) and Count Ernest of Mansfield (d. 1626), 'brothers' in arms on the Protestant side in the Thirty Years War; but Bush (*Variorum*, i. 67–8) raises serious objections and proposes as a more likely pair James I, who died in Mar. 1625, and his almost exact contemporary Maurice, Prince of Orange, who died a month later.

l. 12. *Belgia.* The Netherlands.

l. 16. *Tartarean Jove.* Pluto, ruler of the underworld.

l. 20. *Cypris.* Venus.

l. 26. *Proteus.* The metamorphic god was the herdsman of Neptune's seals.

97 l. 32. *Hesperus.* The evening star.

l. 33. *western wave.* Atlantic Ocean; *Tartessiaco*, in the Latin, alludes to the ancient Spanish city Tartessus.

l. 41. *Iris.* The rainbow.

l. 44. *Chloris.* Or Flora, goddess of flowers; for her wooing by Zephyrus, the west wind, see Ovid, *Fasti*, v. 195–378, and Ben Jonson's masque *Chloridia.*   *garden of Alcinous.* A mythical paradise; see *Od.*, vi. 292 ff. and *PL*, v. 341, ix. 441.

97 l. 46. *Tagus*. River in Spain celebrated for its golden sand.

l. 47. *Favonius*. Zephyrus, the west wind.

l. 50. *Lucifer*. Lit. 'light-bearer'; here either the sun or the morning star.

l. 54. *face . . . light*. Like that of Moses (see Exod. 34: 29–35). The description that follows owes much to Rev. 14.

l. 67. *mistress of Cephalus*. Aurora, the Dawn, carried off by Cephalus.

l. 68. *dreams . . . return*. Paraphrasing Ovid, *Amores*, i. v. 26, wishing for the return of a day like the one spent with Corinna.

99 *Elegy 4. To His Tutor, Thomas Young*. Thomas Young (*c.*1587–1655), a Scottish schoolmaster and clergyman, had been Milton's boyhood tutor from 1618 to 20; in 1622 he moved to Hamburg, as chaplain to the community of English merchants there, and in 1628 returned to a church living in Stowmarket, in Suffolk. In the early 1640s Young was one of the Presbyterians calling themselves Smectymnuus with whom Milton allied himself, though after this time he and Milton were increasingly on opposing sides. The poem probably dates from 1627.

l. 7. *Doris*. Wife of Nereus and mother of the sea nymphs, the Nereids.

l. 10. *Medea*. After killing their children, Medea fled from Jason in a chariot drawn by dragons.

l. 11. *Triptolemus*. Sent by Demeter from Eleusis to sow the earth with seed; like Medea, he rode in a chariot drawn by dragons.

l. 15. *Hama*. A mythical Saxon champion killed by a Danish ('Cimbrian', l. 16) giant.

ll. 19–20. *half my soul*. As Horace refers to Virgil, *Odes*, i. iii. 8.

ll. 23–4. *Alcibiades . . . Telamon*. Alcibiades claimed descent from Telamon, the father of Ajax.

ll. 25–6. *Stagirite . . . pupil*. Aristotle (from his birthplace at Stagira) and Alexander, whose mother Olympias came from Chaonia, and was said to have conceived him after Jove made love to her.

l. 27. *son of Amyntor . . . son of Philyra*. Phoenix and Chiron the centaur, teachers of Achilles ('king of the Myrmidons', l. 28).

l. 29. *Aonian shades*. The Muses' haunt near Mounts Helicon and Parnassus.

l. 31. *Pierian water*. Flowing by Mount Pierus, sacred to the muses, and source of poetic inspiration.   *Clio*. The muse of history.

l. 32. *Castalian wine*. The water of the Castalian spring near Mount Parnassus, also regarded as a source of inspiration. The three occasions on which he tasted it may refer to his three previous elegies.

ll. 33–6. *thrice . . . Ram*. A third springtime (the Ram, Aries) has arrived (two springs—twice Chloris—and two autumns—twice Auster—have passed) since he last saw Young. Milton seems to be alluding to a meeting with Young three years earlier; if so, this poem is the only evidence that Young visited England during his Hamburg years. But it is also possible that Milton's date is wrong, and the poem was written three years after Young left England in 1622.

101 l. 43. *Fathers.* The Church Fathers.

l. 51. *battles.* Of the Thirty Years War.

l. 55. *husband.* Odysseus, who took ten years to make his way home after the Trojan War.

l. 75. *Enyo.* Goddess of war in the *Iliad*; the Roman Bellona.

103 l. 78. *Odrysian.* Thracian; Thrace was considered Mars' homeland.

l. 80. *goddess of peace.* Eirene.

l. 81. *just virgin.* Astraea, the Golden Age goddess of justice, who abandoned the earth during the Iron Age.

l. 95. *Stygian.* Hellish.

l. 97. *Tishbite prophet.* Elijah, who fled from Ahab and his wife Jezebel (see 1 Kgs. 16: 31, 19: 1–4).

l. 102. *Cilician Paul.* St Paul, from Tarsus in Cilicia; the 'Emathian city' is Philippi in Macedonia, where Paul was tortured and imprisoned (see Acts 16: 22–40).

l. 103. *Gergessa.* A town in Galilee (see Matt. 8: 28–34).

l. 114. *citadel of Zion.* Jerusalem, when attacked by Sennacherib (see 2 Kgs. 19: 35–6). The description of the Syrian assault on Samaria that follows is based on 2 Kgs. 7: 6–7.

105 *Elegy 5. On the Approach of Spring.* Date: spring 1629.

ll. 9–10. *Castalian . . . Pirene.* Springs associated with the muses and poetic inspiration.

l. 13. *Phoebus . . . Daphne.* Apollo ('*Delius*', from his birthplace Delos) and the nymph ('*Peneide*', daughter of Peneus) who fled his advances and was transformed into the laurel (see *Met.*, i. 452–567).

107 l. 25. *Philomela.* The nightingale, into which Philomela was transformed after having been ravished by her brother-in-law Tereus (see *Met.*, vi. 424–674).

l. 31. *Tithonian.* From Tithonus, husband of Aurora, the dawn; his lands are in the east. The sun is moving north; it is the vernal equinox.

l. 35. *Boötes . . . wain.* Boötes drives the northern constellation, the Great Bear, '*Lycaonius*' because it is the metamorphosed nymph Callisto, daughter of Lycaon; the constellation is also the wain, or carriage ('*plaustrum*'), of Charles's Wain, its alternative name.

l. 40. *giants.* During the Iron Age, the giants threatened Olympus (see *Met.*, i. 151 ff.).

l. 46. *Cynthia.* Diana, goddess of the moon and the hunt, sister of Apollo, god of the sun (the 'light-bringer' Lucifer).

107 l. 51. *hunter*. Cephalus, her lover, whom she first saw on Mount Hymettus (l. 52); see *Met.*, vii. 700–13.

l. 60. *Paphian*. From Paphos, sacred to Venus.

l. 62. *Ops*. Wife of Saturn and goddess of fertility; she was depicted wearing a turreted headdress.

109 l. 65. *Sicanian goddess*. Proserpina, who was abducted at Enna in Sicily (= Sicania) by Pluto, god of the underworld ('the Taenarian god', l. 66; Taenarus was one of the entrances to hell).

l. 82. *cerulean mother*. Tethys, sea goddess (hence cerulean, or blue), mother of the rivers.

l. 83. *Tartessian waves*. The Western, or Atlantic ocean, after the ancient Spanish city Tartessus.

l. 91. *Semele*. Destroyed by Zeus when he made love to her in his full glory and she was consumed by fire (see *Met.*, iii. 252–315).

l. 92. *Phaethon*. Son of Apollo, he burned to death when he attempted to drive the chariot of the sun (see *Met.*, ii. 19–328).

ll. 103–4. *Venus . . . sea*. Venus was born of sea foam.

111 ll. 105–6. *Hymenaee . . . Hymen*. Refrain of an epithalamion in praise of the god of marriage, Hymen.

l. 112. *Cytherea*. Venus.

l. 114. *Phyllis*. A generic name in pastoral for a shepherdess-lover.

l. 116. *dolphins*. Susceptible to music, as demonstrated in the story of Arion, who saved himself from drowning by charming them with his songs (Ovid, *Fasti*, ii. 83 ff.).

l. 121. *Silvanus*. God of the fields and forests, he wears the cypress in token of his lover Cyparissus, who died of grief after Silvanus killed his pet deer and was transformed into the cypress tree. The story is recounted by Servius in his gloss on Virgil, *Georgics*, i. 20; in Ovid's version, *Met.*, x. 106 ff., Sylvanus is not involved.

l. 125. *Maenalian Pan*. Pan is named after Maenalus, the Arcadian mountain he frequented.

l. 126. *Cybele and Ceres*. Both figures of mother earth.

l. 127. *Faunus . . . oread*. Faunus is, like Sylvanus and Pan, a wood god; an oread is a mountain nymph.

l. 136. *armoury*. The clouds are an armoury because Jove unleashes his thunderbolts from them.

113 *Elegy 6. To Charles Diodati, Staying in the Country*. As the prefatory note indicates, sent to Diodati soon after Christmas 1629, in response to a letter from him; Milton also announces the composition of the 'Nativity Ode'.

l. 8. *halting feet*. Because of the alternating hexameters and pentameters of the elegiac verse form.

113 l. 17. *Euoe.* Cry of Bacchic celebrants.

l. 19. *Naso.* Ovid in exile at Tomis on the Black Sea; the Coralli were a local tribe.

l. 22. *Teian bard.* Anacreon, born in Teos.

l. 23. *Teumesian Euan.* Boeotian Bacchus.

l. 26. *Elean.* After Elis, where the Olympic games, celebrated by Pindar, were held.

l. 27. *Roman lyrist.* Horace. Glycere and Chloe are women who figure in his lyrics (see e.g., *Odes*, i. 19 and 23).

l. 31. *Massic.* After Mount Massica, a wine producing region in Campania.

115 l. 37. *Thracian.* After Orpheus' homeland.

l. 43. *ivory keys.* Of a keyboard instrument like the harpischord or virginal, although the plectrum used to stroke the lyre could also be meant.

l. 48. *Thalia.* Muse of comedy and lyric poetry.

l. 51. *Erato.* Muse of love poetry.

l. 52. *Love.* Cupid.

l. 58. *dog.* Cerberus, watchdog of hell.

l. 59. *Samian master.* Pythagoras, ascetic philosopher born in Samos.

l. 65. *cleansing waters.* Holy water used in ancient purificatory rites.

l. 68. *Tiresias.* The soothsayer of Thebes, blinded for revealing the secrets of the gods.   *Linus.* A mythical bard of Thebes (Ogygia), teacher of Orpheus and Hercules.

l. 69. *Calchas.* The Greek prophet of the Trojan War.

l. 73. *Perseian Circe's.* Circe was the daughter of Phoebus and Perseis. Episodes from Books x–xii of the *Odyssey* are recalled.

117 *Elegy 7.* Although placed last in both 1645 and 1673, this seems to have been written before Elegy 6. The dating provided by Milton is ambiguous; *'Anno aetatis undevigesimo'* may mean either 'in the nineteenth year of his age' (i.e. at the age of 18), or 'at the age of 19'—Milton nowhere else uses an ordinal numeral for his age. The date of the poem would thus be either 1627 or 1628; Elegy 6 dates from 1629. Parker believes, however, that *'undevigesimo'* is a misreading of Milton's manuscript *'uno&vigesimo'*, twenty-one.

l. 1. *Amathusia.* Venus, after her shrine at Amathus on Cyprus.

l. 2. *Paphian.* Of Venus (from her temple at Paphos, on Cyprus).

l. 11. *Cyprian boy.* Cupid, so called from his mother Venus' association with Cyprus, but the epithet is not used by classical authors.

119 l. 21. *Sigeian youth.* The Trojan (= Sigeian) Ganymede, whom Jove loved and made his cupbearer (see *Met.*, x. 155–161).

l. 24. *Hylas.* Drowned in a pool by an amorous water nymph; see Theocritus, xiii.

119 l. 32. *Phoebus.* His killing of the monstrous python that had persecuted his mother Latona is recounted in Ovid, *Met.*, i. 438; his unsuccessful pursuit of Daphne is in *Met.*, i. 452–567.

l. 36. *Parthian horseman.* Famous for their tactic of firing while pretending to retreat; see *PR*, iii. 322.

l. 37. *Cydonian.* Cretan; the Cretans were famous archers.

l. 38. *wife's death.* Cephalus, while hunting, mistook his wife Procris for an animal rustling the trees (see *Met.*, vii. 835–62).

l. 39. *Orion.* A giant; his erotic adventures are recounted in Apollodorus, *Bibliotheca*, I. iv. 3–5; he was killed by Diana for attempting to rape one of her handmaids.

l. 40. *Heracles.* Notorious for his sexual prowess, as well as for his subjection to Queen Omphale, for whose love he wore women's clothes and performed her household tasks.   *Heracles' friend.* The reference is not specific and could apply to numerous figures, e.g. Hylas (see above, l. 24), or Theseus, the faithless lover of Ariadne.

l. 46. *serpent.* Aesculapius, the son of Apollo, who took the form of a serpent when he saved Rome from a plague (*Met.*, xv. 626 ff.).

l. 47. *gold-pointed arrow.* Cupid was said to have gold-tipped arrows to cause love, lead-tipped ones to cause hate (see *Met.*, i. 468–71).

121 l. 64. *queen.* Juno.

l. 81. *Juno's son.* Vulcan (or Hephaistos), cast out of heaven by Jove (see *Il.*, i. 590–3 and *PL*, i. 740–5).

l. 84. *Amphiaraus.* Greek prince and seer, forced by the Athenians to join in the war of the Seven against Thebes, and saved from disgrace by Zeus, who caused the earth to open and receive him.

123 *Epilogue to the Elegies ('Haec ego mente . . .').* Appended to Elegy 7 in 1645 and 1673; apparently intended as an epilogue to the whole series.

l. 5. *Academy . . . streams.* i.e. 'I studied Platonic philosophy'.

l. 10. *Diomedean strength.* When Aphrodite went to the aid of her son Aeneas in battle, she was wounded by Diomedes; see *Il.*, v. 334–417.

125 *On the Fifth of November.* 5 November is Guy Fawkes Day, the anniversary of the Gunpowder Plot. The poem was probably composed for Cambridge festivities in 1626.

l. 2. *Troy-sprung people.* According to the myth recorded in Geoffrey of Monmouth, the English were descended from Brutus, grandson of Aeneas (in the Latin; 'Teucrigenas' = Trojan, from Teucer, founder of Troy).

l. 3. *kingdom of Albion.* Albion was a legendary early ruler of Britain, the son (or in some versions, the descendant) of Neptune (see below); as far back as Aristotle, the name was used for Britain.

l. 7. *fierce tyrant.* Satan, depicted as Pluto, ruler of the underworld. *Acheron.* One of the rivers of Hades.

125 l. 12. *mid-air.* Traditional locale of demons; see *PL*, i. 39.

l. 23. *Summanus.* A nocturnal deity associated with lightning, often conflated with Pluto.

l. 25. *cliffs.* Of Dover, on the English Channel, the usual place of arrival for travellers from the continent.

l. 28. *Amphitryon's fierce son.* Hercules; Jove was his father, but his mother, Alcmena, was married to Amphitryon, and he is often called Amphitryonides in classical literature. For his fight with Albion, see *FQ*, IV. x. 11.

l. 32. *Ceres.* Goddess of agriculture.

127 l. 37. *Typhoeus.* One of the giants defeated in the rebellion against the Olympian gods; see *Met.*, v. 346–8 for the burial of Typhoeus beneath Sicily (= 'Trinacrian Etna').

l. 49. *Ausonia.* Italy.

l. 52. *Thetis.* The sea goddess, used for the sea into which the Tiber empties.

l. 53. *Quirinus.* Romulus; Satan enters Rome while the pope (the 'wearer of the triple crown', l. 55) celebrates St Peter's day (28 June 1605).

l. 56. *gods made of bread.* The Eucharist, which, according to Roman Catholics, is the body of Christ.

l. 60. *Cimmerian.* Cimmeria was a land of perpetual darkness visited by Odysseus (*Od.*, xi. 13–22).

l. 65. *Boeotian Aracynthus.* The Theban mount Aracynthus.

l. 66. *Asopus.* A river in the same region, personified as the river god.

l. 67. *Cithaeron.* A range of mountains dividing Boeotia from Attica, site of Bacchic rituals.

l. 69. *Erebus.* Husband and brother of Night; the traditional names for the horses of Night follow.

l. 74. *subduer of kings.* The pope.

129 l. 79. *false shape.* Satan appears disguised as a Franciscan.

l. 92. *Are you asleep* . . . Cf. *PL*, v. 674.

l. 97. *Roman emperor.* The Holy Roman Emperor.

l. 101. *apostolic keys.* The ecclesiastical authority derived from Christ's giving Peter the keys to the kingdom of heaven (Matt. 16: 19).

l. 102. *Hesperian fleet.* The Spanish Armada, defeated in 1588; Hesperian = western, but Horace uses Hesperia specifically for Spain, *Odes*, i. xxxvi. 4.

l. 105. *Thermodontean virgin.* Elizabeth I as an Amazon (after the river Thermodon, in Pontus, said to be the home of the Amazons); the allusion is to the persecution of Catholics in England under Elizabeth.

l. 108. *Tyrrhenian sea.* The Mediterranean west of Italy.

l. 109. *Aventine hill.* The southernmost of the seven hills of Rome.

131 l. 117. *dignitaries . . . peers.* Members of the Houses of Commons and Lords respectively.

l. 118. *sages . . . state.* Bishops (who sat in the House of Lords) and Privy Councillors.

l. 126. *Gaul . . . Iberian.* French, Spanish.

l. 127. *Marian.* Punning on the reign of both the Catholic Mary Tudor and Marius, the Roman tyrant.

l. 130. *festivals.* The calendar of saints.

l. 133. *porter.* The pope, as holder of the keys of heaven.

l. 137. *rosy Dawn.* Aurora; the Ethiopian Memnon was her 'swarthy offspring' (l. 135).

l. 139. *a place.* Milton amalgamates personifications from classical poetry to populate this cave of night; cf., e.g., Hesiod, *Theogeny*, 225–30, Virgil, *Aen.*, vi. 274–81.

l. 156. *priest of Babylon.* The pope, associated with the Babylon of Rev. 14: 8, 17: 5.

133 l. 168. *smiles.* Cf. Ps. 2:4 and *PL*, ii. 731, v. 736–7.

l. 170. *a place.* As in Chaucer's *Hous of Fame*, 715, or Ovid, *Met.*, xii. 39–42, the tower of Fame (= Rumour) is located in an unspecified middle position.

l. 171. *Mareotis.* A lake in Egypt, here standing for Africa.

l. 174. *Athos . . . Ossa.* Mountains deployed by the giants in their attack on the gods.

l. 181. *mother.* Terra, mother earth, who gave birth to Fame to avenge the defeat of the giants, her sons.

l. 185. *Argus.* The hundred-eyed watchman set by Juno to guard Jove's mistress Io, whom she had transformed into a heifer. Io, who fled to Egypt, was identified with the Egyptian goddess Isis, represented as a woman with the horns of a cow; see *Met.*, i. 568–746.

135 l. 204. *Thunderer.* Jove.

l. 207. *Temesan.* From Temesa, in Italy, a city famous for its copper mines.

To my Father. Arguments dating this poem as early as 1631 or as late as 1645 have been made; most commentators prefer a date in the mid 1630s.

l. 1. *Pierian fountains.* The spring associated with the muses and poetic inspiration.

l. 3. *twin peaks.* Of Mount Parnassus, beside which flows the Castalian spring, similarly sacred to the muses.

137 l. 14. *Clio.* The muse of history, the chief muse.

l. 32. *crowned with gold.* As prophesied in Rev. 4: 4, 14: 2.

137 l. 35. *the fiery spirit.* Unspecified, perhaps an angel, perhaps Milton's own disembodied spirit.

l. 38. *serpent.* The constellation; the time of year, as indicated by the constellations, is springtime.

l. 40. *Maurusian.* Mauretanian (or Moroccan), from the location of Mount Atlas.   *burden . . . stars.* Atlas was said to carry the heavens on his shoulders.

l. 41. *Poems were wont.* Recalling bardic performances, as in *Od.*, viii. 62 ff., *Aen.*, i. 740–6, *Eclogues*, vi. 31–40.

l. 48. *creeping gods.* Gods in their infancy, or in animal form.   *acorns.* Primitive food.

l. 49. *thunderbolt . . . Aetna.* Forged by Vulcan for Jove; his smithy was in Mount Etna in Sicily.

139 l. 60. *Arion.* The musician whose songs so charmed the dolphins that they rescued him from drowning. Milton's father was a composer.

l. 64. *Phoebus.* Apollo, god of music and poetry.

l. 71. *bar.* Milton's younger brother Christopher became a lawyer.

l. 75. *Aonian stream.* The Castalian spring (in Aonia), i.e., the springs of classical learning; the removal is presumably to study at Cambridge (which would date the poem before 1632 to 1635), although the family house at Hammersmith (where Milton lived from 1632 to 1635) or at Horton (his residence from 1635–8) are also possible.

ll. 83–4. *Italian . . . tumults.* i.e. because of the barbarian invasions, Latin decayed into Italian.

l. 85. *prophet . . . utters.* Old Testament Hebrew.

l. 90. *science.* Natural philosophy, conceived as part of the equipment of the poet as master of all knowledge.

141 l. 94. *Austria . . . Peruvian realms.* The wealth of the Holy Roman Empire, coupled with the gold Spain was bringing back from Peru.

l. 98. *young son.* Phaeton, son of Apollo; he burned to death when he attempted to drive the chariot of the sun (see *Met.*, ii. 19–328).

l. 118. *Orcus.* Hades.

To Salzilli. Giovanni Salzilli was friendly with Milton in Rome. He wrote a quatrain praising Milton above Homer, Virgil, and Tasso that was printed among the commendatory verses in the 1645 poems. Milton's poem responds to it and was probably written during his first Roman visit in 1638.

Scazons. See l. 1.

l. 1. *halting pace.* Of the scazontic metre, which requires a final spondee or trochee, rather than an iamb.   *gait of Vulcan.* Vulcan was lame after his fall from heaven.

141 l. 4. *Deiopea.* A nymph whom Juno promised to the wind god Aeolus in exchange for a storm to harass the Trojan fleet (*Aen.*, i. 65–75).

143 l. 11. *worst of the winds.* Aquilo, the north wind; Milton often comments on the English climate and its harmful effects on the writing of poetry.

l. 19. *bile.* The humour responsible for melancholy.

l. 22. *Lesbian strain.* Lyrics modelled on those of the poets of Lesbos, Sappho and Alcaeus.

l. 23. *Health.* The Roman goddess Salus.   *Hebe.* Goddess of youth.

l. 25. *Paean.* A name for Apollo as god of healing; Salzilli is his priest because Apollo is also the god of poetry. For his killing of the python, see Elegy 7, l. 32.

l. 28. *Evander.* Mythical founder of an ancient Italian kingdom and of the city of Pallanteum on the Tiber. See *Aen.*, viii. 51–584.

l. 34. *Numa.* Legendary king of Rome, married to the nymph Egeria (l. 35).

l. 36. *Tiber.* The river of Rome.

l. 41. *Portumnus.* Or Portunus, Roman god of harbours; here, the mouth of the Tiber.

Manso. Milton's headnote supplies most of the information about the occasion of this poem, composed before he left Naples in 1638. Giovanni Battista Manso (*c.*1560–*c.*1645) wrote a life of Tasso and was a generous patron of the arts; he is mentioned in Milton's *Second Defence* (see below, p. 322). He wrote a complimentary couplet for the prefatory material to Milton's 1645 volume.

145 l. 1. *These verses too.* Milton's is one of many verse tributes to Manso.

l. 2. *Pierides.* The muses, born on Mount Pierus; they are 'Phoebus' choir'.

l. 4. *Gallus.* Poet and friend celebrated in Virgil's *Eclogues*, x.   *Maecenas.* Roman patron of Virgil, Horace, and other poets.

l. 9. *Marino.* the poet Giambattista Marino (1569–1625).

l. 11. *at great length.* L'*Adone* (1623) is a poem of some 6000 lines about Venus and Adonis.

l. 12. *Ausonian.* Italian.

l. 16. *wrought bronze.* His monument in Naples; it is assumed from Milton's lines that Manso and his fellow members of the Academy of Humoristi were charged with the burial and commemoration of Marino, including the composition of a life of Marino, which has not survived.

l. 18. *Orcus.* The underworld.

l. 22. *the eloquent one.* Herodotus; he is no longer considered the author of the *Life of Homer.*   *Mycale.* A promontory in Ionia north of Halicarnassus, Herodotus' birthplace.

l. 24. *Clio.* Muse of history.

145 l. 26. *Hyperborean.* Northern; various northern constellations are named in the lines following.

147 l. 34. *Tityrus.* Chaucer; the name, from Virgil's *Eclogues*, had been given him by Spenser in *The Shepheardes Calender*. He visited Italy in 1372 and 1378.

l. 41. *Druids.* Compare *Lycidas*, l. 53.

l. 46. *they.* The Druids, identified with the Hyperborean nymphs named by Herodotus and Callimachus (Loxo, Upis, Hecaerge, below) as worshippers of Apollo at Delos.

l. 49. *fortunate old man.* Echoing Virgil, *Eclogues*, i. 46.

l. 55. *Cynthius.* Apollo (from Mount Cynthus on Delos, his birthplace).

l. 57. *Pheretiades.* Admetus, son of Pheres, whom Zeus condemned Apollo to serve as his herdsman in punishment for killing the Cyclops.

l. 58. *Alcides.* Hercules, who rescued Admetus' wife, Alcestis, after she died in his stead—this occurred, however, after Apollo's servitude; Milton's lines suggest an earlier occasion.

l. 60. *Chiron.* Tutor of Achilles and Aesculapius, the son of Apollo. No source for Milton's story of Apollo's visit to his cave has been identified.

149 l. 72. *grandson.* Hermes.

l. 75. *Aesonian spindles.* Medea restored Aeson to youth, cheating the Fates (upon whose spindles the threads of human life are woven and cut).

l. 76. *honours . . . unshed.* i.e. Manso has not lost his hair. It is clear from contemporary evidence, however, that Manso was bald and wore a wig. Milton may, of course, have been deceived, but Manso was apparently not shy about the matter, and Milton's allusion to it may be a private joke.

l. 81. *Arthur . . . earth.* Tradition held that Arthur had never died and was waiting underground to return to rule Britain.

l. 84. *I . . . war.* Arthur was celebrated by Geoffrey of Monmouth as the defender of England against Saxon invaders.

l. 92. *Paphian . . . laurel.* Attributes respectively of Venus and Apollo.

Damon's Epitaph. While in Italy, Milton learned of the death of his closest friend, Charles Diodati, in August 1638; this elegy was written upon his return to England in 1639 or 1640, and published privately shortly thereafter. As with *Lycidas*, the conventions of pastoral elegy are followed. Thyrsis, the name Milton chooses for himself, he had also used for the Attendant Spirit in *Comus*; Damon, besides being a common pastoral name, may suggest the pair of archetypal friends, Damon and Pythias.

151 l. 1. *Himera.* A river in Sicily; the nymphs are muses of Greek pastoral verse such as Theocritus' first *Idyll*, the lament of Thyrsis for the death of Daphnis.   *Hylas.* A youth drowned by an amorous nymph; see Elegy 7, l. 24.

151 l. 2. *Bion.* Author of the *Lament for Adonis*, and mourned by Moschus in the *Lament for Bion*, the model for a pastoral elegy on the death of a fellow poet.

l. 9. *Twice.* Two autumns had passed since the death of Diodati.

l. 13. *Tuscan city.* Florence.

l. 18. *Go home* . . . The use of the refrain is modelled on Theocritus, *Idyll* I, while the text derives from Virgil, *Eclogues*, vii. 44.

l. 23. *him . . . souls.* Hermes in his role as psychopomp, conductor of the souls of the dead to Hades.

l. 27. *wolf . . . me.* A superstition dating from before the time of Plato held that anyone who was seen by a wolf before he saw it would be struck dumb; see Virgil, *Eclogues*, ix. 53–4.

l. 32. *Pales.* Goddess of shepherds and cattle.   *Faunus.* A woodland and field deity sometimes identified with Pan.

l. 34. *Palladian arts.* Arts of Athena as goddess of wisdom and learning; Diodati had been a student at Oxford and Geneva.

153 l. 56. *Cecropian wit.* Attic wit, famous for its sharpness (from Cecrops, first king of Athens).

l. 69. *Tityrus.* The first of a series of conventional pastoral names for the mourners of Damon.

155 l. 90. *Idumanian river.* The Chelmer in Essex (called Idumanius in Ptolemy's *Geography*), the only specific locale in the poem; its significance is unclear.

l. 117. *Tityrus . . . it.* In *Eclogues*, i, Tityrus goes to Rome and sees Augustus.

157 l. 128. *Lucca.* From which the Diodatis originally came.

l. 129. *Arno.* The river of Florence.

l. 134. *gifts.* Milton had recited his poems to his Italian hosts, and received books and manuscripts of theirs in return.

l. 138. *Dati and Francini.* Carlo Dati and Antonio Francini, Florentine friends of Milton's, both of whom wrote dedicatory poems for his 1645 volume; they are 'of Lydian blood' because Tuscany was thought to have been settled by Lydian Greeks.

l. 149. *Colne.* A river near Horton.   *Cassivellanus.* Ancient British chieftain whose territory included Horton.

l. 155. *grandly sounding.* In an epic (rather than pastoral) strain, to which he had turned eleven days before, and whose subject matter he describes in the following section of the poem.

159 l. 162. *Dardanian . . . Rutupian Sea.* His subject is the arrival of the Trojans in the straits of Dover (Rutupiae, according to Camden, was Richborough in Kent). The names that follow derive from Geoffrey of Monmouth and later redactions of early English history, such as Spenser's in *FQ*, ii. 10.

159 l. 175. *Ouse.* The first in a list of English rivers. Cf. *FQ*, iv. 11.

l. 180. *bark . . . laurel.* The bark is being used as a writing surface, as in Virgil, *Eclogues*, v. 13–14.

l. 181. *cups.* In pastorals, singing contests often end with the gift of inscribed goblets; here they would appear to stand for writings Milton had received from Manso, as the baskets of l. 135 were the literary tributes of his Florentine friends.

l. 183. *Chalcidian.* Neapolitan.

l. 187. *phoenix.* A legendary bird said to exist only one at a time and at its death to immolate itself and be reborn from its ashes.

161 l. 208. *whatever . . . name.* Either Damon, or Diodati, upon which Milton puns below; gods were invoked 'by whatever name you wish to be called'.

l. 214. *virgin's honours.* As described in Rev. 14: 1–4, a passage recalled in the *Apology* (p. 182). The following lines also depend on Rev. 7: 9–10, 19: 6–8; Cf. *Lycidas*, ll. 176–81.

l. 219. *thyrsus.* The vine-leaved staff of Bacchic celebrants.

GREEK POEM ADDED IN 1673

162 *On the Engraver of his Portrait.* This poem appeared engraved beneath Milton's portrait on the 1645 frontispiece; in 1673 it was printed as the third of the Greek poems. The engraver was the prolific and very successful William Marshall, who did not read Greek. Various syntactical and prosodic problems have been noted and debated, and adjudicated by Bush in the *Variorum*, and have been scrutinized by John K. Hale in 'Milton's Greek, 1644–45: Two Notes', *Milton Quarterly*, 34/1 (2000), 13–16.

l. 4. *of a wretched artist.* i.e. both of (Marshall, not Milton) and by him.

UNCOLLECTED LATIN POEM

163 *Elegiac Verses.* From a sheet found in Milton's Commonplace Book first published in 1876, probably an exercise written during Milton's last years at St Paul's, when he was 15 or 16.

l. 5. *Titan.* The sun.

l. 7. *Daulian bird.* The nightingale: the story of Tereus, Procne, and Philomela is set in Daulis in Greece (*Met.*, vi. 668–74; *Heroides*, xv. 154).

l. 11. *wife.* Chloris, or Flora, goddess of flowers.

PROSE WORKS

165 *The Reason of Church Government.* Milton's 1642 tract argues that the only valid form of church government is Presbyterianism. It includes, as a preface to its second book, this autobiographical section designed both to establish Milton's moral and scholarly credentials and to disarm criticism. Milton's first signed published work, *RCG* is the longest of his anti-prelatical tracts. Its rhetorical strategies have been analysed acutely by S. Fish in *Self-Consuming Artifacts.*

withal. At the same time.

wanted. Lacked.

165 *even . . . gifts.* Cf. Sonnets 7 and 19 and the parable of the talents (Matt. 25: 14–30).

orient. Brilliant, like a pearl of the orient.

put off. Sell

merchants. Anglican prelates are included in this metaphor.

166 *factory.* Trading establishment.

variance. Enmity, disagreement.

Jeremiah. 15: 10, in which the prophet laments his role as the voice of divine wrath.

Revelation. 10: 8–10; the book is 'bitter' in the belly but 'sweet as honey' on the tongue; the passage derives from Ezek. 3: 1–3 and also figures in Dante, *Paradiso*, xvii. 130–2.

electuary. A medicine mixed with honey or syrup.

Sophocles . . . men. Oedipus Rex, ll. 316 ff., 'Alas, how terrible is wisdom when / it brings no profit to the man that's wise' (tr. David Grene).

Jeremiah. Jer. 20: 7–10 is cited and summarized.

stomach. Anger, pride.

167 *talents.* Cf. Matt. 25: 14–30.

timorous and ungrateful. Referring to the speaker.

infancy. Speechlessness.

saints. The elect of God, members of the true (i.e. reformed) church.

168 *charter and freehold.* Property purchased and held by written contract; hence, an unchallenged right.

wayward. Untoward, opposed to the wishes of others.

preventive. Anticipatory and forestalling.

equal. Impartial.

exigent. State of pressing need.

curious. Elegant.

if . . . much. If there is enough time to make the argument substantial, little of the time will be devoted to art.

genial. Vital, naturally disposed.

fancies. Imagination. Cf. Sidney, *Defence of Poetry*, describing the poet 'lifted up with the vigour of his own invention . . . freely ranging only within the zodiac of his own wit' (ed. J. van Dorsten [Oxford 1973], p. 78).

empyreal conceit. Sublime ideas: the empyreum is the outermost sphere of the Ptolemaic universe; a conceit is a concept or thought.

169 *be envy to me.* Cause me to be envied.

169 *been . . . tongues.* Learned languages (Latin, Greek, French, Italian, and Hebrew according to 'Ad Patrem', ll. 79–85 (p. 139; Cf. the programme of studies in *Of Education*, above pp. 230 ff.).

sciences. Disciplines of knowledge.

suffer. Allow.

latelier. More recently (Milton travelled to Italy in 1638–9).

shifted . . . patch up. Lacking books or other materials, nevertheless contrived to put together; he is describing such poems as 'Manso' written while he was in Italy.

encomiums. Several of these laudatory tributes appeared in the 1645 volume of Milton's poems.

leases. Cf. 'charter and freehold' above, p. 168; leases were often written to be in force for the length of the longest-lived of three persons named on the lease.

Latins. Poets who write in Latin.

Ariosto . . . Bembo. In his 'Life of Ariosto' appended to his translation of *Orlando Furioso*, Sir John Harington writes of Pietro Bembo (1470–1547), the famous Petrarchan poet and language reformer, that 'when *Bembo* would have dissuaded [Ariosto] from writing Italian, alleging that he should winne more praise by writing Latine: his answer was, that he had rather be one of the principall & chiefe Tuscan writers, then scarce the second or third among the Latines.'

mechanics. Ignorant common people (lit. manual labourers).

170 *Time . . . now.* Now is not the time.

Tasso. The reference is to Torquato Tasso's Christian epic *Gerusalemma Liberata* (Jerusalem Freed).

Aristotle. In *Poetics*, xxvi, long and brief epics are mentioned; the 'rules' were the subject of Italian neo-classical critics who debated whether such works as Ariosto's *Orlando Furioso* were consistent with classical models and precepts.

a prince. Alfonso II of Ferrara supposedly chose the theme of the crusades in preference to the Roman general Belisarius's exploits or those of Charlemagne.

climate. Cf. *PL*, ix. 44 for similar worries about whether the English climate was hospitable to creativity.

constitutions. Compositions.

Origen. In *Canticum Canticorum Prologus* (*A Prologue to the Song of Songs*), cited by David Paraeus, a Reformation scholar to whom Milton is frequently indebted, as he indicates below.

end. Aim, intention.

civility. Citizenship.

171 *amiable.* Worthy of love.

171 *admiration.* That which causes awe or wonder.

refluxes. Backward motions.

solid . . . smoothness. Substantial and artistically polished manner.

delicious temper. Temperament pleased with things of the senses.

lively. In a way that is necessary to life.

such . . . since. In the *Book of Sports* (1633), Charles I declared sports, games, and dancing to be lawful on Sunday; for the broad cultural ramifications of the proclamation, see L. Marcus, *The Politics of Mirth* (Chicago, 1986).

Solomon. Prov. 1: 20–1.

paneguries. General assemblies of a festive and religious nature.

porches. Vestibules of churches or public buildings.

172 *abortive . . . discovery.* Premature revelation (alluding to the inner debate described above).

impertinent. Improper, inappropriate.

duncery. Sophistry.

trencher fury. Poetic inspiration (*furor*) arising from the prospect of a dinner (alluding to poets who write merely to satisfy their patrons).

hallowed fire of his altar. Cf. Isa. 6: 6–7 and 'On the morning of Christ's Nativity', l. 28.

club. Gather or collect, trade.

sumpters. Drivers of pack horses.

rhapsody. Disconnected mass of words.

secretary conscience. i.e. the conscience is the human faculty that conveys God's commands to man.

173 *An Apology for Smectymnuus.* Early in 1641, Joseph Hall, Bishop of Norwich—he is known to literary students for his early collection of satires, *Virgidemiarum* (1597), his book of *Characters of the Vertues and Vices* (1608), and a utopian satire, *Mundus Alter et Idem* (1605)—defended the Anglican establishment in *Episcopacie by Divine Right.* Among those who answered his tract were a group of Presbyterian divines who signed themselves Smectymnuus, combining their initials (Stephen Marshall, Edmund Calamy, Thomas Young [Milton's boyhood tutor], Matthew Newcomen, William Spurstowe). Milton joined with them, writing a postscript to their reply, and followed it with a tract, *Animadversions Upon the Remonstrants Defence*, in reply to Hall's reply to the Smectymnuans. The *Apology* responds to the response provoked by *Animadversions*, an anonymous tract entitled *A Modest Confutation of a Slanderous and Scurrilous Libel.* Milton assumed its author to be Hall and/or one of his sons; this is probably correct, but the authorship has never been positively established. The last of Milton's anti-prelatical tracts, the 1642 *Apology* has often been excerpted for the autobiographical passage that we provide here, although its place in

the treatise as a whole is worth study. For an acute reading of the strategies of self-presentation in the *Apology*, see J. Guillory, *Poetic Authority*.

173 *neuter.* Neutral.

Solon. Athenian lawgiver of the sixth century BC who forbade neutrality in matters of public sedition.

174 *confuter.* The anonymous author of the *Modest Confutation*.

175 *those reverent men.* The Smectymnuans (see headnote).

his. Hall's.

author. Milton.

176 *magazine.* Storehouse.

book of characters. Collection of sketches of character types; these were popular in the period, and Hall's *Characters of the Vertues and Vices* (1608) was an early example.

conversation social relations.

envy. Disrepute.

God hath told us. See Luke 6: 26.

his promise. In the beatitudes, Matt. 5: 11–12.

'vomited out thence.' The *Modest Confutation* reads: 'It is like hee spent his youth, in loyterizing, bezelling, and harlotting. Thus being grown to an Impostume in the brest of the University, he was at length vomited out thence into a Suburbe sinke about London: which, since his coming up, hath groaned under two ills, Him, and the Plague.' It is not clear whether 'vomited out' is intended to refer to Milton's rustication or simply to his graduation.

commodious. Convenient, useful.

177 *propense.* Inclined.

if he think to obtain with me. i.e. Milton declines to enter into a debate about the merits of the university.

she or her sister. Cambridge or Oxford.

kecking. Retching.

sink. Cesspool, sewer.

'and . . . not'. 'Where his morning haunts are I wist not; but he that would finde him after dinner, must search the Play-Houses or the Bordelli, for there I have traced him' ('To the Reader').

limbec. Alchemist's distilling flask.

concocting. Digesting.

178 *protestation.* Of 3 May 1641, issued by the House of Commons, declaring their intention to maintain the Church of England 'against all Popery and Popish innovations' and affirming the 'rights and liberties of the subjects, and every person that maketh the protestation, in whatsoever he shall do in the lawful pursuance of the same'.

178 *unfaithful spy.* The spies that Moses sent returned 'and made all the congregation to murmur against him, by bringing up a slander upon the land' (Num. 14: 36).

gin. Trap, snare.

antistrophon. Retort.

liable to. Subject to.

Cephalus or Hylas. Cephalus was taken from his wife by Aurora (*Met.*, vii. 688–768); Hylas was ravished by Hercules (Theocritus, *Idylls*, xiii).

Viraginea. Along with *Aphrodisia* and *Desvergonia* below, countries in Hall's *Mundus Alter et Idem*; they are, respectively, the land of viragos, romance, and debauchery.

tire. Costume.

Trinculos. Perhaps the character in *The Tempest*, but more likely a clown in Thomas Tomkys' *Albumazar*, a 1614 Cambridge University play.

179 *atticism.* Well-turned phrase.

unlawful. It did, in fact, become unlawful in Sept. 1642 when Parliament closed the theatres.

ἀπειροκαλία. Ignorance of the beautiful, want of taste.

180 *numerous.* Metrical.

two famous renowners. Dante in the *Divine Comedy* and *Vita Nuova*, Petrarch in the *Rime Sparse*.

ought ... poem. Cf. Ben Jonson's prefatory epistle to *Volpone*, on 'the impossibility of any man's being the good poet without first being a good man'.

181 *dear.* Strenuous, difficult; costly.

Homer. As charged by Plato, *Republic*. 377e.

Xenophon. Author of *Memorabilia* of Socrates, and the *Cyropaedia*, exampled in Sidney's *Defence of Poetry* for its moral precepts.

sorceress. Perhaps Homer's Circe, or her various reincarnations in Ariosto, Tasso, and Spenser; cf. *Comus*.

Corinthian. A byword for profligacy and dissipation.

182 *'the body ... the body.'* Citing 1 Cor. 6: 13; see 1 Cor. 11: 7–11 for the ensuing discussion.

that place. Rev. 14: 1–5.

for ... defilement. Cf. 1 Cor. 7: 1–2.

The Doctrine and Discipline of Divorce. Appearing first in 1643 (the text we print here), and in a greatly expanded form a year later, *DDD* was followed by three other divorce tracts in the ensuing two years (*The Judgement of Martin Bucer, Concerning Divorce* [1644]; *Tetrachordon* [1645], *Colasterion*

(1645]). At the time Milton was writing these, Mary Powell, whom Milton had married in May or June 1642, had returned to her parents' home, where she remained until 1645. Many commentators have regarded this as evidence of an unsuccessful marriage, and as the determining element behind the divorce tracts. It certainly cannot be discounted. None the less, it is also true that these works address themselves to an important respect in which England was an anomaly among European Protestant nations. Whereas divorce on grounds of adultery or desertion was sanctioned on the continent, and was essentially a civil consideration (marriage is not a sacrament for Protestants, as it is for Roman Catholics), the Anglican Church retained control over the dissolution of marriages. Such factors as desertion or adultery might be allowed to dissolve a marriage, but they did not permit a grant of divorce; divorce was only possible if the marriage could be shown never to have taken place (e.g. if it was not consummated; if the partners were too closely related by blood; if a prior promise to marry had been violated). Annulments of this sort, however, were extremely difficult to obtain. Thus, in the early 1640s, Milton might well have considered the church's position regarding divorce as a prelatical abuse, and as a clear sign of the failure of reformation in England. Even as Milton wrote, the Westminster Assembly was meeting to discuss questions of reform in church government; the timeliness of the tracts was therefore not only personal. It might finally be noted that the task before Milton was formidable; he sought to base his argument for divorce on Scripture, yet the argument he wishes to make (which goes far beyond grounds of adultery and desertion) has little scriptural support. *DDD* is therefore important not only for Milton's views on the subject, but as an instance of his practice of reading Scripture, and is worth comparing with *CD* on that topic, as well as with *Areopagitica*.

182 *fond.* Foolish.

183 *lin.* Cease.

famous man. Jephthah, who vowed to sacrifice the first person to enter his house if he was granted victory in battle; his daughter was the victim (Judg. 11: 30–40), although it is unclear whether she was put to death or condemned to remain a virgin.

sabbath day. For the refusal of the Jews to fight on the sabbath, see e.g. 1 Macc. 2: 31–8.

Moses. Deut. 24: 1 permits divorce on the grounds of the wife's 'uncleanness'; in Matt. 5: 31–2, Jesus interprets the law to mean that divorce is permissible only in cases of adultery, claiming that a woman who remarries after a divorce granted on any other grounds commits adultery.

first ordaining of marriage. In Gen. 2: 18, by creating Eve as 'help meet' for Adam; Gen. 2: 24, 'therefore shall a man cleave unto his wife: and they shall be one flesh'. In Matt. 19: 4–11, Jesus interprets this text in relation to Mosaic law, reiterating statements like those in Matt. 5: 31–2.

conversation. Intimacy, cohabitation.

183 *be . . . handed.* Join hands in marriage.

tembers. Temperaments.

fadge. Fit.

wise man. Solomon, citing Eccles. 5: 13.

canon law. Church law which, although nominally dependent upon Parliament in England, effectively controlled questions of divorce (see headnote).

element. Letter.

184 *Tertullian.* Church Father (*c.*160–*c.*230) whose *Exhortation to Chastity* treats marriage as a form of concupiscence.

Jerome. St Jerome (*c.*340–420), who shared Tertullian's views about marriage.

sacramental. therefore indissoluble except by a special dispensation (virtually the case in England, despite the fact that marriage was not a sacrament).

Moses. See note to p. 183, above.

colourably. Plausibly.

Christian emperors. Who followed Roman law, which permitted divorce by consent or for improprieties.

Hugo Grotius. Dutch jurist, theologian, poet, and statesman (1585–1645), whose commentary on the gospel is alluded to here.

must now be constituted. By the Westminster Assembly, currently in session.

ingenuous. High-minded; open-minded.

apprehensive. Thoughtful.

185 *for that corporal deficiency.* i.e. divorce when a marriage had not been, or could not be consummated.

clue that winds out. Thread that leads us out of; alluding to Ariadne's stratagem for rescuing Theseus from the labyrinth of the Minotaur (see Ovid, *Met.*, viii).

conceit. Conceive.

words of Christ. Citing Matt. 11: 30.

law. Of the Old Testament.

out. Cf. the citation of Prov. 18: 13 on the 1644 *DDD* title-page: 'He that answereth a matter before he heareth it, it is folly and shame unto him.'

equal. Equitable.

exploded. Rejected (the opposite of applauded).

186 *overture.* Disclosure.

follow . . . pipe. Alluding to Matt. 11: 16–19 and Luke 7: 31–5, where Jesus declares that neither his 'piping' nor John the Baptist's asceticism has won followers.

186 *reclaims.* Continually cries out.

187 *generous.* Magnanimous.

   unclosing. Disharmonious.

   complexion. Temperament.

   reprobates. Those rejected by God.

   piece. Patch.

   stews. Brothels.

   preposterous. Putting secondary things first.

188 *quintessence . . . excrement.* Human semen, as the most exalted fluid voided by the body.

   complains him. Laments (inwardly).

   liturgy. Book of Common Prayer, citing the marriage ceremony.

   ingenuous. Honourable.

   influence. Influx.

   fountain. Source

189 *disworship.* Dishonour, disgrace.

   St Paul. Citing 1 Cor. 7: 9.

   sensitive. Sensual; pertaining to the senses.

   cattle. Rubbish (*OED*, citing this passage); but Milton also later quotes St Paul, 'Doth God care for asses and oxen . . .?' (see below, p. 197).

190 *concoction.* Diet, digestion.

   'many waters . . . drown it.' Citing S. of S. 8: 6–7.

   intelligible. Intellectual.

   provender burning. A desire like that of an animal for its food.

   Plato. In the *Symposium*, 203.

   sorts. Agrees.

   Moses tells us. Allegorizing Gen. 2: 18–24.

191 *phlegm.* The humour held responsible for sloth.

   mutin. Mutiny.

   Ecclesiastes. 9: 9.

192 *Malachi.* 2: 16. Milton depends on Calvin's explication (in *Praelectiones in Duodecim Prophetas Minores*), '*Si odio habeas*, quisquis odio habet, *dimittat uxorem, dicet Iehovah Deus Israel*' ('if he [whoever he be] hate her, let him put away his wife, says Jehovah, God of Israel'), which follows the Vulgate, and not the Authorized Version reading, 'For the Lord, the God of Israel, saith that he hateth putting away'; AV does record the Vulgate reading in its margin, 'if he hate her, put her away.'

   liberal. Free.

   divorced. To those who are in effect divorced.

   betimes than still. Immediately, than to continue.

192 *written.* e.g. Rom. 3: 10, 'Love worketh no ill to his neighbour: therefore love is the fulfilling of the law.'

in sorrow. Jewish law limits the priest's activity in acts of mourning; Milton extends priesthood to all believers. Cf. 1 Peter 2: 5, 'Ye also, as lively stones, are built up a spiritual house, an holy priesthood.'

lively sacrifice. Living sacrifice; cf. Rom. 12:1 and the order for Holy Communion in the Book of Common Prayer: 'this our sacrifice of prayse and thanksgiving . . . our selves, our soules, and bodies, to be a reasonable, holy, and lively Sacrifice unto thee.'

crosses. Trials, afflictions.

'to cover . . . any more'. Mal. 2: 13.

193 *'children of wrath'.* Eph. 2: 3, the unregenerate, 'fulfilling the desires of the flesh and of the mind.'

trained. Lured.

parallel. See e.g. Ezra 10: 1–3, where the Israelites put away their non-Israelite wives; cf. the discussion below.

disbanded. Dismissed, discharged.

194 *circumcision.* The circumcised; the Jews who had become Christians.

vision of St Peter. Acts 10: 9–16, 28, 'God hath shewed me that I should not call any man common or unclean.'

St Paul. 1 Cor. 7: 14.

2 Cor 6. Verse 14, continued six lines below.

Isaiah. Isa. 52: 11.

gospelized. Imparted according to the spirit of the gospels.

antagony. Antagonism.

195 *crotchet.* Perversity, peculiarity.

collections. Inferences.

'To the rest . . . Lord'. Citing 1 Cor. 7: 12.

outface. Deny.

'I speak . . . judgment'. Citing 1 Cor. 7: 6, 25.

Beza. Theodore Beza (d. 1605), biblical commentator who insisted that Paul's views merely reiterated Christ's attitudes towards marriage and adultery.

St Austin. St Augustine.

196 *12th verse.* 1 Cor. 7: 12, 'If any brother hath a wife that believeth not, and she be pleased to dwell with him let him not put her away.' Milton comments on the Greek verb translated as 'be pleased' in the Authorized Version, and which he translates below as 'join in consent'.

complacency. Pleasure, satisfaction.

place. Text.

196 *v. 24.* 1 Cor. 7: 24.

clean. Clear, pure.

197 *code and canon.* Both civil and religious laws.

sublunary. Elemental, material.

apostle's words. 1 Cor. 9: 8–10.

198 *noisomeness.* Offensiveness.

unkindly. Unnatural.

Numbers. Num. 30: 6–15.

if man be lord of the sabbath. As Jesus declared himself, working cures on the sabbath; e.g. Matt. 12: 8–13, Luke 6: 5–10, Mark 2: 27–28, 3: 1–5.

199 *assassinated.* Treacherously attacked or destroyed.

first table. First of the tablets of Moses, Exod. 20: 8, 'Remember the Sabbath day, to keep it holy.'

captivity. In Babylon.

text. Mal. 2: 16; see above p. 192.

200 *attested.* Called to witness.

astriction. Restriction.

St Peter. Citing Acts 15: 10.

201 *Anabaptism, Familism, Antinomianism.* Radical Protestant sects; the first was named for its practice of adult baptism; Familists (or the family of Love) shared the antinomian view that morality cannot be legislated.

physic. Medicine; the practice of bloodletting was similarly based on the idea of the necessity of voiding superfluous blood.

202 *inconcileable.* Irreconcilable.

alphabetical. Literal.

words of Christ. Matt. 5: 32, cited above.

convince. Confute.

place. Matt. 5: 28, 'whosoever looketh on a woman to lust after her hath committed adultery with her already in his heart.'

another time. In John 8: 3–11, when he refuses to condemn the woman taken in adultery.

as when . . . straightness. A metaphor also used by Aristotle, *Ethics*, ii. 9, defining moderation.

'one jot or tittle'. Matt. 5: 18, 'Till heaven and earth pass, one jot or one tittle shall in no wise pass from the law, till all be fulfilled.'

203 *convinced.* Convicted.

unequal. Inequitable.

decrees. As prescribed in Lev. 20: 10, Deut. 22: 22.

only. Single.

203 *Austrian.* Alluding to the Catholic Habsburg rulers of Austria and Spain.

204 *Psalm 94: 20.* 'Shall the throne of iniquity have fellowship with thee, which frameth mischief by a law?'

Mark 10: 5. 'For the hardness of your heart he wrote you this precept.'

equal. Equitable.

205 *'do this and live'.* Gen. 42: 18.

'All . . . saying'. Matt. 19: 11.

'Every man . . . gift'. 1 Cor. 7: 7.

to lay . . . bear. Acts 15: 10.

extravagance. Deviation.

admire. Wonder, be amazed.

helpless. That cannot be helped.

206 *Matt. 5.* Matt. 5: 31, 'It hath been said, Whosoever shall put away his wife, let him give her a writing of divorcement'.

chapter 19 and Mark 10. Matt. 19: 8, cited below, 'Moses because of the hardness of your hearts suffered you to put away your wives: but from the beginning it was not so'; Mark 10: 5 cited above, p. 204.

impression. Emphasis.

same chapter. Matt. 19: 16–22. Jesus tells the 'perfect' young man to sell all his possessions, and he balks.

screws him up. As in tightening the strings of a musical instrument.

opinionative. Opinionated.

command in Eden. Gen. 2: 24.

207 *'making . . . for him'.* Gen. 2: 18.

depress. Depreciate.

sudden. Swift, unpremeditated (as opposed to the deliberation behind God's ordinance for man).

at all adventures. At any risk.

individually. Indivisibly, inseparably.

'have ye . . . his wife'. Matt. 19: 4–5.

clog. Fetter.

208 *called least.* Matt. 5: 19, 'Whosoever therefore shall break one of these least commandments, and shall teach man so, he shall be called the least in the kingdom of God.'

209 *another Law.* Deut. 24: 4, which forbids a husband to receive back a wife who has been put away by her second husband, 'Her former husband, which sent her away, may not take her again to be his wife, after that she is defiled.'

Mal. 2: 16. Cited above, p. 192.

209 *intermixed.* i.e. involving more than one husband.

  wiped. Rubbed away.

  peculiar. Own.

  this. The law of divorce.

  But . . . allowed. Milton voices the objection that although divorce was allowed, it was not approved, and then proceeds to answer it, 'as if . . .'.

  individual. Indissoluble.

210 *cleared.* Made clear.

  accident. Event.

  fondly. Foolishly.

  Another . . . them. i.e. at another time, his opponents claim . . . .

  31st verse of Matt. 5. Cf. p. 206, above.

  civilizing. Making proper in a civil community.

  hands and seals. A bill of divorce required the signatures and/or seals of the husband and two witnesses.

  economical. Domestic.

  court-leet. Minor district court.

211 *overdated.* Temporally unlimited.

  advise. Consider.

  Perkins upon this chapter. The theologian William Perkins (d. 1602), in *A Godly and Learned Exposition* (*Works*, 1609–13, iii. 69).

212 *suffered.* Allowed.

  stews. Brothels.

  falter. Hobble.

  circumcised. Sanctioned.

  slubbering. Stained, soiled.

  Beza. See p. 195; Beza is the 'he' answered in the ensuing discussion.

  Rom. 13. Verse 1, 'For there is no power but of God: the powers that be are ordained of God.'

  papal stews. Roman brothels paid taxes, some of which went to the papacy.

213 *makes.* Works.

  he. Beza.

  asserted. Vindicated.

  'take . . . body'. Matt. 26: 26.

  elementally. Literally.

214 *unconvinced.* Unconfuted.

  amuses. Bewilders.

  one flesh. Gen. 2: 24, Matt. 19: 5–6.

214 *infers thus much over.* Implies this in addition.

Mezentius. Virgil, *Aen.*, viii. 485–8 thus describes the notoriously cruel practice of an ancient Etruscan king.

Christ himself. Matt. 19: 6, 'What therefore God hath joined together, let no man put asunder.'

215 *though . . . expositors.* Even if we concede the interpretation of the standard biblical commentaries.

uneasy. Difficult.

sentence . . . follows. Matt. 19: 9.

216 *the other.* The provisions in Gen. 2 reiterated in Matt. 19.

called . . . St. John. John 13: 34, 'A new commandment I give unto you, That ye love one another; as I have loved you, that ye also love one another.'

charity . . . perfection. Col. 3: 14.

halted. Fell short.

217 *1 Cor. 7: 10, 11.* 'And unto the married I command, yet not I, but the Lord, Let not the wife depart from her husband: But and if she depart, let her remain unmarried, or be reconciled to her husband, and let not the husband put away his wife.'

Grotius. as on p. 184, above, Milton relies on Grotius's *Annotationes in Libros Evangeliorum* (1641).

lying forth of. Passing the night away from.

Josephus. In the *Antiquities of the Jews*, v. 2.

Septuagint. Greek text of the Old Testament.

Chaldean. Old Testament paraphrase written in Chaldean (Aramaic).

two other rabbis. Levi ben Gerson and Rashi; along with Kimchi, standard Talmudic commentators.

to fetch her again. To take her back: the concubine, having returned to her father's house, is reclaimed by her Levite husband (Judg. 19: 1–10).

218 *sudden.* Immediate.

our Saviour's language. Matt. 5: 28 cited above, p. 202.

Numb. 5. Verses 11–31 detail these provisions.

tympany. Swelling (caused by the drink administered, and supposed to prove guilt).

verse. Num. 5: 31, 'Then shall the man be guiltless from iniquity, and this woman shall bear her iniquity.'

Ordalium. Trial by ordeal.

exasperated. Rendered more severe.

219 *St Paul.* 1 Cor. 7: 6; 1 Cor. 7: 15 is cited below.

accustoming. Intimacy.

219   *Christ himself.* Matt. 12: 8–12.

    speculative rest. Contemplative holiday.

    overcharged. Overburdened.

220   *he who.* Matt. 18: 12, 'if a man hath an hundred sheep, and one of them be gone astray, doth he not leave the ninety and nine, and goeth into the mountains, and seeketh that which is gone astray?'; cf. Luke 15: 4–5.

    obduring. Remaining obdurate.

    endeavour. Try to fulfill.

    Eph. 4: 14, 15. 'We henceforth be no more children . . . carried about with every wind of doctrine . . . But speaking the truth in love, may grow up into him in all things, which is the head, even Christ.'

    loadstar. Guiding star.

    Gordian. Alluding to the complex knot that Alexander the Great declined to untie, but cut; cf. 'decided' (determined, cut off) below.

    revolve. Consider.

    boisterous. Unyielding.

221   *colour.* Pretext.

    Perkins . . . notes. The reference is to Perkins's *Christian Oeconomie* (*Works*, iii. 672); see above, p. 211.

    'Lead . . . temptation'. Matt. 6: 13, from the Lord's Prayer.

    bolt overshot. Door bolt that no longer works.

    supportless. Insupportable.

    mystery. Business, as well as secret purpose.

    crosses. Afflictions; also, coins.

    equal. Equitable.

222   *our incident extremities.* The difficulties to which we are liable.

    panic. Groundless fear (as aroused by Pan).

    resistless. Irresistible.

223   *Harry VIII.* The annulment was granted in July 1540 on the grounds that the king's 'misliking' had resulted in his inability to consummate the marriage.

    head. Cf. 1 Cor. 11: 3, 'the head of the woman is the man'.

    hired masters of tongue-fence. Lawyers with their rhetorical ploys; cf. 'fee'd gamester', below.

    his brother's wife. Catherine of Aragon, widow of Henry's elder brother Prince Arthur. Cardinals Campeggio and Wolsey presided over the trial in which Henry pleaded that the papal dispensation that had permitted his marriage was invalid because, despite the queen's denials, her previous marriage had in fact been consummated; a chamberlain was called as witness to report Prince Arthur's words to that effect the morning after the wedding night.

223 *familiary.* Domestic.

appeached. Impeached.

utterless. Unutterable, unspeakable.

Paulus Emilius. Third-century Roman consul; the incident is recorded in Plutarch's biography.

fee'd gamester. Sharp lawyer (one of the 'hired masters of tongue-fence' immediately above).

224 *available.* Of advantage.

Malachi. Mal. 2: 14–16.

225 *Ecclesiastes.* Eccles. 7: 16.

atoms. Particles of dust, motes in a sunbeam.

whom . . . years. Luke 13: 16; Jesus describing the woman he healed on the Sabbath.

reduce. Lead back, restore.

226 *'I will . . . sacrifice'.* Matt. 9: 13, Jesus to the Pharisees, 'I will have mercy, and not sacrifice: for I am come not to call the righteous, but sinners to repentance.'

'saying all . . . depend'. Matt. 22: 40, referring to the two commandments, to love God and to love one's neighbour (Matt. 22: 37–9).

put . . . feet. Cor. 15: 27, 'For he hath put all things under his feet.'

Of Education. Appearing anonymously in 1644 (our text here), this was the first of Milton's tracts to be licensed and registered. It was reprinted in the 1673 volume of poems. It is addressed to Samuel Hartlib, an educator and social reformer, follower of the pedagogic theorist John Amos Comenius, who had stayed with Hartlib during his 1641–2 visit to England. Some commentators have aligned Milton's tract with Comenian reform (especially with his emphasis on utilitarian training), while others prefer to set it within the humanistic tradition represented by such predecessors as Ascham's *The Schoolmaster* or Mulcaster's *Positions.* It also has been considered a codification of the practices of a school like St Paul's, which Milton attended, and commentators answering charges that the treatise seems unrealistic point to the fact that Milton had himself had experience teaching. Not surprisingly, then, a synthetic approach to the treatise seems to prevail in the recent critical literature; it might also be worth observing that there are conflicting impulses within the essay that prompt such contradictory readings.

won . . . of. Made me esteem you as; some editors take the 'person' to be Comenius, in which case 'won you with me' would mean that both Milton and Hartlib had won the esteem of Comenius. But it is difficult to see why the actions of Hartlib should have caused Comenius to esteem Milton.

227 *from a far country.* Hartlib, educated at Cambridge and an English resident, was born in Prussia; Milton had made his acquaintance by 1643.

227 *voluntary idea.* Spontaneous, unconstrained conception; *idea*, perhaps in the Platonic sense of an ideal form.

Januas *and* Didactics. Works by Comenius.

flowered off. Come to flower.

ruins. Consequences of the fall.

conning over. Studying.

creature. Created thing.

228 *vacancies.* Vacations.

preposterous. In reverse order; premature.

copious invention. Rhetorical terms; invention involves the knowledge of the materials pertinent to any topic of discussion; *copia* refers to the variety of such material. See T. Cave, *The Cornucopian Text*, for a full discussion.

conversing. Acquaintance.

praxis. Practice.

lessoned. Taught.

arts. Fields of knowledge.

unmatriculated. Before enrolment.

229 *controversy.* Schoolroom exercises usually took the form of debates.

terms. Times when law courts are in session.

shifts. Machinations.

delicious. Sensual.

airy. Flighty.

Orpheus. Archetypal poet and civilizer; cf. *L'Allegro*, ll. 145-50, *Il Penseroso*, ll. 103-8, *Lycidas*, ll. 58-63, *PL*, vii. 32-8.

stocks and stubs. Logs and stumps; i.e. blockheads.

docible. Tractable, educable.

230 *peculiar.* Specialized.

physic. Medicine.

Lily. William Lily, first master of St Paul's School and author of the Latin grammar that was the basic school text from the time of Henry VIII.

absolute. Complete.

civility. The word also meant good citizenship.

convenience of. Number appropriate for.

smatter. Talk without proper knowledge.

law French. The language in which legal reports were written, an archaic and corrupted version of Norman French.

Cebes. A dialogue describing an allegorical picture, the *Table* was ascribed to Cebes, a pupil of Socrates, and was regularly taught in schools, usually in Latin translation.

230 *Plutarch.* Perhaps his tract on education, or other essays in the *Moralia.*

Socratic discourses. Platonic dialogues.

Quintilian. The *Institutes,* a basic pedagogical and rhetorical treatise.

temper. Adapt for.

study. Zeal, devotion (Lat. *studium*).

liberal. 'Becoming of a gentleman' (*OED*).

231 *as . . . was.* Both Plato (*Laws,* 819–20) and Quintilian recommend the use of games as pedagogic tools.

Cato, Varro and Columella. Each wrote a tract *De Re Rustica,* standard Roman works on agriculture.

Hercules. The cleansing of the Augean stables was read, after Pliny (*Natural History,* xvii. 50), as an allegory of the beginning of the manuring of Italian soil.

old . . . new. In Latin and in the vernacular.

physiology of Aristole. Such zoological works as *Historia Animalium* and *De Generatione Animalium.*

Theophrastus. Pupil of Aristotle and author of botanical works.

under contribution. i.e. they will give whatever is required of them.

Vitruvius. Roman authority on engineering and architecture.

Seneca's Natural Questions. Questiones Naturales, a treatise on the physical universe.

Mela . . . Solinus. Roman authors of treatises on physics, geography, etc., including Pliny's *Natural History.*

compact. Summary.

descend. Proceed.

enginery. Military engineering.

institution of physic. Introduction to medicine.

tempers . . . humours . . . seasons. The physics of the four elements (fire, air, earth, water) included four corresponding temperaments (choleric, sanguine, phlegmatic, melancholic) in turn corresponding to four bodily humours (yellow bile, blood, phlegm, black bile); medicine involved a knowledge of these and their seasonal correspondences as well.

crudity. Indigestion.

232 *Orpheus . . . Virgil.* Texts by (or, in the case of Orpheus, ascribed to) ancient poets that depict the natural world, including Hesiod, *Works and Days;* the *Idylls* of Theocritus; Lucretius, *On the Nature of the Universe;* Virgil, *Eclogues* and *Georgics.*

Proairesis. Moral choice based on reasoning; see Aristotle, *Nicomachean Ethics,* III. ii. 17 and III. iii. 19.

Laertius. Diogenes Laertius, to whom *Lives and Opinions of Eminent Philosophers* was attributed.

232 *Locrian remnants.* Texts ascribed to Plato's disciple Timaeus of Locri.

reduced. Led back, recalled (Lat. *reducere*).

determinate sentence. Authoritative doctrine.

economics. Domestic management.

antidote. Warning (about lasciviousness).

Trachiniæ, Alcestis. Dramas by Sophocles (about Deianira, wife of Hercules) and Euripides; for the latter, see Sonnet 23.

Lycurgus . . . Charondas. Lawgive.s respectively of Sparta, Athens, Locri Epizephyrii (a Greek colony in southern Italy), and Sicily; fragments of these codes were preserved in texts by Aristotle, Plutarch, and Xenophon.

tables. The first Roman law code, the Twelve Tables, which survived only as quoted e.g. in Cicero.

Justinian. Sixth-century emperor and codifier of Roman law, his *Corporis Juris Civilis* remained the basic legal text throughout western continental Europe.

233 *Chaldee.* Aramaic, the language of portions of the Old Testament and commentaries.

Syrian. Syriac, the language of various early versions of the New Testament, and of Old Testament translations.

organic arts. Logic, rhetoric, and poetry as enabling and instrumental practices.

fitted. Appropriate, decorous.

topics. The categories used in the discovery, or invention, of arguments.

contracted palm. The closed fist symbolizing logic; rhetoric was represented by an open hand.

Plato . . . Longinus. Including such works as Plato's *Gorgias, Phaedrus*; Aristotle's *Rhetoric*; Demetrius (Phalereus) *On Style*; Cicero's *De Oratore*; Hermogenes' *Ars Rhetorica*; Longinus' *On the Sublime*.

subsequent . . . precedent. Subsequent in study, but precedent in value.

less subtle. Compared to rhetoric, in its arguments.

more . . . passionate. More direct, more appealing to the senses and evocative of the emotions: 'Eloquence the soul, song charms the sense' (*PL*, ii. 556).

Horace. In the *Ars Poetica*.

Castelvetro. Poetica d'Aristotele, a 1570 treatise stressing the neo-classical unities.

Tasso. Discorsi (1587, 1594) on poetics and the epic.

Mazzoni. Author of a 1587 commentary on Dante.

fraught. Equipped.

middleward. The middle line of a troop formation.

234 *embattling.* Preparation for battle.

Cyrene and Alexandria. North African centres of Hellenistic learning.

Plato. In *Laws*, Book i.

these. The Athenians.

gown. Peacetime professions (after legal and clerical garb).

weapon. The sword.

prove and heat. Test and exercise.

single. Simple, unaided (i.e. without weapons).

descant. Improvisations.

symphony. Consort; the entire company of performers.

out. Mistaken.

235 *cherish.* Foster.

concoction. Digestion.

covert. Cover.

to shed away. To desert (because of sickness), alluding to difficulties in the army at the time Milton was writing.

unrecruitable. Incapable of recruiting.

twenty . . . list. i.e. the size of the company is deliberately kept small and the roster padded with false names while the colonel embezzles the pay of both the real and non-existent recruits.   *delusive.* Calculated to deceive.

commodities. Commodious arrangements.

try. Ascertain, determine.

236 *kickshaws.* From Fr. *quelques choses*, somethings; fantastical, frivolous, Frenchified persons.

in. With.

Ulysses. See *Od.*, xxi for the bow that Odysseus alone could string.

assay. Practice.

Areopagitica. As part of the consolidation of Parliamentary and Presbyterian power, the Licensing Order of 1643 had reinstated pre-publication censorship of the sort mandated by the Star Chamber during the years of Charles I's personal rule. Milton's 1644 response takes its title from the *Areopagite Discourse* (*c.*355 BC) of Isocrates, a text written in the form of an oration and directed to the Athenian Court of the Areopagus, urging it to reclaim its former powers to control education and censor behaviour. While the formal model—that of the classical oration, loosely followed by Milton—might support the mainstream Christian-humanist tradition that has read *Areopagitica* as a document of political liberalism, the particular Isocratean example will obviously also support more recent views (such as those of J. Illo in *Radical Perspectives in the Arts*, ed. L. Baxandall, or

F. Barker in *The Tremulous Private Body*) that stress the limits of the argument—that although it opposes pre-censorship, it approves censorship after publication, and that, moreover, its toleration does not extend to Roman Catholic writings. The liberal notion that the tract affirms the rights of the individual is seriously complicated by Barker and by the brilliant reading of C. Kendrick in *Milton: A Study in Ideology and Form*, who demonstrates that the essay's claims of autonomous subjectivity are themselves deeply involved in social and political formations. Although few readers may be prepared to accept the arguments of H. Rapaport in *Milton and the Postmodern* linking Milton's political views to totalitarianism rather than to liberalism, such arguments offer important correctives to the older criticism of Arthur Barker (*Milton and the Puritan Dilemma*), George F. Sensabaugh (*That Grand Whig Milton*), and A. S. P. Woodhouse (*Puritanism and Liberty*).

237 *states.* Both governing bodies and heads of state.

wanting. Lacking.

mean. Ordinary.

success. Outcome.

censure. Judgment.

foremost. Prefatory.

incidental. Naturally likely to occur.

trophy. Monument to a victory.

beyond . . . recovery. i.e. beyond the power of the simple Roman virtues—honesty, courage, frugality—to achieve; but also, the use of *Roman* in conjunction with the 'tyranny and superstition' of the previous line implies the corruption of the classical ideals through the papacy, and the consequent association of Romanness with episcopacy.

238 *him.* Joseph Hall, Bishop of Norwich (compare *Apology*), who, although a royalist, praised Parliament in the *Humble Remonstrance* (1641).

statists. Politicians.

triennial. By an Act of 1641, Parliament was to meet at least every three years, rather than by royal summons.

cabin counsellors. Cabinet ministers: the reference is to Charles I's exclusive reliance on his advisers; no parliaments had been summoned between 1629 and 1640.

as . . . gainsay. i.e. in arguing against the Licensing Act.

him. Isocrates.

239 *Dion Prusaeus.* Greek rhetorician (d. *c.* AD 117).

not . . . latitude. Cf. similar attitudes towards the effect of the English climate on creativity in *PL*, ix. 45, *RCG*, p. 170.

derogated. Subtracted.

239 *that part.* The provisions that no book could be registered without its owner's consent, thereby preserving copyright, and that books registered for the benefit of the poor could not be reprinted without permission.

painful. Painstaking.

quadragesimal. Lenten; the reference is to the right of bishops to give individual dispensations from dietary restrictions during Lent.

matrimonial. Referring to the episcopal authority to exempt marriages from the required publication of the marriage banns.

when . . . expired. The 1642 Bishops Exclusion Bill excluded bishops from the House of Lords; Presbyterianism was not established by law until 1645.

240 *dragon's teeth.* Sown by Cadmus, mythical founder of Thebes; an army sprang from them: see Ovid, *Met.*, iii. 101–30.

spill. Destroy.

whole impression. Entire edition.

fifth essence. The quintessence, the spiritual component beyond the four material elements.

inquisition. Papal suppression of heretical books has a long history; it became widespread under Torquemada, who was made Grand Inquisitor in 1478. Books were licensed in England by the Privy Council from 1538 on; licensing was administered by the Stationer's Company. Charles I's 1637 Star Chamber decree was the most recent and extensive English censorship document before the 1643 order.

Protagoras. Sophist of the fifth century BC.

Vetus comoedia. The Old (Greek) Comedy, as written e.g., by Aristophanes.

quick. Vital, vigorous.

Cicero. In *On the Nature of the Gods*, i. 23.

event. Outcome.

Epicurus. Founder of Epicureanism, which taught that the highest good was to be found in pleasure.

libertine . . . Cyrene. Founded by Aristippus, a student of Socrates, who equated virtue with pleasure; cf. *PR*, iv. 276 ff.

Cynic impudence. Exemplified by Diogenes, who claimed that the reason he carried a lamp in daylight was that he had yet to see a real man—the Spartans being children and the Athenians women.

241 *Chrysostom.* St John Chrysostom (*c.*347–407), Greek Church Father.

Lacedaemon. Sparta.

Lycurgus. The supposed founder of Sparta; Milton draws on Plutarch's life.

Archilochus. Satiric poet of the seventh century BC.

broad. Plainspoken, satiric.

241 *promiscuous conversing.* Spartan men and women exercised together in the nude (conversing = socializing).

Andromache. ll. 595–601:

> No Spartan girl
> Could ever live clean if she wanted.
> They're always out on the street in scanty outfits,
> Making a great display of naked limbs.
> In those they race and wrestle with the boys too—
> Abominable's the word. It's little wonder
> Sparta is hardly famous for chaste women.
>   (tr. J. F. Nims)

twelve tables. Of the ancient Roman laws.

Pontific College. Supreme religious institution of ancient Rome.

augurs. Priests who interpreted omens.

flamens. Sacrificial priests.

Cato . . . Italy. In 155 BC; Cato's distaste is at least partly understandable: Carneades had attempted to illustrate sceptical methodology by delivering a lecture on the nature of justice, and on the following day, delivering another demolishing his own argument.

Scipio. Scipio the Younger (d. 129 BC), commander and patron of the arts.

Sabine austerity. Cato grew up on a Sabine farm and often secluded himself there.

scrupulous. Dubious, full of scruples.

Naevius . . . Philemon. Comic dramatists of the first and second centuries BC who imitated the Greek New Comedy.

242 *Lucretius . . . Memmius . . . Cicero. De Rerum Natura* is addressed to the praetor Memmius; Cicero, who argued against many of Lucretius's ideas, was said nevertheless to have edited the poem.

Lucilius, or Catullus, or Flaccus. Satiric (and in the case of Catullus, sexually explicit) authors; [Quintus Horatius] Flaccus is Horace.

story of Titus Livius. Livy's *History* which, according to Tacitus, took Pompey's side (the section has not survived).

Naso. Ovid (Publius Ovidius Naso).

covert. Cover, pretext.

emperors . . . Christians. Constantine, the first avowedly Christian emperor, reigned AD 306–37.

Porphyrius. His *Against the Christians* was ordered to be burned by Constantine.

Proclus. Fifth-century neo-Platonist.

scrupled more. Had more scruples about.

gentiles. Non-Christians.

242 *Padre Paolo.* Paolo Sarpi (1552–1623), whose *Historie of the Council of Trent* (tr. 1620) is a main source for Milton.

bull. Inter cunctas, a bull of 1418.

243 *Wyclif and Huss.* John Wyclif and John Huss, precursors of the Protestant reformation.

Leo X. Pope from 1513 to 1521.

Council of Trent. Met from 1545 to 1563 to reformulate Roman Catholic doctrine and practices in response to the Reformation. It authorized the *Index of Prohibited Books* first issued in 1559, along with an *Index of Expurgations* from books otherwise allowed.

stay in. Stop with.

keys. Cf. Matt. 16: 19, 'And I will give unto thee the keys of the kingdom of heaven.'

conceit. Idea.

Claudius. In the margin, Milton cites Suetonius on Tiberius' plan to issue an edict legalizing farting at table, *'Quo veniam daret flatum crepitumque ventris in convivio emittendi'.*

Imprimatur. Let it be printed.

shaven. Alluding to the tonsure.

244 *sponge.* eraser.

responsories . . . antiphonies. Responsive parts of church services.

Lambeth House. London residence of the Archbishop of Canterbury.

Paul's. St Paul's cathedral, near which the Bishop of London resided.

Juno. Juno tried to hinder Alcmena from giving birth to Hercules by commanding the goddess of childbirth to attend her in her labour with her legs crossed (in Milton's account, Juno performs the action herself); see Ovid, *Met.,* ix. 281–323.

Radamanth. One of the judges in the classical underworld.

backward into light. i.e. rather than across the river Acheron into Hades.

mysterious iniquity. The papacy, which reformers identified as the whore upon whose forehead 'Mystery' is inscribed in Rev. 17: 5.

minorites. Comparing Anglican chaplains to the Friars Minor.

245 *Lullius.* Raymond Lull (*c.*1234–1315), famous alchemical theorist.

sublimate. Transform base metals into precious ones: technical alchemical language.

Paul. 1 Cor. 15: 33 quotes a Euripidean fragment that had become proverbial, cited also in the Preface to *SA*; Milton's other examples are Acts 17: 28 (from Aratus) and Titus 1: 12 (from Epimenides).

Julian the Apostate. Emperor from 361 to 363, who renounced Christianity.

shifts. Stratagems.

245 *Apollinarii.* Apollinaris of Alexandria and his son, who wrote grammars and rhetorics based on the Bible.

Socrates. Socrates Scholasticus (*c.*385–440), a Church historian.

Decius or Diocletian. Roman emperors who persecuted the Christians.

Jerome. St Jerome (*c.*340–420), translator of the Bible into Latin; his eighteenth epistle, addressed to Eustochium, is the source of the incident recounted here, in which the angel doubts Jerome's faith because of his devotion to Cicero.

246 *Basil . . . Margites.* Basil the Great (*c.*330–79), whose *On the Right Use of Greek Literature* suggests general principles of reading; *Margites* was a mock-heroic poem, of which only fragments survive, ascribed to Homer.

Morgante. A romance by Luigi Pulci (1481).

Eusebius. Church historian (*c.*264–340), who reports the incident about Dionysius Alexandrinus, a mid-third-century bishop of Alexandria.

answerable to. In accordance with.

Thessalonians. 1 Thess. 5: 21.

author. Paul; Titus 1: 15 is cited.

unapocryphal vision. Acts 10: 9–19, in which Peter is permitted to eat foods forbidden by Old Testament dietary restrictions; it is 'unapocryphal' in contrast with the vision of Dionysius Alexandrinus just discussed.

concoction. Digestion.

Selden. John Selden (1584–1654), historian, lawyer, and antiquarian; Milton draws on his *De Jure Naturali et Gentium juxta Disciplinam Ebraeorum* (1640).

exquisite. Choice.

247 *tabled.* Provided food for their tables, i.e. manna (see Exod. 16).

issue out. Cf. Matt. 15: 17–20 and Mark 7: 15, 'There is nothing from without a man, that entering into him can defile him: but the things which come out of him, these are they that defile the man.'

Solomon. Eccles. 12: 12.

Syriac. The Syriac version of Acts 19: 19.

practised the books. Practised what the books taught.

Psyche. Venus, jealous of Psyche's love for her son Cupid, imposed on her the task of separating seeds; see Apuleius, *The Golden Ass*, iv. 6.

warfaring. Texts read 'wayfaring', hand-corrected in presentation copies to 'warfaring'. The emendation has the support of Eph. 6: 11, 'Put on the whole armour of God', and of such texts as Erasmus's, *Enchiridion Militis Christiani* and Spenser, *FQ,* i. i. 1–2.

unbreathed. Unexercised (to the point of breathlessness).

248 *immortal garland.* Cf. Jas. 1: 12, 'the crown of life,' or 2 Tim. 4: 8, 'a crown of righteousness'; see *Comus,* l. 973.

248 *excremental.* Superficial, as an excrescence or outgrowth, not inherent.

Scotus or Aquinas. Duns Scotus or St Thomas Aquinas, as representative medieval philosophers.

Guyon. In *FQ*, ii. 7, Guyon faces Mammon without the Palmer, who does, however, accompany him to the Bower of Bliss (ii. 12). The error about the Cave of Mammon has been discussed from a thematic point of view by E. Sirluck (*MP*, 48 [1950]) and has recently, thanks to H. Bloom's discussion in *A Map of Misreading*, served as a touchstone for Milton's relation to Spenser; see J. Guillory, *Poetic Authority*; J. Goldberg, *Voice Terminal Echo*.

promiscuously. Indiscriminately.

nicely. Fastidiously.

Talmudist . . . chetiv. A Talmudist is a student of the Jewish commentaries on the Old Testament, in which a '*keri*' in the margin provides an alternative word to be read in place of the text ('*chetiv*') that is forbidden, either because it is too holy—e.g. the name of God—or blasphemous.

Clement of Alexandria. Church Father (second century AD), whose *Hortatory Address to the Greeks* describes lascivious pagan rituals in great detail.

Eusebian . . . preparation. For Eusebius, see above, p. 246. His *Evangelical Preparation* is similarly detailed about obscene pagan practices.

Irenaeus, Epiphanius. Church Fathers whose works detail and argue against heretical beliefs.

249 *criticisms.* Fine points.

Petronius. Author of the obscene classic *Satyricon* (d. AD 66).

Arbiter. Tacitus (*Annals*, xvi. 18–19) reports that Nero called Petronius '*arbiter elegantiarum*' (stylistic adviser).

ribald of Arezzo. Pietro Aretino (1492–1557), author of lewd and satiric works.

vicar of hell. Sir Francis Brian, Anne Boleyn's cousin, whose scurrility and blasphemy were said to have earned Henry VIII's esteem.

Cataio. Cathay, China.

Isaiah. In Acts 8: 27–35, Philip expounds a passage from Isaiah for the benefit of a eunuch.

Sorbonists. Roman Catholic scholars at the Sorbonne.

distinct. Acutely discriminating.

Arminius. Jacob Hermanns (1560–1609), who, answering a Calvinistic tract, argued for the election of those among the fallen who would subsequently answer God's call; Milton came to hold the Arminian belief that divine foreknowledge did not foreclose freedom of the human will; cf. *CD*, 1. 4.

cautelous. Tricky, crafty.

pound up. Impound (and hence keep out).

250 *Aristotle. Ethics*, i. 3, where knowledge is said to be unavailable to those controlled by their passions.

Solomon. Prov. 23: 9, on the futility of educating fools.

Saviour. Matt. 7: 6, on casting pearls before swine.

want. Be without.

qualify. Modify.

prevented. Anticipated.

Plato . . . laws. Milton seems to consider Plato's *Laws* to be as utopian as his *Republic*. Book 7 of the *Laws* legislates censorship.

airy burgomasters. Fictitious governors.

academic night-sitting. Plato's school was the Academy; the *Symposium* depicts such a learned drinking party.

251 *Sophron Mimus*. A popular writer of the fifth century BC.

fond. Foolish.

Doric. According to Plato (*Republic*, 399), a manly and militaristic musical mode.

shrewd. Depraved.

visitors. Ecclesiastical censors.

rebec. A three-stringed violin.

gamut. Range of notes.

Arcadias. Imitations of Sidney's pastoral romance.

Montemayors. Alluding to Jorge de Montemayor, author of the Spanish romance *Diana*.

hears ill. Is ill spoken of.

rioting. Excesses, indulgences.

252 *conversation*. Socializing.

Atlantic. Referring to Atlantis, the mythical island depicted in Plato's *Critias* and *Timaeus*.

Plato there. See *Republic*, 424–33; *Laws*, 643–4.

pittance. Rationing, allowance.

gramercy. Merit, approbation.

motions. Puppet shows.

253 *court-libel*. The 'Court Mercury' (*Mercurius Aulicus*), an anti-Parliament newspaper published 1642–5.

wet. Newly printed.

divulged. Made public.

officials. A term applied to ecclesiastical judges.

254 *damnified*. Injured.

254 *perfectly.* Completely.

Seville. Headquarters of the Spanish Inquisition.

story. History.

wafted. Conveyed.

mean. Inconsiderable.

journeywork. Day labour, hackwork.

would not down. Could not be swallowed.

sensible. Sensitive.

255 *pluralities.* The practice of holding more than one Church living.

competency. Sufficient income.

ferula. Schoolmaster's rod.

fescue. Schoolmaster's pointer.

elaborate. Produced through labour.

uttered. Published.

256 *Palladian oil.* Lamp oil consumed in the course of work honouring Pallas Athena, goddess of wisdom.

puny. Minor, schoolboy.

patriarchal. Paternal, but also alluding to the Roman Catholic Church hierarchy.

ding. Fling.

quoit's distance. The distance that the ring is thrown in the game of quoits.

Bacon. Cited from *A Wise and Moderate Discourse Concerning Church-Affairs* (1589; pub. 1640; Spedding, *Bacon*, i. 78).

jeopardy. Uncertainty.

257 *Knox.* John Knox, the Scottish reformer, whose *History of the Reformation in Scotland* was censored in a 1644 edition.

dash. Line drawn through an offending word.

ironmoulds. Discolourations, ink-stains.

twenty. Thirty-four licensers were in fact appointed by Parliament; 'twenty' may mean 'a large number'.

tickets . . . standards. Authorizations and restrictions (cf. 'mark and license', below).

staple commodity. Merchandise whose sale is controlled by royal authority.

Philistines. The Philistines forbade the Israelites to forge tools or weapons (see 1 Sam. 13: 19–20).

coulters. Iron blades on ploughs.

258 *diffident.* Lacking in faith, distrustful.

frequented. Associated.

258 *laic.* Irreligious.

as that. As if.

conceit. Opinion.

enchiridion. The word means both knife and handbook.

St Angelo. Castel Sant' Angelo in Rome, a papal prison.

259 *Galileo.* Galileo Galilei (1564–1642) spent his last years under arrest in a villa near Florence; Milton visited Italy in 1638–9. Galileo is the only contemporary named in *PL* (i. 288).

envy. Ill will.

he. Cicero, who had been quaestor (chief treasury officer) of Sicily and prosecuted Verres, a subsequent praetor (chief judge) of Sicily, who was charged with extortion and cruelty.

cure. Parish.

259–60 *sole . . . art.* The bishops claimed the exclusive authority to ordain ministers and only ordained university graduates for whom ecclesiastical appointments had first been provided.

260 *covenants and protestations.* Various proclamations issued by Parliament, including the Solemn League and Covenant declaring union with the Scottish Presbyterians.

chop an episcopacy. Exchange one episcopacy for another.

palace metropolitan. Residence of the Archbishop of Canterbury.

commuting our penance. Taking payment in lieu of imposing penance, one of the charges against Laud.

To startle thus betimes. One who is so quickly alarmed.

coventicle. Meeting of dissenters.

cruse . . . oil. Alluding to 1 Kgs. 17: 16, in which a widow's jar (cruse) of oil is inexhaustible.

remember. Remind.

Viscount St Albans. Bacon in the text above (p. 256), quoting Tacitus.

in Scripture. E.g. Ps. 85:11, Prov. 18:4, Eccles. 1:5.

261 *assembly.* The Westminster Assembly, which advised Parliament on the religious settlement.

professors. Those who declare their faith.

implicit faith. Faith based simply on authority.

Loreto. A shrine supposed to contain the house in which Mary conceived Jesus.

mysteries. Trades, occupations.

factor. Agent.

commendatory. Recommendation, certification.

261 *dividual.* Separable.

he. Jesus, see Matt. 21: 17–19, Mark 11: 11–14.

publicans. Tax collectors.

tunaging and poundaging. Tunage was a tariff (originally on each *tun* of wine; subsequently on the value—not the weight—of any goods) that Charles I claimed authority to collect without parliamentary approval. (The term is usually, incorrectly, modernized to 'tonnage'.)

262 *parochial.* Both a minister of a parish and narrow-minded.

Hercules' pillars. Limits (of aspiration), alluding to the pillars Hercules set at the westernmost end of the Mediterranean to mark the extent of his travels, and hence the limits of the ancient world.

topic folio. Commonplace book.

harmony . . . catena. Books reconciling scriptural passages and the commentaries of the Church Fathers; the passages were drawn together under themes and topics (their 'uses, marks, and means').

sol-fa. Musical scale.

unspeakably. Ineffably.

interlinearies . . . gear. Further shortcuts to learning, including interlinear translations, abridgements, and summaries.

our . . . Thomas. Churches as stockhouses for books may be meant, or traditional associations between churches and trade (e.g. St Hugh was patron of shoemakers, although there was no London church named after him).

magazine. Storehouse.

impaled. Protected by stakes (pales).

affect. Adopt.

Christ. John 18: 19–20, answering the high priest.

263 *Alcoran.* The Koran.

glass. Cf. 1 Cor. 13: 12, 'For now we see through a glass darkly; but then face to face.'

that story. Of the dismemberment of Osiris, and Isis's attempt to collect his scattered limbs; see 'On the Morning of Christ's Nativity', ll. 213–20, and Plutarch, *On Isis and Osiris* (*Moralia*, v).

feature. Shape.

264 *obsequies.* Rites and services, usually funereal.

combust. Burned up; i.e. invisible because of their proximity to the sun.

economical. Domestic.

Zuinglius. Ulrich Zwingli (1481–1531), founder of Protestantism in Zurich.

syntagma. Systematic doctrine, collection of treatises.

264 *golden rule.* Both the rule of mathematical proportion, and Matt. 8: 12, 'all things whatsoever ye would that men should do to you, do ye even so to them.'

discourse. Reason, discussion.

Pythagoras . . . island. John Selden, in his commentary on Drayton's *Poly-Olbion* (1613, p. 14), credits Lipsius with the suggestion that Pythagoras learned about metempsychosis from the Druids.

Agricola. Roman proconsul in Britain, AD 78–85. The reference is to Tacitus' *Agricola*, xxi.

Hyrcanian wilderness. German forests.

265 *propending.* Inclining.

Jerome. Jerome of Prague (d. 1416), a disciple of Wyclif and Huss.

demeaned. Conducted.

mansion-house. Chief residence.

plates. Armour.

fast. Steadfastly.

we . . . already. Cf. John 4: 35, 'Say not ye, There be yet four months, and then cometh harvest? behold, I say unto you, Lift up your eyes, and look on the fields: for they are white already to harvest.'

266 *Pyrrhus.* Third-century BC king of Epirus, who expressed his admiration for the Romans after he had defeated them. The passage quoted is from Florus' *Epitome*, i. 18.

wish. Num. 11: 29. 'Would God that all the Lord's people were prophets.'

maniples. Bands of soldiers.

267 *admiration.* Provoking wonder.

derives. Conducts.

his. Livy (*History*, xxvi. 11) tells how Hannibal was discouraged to find the Roman morale so strong that his invasion had not reduced the price of land, even of the field where his army was encamped.

strong man . . . locks. Like Samson, although the awakening occurs after he has been shorn: 'And he awoke out of his sleep, and said, I will go out as at other times before, and shake myself' (Judg. 16: 20).

mewing. Renewing (lit. moulting). Medieval bestiaries report that the eagle moults and renews its sight by flying into the sun.

gabble. Chatter.

engrossers. Monopolists, with a pun on its other meaning, scribes.

268 *formal.* Tied to forms.

law. An ancient Roman law (abolished in AD 318) gave fathers the power of life and death over their children.

coat and conduct. Taxes on clothing and troop movement that Charles I attempted to exact.

268 *nobles.* Coins; the noble was worth 6*s.* 8*d.* (33 p.).

Danegelt. Ship money, a tax in support of the navy originally raised to forestall a Danish invasion. Charles's attempt to revive it without parliamentary sanction met with widespread protest.

just immunities. From such illegalities as Charles's imposition of taxes without parliamentary approval.

unequal. Unjust.

one. Robert Greville, second Lord Brooke (1608–43), a member of the House of Lords who died leading a parliamentary army; he was author of *A Discourse Opening the Nature of that Episcopacie, which is Exercised in England* (1641).

his. Jesus'; e.g. John 14: 21.

269 *the time in special is.* This is the particular moment (because the Westminster Assembly was meeting and Parliament was in session).

Janus. The gatekeeper god, whose two faces looked forward and back (hence 'controversial'); the doors of his temple in the Roman forum stood open in time of war.

winds of doctrine. Citing Eph. 4: 14.

discipline of Geneva. Calvin's doctrine, an essential model for English Presbyterianism.

'to seek . . . treasures'. Paraphrasing Prov. 2: 4 'if thou seekest her [wisdom] as silver, and searchest for her as for hid treasures . . .'

battle. Battalion, army.

Proteus. A metamorphic sea god with the gift of prophesy. In *Od.*, iv. 384 ff. Menelaus describes how he captured and bound Proteus so that he could not change his shape and compelled him to reveal what the hero must do to return home.

Micaiah. See 1 Kgs. 22: 1–36.

270 *'those ordinances . . . cross'.* Paraphrasing Col. 2: 14, 'Blotting out the handwriting of ordinances that was against us, which was contrary to us, and took it out of the way, nailing it to his cross.'

Christian liberty. A Pauline concept; e.g. Gal. 5: 1, 'the liberty wherewith Christ hath made us free'; compare the discussion of law and liberty in Romans, esp. the consideration of indifferent matters in Rom. 14: 1–13, the 'doctrine' alluded to below; see *CD* (p. 723 ff.).

he . . . Lord. See Rom. 14: 1–13.

linen decency. Alluding to the bishops' justification of ceremonial garb.

'wood . . . stubble'. Citing 1 Cor. 3: 12, on the materials each person brings to 'God's building'; the passage is also cited below ('gold . . . stones').

wheat from the tares. Alluding to the parable in Matt. 13: 24–30, 36–43.

'the unity . . . peace'. Citing Eph. 4: 3.

271 *shakes*. Cf. Hag. 2: 6–7, 'For thus saith the Lord of hosts; Yet once, it is a little while, and I will shake the heavens, and the earth . . . and I will shake all nations.'

Convocation House. The chapter-house in Westminster Abbey; the Long Parliament moved powers of convocation from it to the Chapel of Henry VII in Westminster Abbey.

272 *Moses*. Num. 11: 29, cited above.

Saviour. Luke 9: 50, 'he that is not against us is for us.'

let. Obstruction.

Dominican part. The Inquisition's licensers were usually Dominican friars.

order. Of 29 Jan. 1642.

fire and the executioner. Condemned books were burned by the executioner, who also inflicted whatever corporal punishment had been ordered for the author or printer (commonly ear-cropping or nose-slitting).

Star-Chamber decree. Of 1637; the Star Chamber was abolished in 1641.

Lucifer. Alluding to Isa. 14: 12, 'How art thou fallen from heaven, O Lucifer, son of the morning!'

273 *doubted*. Suspected.

copy. Copyright.

glosing colours. False interpretations (promulgated by the Stationers).

but colours. Merely superficial.

event. Outcome.

sophisms and elenches. Fallacious arguments and refutations.

equally almost incident. Almost as likely to occur.

advertisement. Notification.

The Tenure of Kings and Magistrates. In Jan. 1649, Charles I was tried by a Rump Parliament (so called because all Royalist and Presbyterian supporters had been forcibly ejected from it in 'Pride's Purge', when on 6 Dec. 1648 Colonel Pride entered the House with troops and took control); the trial proceeded despite protests by the House of Lords, the king, prelates, and presbyters that it was clearly illegal and opposed to Scripture, and that the reconstituted House of Commons was itself an illegal body. Milton wrote *TKM* at this time, and it appeared within weeks of the execution of Charles I on 30 Jan. It was, of course, necessary for Milton to make the best case possible for the Independent cause, but it is important to observe that the account he gives here does not address what would have been, to the opposing side, the crucial issue: the question of the legality of the tribunal by which the king was tried, and of the new Parliament. By Mar. 1649, Milton had been appointed Secretary for Foreign Tongues by the new government, a commonwealth in which kingship and the House of Lords had been abolished. Milton's official job involved translation and correspondence, but he also served as a spokesman for the positions first articulated in *TKM*, for example in *Eikonoklastes* (1649/50), his point-by-point refutation of *Eikon Basilike: The Portraiture of His Sacred Majesty* (which had appeared a week after Charles I's death and was supposed to have been written by him), and in the Latin defences that Milton wrote in the 1650s. The second edition of *TKM* (dated 1649/50, published 1650), expanded mainly through the addition of supporting citations at the end of the treatise, is our text here.

274 *offended.* Attacked.

in whom. i.e. in those whom.

endued. Endowed.

written. Jer. 48: 10, 'Cursed be he that doeth the work of the Lord deceitfully.'

these men. The Presbyterians, with whom Milton had broken, allying himself with the Independents and the army.

paltered. Equivocated.

bandied. Both banded together and contended.

faction. In the Engagement of 26 Dec. 1647, Charles had agreed to establish Presbyterianism for three years, and to suppress the Independents.

275 *of industry.* Industriously.

we read. Prov. 12: 10, 'the tender mercies of the wicked are cruel.'

Agag. Amalekite king whom Samuel 'hewed . . . in pieces' (1 Sam. 15: 33).

Jonathan. Son of King Saul, who was rescued by the Israelites when the king attempted to kill him (1 Sam. 14). Saul was subsequently rejected by God, and David was anointed king (1 Sam. 16).

niceness. Exaggerated punctiliousness.

unnecessariest clause. The clause affirmed loyalty to the king and pledged his defence and preservation.

wrested. Misapplied; also exacted from them, and wrenched from its context.

compliments. Both flattering words and additions (complements): the words were not distinguished in the seventeenth century.

voice. Vote.

startle. Swerve, deviate from their purpose.

276 *mementoes.* Alluding to William Prynne's *A Briefe Memento* (1649), which argued against the trial of the king.

envy. Ill will, malice.

classic and provincial. The Westminster Assembly had organized Presbyterian government into provinces subdivided into classes.

pluralities. Multiple clerical holdings.

276 *impeached members.* Eleven Members of Parliament charged with conspiring with the queen in 1647.

Korah, Dathan, and Abiram. Rebels against Moses and Aaron (Num. 16: 1–35).

277 *such a one.* Charles I, in his dealings with the Irish.

not to be resisted. To justify the actions of the army and the Rump, Milton draws on St Paul's injunction that the power ordained by God cannot be resisted (Rom. 13: 1–2).

doubling Duplicitous (cf. 'apostate scarecrows' and 'idol with two faces', above).

born to command. Man was created in the image of God, with 'dominion . . . over all the earth' (Gen. 1: 26, 28–9).

278 *partial.* Prejudiced.

279 *Claudius Sesell.* Claude de Seissel, from whose *La Grande Monarchie de France* (1519) Milton quotes.

stories. Histories.

conqueror. Royalist arguments derived the king's authority from conquest rather than from consent.

Aristotle. Nicomachean Ethics, viii. 10 declares that a king should look to his subjects' interests, not his own.

Isa. 26: 13. 'O Lord our God, other lords beside thee have had dominion over us: but by thee only will we make mention of thy name.'

Tertullian. In *On the Crown,* this Church Father reports that even Augustus questioned being called lord, as if he were God.

king. Saul, against whom Samuel warned them (1 Sam. 8); defenders of royal prerogative (including James I in the *The Trew Law of Free Monarchies*) argued that acceptance of a king included his rights over persons and property, as Samuel had detailed them. Milton returns to this question below.

crimes proportional. i.e. proportionately greater than those of ordinary men, as the king is greater then they are.

280 *51st Psalm.* Verse 4, 'Against thee, thee only, have I sinned.'

to murder Uriah. By placing him at the front of the army; Bathsheba was his adulterous wife (see 2 Sam. 1: 2–17).

Deut. 17. Verses 19–20, 'that he may learn to fear the Lord his God, to keep all the words of this law and these statutes, to do them: That his heart be not lifted up above his brother.' The provisions in Duet. 17 are detailed below.

pathetical. Emotional.

Euripides. Heraclidae, ll. 418–21.

Trajan. As reported by Dio Cassius ('Dion', below) in *Roman History,* lxviii. 16.

281 *Theodosius.* Eastern emperor of the fifth century.

Code of Justinian. The Codex, basic compilation of Roman Law that prevailed throughout western Europe.

l. For *liber*, book.

he. 1 Sam. 8: 7, 'And the Lord said unto Samuel, Hearken unto the voice of the people in all that they say unto thee: for they have not rejected thee, but they have rejected me, that I should not reign over them.'

Rehoboam. 1 Kgs. 12 describes this successor to King Solomon, who refused to be a 'servant' to the Jews and vowed to make their burdens heavy; their response (v. 16) is quoted below.

deposed Samuel. When they demanded a king as their ruler in 1 Sam. 8: 1–5.

282 *Livy.* In the opening of the second book of his history.

Numa. Legendary king and lawgiver.

1 Pet. 2: 13. 'Submit yourselves to every ordinance of man for the Lord's sake: whether it be to the king, as supreme.' Milton quotes 1 Pet. 2: 16, below, 'as free, and not using your liberty for a cloak of maliciousness, but as the servants of God.'

Rom. 13. Verses 1–2, as noted above, p. 277.

else. Elsewhere.

he. The devil, during the temptations in the wilderness.

Revelation. 13: 2, cited below.

283 *abstract.* i.e. of kingship in general, but not of every king in particular.

Chrysostom. St John Chrysostom (345–407), in a homily on Romans usually cited by royalists. Milton emphasizes that even Chrysostom makes the 'logical' distinction invoked above.

holding it immediately of God. i.e. the claim of divine right.

demerit. Merit, desert.

284 *St Basil.* St Basil the Great, bishop of Cappadocia, 370–9. Milton's reference is unclear, but in his Commonplace Book he cites a similar passage from Basil's commentary on the Wisdom of Solomon (*Prose Works*, i. 453).

look. Consider.

Hercules. Hercules Furens, ll. 922–4; Hercules speaks after killing the tyrant Lycus.

Ehud. Judg. 3: 14–30 descibes Ehud, the 'deliverer' (v. 15) of Israel from Moabite rule, who presents King Eglon with a knife as 'a message from God' (v. 20).

outlandish. Foreign.

285 *second.* Second objection raised on p. 284.

286 *Agag.* See p. 275, above; Milton cites 1 Sam. 15: 33, the words Samuel speaks before hewing the king in pieces.

286 *Jehu.* Anointed king of Israel, he is charged to slay the reigning king, Jehoram, son of Ahab; 2 Kgs. 9: 6–7, 'Thus saith the Lord God of Israel, I have anointed thee king . . . And thou shalt smite the house of Ahab thy master.'

anointed. King Saul; see 1 Sam. 24: 10, 'I will not put forth my hand against my lord', and again 1 Sam. 26: 8–9.

benefactors. Luke 22: 25–6, 'The kings of the Gentiles exercise lordship over them; and they that exercise authority upon them are called benefactors. But ye shall not be so: but he that is greatest among you, let him be as the younger.'

Luke 13. Verse 22, spoken of Herod.

Mary. Luke 1: 52, 'He hath put down the mighty from their seats, and exalted them of low degree.'

287 *Ludovicus Pius.* Louis the Pious, Holy Roman Emperor AD 814–40.

Charles the Great. Charlemagne.

du Haillan. Bernard de Girard, sieur du Haillan, author of a history of France.

room. Place.

Constantinus Leo. Leo III, author of *Eclogue,* or *Delectus Legum Compendiarus* (AD 726), here cited from Johann Leunclavis, *Juris Graeco-Romani* (1596).

Matthew Paris. Thirteenth-century historian, an important source for Holinshed's *Chronicles.*

288 *baron.* The title originally applied to those called by the king to Parliament.

circumstantial. Pompous; distinguished solely by their position.

Peter Martyr. (1500–62), in his commentary on the book of Judges.

Sir Thomas Smith. Sixteenth-century political theorist. *The Commonwealth of England* appeared in 1583.

Gildas. Sixth-century historian of Britain, author of *Liber Querulus de Excidio Britannieae,* published in English in 1638 as *The Book of Critical Inquiry into the Fall of Britain.*

room. Place.

keys. Alluding to the power given to Peter with the keys of the kingdom of heaven, 'and whatsoever thou shalt bind on earth shall be bound in heaven' (Matt. 16: 19).

indifferently. Indiscriminately.

289 *Sleidan.* Or Johann Philippson (1506–56), *The General History of the Reformation.*

queen-regent. Mary of Guise, widow of James V.

Buchanan. George Buchanan, *Rerum Scoticarum Historia* (1582).

John Knox. Presbyterian reformer and historian of the Church in Scotland (1505–72).

289 *Lethington.* William Maitland of Lethington, who defended Mary Queen of Scots.

fact. Action.

affection. Passion.

Answerable. Equivalent, corresponding.

John Craig. (1512–1600), a supporter of Knox.

290 *Ecclesiastical History of Scotland.* The reference is to Knox's *History of the Reformation of the Church of Scotland* (1644).

same year. 1567.

Gibson. James Gibson, who in 1586 warned James VI against opposing the Presbyterians.

coronation. As king of Scotland, 1567.

291 *Thuan.* Jacques-August de Thou (1553–1617), *Historiarum Sui Temporis* (1604).

eye. The Dutch had protested the trial of Charles I.

Waldenses. See Sonnet 18.

round. Straightforwardly, freely.

doubt. Hesitate, scruple.

two oaths. Required of English citizens, declaring their allegiance to the crown and the monarch's supremacy over the Church.

seven years. Dating from the Grand Remonstrance of Nov.–Dec. 1641, which shifted power to the House of Commons.

292 *sometimes.* Alluding to the shifting allegiances of the Presbyterians, some-times voting with the Independent minority, sometimes against them and with the king.

fine clause. Subtle or cunning clause in the Solemn League and Covenant (1643); see p. 275, above.

relatives. Related terms: Milton ironically plays with a linguistic and philosophical argument.

293 *denied to treat.* In the vote of 'No More Addresses' forbidding further negotiation with Charles, passed by both houses on 3 Jan. 1648 and rescinded in November.

their power. The extent of their power.

294 *supererogating.* Beyond what is necessary.

like occasion. When the Dutch Protestants established the United Provinces of Holland.

whose. Oliver Cromwell's.

294–5 *chancellor.* John Campbell, Earl of Loudon; the encounter took place at Newcastle-upon-Tyne in May 1646, when Charles was taken prisoner.

295 *treaty.* The Treaty of Newport (Nov. 1648) rescinding 'No More Addresses' (see p. 293, above).

specifical. Species of.

obnoxious. Liable to punishment.

Newport. The preamble of the treaty declared the war against the king a 'just and lawful defence'. Charles agreed to accept this article only if the negotiations settled all differences between himself and Parliament, a condition he claimed was never satisfied.

devoted. Doomed.

Antiochus. Persecutor of the Jews overthrown by Judas Maccabaeus in 166 BC.

Meroz. Cursed in the Song of Deborah (Judg. 5: 23) for failing to support the Israelites.

unconfound. Restore.

296 *exasperating.* Incensing.

supreme magistracy. Usually explained as a reference to the Commons, although God could also be meant.

economize. Lit. conduct domestic management.

297 *pismires.* Ants.

unforcible things. Matters of conscience, indifferent matters.

discover. Reveal.

298 *old and perfect enemy.* The Antichrist, 'that old serpent, called the Devil, and Satan' (Rev. 12: 9); here, King Charles.

event. Outcome.

Stories. Histories; Buchanan's *History of Scotland* provides the example of Christiern II (1481–1559).

Maximilian. Maximilian I (1459–1519), Holy Roman Emperor, took the revenge described on Bruges in 1490.

massacre at Paris. The St Bartholomew's Day massacre (24 Aug. 1572).

Naples. The Spanish put down a rebellion there in 1648.

twice promised. 1 Sam. 19: 6; 1 Sam. 26: 21.

chair. Pulpit.

298-9 *in season and out of season.* 2 Tim. 4: 2, 'Preach the word; be instant in season, out of season.'

299 *pragmatical sidesmen.* Lit. dogmatic or opinionated assistants to a church warden; here, those who take sides, partisans.

conversation. Social relations.

progging. Begging.

oblations. Offerings.

commodity. Profit.

299 *consistory.* Court of Church elders.

bellycheer. Feast.

Sion. Sion College, meeting place of Presbyterian assemblies.

characters. Letters; i.e. the capital letters on their pamphlets.

considerable. Worth consideration.

'Curse ye Meroz'. Judg. 5: 23. Cf. p. 295, above.

people. The first edition of *TKM* ends here.

300 *Lib. . . . Sleidan.* Luther's *Book Against the Peasants* as extracted in Sleidan (see p. 289 above).

De Bello contra Turcas. Of the War against the Turks (tr. 1560 as *A Famous Chronicle*).

Cochlaeus. Johannes Dobeneck (1479–1552), Roman Catholic opponent of Luther.

stay. Stop.

Phalaris. King of Agrigentum (565–549 BC), notorious for his cruelty. He was said to have roasted his enemies alive inside a brass bull.

Zwinglius. Huldrich Zwingli (1484–1531), Swiss reformer.

301 *on Daniel. Joannis Calvini Praelectione in Librum Prophetiarum Danielis* (1561).

Bucer. Martin Bucer (1491–1551), follower of Luther and Professor of Theology at Cambridge during the reign of Edward VI; quoted from a commentary on Matt. 5: 39, 'resist not evil: but whosoever shall smite thee on the right cheek, turn to him the other also.'

302 *Paraeus.* David Paraeus (1548–1622), Calvinist commentator frequently cited by Milton.

Knox's Appeal. The Appellation of John Knox (1558).

Cartwright. Thomas Cartwright (1535–1603), Lady Margaret Professor of Divinity at Cambridge; later exiled and imprisoned.

Fenner. Dudley Fenner (d. 1587) led a protest against the Act of Supremacy; he was exiled with Cartwright.

Gilby. Anthony Gilby, another Marian Exile; the quotation is misattributed to Gilby in Milton's source, Sir Thomas Aston's *A Remonstrance, against Presbitery* (1641); its author was John Ponet (1514–56).

Christopher Goodman. (1520–1603), another Marian exile; he had taught divinity at Oxford. Milton cites *How Superior Power Ought to Be Obeyed* (1558).

303 *instance.* Urgency.

Whittingham. William Whittingham (1524–79), Marian exile and close associate of Knox.

304 *phylactery.* See 'On the New Forcers of Conscience', l. 17.

304 *Scripture and Reason.* A 1643 royalist pamphlet, by Herbert Palmer and others.

Romans. Rom. 13., as discussed earlier.

amerce. Punish.

305 *Apollonius.* Apollonius of Perga, second-century BC mathematician.

condign. Deserved.

St Peter's rule. 1 Pet. 2: 13–14, discussed earlier.

306 *commodity.* Profit.

Jebusites. Enemies of King David (see e.g. 2 Sam. 5: 8).

Adonibezec. Canaanite ruler (Judg. 1: 5–7) mutilated by the Israelites.

root. Scion, offshoot; here, Christ.

307 *considerable.* Worth consideration.

Simon Magus. Prototype of simony for offering to pay Peter and John so that he might acquire their power (Acts 8: 18–19).

advowsons . . . augmentations. Various appointments to office.

Daniel. In the apocryphal Book of Bel, he revealed how the priests pocketed gifts.

fellow-locusts. The bishops before them, likened to the plague of locusts (Exod. 10: 12–15) prophesied in Rev. 9: 1–3, 'I saw a star fall from heaven . . . And he opened the bottomless pit . . . And there came out . . . locusts upon the earth.'

impetuous. Violent.

308 *Second Defence of the English People.* In addition to handling official correspondence as Secretary for Foreign Tongues, Milton was called upon to censor books and to serve as respondent to attacks on the new government. Milton's first *Defence of the English People* (1651) was written by order of the Council of State in reply to Claude Salmasius's *Defensio Regia*. Salmasius (1588–1653), professor at the University of Leyden, a French classical scholar of great distinction, had a large continental reputation, and his treatise was a widely respected response to the threat to monarchy posed by the English revolution. In answer to Milton's tract, *Regii Sanguinis Clamor* (*The Cry of the Royal Blood*) appeared anonymously in 1652; Milton took it to have been written by Alexander More, a protégé of Salmasius who had been professor of Greek in Geneva until both theological and sexual scandals forced him to leave the city; Salmasius then secured him a position as professor of theology in Middelburg, in Holland, where, once again, scandal overcame him. The tract, was, in fact, written by Pierre du Moulin, an Anglican clergyman, although the preface, signed by the printer, Adrian Vlacq, was written by More, through whose hands the manuscript had passed. Milton's *Second Defence* appeared (in Latin) in 1654; More responded and Milton answered him in the third of his Latin defences, *Pro Se Defensio* (1655).

The Second Defence has frequently been excerpted, as it is here, for its autobiographical passages; as is the case with the *Apology*, these ought to be read within the context of the entire tract. The translation is by Helen North, from the Yale Milton.

308 *one man.* Claude Salmasius. He had been invited to the court of Queen Christina of Sweden in 1650 and left the following year.

trouble. His unfinished *Ad Johannem Miltonum Responsio* appeared posthumously in 1660.

rogues. More and Vlacq.

309 *own vote and decision.* There is no record extant to support the claim that the *Second Defence*, like the first *Defence*, was commissioned by the Council.

exordium. The first part of a Latin oration, Milton's formal model here.

foreign tongue. Latin, the language in which all three defences were written.

310 *Pillars of Hercules.* Gibraltar, westernmost limit of the Mediterranean Sea and the boundary of ancient man's aspirations supposedly set by Hercules.

Father Liber. Bacchus, who travelled as far as India.

Triptolemus. Sent by Ceres to teach the Scythians the sowing of wheat; see *Met.*, v. 643–50.

he. Salmasius.

fable. Erotic tale.

311 *More.* Alexander More (1616–70), born in France, had a Scottish father and a French mother.

Morus. Greek for 'fool'.

the church. In Geneva, where he was professor of theology and a pastor; he left Geneva in 1649 under accusations of unorthodox beliefs and licentious behaviour.

Alcinous or Adonis. Edenic gardens, in *Od.*, vii. 125–8 and in *FQ*, iii. 6.

mulberry on the fig. Punning on Lat. *morus*, mulberry, and *ficus*, fig and vagina.

public library. MS. Fr. 468, 'Affaire Alexander Morus', remains there.

Spanheim. Frederick Spanheim, who also served as a pastor in Geneva in More's time, and later in Leiden until his death in 1649.

312 *Middleburg* [now Middelburg]. More, in fact, held the chair from 1649, two year's before Milton's first *Defence* appeared.

Pyramus. The story, familiar from *Midsummer Night's Dream*, derives from *Met.*, iv.

Pliny. Alluding to Salmasius's most famous book, *Plinianae Excertationes in Caii Julii Solini Polyhistora* (1629), as if it too were a bastard offspring.

Belgium. The Netherlands. The 'Orange party' below was the royalist faction.

312 *magistrates.* The claims of Pontia (her name in the Salmasius household was Bontia; her legal name was Elizabeth Guerret) were rejected by the Synod of Utrecht, and More was exonerated.

313 *Salmacis.* The nymph in *Met.*, iv responsible for the transformation of Hermaphroditus into an androgyne.

Cyclops. Or Polyphemus; his single eye was gouged out by Odysseus (*Od.*, ix. 375–98); see also Virgil, *Aen.*, iii. 658; the comparison of Milton with the Cyclops is explicit in *Clamor.*

314 *Tiresias . . . Phineus.* Blind prophets. In both instances, the blindness was traditionally explained as a punishment, in the case of Phineus, for his prophetic power; but Milton denies that any criminal act is implied. cf. *PL.*, iii. 36.

Apollonius. Third-century Alexandrian poet; the citation is from *Argonautica*, ii. 181–4.

315 *Timoleon.* Statesman and military commander, fourth-century BC; his life ended in blindness. See Plutarch's biography of him, *Lives*, xxxvii.

Appius Claudius. Roman censor, fourth-century BC; his resistance to the incursion of Pyrrhus is recounted in Plutarch, *Lives*, xviii.

Caecilius Metellus. Third-century BC, a general in the first Punic war and successively magister equitum, consul, and pontifex maximus; his rescue of the Palladium, an image of Athena whose possession was believed to confer invincibility, occurred in 241 BC.

Dandolo. Enrico Dandolo, doge from 1193 to 1205.

Zizka. John Zizka, *c.*1376–1424, a military leader of the Bohemian Hussites who lost his sight in battle.

Zanchius. Jerome Zanchius (1516–1590), an early follower of Calvin.

Isaac. See Gen. 27: 1.

Jacob. Milton is undertaking to deal with a contradiction in the story. Gen. 48: 10 says that Jacob's eyes 'were dim for age, so that he could not see', but in the following verse, Jacob says that he does see Joseph and his children.

the man who was healed. See John 9, in which Jesus pronounces the blindness no mark of sin (9: 3), declares that he 'must work the works of him that sent me while it is day' (9: 4) and that he is 'the light of the world' (9: 5), puts spittle and clay on the blind man's eyes (9: 6), and commands him to bathe in 'the pool of Siloam' (9: 7). The passage is recalled also in Milton's early letter to a friend and in *PL*, i. 11.

316 *Aesculapius.* The god of medicine whose shrine was in Epidaurus.

son of Thetis. Achilles; *Il.*, ix. 411–16, cited below.

317 *the apostle.* St Paul, in 2 Cor. 12: 9, 'my strength is made perfect in weakness', a motto that Milton adopted as his own in the 1650s.

conversation. Citing Euripides, *Orestes*, 795, *Hercules Furens*, 1398, 1402.

318 *Prytaneum.* The dining hall where distinguished Athenians were banqueted; Socrates had proposed this treatment as his 'punishment' in the *Apology*. Milton is insisting that his blindness did not lose him his official position.

Only one man. Milton is citing the *Defensio Regia*, answering its charges against him.

noxious. The Latin proverb says '*heroüm filii noxae*', the sons of heroes are criminals, a translation of *Od.*, ii. 315, expounded by Erasmus in the *Adagia*.

Andraemon. See Martial, *Epigrams*, x. 9, where the poet says he is as well known as the horse.

David. Ps. 22: 6, 'I am a worm, and no man.' In Mark 9: 48, Jesus quotes Isa. 66: 24 on the undying worm of damnation.

319 *Saturn.* Deposed as king of heaven by his son Jupiter, he fled to Italy.

Bucer. Martin Bucer (1491–1551), friend of Luther and late in life professor of theology at Cambridge, whose work was summarized and translated in Milton's *The Judgement of Martin Bucer, Concerning Divorce*.

Fagius. Paulus Fagius (1504–49) accompanied Bucer to England and became professor of Hebrew at Cambridge.

Curius. M. Annius Curius Dentatus, third-centruy BC, famous exemplar of Roman frugality and incorruptibility; Milton argues that the author of *Clamor* has thus misrepresented himself.

321 *Thomas Scudamore.* Actually, John Scudamore; he had been Charles I's ambassador in Paris since 1634.

Hugo Grotius. (1583–1645), legal theorist and author of religious plays, including *Adamus Exul* and *Christus Patiens*.

academies. Literary and social societies, with which the persons mentioned below were associated: the Academy of the Svogliati was founded by Jacopo Gaddi; the Apatisti met in the home of Agostino Coltellini; Carlo Dati was a member of the Florentine Academy, and he is mentioned in the *Ep. Dam.* Letters of Milton to a number of these Florentines and to those mentioned below are extant in the *Familiar Letters*.

Holste. Luc Holste or Holstenius (1596–1661), German theologian, librarian to Cardinal Francesco Barberini and later Vatican librarian.

322 *Manso.* Giovanni Battista Manso, *c.*1560–*c.*1645, patron of Tasso and a poet in his own right; he was hospitable to Milton in Naples and contributed a prefatory poem to the 1645 *Poems*. He is mentioned in *Ep. Dam.* and addressed in 'Manso'.

Diodati. Giovanni Diodati (1576–1649), uncle of Milton's friend Charles Diodati and an eminent theologian.

second Bishops' War. August 1640; the war lasted little more than a week.

323 *two books . . . church.* i.e. the two books of *Of Reformation*.

323 *two bishops.* James Ussher, archbishop of Armagh, and Joseph Hall, who attacked the Smectymnuans (see *Apol.*, headnote).

324 *Selden.* John Selden (1584–1654), legal historian and antiquarian, author of *Uxor Ebraica* (1646).

325 *This book. The Tenure of Kings and Magistrates.*

the history. Milton's *History of Britain* was published in 1670; it begins in legendary times and ends with the Norman Conquest.

326 *unclean More.* Paraphrasing Jesus' encounter with 'a man with an unclean spirit' (Mark 1: 23) whom he rebukes; 'Hold thy peace, and come out of him' (1:25).

328 *liberating Brutuses.* Lucius Junius Brutus (sixth-century BC) expelled the Tarquin kings from Rome.

329 *Crescentius Nomentanus.* Roman aristocrat, he seized power in the name of Roman republican principles after the death of the Holy Roman Emperor Otto II (983) and deposed Pope Gregory V; he was defeated and executed by the Emperor Otto III.

Cola di Rienzi. A friend of Petrarch's, his attempt to seize power in the name of Roman liberty met defeat in 1354.

borne arms. i.e. by writing in Latin.

330 *erected a monument.* Alluding to Horace, *Odes*, iii. 30.

The Ready and Easy Way. From 1658, when Oliver Cromwell died, until 1660, when Charles II was restored, the government of England was in continual crisis. Richard Cromwell had succeeded his father, but only for a few months. The Rump Parliament (which Oliver Cromwell had disbanded in 1653) was recalled, and disbanded, three times, with the army and Parliament in fierce contention throughout the period. General George Monck, leader of the Scottish army, emerged as the central figure through the various shifting political accommodations, promoting a parliament to which those previously excluded (in Pride's Purge of 1648) would be readmitted, thereby paving the way to the restoration of Charles II, which Monck ultimately supported.

During these two years, Milton wrote eight pamphlets responding to the heated political climate, among them *A Treatise of Civil Power* and *Considerations Touching the Likeliest Means to Remove Hirelings. REW* was the last of these; it appeared first early in 1660 and again in a second edition (our text here) in April 1660, shortly before the restoration of Charles II on 1 May 1660. Milton's idea of a perpetual parliament is indebted to the commonwealth proposed in James Harrington's *Oceana* (1656) and in several tracts of 1659–60 written by Harrington and his followers in the newly formed Rota Club, dedicated to the exploration of republican political theory.

[Motto] *Et nos . . . nunc.* Juvenal, *Satires*, i: 'And we have given counsel to Sulla, now let us give it to the people.' (Milton's *The Present Means* had been written as a letter to General Monck.)

330 *new elections.* Mandated by a vote of the Rump, the elections were 'recalled' when its membership had been enlarged by those previously excluded in Pride's Purge; Parliament had ordered elections for a new session to meet in April.

331 *resolution . . . in power.* Monck, the army officers, and the Commons all were avowedly resolved on restoring the commonwealth; in the interval between sittings of Parliament, the Council of State was the ruling body, controlled by the army.

to bondage. i.e. to monarchy.

or. Before.

shroving-time. Shrovetide, the period set aside for confession—and carnival—before Ash Wednesday and the beginning of Lent.

suddenly dispersed. Quickly distributed.

judging kingship. A resolution of Feb. 1649 had abolished kingship as 'unnecessary, burdensome and dangerous'.

covenant. i.e. the Solemn League and Covenant of 1643, pledging the king's safety (quoted below).

332 *Job.* Alluding to Job 13: 15, 'Though he slay me, yet will I trust in him.'

engagement. The oath of loyalty to the commonwealth required of Members of Parliament after Oct. 1649.

protestation. Of 3 May 1641, in which the defence of religion was linked to the defence of the king.

many were excluded. By Pride's Purge.

many fled. Earlier, in 1643–4, royalists had set up their own parliament in Oxford.

church . . . rules. This is the argument of Milton's religious tracts of 1659–60.

positive. Posited, thus arbitrary, artificial.

under force. Alluding to the allegation that the commonwealth derived its power from the army.

legal parliament. The Oxford Parliament of king, lords, and commons, as opposed to the Long Parliament, from which the king was excluded.

intentions. e.g. to support the king, as the Long Parliament at first declared it would do.

333 *Iscariot.* Judas, who betrayed Christ for payment, but who also protested at the waste of oil used to annoint Jesus' feet because it might have been sold to relieve the poor (John 12: 3–6).

Simon. Simon Magus, who offered to pay to be able to perform the apostolic office (Acts 8: 9–23).

333 *Saul.* St Paul's original name, when he persecuted the Jews (Acts 8: 3, 9: 1–9).

were not to learn. They already knew (that many Presbyterians and many citizens sided with the king).

treaty. The Newport Treaty (1648) allowed for parliamentary control of the militia for twenty years, and established Presbyterianism for three years.

put to shift. At odds.

An Inquisition for Blood. *An Inquisition After Blood,* a royalist pamphlet of July 1649 written by James Howell, argued in effect that the king need not, and in fact did not, feel bound by the treaty.

bishops . . . removed. Since Presbyterianism was settled only temporarily.

alienated. Transferred.

rented. Charles had agreed to the use of episcopal lands only on 99-year leases.

'sacrilege.' As Charles I declared in Nov. 1648.

delinquents. Those who raised arms against Parliament.

condign. deserved

author. Charles I.

swore. In the Solemn League and Covenant.

event. Outcome.

defer. Delay.

334 *adversary.* Salamasius (See *Second Defence*).

Saviour. Luke 14: 28–30, 'For which of you, intending to build a tower, sitteth not down first, and counteth the cost . . . lest haply, after he hath laid the foundation, and is not able to finish it, all that behold it begin to mock him.'

335 *United Provinces.* The Netherlands.

equallest. Most equitable.

gave a king. Saul; see *TKM* for discussion of 1 Sam. 8: 5–7.

Christ. Luke 2:25–6 is quoted.

336 *Zebedee's two sons.* James and John: in Mark 10: 42–5, a version of Luke 22: 25–6 (cited above) is offered in answer to them when they ask to sit next to Jesus in his glory (Mark 10: 35–7).

outlandish. Foreign, like Henrietta Maria, who was a French Catholic, and Charles II's Portuguese fiancée Catherine of Braganza.

close-stool. Chamber-pot; Charles II did provide for a Groom of the Stool.

French court. Of Louis XIV, although at the time in the hands of the queen mother, Anne of Austria, and of Cardinal Mazarin.

cheapening. Both bargaining about and lowering the price of.

337 *late court poet.* Davenant and Chapman have been proposed as the referent.

cipher. The arithmetical symbol 'o' that acts as a multiplier although it has no value itself.

Solomon. Citing Prov. 6: 6–8.

pismire. Ant.

338 *admirable.* To be wondered at, astonishing.

heartless. Lacking courage.

339 *interruptions.* Cromwell has 'interrupted' Parliament in 1653 by expelling the Rump; he dissolved the Barebones (or Nominated) Parliament that succeeded it; in 1658–60, Parliament was dismissed three times as the army and Parliament wrestled over questions of membership.

Writs. Of 16 Mar. 1660 for the convening of Parliament on 25 April 1660.

knights and burgesses. Knights were representatives of counties and shires, burgesses of towns, boroughs, and the universities of Oxford and Cambridge.

qualifications. Laid out by the restored Rump in Jan–Feb. 1660, provisions barring Roman Catholics and royalists; these provisions were, in fact, nullified in the March meeting.

340 *council of state.* Such councils had been formed in May 1659, Dec. 1659, and Feb. 1660 in an attempt to limit the power of the army and control the factions in Parliament.

prevent. Anticipate, forestall.

suspense. In suspense, suspended.

'partial rotation'. The proposal was that of James Harrington in *Oceana* (1656), and in pamphlets by him and other members of the Rota Club, a political group devoted to republican ideals.

wheel. Extending the image of rotation.

341 *well-affected.* Loyal.

temperament. Modification.

Sanhedrin. The seventy elders appointed by Moses (Num. 11: 16–17) as the ruling legislative and judicial assembly of Israel.

Areopagus. See *Areopagitica*, headnote.

ancients. A permanent council of thirty members over the age of sixty, established by Lycurgus's constitution for Sparta.

Six. The Venetian Council of Six assisted the Doge; its membership changed frequently, but the Grand Council was permanent.

deputed. Delegated.

policy. Government, the state. The 'reasons' are based on Jean Bodin's *De Republica*, iii. 1.

341 *to seek.* Lacking.

342 *acquisite.* Acquired.

event. Outcome.

in fine. In the end.

Marius. Gaius Marius (157–86 BC), general of plebeian origins, seven times consul, who massacred patricians; Cornelius Sulla (see below), his patrician opponent, became dictator when Marius died.

propounded. By Harrington and the Rota.

chargeable. Expensive.

motion . . . session. Both in their journeying and in their meeting.

lieger. Resident.

other senate. Harrington had proposed a senate of about 300 members as lawmakers, and a second house of about 1000 members to ratify or reject their laws in secret ballots.

343 *Tarquins.* The republic was established when the last of the Tarquin kings was banished in 510 BC.

shouting. County elections were determined by voice vote, those shouting loudest prevailing.

voices. Votes.

committees. Local governing bodies, abusive under Charles I as well as during the Protectorate.

referred to time. Deferred for later treatment.

still. Always.

344 *agrarian law.* A major feature of Harrington's *Oceana*, it artificially limited the value of property and abolished primogeniture in favour of distributing property equally among the heirs.

considerable. Worth consideration.

fond conceit. Foolish idea.

lurch. Steal.

house of Nassau. The family of William of Orange, which was able to assume dictatorial powers in times of national emergency in the United Provinces.

345 *voice.* Vote.

346 *Politics. Pol.*, iii. 15, closely paraphrased.

prejudicate. Judge (unfavourably) beforehand.

gentilizing. Desiring to be like pagan nations, as when the Jews asked to have a king 'like all the nations' (1 Sam. 8: 5).

peculiar. Chosen.

346 *Eli's sons.* 1 Sam. 2: 12–17 describes how these 'sons of Belial' appropriated sacrifices.

346–7 *'Ye shall . . . that day'.* 1 Sam. 8: 18.

those . . . individual. i.e. episcopal revenues are inseparable from royal revenues (individual = single, indissoluble).

neuters. Neutrals.

pacification. In 1639, in the pacification of Berwick, Charles I agreed to place control of government and religion in Scotland in the Scots' own hands; he quickly broke the agreement.

tigers of Bacchus. Bacchus, god of wine, was depicted in a chariot drawn by tigers.

sweating-tub. Used to treat venereal disease; preaching tubs were makeshift pulpits.

348 *plough.* Make furrows on, hence lash, whip.

more . . . actors. The Presbyterians, as participants in more than three parts of the drama of establishing the commonwealth.

Rupert. Prince Rupert (1619–82), son of Frederick V and Queen Elizabeth of Bohemia (daughter of James I), who led Charles I's army from 1642 to 1645, and later commanded troops of English exiles and a royalist fleet.

delinquents and compounders. Delinquents, those who had supported the royalists, had been allowed to redeem ('compound'), upon payment of a stipulated sum, property taken from them. Milton assumed (incorrectly, as it turned out) that similar exactions would occur at the Restoration.

this greatest part. Royalist supporters who, as defeated enemies, have lost the right to vote.

349 *another treatise. Treatise of Civil Power in Ecclesiastical Causes* (Feb. 1659).

umbrage. Shadow.

Camden. William Camden (1551–1623) in *The History of the Most renowned and victorious Princess Elizabeth* (1630).

350 *charge of his father.* Quoting ch. 27 of *Eikon Basilike*, written largely by John Gauden, Charles I's chaplain; it appeared a week after Charles's execution and was answered by Milton in *Eikonoklastes*.

the covenant. The Solemn League and Covenant of 1643 had been reinstated on 5 Mar. 1660; it pledged allegiance to the king.

in circuit. In circumference; i.e. according to size.

351 *indifferent.* Unbiased.

equal. Equitable.

peculiar. Separate, individual. Milton follows Aristotle on the *Athenian Constitution*, xxi. 3 ff., describing the institution of Cleisthenes in 510 BC.

ornaments. Trappings.

352 *envy.* Ill-will.

352 *Jews.* Num. 11: 5 reports the desire of the Jews to return to Egypt, although no 'idol queen' is mentioned.

353 *conceit.* Idea.

who . . . circumstances. People who can deal with particulars.

prophet. Jer. 22: 29, 'O earth, earth, earth, hear the word of the Lord.'

MAJOR POEMS

355 *Paradise Lost.* The earliest subjects Milton seems to have considered for an epic were drawn from British history and legend, and his admiration for 'our sage and serious poet Spenser', the obvious English epic model, is expressed in *Areopagitica*—Dryden reports that Milton told him that 'Spenser was his original'. In the early 1640s he was thinking of biblical material as a subject not for epic but for tragedy: the Trinity MS includes four outlines of a drama on the fall, two of which are entitled *Paradise Lost* and *Adam Unparadized*. Milton's nephew Edward Phillips reports being shown some lines of Satan's soliloquy in Book 4 (ll. 32–41) some years before Milton began the composition of his epic; the speech at that time was the beginning of a tragedy. But by the time Milton was writing the epic *Paradise Lost* he was representing the move away from chivalric legend (and, ultimately, from rhymed stanzas) as an affirmation of truth and liberty. As an immediate model of the Protestant biblical epic, he had Guillaume Salluste, Sieur du Bartas' enormously influential *Les Semaines et les Jours* (1578), which appeared in English in Joshua Sylvester's translation as *Divine Weeks and Days* in 1605; Milton admired the poem, and declares his indebtedness to it by many allusions.

Milton clearly worked on some version of *Paradise Lost*, however intermittently, from the early 1640s on. John Aubrey reports that the composition of the poem in its final form took Milton four or five years, roughly from 1658 to 1663. This was a period of both total blindness and considerable danger for Milton; his sense of his situation is keenly conveyed in the opening section of Book 7. He worked by dictating to whatever willing scribe was at hand; Phillips corrected the spelling and punctuation of at least some of the manuscript. By 1667 it was ready for the printer—Milton's early biographer John Toland reports that the censor objected to it because of a passage in Book 1 (ll. 597–9) about the ominous implications of solar eclipses for the fate of monarchs, but it nevertheless was duly licensed and appeared in a first edition of six variant issues in 1667, 1668, and 1669, and in a second edition in 1674, the year of Milton's death. It sold relatively quickly, and by the time Dryden approached Milton, in the last year of his life, to declare his intention of turning the poem into an opera, it had established itself as a classic.

In its first published version, *Paradise Lost* was a poem in ten books; it did not include either Milton's introductory note on the verse or the arguments of the individual books, and had no prefatory commendatory poems. The note on the verse and the arguments, all grouped together at the beginning, were added in 1668, apparently at the request of the publisher. For the second edition of 1674, Milton had revised the poem into twelve books. To accomplish this, Books 7 and 10 were simply split in two; the rewriting involved was small, but not insignificant (it is indicated in our notes), and a few other minor revisions were made. The volume included a Latin prefatory poem by Milton's friend the physician Samuel Barrow, and Andrew Marvell's 'On Paradise Lost'. Some commentators have seen in the ten-book version a vestige of Milton's original dramatic scheme, a double five-act structure; the change to twelve books (like the opening lines of *Paradise Regained*) clearly reflects Milton's Virgilian model.

Some important recent critical works on the poem are discussed in the general introduction.

The Verse

355 *invention of a barbarous age.* In Latin poetry, rhyme first began to be used regularly in Christian hymns of the fifth and sixth centuries.

apt numbers. Appropriate rhythm.

BOOK I

The Argument
not in the centre. Not at the centre of the earth (which had not yet been created).

utter. Both absolute and outer.

356 *Pandaemonium.* Lit. 'all the demons'; the name is Milton's coinage.

l. 4. *one greater man.* Jesus, as the Messiah.

l. 6. *heavenly muse.* Urania, the muse of astronomy, and therefore of heavenly matters generally, invoked by name in Book 7: as the inspiration of Moses, she is identified here with the divine word.   *secret top.* Summit hidden from public view, where God spoke alone with Moses.

l. 7. *of Oreb, or of Sinai.* God delivered the Ten Commandments to Moses either on Mount Horeb (Deut. 4: 10) or on nearby Mount Sinai (Exod. 19: 20). Here, as throughout, Milton uses the Vulgate form of biblical names.

l. 8. *shepherd.* Moses is identified as the shepherd of Jethro's flock in Exod. 3, but the term is also used figuratively for him as leader of his people.   *seed.* Literally translating *semen*, God's offspring, the children of Israel.

l. 9. *In the beginning.* The opening words of Genesis and John.

l. 10. *out of chaos.* Technically a heretical position: orthodox doctrine held that God created the world not out of unformed matter (the *chaos* of Neoplatonic philosophy) but *ex nihilo*, out of nothing, the 'void' of Gen. 1: 2. See *CD* i. 7.   *Sion hill.* The sacred Mount Zion, on which Solomon's Temple stood.

l. 11. *Siloa's brook.* The Pool of Siloam, which flows alongside the Temple mountain, and with whose waters Jesus cured a blind man (John 9: 7).

356 l. 12. *Fast by.* Close.

l. 15. *Aonian mount.* Helicon, in Aonia in Boeotia, sacred to the classical muses.

ll. 17–22. *And chiefly thou . . . pregnant.* The Holy Spirit, that in Gen. 1: 2 'moved upon the waters' and was the agent of creation. Milton's 'brooding' (l. 21) gives a more precise translation of the Hebrew.

l. 21. *Dove-like.* The Holy Spirit is a dove descending on Jesus in John 1: 32. Cf. *PR*, i. 30–1.

l. 24. *height.* Milton's normal spelling, and standard usage in the seventeenth century, is 'highth'.   *argument.* Subject.

l. 28. *Nor.* Not even.

357 l. 36. *what time.* When; the diction is Latinate, but the expression was in common English usage.

l. 48. *adamantine.* Unbreakable: adamant was a mythical substance of impenetrable hardness.

l. 50. *Nine times . . . night.* The nine days of the rebel angels' fall is based not on biblical authority but on Hesiod's account of the fall of the Titans who rebelled against Zeus (*Theogony*, 664–735), which was considered another version of the same event.

l. 56. *baleful.* Both malign and full of pain.

l. 57. *witnessed.* Both regarded and testified to.

l. 60. *dismal.* Ominous, disastrous.

l. 66. *hope never comes.* Recalling Dante's inscription on the gate of hell, '*Lasciate ogni speranza, voi ch'entrate*' ('Abandon all hope, you who enter', *Inferno*, iii. 9).

l. 68. *Still urges.* Continuously presses.

l. 72. *utter.* Both total and outer.

l. 74. *As from the centre . . . pole.* Milton imagines a Ptolemaic universe with the earth at the centre of nine concentric spheres. The distance from hell to heaven is three times as far as the centre of the earth is from a point on the outermost sphere.

358 l. 78. *weltering.* Writhing.

l. 81. *Beelzebub.* The name in Hebrew means 'god of flies'.

l. 82. *And thence . . . called Satan.* The name means 'enemy'; his original name was Lucifer, 'bringer of light'.

l. 84. *If . . . changed.* The words contain a double echo, of Aeneas seeing a vision of the dead Hector on the night Troy fell, '*quantum mutatus ab illo / Hectore*' ('how changed from that other Hector', *Aen.*, ii. 274–5), and of Isa. 14: 12, 'How art thou fallen from heaven, Lucifer, son of the morning.'

l. 87. *if he.* 'Thou beest' is understood.

l. 104. *dubious.* 'Of uncertain issue or result' (*OED*).

358 l. 107. *study of.* Zeal for (Lat. *studium*).

l. 114. *Doubted.* Feared for.

359 l. 117. *empyreal.* Heavenly (lit. made of fire, the purest element).

l. 132. *proof.* Test.

l. 144. *Of force.* Perforce.

l. 148. *suffice.* Satisfy.

360 l. 158. *Doing or suffering.* Whether active or passive.

l. 167. *fail.* Mistake.

l. 172. *laid.* Put down.

l. 178. *slip.* Neglect.

l. 186. *afflicted.* lit. 'cast down'.

l. 187. *offend.* Injure.

l. 196. *rood.* Or rod, a variable measure, from six to eight yards.

361 ll. 198–9. *Titanian . . . Typhon.* The hundred-armed Briareos was a Titan, the monster Typhon (or Typhoeus) a giant with a hundred serpent-heads. Both Titans and giants made war on the Olympian gods and were thrown back to earth and crushed or cast into the classical hell, Tartarus. See Hesiod, *Theogony*, 713–16 and 819–85, and Ovid, *Met.*, v. 325–31 and 346–58. The Typhon story was moralized by Renaissance mythographers as an allegory of the destructive potential of ambition (Conti, *Mythologiae*, vi. 22).

l. 200. *Tarsus.* According to Pindar, Typhon dwelt in a cave in Cilicia, of which Tarsus was the principal city (*Pythian Odes*, i. 17).

l. 201. *Leviathan.* A mysterious sea-monster in Job 41, a 'piercing' and 'crooked serpent' in Isa. 27: 1, hence associated with Satan; also frequently identified as a whale. The story of the whale appearing a safe haven to unwary sailors was often cited as a parallel to the dangerous deceptiveness of Satan.

l. 206. *rind.* The skin of an animal.

l. 207. *under the lee.* In its shelter.

l. 208. *Invests.* Envelops.

l. 210. *Chained on.* Confined to.

l. 226. *incumbent.* Lying (lit. 'pressing upon'; see l. 227).

l. 228. *lights.* Alights.   *ever.* Always.

l. 231. *subterranean wind.* Ovid describes underground winds creating a hill in *Met.*, xv. 296–377; seventeenth-century meteorology held that the earth is 'full of wind . . . which, sometimes breaking out, causeth horrible earthquakes' (Burton, *Anatomy of Melancholy*, II. ii. 3).

ll. 232–3. *Pelorus . . . Aetna.* Cape Faro, in north-east Sicily, and the volcano nearby.

l. 235. *Sublimed with mineral fury.* Vaporized by the volcano's violence.

362 l. 239. *Stygian flood.* The Styx, one of the four rivers of hell. *Stygian* implies impenetrable darkness.

l. 256. *What matter where.* 'I am' understood.

l. 266. *astonished.* Stunned.   *oblivious.* Producing forgetfulness.

l. 268. *mansion.* Dwelling-place (not necessarily a building).

l. 276. *edge.* Front line (Lat. *acies*).

363 l. 282. *pernicious.* Ruinous, fatal.

l. 285. *Ethereal temper.* Tempered in heavenly fire.

l. 288. *optic glass.* Telescope.   *Tuscan artist.* Galileo, who first devised a telescope sufficiently powerful to reveal the surface of the moon. Milton alludes to a visit to him in *Areopagitica* (see p. 259).

l. 289. *Fesole.* Fiesole, a hill-town near Florence.

l. 290. *Valdarno.* The Arno valley, in which Florence is located.

l. 294. *admiral.* Flagship.

l. 296. *marl.* Soil.

l. 299. *Natheless.* Nevertheless.

l. 303. *Vallombrosa.* Lit. 'valley of shadows', near Florence.   *Etrurian shades.* Tuscan foliage.

l. 304. *sedge.* Seaweed.

l. 305. *Orion.* One of the giants, a great hunter slain by Diana and transformed into a constellation. It was associated with storms because its evening rising during autumn signals the approach of winter.

ll. 306–7. *whose waves . . . chivalry.* After Moses parted the Red Sea and the Israelites passed safely to the opposite shore, the waters closed over the pursuing Egyptians, destroying Pharaoh's army (Exod. 14: 21 ff.). *Busiris.* Pharaoh, here given the name of a legendary Egyptian tyrant.

l. 307. *Memphian chivalry.* Egyptian cavalry.

l. 309. *Goshen.* The area in Egypt where Jacob and his descendants settled, and from which the Israelites were fleeing.

l. 313. *amazement.* Stupefaction.

l. 317. *astonishment.* 'Loss of sense . . . mental prostration, stupor' (*OED*; cf. l. 266).

l. 320. *virtue.* Strength.

364 l. 324. *Cherub and seraph.* The two highest orders of angels, first established by Dionysius the Pseudo-Areopagite (fourth-century AD) in *De Coelesti Hierarchia*, vi. 2

l. 333. *whom.* The one whom.

l. 339. *Amram's son.* Moses, whose 'potent rod' invoked the plague of locusts on the Egyptians (Exod. 10: 12–15).

l. 341. *warping.* Whirling.

364 l. 345. *cope.* Canopy.

l. 353. *Rhene . . . Danaw.* Rhine, Danube.

l. 360. *erst.* Formerly.

365 l. 363. *books of life.* The term is used in the Old and New Testaments for the record of God's faithful, those destined for eternal life in heaven.

l. 365. *Got them new names.* The transformation of the fallen angels into pagan deities is attested by many Church Fathers; see e.g. Tertullian, *Apologeticum*, xx. 22–4.

l. 372. *religions.* Religious rites.

l. 373. *devils . . . deities.* 'They sacrificed unto devils, not to God' (Deut. 32: 17).

l. 376. *then.* i.e. subsequently, in the 'heathen world' of l. 375.

l. 380. *promiscuous.* 'Massed together without order' (*OED*).

l. 392. *Moloch.* The name means *king*; cf. 'Nativity Ode', ll. 205 ff.

ll. 394–5. *Though for the noise . . . unheard.* The cries of sacrificial children were drowned out by the sound of drums and timbrels.

l. 396. *Ammonite.* The Ammonites were enemies of Israel, ultimately conquered by Jephtha.

l. 397. *Rabba.* Rabbah, the Ammonite capital; modern Amman, in Jordan.

ll. 398–9. *Argob . . . Basan . . . Arnon.* The lands east of the Dead Sea, roughly the northern section of modern Jordan. Argob was the southern part of the region of Bashan, in the north, and the area in which Moloch was worshipped extended into Ammon, as far south as the Arnon river.

365–6 ll. 401–3. *Of Solomon . . . that hill.* 'Solomon loved many strange [i.e. foreign] women'; among his seven hundred wives were Ammonites and Moabites, who 'turned away his heart after other gods', and he built a temple 'for Moloch, the abomination of the children of Ammon' on the Mount of Olives, hence 'that opprobrious hill' (1 Kgs. 11: 1–7).

366 ll. 404–5. *Hinnom, Tophet . . . Gehenna.* The valley of Hinnom runs along the western and southern edges of Jerusalem. *Tophet*, in the valley's south, was the site of Moloch's shrine where the child sacrifices of ll. 394–5 were performed. The Hebrew name of the valley, Ge-hinnom, was transliterated into Greek as Geenna, in its English form *Gehenna*, and, because of the abominations practised there, this became the New Testament word for hell.

l. 406. *Chemos.* 'Chemosh, the abomination of Moab', also worshipped at Solomon's shrine (1 Kgs. 11: 7).

l. 407. *Aroar.* Aroer (modern Arair, in Jordan), an important northern Moabite city.   *Nebo.* The name of both a southern Moabite town and the mountain in Moab from which Moses saw the promised land of Canaan.

366 ll. 408–9. *Abarim.* A range of hills, including Mount Nebo, at the western edge of Moab, overlooking the Jordan valley and the Dead Sea. *Hesebon . . . Horonaim . . . Seon's realm.* Heshbon and Horonaim were Amorite cities; Sihon (*Seon*) was king of the Amorites.

ll. 410–11. *Sibma . . . Eleale.* Sibma, east of the Jordan in the Moabite hills, was famous for its wine; Elealeh was a nearby city.   *the Asphaltic Pool.* The Dead Sea, which casts up bitumen, or asphalt.

l. 412. *Peor.* More fully Baal-Peor, the Moabite deity identified with Chemosh.

ll. 413–14. *Sittim . . . wanton rites.* Shittim, on the east bank of the Jordan opposite Jericho, the last encampment of the Israelites before crossing into Canaan, where 'the people began to commit whoredom with the daughters of Moab . . . and Israel joined himself unto Baal-peor' (Num. 25: 1–3).

ll. 415–16. *Yet thence . . . hill of scandal.* The Mount of Olives, the 'opprobrious hill' of l. 403 (see note to ll. 404–5).

l. 417. *hard by.* Adjacent to.

l. 418. *good Josiah.* Extirpated idolatry from Israel and destroyed the shrine of Topheth (2 Kgs. 23: 10).

ll. 420–1. *Euphrates . . . Syrian ground.* From the northernmost to the southernmost border of Syria (the River Besor), including modern Jordan.

l. 422. *Baalim and Ashtaroth.* Baal (plural Baalim) was the general name given to the chief god of the Canaanite pantheon, particularized in various cults by the addition of a surname (e.g. Baal-peor; cf. l. 412); Ashtoreth (plural Ashtaroth) is the biblical form of Ishtar or Astarte, analogous to Venus in the Roman pantheon, goddess of sex and, in the middle-eastern cults, of war. Cf. 'Nativity Ode', ll. 197 ff.

l. 428. *cumbrous.* Cumbersome.

l. 433. *their living strength.* i.e. the God of Israel.

l. 435. *bestial.* Because they were worshipped in the form of animals.

ll. 438–9. *Astoreth . . . Astarte.* Worshipped as the moon goddess, hence 'with crescent horns', l. 439.

l. 441. *Sidonian.* Phoenician (from Sidon, the chief city of Phoenicia).

367 l. 444. *uxorious king.* Solomon, who had seven hundred wives.

ll. 446–9. *Thammuz . . . summer's day.* Astarte's lover Tammuz, a god of fertility and vegetation, was identified with Adonis. His death was annually celebrated at the summer solstice.

ll. 450–1. *Adonis . . . purple.* The River Adonis, in Lebanon, becomes discoloured with reddish mud each summer.

l. 455. *Ezekiel . . . led.* For Ezekiel's vision of the Israelite 'women weeping for Tammuz' see Ezek. 8: 14.

367 ll. 457–9. *came one . . . brute image.* The Philistines placed the captured ark of the Lord in the temple of their god Dagon; the next morning the idol of Dagon was found destroyed (1 Sam. 5: 4). Cf. *SA*, 13.

l. 460. *groundsel.* Threshold.

ll. 464–6. *Azotus . . . Ascalon . . . Accaron.* Vulgate names of the Authorized Version's Ashdod, Askelon, Ekron; these, with Gath and Gaza, were the five principal Philistine cities. *coast.* Philistia lay along the Mediterranean coast. *frontier bounds.* Ekron was the northernmost of the five cities, Gaza the southernmost.

l. 467. *Rimmon.* The chief Syrian deity.

l. 471. *A leper once he lost.* When Elisha told the Syrian general Naaman that washing in the Jordan would cure his leprosy, Naaman scoffed, but when he subsequently followed the prophet's advice and was cured, he acknowledged the God of Israel (2 Kgs. 10 ff.).

ll. 471–6. *a king . . . vanquished.* King Ahaz in alliance with the king of Assyria conquered Damascus, but he then converted to the cult of Rimmon and placed a Syrian altar in the temple of Jerusalem (2 Kgs. 16: 9–17).

l. 472. *sottish.* Foolish.

l. 478. *Osiris, Isis, Orus.* Isis, Egyptian moon goddess, represented with the horns of a cow, was the mother of Orus (or Horus), a hawk-headed god, and wife and mother of the sun god Osiris. See the 'Nativity Ode', ll. 211–20 and notes.

ll. 483–4. *borrowed gold . . . Oreb.* While Moses was on Mount Sinai receiving the ten commandments, his brother Aaron, the high priest, erected a golden idol of a calf, claiming it as the god who had delivered Israel from Egypt. The worship of the golden calf so enraged Moses when he returned that he broke the tablets of the law and destroyed the idol (Exod. 32: 1–20).

367–8 ll. 484–5. *rebel king . . . Dan.* When Jereboam led the rebellion of the Ten Tribes of Israel against King Rehoboam, he set up two golden calves, in Bethel and Dan, as alternative centres of worship to the temple at Jerusalem (1 Kgs. 28–32).

368 ll. 487–9. *Jehovah . . . bleating gods.* For God's destruction of the Egyptian firstborn, see Exod. 12: 12.

l. 488. *equalled.* i.e. made equal by destroying.

l. 490. *Belial.* Not a god in the Old Testament, but a personification: the Hebrew word means 'worthless', and the biblical 'sons of Belial' were not worshippers at a particular shrine but good-for-nothings. Milton is partly aware of this: see ll. 492–3. Cf. *PR*, ii. 150 ff. and note.

ll. 495–6. *Eli's sons . . . God.* Eli was a priest at Shiloh, who took the young Samuel into his care. His two profligate sons 'lay with the women that assembled at the door of the tabernacle'; for this iniquity God pronounced the irremediable doom of Eli's house (1 Sam. 2–4).

l. 502. *flown.* Swollen.

368 ll. 503–5. *Sodom . . . rape.* The story is in Judg. 19: a Levite travelling with his concubine was given shelter by an old man in the city of Gibeah, and 'certain sons of Belial beset the house round about, and beat at the door' demanding to be allowed to rape the Levite. They were given the concubine instead (the 'matron' of l. 505) and raped her to death. Milton's notion that there are preferable kinds of rape is entirely consistent with the biblical account.

l. 508. *Ionian.* Greek.   *Javan.* son of Japhet and grandson of Noah, here identified with Ion, progenitor of the Ionian Greeks.

ll. 509–10. *Heaven and Earth . . . parents.* Uranus and Ge (in Latin, Coelus and Terra) were the parents of the Titans, and grandparents of Zeus (Jove) and the Olympian gods.

ll. 510–13. *Titan . . . found.* Titan, the oldest of Uranus' children, was overthrown by his younger brother Saturn, who in turn was overthrown by his son Jove.   *Rhea.* Saturn's wife, Jove's mother.

ll. 514–15. *Crete . . . Ida.* Jove was born on Mount Ida in Crete.

ll. 517–18. *Delphian cliff . . . Dodona.* The oracle of Apollo was at Delphi, that of Zeus at Dodona.

l. 519. *Doric land.* Greece.   *Saturn . . . fled.* Saturn was banished from heaven by Jove, and roamed the earth.

l. 520. *Adria.* The Adriatic Sea.

l. 520. *Hesperian fields.* Italy.

l. 521. *Celtic.* French.   *utmost isles.* Britain and Ireland.

l. 523. *damp.* Depressed, 'with dampened spirits'.

369 l. 528. *recollecting.* Summoning up, rallying.

l. 532. *clarions.* Shrill-sounding trumpets with a narrow tube, 'formerly much used as a signal in war' (*OED*).

l. 534. *Azazel.* Not an angel in the Bible, but in Cabbalistic writers one of four standard-bearers of Satan's army; the name means 'scapegoat' (see Lev. 16: 8, 20).

l. 537. *meteor.* In the seventeenth century both a shooting star and a comet.

l. 538. *emblazed.* 'Adorned with heraldic devices' (*OED*).

l. 542. *concave.* Vault.

l. 543. *reign . . . Night.* In ii. 894 ff. Chaos and Night rule over a Kingdom of 'eternal anarchy', the formless void between hell and heaven.

l. 546. *orient.* Bright.

l. 547. *helms.* helmets.

l. 550. *phalanx.* 'A body of heavy-armed infantry drawn up in close order, with shields joined and long spears overlapping' (*OED*).   *Dorian mode.* The gravest of the Greek musical modes, considered especially suitable to men preparing for battle (Plato, *Republic*, x. 389).

l. 556. *swage.* Assuage.

369 l. 563. *horrid.* The word retains its etymological sense of 'bristling' (with the 'forest huge of spears' of l. 546).

370 l. 568. *traverse.* All across.

l. 573. *created man.* Man was created.

ll. 575–6. *small infantry . . . cranes.* Homer describes the pygmies slaughtered by cranes in *Il.*, iii. 1–5.   *infantry.* The word also meant a group of infants and puns on their size.

ll. 576–7. *Giant . . . Phlegra.* The giants battled the gods on the plains of Phlegra in Macedonia (Ovid, *Met.*, x. 151).

ll. 577–8. *heroic race . . . Ilium.* The Seven Against Thebes, heroes of the Trojan War and epic subject of Statius' *Thebaid* and of Aeschylus' play.

l. 579. *auxiliar.* Assisting.

l. 580. *Uther's son.* King Arthur, son of Uther Pendragon.

l. 581. *Armoric.* From Brittany.

l. 583. *Aspramont or Montalban.* Castles in the chivalric romances.

l. 584. *Damasco* [Damascus] . . . *Morocco, or Trebizond.* Scenes of jousts between Christian and pagan knights in chivalric romances. Trebizond was a Byzantine city on the Black Sea taken by the Turks in 1461.

l. 585. *whom Bizerta sent.* The Saracens who invaded Spain and defeated Charlemagne's army embarked from Bizerta, in Tunisia.

ll. 586–7. *Charlemagne . . . Fontarabia.* Charlemagne did not fall, but his troops led by Roland were destroyed at Roncesvalles near Fontarabia (the modern Fuenterrabia) in Spain.

ll. 598–9. *with fear . . . monarchs.* Solar eclipses were from earliest times taken to be premonitions of the death of kings, as the king was identified with the sun.

l. 603. *considerate.* Deliberate.

371 ll. 609–10. *amerced / Of heaven.* Both 'deprived of heaven' and 'punished by heaven'.

l. 613. *scathed.* Injured.

l. 617. *From wing to wing.* From one end of the phalanx to the other.

l. 624. *event.* Outcome.

l. 636. *different.* Disagreeing; *counsels* and *danger* are both objects of *shunned*: Satan denies that he either ignored alternative proposals or avoided danger.

l. 641. *still.* Always.

l. 646. *close.* Secret.

372 l. 651. *fame.* Rumour.

l. 656. *eruption.* Lit. 'breaking out'.

l. 672. *scurf.* Crust.

372 l. 673. *his.* Its.

l. 674. *The work of sulphur.* Sulphur was a basic ingredient in the refining of metals.

l. 676. *pioneers.* Lit. 'diggers', originally the foot-soldiers who preceded the main body of the army to dig protective trenches.

l. 678. *Mammon.* Not a biblical devil but Aramaic for 'wealth', and this is how the word appears in the New Testament. But as a personification, the figure was associated with the Greek god of wealth, Plutus, and in turn identified with Pluto, god of the underworld. Milton's account of him is heavily indebted to Spenser's Cave of Mammon episode in *FQ,* ii. 7.

l. 686. *Ransacked the centre.* Mined the earth for precious metals.

373 l. 690. *ribs.* Veins.   *admire.* Marvel.

l. 694. *Of Babel . . . kings.* The tower in Nimrod's capital (Gen. 11: 4, and see *PL*, xii. 38–62), and the Egyptian pyramids, monuments to earthly vanity.

l. 697. *reprobate.* 'Rejected by God' (*OED*).

l. 700. *cells.* Individual containers.

l. 703. *founded.* Melted down (as in a foundry).

l. 706. *various.* Complex.

l. 707. *strange.* Wonderful.

l. 710. *fabric.* Edifice.

l. 711. *exhalation.* Mist.

l. 712. *symphonies.* Harmonious music; the city is built as the walls of Thebes were raised by the songs of the legendary musician Amphion.

l. 713. *pilasters.* Columns attached to the walls.

l. 714. *Doric pillars.* The least ornate and most dignified of the Greek columns: cf. Satan's martial music in the Dorian mode, l. 550; but note also the elaborate ornamentation of the building as a whole.

l. 715. *architrave.* The beam resting on the columns that supports the roof; the lowest section of the entablature.

l. 716. *Cornice or frieze.* The decorative upper sections of the entablature. *bossy . . . graven.* Sculptures carved in relief.

l. 717. *fretted.* Ornamented with decorative patterns in relief.

l. 718. *Alcairo.* Modern Cairo, famous for its luxurious buildings.

l. 720. *Belus.* Babylonian version of Baal.   *Serapis.* Osiris as god of the underworld.

l. 724. *folds.* 'The leaves of a folding door' (*OED*).   *discover.* Reveal.

l. 728. *cressets.* Iron baskets used as lanterns.

l. 729. *naphtha and asphaltus.* Lamp oil and pitch, fuel for the lamps and lanterns.

374 l. 739. *Ausonian land.* Italy.

374 l. 740. *Mulciber.* Or Vulcan (the Greek Hephaestos), smith and artisan of the gods.

ll. 740–1. *how . . . fabled.* For Hephaestos' fall see *II.,* i. 588–95.

l. 750. *engines.* Devices.

l. 756. *Pandaemonium.* Milton's coinage from the Greek, meaning 'all the devils'.

l. 758. *squarèd regiment.* Squadron.

l. 764. *Wont.* Were wont to.   *soldan's.* Sultan's.

l. 765. *paynim.* Pagan.

l. 766. *To . . . lance.* Either a fight to the death or a joust for a prize. *career.* Gallop.

l. 769. *sun . . . rides.* The sun enters Taurus in April.

375 l. 774. *expatiate.* Both walk about and talk at length.   *confer.* Discuss.

l. 785. *arbitress.* As judge.

l. 795. *close.* Private.

l. 797. *Frequent.* Crowded.

l. 798. *consult.* Consultation.

BOOK 2

The Argument

discover. Reveal

power. Ruler.

376 l. 2. *Ormuz.* An island in the Persian Gulf, a rich trading port.   *Ind.* India.

l. 9. *success.* The outcome (with an ironic overtone of the usual meaning).

l. 11. *Powers and dominions.* Two orders of angels, according to St Paul (Col. 1: 16).

l. 15. *virtues* Another of Dionysius' orders of angels (see i. 324, and note).

l. 21. *of merit.* By merit.

l. 27. *whom.* Him whom.

l. 28. *the thunderer.* An epithet for Jupiter.

377 l. 50. *recked not.* Took no notice.   *thereafter.* Therefore.

l. 51. *sentence.* Judgment.

l. 52. *unexpert.* Inexperienced.

l. 65. *engine.* War machine.

l. 69. *Tartarean.* Of Tartarus, the classical hell.

l. 73. *drench.* Soporific drink; the word had its modern meaning in Milton's time only as a verb, though a slangy or punning usage may be intended.

l. 74. *forgetful lake.* The 'oblivious pool' of i. 266.

377 l. 75. *our proper motion.* The motion that is naturally ours.

l. 79. *Insulting.* Both exulting and attacking.

l. 81. *The ascent is easy.* Reversing the sibyl's warning to Aeneas about the descent to hell, '*facilis descensus Averno*' (implying that the way back, however, is very difficult), *Aen.*, vi. 126–9.

l. 82. *event.* Outcome.

378 l. 83. *Our stronger.* He who is stronger than we.

l. 89. *exercise.* Afflict; subject to ascetic discipline (leading to the 'penance' of l. 92).

l. 94. *what doubt we.* Why do we hesitate.

l. 97. *essential.* Essence.

ll. 100–1. *at worst . . . nothing.* We are as badly off as we can be, short of annihilation.   *proof.* Experience.

l. 104. *fatal.* Both maintained by fate and dire.

l. 106. *denounced.* Proclaimed.

l. 113. *manna.* Divine sustenance (from the nourishment God provided the Israelites in the wilderness, Exod. 16).

379 l. 124. *fact.* Feats.

l. 127. *scope.* Lit. target.

l. 139. *ethereal.* Made of pure fire (as opposed to the 'baser fire' of l. 141).

l. 156. *Belike.* Doubtless.   *impotence.* Violent passion: the suggestion is sarcastic.

380 l. 165. *What when.* What was it when.   *amain.* With all our strength.

l. 169. *Chained on.* Confined to (see i. 210).

l. 174. *red.* Fiery, bloody; 'red right hand' translates Horace's 'rubente dextera', Jupiter's red right hand afflicting Rome with the thunderbolts of war (*Odes*, i. ii. 1–4).

l. 184. *converse.* Including its original meaning, dwell.

ll. 188–9. *what can . . . With him.* How can force or guile affect him.

l. 191. *motions.* Proposals.

l. 199. *To suffer, as to do.* Passive or active.

381 l. 212. *Not mind.* Ignore.

l. 220. *light.* Both bright and easy to bear.

l. 224. *For happy.* In degrees of happiness.

382 l. 250. *by leave obtained.* If we were granted permission by God.

l. 271. *Wants.* Lacks.

ll. 274–5. *Our . . . elements.* i.e. we shall truly be in our element; we shall be composed of fire.

382 ll. 276–7. *temper . . . temper.* Playing on the senses of tempering steel and of temperament.

l. 278. *The sensible of pain.* What we feel of pain through the senses.

l. 281. *Compose.* Adjust our minds to.

383 l. 288. *o'erwatched.* Worn out with waking.

l. 291. *sentence.* Opinion.

l. 297. *policy.* Political strategy, with Machiavellian implications.

l. 302. *front.* Forehead or face.

l. 306. *Atlantean.* The Titan Atlas was condemned by Jove to bear the heavens on his shoulders.

ll. 310–11. *Thrones . . . powers . . . virtues.* Angelic orders (see i. 324, ii. 11, and notes).

l. 312. *style.* Title.

384 l. 329. *What.* Why.

l. 334. *stripes.* Lashes.

l. 336. *to our power.* To the extent of our power.

l. 337. *reluctance.* Resistance, 'the act of struggling against something' (*OED*).

l. 341. *want.* Be lacking.

l. 359. *arbitrator.* Judge.

l. 367. *puny.* Lit. 'born since us' (*puis nê*).

385 l. 372. *confusion.* Destruction.

ll. 379–80. *first . . . proposed.* See i. 651 ff.

l. 383. *root.* The metaphor is of a family tree.

l. 384. *involve.* Entangle, 'beset with difficulty or obscurity' (*OED*).

l. 387. *states.* Estates, the hierarchy of the realm.

l. 391. *Synod.* Assembly.

l. 404. *tempt.* Try, attempt, with overtones of the usual sense.

l. 407. *uncouth.* Unknown.

l. 409. *abrupt.* Chasm (*OED*'s only instance of its use as a noun). *arrive.* Reach.

386 l. 415. *Choice in our suffrage.* Care in choosing whom we vote for.

l. 418. *suspense.* In suspense.

l. 423. *Astonished.* 'Filled with consternation, dismayed' (*OED*).

ll. 432–3. *long . . . light.* Another echo of the sibyl's words to Aeneas about to descend to hell; see l. 81.

l. 434. *convex.* Vault.

l. 435. *Outrageous to devour.* Violently destructive.

386 l. 436. *adamant.* The hardest substance.

l. 439. *unessential.* Having no substance, uncreated.

l. 441. *abortive.* Probably not 'causing abortion', but an adjective derived from the noun, hence monstrous, formless. Alternatively, 'perhaps Satan thinks of the gulf as a miscarrying womb . . . from which the traveller may never be born, or which may render him as if unborn' (Fowler). An etymological sense, 'away from birth', hence anti-creative, may also be intended. The word has provoked much inconclusive editorial debate.

l. 448. *moment.* Importance.

387 l. 457. *intend.* Consider.

l. 462. *mansion.* Dwelling.   *intermit no watch.* Keep uninterrupted watch.

l. 467. *prevented.* Forestalled.

l. 468. *raised.* Made bold.

l. 470. *erst.* At first.

l. 478. *awful.* Awestruck.

l. 485. *close.* Secret.

l. 490. *louring element.* Threatening sky.

l. 492. *chance.* By chance.

388 l. 495. *that.* So that.

l. 508. *paramount.* Chief.

l. 512. *globe.* 'A compact body (of persons)' (*OED*), hence the phalanx.

l. 513. *emblazonry.* Heraldry.   *horrent.* Bristling.

l. 517. *alchemy.* 'A metallic composition imitating gold', hence 'a trumpet of such metal, or of brass' (*OED*).

l. 521. *raised.* Cheered, made bold.

l. 528. *sublime.* High above.

l. 530. *Pythian fields.* Near Delphi, where the Pythian games, celebrating Apollo's victory over the Python, were held.

l. 531. *shun the goal.* Avoid touching the track posts as they take the turn in their chariots.

l. 532. *fronted.* Facing each other.

389 l. 535. *van.* Vanguard.

l 536. *Prick.* Spur their horses.   *couch.* Lower into the attack position.

l. 537. *close.* Engage in battle.

l. 538. *welkin.* Sky.

l. 539. *Typhoean.* Monstrous, from Typhon or Typhoeus (see i. 198–9 and note, and see below, l. 541).   *fell.* fierce, cruel.

389 l. 541. *whirlwind.* The word for a whirlwind was *typhon* (not cognate with *typhoon,* but later associated with it).

l. 542. *Alcides.* Hercules (from his grandfather Alcaeus).

ll. 542–6. *from Oechalia . . . Euboic sea.* Returning victorious from Oechalia, in Laconia, Hercules was brought a gift of the cloak of the centaur Nessus, whom he had years earlier fought and killed. The cloak, however, was poisoned, and destroyed him, and in his death agony he hurled Lichas, the innocent deliverer of the gift, into the sea. See Ovid, *Met.,* ix. 134 ff., Sophocles' *Trachiniae,* and Seneca's *Hercules Furens.* l. 545. *Oeta.* A mountain in Thessaly, now called Banina. l. 546. *Euboic.* Euboean; Milton combines two versions of the story, the dramatists', in which the action takes place on the island of Euboea, and Ovid's, in which it is in Thessaly.

l. 552. *partial.* In parts, i.e. harmonized, with a pun on 'prejudiced'.

l. 554. *Suspended.* Enraptured.

l. 564. *apathy.* The Stoic ideal, to be free from passion and unmoved by suffering.

l. 568. *obdurèd.* Obdurate, 'hardened in wickedness or sin; persistently impenitent' (*OED*).

l. 570. *gross.* Large.

390 ll. 577–83. *Abhorrèd Styx . . . oblivion.* Etymologizing the names of the rivers of the classical underworld.

l. 590. *heap.* Into heaps.

l. 591. *pile.* Building.

l. 592. *Serbonian bog.* The quicksands surrounding Lake Serbonis, in Egypt.

l. 593. *Damietta.* A city at the mouth of the Nile.

l. 595. *frore.* Frozen, an archaic past participle.

l. 596. *harpy-footed Furies.* The harpies, who attacked Aeneas and his men, had the faces and breasts of young women, the wings and bodies of birds, and talons for hands (see *Aen.,* iii. 211 ff.). The Furies were the classical agents of divine retribution.

l. 597. *certain revolutions.* See l. 603.

l. 600. *starve.* Cause to die.

l. 604. *sound.* Strait.

l. 611. *Medusa with gorgonian terror.* Medusa, one of the three gorgons, had snakes for hair and a look so terrible that it turned mortals to stone.

l. 613. *wight.* Person.

l. 614. *Tantalus.* Condemned in hell to suffer intense thirst in a pool whose water was just out of reach.

391 l. 625. *prodigious.* Unnatural, abnormal.

391 l. 628. *Gorgons . . . hydras . . . chimeras.* The hydra was a nine-headed dragon, the chimera breathed fire; for gorgons, see l. 611.

l. 632. *Explores.* Tries, puts to proof.

l. 638. *Bengala.* Bengal: the ships are following the spice route, from India south and west around the Cape of Good Hope.

l. 639. *Ternate and Tidore.* Two of the Moluccas, or Spice Islands, near New Guinea.

l. 641. *Ethiopian.* The Indian Ocean.

l. 642. *stemming.* Making headway.

l. 645. *folds.* Layers.

l. 647. *impaled.* Surrounded.

l. 653. *mortal.* Deadly.

ll. 653–4. *about . . . hounds.* Milton's figure of Sin is based on the classical Scylla (see 1. 660), a nymph who was changed by the witch Circe into a monster with ferocious dogs sprouting from her lower body.

l. 654. *cry.* Pack.

l. 655. *Cerberian.* From Cerberus, three-headed watchdog of hell.

l. 656. *list.* Wished.

392 ll. 660–1. *Scylla . . . shore.* Scylla ultimately became a dangerous rock off the Sicilian coast.   l. 661. *Trinacrian.* Sicilian.

l. 662. *Night-hag.* The chief witch, or Hecate, goddess of the underworld. *called.* Invoked.

l. 665. *Lapland.* Especially associated with witches.   *labouring.* Suffering (because in eclipse, l. 666).

l. 677. *admired.* Wondered.

l. 686. *proof.* Experience.

l. 688. *goblin.* Demon.

l. 693. *Conjured.* Sworn together (Lat. *coniuro*).

393 l. 706. *deform.* Deformed.

l. 709. *Ophiuchus.* The constellation of the Serpent-Bearer, in the northern sky.

l. 710. *horrid hair.* Horrid retains its etymological meaning of 'bristling'; *hair* alludes to the etymology of *comet*, from the Greek for long-haired.

l. 711. *Shakes . . . war.* Comets were considered omens of disaster.

l. 735. *pest.* Plague.

394 l. 739. *spares.* Forbears.

ll. 757–8. *a goddess . . . sprung.* The birth of Sin from the head of Satan parallels the birth of Athena from the head of Zeus.

l. 761. *Portentous.* Ominous.

394 l. 772. *pitch*. Height.

395 l. 783. *that*. So that.

l. 798. *list*. Wish.

l. 801. *conscious terrors*. Terrors born of knowledge.

l. 813. *mortal dint*. Death-dealing blow.

l. 815. *lore*. Lesson.

396 l. 825. *pretences*. Claims.

l. 827. *uncouth*. Unfamiliar, uncertain.

l. 829. *unfounded*. Bottomless.

l. 833. *purlieus*. Outskirts.

l. 835. *removed*. Distant.

l. 836. *surcharged*. Overcrowded.

l. 837. *hap . . . broils*. Chance to precipitate new quarrels.

l. 842. *buxom* unresisting, a Spenserian usage.   *embalmed*. Balmy, perhaps with an overtone of the usual sense associating the word with death.

l. 847. *famine*. Hunger.   *maw*. Voracious appetite.

l. 859. *office*. Service.

397 l. 874. *portcullis*. Outer grate.

l. 877. *wards*. The notches in a key, which correspond to those of the lock and permit it to be opened.

l. 883. *Erebus*. Hell.

l. 885. *That*. So that.   *wings*. Flanks of the squadron.

l. 889. *redounding*. Overflowing.

l. 898. *Hot . . . Dry*. The characteristics of the four humours, corresponding to the four elements of fire, earth, water, and air.

l. 900. *embryon*. As yet unformed.

398 l. 904. *Barca . . . Cyrene*. Cities in the Libyan desert.

ll. 905–6. *Levied . . . wings*. The atoms are used as ballast for the winds. *poise*. Add weight to.

l. 919. *frith*. Firth, inlet.

l. 920. *pealed*. Deafened.

l. 922. *Bellona*. Goddess of war.

l. 927. *vans*. Fans, i.e. wings.

l. 930. *cloudy chair*. The cloud machinery of masque scenery, in which deities ascended to the stage's heaven.

l. 933. *pennons*. Feathers, wings.   *plumb*. Directly, like a plumb line.

398 l. 937. *Instinct.* Infused.

l. 939. *Syrtis.* Dangerous shifting sands on the North African coast.

l. 943. *griffin.* A fabulous monster with the body of a winged lion and the head of an eagle.

399 l. 944. *moory.* Marshy.

ll. 945–7. *Pursues . . . gold.* Griffins were the guardians of hoards of gold, which the Arimaspi, a Scythian tribe, continually attempted to steal. The well-known story is first told in Herodotus, iii. 16.

l. 961. *wasteful.* Desolate.

l. 964. *Orcus and Ades* [Hades]. Gods of the underworld.

l. 965. *Demogorgon.* The mysterious primal god of pagan mythology, dreadful and unknowable; first mentioned in a late classical gloss on Statius (the name is perhaps an error for the Platonic Demiurgos, the creator), and described as the original god by Boccaccio in the *Genealogiae Deorum.*

l. 977. *Confine with.* Border on (lit. 'share a boundary with').

l. 982. *behoof.* Benefit.

400 l. 988. *anarch old.* Chaos.

l. 989. *incomposed.* Discomposed.

l. 1001. *intestine.* Internal.

ll. 1005–6. *linked . . . heaven.* The notion of the world hanging by a golden chain from the floor of heaven derives originally from Homer (*Il.*, viii. 23–4), and was greatly elaborated in Platonic and neo-Platonic philosophy. See ll. 1051–2.

l. 1008. *speed.* The word also means 'succeed'.

ll. 1017–18. *Argo . . . rocks.* When the Argo, the ship of Jason and the Argonauts, passed through the Bosphorus, it was nearly crushed by the huge floating islands of the Symplegades (see Apollonius Rhodius, *Argonautica*, ii. 552–611).

l. 1019. *larboard.* Port, or left side (as he sailed through the Straits of Messina, between Italy and Sicily).

l. 1020. *Charybdis.* The whirlpool on the Italian side of the Straits, opposite Scylla, the 'other whirlpool' (see *Od.*, xii. 73–100, 234–59).

l. 1024. *amain.* At full speed.

401 l. 1043. *holds.* Approaches.

l. 1044. *shrouds.* Sails.

l. 1048. *undetermined . . . round.* i.e. Satan cannot make out its shape.

l. 1050. *Of.* With.   *living.* 'Native, in its natural condition' (*OED*).

l. 1051. *fast by.* Beside it.

l. 1052. *This pendent world.* Not the earth, but the whole created universe.

BOOK 3

402 ll. 2–3. *Or . . . unblamed?* Or may I, without incurring blame, call you equally eternal with God? *express*. Describe. *since God is light*. Quoting the First Epistle of John 1: 5.

l. 6. *effluence*. Radiance. *increate*. Never created.

l. 7. *hear'st thou rather*. Would you rather be called.

l. 8. *fountain*. Source.

l. 10. *invest*. Envelop.

ll. 17–18. *Orphean . . . Night*. The poet Orpheus went to the underworld and succeeded in recovering his dead wife Eurydice. He was the legendary founder of the Orphic mystical tradition and a *Hymn to Night* was ascribed to him.

l. 19. *the heavenly Muse*. Urania, Muse of astronomy (see i. 6, and vii. 1).

l. 23. *Revisit'st not these eyes*. Milton had been totally blind since 1652.

403 ll. 25–6. *drop serene . . . suffusion*. Medical terms for Milton's blindness: the *gutta serena*, in which the eye appears normal, and the cataract, which covers it with an opaque film.

l. 30. *Sion*. The sacred mountain, source of Hebrew poetry (as opposed to the Greek spring Helicon and Mount Parnassus).

l. 34. *So were I*. If I were.

l. 35. *Thamyris*. Legendary bard mentioned by Homer (*Il.*, ii. 594). *Maeonides*. Homer, said to have been born in Maeonia (or Lydia) in Asia Minor.

l. 36. *Tiresias*. The blind prophet in the Oedipus story. *Phineus*. Blind Thracian prophet-king; Milton invokes the same examples in the *Second Defence* (see p. 314).

l. 37. *voluntary*. Freely; of their own volition.

l. 38. *numbers*. Poetic units, hence verses. *wakeful bird*. The nightingale.

l. 39. *darkling*. In the dark.

l. 60. *sanctities*. Sacred creatures, the angels.

l. 61. *his sight*. Both from his eyes, and from seeing him.

404 l. 72. *sublime*. Aloft.

l. 73. *stoop*. Descend.

l. 74. *outside of this world*. .Outer shell of the universe.

l. 75. *embosomed*. Enclosed. *firmament*. Sky.

l. 76. *Uncertain . . . air*. i.e. it is unclear to Satan whether the land is surrounded by water or air.

l. 84. *interrupt*. 'Forming an interval or breach' (*OED*).

l. 93. *glozing*. Flattering, cajoling.

404 l. 106. *would.* Wished to do.

405 l. 120. *least impulse.* In any way being forced.

l. 129. *first sort.* i.e. the fallen angels.   *suggestion.* Temptation.

l. 136. *spirits elect.* The unfallen angels, who are therefore God's chosen.

l. 140. *Substantially.* In his substance; i.e. he partakes of the divine nature.

406 l. 170. *effectual might.* My agent, through whom my power takes effect.

l. 174. *of.* Through.

l. 176. *lapsèd.* Lit. 'fallen'.

l. 177. *exorbitant.* 'Erring, faulty, transgressing' (*OED*).

l. 179. *mortal.* Deadly.

407 l. 204. *fealty.* Obligation, fidelity: a feudal term.

l. 206. *Affecting godhead.* Assuming divinity.

l. 208. *sacred and devote.* Dedicated and condemned.

l. 219. *Patron.* Protector, advocate.

l. 222. *redemption.* Lit. 'buying back'; compare *ransom*, l. 221.

l. 224. *doom.* Sentence.

408 l. 231. *unprevented.* Unanticipated.

l. 234. *meet.* Suitable.

l. 248. *unspotted.* Untainted.

l. 251. *spoiled.* Despoiled.

l. 255. *maugre.* In spite of.

l. 270. *attends.* Both awaits and serves.

409 l. 276. *complacence.* Source of pleasure.

ll. 281–2. *Thou . . . join.* The syntax is, 'therefore join to thy nature the nature of those whom only thou canst redeem'.

l. 285. *room.* Place.

ll. 290–4. *His . . . life.* Paraphrased from Rom. 5: 17–19.

l. 291. *Imputed.* Assigned, transferred; technical theological language, alluding to the doctrine of imputed righteousness, whereby Christ's virtue is transferred to Christians through their faith.

l. 299. *Giving.* Both yielding and giving (Christ) to.

l. 303. *assume.* Take on.

l. 307. *fruition.* 'Enjoyment . . . the pleasure arising from possession' (*OED*), possibly with a pun on *fruit* (cf. i. 1), though the words are etymologically unrelated.

410 ll. 318–19. *assume / Thy merits.* Take on the honours you merit.

410 l. 320. *Thrones . . . dominions.* Angelic orders, with *princedoms* replacing its synonym *principalities.*

ll. 324 ff. The account of judgement and paradise liberally paraphrases Revelation.

l. 326. *from all winds.* i.e. from the four points of the compass.

l. 327. *cited.* Summoned.

l. 328. *doom.* Judgement.

l. 340. *need.* Be needed.

l. 341. *gods.* Angels.

l. 348. *jubilee.* Jubilation.

l. 352. *amaranth.* Lit. 'unwithering', a legendary deathless purple flower; subsequently applied to a large genus of purple-flowered plants and the colour deep purple.

411 l. 354. *fast by.* Right next to.

l. 359. *Elysian . . . stream.* The river that runs through the Elysian Fields, paradise of the virtuous and brave (see *Aen.,* vi. 656–9).   *amber.* Connoting both clarity and beauty.

l. 377. *but.* Except.

l. 380. *bright.* Brightness.   *thy skirts appear.* i.e. then your robes are visible.

l. 381. *that.* So that.

l. 385. *conspicuous.* Clearly visible.

l. 392. *aspiring dominations.* Rebel angels.

412 l. 397. *thy powers.* The loyal angels.

l. 418. *opacous.* Opaque.

l. 419. *first convex.* The outer shell of the created universe, 'the bare outside of this world' where Satan was about to land at l. 72.

l. 420. *luminous inferior orbs.* The inner spheres of the stars, planets, sun, and moon.

l. 431. *Imaus.* The Himalayas.

l. 434. *yeanling.* Newborn.

413 l. 436. *Hydaspes.* Now the Jhelum river, a tributary of the Indus.

l. 438. *Sericana.* China; the 'barren plains' (l. 437) are the Gobi Desert.

l. 444. *store.* Many.

l. 449. *fond.* Foolish.

l. 452. *painful.* Including the sense of laborious.

l. 456. *unkindly.* Unnaturally.

l. 457. *fleet.* Fly.

413 l. 459. *in . . . dreamed.* Giordano Bruno, Jerome Cardan, and Henry More had seriously postulated lunar inhabitants, and the idea was satirized by Ariosto, who located a fool's paradise in the moon in *Orlando Furioso* (1532), and by Ben Jonson's masque *News from the New World Discovered in the Moon* (1620).

l. 460. *argent.* Silver.

l. 461. *Translated saints.* Such Old Testament heroes and prophets as Enoch and Elijah, who were transported to heaven.

ll. 462-4. *Betwixt . . . came.* Gen. 6: 4 describes how 'the sons of God came in unto the daughters of men', who bore their children, a race of giants. The story is told in more detail in xi. 573-627.

l. 467. *Sennaar.* Shinar; the story is in Gen. 10: 10.

l. 470. *fondly.* Foolishly.

l. 471. *Empedocles.* Sicilian pre-Socratic philosopher (fifth century BC).

l. 473. *Cleombrotus.* A youth said to have drowned himself after reading the *Phaedo.*

l. 474. *eremites.* Hermit friars.

l. 475. *White, black and grey.* Carmelite, Dominican, and Franciscan, from the colour of their habits.

414 l. 477. *Golgotha.* Site of Christ's crucifixion and burial.

l. 479. *weeds.* Garments.

l. 481. *the fixed.* The sphere of the fixed stars.

ll. 482-3. *that crystalline . . . talked.* The crystalline sphere contains the constellation Libra, 'the balance'; this is said to measure the amount of 'trepidation', i.e. irregular motion in the Ptolemaic system.   *talked.* So-called.   *that first moved.* The *primum mobile*, the tenth and outermost sphere.

l. 484. *wicket.* Gate; the diminutive term is ironic.

l. 489. *devious.* Both distant and erratic.

l. 491. *beads.* Rosaries.

l. 492. *dispenses.* Dispensations.   *bulls.* Papal decrees.

l. 495. *limbo.* Lit. border region.

l. 506. *frontispiece.* Façade.

l. 507. *orient.* Lustrous, brilliant.

ll. 510-15. *The stairs . . . heaven.* After Jacob had deceived his father Isaac into giving him the blessing intended for his older brother Esau, and supplanted him as the heir, he had a dream of angels upon a ladder reaching to heaven, and a vision of God promising to make him prosper (Gen. 26-8).

l. 513. *Padan-Aram.* In Syria, where Jacob was fleeing to the protection of his uncle Laban in order to escape Esau's rage.   *Luz* in the Judaean hills; after the vision Jacob renamed the place Bethel.

414 l. 516. *stair.* Step.   *mysteriously.* Symbolically; allegorical interpretations of Jacob's ladder commonly related it to the golden chain of Jupiter (see ii. 1005 and 1051), linking heaven to earth and establishing and justifying the natural and social hierarchies.

415 l. 522. *Rapt.* Transported.

l. 534. *choice.* Careful.

l. 535. *Paneas.* Greek name for the city of Dan, at the source of the Jordan, and the northern boundary of Canaan.

l. 536. *Beersaba.* Beersheba, the southern boundary.

l. 546. *Obtains.* Reaches.

l. 547. *discovers.* Reveals.

l. 552. *though after heaven seen.* Though he had seen heaven.

416 l. 558. *Libra . . . star.* The constellations of the scales and Aries.

l. 559. *Andromeda.* The constellation next to Aries.

l. 562. *world's first region.* Uppermost region of the atmosphere.

l. 563. *precipitant.* Precipitous.

l. 564. *marble.* The relevant connotations are cold, smooth, shining.

l. 566. *nigh hand.* Nearby.

l. 568. *Hesperian gardens.* The earthly paradise, where the daughters of Hesperus kept the golden apples of immortality (see Ovid, *Met.*, iv. 637–8; and cf. *Comus*, l. 393).

l. 575. *By centre, or eccentric.* i.e. depending on whether the earth is at the centre of the universe or not: Milton declines to choose between the Ptolemaic and Copernican systems.

l. 576. *longitude.* How far he flew horizontally (as opposed to 'up or down', l. 574).

l. 577. *Aloof.* Standing apart from.

l. 580. *numbers.* (Musical) measures.

l. 586. *virtue.* Force.

ll. 588–90. *a spot . . . saw.* Galileo had reported his observation of sunspots in 1613.

l. 595. *clear.* Bright.

l. 596. *carbuncle.* Used for a variety of red stones, including the garnet and ruby, and also 'applied to a mythical gem said to emit light in the dark' (*OED*).   *chrysolite.* Used for various green stones, including tourmaline, zircon, and topaz; the two terms may be in apposition with *Ruby or topaz*, l. 597.

l. 597. *to.* i.e. and so on, to.

l. 598. *Aaron's breastplate.* The ceremonial raiment of Moses' brother, the high priest. Each stone was inscribed with the name of one of the twelve tribes (Exod. 28: 17–24).

417 ll. 600–1. *that which . . . sought.* The Philosopher's Stone, which was said by alchemists ('philosophers') to be able to change base metal into gold.

l. 603. *Hermes.* Or mercury, the crucial element in alchemical processes.

l. 604. *Proteus.* Sea-god capable of infinite changes of shape.

l. 605. *limbeck.* Chemical retort.

l. 607. *elixir pure.* The final product of the alchemical process, which would effect the transformation into gold.

l. 608. *Potable.* Liquid.   *virtuous.* Powerful.

l. 609. *arch-chemic.* Archetypical alchemist.

ll. 610–12. *Produces . . . glorious.* The theory was that precious stones are created by the action of the sun's rays penetrating underground. See vi. 479–81.

l. 610. *terrestrial humour.* Earthly moisture.

l. 617. *Culminate from the equator.* Shine directly overhead, from the celestial equator (and hence produce no shadows to interfere with Satan's view).

l. 622. *ken.* Range of vision.

l. 623. *The same whom John saw.* See Rev. 19: 17.

l. 625. *tiar.* Crown.

l. 627. *Illustrious.* Lustrous.   *fledge.* Feathered.

l. 634. *casts.* Both casts about and casts off his present shape.

l. 637. *Not of the prime.* (1) Not yet mature; (2) not one of the important angels.

418 l. 643. *succinct.* Girded up, not voluminous.

l. 644. *decent.* Both graceful and decorous, modest.

l. 648. *Uriel.* Lit. 'light of God', a cabbalistic name, not in the Bible.

l. 656. *authentic.* Authoritative.

419 l. 690. *held.* Considered.

l. 694. *tends.* Intends.

l. 699. *mansion.* Dwelling.

l. 712. *his second bidding.* God's second command was 'Let there be light.'

l. 717. *spirited.* Inanimate.

l. 718. *orbicular.* In a circle.

420 l. 729. *still . . . still.* Always . . . always.

l. 730. *countenance triform.* The moon has three faces, or phases, the new crescent, the full moon, and the waning crescent. Its three forms were analogously personified by three goddesses, Diana, Lucina (or Luna), and Hecate.

l. 731. *Hence.* From here (i.e. the sun).

420 l. 732. *checks.* Restrains.

l. 740. *ecliptic.* The path of the sun.

l. 742. *Niphates.* A mountain in Armenia, near the Assyrian border.

BOOK 4

421 ll. 1–3. *which . . . rout.* St John's vision of a new battle in heaven culminating in another defeat of the dragon Satan is in Rev. 12: 3–12.

l. 6. *while time was.* While there was still time.

l. 11. *wreak.* Avenge.

l. 17. *engine.* Cannon.

ll. 20–3. *The hell . . . place.* As Mephistopheles tells Faustus in Marlowe's *Doctor Faustus*, I. iii. 76 and II. i. 122–4.

ll. 27–8. *Eden . . . Lay pleasant. Eden* means 'pleasure' in Hebrew.

l. 30. *meridian.* Noon.

l. 31. *revolving.* Contemplating.

421–2 ll. 32–41. *O thou . . . king.* Milton's nephew Edward Phillips wrote in his *Life of Milton* that Milton showed him these lines 'several years before the poem was begun' (i.e. in the early 1640s) as the opening speech of a projected tragedy on the fall.

l. 50. *'sdained.* Disdained.

l. 51. *quit.* Cancel.

ll. 53–4. *still.* Always.

l. 56. *still.* Nevertheless.

423 l. 87. *dearly.* Painfully.　　*abide.* Abide by, or await the issue of; suffer, bear.

l. 94. *By act of grace.* By a concession of God's.

ll. 114–15. *each passion . . . despair.* i.e. each of the three passions brought pallor ('*pale*') to his face.

424 l. 118. *distempers.* Disorders.

l. 123. *couched.* (Lying) hidden.

l. 126. *the Assyrian mount.* Niphates (see iii. 742).

l. 134. *champaign head.* Open country.

l. 136. *grotesque.* Like a grotto.

l. 149. *enamelled.* Bright.

l. 151. *humid bow.* Rainbow.

l. 153. *of.* From.

425 l. 157. *odoriferous.* Scent-bearing.

l. 160. *Cape of Hope.* Cape of Good Hope: the ships are travelling the spice route to Asia.

l. 162. *Sabean.* From Sheba (modern Yemen), in southern Arabia.

425 l. 163. *Araby the blest*. Or *Arabia Felix*, applied to the main part of the Arabian peninsula and particularly to Yemen.

l. 165. *grateful*. Gratifying.   *Ocean*. Oceanus, one of the Titans, father of the rivers and in Homer the progenitor of the Olympian gods (*Il.*, xiv. 201 ff.).

l. 167. *bane*. Poison.

ll. 168–71. *Asmodeus . . . bound*. The story is from the apocryphal Book of Tobit: Tobit's son Tobias, travelling in Media, in Persia, on the advice of the archangel Raphael married Sara, whose seven previous husbands had been murdered on their wedding night by her incubus Asmodeus. Raphael enabled Tobias to escape their fate by instructing him to burn the heart and liver of a fish, and the smell drove the demon 'into the utmost parts of Egypt, and the angel bound him' (Tobit 8: 3).   *post*. Quickly (cf. posthaste).

l. 175. *brake*. Thicket.

l. 176. *had perplexed*. Would have perplexed, rendered impassible.

l. 182. *sheer*. Entirely.

l. 186. *hurdled cotes*. Fenced shelters.   *secure*. With an ironic overtone: the sheep are secured, the shepherds too sure of themselves.

l. 192. *clomb*. Climbed; a Spenserian archaism.

l. 193. *lewd*. The original meaning was 'lay or non-clerical', generalized to 'ignorant' and thence to 'wicked, unprincipled'.   *hirelings*. Mercenaries (i.e. salaried ministers).

426 l. 198. *virtue*. Power.

l. 211. *Auran*. Haran, on the eastern boundary of ancient Israel.

l. 212. *Seleucia*. In modern Iraq, on the Tigris.

l. 214. *Telassar*. A city in Eden (2 Kgs. 19: 12, Isa. 37: 12).

l. 228. *kindly*. Natural.

l. 237. *crispèd*. Rippling.

427 l. 239. *error*. Wandering.

l. 241. *nice*. Meticulous, delicate.

l. 242. *curious knots*. Complex designs.   *boon*. Bountiful.

l. 250. *Hesperian fables*. The golden apples of Hesperus, which conferred immortality. See iii. 568 and *Comus*, l. 393.

l. 255. *irriguous*. Well-watered.

l. 257. *umbrageous*. Shady.

l. 264. *apply*. Both join and practise (as in 'applied art').   *airs*. Both breezes and melodies.

l. 266. *Pan*. God of nature; the word in greek means 'all'.

l. 267. *Graces . . . Hours*. Or Charites and Horae, goddesses respectively of natural beauty and of the seasons.

427 ll. 269–72. *Enna . . . world.* Dis, or Pluto, god of the underworld, abducted
Proserpina, daughter of the grain goddess Ceres, from the meadow of
Enna, in Sicily. Ceres, in mourning, searched for her, and during this time
no crops would grow. Dis agreed to return Proserpina to her mother for
half of each year, and in this period the earth is fertile. The story was considered a pagan analogue to Eve's fall (Ovid, *Met.*, v. 391 ff., *Fasti*, iv.
417 ff., and the Homeric *Hymn to Demeter*; see below, ix. 432).

ll. 273–4. *Daphne . . . spring.* The grove of Daphne on the river Orontes in
Syria had a spring named for the Castalian Spring of the Muses on Mount
Parnassus, and an oracle of Apollo (hence '*inspired*').

ll. 275–9. *Nyseian . . . eye.* Diodorus records how Ammon, the son of
Saturn and king of Lybia, loved the nymph Amalthea and had a son,
Bacchus, by her. To protect them from the jealousy of his wife Rhea, he
hid them on the island of Nysa, in the River Triton, in modern Tunisia
(*Library of History*, iii. 67 ff.). Ammon was identified by the Romans with
Jove, and by Christian commentators with Noah's son Ham, or Cham in
the Vulgate.

l. 278. *florid.* Ruddy: Bacchus is god of wine.

428 l. 280. *Abassin.* Abyssinian.   *issue.* Children.

ll. 281–2. *Mount . . . line.* Amara, a sandstone hill in modern Ethiopia, was
thought in Milton's time to be on or near the Equator, the 'Ethiop line',
and sometimes identified with Eden.

l. 283. *Nilus' head.* The source of the Nile.

l. 294. *filial freedom.* Freedom deriving from their status as God's children.

l. 295. *Whence.* i.e. from God.

l. 300. *front.* Forehead.   *sublime.* 'Of lofty . . . aspect' (*OED*).

l. 301. *hyacinthine locks.* Hair as beautiful as that of Hyacinthus, the youth
loved by Apollo.

l. 306. *wanton.* Here, luxuriant, unrestrained, but the word is most often
used pejoratively in the period.

l. 310. *coy.* 'Shyly reserved' (*OED*), perhaps again with an ironic overtone.

l. 312. *mysterious.* Both secret and sacred, as in a religious mystery.

l. 313. *dishonest.* Including the sense 'unchaste'.

429 ll. 323–4. *since . . . sons.* Since his descendants were born (before which
time there was no one to compare him with).   *her daughters.* i.e. all
women.

l. 329. *zephyr.* The west wind.

l. 332. *Nectarine.* Sweet as nectar.

l. 333. *recline.* Reclining.

l. 337. *gentle.* Both kindly and noble.   *purpose.* Conversation.

l. 341. *chase.* Hunting ground.

429   l. 343. *ramped*. Reared up.

l. 344. *ounces, pards*. Lynxes (or any similar small wildcats), leopards.

l. 347. *sly*. The word could mean merely clever or skilful, but the pejorative sense was the primary one by Milton's time.

l. 348. *Insinuating*. Moving sinuously; like '*sly*', with both neutral and pejorative implications.   *with Gordian twine*. As convoluted as the Gordian knot (which could not be untied, and was only undone when it was cut by Alexander).

l. 349. *braided*. Tangled, intricate.

l. 352. *ruminating*. Chewing the cud.

l. 353. *prone career*. Sinking course.

l. 354. *Ocean Isles*. In the western Atlantic, identified as the Azores in l. 592.

l. 359. *room*. Place.

431   l. 404. *purlieu*. 'A place where one has the right to range at large . . . or which one habitually frequents' (*OED*).

l. 410. *Turned . . . ear*. The syntax is ambiguous: either Adam's speech compelled Satan's full attention, or Eve turned fully attentive to Adam ('him' in the latter case would be dative). The first gives the easier sense, but both constructions are elliptical, and in any case the confusion of Eve's attention with Satan's may be part of the point.

l. 411. *sole part*. Unrivalled part, with the additional implication that Eve is all his joy.

432   l. 447. *odds*. 'The amount . . . by which one thing exceeds, or excels . . . another' (*OED*); like *news*, a plural substantive treated as a singular noun.

ll. 460–9. *As . . . goes*. Recalling Ovid's Narcissus, vainly yearning for his own image reflected in a pool (*Met.*, iii. 402 ff.).

l. 470. *shadow stays*. Image awaits.

l. 478. *platan*. Plane tree.

433   l. 486. *individual*. Inseparable.

l. 500. *impregns*. Impregnates.

l. 511. *pines*. Torments (me).

434   l. 530. *A . . . chance*. A bit of mere luck.

l. 539. *in utmost longitude*. At the greatest distance, 'the ends of the earth'.

ll. 541–2. *with . . . Against*. i.e. directly facing.

l. 548. *Still*. Always.

l. 549. *Gabriel*. With Michael, Uriel, and Raphael, one of the four archangels; the name means 'strength of God'.

l. 557. *thwarts*. Both crosses (the literal meaning) and defeats.   *vapours fired*. Fiery exhalations from the earth, thought to be the cause of shooting stars.

435　l. 567. *described.* Descried.

l. 568. *gait.* Course, bearing.

l. 590. *now raised.* The beam points upward because the sun has now moved below the horizon.

ll. 592–5. *whether . . . there.* Whether through the movement of the sun or the earth; Milton once again declines to choose between the Ptolemaic and Copernican systems.　　　l. 594. *Diurnal.* In a single day.　　　*voluble.* 'Capable of ready rotation on a centre or axis' (*OED*).

l. 600. *Silence accompanied.* Both an absolute construction, for 'silence accompanied evening', and an oxymoron, 'silence was accompanied', by the song of the nightingale of l. 602.

l. 603. *descant.* 'A melodious accompaniment to a simple musical theme' (*OED*).

l. 605. *Hesperus.* The evening star.

436　l. 608. *Apparent.* Manifest, and playing on 'heir apparent'.

l. 612. *Mind us.* Put us in mind.

l. 628. *manuring.* Cultivation (lit. 'working with the hands').

l. 632. *Ask riddance.* Need to be cleared.

l. 635. *author.* One 'who originates or gives existence'; 'one who authorizes or instigates'; 'an authority, an informant' (*OED*).

l. 640. *seasons.* Not seasonal changes, which began only after the fall, but times of day, as the next eight lines indicate (usage not recorded in *OED*).

l. 642. *charm.* Including senses derived from its double etymology, from Anglo Saxon *cierm*, magic spell, and Lat. *carmen*, song.

437　l. 669. *foment.* 'Cherish with heat' (*OED*).

l. 676. *want . . . want.* Lack . . . lack.

438　l. 698. *jessamine.* Jasmine.

l. 699. *flourished.* Flowered.

l. 703. *emblem.* Both inlaid work and symbolic image.

l. 706. *feigned.* Invented (by poets).

l. 707. *Pan . . . Sylvanus.* Gods respectively of all nature and of woods and gardens.

l. 708. *Faunus.* Roman farm and forest deity.

l. 711. *hymenean.* Marriage song (from Hymen, god of marriage).

l. 712. *genial.* Presiding over marriage, generative.

l. 714. *Pandora.* Lit. 'all gifts'; the first woman, created at Jove's command and sent with Hermes as a gift for Epimetheus ('hindsight') to avenge the audacity of his brother Prometheus ('foresight'), who had stolen fire from the gods to give to man. Pandora came with a box filled with evils; when Epimetheus opened the box, these were let loose throughout the world.

438 l. 716. *event.* Outcome.

l. 717. *Japhet.* The Titan Iapetus, father of Prometheus and Epimetheus; he was identified with Noah's son Japhet.

l. 719. *authentic.* Original.

l. 724. *pole.* Sky, heavens.

l. 730. *wants.* Lacks.

439 l. 736. *unanimous.* Lit. 'with one mind'.

l. 739. *Handed.* Holding hands.   *eased the putting off.* Not needing to take off.

l. 743. *Mysterious.* Sacred.

l. 747. *commands to some.* In 1 Cor. 7, marriage is enjoined upon those who otherwise would be unable to avoid fornication (see l. 753).

l. 748. *Our . . . increase.* In Gen. 1: 28.

l. 751. *sole propriety.* i.e. marriage was the only property exclusively ordained for Adam and Eve in paradise—the relation of husband to wife is conceived as a property relationship.

l. 756. *charities.* Natural affections.

l. 763. *Love.* Personified as Cupid.   *shafts.* Arrows.

l. 764. *purple.* Imperial, royal; also bright-hued, brilliant, splendid.

l. 769. *starved.* Deprived (of love).

440 l. 773. *repaired.* Renewed on the branches.

l. 777. *sublunar.* Beneath the moon.

l. 778. *port.* Gate.

l. 782. *Uzziel.* Lit. 'strength of god'; a human name in the Bible, an angel in the cabbalistic tradition.

l. 785. *shield . . . spear.* The sides on which these were held, left and right.

l. 786. *these.* The latter.

l. 788. *Ithuriel and Zephon.* Lit. 'discovery of God' and 'searcher'. Ithuriel is not a biblical name, and the biblical Zephon is not an angel.

l. 791. *secure.* 'Feeling no care or apprehension' (*OED*).

l. 793. *Who.* One who.

l. 805. *animal spirits.* Burton explains the relationship of the bodily spirits: 'The natural are begotten in the liver, and thence dispersed through the veins . . . The vital spirits are made in the heart . . . The animal spirits formed of the vital, brought up to the brain, and diffused by the nerves, to the subordinate members, give sense and motion to them all.' (*Anatomy of Melancholy*, I. i. 2. 2.) *Animal* = of the spirit or soul.

l. 809. *high conceits.* Fanciful, excessive conceptions.

l. 812. *celestial temper.* Both the weapon, tempered in heaven, and Ithurial's angelic nature.

441 l. 813. *Of force.* Perforce, necessarily.

l. 815. *nitrous powder.* Gunpowder.

l. 816. *Fit for the tun.* Ready for storage; *tun* = barrel.   *magazine.*
Storehouse for explosives.

l. 817. *Against.* In anticipation of.   *smutty.* Black; smut is a fungus
disease affecting grain that turns it to black powder.

442 l. 879. *transgressions.* The word includes its etymological sense of crossing
boundaries.   *charge.* Both the duty and those whom the angels are
charged to care for, Adam and Eve.

l. 886. *hadst . . . wise.* Were considered wise.

443 l. 899. *durance.* Imprisonment.   *thus . . . asked.* So much for your
question.

l. 904. *O . . . wise.* 'What a judge of wisdom you are, what a loss to heaven'.

l. 911. *However.* In whatever way he can.

l. 930. *at random.* i.e. missing the point.

444 l. 939. *afflicted powers.* Weakened forces—both his own diminished
strength and his crippled army.

l. 942. *gay.* Showy, gaudy.

l. 945. *practised distances.* Keeping a deferential distance.

ll. 947–9. *To say . . . traced.* Gabriel is mistaken (as he is again at
ll. 1011–12): Satan's two claims do not contradict each other.

l. 962. *aread.* Warn.   *avaunt.* Begone.

l. 967. *facile.* Easily opened.

l. 971. *limitary.* Stationed on the boundary; also, setting limits, and limited.

l. 976. *progress.* Ceremonial procession.

445 l. 978. *moonèd horns.* Formation like the crescent moon.

l. 980. *ported spears.* Spears carried 'diagonally across and close to the body,
so that the blade is opposite the middle of the left shoulder'; the military
command is 'port arms' (*OED*). The point is that the spears therefore are
not in the attack position.

l. 981. *Ceres.* The grain goddess.

l. 983. *careful.* Worried.

l. 987. *Tenerife or Atlas.* Mountains in the Canary Islands and Morocco respectively.   *unremoved.* 'Fixed in place, firmly stationed' (*OED*).

l. 989. *wanted.* Lacked.

ll. 997–8. *scales . . . Scorpion.* The constellation Libra, between Virgo and
Scorpio; cf. Zeus weighing the fates of Greeks and Trojans (*Il.*, viii. 69 ff.)
and of Achilles and Hector (xxii. 209), and the Virgilian version, Jove
weighing Aeneas' and Turnus' fates (*Aen.*, xii. 725 ff.).   *Astraea.*
Goddess of justice, who fled from earth after the Golden Age, identified
here with the constellation Virgo.

445 l. 1001. *ponders*. Lit. weighs.

l. 1004. *kicked the beam*. Struck the crossbar.

ll. 1011–13. *read . . . resist*. Gabriel misinterprets the sign, which does not weigh Satan against the angels but fighting against parting, and shows parting to be preferable—for Gabriel as well as for Satan.

ll. 1013–14. *knew . . . scale*. Satan accepts Gabriel's interpretation.

BOOK 5

446 ll. 5–7. *which . . . dispersed*. i.e. the mere sound of wind in the leaves and water was enough to wake Adam.   *Aurora*. Goddess of dawn.

l. 12. *cordial*. Lit. from the heart.

l. 15. *peculiar*. Special, all its own.

l. 16. *Zephyrus . . . Flora*. The west wind and the goddess of flowers.

l. 21. *prime*. The first morning hour, beginning at six o'clock.

l. 22. *blows*. Blooms.

l. 23. *balmy reed*. Balsam.

447 l. 41. *love-laboured*. Produced with love.

l. 47. *still*. Always.

l. 61. *reserve*. Restriction.

448 l. 66. *vouched with*. Confirmed by.

l. 98. *uncouth*. Strange, with an overtone of distasteful.

l. 102. *fancy*. Fantasy, in Renaissance psychology that branch of the imaginative faculty with the power to create and interpret images.

449 l. 109. *cell*. Compartment of the brain.

l. 127. *bosomed*. Hidden.

l. 145. *orisons*. Prayers.

l. 146. *various style*. A mixture of styles.

449–50 ll. 146–8. *neither . . . maker*. i.e. their prayers included both formal and spontaneous elements.

450 l. 150. *numerous*. Rhythmical.

l. 151. *tuneable*. Tuneful.

l. 166. *Fairest of stars*. The morning star, called both Venus and Lucifer ('light-bringer').

l. 176. *orb that flies*. Revolving sphere.

l. 177. *five . . . fires*. The five planets ('other' is a slip on Milton's part, since Venus has already been invoked at l. 166).

l. 178. *not without song*. The music of the spheres.

l. 181. *quaternion*. A group of four.

l. 185. *exhalations*. Vapours.

451 l. 191. *still.* Ever.

ll. 222–3. *Tobias . . . maid.* See iv. 167–71.

452 l. 238. *too secure.* Overconfident of his safety.

l. 249. *ardours.* Effulgent spirits; biblical usage.

l. 259. *unconform.* Dissimilar.

l. 264. *Cyclades.* An island group in the Aegean.

l. 265. *Delos.* The central Cycladic island.   *Samos.* An island north-east of the Cyclades.   *kens.* Perceives.

l. 266. *prone.* Moving downward.

l. 269. *fan.* Wing.

l. 270. *buxom.* Unresisting.   *soar.* The range of altitude.

453 ll. 272–4. *phoenix . . . flies.* The mythical phoenix existed only one at a time; it reproduced by immolating itself, and a new phoenix, born from the ashes, flew to the Temple of the Sun in Heliopolis to offer up the remains to the god (see Ovid, *Met.*, xv. 391–407). Milton, like other Renaissance writers, identified Heliopolis with the nearby Egyptian city of Thebes.

l. 281. *zone.* Belt.

l. 285. *Sky-tinctured grain.* Dyed blue (*grain* was technically crimson dye, but by Milton's time the word also signified any fast colour).   *Maia's son.* Mercury, the heavenly messenger.

l. 288. *state.* Rank.

l. 289. *message.* The word also meant mission, errand.

l. 293. *cassia.* A plant with a cinnamon odour.   *nard.* Spikenard, source of a fragrant ointment.

l. 295. *Wantoned.* Playcd (innocently)—the word is used of children's games—but with ominous overtones.

l. 297. *enormous.* Unfettered (lit. 'outside of the rules'); like *wantoned*, usually pejorative, but here still innocent: Edenic wildness was superior to postlapsarian art.

l. 306. *milky.* Nourishing, juicy, sweet (modifying *Berry or grape* as well as *stream*).

454 l. 324. *frugal.* Prudent, careful: there is always plenty to eat in Eden, but some food is better if dried.

l. 336. *upheld.* Continued.   *kindliest.* Most natural.

l. 339. *middle shore.* Literally translating Mediterranean.

l. 340. *Pontus.* On the Black Sea.   *Punic.* Carthaginian, the north-east African coast of the Mediterranean.

l. 341. *Alcinous reigned.* Alcinous ruled the Phaeacians on the legendary island of Scheria, in the extreme west. Odysseus visited him and saw his superb gardens (*Od.*, vii. 113 ff.).

454 l. 345. *inoffensive must*. Unfermented grape juice.   *meads*. Drinks sweetened with honey.

l. 347. *tempers*. Mixes.   *dulcet*. Sweet.

l. 348. *Wants*. Lacks.

l. 349. *unfumed*. Not burned (to produce incense).

455 l. 359. *submiss*. Submissive: the diction is formal or legal.

l. 365. *want*. Be parted from.

l. 369. *meridian*. Midday.

l. 371. *virtue*. Power; also, the Virtues were one of the angelic orders (see i. 128–9 and ii. 15).

l. 378. *Pomona*. Goddess of fruit.

ll. 381–2. *fairest . . . strove*. Venus, the invidious comparison with Eve providing another ominous overtone: the Trojan prince Paris was chosen to award a golden apple to the fairest of the three goddesses Juno, Minerva, and Venus. He selected Venus; his reward was the most beautiful woman on earth, Helen, whom he abducted from her husband Menelaus, and thus precipitated the Trojan War. The Judgment of Paris took place on Mount Ida (now Kaz Daghi, in northern Turkey).

l. 384. *virtue-proof*. Taken in context, this must mean 'armed with virtue'; but the natural interpretation would be 'armed *against* virtue', and Eve is again being praised in a way that simultaneously calls her virtue into question.   *infirm*. Irresolute, of weak character.

456 ll. 394–5. *spring . . . hand*. As in Spenser's Garden of Adonis, growth and harvest are simultaneous and perpetual (*FQ*, III. vi. 42).

l. 396. *No . . . cool*. Miltonic literalism: paradisal meals must be uncooked, since Adam and Eve learned the use of fire only after the fall (see x. 1078 ff.).

l. 397. *author*. Progenitor.

l. 406. *of*. By.

l. 407. *No ingrateful*. i.e. pleasing.

l. 408. *Intelligential substances*. Angelic intelligences.

l. 409. *rational*. Contrasted with the pure spiritual ('intelligential') substance of the angels.

l. 412. *concoct, digest, assimilate*. The three stages of digestion, consisting of the processing of food in the stomach, its conversion to blood, and its incorporation into the body.

l. 418. *lowest . . . moon*. The moon occupied the lowest of the heavenly spheres.

ll. 419–20. *spots . . . turned*. The moon's markings here are not elements of the lunar landscape, as in ll. 290–1, but exhalations from earth remaining on the moon's surface, as yet unassimilated.

l. 429. *mellifluous*. Sweet as honey.

456 l. 433. *nice.* 'Fastidious, difficult to please' (*OED*).

456–7 ll. 434–6. *nor . . . theologians.* i.e. angels are material beings: Milton rejects the orthodox view, which holds that angels are immaterial but assume slightly material bodies to converse with mortals (as, for example, in Donne's 'Air and Angels', l. 3).

457 l. 437. *concoctive heat.* Digestive energy.

l. 438. *transubstantiate.* Turn one substance into another, with a pun on the theological sense, the Roman Catholic doctrine of the Eucharist, which Milton and the Reformers rejected. *redounds.* Is excessive.

l. 440. *empiric.* Experimental, usually with pejorative implications—the noun was a term for a charlatan or quack. But since Milton's point about the angels depends on the validity of the analogy, the comparison reveals either a belief in the authenticity of empiric alchemy or an unacknowledged ambivalence about angelic transubstantiation.

l. 445. *crowned.* Filled to overflowing.

l. 467. *what compare?* How can they be comparable?

l. 468. *hierarch.* Archangel (lit. 'holy leader').

l. 472. *one first matter.* i.e. the world was created not *ex nihilo*, out of nothing, but of an original essential matter (see i. 10, and *CD*, i).

458 ll. 478–9. *bounds . . . kind.* Stages appropriate to each form of life.

l. 481. *consummate.* Perfected.

l. 483. *sublimed.* Refined; an alchemical term.

ll. 484–5. *vital . . . intellectual.* The three kinds of fluids that enable and control the bodily and intellectual functions.

l. 488. *Discursive.* Through the reasoning process.

l. 493. *proper.* My own.

l. 498. *tract.* Length.

l. 514. *want.* Lack.

459 l. 557. *Worthy . . . silence.* Translating Horace's '*sacro digna silentio*', referring to the attentiveness of the spirits in the underworld to the songs of Sappho and Alcaeus (*Odes*, ii. xiii. 29).

460 l. 566. *remorse.* Sorrow, compassion.

ll. 574–6. *earth . . . like.* The Platonic doctrine that earth is formed on the model of heaven and that what we perceive as real is merely a shadow of the divine is from *Republic*, x; but Milton's materialist version stresses the likeness of earth to heaven, not their differences.

l. 581. *things durable.* Things that last at all, that have any extension in time.

l. 583. *great year.* The period when an entire cycle of the heavens is completed, and the heavenly bodies have returned to their original positions; Plato's estimate of its length is unclear, but is usually given as 36,000 years (*Timaeus*, 39D).

460 l. 589. *gonfalons.* Banners.   *van.* Front.

l. 593. *memorials.* Records, commemorations.

461 ll. 603–4. *This . . . son.* The begetting on 'this day' is metaphorical, alluding to Ps. 2: 6 ff.; Milton in *CD* takes 'begotten' to include the sense 'made him a king' (i. 5).

l. 609. *vicegerent.* Deputized, exercising God's authority.

l. 610. *individual.* Inseparable.

l. 623. *Eccentric.* Slightly irregular; a technical astronomical term for an off-centre stellar motion (see viii. 83 n.).   *intervolved.* Intertwined.

461–2 ll. 637–40. *They . . . showered.* In the first (1667) edition, these lines read, 'They eat, they drink, and with refection sweet / Are filled, before the all bounteous king, who showered'.

l. 646. *roseate.* Rose-scented, punning on *ros*, Latin for 'dew'.

l. 658. *his former name.* Lucifer, according to Isa. 14: 12.

l. 664. *anointed.* Literally translating 'messiah'.

l. 665. *impaired.* Damaged, injured.

l. 669. *dislodge.* Both move (himself) and displace (God's throne, l. 670).

l. 671. *his next subordinate.* Identified as Beelzebub in i. 79–81.

463 l. 697. *several.* Separately.

l. 708. *morning star.* Lucifer, lit. 'light-bringer'.

l. 712. *Abstrusest.* Most hidden.

l. 721. *Nearly.* Significantly, intimately.

464 l. 729. *advise.* Deliberate, consider together.

l. 736. *Justly . . . derision.* Alluding to God's laughter in Ps. 2: 4.

l. 739. *Illustrates.* Used in its literal sense of 'renders illustrious'.

l. 740. *in event.* In the outcome.

l. 741. *dextrous.* Capable, alluding to his place *ad dextram*, at God's right hand.

l. 749. *potentates.* Angelic powers, one of the orders of angels.

l. 750. *triple degrees.* Alluding to Dionysius' system of angelic hierarchies; see i. 128–9.   *to.* In comparison with.

ll. 753–4. *globose . . . longitude.* Flattened sphere (as in maps drawn on Mercator's projection).

465 l. 763. *Affecting.* Claiming, aspiring to.

l. 766. *The . . . called.* For Lucifer's inauguration of his holy mountain see Isa. 14: 13.

l. 788. *supple.* Lit. 'submissive', suppliant.

l. 793. *well consist.* Are fully consistent.

466 l. 805. *Abdiel.* Lit. 'Servant of God'; not an angel in the Bible.

466 l. 821. *unsucceeded.* Eternal, with no successor.

467 l. 861. *fatal.* Ordained by fate, inevitable.

468 l. 890. *devoted.* 'Formally or surely consigned to evil; doomed' (*OED*). *lest.* i.e. but rather lest.

l. 901. *with him wrought.* Persuaded him.

l. 906. *with retorted scorn.* Having returned their scorn.

BOOK 6

l. 2. *champaign.* Plain.

469 l. 3. *Hours.* The Horae, goddesses of the seasons and gatekeepers of heaven (see *Il.*, v. 749 and Spenser, *FQ*, VII. vii. 45).

l. 5. *fast by.* Next to.

l. 8. *vicissitude.* Change.

l. 10. *Obsequious.* Obedient, with an overtone of its literal sense, 'following'.

l. 16. *embattled.* Ready for battle.

l. 19. *procinct.* Readiness.

l. 29. *Servant of God.* Translating 'Abdiel'.

470 l. 58. *reluctant.* With an overtone of its literal sense, 'struggling, writhing'.

l. 62. *quadrate.* Square formation.

l. 69. *obvious.* Lit. 'in the way'.

l. 70. *straitening.* Narrowly confining.

l. 78. *terrene.* Earth.

l. 80. *skirt to skirt.* End to end.

l. 84. *argument.* Heraldic emblems.

471 l. 86. *expedition.* Speed.

l. 90. *fond.* Foolish.

l. 93. *hosting.* Enmity.

l. 107. *cloudy.* Ominous.   *van.* Vanguard.

l. 110. *adamant.* A mythical substance of impenetrable hardness.

l. 115. *realty.* Sincerity, honesty; reality.

l. 118. *to sight.* Seemingly.

l. 120. *tried.* Tested (and found).

472 l. 126. *Most reason is.* It is most reasonable.

l. 129. *prevention.* 'The action of . . . baffling or stopping another person in the execution of his designs' (*OED*).

l. 130. *securely.* Confidently.

l. 141. *whelmed.* Overthrown and buried.

l. 143. *who.* Those who.

472 l. 147. *sect.* Abdiel ironically applies the royalist term for religious schismatics to himself.

l. 153. *assay.* Trail.

l. 156. *synod.* Assembly.

l. 161. *thy success.* How you succeed: 'success' means, literally, simply the outcome of an action, whether good or bad; but given its more usual sense, Satan's usage is unintentionally ironic.

l. 162. *pause between.* i.e. between our meeting and your destruction.

l. 163. (*Unanswered . . . boast*). Lest you boast that I was unable to answer you.

473 l. 168. *minstrelsy.* Minstrels; cognate with 'ministering', l. 167.

l. 174. *deprav'st.* Distorts, perverts.

l. 182. *lewdly.* Combining the senses of foolishly and wickedly.

474 l. 210. *madding.* Furiously whirling.

l. 215. *cope.* Sky.

l. 216. *battles main.* Both mighty troops and the bulk or main body of both armies; also, a 'main battle' is 'a pitched battle, as opposed to mere skirmishing' (*OED*).

l. 225. *combustion.* Conflict.

l. 229. *numbered such.* So numerous.

ll. 232–3. *leader . . . chief.* Every single warrior seemed like a leader.

l. 239. *As.* As if.   *moment.* Deciding factor.

l. 243. *main.* Powerful.

475 l. 251. *sway.* Swinging motion.

l. 259. *Intestine war.* Civil war.

l. 288. *err not.* Do not mistakenly believe.

476 l. 296. *parle.* Parley.   *addressed.* Prepared.

l. 308. *erst.* Formerly.

l. 313. *aspect malign.* Opposed positions (hence shedding evil influence).

l. 318. *determine.* Decide the outcome.   *repeat.* Be repeated.

l. 319. *As . . . once.* It would not have been possible to repeat such a blow right away.

l. 320. *prevention.* Anticipation.

l. 329. *griding.* Cutting.   *discontinuous wound.* The technical medical term for an open wound.

477 l. 332. *humour.* Fluid.

l. 333. *Sanguine.* Red, and analogous to blood in mortals.

l. 346. *reins.* Kidneys.

l. 353. *condense or rare.* Dense or airy.

477 l. 362. *uncouth.* (Hitherto) unknown.

ll. 362-3. *On . . . foe.* i.e. each had his foe. Raphael describes his own actions without identifying himself.

l. 365. *Adramelec.* Adramelech, Babylonian sun god (2 Kgs. 17: 31). *Asmadai.* The evil spirit Asmodeus of the Tobit story; see iv. 168.

l. 369. *annoy.* Harass, injure.

l. 370. *atheist.* Lit. 'godless'.

l. 371. *Ariel.* Though in the Bible this is an epithet for Jerusalem (lit. 'lion of God', Isa. 29: 1), in the cabbalistic tradition it is the name of an evil angel, formerly a pagan god. The name also appears as a spirit of earth in many magical texts, e.g. H. C. Agrippa's *De Occulta Philosophia* (Shakespeare's airy spirit is apparently without precedent).   *Arioch.* Lit. 'lion-like'; a king against whom Abraham fought (Gen. 14), and a Babylonian captain hostile to the Jews (Daniel 2: 14). But Milton seems to be relying on Renaissance demonology, in which the name is that of a vengeful spirit.

478 l. 372. *Ramiel.* 'Thunder of God', not a biblical name; an evil angel in the pseudepigraphic Book of Enoch, and the name of a devil in various cabbalistic texts.

l. 382. *Illaudable.* Not worthy of praise.

l. 393. *Defensive scarce.* Hardly able to defend themselves.

l. 404. *unobnoxious.* Lit. 'not subject to injury'.

l. 410. *foughten field.* Battlefield.

l. 411. *prevalent.* Having prevailed, victorious.

479 l. 421. *mean pretence.* Modest ambition, but with an overtone of the modern sense.   *affect.* Aim at; 'put on a false appearance of' (*OED*).

l. 429. *Of future.* In future.

l. 447. *Nisroch.* An Assyrian god in 2 Kgs. 19: 37.

480 l. 455. *impassive.* Not subject to pain.

l. 458. *remiss.* Weak.

l. 465. *offend.* Attack.

l. 477. *mind.* Remember.

l. 485. *touch.* Both contact and touch-powder, fine gunpowder.

481 l. 496. *cheer.* Spirits.

l. 511. *originals.* Basic elements.

l. 514. *Concocted and adusted.* Heated and dried, alchemical processes.

l. 518. *found.* Cast (as in a foundry).   *engines.* War machines, specifically cannons.

l. 519. *missive.* Missile.   *incentive.* Igniting.

481 l. 520. *pernicious.* The word, from two separate Latin roots, means both swift and destructive.

l. 521. *conscious.* Both aware and guilty; but also indicating their own unnatural wakefulness.

l. 524. *orient.* Both bright and rising.

l. 535. *Zophiel.* Lit. 'spy of God'; not a biblical name.

482 l. 541. *Sad.* Serious.   *secure.* Confident.

l. 549. *took alarm.* Responded to the alarm, or call to battle.

l. 553. *Training.* Drawing behind.   *impaled.* Surrounded, fenced in.

l. 555. *interview.* Mutual view.

l. 560. *composure.* Composition, settlement.

l. 568. *ambiguous words.* Calling attention to the miltary puns in ll. 560–7, including, in addition to 'composure', 'breast' (heart and the front line of the company), 'overture' (opening of negotiations and aperture, orifice) 'discharge' (perform and fire off), 'appointed' (chosen and equipped), 'have in charge' (have been charged to do and are ready to fire, as a loaded weapon), 'touch' (mention and ignite).

l. 571. *discovered.* Revealed.

l. 576. *mould.* Moulded out of (brass, etc.).

483 l. 578. *hollow.* False.

l. 580. *suspense.* Suspended, in suspense.

l. 581. *amused.* Bemused, puzzled.

l. 589. *chained thunderbolts.* Satan's troops are using chain shot, cannonballs linked together with chains.

l. 597. *quick contraction or remove.* Quickly diminishing their size or departing.

l. 598. *dissipation.* Dispersal.

l. 601. *indecent.* Shameful.

l. 605. *displode . . . tire.* Fire . . . volley.

484 l. 623. *amused.* Baffled.

l. 624. *stumbled.* Caused to stumble.

l. 625. *understand.* Both comprehend and support themselves.

l. 644. *seated.* Fixed.

l. 654. *Main.* Whole.

485 l. 665. *jaculation.* Throwing.

l. 668. *To.* Compared with.

l. 673. *Consulting.* Deliberating.   *foreseen.* Having foreseen.

l. 674. *advised.* Advisedly, in full knowledge.

485 l. 679. *assessor*. 'One who sits beside; hence one who shares another's rank, position or dignity' (*OED*).

l. 692. *Insensibly*. Imperceptibly.

l. 698. *main*. Whole.

486 l. 701. *suffered*. Permitted.

l. 709. *unction*. Anointing.

487 ll. 749–59. For the source of Milton's chariot in the whirlwind see Ezek. 1: 4 ff.

l. 752. *instinct*. Impelled.

l. 761. *urim*. The mystical stones incorporated, along with the *thummim*, into the breastplate of Aaron the High Priest (see iii. 597–8 and Exod. 28: 30).

l. 766. *bickering*. Flashing.

l. 771. *sublime*. Including its literal sense, aloft.

l. 773. *Illustrious*. Luminous, clearly manifest.

l. 777. *reduced*. Lit. 'led back'.

l. 778. *circumfused*. Diffused.   *wing*. Flank.

l. 779. *embodied . . . one*. Regrouped into a single body, or *corps*.

488 l. 783. *Obsequious*. Obedient; however the word had its pejorative connotations by Milton's time.

l. 785. *obdured*. Hardened.

l. 787. *Insensate*. Senselessly.

l. 788. *In . . . dwell?* Paraphrasing Virgil's wonder at Juno's implacable enmity toward Aeneas, *Aen.*, i. 11.

l. 793. *height*. Milton's form, as always, is 'highth'; the line is not a rhyme in seventeenth-century English.

ll. 809–10. *Number . . . multitude*. i.e. Christ alone will be the agent of God's vengeance.

489 l. 823. *vouchsafe*. 'Condescend to engage in' (*OED*).

l. 827. *the four*. The 'cherubic shapes' of l. 753.

l. 836. *thunders*. Thunderbolts.

l. 838. *Plagues*. Scourges (lit. 'wounds').

l. 845. *fourfold-visaged four*. See ll. 753–4.

l. 846. *Distinct*. Decorated.

l. 849. *pernicious*. Both swift and destructive.

l. 862. *wasteful*. Desolate.

491 l. 909. *weaker*. Weaker vessel, alluding to 1 Pet. 3: 7, 'honour unto the wife, as unto the weaker vessel'.

BOOK 7

491 l. 1. *Urania.* Classical muse of astronomy, but here used in a more literal sense: the name means 'heavenly', from Greek *ouranos*, the sky, and Milton invokes 'The meaning, not the name' (l. 5).

l. 3. *Olympian hill.* Olympus, a favourite haunt of the muses and the home of the classical gods.

l. 4. *Pegasean wing.* The winged horse Pegasus, who created the muses' sacred fountain Hippocrene by stamping his hoof on Mount Helicon, and was therefore associated with poetic inspiration. His rider was Bellerophon (l. 18).

l. 9. *converse.* The word retains its literal meaning, 'dwell'.

l. 15. *Thy tempering.* Tempered by you.

ll. 17–18. *as once Bellerophon.* Bellerophon attempted to fly to heaven on Pegasus, and Zeus punished him by sending a gadfly to sting the horse and cause it to throw its rider; though he survived his fall he lived out his last years, according to the mythographers, in blindness and alone (hence perhaps Milton's choice of him as an appropriate heroic model).

l. 19. *Aleian field.* In Lycia, in modern Turkey, where Bellerophon fell.

l. 20. *Erroneous.* Lit. 'wandering'.

l. 22. *visible diurnal sphere.* The visible universe, which revolves diurnally, or daily, around the earth.

492 l. 23. *rapt.* Transported.

ll. 25–6. *though fallen . . . tongues.* Milton, as an important spokesman for the revolution, was under attack in the last year of the Commonwealth, and in danger of arrest and indictment after the restoration of the monarchy in 1660.

l. 27. *In darkness.* Milton had been totally blind since 1652.

l. 33. *Bacchus.* The Greek Dionysus, god of wine, theatre, and ecstatic poetry, patron of the legendary poet Orpheus, but also leader of the 'barbarous . . . rout' of Bacchantes, his murderers.

ll. 34–8. *Thracian bard . . . son.* Orpheus had offended the Bacchantes by spurning women after the death of his wife Eurydice and his failure to bring her back from Hades. Instead he turned to boys, and was credited with the introduction of pederasty into Greece. In revenge, the Thracian maenads attacked him and tore him to pieces. See *Met.*, xi. 1 ff., and *Lycidas*, ll. 58–63.

l. 35. *Rhodope.* A Thracian mountain.

ll. 35–6. *woods . . . rapture.* According to Ovid, nature was so entranced with Orpheus' songs that not only the animals but the rocks and trees stopped to listen, and wept at his fate.

l. 37. *muse.* Calliope, muse of epic poetry and mother of Orpheus.

l. 50. *consorted.* Associated, leagued, united as consorts.

492 l. 52. *admiration.* Wonder.

l. 59. *repealed.* Abandoned (lit. 'called back').

l. 63. *conspicuous.* Visible (as opposed to the world of God and the angels beyond the visible spheres).

493 l. 67. *current.* Running.

l. 90. *florid.* Flourishing, beautiful; lit. 'full of flowers'.

l. 94. *Absolved.* Completed.

l. 99. *suspense.* Both suspended and attentive.

l. 102. *His generation.* How he was created.

l. 103. *unapparent.* Invisible.

494 l. 106. *watch.* Stay awake.

l. 116. *infer.* Render.

l. 121. *inventions.* Speculations, inventiveness.

l. 132. *So call him.* Satan lost his original name Lucifer ('light-bringer') after his rebellion; see v. 658.

l. 133. *that star.* Lucifer is the name of Venus as the morning star.

l. 142. *us dispossessed.* Once he had dispossessed us.

l. 143. *into fraud.* i.e. into his own fraud.

495 l. 152. *fondly.* Foolishly.

l. 162. *inhabit lax.* Spread out, relax.

l. 179. *earthly notion.* Human understanding.

496 l. 212. *Outrageous.* Both enormous and violent.

l. 217. *omnific.* All-creating; apparently a Miltonic coinage.

l. 224. *fervid.* Burning (cf. vi. 832).

497 l. 236. *virtue.* Power.

l. 238. *tartareous.* Gritty, crusty, with an overtone of Tartarus, the classical hell.

l. 239. *founded.* Gave shape to.   *conglobed.* Made into globes or spheres.

ll. 243 ff. The account of creation paraphrases Gen. 1: 4–8.

498 l. 273. *distemper.* Disturb the order of.

l. 277. *embryon.* Embryo.   *involved.* Lit. 'enveloped, surrounded'.

l. 279. *Main.* Mighty; 'said of a considerable uninterrupted stretch of land or water' (*OED*).

l. 280. *Prolific humour.* Fertile liquid.

l. 282. *genial.* Generative.

l. 288. *tumid.* Swollen.

l. 292. *conglobing.* Becoming spheres.

498 l. 299. *rapture*. Forceful movement.

l. 302. *serpent error*. Winding like a serpent.

498–9 ll. 307–12. *The dry land . . . earth*. The account follows Gen. 1: 10 ff.

499 l. 321. *swelling*. Bentley's emendation for the first and second editions' 'smelling' (cf. l. 319) has been almost universally accepted.

l. 322. *humble*. 'Of plants: low-growing; (*OED*), but including the suggestion of a natural hierarchy analogous to the social hierarchy.

l. 323. *implicit*. Tangled.

l. 325. *gemmed*. Budded.

ll. 339 ff. The account depends on Gen. 1: 14–18.

l. 348. *altern*. Alternately.

500 l. 351. *vicissitude*. Alternation.

l. 360. *clouäy shrine*. See l. 248.

l. 366. *morning . . . horns*. Venus was known, most recently through Galileo's observations, to have phases, like the moon; 'her' is Milton's emendation of the first edition's 'his', referring to Lucifer as the morning star.

l. 367. *tincture*. Absorption (of the sun's light).

l. 368. *small peculiar*. Own small light.

l. 374. *Pleiades*. The seven daughters of Atlas, who were transformed into the constellation of seven stars in Taurus.

l. 377. *His*. The sun's.

l. 382. *dividual*. Shared.

500–1 ll. 387–98. *And God said . . . earth*. The account paraphrases Gen. 1: 20–3.

501 l. 403. *Bank*. Make a bank in (because they are so numerous).

l. 406. *dropped*. Spotted, a heraldic usage.

l. 407. *attend*. Await.

l. 409. *smooth*. Calm water.

l. 412. *Tempest*. Make stormy.

l. 412–15. *leviathan . . . land*. The great sea creature has not yet become Satanic (see i. 200 ff.).

l. 419. *kindly*. Natural.

l. 420. *callow*. Unfledged, not ready to fly.   *fledge*. Fledged.

l. 421. *summed their pens*. Had all their feathers.

l. 422. *clang*. From Latin *clangor*, the harsh cry of a bird.

ll. 422–3. *under . . . prospect*. Viewed from below ('in prospect') the earth seemed under a cloud (so numerous were the birds).

l. 426. *ranged . . . way*. Fly in a wedge-shaped formation.

l. 427. *Intelligent*. Aware.

501 l. 432. *Floats.* Undulates.

502 l. 439. *mantling.* Forming a mantle.

l. 440. *state.* Dignified bearing.

l. 441. *dank.* Water.

l. 444. *the other.* The peacock.

l. 451. *soul.* Bentley's emendation of the first and second editions' 'Fowle' and 'Foul' has been universally accepted.

l. 454. *teemed . . . birth.* Bore in a single delivery.

l. 455. *perfect.* Complete.

l. 457. *wons.* Dwells.

l. 463. *clods.* Earth.

l. 466. *brinded.* Brindled (streaked or flecked).   *ounce.* Lynx.

l. 471. *Behemoth.* A huge biblical beast mentioned in Job 40: 15, usually identified in Milton's time as the elephant.

l. 473. *ambiguous.* Amphibious.

503 l. 474. *river horse.* Literally translating hippopotamus.

l. 482. *Minims.* Smallest creatures.

l. 483. *involved.* Coiled.

l. 484. *added wings.* i.e. some serpents were winged before the fall.

l. 485. *parsimonious emmet.* Thrifty ant.

ll. 487–9. *Pattern . . . commonality.* i.e. the ants may serve as a model for future democratic societies.

l. 497. *mane terrific.* Recalling Virgil's account of the splendid sea-serpents coming to destroy Laöcoön (*Aen.*, ii. 203–7).

l. 502. *Consummate.* Completed.

l. 504. *Frequent.* In great numbers.

l. 505. *end.* Both completion and object.

l. 509. *front.* Brow.

l. 511. *Magnanimous.* Lit. 'great-souled'; magnanimity was the Aristotelian virtue to be aspired to by monarchs.

504 ll. 519–34. *Let . . . earth.* Adapted from Gen. 1: 26–8 and 2: 7.

l. 528. *Express.* Exact.

ll. 542–4. *but . . . diest.* The proscription of the Tree of Knowledge and the warning of the death penalty are in Gen. 2: 16–17.

l. 553. *heaven of heavens.* Highest heaven.

505 l. 557. *Answering.* Corresponding to.

l. 559. *Symphonious.* Harmonious.   *tuned.* Performed.

505 l. 564. *pomp.* 'A triumphal or ceremonial procession' (*OED*).

506 l. 597. *sounds on fret.* Sounds determined by fingering the frets, or bars, that regulate the notes on the finger-boards of lutes and similar instruments. *string.* Gut.

l. 605. *giant angels.* Satan's rebellion, as often in the period, is a version of the attempt by the Giants to overthrow Jove.

l. 619. *hyaline.* Transliterating the Greek word for 'glassy', and referring to the 'sea of glass like unto crystal' before God's throne in Rev. 4: 6.

l. 620. *immense.* Infinite (lit. 'unmeasurable').

l. 636. *face.* Appearance.

BOOK 8

507 ll. 1–4. *The angel . . . replied.* These lines were added in the 1674 edition, when the 10–book poem became 12; l. 4 originally read, 'To whom thus Adam gratefully replied.'

l. 2. *charming.* Including its literal sense 'spell-binding'.

l. 9. *condescension.* The sense is certainly positive ('affability to one's inferiors, with courteous disregard of difference of rank': *OED*); but the word had started to have its modern pejorative sense by the 1640s. Cf. l. 649, below.

l. 22. *officiate.* Supply, with a religious overtone from its literal meaning, perform a divine service.

l. 23. *opacous.* Dark.   *punctual.* Tiny (like a point).

l. 25. *admire.* Wonder.

508 l. 32. *sedentary.* Motionless.

l. 36. *sumless.* Immeasurable.

l. 37. *Of incorporeal speed.* With the swiftness of the spirit (since nothing physical could move so quickly), as in l. 110, 'speed almost spiritual'.

l. 45. *visit.* 'Inspect or examine' (*OED*); the etymological meaning is 'see'.

l. 46. *Her nursery.* The objects of her care.

l. 47. *tendance.* Tending.

l. 61. *pomp.* Procession.   *still.* Always.

l. 65. *facile.* Affable, courteous (*OED*); the word did not yet have its pejorative implications.

509 l. 78. *wide.* Erring.

l. 82. *To save appearances.* Like 'to save the phenomena', a standard term for attempts to reconcile observed celestial phenomena with astronomical theory.

l. 83. *centric and eccentric.* Orbits with the earth at the centre and off-centre respectively: eccentric spheres were a necessary element in both Ptolemaic and Copernican explanations of celestial motion.

509 l. 84. *epicyle.* A smaller orbit, whose centre is on the circumference of the main orbit; also essential to Ptolemaic and Copernican theories.

l. 91. *infers.* Implies (*OED*): the modern distinction had not yet developed.

l. 99. *Officious.* Dutiful.

510 l. 124. *attractive virtue.* Power of attraction.

l. 126. *wandering course.* Etymologizing 'planet', from the Greek for 'wanderer'.

l. 130. *three different motions.* The daily rotation, the yearly rotation around the sun, and the rotation of the earth's axis itself.

l. 132. *thwart obliquities.* The spheres moving 'athwart' each other in the Ptolemaic system.

l. 134. *Nocturnal . . . rhomb.* The outermost tenth sphere, or *primum mobile*, which in Ptolemaic astronomy revolved around the universe.

l. 141. *transpicuous.* Transparent.

l. 142. *terrestrial moon.* Raphael suggests that the moon is another earth, with 'fields and inhabitants' (l. 145).

l. 150. *male . . . light.* The light of the sun is conceived as male, that of the moon female, just as in mythology the sun was a god, Apollo, the moon a goddess, Diana.

511 l. 158. *obvious.* 'Exposed or open' (*OED*). Milton himself debated the point as a Cambridge undergraduate in his Seventh Prolusion.

l. 164. *inoffensive.* Harmless, not dangerous.

l. 167. *Solicit.* Disturb.

ll. 180–1. *pure / Intelligence.* Angelic creature.

512 l. 194. *fume.* 'Something comparable to smoke or vapour as being unsubstantial, transient, imaginary' (*OED*).

l. 195. *fond impertinence.* Foolish irrelevance ('impertinence' did not yet have its modern sense of 'taking liberties').

l. 197. *still to seek.* Always searching.

l. 230. *uncouth.* Strange, unfamiliar.

513 l. 239. *state.* Dignity.   *inure.* Exercise, make habitual.

l. 247. *relation.* Story.

l. 256. *reeking.* Vaporous (without its modern pejorative sense).

l. 263. *lapse.* Lapping, flow.

l. 268. *went.* Walked.

514 l. 296. *mansion.* Dwelling (not necessarily a building).   *wants.* Lacks.

l. 299. *seat.* Residence.

515 l. 316. *Submiss.* Submissive.

ll. 320–30. *To till . . . die.* Paraphrasing Gen. 2: 15–17.

515 l. 337. *purpose.* Matter, discourse.

516 l. 371. *Replenished.* 'Abundantly stocked' (*OED*).

   l. 387. *intense . . . still remiss.* High-tuned . . . always weak or low (continuing the musical metaphor of tighter and more slack strings on an instrument).

   l. 396. *converse.* 'Consort, keep company' (*OED*); the original senses include 'dwell' and 'have sexual intercourse'; cf. l. 418.

517 l. 399. *nice.* Delicate, fastidious.

   l. 402. *in pleasure.* Eden etymologically means 'pleasure'.

   l. 421. *through . . . absolute.* Both 'perfect in all your parts' and 'containing all numbers in your unity'.

   l. 423. *His single imperfection.* His incompleteness in being single.

   l. 425. *unity.* Singleness.

   l. 432. *these.* The animals.

   l. 433. *complacence.* Pleasure, satisfaction.

   l. 435. *Permissive.* Which was permitted.

518 l. 453. *earthly.* i.e. earthly nature.

   l. 462. *Abstract.* From a distance, carried away.

   l. 466. *cordial.* Vital (lit. 'from the heart').

   l. 476. *air.* (1) Demeanour; (2) breath; the latter sense is continued in 'inspired', lit. 'breathed in'.

519 l. 481. *out of hope.* Hopeless.

   l. 490. *aloud.* Speaking aloud.

   l. 494. *enviest.* i.e. 'you do not begrudge me the gift'.

   ll. 495–9. *Bone . . . soul.* Paraphrasing Gen. 3: 23–4, repeated in Matt. 19: 4–6 and Mark 10: 6–8.

   l. 502. *conscience.* Consciousness.

   l. 504. *obvious.* Flaunting herself.

   l. 509. *obsequious.* Compliant, dutiful; the word had just begun to acquire its modern pejorative sense.

   l. 514. *gratulation.* Rejoicing.

   l. 516. *their wings.* Those of the personified airs.

   l. 518. *bird of night.* Nightingale.

520 l. 526. *vehement.* Lit. 'deprived of mind' (in contrast with l. 525).

   l. 529. *transported.* Ecstatic.

   l. 533. *charm.* Spell.

   l. 535. *proof.* Combining the senses of experienced and armed.   *sustain.* Withstand.

   l. 536. *subducting.* Removing.

520 l. 539. *exact*. Perfect; cf. ix. 1017.

l. 550. *discreetest*. Most discerning, showing best judgement.

l. 556. *Occasionally*. For an occasion, i.e. to satsify Adam's desire for a companion.

521 l. 562. *diffident*. Mistrustful.

l. 576. *adorn*. Adorned (cf. 'elaborate', l. 539); the adjective is apparently Milton's coinage.

l. 577. *awful*. Awe-inspiring.

l. 598. *genial*. Relating to generation, hence nuptial.

522 l. 607. *subject not*. Do not make me subject to her.

l. 608. *foiled*. Overcome.

ll. 609–10. *from . . . representing*. Variously presented to me by my senses.

l. 617. *virtual*. 'In essence or effect, though not formally or actually' (*OED*). *immediate*. Through actual contact (to make love by looks would be virtual, to 'mix irradiance' would be immediate).

l. 624. *In eminence*. To the highest degree.

l. 628. *restrained conveyance*. Restrictions on the manner of expression.

l. 631. *verdant isles*. The Cape Verde Isles, off West Africa.

l. 632. *Hesperian*. In the west.

BOOK 9

523 l. 2. *familiar*. Including the sense of familial.

l. 5. *Venial*. Pardonable (not 'permissible' or 'blameless', as the *OED* claims [*s.v.* 3], in which case 'unblamed' would make no sense): the implication is that Adam is at fault (e.g. for his inquisitiveness about astronomy), but not seriously.

524 l. 13. *argument*. Subject.

l. 15. *his foe*. Hector.

l. 16. *fugitive*. Fleeing; for Achilles' pursuit of and victory over Hector see *Il.*, xxii.

ll. 16–17. *rage . . . disespoused*. Lavinia, the daughter of the king of Latium, was betrothed to Turnus, King of the Rutuli. Her father Latinus, however, in deference to a divine warning that he should marry her to a stranger, gave her to Aeneas instead, thus precipitating hostility and conflict between the Rutuli and the Trojans (*Aen.*, vii).

l. 19. *the Greek . . . son*. Odysseus and Aeneas, son of Venus or Cytherea, so-called from her association with the island of Cythera.

l. 20. *answerable*. Appropriate.

l. 21. *celestial patroness*. Urania, muse of astronomy (see vii. 1 ff.).

ll. 25–6. *this . . . late*. Milton's earliest sketches for *Paradise Lost* were in the early 1640s, as the subject of a drama.

524 l. 27. *sedulous.* Eager, diligent.

l. 28. *argument.* Subject matter.

l. 29. *dissect.* Analyse.

l. 31. *feigned.* Invented, as in the *Faerie Queene*; cf. Milton's more favourable attitude toward the chivalric epic in *RCG* (p. 170).

l. 34. *tilting furniture.* Jousting weapons.

l. 35. *Impresas quaint.* Complex heraldic symbols.   *caparisons.* Ornamental coverings for horses.

l. 36. *Bases.* Cloth coverings for horses.

l. 38. *sewers, and seneschals.* The sewer (lit. 'seater') 'superintended the arrangement of the table, the seating of the guests, and the tasting and serving of the meal' (*OED*); the seneschal was the major-domo, or chief steward of the household.

l. 44. *That name.* Of epic.

ll. 44–5. *cold / Climate.* Milton discusses the effects of the English climate on creativity in *RCG* (see p. 170).

525 l. 49. *Hesperus.* Venus as the evening star.

l. 54. *improved.* Increased, aggravated (*OED*).

l. 56. *maugre.* Despite.

ll. 64–5. *thrice . . . circled.* Satan circles the earth at the equator, keeping ahead of the sun and thereby remaining in darkness.

l. 66. *colure.* The coloures are two longitudinal circles intersecting at right angles at the poles and dividing the ecliptic into four equal parts.

l. 77. *Pontus.* The Black Sea.

l. 78. *Maeotis.* The Sea of Azov.   *river Ob.* In the Siberian arctic.

l. 80. *Orontes.* A river in Lebanon, Syria, and Turkey.

l. 81. *Darien.* Panama.

526 l. 90. *suggestions.* Temptations to evil.

l. 95. *Doubt.* Suspicion.

l. 104. *officious.* Dutiful, though here perphaps with its modern pejorative overtone.

l. 112. *gradual.* Gradated, in stages.

l. 121. *siege.* Both seat and attack.

527 l. 145. *virtue.* Power.

ll. 146–7. *if . . . created.* i.e. if the angels are not self-created, or did not always exist; cf. v. 860.

l. 148. *room.* Place.

l. 150. *original.* Origin.

527–8 ll. 170–1. *obnoxious . . . To.* Exposed to harm from; the modern sense was apparently not yet in use.

528 l. 173. *reck.* Care.

l. 174. *higher.* i.e. when I aim at God.

l. 186. *Nor nocent.* Both not harmful and innocent.

l. 188. *brutal.* Animal.

l. 191. *close.* Secretly.

l. 197. *grateful.* Including the meaning 'pleasing'.

l. 199. *wanting.* Lacking.

l. 209. *Luxurious.* Luxuriant, though the word was most commonly pejorative, and must have such an overtone here.

l. 211. *wanton.* Unrestrained; like *luxurious* above, with pejorative overtones.

529 l. 218. *spring.* Grove.

l. 219. *redress.* 'Set upright again' (*OED*).

l. 229. *motioned.* Suggested.

530 l. 265. *Or . . . worse.* Whether his intention be this or something worse.

l. 270. *virgin.* Innocent.

l. 292. *entire.* 'Free from reproach, unblemished, blameless' (*OED*).

531 l. 296. *asperses.* Slanders.

l. 310. *Access.* Increase.

l. 326. *still.* Always.

l. 330. *front.* Lit. 'face', but punning on 'affronts', l. 328.

l. 334. *event.* Outcome.

532 l. 353. *still erect.* Always alert.

l. 358. *mind.* Both remind, admonish, and pay attention to.

l. 361. *specious.* Deceptively attractive.

l. 367. *approve.* Prove, test.

l. 371. *securer.* Less careful.

533 l. 387. *Oread or dryad.* Mountain or wood nymph.   *Delia.* Diana, so called from her birthplace on Delos.

l. 390. *bow and quiver.* Diana was goddess of the hunt.

l. 392. *Guiltless.* Innocent, without experience.

l. 393. *Pales.* Goddess of pastures.   *Pomona.* Goddess of orchards.

l. 395. *Vertumnus.* More properly Vortumnus, god of gardens, who presided over the changes of the year. Variously disguised, he pursued and wooed Pomona, ultimately successfully; see *Met.*, xiv. 628 ff.   *Ceres.* Goddess of agriculture (cf. iv. 268 ff.).

l. 396. *Proserpina.* Child of Ceres by Jove.

l. 405. *event perverse.* Evil outcome.

533 l. 413. *Mere.* Wholly a.

534 l. 419. *Their tendance.* The object of their care.

l. 431. *mindless.* Both unaware and inattentive (cf. l. 358).

l. 436. *voluble.* Undulating.

l. 437. *arborets.* Shrubs.

l. 438. *hand.* Handiwork.

ll. 439–40. *gardens . . . Adonis.* Adonis was the lover of Venus. When hunting he was killed by a boar, and Venus made the anemone (or in some versions the rose) spring from his blood. After his death, in response to the pleas of both Venus and Proserpina, Jove restored him to life and allowed him to live half the year with each—the myth, like that of Proserpina herself, was from the earliest times said to allude to the cycles of the crops. The Garden of Adonis became a proverbial expression for the swift passing of earthly beauty; however, in Spenser's version of the tale, it is the secret garden where Adonis and Venus make love, a place of 'perpetual spring and harvest' (*FQ*, III. vi. 29).

l. 441. *Alcinous . . . son.* Homer describes the visit of Odysseus, son of Laertes, to Alcinous, king of the Phaeacians, and his marvellous gardens, in *Od.*, vii. 112 ff.; cf. v. 341.

l. 442. *not mystic.* Real, not fabled or allegorical.   *sapient king.* Solomon.

l. 443. *Egyptian spouse.* Solomon married the daughter of Pharaoh (1 Kgs. 3:1); for Solomon's garden see S. of S. 6: 2.

l. 450. *tedded.* Cut and dried, for use as hay.   *kine.* Cattle.

l. 453. *for.* Because of.

l. 456. *plat.* Plot of ground.

535 l. 472. *gratulating.* Rejoicing.

l. 476. *for.* In exchange for.

l. 481. *opportune.* Open, conveniently located.

l. 483. *intellectual.* Intellect.

l. 484. *haughty.* Lofty, high-minded.

l. 488. *to.* In comparison with.

536 l. 500. *carbuncle.* 'A mythical gem said to emit light in the dark' (*OED*).

l. 502. *spires.* Coils.

l. 503. *redundant.* The word had the senses of both 'wavelike' and 'copious'.

ll. 505–6. *those . . . Cadmus.* For the metamorphosis of Harmonia (or Hermione) and Cadmus into serpents see *Met.*, iv. 563 ff.

ll. 506–7. *god . . . Epidaurus.* Aesculapius, god of healing, who appeared in his shrine at Epidaurus in the form of a serpent (*Met.*, xv. 760–4).

536 ll. 508–10. *Ammonian . . . Scipio.* Jupiter Ammon made love to Olympias, the mother of Alexander the Great, in the form of a serpent, as Jupiter Capitolinus (so named from his shrine on the Capitoline in Rome) did to the mother of the Roman hero Scipio Africanus.   *height of Rome.* Greatest Roman.   *tract.* Path, course.

l. 522. *at . . . disguised.* The sorceress Circe transformed her victims into fawning animals (*Od.*, x. 212–19).

l. 530. *Organic.* Being used as an organ or instrument (of speech, because snakes have no vocal chords).   *impulse . . . air.* Impelling the air to make the sounds of speech.

537 l. 549. *glozed.* Flattered.

l. 558. *demur.* Am doubtful about.

l. 580. *Grateful.* Pleasing.

538 l. 581. *fennel . . . teats.* Snakes were said to be especially fond of fennel, and of milk sucked directly from the teat.

l. 586. *defer.* Delay.

l. 601. *Wanted.* Lacked.

l. 605. *middle.* The air between.

l. 616. *virtue.* Combining the meanings of power, innate excellence, and nature.   *proved.* Tested.

539 l. 623. *their provision.* What they provide.

l. 624. *birth.* Milton uses 'bearth', an etymologizing spelling not in normal usage, but appropriate to trees which 'bear' fruit.

l. 629. *blowing.* Blooming.

l. 635. *Compact . . . vapour.* Composed of oily gases; referring to the *ignis fatuus*, or will o' the wisp.

540 l. 668. *Fluctuates.* Changes his aspect.

ll. 675–6. *Sometimes . . . brooking.* i.e. began at the height of the argument, without any preface.

l. 680. *science.* Knowledge.

ll. 685–7. *ye . . . knowledge.* Paraphrasing Gen. 3: 4–5.   *To knowledge.* Eventuating in knowledge.

l. 695. *denounced.* Threatened.

541 l. 717. *participating.* Partaking of.

l. 722. *they.* 'Produce' understood.

l. 732. *humane.* Both benevolent and human: the spellings were not yet fully distinguished in the seventeenth century.

l. 737. *impregned.* Impregnated.

l. 742. *Inclinable.* Inclined, disposed.

542 l. 754. *infers.* Implies.

542 l. 758. *In plain.* In plain words.

l. 771. *author unsuspect.* Trustworthy authority.

543 l. 793. *boon.* Jovial.

l. 797. *To sapience.* In producing knowledge, with a pun on the etymological meaning of sapience, 'taste' (*sapere*, taste, know).   *infamed.* Slandered.

l. 821. *wants.* Is wanting.

544 l. 837. *sciential.* Endowed with or bestowing knowledge.

l. 845. *divine of.* Divining.

l. 846. *faltering measure.* Of his heart, which 'misgave him'.

545 l. 876. *erst.* Formerly.

l. 887. *distemper.* Disorder, intoxication.

l. 890. *Astonied.* Stunned (lit. 'turned to stone').   *blank.* Speechless, nonplussed, helpless.

l. 901. *devote.* Comdemned.

546 l. 928. *fact.* Crime, the most usual seventeenth-century sense.

547 l. 951. *Matter . . . foe.* 'He would not give the enemy grounds for contempt.'

l. 953. *Certain.* Resolved (Lat. *certus*).

l. 980. *oblige thee.* Make you subject to a penalty, involve you in guilt. *fact.* Deed.

l. 984. *event.* Outcome.

l. 987. *to.* In comparison with.

548 l. 999. *fondly.* Foolishly.

l. 1016. *dalliance.* Sport, trifling, with implications of wanton or lascivious flirtation.

l. 1018. *elegant.* Refined.

l. 1019. *each meaning.* Of 'taste', judgment, and savour; cf. l. 797, above.

l. 1028. *meet.* Appropriate.

549 l. 1034. *toy.* 'Light caress' (*OED*).

l. 1047. *bland.* 'Pleasing to the senses' (*OED*).

l. 1050. *unkindly.* Both unnatural and immoral.   *conscious.* Guilty.

ll. 1059–62. *so rose . . . strength.* For Delilah's treachery in cutting off Samson's hair see Judg. 16.   *Danite.* Samson was from the tribe of Dan. *Dalilah.* Milton uses a variant of the Vulgate form Dalila.

550 l. 1078. *evil store.* A multitude of evils.

l. 1081. *erst.* Formerly.

l. 1094. *obnoxious.* Exposed (to evil or harm).

l. 1101. *fig-tree.* The banyan, or *ficus indica*.

550 l. 1111. *Amazonian targe*. The shields of Amazons: Milton found the simile (and the 'loop-holes' of the previous line) in the description of the banyan in Gerard's *Herbal* (1597), 1330.

551 l. 1140. *approve*. Test, demonstrate.

l. 1141. *owe*. Either possess, or are obliged to render.

552 ll. 1164–5. *expressed / Immutable*. (My love) which I declared was unalterable.

l. 1175. *secure*. Over-confident.

BOOK 10

553 l. 10. *Complete*. Fully able.

l. 12. *still*. Always.

l. 19. *by this*. By this time.

554 ll. 28–9. *they . . . Accountable*. i.e. those who were responsible (for the vigilance of l. 30).

l. 31. *approved*. Justified, vindicated (modifying *vigilance*).

l. 40. *speed*. Succeed.

l. 48. *rests*. Remains.

l. 49. *denounced*. Formally proclaimed (as 'the mortal sentence').

l. 53. *acquittance*. Acquittal.

l. 54. *Justice . . . return as*. My justice must not be repaid with (but the syntax is curiously obscure as God justifies himself).

555 l. 77. *On me derived*. Diverted on to me.

l. 78. *illustrate*. Show.

l. 79. *Them*. Both justice and mercy (l. 78) and Adam and Eve.

l. 80. *train*. Attendants.

l. 82. *the third*. Satan.

l. 83. *Convict*. Convicted.

l. 84. *Conviction*. In the legal sense, a formal determination of guilt. *none belongs*. Is not appropriate to.

l. 92. *cadence*. Setting, sinking, with an overtone of the musical sense—cf. 'airs', l. 93.

l. 97. *voice of God*. As viceregent, Christ speaks with God's voice, and is called God throughout the scene.

556 l. 118. *revile*. Abuse.

557 ll. 155–6. *part / And person*. Theatrical terms, role and character.

l. 157. *in few*. In few words.

557 ll. 165–7. *unable . . . mischief.* Since the serpent cannot speak, he cannot accuse Satan; and hence the first instance of God's justice after the fall is the condemnation of the only wholly innocent party to the crime. Milton undertakes no mitigation of the biblical account in Gen. 3: 14–15, though he acknowledges its 'mysterious terms' (l. 173).

558 l. 184. *Saw . . . heaven.* Jesus reports Satan's fall in Luke 10: 18.

ll. 186–7. *Spoiled . . . show.* Cf. St Paul's account of Christ's victory, Col. 2:15.

ll. 187–8. *with ascension . . . captive.* Alluding to Ps. 68: 18.

ll. 198–208. The passage quotes Gen. 3: 17–19 almost verbatim.

l. 210. *denounced.* Pronounced (as a judge passing a sentence).

l. 215. *washed . . . feet.* Jesus washes his disciples' feet in John 13: 5.

ll. 217–18. *or slain . . . repaid.* Milton offers alternative possibilities for the source of the first clothing, a subject on which the scripture gives no guidance: either Christ killed animals for their pelts, or the animals sloughed off their skins as snakes do.   *repaid.* recompensed (for losing its skin).

559 l. 231. *In counterview.* Opposite each other.

ll. 241–2. *no place . . . fit.* i.e. no other place is so suitable.

l. 246. *Or . . . or.* Whether . . . or.   *connatural force.* Innate force linking us.

l. 249. *conveyance.* Communication.

l. 257. *main.* The ocean of Chaos: see ii. 919.

l. 260. *intercourse.* Coming and going.

l. 261. *transmigration.* Permanent emigration.

560 l. 272. *snuffed.* Inhaled.

l. 275. *Against.* In anticipation of.

l. 277. *designed.* Designated.

l. 279. *feature.* Form, creature.

l. 281. *Sagacious.* On the scent, 'acute in . . . the sense of smell' (*OED*).

l. 284. *diverse.* In different directions.

l. 288. *shoaling.* Crowded.

l. 290. *Cronian sea.* Arctic Ocean (from Cronos, or Saturn, the oldest and therefore the coldest of the gods).

l. 291. *the imagined way.* The fabled northern passage to Asia.

l. 292. *Petsora.* Or Pechora, Siberian river.

l. 294. *petrific.* That turns things to stone.

l. 295. *trident.* The three-pronged weapon of Neptune.

560 l. 296. *Delos floating*. When Leto, or Latona, was pregnant by Jupiter, Neptune created the floating island of Delos as a haven for her from the anger of Juno, and there she gave birth to the twins Apollo and Diana. Jupiter later anchored the island among the Cyclades.

l. 297. *Gorgonian rigor*. The look of the Gorgons turned people to stone.

l. 298. *asphaltic slime*. Pitch, used by the devils in the construction of Pandaemonium (i. 729).

l. 300. *mole*. Massive pier.

l. 302. *wall*. The outer shell of the universe (see ii. 1029–30).

l. 303. *fenceless*. Defenceless.

l. 305. *inoffensive*. Without obstacles.

561 ll. 307–11. *Xerxes . . . waves*. When a storm destroyed the bridge of ships that Xerxes had created across the Hellespont, he ordered the sea to be beaten.

l. 308. *Susa*. The biblical Shushan, in Persia, Xerxes' winter capital. *Memnonian*. Susa was founded by Tithonus, the lover of Aurora, whose son Memnon was the first king.

l. 309. *Hellespont*. The Dardanelles, the Turkish strait connecting the Sea of Marmara with the Aegean, and the dividing line between Europe and Asia.

l. 313. *Pontifical*. Lit. 'bridge-making'.

l. 314. *vexed*. Stormy.

l. 318. *adamant*. The mythical substance of impenetrable hardness.

l. 321. *confines*. Boundaries.

l. 328. *Centaur . . . Scorpion*. The constellations Sagittarius and Scorpio.

l. 332. *unminded*. Unnoticed.

562 l. 348. *pontifice*. Bridge.

l. 370. *fortify*. Grow strong; also making the bridge strong.

l. 371. *portentous*. Both ominous and prodigious.

l. 372. *virtue* . Strength, valour, with an ironic overtone of the moral sense.

l. 374. *odds*. Advantage.

l. 375. *foil*. Defeat.

l. 378. *doom*. Sentence.

l. 381. *quadrature*. Heaven is here conceived as a square, apparently on the authority of Rev. 21: 16, where the New Jerusalem is described as 'four-square'. In ii. 1048, however, heaven in Satan's view was 'undertermined square or round'.

l. 382. *try thee*. Find you to be.

l. 384. *son and grandchild*. Because Death is the child of Satan's incest with his daughter Sin.

562 l. 387. *Antagonist.* Literally translating Satan.

563 l. 404. *Plenipotent.* Deputies with full authority, parallel with Christ as God's agent on earth.

l. 413. *planet-struck.* Stricken by their malignant influence as they wander through the heavens: *'planet struck'* = suffering from the unfavourable astrological influence of a malignant planet.   *real eclipse.* i.e. not merely apparent, a function of the view of the heavens from earth.

l. 418. *his.* Chaos's.

l. 426. *paragoned.* Compared (in Isa. 14: 12: 'How art thou fallen from heaven, Lucifer, son of the morning').

l. 428. *solicitous.* Apprehensive about.

564 l. 432. *Astrakhan.* Tartar city on the Volga, near the Caspian Sea.

l. 433. *Bactrian Sophy.* The Persian Shah.

ll. 433–4. *horns . . . crescent.* Both the Turks' insignia and their battle array.

l. 435. *Aladule.* Armenia.

l. 436. *Tauris or Casbeen.* Tabriz, Kazvin, both in northern Iran.

l. 437. *left . . . hell.* Left the outermost reaches of hell deserted.

l. 438. *reduced.* Retreated.

l. 442. *show.* Appearance.

l. 444. *Plutonian.* Underworld (from Pluto, the classical god of the underworld).

l. 445. *state.* Canopy.

l. 449. *fulgent.* Radiant.

l. 457. *divan.* Council; originally the Turkish privy council.

565 l. 475. *uncouth.* Both strange and solitary.

l. 477. *unoriginal.* Eternal, without any origin.

l. 478. *fiercely opposed.* In fact, Night offered no opposition, and Chaos aided Satan: see ii. 990–1009.

l. 481. *fame.* Rumour.

l. 499. *when is not set.* The time is not yet determined.

566 l. 513. *supplanted.* Overthrown (lit. 'tripped up').

l. 515. *Reluctant.* Lit. 'struggling'.

l. 517. *his doom.* Both Satan's fate and God's judgement.

l. 521. *riot.* Rebellion.

l. 523. *complicated.* Intertwined.

l. 524. *amphisbaena.* A fabulous serpent with a head at either end.

l. 525. *Cerastes.* A four-horned serpent.   *hydrus and ellops.* Water snakes.

l. 526. *dipsas.* A mythical snake whose bite caused violent thirst.

566 ll. 526–7. *soil . . . Gorgon.* After Perseus slew Medusa, serpents sprang from the blood that dropped from her severed head.

l. 528. *Ophiusa.* Lit. 'snake-filled', an ancient name for Rhodes and several other Greek islands.

l. 529. *whom.* Him whom.

ll. 529–31. *the sun . . . Python.* For the birth of the great Python from the slime of the universal flood, see *Met.*, i. 438–40.

l. 535. *in . . . array.* At their posts, or in review formation.

l. 536. *Sublime.* Raised up.

l. 546. *exploding.* With an overtone of its etymological meaning, 'driving them off the stage' (from *explaudo*, the opposite of *plaudo*, applaud).

567 l. 560. *Megaera.* One of the three avenging Furies.

l. 565. *gust.* Relish.

l. 568. *drugged.* Nauseated, a usage apparently originating with Milton.

ll. 571–2. *not . . . lapsed.* Implying both that unlike man, they fell over and over again, and that man, once he had fallen, was not deceived again by 'the same illusion'. *triumphed.* Triumphed over.

l. 579. *purchase.* Plunder.

l. 581. *Ophion with Eurynome.* The original king and queen of Olympus; Ophion means 'serpent', Eurynome 'wide-ruling' (hence 'the wide-encroaching Eve').

l. 584. *Ops.* Or Rhea, wife of Saturn. *Dictaean.* From Dicte, the mountain in Crete where Jupiter was raised.

l. 586. *in power.* Potentially.

l. 587. *Once actual.* Once sin has been committed: 'actual sin' is the theological term for a willed sinful act, as opposed to the general human condition of original sin—in the case of Adam and Eve, these are the same.

ll. 589–90. *mounted . . . horse.* For Death on his pale horse see Rev. 6: 8.

568 l. 599. *ravin.* Prey.

l. 601. *unhide-bound.* Shapeless, not bound or limited in size by any outer skin (see ii. 667).

l. 624. *conniving.* Lit. 'winking, shutting the eyes', with implications of complicity.

l. 627. *quitted.* Given over.

l. 630. *draff.* Dregs.

569 l. 640. *precedes.* i.e. God's curse takes precedence until Christ's victory.

l. 645. *extenuate.* Diminish.

l. 651. *sorted best with.* Was most appropriate to.

l. 656. *blank.* Pale, white (French *blanc*).

l. 657. *the other five.* i.e. planets.

569 l. 658. *aspects.* Astrological positions, the *sextile, square, trine,* and *opposite* of l. 659.

l. 660. *noxious efficacy.* In these four positions, the planets were said to have harmful effects on earth.

l. 661. *synod.* Conjunction.   *fixed.* i.e.stars.

ll. 664–5. *winds . . . corners.* Alluding to the notion that the winds blow from the four corners of the earth.

569–70 ll. 668–80. To account for the prelapsarian 'eternal spring', Milton assumes that before the fall the sun's course coincided with the celestial equator. Alternative explanations are given for its present course, moving between the tropics of Cancer in the spring and Capricorn in the autumn, and the consequent change of the seasons: if the universe is heliocentric, the earth was tilted on its axis; if geocentric, the sun changed its route.

l. 671. *centric globe.* Earth.

l. 672. *equinoctial road.* Equator.

l. 673. *Like distant breadth.* A similar distance.

ll. 673–4. *Taurus . . . Sisters.* In spring, the sun reaches Taurus, which includes the stars of the Pleiades, or Seven Sisters, daughters of Atlas, hence 'Atlantic'.   *Spartan twins.* Gemini, the twins Castor and Pollux.

l. 675. *tropic Crab.* Tropic of Cancer.

570 l. 676. *Virgin . . . Scales.* The constellations Virgo and Libra.

l. 679. *vernant flowers.* Flowers specific to spring.

l. 686. *Estotiland.* In northern Labrador.

l. 687. *Magellan.* The Straits of Magellan, below South America.

ll. 688–9. *sun . . . intended.* Thyestes seduced the wife of his brother Atreus. In revenge, Atreus killed Thyestes' sons and served their flesh to their unsuspecting father at a banquet. In Seneca's *Thyestes* the sun is represented as turning aside in horror (ll. 776 ff.).

l. 693. *sideral blast.* Evil influence from the stars.

l. 696. *Norumbega.* Roughly, northern New England and Nova Scotia.   *Samoed.* Siberian.

l. 698. *flaw.* Wind squall.

ll. 699 ff. *Boreas . . . Caecias, etc.* Names of the various winds.

l. 703. *Serraliona.* Sierra Leone.   *thwart.* i.e. blowing across the north–south winds from east and west.

l. 704. *Levant . . . ponent.* East and west (lit. 'rising and setting', hence from the directions of sunrise and sunset).

l. 706. *Sirocco, and Libecchio.* Italian names for south-east and south-west winds respectively.

571 l. 729. *Is propagated curse.* Extends the curse.

571 l. 738. *Mine own.* Curses.

l. 748. *equal.* Just.

572 l. 764. *election.* Choice.

l. 766. *of choice.* By choice.

l. 783. *all I cannot.* I cannot entirely.

l. 795. *be it.* Even if it is.

573 ll. 806–8. *all . . . sphere.* Adam uses a scholastic argument, which holds that 'an agent's action is limited by the recipient's capacity to be acted upon; so although God's wrath might be infinite, the fact that man is finite means that there must be a limit to his suffering' (J. Martin Evans, *Paradise Lost Books 9 and 10*, Cambridge, 1973).

l. 816. *incorporate.* Both embodied, and together in one body.

l. 817. *Nor . . . single.* Nor am I only a single body either.

l. 834. *So . . . wrath.* 'I wish the wrath would also', or 'perhaps the wrath will also'.

574 l. 853. *denounced.* Proclaimed.

l. 867. *thou serpent.* It had been noted as early as the ancient rabbinic commentators that the name Eve is related to old Semitic words, e.g. in Phoenician and Aramaic, for 'serpent'.

l. 869. *wants.* Is missing.

ll. 872–3. *pretended / To.* 'Feigned by', with overtones of its etymological sense 'held out [e.g. as a screen] before'.

ll. 878–9. *him . . . over-reach.* Arrogantly thinking to outsmart him.

575 l. 886. *part sinister.* Left side, with ominous overtones.

ll. 887–8. *supernumerary . . . number.* Some commentators, including Calvin, argued that Eve was created from an extra rib, since Adam was created perfect.

l. 898. *strait conjunction.* Close connection: *conjunction* was used in the period for both the marriage union and sexual intercourse.

576 l. 926. *doom express.* Christ's sentence, delivered at ll. 179–80.

577 l. 965. *derived.* Passed down.

l. 978. *As . . . evils.* In evils such as ours.

l. 979. *descent.* Descendants.

l. 989. *so death.* In the first five editions, these words appear at the beginning of the following line. All editors have moved it back to regularize the metre, with the exception of Fowler, who argues that 'the line division . . . is perhaps intended to mime first the deficiency of childlessness . . . then the glut denied to Death.'

l. 990. *deceived.* Cheated of.

l. 993. *Conversing.* Lit. 'cohabiting'.

577   l. 996. *present object*. Object in your presence, i.e. Eve.

    l. 1000. *make short*. Be quick.

578   l. 1027. *contumacy*. Wilful disobedience.

579   l. 1045. *Reluctance*. Resistance.

    l. 1053. *aslope*. Falling aslant, missing its true mark.

    l. 1068. *shroud*. Shelter.   *cherish*. Keep warm, comfort.

    l. 1069. *this diurnal star*. The sun.

    l. 1070. *how*. Seek how.

    l. 1071. *with . . . foment*. Kindle in dry matter (*fire*, l. 1073).

    l. 1073. *attrite*. By friction.

    l. 1075. *Tine*. Ignite.   *thwart*. Slanting.

    l. 1078. *supply*. Replace.

    ll. 1081–2. *of . . . him*. Asking him for grace.

580   l. 1091. *Frequenting*. Filling.

BOOK 11

    l. 3. *Prevenient grace*. The grace that precedes and makes possible repentance.

581   ll. 12–14. *Deucalion . . . devout*. Deucalion was the Noah of Greek myth. He and his wife Pyrrha were instructed by the oracle of Themis, goddess of Justice, to repopulate the earth after the universal flood by throwing stones behind them, from which grew men and women; see *Met.*, i. 321–80.

    l. 17. *Dimensionless*. Non-corporeal, immaterial.

    l. 28. *manuring*. Cultivating (lit. 'working with the hands'); see iv. 628.

    l. 38. *smell*. First suggestion; also, the prayers are 'clad with incense', ll. 17–18.

582   l. 53. *gross . . . gross*. i.e. from the pure air of paradise to air as impure as Adam has become.

    l. 59. *that*. The former, happiness.   *fondly*. Foolishly.

    l. 67. *synod*. Meeting, specifically of an ecclesiastical council.

    l. 70. *peccant*. Sinning.

    l. 74. *Oreb*. Horeb, where the trumpet signalled the descent of God to Mount Sinai to give Moses the Ten Commandments. Cf. 'Nativity Ode', ll. 155–9.

    l. 76. *general doom*. The Judgment Day.

    l. 78. *amarantine*. Immortal (from the amaranth, the legendary flower that never fades: see iii. 353 ff.).

    l. 86. *defended*. Forbidden.

    l. 91. *motions*. Workings, influence.

583 l. 93. *Self-left.* If left to itself.

ll. 102–3. *invade . . . possession.* i.e. become a squatter on my untenanted land (in which case, under English law, the squatter would have a legal right to remain).

l. 106. *denounce.* Announce.

l. 111. *excess.* Transgression.

l. 129. *double Janus.* Janus, guardian of gateways, had two faces looking forward and back; the double Janus, or Janus Quadrifrons, had four faces looking towards the four compass points.

l. 131. *Argus.* A hundred-eyed monster set by Juno to watch Io, with whom Jove was in love. He was charmed to sleep and killed by Hermes / Mercury; see *Met.*, i. 625 ff.

584 l. 135. *Leucothea.* Goddess of the dawn.

l. 144. *prevalent.* Forceful.

ll. 159–60. *rightly . . . living.* Etymologically, Eve (in Hebrew *Chava*) is cognate with *chai*, life. Cf. Gen. 3: 20.

585 l. 185. *bird of Jove.* Eagle.   *stooped.* Having swooped down.
tower. High flight.

l. 187. *beast . . . woods.* Lion.

l. 188. *brace.* Pair.

l. 196. *secure.* Confident.

l. 205. *orient.* Bright.

l. 208. *by this.* By this time.

l. 209. *lighted.* Alighted.

l. 210. *made alt.* Halted; a technical military expression.

l. 212. *carnal.* Unholy, deriving from his sinful nature.

l. 214. *Mahanaim.* Lit. 'armies', 'encampments', the name given by Jacob to the place where he saw the army of angels (Gen. 32: 1–2).

586 ll. 216–20. *that . . . unproclaimed.* When the Syrian king attempted to seize the prophet Elisha, who had warned the Israelites against him, an angelic army 'full of horses and chariots of fire' appeared to protect him (2 Kgs. 6: 13–17).   l. 216. *Dothan.* Modern Tell Dotha, strategic town near Samaria.   l. 220. *princely hierarch.* Michael (see l. 99).

l. 221. *stand.* Station, another technical military term.

l. 240. *lucid.* Shining.

l. 242. *Meliboean.* Meliboea, in Thessaly, supplied the ancient world with the finest purple dye.   *grain.* Dye.

l. 243. *Sarra.* Tyre, also famous for its dyes; Tyrian purple was the colour of Roman imperial robes.

586 l. 244. *Iris . . . woof.* Thereby making the cloth *iridescent*; Iris was goddess of the rainbow.

l. 247. *zodiac.* The heavenly sphere containing the constellations.

587 l. 264. *gripe.* Spasm, pang.

l. 267. *Discovered.* Revealed.   *retire.* Withdrawal.

l. 272. *respite.* 'Time granted . . . until the coming of' (*OED*), a usage apparently peculiar to Milton; the word was normally used in the sense of reprieve, postponement, cessation of labour.

l. 283. *to.* In comparison with.

l. 293. *damp.* 'Dazed or stupefied condition', 'state of dejection, depression of spirits' (*OED*).

589 l. 338. *Fomented.* Fostered, cherished.   *virtual.* Strong, effective.

l. 359. *supernal.* Heavenly.

l. 374. *obvious.* Exposed.

590 l. 379. *ken.* View.

ll. 382–4. *tempter . . . glory.* For Satan's temptation of Christ in the wilderness see Matt. 4: 8, Luke 4: 5, and *PR*, iii. 251 ff.

l. 388. *Cambalu.* Cambaluc, capital of Mongolian Cathay.

l. 389. *Oxus.* Or Amu Darya, central Asian river.   *Temir.* Timur or Tamburlaine, the Tartar king.

l. 390. *Paquin.* Peking, or Beijing.   *Sinaean.* Chinese (as distinct from that part of Cathay ruled by the Mongols).

l. 391. *Agra and Lahore.* Mughal capitals in northern India.

l. 392. *golden Chersonese.* Rich Malacca and Thailand.

l. 393. *Ecbatan.* Ecbatana, ancient capital of the Persian kings.

ll. 393–4. *since . . . Hispahan.* Isfahan became the Persian capital around 1600.

l. 395. *Bizance.* Byzantium, or Constantinople, which fell to the Turks in 1453.

l. 397. *Negus.* Title of the king of Abyssinia.

l. 398. *Ercoco.* Archico a Red Sea port in modern Ethiopia.

l. 399. *Mombasa . . . Melind* [Malindi]. Ports on the coast of Kenya. *Quiloa.* The modern Kilwa, on the coast of Tanzania.

l. 400. *Sofala.* Now Beira, in Mozambique.   *thought.* Thought to be. *Ophir.* The biblical kingdom from which Solomon's ships brought gold and jewels (1 Kgs. 10: 11).

l. 403. *Almansor.* 'The victorious', a title of Mohammedan princes; specifically here the Amir Mohammed of Cordova (939–1002), king of Andalusia, who consolidated and greatly extended the Muslim control of Spain and North Africa.   *Fez.* In Morocco.   *Sus.* Tunis.

590 l. 404. *Tremisen.* The modern Tlemcen, in Algeria.

l. 406. *in spirit.* Not physically, because of the earth's curvature.

l. 409. *Atabalipa.* Atahuallpa, defeated by Pizarro in 1533.

l. 410. *Geryon's sons.* The Spanish. Geryon was a three-headed (or three-bodied) monster who inhabited an island off the Spanish coast. To kill him and bring back his oxen was one of the labours of Hercules. He is identified in Dante with Fraud, and Spenser uses him specifically as an allegory of Spanish oppression (*FQ*, v. x. 8).

l. 414. *euphrasy.* Or eyebright, a herb used in poultices for the eyes. *rue.* Also said to improve eyesight.

591 l. 426. *excepted.* Forbidden.

ll. 429–47. *His eyes . . . effused.* For the murder of Abel by Cain see Gen. 4.

l. 430. *tilth.* Cultivated land.

l. 436. *Unculled.* Unselected, i.e. picked at random (as opposed to Abel's 'choicest and best' offering, l. 438).

l. 442. *nimble glance.* Quick flash.   *grateful.* Pleasing.

l. 457. *fact.* Deed; generally used in the period for a criminal act.

592 l. 479. *lazar-house.* Hospital, especially one for lepers, but here (as the next lines make clear) for all diseases.

l. 481. *qualms.* Fits.

ll. 485–7. *Demoniac . . . pestilence.* Lines added in 1674.   *moon-struck madness.* Literally translating 'lunacy'.   *Marasmus.* Diseases that cause the body to waste away.

l. 496. *Though . . . born.* Echoing *Macbeth*, IV. i. 80, and elsewhere in the play, referring to Macduff; the implication here is that compassion is a female quality deriving from the mother, and is essentially unmanly—Macduff disputes the point in IV. iii. 220 ff.

593 l. 519. *Inductive . . . to.* Leading directly to (a repetition of).

l. 541. *Obtuse.* i.e. no longer acute.

594 l. 544. *damp.* Depression.   *cold and dry.* In the old physiology, the humours of phlegm and black bile, producing a melancholic temperament.

ll. 551–2. *Of rendering . . . replied.* In 1667 the passage reads 'Of rend'ring up. Michael to him replied'.   *attend.* Await.

ll. 556 ff. The scene is based on Gen. 4: 19–22, the account of the three sons of Cain's descendant Lamech: Jabal, 'father of such as dwell in tents and have cattle', Jubal, 'father of all such as handle the harp and organ', and Tubal-cain ('Tubal the smith'), 'an instructor of every artificer in brass and iron'.

l. 561. *volant.* Flying.

l. 562. *Instinct.* Both impelled and innate, intuitive.   *proportions.* Harmonies, musical relationships.

l. 563. *fugue.* Lit. 'flight'.

594 ll. 564 ff. Milton's account of the discovery of metals derives from Lucretius, *De Rerum Natura*, v. 1241–68.

l. 566. *casual.* Accidental.

l. 573. *fusile.* By melting.   *After these* . . . The vision (ll. 573–627) of the 'sons of God' (see l. 622) alludes to Gen. 6: 2–4, but depends largely on patristic commentators. See also iii. 461–4.

l. 574. *the hither side.* The west; Cain's descendants lived east of Eden.

595 l. 588. *evening star.* Venus.

l. 591. *Hymen.* God of marriage.

l. 595. *symphonies.* Harmonies.   *attached.* Seized.

l. 619. *appetence.* Appetite.

l. 620. *troll.* Wag.

l. 624. *trains.* Wiles.

596 ll. 638 ff. *He looked* . . . The fourth vision (ll. 638–73) recalls Homer's description of the shield made by Hephaestos for Achilles, *Il.*, xviii. 478–616.

l. 641. *Concourse.* 'Hostile encounter' (*OED*).

l. 642. *emprise.* Undertaking, with chivalric overtones.

l. 647. *beeves.* Cattle (plural of 'beef').

l. 654. *ensanguined.* Bloody.

l. 656. *scale.* Ladder.

l. 665. *Of middle age one.* Enoch, the father of Methusaleh, a just man who was 'translated' to heaven in 'middle age', i.e. at the age of 365 years, half the lifespan of the patriarchs. See Gen. 5: 17–24 and the pseudepigraphical Book of Enoch, which was partly known to Milton.

597 l. 669. *Exploded.* Lit. 'hissed off the stage' (opposite of applauded).

l. 700. *he the seventh from thee.* Enoch was seven generations removed from Adam.

598 l. 715. *luxury.* Lasciviousness.

l. 717. *passing fair.* Both surpassing beauty and pretty passers-by.

ll. 719 ff. For the flood see Gen. 6: 9–9: 17 and the analogous account of Deucalion's flood in *Met.*, i. 262–347.

l. 731. *Smeared . . . pitch.* In order to caulk the ark.

l. 735. *sevens, and pairs.* Noah was ordered to take seven pairs of clean beasts and two of unclean beasts (Gen. 7: 2).

l. 741. *exhalation dusk.* Dark fog.

l. 742. *amain.* Violently.

599 l. 753. *bottom.* Boat.

l. 777. *Man is not whom.* There is no man left.

600 l. 805. *tried.* Tested.

l. 815. *denouncing.* Proclaiming.

l. 821. *devote.* Doomed.   *rack.* Ruin.

601 l. 831. *hornèd.* Branching.

l. 835. *orcs.* Whales; also applied 'to more than one vaguely identified fero-cious sea-monster' (*OED*).   *seamew's clang.* Gull's cry.

l. 840. *hull.* Drift.

l. 847. *tripping.* Running.

ll. 865–6. *bow . . . gay.* The rainbow, striped ('*listed*') with the three primary colours red, yellow, and blue.

602 l. 880. *Distended.* Spread (as God's brow is now relaxed).

ll. 886–7. *repenting . . . heart.* Milton's syntax is much more ambiguous than his source, Gen. 6: 6: 'it repented the Lord that he had made man on the earth, and it grieved him at his heart.'

BOOK 12

603 ll. 1–5. Added in 1674, when Book 10 of the first edition became Books 11 and 12 of the second.   l. 1. *bates.* Pauses.

l. 24. *one.* Nimrod; the account alludes to Gen. 10: 8–10, but Nimrod's connection with the Tower of Babel derives from later commentators, beginning with Josephus, *Antiquities*, 1. iv. 2.

l. 36. *from . . . name.* Nimrod was etymologized (incorrectly) from the Hebrew verb 'to rebel'.

604 l. 41. *gurge.* Whirlpool.

l. 43. *cast.* Determine.

l. 53. *various.* Changeable; 'calculated to cause difference or dissimilarity' (*OED* 5b, the only citation for the latter sense).   *rase.* Erase.

l. 62. *Confusion.* Incorrectly thought to be the etymological meaning of Babel.

605 l. 81. *affecting.* Presuming.

l. 84. *right reason.* The inherent ability to perceive the good; conscience.

l. 85. *dividual.* Separate.

ll. 101–4. *irreverent . . . race.* Ham, Noah's son, whose irreverence con-sisted of seeing his father drunk and naked; in punishment Noah con-demned Ham's son Canaan to permanent servitude, Gen. 9: 25.

l. 111. *peculiar.* Particular.

l. 114. *Him.* Abraham; the biblical account is in Gen. 11: 27 ff.

l. 117. *the patriarch . . . flood.* Noah.

606 l. 130. *Ur.* On the west bank of the Euphrates.

ll. 130–1. *ford . . . Haran.* Haran is east of the Euphrates, about 400 miles north-west of Ur.

606 l. 132. *servitude*. Servants.

l. 136. *Sechem*. Or Shechem, near Mount Gerizim and Mount Ebal, site of Abraham's first encampment in Canaan. The account of the journey is based on Gen. 12: 5–6.

l. 139. *Hamath*. On the River Orontes in Syria, 120 miles north of Damascus. It marked the northern border of the Promised Land (see Num. 34: 8 and Josh. 13: 5–6).   *desert south*. The Wilderness of Zin, the southern border.

l. 141. *Hermon*. The sacred mountain, the eastern boundary.   *great western sea*. The Mediterranean.

ll. 144–5. *double-founted . . . Jordan*. Milton relied on an incorrect tradition that the Jordan springs from two streams called the Jor and the Dan.

l. 146. *Senir*. A peak (not a ridge) of Mount Hermon.

l. 153. *son . . . grandchild*. Isaac and Jacob.

607 l. 160. *younger son*. Joseph; the subsequent account follows Exodus.

l. 165. *Suspected to*. Distrusted by.

l. 173. *denies*. Refuses.

ll. 176 ff. *to blood* . . . The ten plagues are described in Exod. 7–12.

l. 180. *blains*. Swollen sores.   *emboss*. Cover with swellings.

l. 191. *river dragon*. The epithet is from Ezek. 29: 3.

l. 200. *saint*. Holy man, Moses.

608 ll. 202–3. *Before . . . fire*. From Exod. 13: 21.

l. 207. *defends*. Wards off attack, protects; syntactically 'between' precedes the verb.

l. 210. *craze*. Crack; the account is in Exod. 14.

l. 214. *war*. Army.

ll. 216–19. *not the readiest way . . . rather*. Milton's explanation for the Israelites' 38 years in the desert is from Exod. 13: 17–18.

l. 225. *great senate*. The Seventy Elders (Exod. 24: 1–9 and Num. 11: 16–30).

ll. 237–8. *That . . . cease*. 'Speak thou with us and we will hear: but let not God speak with us, lest we die' (Exod. 20: 19).

ll. 240–1. *mediator . . . bears*. i.e. Moses prefigures Christ as a mediator between God and man.

609 l. 247. *tabernacle*. See Exod. 25–6.

l. 253. *mercy-seat*. The gold covering over the ark, conceived as the seat of God.

ll. 263–4. *the sun . . . entire*. When Joshua defeated the Amorites (Josh. 10: 13). They had negotiated a treaty with Joshua under false pretences, and when the deception was discovered Joshua commanded the sun and moon to stand still 'until the people had avenged themselves upon their enemies'.

609 l. 265. *Gibeon.* Now el-Jib, about five miles north of Jerusalem, capital of the Hivites, an Amorite tribe.

l. 266. *Aialon.* Or Aijalon, a town and valley about fourteen miles north of Jerusalem.

l. 267. *so call the third.* Jacob was given the name Israel after his fight with the angel (Gen. 32: 28); the name was interpreted to mean 'he wrestles with God', though more properly it would mean 'God wrestles'; neither etymology, however, has any sound basis.

610 l. 287. *evince.* 'Make manifest' (*OED* 5); 'overcome' (*OED* 1).

l. 288. *natural pravity.* Original sin.

l. 295. *imputed.* Vicariously imparted (alluding to the doctrine of imputed righteousness, whereby Christ's virtue is transferred to Christians through their faith: see iii. 291).

l. 301. *resign.* Consign.

l. 303. *From . . . truth.* From the prefigurings of the Old Testament to Christian truth. On the Christian notion of typology, see Erich Auerbach, 'Figura', in *Scenes from the Drama of European Literature*; as applied to Milton, see William Madsen, *From Shadowy Types to Truth*, and Edward Tayler, *Milton's Poetry*.

ll. 310–14. *Joshua . . . rest.* Moses was not permitted to lead the Israelites into Canaan; the charge fell to his successor Joshua. Joshua thus was taken to prefigure Jesus, an identification confirmed by the fact that the name Jesus is the Greek version of Joshua, meaning 'God the saviour'.

l. 316. *but.* Except.

611 l. 327. *A son.* Jesus' human ancestry was traced back to David.

l. 332. *his next son.* Solomon.

l. 338. *Heaped . . . sum.* On top of those of the people; Solomon's idolatry and subjection to women are described in i. 399–405.

ll. 348–50. *by leave . . . re-edify.* The Persian kings under whom the Temple was rebuilt are Cyrus, who permitted the Jews to return to Palestine in 538 BC and authorized the reconstruction, Darius Hystaspis, in whose reign the Temple was completed, and Artaxerxes, who in 458 BC allowed Ezra to lead a large group of exiles back to Jerusalem (recounted in Ezra).

l. 351. *In mean estate.* Temperately, in moderation.

ll. 355–7. *strife . . . sceptre.* 2 Macc. 3–4 records the conflicts over the high priesthood in the second century BC. The usurpation of ll. 356–7, by which the Jewish theocracy was changed into a kingship, is that of Aristobulus I, of the priestly Asmonean family, who succeeded to the high priesthood on his father's death in 104 BC but then proclaimed himself king.

l. 358. *stranger.* Antipater the Idumean, governor of Jerusalem under the Romans from 61 BC and Procurator of Judaea from 47 BC. Jesus was born during the reign of his son Herod the Great.

612 l. 373. *as . . . been.* Which would have been, like grief.

ll. 375–6. *finisher / Of.* i.e. who has ended with.

l. 383. *capital.* Both mortal, and on his head.

l. 393. *recure.* Cure.

l. 396. *want.* Lack.

l. 401. *apaid.* Satisfied.

613 l. 409. *Imputed.* Vicariously imparted (see l. 295).

l. 410. *though . . . works.* Though all that they did was in accordance with the law; the point is that salvation comes through faith, not works.

l. 419. *satisfaction.* i.e. of God's justice; technical theological language.

l. 433. *temporal.* In time, temporary, referring not only to the death of the body, but, as Milton argues in *CD*, of the soul too.

l. 439. *Still.* Always.

l. 442. *profluent.* Running.

614 l. 460. *quick.* living.

l. 467. *period.* Ending.

l. 469. *immense.* Lit. 'without measure'.

l. 486. *a comforter will send.* The Holy Spirit (see John 15: 26).

615 l. 507. *room.* Place.

l. 508. *grievous wolves.* Quoting Acts 20: 29; Milton applies the prophecy to the history of the Church in *Of Reformation*.

ll. 522–3. *none . . . enrolled.* Which will not be found recorded for them (i.e. in the Scriptures); cf. *CD*, i. 30.

616 l. 540. *respiration.* Respite, a breathing-space.

l. 546. *dissolve.* Destroy.

617 ll. 588–9. *top / Of speculation.* Both mountain-top vantage point and high philosophical inquiry.

ll. 591–2. *expect . . . motion.* Await their orders to move.

618 l. 629. *meteorous.* Meteoric.

l. 630. *marish.* Marsh.

l. 635. *adust.* Scorched.

l. 640. *subjected.* Lying below.

619 *Paradise Regained. Paradise Regained* was printed in 1671 in a volume that also included *Samson Agonistes*. The poem is presumed to have been written after *Paradise Lost*, largely because of the testimony of Thomas Ellwood, who was Milton's pupil and reader in the early 1660s. Ellwood was given the completed manuscript of *Paradise Lost* sometime after 1663, and, having read it, reports that he remarked to Milton: 'Thou hast said much of paradise lost, but what hast thou to say of paradise found?', a comment to which Milton is reported to have alluded when presenting Ellwood

with a copy of *Paradise Regained*. Parker argues that it is probably taking Ellwood too literally (as Edward Phillips did in his biography of Milton) to believe that the entire poem was undertaken only after the publication of *Paradise Lost*; there are, however, no extant plans or sketches of the sort that survive for the earlier poem. Milton preferred his final epic to *Paradise Lost*, and could not bear to hear it disparaged; it was, however, less popular when it appeared, and has remained so throughout its critical history. The plot of *Paradise Regained* is based on the gospels' account of the Temptation of Christ in the wilderness: Milton depends mainly, but not exclusively, upon Luke; our notes record the relationship between his account and those found in the gospels. The critical literature on the poem includes several books exploring its relationship to received theology, notably Elizabeth Pope's *Paradise Regained: The Tradition and the Poem* and Barbara Kiefer Lewalski's *Milton's Brief Epic*, which also treats generic questions; Arnold Stein's New Critical *Heroic Knowledge* focuses on epistemological issues; notable essays include Northrop Frye's 'The Typology of *Paradise Regained*', *MP*, 53 (1956), and Stanley Fish's brilliant study of the import of the inaction of the plot, 'Things and Actions Indifferent: The Temptation of Plot in *Paradise Regained*', *Milton Studies*, 17 (1983), whose argument follows from 'The Temptation to Action in Milton's Poetry', *ELH*, 48 (1981). David Quint has recently commented on the politics of the poem in 'David's Census: Milton's Politics and *Paradise Regained*', in *Re-Membering Milton*, ed. Margaret Ferguson and Mary Nyquist.

THE FIRST BOOK

619 l.1. The earliest surviving MSS of Virgil's *Aeneid* include the opening lines ' I am he who once made my song on a slender reed . . .'. Modern scholars consider these either spurious, or an early version subsequently cancelled by Virgil or by his literary executors, but they were thought genuine in Milton's time, and appear in Renaissance editions of the *Aeneid*. Milton is also imitating Ovid's *Tristia*, IV. x. 1, 'I am he who once wrote of soft loves', and the opening of the *Faerie Queene*, 'Lo I the man, whose Muse whilome did maske, / As time her taught, in lowly Shepheards weeds . . .'

ll. 2–4. *By One . . . tried.* cf. Rom. 5: 19.

l. 7. *waste.* Desolate, dreary (Latin *vastus*).

l. 8 *spirit.* Perhaps the Holy Ghost as in Luke 4: 1, but unspecified, as in Matt. 4: 1.: 'Then was Jesus led up of the Spirit into the wilderness to be tempted of the devil'; cf. Mark 1: 12.   *eremite.* Hermit (Gk., lit. 'desert dweller').

l. 11. *proof.* Trial.

ll. 12–17. Cf. *PL*, ix. 13–33.

l. 14. *prosperous.* 'conducing to success' (OED).   *full summed.* Fully feathered, ready for flight.

l. 16. *unrecorded.* Not 'unwritten', since there are the gospel accounts, but 'unsung' (l. 17), or uncelebrated.

619 l. 18. *great proclaimer.* John the Baptist, 'the voice of one crying out in the wilderness' (Matt. 3: 3, Mark 1: 3, Luke 3: 4, John 1: 23) 'saying, Repent ye: for the kingdom of God is at hand' (Matt. 3: 2). For accounts of the baptism, see Matt. 3, Mark 1: 3–11, Luke 3: 3–22, John 1: 19–34; see also ll. 269 ff., below.

l. 24. *as then.* As he was then.

l. 27. *his worthier.* The fact that he was more worthy (than John).

l. 33. *adversary.* Literally translating the Hebrew 'Satan'. *still.* Always.

620 l. 42. *gloomy consistory.* Aeneas describes the Cyclops as '*concilium horrendum*' (*Aen.* iii. 679). *Consistory* = council, with papal overtones.

l. 48. *as . . . men.* According to human computation.

l. 50. *In . . . will.* In whatever way we wished.

l. 51. *facile.* Easily led, compliant.

l. 53. *attending.* Awaiting (the fulfilment of the curse in Gen 3: 15, interpreted in *PL*, xii. 386 ff.

l. 54. *seed.* Progeny, alluding to Gen. 3: 15, 'I will put enmity between thee and the woman, and between thy seed and her seed.'

l. 56. *longest . . . short.* 'One day is with the Lord as a thousand years, and a thousand years as one day' (2 Pet. 3: 8).

l. 62. *infringed.* Broken, defeated (Lat. *infringere*).

l. 65. *late.* Lately.

l. 73. *Pretends.* Professes (not necessarily falsely).

621 l. 83. *A perfect dove.* 'The Holy Ghost descended in bodily shape like a dove' (Luke 3: 22). 'Perfect' can imply either an ideal natural object or a convincing mimetic representation.

l. 87. *obtains.* Possesses.

l. 89. *first-begot.* In *PL*, the naming of God's 'only son' (v. 604) instigates Satan's rebellion.

ll. 94–5. *utmost . . . hazard.* Most extreme peril.

l. 97. *well-couched.* Both well-expressed and well-concealed.

l. 100. *sole undertook.* See *PL*, ii. 430–66.

l. 107. *amazement.* Perplexity.

l. 109. *no time was.* There was no time.

l. 112. *main.* Very important.

l. 113. *dictator.* A temporary ruler 'invested with absolute authority, elected in seasons of emergency by the Romans, and by other Italian states' (*OED*); the practice was recommended by Machiavelli and other Renaissance political theorists, but Milton, in the *The Ready and Easy Way*, opposed it.

622 l. 119. *coast.* Border.

622 l. 128. *frequence.* Crowd, assembly.

l. 129. *Gabriel.* Angel of the Annunciation in Luke 1: 19–38.

l. 146. *apostasy.* Apostate followers.

l. 147. *Job.* Many critics have found Milton's reference to Job as a 'brief epic' in *RCG* (p. 170) suggestive for the form of *PR*; Job is alluded to at i. 369, 425, iii. 64–7, 95 below.

l. 155. *By fallacy surprised.* Overcome by deception or delusion in reasoning or logic.

l. 156. *exercise.* This is the function of what Milton calls 'a good temptation' in *CD*, i. 8.

623 l. 159. *Sin and Death.* Represented as allegorical figures in *PL*, ii. 648–833, x. 585–640.

l. 161. *weakness shall o'ercome.* A paradox emphasized by St Paul (e.g. 1 Cor. 1: 27, 2 Cor. 13: 41) and Heb. 11: 34.

l. 166. *by merit.* A point also emphasized in *PL*, iii. 309.

l. 171. *the hand.* Instrumental music.

l. 172. *argument.* Theme or subject.

l. 176. *The Father knows the Son.* Jesus says in John 10: 15, 'As the Father knoweth me, even so know I the Father.'   *secure.* Free from care.

l. 180. *frustrate.* Frustrated.

l. 182. *vigils.* Nocturnal prayers.

l. 184. *Bethabara.* The place of the baptism in John 1: 28.

l. 188. *Publish.* Make public.

ll. 190–1. *converse / With.* Lit. 'keep company with'.

l. 197. *swarm.* Cf. *SA*. l. 19.

624 l. 200. *sorting.* Agreeing, suiting.

l. 201. *When . . . child.* Cf. 1 Cor. 11. Christ's childhood is recounted in Luke 2; many commentators have noted that the account also resembles Milton's autobiographical statements in the prose.

l. 203. *Serious.* Seriously.

l. 205. *Born . . . truth.* See Jesus' response to Pilate, John 18: 37.

l. 210. *great feast.* Of the Passover; see Luke 2: 41–50.

l. 214. *admired.* Wondered at.

l. 224. *erring.* The word retains its literal sense of straying, wandering.

l. 233. *express.* Make manifest.

l. 238. *A messenger.* For the annunciation to Mary, see Luke 1: 28–56; in Matt. 1: 20–3, the angel appears to Joseph; Luke 2: 1–20 describes the nativity; Matt. 2: 7–11 the visit of the Magi.

625 l. 253. *new graven.* Either newly carved or indelibly fixed.

625 l. 255. *Simeon . . . Anna.* 'Simeon . . . was just and devout' (Luke 2: 25), and was rewarded for his faith by seeing Jesus, whom he acknowledged as the messiah; 'Anna, a prophetess' (Luke 2: 36) testified to Christ as the redeemer when he was brought to the temple.

l. 259. *This having heard . . .* Christ resumes his narrative.   *revolved.* Searched through, thought over.

l. 264. *assay.* Trial.

l. 279. *hardly won.* Persuaded with difficulty.

626 l. 283. *sum.* Ultimate end, highest point.

l. 290. *strong motion.* Cf. Samson's 'rousing motions' (*SA*, l. 1382).

l. 292. *I need not know.* Citing Matt. 24: 36 and Mark 13: 32, Milton argues in *CD*, i. 5 that God's knowledge exceeds Christ's.

l. 294. *morning star.* Christ's name for himself in Rev. 22: 16; also Satan's (Lucifer, light-bringer); cf. 'Nativity Ode', l. 74 n.

l. 296. *horrid.* Causing terror (lit. 'bristling').

l. 302. *solitude . . . society.* Cf. Cicero, *De Officiis* iii. 1., 'Never less alone than when alone'; echoed in Marvell, 'The Garden', 'Society is all but rude / To this delicious solitude'.

l. 303. *forty days.* As in Matt. 4: 2; in the other gospel accounts (Luke 4: 2, Mark 1: 13) the temptation itself lasts forty days.

l. 305. *covert.* Covering, shelter or hiding place; cf. ii. 262, below.

l. 310. *wild beasts.* A detail from Mark 1: 13.

l. 312. *noxious.* Injurious or harmful.   *worm.* Any animal that creeps or crawls.

l. 314. *agèd . . . weeds.* Cf. the disguise of Archimago in *FQ*, I. 29, and of Comus.

l. 319. *curious.* Attentive, solicitous.

627 l. 325. *pined.* Wasted.

l. 326. *admire.* Marvel.

ll. 333–4. *aught . . . What.* Anything that.   *fame.* Rumour, report (Lat. *fama*).

l. 339. *stubs.* Stumps of trees or shrubs.

l. 349. *Man lives not . . .* Cf. the similar response in Matt. 4: 4, Luke 4: 4; the response quotes Deut. 8: 3, relating to the provision of manna in the wilderness.

l. 352. *Moses.* Citing Exod. 34: 28.

l. 353. *Elijah.* After eating, Elijah 'went in the strength of that meat forty days and forty nights unto Horeb the mount of God' in the wilderness near Beersheba (1 Kgs. 19: 8).

628 l. 363. *unconniving.* Tacitly permitting it.

l. 365. *round.* Encircle, i.e. go everywhere on.

628 l. 368. *I . . . God.* In Job 1: 6., 2: 1, 'the sons of God came to present themselves before the Lord, and Satan came also'; God asks Satan to consider 'my servant Job' (1: 8, 2: 3) and delivers him 'in thine hand' (2: 6) to test him and show 'that there is none like him in the earth, a perfect and an upright man' (1: 8, 2: 3).

l. 369. *Uzzean.* Job lived in Uz, 'a land . . . obscure' (see iii. 94. below).

l. 370. *prove.* Test, try.   *illustrate.* Bring to light, display to advantage, render illustrious.

l. 372. *Ahab.* See 1 Kgs. 22: 19–35 for the story of how Ahab was lured to defeat through a 'lying spirit' (22: 22) sent by God.   *fraud.* Being defrauded.

l. 373. *they demurring.* As the angels temporized.

l. 375. *glibbed.* Made glib.

l. 383. *What can be then less in me.* How can I have anything less, probably with a *double entendre*: there is nothing I like less than to have to deal with Christ. Cf. l. 404 below for a similar construction.

l. 385. *attent.* Attentively.

l. 400. *proof.* Experience, trial.

l. 401. *smart.* Pain.

629 l. 413. *prime.* Principal, most exalted (angels).

l. 414. *gazed.* Gazed at (in scorn).

l. 428. *four hundred.* The number of prophets that led Ahab to destruction in 1 Kgs. 22: 6. See above, l. 372.

ll. 430–5. *oracles . . . deluding.* The oracles of Apollo and Zeus were notoriously ambiguous. The conflation of the pagan gods and fallen angels is detailed in *PL*, i and goes back to patristic sources.

l. 439. *instruct.* Instructed.

630 l. 447. *president.* Presiding.

l. 454. *retrenched.* Cut short.

l. 456. *oracles are ceased.* Cf. 'Nativity Ode', l. 173.

l. 458. *Delphos.* Delphi, site of Apollo's oracle, was regularly called Delphos in the period, though the two places were not confused.

l. 460. *hath now sent.* Perhaps echoing 1 John 9, 'God sent his only begotten Son into the world, that we might live through him'; and 1 John 13, 'we dwell in him, and he in us, because he hath given us of his Spirit.'

l. 476. *submiss.* Submissively (lit. 'placed beneath').

l. 477. *quit.* Acquitted.

l. 480. *tuneable.* Melodious.

631 l. 487. *atheous.* Impious.

l. 491. *Balaam.* See Num. 22–4 for the story of the reprobate priest Balaam who none the less prophesied God's will.

631 l. 494. *scope*. Aim, purpose.

l. 499. *Into thin air*. As the spirits disappear in *The Tempest*, IV. i. 150.

l. 500. *sullen*. Dark, gloomy.   *double-shade*. Cf. *Comus*, l. 334.

THE SECOND BOOK

l. 7. *Andrew and Simon*. The first two apostles called, disciples of John (see Matt. 4: 18 and John 1: 35–42).

l. 11. *Began to doubt*. The apostles' doubt is not reported in the gospels, but Milton may be adapting such episodes as the unbelief of the apostles in Mark 16: 10, and Thomas' doubt in John 20: 25.

l. 14. *caught up*. Cf. St Paul's description of himself as 'one caught up to the third heaven' (2 Cor. 12: 2), and 'caught up into paradise' (12: 4).

l. 15. *Moses*. His absence on Mount Sinai caused doubt and idolatry; see Exod. 32: 1.

l. 16. *Thisbite*. Elijah; 2 Kgs. 2: 11 describes his ascent in a chariot of fire. Moses and Elijah are also grouped together above, I. 352–3. The promise of Eljiah's second coming (made in Mal. 4: 5) is attached to John the Baptist in Matt. 11: 14 and to Christ in Matt. 16: 14, Mark 8: 28, and Luke 9: 19.

l. 19. *Sought lost Elijah*. The 'sons of the prophets' who saw the ascension at Jericho, along with fifty others, 'sought three days, but found him not' (2 Kgs. 2: 15–17).

632 ll. 20–1. *Jericho . . . palms*. Cf. Deut. 34: 3.

l. 21. *Aenon, and Salem old*. See John 3: 23, where the Baptist was 'in Aenon near to Salim'. Milton appears to be associating Salim with Salem, where Melchizedek ruled (hence 'old', Gen 14: 18). Cf. 'The Passion', l. 40.

l. 22. *Machaerus*. A fortress in Peraea, north-east of the Dead Sea.

l. 23. *this side*. The north-west, location of the Sea of Galilee (Gennesaret in Luke 5: 1).

l. 27. *fishermen . . . call*. Jesus calls the disciples 'fishers of men' (Matt. 4: 19); cf. Spenser, *Shepheardes Calender*, 'A Shepheards boye (no better doe him call)' ('Januarye', l. 1).

l. 34. *full of grace and truth*. Cf. John 1: 14.

l. 38. *amaze*. Bewilderment.

l. 40. *rapt*. Carried off.

l. 44. *kings of the earth*. Cf. Acts 4: 26.

633 ll. 66 ff. *O what . . . events*. Like the disciples' complaint above, Mary's (ll. 66–104) has no scriptural precedent, although it is perhaps suggested by her sorrowing discovery of Christ in the temple (Luke 2: 48) and its consequence: 'his mother kept all these sayings in her heart' (cf. ll. 103–4, below). The complaint rehearses materials narrated by God above (i. 130–40) and remembered by Christ (i. 229–58). The narrative depends upon and conflates the accounts offered in Luke 2 and Matt. 2.

ll. 67–8. *salute . . . blessed*. Gabriel's greeting (Luke 1: 28).

633 l. 76. *the murderous king.* Herod, who, hearing of the Wise Men's prophecy that a child destined to be king of the Jews had been born in Bethlehem, ordered the destruction of 'all the children that were in Bethlehem' (Matt. 2: 16).

l. 87. *Simeon plain foretold.* In Luke 2: 34–5: see i. 255.

l. 94. *argue.* Dispute.

l. 99. *His father's business.* The account is in Luke 2: 48–9.   *mused.* Both pondered and wondered.

l. 101. *obscures.* Leaves unexplained.

634 l. 106. *remarkably.* Worth remarking, remarkable.

l. 109. *tracing.* Wandering.

l. 115. *preface.* Lit. 'previous statement'; i.e. Satan's promise to return (i. 483–5).

l. 116. *vacant.* Unoccupied.

l. 120. *Solicitous.* Full of care.   *blank.* Nonplussed; cf. *PL*, ix. 890.

ll. 122–4. *Demonian . . . earth.* Cf. *Il Penseroso*, l. 93 and note.

l. 130. *frequence.* Assembly.

l. 131. *tasted.* Experienced.

l. 139. *amplitude of mind.* Both Aristotle's *magnanimity (Nicomachean Ethics*, iv. 7), the virtue of princes, and Cicero's *amplitudinem animi Tusculan Disputations*, ii. 26), the stoic virtue of imperturbability.

635 l. 147. *the old serpent.* So called in Rev. 12: 9.

l. 150. *Belial.* The word appears frequently as a common noun meaning worthlessness in the Old Testament. Milton, drawing on a long post-biblical tradition that made Belial a Satanic spirit, associates him with lewdness. Cf. *PL*, i. 490–505 and note, ii. 109–17.

l. 151. *Asmodai.* In the apocryphal Tobit 3: 8, he is the 'evil spirit' who slays the seven successive husbands of his beloved Sarah on their wedding nights.

l. 152. *incubus.* A demon who has sexual intercourse with women in their sleep.

ll. 153 ff. *Set woman . . . wives.* With Belial's speech (ll. 153–71) cf. both the pleasures anatomized in Milton's elegies (esp. 1 and 7) and the dangers of Dalila's snares.

l. 164. *temper.* Temperament.

l. 165. *Enerve.* Enervate.

l. 168. *magnetic.* Magnet.

l. 170. *Solomon.* In his old age, he was led by his pagan wives into idolatry (1 Kgs. 11: 408); the Song of Solomon also contributes to Belial's argument.

635 ll. 178–81. *Before the flood . . . race.* Cf. Gen. 6: 2, 'the sons of God saw the daughters of men that they were fair; and they took them wives of all which they chose.' This is the race destroyed by the flood; cf. *PL*, xi. 556–626.

636 ll. 186–8. *Calisto . . . Syrinx.* Nymphs involved with the lusts of the gods; see Ovid, *Met.*, ii. 409–40 for Calisto and Jove, i. 765–75 for Clymene and Apollo, i. 452–567 for Daphne and Apollo, iii. 253–315 for Semele and Jove, i. 689–712 for Syrinx and Pan; for Anymone and Neptune, see Ovid, *Amores*, 1. x. 5. Satan's argument about the demonic sources of classical myth is also Milton's in *PL*, i. 507 ff.

l. 189. *Too long.* Too many to mention.   *scapes.* Sexual transgressions.

l. 191. *haunts.* Habits.

l. 196. *Pellean conqueror.* Alexander the Great, born at Pella; Plutarch reports his sexual abstinence in his *Life*, xxi.

l. 198. *slightly.* Slightingly.

l. 199. *he . . . Africa.* Scipio Africanus, who restored a beautiful captive woman to her fiancé (Livy, xxvi. 50).

l. 201. *For.* As for.

l. 205. *wiser far.* Cf. Matt. 12: 42, 'behold, a greater than Solomon is here'.

l. 211. *fond.* Foolish.

l. 214. *zone of Venus.* The belt of Venus, or Aphrodite, which Hera obtained in order to beguile Zeus (*Il.*, xiv. 197 ff.).

l. 219. *deject.* Cast down, humble.

637 l. 242. *from shade to shade.* Either from nightfall to nightfall, or passing from shelter to shelter.

l. 255. *so.* So long as.

ll. 258–9. *fed . . . will.* Christ says in John 4: 34, 'My meat is to do the will of him that sent me.'

638 l. 266. *Him thought.* It seemed to him.   *brook of Cherith.* Where God commands Elijah to hide, and where he drinks and is fed by ravens (see 1 Kgs. 17: 17), and before his forty-day fast, is fed twice by angels (see 1 Kgs. 19: 4–8; cf. i. 353, above.

l. 278. *Daniel.* He refused Nebuchadnezzars's food, preferring a diet of pulses (legumes, beans, lentils, and the like) (Dan. 1: 8–19).

l. 289. *bottom.* Valley, dell.

l. 292. *noon.* A critical time in Milton; e.g. the fall takes place at noon (*PL*, ix. 739) as does Samson's death (*SA*, l. 1612); perhaps to be related to the spectre of the noontime devil, 'the destruction that walketh at noonday' (Ps. 91: 6).

l. 293. *brown.* Shaded, dark.

l. 302. *officious.* Here, ready to serve; the pejorative meaning was also current.

639 ll. 308–10. *fugitive . . . angel.* Hagar and her son Ishmael, cast out by Abraham and Sarah, were shown a well by an angel (Gen. 21: 19); Nebaioth was Ishmael's first son (Gen. 25: 13), the progenitor of an important and powerful Ishmaelite tribe. Perhaps the promise to make Ishmael 'a great nation' accounts for the substitute name. In editions subsequent to 1671, 'he' in l. 309 has been emended to 'here'.

l. 312. *manna.* Provided for the Jews' forty years of wandering in the wilderness (Exod. 16: 35).   *that prophet.* Elijah.

l. 328. *Meats . . . unclean.* Foods prohibited to Jews are listed in Lev. 11: 2–31 and Deut. 14: 3–20; several of the foods subsequently offered (ll. 341 ff., below) violate these prohibitions: only animals that chew the cud are allowed, hence the game animals of l. 342 are forbidden, as are many fowl, the shellfish of l. 345, and all other fish without scales. Christianity, of course, took the position that the dietary laws had been superseded, and Milton rejects them in *CD.*

l. 329. *Daniel.* Cf. l. 278 n, above.

ll. 337 ff. *He spake . . .* The banquet scene has no biblical precedent and, as the final allusion to the harpies (at l. 403) suggests, seems indebted to *The Tempest* (III. iii. 19–84), itself indebted to the *Aen.* (iii. 219 ff.), and to other tempting banquets in classical and Renaissance literature, e.g. Armida's feast in Tasso's *Jerusalem Delivered*, x. 64.

l. 343. *In pastry built.* A regular feature of Renaissance banquets.

l. 344. *Grisamber.* Ambergris, from the sperm whale, used to perfume dishes.

l. 345. *Freshet.* A small fresh water stream.

l. 347. *Pontus and Lucrine bay.* The Black Sea, and the lagoon near Naples famed for its oysters and other shellfish.

640 l. 348. *cates.* Delicacies.

l. 349. *crude.* Both raw and commonplace.   *diverted.* lead astray.

l. 353. *Ganymede.* Jove's cupbearer and lover (see Ovid, *Met.*, x. 155–61, and Milton's Elegy 7, ll. 21 ff.).   *Hylas.* Hercules' lover, drowned by an amorous sea nymph. He is also paired with Ganymede in Elegy 7, ll. 21–34.

l. 355. *Naiades.* Nymphs of rivers, streams, and springs.

l. 356. *Amalthea's horn.* The horn of plenty, cornucopia.

l. 357. *Hesperides.* Daughters of Hesperus, guardians of the golden apples in his garden (Milton here uses Hesperides as the name of the garden); in *PL*, iv. 250, Eden is compared to the Hesperides, and the Attendant Spirit flies there in *Comus*, ll. 980–1.

l. 360. *Logres . . . Lyonesse.* Ancient names of locales in Arthurian Britain; in medieval romances the latter is Arthur's birthplace.

l. 361. *Lancelot . . . Pellenore.* Arthurian knights noted for their amorous adventures.

640 l. 364. *Arabian odours.* Arabia was the source of perfumes, especially the biblical frankincense and myrrh.

l. 365. *Flora.* Roman goddess of flowers.

l. 368. *What doubts.* Why hesitates.

l. 370. *Defends.* Prohibits.

l. 371. *works.* Produces (in contrast to the forbidden fruit of the Tree of Knowledge).

l. 382. *likes.* Pleases.

l. 384. *Command a table.* Cf. the impious question in Ps. 78: 19, 'Can God furnish a table in the wilderness?'

l. 386. *my cup.* Cf. Matt. 20: 22 (also Mark 10: 38); and 1 Cor. 11: 25 (quoting Luke 22: 20).

l. 387. *diligence.* Persistent effort to please.

641 l. 401. *far-fet.* Brought from afar.

ll. 402–3. *vanished . . . harpies' wings.* Cf. *The Tempest*, III. iii. 53, stage direction 'Enter Ariel like a Harpy; claps his wings upon the table; and, with a quaint device, the banquet vanishes'.

l. 404. *importune.* Importunate, insistent.

l. 408. *besides.* In all other respects.

l. 422. *Money.* Cf. Mammon's praise of money in *FQ*, II. vii. 11; his temptation of Guyon is an important source for *PR* throughout.

l. 423. *Antipater.* According to Josephus, both he and his son Herod rose to power through their wealth.

642 l. 439. *Gideon.* Though of a poor family, he rose to lead the army that defeated the Midianites (Judg. 6, 7).   *Jephtha.* The son of a harlot who delivered the nation from the Ammonites (Judg. 11).   *shepherd lad.* David. Gabriel prophesies Christ's succession to David's throne, Luke 1: 33.

l. 446. *Quintius.* L. Quintus Cincinnatus; called from his farm to deliver Rome from the invading Aequians, he resigned his dictatorship fifteen days after the victory and returned home.   *Fabricius.* G. Fabricius Luscinus, famed for his austerity, and for rejecting the bribes of Pyrrhus to change sides and fight against Rome.   *Curius.* Manius Curius Dentatus, hero of the wars against the Sabines, Samnites, and Pyrrhus, turned all his captured booty over to the Republic.   *Regulus.* M. Atilius Regulus, captured by the Carthaginians and sent to Rome with conditions for peace, persuaded the Romans to reject the conditions, and, according to his promise, returned to Carthage to his death.

l. 453. *toil.* Snare.

l. 456. *aught may.* Anything that may.

l. 458. *for that.* Because. The lines recall Henry V's soliloquy on the burdens of kingship, *Henry V*, IV. i. 235 ff.

642 l. 466. *reigns within himself.* The stoic doctrine of self-control has its biblical counterpart in Prov. 16: 32, 'he that ruleth his spirit [is greater] than he that taketh a city'.

643 l. 482. *lay down.* Renounce; a recurrent phrase in John, e.g. 'I lay down my life' (10: 17; cf. 10: 15, 10: 18, 13: 37, 15: 13).

THE THIRD BOOK

l. 14. *Urim and Thummim.* Objects in the high priest's breastplate (see Exod. 28: 30) with oracular properties.

l. 16. *sought to.* Called on for.

l. 19. *sustain.* Withstand.

644 l. 27. *erected.* Noble, exalted.

ll. 27–8. *most tempered pure / Ethereal.* The most purely spiritual constitution.

l. 31. *Thy years.* Thirty, according to Luke 3: 23. For Milton's sense of that age as 'over-ripe', see Sonnet 7, ll. 6–7.

ll. 31–3. *son . . . held.* By the age of 26, Alexander had conquered the Persian empire.

ll. 34–6. *Scipio . . . king.* Satan is not entirely correct: Scipio commanded the armies against Carthage while still in his twenties, but his decisive victory at Zama occurred when he was past thirty; Pompey was in his forties when he defeated Mithridates, King of Pontus, and returned in triumph to Rome.

l. 37. *to.* Along with.

ll. 39–41. *Julius . . . wept.* In his *Life of Caesar*, xi. 3, Plutarch reports that at the age of 30, Julius Caesar wept on reading that the youthful Alexander had accomplished so much more than he.

l. 47. *blaze of fame.* Cf. *Lycidas*, l. 74.

l. 51. *well weighed.* If they were properly judged.

l. 62. *divulges.* Proclaims; cf. *Lycidas*, ll. 78–84.

645 l. 67. *Hast . . . Job?* See Job 1: 8, and i. 369–70, above.

l. 84. *son of Jove.* Both Alexander and Scipio claimed this lineage.   *of Mars.* Romulus was said to have been Mars' son.

l. 86. *Rolling . . . vices.* Alexander died after a bout of drunkenness.

ll. 96–8. *Socrates . . . unjust.* Condemned for corrupting the youth and for blasphemy, he refused to break the law by fleeing from Athens and so escape death. Plato's *Apology* provides the fullest account of the accusations.

l. 101. *African.* Scipio Africanus.

646 l. 106. *I . . . his.* Cf. John 8: 50, 7: 18.

l. 110. *he seeks glory.* Satan's argument can also be found in Milton's *De Doctrina*, i. 7–8, and has wide biblical support. The Westminster Shorter Catechism reads, 'Man's chief end is to glorify God'.

646 l. 118. *Promiscuous.* Of all kinds, without distinction.

l. 119. *barbarous.* Preserving the Greek meaning, foreign.

l. 138. *ingrate.* This is also God's charge against humankind in *PL*, iii. 97; in *PL*, iv. 42–8, Satan acknowledges his indebtedness to God.

647 l. 146. *not to answer.* Nothing to answer.

l. 153. *father.* Ancestor.

l. 154. *By mother's side.* In Luke 3: 24–38 and Matt. 1: 2–17, Jesus' genealogy relates him to David on Joseph's side. Luke ambiguously places Mary in this family line: 'a virgin espoused to a man whose name was Joseph, of the house of David' (1: 27).

l. 161. *The Temple.* Violated by Pompey, Crassus, Herod, and Pilate.

l. 163. *Antiochus.* Antiochus Epiphanes, King of Syria. 1 Macc. 1: 21–4 describes his capture of Jerusalem (169 BC) and his plunder and desecration of the temple.

ll. 165–70. *Maccabaeus ... content.* The career of Judas Maccabaeus is detailed in 1 Macc. 2–9, as well as in Josephus.   *king.* Antiochus, defeated in 166 BC.   *Modin.* Maccabaeus' birthplace; its location is unknown.

l. 173. *forelock.* A common iconographical attribute of Occasion, or Opportunity; she was otherwise bald. To seize Occasion's forelock was to make the best use of an opportunity.

l. 182. *due time.* John is the gospel most concerned with this issue; e.g. 2: 4, 'mine hour is not yet come'. Cf. John 7: 6 and ll. 396–7, below.

l. 183. *time ... said.* See Eccles. 3: 1.

l. 185. *never end.* According to the prophecy in Isa. 9: 7, quoted in Luke 1: 33.

648 l. 213. *whatever.* Whatever it was.

649 l. 242. *he ... kingdom.* Saul, first king of the Jews, seeking his father's stray asses, was anointed by Samuel (1 Sam. 9: 3, 15–16).

l. 246. *monarchies of the earth.* The temptation of the kingdoms is the second temptation in Matt. 4: 8–10 and Luke 4: 58.

l. 247. *inform.* Train, discipline.

l. 249. *mysteries.* Combining the senses of skills and secrets.

l. 250. *their opposition.* That of the monarchies, l. 246.

l. 252. *mountain high.* Cf. Luke 4: 5, Matt. 4: 8, and the hill of Adam's vision in *PL*, xi. 381–4.

l. 255. *his.* Its.   *two rivers.* Presumably the winding Euphrates and the straight Tigris.

l. 257. *champaign.* Flat open land.

l. 259. *glebe.* soil.

650 l. 269. *Cut shorter.* i.e. than an overland journey would have been.

650 l. 271. *Araxes.* The Aras, a river of Armenia that empties into the Caspian Sea.

l. 274. *drouth.* Desert.

l. 275. *Nineveh.* Capital of Assyria.

l. 276. *Ninus old.* Legendary King of Assyria, husband of Semiramis and, according to pagan writers, the eponymous founder of Nineveh; in Gen. 10: 11, however, the founder is Asshur.

l. 278. *Salmanassar.* Or Shalmaneser, King of Assyria 727–722 BC, who carried the Israelites into captivity (see 2 Kgs. 17: 3–6).

l. 281. *him.* Nebuchadnezzar; he twice sacked Jerusalem and led the Jews into slavery (see 2 Kgs. 24: 10–17, 25: 1–22, Dan. 1: 1–2, Jerem. 39: 1–9).

l. 284. *Cyrus.* See Ezra 1–2 for an account of the Persian conquest of Babylon.   *Persepolis.* Capital of Persia.

ll. 285–8. *Bactra . . . Susa.* Persian cities in Bactria, Media, Parthia, and Susiana.

l. 290. *Emathian.* Macedonian. The cities listed in ll. 291 ff. were built after the time of Alexander the Great.   *Parthian.* The Parthian empire eventually extended over much of western Asia.

l. 295. *Arsaces.* Name of several early Parthian kings, from *c.*250 BC.

l. 301. *Scythian.* Scythia comprised much of modern Russia and Siberia; 'Scythian' was synonymous with 'barbarian'.

l. 302. *Sogdiana.* Modern Turkestan and Bokhara.

651 l. 309. *rhombs.* Lozenge-shaped battle formations.   *wedges.* Half-rhombs.

l. 310. *numberless.* Innumerable.

ll. 316–21. *Arachosia . . . haven.* The lines list provinces and regions in the Parthian empire, from its easternmost areas near the Indus River to its northern, western, and southern reaches along the Persian gulf.

l. 327. *horn.* Wing of the battle formation.

l. 328. *Cuirassiers.* Horsemen in cuirasses, or breast- and backplates.

l. 329. *endorsed with towers.* With turrets (or howdahs) on their backs.

l. 330. *pioneers.* Advance foot-soldiers.

l. 338–43. *Agrican . . . Charlemagne.* Agrican is a Tartar king in Boiardo's *Orlando innamorato,* who brings 2,200,000 men to Albracca to win Angelica, Orlando's faithless lover, the daughter of Galfrone (Milton's Gallaphrone), King of Cathay.   *prowest.* Bravest.   *paynim.* Pagan.

l. 344. *chivalry.* Army.

ll. 347–9. *That thou . . . safety.* 'It is not my intention to rouse your courage without providing adequately for your safety.'   *virtue.* Lit. 'manliness'; strength, courage.

652 l. 353. *father.* Cf. l. 154 above. David fought a long war against the house of Saul before coming to power (see 2 Sam. 3, 5).

l. 358. *opposite.* Opposing.

l. 365. *annoy.* Harass.

ll. 366–7. *captive . . . bound.* Milton here misremembers, or has Satan misrepresent, Josephus (*Antiquities*, xiv). Hyrcanus II, King of Judaea, was deposed by the Parthians, but his nephew Antigonus, who was allied with them, became king in his place.

l. 368. *Maugre.* Despite.

l. 369. *at dispose.* At your disposition.

l. 374. *ten tribes.* These comprised the kingdom of Israel, as opposed to the two tribes of Judah and Benjamin, the kingdom of Judah (see 1 Kgs. 12: 15–21). The ten tribes were led into captivity in Assyria by Shalmaneser (see above, l. 278) and never returned; whence the ten 'lost' tribes (l. 377).

l. 376. *Habor.* An Assyrian river, a tributary of the Euphrates, but used here to refer to the region around it in which the captive Israelites settled.

l. 377. *Ten . . . Joseph.* i.e. the ten tribes are all descended from Jacob, and two of them are descended from Jacob's son Joseph.

l. 384. *From Egypt to Euphrates.* Repeating God's covenant with Abraham, giving him the land 'from the river of Egypt unto the great river, the river Euphrates' (Gen. 15: 18).

653 l. 391. *policy.* Politics.

l. 410. *numb'ring Israel.* David's order for a census constituted a sin of pride; see 1 Chron. 21: 1; in the ensuing plague sent by God as punishment, 70,000 died.

ll. 414–15. *captive . . . captivity.* See 2 Kgs. 17: 7–18.

l. 416. *calves.* Jeroboam instituted the worship of golden calves in Bethel and Dan; see 1 Kgs. 12: 28, 2 Kgs. 17: 16, and l. 431, below.

l. 417. *Baal.* The Canaanite sun god. Cf. 'Nativity Ode', l. 197.   *Ashtaroth.* Plural form of Ashtoreth, or Astarte, the Syrian moon goddess. Cf. 'Nativity Ode', ll. 200–2.

l. 430. *would . . . gods.* i.e. would follow their forefathers and revert to their false gods.

654 ll. 435–8. *bring . . . cleft.* Cf. Isaiah's prophecy (11: 16).

THE FOURTH BOOK

l. 1. *Perplexed.* Deeply distressed, perhaps also with its Latin sense, entangled.   *success.* Result.

l. 5. *sleeked.* Smoothed.   *won so much on.* Gained such advantage over.

l. 7. *This.* Jesus.   *who.* Refers back to 'his' (Satan's), although the syntax is characteristically ambiguous.

654 ll. 15–18. *flies . . . rock.* Both the flies and wine and the rock similes are common from Homer onward to express annoyances or temptations and steadfastness respectively; they also recall Christological metaphors of the vine and the rock, e.g. 'I am the true vine' (John 15: 1), 'that Rock was Christ' (1 Cor. 10: 4), or of Christ as 'chief corner stone' (1 Pet. 2: 4–8); for the latter, cf. iv. 149, below.

l. 16. *must.* New wine.

l. 19. *to shivers dashed.* Utterly dispersed.

655 ll. 27–33. *plain . . . city.* The plain of Latium (Lazio) in Italy, sheltered from the northern winds ('Septentrion blasts') by the Apennines; Rome is the 'imperial city' through which the Tiber flows.

l. 36. *Porches.* Porticos.

l. 37. *trophies.* Spoils of war.

l. 40. *parallax.* Here, an apparent change in position of an object because of the refraction of light through a medium.

l. 42. *curious.* Unnecessary, beyond acceptable limits.

l. 49. *Tarpeian rock.* The steep cliff of the Capitoline hill.

l. 50. *Mount Palatine.* One of the seven hills of Rome, the location of the imperial palace, although the 'battlements', 'turrets', and 'spires' correspond less to elements of Roman architecture than to Renaissance palatial design.

l. 59. *hand.* Handiwork.

l. 63. *Praetors.* Magistrates.   *proconsuls.* Provincial governors.

l. 65. *Lictors and rods.* Lictors were the attendants of magistrates and executors of their orders; they bore the fasces, a bundle or rods, as the symbol of their authority.

l. 66. *cohorts.* Infantry units; ten cohorts made up a legion.   *turms.* Cavalry units.   *wings.* Cavalry formations (from their position on the flanks of the battle array).

656 l. 68. *Appian road.* The Via Appia, the main road leading from the port of Brindisium north to Rome.

l. 69. *Aemilian.* The Via Aemilia, leading north from Rome to Aquileia on the Adriatic.

l. 70. *Syene.* Assuan in Egypt, the southernmost extension of Roman power.   *where . . . falls.* At the equator.

l. 71. *Meroe.* The capital of Ethiopia, on a peninsula (thought by Pliny and other ancient geographers to be an island) in the Nile.

l. 72. *realm of Bocchus.* Mauretania, modern Morocco; Bocchus, father-in-law of Jugurtha, was its king during the Jugurthine War.   *Blackmoor Sea.* The Mediterranean off Morocco, by the Barbary coast.

l. 74. *Chersoness.* The Malay peninsula, said by Josephus (*Antiquities*, viii. 6) to have been the source of Solomon's gold.

656 l. 75. *Taprobane.* The name was used for both Sri Lanka (Ceylon) and Sumatra.

l. 77. *Gallia.* Gaul (France). *Gades.* Cadiz, in Roman times chief city of the Iberian peninsula.

l. 78. *Sarmatians.* Inhabitants of the territory north of the Scythians, modern Poland and western Russia.

l. 79. *Danubius.* The Danube, the north-eastern boundary of the Roman empire. *Tauric pool.* Sea of Azov.

l. 90. *This emperor.* Tiberius (ruled AD 14–37); his sons Germanicus and Drusus had died in AD 19 and 23 respectively. He retired to Capri in AD 27, and was notorious for his sexual excesses. Suetonius and Tacitus give accounts of his reign.

l. 95. *favourite.* Aelius Sejanus; his fall is the subject of Ben Jonson's *Sejanus.*

l. 103. *to me the power.* Cf. Luke 4: 6, and ll. 164–5, below.

657 l. 108. *David's throne.* Cf. above, i. 240–1, ii. 440 ff., iii. 150 ff. and below, iv. 151, 379.

l. 115. *citron tables.* African citrus wood was highly valued for its hardness and beauty. *Atlantic stone.* Probably Libyan marble (*Atlantic* = from the area of Mount Atlas).

l. 117. *Setia, Cales, and Falerne.* Famous Roman vineyards; l. 118, below, lists their Greek counterparts.

l. 119. *myrrhine.* Probably porcelain (Lat. *murra* or *murrha*, a rare clay used for fine pottery).

l. 132. *people . . . once.* The Romans, triumphant during the republic.

l. 136. *Peeling.* Plundering.

l. 138. *Of . . . vanity.* For vain and contemptuous celebrations of victory.

l. 139. *sports.* Gladitorial combats.

l. 142. *scene effeminate. Scene* = Lat. *scaena*, theatre. The charge that theatre effeminizes both perfomers and audience goes back at least as far as Plato, and was frequently made in sixteenth- and seventeenth-century anti-theatrical tracts.

l. 147. *like a tree.* Cf. Nebuchadnezzar's dream of a tree extending from heaven to earth (Dan. 4: 11) interpreted by Daniel to reveal the absolute-ness of God's rule; also Isaiah's prophecy that 'there shall come forth a rod out of the stem of Jesse' (Isa. 11:1).

658 l. 149. *as a stone.* This also corresponds to a dream of Nebuchadnezzar's, of a stone smashing an idol and becoming a great mountain, which Daniel interprets as the triumph of God's kingdom (Dan. 2: 44).

l. 151. *of . . . end.* Cf. Luke 1:33.

l. 157. *difficult and nice.* Obstinate and hard to please or fastidious.

l. 158. *still.* Always.

658 l. 176. *first of all commandments.* The ten commandments are in Exod. 20: 3–5, Deut. 5: 7–9, 6: 13; the first is quoted, as here, in Matt. 4: 10.

l. 184. *donation.* Grant, unforced gift.

659 l. 193. *Get thee behind me.* Quoting Luke 4: 8.

l. 197. *sons of God.* The angels, including Satan, are so called in Job 1: 6, 2: 1, and the term is extended to all those who believe in Christ in John 1: 12 and Rom. 8: 14.

l. 201. *Tetrarchs.* Subordinate rulers; a tetrarch was literally the ruler of a fourth part, used of the governor of a district of the Roman empire (e.g., Herod in Palestine); here, applied to the rulers of each of the four elements.

l. 219. *Moses' chair.* The place of judgment and legal interpretation in Exod. 18: 13–16 and Matt. 23: 2.

l. 226. *The Pentateuch.* The first five books of the Old Testament, the five books of Moses.

l. 228. *To admiration.* Admirably.

660 l. 232. *conversation.* The word retained its broader sense of social intercourse.

l. 234. *idolisms.* False images or ideas (like Bacon's idols, *Novum Organum,* i. 38). *paradoxes.* Used to teach moral philosophy, especially in the Stoic tradition.

l. 235. *evinced.* Convinced, overcome in argument.

l. 236. *specular.* From Lat. *specula,* watch-tower, lookout; cf. *PL*, xii. 588–9.

l. 240. *the eye.* As locus of intelligence and illumination.

l. 242. *recess.* Place of retirement or seclusion.

l. 243. *studious.* Conducive to study.

l. 244. *Academe.* The Academy, a gymnasium and place of study associated especially with Plato and his followers.

l. 245. *Attic bird.* Nightingale; the birds were found in profusion around Athens.

l. 247. *Hymettus.* A mountain south of Athens noted for its honey.

l. 249. *Ilissus.* A stream near Athens; the setting for Plato's *Phaedrus.*

ll. 251–2. *his . . . Alexander.* Aristotle was the tutor of Alexander the Great.

l. 253. *Lyceum.* Aristotle's school. *Stoa.* The colonnade in the market-place, decorated with paintings by Polygnotus, a favourite meeting-place of Zeno and his followers (whence 'Stoic').

ll. 254–5. *secret . . . harmony.* Cf. *L'Allegro*, l. 144.

l. 257. *Aeolian . . . Dorian.* The two chief Greek lyric modes; Sappho and Alcaeus wrote in the Aeolian dialect, Pindar in the Dorian. *charms.* Songs (Lat. *carmen*).

660 l. 259. *Melesigenes.* Homer, said to have been originally named for his birth-place on the river Meles, but renamed in token of his blindness (Gk. *homeros* = blind).

l. 260. *Phoebus . . . own.* In an epigram in the *Greek Anthology* (ix. 455), Apollo says, 'The poem is mine, but divine Homer wrote it down'.

l. 262. *chorus or iambic.* In Greek tragedy, the chorus is composed in a variety of complex metres; the dialogue is usually written in iambic hexametre. With the description of Greek tragedy, compare the preface to *SA.*

l. 264. *sententious.* Aphoristic, full of wisdom (not pejorative).

l. 268. *resistless.* Irresistible.

l. 269. *Wielded.* Ruled.   *democraty.* Democracy.

l. 270. *Shook the Arsenal.* The construction of the famous naval arsenal in Piraeus was suspended in 339 BC at the insistence of Demosthenes, who urged that all civic resources be committed to the war against Philip of Macedon.   *fulmined.* Fulminated, spoke passionately (lit. 'emitted thunder and lightning').

l. 271. *Artaxerxes.* King of Persia.

661 l. 274. *tenement.* Dwelling.

ll. 275–6. *oracle . . . men.* As reported in the *Apology*, xxi; Socrates was declared the wisest of men because he alone knew his ignorance. Cf. ll. 293–4, below.

ll. 277 ff. *all the schools . . .* These are the Old Academy of Plato and the New Academy, its more sceptical successor, the Peripatetic school of Aristotle (named from the habit of arguing while walking in the Lyceum), the Epicureans, named after Epicurus, whose teaching developed from that of Socrates' disciple, Aristippus; Antisthenes, another disciple, founded the Cynics, and from his doctrines Zeno founded the Stoics.

l. 281. *revolve.* Consider, turn over in your mind.

l. 295. *The next.* Plato, who introduces numerous fables and allegories in his dialogues, here characterized as specious ('smooth') and far-fetched in their arguments ('conceits').

l. 296. *A third.* The Sceptics, who doubted both rational and sensory knowledge.

ll. 297–8. *Others . . . life.* Aristotle and his followers; *Nicomachean Ethics*, i. 11 describes the highest good as a combination of virtuous self-possession and external comfort.

l. 299. *he.* Epicurus, who maintained that pleasure of mind and body was the one indisputable good.

l. 303. *shames not to prefer.* i.e. he is not ashamed to prefer himself to God.

l. 306. *lists.* Pleases.

662 ll. 317–18. *regardless . . . Of.* Quite without concern for.

l. 322. *Wise men.* See Eccles. 12: 12.

662 l. 325. *what . . . seek.* A significant qualification, not found in the attitudes towards reading expressed in *Areopagitica.*

l. 328. *Crude.* Raw, immature (Lat. *crudus*); 'lacking power to digest' (*OED*). *toys.* Trivia.

l. 329. *worth a sponge.* Either having no more value than a sponge, incapable of lasting absorption; or fit only to be expunged, because such learning is of no value.

l. 334. *All our Law.* Cf. *Reason of Church Government* (p. 170), for a similar view of the Bible as a storehouse of poetic forms.

l. 335. *artful terms.* Either skilful language, or possibly an allusion to the headings of certain psalms that seem to indicate the occasion and nature of their composition (see e.g. Pss. 34, 39, 42, 51, 54, 60).

ll. 336–7. *Hebrew . . . ear.* Cf. Ps. 137: 1–3.

l. 343. *swelling.* Pretentious, hyperbolic.

l. 344. *varnish.* Cosmetics; the term was loosely applied to any speciously attractive surface.

l. 351. *Unless . . . .* This closes the syntactic unit begun at l. 346 above: Greek poetry is 'unworthy to compare' with Scripture except when it expresses moral virtue in accordance with reason and natural law.

663 l. 354. *statists.* Statesmen, politicians.

l. 377. *Nicely.* Fastidiously.

l. 380. *fulness of time.* Cf. Gal. 4: 4.

ll. 384–5. *Voluminous . . . spell.* Whether the stars are read ('spell' = decipher) as a volume or as individual letters joined together in a zodiac ('conjuction').

l. 388. *stripes.* Whipmarks, as from flagellation.

l. 393. *rubric.* Lit. a chapter heading or title (continuing the book metaphor above); here, a direction or explanatory gloss.

664 ll. 399–400. *unsubstantial . . . day.* i.e. darkness and night are not substances or entities, they are merely the absence of light and day.

l. 402. *jaunt.* A tiresome or troublesome journey.

l. 407. *at his head.* Cf. Eve's dream, *PL*, iv. 799 ff.

l. 409. *either tropic.* Both the northern and southern skies.

l. 411. *abortive.* Not life-giving, destructive.

l. 413. *ruin.* Destruction, including its literal sense, the act of falling.

l. 415. *hinges.* The cardinal points (Lat. *cardo*, hinge).

l. 420. *only.* Alone.

l. 421. *stayed.* Stopped.

l. 427. *amice.* An ecclesiastical hood or cape.

l. 428. *radiant finger.* Recalling the Homeric rosy-fingered dawn.

665 l. 437. *Cleared up.* Sang out clearly.

l. 438. *gratulate.* Welcome, express joy for.

l. 449. *in wonted shape.* In his usual form (which may imply either that he is no longer in disguise, or that he remains in the disguise he has adopted throughout).

l. 450. *careless.* Seemingly untroubled or negligent, perhaps suggesting recklessness.

l. 452. *rack.* Destructive storm.

l. 454. *flaws.* Squalls.

l. 457. *main.* Universe as a whole, macrocosm (as compared to the 'less universe', the microcosm, l. 459 below).

l. 458. *sneeze.* Renaissance medical treatises commonly followed Aristotle in the belief that sneezing beneficially purges the brain.

667 l. 524. *collect.* Infer, conclude.

l. 525. *fatal.* Both destined and mortal.

l. 529. *parle.* Parley.   *composition.* Agreement to cease hostilities; these are military terms.

l. 532. *sift.* Make trial of (cf. Luke 22: 31).

l. 534. *adamant.* A legendary substance of impenetrable hardness. *centre.* Fixed point of rotation.

l. 542. *hippogriff.* Mythical creature, half horse, half griffin, who transports Astolfo to the moon in Ariosto, *Orlando Furioso*, iv. 18.   *sublime.* Aloft.

l. 547. *pile.* Mass.

ll. 547–8. *like . . . alabaster.* So described by Josephus, *Jewish War*, v. v. 6.

l. 549. *pinnacle.* In Luke, as here, this is the final temptation; Matthew places it second.

l. 554. *progeny.* Lineage, parentage.

l. 556. *it is written.* Ps. 91: 11–12.

668 l. 560. *Also . . . written.* Deut. 6: 16, 'Ye shall not tempt the Lord your God.' Critics have debated whether Christ's response reveals his belief in God or (answering Satan's demand) proves that he is God, questions complicated by Milton's Arianism (which denied that the Son was equal to God). It is worth noting, however, that the gospel accounts are equally ambiguous about the declaration; S. Fish's argument in 'Things and Actions Indifferent: The Temptation of Plot in *Paradise Regained*', *Milton Studies* (1983), that the moment is no more or less elucidatory than any of the previous cryptic encounters, is salutary.

l. 563. *Antaeus.* The Libyan ruler and giant son of mother Earth, he was overcome by Hercules ('Alcides', l. 565 below), who crushed him in his grip while holding him aloft so that he could not draw strength from the ground.

668 ll. 563–4. *to compare . . . greatest.* A Virgilian formula (e.g. *Ecl.*, i. 24) also found in *PL* (see ii. 921–2).   *Irassa.* A district in Libya.

l. 565. *Jove's Alcides.* Hercules was called Alcides after his maternal grandfather Alcaeus; his father was Jove.

l. 572. *Theban monster.* The Sphinx, who asked the riddle about a creature that goes on four, then on two, finally on three legs, and who devoured all those unable to answer it, until Oedipus replied 'Man', and the Sphinx threw herself into the River Ismenus.

l. 578. *triumphals.* Tokens of triumph.

l. 581. *globe.* From Lat. *globus*, a compact group of people.

l. 583. *vans.* Wings.   *him.* Satan appears to be the grammatical antecedent. This astonishing example of the conflict of syntax and sense has gone almost unremarked by editors and critics.

l. 585. *blithe.* Mild.

l. 589. *Ambrosial.* Ambrosia was the gods' food; the tree of life (Gen. 2: 9) similarly confers immortality, of which it is a token in the final vision in Rev. 22: 2, 14.

l. 590. *fount of life.* Cf. Rev. 21: 6.

ll. 596–7. *True . . . light.* Cf. Heb. 1: 3, which describes Jesus as 'the express image' of God; John 1: 9 describes Jesus as 'the true Light' and places him 'in the bosom of the Father' at 1: 18.

l. 598. *Conceiving.* Receiving, taking on; like 'image' in l. 596 above, or 'godlike' (l. 602, below), a hierarchical relationship between Father and Son seems to be implied.

669 l. 600. *whatever place.* In whatever place.

l. 605. *debel.* Conquer in war, vanquish by arms, a rare word probably alluding to Anchises' prophecy that Rome would 'overthrow the proud' (*debellare superbos*) and establish the rule of universal law (*Aen.*, vi. 853).

l. 607. *Supplanted Adam.* The typology is Pauline, e.g. 1 Cor. 15: 22, 'As in Adam all die, even so in Christ shall all be made alive.'

l. 612. *be failed.* Has ceased to exist.

ll. 618–21. *serpent . . . feet.* Cf. Rev. 8: 10, 'there fell a great star from heaven' (Lucifer, the morning star). Satan is described as lightning in Luke 10: 18, and in 10: 19 Christ gives his followers 'power to tread on serpents and scorpions'; in Rom. 16: 20, 'The God of peace shall bruise Satan under your feet.' The prophecy is recalled in *PL*, x. 190.

l. 622. *Thy wound.* The final wound to Satan's head is prophesied in Gen. 3: 15.

l. 624. *Abaddon.* Here, hell; in Job. 26: 6 and Rev. 9: 11, it is the name of 'the angel of the bottomless pit.'

669 l. 628. *holds.* Dwellings, strongholds.

ll. 630-1. *herd . . . deep.* When Jesus met a man possessed of devils, he cast the devils into swine, who then plunged over a cliff into the sea (Mark 5: 1-13, Matt. 8: 28-32). There is a similar incident in Luke 8: 27-33.

671 *Samson Agonistes. SA* appeared in 1671, in the same volume with *PR.* Some critics, notably W. R. Parker, have argued for dating the poem in the late 1640s or early 1650s, citing the evidence of the title-page that it is presented as an addendum ('*Paradise Regain'd* . . . to which is added *Samson Agonistes*'), the fact that there is not, as there is for *PR*, any external evidence that it was composed after *PL*, and the strong autobiographical elements relating to Milton's first marriage and the divorce tracts. It is certainly possible that work on the poem was begun at that time (the same is arguable for *PL*), but the fact that the poem appeared as the last of Milton's works, and that it bears numerous verbal parallels to *PR*, argues in favour of a late date at least for its final version. In the title, *agonistes* means both an actor and a combatant (the double sense is implied in the Argument by the command that Samson 'play or show his strength', ll. 70-1). The plot depends upon the narrative in Judg. 13-16, a summary of which follows:

Manoah's barren wife is told by a visitor that if she abstains from wine and all unclean foods, she will bear a child. The child's hair must never be cut—he will be a Nazarite, a man dedicated to God, and will begin the delivery of Israel from the Philistines (13: 5); these commands are reiterated to Manoah and his wife on a second visit (13: 13). When Manoah sacrifices to God, the visitor reveals himself as an angel, who ascends in flames from the altar (13: 20). In due time Samson is born.

When he reaches manhood, Samson is prompted by God to marry a Philistine woman of Timnath because God 'sought an occasion against the Philistines' (14: 14). At the marriage feast, Samson proposes a riddle: 'out of the eater came forth meat, and out of the strong came forth sweetness' (14: 14). This alludes to a lion he slew when he came to woo his bride; when he returned to claim her he found in the lion's carcase a honeycomb (14: 5-8). The Philistines are unable to solve the riddle, and urge Samson's wife to extract the solution from him; her tears move Samson to divulge it (14: 17), and she reveals the answer to her countrymen. Realizing he has been tricked, Samson tells the Philistines that 'If ye had not plowed with my heifer, ye had not found out my riddle' (14: 18). In order to fulfil his pledge to provide new clothing to the Philistines if they solve the riddle, imbued with the Lord's spirit he slays thirty men of Ashkelon and gives their garments to the Philistines; but 'his anger was kindled' (14: 19).

In his absence, his father-in-law gives his wife away to another husband, and Samson in retaliation sets fire to the tails of 300 foxes, who burn the Philistines' corn (15: 4); the Philistines in revenge burn Samson's wife and father-in-law to death (15: 6), and Samson slays a great many of them and returns to his own people. The Philistines demand that the Jews deliver Samson to them; they do so, but he breaks his bonds and slays a thousand Philistines with the jawbone of an ass (15: 16). In Gaza, he sleeps with a harlot, and while the inhabitants prepare to kill him when morning comes, he leaves her at midnight and carries away the gates of the city (16: 1–3).

In the valley of Sorek, he meets and loves the Philistine woman Delilah. The Philistines offer her eleven hundred pieces of silver to discover the secret of his strength (16: 5). Three times he lies to her, and foils the Philistines' attempts on his life (16: 6–15). At last he succumbs, telling her that he is a Nazarite whose strength is in his hair. While he is asleep, she summons a man to shave his head, and he is taken and blinded (16: 21), and carried off to turn a millstone in the prison at Gaza. Commanded to provide entertainment at the celebration of the god Dagon, Samson is set between two pillars (16: 25–6); his hair has begun to grow again, and he prays that his strength will return (16: 28). He takes hold of the pillars and 'bowed himself with all his might', and brings the house down on the Philistines and himself (16: 30). He is buried 'in the buryingplace of Manoah his father' (16: 31).

Preface: 'Of that Sort of Dramatic Poem . . .'

671 *Aristotle.* In *Poetics*, vi, describing the cathartic effect of tragedy.

a verse of Euripides. 'Evil communications corrupt good manners' (1 Cor. 15: 33), a Euripidean fragment that became proverbial in late classical times.

Paraeus. David Paraeus (1548–1622), German Calvinist; his commentary on Revelation was translated into English in 1644 and is frequently cited in Milton's prose.

Dionysius the elder. Tyrant of Syracuse (431–367 BC), author of a tragedy awarded first prize in the Athenian competition.

Augustus Caesar. Suetonius reports (*Caesars*, ii. 85) that Augustus destroyed his incomplete tragedy.

Seneca. There was debate over whether the ten tragedies ascribed to Seneca were the work of the philosopher or of a dramatist with the same name.

Gregory Nazianzen. Fourth-century bishop of Constantinople and supposed author of *Christ Suffering*.

intermixing . . . gravity. Sidney in the *Defence of Poetry* similarly condemns mixed genres.   *sadness.* Seriousness.

prologue. Prefatory address, apology.

Martial . . . epistle. Ad Lectorem, prefaced to his first book of Epigrams.

monostrophic . . . apolelymenon. A single stanza employing a free strophic pattern, rather than the usual strict pattern of strophe, antistrophe, epode.

672 *alleostropha.* Irregular strophes.

produced . . . act. Extended beyond the action that would be appropriate to the final act of a traditional tragedy.

plot, . . . explicit. Aristotle classes plots as simple and complex in *Poetics*, vi.

672 *rule.* A neo-classic dictum (deriving in part from Aristotle, but more significantly from Horace's *Ars Poetica*) that the action of a drama should take place in a single day. For a brilliant study of the idea and its consequences, see D. Riggs, 'The Artificial Day and The Infinite Universe', *Journal of Medieval and Renaissance Studies*, 5 (1975).

The Argument. While the 'fable' behind *SA* is the story in Judges, the 'argument' summarizes the play, emphasizing its classic form—it most resembles Sophocles' *Oedipus at Colonus*, the story of the final days of Oedipus, blind and in banishment.

Manoa. Here as throughout, Milton uses the Vulgate form of proper names.

catastrophe. The event that produces the denouement of the drama.

by accident. As a secondary effect; in Judg. 16: 30, Samson prays, 'Let me die with the Philistines'; Milton is perhaps concerned to remove the implication that the hero's intentions include suicide.

673 l. 6. *else.* Otherwise.

l. 11. *day-spring.* Dawn.

l. 13. *Dagon their sea-idol.* The chief Philistine deity, described in *PL*, i. 462–3, as a 'sea monster, upward man / And downward fish.'

l. 16. *popular noise.* Noise of the populace.

ll. 19–20. *thoughts . . . hornets.* Cf. *PR*, i. 196–7.

ll. 23–4. *foretold / Twice.* In Judg. 13: 3–5 and 10–23; cf. ll. 361, 635, below.

l. 27. *charioting.* Carrying off as if in a chariot.

l. 31. *separate.* Literally translating Nazarite, one who is set apart and dedicated to God's service, as his uncut hair witnesses (from Hebrew *nazar*, to separate; cf. Num. 6: 2).

l. 34. *gaze.* Spectacle; cf. l. 112, below.

l. 38. *Promise was.* See Judg. 13: 5.

674 ll. 50–1. *to . . . tears.* Milton conflates Dalila's treachery with Samson's earlier betrayal by the woman of Timnath (Judg. 14: 17).

l. 55. *secure.* Overconfident.

l. 63. *bane.* Evil, destruction.

ll. 65–6. *each . . . wail.* Each by itself would require a lifetime to deplore.

l. 70. *prime work.* First creation; see Gen. 1: 3, and cf. ll. 83 ff., below. *extinct.* Extinguished.

l. 77. *still.* Always.

675 l. 87. *silent.* 'Of the moon: Not shining' (*OED*, first recorded in 1646); see l. 89.

l. 89. *vacant interlunar cave.* The moon is conceived as resting in a dark cave in the period between the old and new moon; *vacant* = not at work (cf. 'vacation'). According to Pliny (*Natural History*, xvi. 74), 'interlunar' or 'silent' was the Roman designation for the moon in conjunction with the sun.

675 l. 93. *She . . . part.* i.e. the soul is diffused throughout the body; the idea, from Augustine's *De Trinitate*, v. 6, is accepted in *CD*, where it is credited to Aristotle.

l. 95. *obvious.* Exposed.

l. 106. *obnoxious.* Exposed to harm.

l. 118. *at random.* In disorder.   *diffused.* Spread out.

l. 122. *In slavish habit.* Dressed like a slave.   *weeds.* Clothing.

676 l. 128. *tore the lion.* See Judg. 14: 5–6.

l. 129. *embattled.* Ready for battle.

l. 131. *forgery.* Forging.

l. 132. *cuirass.* Breastplate.

l. 133. *Chalybean.* The Chalybes were famous metal workers, celebrated, e.g. in Virgil, *Georgics*, i. 58.

l. 134 *Adamantean proof.* Capable of withstanding adamant, a substance of 'impregnable hardness' (*OED*).

l. 136. *insupportably.* Irresistibly.

l. 138. *Ascalonite.* Ascalon (Ashkelon) was one of the five principal Philistine cities, where Samson slew thirty men (Judg. 14: 19).

l. 139. *lion ramp.* Leonine attack.   *old.* Experienced.

l. 140. *plated.* Armoured.

ll. 142–3. *trivial . . . ass.* See Judg. 15: 15–16.

l. 144. *foreskins.* The Philistines were uncircumcised.

l. 145. *Ramath-lehi.* Identified in Judg. 15: 17 as the place where Samson discarded the jawbone.

l. 147. *Azza.* Variant form of Gaza; see Judg. 16: 3.

l. 148. *Hebron . . . giants.* See Num. 13: 33.

l. 149. *journey of a sabbath-day.* The sabbath's day journey—the distance permissible to travel on the sabbath—was variously computed at 2000, 3000, and 4000 cubits (a cubit was a various times from 18 to 22 inches); the point is that Samson carried the massive gates a considerable distance.

l. 150. *whom . . . heaven.* Atlas, the Titan who bore the sky on his shoulders.

l. 161. *incorporate.* Become one with.

l. 163. *visual beam.* Ancient and Renaissance science held that sight derives from rays emitted by the eye.

677 ll. 164–5. *O mirror . . . unparalleled.* i.e. there has been no symbol of the uncertainty of the human condition to equal Samson since the time that man first appeared on earth.

677 l. 170. *in high estate*. A necessary quality of the tragic hero according to Aristotle, *Poetics*, xiii.

l. 181. *Eshtaol . . . Zora*. Danite cities. Samson's father Manoah was of the tribe of Dan; Samson was born in Zora (Judg. 13: 2).

l. 185. *tumours*. Lit. 'swellings', often applied to the effects of passion on the mind.

l. 190. *superscription*. Lit. 'the inscription on a coin'.

ll. 190–1. *of . . . understood*. i.e. this applies to most people.

678 l. 207. *mean*. Average.

l. 208. *paired*. Been equal.

l. 209. *transverse*. Off course.

l. 210. *Tax*. Blame.

l. 212. *pretend . . . wise*. However wise they may claim to be.

l. 219. *first . . . Timna*. See Judg. 14: 1–20 and ll. 382 ff., below.

l. 223. *intimate*. Inmost, deep-seated.

l. 228. *fond*. Foolish.

l. 229. *Sorec*. Cf. Judg. 16: 4–20.

l. 230. *specious*. Deceptively attractive.   *accomplished*. Both effective and cultured.

l. 235. *peal*. Discharge (as of artillery).

679 l. 247. *ambition*. The word retains its Latin sense, from *ambitio*, going about to seek votes or support.

l. 253. *rock of Etham*. See Judg. 15: 8.

l. 254. *forecasting*. Planning.

l. 258. *on some conditions*. The Israelites agreed that they would not attack him themselves; see Judg. 15: 12.

l. 263. *trivial weapon*. The jaw bone of an ass; cf. l. 142 above.

l. 266. *by this*. By this time.   *Gath*. One of the five principal Philistine cities.

l. 275. *frequent*. Usual.

l. 278. *Succoth and . . . Penuel*. Their inhabitants refused to aid Gideon in pursuit of the kings of Midian (see Judg. 8: 5–9).

l. 282. *ingrateful Ephraim*. The Ephraimites refused to aid Jephtha and his Gileadite supporters against the Ammonites (Judg. 11: 12–33, 12: 1–6); Jephtha slaughtered the Ephraimites, who revealed themselves by their inability to pronounce the word 'shibboleth' (Judg. 12: 5–6).

680 l. 291. *mine*. My countrymen.

l. 295. *think not God*. Think that there is no God.

l. 298. *the fool*. Cf. Ps. 14: 1.

680 l. 299. *doctor.* Teacher.

l. 300. *doubt.* Suspect.

l. 305. *ravel.* Become entangled.

l. 307. *interminable.* Infinite.

l. 312. *obstriction.* Obligation (to marry only Jewish women); the word is Milton's coinage.

l. 313. *legal debt.* What is owed to the (Mosaic) law.

l. 320. *fallacious.* Deceitful.

l. 324. *quits . . . unclean.* Acquits her of the charge that she was unclean: a gentile marriage partner was, according to Mosaic law, unclean (see Deut. 7: 3), however impeccable her moral or sexual behaviour.

l. 327. *careful.* Full of care.

681 l. 333. *uncouth.* Strange, unknown.

l. 335. *informed.* Directed.

l. 338. *signal.* Conspicuous, remarkable.

l. 352. *I prayed . . . children.* See Judg. 13.

l. 360. *graces.* Favours.

682 l. 373. *Appoint not.* Either 'do not attempt to prescribe', or 'do not dispute'.

l. 377. *profaned.* Retains its original sense, 'sacrilegiously made public' (from Lat. *profanus*, outside the temple).

l. 384. *secret.* The riddle of the lion and the honeycomb; see Judg. 14:8–9, 12–18. For the subsequent narrative, see Judg. 16: 6–20.

l. 389. *vitiated.* Corrupted.

ll. 390–1. *by . . . treason.* i.e. the mere smell of gold caused her to 'give birth to' treason.

l. 394. *capital.* Of the head; principal; fatal.

l. 395. *summed.* Concentrated.

l. 405. *over-watched.* Exhausted by staying awake too long.

683 l. 423. *infest.* Plague.

l. 424. *state not.* Do not comment upon.

l. 430. *Tacit.* Silent.

l. 433. *rigid score.* Stiff (Lat. *rigidius*) debt; 'score' also connotes cutting or marking.

l. 434. *popular.* Public.

l. 439. *Them out of thine.* The Philistines out of Samson's hands.

684 l. 454. *diffidence.* Distrust.

l. 455. *propense.* Inclined.

l. 466. *connive.* Shut his eyes, pretend ignorance (Lat. *conniveo*).

684 l. 469. *discomfit.* Defeat.

l. 471. *blank.* Confound.

ll. 481–3. *I already . . . ransom.* Manoa's negotiation with the Philistines and the plan to ransom Samson have no basis in the biblical account.

685 l. 493. *fact.* Deed.

l. 496. *front.* Forehead.

ll. 500–1. *Gentiles . . . confined.* Tantalus was condemned to eternal punishment in Hades for revealing divine secrets (see Ovid, *Met.,* iv. 457).

l. 509. *quit thee.* Cancel.

l. 514. *argues over-just.* Shows one to be excessively just.

l. 515. *self-offence.* Offence against oneself.

l. 516. *what . . . knows.* Whatever means are offered which, for all one knows . . .

l. 526. *instinct.* Impulse.

l. 528. *sons of Anak.* The giants of l. 148, above.   *blazed.* Celebrated.

686 l. 533. *fallacious.* Deceptive.   *venereal trains.* Sexual traps.

l. 535. *pledge.* Sign, i.e. his unshorn hair, the token of his status as a Nazarite (see Judg. 13: 5).

l. 537. *shore me.* In Judg. 16: 19, the shearing is done not by Delilah but by a man she summons for the purpose.

l. 538. *wether.* Castrated ram.

l. 541. *wine.* Nazarites were required to abstain from wine (see Num. 6: 3 and Judg. 13: 4).

l. 549. *fiery rod.* Sunbeam.

l. 550. *milky juice.* Water (as nourishment); cf. *PL,* v. 306.

l. 557. *liquid.* Clear.

l. 560. *What boots it . . .* Of what use is it.

l. 567. *gaze.* Spectacle.

l. 568. *redundant.* Both superfluous and flowing or abundant.

l. 569. *Robustious.* Strong.

l. 571. *craze.* Render infirm.

687 l. 574. *draff.* Garbage, swill.

l. 578. *annoy.* Injure.

l. 581. *a fountain.* See Judg. 15: 18–19; in the Authorized Version the water comes from the jawbone, but the text is ambiguous and may mean (as Milton interprets it) that the fountain came from the place named for the jawbone.

l. 591. *treat.* Have to do (lit. 'negotiate').

l. 594. *genial.* Vital.

687 l. 600. *humours black.* In the old physiology, an excess of the black bile humour caused a disposition to melancholy.

l. 601. *fancy.* Imagination.

l. 603. *prosecute.* Pursue.

l. 604. *how else.* Whatever other means.

l. 609. *reins.* Kidneys.

l. 612. *accidents.* Symptoms of a disease.

688 l. 615. *answerable.* Corresponding.

l. 622. *mortification.* 'The death of a part of the body while the rest is living' (*OED*); synonymous with gangrene.

l. 624. *apprehensive.* Sensate.

l. 625. *exasperate.* Irritate.   *exulcerate.* Cause ulcers.

l. 628. *alp.* High mountain.

l. 635. *message.* Messenger, angel (see Judg. 13 and ll. 23–29, above).

l. 639. *nerve.* Strength.

l. 645. *repeated.* Repeatedly.

689 l. 657. *Consolatories.* Consoling treatises.

l. 659. *Lenient.* Soothing.

l. 677. *Heads without name.* Unknown people.

l. 687. *remit.* Send them back.

l. 688. *dismission.* Dismissal.

690 l. 700. *crude.* Premature.

l. 701. *Though not disordinate.* Though they have not been intemperate.

l. 702. *in fine.* In conclusion.

l. 706. *minister.* Servant, agent.

ll. 714–15. *ship / Of Tarsus.* A common biblical phrase exemplifying pride (e.g. Isa. 23: 1, 14); Tarsus was a Spanish port.

l. 716. *Javan.* Greece (after Noah's grandson Javan, who supposedly sired the Ionians; cf. *PL*, i. 505).   *Gadire.* Cadiz.

l. 717. *bravery.* Finery.

l. 719. *hold them play.* Keep them in play.

l. 720. *amber.* Ambergris, the basis of perfume.

l. 731. *makes address.* Prepares.

l. 736. *fact.* Deed.

l. 737. *perverse event.* Untoward or unexpected outcome.

691 l. 748. *hyena.* Proverbial example of deceitfulness (cf. Jonson, *Volpone*, IV. vi. 2–3).

l. 752. *move.* Propose.

691 l. 769. *with . . . surcharged.* Not overburdened with exaggerations.

l. 775. *importune.* Persistent in solicitation.

692 l. 785. *parle.* Parley (discussion of truce).

l. 786. *the . . . kind.* Of the same nature.

l. 794. *fancy.* Affection.

ll. 800–2. *I . . . custody.* In Judg. 15: 5, the Philistines tell Delilah their aim is to 'bind him to afflict him'.

l. 803. *made for me.* Suited me.

l. 812. *fond.* foolish.

693 l. 826. *which.* Refers to pardon, l. 825.

l. 847. *awed.* Struck with fear.

694 l. 865. *grounded.* Established.

l. 897. *acquit themselves.* Perform their offices.

l. 901. *varnished colours.* False rhetoric.

695 l. 906. *worried.* Assailed.   *peals.* Outbursts (cf. l. 235, above).

l. 910. *place.* Opportunity.

l. 913. *sensibly.* Intensely.

l. 916. *want.* Lack.

l. 926. *grateful.* Pleasing.

ll. 932–3. *trains . . . gins . . . toils.* All words for traps.

l. 934. *enchanted . . . charms.* Dalila is compared with Circe and various Renaissance descendants of the sorceress; see *Comus*, ll. 50 ff.   *charms.* Including the Latinate sense, songs.

l. 936. *adder.* Proverbially deaf, as in Ps. 58: 4.

696 l. 944. *insult.* 'Exult proudly or contemptuously' (*OED*).

l. 948. *gloss upon.* Comment on.

l. 950. *To.* Compared to.

l. 967. *evil omen.* The sarcastic prediction that she will be 'memorable/ Among illustrious women', ll. 956–7.

l. 968. *denounced.* Pronounced.

l. 969. *concernments.* Concerns.

ll. 971–3. *Fame . . . white.* Fame is the Latin *fama*, rumour, unreliable and hence 'double-mouthed'. In all classical and Renaissance sources, however, the figure is female; the black and white wings are also Milton's invention.   *blast.* As of a trumpet.

l. 975. *circumcised.* Israelites.

l. 981. *Ecron . . . Gath.* Major Philistine cities.

697 l. 987. *odours.* Incense.

697 ll. 988–90. *Mount Ephraim . . . nailed.* The reference is to the song of the prophetess Deborah, who lived on Mount Ephraim (Judg. 4: 5), a hymn of praise for Jael, who slew the Canaanite general Sisera when she had given him refuge after his defeat by the Israelites (see Judg. 4: 17–21, 5: 24).

l. 1000. *aggravate.* Lit. 'add to the weight of'.

l. 1012. *inherit.* Possess.

l. 1016. *thy riddle.* The riddle proposed at his first wedding to the woman of Timnath, 'Out of the eater came forth meat, and out of the strong came forth sweetness' (Judg. 14: 14); Samson gave the Philistines seven days to find the solution.

l. 1018. *any of these.* Any of the virtues in ll. 1010–11.

l. 1020. *paranymph.* Best man, friend of the groom; in Judg. 14: 20, the woman of Timnath is, in Samson's absence, 'given to his companion, whom he had used as his friend'.

l. 1022. *both.* Both wives.   *disallied.* Dissolved; Milton's coinage.

698 l. 1025. *for that.* Because.

l. 1037. *joined.* Married.

l. 1038. *Intestine.* Internal; here, domestic.

l. 1039. *cleaving.* Clinging, but also self-dividing.

l. 1048. *in . . . combines.* Joins (with him) in domestic happiness.

l. 1058. *confusion.* Ruin, destruction.

l. 1062. *contracted.* Suffered (as in 'contract a disease').

699 l. 1068. *Harapha.* Not in the scriptural narrative; the name appears to derive from the Hebrew *ha raphah*, the giant, sometimes treated by biblical commentators as a proper name.

l. 1069. *pile.* Mass, stature (as of a building); cf. l. 1239 below.

l. 1073. *habit.* Clothing (he is unarmed).

l. 1075. *fraught.* Freight, i.e. what he brings.

l. 1076. *condole thy chance.* Lament your fate.

l. 1080. *Og . . . Anak . . . Emims.* Biblical giants (see Deut. 2: 10–11, 3: 11; Num. 13: 33); cf. ll. 148, 528, above.

l. 1081. *Kiriathaim.* In Gen. 14: 5, where the Emims dwelt.

l. 1082. *If . . . known.* If you know anything at all; but cf. also Satan to Ithuriel, 'Not to know me argues yourself unknown' (*PL*, iv. 830).

l. 1087. *camp . . . field.* Either on the battlefield or in the lists, at a tournament.

ll. 1088–9. *noise . . . about.* Reports have circulated.

l. 1092. *single.* Challenge to single combat.

l. 1105. *in thy hand.* Within reach.

700 l. 1109. *assassinated.* Treacherously stricken.

700 l. 1113. *Close-banded.* Secretly leagued together.

l. 1120. *brigandine.* Body armour.   *habergeon.* Sleeveless coat of chain mail.

l. 1121. *Vantbrace and greaves.* Arm and leg armour.   *gauntlet.* Mailed glove.

ll. 1121–2. *spear / A weaver's beam.* Spear as big as the roller on a loom; cf. the description of Goliath in 1 Sam. 17: 7.   *seven-times-folded.* Made of seven layers of hide.

l. 1138. *chafed.* Enraged.   *ruffled.* both angered, and with their quills standing on end.

l. 1147. *spread.* Lay.

701 l. 1164. *boisterous.* Coarse-growing, rank (*OED* 6).

l. 1169. *thine.* Thy people.

ll. 1183–5. *took . . . hands.* See Judg. 15: 11–13, and ll. 253 ff., above.

ll. 1186–8. *murder . . . robes.* At his wedding feast, Samson had promised thirty Philistines new garments if they could solve the riddle he proposed. They succeeded by persuading his wife to extract the answer from him, and to fulfil his vow he slew thirty men of Askalon and gave their garments to the Philistines. See Judg. 14: 12, 19, and ll. 382 ff., above.

702 ll. 1196–7. *Under . . . spies.* Josephus adds this detail to the story, that the thirty men were offered to Samson 'in pretence to be his companions, but in reality to be a guard upon him' (*Antiquities*, v. 8).   *await.* Wait upon.

ll. 1201–3. *When . . . hostility.* 'When I saw that everyone was determined to be my enemy, I was hostile at every opportunity, as I would be with my enemies.'

l. 1204. *underminers.* Betrayers.

l. 1220. *appellant.* Challenger to combat.

l. 1221. *maimed for.* Rendered incapable of.

l. 1223. *of small enforce.* Easy to perform.

703 l. 1231. *Baal-zebub.* Lit. 'god of flies', one of the many forms of the Philistine sun god Baal, whose shrine was in Ekron, the northernmost Philistine city; he appears as Satan's companion Beelzebub in *PL*.   *unused.* i.e. to hearing 'dishonours' (l. 1232).

l. 1234. *van.* Vanguard, first line of battle; i.e. start fighting.

l. 1237. *baffled.* Publicly disgraced (*OED* I. 1).

l. 1238. *vast.* The adjective modifies 'bulk'.

l. 1242. *Astaroth.* Collective name for the many forms of Astarte, the fertility goddess and female counterpart of Baal; cf. 'Nativity Ode', ll. 200–2.

l. 1243. *braveries.* Boasts.

l. 1245. *unconscionable.* Excessive.

703 l. 1248. *divulge.* Proclaim.

l. 1249. *Goliah.* The Authorized Version's Goliath; for his genealogy, see 1 Sam. 17: 4, and for the sons of the giant (Heb. 'ha raphah') of Gath, 2 Sam. 21: 22.

704 l. 1277. *ammunition.* War supplies.

l. 1283. *expedition.* Speed.

l. 1287. *patience.* The word literally means suffering; cf. *PL.*, ix. 31–3.

l. 1288. *saints.* In the Protestant sense, holy persons, especially 'the elect', those chosen for salvation; the term was regularly used by seventeenth-century puritans self-referentially; cf. Sonnet 23.

l. 1300. *behind.* Yet to come.

l. 1303. *quaint.* Curious.

l. 1305. *habit.* dress.

l. 1307. *voluble.* Fluent.

l. 1309. *remark.* Mark out, distinguish.

705 l. 1317. *heartened.* Refreshed.

l. 1320. *law forbids.* The second commandment forbids worship of idols or service to other gods (Exod. 20: 4–5).

l. 1325. *antics.* Clowns.   *mummers.* Mimes.

l. 1333. *Regard thyself.* Look to your own interests.

l. 1342. *Joined.* Enjoined, imposed.

l. 1344. *Brooks.* Permits.

l. 1346. *sorry what.* Sorry to think what.   *stoutness.* Obstinacy, defiance.

706 l. 1369. *sentence holds.* Maxim holds true.

l. 1375. *jealousy.* Cf. Exod. 20: 5, 'I the Lord thy God am a jealous God'.

ll. 1377–8. *dispense . . . Present.* Give a dispensation for me or thee to be present.

l. 1380. *come off.* Escape.

707 l. 1399. *art.* Skill.

l. 1402. *Because.* So that.

l. 1420. *aught.* At all (modifying 'concerned').

ll. 1431–3. *angel . . . flames.* See Judg. 13: 8–25.

708 l. 1450. *I had no will.* I had no will to go there.

l. 1453. *give ye part.* Let you share.

l. 1454. *With good success.* Successfully.

l. 1457. *attempted.* Entreated.

l. 1459. *With supplication prone.* Prostrating myself as I pleaded.

708 l. 1470. *The . . . remit.* To give up the rest (of their revenge) would be magnanimous.

709 l. 1478. *numbered down.* Counted out.

l. 1484. *wanting.* Lacking.

l. 1503. *to.* In addition to.

l. 1507. *next.* Next of kin, tribesmen (like Samson, they are Danites).

l. 1515. *ruin.* In its literal sense, collapse.

710 l. 1529. *dole.* Grief, pain, with a pun on dole as what is dealt.

l. 1535. *subscribe.* Agree.

l. 1536. *stay.* Pause.

l. 1538. *post.* Quickly (as on post horses).   *baits.* Travels slowly ('to bait' originally meant to pause on a journey to feed the horses).

l. 1539. *to.* In accordance with.

l. 1543. *erst.* Just now.

l. 1552. *accident.* Occurrence (lit. 'happening').

711 l. 1567. *irruption.* Bursting in.

l. 1574. *windy.* Empty.

l. 1585. *at variance.* In conflict.

712 l. 1596. *Occasions.* Business.

l. 1599. *little I had dispatched.* I had accomplished little.

l. 1603. *minded.* Intended.

l. 1605. *theatre.* The temple of Dagon is called a 'house' in Judg. 16: 26–7; but the pillars (16: 25–9) and the presence of 3000 spectators (16: 27) may have suggested a theatrical structure to Milton.

ll. 1607–8. *each . . . sort.* Everyone of high rank.

l. 1610. *banks.* Benches.   *scaffolds.* Platforms.

l. 1619. *cataphracts.* Soldiers in full armour.   *spears.* Spearsmen.

l. 1627. *stupendious.* Stupendous.

l. 1630. *his guide.* A boy in Judg. 16:26; cf. Milton's ensuing account with that in Judg. 16:28–30.

713 l. 1646. *nerves.* Sinews.

ll. 1647–8. *with . . . tremble.* Earthquakes and volcanoes were explained as the effects of the volatile elements trapped underground; cf. *PL*, i. 230–7, vi. 195–8.

l. 1659. *vulgar.* Common people.

l. 1669. *sublime.* Elated.

l. 1671. *regorged.* Regurgitated.

l. 1674. *Silo.* Shiloh, where the ark of the covenant was kept (Josh. 18: 1).

714 l. 1682. *fond.* Foolish.

l. 1685. *Insensate . . . reprobate.* Left senseless, or left to a godless ('reprobate') sense.

l. 1692. *evening dragon.* Firedrake, a meteorological phenomenon similar to the will-o'-the-wisp (see Edward Tayler, 'Milton's Firedrake', *Milton Quarterly* 6, 3 [October 1972], 7–10).

l. 1695. *villatic.* Farmyard; Milton's coinage.

l. 1699. *self-begotten bird.* The phoenix, a mythical bird continually reborn out of its own ashes; cf. 'Damon's Epitaph', 185–7; *PL*, v. 272–4.

l. 1700. *embossed.* Imbosked, hidden in the woods.

l. 1701. *no . . . third.* Only one phoenix existed at a time.

l. 1702. *lay . . . holocaust.* Was a short while ago wholly consumed by fire.

l. 1703. *teemed.* Born.

l. 1707. *secular.* Lasting for ages.

l. 1709. *quit.* Acquitted.

l. 1713. *sons of Caphtor.* The Philistines, who emigrated to Canaan from Caphtor, generally thought to be Crete.

l. 1715. *hath.* He hath.

715 l. 1727. *lavers.* Washbasins

l. 1728. *what speed.* With as much speed as possible.

l. 1729. *plight.* Condition.

ll. 1736–7. *enrolled . . . legend.* Fully written out (*legend* = something to be read).

l. 1746. *dispose.* Disposition.

l. 1751. *in place.* Here.

l. 1753. *band them.* Band together.

l. 1755. *acquist.* Acquisition.

FAMILIAR LETTERS (1674)

Thirty-one Latin personal letters of Milton, along with a group of his college rhetorical exercises (prolusions), were published in 1674 (*Joannis Miltonii Angli Epistolarum Familiarium Liber Unus*). The fact that they appeared together and that copies of the letters—some written as much as forty years before—had been preserved indicates that they, like the prolusions, were considered models of rhetorical composition. The letters are addressed to Milton's schoolteachers, friends, Florentine associates, and political allies. Several additional letters (as well as a number of letters to Milton) have since come to light; all of them may be found in the Yale edition. We print one of the letters to Diodati, one letter written in Florence, and a letter describing the course of Milton's blindness. The translations are those of the Yale edition.

To Charles Diodati, 1637. For Diodati, see note to Sonnet 6. Milton responds to a letter of Diodati's, no longer extant.

717 *your art.* Diodati had just started practising medicine.

718 *Ceres.* Ceres pursued her daughter Proserpina to Hades, where she had been abducted by the god of the underworld.

'for . . . divine'. Milton quotes a Euripidean formula appearing at the end of, e.g., *Alcestis, The Bacchae, Helen.*

Pegasus. The winged horse of the muses, emblematic of poetry.

Inns of Court. Where lawyers were trained; in 1637 Milton's brother Christopher resided in the Inner Temple. Young men seeking a career in public life could also live in the Inns of Court.

stepmotherly warfare. Diodati's father had remarried, and the children of the first marriage were not on speaking terms with their stepmother.

Dacian or Sarmatian. Fierce opponents of their Roman rulers.

719 *Giustiniani . . . Veneti.* Bernardo Giustiniani, *De Origine Urbis Venetiarum* (1492).

To Benedetto Buonmattei, 1638. The recipient was one of the Florentine academicians whom Milton met on his Italian journey, an authority on the Tuscan language whose *Della Lingua Toscana,* alluded to in the opening phrase of the letter, appeared in 1643.

Romulean. Romulus killed his brother Remus when Remus, to ridicule its inadequacy, leapt over the wall Romulus was building around Rome; the 'Romulean law' mandated the same punishment to all other intruders.

Athens. No particular episode seems to be alluded to; the general sense is that Athenian glory went hand in hand with the purity of the language, and with resistance to 'barbarian' tongues.

Plato. Laws, vii. 797.

720 *Etruscan tongue.* Milton confers an antique origin upon Tuscan Italian.

Arno . . . Fiesole. Cf. the Florentine scene in *PL,* i. 288 ff.

721 *Cicero and Fabius.* In *Brutus,* Cicero describes the major Greek and Latin orators; a similar survey is found in Quintilian's *Institutio Oratio,* x. Buonmattei did not take Milton's advice.

daughter's cause . . . Latium. i.e. the Italian language is the daughter of the mother tongue, Latin, named from Latium, the ancient name for Italy.

To Leonard Philaras, 1654. Philaras, an Athenian by birth (*c.*1600), was serving as the envoy from Parma to the French court when he introduced himself by letter to Milton in 1652. He visited England in 1654, and offered to enlist the services of the Parisian physician Thévenot, who specialized in diseases of the eye, on Milton's behalf. Milton's letter replies to the offer and details the progress of his blindness.

more despicable . . . many. Cf. his discussion of the attack on his blindness in *Second Defence.*

722 *Argonauts.* Apollonius Rhodius, *Argonautica*, ii. 205–8.

the wise man. Eccles. 11: 8, 'But if a man live many years, and rejoice in them all; yet let him remember the days of darkness; for they are many. All that cometh is vanity.'

as it is written. Deut. 8: 3, 'man doth not live by bread only, but by every word that proceedeth out of the mouth of the Lord doth man live.' The verse is quoted by Jesus in response to Satan's temptation in Luke 4: 4 and Matt. 4: 4.

723 *Lynceus.* One of the Argonauts, notable for his keen sight.

Christian Doctrine. The bulk of the writing of *De Doctrina Christiana* probably took place between 1640 and 1660, although additions to the manuscript were made until Milton's death. In 1675, Daniel Skinner, in whose hand the first third of the manuscript is written, attempted to have the work published in Amsterdam; it was rejected, probably because of its heretical character. Sir Joseph Williamson, the Secretary of State, refused to allow publication of the work in England, and demanded the manuscript, which he deposited in Whitehall. The manuscript, in a packet labelled 'To Mr Skinner, Merchant', was found in the Old State Paper Office at Whitehall in 1823 and was published, along with an English translation, by Charles R. Sumner in 1825. This is the version of the treatise that was read until John Carey provided a new and far more accurate translation for the Yale edition, which has served as our copytext here, and is used with his generous permission and that of the Yale University Press. The treatise is worth close study; the first book is of especial interest to readers of the epics in its treatment of the question of the relation of foreknowledge to free will, as well as discussions of the fall, the nature of temptation, and the nature of Christ. Milton's heretical beliefs—the inequality of Father and Son, the rejection of the Trinity, the material basis of creation, the belief in mortalism (the death of the soul)—are amply displayed. There are, moreover, chapters on such abiding concerns as the nature of Christian liberty and the reading of scripture. Limitations of space have made it impossible to include more than the briefest sampling from the treatise. For a summary of *Christian Doctrine* that will help locate important passages, the student may turn to J. Max Patrick's account in his edition of *The Prose of John Milton*. For a discussion of the parallels between *CD* and *PL*, Maurice Kelley's *This Great Argument* remains the standard study; his introduction and notes in the Yale edition are also invaluable. Christopher Kendrick's use of the passages about free will in his *Milton: A Study in Form and Ideology* contributes significantly to an account of the relationship between the treatise and *PL*.

FURTHER READING

THERE is no authoritative edition of Milton's poetry; frequently cited are Merritt Y. Hughes (ed.), *John Milton: Complete Poems and Major Prose* (New York, 1957) and John Carey and Alastair Fowler (eds.), *The Poems of John Milton* (New York and London, 1968, 1997). A more recent edition is Roy Flannagan (ed.), *The Riverside Milton* (Boston, 1998). All these offer annotations fully in tune with traditional Milton scholarship. A summary of such criticism on the shorter poems and on *Paradise Regained* can be found in Douglas Bush and A. S. P. Woodhouse, *A Variorum Commentary on the Poems of John Milton* (New York, 1970). The standard edition of the prose is the Yale edition, *The Complete Prose Works of John Milton*, 8 vols. (New Haven, 1953–82), which offers much information on the historical contexts. A full-scale modern biography is William Riley Parker, *Milton: A Biography* (Oxford, 1968); revised edn. Gordon Campbell (Oxford, 1997); another is Barbara K. Lewalski, *The Life of John Milton: A Critical Biography* (Oxford, 2000). These are worth supplementing with the seven volumes of David Masson, *The Life of John Milton* (Cambridge and London, 1859–94), and Helen Darbyshire (ed.), *The Early Lives of Milton* (London, 1932).

A strong collection of original essays is Mary Nyquist and Margaret W. Ferguson (eds.), *Re-Membering Milton* (New York and London, 1987); a convenient collection of previously published work is Annabel Patterson (ed.), *John Milton* (London, 1992). Other recommended studies:

Sharon Achinstein, *Milton and the Revolutionary Reader* (Princeton, 1994).

Denise Albanese, *New Science, New World* (Durham, NC, 1996).

Francis Barker, *The Tremulous Private Body* (New York and London, 1984; Ann Arbor, 1995); excerpted in Patterson.

Catherine Belsey, *John Milton: Language, Gender, Power* (Oxford and New York, 1988).

Harold Bloom, *The Anxiety of Influence* (London and New York, 1973).

—— *A Map of Misreading* (London and New York, 1975).

Gregory W. Bredbeck, *Sodomy and Interpretation* (Ithaca, NY, 1991).

Anthony Easthope, 'Towards the Autonomous Subject in Poetry: Milton's "On His Blindness"', in Richard Machin and Christopher Norris (eds.), *Post-Structuralist Readings of English Poetry* (Cambridge, 1987).

William Empson, *Milton's God* (London, 1961, 1965; Cambridge, 1981).

—— *Some Versions of Pastoral* (London, 1935).

Stephen M. Fallon, *Milton Among the Philosophers: Poetry and Materialism in Seventeenth-Century England* (Ithaca, NY, 1991).

Stanley Fish, *Surprised by Sin: The Reader in Paradise Lost* (London and Berkeley, 1967).

—— *How Milton Works* (Cambridge, Mass., 2001).

Angus Fletcher, *The Transcendental Masque: An Essay on Milton's Comus* (Ithaca, NY, 1971).

Jonathan Goldberg, 'Dating Milton', in Elizabeth D. Harvey and Katharine Eisaman Maus (eds.), *Soliciting Interpretation: Literary Theory and Seventeenth-Century Poetry* (Chicago, 1990); reprinted in Patterson.

—— *Voice Terminal Echo: Postmodernism and English Renaissance Texts* (New York and London, 1986).

Linda Gregerson, *The Reformation of the Subject: Spenser, Milton and the English Protestant Epic* (Cambridge, 1995).

Kenneth Gross, '"Each heav'nly close": Mythologies and Metrics in Spenser and the Early Poetry of Milton,' *PMLA* 98 (1983), 21–36.

John Guillory, 'Dalilah's House: *Samson Agonistes* and the Sexual Division of Labor', in Margaret W. Ferguson, Maureen Quilligan, and Nancy J. Vickers (eds.), *Rewriting the Renaissance* (Chicago, 1986).

—— 'From the Superfluous to the Supernumerary: Reading Gender into *Paradise Lost*', in Elizabeth D. Harvey and Katharine Eisaman Maus (eds.), *Soliciting Interpretation* (Chicago, 1990).

—— 'The Father's House: *Samson Agonistes* in its Historical Moment', in *Re-Membering Milton*; repr. in Patterson.

—— *Poetic Authority: Spenser, Milton, and Literary History* (New York, 1983).

Janet E. Halley, 'Female Autonomy in Milton's Sexual Poetics', in Julia M. Walker (ed.), *Milton and the Idea of Woman* (Champaign, Ill., 1988).

Richard Halpern, 'Puritanism and Maenadism in *A Mask*', in Margaret W. Ferguson, Maureen Quilligan, and Nancy J. Vickers, *Rewriting the Renaissance* (Chicago, 1986).

—— 'The Great Instauration: Imaginary Narratives in Milton's "Nativity Ode"', in *Re-Membering Milton*.

Geoffrey Hartman, 'Adam on the Grass with Balsamum' and 'Milton's Counterplot', in id., *Beyond Formalism* (New Haven, 1970).

Christopher Hill, *Milton and the English Revolution* (London and New York, 1978).

Christopher Kendrick, Milton: *A Study in Ideology and Form* (New York and London, 1986).

—— 'Milton and Sexuality: A Symptomatic Reading of *Comus*', in *Re-Membering Milton*.

William Kerrigan, 'The Heretical Milton: From Assumption to Mortalism', *English Literary Renaissance*, 5 (1975), 125–66.

—— *The Prophetic Milton* (Charlottesville, Va., 1974).

—— *The Sacred Complex: On the Psychogenesis of 'Paradise Lost'* (Cambridge, Mass., 1983).

Edward Semple LeComte, *Milton's Unchanging Mind* (Port Washington, NY, 1973).

Mary Nyquist, 'Fallen Differences, Phallologocentric Discourses: Losing *Paradise Lost* to History', in Derek Attridge, Geoff Bennington, and Robert Young (eds.), *Post-Structuralism and the Question of History* (Cambridge, 1987); reprinted in Patterson.

—— 'The Father's Word/Satan's Wrath', *PMLA* 100 (1985), 187–202.

—— 'Textual Overlapping and Dalilah's Harlot-Lap', in Patricia Parker and David Quint (eds.), *Literary Theory/Renaissance Texts* (Baltimore, 1986).

Mary Nyquist, 'The Genesis of Gendered Subjectivity in the Divorce Tracts and in *Paradise Lost*', in *Re-Membering Milton*.

Patricia Parker, *Inescapable Romance* (Princeton, 1979).

C. A. Patrides (ed.), *Milton's Lycidas: The Tradition and the Poem* (Columbia, Mo., 1983).

Maureen Quilligan, 'Freedom, Service, and the Trade in Slaves: The Problem of Labor in *Paradise Lost*', in Margreta de Grazia, Maureen Quilligan, and Peter Stallybrass (eds.), *Subject and Object in Renaissance Culture* (Cambridge, 1996).

Balachandra Rajan and Elizabeth Sauer (eds.), *Milton and the Imperial Vision* (Pittsburgh, Pa., 1999).

John Rogers, *The Matter of Revolution: Science, Poetry, and Politics in the Age of Milton* (Ithaca, NY, 1996).

John Shawcross, 'Milton and Diodati: An Essay in Psychodynamic Meaning', *Milton Studies*, 7 (1975), 127–63.

Victoria Silver, *Imperfect Sense: The Predicament of Milton's Irony* (Princeton, 2000).

INDEX OF TITLES AND FIRST LINES

POEMS

A book was writ of late called *Tetrachordon*   78
A little onward lend thy guiding hand   673
Ad Patrem   200
Another on the Same   21
Arcades   36
At a Solemn Music   17
At a Vacation Exercise   75
Avenge O Lord thy slaughtered saints, whose bones   80

Because you have thrown off your prelate lord   83
Before the starry threshold of Jove's court   45
Blest pair of sirens, pledges of heaven's joy   17

Captain or colonel, or knight in arms   35
Canzone   32
'Comus' (*A Masque . . . Presented at Ludlow Castle*)   44
Cromwell, our chief of men, who through a cloud   85
Curre per immensum subito, mea littera, pontum   98
Cyriack, this three years' day these eyes, though clear   86
Cyriack, whose grandsire on the royal bench   82

Damon's Epitaph   148
Daughter to that good earl, once president   36
Diodati, e te'l dirò con maraviglia   32
Donna leggiadra il cui bel nome onora   30

Elegiac Verses   163
Elegy 1. To Charles Diodati   88
Elegy 2. On the Death of the Cambridge University Beadle   92
Elegy 3. On the Death of the Bishop of Winchester   94
Elegy 4. To His Tutor, Thomas Young   98
Elegy 5. On the Approach of Spring   104
Elegy 6. To Charles Diodati, Staying in the Country   112
Elegy 7. ('Nondum blanda tuas leges')   116
Epilogue to the Elegies   122
Epitaph on the Marchioness of Winchester, An   17
Erewhile of music, and ethereal mirth   13

Fairfax, whose name in arms through Europe rings   85
Fifth Ode of Horace, The   83
Floribus et visa est posse placere suis   108
Fly envious Time, till thou run out thy race   15

Giovane piano, e semplicetto amante   34

Haec ego mente olim laeva, studioque supino   122
Haec quoque, Manse, tuae, meditantur carmina laudi   144
Hail native language, that by sinews weak   75
Harry, whose tuneful and well-measured song   79
Hence loathèd Melancholy   22
Hence vain deluding joys   25
Here lies old Hobson, Death hath broke his girt   20
Here lieth one who did most truly prove   21
Himerides Nymphae—nam vos et Daphnin et Hylan   150
How soon hath time the subtle thief of youth   34

I did but prompt the age to quit their clogs   79
I who erewhile the happy garden sung   619
Iam pius extrema veniens Iacobus ab arcto   124
Il Penseroso   25
In Effigiei eius Sculptor   162
In Quintum Novembris   124
In se perpetuo Tempus revolubile gyro   104

Lady, that in the prime of earliest youth   35
L'Allegro   22
Lawrence of virtuous father virtuous son   81
Let us with a gladsome mind   11
Look nymphs, and shepherds look   36
Lycidas   39

Manso   142
Masque . . . Presented at Ludlow Castle, A ('Comus')   44
Methought I saw my late espousèd saint   82
Mitto tibi sanam non pleano ventre salutem   112
Moestus eram, et tacitus, nullo comitante, sedebam   94

Nondum blanda tuas leges, Amathusia, noram   116
Now the bright morning star, day's harbinger   19
Nunc mea Pierios cupiam per pectora fontes   134

O fairest flower no sooner blown but blasted   73
O Musa gressum quae volens trahis claudum   140
O nightingale, that on yon bloomy spray   30
Of man's first disobedience and the fruit   356
On Shakespeare   20
On the Death of a Fair Infant   73
On the Engraver of his Portrait   162
On the Fifth of November   124
On the Lord General Fairfax   85
On the Morning of Christ's Nativity   3
On the New Forcers of Conscience   83
On the University Carrier   20
On Time   15

Paradise Lost   355
Paradise Regained   619
Paraphrase on Psalm 114, A   10
Passion, The   13
Per certo i bei vostr'occhi, donna mia   33
Psalm 136   11

Qual in colle aspro, al' imbrunir di sera   31

Ridonsi donne e giovani amorosi   32

Samson Agonistes   671
Song. On May Morning   19
Sonnet 1 ('O nightingale')   30
Sonnet 2 ('Donna leggiadra')   30
Sonnet 3 ('Qual in colle aspro')   31
Sonnet 4 ('Diodati, e te'l dirò')   32
Sonnet 5 ('Per certo')   33
Sonnet 6 ('Giovane piano')   34
Sonnet 7 ('How soon hath time')   34
Sonnet 8 ('Captain or colonel')   35
Sonnet 9 ('Lady, that in the prime')   35
Sonnet 10 ('Daughter to that good earl')   36
Sonnet 11 ('A book was writ of late')   78
Sonnet 12. On the Same ('I did but prompt the age')   79
Sonnet 13. To Mr H. Lawes ('Harry whose tuneful')   79
Sonnet 14 ('When faith and love')   80
Sonnet 15. On the Late Massacre in Piedmont   80
Sonnet 16 ('When I consider how my light is spent')   81
Sonnet 17 ('Lawrence of virtuous father')   81
Sonnet 18 ('Cyriack, whose grandsire')   82
Sonnet 19 ('Methought I saw my late espousèd saint')   82
Surge, age, surge, leves, iam convenit, excute somnos   163

Tandem, care, tuae mihi pervenere tabellae   88
Te, qui conspicuus baculo fulgente solebas   92
This is the month, and this the happy morn   3
This rich marble doth inter   17
To Mr Cyriack Skinner Upon his Blindness   86
To my Father   134
To Salzilli   140
To Sir Henry Vane the Younger   86
To the Lord General Cromwell   85

Upon the Circumcision   16

Vane, young in years, but in sage counsel old   86

What needs my Shakespeare for his honoured bones   20
What slender youth bedewed with liquid odours   83

When faith and love which parted from thee never   80
When I consider how my light is spent   81
When the blest seed of Terah's faithful son   10

Ye flaming powers, and wingèd warriors bright   16
Yet once more, O ye laurels, and once more   39

PROSE WORKS

Apology for Smectymnuus, An   173
Areopagitica   236

Christian Doctrine   723

Doctrine and Discipline of Divorce, The   182

Letter (1633)   1

Of Education   226

Ready and Easy Way, The   330
Reason of Church Government, The   165

Second Defence of the English People   308
Tenure of Kings and Magistrates, The   273

To Benedetto Buonmattei   719
To Charles Diodati   717
To Leonard Philaris   721

A SELECTION OF OXFORD WORLD'S CLASSICS

An Anthology of Elizabethan Prose Fiction

An Anthology of Seventeenth-Century Fiction

Early Modern Women's Writing

Three Early Modern Utopias (Utopia; New Atlantis; The Isle of Pines)

FRANCIS BACON — Essays

APHRA BEHN — Oroonoko and Other Writings
The Rover and Other Plays

JOHN BUNYAN — Grace Abounding
The Pilgrim's Progress

JOHN DONNE — The Major Works
Selected Poetry

BEN JONSON — The Alchemist and Other Plays
The Devil is an Ass and Other Plays
Five Plays

JOHN MILTON — Selected Poetry

SIR PHILIP SIDNEY — The Old Arcadia

IZAAK WALTON — The Compleat Angler

A SELECTION OF   OXFORD WORLD'S CLASSICS

The Anglo-Saxon World

Beowulf

Lancelot of the Lake

The Paston Letters

Sir Gawain and the Green Knight

Tales of the Elders of Ireland

York Mystery Plays

GEOFFREY CHAUCER   The Canterbury Tales
                         Troilus and Criseyde

HENRY OF HUNTINGDON   The History of the English People
                            1000–1154

JOCELIN OF BRAKELOND   Chronicle of the Abbey of Bury
                            St Edmunds

GUILLAUME DE LORRIS   The Romance of the Rose
and JEAN DE MEUN

WILLIAM LANGLAND   Piers Plowman

SIR THOMAS MALORY   Le Morte Darthur

Bhagavad Gita

The Bible Authorized King James Version
  With Apocrypha

Dhammapada

Dharmasūtras

The Koran

The Pañcatantra

The Sauptikaparvan (from the
  Mahabharata)

The Tale of Sinuhe and Other Ancient
  Egyptian Poems

Upaniṣads

ANSELM OF CANTERBURY	The Major Works
THOMAS AQUINAS	Selected Philosophical Writings
AUGUSTINE	The Confessions On Christian Teaching
BEDE	The Ecclesiastical History
HEMACANDRA	The Lives of the Jain Elders
KĀLIDĀSA	The Recognition of Śakuntalā
MANJHAN	Madhumalati
ŚĀNTIDEVA	The Bodhicaryàvatàra

A SELECTION OF   OXFORD WORLD'S CLASSICS

	Classical Literary Criticism
	The First Philosophers: The Presocratics and the Sophists
	Greek Lyric Poetry
	Myths from Mesopotamia
APOLLODORUS	**The Library of Greek Mythology**
APOLLONIUS OF RHODES	**Jason and the Golden Fleece**
APULEIUS	**The Golden Ass**
ARISTOPHANES	**Birds and Other Plays**
ARISTOTLE	**The Nicomachean Ethics** **Physics** **Politics**
BOETHIUS	**The Consolation of Philosophy**
CAESAR	**The Civil War** **The Gallic War**
CATULLUS	**The Poems of Catullus**
CICERO	**Defence Speeches** **The Nature of the Gods** **On Obligations** **The Republic and The Laws**
EURIPIDES	**Bacchae and Other Plays** **Medea and Other Plays** **Orestes and Other Plays** **The Trojan Women and Other Plays**
GALEN	**Selected Works**
HERODOTUS	**The Histories**
HOMER	**The Iliad** **The Odyssey**

A SELECTION OF **OXFORD WORLD'S CLASSICS**

HORACE   **The Complete Odes and Epodes**

JUVENAL   **The Satires**

LIVY   **The Dawn of the Roman Empire**
                  The Rise of Rome

MARCUS AURELIUS   **The Meditations**

OVID   **The Love Poems**
                  Metamorphoses
                  Sorrows of an Exile

PETRONIUS   **The Satyricon**

PLATO   **Defence of Socrates, Euthyphro, and Crito**
                  Gorgias
                  Phaedo
                  Republic
                  Symposium

PLAUTUS   **Four Comedies**

PLUTARCH   **Greek Lives**
                  Roman Lives
                  Selected Essays and Dialogues

PROPERTIUS   **The Poems**

SOPHOCLES   **Antigone, Oedipus the King, and Electra**

STATIUS   **Thebaid**

SUETONIUS   **Lives of the Ceasars**

TACITUS   **Agricola and Germany**
                  The Histories

VIRGIL   **The Aeneid**
                  The Eclogues and Georgics

Women's Writing 1778–1838

WILLIAM BECKFORD   Vathek

JAMES BOSWELL   Life of Johnson

FRANCES BURNEY   Camilla
Cecilia
Evelina
The Wanderer

LORD CHESTERFIELD   Lord Chesterfield's Letters

JOHN CLELAND   Memoirs of a Woman of Pleasure

DANIEL DEFOE   A Journal of the Plague Year
Moll Flanders
Robinson Crusoe
Roxana

HENRY FIELDING   Joseph Andrews and Shamela
A Journey from This World to the Next and
     The Journal of a Voyage to Lisbon
Tom Jones

WILLIAM GODWIN   Caleb Williams

OLIVER GOLDSMITH   The Vicar of Wakefield

MARY HAYS   Memoirs of Emma Courtney

ELIZABETH HAYWOOD   The History of Miss Betsy Thoughtless

ELIZABETH INCHBALD   A Simple Story

SAMUEL JOHNSON   The History of Rasselas
The Major Works

CHARLOTTE LENNOX   The Female Quixote

MATTHEW LEWIS   Journal of a West India Proprietor
The Monk

HENRY MACKENZIE   The Man of Feeling

ALEXANDER POPE   Selected Poetry

A SELECTION OF OXFORD WORLD'S CLASSICS

ANN RADCLIFFE	The Italian The Mysteries of Udolpho The Romance of the Forest A Sicilian Romance
SAMUEL RICHARDSON	Pamela
FRANCES SHERIDAN	Memoirs of Miss Sidney Bidulph
RICHARD BRINSLEY SHERIDAN	The School for Scandal and Other Plays
TOBIAS SMOLLETT	The Adventures of Roderick Random The Expedition of Humphry Clinker Travels through France and Italy
LAURENCE STERNE	The Life and Opinions of Tristram Shandy, Gentleman A Sentimental Journey
JONATHAN SWIFT	Gulliver's Travels A Tale of a Tub and Other Works
HORACE WALPOLE	The Castle of Otranto
MARY WOLLSTONECRAFT	Mary and The Wrongs of Woman A Vindication of the Rights of Woman

A SELECTION OF   **OXFORD WORLD'S CLASSICS**

JANE AUSTEN	Emma
	Persuasion
	Pride and Prejudice
	Sense and Sensibility
MRS BEETON	Book of Household Management
ANNE BRONTË	The Tenant of Wildfell Hall
CHARLOTTE BRONTË	Jane Eyre
EMILY BRONTË	Wuthering Heights
WILKIE COLLINS	The Moonstone
	The Woman in White
JOSEPH CONRAD	Heart of Darkness and Other Tales
	Nostromo
CHARLES DARWIN	The Origin of Species
CHARLES DICKENS	Bleak House
	David Copperfield
	Great Expectations
	Hard Times
GEORGE ELIOT	Middlemarch
	The Mill on the Floss
ELIZABETH GASKELL	Cranford
THOMAS HARDY	Jude the Obscure
	Tess of the d'Urbervilles
WALTER SCOTT	Ivanhoe
MARY SHELLEY	Frankenstein
ROBERT LOUIS STEVENSON	Treasure Island
BRAM STOKER	Dracula
WILLIAM MAKEPEACE THACKERAY	Vanity Fair
OSCAR WILDE	The Picture of Dorian Gray

The Oxford World's Classics Website

www.worldsclassics.co.uk

- Information about new titles
- Explore the full range of Oxford World's Classics
- Links to other literary sites and the main OUP webpage
- Imaginative competitions, with bookish prizes
- Peruse the Oxford World's Classics Magazine
- Articles by cditors
- Extracts from Introductions
- A forum for discussion and feedback on the series
- Special information for teachers and lecturers

www.worldsclassics.co.uk

American Literature

British and Irish Literature

Children's Literature

Classics and Ancient Literature

Colonial Literature

Eastern Literature

European Literature

History

Medieval Literature

Oxford English Drama

Poetry

Philosophy

Politics

Religion

The Oxford Shakespeare

A complete list of Oxford Paperbacks, including Oxford World's Classics, Oxford Shakespeare, Oxford Drama, and Oxford Paperback Reference, is available in the UK from the Academic Division Publicity Department, Oxford University Press, Great Clarendon Street, Oxford OX2 6DP.

In the USA, complete lists are available from the Paperbacks Marketing Manager, Oxford University Press, 198 Madison Avenue, New York, NY 10016.

Oxford Paperbacks are available from all good bookshops. In case of difficulty, customers in the UK can order direct from Oxford University Press Bookshop, Freepost, 116 High Street, Oxford OX1 4BR, enclosing full payment. Please add 10 per cent of published price for postage and packing.